Association of Southeast Asian Nations (ASEAN) page 161
http://www.asean.or.id

CHAPTER 6

World Trade Organization page 185
http://www.wto.org

World Climate Facts Organization page 191
http://www.climatefacts.org

United States Treasury page 193
http://www.ustrest.gov

Journal of Commerce page 194
http://www.joc.com

U.S. Department of Commerce page 199
http://www.doc.gov/services/doc.services.html/

Export-Import Bank of the United States (Ex-Im Bank) page 199
http://www.exim.gov

CHAPTER 7

Transparency International page 226
http://www.is.in-berlin.dc/service/ti.html

Organization for Economic Cooperation and Development page 232
http://www.oecd.org/

National Association of Manufacturers page 232
http://www.nam.org

USA Engage page 232
http://www.engage.org

Global Risk Assessment, Inc. page 243
http://www.global-riskassessment.com

World Trade Organization (WTO) page 243
http://www.wto.org

CHAPTER 8

3M page 257
http://www.3m.com/intl

H. J. Heinz page 272
http://www.hjheinz.com

American Feng Shui Institute page 275
http://www.amfengshui.com

CHAPTER 9

Forbes Magazine page 304
http://www.forbes.com

McKinsey Quarterly page 314
http://www.mckinsey.com

The Conference Board page 318
http://www.conference-board.org

CHAPTER 10

Global Trade Information Services, Inc. page 351
http://www.gtis.com

Commission of the European Union to the United States page 358
www.eurunion.org

The Washington Post page 364
http://www.washingtonpost.com

Marketing News page 368
http://www.ama.org

CHAPTER 11

World Trade page 386
http://www.worldtrademag.com

CHAPTER 12

Sharper Image page 423
http://www.sharperimage.com

Organization for Ecnomic Cooperation and Development page 445
http://www.oecd.org

Advertising Age page 446
http://www.adage.com

The Wall Street Journal page 447
http://www.wsj.com

Manpower page 447
http://www.manpower.com

CHAPTER 13

Port Import Export Reporting Service (PIERS) page 463
http://www.piers.com

Journal of Commerce page 464
http://www.joc.com

Sea-Land Service, Inc. page 465
http://www.sealand.com

International Civil Aviation Organization page 468
http://www.cam.net/~icao/index.html

Port Authority of New York and New Jersey page 470
http://www.panynj.gov

National Insurance Crime Bureau page 479
http://www.nicb.com

Mobil Corporation page 481
http://www.mobil.com

McDonnell Douglas Part 4 Cases page 502
http://www.dac.mdc.com

McDonalds Part 4 Cases page 510
http://www.mcdonalds.com

CHAPTER 14

American Countertrade Association page 521
http://www.i-trade.com

U.S. General Accounting Office page 526
http://www.gao.gov

CHAPTER 15

World Trade Organization (WTO) page 561
http://www.wto.org

Ford Motor Company page 564
http://www.ford.com

Boeing page 565
http://www.boeing.com

Global Business
Second Edition

MICHAEL R. CZINKOTA
Georgetown University

ILKKA A. RONKAINEN
Georgetown University

MICHAEL H. MOFFETT
Thunderbird—The American Graduate School of International Management

EUGENE O. MOYNIHAN
Rockland Community College State University of New York

The Dryden Press
Harcourt Brace College Publishers
Fort Worth Philadelphia San Diego New York Orlando Austin San Antonio
Toronto Montreal London Sydney Tokyo

Publisher George Provol
Acquisitions Editor John Weimeister
Product Manager Lisé Johnson
Developmental Editor Karen Hill
Project Editor Sandy Walton
Art Director Scott Baker
Production Manager Eddie Dawson

ISBN: 0-03-024888-4
Library of Congress Catalog Card Number: 97-77736

Address for Orders
The Dryden Press, 6277 Sea Harbor Drive, Orlando, FL 32887-6777
1-800-782-4479

Address for Editorial Correspondence
The Dryden Press, 301 Commerce Street, Suite 3700, Fort Worth, TX 76102

Web Site Address
http://www.hbcollege.com

Printed in the United States of America

8 9 0 1 2 3 4 5 6 032 9 8 7 6 5 4 3 2

The Dryden Press
Harcourt Brace College Publishers

To all the Czinkotas: Ilona, Ursula, Mihaly, Birgit, and Thomas—MRC
To my family: Sanna, Sirkka, Susan, Alex and Alpo—IAR
To Bennie Ruth and Hoy Moffett—MHM
To Regina, Colleen, and Brian Moynihan—EOM

The Dryden Press Series in Management

Anthony, Perrewé, and Kacmar
Strategic Human Resource Management
Second Edition

Bereman and Lengnick-Hall, Mark
Compensation Decision Making: A Computer-Based Approach
Second Edition

Bergmann, Scarpello, and Hills
Compensation Decision Making
Second Edition

Bourgeois
Strategic Management: From Concept to Implementation

Bracker, Montanari, and Morgan
Cases in Strategic Management

Brechner
Contemporary Mathematics for Business and Consumers

Calvasina and Barton
Chopstick Company: A Business Simulation

Costin
Readings in Total Quality Management

Costin
Managing in the Global Economy: The European Union

Costin
Economic Reform in Latin America

Costin
Management Development and Training: A TQM Approach

Costin
Readings in Strategy and Strategic Management

Czinkota, Ronkainen, and Moffett
International Business
Fourth Edition

Czinkota, Ronkainen, Moffett, and Moynihan
Global Business
Second Edition

Daft
Management
Fourth Edition

Daft
Understanding Management
Second Edition

DeSimone and Harris
Human Resource Development
Second Edition

Foegen
Business Plan Guidebook
Revised Edition

Gatewood and Feild
Human Resource Selection
Fourth Edition

Gold
Exploring Organizational Behavior: Readings, Cases, Experiences

Greenhaus and Callanan
Career Management
Second Edition

Higgins and Vincze
Strategic Management: Text and Cases
Fifth Edition

Hodgetts
Modern Human Relations at Work
Sixth Edition

Hodgetts and Kroeck
Personnel and Human Resource Management

Hodgetts and Kuratko
Effective Small Business Management
Sixth Edition

Holley and Jennings
The Labor Relations Process
Sixth Edition

Jauch and Coltrin
The Managerial Experience: Cases and Exercises
Sixth Edition

Kindler and Ginsburg
Strategic & Interpersonal Skill Building

Kirkpatrick and Lewis
Effective Supervision: Preparing for the 21st Century

Kuratko and Hodgetts
Entrepreneurship: A Contemporary Approach
Fourth Edition

Kuratko and Welsch
Entrepreneurial Strategy: Text and Cases

Lengnick-Hall, Cynthia, and Hartman
Experiencing Quality

Lewis
Io Enterprises Simulation

Long and Arnold
The Power of Environmental Partnerships

Morgan
Managing for Success

Ryan, Eckert, and Ray
Small Business: An Entrepreneur's Plan
Fourth Edition

Sandburg
Career Design Software

Vecchio
Organizational Behavior
Third Edition

Walton
Corporate Encounters: Law, Ethics, and the Business Environment

Zikmund
Business Research Methods
Fifth Edition

Preface

Global Business is designed specifically as an introductory international text for use at the undergraduate level. Its comprehensive coverage of the subject also makes it appropriate for use in MBA programs.

From the outset, it was intended that *Global Business* would be both an improvement and simplification of the array of international business texts now available but still be rigorous and demanding enough to satisfy the professional integrity of the instructor.

The ever-growing cultural diversity of students attending U.S. colleges and universities has also influenced the development of this text. These students not only bring to the classroom a richness in cultural backgrounds but also exhibit a wide range of learning experiences. The authors of *Global Business* are sensitive to these conditions and to the educational opportunities they present to instructors.

Coverage

The text emphasizes global consideration of the international activities of small and medium-sized firms as well as those of large multinational corporations. It presents a balanced coverage of the subject matter that one would expect from authors with extensive business, consulting, writing, and teaching experience. Important topics only marginally or rarely discussed in most international business texts are given more-than-adequate exposition; these include physical distribution (logistics), countertrade, north–south economic integration, the development of global management talent, and future career roles for women in global business.

Organization

Global Business contains 15 streamlined chapters, which translates into one chapter per week for the traditional 15-week semester. Five parts of two to four chapters each organize the text to flow logically from introductory material to the global environment to marketing and financial considerations in the global marketplace.

Up-to-Date Research

Extra effort has been made to provide extensive current research information. Chapter notes are augmented by lists of relevant recommended readings. These resources enable the instructor and the student to incorporate additional information where it is useful and desirable. The data are current through July 1997.

Dramatic Illustrations

The text contains many dramatic illustrations to help the student understand complex concepts, such as the global integration of manufacturing and marketing of the Ford

Global Car Program in Chapter 1 and the logistical solutions presented by the use of third-generation shipping vessels and related equipment in Chapter 13.

Cultural Sensitivity

Global Business is sensitive to the diverse cultural backgrounds of students. For example, Global Learning Experience 8.3 highlights the Mexican celebration of "the Day of the Dead" with quotations from the renowned Mexican poet Octavio Paz. In a similar manner Chapter 5 focuses on Latin American economic integration and provides statistical data relevant to NAFTA, Mercosur, and other initiatives at economic integration is the Americas.

In-Depth Tables and Figures

Many of the tables and figures have been specifically designed and developed to enhance student understanding of the text material. In addition to trade data provided by the U.S. Department of Commerce, data collected by Statistics Canada is also utilized. The development and analysis of data was supported by Global Trade Information Services, Inc., using their extensive trade database.

Marginal Glossary

An extensive marginal glossary makes it easier for students to define and understand key terms. An end-of-the-book glossary contains all key terms and definitions in a convenient alphabetical form.

Latin American Spanish Glossary

The end-of-the-book glossary in English is complemented by a Latin American Spanish Glossary, included to assist students who have recently arrived in the United States and are still in the process of acquiring a mastery of English.

Cases and Video Support

The text is supported by seventeen cases, eight of which are accompanied by a supporting video case. Challenging questions for each case encourage in-depth discussions of the material covered in chapters and allow students to apply their knowledge.

Maps

To increase the geographic literacy of students, the text contains excellent maps that provide the instructor with the means to demonstrate concepts visually, such as political blocs, socioeconomic variables, and transportation routes. In addition, the text includes a 16-page, 4-color world atlas insert for each reference by both instructor and student.

Geographic Quiz Questions

Interspersed throughout the text are geographic quiz questions and answers. The focus is on interesting facts about the planet we live on. These "brain teasers" provide additional reinforcement for the text maps and 4-color world atlas.

Culture Tips

Chapter 8, "The Cultural Environment" (and middle chapter in the text), temporarily breaks from the geography quiz to feature culture tips—about one every other page.

Contemporary Realism

Each chapter offers a number of Global Learning Experience boxes that highlight actual contemporary business situations. Global Learning Experiences can be used to reinforce chapter examples, or as mini-cases. As such, they assist the instructor in stimulating class discussion and aid the student in understanding and absorbing the text material. Many feature discussions of recent and critical events in global business.

Simplified Language

Throughout the text every effort has been made to present complex ideas in easy-to-understand language, with the aim of making *Global Business* very reader-friendly.

COMPREHENSIVE LEARNING PACKAGE

Instructor's Manual and Test Bank

The text is accompanied by an *Instructor's Manual* designed to provide in-depth assistance to the professor. For each chapter of the text, the manual provides chapter objectives, suggestions for teaching, suggestions for group projects, and questions for discussion, along with answers. Answers are provided for all the questions that follow the end-of-part cases. Video teaching notes are provided for each video case that appears in the text. In addition, an annotated list of suggested films and videos is provided as an extra resource. The *Test Bank* portion of the manual provides over 700 questions with a wide range of incisive true/false, multiple choice, and short answer questions for each chapter.

Computerized Test Bank and RequesTest

All the questions in the printed Test Bank are available on computer diskette in DOS, Windows, and Macintosh-compatible form. Adopters also can request customized tests with Dryden's special service, RequesTest, by simply calling the toll-free number, 1-800-447-9457. Dryden will compile test questions according to a requestor's criteria and then either mail or fax the test master to the user within 48 hours.

Acetate Package

A package of 75 transparency acetates, which features text art and maps, is available. The acetates are accompanied by detailed teaching notes that include summaries of key concepts.

Videos

New and re-edited videos are available to accompany *Global Business.* The video package features segments from popular Dryden videos such as Esprit and Lakewood Forest Products. Each of the eight segments provides video support for the cases in the text.

Acknowledgments

We are grateful to a number of reviewers for their imaginative comments and criticisms and for showing us how to get it even more right:

Turgut Guvenli
Mankato State University

Bradford Knipes
Westfield State College

Thomas W. Lloyd
Westmoreland County Community College

Francine Newth
Providence College

Scott Norwood
San Jose State University

Gregory K. Stephens
Texas Christian University

Hsin-Min Tong
Radford University

We would also like to thank those who helped shape the first edition:

Joe Anderson
Northern Arizona University

Ellen Cook
University of San Diego

Massoud Farahbaksh
Salem State College

Antonio Grimaldi
Rutgers, The State University of New Jersey

Htien Han
University of La Verne

Benjamin M. Hawkins
Berry College

Andre Honoree
Delgado Community College

Robert J. Hopkins
St. Andrew's Presbyterian College

Bruce Hyland
City College of San Francisco

Thomas Jay
Flathead Community College

Patricia Matthews
Mount Union College

William Motz
Lansing Community College

Renee Prim
Piedmont Community College

Edward Raupp
Anoka-Ramsey Community College

Douglas Tseng
Portland State University

Robert Unterman
Glendale Community College

Heidi Vernon-Wortzel
Northeastern University

Dennis Wahler
San Jose City College

Steve Walters
Davenport College

George H. Westacott
SUNY-Binghamton

Many thanks to those faculty members and students who helped us in sharpening our thinking by cheerfully providing challenging comments and questions. Several individuals had particular long-term impact on our thinking. These are Professor Bernard LaLonde, Ohio State University, a true academic mentor; the late Professor Robert Bartels, also of Ohio State; Professor Arthur Stonehill, Orgeon State University; Professor James H. Sood, American University; Professor Arch G. Woodside, Tulane University; Professor David Ricks, Thunderbird; Professor Brian Toyne, St. Mary's University; and Professor John Darling, Mississippi State University. They are our academic ancestors.

Many colleagues, friends, and business associates graciously gave their time and knowledge to clarify concepts; provide us with ideas, comments, and suggestions; and deepen our understanding of issues. Without the direct links to business and policy that you have provided, this book could not offer its refreshing realism. In particular, we are grateful to Secretaries C. William Verity, Clayton Yeutter, William Brock, and the late Malcolm Baldrige for the opportunity to gain international business policy experience and to William Morris, Paul Freedenberg, H.P. Goldfield, and J. Michael Farrell for enabling its implementation. We also thank William Casselman, Robert Conkling Associates, Lew Cramer of US WEST, Joseph Lynch of ADI, and Reijo Luostarinen of HSE.

A very special word of thanks to the people at The Dryden Press. John Weimeister and Yvette Rubio made the lengthy process of writing a text bearable with their enthusiasm, creativity, and constructive feedback. Major assistance was also provided by the friendliness, expertise, and help of Karen Hill of Elm Street Publishing Services.

Foremost, we are grateful to our families, who have had to tolerate late-night computer noises, weekend library absences, and curtailed vacations. The support and love of Ilona Vigh-Czinkota, Susan and Sanna Ronkainen, Megan Murphy, and Regina Moynihan gave us the energy, stamina, and inspiration to write this book.

Michael R. Czinkota
Ilkka A. Ronkainen
Michael H. Moffett
Eugene O. Moynihan
October 1997

Contents in Brief

Detailed Contents

Part Five **International Finance and the Future**

Global Business

Second Edition

PART ONE

Introduction to Global Business Theory and Practice

Changes in the world environment are bringing totally new opportunities and threats to firms and individuals. The challenge is to compete successfully in the global marketplace as it exists today and develops tomorrow.

Part 1 sets the stage and then provides theoretical background for global trade and investment activities. Key classical concepts such as absolute and comparative advantage are explained and expanded to include modern-day realities. The intent is to enable the reader to understand both the theoretical and practical rationale for global business activities.

The Global Business Imperative

LEARNING OBJECTIVES

To understand the history and importance of global business.

To learn the definitions of domestic, global, and multinational businesses.

To recognize the growth of global linkages today.

To understand the U.S. position in world trade and the impact international business has on the country.

To appreciate the opportunity offered by global business.

The Real Fast Track Is Overseas

"Foreign assignments are shedding their dead-end image and promise an enormous career boost," writes Marshall Loeb of *Fortune Magazine.* An assignment abroad, once thought to be a career dead end, has become a ticket to speedy advance. Headhunters are already putting a premium on people with global business experience, he notes. Loeb points out that "it's no coincidence that the CEOs of the Big Three automakers all headed key international divisions." These days all kinds of companies—drugmakers, computer outfits, and manufacturers of other stripes—are actively globalizing their execs.

Loeb offers the following advice on landing a choice foreign assignment:

- Most importantly, tell your boss you want to go and bring up the subject at every performance review.
- It helps to take courses in international business and politics (and let people know you're doing so).
- Keep up to date on what your company is doing abroad and where.
- Get to know the international team, not only those who work in your building but also the ones visiting from foreign outposts. Maybe they will put your name forward, knowing your enthusiasms.
- A second or third language can only help.

Many companies are facing the realization that business is no longer limited by geographic boundaries, and they now include overseas assignments when developing career programs for their executives. For global companies, and those companies with global aspirations, it is becoming increasingly clear that the fast track to senior-level jobs almost requires some degree of foreign experience.

Individual Tax Returns Filed by U.S. Citizens Abroad (excludes Puerto Rico and Members of U.S. Military)

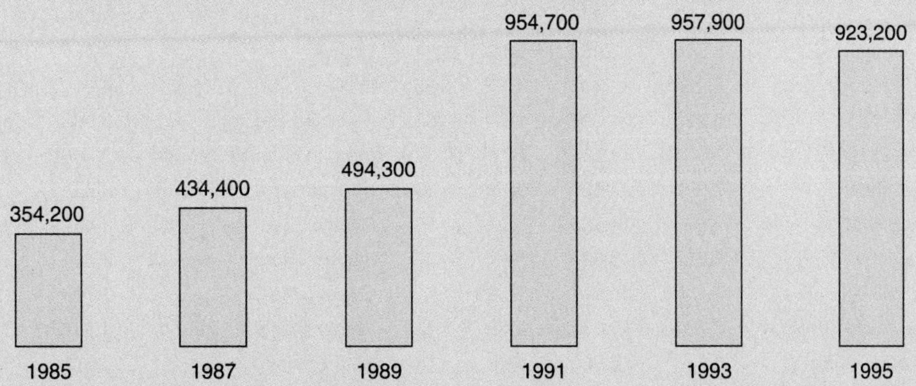

NOTE: The total number of Americans working abroad is not certain, but some idea of the number can be obtained from data provided by the Internal Revenue Service. According to the *IRS Data Book* (published annually), the number of U.S. Individual Tax Returns received from international locations increased from 1985 to 1995. In 1985 approximately 354,000 of these returns were filed. In contrast, in 1995 the number of returns received was about 923,000.

SOURCES: Marshall Loeb, "The Real Fast Track Is Overseas," *Fortune,* September 21, 1995: 129. U.S. Internal Revenue Service

TABLE 1.1 **Total and Foreign Revenues of the 100 Largest U.S. Multinational Companies, 1996 (in millions—ranked by foreign revenues)**

		Revenue					Revenue		
Rank	Company	Foreign ($mil)	Total ($mil)	Foreign as % of Total	Rank	Company	Foreign ($mil)	Total ($mil)	Foreign as % of Total
1	Exxon	89,608	116,728	76.8	41	CPC International	5,962	9,844	60.6
2	General Motors	51,000	164,069	31.1	42	International Paper	5,915E	20,143	29.4
3	Mobil	48,533[1]	72,267[1]	67.2	43	Aflac	5,849	7,100	82.4
4	Ford Motor	48,104	146,991	32.7	44	Alcoa	5,815	13,061	44.5
5	IBM	46,552	75,947	61.3	45	American Home Products	5,753	14,088	40.8
6	Texaco[1]	31,385	59,205	53.0	46	UAL	5,600	16,362	34.2
7	General Electric	23,361	79,179	29.5	47	Texas Instruments	5,451	9,940	54.8
8	Chevron[1]	22,220	47,798	46.5	48	Pfizer	5,365	11,306	47.5
9	Hewlett-Packard	21,379	38,420	55.6	49	Crown Cork & Seal	5,005	8,332	60.1
10	Citicorp	19,772	32,605	60.6	50	Wal-Mart Stores	5,002	104,859	4.8
11	Phillip Morris Cos	19,628	54,553	36.0	51	Pharmacia & Upjohn	4,858	7,286	66.7
12	Procter & Gamble	17,682[2]	35,284	50.1	52	American Express	4,800E	17,280	27.8
13	El du Pont de Nemours	16,525	38,349	43.1	53	BankAmerica	4,755	21,924	21.7
14	American Intl Group	14,991[2]	28,205	53.2	54	AMR	4,741	17,753	26.7
15	Motorola	12,600E	27,973	45.0	55	Electronic Data Systems	4,685	14,441	32.4
16	Coca-Cola	12,449[2]	18,546	67.1	56	Apple Computer	4,577	9,833	46.5
17	Intel	12,179	20,847	58.4	57	Bankers Trust New York	4,360	9,565	45.6
18	Xerox[1]	12,038	20,621	58.4	58	ITT Industries	4,329	8,718	49.7
19	Dow Chemical	11,264	20,053	56.2	59	Manpower	4,306	6,080	70.87
20	Johnson & Johnson	10,721	21,620	49.6	60	Fluor	4,232	11,015	38.4
21	United Technologies	10,080[1]	23,512[1]	42.9	61	Abbott Laboratories	4,227	11,013	38.4
22	Digital Equipment	9,436	14,563	64.8	62	Rhone-Poulenc Rorer	4,141	5,421	76.4
23	PepsiCo	9,197	31,645	29.1	63	Warner-Lambert	4,058	7,231	56.1
24	Eastman Kodak	8,515	15,968	53.3	64	Unisys	4,021	6,371	63.1
25	Compaq Computer	8,428[2]	18,109	46.5	65	NCR	4,019	6,963	57.7
26	Chrysler	8,226	61,397	13.4	66	Emerson Electric	3,982	11,150	35.7
27	Amoco	7,971[1]	32,726[1]	24.4	67	Morgan Stanley, DW, D[2]	3,900E	22,172	17.6
28	Chase Manhattan	7,932	27,421	28.9	68	HJ Heinz	3,876	9,112	42.5
29	Minn Mining & Mfg	7,556	14,236	53.1	69	Costco Cos	3,857	19,566	19.7
30	Sara Lee	7,387	18,624	39.7	70	Ingram Micro	3,734	12,023	31.1
31	Merrill Lynch	7,150E	25,011	28.6	71	General Re	3,703	8,296	44.6
32	JP Morgan & Co	6,754[2]	15,866	42.6	72	Archer Daniels Midland	3,581	13,314	26.9
33	Bristol-Myers Squibb	6,614	15,065	43.9	73	Walt Disney	3,571	18,739	19.1
34	Kimberly-Clark[1]	6,470E	14,108	45.9	74	Deere & Co	3,515	11,229	31.3
35	Colgate-Palmolive	6,263[2]	8,749	71.6	75	Safeway	3,472	17,269	20.1
36	RJR Nabisco	6,170E	17,063	36.2	76	Halliburton	3,432	7,385	46.5
37	Gillette	6,117	9,698	63.1	77	Northwest Airlines	3,390	9,881	34.3
38	Goodyear Tire & Rubber	6,103	13,113	46.5	78	Sears, Roebuck	3,388	38,236	8.9
39	McDonald's	6,096	10,687	57.0	79	TRW	3,388	9,857	34.4
40	Merck	5,989	19,829	30.2	80	Atlantic Richfield	3,367	18,592	18.1

Rank	Company	Revenue Foreign ($mil)	Revenue Total ($mil)	Foreign as % of Total	Rank	Company	Revenue Foreign ($mil)	Revenue Total ($mil)	Foreign as % of Total
81	Monsanto	3,322	9,262	35.9	91	ITT	3,096	6,597	46.9
82	Sun Microsystems	3,304	7,095	46.6	92	Eli Lilly	3,081	7,347	41.9
83	Rockwell International	3,270E	10,373	31.5	93	AMP	3,053	5,468	55.8
84	Johnson Controls	3,243	9,210	35.2	94	Lear	3,050E	6,249	48.8
85	Whirlpool	3,223[2]	8,696	37.1	95	Dresser Industries	3,035E	6,562	46.3
86	Caterpillar	3,211	16,522	19.4	96	Woolworth	3,008	8,092	37.2
87	AlliedSignal	3,197	13,971	22.9	97	Salomon	2,901[2]	9,046	32.1
88	Avon Products	3,142	4,814	65.3	98	Kellogg	2,897	6,677	43.4
89	Cigna	3,125	18,950	16.5	99	Applied Materials	2,874	4,145	69.3
90	Ralston Purina	3,120	6,114	51.0	100	Honeywell	2,834	7,312	38.8
						Totals	928,313	2,301,902	40.3%

[1]Includes other income.
[2]Excludes Canadian operations.
E: Estimate.
Source: Forbes, July 28, 1997.

WHY STUDY GLOBAL BUSINESS?

Welcome to the world of global business. You are about to begin the study of one of the most important aspects of business. Although the United States has always engaged in some degree of international business, most U.S. business firms have ignored global markets in favor of a growing U.S. market. However, since the 1950s and particularly over the last 20 years, the U.S. market has become saturated with foreign-made products. Accordingly, U.S. companies are now fighting to keep or increase their share of the domestic market and are also beginning to seek new markets abroad. It is understandable, then, that as more and more U.S. business firms "go global," it will be necessary for their employees to understand how different doing business in the United States is compared with doing business almost anywhere else in the world. Many students think that just because many foreigners speak English, they understand American culture. Nothing could be further from the truth! Behavior and actions that seem perfectly acceptable in the United States can be an insult in a foreign country and ruin a business deal.

Global business causes the flow of goods, services, culture, and ideas around the world. It also facilitates the movement of the factors of production (except land) and, as Global Learning Experience 1.1 indicates, provides challenging employment opportunities as well.

Continuous changes in the economies of countries have made **isolationism** for them impossible. No nation can go it alone or exist without interacting with other nations, and a nation's failure to become part of the global community and participate in global markets virtually ensures that it will suffer declining economic influence and a lower standard of living for its citizens. On the other hand, a country's successful participation in global business and global markets should lead to a better life and society for its citizens.

isolationism
a policy that a nation can exist without interacting with other nations

Table 1.1 will give you some idea of the importance of global operations to many of the largest U.S. multinational companies.

As you can see from Table 1.1, these 100 U.S. companies had combined total sales in 1996 of $2,301,902 million, 40.3 percent of which was from foreign sales. Given numbers such as these, it is clear that U.S. businesses must participate in world markets to stay competitive. There are many reasons for doing business internationally, including creating new markets and/or increasing profits; finding and acquiring new products and technology for use in the home market; protecting domestic markets; improving intracompany communications; finding new sources of supply; developing geographic diversification; and maximizing shareholder wealth.

Even if a U.S. company cannot enter foreign markets for some reason, its officers and employees should be well schooled in global business. Because so many foreign business firms have entered, and are continuing to enter, the U.S. market, soon it will be the rare U.S. business that does not have foreign competition in the United States.

Understandably, foreign ownership of a portion of U.S. manufacturing assets could raise concerns as to whether those assets were being managed in the best interests of the U.S. economy. It also raises concerns for the job stability of individuals employed by foreign-owned businesses in the United States.

Finding and holding a job is of concern to many Americans today. Scarcely a week goes by without some announcement that a major U.S. firm is restructuring itself to be more competitive in global markets and that thousands of jobs will be affected. Table 1.2 provides an interesting perspective on employment in U.S. manufacturing industries. As of 1994, about 11.8 percent of the 18.3 million employees in U.S. manufacturing worked for companies that were U.S. **affiliates of foreign corporations.** Table 1.2 shows the relative degree of employment concentration for selected industries: almost 34 percent in chemicals and allied products and 20 percent in stone, clay, and glass products.

affiliates of foreign corporations
affiliates are U.S. companies owned 10 percent or more by foreigners

It is hoped the reader is beginning to grasp how important an understanding of the basic principles of global business already is and why it will continue to be important in the future. Global business *is* the future, and a study of it will help the reader prepare for that future.

ACTIVITIES THAT DEFINE GLOBAL BUSINESS

One might wonder exactly what business activities are included in the area of global business. Most people initially tend to think of global business as the **exporting** and **importing** of merchandise. However, one soon learns that global business may be divided into four much broader categories: merchandise, services, portfolio capital, and direct investment.

exporting
the sale and delivery of tangible goods to another country

importing
the purchase and receipt of tangible goods from another country

merchandise
tangible goods such as automobiles, machinery, and chemicals

services
the export and import of all types of services

portfolio capital
flows of money resulting from financial investments

Merchandise consists of tangible goods such as televisions, VCRs, automobiles, machinery, and chemicals.

When we speak of **services,** we mean the sale (export) and purchase (import) of all types of services including accounting, advertising, banking, communications, computer programming, distribution rights for motion pictures and TV shows, education and training, financial, insurance, transportation, and travel and tourism. This is just a partial list of what is included in the services category and is intended to give you some idea of the vast scope of the global trade in services.

Portfolio capital is a term used to define flows of capital (money) resulting from the purchase or sale of various types of financial investments. Portfolio capital includes:

1. Marketable Securities:
   - Bonds and commercial paper
   - Common stock (in amounts that do not constitute control of the business organization)
2. Nonmarketable Investments:
   - Bank accounts (for example, an American citizen who has a Swiss bank account)

TABLE 1.2

Total Employment of U.S. Affiliates of Foreign Corporations and U.S. Business in Manufacturing, 1994 (in thousands of employees)

Manufacturing Product Category	All Business in the United States	Foreign Affiliates[1]	Foreign Affiliates as a Percent of All U.S. Businesses
Chemicals and allied products	1,059	356	33.6
Petroleum and coal products	NA	59	NA
Stone, clay, and glass products	536	105	19.6
Primary metal industries	701	117	16.7
Electronic and other electric equipment	1,578	262	16.6
Rubber and plastics products	950	134	14.1
Instruments and related products	869	113	13.0
Motor vehicles and equipment	899	107	11.9
Industrial machinery and equipment	1,991	227	11.4
Food and kindred products	1,685	187	11.1
Fabricated metal products	1,386	115	8.3
Paper and allied products	699	51	7.3
Printing and publishing	1,571	110	7.0
Textile mill products	672	45	6.7
Apparel and other textile products	984	60	6.1
Other transportation equipment	850	34	4.0
Lumber, wood, furniture, and fixtures	1,259	34	2.7
Other	564	57	10.1
All manufacturing	18,253	2,172	11.8

[1]Affiliates are U.S. companies owned 10 percent or more by foreigners.

NA: not available

SOURCE: U.S. Department of Commerce, *Survey of Current Business* (Washington, DC: U.S. Government Printing Office, July 1996), Table 13, p. 113.

Direct investment refers to the ownership (or control) of a company in a foreign land. In place of total (100 percent) ownership, control is said to exist when U.S. shareholders of any type own more than 50 percent of the combined voting power of the foreign company. A U.S. shareholder is defined as a U.S. person owning 10 percent or more of the voting power. The U.S. government regards ownership of 10 to 50 percent of the voting power of a foreign company sufficient to exercise some degree of control of the company and considers it to be a direct investment.

direct investment ownership or control of a company in another country

The Export of Culture and Ideas

Another aspect of global business activity relates to the exportation (and importation) of culture and ideas. There is probably no way anyone can keep figures on how people around the globe interact with each other, but it is nevertheless a significant and important aspect of global activity.

QUESTION *What is the world's highest mountain?*

ANSWER *Mount Everest, in the Himalayas Range between Tibet and Nepal rises to 29,108 ft. or about 5.5 miles high. The second highest mountain is K-2 in the Karakoram Range of nearby Pakistan. The Himalayas and Karakoram Ranges hold almost all of the tallest mountains in the world. The volcanic Mauna Kea in Hawaii measures 33,746 feet high, taller than Mount Everest, but only 13,680 feet is visible above the surface of the ocean.*

Taco Bell restaurants feature foods inspired by Mexican culture.

Exporting and Importing Culture

Over the past few decades, the U.S. culture and "way of life" have been exported extensively about the globe. In a similar manner, the United States has imported various aspects of foreign cultures. This has been the result of merchandise and service trade activities undertaken for business reasons. Intended, or unintended, these activities have had the result of exposing citizens of foreign lands to U.S. culture and the American "way of life," and vice versa.

It is indeed difficult to go to a foreign land and not find a McDonald's fast-food restaurant, be it City Hall Park in Toronto, Canada, on the Champs Elysées in Paris, in Moscow, Russia, Bejing, China, or Tokyo, Japan. Levi Strauss jeans are "in" clothing around the world, while the U.S. television and motion picture industry film and video presentations have been well received and have exposed untold hundreds of millions of foreign citizens to the American way of life and U.S. culture. A classic example is given in Global Learning Experience 1.2. "Baywatch" is the most watched television program in the world.

In the United States, a growing portion of the population with Mexican origins has led to an appreciation for Mexican-style food products and cooking techniques. Indicative of how the United States has adopted "Tex-Mex" is the Taco Bell restaurant chain, with over 5,500 locations in the United States, serving flavorful tacos, fajitas, and other Mexican inspired treats.

Exporting Ideas

As businesses and peoples about the globe travel and interact with each other, there is an exchange of ideas with respect to fundamental institutions that have an impact on the quality of life. Two examples are the ideas of a "free market economy" and the concept of "democracy."

It was not too many years ago that many foreign nations were operating under a communist form of government. Americans were thought to be "capitalistic warmongers" and referred to as "ugly Americans." Over time as companies began to do business on a global scale, people traveled internationally, and with student exchange and other similar programs, people from nondemocratic countries began to understand what a free market economy was all about: That the thing called democracy (with all its imperfections) had some advantages after all, and that those "ugly Americans" were really nice people.

Regarding democracy, in a prophetic statement Sir Winston Churchill once noted, "No one pretends that democracy is perfect or all-wise. Indeed, it has been said that democracy is the worst form of government except all those other forms that have been tried from time to time."

"Baywatch"—The Most Watched TV Show on Earth

On the sparkling shoreline of Southern California, a small group of lifeguards patrols its surfside beat—a patch of soft sand, less than one mile long and only several hundred feet wide. Their workdays are packed with action while their off-duty hours are filled with matters of love, relationships, and compelling human drama. Through it all, the whole world is watching. On every continent of the globe, with the exception of Antarctica, a combined total of more than one billion viewers in more than 144 countries and 210 U.S. cities keep a weekly appointment with the men and women of "Baywatch."

Translated into fifteen languages, the show has become a national viewing pastime in the United Kingdom, Germany, Norway, Sweden, Denmark, Australia, New Zealand, South Africa, South America, Asia, and Africa. Amazingly, "Baywatch" crosses all cultures, airing in such Islamic countries as Saudi Arabia, Iran, and Iraq and in the Peoples Republic of China without negative repercussions.

As people of the world view "Baywatch," they are absorbing U.S. culture—in particular California beach culture. This is the California where everyone is athletic, tanned, and attractive; drives a car; has a beautiful home; and enjoys all the good things of life. This is America.

SOURCE: Baywatch—All American Televison, Inc.

QUESTION *What is the world's largest continent?*

ANSWER *Asia, it measures 17 million square miles, nearly a third of the Earth's land surface, with a combined population of about 2.5 billion people. North America is the third largest continent—9,360,000 square miles covering the U.S., Canada, Mexico, Greenland and the Caribbean Islands.*

Once the ideas of "free markets" and "democracy" became understood around the globe, the logic of simple economic theory took over, and in one stunning month the entire Soviet-dominated communist portion of the world disintegrated and began the task of embracing free market and democratic concepts.

A Definition of Global Business

domestic company
a company that operates only within its own nation

global company
a business organization that operates in more than one country

multinational company
a company that operates internationally to earn profits on a global basis

Having just identified some of the activities associated with global business, we now define the term *global business.* To do so, we will consider three different types of companies: domestic, global, and multinational. A **domestic company** is one that operates within its own national borders. A **global company** is a business organization that operates beyond its national borders; that is, it operates in more than one country. A **multinational company (MNC),** generally speaking, refers to a company that operates internationally, but with important differences. A multinational not only operates in many countries but also conducts itself in such a manner that it owes allegiance to no country, views itself as a citizen of the world, and seeks to earn profits on a global basis. (Note: at this point, it is important to understand that there are many definitions of what an MNC is and that the terms *multinational corporation* (MNC), *multinational enterprise* (MNE), and *worldwide company* (WWC) are essentially interchangeable.)

Multinational companies have advantages not available to the typical company doing business on an international basis, which will be discussed in detail later in the text. Until then, it is sufficient to summarize a few of them.

1. *Advanced technology*—Generally speaking, MNCs have access to advanced levels of technology that makes it possible for them to be extremely competitive when entering new foreign markets.
2. *Product development*—MNCs can capitalize on the development of products in one market and, if successful, use that success to exploit foreign markets.
3. *Financial strength*—Because of their sheer size (many MNCs are financially stronger than the governments of some of the countries in which they operate) MNCs are able to obtain capital easier, and at lower cost, than smaller, local, foreign competitors.
4. *Management*—Being large organizations, MNCs have depth in their management ranks. They also can afford to employ individuals with specialized business skills to enhance company profits and/or effectiveness.
5. *Reduced political risk*—Doing business in a foreign land carries some degree of risk due to changes in a country's political system. Because MNCs tend to do business in many countries, the political risk is spread over many locations, thus lessening the relative degree of risk in any one location.

GLOBAL LINKAGES TODAY

International business has forged a network of global linkages around the world that binds us all—countries, institutions, and individuals—much closer than ever before.

The Ford Global Car Program

Ford's CDW-27 program is a classic case of the use of global integration of suppliers and corporate resources (employees and equipment) to design and produce automobiles for global markets. The most visible results of the program are three all-new midsize, advanced-technology cars (Mondeo, Ford Contour, and Mercury Mystique), available with right-hand or left-hand drive; three versions of a new four-cylinder engine; an all-new V-6 engine; an all-new automatic transmission; and the retooling of six component plants and three assembly plants in Europe and North America.

Mondeo was introduced in Europe in March 1993 and in Asian Pacific markets (Taiwan, Hong Kong, Thailand, Singapore) in the fall of 1993. The Contour and Mystique were introduced in North America during September 1994. The company plans to sell 800,000 Mondeos, Contours, and Mystiques annually in 59 countries.

Mondeo, Ford Contour, and Mercury Mystique —all based on a common platform, sourced worldwide, and built in three countries—are targeted at multiple markets, including Europe, North America, Asia, South America, and the Middle East.

Designing one automobile for the world presented Ford with some unusual challenges. The basic car, or platform, had to be engineered from the start to meet both safety and legal requirements for all 59 markets in which the cars will be sold. Although the three cars share a high degree of commonality in the underbody, chassis, suspension, engine, and transmission—the parts of the cars that can be seen—the sheet metal, trim, interior, and seats are unique because of different cultural and consumer style and option preferences between Europe and North America. For example, Europeans like to hold the steering wheel with their arms outstretched; North Americans are more relaxed and hold the wheel closer to their bodies. In parts of Europe, heated seats are a "must" option but are not even offered in North America.

The result is that each of the cars has a "personality" designed to appeal to the target customers of each market. For example, the Mondeo is concise and formal—very much in keeping with the needs of European drivers as well as Middle Eastern and Asian customers. Contour is a little sportier, with somewhat more flowing lines and shapes. Mystique is slightly more formal, with a more sophisticated look.

Figure 1.1 gives an indication of the magnitude of Ford's global integration effort. The illustration shows the integration of sources of supply by country and major component, manufacturing plants, and markets.

Mercury Mystique: A version of the Ford global car designed for U.S. markets.

SOURCE: Ford Motor Company.

continued

FIGURE 1.1 Ford Global Car Program—The Integration of Suppliers, Manufacturing Facilities, and Markets

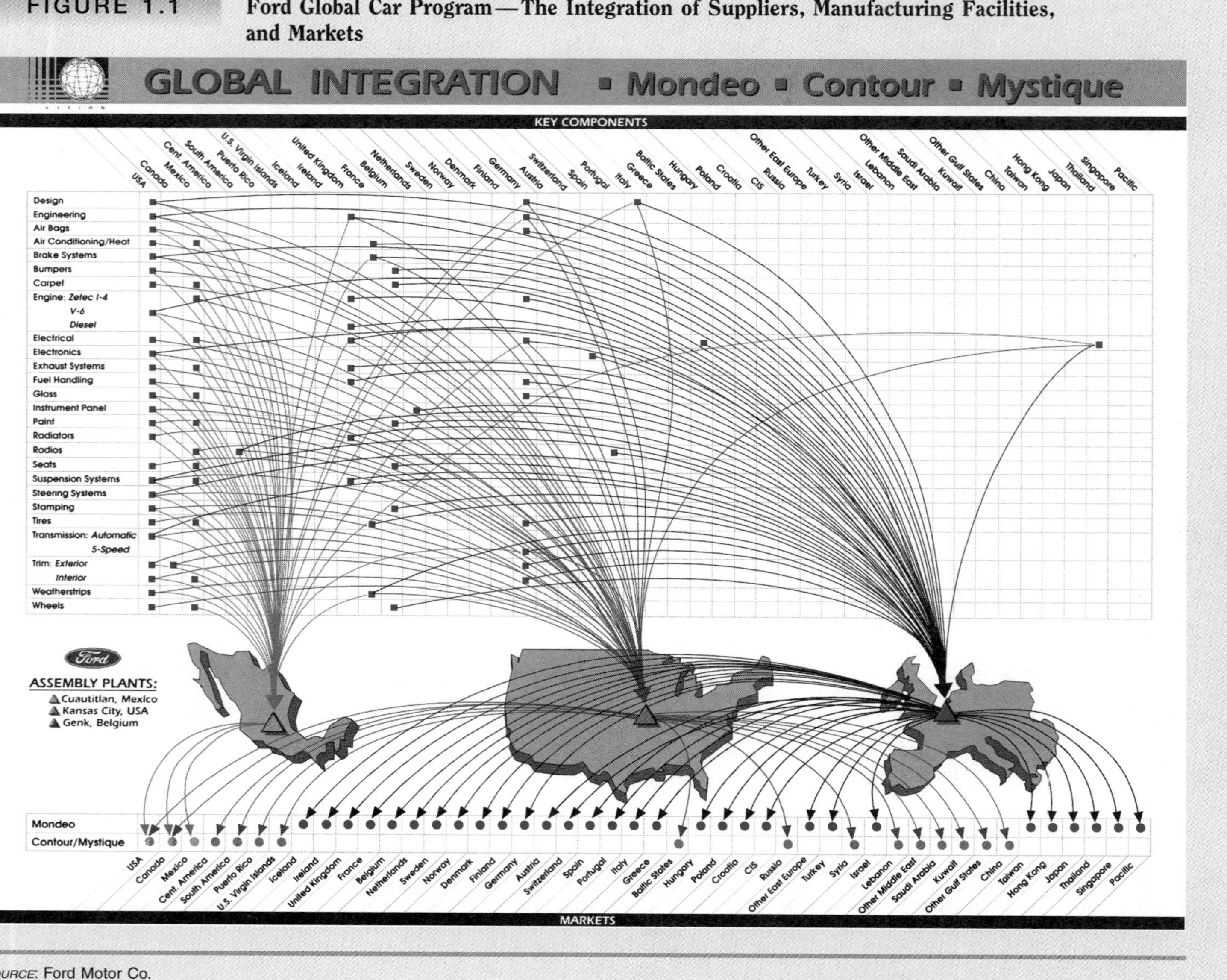

SOURCE: Ford Motor Co.

These linkages tie together trade, financial markets, technology, and living standards in an unprecedented way. They were first widely recognized during the worldwide oil shock of the 1970s and have been apparent since then. A freeze in Brazil and its effect on coffee production are felt around the world. The sudden decline in the value of the Mexican peso affected financial markets in all emerging economies and had an impact in Poland, Hungary, and the Czech Republic. Iraq's invasion of Kuwait and the resulting Persian Gulf War affected oil prices, stock markets, trade, and travel flows in all corners of the earth.

International business has also brought a global reorientation in production strategies. Only a few decades ago, for example, it would have been thought impossible to produce parts for a car in more than one country, assemble it in another, and sell it in yet other countries around the world. Yet such global strategies, coupled with production and distribution sharing, are common today. Firms are also linked to each other through global supply agreements and joint undertakings in research and development. The Ford Motor Co. "Global Car" program as discussed in Global Learning Experience 1.3 is one example of the scope and complexity involved in worldwide supply, production, and marketing.

Firms and governments are recognizing production's worldwide effects on the environment common to all. For example, high acid production in one area may cause acid rain in another. Pollution in one country may result in water contamination in another. These concerns result in global action by some firms and heightened awareness by governments and consumers.

It is not just the production of products that has become global. Increasingly, service firms are part of the global scene. Banks and their financial services, insurance companies, software firms, and universities are participating to a growing degree in the global marketplace.

In the past, most of the global business conducted by U.S. companies was done by the largest firms. Now, aided by the continuing weakness of the U.S. dollar, small and midsize U.S. companies are beginning to see the profit potential in foreign markets. Global Learning Experience 1.4 indicates the reasons for a shift in strategy by small and midsize U.S. firms.

The level of international investment is at an unprecedented high. Multinational corporations making these investments have become corporate giants which, in terms of annual sales, can be greater than the gross national product of some nations. If one were to rank the large multinational companies, using annual sales, together with the countries of the world, using gross national product, it would be evident that General Motors, Ford, and IBM, to mention only a few companies, are probably larger than half the nations of the world.

The level of international investment is at an unprecedented high. The United States, after having been a net creditor to the world for many decades, has been a world debtor since 1985. This means that the United States owes more to foreign institutions and individuals than it owes to U.S. entities. The shifts in financial flows have had major effects on international direct investment into plants as well. As Table 1.2 shows, the U.S. affiliates of foreign companies employ 12 percent of U.S. manufacturing employees. Many U.S. office buildings are held by foreign landlords. The opening of plants abroad and in the United States increasingly takes the place of trade. All these developments make us more and more dependent on one another.

QUESTION *This, the fourth largest continent in the world with an area of 6,883,000 square miles is home to 302 million people. (Hint: virtually the whole continent lies east of Savannah, Georgia.)*

South America.

Small U.S. Firms Are Moving Forward in the Global Marketplace

A report by the United Nations confirms what the U.S. business community is all too aware of: small and medium-size companies in the United States are far behind their counterparts in other countries in setting up foreign operations. Compared with Japan and Western Europe, the United States has a relatively small percentage of corporate direct investment abroad from companies with less than 500 employees at their home sites. Small and medium-size U.S. companies had $15 billion in foreign direct investments, 3 percent of the U.S. total. Japanese companies of similar size had $40 billion (15 percent) and developed European countries had about $43 billion (7.5 percent), according to the report.

Hopes are, however, that this tendency within the United States will shift as global business accelerates. There are some encouraging signs. The larger size of the U.S. marketplace was the main reason so many smaller companies tended to stay home, according to one of the authors of the report. Now, U.S. overseas presence has taken a big jump since the early 1980s because even small and medium-size companies are beginning to feel competition from less developed countries. In addition, more firms are finding it easier to manage foreign operations or a joint venture because "recent technological developments in communications, transportation, and financial services have enabled firms of all sizes to better exploit international opportunities."

The growth in exports by U.S. companies of all sizes may well accelerate the pace of direct investments, according to John Williams, chief global economist of Bankers Trust Company. The weakness of the dollar, which makes U.S. goods cheaper for foreign customers, is giving many companies their first taste of foreign sales, he noted. "In the mid-1980s, when the dollar was much stronger, far fewer U.S. companies could compete."

Adds John Endean, vice president of the American Business Conference, "What we found with our members was that they start as exporters and move very quickly to rolling out direct investments to enhance or supplant their export strategy."

SOURCE: Fred R. Beakley, "Smaller Firms in U.S. Avoid Business Abroad," *The Wall Street Journal*, August 24, 1993, p. A7.

This interdependence, however, is not stable. On virtually a daily basis, realignments take place on both micro and macro levels that make past orientations at least partially obsolete. For example, for its first 200 years, the United States looked to Europe for markets and sources of supply. Despite the maintenance of this orientation by many individuals, firms, and policymakers, the reality of trade relationships is gradually changing.

At the same time, entirely new areas for international business activities have opened up. While the East-West juxtaposition had for more than 40 years effectively separated the "Western" economies from the centrally planned ones, the lifting of the Iron Curtain presented a new array of trading and investment partners. As a result, trade and investment flows may again be realigned in different directions. Already, new products and services are being exchanged, and the volume is likely to increase.

Concurrently, an increasing regionalization is taking place around the world, resulting in the split-up of countries in some areas of the world and the development of country and trading blocs in others. Over time, firms may find that the free flow of goods, services, and capital encounters more impediments as regions become more inward-looking.

FIGURE 1.2 The Changing U.S. Share of World Trade

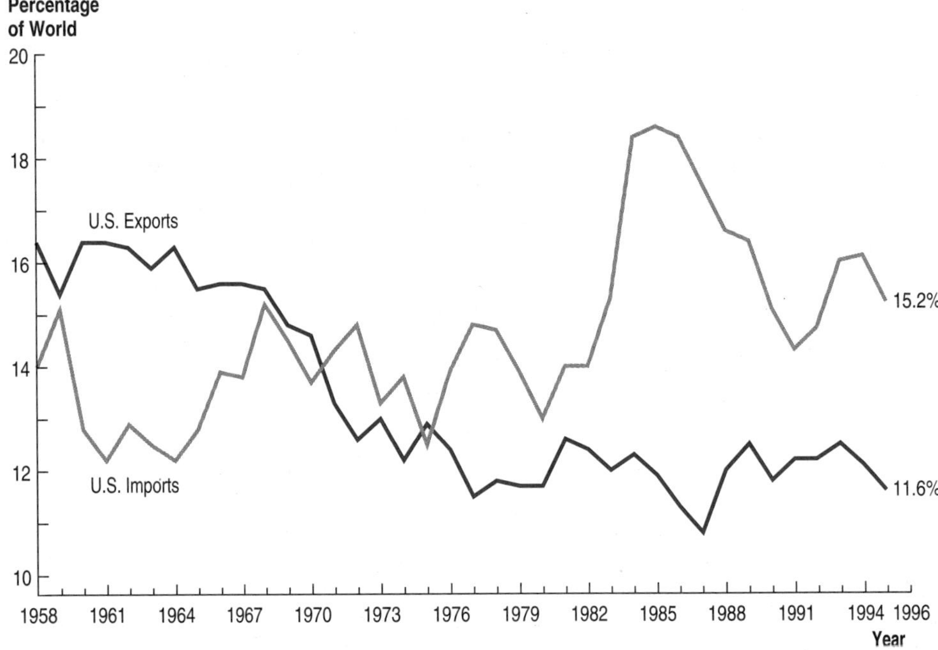

SOURCE: International Monetary Fund (IMF), September 1996.

Not only is the environment changing, but the pace of change is accelerating. "A boy who saw the Wright brothers fly for a few seconds at Kitty Hawk in 1903 could have watched the Apollo II land on the moon in 1969. The first electronic computer was built in 1946; today, the world rushes from the mechanical into the electronic age. The double helix was first unveiled in 1953; today biotechnology threatens to remake mankind."[2]

These changes and the speed with which they come about significantly affect countries, corporations, and individuals. During the past few decades, the United States was seen as the hub of world trade. While the United States is still the locomotive that drives market flows, its participation in world trade measured as a portion of world market share in exports has declined drastically as shown in Figure 1.2. In the late 1950s the United States accounted for approximately 19 percent of the world's exports; by 1995 this figure had declined to the 11 percent level. During the same period the U.S. share of world imports increased from 12 percent to 15 percent. As a result, from a global perspective, the United States has lost some of its importance as a supplier to the world but has gained importance as a market for the world.

THE CURRENT U.S. INTERNATIONAL TRADE POSITION

Table 1.3 indicates the dollar value of U.S. exports and imports of merchandise and services from 1970 through 1996. As shown in the table, U.S. exports of merchandise and services have increased from $56.7 billion in 1970 to more than $848.8 billion in 1996. This represents an increase of $792.1 billion over the 26-year period. Imports of merchandise and services, on the other hand, have increased more rapidly, rising from $54.4 billion in 1970 to $959.8 billion in 1996—an increase of 1,964 percent. The result is that the United States, which had realized a trade surplus in the early to mid-1970s, is now experiencing significant trade deficits in merchandise: $191.1 billion in 1996, partially offset by a $80.1 billion surplus in services—a net deficit of $111.0 billion.

TABLE 1.3 **U.S. International Merchandise and Services Transactions, 1970, 1975, 1980, 1985 and 1990–1996 (in billions of dollars)**

	1970	1975	1980	1985	1990	1991	1992	1993	1994	1995	1996
Exports											
Merchandise	42.5	107.1	224.3	215.9	389.3	416.9	440.4	456.8	502.4	575.9	612.1
Services	14.2	25.5	47.6	73.2	147.8	164.2	177.2	186.7	197.2	218.7	236.7
Total	56.7	132.6	271.9	289.1	537.1	581.1	617.6	643.5	699.6	794.6	848.8
Imports											
Merchandise	39.9	98.2	249.8	338.1	498.3	491.0	536.5	589.4	668.6	749.4	803.2
Services	14.5	22.0	41.5	72.9	120.0	121.2	120.3	126.4	135.5	147.0	156.6
Total	54.4	120.2	291.3	411.0	618.3	612.2	656.8	715.8	804.1	896.4	959.8
Trade Surplus (Deficit)											
Merchandise	2.6	8.9	(25.5)	(122.2)	(109.0)	(74.1)	(96.1)	(132.6)	(166.2)	(173.5)	(191.1)
Services	(.3)	3.5	6.1	.3	27.8	43.0	56.9	60.3	61.8	71.7	80.1
Total	2.3	12.4	(19.4)	(121.9)	(81.2)	(31.1)	(39.2)	(72.3)	(104.4)	(101.8)	(111.0)
Memo:											
Balance on Current Account	2.3	18.1	2.3	(124.2)	(94.7)	(9.5)	(62.6)	(99.9)	(148.4)	(148.2)	(165.6)

SOURCE: U.S. Department of Commerce, *Survey of Current Business* (Washington, DC: U.S. Government Printing Office, July 1997) 64 and 65.

It should also be noted that the merchandise trade deficit declined from a temporary high point of $159.6 billion in 1987 (not shown) by approximately one-half, to $74.1 billion, in 1991. Since 1991, the merchandise trade deficit grew significantly to $191.1 billion in 1996—an increase of $117.0 billion in just 5 years.

Throughout the 1970–1996 period, the United States has realized satisfactory balances in services. As shown in Table 1.3, services balance improved from a nominal deficit of $0.3 billion in 1970 to a surplus of $80.1 billion in 1996. Despite the dramatic improvement in services, it has not been sufficient to offset the deficit in merchandise. Essentially, the data in Table 1.3 indicate that the United States is buying more from foreigners than it is selling to them. The result is that the United States has experienced an overall trade deficit every year since 1976—a total of 20 years of consecutive trade deficits—reaching a level of $111.0 billion in 1996. The implications of this situation for the future of the United States will be covered in detail in Chapter 3.

An occasional merchandise trade deficit is normally not a cause for concern. However, continuous, long-run U.S. trade deficits of the large amounts shown in Table 1.3, can become a major problem for the United States for two reasons. First, large trade deficits add to the U.S. international debt which must eventually be repaid. Second, and of more immediate significance, is the loss of potential jobs for U.S. citizens. It is estimated that $1 billion in exports creates approximately 22,800 jobs.[3] Thus, an increase in exports is not only good for the United States in the long run, but would help to reduce unemployment as well. U.S. exports are increasing, but not fast enough. It is estimated that 2,500 companies account for most U.S. exports and that tens of thousands of U.S. companies are capable of entering export markets but are not doing so. As noted in Global Learning Experience 1.5, the Avon Company has found that there are profits to be made overseas in the most unlikely business ventures.

When the Avon Lady Calls—Globally

Avon began in 1886 as a regional U.S. company. Today, it is a global enterprise serving the cosmetic and beauty needs of consumers in 125 countries. When many companies are just beginning to discover the virtues of "going global," Avon can speak from experience about the inherent benefits of being a global enterprise.

A key to Avon's global success is the strategy of using and building on the remarkable strength of direct selling to customers. Throughout the world, there are nearly 2,000,000 Avon representatives: 445,000 in the United States and, surprisingly, 25,000 in China. In Brazil alone there are 400,000 representatives, about twice as many as the 200,000 people in the Brazilian army.

In 1996, Avon representatives around the world generated over 650 million customer transactions, earning nearly $2 billion for themselves in the process. In some developing countries, many Avon representatives are the principal source of family support and often earn well above the median income level.

Supporting the global direct selling effort is the Avon "Store," the sales brochure that representatives bring to customers for each selling campaign. Avon prints more than 650 million brochures annually in more than a dozen different languages.

Avon's strategy of aggressive global expansion anticipates increased growth in emerging markets like China, Indonesia, and Eastern Europe, and the penetration of new markets, such as India, South Africa, Romania, and the Ukraine.

Eventually every woman in the world will probably be called on by an Avon representative, and someday in the future, should humans inhabit distant planets, don't be surprised if the telephone in outer space rings and the voice says, "Avon calling."

SOURCE: Avon Products Co.

FIGURE 1.3 **Exports and Imports Per Capita for Selected Countries, 1995**

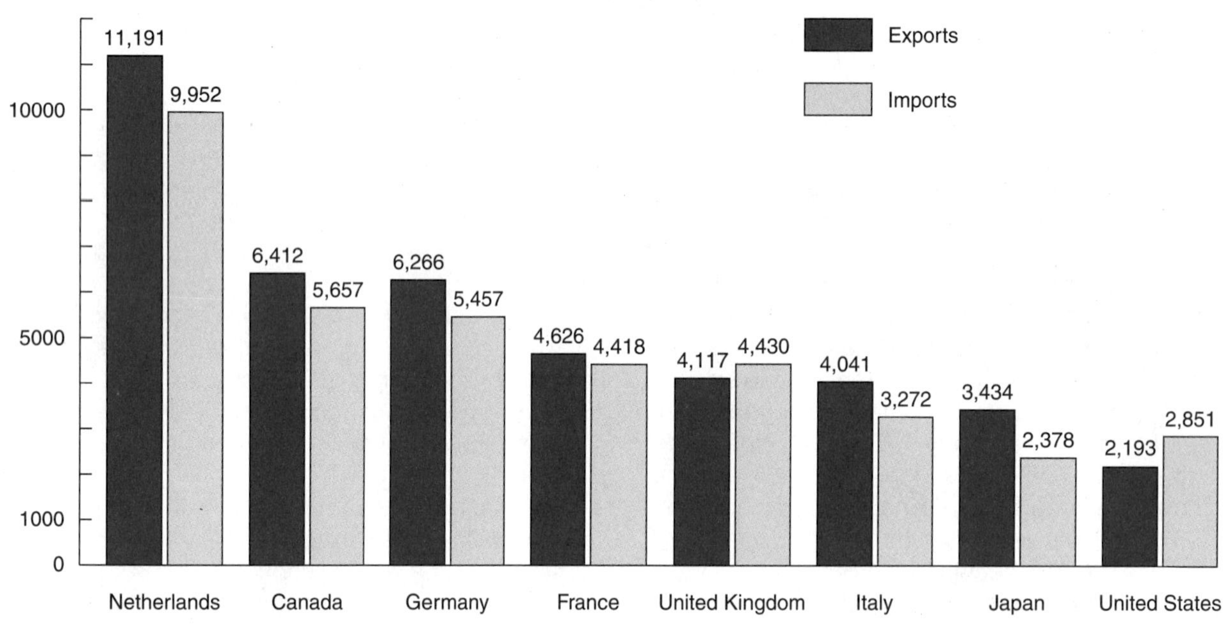

SOURCE: *IMF International Financial Statistics,* August, 1996, Washington, D.C.

per capita
the average dollar value of exports and imports for each person in a country

The authors take the position that the realities of economic life will force most of these export-capable firms to "go global"; they will either "export or die." This is the basis for our belief that *global business is the future* and that students who prepare for global business careers now will be well rewarded in the years ahead.

Another way to look at how competitive the United States is in the global export market is to compare the dollar value of exports and imports **per capita** (for each person in a country) with those of other countries. Figure 1.3 indicates the 1995 per capita exports and imports for the United States and selected countries. The data make the point clear that the value of U.S. exports for each person in the country is lower than that of any of the other countries shown. While the United States exports $2,193 per capita, the Germans export $6,266, the Canadians $6,412, and the Netherland Dutch $11,191. In terms of percentages, the United States exports only 34 percent of what Canada does on a per capita basis and 20 percent of what the Netherlands does. These data do not paint a pretty picture of U.S. export activity, at least at the moment. If and when U.S. businesses aggressively embrace the "export or die" philosophy, they can take advantage of the tremendous amount of potential business that is possible, as shown by the data in Figure 1.3. For example, based on the data presented so far in this chapter, if U.S. exports per capita could be increased by $1,000, say, from $2,193 to $3,193, approximately 5,700,000 new jobs would be created in the United States—more than enough to solve this country's unemployment problems.

The U.S. Merchandise Trade Deficit

To further understand the nature of the U.S. merchandise trade deficit, the reader is directed to Table 1.4. As analysis of 1996 trade data reveals, most of the U.S. merchan-

TABLE 1.4

Analysis of 1996 U.S. Merchandise Trade Surplus/(Deficit) (in millions of dollars)

	U.S. Exports To	U.S. Imports From	U.S. Trade Surplus/ (Deficit)	Percent of U.S. Total Surplus/(Deficit)
Pacific Rim Countries				
Japan	$ 65,954	$115,167	$ (49,213)	(25.7%)
China	11,938	51,511	(39,573)	(20.7)
Subtotal	77,892	166,678	(88,786)	(46.4)
Other Pacific Rim Countries	113,090	134,605	(21,515)	(11.3)
Total Pacific Rim	190,982	301,283	(110,301)	(57.7)
NAFTA Countries				
Canada	134,609	158,640	(24,031)	(12.6)
Mexico	56,735	75,108	(18,373)	(9.6)
Total NAFTA Countries	191,344	233,748	(42,404)	(22.2)
Other Major Countries				
United Kingdom	30,246	28,832	1,414	0.7
Germany	22,970	38,831	(15,861)	(8.3)
France	14,454	18,630	(4,176)	(2.2)
Netherlands	16,501	7,473	9,028	4.7
Italy	8,621	18,294	(9,673)	(5.1)
Belgium and Luxembourg	12,685	9,499	3,186	1.7
Saudi Arabia*	7,311	10,467	(3,155)	(1.7)
Brazil	12,347	8,773	3,574	1.9
Total Other Major Countries	125,135	140,799	(15,663)	(8.3)
All Other Countries	104,608	127,409	(22,801)	(11.9)
Total United States	$612,069	$803,239	$(191,170)	100.0

Other Pacific Rim includes: Hong Kong, S. Korea, Singapore, Taiwan, Indonesia*, Malaysia*, Philippines*, Thailand*, Australia, New Zealand, Brunei*, Macao* and Papua New Guinea*.

SOURCE: U.S. Department of Commerce, *Survey of Current Business*, July 1997, Tables 1 and 2, p. 64–65 and 74–76. Data marked * from *Report FT-900*, Annual Revision for 1996.

WWW

dise trade deficit originates in countries commonly referred to as the **Pacific Rim.** The total 1996 U.S. trade deficit with the entire world was $191.1 billion. Table 1.4 shows that the U.S. merchandise trade deficit with the Pacific Rim countries was $110.3 billion, or 58 percent of the total. Over 46 percent of the total deficit is the result of trade with Japan and China. Another area of interest is trade with Canada and Mexico; combined they accounted for approximately 22 percent of the U.S. merchandise trade deficit. The United States had 1996 trade deficits with other countries, but those deficits were smaller than those with Japan and China, and Canada and Mexico.

Pacific Rim
developed and newly industrialized countries (NIC) of the Far East, including Japan, China, Hong Kong, South Korea, Singapore, Taiwan, Indonesia, Malaysia, Philippines, Thailand, Australia, New Zealand, Brunei, Macao, and Papua New Guinea

Trade with Japan and China

Figure 1.4 presents the record of U.S. merchandise trade with Japan and China for the 1985–1996 period. The deficit with Japan, which was $43.5 billion in 1985, appears to have peaked in 1994 at $67.3 billion and since then declined to $60.4 billion in 1995 and $49.2 billion in 1996.

FIGURE 1.4 **The Growth of the U.S. Merchandise Trade Deficit with Japan and China, 1985–1996 (in billions of dollars)**

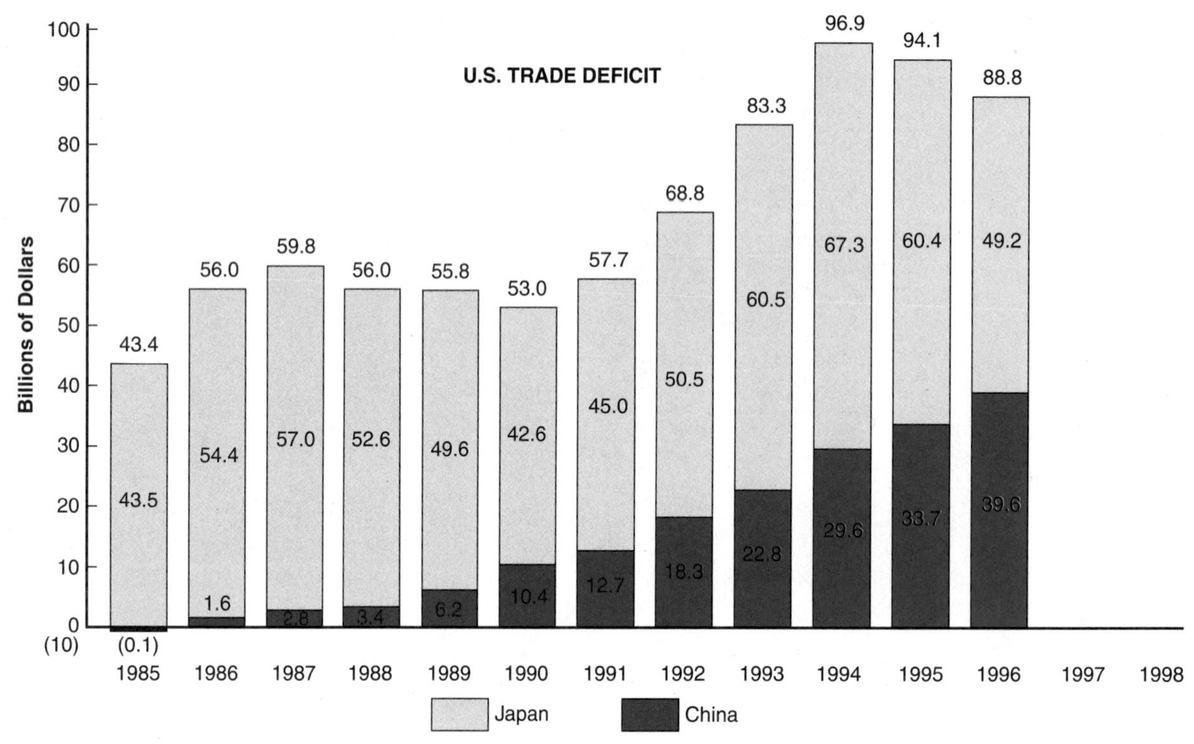

SOURCE: U.S. Department of Commerce, *Survey of Current Business,* July 1997, Tables 1 and 2, p. 64–65 and 74–76.

During 1985–1996, the Japanese spread financial influence, investment, technology, and manufacturing know-how to many of its Pacific Rim neighbors. In effect the United States is not dealing with one Japan, but a number of Japans of various sizes. Indeed the trade data hide the fact that many Japanese companies have invested in manufacturing facilities in other Pacific Rim countries that export to the United States. However, those exports are not identified as Japanese exports, and the result is that the total amount of exports to the United States that is under Japanese control is probably much greater than the trade data indicate.

Of equal importance is U.S. trade with the Peoples Republic of China. In 1985, the United States had a slight trade surplus with China that has reversed dramatically to the 1996 deficit level of $39.6 billion. This compared with the U.S. trade deficit of $49.2 billion with Japan. The declining U.S. trade deficit with Japan and the increasing deficit with China suggest that in 1997 the deficit with China will be the greater of the two.

China, with its large supply of low-cost labor and improving technological base, is becoming increasingly competitive in global markets and, as noted in Global Learning Experience 1.6, is showing its newly found global financial and trade power.

The World's Tallest Building—in Shanghai?

Americans, and particularly New Yorkers, have long regarded New York City as the only appropriate place to erect the world's tallest buildings. The Empire State Building and the Twin Towers of the World Trade Center symbolize New York as a place of power and influence; a place where big deals are put together by the financial wizards of Wall Street and the most powerful people in the United States. This demanded, not just tall buildings, but the tallest in the world, consistent with the city's image. Now the centers of power are moving to the Pacific Rim and with them the symbols of that power—tall buildings. The new tall buildings in Asia are reminders that the economies of the Pacific Rim are more robust and growing faster than any other area of the globe. They signal the rise of dynamic forces that are propelling the Pacific Rim economies to the center stage of global business. Construction of the tallest skyscraper in the world, the Shanghai World Financial Tower, has just begun to be completed in 2001. The 10 tallest buildings in the world are:

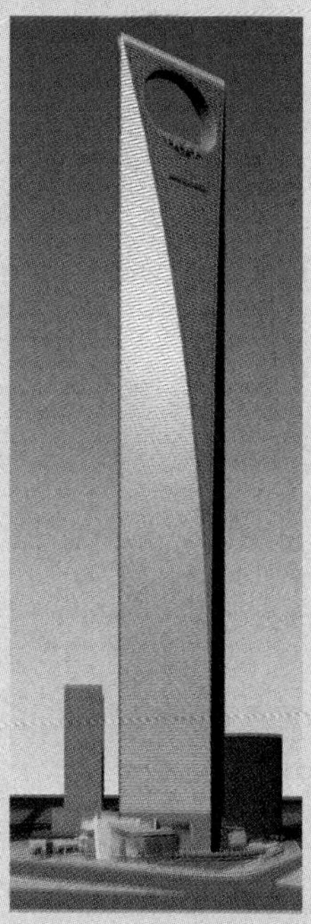

The Shanghai World Financial Tower. The tower is under construction and scheduled for completion in 2001.

Rank	Building	City	Year Completed /Scheduled Completion	Stories	Height (in feet)
1.	Shanghai World Financial Tower	Shanghai, China	2001	95	1,509
2.	Petronas Tower 1	Kuala Lumpur, Malaysia	1996	88	1,483
3.	Petronas Tower 2	Kuala Lumpur, Malaysia	1996	88	1,483
4.	Sears Tower	Chicago, USA	1974	110	1,450
5.	Jin Mao Building	Shanghai, China	1998	88	1,379
6.	World Trade Center, One	New York, USA	1972	110	1,368
7.	World Trade Center, Two	New York, USA	1973	110	1,362
8.	Empire State Building	New York, USA	1931	102	1,250
9.	Central Plaza	Hong Kong, China	1992	78	1,227
10.	Bank of China Tower	Hong Kong, China	1989	70	1,209

Data furnished by Council on Tall Buildings and Urban Habitat, Lehigh University.
Photo by Kohn Pedersen Fox Associates, Architects.

FIGURE 1.5 **The Growth of the U.S. Merchandise Trade Deficit with Canada and Mexico, 1985–1996 (in billions of dollars)**

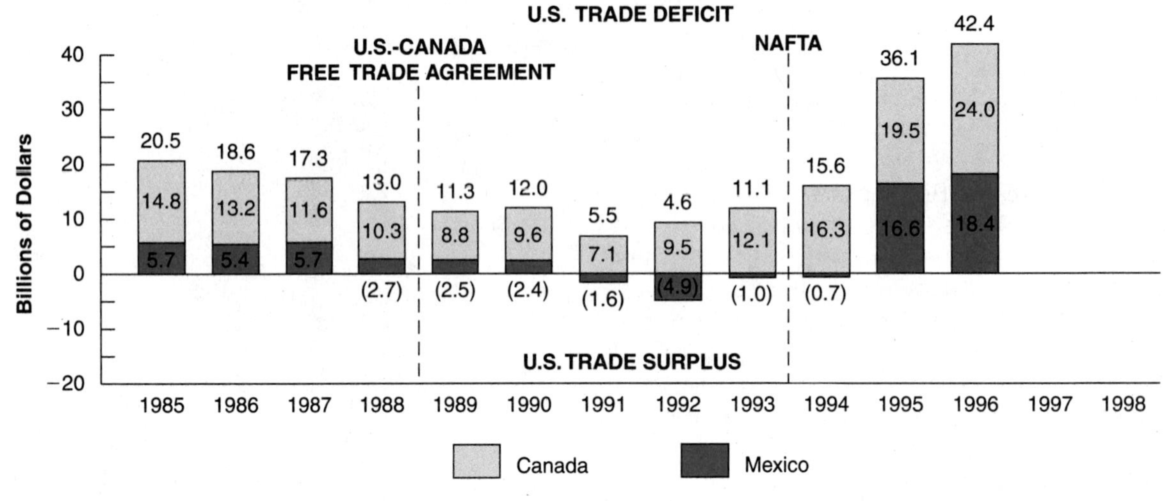

SOURCE: U.S. Department of Commerce, *Survey of Current Business,* July 1997, Tables 1 and 2, p. 64–65 and 74–76.

Trade with Canada and Mexico

NAFTA
North American Free Trade Agreement; agreement among Canada, the United States, and Mexico to lower and/or eliminate tariff barriers among the three countries in order to stimulate trade

Figure 1.5 illustrates the magnitude of U.S. merchandise trade deficits with Canada and Mexico from 1985 through 1996. In the evaluation of these data, the reader is asked to consider that **NAFTA** (the North American Free Trade Agreement among the United States, Canada, and Mexico) went into effect on January 1, 1994.

U.S. merchandise trade with Canada, during the period under study, resulted in a U.S. trade deficit each of the 12 years. From 1985 through 1992, the deficit declined from $14.8 billion to $7.1 billion—a decrease of approximately 50 percent. However, it is interesting to note that since 1991, the downward trend in the deficit with Canada reversed course and increased significantly from the 1991 level of $7.1 billion to a record of $24.0 billion in 1996. Further, the U.S. deficit with Canada rose from the pre-NAFTA level of $12.1 billion in 1993 to $24.0 billion in 1996, an increase of $11.9 billion or almost 100 percent in just three years.

Merchandise trade with Mexico during the same period followed a pattern similar to that of Canada, but much more dramatic. In 1985 the United States realized a merchandise trade deficit with Mexico of $5.7 billion. That deficit declined over the 1985–1996 period, becoming a U.S. trade surplus of $1.6 billion in 1991 and $4.9 billion in 1992. From that point, the U.S. surplus position diminished to $0.7 billion in 1994—the first year of the NAFTA agreement. In 1995, the 1994 surplus of $0.7 billion became a large deficit of $16.6 billion, a change of almost $17 billion, and then increased dramatically to $18.4 billion in 1996—also a record deficit level. Combined deficits with Canada and Mexico amounted to $42.4 billion, or 22 percent of the U.S. merchandise trade deficit in 1996.

TRADING PARTNERS

In this final section of Chapter 1, we briefly consider those countries with which the United States does most of its international business. The large volume of business that the United States does with its **trading partners** can have important implications for a variety of U.S. commercial and foreign policies relative to those countries.

trading partners
other countries with which a country does business

Table 1.5 indicates the total volume of merchandise trade between the United States and its major trading partners during 1996. The data at the very top of Table 1.5 are the basis for some of the most important U.S. initiatives in commerce and diplomacy. It is interesting to note that of the three top U.S. trading partners, two, Canada and Mexico, are the United States' neighbors to the north and south. The large dollar value of business among the United States, Canada, and Mexico is the basis for the North American Free Trade Agreement. This agreement has been accepted by the three governments and it is thought that it will have a far-reaching impact on employment in the United States.

Another area of policy concern for the United States is that with China. Table 1.5 shows that the U.S. trade deficit with that country (39.5 billion) is one of the largest,

TABLE 1.5

Major U.S. Trading Partners Based on 1996 Merchandise Exports and Imports (in millions of dollars)

Country	Rank	U.S. Exports	U.S. Imports	Total Merchandise Trade	Memo: U.S. Trade Surplus/(Deficit)
Canada	1	$134,609	$158,640	$293,249	$(24,031)
Japan	2	65,954	115,167	181,121	(49,213)
Mexico	3	56,735	75,108	131,843	(18,373)
China	4	11,938	51,511	63,449	(39,573)
Germany	5	22,970	38,831	61,801	(15,861)
United Kingdom	6	30,246	28,832	59,078	1,414
Korea	7	25,653	22,611	48,264	3,042
Taiwan	8	17,540	29,902	47,442	(12,362)
Singapore	9	16,253	20,338	36,591	(4,085)
France	10	14,454	18,630	33,084	(4,176)
Italy	11	8,621	18,294	26,915	(9,673)
Malaysia*	12	8,546	17,829	26,375	(9,283)
Netherlands	13	16,501	7,473	23,974	9,028
Hong Kong	14	13,873	9,854	23,727	4,019
Belgium/Luxembourg	15	12,685	9,499	22,184	(4,138)
Brazil	16	12,347	8,773	21,120	3,574
Thailand*	17	7,198	11,336	18,534	(4,138)
Venezuela	18	4,665	13,171	17,836	(8,506)
Saudi Arabia*	19	7,311	10,467	17,778	(3,155)
Switzerland*	20	8,373	7,793	16,166	580

SOURCE: U.S. Department of Commerce, *Survey of Current Business,* July 1997. 64–65 and 74–76. Data marked * from *Report FT-900,* Annual Revision for 1996.

QUESTION *São Paulo is a major industrial city in this country.*

Brazil.

McDonald's is one example of a U.S. business organization that realized early the opportunities available through international activities. McDonald's actively continues expansion. The company has restaurants in 66 countries with a total of 13,000 restaurants worldwide: 9,000 domestically and 4,000 internationally.
SOURCE: © 1987 David Pollack/ The Stock Market.

second only to Japan. China benefits from a growing volume of trade with the United States. In exchange for access to U.S. markets, American diplomats are putting pressure on China to correct what are believed to be violations of human rights by the Chinese government; for example, political suppression and slave labor. These matters are of concern to democratic governments around the world and are reported widely in the press and on radio.

With respect to Japan, scarcely a day goes by without some mention in newspapers or on radio of U.S. efforts aimed at getting the Japanese to open their markets to American-made goods.

STRUCTURE OF THE BOOK

This book was written to help students become more knowledgeable and thus better prepared for careers in a globally oriented business world. It is also the authors' intention that the text serve as a foundation for other individuals seeking to expand their understanding of the world around them. The text blends theory and practice in an easy-to-read and understand style of writing. It provides a balance between theoretical concepts and practical knowledge that can be useful in understanding how global business firms function day to day. The book addresses the needs of not just the large global and multinational business firms but also the many thousands of small U.S. businesses that will be entering the global marketplace in the years to come.

SUMMARY

Although trade among nations has been conducted for thousands of years, the importance of international trade to U.S. business firms, both large and small, is something that has been recognized in just the past few years. As markets in the United States have become saturated with U.S. and foreign-made goods, American companies are being forced to look for new markets. The reality of the saturation is that if U.S. firms do not involve themselves in global business, they probably will not survive. Rallying under the battle cry of "export or die," more and more U.S. companies are turning their attention to global business opportunities. However, the total number of companies involved is still too few.

On a national policy level, increased exports will mean more jobs for American workers, which in turn will help improve the standard of living for all Americans. The pressure of having large U.S. trade deficits with its trading partners (and the related loss of U.S. jobs) has placed political pressures on the current administration. These pressures have led to a variety of commercial and diplomatic initiatives by the U.S. government intended to create a more level balance of trade.

Key Terms and Concepts

isolationism
affiliates of foreign corporations
exporting
importing
merchandise
services
portfolio capital
direct investment
domestic company
global company
multinational company
per capita
Pacific Rim
NAFTA

Questions for Discussion

1. Will future expansion of global business be similar to that in the past? Why or why not?
2. Discuss the reasons for the decline in the U.S. world trade market share.
3. Does increased global business mean increased risk?
4. Is it beneficial for nations to become dependent on one another?
5. With wages in some countries at one-tenth of U.S. wages, how can the United States compete?
6. What makes a multinational firm different from a global firm?
7. What contribution could increased exports make in lowering unemployment in the United States?
8. Look in your local newspaper and find an article on global business and bring it to class for discussion.

Recommended Readings

Czinkota, Michael R., Ilkka A. Ronkainen, and John J. Tarrant. *The Global Marketing Imperative.* Chicago: NTC, 1995.

Hassan, Salah S., and Erdener Kaynak. *Globalization of Consumer Markets: Structures and Strategies.* New York: International Business Press, 1994.

Marquardt, Michael J., and Angus Reynolds. *The Global Learning Organization.* Burr Ridge, Ill.: Irwin, 1994.

Naisbitt, John. *Global Paradox.* New York: William Morrow, 1994.

Porter, Michael E. *The Competitive Advantage of Nations.* New York: The Free Press, 1990.

Reich, Robert B. *The Work of Nations: Preparing Ourselves for 21st-Century Capitalism.* New York: Random House, 1992.

Tyson, Laura D. *Who's Bashing Whom? Trade Conflict in High-Technology Industries.* Washington, D.C.: Institute of International Economics, 1992.

Wolf, Charles, Jr. *Linking Economic Policy and Foreign Policy.* New Brunswick, N.J.: Transaction Publishers, 1991.

Notes

1. *Oxford Dictionary of Quotations,* New Edition, 4th Edition. Edited by A. Partington (Oxford University Press, Oxford, England, 1992), 202–23.
2. Arthur M. Schlesinger, Jr., *The Cycles of American History* (Boston: Houghton Mifflin, 1986), xi.
3. Lester A. Davis, *Contribution of Exports to U.S. Employment: 1980–87* (Washington, D.C.: U.S. Government Printing Office, 1989).

The Theory of Global Trade and Investment

LEARNING OBJECTIVES

To understand the traditional arguments as to how and why global trade improves the welfare of all countries.

To review the history and compare the implications of trade theory from the original work of Adam Smith to the contemporary theories of Michael Porter.

To examine the criticisms of classical trade theory and examine alternative viewpoints of what business and economic forces determine trade patterns between countries.

To understand how the trade in goods is directly related to issues of international investment.

GLOBAL LEARNING EXPERIENCE 2.1

The Spanish Treasure Fleets—Bringing Treasure from the New World

The Spanish exploration of the New World in search for precious metals was very successful. In addition to gold, the discovery of vast deposits of silver in Potosi Mountain in Peru (now Bolovia), emeralds in Colombia, and pearls on the Island of Margarita were to provide the Spanish Crown with desperately needed financing. Between 1492 and 1830, the Spaniards minted a total of 4,035,156,000 pesos of gold and silver from the mines of the New World.

To bring this treasure to the Port of Seville, the Spanish developed the *flota* system—or convoys of galleons. These treasure ships would pick up their precious cargo in various locations in the Americas, rendezvous at Nombre deDios in Panama, and become a vast treasure-laden convoy for the return trip across the Atlantic Ocean to Spain. By all accounts, there was so much silver bullion to be shipped that it was literally stacked on the streets of Nombre deDios. The concentration of so much treasure in one place created a problem—pirates. In one account, the British pirate Francis Drake invaded and seized Nombre deDios. There in the governor's house he found silver awaiting shipment to Spain. The stack of 35- to 70-pound silver bars measured 70 feet long, 10 feet high, and 12 feet deep. Unfortunately for pirate Drake, the quantity of silver was too great for his small ships to carry, and he left with a few chests of gold, precious stones, and pearls.

The voyage of the treasure fleet to Spain was a hazardous undertaking at best. The combination of heavily loaded and top heavy ships, the treacherous waters of the Caribbean and Florida, poor navigation, and the Atlantic hurricane season took its toll on the treasure galleons, many of which were lost at sea or delayed in reaching Spain. The importance of the treasure from the New World to Spain can be readily understood from the following dispatch sent by the Venetian ambassador in Spain to the doge in September 1567:

> At the time of writing my last dispatch to you, I informed you that there was great anxiety all over Spain, over the delay of the arrival of the treasure fleet from the Indies and, when the Genoese bankers informed the King that unless the fleet reached port shortly, that they would be unable to negotiate any further loans for him, Philip II fell into such a state of shock that he had to be confined to bed by his physicians. The King then ordered about 10,000 Ducats, which was about all the treasure left in his royal coffers, to be sent all over his realm and distributed to various churches and monasteries for the saying of masses for the safe arrival of the treasure fleet. I am happy to inform you that news has just arrived from Seville that the fleet has made port safely and there is now great rejoicing not only here in the Royal Court, but all over the land as well.

The above account was by no means exceptional; in fact, it was almost a yearly occurrence over a period of three centuries. The importance of the Indies treasure was such that any delay in its arrival damaged Spanish credit disastrously and caused concern in all the major financial centers of Europe. The Spanish Crown was constantly in debt to international bankers, sometimes pledging its share of the Indies treasure to these bankers for as much as four or five years in advance.

The treasure from the New World also benefitted other European nations as well. About 95 percent of it ended in the hands of other European nations in payment for their exports to Spain and became the precious metals on which their monetary systems were based.

SOURCE: Adapted from Marx, Robert E., *Shipwrecks of the Western Hemisphere: 1492–1825,* David McKay Co., Inc., New York, 1971.

Global trade is one of the oldest and most fundamental concepts in business or economics. The debates, the costs, the benefits, and the dilemmas of global trade have, in many ways, not changed significantly from the time when Marco Polo crossed the wilderness of Eurasia. Currently, global trade has been hotly debated with the agreement among the United States, Canada, and Mexico for the elimination of tariffs on imports under NAFTA (the North American Free Trade Agreement). Although the agreement was reached in anticipation of increasing total economic activity in North America, its effects are still in dispute.

Fundamental to the study of global business is the attempt to understand the nature of global trade; how it changes over time and how it affects the societies participating in the trading process. This chapter provides a path through hundreds of years in the development of thought on why and how trade and investment across national boundaries occurs.

THE AGE OF MERCANTILISM

mercantilism
political and economic policy encouraging the export of goods in return for gold

barter economy
system of trading one commodity for another

exchange economy
system of trading in which a commodity is exchanged for precious metal equal to the worth of the commodity

The theories, practices, and policies of **mercantilism** spanned a period of approximately 300 years—from about 1500 to about 1800. When Columbus made his historic voyage to the New World (1492), the nations of Europe were in a state of economic stagnation due to a transition from **barter economies** to **exchange economies.** Barter, the old system of trading one commodity for another, had become outmoded and was being replaced by one in which gold and silver coins had been found satisfactory as a medium of exchange.

During the period, international commerce was largely conducted under the authority of governments. The goals of trade were, therefore, the goals of governments. The major European nations of the time were also absorbed with supporting and expanding great colonial possessions around the world. These colonial possessions required fleets, armies, food, and all the other resources the nations could muster. Trade was therefore conducted in a fashion that would fill the government's treasuries to provide the wealth necessary to purchase the resources needed. This was mercantilism.

Though it is rather difficult to generalize concerning the theories and policies of mercantilism, this much may safely be said: One great purpose dominated it, namely, the desire to make the state strong, and the economic basis for strength—wealth—was given great weight. The most important form of wealth was considered to be the precious metals or "treasure." Foreign trade was generally preferred above other forms of industry as best furnishing a supply of the desired form of wealth, and in measuring the success of this policy and of foreign trade, great importance was attached to the so-called "balance of trade."[1]

Several quotes from writers of the mercantilist era are provided to give the reader a sense of the attitudes of that time.

> To Sir Josiah Child, the most important question was, what is to be done to improve the nation's trade to such a degree as to equalize or overbalance our neighbors in our national profit by foreign trade.[2]
>
> Sir William Perry wrote that the great and ultimate effect of trade is not wealth at large, but particular abundance of silver, gold, and jewels, which are not permissible, nor so mutable as other commodities, but are wealth at all times, and all places.... So as the raising of such, and the following of such trade, which does store the country with gold, silver, jewels, etc., is profitable before others.[3]
>
> Thomas Mun noted that "the ordinary means to increase our wealth and treasure is by foreign trade."[4]

In an effort to fill their treasuries with gold and silver, the countries of Europe used a variety of tactics. *Foreign trade,* that is, exporting more than was imported, would result in a net increase in gold. *Restriction of imports* of a variety of goods wanted by the people were used to restrict the out flow of gold from a country. The French government forbade the importation of luxury items on a number of occasions and, in an edict of 1549, forbid the importation of luxury fabrics. Cloth of gold, cloth of silver, embroideries, fringes, velvets and the like were, therefore, to be worn by no one, save only members of the royal family.[5] Import duties, tariffs, and subsidization of exports were also used to maximize the gains from exports over the cost of imports.

Exploration

New sources of gold and silver were also sought. Typical is Spain which, during the period, had virtually no industry and was totally dependent on other nations for manufactured goods. When Columbus brought back small quantities of gold from the New World, the Spanish Crown immediately set about colonizing the newly found territories. Florida and Central and South America were intensely explored by the Spanish Conquistadors in the search for precious metals.

One of the real problems with mercantilism and its fixation on the accumulation of "gold and treasure" was its win-lose logic. Through trade, a nation that exported more than it imported built up a stock of gold (the winner), while the country with imports greater than exports gave up gold (the loser). What never occurred to the mercantilists for approximately 300 years was that two countries could trade and both could gain from trade—a win-win situation.

The demise of mercantilism was inevitable given class structure and the distribution of society's product. As the Industrial Revolution introduced the benefits of mass production to the people, lowering prices and increasing the supplies of goods to all, the exploitation of colonies and trading partners diminished. The eighteenth century saw the development of new types of production and exchange that are more familiar to us today, but the limbs and branches of the international trade tree have never spread very far from its roots. Governments still exercise considerable power and influence on the conduct of trade. Countries such as Taiwan, Japan, and China even today follow policies that are termed neo-mercantilist, attempting to maintain net trade surpluses in all products while accumulating massive amounts of foreign currency reserves and gold.

CLASSICAL TRADE THEORY

Why Do Countries Trade? Although seemingly a simple question, it has proven to be a quite complex one. Since the latter half of the eighteenth century, academicians have been not only struggling to understand what are the motivations and benefits of international trade, but also attempting to identify the causes of why some countries grow faster and wealthier than others through trade.

Figure 2.1 provides an overview of the path of evolution of international trade theory. Although somewhat simplified, it shows the line of development of the major theories put forward over the past two centuries. The line of evolution, which began with the work of Adam Smith and David Ricardo, has continued to advance understanding significantly. The trade theories up through those of Eli Heckscher and Bertil Ohlin were theories of national competition. More recent developments, however, have focused on the industry, the products, and how it may influence which country holds the advantage at certain points in time.

In this chapter, we will examine the following theories of international trade: absolute advantage (Adam Smith, 1776); comparative advantage (David Ricardo, 1817); factor proportions (Eli Heckscher/Bertil Ohlin, 1949–1977); Leontief paradox (Wassily

FIGURE 2.1 **The Evolution of International Trade Theory**

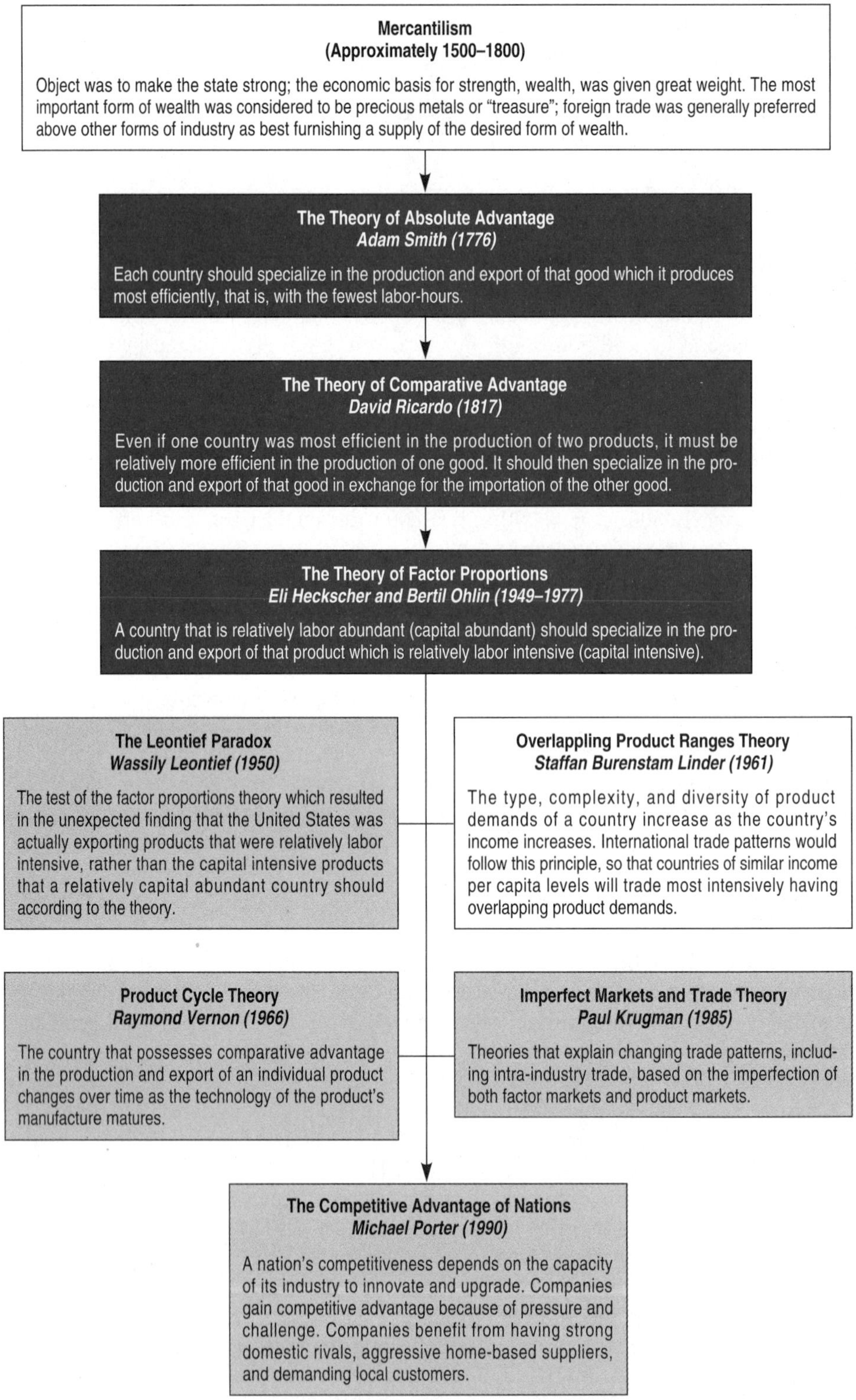

Mercantilism
(Approximately 1500–1800)

Object was to make the state strong; the economic basis for strength, wealth, was given great weight. The most important form of wealth was considered to be precious metals or "treasure"; foreign trade was generally preferred above other forms of industry as best furnishing a supply of the desired form of wealth.

↓

The Theory of Absolute Advantage
Adam Smith (1776)

Each country should specialize in the production and export of that good which it produces most efficiently, that is, with the fewest labor-hours.

↓

The Theory of Comparative Advantage
David Ricardo (1817)

Even if one country was most efficient in the production of two products, it must be relatively more efficient in the production of one good. It should then specialize in the production and export of that good in exchange for the importation of the other good.

↓

The Theory of Factor Proportions
Eli Heckscher and Bertil Ohlin (1949–1977)

A country that is relatively labor abundant (capital abundant) should specialize in the production and export of that product which is relatively labor intensive (capital intensive).

The Leontief Paradox
Wassily Leontief (1950)

The test of the factor proportions theory which resulted in the unexpected finding that the United States was actually exporting products that were relatively labor intensive, rather than the capital intensive products that a relatively capital abundant country should according to the theory.

Overlappling Product Ranges Theory
Staffan Burenstam Linder (1961)

The type, complexity, and diversity of product demands of a country increase as the country's income increases. International trade patterns would follow this principle, so that countries of similar income per capita levels will trade most intensively having overlapping product demands.

Product Cycle Theory
Raymond Vernon (1966)

The country that possesses comparative advantage in the production and export of an individual product changes over time as the technology of the product's manufacture matures.

Imperfect Markets and Trade Theory
Paul Krugman (1985)

Theories that explain changing trade patterns, including intra-industry trade, based on the imperfection of both factor markets and product markets.

↓

The Competitive Advantage of Nations
Michael Porter (1990)

A nation's competitiveness depends on the capacity of its industry to innovate and upgrade. Companies gain competitive advantage because of pressure and challenge. Companies benefit from having strong domestic rivals, aggressive home-based suppliers, and demanding local customers.

Leontief, 1950); overlapping product ranges theory (Staffan Burenstam Linder, 1961); product cycle theory (Raymond Vernon, 1966); imperfect markets and trade theory (Paul Krugman, 1985); and competitive advantage of nations (Michael Porter, 1990).

It should be noted that the various theories of international trade are being presented in an approximate chronological sequence. As is true with most theories, each new theory tries to expand or explain our knowledge of some phenomenon. Accordingly, the reader is urged to view these theories as building blocks in our knowledge of how and why international trade works.

Adam Smith—The Theory of Absolute Advantage

Generally considered to be the Father of Economics, Adam Smith published *The Wealth of Nations* in 1776 in London. In this book, Smith examined the mercantilistic policies of accumulating wealth (gold and silver) and attempted to explain the process by which markets and production actually operate in society. His studies led him to a number of striking results. He concluded that the true wealth of a nation lies not in building a huge stockpile of gold and silver in its treasury, but rather, the real wealth of a nation is an increase in the quality of living of the citizens of that nation—that is, by an increase in *per capita income.*

per capita income
the income of a country divided by the number of its citizens

> The annual labour of every nation is the kind which originally supplies it with all the necessities and conveniences of life which it annually consumes, and which consist always either in the immediate produce of that labour, or in what is purchased with that produce from other nations.
>
> According therefore, as this produce, or what is purchased with it, bears a greater or smaller proportion to the number of those who are to consume it, the nation will be better or worse supplied with all the necessities and conveniences for which it has occasion.

and

> The reasons and causes which have induced almost all modern governments to mortgage some part of this revenue, or to contract debts, and what have been the effects of those debts upon the real wealth, the annual produce of the land and labour of the society.[6]

Production, the creation of a product for exchange, always requires the use of society's primary element of value, human labor. Smith noted that some countries, owing to the skills of their workers or the quality of their natural resources, could produce the same products as others with fewer labor-hours. He termed this efficiency **absolute advantage.**

absolute advantage
the ability to produce a good or service more cheaply than it can be produced elsewhere

Adam Smith observed the production processes of the early stages of the Industrial Revolution in England and recognized the fundamental change that had occurred in production. In previous states of society, a worker performed all stages of a production process, with resulting output that was little more than sufficient for the worker's own needs. The factories of the industrializing world were, however, separating the production process into distinct stages, in which each stage would be performed exclusively by one individual. Smith termed this **division of labor.** This specialization increased the production of workers and industries. Smith's description of the pin factory has long been considered the recognition of one of the most significant principles of the industrial age.

division of labor
assigning stages of production to several individuals rather than each producing an entire good or service

Readers should note that Smith wrote almost 100 years prior to the invention of zippers and Velcro closures so common on modern clothing. In 1776, people used buttons

QUESTION *What is the longest river in South America?*

ANSWER

The Amazon River. At 4,050 miles, it is the longest river in South America, and second longest in the world, after the Nile (4,145 miles), but its volume of water is far more impressive. The Nile carries less than 2 percent of the Amazon's volume. The Amazon contains more water than the Nile, Yangtze and Mississippi Rivers combined—nearly one fifth of the earth's running fresh water. The outpouring of the Amazon River, whose source is in the Peruvian Andes, is so great that the open sea is freshwater for over two hundred miles beyond the mouth of the Amazon. At its broadest as it nears the ocean, the Amazon is forty miles wide. Seasonal tides—called the Pororoca*—send its waters running up river in large waves at thirty-five kilometers per hour. Oceangoing vessels can travel the Amazon all the way to the city of Iquitos in Peru.*

or pins to keep their clothing in place, thus pin making was of some importance at that time. In analyzing the operations of a pin factory employing 10 workers, Smith observed that some workers, each making an entire pin, could make as few as 1 pin a day while the best workers might make only 20 pins a day. The total maximum production would not exceed 200 pins a day. If, however, the pin-making process was divided up and each worker specialized in performing one portion of the process, the daily output could be increased to as many as 48,000 pins.

Adam Smith then extended his division of labor in the production process to a division of labor and specialized product across countries. Each country would specialize in products for which it was uniquely suited. More would be produced for less. Thus, by each country specializing in products for which it possessed absolute advantage, countries could produce more in total and exchange products—trade—for goods that were cheaper in price than those produced at home, and in the process maximize the nation's income and thus per capita income.

David Ricardo—The Theory of Comparative Advantage

Although Smith's work was instrumental in the development of economic theories about trade and production, it did not answer some fundamental questions about trade. First, Smith's trade theory relied on a country possessing an absolute advantage in production but did not explain what caused the production advantages. Second, if a country did not possess an absolute advantage in any product did this mean that it could not (or would not) be able to successfully trade in the global marketplace?

David Ricardo, in his work entitled *The Principles of Political Economy and Taxation,* 1817, sought to take the basic ideas set down by Adam Smith a few logical steps further. Ricardo noted that even if country A possessed an absolute advantage in the production of two products compared with country B, also capable of producing both products, each country might be relatively more efficient in one of the products than the other—what is termed **comparative advantage.** Each country would then possess comparative advantage in the production of one of the two products, and both countries would then benefit by specializing completely in one product and trading for the other. In providing an example of the production of wine and cloth by England and Portugal, Ricardo noted:

comparative advantage
the ability to produce a good or service more cheaply, relative to other goods and services, than other countries

> England may be so circumstanced that to produce the cloth must require the labour of 100 men for one year; and if she attempted to make the wine, it might require the labour of 120 men for the same time. England would therefore find it in her interest to import wine, and to purchase it by the exportation of cloth.
>
> To produce the wine in Portugal might require only the labour of 80 men for one year, and to produce the cloth in the same country might require the labour of 90 men for the same time. It would therefore be advantageous to her to export wine in exchange for cloth. This exchange might even take place notwithstanding that the commodity imported by Portugal could be produced there with less labour than in England. Though she could make the cloth with the labour of 90 men, she would import it from a country where it required the labour of 100 men to produce it, because it would be advantageous to her rather to employ her capital in the production of wine, for which she would obtain more cloth from England, than she could produce by diverting a portion of her capital from the cultivation of vines to the manufacture of cloth.[7]

Unlike mercantilism, which was a win-lose situation, Ricardo's work was significant because it presented the logic of how a country, at an apparent disadvantage relative to other countries, could engage in foreign trade and both countries could gain—a *win-win* situation.

A Numerical Example of Classical Trade Theory

To fully understand the theories of absolute and comparative advantage, consider the following example shown in Table 2.1. Two countries, Germany and Italy, fully using their national resources, are both capable of producing the same two products, machine tools and trucks. As shown, Germany can outproduce Italy in both products—thus, possessing an absolute advantage over Italy in both products. This might lead to the conclusion that Italy would not be able to trade. However, those clever Italians are twice as efficient in the production of trucks relative to machine tools as the Germans. They have a comparative advantage, which they will be able to exploit and gain from international trade. Ricardo pointed out that both countries would be better off if they specialized in what they did best and exchanged the resulting products for what they wished to consume.

Comparative advantage, according to Ricardo, was based on what was given up or traded off in producing one product instead of both. A country cannot possess comparative advantage in the production of both products, so each country has an economic role to play in international trade.

National Production Possibilities Curve

Given that each nation has a limited amount of resources and is capable of producing only two products, a **production possibilities curve** may be constructed which will show all of the possible combinations of the two products that can be produced with the nation's limited resources. If, however, a nation can produce and trade in a way that will yield a quantity of goods and services that is beyond the limits of its production possibilities curve, the gain would be equivalent to an improvement in level of living of that country—an increase in per capita income. Figure 2.2 illustrates the production possibilities curves for Germany and Italy from the preceding example in Table 2.1. If Germany did not trade with any other country, it could only consume the products that it produced itself. It would probably produce and consume some combination of 60 machine tools or 60 trucks. Such as point A in Figure 2.2 (44 units of machine tools and 16 trucks).

production possibilities curve curve designed to show all possible combinations of two products (or output) that can be produced with a nation's limited resources; how much of one product is "traded off" in order to produce another

Italy's production possibilities curve is constructed in the same way. Italy, by itself, can produce and consume some combination of 15 machine tools or 30 trucks, shown

TABLE 2.1 Absolute and Comparative Advantage

	Production Possibilities (Units)		Trade-Off	Production Before Trade		International Trading	Assumed Consumption After Trade		Gains from Trade	
	Machine Tools	Trucks	Ratio	Machine Tools	Trucks	Rate	Machine Tools	Trucks	Machine Tools	Trucks
Germany	60	or 60	1:1	60	—	1:1.5	44	24	—	8
Italy	15	or 30	1:2	—	30	1:1.5	16	6	4	
							60	30		

- Germany has an absolute advantage in the production of both machine tools and trucks. With its national resources, it can outproduce Italy in both products. Italy on the other hand is relatively more efficient in the production of trucks than Germany—it can produce 2 trucks for each machine tool, while Germany can only produce 1 truck for each machine tool. Thus, Italy has a comparative advantage in the production of trucks.
- Germany should concentrate on what it does best—machine tools; Italy should concentrate its resources on the production of trucks, where it is more efficient. The surplus production not needed for home consumption would be traded for products that are needed.
- Assuming that the two countries agree on a satisfactory international trading rate, i.e., 1 machine tool for $1\frac{1}{2}$ trucks (1:1.5) and that Germany required 44 machine tools for its own internal use, and Italy required 6 trucks for its own internal use, the surplus production of each country would be traded.
- The gains from trade would be as follows:

Germany, having produced 60 machine tools, would retain 44 for its own use and trade the surplus of 16 tools. In return it would receive 24 trucks from Italy (1 machine tool for $1\frac{1}{2}$ trucks). If Germany had desired to make its own trucks, it could have only produced 16 trucks at the trade-off ratio of 1:1. By trading with Italy, Germany now has 24 trucks—8 more than it could have produced itself.

Italy concentrated its resources on the production of 30 trucks, its area of greatest efficiency, keeping 6 trucks for its own use and trading 24 in return for 16 machine tools, and in the process gained 4 more machine tools than the 12 it could have made by itself.

Production Possibilities Curves, Specialization of Productions, and the Benefits of Trade

FIGURE 2.2

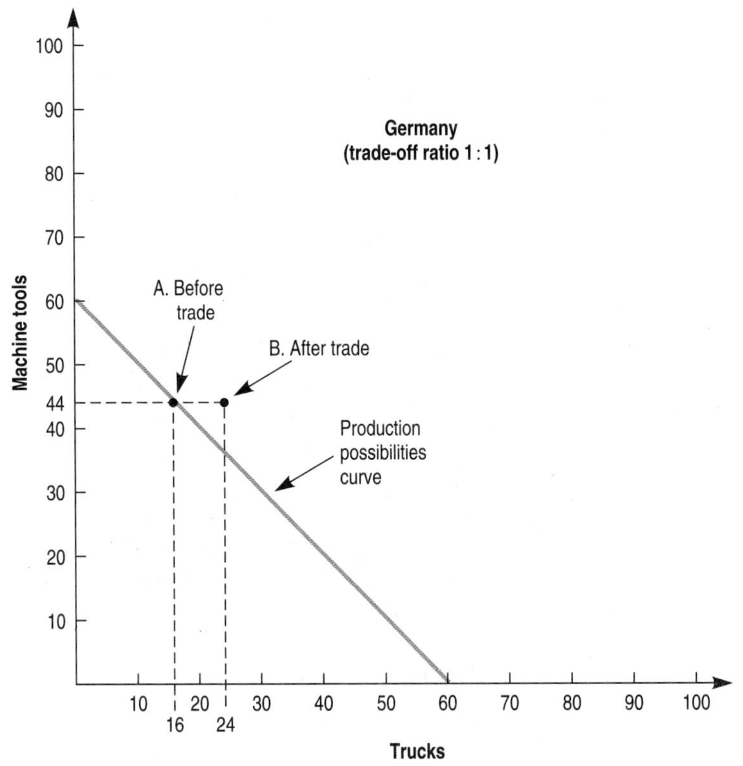

1. Germany gives up production of one truck to produce one machine tool.
2. In producing 44 machine tools it can only produce 16 trucks (1 : 1)
3. By concentrating on machine tools and trading it receives 24 trucks (1 : 1.5) a gain of 8 trucks.

Germany's Production Possibilities Curve

Machine Tools	Trucks
60	0
50	10
44	16
40	20
30	30
20	40
10	50
0	60

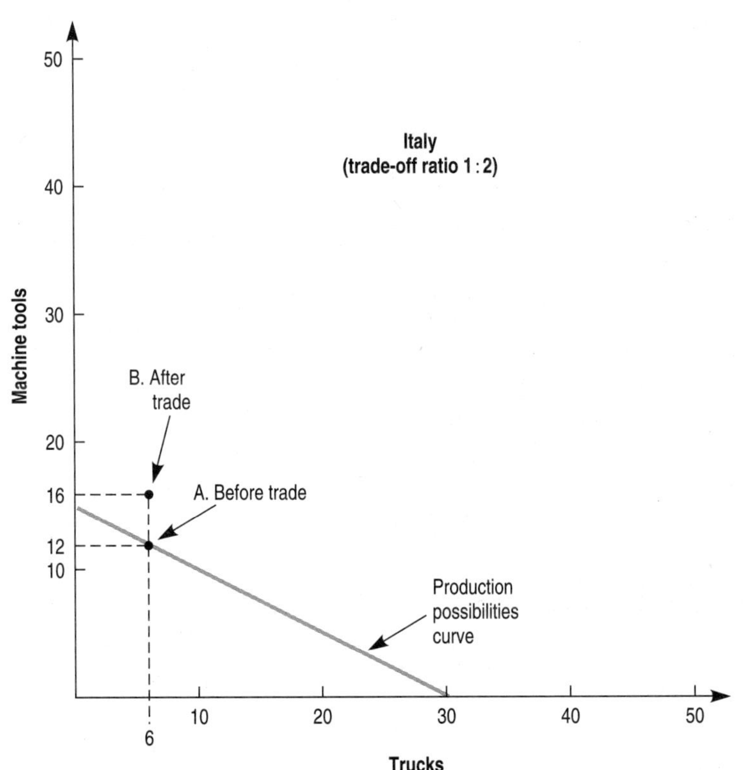

Italy's Production Possibilities Curve

Machine Tools	Trucks
15	0
14	2
13	4
12	6
11	8
10	10
9	12
8	14
7	16
6	18
5	20
4	22
3	24
2	26
1	28
0	30

1. Italy gives up production of one machine tool to produce 2 trucks (1 : 2)
2. In producing 6 trucks it is limited to the production of 12 machine tools.
3. By concentrating on trucks and trading it receives 16 machine tools—a gain of 4 machine tools.

autarky
a country that does not participate in international trade

opportunity costs
additional cost of taking one action compared to another

as point A in Figure 2.2—an assumed combination of 12 machine tools and 6 trucks. These curves depict what each country could produce in isolation, that is without trade (sometimes referred to as **autarky**). The slope of the curve reflects the "trade-off" of producing one product over the other; these trade-offs represent prices, or **opportunity costs.** Opportunity cost is the foregone value of a factor of production in its next best use. In the example, if Germany gives up the production of one machine tool, it will be able to produce one truck—a trade-off ratio of 1:1. If Italy decides not to produce one machine tool, it will have resources that can be used to produce two trucks—a trade-off ratio of 1:2. According to the theory of comparative advantage, both countries should specialize completely in the production of the product that they do best or that has the most advantage—Germany should produce machine tools and Italy should produce trucks.

Are both countries better off as a result of trade? Yes, the final step to understanding the benefits of classical trade theory is to note that each country is now consuming beyond its own production possibilities curve. This final point summarizes the work of Smith and Ricardo. The real wealth of a nation is an improvement in its standard of living, which is normally measured in its ability to have, and be able to consume, increasing amounts of goods and services. Figure 2.2 shows that both Germany and Italy were able to use their limited resources by means of international trade to obtain more goods and services than they could have produced for themselves. In other words, more goods and services is better, and global trade provides more goods and services.

Concluding Points about Classical Trade Theory

Classical trade theory contributed much to the understanding of how production and trade operate in the world economy. Although like all economic theories it is often criticized for being unrealistic or out-of-date, the purpose of a theory is clearly to simplify reality so that the basic elements of the logic can be seen. Several of these simplifications have continued to provide insight in understanding global business.

- *Division of labor*—Adam Smith's explanation of how industrial societies can increase output using the same labor-hours as in preindustrial society is fundamental to our thinking even today. Smith extended this specialization of the efforts of a worker to the specialization of a nation.
- *Comparative advantage*—David Ricardo's extension of Smith's work for the first time explained how countries that seemingly had no obvious reason for trade could individually specialize in whichever production they "did best," and trade for the product they did not produce.
- *Gains from trade*—The theory of comparative advantage argued that nations could improve the welfare of their populations through international trade. A nation could actually achieve consumption levels beyond what it could produce by itself. To this day, this is one of the fundamental principles underlying the arguments for all countries to strive to expand and "free" world trade.

FACTOR PROPORTIONS THEORY

Trade theory, like all of economic theory, changed drastically in the first half of the twentieth century. The factor proportions theory developed by the Swedish economist Eli Heckscher and later expanded by his former graduate student Bertil Ohlin formed the major theory of international trade that is still widely accepted today. Whereas Smith and Ricardo emphasized a *labor theory of value* (the amount of labor involved in manufacturing which gives it its value), the *factor proportions theory* (or the

Heckscher-Ohlin theory) was based on a more modern concept of production that raised capital to the same level of importance as labor.

Factor Intensity in Production

The factor intensity in production theory considered two **factors of production,** labor and capital. Technology determines the way they combine to form a product. Different products required different proportions of the two factors of production.

factors of production
all inputs into the production process, including capital, labor, land, and technology

Figure 2.3 illustrates what it means to describe a product by its "factor proportions." The production of 1 unit of good X requires 4 units of labor and 1 unit of capital. At the same time, to produce 1 unit of good Y requires 4 units of labor and 2 units of capital. Good X therefore requires more units of labor per unit of capital (4 to 1) relative to Y (4 to 2). X is therefore classified as a "relatively labor-intensive" product, and Y is "relatively capital-intensive." These *factor intensities* or *proportions* are truly relative and are determined only on the basis of what product X requires relative to product Y and not to the specific numbers of labor to capital.

It is easy to see how the factor proportions of how a product is produced differs substantially *among groups of products.* For example, the manufacturing of leather footwear is still a relatively labor-intensive process, even with the most sophisticated leather-treatment and patterning machinery. Other products, such as computer memory chips, however, although requiring some highly skilled labor, require massive quantities of capital for production. These large capital requirements include the enormous sums needed for research and development and the manufacturing facilities needed for clean production to ensure the extremely high quality demanded in the industry. The concept of factor proportions is very useful in the comparison of the production processes of goods.

According to factor proportions theory, factor intensities depend on the state of technology, the current method of manufacturing a product. The theory assumed that the same technology of production would be used for the same goods in all countries. It is not, therefore, differences in the efficiency of production that will determine trade between countries as it did in classical theory. Classical theory implicitly assumed that technology or the productivity of labor is different across countries. Otherwise, there would be no logical explanation as to why one country requires more units of labor to produce a unit of output than another country. Factor proportions theory assumes no such productivity differences.

Factor Endowments, Factor Prices, and Comparative Advantage

If there is no difference in technology or productivity of factors across countries, what then determines comparative advantage in production and export? The answer is that factor prices determine cost differences. And these prices are determined by the endowments of labor and capital the country possesses. The theory assumes that labor and capital are immobile, meaning they cannot move across country borders. Therefore, the country's endowment determines the relative costs of labor and capital as compared to other countries.

Each country is defined or measured by the amount of labor and capital that it possesses. If a country has, when compared with other countries, more labor and less

What is the difference between the United Kingdom and Great Britain?

ANSWER

The United Kingdom is made up of England, Scotland, Wales and Northern Ireland. Great Britain is the main island in the United Kingdom, on which England, Scotland and Wales are located.

capital, it would be characterized as relatively labor-abundant. That which is more plentiful is cheaper; so a labor-abundant country would therefore have relatively cheap labor.

For example, a country such as China possesses a relatively large endowment of labor and a relatively smaller endowment of capital. At the same time, Japan is a relatively capital-abundant country, with a relatively smaller endowment of labor. China possesses relatively cheaper labor and should therefore specialize in the production and export of labor-intensive products (such as good X in Figure 2.3). Japan possesses relatively cheap capital and should specialize in the production and export of capital-intensive products (such as good Y in Figure 2.3). Comparative advantage is derived not from the productivity of a country, but from the relative abundance of its factors of production.

Using these assumptions, factor proportions theory stated that a country should specialize in the production and export of those products that use intensively its relatively abundant factor.

- A country that is relatively labor-abundant should specialize in the production of relatively labor-intensive goods. It should then export these labor-intensive goods in exchange for capital-intensive goods.
- A country that is relatively capital-abundant should specialize in the production of relatively capital-intensive goods. It should then export these capital-intensive goods in exchange for labor-intensive goods.

FIGURE 2.3 **Factor Proportions in Production**

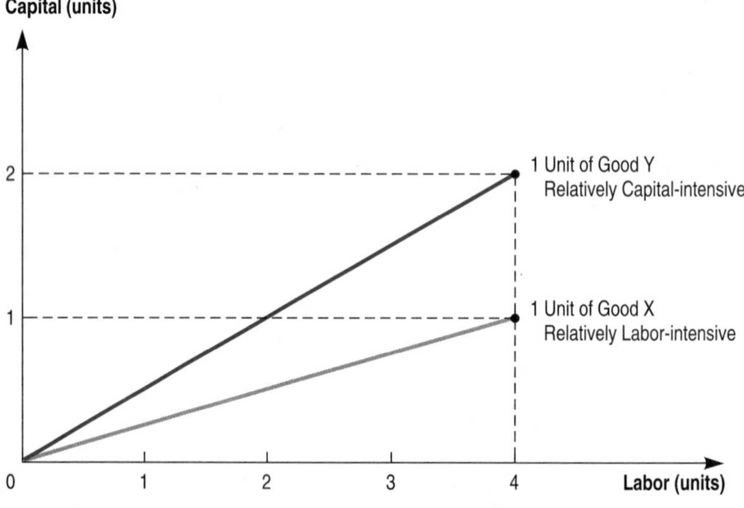

The Leontief Paradox

One of the most famous tests of any economic or business theory occurred in 1950, when economist Wassily Leontief tested whether the factor proportions theory could be used to explain the types of goods the United States imported and exported. Leontief's premise was based on a widely shared view that some countries such as the United States were endowed with large amounts of capital equipment, while other countries were short on capital but well endowed with large amounts of labor. Thus it was thought that a country with significant capital would be more efficient in producing capital-intensive products, and that a country with large amounts of labor would be more efficient in producing labor-intensive products.

Leontief first had to devise a method to determine the relative amounts of labor and capital in a product. His solution, known as **input-output analysis,** was an accomplishment on its own. Input-output analysis is a technique of breaking down products into the amounts and costs of the labor, capital, and other potential factors employed in the product's manufacture. Leontief then used this methodology to analyze the labor and capital content of all U.S. merchandise imports and exports. The hypothesis was relatively straightforward: U.S. exports should be relatively capital-intensive (use more units of capital relative to labor) than U.S. imports. Leontief's results were, however, a bit of a shock.

Input-output analysis
technique for studying an economy by breaking it down into industry groups and establishing the relationship between an industry's total output and the size of its inputs (labor, raw materials, machinery, etc) purchased from other industries

Leontief found that the products that U.S. firms exported were relatively more labor-intensive than the products the United States imported.[8] It seemed that if the factor proportions theory were true, the United States is a relatively labor-abundant country! Alternatively, the theory could be wrong. Neither interpretation of the results was acceptable to many in the field of international trade research.

A variety of explanations and continuing studies have attempted to solve what has become known as the **Leontief Paradox.** At first, it was thought to have been simply a result of the specific year (1947) that the data were for. However, the same results were found with different years and data sets. Second, it was noted that Leontief did not really analyze the labor and capital contents of imports, but rather the labor and capital contents of the domestic equivalents of these imports. It was possible that the United States was actually producing these products in a more capital-intensive fashion than were the countries from which it also imported these manufactured goods.[9] Finally, the debate turned to the need to distinguish different types of labor and capital. For example, several studies attempted to separate labor factors into skilled labor and unskilled labor. These studies have continued to show results more consistent with what the factor proportions theory would predict for country trade patterns. Finally, in the 1970s, a number of studies expanded the factors of production to include energy, particularly oil, as a factor of production that would explain the paradox. The results to date have been mixed at best.

Leontief Paradox
the general belief that the United States was capital-abundant against Leontief's findings that the country is labor-abundant

Linder's Overlapping Product Ranges Theory

The difficulty in confirming the factor proportions theory led many scholars in the 1960s and 1970s to search for new explanations of why countries trade with each other. The work of Staffan Burenstam Linder focused on the preferences of consumers—the demand side, rather than the production or supply side.

Linder argued that trade in manufactured goods was dictated not by cost but rather by the demand for similar type products across countries. His theory was based on two principles:

1. As per capita income rises, the complexity and quality level of products demanded by a country's residents also rises. The range of product sophistication demanded by a country's residents is largely determined by its level of income.

2. The business firms that produce a society's needs are more knowledgeable about their own domestic markets than about foreign markets. The firms could not be expected to effectively service a foreign market that is significantly different from the domestic market because the ability to compete comes from experience in the home market. A logical pattern would be for the firm to gain success and market share at home first, and then expand to foreign markets that have a demand for similar products.

Global trade in manufactured goods among nations would then be influenced by the demand for similar products. The countries that would engage in the most intensive trade would be those with similar per capita income levels, for they would possess a greater likelihood of overlapping product demands. For example, the United States and Canada have similar per capita income levels and in both countries consumers demand similar products, both in complexity and quality.

By comparison, the United States and Mexico have significantly different per capita income levels and, as might be anticipated, have dissimilar consumer product demands. The conclusions drawn from Linder's theory differed from the cost-oriented theories that preceded it. First, the most intensive trade would exist between countries of the same income or industrialization levels. Second, the theory implied a large part of global trade would be what is commonly referred to as **intraindustry trade,** which is the exchange of essentially identical goods between countries; for example, the United States exporting automobiles to Europe and, at the same time, Europe exporting automobiles to the United States.

intraindustry trade
two-way exchange of the same goods

INTERNATIONAL INVESTMENT AND PRODUCT CYCLE THEORY

A very different path was taken by Raymond Vernon in 1966 with what is now termed **product cycle theory.*** Diverging significantly from traditional approaches, Vernon focused on the product (rather than the country and the technology of its manufacture), not its factor proportions. But most striking was the appreciation of the role of information, knowledge, and the costs and power that go hand-in-hand with knowledge.

product cycle theory
views the manufacturing of products as passing through three stages: new product, maturing product, and standardized product

> . . . .we abandon the powerful simplifying notion that knowledge is a universal free good, and introduce it as an independent variable in the decision to trade or to invest.

Using many of the same basic tools and assumptions of factor proportions theory, Vernon added two technology-based premises to the factor-cost emphasis of existing theory:

product life cycle theory
marketing theory illustrating that a product goes through four stages: introductions, growth, maturity, and decline

*Note: Readers may find Vernon's **product cycle theory** somewhat confusing because of the similarity of the terminology with the **product life cycle theory** that was learned in a marketing course. Vernon's theory with its three stages (new product, mature product, and standardized product) is concerned with the *manufacturing* cycle of a product, that is, where the product is manufactured and the cost of that production. The product life cycle theory with its four stages (introduction, growth, maturity, and decline) relates to *marketing (sales) activity* and profitability over the life of a product. This situation is indicative of the complexity of conducting business on a global scale. The company's manufacturing function is focused on the improvement of profits by lowering the cost of production, wherever in the world that may take place. The marketing function aims to increase profits by maximizing sales in the countries and markets that the company serves. Additionally, it should be noted that a product may simultaneously be in different stages of its product life cycle in different markets, i.e., in a declining stage in the United States, but in the introduction and growth stages in various Asian markets.

1. Technical innovations leading to new and profitable products require large quantities of capital and highly skilled labor. These factors of production are predominantly available in highly industrialized capital-intensive countries.
2. These same technical innovations, both the product itself and, more importantly, the methods for its manufacture, go through three stages of maturation as the product becomes increasingly commercialized. As the manufacturing process becomes more standardized and low-skill labor-intensive, the comparative advantage in its production and export shifts across countries.

The Stages of the Product Cycle

Product cycle theory is both supply-side (cost of production) and demand-side (income levels of consumers) in its orientation. Each of these three stages that Vernon described combines differing elements of each.

Stage I: The New Product Innovation requires highly skilled labor and large quantities of capital for research and development. The product will normally be most effectively designed and initially manufactured near the parent firm and therefore in a highly industrialized market due to the need for proximity to information; communication between the many different skilled-labor components is required. In this development stage, the product is nonstandardized. The production process requires a high degree of flexibility (meaning continued use of highly skilled labor). Costs of production are therefore quite high.

Stage II: The Maturing Product As production expands, its process becomes increasingly standardized. The need for flexibility in design and manufacturing declines, and therefore the demand for highly skilled labor declines. The innovating country increases its sales to other countries. Competitors with slight variations develop, putting downward pressure on prices and profit margins. Production costs are an increasing concern.

As competitors increase, as well as their pressures on price, the innovating firm faces critical decisions as to how to maintain market share. Vernon argues that the firm faces a critical decision at this stage, to either lose market share to foreign-based manufacturers utilizing lower-cost labor or invest abroad to maintain its market share by exploiting the comparative advantages of factor costs in other countries. This is one of the first theoretical explanations of how trade and investment become increasingly intertwined.

Stage III: The Standardized Product In this final stage, the product is completely standardized in its manufacture. Thus, with access to capital on world capital markets, the country of production is simply the one with the cheapest unskilled labor. Profit margins are thin, and competition is fierce. The product has largely run its course in terms of profitability for the innovating firm.

The country of comparative advantage has therefore shifted as the technology of the product's manufacture has matured. The same product shifts in its location of production. The country possessing the product during this stage enjoys the benefits of net trade surpluses. But such advantages are fleeting, according to Vernon. As knowledge and technology continually change, so does the country of that product's comparative advantage.

Trade Implications of the Product Cycle

Product cycle theory shows how specific products were first produced and exported from one country, but through product and competitive evolution, shifted their location of production and export to other countries over time. Figure 2.4 illustrates the trade patterns that Vernon visualized as resulting from the maturing stages of a

FIGURE 2.4 **Trade Patterns and Product Cycle Theory**

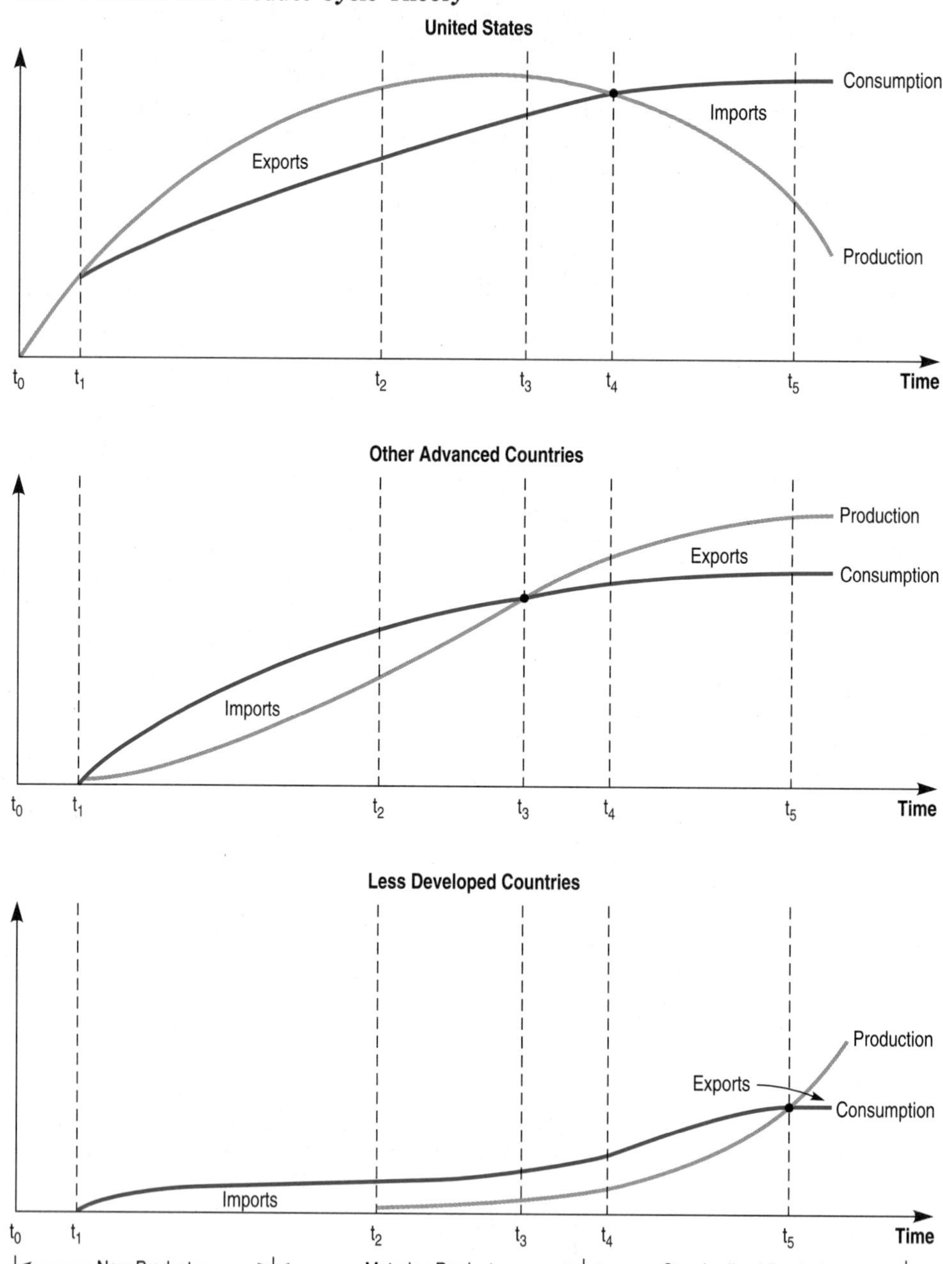

SOURCE: Raymond Vernon, "International Investment and International Trade in the Product Cycle," *Quarterly Journal of Economics* (May 1966) 199.

specific product's cycle. As the product and the market for the product mature and change, the countries of its production and export shift.

The product is initially designed and manufactured in the United States. In its early stages (from time t_0 to t_1), the United States is the only country producing and consuming the product. Production is highly capital-intensive and skilled labor-intensive at this time. At time t_1, the United States begins exporting the product to Other Advanced Countries, as Vernon classified them. These countries possessed the income to purchase the product in its still New Product Stage, in which it was relatively high-priced. These Other Advanced Countries also commence their own production at time t_1, but continue to be net importers. A few exports, however, do find their way to the Less Developed Countries at this time as well.

As product moves into the second stage, the Maturing Product Stage, production capability expands rapidly in the Other Advanced Countries. Competitive variations begin to appear as the basic technology of the product becomes more widely known and the need for skilled labor in its production declines. These countries eventually also become net exporters of the product near the end of the stage (time t_3). At time t_2, the Less Developed Countries begin their own production, although they continue to be net importers. Meanwhile, the lower-cost production from these growing competitors turns the United States into a net importer by time t_4. The competitive advantage for production and export is clearly shifting across countries at this time.

The third and final stage, the Standardized Product Stage, sees the comparative advantage of production and export now shifting to the Less Developed Countries. The product is now a relatively mass-produced product that can be produced with increasingly less skilled labor. The United States continues to reduce domestic production and increase imports. The Other Advanced Countries continue to produce and export, although exports peak as the Less Developed Countries expand production and become net exporters themselves. The product has run its course, or life cycle, in reaching time t_5.

A final point. Note that throughout this product cycle, the countries of production, consumption, export, and import are identified by their labor and capital levels, not firms. Vernon noted that it could very well be the same firms that are moving production from the United States to Other Advanced Countries to Less Developed Countries. The shifting location of production was instrumental in the changing patterns of trade, but not necessarily in the loss of market share, profitability, or competitiveness of the firms. The country of comparative advantage changes.

The Contributions of Product Cycle Theory

Although interesting in its own right for increasing emphasis on technology's impact on production costs, product cycle theory was most important because it helped to explain why international investment takes place. Not only did the theory recognize the mobility of capital across countries (breaking the traditional assumption that capital is immobile), it shifted the focus from the country to the product. This made it important to match the product by its maturity stage with its production location to examine competitiveness.

Of course, product cycle theory has many limitations. It is obviously most appropriate for technology-based products. These are the products that are most likely to experience changes in the production process as they grow and mature. Other products, either resource-based (like minerals and other commodities) or services (which employ capital but mostly in the form of human capital), are not so easily characterized by stages of maturity. And product cycle theory is most relevant to products that eventually fall victim to mass production and therefore cheap labor forces. Global Learning Experience 2.2 provides an interesting perspective on the use of cheap labor. But, all things considered, product cycle theory served to breach a wide gap between the trade theories of old and the intellectual challenges of a new, more globally competitive market in which capital, technology, information, and firms themselves were more mobile.

Fair Trade: The Use of Child Labor in Producing Products for the Global Marketplace

While the nations of the world debate the elimination of trade barriers in the movement toward *free trade,* another concept of global trade is beginning to be recognized. The new concept, called *fair trade,* focuses on a notion of global trade without the abuse and exploitation of workers in developing nations. The major concern of the fair trade movement is the use, abuse, and poor working conditions of an estimated 200 million children worldwide, under the age of 14, who are working full time and not attending school. About one-third of these underage workers are in Pakistan and India where they make bricks, weave rugs, and sew athletic equipment and clothing. Child labor can also be found in sugarcane fields in Haiti, garment factories in Honduras, the orange groves of Brazil, toy factories in China and Thailand, and on sporting-goods assembly lines in Indonesia. In Pakistan, for example, a child of 5 to 10 years might be sold by parents into years of bonded servitude—called a *pesghi*—perhaps to a carpet master, for a sum of money ($15 to $150). Once bonded to a master in this manner, the child can expect to work up to 14 hours a day, 6 days a week, weaving carpets in inhumane living and working conditions. The pay is pennies per hour. Doing anything to displease the master may result in punishment. Without going into the nature and severity of punishment, it is sufficient to mention that "the punishment room is a standard feature of a Pakistani factory, as common as a lunchroom at a Detroit assembly plant."

"The low cost of child labor gives manufacturers a significant advantage in the Western marketplace, where they undersell their competitors from countries prohibiting child labor, often by improbable amounts." Not surprisingly, American and European consumers are attracted to the low price, high quality products made with child labor. The fair trade movement seeks to set global "anti-sweatshop" standards for child labor. Manufacturers who adopt the standards would be permitted to use a "No Sweat" label on their products.

The fair trade movement has some problem areas. If producers adhere to anti-sweatshop standards, production costs will rise, raising the question of whether consumers would be willing to pay the resulting higher selling price. In this regard, a poll of Americans indicated that 84 percent of those responding would be willing to pay $1 more for a $20 garment if they knew it was not made in a sweatshop. Another concern is whether industries in emerging economies that use large inputs of child labor would lose their competitive cost advantage and fail to survive in the global marketplace—causing increased unemployment and financial hardship in already depressed economies.

SOURCE: "Child Labor in Pakistan," J. Silvers, *The Atlantic Monthly,* February 1996, pp. 79–92. There are many other reports on the abuse of child labor; also see: "Six Cents an Hour," S. Schanberg, *Life,* June 1996, pp. 38–48; "Cause Celeb," N. Gibbs, *Time,* June 17, 1996, pp. 28–30; "Child Labor and Sweatshops," C. Clark, *CQ Researcher,* Aug. 16, 1996, pp. 721–723.

THE NEW TRADE THEORY

The 1980s brought many of the questions regarding the validity of modern trade theory to the surface. The rapid growth of world trade, coupled with the sudden expansion of the U.S. merchandise trade deficit in the 1980s, forced many academics and policymakers to take another look at the determinants of international trade. The issues included:

- Continuing frustration in verifying the factor proportions theory of international trade. Although tests continued, the results were still unconvincing in proving the basic theory to be sound.
- The inability of the theory to explain intraindustry trade, the two-way exchange of the same goods; for example, the United States exporting automobiles to Europe, and at the same time Europe exporting automobiles to the United States. Either they were not actually the same product, or there were factors in trade that could not be explained by theories of relative prices.
- The demonstrated ability of governments to influence positively and negatively the competitiveness of specific trade sectors of their economies. For example, a number of newly industrializing countries in the Asian Pacific had successfully nurtured and protected industries purely for export purposes, some with great success.

There were two major developments in the 1980s largely in response to these and other issues: first, the work of many trade theorists like Paul Krugman at MIT in analyzing international trade for real-world economies, economies that do not possess perfect competition, free trade, or unregulated markets; second, the works of people like Michael Porter at Harvard, who attempted to examine the competitiveness of industries on a global basis rather than relying on country-specific factors to determine their competitiveness, the so-called competitive advantage.

Economies of Scale and Imperfect Competition

Paul Krugman's theoretical developments once again focused on cost of production and how cost and price drive international trade. Using theoretical developments from microeconomics and market structure analysis, Krugman focused on two types of economies of scale, *internal economies of scale* and *external economies of scale.*[10]

Internal Economies of Scale When the cost per unit of output depends on the size of an individual firm, the larger the firm the greater the scale benefits, and the lower the cost per unit. A firm possessing internal economies of scale could potentially monopolize an industry (creating an *imperfect market*), both domestically and internationally. If it produces more, lowering the cost per unit, it can lower the market price and sell more products, because it *sets* market prices.

The link between dominating a domestic industry and influencing international trade comes from taking this assumption of imperfect markets back to the original concept of comparative advantage. For this firm to expand sufficiently to enjoy its economies of scale, it must take resources away from other domestic industries in order to expand. A country then sees its own range of products in which it specializes narrowing, providing an opportunity for other countries to specialize in these so-called abandoned product ranges. Countries again search out and exploit comparative advantage.

A particularly powerful implication of internal economies of scale is that it provides an explanation of intraindustry trade, one era in which traditional trade theory had indeed seemed bankrupt. Intraindustry trade, when a country seemingly imports and exports the same product, is an idea obviously inconsistent with any of the trade theories put forward in the past three centuries. According to Krugman, internal economies of scale may lead a firm to specialize in a narrow product line (to produce the volume necessary for economies of scale cost benefits); other firms in other countries may produce

QUESTION *This is the world's largest freshwater lake and one of the five Great Lakes.*

ANSWER **Lake Superior, bordered by Ontario (Canada), Michigan, Wisconsin and Minnesota. (If you want to remember the names of all of the Great Lakes in order by size, just think of SHMEO—Superior, Huron, Michigan, Erie, Ontario).**

products that are similarly narrow; yet extremely similar: *product differentiation.* If consumers in either country wish to buy both products, they will be importing and exporting products that are, for all intents and purposes, the same.[11]

External Economies of Scale When the cost per unit of output depends on the size of an industry, not the size of the individual firm, the industry of that country may produce at lower costs than the same industry that is smaller in size in other countries. A country can potentially dominate world markets in a particular product, not because it has one massive firm producing enormous quantities (for example, Boeing), but rather because it has many small firms that interact to create a large, competitive, critical mass (for example, fine crystal glassware in eastern Germany). No one firm need be all that large, but all small firms in total may create such a competitive industry that firms in other countries cannot ever break into the industry on a competitive basis.[12]

Unlike internal economies of scale, external economies of scale may not necessarily lead to imperfect markets, but they may result in an industry maintaining its dominance in its field in world markets. This provides an explanation as to why all industries do not necessarily always move to the country with the lowest-cost energy, resources, or labor. What gives rise to this critical mass of small firms and their interrelationships is a much more complex question. The work of Michael Porter provides a partial explanation of how these critical masses are sustained.

The Competitive Advantage of Nations

In many ways, the study of international trade has come full circle. The focus of early trade theory was on the country or nation and its inherent, natural, or endowment characteristics that may give rise to increasing competitiveness. As trade theory evolved, it shifted its focus to the industry and product level, leaving the national-level competitiveness question somewhat behind. Recently, many have turned their attention to the question of how countries, governments, and even private industry can alter the conditions within a country to aid the competitiveness of its firms.

The leader in this area of research has been Michael Porter of Harvard. As he states:

> National prosperity is created, not inherited. It does not grow out of a country's natural endowments, its labor pool, its interest rates, or its currency's values, as classical economics insists.
>
> A nation's competitiveness depends on the capacity of its industry to innovate and upgrade. Companies gain advantage against the world's best competitors because of pressure and challenge. They benefit from having strong domestic rivals, aggressive home-based suppliers, and demanding local customers.
>
> In a world of increasingly global competition, nations have become more, not less, important. As the basis of competition has shifted more and more to the creation and assimilation of knowledge, the role of the nation has grown. Competitive advantage is created and sustained through a highly localized process. Differences in national values, culture, economic structures, institutions, and histories all contribute to competitive success. There are striking differences in the patterns of competitiveness in every country; no nation can or will be competitive in every or even most industries. Ultimately, nations succeed in particular industries because their home environment is most forward-looking, dynamic, and challenging.[13]

Porter argued innovation is what drives and sustains competitiveness. A firm must avail itself of all dimensions of competition, which he categorized into four major components of "the diamond of national advantage":

1. *Factor conditions*—The appropriateness of the nation's factors of production to compete successfully in a specific industry. Porter notes that although these factor conditions are very important in the determination of trade, they are not the only source of competitiveness as suggested by the classical or factor proportions theories of trade. Most importantly for Porter, it is the ability of a nation to continually create, upgrade, and deploy its factors (such as skilled labor) that is important, not the initial endowment. (See Global Learning Experience 2.3.)

Being Competitive in the Automobile Industry

In the automobile industry, being competitive can be measured in pennies and minutes. A few minutes of labor saved on the power train (engine and transmission) and assembly of each vehicle, in the production of millions of vehicles, can have a significant impact on its total cost, selling price, share of market, profits, and a company's ability to compete in the industry. This analysis presents U.S. auto industry rankings for the most productive plants, in each of the categories shown, for 1996. The data are in terms of workers per unit (vehicle, engine, or transmission) and an estimate of the total number of hours needed to build each unit. Although the differences in productivity from plant to plant may not appear to be significant, they take on a new meaning when one considers that the average cost of labor in this industry is $43 per hour.

The manufacturer with the lowest cost has a definite advantage over its competitors. With lower costs, it has several options including selling the vehicle for less and, thereby, gaining a

Motor Vehicle Manufacturing Productivity in the United States—1996 Plant Productivity Rankings in Selected Categories

Vehicle Assembly Operations					
Automobile Assembly			Truck Assembly		
Plant	Workers per Unit	Total Hours Needed to Build	Plant	Workers per Unit	Total Hours Needed to Build
1. Nissan (Smyrna, TN)	2.22	17.76	1. Nissan (Smyrna, TN)	2.25	18.00
2. Toyota (Cambridge, Ontario)	2.35	18.80	2. Nummi (Fremont, CA)*	2.54	20.32
3. Honda (East Liberty, OH)	2.38	19.04	3. Ford (Minneapolis, MN)	2.64	21.12
4. Toyota #1 (Georgetown, KY)	2.50	20.00	4. Ford (Louisville, KY)	2.66	21.28
5. Chrysler (Bramalea, Ontario)	2.54	20.32	5. Ford Kentucky (Louisville)	2.83	22.64
6. Honda (Marysville, OH)	2.57	20.56	6. Ford (Oakville, Ontario)	2.85	22.80
7. Ford (Atlanta, GA)	2.63	21.04	7. Chrysler	2.94	23.52
8. Ford (Chicago, IL)	2.66	21.28	8. Ford (Edison, NJ)	2.96	23.68
9. Chrysler (Belvidere, IL)	2.68	21.44	9. GM (Oshawa, Ontario)	3.06	24.48
10. GM #1 (Oshawa, Ontario)	2.68	21.44	10. GM (Fort Wayne, IN)	3.07	24.56

*Nummi is a joint venture between General Motors Corp. and Toyota Motor Corp.

continued

Power Train Manufacturing

Engine Manufacturing

Plant	Workers per Unit	Total Hours Needed to Build
1. Toyota (Georgetown, KY)	0.33	2.64
2. Ford (Dearborn, MI)	0.41	3.27
3. Ford (Romeo, MI)	0.46	3.66
4. Ford (Lima, OH)	0.47	3.73
5. Honda (Anna, OH)	0.48	3.80
6. GM (Spring Hill, TN)	0.53	4.26
7. Ford (Essex, Ontario)	0.59	4.71
8. GM (Flint, MI)	0.59	4.75
9. GM (Tonawanda, NY)	0.59	4.75
10. GM (Lansing, MI)	0.66	5.24

Transmission Manufacturing

Plant	Workers per Unit	Total Hours Needed to Build
1. Ford (Livonia, MI)	0.54	4.28
2. GM (Toledo, OH)	0.58	4.60
3. Ford (Sharonville, OH)	0.63	5.04
4. Ford (Van Dyke, MI)	0.64	5.11.
5. Chrysler (Kokomo, IN)	0.65	5.22

larger share of the market or improving its profits. The less productive and higher cost producers pay a penalty in terms of lost sales and/or reduced profits. The highly regarded *Harbour Report* contains estimates of the productivity cost penalty and provides some insight as to the competitiveness of the various companies in the U.S. automobile industry compared with the lowest cost producer.

Based on these data, it is clear that in terms

U.S. Automobile Industry
Productivity Cost Penalty 1996

Producer	Labor Hours per Vehicle	Labor Cost per Vehicle ($43. per hour)	Labor Cost Penalty per Vehicle	Annual Volume (million)	Annual Cost Penalty (millions)	Estimated Excess Workers
Nissan	28.32	$1,218	—	0.414	—	—
Toyota	29.54	1,270	52	0.483	25	313
Honda	30.88	1,328	110	0.664	73	905
Ford	37.59	1,616	398	4.271	1,702	21,062
Chrysler	40.53	1,743	525	2.767	1,453	17,968
General Motors	44.59	1,917	700	5.039	3,525	43,610

SOURCE: *Harbour Report,* 1997.

of labor, Nissan is the most productive company in the industry; having a competitive cost advantage over GM of approximately $700 per vehicle. If GM had been as labor productive as Nissan, it could have reduced its annual labor cost by an estimated $3,525,000,000 (yes, you read the number correctly—$3.5 billion) in 1996, according to the *Harbour Report.* It should also be noted that a company's strength, productivity advantages, and market success in such an intensely competitive industry will be transfered to and exploited in global markets.

SOURCE: *The Harbour Report,* 1997; Harbour and Associates, Inc.

GLOBAL LEARNING EXPERIENCE 2.4

ISO 9000—A Worldwide Standard of Quality

In order to be competitive in today's modern world, it is not enough to produce a product at a low cost. What is required is low cost *and* high, consistent quality. ISO 9000 is a set of international standards for a quality assurance management system.

The ISO (International Organization for Standardization) was founded in 1946 to facilitate the exchange of goods and services worldwide. Based in Geneva, Switzerland, it is composed of member bodies from over 100 countries. The purpose of this standard is to assure that firms have a quality assurance system in place and are complying with it. This should result in the delivery of a quality product in a repeatable and consistent manner.

The European Union (EU) has adopted ISO 9000 as its quality standard and is requesting compliance with ISO 9000 by its suppliers. This means that in order to sell to a European firm, a U.S. company must be ISO 9000 certified. High quality is mandatory to compete in today's global environment and ISO 9000 certification is gaining global acceptance. In receiving ISO 9000 registration, a firm benefits in several ways:

- higher customer satisfaction
- lower cost through internal efficiencies
- greater market share

An important benefit of ISO 9000 registration is that customer perception of and confidence in the firm is improved due to recognition of the ISO registration. This can lead to competitive marketing advantages and/or help to differentiate among suppliers selling similar products.

The basic precept of ISO is that an organization should have a uniform and disciplined quality assurance process, properly document that process, and conduct audits to ensure conformance to that process. The guiding principle for ISO is: "Say what you do, do what you say, and prove it"—in other words, walk the talk.

SOURCE: Adapted from Ford Motor Co., Automotive Components Division, *ISO 9000 Awareness Training Manual,* 1995.

2. *Demand conditions*—The degree of health and competition the firm must face in its original home market. Firms that can survive and flourish in highly competitive and demanding local markets are much more likely to gain the competitive edge. Porter notes that it is the character of the market, not its size, that is paramount in promoting the continual competitiveness of the firm. And Porter translates *character* as demanding customers. (See Global Learning Experience 2.4)
3. *Related and supporting industries*—The competitiveness of all related industries and suppliers to the firm. A firm that is operating within a mass of related firms and industries gains and maintains advantages through close working relationships, proximity to suppliers, and timeliness of product and information flows. The constant and close interaction is successful if it occurs not only in terms of physical proximity but also through the willingness of firms to work at it.

What is the largest lake in the world?

ANSWER *The Caspian Sea (143,550 square miles is technically a lake) lies between Russia and Iran. It is 92 feet below sea level and is the lowest point in Europe. The second largest lake, Lake Superior is only 31,800 square miles.*

4. *Firm strategy, structure, and rivalry*—The conditions in the home nation that either hinder or aid in the firm's creation and sustaining international competitiveness. Porter notes that no one managerial, ownership, or operational strategy is universally appropriate. It depends on the fit and flexibility of what works for that industry in that country at that time.

These four, as illustrated in Figure 2.5, constitute what nations and firms must strive to "create and sustain through a highly localized process" to ensure themselves of success.

The work of Porter is in many ways a synthesis of all that came before it. The emphasis on innovation as the source of competitiveness reflects the increased focus on the industry and product that we have seen in the past three decades. The acknowledgement that the nation is "more, not less, important" is to many eyes a welcome return to a positive role for government and even national-level private industry in encouraging international competitiveness. Including factor conditions as a cost component, demand conditions as a motivator of firm actions, and competitiveness all combine to include the elements of classical, factor proportions, product cycle, and imperfect competition theories in a pragmatic approach to the challenges that the global markets of the twenty-first century present the firms of today.

THE THEORY OF INTERNATIONAL INVESTMENT

To understand international investment, its motivation, process, and implications, we return to the basic premise of international trade.[14] Trade is the production of a good

FIGURE 2.5 **Determinants of National Competitive Advantage: Porter's Diamond of National Advantage**

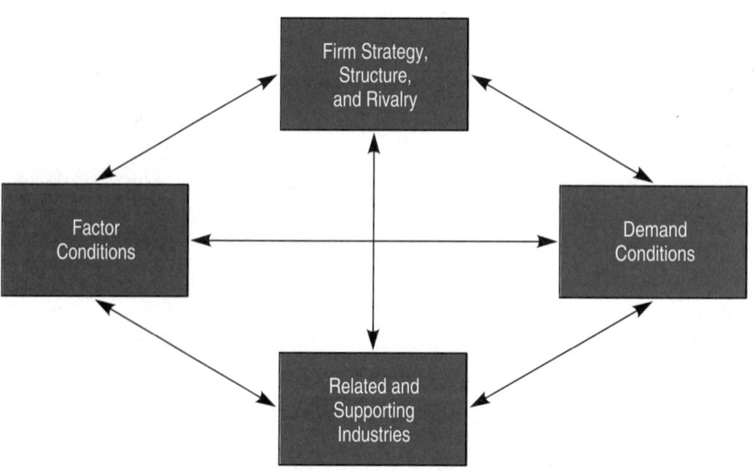

or service in one country and its sale to a buyer in another country. In fact, we specifically note that it is a firm (not a country) and a buyer (not a country) that are the subjects of trade, domestically or internationally. A firm therefore is attempting to access a market and its buyers. The producing firm wants to utilize its competitive advantage for growth and profit.

Although this sounds easy enough, consider any of the following potholes on this smooth freeway to investment success. Any of the following potholes may be avoided by producing within another country.

- Sales to some countries are difficult because of tariffs imposed on your product when it is entering that country. If you were producing within the country, your product would no longer be an import.
- Your product requires natural resources that are available only in certain areas of the world. It is therefore imperative that you have access to these natural resources. You can buy them from that country and bring them to your production process (import) or simply take the production to them.
- Competition is constantly pushing you to improve efficiency and decrease the costs of producing your product. You therefore may wish to produce where it will be cheaper—cheaper capital, cheaper energy, cheaper natural resources, or cheaper labor. Many of these factors are still not mobile, and therefore you will go to them instead of bringing them to you.

There are thousands of reasons why a firm may want to produce in another country, and not necessarily the country that is cheapest for production or the country where the final product is sold. And there are many shades of gray between the black and white of exporting or investing directly in the foreign country.

The subject of international investment arises from one basic idea: the mobility of capital. Although many of the traditional trade theories assumed the immobility of the factors of production, it is the movement of capital that has allowed **foreign direct investments** across the globe. If there is a competitive advantage to be gained, capital can get there.

foreign direct investments the establishment or expansion of operations in a foreign country with transfer of capital

The Foreign Direct Investment Decision

Consider a firm that wants to exploit its competitive advantage by accessing foreign markets as illustrated in the decision-sequence tree of Figure 2.6.

The first choice is whether to exploit the existing competitive advantage in new foreign markets or to concentrate resources in the development of new competitive advantages in the domestic market. Although many firms may choose to do both as resources will allow, more and more firms are choosing to go international as at least part of their expansion strategies.

Second, should the firm produce at home and export to the foreign markets or produce abroad? Customarily, the firm will choose the path that will allow it to access the resources and markets it needs to exploit its existing competitive advantage. That is the minimum requirement. But it also should consider two additional dimensions of each foreign investment decision: (1) the degree of control over assets, technology, information, and operations, and (2) the magnitude of capital that the firm must risk. Each decision increases the firm's control at the cost of increased capital outlays.

For some reason, possibly one of the potholes described previously, the firm decides to produce abroad. There are, however, many different ways to produce abroad. The distinctions among different kinds of foreign direct investment (branch 3 and downward in Figure 2.6), licensing agreements to greenfield construction (building a new facility from the ground up), vary by degrees of ownership. The licensing management

FIGURE 2.6 **The Direct Foreign Investment Decision Sequence**

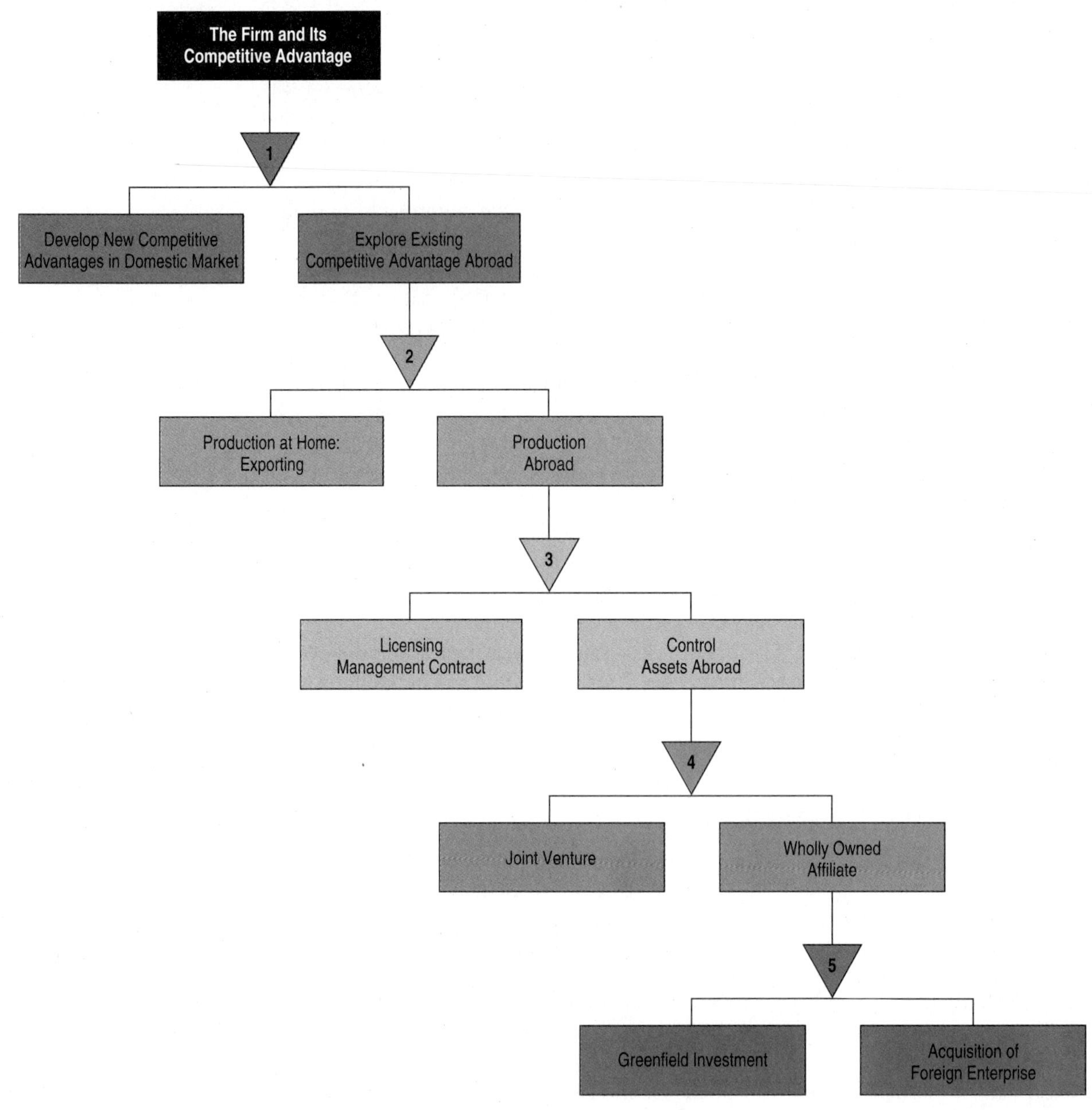

SOURCE: Adapted from Gunter Dufey and R. Mirus, "Foreign Direct Investment: Theory and Strategic Considerations," unpublished. University of Michigan, May 1985.

contract is by far the simplest and cheapest way to produce abroad; another firm is actually doing the production, but with your firm's technology and know-how. The question for most firms is whether the reduced capital investment of simply licensing the product to another manufacturer is worth the risk of loss of control over the product and technology.

The firm that wants direct control over the foreign production process next determines the degree of equity control, to own the firm outright or as a joint investment with another firm. Trade-offs with shared ownership continue the debate over control of assets and other sources of the firm's original competitive advantage. Many countries, trying to ensure the continued growth of local firms and investors, may require that foreign firms operate jointly with local firms.

The final decision branch between a "greenfield investment"—building a firm from the ground up—and the purchase of an existing firm, is often a question of cost. A greenfield investment is usually the most expensive of all foreign investment alternatives. The acquisition of an existing firm is often lower in initial cost but may also contain a number of customizing and adjustment costs that are not apparent at the initial purchase. The purchase of a going concern may also have substantial benefits if the existing business possesses substantial customer and supplier relationships that can be used by the new owner in the pursuit of its own business line.

The Theory of Foreign Direct Investment

What motivates a firm to go beyond exporting or licensing? What benefits does the multinational firm expect to achieve by establishing a physical presence in other countries? These are the questions that the theory of foreign direct investment has sought to answer. As with trade theory, the questions have remained largely the same over time while the answers have continued to change. With hundreds of countries, thousands of firms, and millions of products and services, there is no question that the answer to such an enormous question will likely get messy.

The following overview of investment theory has many similarities to the preceding discussion of international trade. The theme is a global business environment that continues to attempt to satisfy increasingly sophisticated consumer demands, while the means of production, resources, skills, and technology needed become more complex and competitive. A more detailed analysis of foreign direct investment theory is presented in Chapter 12.

Firms as Seekers

There is no question that much of the initial foreign direct investment of the eighteenth and nineteenth centuries was the result of firms seeking unique and valuable natural resources for their products. Whether it be the copper resources of Chile, the linseed oils of Indonesia, or the petroleum resources spanning the Middle East, firms established permanent presences around the world to get access to the resources at the core of their business. The twentieth century has seen the expansion of this activity combined with a number of other objectives sought by multinationals.

The resources needed for production are often combined with other advantages that may be inherent in the country of production. The same low-cost labor that was used as the source of international competitiveness in labor-intensive products according to factor proportions trade theory provides incentives for firms to move production to countries possessing those factor advantages. And, consistent with the principles of Vernon's product cycle, the same firms may move their own production to locations of factor advantages as the products and markets mature.

Seeking may also include the search for knowledge. Firms may attempt to acquire firms in other countries for the technical or competitive skills they may possess.

QUESTION *This island, first visited by the notorious Viking, Eric the Red, is the world's largest.*

ANSWER *Greenland, with an area of 840,000 square miles. New Guinea is second largest with 306,000 square miles. Australia, often called an island, is a continent.*

Alternatively, companies may locate in and around centers of industrial enterprise unique to their specific industry, such as the footwear industry of Milan or the semiconductor industry of the Silicon Valley of California.

Finally, firms may seek markets. The ability to gain and maintain access to markets is of paramount importance to multinational firms. The need to grow beyond the domestic market is central to all of global trade and business theory. Whether following the principles of Linder, in which firms learn from their domestic market and use that information to go global, or the principles of Porter, which emphasized the character of the domestic market as dictating global competitiveness, foreign-market access is necessary. As governments have become more intertwined in the business affairs of their constituents, multinational firms have often been forced to position themselves against the potential loss of market access by establishing permanent physical presence. The reaction of North American and East Asian firms to the Single European Market pushed forward in 1986 was to increase their level of investment in the European Union to ensure that they would not fall victim to a "Fortress Europe" if it were to arise (it did not).

Firms as Exploiters of Imperfections

Much of the investment theory developed in the past three decades has focused on the efforts of multinational firms to exploit the imperfections in factor and product markets created by governments. The work of Stephen Hymer (1960), Charles Kindleberger (1969), and Richard Caves (1971) noted that many of the policies of governments create imperfections. These market imperfections cover the entire range of supply- and demand-related principles of the market: trade policy (tariffs and quotas), tax policies and incentives, preferential purchasing arrangements established by the governments themselves, and financial restrictions on the access of foreign firms to domestic capital markets.

import substitution restriction of imports in order to allow domestic firms an opportunity to grow and prosper

For example, many of the world's developing countries long have sought to create domestic industry by restricting imports of competitive products in order to allow smaller, less competitive domestic firms to grow and prosper—so-called **import substitution** policies. Multinational firms have sought to maintain their access to these markets by establishing their own production presence within the country, effectively bypassing the tariff restriction but at the same time fulfilling the country's desire to stimulate domestic industrial production (and employment) in that area.

Other multinational firms have exploited the same sources of comparative advantage identified throughout this chapter: the low-cost resources or factors often located in less developed countries or countries with restrictions in place on the mobility of labor and capital. It should once again be noted that it is mobility of capital, international investment and foreign direct investment, that is the topic. The combining of the mobility of capital with the immobility of low-cost labor has characterized much of the foreign investment seen throughout the developing world over the past 30 years.

The ability of multinational firms to exploit or at least manage these imperfections will still rely on their ability to gain an advantage. Market advantages or powers are seen in international markets in the same way as in domestic markets: cost advantages, economies of scale and scope, product differentiation, managerial or marketing technique and knowledge, and financial resources and strength. All are the things of which competitive dreams are made. The multinational firm needs to find these in some form or another to justify the added complexities and costs of international investments.

Firms as Internalizers

The question that has plagued the field of foreign direct investment is why can't all of the advantages mentioned above be achieved through management contracts or licensing agreements (the choice available to the international investor at step 3 in Figure 2.6). Why is it necessary for the firm itself to establish a presence in the country? What pushes the multinational firm farther down the investment-decision tree?

The research and writings of Peter Buckley and Mark Casson (1976) and John Dunning (1977) have attempted to answer these questions by focusing on nontransferable sources of competitive advantage—proprietary information possessed by the firm and its people. Many of the true advantages possessed by firms center on their hands-on knowledge of producing a product or providing a service. By establishing their own multinational operations, they can internalize the production, thus keeping within the firm the information that is at the core of the firm's competitiveness. **Internalization** is preferable to the use of arm's-length investment arrangements, such as management contracts or licensing agreements. They either do not allow the effective transmission of the knowledge or represent too serious a threat to the loss of the knowledge to allow the firm to achieve the benefits of international investment.

internalization
action by a firm to keep all production related to a product inside the organization in order to protect manufacturing know-how or secrets from competition

As stated, these are theories. The synthesis of motivations provided by Dunning and others has only sought to partially explain, in the manner of Porter, many of the facts and forces leading firms to pursue international investment. To date, there is scant empirical evidence to support or refute these theories.

SUMMARY

The theory of international trade has changed drastically from that first put forward by Adam Smith. The classical theories of Adam Smith and David Ricardo focused on the abilities of countries to produce goods more cheaply than other countries. The earliest production and trade theories saw labor as the major factor expense that went into any product. If a country could pay that labor less, and if that labor could produce more physically than labor in other countries, the country might obtain an absolute or comparative advantage in trade.

Subsequent theoretical development led to a more detailed understanding of production and its costs. Factors of production are now believed to include labor (skilled and unskilled), capital, natural resources, and other potentially significant commodities that are difficult to reproduce or replace, such as energy. Technology, once assumed to be the same across all countries, is now seen as one of the premier driving forces in determining who holds the competitive edge or advantage. International trade is now seen as a complex combination of thousands of products, technologies, and firms that are constantly innovating to either keep up with or get ahead of the competition.

Modern trade theory has looked beyond production to cost to analyze how the demands of the marketplace alter who trades with whom and which firms survive domestically and internationally. The abilities of firms to adapt to foreign markets, both in the demands and the competitors that form the foreign markets, have required much of international trade and investment theory to search out new and innovative approaches to what determines success and failure.

Finally, as world economies grew and the magnitude of world trade increased, the simplistic ideas that guided international trade and investment theory have had to grow with them. The choices that many firms face today require them to directly move their capital, technology, and know-how to countries that possess other unique factors or market advantages that will help the firm keep pace with market demands.

Key Terms and Concepts

mercantilism
absolute advantage
division of labor
comparative advantage
production possibilities curve
autarky
opportunity cost
factors of production
Leontief Paradox
intraindustry trade
input-output analysis
barter economy
exchange economy
per capita income
product cycle theory
product life cycle theory
foreign direct investment
import substitution
internalization

Questions for Discussion

1. According to the theory of comparative advantage as explained by Ricardo, why is trade always possible between two countries, even when one is absolutely inefficient compared to the other?
2. What is meant by the national production possibilities curve?
3. Explain the Leontief Paradox.
4. Review the three stages in Vernon's product cycle theory.
5. Discuss the four major components of Porter's "diamond of national advantage."

Recommended Readings

Buckley, Peter J., and Mark Casson. *The Future of the Multinational Enterprise.* London: Macmillan, 1976.

Caves, Richard E. "International Corporations: The Industrial Economics of Foreign Investment." *Economica* (February 1971): 1–27.

Dunning, John H. "Trade Location of Economic Activity and the MNE: A Search for an Eclectic Approach," in *The International Allocation of Economic Activity.* Bertil Ohlin, Per-Ove Hesselborn, and Per Magnus Wijkman, editors. New York: Homes and Meier, 1977, 395–418.

Heckscher, Eli. "The Effect of Foreign Trade on the Distribution of Income," in *Readings in International Trade.* Howard S. Ellis and Lloyd A. Metzler, editors. Philadelphia: The Blakiston Company, 1949.

Helpman, Elhaman, and Paul Krugman. *Market Structure and Foreign Trade.* Cambridge, Mass.: MIT Press, 1985.

Husted, Steven, and Michael Melvin. *International Economics.* New York: Harper & Row, 1990.

Hymer, Stephen H. *The International Operations of National Firms: A Study of Direct Foreign Investment.* Cambridge, Mass.: MIT Press, 1976.

Linder, Staffan Burenstam. *An Essay on Trade and Transformation.* New York: John Wiley & Sons, 1961.

Maskus, Keith E., Deborah Battles, and Michael H. Moffett. "Determinants of the Structure of U.S. Manufacturing Trade with Japan and Korea, 1970–1984," in *The Internationalization of U.S. Markets.* David B. Audretch and Michael P. Claudon, editors. New York: New York University Press, 1989, 97–122.

Ohlin, Bertil. *Interregional and International Trade.* Boston: Harvard University Press, 1933.

Porter, Michael. "The Competitive Advantage of Nations." *Harvard Business Review* (March–April 1990).

Ricardo, David. *The Principles of Political Economy and Taxation.* Cambridge. United Kingdom: Cambridge University Press, 1981.

Root, Franklin R. *International Trade and Investment,* sixth edition. Chicago: South-Western Publishing, 1990.

Smith, Adam. *The Wealth of Nations.* New York: The Modern Library, 1937.

Vernon, Raymond. "International Investment and International Trade in the Product Cycle." *Quarterly Journal of Economics* (1966): 190–207.

Wells, Louis T., Jr. "A Product Life Cycle for International Trade?" *Journal of Marketing* 22 (July 1968): 1–6.

Notes

1. Haney, L. H., *History of Economic Thought,* The Macmillan Co.: New York, 1949.
2. Ibid., p. 118
3. Ibid., p. 119
4. Ibid., p 121
5. Cole, C. W., *French Mercantilist Doctrines Before Colbert,* Octagon Books: New York, 1969 p. 11.
6. Smith, Adam, *An Inquiry into the Nature and Causes of the Wealth of Nations,* edited by Edwin Cannan, Modern Library Edition, Random House, New York, 1994, lix, lxii
7. Ricardo, David, The Principles of *Political Economy and Taxation,* J. M. Dent & Sons, Ltd., Everyman's Library, London, 1948, p. 82.
8. Leontief, Wassily "Domestic Production and Foreign Trade: the American Capital Position Re-Examined," *Proceedings of the American Philosophical Society,* vol. 97, no. 4, September 1953, as reprinted in Wassily Leontief, *Input-Output Economics* (New York: Oxford University Press, 1966)
   In Leontief's own words: "These figures show that an average million dollars' worth of our exports embodies considerably less capital and somewhat more labor than would be required to replace from domestic production an equivalent amount of our competitive imports. . . . The widely held opinion that—as compared with the rest of the world—the United States' economy is characterized by a relative surplus of capital and a relative shortage of labor proves to be wrong. As a matter of fact, the opposite is true." Leontief, 1953, 86.
9. If this were true, it would defy one of the basic assumptions of the factor proportions theory, that all products are manufactured with the same technology (and therefore same proportions of labor and capital) across countries. However, continuing studies have found this to be quite possible in our imperfect world.
10. For a detailed description of these theories see Helpman Elhanan and Paul Krugman. *Market Structure and Foreign Trade,* (Cambridge: MIT Press, 1985).
11. This leads to the obvious debate as to what constitutes a "different product" and what is simply a cosmetic difference. The most obvious answer is found in the field of marketing: If the consumer believes the products are different, then they are different.
12. There are a variety of potential outcomes from external economies of scale. For additional details see Paul R. Krugman and Maurice Obstfeld, *International Economics: Theory and Policy,* 3rd ed. (Harper-Collins, 1994).
13. Michael E. Porter, "The Competitive Advantage of Nations," *Harvard Business Review* (March–April 1990): 73–74.
14. The term "international investment" will be used in this chapter to refer to all nonfinancial investment. International financial investment includes a number of forms beyond the concerns of this chapter, such as the purchase of bonds, stocks, or other securities issued outside the domestic economy.

CASES PART ONE

VIDEO CASE

International Vendor Relations at Pier 1 Imports

Over 200,000 pieces of stainless steel flatware are just sitting in a Pier 1 Imports warehouse. Where did these come from? Most recently they were stocked in Pier 1 stores—that is until a couple of customers informed store managers that the stainless steel pieces rusted. The company response? After a very rapid testing process that confirmed the customers' observations, the offending product was pulled from all stores and sent to its "resting place"—all within a two-week period.

The people in merchandising at company headquarters in Fort Worth, Texas, and the local Pier 1 agent in China now have ascertained that while there are 47 different types of stainless steel, only one—referred to as 18-8—can be used to make serviceable flatware that won't rust. This newly recognized quality specification has been quickly communicated to all other company agents who purchase flatware assuring that this product quality issue will not arise again.

It is John Baker's responsibility to oversee the network of corporate buyers and on-site agents who are directly responsible for finding, choosing, and assuring the quality of merchandise imported from around the world. Baker, the Senior Manager of Merchandise Compliance, accepted a position at Pier 1 Imports over 20 years ago after working for various department stores purchasing "table-top" and kitchen wares. When he first came on board as a buyer, he spent nearly 6 months of the year on the road, working with the agent network and finding new vendors for Pier 1 merchandise. Today, Baker also handles the increasingly complex area of government regulations of merchandise.

Because such a high percentage of Pier 1 Imports' merchandise is imported (over 85 percent), it is especially critical that U.S. government regulations regarding various product categories be studied and communicated to the manufacturers in other countries. These government regulations form one of the two measures of quality assurance for Pier 1 products. The second is that the products must conform to aesthetic standards that guarantee that the product fits the Pier 1 image and Pier 1 customer desires. It is in large part the buyer's expertise that assures that these standards are met.

What is the process for finding and selecting vendors in countries other than the United States? First of all, Pier 1 depends upon a well- and long-established network of agents in every country from which they import. In some lesser-developed regions, Pier 1 agents work with governments to help locate professional exporters. Some exporters are found at international trade fairs as well. The bulk of Pier 1 agents are native to the country in which they work, and some have been in place for as long as 30 years with their children now taking over the local positions.

The agents' jobs include finding local producers of handcrafted items that fit the Pier 1 customer needs. Buyers look for new sources of products at local craft fairs and even flea markets. Right now, for example, local agents in several countries are looking for sources of wooden furniture—primarily chests and tables—because Pier 1 would like to add to this in-store category. Based upon the location of raw materials, in this case in Italy, South America, Indonesia, and Thailand, agents are searching for just the right manufacturers to be brought to the buyers' attention.

Because it is the agents based within the various exporting countries who must enforce quality requirements, it is critical that John Baker and his colleagues carefully communicate both governmental and aesthetic product requirements to the agents. The agents can then "sit down at the table" with the manufacturers and work out the quality issues. If misunderstandings occur, Pier 1 is always ready to accept some of the responsibility because they view their manufacturers and agents as their partners in this business.

Because Pier 1 Imports has carefully carved out a unique niche in the specialty retail store industry, buyers are hard to hire from outside the company. As Baker noted, "The bulk of our staff has come out of our stores. It is easy for a buyer to move from Macy's to Hudson's—the products are the same as are most of the vendors. The Pier 1 buyer, however, must understand the Pier 1 store in order to be able to effectively and efficiently buy for it." These Pier 1 buyers, along with their agents onsite around the globe, serve as the company's primary link to product quality.

Questions for Discussion

1. What are the implications for sales, customer satisfaction, and profits for companies like Pier 1 when low quality merchandise is not identified early in the purchasing process?
2. Do you think that Pier 1 might have avoided this problem if it had a very aggressive quality assurance program, i.e., ISO 9000, in place?

Hong Kong: The Market of the Future or No Future

The People's Republic of China (PRC) and the British Crown Colony of Hong Kong are inextricably linked. Looking at the past, there are abundant reasons for the relationship to be one of price and fear (see Table 1 for a time line). In fact, many argue that Beijing never fully recognized Hong Kong's separation from the mainland after the Opium War in 1842. As a result of long-standing economic and cultural relationships—primarily between southern China and Hong Kong—some viewed the reunification on July 1, 1997, mainly as a symbolic flag-raising ceremony. What that symbolism means is debated. "Hong Kong has taken over China, not the other way around," says a representative of the Hong Kong Trade Development Council, while an American businessman well entrenched in China and its system warns: "Hong Kong is the scapegoat for what Chinese leaders perceive as Western injustice."

Although recent Eastern European history offers numerous examples of command economies giving way to market-oriented systems, it is difficult to predict what will happen now that a command economy—the PRC—has taken over an unbridled bastion of capitalism—Hong Kong. "There are bound to be, on both sides, uncertainties, and there are bound to be suspicions," said Sir David Wilson, governor of Hong Kong from 1987 to 1992. "This whole process is something which is unprecedented in terms of world history. There are no international historical blueprints to go by. We have to find our own way."

The 1984 Sino-British Joint Declaration and Basic Law which has returned Hong Kong to Chinese sovereignty makes it a Special Administrative Region (SAR) of China for at least fifty years, presumably enough time for the two political and economic systems to mesh. China has also pledged that now that the British have departed, Hong Kong will be run largely by its own people under the concept of "one country, two systems." This means continuing the system of an elected government, rule of law, independent courts, and wide personal freedoms. The SAR is run by a chief executive selected among longtime Chinese residents of Hong Kong. Hong Kong remains a free port and separate customs territory and is able to decide on and conduct its own economic policies. This is evident in practice through Hong Kong keeping its own currency and retaining its separate membership in the General Agreement on Tariffs and Trade (GATT).

HONG KONG AS A BUSINESS CENTER

Hong Kong is the world's tenth largest trading nation and the third-largest financial center. In an area of just over 400 square miles, it has a population of 6.2 million. Its per capita income is over $25,300, second in Asia after Japan. It's the world's largest free port and top-ranking manufacturer and exporter of textiles, clothing, and toys. No other business center in the Asia-Pacific is as friendly to business, offering free trade, free enterprise, a well educated work force, a policy of "positive nonintervention" in trade matters, and low taxes. Hong Kong was ranked by the Heritage Foundation as the freest economy in the world in 1996. For a summary of Hong Kong economic facts, see Table 2.

SOURCE: This case study was written by Ilkka A. Ronkainen and funded in part by a grant from the Business and Source: International Education Program of the U.S. Department of Education. The assistance of the U.S. Consulate in Hong Kong, Inchcape Pacific, the Customs and Excise Department of the Hong Kong Government, the Hong Kong Trade Development Council is also appreciated. For additional information, see http://www.info.gov.hk., and the Hong Kong Economic and Trade Office in Washington, DC.

TABLE 1

Hong Kong and China: A Time Line

214 B.C.	*China Takes Hong Kong* China colonized Hong Kong under emperor Qin Shi Huangdi—the powerful ruler in the north credited with first uniting the kingdom. However, Hong Kong remained a backwater.
1842	*The Opium War* China ceded Hong Kong island to the British under the Treaty of Nanjing. Subsequent treaties gave Britain permanent use of Kowloon Peninsula in 1860 and a ninety-nine-year lease of the New Territories starting in 1898. Chinese consider this period one of national shame and weakness.
The 1900s	*Hong Kong Emerges as a Port* Hong Kong's role as a transit port to China grew, as did its population, swelled by refugees fleeing civil war and the Japanese invasion of the mainland. Hong Kong boomed in the post–World War II era, and a class of Chinese business leaders emerged.
1949	*Communism Sweeps the Mainland* The Communist victory on the mainland resulted in an exodus to Hong Kong of many of China's capitalists, landowners, and entrepreneurs. Later, China's failed economic policies cause more people to cross the border.
1978	*China Opens Up, Hong Kong Cashes In* Economic reforms by Deng Xiaoping included special economic zones, one of which is across the border from Hong Kong, and businesses from the territory were the first to invest there. While benefiting from the transit trade, Hong Kong started changing into a financial center.
1984	*The Sino-British Joint Declaration* The agreement between China and Britain provided for the return of Chinese rule under a "one country–two systems" scheme. Hong Kong is to pay no taxes to Beijing and will remain a free port and financial center, with laws left unchanged for fifty years.
1989	*Tiananmen* Beijing's military crushed pro-democracy protests and cast a dark shadow across Hong Kong's return to China.
1990	*The Basic Law* The National People's Congress—China's lawmaking body—passed the Basic Law for Hong Kong, which is to become the constitution after the changeover. A broad article on treason could undermine other promises made in the document.
1992	*Face-off with Beijing* Electoral reforms made by Governor Chris Patten turned relations with Beijing sour, complicating projects such as the new airport at Chek Lap Kok.
1993	*A Key Arrest* Beijing arrested Hong Kong-based journalist Xi Yang while he was reporting in the mainland and sentenced him to twelve years for subversion. This sent chills through the press in Hong Kong.
1995	*Democrats Win Elections* Under the new election scheme, Democrats won sixteen of the twenty directly elected seats in the sixty-member Legislative Council. Beijing swore to disband the council in 1997.
1996	*The Shadow Government* Beijing's response to the election was to form the Preparatory Committee—a group of 150 handpicked mainland officials and Hong Kong residents. Working in parallel with the Legislative Council, it is to select a 400-strong body of Hong Kong people who will, in turn, choose the post-1997 chief executive to replace the governor of Hong Kong.
1997	*The Handover* On midnight July 1, a joint ceremony in the new convention center marked the "dignified departure" of the British. A provisional legislature, chosen by the Preparatory Committee, took the place of the Legislative Council.
1998	*Hong Kong Elections* The first major test of Beijing's hands-off promise when Hong Kong residents go to the polls for the first time in the postcolonial era.
1999	*Portugal Returns Macao to Hong Kong* Macao returns to China December 31, 1999. Beijing is trying hard, alternating with carrot and stick, to forge a reunification agreement with Taiwan.

SOURCE: "Coming Full Circle," *MSNBC,* October 21, 1996.

TABLE 2 **Hong Kong Essential Facts, 1996**

Population	6.2 million
GDP per Capita	$25,300
Foreign Exchange Reserves	$57 billion
Total Exports	173.4 billion
Domestic Exports	29.5 billion
Re-exports	143.9 billion
Imports	193.3 billion
U.S. Exports to Hong Kong	11.6 billion
U.S. Imports from Hong Kong	35.2 billion
Principal U.S. Exports	Electrical machinery, resins and plastic materials, transport equipment, office machines, tobacco manufactures
Principal U.S. Imports	Garments, electronics, office machines, photographic apparatus, electrical machinery
U.S. Investment in Hong Kong	$13 billion
U.S. Expatriates in Hong Kong	23,500
U.S. Firms with Offices/ Plants in Hong Kong	900
Chinese Investment in Hong Kong	$25 billion
Hong Kong Investment in China	$133 billion

The economy as a whole is externally oriented and its growth and well-being depend mainly on its trade performance. Apart from trade in goods, trade in services also contributes significantly to Hong Kong's growth. Given its strategic location and well established infrastructure and business contacts, Hong Kong has developed into a center for trade, finance, communications, and business services for the entire Asia-Pacific region.

The Hong Kong government plays no favorites, putting foreign policy and locally owned companies on the same footing. While there are no special incentives offered to overseas business to relocate, formalities to setting up a business are kept to as few as possible. There are no regulations concerning the minimum capital requirement of a company, or any regulations concerning the relative degree of local/overseas participation in the ownership of the company. The Hong Kong government assists in finding suitable local partners for joint ventures. Likewise, there are no regulations concerning the relative proportion of local to overseas staff that may be employed. Typically, however, the high cost of living (i.e., mainly housing) discourages companies from using a large number of expatriates. There are no restrictions on foreign exchange or on transferring capital or profits in or out of the colony.

THE ECONOMIC INTERDEPENDENCE OF HONG KONG AND CHINA

Existing Hong Kong–PRC economic ties will set the pattern for future developments. The PRC is currently Hong Kong's largest trading partner and its main source of investment capital. Hong Kong has evolved as the "International Division of China Inc."—both in managing China's exports and importing foreign goods for re-export to China. Approximately 70 percent of China's annual exports to the United States pass through Hong Kong in the form of re-exports. Hong Kong's established business and social connections with both China and the rest of the world, excellent telecommunications and transportation facilities, and financial sophistication make it uniquely suited to its role as facilitator. An important part of this facilitation is to serve as an intermediary in trade between China and Taiwan.

Since the PRC implemented an "open door" policy in the last decade, Hong Kong's and outsiders' economic importance to China has increased. There are now 84,000 foreign-funded enterprises in China, most of them in the south. These enterprises are estimated to account for 25 percent of all of China's foreign trade. The economic development of southern China—especially the Pearl River Delta in Guangdong Province and the coastal economic zones—has been the catalyst for China's economy to grow by almost 10 percent a year since 1978.

Guangdong Province itself has for the last ten years averaged real annual growth of a stunning 15 percent. Although the province has less than half a percent of China's land, a mere 16 million of its 1.2 billion people and it accounts for 5 percent of total industrial output and 10 percent of exports. Per capita income in Guangdong Province is roughly $600, double that of China as a whole. The star of the province is Shenzhen, a city across the border from Hong Kong, set up as a special economic zone by Beijing in 1979. Shenzhen residents enjoy rapidly increasing per capita incomes of $800, which is expected to increase to $2,800 by the year 2000. Figure 1 provides a summary of the major business centers of the Pearl River Delta.

During its thirty-year-old drive to attract foreign direct investment, estimated total realized investment reached $220 billion (1995). About 60 percent is estimated to have come from or through Hong Kong. A full 80 percent of Hong Kong manufacturers have set up labor-intensive production facilities across the border. Hong Kong companies operating in Southern China now employ about 4 million people—more than ten times the number of manufacturing sector workers in Hong Kong itself. More than 60,000

The Fastest-Growing Economy on Earth **FIGURE 1**

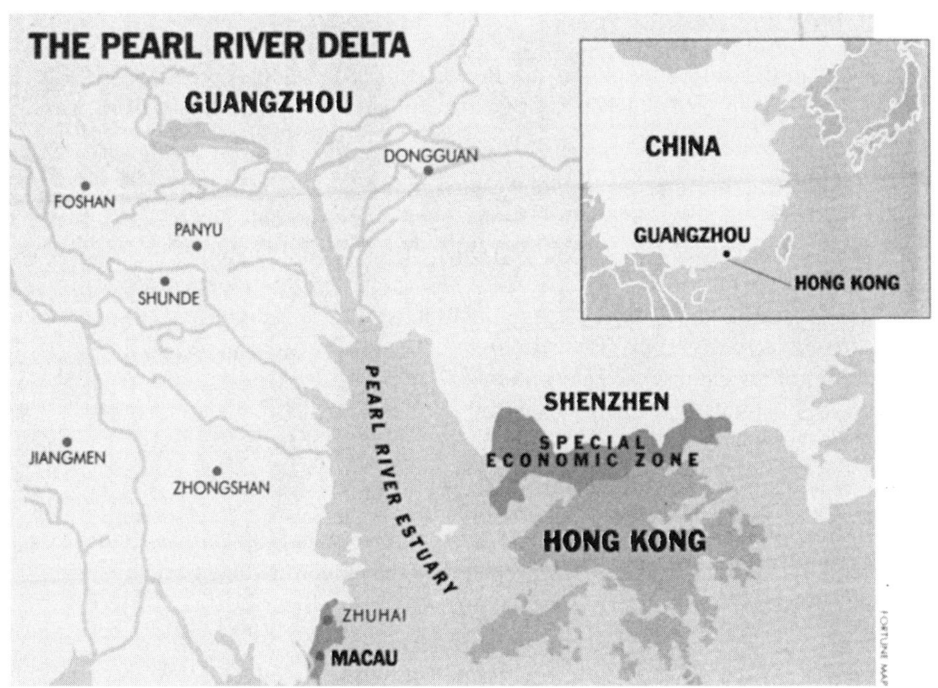

SOURCE: Ford W. Worthy, "Where Capitalism Thrives in China," *Fortune,* March 9, 1992, 71.

Hong Kong managers, professionals, technicians, and supervisors are currently working in China. In addition, 20 percent of Hong Kong's currency circulation takes place in Guangdong Province.

At the same time, China is increasing its stake in Hong Kong. China is the biggest investor ($25 billion) in the economy ahead of the United States and Japan, with major investments in the aviation sector (e.g., a majority ownership in Cathay Pacific), telecommunications, and property. As a matter of fact, it is estimated that PRC buyers controlled 20 percent of the Hong Kong property market by the time the takeover occured. The Bank of China, which is the second largest banking group (after Hong Kong Bank) in Hong Kong, has started issuing in the colony's currency notes, fully backed by foreign exchange deposits with the Hong Kong government.

CHINA'S ECONOMIC AND CONSUMER BOOM

Economic growth in China has been rapid: GNP growth has been over 10 percent consistently in the 1990s. China's exports totaled $121 billion, imports $116 billion, resulting in a trade surplus of $5 billion in 1994.

Despite the austerity measures introduced in the summer of 1993 to cool down the economy, strong growth is still continuing. This growth is bringing affluence to many parts of China, not just the major cities, such as Guangzhou, Shanghai, and Beijing. Examples of the changes this growth is bringing include:

- Retail sales in China surged 10 percent in the early 1990s to approximately $200 billion. By the year 2000, annual retail sales are projected to have reached $600 billion.
- Department stores display a wide variety of consumer goods and are overflowing with eager consumers. Traffic through some of China's department stores is well over 100,000 people per day.
- For a working couple in Guandong Province, monthly household income may be 1,200 yuan ($210). Although Ferrero Rochet chocolates sell for 68 yuan, and a pack of Brand's Essence of Chicken is priced at 100 yuan, they sell very well to a broad range of customers.

While incomes in China are low by Western standards and by those in the developed economies of the Asia-Pacific region, the proportion of disposable income is high as are savings. Living expenses take only 5 percent or less of family income in China, while the comparable figure in Hong Kong is 40 percent. There is tremendous pent-up demand for consumer goods among the population who have had nothing to spend their money on for many years. Private savings are high even by Asian standards and amount to one-third of an average worker's annual income.

Chinese consumers are quality conscious. Joint-venture products (such as Head & Shoulders, Tang, and Pepsi-Cola) are perceived as quality items and often command double or triple the price of goods produced solely by Chinese companies.

In developing a strategy for China, companies such as Inchape Pacific (which acts as a marketer and distributor for many companies including Cadbury's, SmithKline-Beecham, and Kellogg's) consider approaching China as one big market a mistake. Inchape's priority markets are Southern China (Pearl River Delta), Eastern China (Shanghai, Nanjing, and Hangzhou), and North China (Beijing, Tianjin, and Dalian). The rationale is that each is a very separate and different market from the others in terms of people, culture, dialect, way of life, climate, and diet. Most importantly, each is a huge consumer market in its own right. The sheer size and the logistics problems make national distribution in China an impossibility.

Taking advantage of this opportunity requires flexibility. Changes in the regulatory environment create both opportunities and challenges. Contacts have to be cultivated beyond the central government in Beijing. Provincial and municipal authorities enjoy autonomy and influence and tend to be quite entrepreneurial. The municipal government usually supports or has very close links with a few companies in its area. A potential entrant needs to develop good relations with these officials and the business leaders in the local companies.

HONG KONG–U.S. BUSINESS LINKS

The overall key to Asia is access—access to markets and market information. For many U.S. companies, Hong Kong's strategic location, developed infrastructure, and commercial expertise provide the best bang for the buck in Asia. Markets in Asia, China in particular, lack a solid legal framework for business and rely more on personal relationships. Leading Overseas Chinese entrepreneurs can be invaluable facilitators because they operate through a network of personal contacts. Procter & Gamble, for example, got into the Chinese market in 1988 by forming an alliance with Hong Kong businessman Li Ka-shing.

More than 900 U.S. companies have operations in Hong Kong at present, more than double the number of five years earlier. Virtually every Fortune 500 company that does business in the Asia-Pacific region has maintained a presence in Hong Kong, usually a regional headquarters. A good example of this is Polaroid Far East Limited. A wholly owned subsidiary of Polaroid Corporation, Polaroid Far East Limited's Hong Kong office is headquarters for a region that covers South Korea, Singapore, Malaysia, Taiwan, China, Indonesia, Thailand, and India. The Hong Kong office, which opened in 1971 and now has sixty-nine employees, controls finance, sales and marketing, and personnel.

Hong Kong is a major market for U.S.-made goods in its own right. As a matter of fact, Hong Kong imports more U.S. goods per capita than any country in the world—four times the level of Japan, five times that of Europe. Some of the major categories of traded goods can be found in Table 2.

Hong Kong also represents a convenient stepping-stone to China. Polaroid recently announced a manufacturing joint venture in Shanghai to produce consumer cameras for export. In addition to manufacturing cameras, Polaroid hopes to develop the Chinese domestic market for document photography. Hong Kong's role is to provide training for the new operation in China as well as sales and marketing support. C. C. Chan, sales and marketing manager for the Polaroid Far East China Trade Department, thinks most people in the PRC are still unfamiliar with free market Western-style business. "Hong Kong brings China closer to the world," says Chan.

Some of the other firms in the market are:

- Campbell Soup, which opened a $500,000 R&D center to spearhead its thrust into the Asia-Pacific region. The new center will be developing a wide range of canned products for the Chinese palate. The operation is also intended as a springboard into China.
- Motorola, the world's fourth largest semiconductor manufacturer, opened a multimillion-dollar state-of-the-art chip-manufacturing plant in Hong Kong. The plant will supply the entire Pacific Rim, which is a $14 billion market for semiconductors.
- Waste Management International has a 70 percent stake in a consortium that won a multimillion-dollar contract to build and operate Asia's first chemical waste treatment facility in Hong Kong.

THE OTHER SIDE OF THE COIN: MACRO AND MICRO CHALLENGES

Hong Kong's economy suffered badly as a result of the June 4, 1989, crackdown on student dissidents on Tiananmen Square. "The events reminded people of the uncertainty, risk, and lack of predictability in dealing with Beijing," says Robert Dorsee, vice president and managing director of Tyco (Hong Kong) Ltd., a division of American-owned Tyco Toys Inc.

Others are also considering changes as a result of growing concern over Hong Kong–China relations. In October 1992, the present governor of Hong Kong, Chris Patten, put forth proposals that would further democratic reform in Hong Kong by allowing more participation by the Hong Kong Chinese in the selection of members of the local legislature (the Legislative Council). The Chinese government has objected ferociously on the grounds that major changes are a violation of the Joint Declaration, and that the proposed reforms are in breach of the Basic Law. Before the handover in 1997, rhetoric from Beijing went as far as to suggest that the treaty with Britain be "scattered to the wind," and even that China might grab control over the colony before 1997. Although discussions were held to resolve the disagreement, the confidence of people both in Hong Kong and those interested in investing there was shaken. For example, the Hong Kong Electronics Association, whose members do most of their manufacturing in Hong Kong, has sponsored trips to the Philippines, Malaysia, and Thailand to study the climate for new investments in those Asian nations. One of their concerns is that export control rules will cut their access to Western technology now that China has taken over. China's rough tactics may also endanger its already shaky most-favored-nation (MFN) status with the United States which was renewed after some controversy in June 1994.

The latter concern points out the fact that the greatest threat to Hong Kong may not come from China but from the United States. China's trade surplus with the United States reached $39.6 billion in 1994 (up from 33.7 billion the year before), a major irritant in the countries' trade relations. In October 1992, the two governments reached an agreement on market access (so-called 301 investigation), under which China pledged to liberalize its foreign trade regime. About 75 percent of the nontariff barriers were eliminated by 1994, the rest by 1997. Tariffs will also be reduced. The agreement did not, however, clear the way for China to join WTO, as differences of opinion still remain between China and the United States.

If China loses its MFN status with the United States because of its human rights record or concerns over protectionism, military goods exports, and intellectual property, Hong Kong will suffer the most. This is why a special Hong Kong Business Mission has lobbied in Washington for the renewal of China's MFN status every time it has been up. U.S. exports would also suffer as China would undoubtedly retaliate with higher tariffs. When China lost its bid to host the 2000 Olympic Games, U.S. exporters worried about negative trade measures as a response to the opposition to the bid by the U.S. Congress.

Although many Hong Kong–based U.S. executives are not planning to leave, their confidence is flagging. What is required for both the Chinese government and the Hong Kong government is to improve the investment climate. The Chinese government mainly has to confirm its commitment to living up to agreements in the eyes of U.S. and European firms.

Many hope that the statement by Lu Ping, director of China's Hong Kong and Macau Affairs office, holds true in the positive sense: "Hong Kong is bound up with its Motherland. It will serve as a bridge, channel, and window between China and the rest

TABLE 3

Hong Kong's Possible Roles (before and after 1997)

- Hong Kong will continue developing its entrepôt role—as the international marketing arm of China.
- Hong Kong is not just the world's gateway to China, it is also China's springboard to the world.
- Hong Kong has the knowledge and experience of international business; through Hong Kong, China can better understand how international business operates and what the expectations are.
- Hong Kong will continue acting as a broker for international firms looking to set up in China, often in three-way joint ventures.
- Hong Kong will continue to provide a secure base for capital.
- Hong Kong could also develop as China's own "Silicon Valley," providing R&D for China's expanding industrial sector. It can also train mainland staff in Hong Kong or provide on-the-job training in China.
- Hong Kong's role as the link between Taiwan and China will also continue in the foreseeable future.

SOURCE: Stephen Clark, "Hong Kong's Role in the Development of Greater China," presentation given July 30, 1993. Chinese University of Hong Kong.

of the world, and play its unique and positive role in China's development in the next century."

Now that Hong Kong has formally become the Hong Kong Special Administrative Region of the People's Republic of China. Beijing will determine whether Hong Kong remains and grows as an open international business hub. It is already the unofficial commercial capital of the Overseas Chinese. For U.S. firms, Hong Kong will be the place to find appropriate partners and connections to enter the Chinese market. In many ways, Hong Kong's roles are, and continue to be, critical as seen in the summary provided in Table 3.

However, if Beijing reneges on its guarantee that Hong Kong can retain its position as China's capitalist gateway to the world, not only will Hong Kong become a backwater for global business, but China itself will be hurt in terms of attracting foreign direct investment and its most-favored-nation status with the United States.

Questions for Discussion

1. Would you agree or disagree with the following statement from the U.S. Information Agency in Hong Kong: "The reality, beyond the newspaper headlines, is that China is not going to kill the golden goose."
2. What are Hong Kong's benefits for a Western company that would make a move to the Philippines or Thailand undesirable or difficult?
3. Provide a possible strategy for a U.S. company operating in Hong Kong to leverage against political risk.
4. What are the benefits of using Hong Kong as a base for entering and marketing in the Chinese market?

References

Auerbach, Stuart. "Toy-Making Losing in China Some Appeal." *The Washington Post,* December 2, 1989, D11–13.

The Basic Law of the Hong Kong Special Administrative Region of the People's Republic of China. Hong Kong: The Consultative Committee for the Basic Law of the Hong Kong Special Administrative Region of the People's Republic of China, April 1990.

"Campbell Soup Targets Asia with New R&D Center." *Business International.* January 27, 1992.

Cheng, Paul M. F. "Gateway to Greater China." Sydney, Australia: Presentation made to the 36th CIES Annual Executive Congress, April 22–24, 1993.

"China at a Boiling Point." *The Economist,* July 10, 1993, 15.

Conley, Kirsta, "Hong Kong: Business Center of the Future." *Export Today* 7 (February 1991): 20–22.

Country Report: China, Mongolia, second quarter. The Economist Intelligence Unit, 1993.

Establishing an Office in Hong Kong. 6th ed. Hong Kong: The American Chamber of Commerce in Hong Kong, 1989.

Johnson, W. Todd. "Hong Kong Exporter's Gateway to China." *Export Today* 7 (June, 1991): 18–22.

Joint Declaration of the Government of the United Kingdom of Great Britain and Northern Ireland and the Government of the People's Republic of China on the Question of Hong Kong. Hong Kong: Hong Kong Government Information Services. December 1984.

Kraar, Louis. "Asia 2000." *Fortune,* October 5, 1992, 111–142.

——. "Storm over Hong Kong." *Fortune,* March 8, 1993, 98–105.

——. "Strategies that Win in Asia." *Fortune,* Fall 1991, 49–56.

Mutch, Andrew J. "Hong Kong: Tapping into the Dynamic Dragon." *Export Today* 9 (January/February 1993): 30–34.

Setting Up Business in Hong Kong. Hong Kong: Hong Kong General Chamber of Commerce, 1990.

Worthy, Ford S. "Where Capitalism Thrives in China." *Fortune,* March 9, 1992, 71–75.

The World Automobile Market

Cars are as essential to people as the clothes they wear; after a home, a car is the second-largest purchase for many. The car provides more than just instant and convenient personal transportation: it can be a revered design or a sign of success. Developers estimate that 200 yards is the maximum distance an American is prepared to walk before getting into a car. When the Berlin Wall came down, one of the first exercises of a newfound freedom for the former East Germans was to exchange their Trabants and Wartburgs for Volkswagens and Opels.

Western Europe is the largest car market in the world (see Figure 1). But while the car markets of Western Europe, North America, and Japan account for 90 percent of the vehicles sold, these markets are quite saturated. By the year 2000, for example, there will probably be one car per person aged 20–64 in North America.

Two general approaches will become evident. First, car manufacturers need to sell fewer cars, but more profitably. Secondly, they need to look for new markets. In the coming decades market growth will come from Asia, Eastern and Central Europe, and Latin America. China and India will eventually provide millions of new drivers. These new realities will have a profound impact on the car market and its players in the future. For a long time, U.S. and European car makers neglected Asian markets, allowing them to become largely a Japanese preserve, but belatedly they are attempting to gain lost ground. General Motors is using its European Opel division to spearhead expansion into Asia. Assembly operations have started in Taiwan, Indonesia, and India. All leading producers are lining up to start or expand their operations in China.

SOURCES: This case was prepared by Ilikka A. Ronkainen. It is largely based on "The Endless Road," *The Economist,* October 17, 1992, 1–18; "On Guard, Europe," *Business Week,* December 14, 1992, 54–44; Carla Rapoport, "Europe Takes on the Japanese," *Fortune,* January 11, 1993, 14–18; "Back to the Way We Were," *The Economist,* November 6, 1993, 83–84; "World Car Industry," *Financial Times Survey,* October 4, 1994; "Asian Carmakers' European Plan," *Business Week,* November 7, 1994; Louis Kraar, "Korea's Automakers," *Fortune,* March 6, 1995, 152–164; "Detroit is Getting Sideswiped by the Yen," *Business Week,* November 11, 1996, 54: and Louis Kraar, "Korea's Automakers," *Fortune,* March 6, 1995, 152–164.

FIGURE 1

World Car Sales by Region, 1992–2002 (in Millions of Cars)

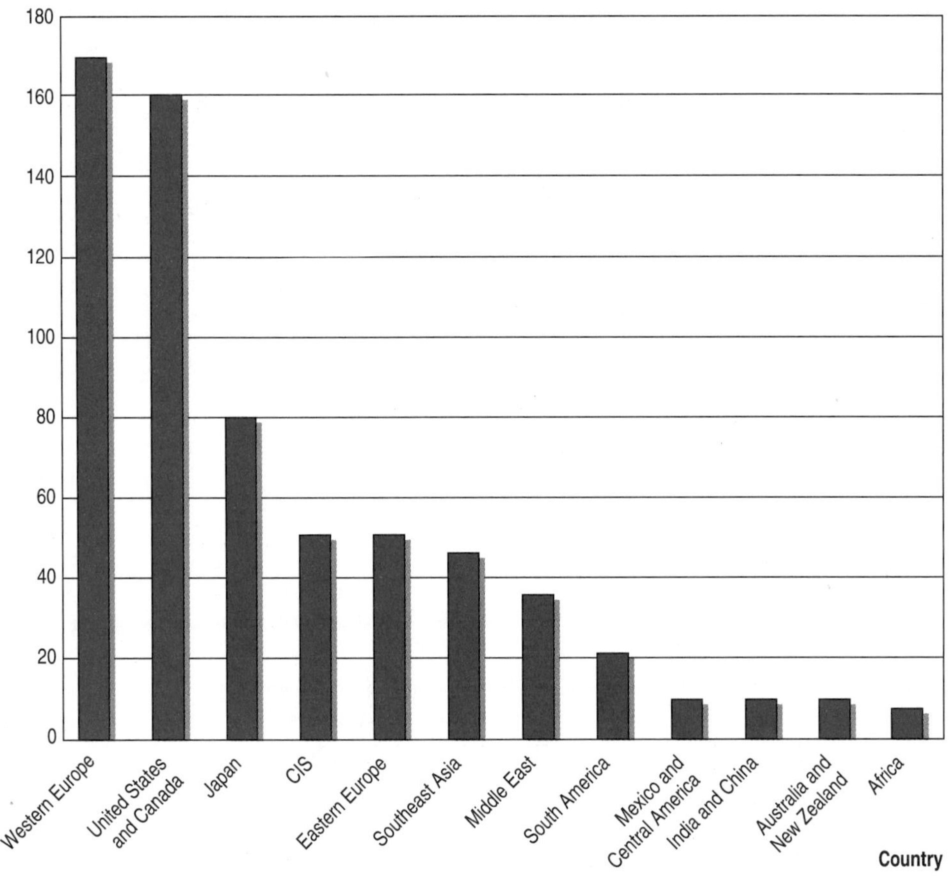

SOURCE: "The Car Industry: In Trouble Again," *The Economist*, October 17, 1992, 4.

In 1986, the Massachusetts Institute of Technology started a study that was published in a book, *The Machine that Changed the World.* The results showed that the Japanese took less time to make a car with fewer defects than the Americans or the Europeans. The main differences were due to the way factories were organized as shown in Table 1. The higher productivity of the Japanese has given them an overwhelming advantage: though they have not used it to cut prices, it has given them more profit per car than competitors get. As earnings mount, they can spend more to develop better cars or build the sales networks they need to expand sales. For example, Japanese car companies cut prices by 1.1 percent in the 1997 model year, while Detroit hiked them up an average 2.8 percent.

Cars have also become a global business on the manufacturing front as seen in Table 2. Japanese vehicle manufacturers have transferred more and more of their production abroad, first to North America, then Europe, and then to southeast Asia. Economic pressures and the appreciation of the yen have accelerated the Japanese expansion overseas. For example, since the 1980s the Japanese have built in the United States an auto industry larger than that of the United Kingdom, Italy, or Spain (15 percent of U.S. car

TABLE 1 **Differences in Car Manufacturing**

	Average* for Car Plants In: Japan	United States	Europe
Performance			
Productivity (hours per car)	16.8	25.1	36.2
Quality (defects per 100 cars)	60	82	97
Layout			
Factory space (per sq ft per car per year)	5.7	7.8	7.8
Size of repair area (as % of assembly space)	4.1	12.9	14.4
Stocks**	0.2	2.9	2
Employees			
Workforce in teams (%)	69.3	17.3	0.6
Suggestions (per employee per year)	61.6	0.4	0.4
Number of job classifications	12	67	15
Training of new workers (hours)	380	46	173
Automation (% of process automated)			
Welding	86	76	77
Painting	55	34	38
Assembly	2	1	3

*1989

**for eight sample parts

SOURCE: "The Secrets of the Production Line," *The Economist,* October 17, 1992, 6.

TABLE 2 **Leading World Passenger Automobile Producers (in millions)**

Country	1994	1995
Japan	7,801.3	7,613.1
United States	6,601.0	6,329.7
Germany	4,093.7	4,360.2
France	3,175.2	3,050.9
Spain	1,497.6	1,958.2
South Korea	1,453.6	1,892.5
Great Britain	1,466.8	1,532.1
Italy	1,111.0	1,422.4
Canada	1,215.8	1,348.3
Brazil	1,249.3	1,307.7
Belgium	798.9	1,189.7
Mexico	840.0	710.1

SOURCE: David J. Wallace, "Specialize or Perish," *World Trade,* October 1996, 30.

production is now coming from Japanese-owned plants). Japanese producers account for a quarter of U.K. car production. The big three U.S. manufacturers have themselves restructured to remain competitive. Ford has undertaken a sweeping restructuring of its operations hoping to run it as a single automotive company to reap benefits of scale and scope. The Europeans are following suit. The Volkswagen Group, Europe's biggest maker, is planning to reduce the number of platforms (from which all of its car ranges are derived) from a present sixteen to four to cut costs and to simplify global manufacturing activities. Mercedes-Benz has launched a range of cars into new segments of the world market including a four-wheel drive sports utility vehicle assembled in the United States. Inevitably the restructuring in the car industry will lead to new alliances and mergers, although the progress has not been smooth in the past for such endeavors.

THE EUROPEAN CAR MARKET

The "1992" process was to have opened up European car market to competition by December 31, 1992. However, largely due to the performance gap between the Europeans and the Japanese producers, the European Commission has pushed the dismantling of trade barriers to the end of 1999. This has taken the form of voluntary quotas which for 1995 was 993,000 cars. The Europeans fear that while all the Japanese car makers together just barely equal the share of no. 2 General Motors, things could change rapidly in a market where no one company has even 20 percent market share (see Figure 2).

Japanese car manufacturers are also hindered in Europe due to exclusive dealerships; that is, dealers are not allowed to sell competing brands. Car manufacturers argue that such arrangements are critical in protecting the character, quality and service of their cars. In practice, this means that outsiders would have to develop distribution systems from scratch. The European Commission has granted a block exemption for this practice from the antitrust provisions of the Treaty of Rome.

Europe's Fiercely Contested Car Market FIGURE 2

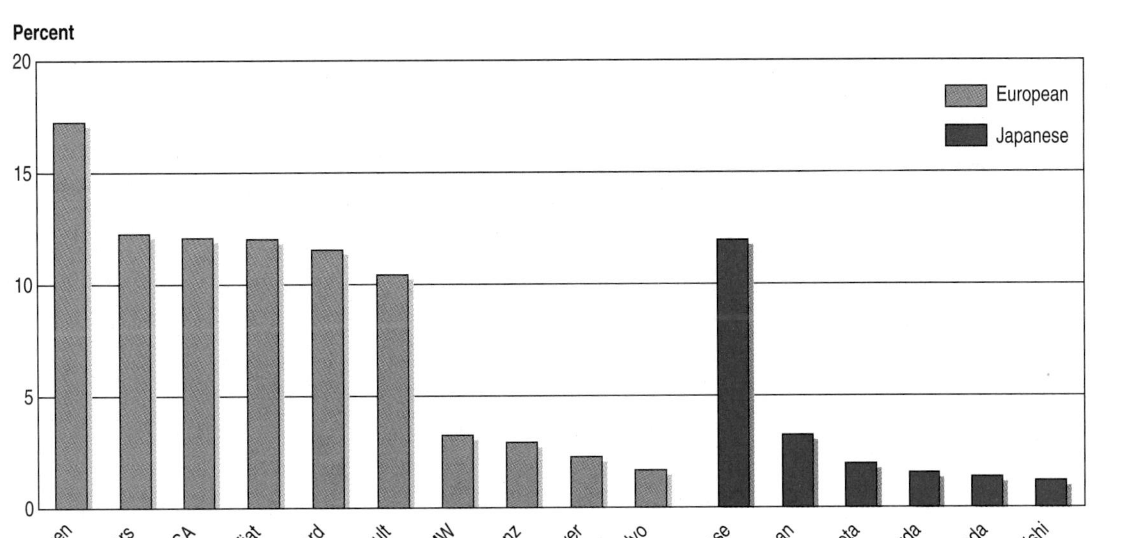

SOURCE: Carla Rapoport, "Europe Takes on the Japanese," *Fortune,* January 11, 1993, 14.

Behind the protectionism is that European car makers want to avoid the fate of their American counterparts a decade earlier, when Japanese market share jumped from 20 to 32 percent in the United States. By the end of the 1990s, the Japanese could be producing more than 1.5 million cars in Europe. Added to growing imports from Japan, Japanese market share could grow to 18 percent of the market from 12 percent in 1993. In addition, the Brussels-based European Automobile Association fears that 360,000 autos could be imported into the European Union by the year 2000—almost triple of 1993. These prospects have stirred both protectionist impulses, especially in France and Italy, and new competitiveness by the European producers.

Both in France and in Italy the car industry is one of the national champions that have fared well in protected markets but are relative weaklings in the global marketplace. Italy's Fiat, for example, produces about 4 percent of the country's GNP, which makes it impossible for the government to let it go down. In France, Jacques Calvet, the chairman of PSA (producer of Peugeot and Citroen) has repeatedly called for prohibiting new Japanese transplant factories in Europe, strict quotas, and freezing Japanese market share within the European Union.

More alarming for the Europeans is their loss of share outside of Europe. France's Renault and PSA have completely written off the U.S. market, believing that they can prosper with a strong European base while holding off the Japanese. Even some of the European specialists, such as Mercedes-Benz and Volvo, have been steadily losing share in the growing luxury segment of the U.S. market. Some have faith in their own markets. One auto executive forecast by saying: "The French are, well, so French. I don't think foreign cars, especially Japanese cars will do well in France. Not in our lifetime."

Questions for Discussion

1. The CEO of BMW Eberhard von Kuenheim commented on the Japanese threat by saying: "Where is the rule that the Japanese must win? The story of their endless success just may be ending." Is he realistic?
2. What must the European car manufacturers do to face the global realities of their industry to survive and succeed? Would you agree with Paul Ingrassia and Joseph White, authors of *Comeback: The Fall and Rise of the American Automobile Industry,* who state that "while Detroit decried free trade as a threat to its existence, free trade is what saved Detroit by forcing it to improve"?
3. Two of the largest car manufacturers in Europe are General Motors and Ford. Neither has been targeted by European Commission moves and are not generally seen as a threat. Why?

VIDEO CASE

Old Ways, New Games

American business is in transition. The end of World War II witnessed the emergence of the United States as the world's only economic superpower. The defeated Axis powers, Germany and Japan, literally lay in ruins and could only look to America for the funds and assistance to pick up the pieces.

Dramatic changes have occurred over the past half-century. The defeated countries rebuilt their economies and have emerged as economic superpowers themselves, and much of their advance has come at the expense of the United States. Sadly, how this shift in economic clout came about may have as much to do with the attitude of the majority of U.S. companies as it does perseverance on the part of economic competitors.

German and Japanese companies differ in many respects from their counterparts in the United States. Japanese managers tend to take a much longer view, especially in the area of product development. Both German and Japanese companies also contrast starkly with U.S. firms when it comes to labor relations. Perhaps more importantly, German and Japanese companies seem to have devised methods that accomplish two goals: Workers have been made to feel that the company cares about them and is willing to make an investment to make them more productive and better at their jobs. This not only engenders loyalty, but raises the overall quality and productivity of the company as a whole.

We will examine some of the methods German and Japanese firms have used in rising to the status of major economic global players. But first, we should review what has been happening to two big U.S. companies over the last three decades. We'll try to discover what American businessmen overlooked as they were losing market share to the competition. Then perhaps we can figure out what they did wrong, and what methods might be helpful in making a comeback.

Perhaps no company stands as a better metaphor of the declining fortunes of U.S. business than International Business Machines. The company that once offered a de facto guarantee of lifetime employment has laid off 190,000 workers, and recently lost $13 billion over one 24-month period.

Just three decades ago profits generated by mainframe sales enabled Big Blue to dominate the computer industry. But the vast hierarchal structure that grew up at IBM hid what should have been obvious. While management rested on mainframe laurels, the computer market veered sharply in the direction of personal computers and software.

Almost before its stodgy upper managers noticed, IBM had 100,000 fast moving, technology-driven competitors. Though caught flat-footed, IBM was finally able to grind into action. The company's Boca Raton–based PC business—with the help of IBM's super-talented R&D engineers—soon developed a host of solid, technologically advanced products. But management clung to its anachronistic methods of doing things and insisted that the PC subsidiary be brought to the corporate headquarters in Armonk, New York. Very shortly the company mentality, stifling bureaucracy, and plodding-paced operations had stunted innovative thinking.

By 1991 even IBM's top brass knew the company's structure had to be altered. The decision was made to break Big Blue into 14 "baby blues." The company had finally taken a critical look at factors that made it uncompetitive. Basic decision making required time-consuming meetings, followed by orders that flowed up and down the chain of command. All too frequently, by the time new products or policy changes reached the market or the customer, they were either obsolete or had already been matched by competitors.

Perhaps more damaging, IBM managers tended to make decisions that did not consider its customer's needs. The company culture appeared finally to have achieved a fatal level of arrogance. Management acted as though customers should accept whatever products IBM offered simply because the company had once dominated the industry.

IBM was operating with a hierarchal, highly stratified structure that made fast decision making impossible. This dense bureaucracy also made it difficult to react to shifts in the market and changes in customer preferences. And that problem was exacerbated by a company culture steeped in a top-down managed, chain-of-command structure with product development far removed from the market. Without changes in each of these areas, it wasn't likely IBM would ever return to competitiveness.

Questions for Discussion

1. What are the primary reasons that large U.S. companies like IBM have lost market share to the Germans and Japanese?
2. How are IBM's problems indicative of the overall problems that have led to a decline of U.S. competitiveness?
3. IBM's new chairman Louis Gerstner, Jr. has been charged with the task of returning the company to its former glory. What strategies should he emphasize?

In many ways, the Silicon Valley represents a microcosm of the best and brightest the United States has to offer. It has long been a technological hotbed of inventions and innovations. But too often, American companies have failed to commercialize on potentially profitable ideas.

But those ideas haven't had difficulty finding a home across the Pacific in Japan. And Japanese industry takes an entirely different view of capitalizing on technology. They also have a markedly different way of treating their employees.

There are plenty of examples of how abandoned U.S. technology was taken over and exploited by Japanese industry. A talented group of RCA engineers far ahead of their time developed the first flat panel liquid crystal display. But short-sighted RCA managers feared they were facing an on-going investment black hole with an uncertain payback. They ordered the project abandoned. The Japanese had no such reservations. They patiently nurtured the technology, and today produce 98 percent of the world's flat panel displays.

As for those best and brightest Americans back in the Silicon Valley—the ones who worked for managers who focused on short-term profits—many are unemployed today. Layoffs still occur without warning, and hordes of PhDs, engineers, and other highly talented and educated people are searching for work. One industry that is thriving is self-help groups. It's at such meetings that the lament can frequently be heard that the next generation likely won't be able to live as well as this one.

During the immediate post-war period, the United States led the world in plant reinvestment, capital improvements, and R&D expenditures. That is no longer the case. And in one instance where a major U.S. car maker attempted to out-automate the Japanese, the result has been disastrous.

For two decades General Motors witnessed the steady erosion of its market share to the Japanese. And by the 1980s, chairman Roger Smith decided to do something about it.

Weary of labor difficulties and hopeful of gaining a competitive advantage over Toyota and Nissan, he oversaw the purchase of state-of-the-art plant robotics and technology. Smith's reasoning went along the lines that robots didn't require overtime pay and they didn't go out on strike. Thousands of embittered workers were laid off.

While Smith's capital improvements were taking shape at GM, Japanese automakers were employing a diametrically opposite, people-centric approach. Teamwork and kaizan worker self- and job-improvement methods were emphasized. Workers were encouraged not only to make the best product, but to become the best worker they could. And unlike their American counterparts, Japanese workers could depend on the company to either employ them for life, or find them other employment if a layoff did occur.

Workers at Mercedes-Benz in Germany also are organized in self-directed work teams. Instead of the assembly-line approach used in the United States, teams complete subassembly portions of the automobile. Management vests these workers with the responsibility to accomplish their jobs well, the first time, and without oversight. Essentially, they place a great deal of faith in the individual excellence of individual workers, and their teams as a whole.

This is not the attitude GM management takes with the rank and file in U.S. auto plants. The teamwork concept is employed, but many workers claim it exists in theory but not actual practice. The element of trust is wholly lacking, and instead of delegating responsibility, finger pointing is the norm. Perhaps worst of all and reminiscent of IBM, management has insulated itself from the group it should be focused on: the customer.

Roger Smith's remake of General Motors cost a staggering $77 billion. It created plants that could mass manufacture cars around the clock. But when all the capital improvements were complete and in place, there weren't enough customers for all the cars GM was suddenly capable of producing. The state-of-art plants had to be run at 50 percent capacity, or even less. In one more parallel to another fallen industry titan IBM, General Motors assumed that if it mass produced the Chevrolet Grand Prix and Oldsmobile Cutlass as fast as it could, consumers would flock to purchase them.

They did not.

Questions for Discussion

4. What lessons could General Motors have learned from its German and Japanese counterparts that might have prevented its problems?

5. If GM were to try to emulate some of the German and Japanese management techniques, how could it ensure that the theories were actually put into practice?

6. How would you suggest that GM improve its labor relations given its dismal record?

PART TWO

The Global Economic Environment and Institutions

As nations and businesses engage in global trade and investment, they operate within the framework of an *international monetary system. Accounting systems* measure economic activity amid the continuous efforts of nations to *integrate and coordinate* these economic activities with *changing trade policies* of individual countries.

Part 2 examines each of these four areas and is intended to provide the reader with a global economic and institutional perspective of the setting for conducting international trade.

The International Economic Activity of the Nation: The Balance of Payments

LEARNING OBJECTIVES

To understand the fundamental principles of how countries measure international business activity, the balance of payments.

To examine the similarities of the current and financial accounts of the balance of payments.

To understand the critical differences between trade in merchandise and services, and why international investment activity has recently been controversial in the United States.

To review the mechanical steps of how exchange rate changes are transmitted into altered trade prices and eventually trade volumes.

U.S. Excels in Service Productivity Poll

U.S. workers in major service industries are more productive than their counterparts overseas—except in restaurants, where the French excel.

A study by an affiliate of McKinsey & Co., a management consulting firm, concludes that the U.S. edge largely reflects both the way management organizes operations and the degree to which government allows competition to force businesses to be efficient. Workers' skills and the amount of financial investment make suprisingly little difference.

The report by the McKinsey Global Institute was prepared with advice from several economists, including Nobel laureate Robert Solow of the Massachusetts Institute of Technology. The study concludes that "the U.S. has a slightly higher level of overall productivity than Germany and France and a significantly higher level than Japan and the U.K."

Productivity, a measure of how much output is produced for an hour of work, is the key to rising standards of living.

In service industries, which represent a growing share of world employment, productivity is notoriously difficult to measure. The McKinsey report took a case-study approach to evaluate airlines, banks, and restaurants, as well as retailing and telecommunication industries. Japan was included in only the last two categories; Europe was included in all five.

The study urges governments to lower barriers so that new companies can more easily enter service industries; encourage foreign investment, particularly in airlines; relax regulations that prevent firms from laying off workers when the technologies of markets change; and aggressively combat anticompetitive practices.

SOURCE: Abstracted from "U.S. Excels in Service Productivity Poll," by David Wesser, *The Wall Street Journal*, October 13, 1992.

Global business transactions occur in many different forms over the course of a year. The measurement of all global economic transactions between the residents of a country and foreign residents is called the **balance of payments (BOP).**[1] Government policymakers need such measures of economic activity in order to evaluate the general competitiveness of domestic industry, set exchange rate or interest rate policies or goals, and for many other purposes. Individuals and businesses use various BOP measures to gauge the growth and health of specific types of trade or financial transactions by country and regions of the world with the home country.

balance of payments international economic transactions between one country and another

Global transactions take many forms. Each of the following examples is a global economic transaction that is counted and captured in the U.S. balance of payments:

- U.S. imports of Honda automobiles, which are manufactured in Japan.
- A U.S.-based firm, Bechtel, is hired to manage the construction of a major water-treatment facility in the Middle East.
- The U.S. subsidiary of a French firm, Saint Gobian, pays profits (dividends) back to the parent firm in Paris.

QUESTION *How many nations are there in the world?*

According to the most recent count there are 178 members of the United Nations and 11 non-members. A total of 189 nations.

- Daimler-Benz, the well-known German automobile manufacturer, purchases a small automotive parts manufacturer outside Chicago, Illinois.
- An American tourist purchases a hand-blown glass figurine in Venice, Italy.
- The U.S. government provides grant financing of military equipment for its NATO (North Atlantic Treaty Organization) military ally, Turkey.
- A Canadian dentist purchases a U.S. Treasury bill through an investment broker in Cleveland, Ohio.

These are just a small sample of the hundreds of thousands of global transactions that occur each year. The balance of payments provides a systematic method for the classification of all of these transactions. There is one rule of thumb that will always aid in the understanding of BOP accounting: Watch the direction of the movement of money.

FUNDAMENTALS OF BALANCE OF PAYMENTS ACCOUNTING

There are three main elements to the process of measuring global economic activity: (1) identifying what is and is not an international economic transaction; (2) understanding how the flow of goods, services, assets, and money creates changes in the BOP; and (3) understanding the bookkeeping procedures for BOP accounting.

Defining International Economic Transactions

Identifying international transactions is ordinarily not difficult. The export of merchandise, goods such as trucks, machinery, computers, telecommunications equipment, and so forth, is obviously an international transaction. Imports such as French wine, Japanese cameras, and German automobiles are also clearly international transactions. But this merchandise trade is only a portion of the thousands of different international transactions that occur in the United States or any other country each year.

Many international transactions such as service transactions are not so obvious. The purchase of a glass figure in Venice, Italy, by an American tourist is classified as a U.S. merchandise import. In fact, all expenditures made by American tourists around the globe that are for goods or services (meals, hotel accommodations, and so forth) are recorded in the U.S. balance of payments as imports of travel services in the current account. As noted in Global Learning Experience 3.1, services is an area where the U.S. excels—and will most likely have major implications for the future. The purchase of a U.S. Treasury bill by a foreign resident is an international financial transaction and is dutifully recorded in the financial account of the U.S. balance of payments.

The BOP as a Flow Statement

The BOP is often misunderstood because many people believe it to be a balance sheet, rather than a cash flow statement. By recording all international transactions over a period of time, it is tracking the continuing flow of purchases and payments between a country and all other countries.

There are two types of business transactions that dominate the balance of payments:

Real assets—The exchange of physical goods and all types of services for the payment of money. (Note: When the payment is other goods or services, it is referred to as barter.)

Financial assets—The exchange of financial claims (stocks, bonds, loans, purchases, or sales of companies) in exchange for other financial claims or money.

Generally speaking, the export and import of goods and services are recorded in the current account while financial transactions are recorded in the financial account. The balance of payments is composed of two main groups of accounts:

1. The current account
2. The capital and financial account

These accounts are most important and are closely watched and studied by investors, politicians, business people, and students of global business.

Although assets can be separated as to whether they are real (merchandise and services) or financial (stocks and bonds), it is often easier to simply think of all assets as being goods that can be bought and sold. An American tourist's purchase of a hand-woven area rug in a shop in Bangkok is not all that different from a Wall Street banker buying a British government bond for investment purposes.

Before describing the BOP subaccounts and the balance of payments as a whole, it is necessary to understand how balance of payments accounting is carried out.

BOP ACCOUNTING: DOUBLE-ENTRY BOOKKEEPING

The balance of payments employs an accounting technique called **double-entry bookkeeping,** which is a method of accounting in which every transaction produces both a **debit** and a **credit** of the same amount. A debit (−) is created whenever an asset is increased, a liability is decreased, or an expense is increased. A credit (+) is created whenever an asset is decreased, a liability is increased, or an expense is decreased. The theory is that every transaction causes both a debit and a credit entry in some account in the balance of payments. What is done to one side of the BOP must be done to the other side. Thus, when both sides of the balance of payments are added up, they are equal—they are in balance.

double-entry bookkeeping
a method of accounting in which every transaction produces both a debit and a credit of the same amount

debit
created when an asset is increased, a liability is decreased, or an expense is increased

credit
created when an asset is decreased, a liability is increased, or an expense is decreased

Individuals experience this same type of double-entry bookkeeping when they decide to purchase any good or service. For example, when a person decides to purchase a package of chewing gum for $1, the clerk behind the counter hands him the gum which he puts in his left pocket. This increases his inventory of gum (an increase in assets). He removes $1 from his right-hand pocket and pays for the gum (a decrease in financial assets). He has added (debited) $1 in gum to his physical assets and simultaneously reduced (credited) his financial assets by $1, so there are two entries.

It may be useful for readers to consider their left-hand pocket as the current account where all assets (such as chewing gum) are stored and to think of their right-hand pocket as where financial transactions (money) are stored. The balance of payments is exactly the same except that it is done at the national level with large numbers of transactions. Let's consider two international transactions examples: (A) A U.S. retail store buys (imports) $2 million worth of TVs and VCRs from a Japanese manufacturer and (B) A U.S. machine tool manufacturer sells (exports) $3 million worth of automated machine tools to an Italian company. These transactions would be recorded in the BOP as follows:

Current Account

Debit (−)		Credit (+)	
A. Import of TVs and VCRs (Increase in Assets)	$2,000,000	B. Export of Machine Tools (Decrease in Assets)	$3,000,000

Capital Account

Debit (−)		Credit (+)	
B. Receipt of Payment for MachineTools from Italian Company (Increase in Cash)	$3,000,000	A. Payment to Japan for TVs and VCRs (Decrease in Cash)	$2,000,000
Total BOP	$5,000,000		$5,000,000

The reader should note two important points in the BOP account illustrated above: (1) While there may be imbalances in the current and financial accounts individually, the sum of both accounts balance and (2) Imbalances in the current account tend to be offset by an equal imbalance in the financial account.

THE CURRENT ACCOUNT

The current account includes all international economic transactions with income or payment flows occurring within the year, the current period. The current account consists of four subcategories:

merchandise trade
funds used for merchandise imports and funds obtained from merchandise exports

1. *Merchandise trade*—This is the export and import of goods. **Merchandise trade** is the oldest and most traditional form of international economic activity. Although many countries depend on imports of many goods (as they should according to the theory of comparative advantage), they also normally work to preserve either a balance of merchandise trade or even a surplus. As illustrated in Table 3.1, the United States has a deficit of more than $186.2 billion in mer-

TABLE 3.1 **The Current Account, 1996 (billions of U.S. dollars)**

	1996
Exports of merchandise	$613.5
Imports of merchandise	−799.8
Trade Balance	−186.2
Exports of services	221.8
Imports of services	−148.5
Service trade balance	73.3
Income receipts on investments	197.1
Income payments on investments	−206.7
Income balance	−9.6
Net unilateral transfers	−43.0
Balance on current account	−165.6

SOURCE: International Monetary Fund. *Balance of Payments Statistics Yearbook,* 1997.

chandise trade in 1996. This is a considerable sum, and it represents a significant increase in the deficit compared with the $74.1 billion deficit of 1991 and $96.1 billion deficit of 1992.

2. *Service trade*—This is the export and import of services. Common international services include financial services provided by banks to foreign importers and exporters, travel services of airlines, and construction services of U.S. firms building pipelines or bridges in other countries. For the major industrial countries, this subaccount has shown the fastest growth in the past decade. The United States has gross exports of **service trade** of $221.8 billion in 1996, service imports of $148.5 billion, with a balance on service trade of a surplus of $73.3 billion. The service sector, both in domestic trade and international trade, continues to be a major growth sector for the U.S. economy.
3. *Investment income*—This is the current income associated with investments that were made in previous periods. If a U.S. firm created a subsidiary in South Korea to produce metal parts in a previous year, the proportion of net income that is paid back to the parent company this year (the dividend) constituents current *investment income* on a U.S. asset abroad. Conversely, if a foreign company has a subsidiary in the United States, dividends sent to the foreign company result in income payments on foreign assets in the United States. The United States experienced deficit of $9.6 billion in the investment category in 1996.
4. *Current Transfers*—A transfer between countries that is one way; a humanitarian type gift or grant that reduces the income and consumption of the donor and increases the income and consumption of the recipient. Examples are gifts of food, clothing, other consumer goods, medical supplies, etc. associated with relief efforts resulting from earthquakes, famine, and other natural disasters. In 1996, the United States recorded a deficit in current transfers of $43.0 billion. In total, the United States experienced a deficit of $165.6 billion in its current account.

service trade
the international exchange of personal or professional services

All countries possess some amount of trade, most of which is merchandise. Many smaller and less developed countries have little service trade and may also have very little international financial transactions that would be classified under the financial account.

The current account is typically dominated by the export and import of merchandise. For this reason, the balance of trade (BOT), which is so widely quoted in the business press in most countries, refers specifically to the balance of exports and imports of merchandise trade only. For larger industrialized countries, however, the BOT is somewhat misleading in that service trade is not included, and that trade may actually be fairly large as well. Although the merchandise-trade deficit has been a continuing source of concern for the United States since the early 1980s, the other three major subaccounts of the current account should not be ignored.

Merchandise Trade

Figure 3.1 places the current account values of 1996 in perspective over time by dividing the current account into its two major components: (1) merchandise trade and (2) services trade and investment income. The first and most striking message is the suddenness and magnitude with which the merchandise-trade deficit increased beginning

QUESTION *Which of the world's cities has the largest population?*

ANSWER *Mexico City, with a population of 15 million, is built on a filled-in lake, at a height of 7,350 feet. Some estimates indicate that Mexico City's population will double by the year 2025. São Paulo, Brazil is the second largest city with a population of 21.1 million. Next comes Tokyo/Yokohama with 20.9 million; New York, 15.7 million; Calcutta, 13.7 million; Shanghai, 13.4 million; Bombay, 13.1 million; Buenos Aires, 12.3 million; and Rio De Janeiro with 12.1 million.*

in 1982. The balance on services and income, although not large in comparison to net merchandise trade, has with few exceptions run a surplus over the past two decades. The merchandise-trade deficit of the United States hit an all-time high of $160 billion in 1987. The 1988-1993 period, however, showed a remarkable improvement as U.S. exports grew at a much more rapid pace than U.S. merchandise imports, and the merchandise-trade deficit in 1991 declined to $74.1 billion. Since then imports resumed growing at a more rapid pace than exports. By the end of 1996, the merchandise-trade deficit increased to $186.3 billion. The post-1987 period has also seen a surge in

FIGURE 3.1 **The Components of the U.S. Current Account Balance: Merchandise-Trade Balance and Services and Income Balance, 1970–1996**

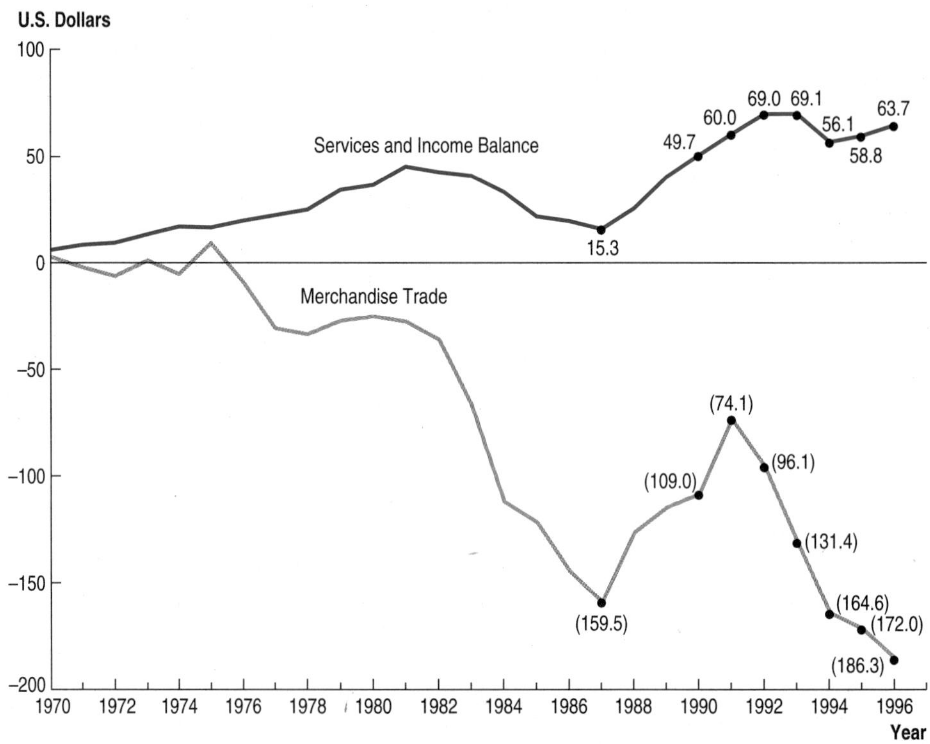

SOURCE: The International Monetary Fund, *Balance of Payments Statistics Yearbook,* 1997

FIGURE 3.2

U.S. Merchandise Imports and Exports, 1970–1996

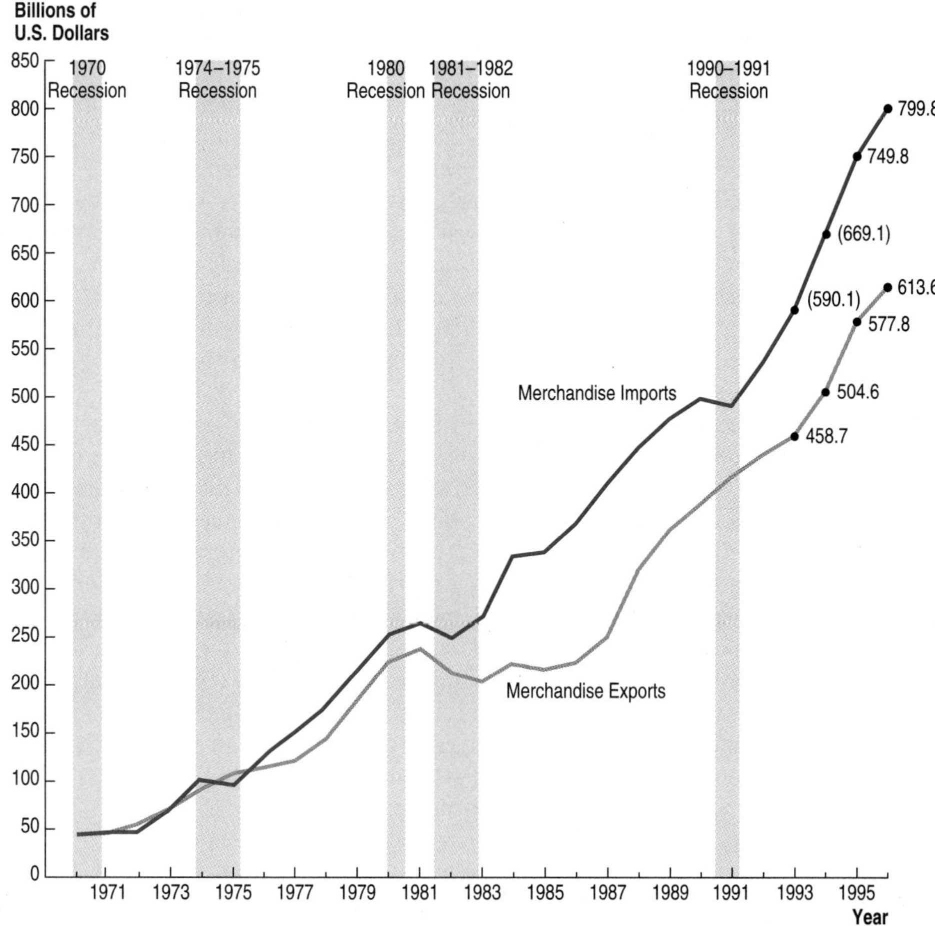

SOURCE: The International Monetary Fund, *Balance of Payments Statistics Yearbook,* 1997.

the service-trade surplus and net income balance which reached the $69.1 billion level in 1993 and then declined to the 1996 level of $63.7 billion due to an increasing U.S. deficit in the investment income sector.

The merchandise-trade deficits of the past decade have been an area of considerable concern for the United States, in both the public and private sectors. Merchandise trade is the original core of international trade. The manufacturing of goods was the basis of the Industrial Revolution and the focus of the theory of international trade described in the previous chapters. Manufacturing is traditionally the sector of the economy that employs most of a country's workers. The merchandise-trade deficit of the 1980s saw the decline in traditional heavy industries in the United States, industries that have historically employed many of America's workers. Declines in the net trade balance in areas such as steel, automobiles, automotive parts, textiles, shoe manufacturing, and others have caused massive economic and social disruption. The problems of dealing with these shifting trade balances will be discussed in detail in a later chapter.

The most encouraging news for U.S. manufacturing trade is the growth of exports in the latter half of the 1980s and the 1990s, as shown in Figure 3.2. A number of factors contributed to the growth of U.S. exports, such as the weaker dollar (which made

U.S.-manufactured goods cheaper in terms of the currencies of other countries) and more rapid economic growth in Europe in the latter part of the 1980s. Understanding merchandise import and export performance is much like analyzing the market for any single product. The demand factors that drive both imports and exports are income, the economic growth rate of the buyer, and the price of the product in the eyes of the consumer after passing through an exchange rate. For example, U.S. merchandise imports reflect the income level and growth of American consumers and industry. As income rises, so does the demand for imports. As shown in Figure 3.2, when the United States came out of the 1981–1982 recession, imports rose dramatically as the U.S. economy recovered. With the 1990–1991 recession over and the U.S. economy recovering, the pattern of increasing imports is evident once again. Of course supply-side factors, such as the cost of production and the eventual cost of the product, are also important. Many exports argue that in the early to middle 1980s, the U.S. economy had no reasonably priced competitive products for much of the merchandise that was imported in larger and larger volumes.

Exports follow the same principles but in the reversed position. U.S. manufacturing exports depend not on the incomes of U.S. residents, but on the incomes of buyers of U.S. products in all other countries. The major markets for U.S. exports are the industrialized nations such as Canada, Japan, and Western Europe. When these economies are growing, the demand for U.S. products rises. The rapid growth of the Western European economies in the later 1980s, as well as the falling dollar making U.S. products relatively cheaper to European consumers, aided greatly in the growth of U.S. merchandise exports beginning in 1987.

The service component of the U.S. current account is one of mystery to many. Figure 3.3 shows the recent growth in total U.S. service imports and exports, but also the much appreciated increasing surplus in the U.S. service-trade balance. The major categories of services include travel and passenger fares, transportation services, expenditures by U.S. students abroad and foreign students pursuing studies in the United States, telecommunications services, and financial services.

Of the remaining components of the current account, net investment income and unilateral transfers, net investment income was neutral (a deficit of $9.6 billion) in 1996 while **current transfers** was negative ($43.0 billion).

current transfers
transfers, gifts, or grants of humanitarian goods and services

THE CAPITAL AND FINANCIAL ACCOUNT

The *capital and financial account* has two major components—the *capital account* and the *financial account.*

capital account
transfers of capital assets and debt forgiveness amount countries without compensation

The **capital account** measures the transfers of fixed assets (land, buildings, etc.) and items like debt forgiveness among nations when they are undertaken without payment or compensation. In 1996 the U.S. realized a favorable balance of $0.5 billion in the capital account.

direct investment
transactions between investors and enterprises in the control or ownership of assets in a foreign economy

portfolio investment
the net balance of capital that flows in and out of the United States less than 10 percent ownership

Of greater significance for the United States is the *financial account* which measures all International transactions of financial assets. Financial assets can be classified in a number of different ways, including the length of the life of the asset (its maturity), by nature of the ownership (public or private), or by the degree of control over assets or operations that the claim represents (portfolio, with no control, or direct investment, with some degree of control).

Table 3.2 shows the major subcategories of the U.S. financial account balance for 1996: **direct investment, portfolio investment,** and other investment assets.

1. *Direct investment*—This is the net balance of capital that flows out of and into the United States for the purpose of exerting control over assets. For example, if

U.S. Imports and Exports of Services, 1984–1996 FIGURE 3.3

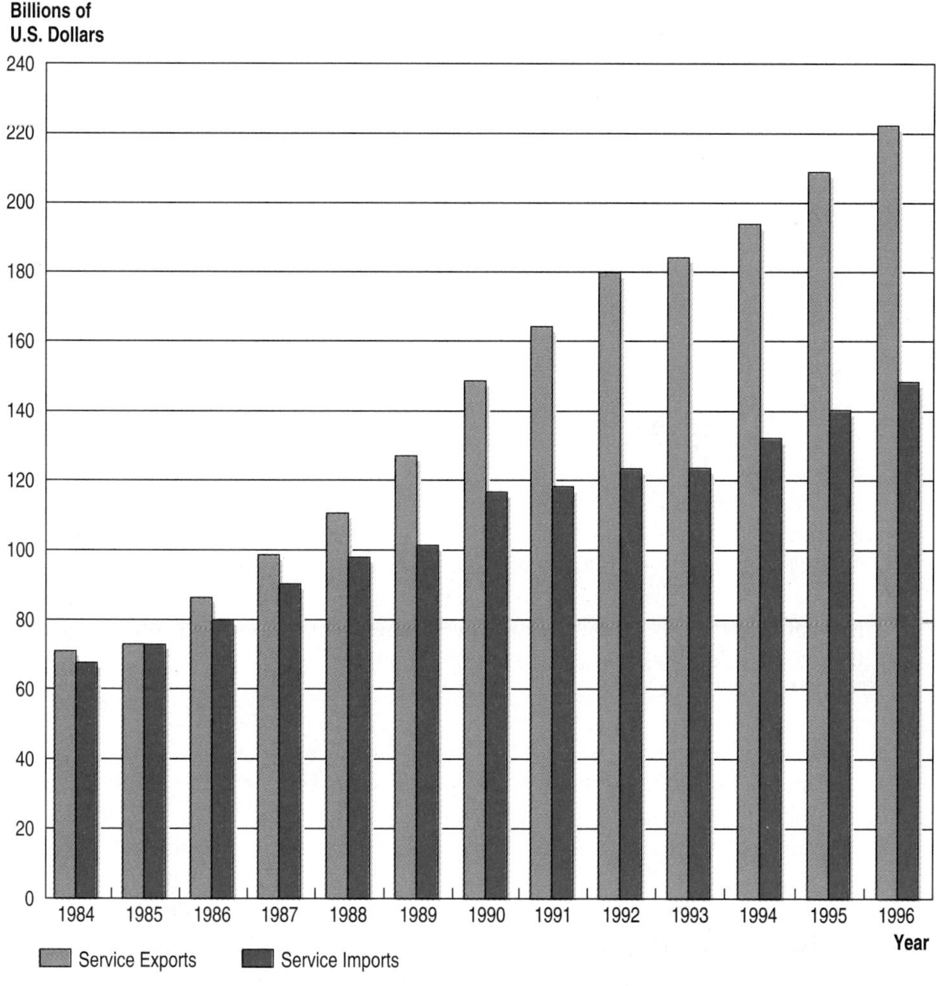

SOURCE: The International Monetary Fund, *Balance of Payments Statistics Yearbook,* 1997.

a U.S. firm either builds a new automotive parts facility in another country (Ford built a fuel-handling part facility in Hungary) or purchases a company in another country, this would fall under direct investment. When the capital flows out of the United States, as in the two examples just used, it enters the balance of payments as a negative cash flow. If, however, foreign firms purchase firms in the United States (for example, Sony of Japan purchased Columbia Pictures in 1989), it is a capital inflow and enters the balance of payments positively. Whenever 10 percent or more of the voting shares in a U.S. company are held by foreign investors, the company is classified as the U.S. affiliate of a foreign company and a foreign direct investment. Similarly, if U.S. investors hold 10 percent or more of

QUESTION

This is the lowest point on land.

The shores of the Dead Sea. It is 1,312 feet below sea level in Israel and Jordan.

the control in a company outside the United States, that company is considered the foreign affiliate of a U.S. company. The United States experienced a deficit of $4.4 billion in direct investment in 1996.

2. *Portfolio investment*—This is net balance of capital that flows in and out of the United States but that does not reach the 10 percent ownership threshold of direct investment. If a U.S. resident purchases shares in a Japanese firm but does not attain the 10 percent threshold, it is considered a portfolio investment (and in this case an outflow of capital). The purchase or sale of debt securities (like U.S. Treasury bills or bonds) across borders is always classified as portfolio investment because debt securities by definition do not provide the buyer with ownership or control. Net portfolio investment for the United States was a positive $274.2 billion for 1996, indicating that foreign citizens and financial institutions purchased more U.S. portfolio instruments than U.S. citizens did of foreign investments.
3. *Other investments*—This category consists of various bank loans extended by U.S. resident banking operations as well as net borrowing by U.S. firms from financial institutions outside the United States. The net balance on other long-term capital in 1996 was a deficit of $57.8 billion.

Direct Investment

Figure 3.4 shows how the two major subaccounts of the U.S. financial account, net direct investment and portfolio investment, have changed since 1980. Net direct investment started the 1980s with a slight deficit in 1980 but showed a surplus every year between 1981 and 1990. The balance on net direct investment went negative in 1991 for the first time in a decade and continued to be negative through 1996. It appears the world's enthusiasm for the acquisition of U.S. firms and other foreign-controlled investment (direct investment) in the United States has been exceeded by an acquisition of foreign firms and assets by U.S. firms.

TABLE 3.2 **The U.S. Financial Account, 1996 (billions of U.S. dollars)**

Capital Account	$0.5
Financial Account	
Direct Investment Abroad	$(88.3)
Direct Investment in the United States	83.9
Net Direct Investment	(4.4)
Net Portfolio Investment	274.2
Other Investments	(57.8)
Reserves and Related Items	6.7
Total Capital and Financial Account	$218.7

SOURCE: International Monetary Fund, *Balance of Payments Statistics Yearbook,* 1997.

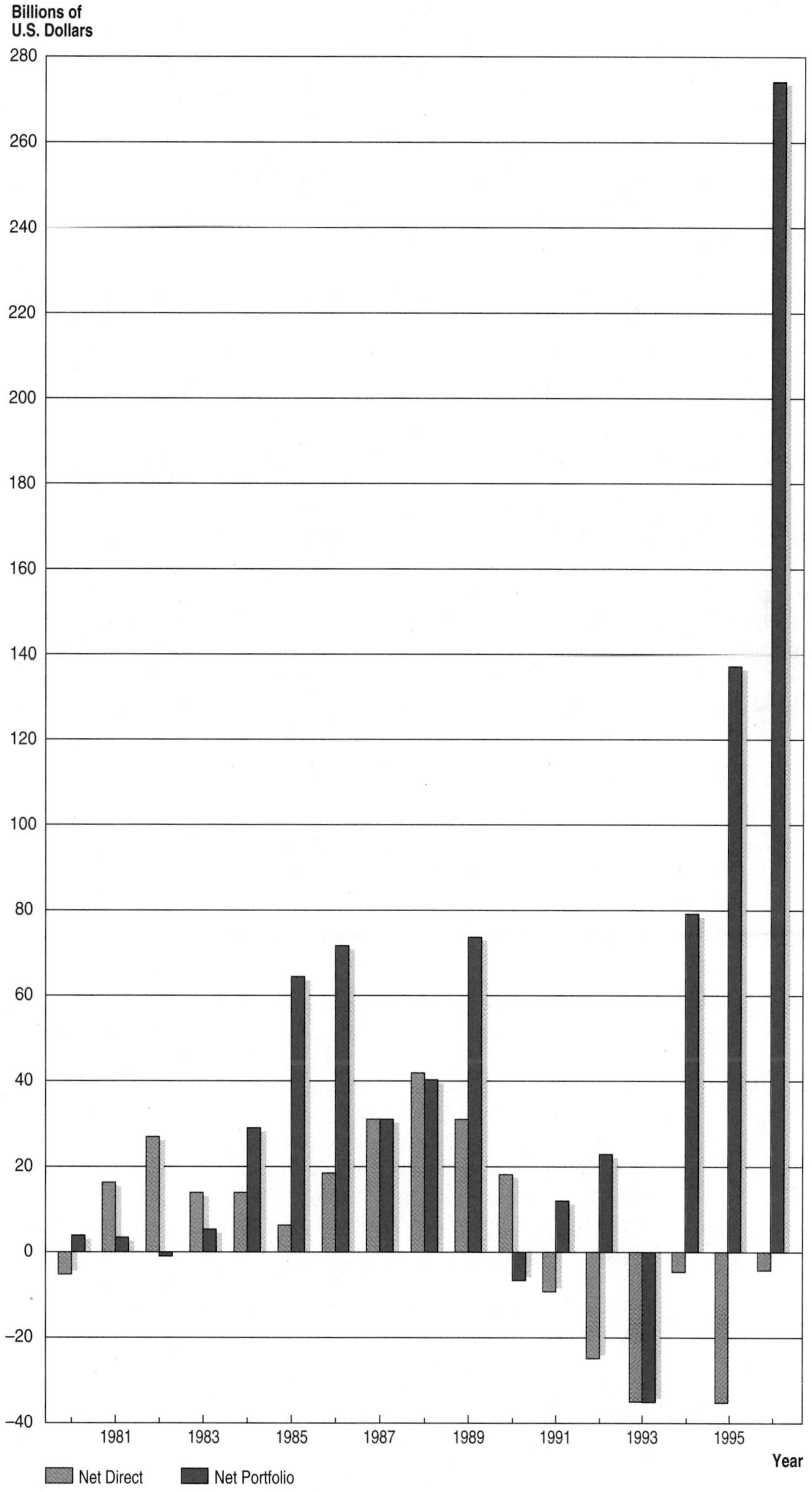

FIGURE 3.4

U.S. Financial Account Components, 1974–1993: Net Direct Investment and Net Portfolio Investment, 1980–1996

SOURCE: The International Monetary Fund, *Balance of Payments Statistics Yearbook*, 1997.

"They Don't Let Just Anyone Buy a Defense Contractor"

Alain Gomez, the dapper chairman of France's Thomson-CSF, lined up some of the best string-pullers money can buy to help acquire bankrupt LTV Corp.'s missile business. The defense-electronics giant, 58 percent-owned by the French government, joined with the Carlyle Group, a well-connected Washington investment bank whose vice chairman is former Defense Secretary Frank C. Carlucci. For public relations, Gomez tapped Carter Administration Press Secretary Jody Powell's high-powered spin-ship, Powell Tate, as well as a legion of K Street lawyers.

But the pricey talent couldn't overcome the volatile politics of selling sensitive U.S. defense assets to foreigners, particularly in an election year. On July 5, Thomson withdrew its $450 million joint bid with Carlyle to buy LTV's missile and aircraft businesses. Small wonder. The U.S. defense establishment carried out a blistering behind-the-scenes assault on Thomson over its status as a French government holding and its past business dealings with Iraq.

Even if Thomson can pull together a new proposal, it will still face heated opposition from Martin Marietta Corp. and Lockheed Corp., whose rival $385 million offer lost out to the French in April. Martin Marietta Chairman Norman R. Augustine objects to Thomson's taking even a minority stake. Augustine has friends in high places: He was on Bush's short list of potential defense secretaries back in 1988.

Ironically, Thomson's association with the Carlyle Group also hurt the deal. Roughly one-third of the $150 million Carlyle planned to put up for LTV's aircraft unit was bankrolled by state-backed Credit Lyonnais. So the group was viewed as "a front" for the French government, says an administration source. Such rough treatment speaks volumes about the U.S. defense industry's inevitable post-cold-war consolidation. Foreigners serious about buying their way in had better be combat-ready.

SOURCE: Brian Bremner, Seth Payne, and Jonathan B. Levine, "They Don't Let Just Anyone Buy a Defense Contractor," *Business Week,* July 20, 1992, 41–42.

The boom in foreign investment in the United States during the 1980s was, however, extremely controversial. Historically, it has typically been the case that U.S. firms invested abroad. The rapid growth of the U.S. economy and the expansion of many U.S. firms to build manufacturing, mining, refining, and many other industrial facilities around the world had become the norm. With the 1980s came a complete reversal in the direction of these net capital flows. Foreign investors were pouring more long-term capital into the United States that U.S. firms invested abroad. Many Americans worried about this increasing foreign presence in the U.S. marketplace, not just in selling products to U.S. consumers as has become so common with merchandise imports, but with foreign investors actually exercising significant control over U.S. firms, U.S. workers, and U.S. assets. (See Global Learning Experience 3.2.)

The source of concern over foreign investment in any country, including the United States, normally focuses on one of two major topics, control and profit. Most countries have restrictions on what foreigners may own. This is based on the premise that domestic land, assets, and industry in general should be held by residents of the country. For example, until 1990 it was not possible for a foreign firm to own more than 20 percent of any company in Finland. And this is the norm, rather than the exception. The

United States has traditionally had few restrictions on what foreign residents or firms can own or control in the United States, with most restrictions remaining today being related to national security concerns. As opposed to many of the traditional debates over whether international trade should be free or not, there is not the same consensus for unrestricted international investment. This is a question that is still very much a domestic political concern first and an international economic issue second.

The second major source of concern over foreign direct investment is who ultimately receives the profits from the enterprise. Foreign companies owning firms in the United States will ultimately profit from the activities of the firms, or put another way, from the efforts of American workers. In spite of evidence that indicates foreign firms in the United States reinvest most of the profits in the United States (in fact, at a higher rate than domestic firms), the debate has continued on possible profit drains. Regardless of the choices made, workers of any nation usually feel the profits of their work should remain in the hands of their own countrymen. Once again, this is in many ways a political and emotional concern more than an economic one.

A final note regarding the massive capital inflows into the United States in the 1980s. The choice of which words are used to describe this increasing foreign investment can alone influence public opinion. If these massive capital inflows are described as "capital investments from all over the world showing their faith in the future of American industry," the net capital surplus is represented as decidedly positive. If, however, the net capital surplus is described as resulting in "the United States as the world's largest debtor nation," the negative connotation is obvious. But which, if either, is correct? The answer is actually quite simple. Investment, whether short-term or long term, flows to where it believes it can earn the greatest return for the level of risk. And although in an accounting sense this is "international debt," when the majority of the capital inflow is in the form of direct investment, a long-term commitment to jobs, production, services, technological, and other competitive investments, the competitiveness of American industry (industry located within the United States) is increased. The "net debtor" label is also misleading in that it invites comparison with large "debtor-nations" like Mexico and Brazil. But unlike Mexico and Brazil, the majority of this foreign investment is not bank loans that will have to be paid back in regular installments over 8 to 10 years, and it is not bank loans denominated in a currency that is foreign. Mexico and Brazil owe U.S. dollars; the United States "owes" U.S. dollars. Therefore, the profitability of the industry and the economy in the United States will be the source of repaying the investments.

Portfolio Investment

Portfolio investment is capital that is invested in activities that are purely profit-motivated (return), rather than ones made in the prospect of controlling or managing or directing the investment. Investments that are purchases of debt securities, bonds, interest-bearing bank accounts, and the like are only intended to earn a return. They provide no vote or control over the part issuing the debt. Purchase of debt issued by the U.S. government—U.S. Treasury bills, notes, and bonds—by foreign investors constitute net portfolio investment in the United States.

As illustrated in Figure 3.4, portfolio investment has shown a similar pattern to net direct investment over the past decade. Many U.S. debt securities, such as U.S. Treasury securities and corporate bonds, were in high demand throughout the 1980s. The primary reason for the surge in net portfolio investment resulted from two different forces, return and risk.

In the early 1980s, interest rates were quite high in the United States, the result of high inflation in the late 1970s and the "tight money policy" (slow money supply growth) of the U.S. Federal Reserve. The rate of inflation fell rapidly in the early 1980s, while interest rates

Emerging Market Firms Innovate to Raise Funds

Raising capital used to be a cinch for emerging-market companies, as foreign investors couldn't seem to buy enough of their stocks and bonds. Then U.S. rates skyrocketed in the last year and the Mexican peso fell, and suddenly the flush days were gone.

Today's hard times mean "portfolio investment is out and direct investment is in," said Roberto Danino, chairman of the Latin American practice group at the law firm Rogers & Wells in Washington. There are two basic routes to direct investing. First, there's "securitization," or buying securities that are backed by specific company assets. Alternatively, there is venture capital, which involves taking a direct stake in a company through a privately negotiated transaction.

Throughout the world's emerging markets, "it's cheaper to get deals" today, said Joseph Fogg, head of the venture capital firm JG Fogg & Co. in Westbury, Conn. A former executive at Morgan Stanley & Co., Mr. Fogg has already launched two $50 million venture funds, one to invest exclusively in Peru, the other in Vietnam. In both funds, he is focusing on "very simple basic stuff, appropriate to economies at early stages of development like bottled water and real estate."

SOURCE: Thomas T. Vogel, Jr., and Jose de Cordoba, "Emerging Market Firms Innovate to Raise Funds," *The Wall Street Journal,* February 13, 1995, C1, C17.

did not. This resulted in very high "real rates" of interest (interest less inflation), which were much higher than what could be earned in many other nations. Capital flowed into the U.S. economy in order to take advantage of these relatively high *real returns.*

At the same time, many of the major industrial countries were suffering prolonged recessions or very slow economic growth. This meant that profitable investments for capital were hard to find. And many of the major borrower countries, like Mexico and Brazil, were turning out to be bad borrowers, unable to repay their debts. Capital was therefore looking for a *safe haven,* a place where the political and economic systems were dependable and secure. The safe haven for world capital in the early to middle 1980s was the United States.

As shown in Figure 3.4, the balance on portfolio investment was positive for every year between 1980 and 1989, except for a slight deficit in 1982. The net surplus of portfolio investment in the 1980s peaked in 1986 at more than $70 billion. By 1990, however, interest rates and other motivations for portfolio investment in the United States had waned, as did the flow of portfolio investment. The balance on portfolio investment in 1990 saw a shift to the negative, with a net outflow of capital of approximately $6.8 billion. In 1991, it returned to a slight surplus once again, this time approximately $11.8 billion, and in 1992 it rose to $22.8 billion as shown in Figure 3.4. It returned to a negative $35.3 billion in 1993, but then turned positive through 1996 as foreign investors took large positions in the ownership of U.S. debt and as net portfolio investment increased to $274.2 billion in 1996. Global Learning Experience 3.3 provides an example of how portfolio investment changes over time.

Current and Financial Account Balance Relationships

Figure 3.5 illustrates the current and financial account balances for the United States in recent years. What the figure shows is one of the basic economic and accounting relationships of the balance of payments: the inverse relation between the current and fi-

U.S. Current and Financial Account Balances, 1984–1996 (billions of U.S. dollars) FIGURE 3.5

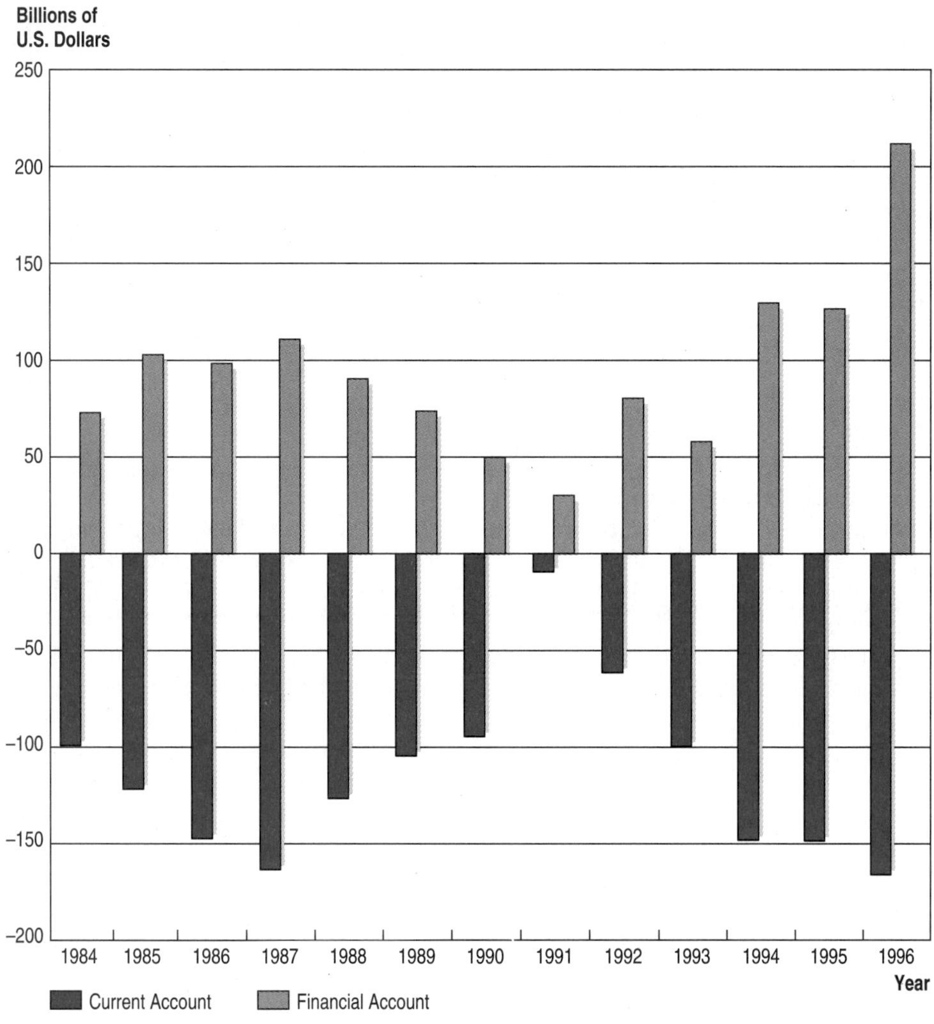

SOURCE: International Monetary Fund, *Balance of Payments Statistics Yearbook,* 1997.

nancial accounts. This inverse relationship is not accidental. The methodology of the balance of payments, double-entry bookkeeping, requires that the current and financial accounts be offsetting.

The U.S. current account deficits of the 1980s, resulting primarily from massive merchandise-trade deficits, were "financed" by equally large surpluses in the financial account. This is the typical way it is represented: Current account activities cause financial account entries. There are experts who believe, however, that it could very well be the other way around. The truth is probably some combination of the two.

The last year for which balance of payments data are available, 1996, shows a continuation of the inverse relationship.

NET ERRORS AND OMISSIONS

As noted before, because current account and financial account entries are collected and recorded separately, errors or statistical discrepancies will occur. The net errors and omissions account (the title used by the International Monetary Fund) makes sure that the BOP actually balances.

For the United States, the size of the net errors and omissions account has varied substantially over recent times. The United States recorded surpluses in "errors" of $55.8 billion and $46.5 billion in 1989 and 1990, followed by negative values of $26.8 billion and $23.1 billion in 1991 and 1992 respectively. Surpluses occurred again in 1993 through 1995 but became negative—$53.1 billion in 1996. There are a variety of potential explanations for this, including underreporting of exports and the underground or illegal economy's impacts on the flows of assets values across borders.

OFFICIAL RESERVES ACCOUNT

official reserves account total currency and metallic reserves held by official monetary authorities within a country

The **official reserves account** is the total currency and metallic reserves held by official monetary authorities within the country. These reserves are normally composed of the major currencies used in international trade and financial transactions (so-called "hard currencies" like the U.S. dollar, German mark, Japanese yen, British pound, Swiss franc, French franc, and Canadian dollar) and gold.

The significance of official reserves depends generally on whether the country is operating under a fixed exchange rate regime or a floating exchange rate system. If a country's currency is fixed, this means that the government of the country officially declares that the currency is convertible into a fixed amount of some other currency. For example, for many years the South Korean won was fixed to the U.S. dollar at 484 won equal to 1 U.S. dollar. If the exchange rate is fixed, the government accepts responsibility for maintaining this fixed rate (also called parity rate). If for some reason there is an excess of Korean won on the currency market, to prevent the value of the won from falling, the South Korean government must "support the won." Supporting a currency is identical to supporting any price. To push a price up you must increase demand. Under these conditions, the South Korean government would go to the currency markets and purchase its own currency until it eliminated the excess supply. But what does the South Korean government use to purchase South Korean won? It uses other major currencies like the dollar, the mark, the yen, or even gold. Therefore, in order for a country with a fixed exchange rate to be able to support its own currency, the country needs to maintain substantial reserves of foreign currencies and gold, official reserves.

Many countries still use fixed exchange rate systems. For them, it is still critically important to maintain official reserves in sufficient quantity to support their own currencies in case of need. However, many of the major industrial countries, such as the United States and Japan, no longer operate under fixed exchange rates. For these countries, holdings of official reserves are not as critically important and have, in fact, declined substantially over the past two decades in proportion to the volume of international trade and investment.

In 1991, the United States and several other major countries agreed that their holdings of foreign currencies were excessive and agreed to reduce them. The United States reduced the level of its official foreign reserves by buying dollars with these foreign currencies.

GLOBAL COMPARISON MAPS

Every business operation, from the large multinational corporation to the small entrepreneurial firm, is affected by the political, economic, and geographical realities of the world as a whole. The maps in this special section are intended to give readers a visual appreciation for those realities as they pursue the study of international marketing.

International Trade as a Percentage of Gross Domestic Product

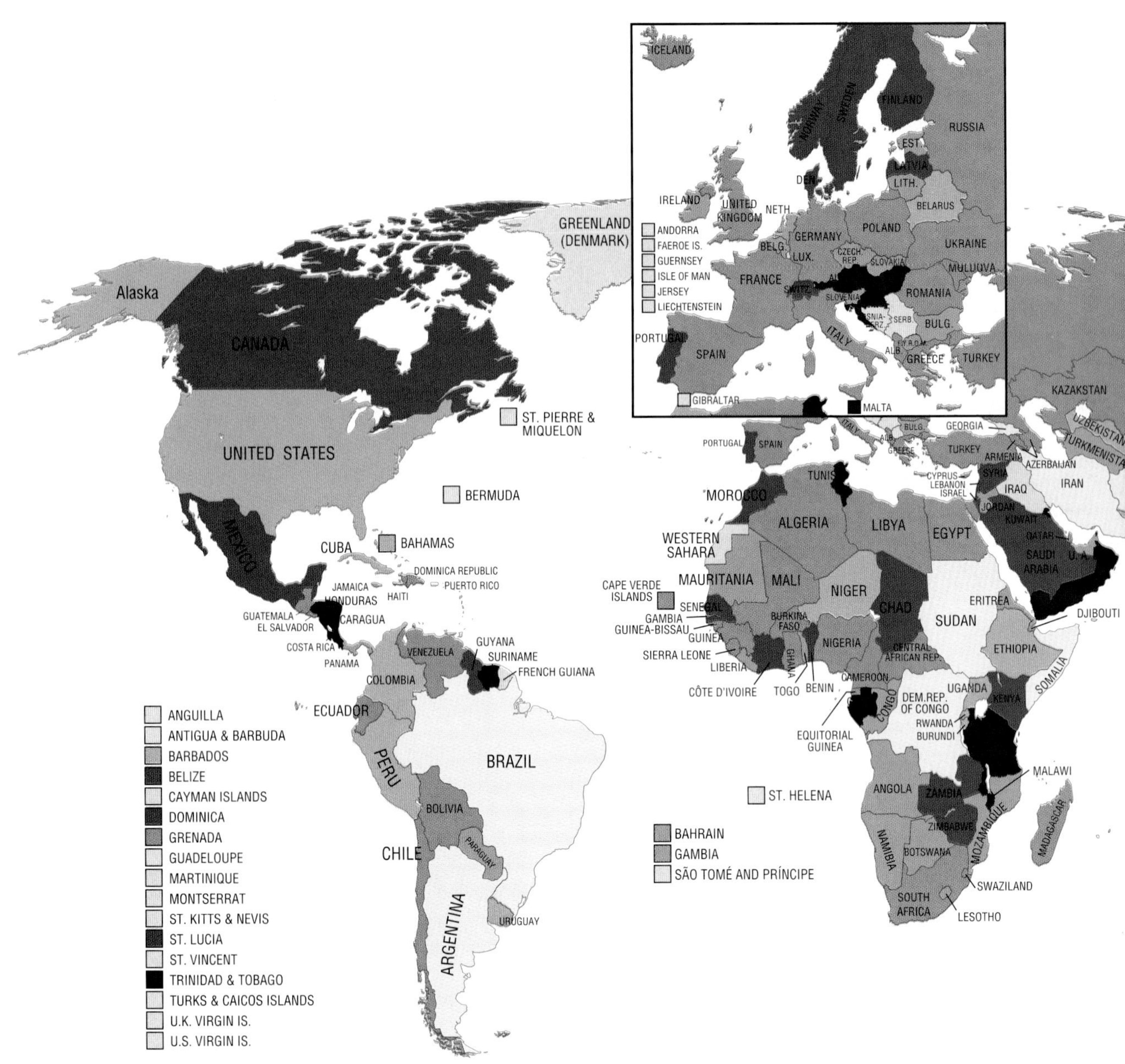

Note: $\frac{\text{Exports + Imports}}{\text{GDP}}$ = International Trade Percentage

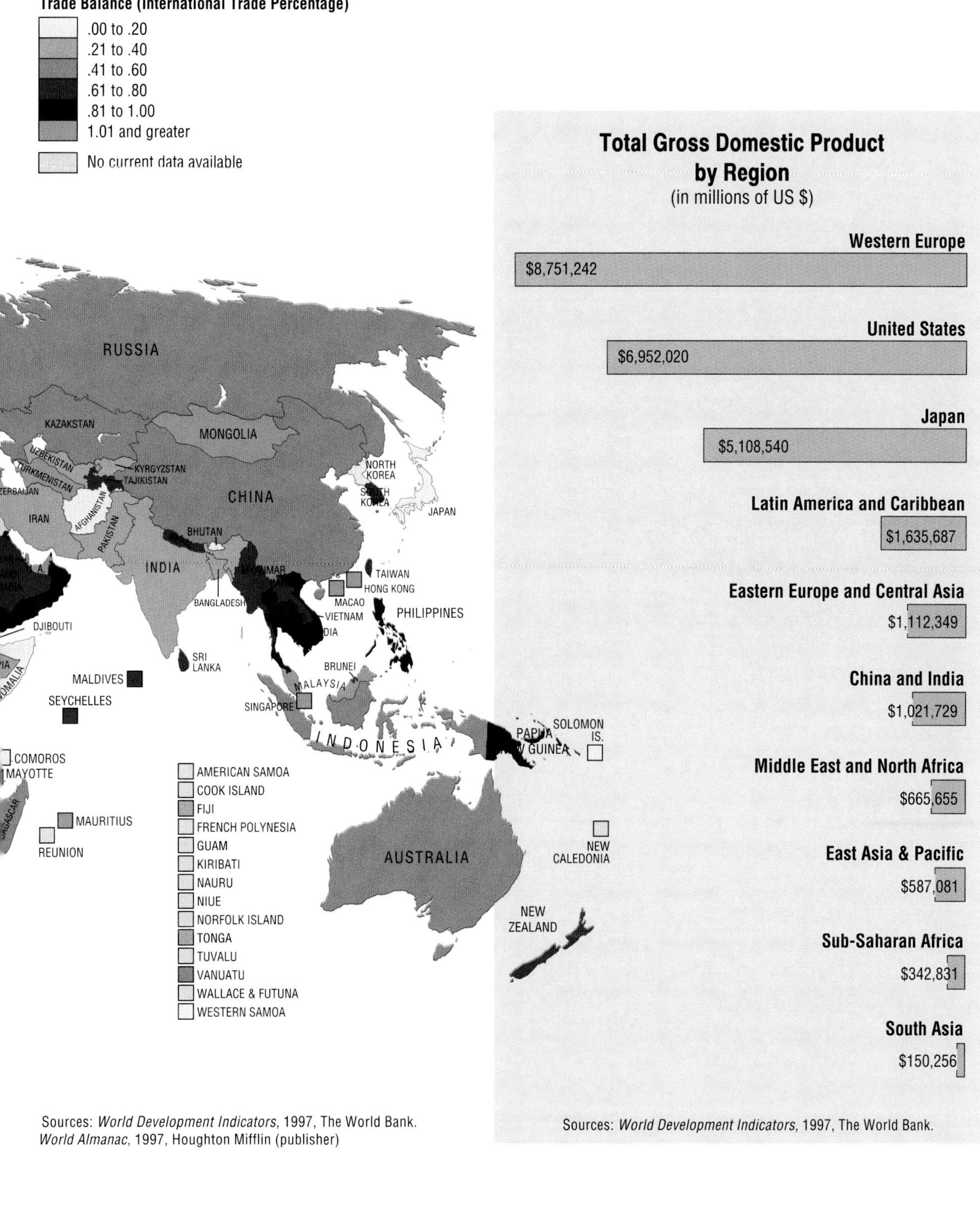

Trade Balance (International Trade Percentage)
.00 to .20
.21 to .40
.41 to .60
.61 to .80
.81 to 1.00
1.01 and greater
No current data available
RUSSIA
KAZAKSTAN
MONGOLIA
UZBEKISTAN
TURKMENISTAN
KYRGYZSTAN
TAJIKISTAN
NORTH KOREA
SOUTH KOREA
JAPAN
CHINA
IRAN
AFGHANISTAN
PAKISTAN
BHUTAN
INDIA
BANGLADESH
TAIWAN
HONG KONG
MACAO
VIETNAM
PHILIPPINES
DJIBOUTI
SRI LANKA
BRUNEI
MALDIVES
SEYCHELLES
MALAYSIA
SINGAPORE
INDONESIA
SOLOMON IS.
COMOROS
MAYOTTE
MAURITIUS
REUNION
AMERICAN SAMOA
COOK ISLAND
FIJI
FRENCH POLYNESIA
GUAM
KIRIBATI
NAURU
NIUE
NORFOLK ISLAND
TONGA
TUVALU
VANUATU
WALLACE & FUTUNA
WESTERN SAMOA
AUSTRALIA
NEW CALEDONIA
NEW ZEALAND
Sources: *World Development Indicators*, 1997, The World Bank.
World Almanac, 1997, Houghton Mifflin (publisher)
Total Gross Domestic Product by Region
(in millions of US $)
Western Europe
$8,751,242
United States
$6,952,020
Japan
$5,108,540
Latin America and Caribbean
$1,635,687
Eastern Europe and Central Asia
$1,112,349
China and India
$1,021,729
Middle East and North Africa
$665,655
East Asia & Pacific
$587,081
Sub-Saharan Africa
$342,831
South Asia
$150,256
Sources: *World Development Indicators*, 1997, The World Bank.

Economic Strength

Top World Economies (GDP in million dollars U.S.)

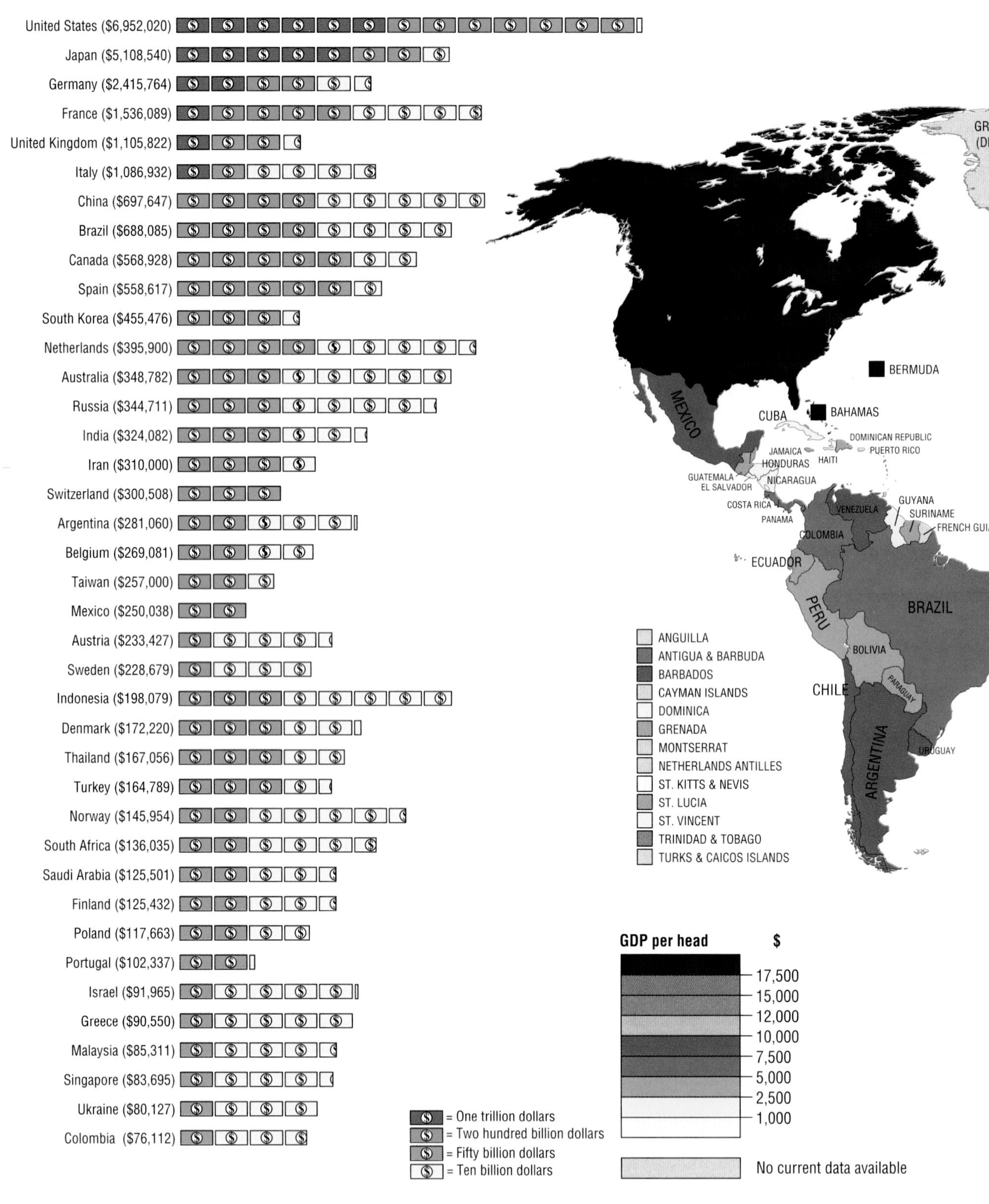

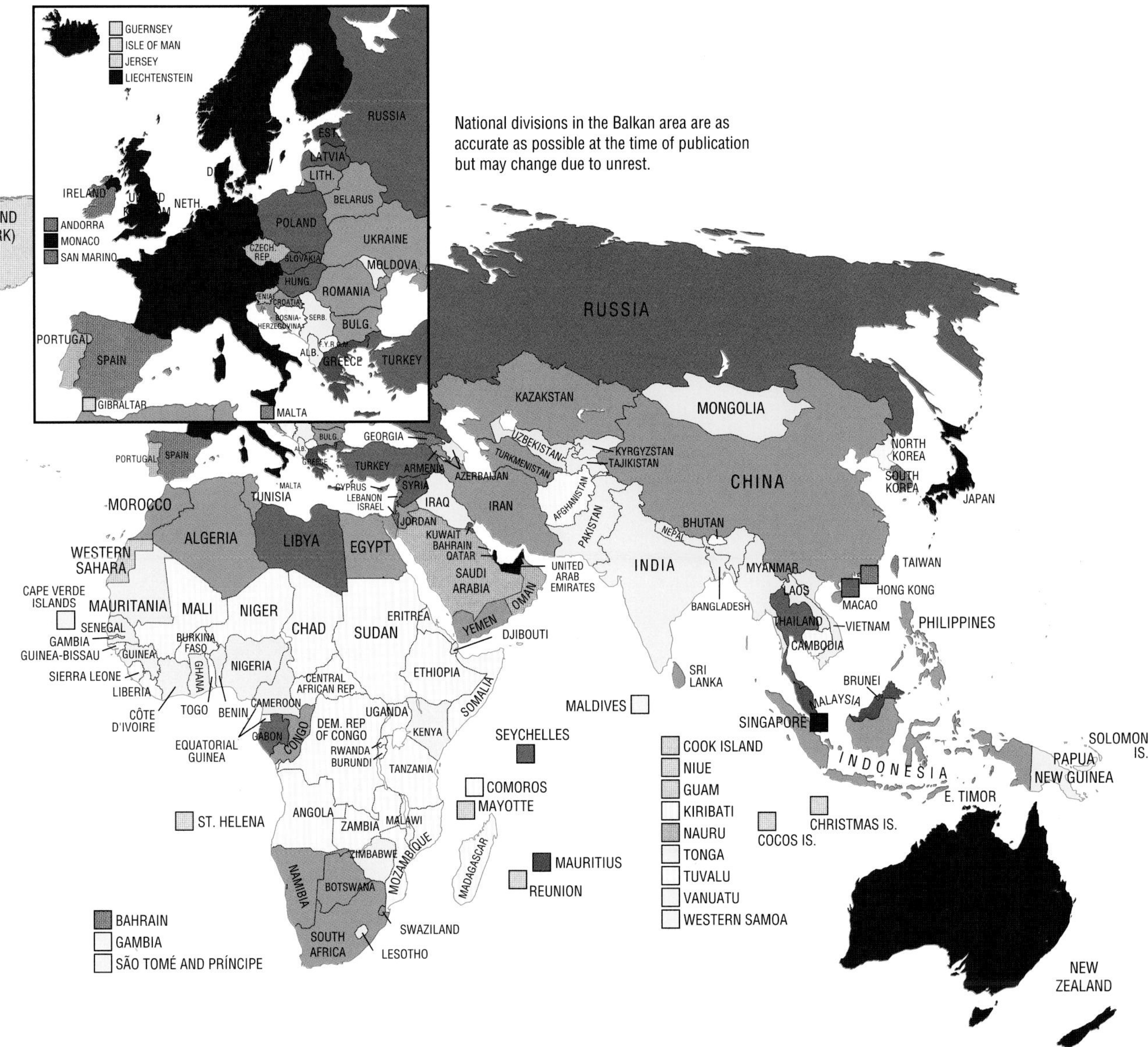

Source: The *World Factbook*, 1997.

International Groupings

OECD Organization for Economic Co-operation and Development
OPEC Organization of the Petroleum Exporting Countries
Commonwealth

Sources: *Statesman Yearbook , 1996; The World Factbook, 1996.*
Note: Countries that have only observer status or other partial membership in these organizations are not identified. Dependencies and non-sovereign states are not identified. For a fuller explanation of these terms, and of the aims of the organizations shown, see relevant sections of the *World Encyclopedia* and the *Statesman Yearbook.*

MIDDLE-EAST

OAPEC Organization of Arab Petroleum Exporting Countries
Gulf Co-operation Council
The Arab League

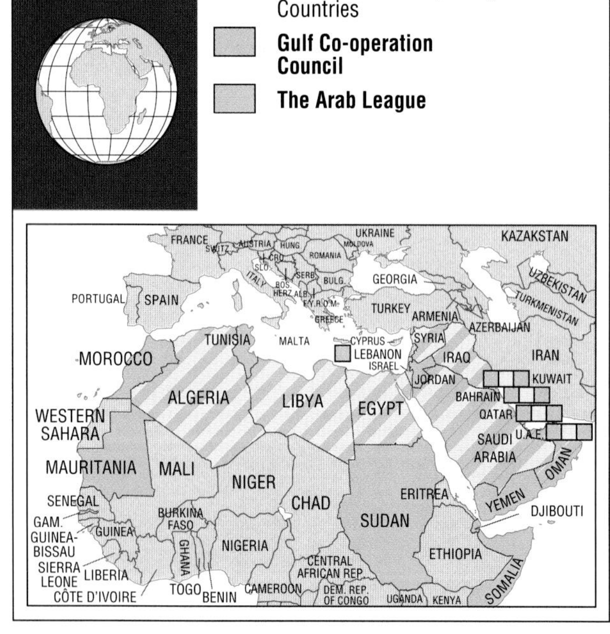

EUROPE-TRADE

EU European Union
EFTA European Free Trade Agreement
Associate membership in EU

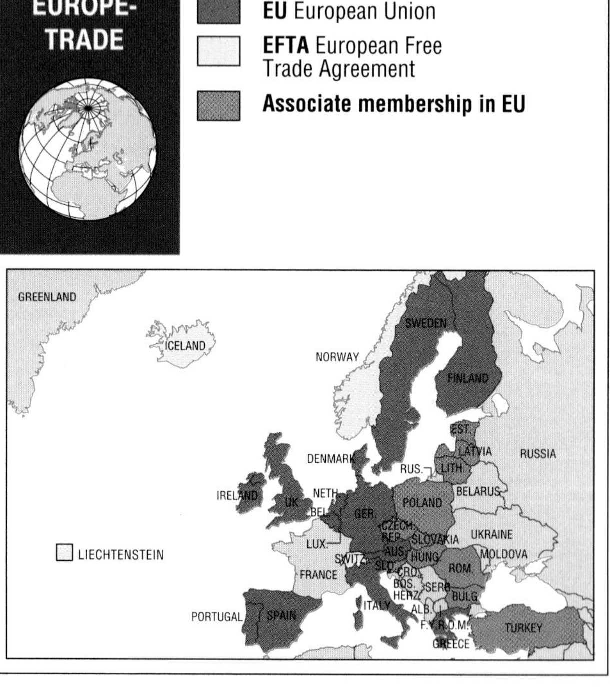

PACIFIC BASIN
AFTA ASEAN (Association of South East Asian Nations) Free Trade Area

MYANMAR
LAOS
THAILAND
CAMB.
VIETNAM
PHILIPPINES
BRUNEI
MALAYSIA
SINGAPORE
INDONESIA
PAPUA NEW GUINEA

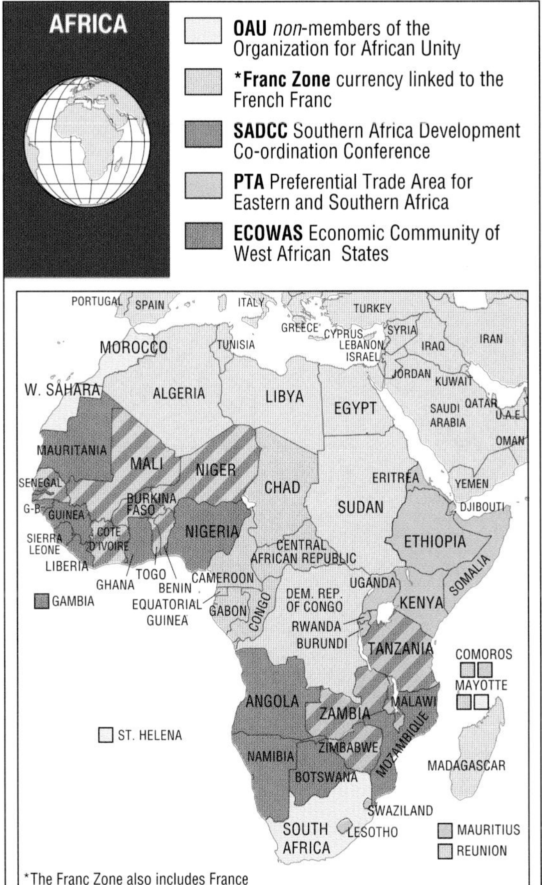

AFRICA
OAU *non*-members of the Organization for African Unity
*Franc Zone currency linked to the French Franc
SADCC Southern Africa Development Co-ordination Conference
PTA Preferential Trade Area for Eastern and Southern Africa
ECOWAS Economic Community of West African States
PORTUGAL
SPAIN
ITALY
TURKEY
GREECE
CYPRUS
SYRIA
LEBANON
ISRAEL
IRAQ
IRAN
MOROCCO
TUNISIA
JORDAN
KUWAIT
W. SAHARA
ALGERIA
LIBYA
EGYPT
SAUDI ARABIA
QATAR
U.A.E.
OMAN
MAURITANIA
MALI
NIGER
CHAD
SUDAN
ERITREA
YEMEN
SENEGAL
G-B
GUINEA
BURKINA FASO
DJIBOUTI
SIERRA LEONE
COTE D'IVOIRE
NIGERIA
ETHIOPIA
LIBERIA
CENTRAL AFRICAN REPUBLIC
TOGO
GHANA
BENIN
CAMEROON
SOMALIA
GAMBIA
EQUATORIAL GUINEA
GABON
CONGO
DEM. REP. OF CONGO
UGANDA
KENYA
RWANDA
BURUNDI
TANZANIA
COMOROS
MAYOTTE
ANGOLA
ZAMBIA
MALAWI
ST. HELENA
NAMIBIA
ZIMBABWE
MOZAMBIQUE
MADAGASCAR
BOTSWANA
SWAZILAND
SOUTH AFRICA
LESOTHO
MAURITIUS
REUNION
*The Franc Zone also includes France and its overseas territories

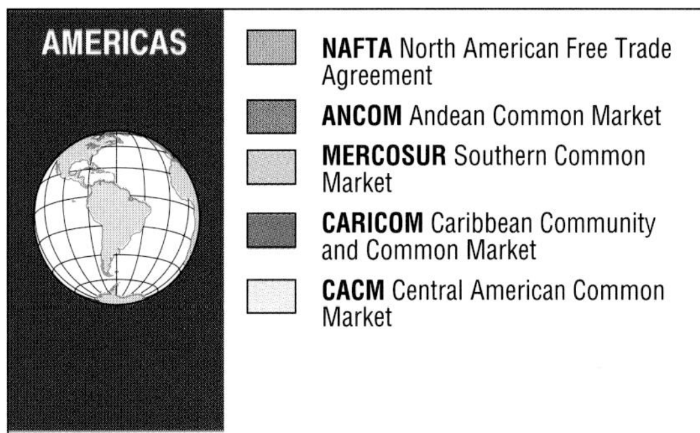

AMERICAS
NAFTA North American Free Trade Agreement
ANCOM Andean Common Market
MERCOSUR Southern Common Market
CARICOM Caribbean Community and Common Market
CACM Central American Common Market

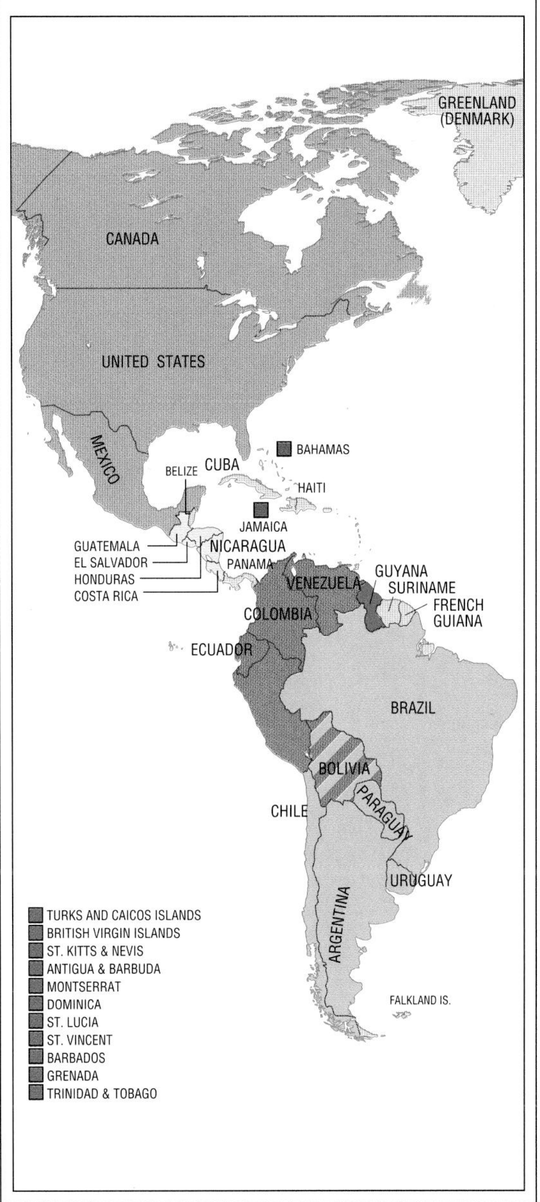

GREENLAND (DENMARK)
CANADA
UNITED STATES
MEXICO
BAHAMAS
BELIZE
CUBA
HAITI
JAMAICA
GUATEMALA
EL SALVADOR
HONDURAS
COSTA RICA
NICARAGUA
PANAMA
VENEZUELA
GUYANA
SURINAME
FRENCH GUIANA
COLOMBIA
ECUADOR
BRAZIL
BOLIVIA
CHILE
PARAGUAY
URUGUAY
ARGENTINA
FALKLAND IS.
TURKS AND CAICOS ISLANDS
BRITISH VIRGIN ISLANDS
ST. KITTS & NEVIS
ANTIGUA & BARBUDA
MONTSERRAT
DOMINICA
ST. LUCIA
ST. VINCENT
BARBADOS
GRENADA
TRINIDAD & TOBAGO

Population Density and Growth

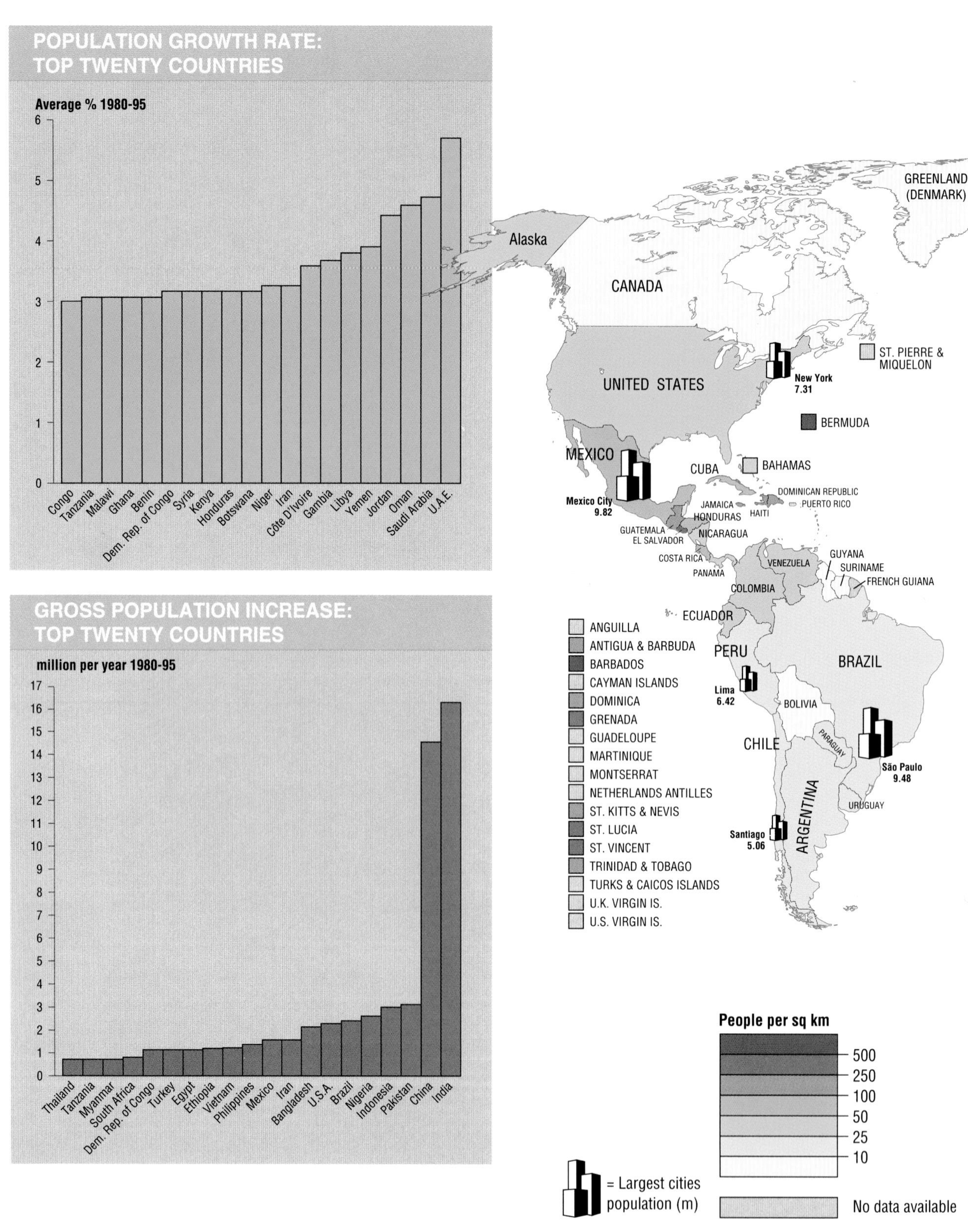

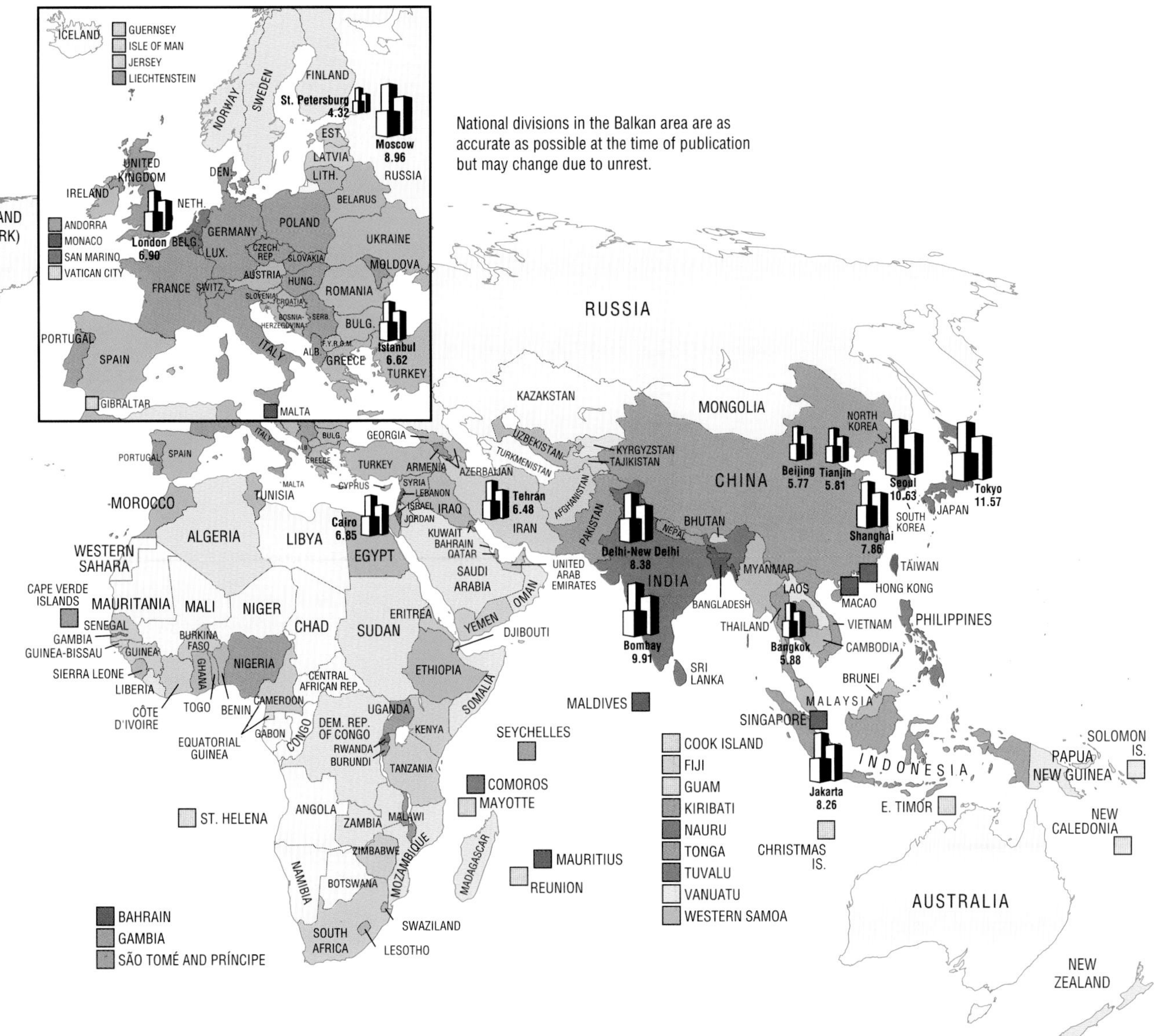

National divisions in the Balkan area are as accurate as possible at the time of publication but may change due to unrest.

Sources: *World Development Indicators, 1997; The World Factbook, 1996; National Geographic Atlas of the World, 6th Edition.*

The Global Environment: A Source of Conflict Between Developed and Less-Developed Nations

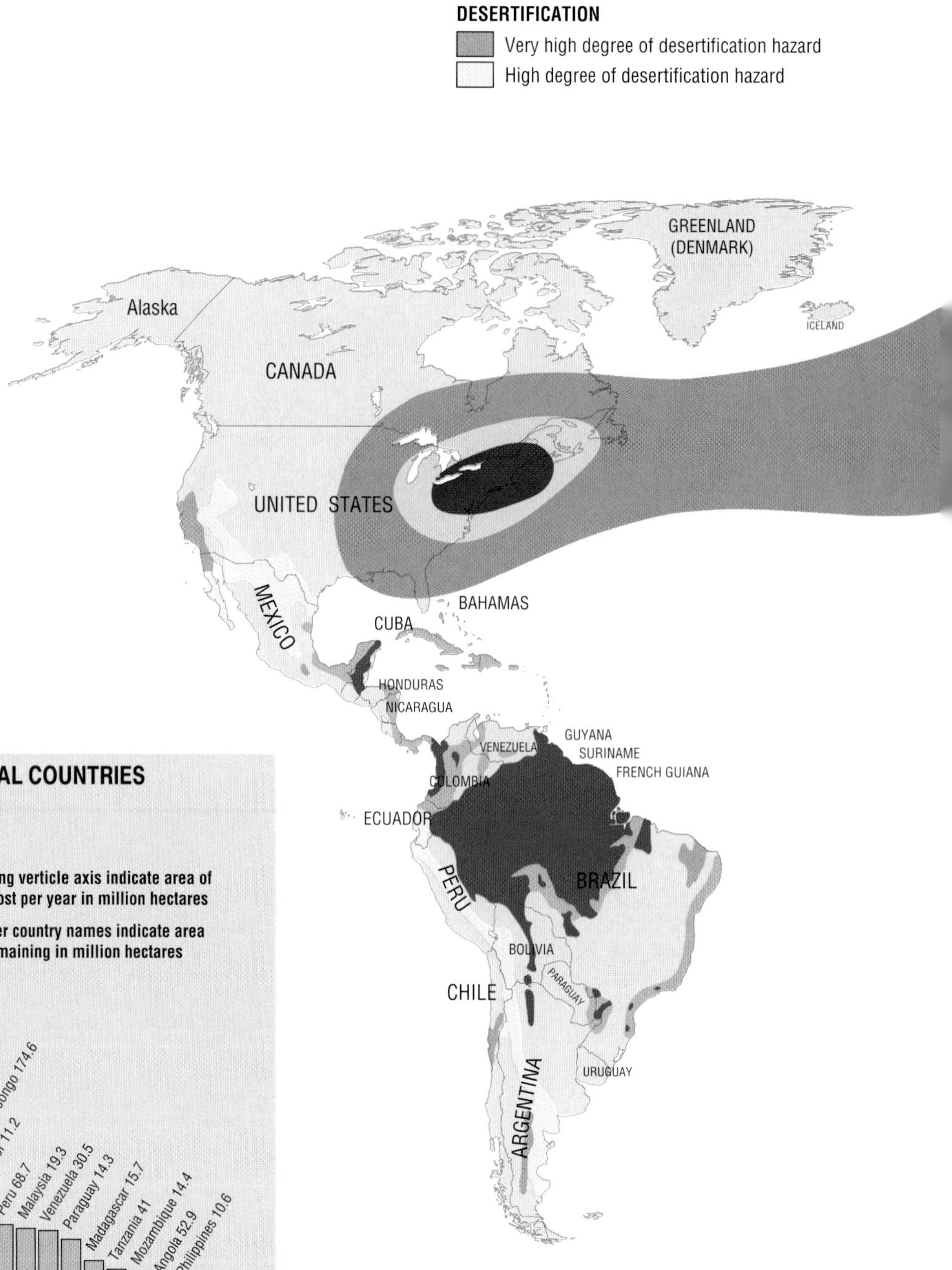

DESERTIFICATION
Very high degree of desertification hazard
High degree of desertification hazard
GREENLAND
(DENMARK)
ICELAND
Alaska
CANADA
UNITED STATES
MEXICO
BAHAMAS
CUBA
HONDURAS
NICARAGUA
GUYANA
SURINAME
FRENCH GUIANA
VENEZUELA
COLOMBIA
ECUADOR
PERU
BRAZIL
BOLIVIA
PARAGUAY
CHILE
URUGUAY
ARGENTINA

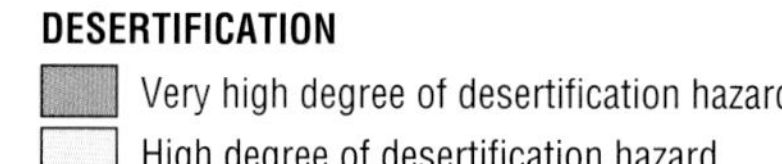

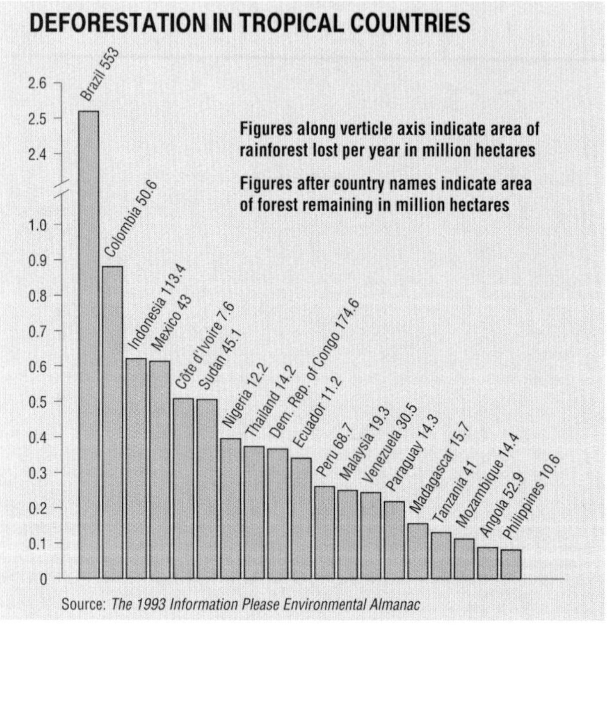

DEFORESTATION IN TROPICAL COUNTRIES
Figures along verticle axis indicate area of rainforest lost per year in million hectares
Figures after country names indicate area of forest remaining in million hectares
2.6
2.5
2.4
1.0
0.9
0.8
0.7
0.6
0.5
0.4
0.3
0.2
0.1
0
Brazil 553
Colombia 50.6
Indonesia 113.4
Mexico 43
Côte d'Ivoire 7.6
Sudan 45.1
Nigeria 12.2
Thailand 14.2
Dem. Rep. of Congo 174.6
Ecuador 11.2
Peru 68.7
Malaysia 19.3
Venezuela 30.5
Paraguay 14.3
Madagascar 15.7
Tanzania 41
Mozambique 14.4
Angola 52.9
Philippines 10.6
Source: The 1993 Information Please Environmental Almanac

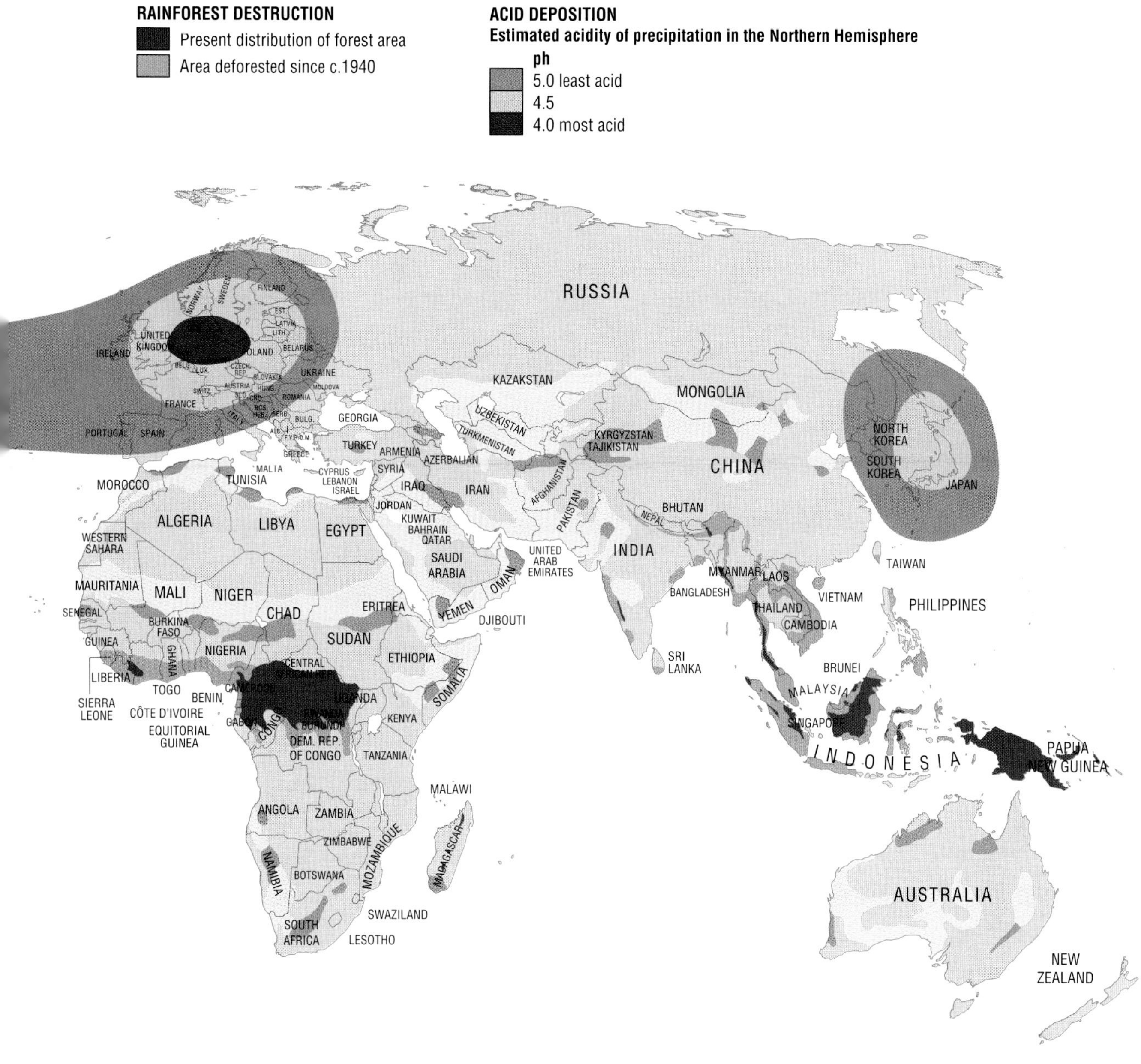

RAINFOREST DESTRUCTION
Present distribution of forest area
Area deforested since c.1940
ACID DEPOSITION
Estimated acidity of precipitation in the Northern Hemisphere
ph
5.0 least acid
4.5
4.0 most acid
RUSSIA
KAZAKSTAN
MONGOLIA
CHINA
INDIA
JAPAN
NORTH KOREA
SOUTH KOREA
ALGERIA
LIBYA
EGYPT
MALI
NIGER
CHAD
SUDAN
ETHIOPIA
NIGERIA
ANGOLA
ZAMBIA
SOUTH AFRICA
INDONESIA
PAPUA NEW GUINEA
AUSTRALIA
NEW ZEALAND
PHILIPPINES
VIETNAM
IRAN
SAUDI ARABIA
TURKEY

Sources: *Atlas of the Environment.*
The Economist World Atlas and Almanac.

Trade and Travel Networks

Civilization depends on trade for growth, and travel makes this possible. Shipping is the most important method of world transport, but economic progress and mobility are constantly being improved by the development of new routes and new methods of transport.

Road and Rail

Integrated road and rail networks are the basis of industrial society. Containerization and the extension of modern highway systems have increased flexibility and reduced the emphasis on railways transporting freight.

Roads

Bar length equals the total road network in log scale.
Number next to country name is the total road network in thousands of kilometers.

Source for total road network figures: *The World Factbook*, 1996.
Source for vehicle figures: *Statistical Yearbook*, 41st Issue, United Nations, 1996.

Country	Total road network (thousands of km)	Number of vehicles per km of road	Density of population per length of road (100km/1 million people)	Road density (km/100km²)
USA	6248	31	68	277
India	2037	3	49	23
Brazil	1662	6	16	115
Japan	1113	57	296	95
China	1029	1	9	9
Canada	849	20	9	367
Australia	810	13	11	552
France	1511	19	146	149
Russia	934	12	6	53
Germany	636	67	172	78
UK	386	64	154	63
Poland	367	23	96	83
Italy	305	106	98	51
Argentina	216	26	7	74

Density of population per length of road (100km/1 million people): High, Medium, Low

Road density (km/100km²): High, Medium, Low

Number of vehicles per km of road

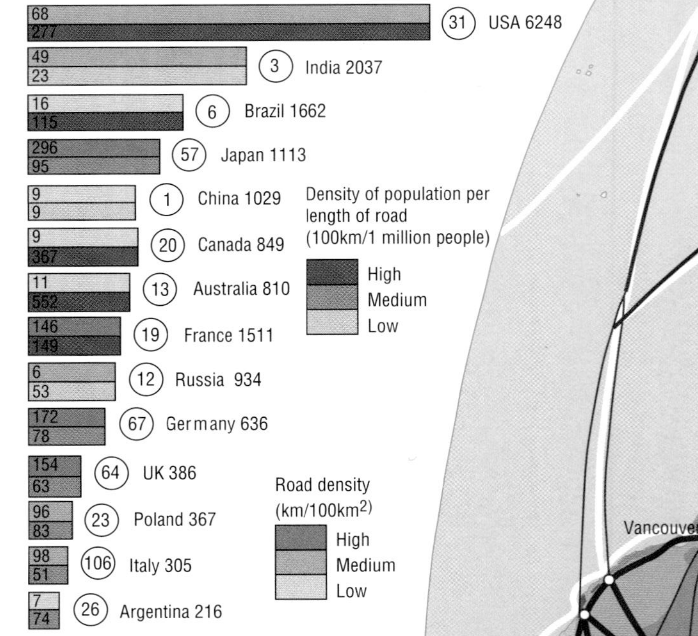

Railways

Country	Total railway network (thousands of km)	Density of population per length of road	Rail density
UK	17.6	8	3
Italy	19.0	7	4
Poland	25.2	8	7
Japan	26.5	7	2
Brazil	27.4	0.4	3
France	33.9	6	6
Argentina	37.9	2	12
Australia	38.6	0.5	27
Germany	44.0	.3	5
China	58.4	0.5	1
India	62.5	2	1
Canada	70.2	7	28
Russia	154	0.5	6
USA	240	3	14

Density of population per length of road (100km/1 million people): High, Medium, Low

Rail density (km/100km^2): High, Medium, Low

Bar length equals the total road network in log scale.
Number next to country name is the total railway network in thousands of kilometers.

Source for total railway network figures: *The World Factbook*, 1996.

San Francisco
Los Angeles
Mexico
Dallas
Houston
Chicago
Montreal
East Coast U.S.A.
Miami
Caribbean
Panama
Caracas
Recife
Rio de Janeiro
São Paulo
Montevideo
Buenos Aires
Moscow
Stockholm
Copenhagen
Amsterdam
London
Frankfurt
Zürich
Paris
Rome
Istanbul
Beirut
Amman
Cairo
Kuwait
Dubai
Abu Dhabi
Djibouti
Accra
Lagos
Abidjan
Matadi
Nairobi
Mombasa
Dar es Salaam
Johannesburg
Durban
Cape Town
Port Elizabeth

Journey Time

The Suez Canal cuts 3600 nautical miles off the London-Singapore route, while the Concorde halves the London-New York journey time.

Air and Sea Routes

A complex network of primary air routes centered on the Northern Hemisphere provides rapid transit across the world for mass travel, mail, and urgent freight.

Ships also follow these principal routes, plying the oceans between major ports and transporting the commodities of world trade in bulk.

Source: *Bartholomew*, 1993

Religions of the World: A Part of Culture

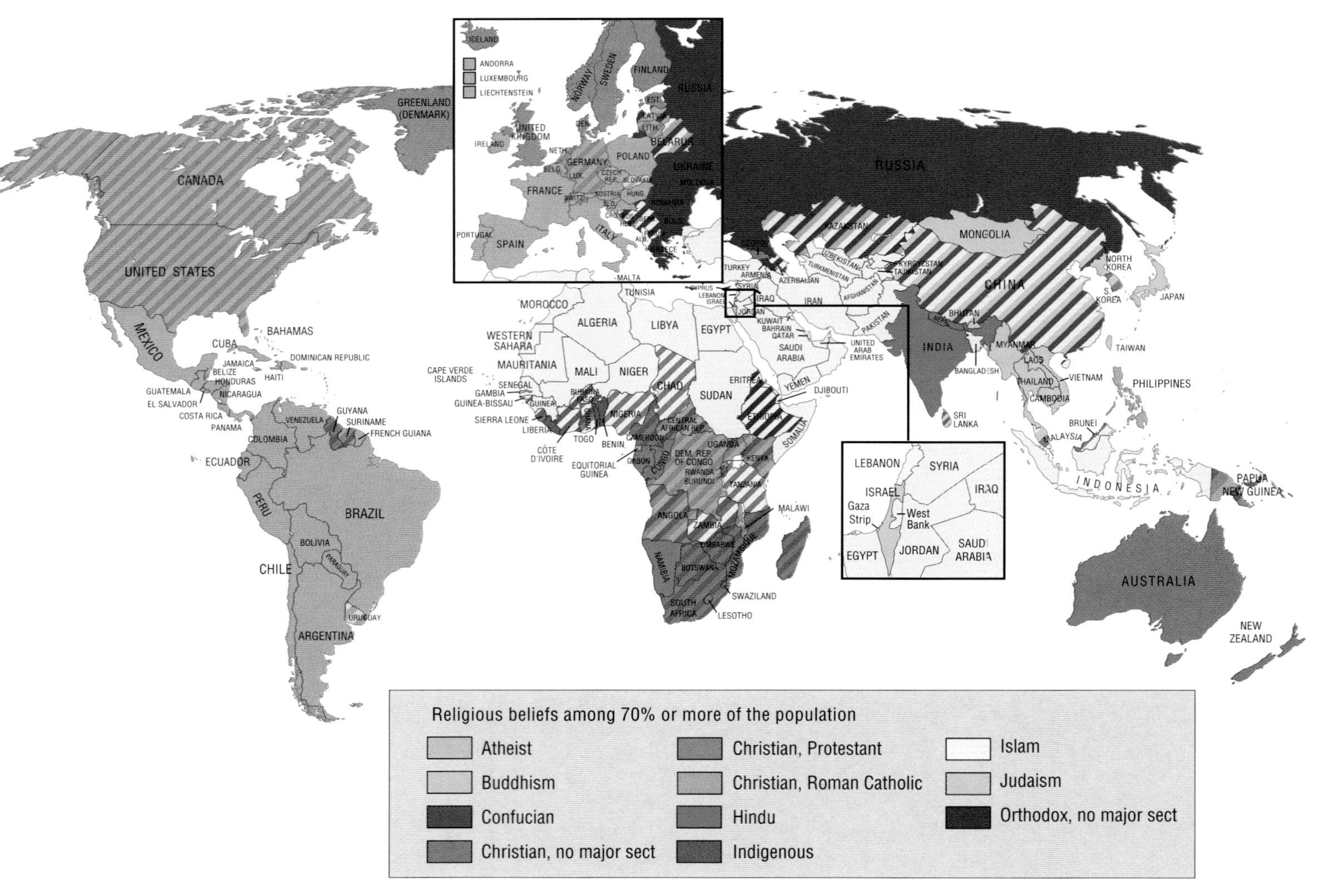

Source: *The World Factbook 1996.*

Services as a Portion of Gross Domestic Product

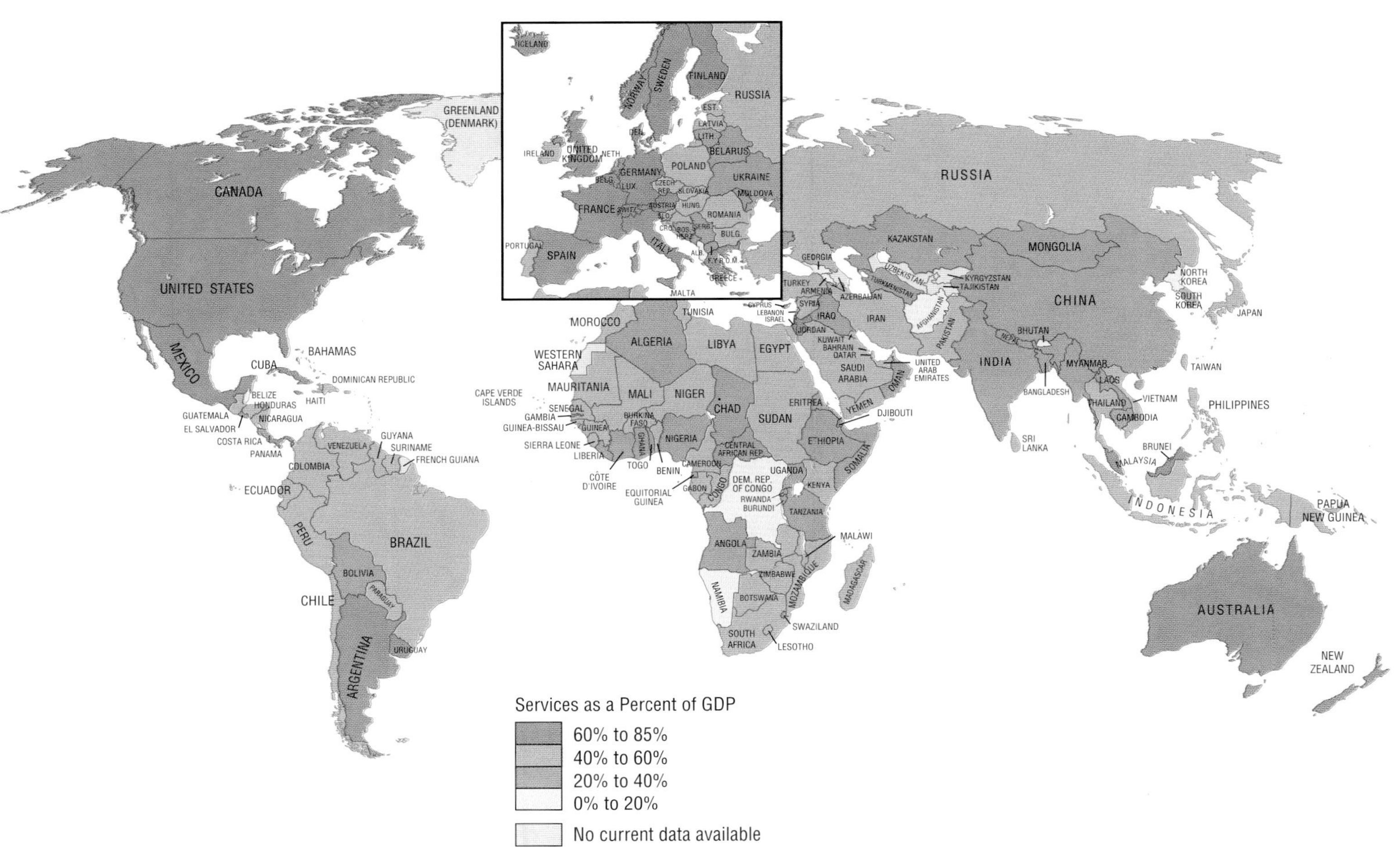

Source: *World Fact Book*, 1996.

THE BALANCE OF PAYMENTS IN TOTAL

Table 3.3 provides the official balance of payments as presented by the International Monetary Fund (IMF), the multinational organization which collects these statistics for more than 160 countries. Now that the individual accounts and the relationships between the accounts have been discussed, Table 3.3 allows an overview of how the individual accounts are combined to create useful summary measures.

The international investment position of a country (external assets less external liabilities) is used to evaluate the performance of that economy compared with other countries of the world. The international investment position indicates what the economy owns relative to what it owes. The *financial account* of the balance of payments measures the changes in its external assets and liabilities and thus the change in the country's international investment position. As noted previously, changes in the *current account* tend to be offset by like changes in the *financial account,* and thus have an impact on the economy's international investment position.

The *investment income* component of the *current account* may be used to analyze a country's rate-of-return, or yield, on its external financial assets and liabilities.

The meaning of "the balance of payments" has changed over the past 25 years. As long as most of the major industrial countries were still operating under fixed exchange rates, the interpretation of the BOP was relatively straightforward. A surplus in the BOP implied that the demand for the country's currency exceeded the supply, and the government should either allow the currency value to increase (revalue) or intervene and accumulate additional foreign currency reserves in the official reserves account. This would occur as the government sold its own currency in exchange for other currencies, thus building up its stores of hard currencies. A deficit in the BOP implied an excess supply of the country's currency on world markets, and the government would then either devalue the currency or expend its official reserves to support its value.

But the major industrial nations such as Japan, the United States, and Germany are no longer operating in a world of fixed exchange rates. Now, major industrial governments and other authorities no longer refer to the balance of payments for their country, but instead monitor and measure balances on trade, current account, net direct and portfolio investments, and sometimes basic balances. The two major subaccounts of the BOP, the current and financial accounts, are watched individually for the magnitude of their imbalances, if imbalanced. However, it is not at all clear that they should be balanced individually or that a balance in either (actually, if one is in balance the other must be) is desirable.

Although economists do not really agree on what is best or what is sustainable, the bilateral relationship between the United States and Japan serves to demonstrate the trade-offs. The United States ran substantial current account deficits and capital account surpluses throughout the 1980s. Japan ran sizable current account surpluses and capital account deficits over the same period. And much of these respective imbalances were with each other (bilateral). But which is better off? There is no clear answer to this. Many have argued that the U.S. current account deficit, more specifically the U.S. merchandise-trade deficit, was unsustainable. But this also allowed massive capital inflows into the United States, aiding in the expansion and modernization of many industries.

Merchandise-Trade and Foreign Exchange Rate Dynamics

Merchandise trade, exports and imports, is sensitive to foreign exchange rate changes. Many countries in the not too distant past have intentionally devalued their currencies

TABLE 3.3 **The U.S. Balance of Payments: Aggregated Presentation, Transactions Data, 1989–1996 (in billions of dollars)**

	1989	1990	1991	1992	1993	1994	1995	1996
A. Current Account*	−104.26	−94.26	−9.26	−61.36	−99.72	−147.77	−148.23	−165.59
Goods: exports f.o.b.	362.16	389.31	416.91	440.35	458.73	504.55	577.82	613.58
Goods: imports f.o.b.	−477.30	−498.34	−490.98	−535.45	−590.10	−669.15	−749.81	−799.84
Balance on Goods	*−115.14*	*−109.03*	*−74.07*	*−96.10*	*−131.37*	*−164.60*	*−171.99*	*−186.26*
Services: credit	127.72	147.35	163.67	177.14	184.09	193.62	208.55	221.83
Services: debit	−102.54	−117.64	−118.46	−118.29	−123.62	−132.23	−140.43	−148.52
Balance on Goods and Services	*−89.96*	*−79.32*	*−28.86*	*−37.25*	*−70.91*	*−103.21*	*−103.87*	*−112.96*
Income: credit	152.65	160.42	137.14	119.21	120.05	141.87	182.85	197.08
Income: debit	−139.68	−140.54	−122.33	−109.04	−111.42	−147.17	−192.02	−206.72
Balance on Goods, Services, and Income	*−76.99*	*−59.44*	*−14.05*	*−27.09*	*−62.27*	*−108.51*	*−113.04*	*−122.60*
Current transfers: credit	4.09	8.79	46.84	6.50	5.20	5.22	5.65	5.77
Current transfers: debit	−31.37	−43.61	−42.05	−40.77	−42.65	−44.48	−40.84	−48.76
B. Capital Account*	.24	.26	.28	.43	−.20	−.61	.10	.52
Capital account: credit	.24	.26	.28	.43	.47	.47	.53	.52
Capital account: debit	...	...	...	...	−.67	−1.08	−.43	...
Total, Groups A Plus B	*−104.02*	*−94.00*	*−8.98*	*−60.93*	*−99.92*	*−148.38*	*−148.13*	*−165.07*
C. Financial Account*	73.46	49.69	30.06	80.11	57.76	129.34	126.33	211.52
Direct investment abroad	−36.83	−29.95	−31.38	−42.66	−78.17	−54.47	−95.53	−88.30
Direct investment in United States	67.73	47.92	22.01	17.58	43.01	49.76	60.23	83.95
Portfolio investment assets	−22.10	−28.80	−45.69	−49.17	−146.26	−60.29	−98.96	−104.54
Equity securities	−17.22	−7.41	−30.64	−32.40	−63.38	−48.09	−50.70	−57.76
Debt securities	−4.88	−21.39	−15.05	−16.77	−82.88	−12.20	−48.26	−46.77
Portfolio investment liabilities	95.70	22.02	57.53	72.00	110.97	139.45	236.18	378.73
Equity securities	6.96	−14.52	9.47	−4.17	20.92	.91	16.41	11.51
Debt securities	88.74	36.54	48.06	76.17	90.05	138.54	219.77	367.22
Other investment assets	−83.40	−13.73	13.81	17.79	31.18	−41.31	−103.63	−120.66
Monetary authorities	....	....	...	...	...	...	...	...
General government	2.39	1.71	3.32	−3.16	−.34	−.35	−.28	−.67
Banks	−40.12	15.53	−15.08	23.82	29.95	−8.16	−69.14	−88.22
Other sectors	−45.67	−30.97	25.58	−2.87	1.58	−32.80	−34.21	−31.78
Other investment liabilities	52.36	52.24	13.77	64.56	97.02	96.19	128.04	62.34
Monetary authorities	−25.07	6.34	13.56	18.41	49.09	−13.88	34.25	23.50
General government	.16	1.87	1.36	2.19	1.71	2.34	1.08	1.40
Banks	54.26	1.76	2.25	27.09	35.76	115.11	58.14	3.03
Other sectors	23.01	42.27	−3.40	16.88	10.46	−7.38	34.57	34.41
Total, Groups A through C	*−30.56*	*−44.31*	*21.08*	*19.19*	*−42.17*	*−19.04*	*−21.80*	*46.45*
D. Net Errors and Omissions	55.83	46.54	−26.83	−23.11	43.55	13.71	31.54	−53.12
Total, Groups A Through D	*25.27*	*2.23*	*−5.76*	*−3.92*	*1.38*	*−5.34*	*9.74*	*−6.67*
E. Reserves and Related Items	−25.27	−2.23	5.76	3.92	−1.38	5.34	−9.74	6.67
Reserve assets	−25.27	−2.23	5.76	3.92	−1.38	5.34	−9.74	6.67
Use of Fund credit and loans	...	...	...	...	...	...	...	...
Exceptional financing	...	...	...	...	...	...	...	...

*Excludes components that have been classified in the categories of Group E.

to make their export products more competitive on world markets. These competitive devaluations, however, are normally considered self-destructive because, although they do make export products relatively cheaper, they also make imports relatively more expensive. So what is the logic of intentionally devaluing the domestic currency to improve the trade balance?

A country typically devalues its currency as a result of persistent and sizable trade deficits. Economic analysis has usually characterized the trade balance adjustment process as occurring in three stages: (1) the currency contract period, (2) the pass-through period, and (3) the quantity adjustment period.

In the first period, the *currency contract period,* a sudden unexpected devaluation of the domestic currency has a somewhat uncertain impact, simply because all of the contracts for exports and imports are already in effect. Firms operating under these agreements are required to fulfill their obligations, regardless of whether they profit or suffer losses. If the United States experienced a sudden fall in the value of the U.S. dollar (as occurred in the 1985–1987 period), and most exports were priced in U.S. dollars but most imports were contracts denominated in foreign currency, the result of a sudden depreciation would be an increase in the size of the trade deficit. This is because the cost to U.S. importers of "paying their bills" would rise (as they spent more and more dollars to buy the foreign currency they needed), while the revenues earned by U.S. exporters would remain unchanged. Although this is the commonly cited scenario regarding trade balance adjustment, there is little reason to believe that most U.S. imports are denominated in foreign currency and most exports in U.S. dollars.

The second period of the trade balance adjustments process is termed the pass-through period. As exchange rates change, importers and exporters eventually must *pass* these exchange rate changes *through* to their own product prices. For example, a foreign producer selling to the U.S. market after a major fall in the value of the U.S. dollar will have to cover its own domestic costs of production. This will require that the firm charge higher dollar prices in order to earn its own local currency in large enough quantities. The firm must raise its prices in the U.S. market. Import prices rise substantially, eventually passing through the full exchange rate changes into prices. American consumers see higher import-product prices on the shelf. Similarly, the U.S. export prices are now cheaper compared to foreign competitors' because the dollar is cheaper. Unfortunately for U.S. exporters, many of their inputs may be imported, causing them also to suffer slightly rising prices after the fall of the dollar.

The third and final period, the *quantity adjustment period,* achieves the balance of trade adjustment that is expected from a domestic currency devaluation or depreciation. As the import and export prices change as a result of the pass-through period, consumers both in the United States and in the U.S. export markets adjust their demands to the new prices. Imports are relatively more expensive; therefore the quantity demanded decreases. Exports are relatively cheaper, and therefore the quantity of exports rises. The balance of trade, the expenditures on exports less the expenditures on imports, improves.

Unfortunately, these three adjustment periods do not occur overnight. Countries like the United States that have experienced major exchange rate changes also have seen this adjustment take place over a prolonged period. Often, before the adjustment is com-

The population of the world is about 5,300,000,000 and multiplying. What is the most populated country in the world?

The most populated country in the world is the People's Republic of China, with 1.13 billion.

pleted, new exchange rate changes occur, frustrating the total adjustment process. Trade adjustment to exchange rate changes does not occur in a sterile laboratory environment, but in the messy and complex world of international business and economic events.

SUMMARY

The balance of payments is the summary statement of all international transactions between one country and all other countries. The balance of payments is a flow statement, summarizing all the international transactions that occur across the geographic boundaries of the nation over a period of time, typically a year. Because of its use of double-entry bookkeeping, the BOP must always balance in theory, though in practice there are substantial imbalances as a result of statistical errors and misreporting of current account and capital account flows.

The two major subaccounts of the balance of payments, the current account and the financial account, summarize the current trade and international capital flows of the country. Because of the method of accounting, double-entry bookkeeping, the current account and financial account are always inverse on balance, one in surplus while the other experiences deficit. Although most nations strive for current account surpluses, it is not clear that a balance on current or financial account, or a surplus on current account, is either sustainable or desirable. The monitoring of the various subaccounts of a country's balance-of-payments activity is helpful to decisionmakers and policymakers at all levels of government and industry in detecting the underlying trends and movements of fundamental economic forces driving a country's international economic activity.

Key Terms and Concepts

balance of payments (BOP)
double-entry bookkeeping
debit
credit
merchandise trade
service trade
current transfers
capital account
direct investment
portfolio investment
official reserves account

Questions

1. Why must a country's balance of payments always be balanced in theory?
2. What is the difference between the merchandise-trade balance and the current account balance?
3. What is service trade?
4. Why is foreign direct investment so much more controversial than foreign portfolio investment?
5. Should the fact that the United States may be the world's largest net debtor nation be a source of concern for government policymakers?
6. What does it mean for the United States to be one of the world's largest indebted countries?

7. How do exchange rate changes alter trade so that the trade balance actually improves when the domestic currency depreciates?

Recommended Readings

Bergsten, C. Fred, ed. *International Adjustment and Financing: The Lessons of 1985–1991.* Washington, D.C.: Institute for International Economics, 1991.

Evans, John S. *International Finance: A Markets Approach.* New York: Dryden Press, 1992.

Grabbe, J. Orlin. *International Financial Markets.* 3rd ed. Lexington, MA: Elsevier, 1996.

Husted, Steven, and Michael Melvin. *International Economics.* New York: Harper & Row, 1990.

International Monetary Fund. *IMF Balance of Payments Yearbook.* Washington, D.C., annually.

International Monetary Fund. *Balance of Payments Textbook.* Washington, D.C., 1996.

International Monetary Fund. *Balance of Payments Manual.* Washington, D.C., 1997.

International Monetary Fund. *Balance of Payments Compilation Guide.* Washington, D.C., 1995.

Root, Franklin, R. *International Trade and Investment.* 6th ed. Chicago: South-Western Publishing, 1990.

United Nations. *Handbook of International Trade and Development Statistics.* New York, 1989.

Notes

1. The official terminology used throughout this chapter unless otherwise noted is that of the International Monetary Fund (IMF). Since the IMF is the primary source of similar statistics for balance of payments and economic performance worldwide, it is more general than other terminology forms, such as that employed by the U.S. Department of Commerce.

Foreign Exchange, Global Financial Markets, and the International Monetary System

LEARNING OBJECTIVES

To define what an exchange rate is and what its value should be.

To understand how currencies are traded and quoted on world financial markets.

To examine the linkages between interest rates and exchange rates.

To understand the difference between fixed and floating exchange rates.

To understand the similarities and differences between domestic sources of capital and international sources of capital.

To examine how the needs of individual borrowers have changed the nature of the instruments traded on global financial markets in the past decade.

To understand the purpose and future ambitions of the European Monetary System.

GLOBAL LEARNING EXPERIENCE

4.1

A Matter of Exchange Rates

The American manufacturing sector has been getting some pretty good press lately, even from those who were busy writing its obituary just a few years ago. Yes, the numbers are pretty good. But there's a case to be made for at least a second look at this newly acclaimed supremacy of American manufacturing.

Exhibit A is the currency situation. In 1985, the yen was 270 to the dollar. Today, it's roughly 150 percent stronger, at 105. In 1985, the mark was 3.30 to the dollar. It's now about 50 percent stronger, 1.65. How much would we be selling; how bold and innovative would we American managers be; how envious would the world be of our manufacturing prowess if that yen and that mark were at the same strength they were not nine years ago, but only three—about 140 yen to the dollar?

The annual report of Toyota Motor, one of the world's greatest manufacturers, lays out very clearly solution number one to the problem of the yen: "We will cut costs like we have never cut costs before." The Japanese are grimly determined to achieve not incremental performance improvements, but what they call "bullet train," or order-of-magnitude improvements. They put no stock in predictions of a weaker yen, and are preparing themselves to compete at 90 yen to the dollar. I could make the case that the powerful yen is the best thing that ever happened to Japanese competitiveness.

Global competitors are taking actions today that could push U.S. manufacturers from the deceptive tranquillity of the eye back into the turbulence of the hurricane, a hurricane that this time will come with a ferocity that could be intensified should the currency go the wrong way. What happens if the yen swings back over 130, as it was just two years ago, or the mark moves toward 2?

We should not wait that long. There are things that can be done now. If the Japanese are preparing to compete at 90 yen, the U.S. must be ready to compete at 130. Until we are, we delude ourselves if we think we are in control of our own fate.

SOURCE: Excerpts from John F. Welch, "A Matter of Exchange Rates," *The Wall Street Journal,* June 21, 1994, editorial page. Mr. Welch is chairman and CEO of General Electric Co. This is an adaptation of a talk to the Economic Club of Detroit.

Global financial markets serve as links between financial markets of individual countries and as independent markets outside the jurisdiction of any one country. The market for currencies is the heart of this global financial market. This chapter will serve as a guide to the structure, mechanics, and functions of foreign currency markets, international money markets, and international securities markets.

All international export/import transactions are essentially two transactions. The first transaction is the transfer of merchandise, services, or portfolio products and the second transaction is the exchange of currencies. Recall our chewing gum example from Chapter 3. A person buys a package of chewing gum, placing it in his left pocket, while he pays for the gum with $1 taken from his right pocket. This transaction would work in the United States, but let's assume the transaction is taking place in France. As he produces the $1, the clerk shakes his head and says, "I'm sorry, we only accept

QUESTION

What is the world's southernmost city?

Ushuaia, Argentina, the capital of Tierra del Fuego National Territory.

French francs." Because the franc is the currency of France, the clerk obviously doesn't want dollars, he wants francs. In order for the gum chewer to pay for his purchase, he would have to exchange his U.S. dollar for French francs. To do this he (or his bank, travel agent, etc.) would go into the foreign exchange market, sell his dollars, buy francs, and then pay for the gum.

THE PURPOSE OF EXCHANGE RATES

If countries are going to trade with each other, they must be able to exchange currencies. In order to buy wheat, corn, or videocassette recorders, the buyer must first obtain the currency in which the product is sold. An American firm purchasing consumer electronic products manufactured in Japan must first exchange its U.S. dollars for Japanese yen in order to purchase the products. And each country has its own currency.[1] The exchange of one country's currency for another should be a relatively simple transaction, but it's not, as indicated in Global Learning Experience 4.1.

WHAT A CURRENCY IS WORTH

At what rate should one currency be exchanged for another currency? The simplest answer is that the exchange rate should equalize purchasing power. For example, if the price of a movie ticket in the United States is $6, the "correct" exchange rate would be one that exchanges $6 for the number of Japanese yen it would take to purchase a

I am so sorry Monsieur, we only accept French francs!

Purchasing Power Parity and "Le Shuttle"

The Eurotunnel, the tunnel that connects the United Kingdom and France underneath the English Channel, poses a classic problem of purchasing power parity. Also nicknamed *Le Shuttle* and the *Chunnel,* the tube provides two-way transportation for people and products between two different currency markets.

On December 17, 1994, the Eurotunnel announced the fare structure for passenger cars. A one-day return (round-trip ticket) will cost £49, or $76.59 at the exchange rate in effect on that date ($1.5630/£). At a spot exchange rate of FF8.4637/£ between the British pound and the French franc—the currency at the other end of the tunnel—the same return ticket will cost FF414.72—(FF8.4637 × £49). Now every time the spot rate changes between the pound and the franc, a potential passenger on one side of the channel will *win* and one on the other side will *lose.*

Although this is not a unique problem—after all, planes, trains, and automobiles have been crossing borders and paying tolls on both sides for many years—this case poses a particularly tricky problem given that the Eurotunnel is a joint project of investors, private and public, in both countries. For now, with primary administration lying with the United Kingdom, it seems the *fixed price* will be the pound-price.

movie ticket in Japan. If ticket prices are ¥750 (the symbol for the yen is ¥) in Japan, then the exchange rate that would equalize purchasing power would be:

$$\frac{\text{YEN750}}{\$6} = \text{YEN125/USD}.$$

That is, each dollar is equal to 125 yen. Therefore, if the exchange rate between the two currencies is YEN125/USD, regardless of which country the movie-goer is in, he or she could purchase a ticket. This is the theory of **purchasing power parity (PPP),** generally considered the definition of what exchange rates should ideally be. The purchasing power parity exchange rate is simply the rate that equalizes the price of an identical product or service in two different currencies:

purchasing power parity
a theory that the prices of tradable goods will tend to equalize across countries

$$\text{Price in Japan} = \text{Exchange rate} \times \text{price in United States.}$$

This price could be the price of just one good or service, like the movie ticket mentioned previously, or it could be price indices for each country that cover many different goods and services. Either form is an attempt to find comparable products in different countries (and currencies) in order to determine an exchange rate based on purchasing power parity. The question then is whether this theoretical approach to exchange rates actually works in practice. (See Global Learning Experience 4.2.)

THE LAWS OF ONE PRICE

The version of purchasing power parity that estimates the exchange rate between two currencies using just one good or service as a measure of the proper exchange for all goods and services is called the **Law of One Price.** To apply this theory to actual prices across countries, a product must be selected that is identical in quality and content in

Law of One Price
the exchange rate between two currencies based on just one good or service

TABLE 4.1 **"Big Mac" Index of Foreign Currencies, April 1997—The Hamburger Standard**

	Big Mac Prices in Local Currency	in Dollars	Implied PPP* of the Dollar	Actual $ Exchange Rate 4/7/97	Local Currency under(−)/over(+) Valuation,†%
United States‡	**$2.42**	**2.42**	—	—	—
Argentina	Peso2.50	2.50	1.03	1.00	+3
Australia	A$2.50	1.94	1.03	1.29	−20
Austria	Sch34.00	2.82	14.0	12.0	+17
Belgium	BFr109	3.09	45.0	35.3	+28
Brazil	Real2.97	2.81	1.23	1.06	+16
Britain	£1.81	2.95	1.34††	1.63††	+22
Canada	C$2.88	2.07	1.19	1.39	−14
Chile	Peso1,200	2.88	496	417	+19
China	Yuan9.70	1.16	4.01	8.33	−52
Czech Republic	CKr53.0	1.81	21.9	29.2	−25
Denmark	DKr25.75	3.95	10.6	6.52	+63
France	FFr17.5	3.04	7.23	5.76	+26
Germany	DM4.90	2.86	2.02	1.71	+18
Hong Kong	HK$9.90	1.28	4.09	7.75	−47
Hungary	Forint271	1.52	112	178	−37
Israel	Shekel11.5	3.40	4.75	3.38	+40
Italy	Lire4,600	2.73	1,901	1,683	+13
Japan	¥294	2.34	121	126	−3
Malaysia	M$3.87	1.55	1.60	2.50	−36
Mexico	Peso14.9	1.89	6.16	7.90	−22
Netherlands	F15.45	2.83	2.25	1.92	+17
New Zealand	NZ$3.25	2.24	1.34	1.45	−7
Poland	Zloty4.30	1.39	1.78	3.10	−43
Russia	Rouble11,000	1.92	4,545	5,739	−21
Singapore	S$3.00	2.08	1.24	1.44	−14
South Africa	Rand7.80	1.76	3.22	4.43	−27
South Korea	Won2,300	2.57	950	894	+6
Spain	Pta375	2.60	155	144	+7
Sweden	SKr26.0	3.37	10.7	7.72	+39
Switzerland	SFr5.90	4.02	2.44	1.47	+66
Taiwan	NT$68.0	2.47	28.1	27.6	+2
Thailand	Baht46.7	1.79	19.3	26.1	−26

*Purchasing-power parity; local price divided by price in the United States. †Against dollar
‡Average of New York, Chicago, San Francisco and Atlanta ††Dollars per pound
SOURCE: "Big Mac Currencies," *The Economist*, April 12, 1997, p. 71. Distributed by the New York Times Special Features/Syndication Sales.

every country. To be truly theoretically correct, such a product should be produced entirely domestically so that there are no imported factors in its construction.

Where would one find such a perfect product? McDonald's. Table 4.1 presents what *The Economist* magazine calls the "Big Mac Index of Currencies." Here the Big Mac is used as an index because it is a product that is essentially the same the world over and is produced and consumed entirely domestically. By comparing Big Mac prices between the United States and foreign countries, the Big Mac Index compares the exchange rate implied by the purchasing power parity (PPP) measurement with the actual exchange in effect on a given day (April 7, 1997). For example, the average price of a Big Mac in Canada, in Canadian dollars, was \$2.88. On the same date, the price of a Big Mac in the United States was \$2.42. These prices were then used to evaluate the PPP exchange rate:

$$\frac{\text{C\$2.88 per Big Mac}}{\text{\$2.42 per Big Mac}} = \text{C\$1.19 (that is, 1.19 Canadian dollars is equal to 1 U.S. dollar).}$$

The exchange rate between the Canadian dollar and the U.S. dollar should be C\$1.19/\$ according to a PPP comparison of Big Mac prices. The actual exchange rate on the date of comparison (April 7, 1997) was C\$1.39/\$. This means that each U.S. dollar was actually worth 1.39 Canadian dollars, but the index indicates that each U.S. dollar should have been worth 1.19 Canadian dollars. Therefore, if one is to believe the Big Mac Index, the U.S. dollar was being "overvalued" on the markets by about 16 percent.

Besides being entertaining, the Big Mac Index is actually an excellent example of how purchasing power parity should work in determining exchange rates. Few products are identical across so many countries and produced completely within that country. Note that for most currencies listed, the Big Mac Index implies an exchange rate that is fairly close to the actual rate. Although there are many valid criticisms of the Big Mac Index (for example, local taxes, poverty values, and tariffs that affect the prices in each country are not taken into account), it does serve as a measure of what currencies should be worth. Although the use of any single product to determine exchange rates could be similarly criticized, the alternative method of comparing consumer or producer price indices across countries may actually be worse considering how few products actually meet the requirements so clearly fulfilled by the Big Mac.

THE FOREIGN EXCHANGE MARKET

The **foreign exchange market** is an international market that exchanges financial instruments denominated in different currencies. The financial instruments involved range from cash, drafts, checks, and wire and telephone transfers to contracts to buy and sell currency in the future.

foreign exchange market an international market that exchanges financial instruments in a variety of currencies

The most common instrument of foreign exchange is the telephone transfer among banks and usually involves transactions exceeding \$1 million. This part of the foreign exchange market (banks dealing with other banks in large volumes) is known as the **interbank market. Brokers,** who sometimes assist in the transfer of funds between banks, may be used to help find the most favorable prices for currencies and to keep the transfer of funds confidential. Brokers are paid a commission for their efforts. The **central banks** of governments may participate in the foreign exchange (FX) market in order to implement governmental policies regarding the value of their currencies. The other part of the market is the retail market that consists mainly of local banks that sell to nonbank customers such as businesses and tourists.

interbank market banks dealing with other banks in large volumes, with transactions exceeding \$1 million

brokers professionals who assist in the transfer of funds between banks and find the most favorable prices for currencies

central banks national banks that implement governmental policies regarding the value of their currencies

QUESTION *These two countries in South America are land locked, they have no access to the ocean.*

Bolivia and Paraguay.

FOREIGN CURRENCY MARKET STRUCTURE

The market for foreign currencies is a worldwide market that is informal in structure. This means that it has no central place, pit, or floor (like the floor of the New York Stock Exchange) where trading takes place. The "market" is actually the thousands of telecommunications links between financial institutions around the globe and it is open 24 hours a day. Although the FX market has no central location, trading volume is particularly concentrated in the United States, the United Kingdom, and Japan. Figure 4.1 indicates the dominant positions these three countries hold in the FX market.

The structure of the foreign currency market leads to some interesting problems. For example, since there is no one exchange, no one floor, no world central bank, is there a single exchange rate? The answer is no; there is no single agreed upon rate of exchange for all financial institutions. All the banks and financial institutions that are trading currencies are calling and communicating with dozens or hundreds of banks all over the world so they are all seeing or hearing slightly different rates. Global Learning Experience 4.3 illustrates how China is changing its structure.

FIGURE 4.1 **Three Countries Dominate the Foreign Exchange Market**

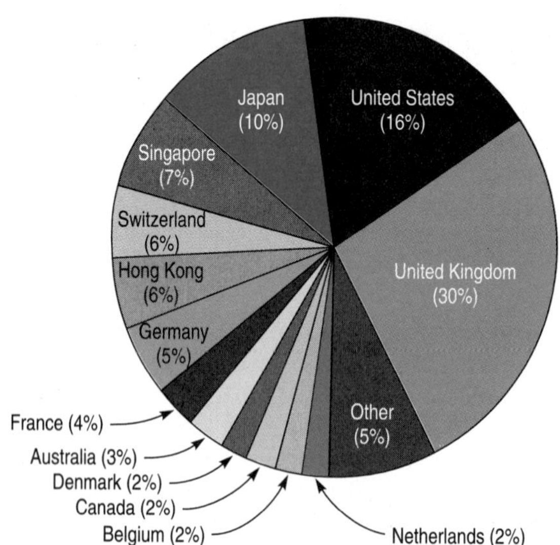

1992 daily average of gross market volume, percentage of world total.

SOURCES: BIS; Federal Reserve Bank of New York.

Yin/Yang Balance with the Yuan

Proving its resolve to become part of the world economy soon, China eliminated its two-tiered exchange rate mechanism on Jan. 1. Instead of an official rate and a swap center rate—the latter normally set at about 45 percent below the former—the swap rate has now become official.

Coming as it did almost a year ahead of schedule, the move is a strong indication of the Chinese government's desire to continue to attract foreign investment. For companies of all sizes, China has become a hotbed of new investment. Currency stability and convertibility are essential to the success of foreign ventures and to the government's efforts to reform the economy.

But the exchange rate realignment has also raised some new concerns for companies with joint ventures in China. The biggest worry: The government continues to hold the reins on the yuan by controlling the supply of hard currency. And just how Beijing will use its discretion is as hard to decipher as the *I Ching*.

SOURCE: "Becoming," *International Business*, March 1994, 120–121.

MARKET SIZE AND COMPOSITION

Until about 20 years ago, there was little data on the actual volume of trading in world foreign currency markets. However, in 1977 the Federal Reserve Bank of New York began to measure the volume of foreign exchange trading in the United States every three years. Starting in 1986, the Bank for International Settlements began conducting similar surveys of world foreign exchange trading activity.

Growth in foreign currency trading has been nothing less than astronomical, as shown in Figure 4.2. The survey results for April 1995 indicated that daily foreign currency trading on world markets exceeded $1.2 trillion, approximately equal to the gross domestic product of Great Britain. This is about $200 of FX trading for each person on the globe—every day!

In the United States, the daily volume of foreign exchange trading was $244 billion in 1995—more than $900 per day for every man, woman, and child in the U.S. In comparison, the annual (not daily) U.S. government budget deficit has never exceeded $300 billion, and the U.S. merchandise trade deficit has never topped $200 billion.

Three reasons typically given for the enormous growth in foreign currency trading are:

1. *Deregulation of international capital flows*—It is easier than ever to move currencies and capital around the world without major governmental restrictions. Much of the deregulation that has characterized government policy over the past 10 to 15 years in the United States. Japan, and the now European Union has focused on financial deregulation.
2. *Gains in technology and transaction cost efficiency*—It is faster, easier, and cheaper to move millions of dollars, yen, or marks around the world than ever before. Technological advancements in not only the dissemination of information, but also in the conduct of exchange or trading, have added greatly to the ability of individuals working in these markets to conduct instantaneous arbitrage (some would say speculation).

FIGURE 4.2 **U.S. and World Daily Foreign Exchange Trading, 1977–1995 (in billions of dollars)**

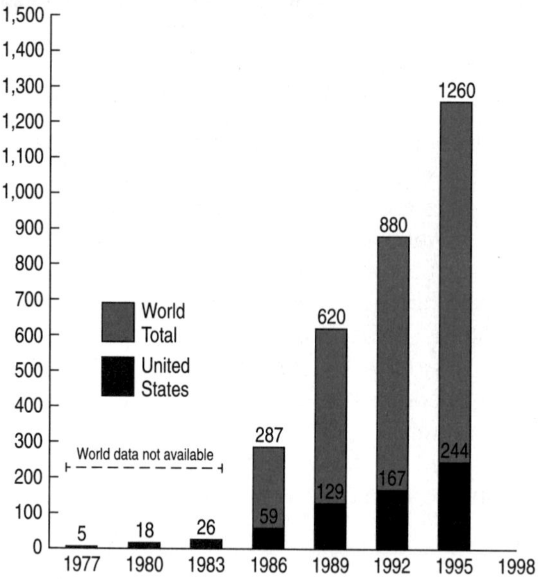

SOURCES: U.S. Data—Federal Reserve Bank of New York—Central Bank Survey of Foreign Exchange Market Activity, April, 1995.
World Data—Bank for International Settlements—Survey of Foreign Exchange Market Activity, April, 1995.
NOTES: All data adjusted for double counting and estimated gaps in reporting except world 1986 (estimated) and U.S. 1977. World data 1977–1983 is not available.

3. *The world is a risky place*—Many argue that the financial markets have become increasingly volatile over recent years, with larger and faster swings in financial variables such as stock values and interest rates adding to the motivations for moving more capital at faster rates.

EXCHANGE RATE QUOTATIONS AND TERMINOLOGY

Figure 4.3 illustrates foreign exchange quotations taken from *The Wall Street Journal,* Thursday, January 22, 1998. The exchange rate between the U.S. dollar (USD) and the German mark (Deutschemark or DEM) can be expressed in two ways:

1. *U.S. terms*—This gives the price of a mark in terms of the U.S. dollar or its U.S. dollar equivalent. Example: USD/DEM or \$/DM = \$.5542. That is, one German mark is equal to (or would cost) \$.5542 USD.
2. *European terms*—This quotation gives the price of a U.S. dollar in terms of its German mark equivalent. Example: DEM/USD or DM/\$ = 1.8043 DM. That is, one U.S. dollar is equal to (or would cost) 1.8043 DM.

In the interbank market, almost all quotations are for sale or purchase of U.S. dollars against a foreign currency using the DEM/USD form. These two exchange rates are actually reciprocals of each other. Once one of the rates is known, the other may be easily calculated from it. A reciprocal is any number divided into 1; thus, if the USD/DEM rate of .5542 is known, one can calculate the DEM/USD rate by dividing .5542 into 1 or $\frac{1}{.5542} = 1.8043$.

Foreign Currency Exchange Rates — FIGURE 4.3

CURRENCY TRADING

Thursday, January 22, 1998

EXCHANGE RATES

The New York foreign exchange selling rates below apply to trading among banks in amounts of $1 million and more, as quoted at 4 p.m. Eastern time by Dow Jones and other sources. Retail transactions provide fewer units of foreign currency per dollar.

Country	U.S. $ equiv. Thu	U.S. $ equiv. Wed	Currency per U.S. $ Thu	Currency per U.S. $ Wed
Argentina (Peso)	1.0001	1.0001	.9999	.9999
Australia (Dollar)	.6592	.6635	1.5170	1.5072
Austria (Schilling)	.07871	.07756	12.705	12.894
Bahrain (Dinar)	2.6525	2.6525	.3770	.3770
Belgium (Franc)	.02682	.02660	37.280	37.592
Brazil (Real)	.8928	.8928	1.1201	1.1201
Britain (Pound)	1.6480	1.6312	.6068	.6130
1-month forward	1.6455	1.6287	.6077	.6140
3-months forward	1.6404	1.6237	.6096	.6159
6-months forward	1.6329	1.6162	.6124	.6188
Canada (Dollar)	.6881	.6918	1.4533	1.4455
1-month forward	.6888	.6925	1.4518	1.4440
3-months forward	.6898	.6935	1.4497	1.4420
6-months forward	.6910	.6946	1.4471	1.4396
Chile (Peso)	.002183	.002183	458.00	458.00
China (Renminbi)	.1208	.1208	8.2786	8.2786
Colombia (Peso)	.0007510	.0007536	1331.48	1327.00
Czech. Rep. (Koruna)	....	....	....	....
Commercial rate	.02845	.02803	35.153	35.681
Denmark (Krone)	.1455	.1443	6.8730	6.9280
Ecuador (Sucre)	....	....	....	....
Floating rate	.0002223	.0002223	4498.00	4498.00
Finland (Markka)	.1831	.1808	5.4617	5.5295
France (Franc)	.1654	.1641	6.0450	6.0925
1-month forward	.1657	.1644	6.0343	6.0817
3-months forward	.1663	.1650	6.0143	6.0622
6-months forward	.1670	.1657	5.9873	6.0345
Germany (Mark)	.5542	.5496	1.8043	1.8195
1-month forward	.5552	.5506	1.8011	1.8163
3-months forward	.5570	.5524	1.7952	1.8103
6-months forward	.5595	.5550	1.7874	1.8019
Greece (Drachma)	.003505	.003487	285.32	286.75
Hong Kong (Dollar)	.1292	.1293	7.7383	7.7358
Hungary (Forint)	.004856	.004817	205.91	207.58
India (Rupee)	.02580	.02577	38.765	38.805
Indonesia (Rupiah)	.00007519	.00008696	13300.00	11500.00
Ireland (Punt)	1.3920	1.3841	.7184	.7225
Israel (Shekel)	.2792	.2799	3.5817	3.5721
Italy (Lira)	.0005631	.0005590	1776.00	1789.00
Japan (Yen)	.007860	.007868	127.23	127.10
1-month forward	.007894	.007903	126.68	126.54
3-months forward	.007960	.007970	125.63	125.47
6-months forward	.008060	.008069	124.07	123.93
Jordan (Dinar)	1.4134	1.4134	.7075	.7075
Kuwait (Dinar)	3.2765	3.2690	.3052	.3059
Lebanon (Pound)	.0006554	.0006554	1525.75	1525.75
Malaysia (Ringgit)	.2203	.2275	4.5400	4.3953
Malta (Lira)	2.5478	2.5413	.3925	.3935
Mexico (Peso)	....	....	....	....
Floating rate	.1208	.1206	8.2770	8.2900
Netherland (Guilder)	.4919	.4881	2.0329	2.0488
New Zealand (Dollar)	.5822	.5841	1.7176	1.7120
Norway (Krone)	.1339	.1332	7.4708	7.5088
Pakistan (Rupee)	.02296	.02296	43.560	43.560
Peru (new Sol)	.3652	.3675	2.7382	2.7213
Philippines (Peso)	.02338	.02395	42.770	41.750
Poland (Zloty)	.2847	.2824	3.5120	3.5405
Portugal (Escudo)	.005421	.005378	184.48	185.95
Russia (Ruble) (a)	.1663	.1665	6.0150	6.0050
Saudi Arabia (Riyal)	.2666	.2666	3.7508	3.7505
Singapore (Dollar)	.5680	.5703	1.7605	1.7535
Slovak Rep. (Koruna)	.02820	.02782	35.455	35.945
South Africa (Rand)	.2026	.2015	4.9365	4.9640
South Korea (Won)	.0005690	.0005809	1757.50	1721.50
Spain (Peseta)	.006537	.006489	152.97	154.11
Sweden (Krona)	.1255	.1244	7.9682	8.0415
Switzerland (Franc)	.6804	.6776	1.4698	1.4758
1-month forward	.6829	.6801	1.4644	1.4704
3-months forward	.6877	.6848	1.4542	1.4603
6-months forward	.6944	.6916	1.4400	1.4460
Taiwan (Dollar)	.02967	.02987	33.706	33.478
Thailand (Baht)	.01867	.01907	53.550	52.450
Turkey (Lira)	.00000468	.0000465	213815.00	214895.00
United Arab (Dirham)	.2723	.2723	3.6725	3.6725
Uruguay (New Peso)	....	....	....	....
Financial	.1002	.1002	9.9800	9.9800
Venezuela (Bolivar)	.001965	.001965	508.80	508.83
SDR	1.3501	1.3415	.7407	.7454
ECU	1.0927	1.0854	....	....

Special Drawing Rights (SDR) are based on exchange rates for the U.S., German, British, French, and Japanese currencies. Source: International Monetary Fund.

European Currency Unit (ECU) is based on a basket of community currencies.

a-fixing, Moscow Interbank Currency Exchange. Ruble newly-denominated Jan. 1998.

The Wall Street Journal daily foreign exchange data for 1996 and 1997 may be purchased through the Readers' Reference Service (413) 592-3600.

Key Currency Cross Rates Late New York Trading Jan 22, 1998

	Dollar	Pound	SFranc	Guilder	Peso	Yen	Lira	D-Mark	FFranc	CdnDlr
Canada	1.4533	2.3950	.98877	.71489	.17558	.01142	.00082	.80546	.24041	....
France	6.0450	9.9622	4.1128	2.9736	.73034	.04751	.00340	3.3503	....	4.1595
Germany	1.8043	2.9735	1.2276	.88755	.21799	.01418	.00102	....	.29848	1.2415
Italy	1776.0	2926.8	1208.3	873.63	214.57	13.959	....	984.32	293.8	1222.0
Japan	127.23	209.68	86.563	62.585	15.372	....	.07164	70.515	21.047	87.546
Mexico	8.2770	13.64	5.6314	4.0715	....	.06506	.00466	4.5874	1.3692	5.6953
Netherlands	2.0329	3.3502	1.3831	....	.24561	.01598	.00114	1.1267	.33629	1.3988
Switzerland	1.4698	2.4222	....	.72301	.17758	.01155	.00083	.81461	.24314	1.0114
U.K.	.60680	....	.41284	.29849	.07331	.00477	.00034	.33631	.10038	.41753
U.S.	....	1.6480	.68036	.49191	.12082	.00786	.00056	.55423	.16543	.68809

Source: Dow Jones

SOURCE: *The Wall Street Journal,* Friday, January 23, 1998, C17.

Cross Rates

Although it is common among exchange traders worldwide to quote currency values against the U.S. dollar, it is not necessary. Any currency's value can be stated in terms of any other currency. When the exchange rate for a currency is stated without using the U.S. dollar as a reference, it is referred to as **cross rate.** For example, the German mark and Japanese yen are both quoted on Thursday, January 22, 1998, versus the U.S. dollar: DEM 1.8043/USD and Yen 127.23/USD. But if the YEN/DEM cross rate is needed, it is simply a matter of division:

cross rate exchange rate quotations that do not use the U.S. dollar

$$\frac{\text{YEN 127.23/USD}}{\text{DEM 1.8043/USD}} = \text{YEN 70.515/DEM}$$

The YEN/DEM cross rate of 70.515 is the third leg of the triangle, which must be true if the first two exchange rates are known. If one of the exchange rates changes due to market forces, the others must adjust for the three exchange rates to all be aligned once again. If they are out of alignment, it would be possible to make a profit simply by exchanging one currency for a second, the second for a third, and the third back to the first. This is known as triangular arbitrage. Besides the potential profitability of arbitrage that may occasionally occur, cross rates have become increasingly common in a world of rapidly expanding trade and investment. The world's financial markets no longer revolve about the U.S. dollar.

Some newspapers with more comprehensive coverage of the financial news provide cross rates for the major currencies, as shown in Figure 4.3.

Using Your Hand-held Calculator to Compute Foreign Exchange Rates

Foreign exchange computations can be simplified when you use a hand-held calculator. The following computational steps will work on most calculators. If you have any trouble, consult the manual that came with the calculator. To compute reciprocals, follow these steps.

1. If your calculator has a reciprocal key $\boxed{1/\chi}$, enter .5542; press $1/\chi$ (reciprocal key). Display is 1.8043.
2. If your calculator does not have the reciprocal key, but has a $\frac{1}{\chi}$ over another key, it indicates a shift operation, $\frac{1}{\chi}/\boxed{\pi}$. The shift key is usually marked or may be in a light color such as yellow or orange. To use the shift, enter .5542; press shift; press key with $\frac{1}{\chi}$ over it. Display is 1.8043.
3. If your calculator does not have reciprocal or shift keys, enter 1.000 (note 4 decimal places); press ÷ (divide); enter .5542; press = (equals). Display is 1.8043.

Percentage Change Calculations

The quotation form is important when calculating the percentage change in an exchange rate. For example, if the spot rate between the Japanese yen and the U.S. dollar changed from YEN 125/USD to YEN 150/USD, the percentage change in the value of the Japanese yen is

$$\frac{\text{YEN 125/USD} - \text{YEN 150/USD}}{\text{YEN 150/USD}} \times 100 = -16.67\%.$$

The Japanese yen has declined in value versus the U.S. dollar by 16.67 percent. This is consistent with the intuition that it now requires more yen (150) to buy a dollar than it used to (125).

The same percentage change result can be achieved by using the inverted forms of the same spot rates (indirect quotes on the Japanese yen) if care is taken to also "invert" the basic percentage-change calculation. Using the inverse of YEN 125/USD (USD 0.0080/YEN) and the inverse of YEN 150/USD (USD 0.0067/YEN), the percentage change is still −16.67 percent:

$$\frac{\text{USD } 0.0067/\text{YEN} - \text{USD } 0.0080/\text{YEN}}{\text{USD } 0.0080/\text{YEN}} \times 100 = -16.67\%.$$

If the percentage changes calculated are not identical, it is normally the result of rounding errors introduced when inverting the spot rates. Both methods are identical, however, when calculated properly.

Bid and Offer Quotes

When asked for a quotation, a foreign exchange trader (bank) actually gives two quotes: a bid—the rate at which the trader is willing to buy the currency and an offer—the rate at which the trader is willing to sell the currency. Since the trader's profit is the difference (or spread) between the two rates, the bid (buy) rate will always be lower than the offer (sell) rate. For example, the DEM/USD quotation discussed previously when given by a foreign exchange trader might actually have been USD/DEM .5665–.5678. Which of these two rates one would use depends on the transaction. If someone had imported merchandise from Germany and had to pay the German firm in marks, he or she would want to buy marks at $.5678, the rate at which the trader is willing to sell marks. Conversely, if someone had received a payment in German marks and wanted to convert it to dollars, he or she would want to sell marks and use .5665; the bid price at which the trader (bank) is willing to buy marks.

Direct/Indirect Quotations

The order in which the foreign exchange (FX) rate is stated is sometimes confusing to the uninitiated. For example, when the rate between the U.S. dollar and the German mark is stated as it was in the preceding section, a **direct quotation** on the German mark was used. This method is simultaneously an **indirect quotation** on the U.S. dollar. A direct quotation on any currency is the form used when that currency is stated first; an indirect quotation is the form used when the subject currency is stated second. Figure 4.3 illustrates both forms, direct and indirect quotations, for major world currencies on Tuesday, July 8, 1997. These are the most commonly read set of exchange rate quotations in use today, the daily currency quotations from *The Wall Street Journal.*

direct quotation
a foreign exchange quotation that specifies the units of home country currency needed to purchase one unit of foreign currency

indirect quotation
foreign exchange quotation that specifies the units of foreign currency needed to purchase one unit of the home currency

TYPES OF FOREIGN EXCHANGE TRANSACTIONS

Foreign exchange transactions can be classified into two groups with respect to the time required for delivery of the currency: spot transactions and forward transactions.

Spot Transactions

Most of the quotations listed in Figure 4.3 are spot rates. A **spot transaction** is the exchange of currencies for immediate delivery. Although it is defined as immediate, in

spot transaction
the exchange of currencies for immediate delivery

In what country is the world's largest pyramid?

ANSWER! *The largest pyramid is that of Quetzalcoatl in Mexico, whose volume is 3.3 million cubic meters. The pyramid of Cheops in Egypt has a volume of only 2.5 million cubic meters.*

practice, settlement actually occurs two business days following the agreed upon exchange date. As shown in Figure 4.3, about half of the transactions in the foreign exchange market are spot transactions.

Forward Transactions

forward transaction the exchange of currencies on a future date at an agreed upon exchange rate

forward outright transactions for maturities of 30, 90, 120, 180, and 360 days

forward swaps exchange of currency for an agreed-length of time at an agreed rate

Forward transactions are contracts that provide for two parties to exchange currencies on a future date at an agreed upon exchange rate. There are two types of forward transactions: outright and swaps. **Forward outrights** are typically traded for the major volume currencies for maturities of 30, 90, 120, 180 and 360 days (from the present date). As shown in Figure 4.4, they represent about 7 percent of foreign exchange transactions.

Forward swaps are the most common type of forward transactions, comprising about 46 percent of all foreign exchange transactions. In a swap transaction, two companies exchange currency for an agreed length of time at an agreed exchange rate. At the end of the time period, each company returns the currencies to the former owner at the agreed exchange rate with an adjustment for differences in interest rates.

The forward, like the basic spot exchange, can be for any amount of currency. Forward contracts serve a variety of purposes, but their primary purpose is to allow firms to lock in a rate of exchange on funds that will be required in the future. In this way, business firms can avoid a potential loss on foreign exchange in the event that the currencies involved change in value between the date the contract was entered into and the date when the merchandise or services were delivered.

FIGURE 4.4 **Spot and Forward Transactions Account for 95 Percent of Trading in the Foreign Exchange Market**

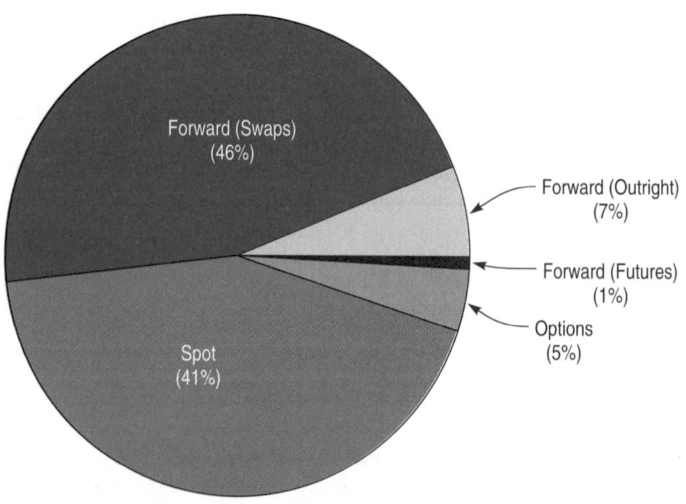

SOURCES: BIS; Federal Reserve Bank of New York.

The quotations listed in Figure 4.3 will also occasionally indicate if the rate is applicable to business trade, the commercial rate, or financial asset purchases or sales, the financial rate. Countries that have government regulations regarding the exchange of their currency may post official rates, while the markets operating outside their jurisdiction will list a floating rate. In this case, any exchange of currency that is not under the control of a government is interpreted as a better indication of the currency's true market value.

The interesting origins of the "dollar," "mark," "peso," and other currencies is presented in Global Learning Experience 4.4.

FIXED AND FLOATING FOREIGN EXCHANGE RATES

Today's foreign exchange rates are said to *float*; **floating foreign exchange rates** respond quickly to market forces of supply and demand for a currency. For the first half of this century, however, foreign currencies were *fixed* to each other by a system called the *Gold Exchange Standard.* Under the Gold Exchange Standard, foreign currencies were linked to each other based on the amount of gold for which they could be exchanged. The major benefit of using gold as a standard was price stability and thus control of inflation. The countries that used gold as a standard for currency exchange agreed to buy and sell gold openly at the **fixed foreign exchange rate.** Since a country's money supply was fixed by the value of the gold it held, the money supply could not be increased unless the country increased its supply of gold. Because the world supply of gold increased slowly, prices were generally stable.

floating foreign exchange rate foreign exchange rates that respond quickly to market forces of supply and demand

fixed foreign exchange rate foreign currencies linked to each other based on gold

Another feature of the gold standard also relied on the ability of the gold to flow. Rapid growth, particularly in imports, could push the balance of payments into deficit (outflows of money and currency exceeding inflows). Because the system relied on fixed exchange rates and *convertibility* of currencies for gold, anyone not wanting to be paid in paper currency could essentially demand gold bullion. Thus, if there was reason to doubt the value of the currency, the government would allow gold to flow, in this case to flow out of the country.

The gold flow out of the country reduced the supply of money (remember the fixed link of paper money to gold), pushing the system back into balance. Having less money in the country's economy would slow business, economic activity, and prices. The fall in prices would then stimulate exports and move the country's balance of payments toward an equilibrium position.

Because of the devastating nature and inflation of World War I, many countries abandoned their individual gold standards, permitting citizens to exchange currency for gold at will. World War I was followed by the Great Depression of the 1930s and what amounted to an international trade war as countries sought to protect their domestic industries. By the early days of World War II, international trade had ground to a halt. The governments of the Allied powers knew that the devastating impacts of World War II would require swift and decisive policies. Therefore, a full year before the end of the war, representatives of 44 nations met in the summer of 1944 in Bretton Woods, New Hampshire. Their purpose was to plan the postwar international monetary system. It was a difficult process, and the final synthesis of viewpoints was shaded by pragmatism and significant doubt.[2] After weeks of meetings, the participants finally came up with a plan called the Bretton Woods Agreement. To structure the postwar international monetary system, the agreement called for:

1. Fixed exchange rates, termed an "adjustable peg" among members;
2. A fund of gold and constituent currencies available to members for stabilization

The Origins of Monies

Currency Name	Representative Currencies	Origins
Krona	Czech Repûblic koruna Danish krone Icelandic krona Norwegian krone Slovak Republic koruna Swedish krona	From the word meaning "crown" and simultaneously that of "gold" from the Latin word *aureus.*
Dollar	Australian dollar Canadian dollar Hong Kong dollar Singapore dollar Taiwanese dollar United States dollar	From the old German *Daler* or *Taler,* an abbreviation of the name given the silver coin—*joachimsthaler*—a coin with the likeness of St. Joachim imprinted upon it and first minted in 1519.
Franc	French franc Swiss franc Belgian franc Luxembourg franc Liechtenstein franc	From the Latin inscription of the coin first minted in 1360 by order of King John II of France which read, *Johannes Dei Gracia Francorum Rex* (John by the Grace of God King of the Franks).
Mark	German mark (Deutschemark) Finnish markka	From an old Norse term for a unit of measure, a mark, used as early as the third century A.D. It was first employed by the Goths and later by the Germans.
Peso	Argentina peso Chilean peso Mexican peso Philippines peso Spanish peseta Uruguay new peso	From the word meaning "weight." The *peso* was established in Spain in 1497 by King Ferdinard and Queen Isabella. The Spanish *peseta* was introduced as a companion coin to the *full peso,* the famous "piece of eight," referring to its value of eight *reales.*
Pound	British pound sterling Italian lira Maltese lira Turkish lira	Pound is from the Roman *libra* or pound, money of account from early medieval times. The British pound is from the eighth century in Anglo-Saxon Britain when the basic monetary unit called the *sterling* was defined as 1/240 of a *pound of sterling silver.* The Italian lira from *libra* was first minted in 1472 by the Doge Nicolas Tron of Venice (also being known as the *testone* or "head" because it depicted the head of Doge Nicolas).
Yen	Japanese yen Chinese yuan	From Japanese meaning "round," and basically borrowed from the Chinese term *yuan* also meaning round.

SOURCE: Adapted by authors from Leslie Dunkling and Adrian Room, *The Guinness Book of Money,* Facts on File Publishing, New York, 1990.

International Monetary Fund gold and constituent currencies available to members for currency stabilization

of their respective currencies, called the **International Monetary Fund (IMF);** and

3. A bank for financing long-term development projects (World Bank).

Fixed Exchange Rates: The Adjustable Peg

All currencies were to establish par values defined in terms of gold. However, unlike the gold standard prior to World War I, there was little if any convertibility of currencies for gold. Each government was responsible for monitoring its currency value to ensure

The London financial district flourished during the decades prior to World War I when the British pound sterling was the dominant world currency and when most currencies were based on the gold standard.
SOURCE: The Bettmann Archive, Reuters/Bettmann.

that it varied by less than 1 percent from its par value. If a country experienced a **fundamental disequilibrium** in its balance of payments, it could alter its peg by up to 10 percent from its initial par value without approval from the IMF. But, as with any fixed-price system, the goal of the system was not to change the par value. The "adjustment" part of the peg was to be kept to a minimum.[3] A country experiencing significant problems could therefore apply to the IMF for temporary loans of gold or convertible currencies for the purpose of defending its par value and adjusting the balance of payments back toward equilibrium.

fundamental disequilibrium persistent imbalances in BOP

The one currency that was convertible to gold was the U.S. dollar. The dollar was pegged at $1 = 1/35 ounce of gold, or $35 per ounce. The U.S. Treasury would, however, convert U.S. dollars for gold only with foreign governments, not with private individuals, domestic or foreign. This was a significant reduction in convertibility compared to that of the old gold standard. But with all currencies pegged to gold, and the dollar convertible to gold, even if only with official authorities, the dollar was considered "good as gold." This was the feature of the system that brought 25 years of success, as well as its eventual collapse.

For example, a country experiencing a balance of payments deficit would normally experience devaluation pressure on its currency value. The country's authorities, normally the central bank, would defend its currency by using its foreign currency reserves, primarily U.S. dollars, to purchase its own currency on the open market to push its value back up and preserve its par value. Once a country used up a large proportion of its currency reserves, it could apply to the IMF for additional funds to stabilize its currency value. Similarly, if the country was experiencing a balance of payments surplus and associated upward pressure on its currency, it could sell additional currency on the open market and accept payment in major convertible currencies like the U.S. dollar. Since the dollar was convertible for gold, the U.S. dollar was quite acceptable.

The International Monetary Fund

The International Monetary Fund (IMF) was created to provide funds to countries in need of additional assistance for economic stabilization. It was initially funded through the contributions from all members. Each country was given a quota in the original agreement at Bretton Woods. Quotas were established on the basis of the size and estimated strengths at the end of the Second World War, in addition to the size of foreign trade the country demonstrated prior to the war.[4] The quotas, once paid, would establish the pool of capital available to the IMF for its economic stabilization lending.

Each quota was payable 25 percent in gold and the remaining 75 percent in the country's own currency.[5] Since most countries possessed currencies that were obviously not convertible and therefore of little value, it was the gold portion of the quota that was considered the true resource of the IMF's lending capabilities.

special drawing right
an index of currencies available to each member in the IMF

A final feature of the IMF, not added until the mid-1960s, was the creation of an index of currencies, the **Special Drawing Right (SDR).** The SDR was intended as an artificial reserve asset for member countries, representing the resources available to each member in the event it were to draw upon IMF funds. The fund of SDRs would represent currency credits between central banks and would aid a country in the management of temporary balance-of-payments problems. The value of the SDR was originally calculated as the average of 16 different world currencies but was later reduced to five major currencies.

The International Bank for Reconstruction and Development

International Bank for Reconstruction and Development
the World Bank intended for reconstruction and development

The third and final part of the Bretton Woods Agreement was the formation of the **International Bank for Reconstruction and Development,** or **World Bank.** As opposed to the other two elements, which were focused on exchange rate stabilization, the World Bank was intended for reconstruction and development. Although initially focused on lending for the reconstruction of the war-torn country members, the World Bank quickly found its focus shifting toward the developing countries of Africa, Asia, the Middle East, and South America.

The Experience under Bretton Woods, 1946–1971

The 1950s were characterized by a dollar shortage on world markets as the United States ran balance-of-payments surpluses, primarily as a result of the strength of U.S. exports. As countries struggled to obtain the U.S. dollars needed for their currency reserves, the U.S. balances on trade and capital accounts slowly shifted from surpluses to deficits as the European and Japanese economies recuperated from the devastation of World War II.

By the late 1960s, the adjustable peg exchange rate system was showing signs of stress. As the United States continued to run larger and larger balance-of-payments deficits, many countries were being forced to intervene to preserve fixed parities. They bought dollars to keep the dollar from falling and their own currencies from rising.

The continued defense of the dollar left central banks around the world with massive quantities of U.S. dollars. These countries, knowing that the dollars they held were in fact convertible into gold with the U.S. Treasury, attempted to hold back, demanding gold in exchange. These central banks knew that if they did demand gold in exchange for the paper balances they held, it could very well send the international monetary system into a tailspin.

In 1970, the United States had gold reserves valued at $11 billion and foreign governments and individuals held $47 billion; in other words, the United States did not have enough gold to cover its obligations to convert dollars to gold. It became painfully clear in 1971 that the U.S. dollar was overvalued, and devaluation of the dollar versus gold was inevitable. More and more central banks began presenting U.S. dollar balances to the U.S. Treasury for conversion to gold. The United States allowed the gold to flow, and it flowed out of the Treasury coffers at an alarming rate.

Collapse and Transition, 1971–1973

On August 15, 1971, former President Richard M. Nixon announced that "I have instructed [Treasury] Secretary [John B.] Connally to suspend temporarily the convertibility of the dollar into gold or other assets." With this simple statement, Nixon effectively ended the fixed exchange rates established at Bretton Woods, New Hampshire, more than 25 years earlier. The closing of the "gold window" by Nixon was in fact not a major surprise to world currency markets. The events of the previous months and years had foretold the need for the dollar to fall. The real question was what would come next? What would the international monetary system look like now?

By March 1973, after many attempts were made to patch up the system and after the world currency markets devalued the dollar from $35 to $38 dollars per ounce of gold and again from $38 to $42.22 per ounce, the system ground to a complete halt. Most major currencies were simply allowed to float, effectively ending the experiment with fixed rates.

FLOATING EXCHANGE RATES, 1973–PRESENT

A floating exchange rate system poses many new and different problems for participants. The biggest is the most obvious: the lack of certainty as to what rate currencies will be exchanged at a year, a month, or a day from now. However, firms worldwide have learned to live and deal with these price-risk issues relatively quickly. A larger crisis in the eyes of many major countries is that floating exchange rates do not allow the same degree of economic policy isolation that they previously enjoyed.

Under the previous fixed exchange rate regime, governments could conduct relatively independent monetary policy. The central bank of a country would normally increase the country's money supply at rates consistent with domestic economic policy goals. If interest rates rose or fell, although they may attract capital into or cause it to flow out of the country, government intervention in the foreign exchange markets could offset negative exchange rate effects. Governments enjoyed this degree of independence; the ability to self-determine domestic economic policy is one of the ways a country might define sovereignty. Floating exchange rates changed all of that. A country's domestic economic policies now translated into immediate impacts on its external relations, its currency's exchange value. There is no better example of this than the events in the United States beginning in 1979.

The Rise of the Dollar, 1980–1985

The United States suffered increasing rates of inflation throughout the 1970s. By 1979, the annual rate of inflation was approaching 12 percent, and the U.S. economy was

In what exact direction do you travel when you go through the Panama Canal from the Caribbean Sea to the Pacific Ocean?

From Northwest to Southeast.

continuing to suffer both inflation and stagnant economic growth. In the summer of 1979, the U.S. Federal Reserve System instituted a tight "monetary growth role." This meant that the Federal Reserve would increase the U.S. money supply at a steady, slow rate regardless of interest rates. Within weeks, interest rates in the United States rose precipitously. Over the following years, the United States suffered a modest recession (1980) and then a severe recession (1981–1982). Inflation was purged slowly from the U.S. economy, but at the cost of increased unemployment and slow economic growth.

The eventual rebound of the U.S. economy in 1983 and 1984 was also characterized by a rapidly rising dollar. The relatively rapid economy growth of the United States compared to other industrial countries, the falling rate of inflation, the still extremely high real rates of interest available in the United States, and the role of the country as a "safe haven" in a world of increasing risk all contributed to the rise of the dollar. Depending on which currencies are used for measurement, the dollar rose roughly 45 percent against currencies of other major industrial countries between the spring of 1980 and early 1985.

Although the dollar rose as a result of many forces, many of which were signs of relative economic health, the degree of the dollar's rise was not healthy for anyone inside or out of the United States. The strong dollar resulted in extreme U.S. purchasing power abroad, which led to rising import bills, while U.S. exports languished. American product prices were increasingly uncompetitive on world markets as a result of the dollar. Before you could buy an American product, you had to buy a dollar. And dollars were very expensive.

The single most powerful argument against freely floating exchange rates has always been the uncertainty it introduces into international commerce. Although the dollar had floated relatively freely throughout the 1970s, the volatility of its movements had not been an insurmountable problem for firms or governments. The first half of the 1980s, however, confronted policymakers around the world with the very thing they had always feared: massive exchange rate movement over a very short period of time.

Intervention in the 1980s: Expectations and Coordination

intervention
government buying and selling of the country's own currency on the open market

The **intervention** of a government in a foreign exchange market has traditionally referred to the actual buying and selling of the country's own currency on the open market. If the magnitude of government sales or purchases relative to the total size of the market at the time of the trades is substantial, the government can literally alter the exchange rate on its own. However, while the world's currency markets grew in size over the 1960s, 1970s, and into the 1980s, the amount of official reserves (major currencies and gold) held by governments did not. It therefore became increasingly difficult for an individual government to intervene successfully.

By the mid-1980s, it was clear that major world currencies like the U.S. dollar, the German mark, or the Japanese yen could only be managed by the coordination of policies among the industrial countries. Governments realized that one of their most powerful tools was their ability to influence the expectations of the market. Currency traders, international speculators, and investors are all moving the world's capital into currencies and assets that they expect to yield the relatively higher returns. Therefore, government economic policies with respect to monetary policy, anti-inflammatory measures, stimulus measures, and so forth alter the actual yields that these investors pursue. If a government can alter what investors believe, it may successfully influence the supply-and-demand forces for its currency—in theory.

The Plaza Agreement, September 1985

Although the U.S. dollar peaked in its rise against most currencies in February 1985, it was September before the **Group of Five,** or G5 countries (United States, Japan, West Germany, United Kingdom, France), could meet at the Plaza Hotel in New York to discuss the issue. The rapidly deteriorating U.S. trade balance had caused a surge of protectionist sentiment in the United States. This renewed call for protection from imports—imports from Japan and Germany—prompted the meeting to aid in the dollar's fall to competitiveness.

Group of Five
the G5 countries: the United States, Japan, West Germany, United Kingdom, and France

The message of the Plaza Agreement to the world's financial markets was clear: The G5 countries wanted the dollar to fall, and they intended to work cooperatively toward that end. It was generally concluded that the countries other than the United States needed to stimulate their own economies (and possibly raise their interest rates relative to dollar rates), and the United States in turn needed to work toward lowering interest rates through concerted efforts to reduce the ballooning U.S. government budget deficit. Although it is difficult to find true coordination of the policies following the Plaza meeting, the dollar did fall considerably over the following 18 months.

The Louvre Accord, February 1987

By February 1987, the dollar was thought to have fallen far enough. A meeting of the **Group of Seven,** or G7 (G5 plus Canada and Italy), was held February 21–22 at the Louvre Museum in Paris to consider the immediate prospects of the international monetary system.[6] The purpose of the meeting was to stop the fall of the dollar; however, the formal and informal agreements reached at the meeting failed to stop the dollar's slide.

Group of Seven
the G5 countries plus Canada and Italy

By the end of March 1987, the U.S. dollar was hitting record lows against the Japanese yen (approximately ¥148/$). Coordinated intervention by all major central banks did succeed in stabilizing the dollar's value over the next few months. Although the degree of coordinated policy was relatively short-lived, the events following the Louvre Accord demonstrated that coordinated policy among industrial countries could gain some temporary degree of success in managing exchange rates.

Recent Currency Movements

The movements of the U.S. dollar, Japanese yen, and German mark have been anything but stable since 1987. Figure 4.5 indicates a continuing downward trend in the dollar versus the yen and mark. As the dollar approached the 100-yen and 1.60-mark levels, the U.S. Federal Reserve and the central banks of other nations began a series of intervention efforts to stop the dollar's slide as indicated in Table 4.2.

The prevailing wisdom is that in the 110–120 yen range, U.S. and Japanese manufacturers would be equally price competitive in global markets and this would bring about an equilibrium in imports and exports between the two countries. If the dollar falls below this theoretical point, U.S. exports would become less expensive to foreign citizens, while U.S. imports would become more expensive for Americans—thus lowering their standard of living. Pushing theory to the limit, if the dollar kept falling it might go into a "free fall" and cause massive increases in the cost-of-living in the United States. Accordingly, intervention is seen as a method of controlling the value of currencies relative to each other. However, intervention by central banks is a risky proposition, which does not always work. The United States and other nations

FIGURE 4.5 **The Recent Movements of the Dollar, Yen, and Mark (monthly, 1987–1998)**

SOURCE: *Federal Reserve Bulletin,* Board of Governors of the Federal Reserve System, monthly.

TABLE 4.2

Intervention Activity in Support of the U.S. Dollar Against the Mark and Yen 1994–1997

	German Mark		Japanese Yen		
Date	**Trading Price**	**Amount of Dollars Purchased (millions)**	**Trading Price**	**Amount of Dollars Purchased (millions)**	**Total U.S. Purchases (millions)**
1994					
January 31 Value of dollar	1.7338	—	108.65	—	—
April 29 U.S. Purchases dollars	1.6440	500	102.00	200	700
May 4 U.S. and 18 countries join in support of U.S. dollar	1.6330	750	101.83	500	1250
June 24 U.S. and 16 foreign central banks purchase dollars	1.5855	980	99.93	610	1560
November 2 U.S. purchases dollars	1.4910	800	96.11	800	1600
November 3 U.S. and one other country support dollar	1.5145	500	97.65	500	1000
December 31 Dollar closes at:	1.5490	—	99.55	—	—
1995					
March 2 U.S. intervenes in foreign exchange market	1.4348	300	94.93	300	600
March 3 U.S. plus 13 other central banks buy dollars	1.4490	450	94.80	370	820
April 3 U.S. in coordinated activity with bank of Japan	1.3735	750	86.50	750	1500
April 5 U.S., Germany, and Japan support dollar	1.3737	850	86.00	250	1100
April 19 Dollar at new low	1.3472	—	79.75	—	—
May 31 U.S. and other G-10 countries purchase dollars against the mark and yen	1.3850	500	82.70	500	1000
July 7 U.S. monetary authorities purchase dollars	—	—	86.20	333.3	333.3
August 2 U.S. and Japan support dollar against yen	—	—	90.15	500	500
August 15 U.S., Germany, and Japan support dollar	1.4795	400	95.02	300	700
December 31 Dollar closes at:	1.4339	—	103.20	—	—
1996					
— No intervention activity in 1996					
December 31 Dollar closes at:	1.5387	—	115.77	—	—
1997					
February 7 U.S. officials indicate end of long U.S. push to support dollar	1.6568	—	125.00	—	—
April 27 G-7 ministers express concern over rise in the dollar	1.7352	—	126.25	—	—
May 9 Dollar in major decline in foreign exchange markets	1.6869	—	120.35	—	—
June 12 U.S. Treasury officials suggest that Japan should not export their way out of an economic slump by depreciating the yen	1.7161	—	110.20	—	—
June 30 Dollar closes at:	1.7438	—	114.61	—	—

SOURCE: Federal Reserve Bank of New York Quarterly Reports of Treasury and Federal Reserve Foreign Exchange Operations.

purchased billions of dollars during the April 1994 to April 1995 period only to watch the dollar continue its slide to a low of 79.80 yen to the dollar on April 19, 1995. The fundamental problem with intervention is that in a global foreign exchange market trading in excess of $1 trillion a day, intervention efforts of $1.0 billion are only a "drop in the bucket" and are insufficient in offsetting an FX market that is moving in the opposite direction. Intervention is a subtle game and at best a weak substitute for sound national policies that would have a positive effect on trade and interest rates.

SOURCE: New York Times, Sunday July 3, 1994, 10E.

The Peso Crisis

In recent years using an occasional intervention, the Mexican government had been able to hold the peso at 3.46 pesos to the U.S. dollar—or 28.9 cents. In the process of intervention, Mexico's reserve of U.S. dollars had fallen to very low levels—to the extent that intervention efforts in the near future would not be possible. On December 21, 1994, several days after being elected, Mexico's new president devalued the peso and allowed it to float freely in the foreign exchange market. The result was immediate and dramatic. The value of the peso declined from 28.9 cents to 17.9 cents in a few days, continued to drop throughout 1995, and stabilized in the 12- to 13-cent range—losing about 56 percent of its value. The peso crisis caused economic chaos in Mexico. In the months following the devaluation, the U.S. government, International Monetary Fund, and Bank for International Settlements put together a $50 billion "bailout package" to rescue the Mexican economy. Some reasons for the peso crisis are provided in Global Learning Experience 4.5.

EUROPEAN EXCHANGE RATES: THE MONETARY SYSTEM

The European Monetary System

European monetary system fixed parity rates among member currencies

Exchange rate mechanism maintenance of European Monetary System member currencies versus other member currencies

In 1979, a formalized structure was put in place among many of the major members of the European Union. The **European Monetary System (EMS)** officially began operation in March 1979 and established a grid of fixed parity rates among member currencies. The EMS consisted of three different components that would work in concert to preserve fixed parities (also termed central rates).

First, all countries that were committing their currencies and their efforts to the preservation of fixed exchange rates entered the **Exchange Rate Mechanism (ERM).**

GLOBAL LEARNING EXPERIENCE 4.5

Spending at Core of Mexico's Woes

WASHINGTON—Here are answers to some basic questions about the Mexican financial crisis:

QUESTION: How did Mexico get into this mess?

ANSWER: For years, both the Mexican government and the Mexican people have been spending beyond their means. The country's trade deficit is high, and the government relies too much on money borrowed from foreigners. In December, a renewed peasant uprising in Chiapas state made investors nervous, with the result that they dumped pesos and called in their debts, causing the currency's value to begin dropping on international markets. The government did not have enough foreign currency reserves to buy pesos and halt the decline. It had to call on its allies for help.

Q: So why is this a problem for the United States?

A: Sales of U.S. goods in Mexico could plunge because the prices of our products are soaring there. This could cost thousands of U.S. jobs as exports are slowed. Also, with the peso's value plunging, more U.S. jobs could shift to Mexico because wages and production costs would be lower there. And many U.S. investors who purchased Mexican stocks or mutual funds holding Mexican stocks could lose much of their investments. There also could be political problems in the United States if the peso remained weak, because a sharp rise in illegal immigration would be expected as more and more Mexicans tried to get dollar-paying jobs.

Q: What are we going to do to help?

A: Originally, President Clinton wanted to extend loan guarantees of $40 billion to Mexico, much the same way the government bailed out Chrysler Corp. But Congress refused to support the idea because it would impose too much of a financial risk on U.S. taxpayers. Clinton is bypassing Congress and going straight to the U.S. Treasury, using his executive power to commit $20 billion for emergency assistance to Mexico. This is not foreign aid or a grant. Instead, it is expected to take the form of currency swaps: The Treasury will exchange dollars for pesos as a way of pumping dollars into Mexican coffers with an agreement to swap them back in the future.

Q: How much will this cost U.S. taxpayers?

A: There's no direct cost. But there is a risk for the Treasury, which will be committing billions of its reserves to the proposition that the value of the peso will stabilize.

Q: What about Mexico's other allies?

A: The International Monetary Fund and Bank of International Settlements will kick in $27 billion in loans, while the Bank of Canada will provide a $1 billion line of credit.

Q: What will Mexico do with the money?

A: Investor confidence has been so shaken that Mexico needs to be able to commit billions of dollars to cover all its obligations if bondholders decide to take the money and run. Hopefully, that won't be necessary. But the Mexican government has to be prepared for the worst.

Q: Is this a bailout for Wall Street?

A: Many in Congress think so. But unlike the Mexican debt crisis in 1982, when just a few big commercial banks were holding bad loans, this crisis has many more potential victims, including millions of Americans who have invested money in bond funds for "emerging nations." According to some estimates, U.S. investors hold as much as $100 billion in Mexican stocks and bonds.

Q: Did the North American Free Trade Agreement cause this crisis?

A: Indirectly. During debate over the agreement in 1993, President Clinton and Mexico's then-President Carlos Salinas de Gortari emphasized the progress Mexico had made in opening and reforming its economy, not its shortcomings. Salinas could have taken steps to reduce imports and pay Mexico's soaring foreign debt, but that would have meant higher inflation and a recession.

SOURCE: Knight-Ridder Tribune, *The Arizona Republic,* February 1, 1995, p. A7.

Although all the currencies of the countries of the European Union would be used in the calculation of important indices for management purposes, several countries chose not to be ERM participants. Participation meant the country would commit itself to the preservation of the agreed upon grid of fixed rates, and several of the member countries were not yet willing to do so. Participation in the ERM technically required that countries accept bilateral responsibility of maintaining the fixed rates. If, for example, the German mark were to start rising to the limits of its allowed band versus another currency, such as the French franc, it would be the responsibility of both countries to undertake actions to preserve the rate. The coordinated bilateral responsibility might include foreign exchange market intervention and possibly monetary policy actions altering interest rates. In the event that the rate was considered to be unsustainable, the ERM allowed necessary realignments of the parity rates.

The second element of the European Monetary System was the actual grid of bilateral exchange rates with their specified band limits.

Euro
name of currency to be introduced as part of the implementation of the European monetary union (EMU)

The third and final element of the European Monetary System was the creation of the European Currency Unit (ECU), later renamed the **Euro**. As illustrated in Figure 4.6, the Euro is a weighted average index of the currencies that are members of the EMS. Each currency is weighted by a value reflecting the relative size of that country's trade and gross domestic product. This allows each individual currency to be defined in units per Euro. The Euro can also serve as a method of value accounting between EMS members without showing preference by using one individual currency.

Events and Performance of the EMS

The need for fixed exchange rates within Europe is clear. The countries of Western Europe trade amongst themselves to a degree approaching interstate commerce in the United

FIGURE 4.6 **The Composition of the Euro**

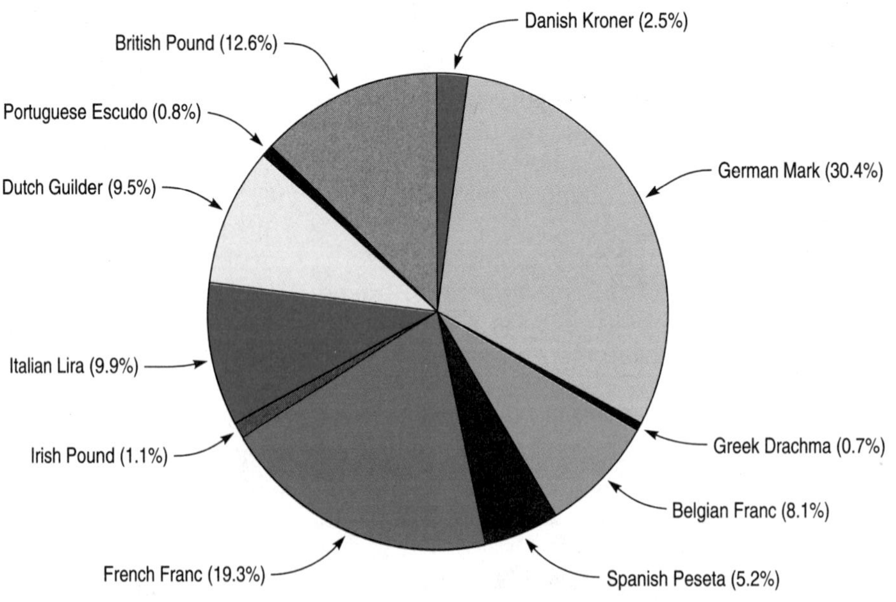

SOURCE: "The ECU and Its Role in the Process Towards Monetary Union," *European Economy*, No. 48, September 1991, p. 125. Used with permission of the Office for Official Publications of the European Community, Luxembourg.

States. It is therefore critical to the economies and businesses of Europe that exchange rates be as stable as possible. Although it has its critics, the EMS has been generally successful in providing exchange rate stability. Between March 1979 and August 1992, there were 11 realignments of central rates, with most occurring in the earlier years.

The EMS, however, suffered several setbacks beginning in September 1992. A number of the political and economic forces that had driven European economies in the past decade started to put new and exceptional pressures on the EMS. These pressures included the rapid growth of German industry and trade, which resulted in the Deutschemark growing in its proportion of world currency trading. Additionally, the merging of West Germany and East Germany in 1989 significantly increased inflationary and budget pressures in Germany. Another factor, the expansion of the EMS to include Greece, Portugal, and Spain, put considerable pressure on the system.

In December 1991, in an attempt to maintain the momentum of European integration, the members of the European Union concluded the Maastricht Treaty. The treaty, besides laying out long-term goals of harmonized social and welfare policies in the Union, specified the criteria that must be met by individual countries in order to be part of the European Monetary Union (EMU) and a timetable for the adoption of a single currency—shown in Figure 4.7.

The first major hurdle for the single currency was the acceptance of the treaty. Denmark had been successful in gaining the right to conduct a popular vote of its citizens to determine whether the degree of integration described by Maastricht was indeed desirable. In May 1992, the Danes voted "nej" (no). The Irish and French immediately scheduled popular votes in their own countries. The Irish vote resulted in a relatively strong show of support, while the French vote conducted on September 20 was an extremely narrow yes vote. The French result was immediately dubbed "le petit oui."

FIGURE 4.7

Criteria for Membership in the European Monetary Union (EMU) and Timetable for Implementation

Criteria for Membership:

1. Country's gross debt should not exceed 60% of GDP.
2. Government budget deficit should not exceed 3% of GDP.
3. Long term interest rates should be within 2 percentage points of the average of the three best performing EU members. (10%)
4. Inflation rate should be within 1 1/2 percentage points of the 3 best performing EU members. (3.0%)
5. Short term interest rates should not exceed 6.8%.
6. Exchange rate-observe the "normal margins" of the exchange rate mechanism (ERM) for two years.

EMU Timetable

Early 1998 - Preparation	January 1st 1999 - Launch	January 1st 2002 - Completion	July 1st 2002
• Decide which countries qualify for monetary union on the basis of economic performance for 1996-97 • Establish the European Central Bank and the network of national central banks	• Fix national exchange rates against the Euro "irrevocably" • Central banks begin to use Euro, as do inter-bank and foreign-exchange markets • Issue new government debt in Euros	• Issue Euro notes and coins • Convert retail payment systems to Euros	• Withdraw old currencies • Euro becomes sole legal tender

SOURCE: European Commission

The EMS Crisis of September 1992

The inflationary pressures of absorbing, employing, and redeveloping the former East Germany led the German central bank, the Bundesbank, to tighten monetary policy in 1992. As interest rates rose in Germany over the summer of 1992, capital continued to flow out of other major European currencies into Deutschemarks. Several EMS currencies experienced downward pressure to the point they were hitting their allowed bands versus the Deutschemark. Although the Bundesbank was well aware of its tight money policy's impact on the exchange markets, its primary responsibility was preserving price stability in Germany, not exchange rate stability.

Even after raising interest rates several times in attempts to defend their currencies, both Italy and Great Britain withdrew their currencies from the ERM the week of September 14, 1992. It was a devastating setback for the European Monetary System. The Spanish peseta and the Portuguese escudo were devalued officially within the EMS grid, although they were able to remain in the ERM. As the lira and pound then floated free of the EMS, their values dropped significantly as the downward pressures on currency values were given free rein. It is not expected that either currency will likely rejoin the ERM soon.

In 1993, the problems only worsened. In the summer of 1993, a number of non-EMS currencies were hit with speculative attacks (Norway, Sweden, and Finland). Finally on July 31, the French monetary authorities were unable to defend the franc any longer. The EMS, knowing that the devaluation of the franc was probably only a temporary solution, made a drastic change in the entire system: all currencies would be allowed to vary by 15 percent, not 2.25 percent (the Netherlands was the sole exception, maintaining the 2.25 percent range) from the standards set by the EMS grid. As the membership of the European Monetary Union continued to move toward the scheduled launching of the Euro on January 1, 1999, it became clear that few, if any, of the countries would be able to meet the Maastricht criteria. By mid-1997, economic "belt tightening" policies to achieve the Maastricht goals were beginning to cause the loss of jobs and elimination of generous employment benefits and social programs in the EMU countries. With unemployment at more than 10 percent in most European countries, voters were demanding more jobs and showed little interest in the single currency. Remembering the old saying that "all economics is local," it remains to be seen if the Euro will actually be launched on January 1, 1999.

The following section describes the fundamental financial forces that drive exchange rate movements and the inherent conflict between domestic economic goals and international economic goals that continue to plague the world's monetary system.

EXCHANGE RATES, INTEREST RATES, AND ECONOMIC POLICY

The global monetary system of the 1990s is a significantly different one than any of the past. The capital markets of major industrialized countries are now linked so closely that significant economic or financial events that used to be "isolated" can now affect capital flows worldwide in minutes. For those who believe in the efficiency of unregulated markets, the trend toward more open financial markets worldwide is a good one. But open markets and freely flowing markets also come at a cost. The cost is the ability of a country to define and determine its domestic economic and monetary policies independently of world markets.

As noted previously, currencies respond to interest rate movements. Assuming all markets and currencies are relatively stable and secure, a country that can lower its domestic interest rates to encourage growth may at the same time find its currency under downward pressure as capital flows out in search of higher interest. This poses a serious problem for the country. If it believes in open and free markets, government policymakers do not wish to restrict capital flows. Yet most countries prefer stable exchange rates. So what is the government to do?

This is the problem now confronting the members of the European Union. Simply put, internal goals and external goals are in direct conflict. The conflict arises from the following three financial policies:

1. *Fixed exchange rates*—A fixed exchange rate is best for the conduct of international commerce. The stability it provides in pricing helps a country's importers and exporters to manage sourcing and sales without dealing with large currency risks.
2. *Freedom of capital flows*—Not only within the European Union, but throughout the world, countries are deregulating financial markets. Capital flows between countries and major financial markets are increasing. As capital moves more freely, it can move in larger quantities and more quickly to take advantage of higher returns (such as higher interest rates). If economic and monetary policies are roughly the same across countries, there is little reason to exchange currency in an attempt to escape inflation or seek out higher interest rates.
3. *Independent monetary policies*—Every country wants to conduct its own economic policy. This means the ability to utilize fiscal policy measures (government spending and taxation) and monetary policy measures (money supply growth, interest rate restricting or *pegging*) to manage domestic economic needs.

It is important to note that Latin America has no monopoly on debt. Brazil, Mexico, and Argentina are still three of the most severely indebted countries, but a number of the emerging nations of Asia and Europe also have incurred significant debt burdens, i.e., China, Indonesia, Korea, India, and Russia.

Figure 4.8 illustrates the key debt-burden ratios for a selected group of heavily indebted nations. The ratio of total external debt to the country's gross domestic product (GDP) is indicative of the relative burden. In 1996, a group of countries had debt that was equal to more than half of the entire annual output of their economies; for example, Peru, 52 percent; Ecuador, 73 percent; Philippines, 53 percent; Hungary, 63 percent, and Bulgaria, 97 percent.

Of more immediate concern, however, is the amount of export earnings that are required to service the debt (pay interest on the debt) in the current year. The ratios of interest expenses to export earnings, also shown in Figure 4.8, indicate a number of countries are well over 20 percent of their total export revenues needed for debt service, income that is in effect already spent.

INTERNATIONAL MONEY MARKETS

A money market is traditionally defined as a market for deposits, accounts, or securities that have maturities of one year or less. The international money markets, often termed the Eurocurrency markets, constitute an enormous financial market that is in many ways outside the jurisdiction and supervision of world financial and governmental authorities.

Eurocurrency Markets

A *Eurocurrency* is any foreign currency-denominated deposit or account at a financial institution outside the country of the currency's issuance. For example, U.S. dollars

FIGURE 4.8 **Relative Debt Burdens of the Most Severely Indebted Countries**

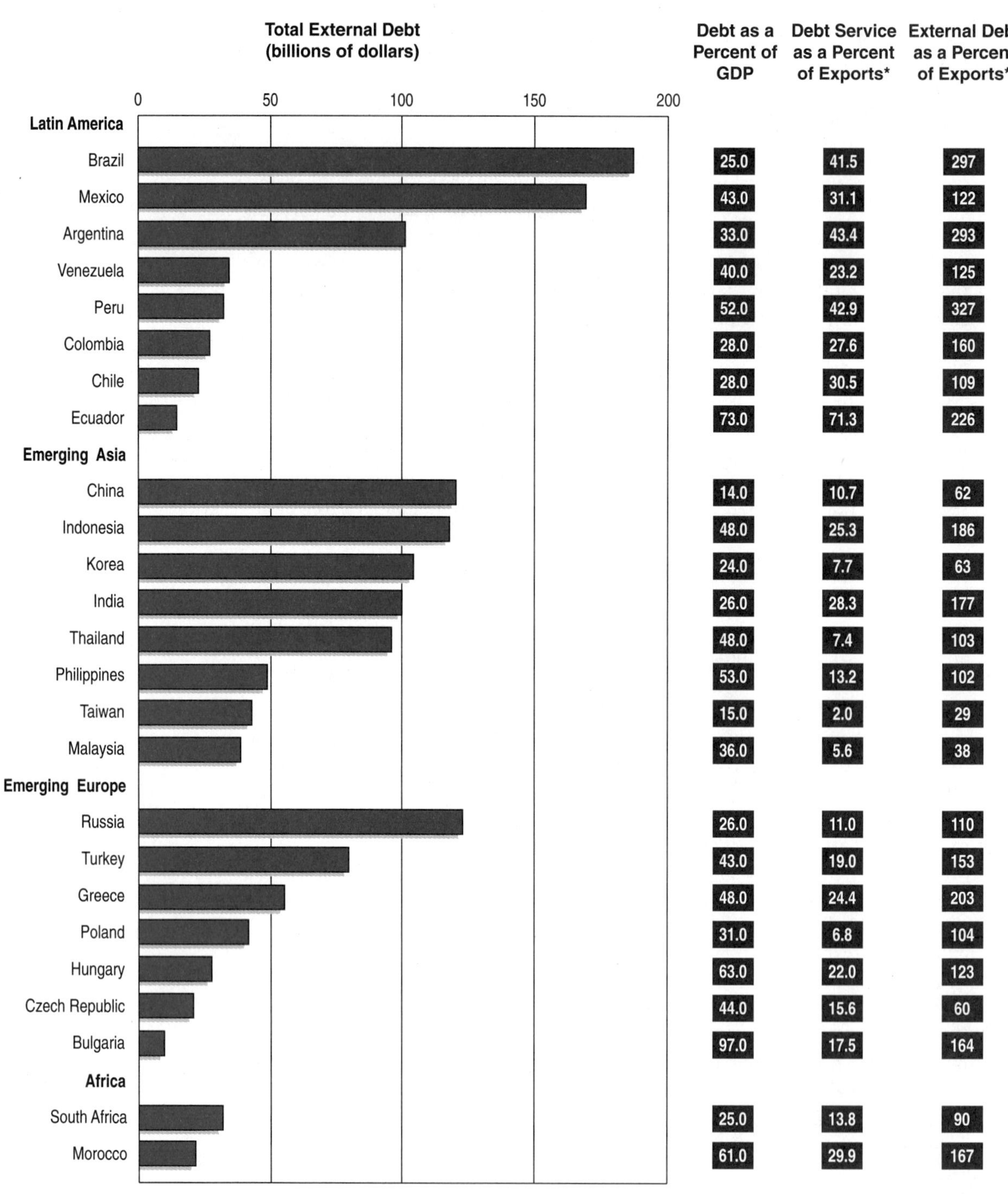

	Debt as a Percent of GDP	Debt Service as a Percent of Exports*	External Debt as a Percent of Exports*
Latin America			
Brazil	25.0	41.5	297
Mexico	43.0	31.1	122
Argentina	33.0	43.4	293
Venezuela	40.0	23.2	125
Peru	52.0	42.9	327
Colombia	28.0	27.6	160
Chile	28.0	30.5	109
Ecuador	73.0	71.3	226
Emerging Asia			
China	14.0	10.7	62
Indonesia	48.0	25.3	186
Korea	24.0	7.7	63
India	26.0	28.3	177
Thailand	48.0	7.4	103
Philippines	53.0	13.2	102
Taiwan	15.0	2.0	29
Malaysia	36.0	5.6	38
Emerging Europe			
Russia	26.0	11.0	110
Turkey	43.0	19.0	153
Greece	48.0	24.4	203
Poland	31.0	6.8	104
Hungary	63.0	22.0	123
Czech Republic	44.0	15.6	60
Bulgaria	97.0	17.5	164
Africa			
South Africa	25.0	13.8	90
Morocco	61.0	29.9	167

*Exports of goods, services and transfers.

NOTE: Debt as a percentage of total gross national product (GNP) and interest expenses as a percentage of total export earnings are frequently used indicators of the burden of foreign currency-denominated debt.
SOURCE: Compiled from data supplied by Morgan Guaranty Trust—Economics Dept.

that are held on account in a bank in London are termed *Eurodollars*. Similarly, Japanese yen held on account in a Parisian financial institution would be classified as *Euroyen*. The Euro prefix does not mean these currencies or accounts are only European, as German marks on account in Singapore would also be classified as a Eurocurrency, a Euromark account.

Eurocurrency Interest Rates

What is the significance of these foreign currency-denominated accounts? Simply put, the purity of value that comes from no governmental interference or restrictions with their use. Because Eurocurrency accounts are not controlled or managed by governments (for example, the Bank of England has no control over Eurodollar accounts), the financial institutions pay no deposit insurance, hold no reserve requirements, and are normally not subject to any interest rate restrictions with respect to these accounts. Eurocurrencies are one of the purest indicators of what these currencies should yield in terms of interest.

There are hundreds of different major interest rates around the globe, but the global financial markets focus on a very few, the interbank interest rates. Interbank rates charged by banks to banks in the major international financial centers such as London, Frankfurt, Paris, New York, Tokyo, Singapore, and Hong Kong are generally regarded as "the interest rate" in the respective market. The interest rate that is used most often in international loan agreements is the Eurocurrency interest rate on U.S. dollars (Eurodollars) in London between banks: the London interbank offer rate (LIBOR). Because it is a Eurocurrency rate, it floats freely without regard to governmental restrictions on reserves or deposit insurance or any other regulation or restriction that would add expense to transactions using this capital. The interbank rates for other currencies in other markets are often named similarly, PIBOR (Paris interbank offer rate), MIBOR (Madrid interbank offer rate), HIBOR (either Hong Kong or Helsinki interbank offer rate), SIBOR (Singapore interbank offer rate). While LIBOR is the offer rate, the cost of funds "offered" to those acquiring a loan, the equivalent deposit rate in the Euromarkets is LIBID, the London interbank bid rate, the rate of interest other banks can earn on Eurocurrency deposits.

How do these international Eurocurrency and interbank interest rates differ from domestic rates? Answer: not by much. They generally move up and down in unison, by currency, but often differ by the percent by which the restrictions alter the rates of interest in the domestic markets. For example, because the Euromarkets have no restrictions, the spread between the offer rate and the bid rate (the loan rate and the deposit rate) is substantially smaller than in domestic markets. This means the loan rates in international markets are a bit lower than domestic market loan rates, and deposit rates are a bit higher in the international markets than in domestic markets. This is, however, only a big-player market. Only well-known international firms, financial or nonfinancial, have access to the quantities of capital necessary to operate in the Euromarkets. But as described in a later chapter on international debt and equity markets, more and more firms are gaining access to the Euromarkets to take advantage of deregulated capital flows.

SUMMARY

The exchange of currency is necessary for global trade and commerce. The purpose of exchange rate systems is to provide a free and liquid market for the world's currencies while providing some degree of stability and predictability to currency values. The modern history of the global monetary system has seen periods of success and failure in the accomplishments of this purpose.

The Bretton Woods Agreement signed in 1944, in anticipation of the reconstruction of the world economy after World War II, was an international monetary system in which the U.S. dollar was the centerpiece and literally "good as gold." Although working well for 25 years, it too saw its natural decline as the world economy changed and world currency markets needed to change with it. The result, the floating exchange rate system in use today, reflects the dominance of market economies, market forces, and the growth in international commerce.

The world's currency markets have expanded threefold in only the past six years, and there is no reason to believe this growth will end. It is estimated that more than $1 trillion worth of currencies changes hands daily, and the majority of it is either U.S. dollars, German marks, or Japanese yen. These are the world's major floating currencies.

But the world's financial markets are much more than currency exchanges. The rapid growth in the global financial markets—both on their own and as linkages between domestic markets—has resulted in the creation of a large and legitimate source of finance for the world's multinational firms. The recent expansion of market economies to more and more of the world's countries and economies sets the stage for further growth for the world's currency and capital markets.

The international flow of capital discussed in Chapter 3 is not without its dangers. Countries with large foreign currency debts have continued to be burdened with the servicing of their debts. The ability of countries to generate sufficient hard currency earnings is still dependent on export earnings. The stability of currency markets, the need for continued free-flowing international trade and export earnings, is integral to the continued health and growth of the world economy.

Key Terms and Concepts

purchasing power parity (PPP)
Law of One Price
foreign exchange market
interbank market
brokers
central banks
cross rates
direct quotation
indirect quotation
spot transaction
forward transaction
forward outright
forward swaps
floating foreign exchange rate
fixed foreign exchange rate
International Monetary Fund (IMF)
fundamental disequilibrium
special drawing right
International Bank for Reconstruction and Development (World Bank)
intervention
Group of Five
Group of Seven
European Monetary System
Exchange Rate Mechanism
Euro

Questions

1. Why has the gold standard always been considered such a solid and dependable system?
2. Why was it so important that the U.S. dollar be convertible to gold for the Bretton Woods system to operate effectively?
3. Why did the major world currencies move from a fixed to a floating exchange rate system in the 1970s?

4. Why is it necessary for the European Union to form a single banking system with a single monetary policy before it can adopt a single currency?
5. How and where are currencies traded?
6. Does it matter whether a currency is quoted as DEM/USD or USD/DEM?
7. Distinguish between spot and forward transactions.
8. What is a Eurocurrency?
9. Are all currencies freely floating on world markets?
10. Are fixed exchanged rates preferable to floating exchange rates?

Foreign Exchange Exercise

The purpose of this exercise is to familiarize readers with the simple mathematics of foreign exchange. A calculator may be used to solve these problems. Refer to page 110 for assistance.

1. Convert each currency from U.S. terms to European terms.

	U.S. Term		European Term	
Deutschemark	$ / DEM	$.6163	DEM / $	________
Swiss franc	$ / SFR	.7014	SFR / $	________
Chinese yuan	$ / Y	.1732	Y / $	________
Brazilian cruzeiro	$ / CR$	.0075	CR$ / $	________

2. For each situation described below, indicate which rate (bid or offer) would apply.
   a. A Pakistani importer wishes to convert rupees to U.S. dollars to pay for a shipment. His bank is quoting R/$ R29.78–29.88.
   b. Assume that in part (a) above the required U.S. dollar payment is $75,000. How many rupees would be required?
   c. An exporting firm in Singapore has just received payment in U.S. dollars and wants to convert it to Singapore dollars. The bank is quoting S$/$ 1.5979–1.5987.
   d. A Japanese manufacturing firm must make a payment in U.S. dollars. The bank has made its quotation in U.S. terms as follows: $/¥ .009430–.009436.
3. Compute the following cross rates for the French franc (FF) and the Danish krone (DKK).
   a. FF5.5660/$
      DKK6.5495/$
   b. From part (a) above, calculate the DKK/FF cross rate.

Recommended Readings

Bank for International Settlements. *Annual Report.* Basle, Switzerland, annually.

"Black Wednesday: The Campaign for Sterling." *The Economist,* January 9, 1993, 52, 54.

Commission of the European Communities. "The ECU and Its Role in the Process Towards Monetary Union." *European Economy* 48 (September 1991):121–138.

Driscoll, David D. *What Is the International Monetary Fund?* Washington, D.C.: External Relations Department, International Monetary Fund, November 1992.

Eiteman, David, Arthur Stonehill, and Michael H. Moffett. *Multinational Business Finance.* 7th ed. Reading, Mass.: Addison-Wesley, 1995.

Evans, John S. *International Finance.* Forth Worth, Tex.: Dryden Press, 1992.

Federal Reserve Bank of New York. *Summary of Results of the U.S. Foreign Exchange Market Turnover Survey.* April 1995.

Giddy, Ian. *Global Financial Markets.* Lexington, Mass: Elsevier, 1994.

Goodhart, C.A.E., and L. Figliuoli, "Every Minute Counts in Financial Markets." *Journal of International Money and Finance* 10 (1991):23–52.

Morgan Guaranty. *World Financial Markets.* New York, various issues.

O'Cleireacain, Seamus. *Third World Debt and International Public Policy.* New York: Praeger, 1990.

The World Bank. *World Debt Tables,* Washington, D.C., annually.

"Treasury and Federal Reserve Foreign Exchange Operations." *Federal Reserve Bulletin,* October 1971, 783–814.

Notes

1. Actually, there are a few exceptions. Panama has used the U.S. dollar as its currency for many years.
2. The student is always led to believe in the study of historical events that policies or laws or decisions were achieved so clearly or with little question or doubt. *Business Week's* issue of July 8, 1944, in its regular editorial news on "The War and Business Abroad," led with the following statement: "The world is watching the monetary conference at Bretton Woods for the first clews to the way the United Nations are prepared to cooperate in shaping the peace—and the results inevitably will be disappointing." Although the Bretton Woods Agreement eventually worked well for more than 20 years, there was considerable debate regarding its prospects in 1944. And, yes, the word was spelled "clews" and not "clues."
3. The participants at Bretton Woods specifically wanted to avoid the devaluation problems experienced on world markets in the 1930s. The competitive devaluations that dominated that period proved disastrous to world trade and economic stability as governments continually attempted to devalue to keep exports cheaper than foreign competitors'. The point of the adjustable peg was ultimately not to have to adjust it.
4. The meetings at Bretton Woods had hardly begun when the delegation from the Soviet Union objected to its preliminary quota as being too small! Soviet delegates argued that prewar trade was not representative of the true size and strength of the Soviet economy, and the postwar era would see a much more powerful trading nation. The quotas were readjusted, with the Soviet quota rising from about $800 million to $1.2 billion.
5. The original proposal was to contribute 25 percent of its quota in gold or 10 percent of its domestic gold stock, whichever the country chose. The Soviet Union as well as a number of other countries opposed this. Everyone was actually quite happy to eliminate the choice and choose the 25 percent of quota approach since it generally required a significantly smaller contribution of gold.
6. The Group of Seven is composed of the United States, Japan, Germany, France, Great Britain, Canada, and Italy. The Italian delegation withdrew from the meetings the first day, however, in protest over being excluded from a G5 (G7 minus Canada and Italy) state dinner the evening before. So the meetings may actually have been classified as the G6.
7. The large increases in oil prices instituted by the Organization of Petroleum Exporting Countries (OPEC) in 1974 and 1979 had also resulted in enormous quantities of capital that needed to be invested in profitable ventures. Because oil is priced and sold on world markets in U.S. dollars, this accumulation of capital, OPEC dollars, provided an enormous supply of one specific currency.

Economic Integration and Emerging Market Economies

LEARNING OBJECTIVES

To review types of economic integration among countries.

To examine the costs and benefits of economic integration among nations.

To understand the European Union (EU) and its implications for firms within and outside Europe.

To explore the emergence of integration agreements in the Americas, especially the North American Free Trade Agreement (NAFTA), the Southern Cone Common Market (Mercosur), and the Free Trade Area of the Americas (FTAA).

To review integration developments in Asia, in particular the Asia Pacific Economic Cooperation (APEC) and the Association of Southeast Asian Nations (ASEAN).

To survey the opportunities for trade offered by emerging market economies.

GLOBAL LEARNING EXPERIENCE 5.1

Economic Integration Does Not Guarantee Jobs

Economic integration, that is the creation of a trading bloc among a group of countries, is intended to improve trade and the standard of living among the member countries. However, that desirable goal may have some undesirable side effects. As the number of trading blocs increases, economists are beginning to examine the risk that regional trading blocs are really protectionism on a grand scale and that productivity-sapping trade diversion will outweigh productivity-enhancing trade creation. In the process, jobs, the underlying strength of an economy, may not be gained but merely shifted from one country to another, as companies in the bloc shift operations to achieve cost, labor, or marketing advantages. Countries that are members of the European Union (EU) are finding that economic integration with the free flow of products, services, labor, and capital across national borders is not a guarantee against the loss of jobs.

In January 1997, the Ford Motor Co., in a first step in turning its unprofitable European operations around, decided to shift the production of the Escort model from its Halewood, England, assembly plant to plants in Germany and Spain. The decision will reduce employment by 1,300 workers, or one-third of the Halewood labor force. Ford cited costs and overcapacity as reasons for the job cuts. Understandably the British government and labor unions were upset by the announcement. The prime minister described the development as a "very surprising decision"; union leaders attributed the move to lax labor compensation laws, which make it less costly to dismiss workers in Britain than in other European countries. Britain did not participate in the so-called **European Social Charter,** which offers strong protection to workers.

Whatever the reason(s), for the Ford Motor Co., the move is intended to make the company more competitive in global markets, particularly in Europe where it sustained a loss in 1996. The European Union is regional, but jobs are local. Every time a company seeks to acquire a competitive advantage by transferring operations from one country to another, local politicians tend to forget the logic of economic integration.

SOURCE: "Ford Plans Cutbacks at British Assembly Plant," *New York Times,* January 17, 1997, D4.

The benefits of free trade and stable exchange rates are available only if nations are willing to give up some measure of independence and autonomy. This has resulted in increased economic integration around the world with agreements among countries to establish links through movement of goods, services, capital, and labor across borders. Some predict, however, that the regional **trading blocs** of the new economic world order will divide into a handful of protectionist superstates that, although liberalizing trade among members, may raise barriers to external trade.

trading blocs
a preferential economic arrangement among a group of countries

Economic integration is best viewed as a spectrum. At one extreme, we might envision a truly global economy in which all countries shared a common currency and agreed to free flows of goods, services, and factors of production. At the other extreme would be a number of closed economies, each independent and self-sufficient. The various integrative agreements in effect today lie along the middle of the spectrum. The most striking example of the promises and pitfalls of integration is the historic economic unification that is taking place in Europe and elsewhere today, as discussed in Global Learning Experience 5.1. Some countries, however, give priority to maintaining economic self-sufficiency and independence. Examples of this latter strategy include the policies of North Korea, Vietnam, and Albania.

European Social Charter establishes and guarantees economic, social, and cultural rights for the nationals of the member states of the council of Europe

This chapter will begin with an explanation of the various levels of economic integration. Next, major arguments both for and against economic integration will be reviewed. The European Union, the North American Free Trade Agreement, and other economic alliances will be discussed. In the second half to the chapter, the newly emerging market economies will be identified and evaluated in terms of their short- and long-term market potential.

LEVELS OF ECONOMIC INTEGRATION

A trading bloc is a preferential economic arrangement among a group of countries. The forms it may take are provided in Table 5.1. From least to most integrative, they are the: free trade area, customs union, common market, and economic union.[1]

The Free Trade Area

free trade area elimination of tariff and quota barriers among member countries, while each country establishes its own tariff and quota barriers against nonmember countries

The **free trade area** is the least restrictive and loosest form of economic integration among countries. In a free trade area, all barriers to trade among member countries are removed. Therefore, goods and services are freely traded among member countries in much the same way that they flow freely between, for example, South Carolina and New York. No discriminatory taxes, quotas, tariffs, or other trade barriers are allowed. Sometimes a free trade area is formed only for certain classes of goods and services. An agricultural free trade area, for example, implies the absence of restrictions on the trade of agricultural products only. The most notable feature of a free trade area is that each member country is free to set any tariffs, quotas, or other restrictions that it chooses for trade with countries outside the free trade area.

The Customs Union

customs union elimination of tariff and quota barriers among member countries; member countries establish common tariff and quota barriers against nonmember countries

The **customs union** is one step further along the spectrum of economic integration. Like members of a free trade area, members of a customs union remove barriers to trade in goods and services among themselves. In addition, however, the customs union establishes a common trade policy with respect to nonmembers. Typically, this takes the form of a common external tariff, whereby imports from nonmembers are subject to the same tariff when sold to any member country. Tariff revenues are then shared among members according to a prespecified formula.

TABLE 5.1 **Forms of International Economic Integration**

Stage of Integration	Abolition of Tariffs and Quotas among Members	Common Tariff and Quota System	Abolition of Restrictions on Factor Movements	Harmonization and Unification of Economic Policies and Institutions
Free trade area	Yes	No	No	No
Customs union	Yes	Yes	No	No
Common market	Yes	Yes	Yes	No
Economic union	Yes	Yes	Yes	Yes

SOURCE: Reproduced from Franklin R. Root, *International Trade and Investment,* Cincinnati, Ohio: South-Western Publishing Company, 1992, p. 254, with the permission of South-Western College Publishing.

The Common Market

Further still along the spectrum of economic integration is the **common market.** Like the customs union, a common market has no barriers to trade among members and has a common external trade policy. In addition, the common market removes restrictions on the movement of the factors of production (labor, capital, and technology) across borders. Thus, restrictions on immigration, emigration, and cross-border investment are abolished. When factors of production are freely mobile, then capital, labor, and technology may be employed in their most productive uses.

common market
like customs union, has no barriers to trade among members and a common external trade policy; further, removes restrictions on the movement of factors of production across member borders

Despite the obvious benefits, members of a common market must be prepared to cooperate closely in monetary, fiscal, and employment policies. Furthermore, while a common market will enhance the productivity of members in the aggregate, it is by no means clear that individual member countries will always benefit. Because of these difficulties, the goals of common markets have proved to be elusive in many areas of the world, notably Central America and Asia. However, the objective of the **Single European Act,** to have a full common market in effect within the European Union at the end of 1992, is really more of a process rather than a fixed date. While many of the directives aimed at opening borders and markets were implemented on schedule, others will take years to put in place.

Single European Act
amended the treaty of Rome; mandates the removal of physical, technical, and tax barriers to the free movement of persons, goods, services, and capital

The Economic Union

The creation of a true **economic union** requires integration of economic policies in addition to the free movement of goods, services, and factors of production across borders. Under an economic union, members would **harmonize** monetary policies, taxation, and government spending. In addition, a common currency would be used by all members. This could be accomplished by member countries agreeing to a common currency or, in effect, by a system of fixed exchange rates. Clearly, the formation of an economic union requires nations to surrender a large measure of their national sovereignty. Needless to say, the barriers to full economic union are quite strong. Our global political system is built on the autonomy and supreme power of the nation-state, and attempts to undermine the authority of the state will undoubtedly always encounter opposition. As a result, no true economic unions are in effect today.

economic union
has all the characteristics of a common market and, in addition, the integration of economic policies: harmonized monetary policies, taxation, government spending, and common currency

harmonize
merging of the policies of several countries into a common, unified policy

ARGUMENTS SURROUNDING ECONOMIC INTEGRATION

A number of arguments surround economic integration. They center on (1) trade creation and diversion; (2) the effects of integration on import prices, competition, economies of scale, and factor productivity; and (3) the benefits of regionalism versus nationalism.

Trade Creation and Trade Diversion

Chapter 2 illustrated that when trade barriers between countries are removed, their country and its industries will concentrate on the most efficient use of resources and trade for those goods that they are inefficient at producing. The result is that both countries will gain from trade—a win-win situation. The question is whether similar gains from trade will be realized when free trade is limited to one group of countries. The answer to this question may be "yes" and "no," depending on whether established trading patterns are disrupted by the establishment of a trading bloc. The entry of Spain into the European Union provides an interesting example of *trade creation* and *trade diversion.*

QUESTION *Except for Canada and Mexico, what country is closest to the United States?*

Russia. In the Bering Strait, Russian, and United States Islands are only three miles apart.

In 1986, Spain formally entered the European Union (EU) as a member. Prior to membership, Spain—like all nonmembers such as the United States, Canada, and Japan—traded with the EU and suffered from the common external tariff imposed by the EU. Imports of agricultural products from Spain or the United States had the same tariff applied to their products, for example, 20 percent. During this period, the United States was a lower-cost producer of wheat compared to Spain. U.S. exports to EU members may have cost $3.00 per bushel, plus a 20 percent tariff of $0.60, for a total of $3.60 per bushel. If Spain at the same time produced wheat at $3.20 per bushel, plus a 20 percent tariff of $0.64 for a total cost to EU customers of $3.84 per bushel, Spain's wheat was more expensive and therefore less competitive.

But when Spain joined the EU as a member, its products were no longer subject to the common external tariffs; Spain had become a member of the "club" and therefore enjoyed its benefits. Spain was now the low-cost producer of wheat at $3.20 per bushel, compared to the price of $3.60 from the United States. Trade flows changed as a result. The increased export of wheat and other products by Spain to the EU as a result of its membership is termed **trade creation.** The elimination of the tariff literally created more trade between Spain and the EU. At the same time, because the United States is still outside of the EU, its products suffer the higher price as a result of the tariff application. U.S. exports to the EU fell. When the source of trading competitiveness is shifted in this manner from one country to another, it is termed **trade diversion.**

trade creation
a benefit of economic integration; the benefit to a particular country when a group of countries trade a product freely among themselves but maintain common barriers to trade with nonmembers

trade diversion
a cost of economic integration; the cost to a particular country when a group of countries trade a product freely among themselves

Whereas trade creation is distinctly positive in moving toward freer trade, and therefore lower prices for consumers within the EU, the impact of trade diversion is negative. Trade diversion is inherently negative because the competitive advantage has shifted away from the lower-cost producer to the higher-cost producer. The benefits of Spain's membership are enjoyed by Spanish farmers (greater export sales) and EU consumers (lower prices). The two major costs are reduced tariff revenues collected and costs borne by the United States and its exports as a result of lost sales.

From the perspective of nonmembers like the United States, the formation or expansion of a customs union is obviously negative. Most damaged will naturally be countries that may need to have trade to build their economies, such as the countries of the Third World. From the perspective of members of the customs union, the formation or expansion of a customs union is only beneficial if the trade-creation benefits exceed trade-diversion costs.

Reduced Import Prices

When a small country imposes a tariff on imports, the price of the goods will typically rise because sellers will increase prices to cover the cost of the tariff. This increase in price, in turn, will result in lower demand for the imported goods. If a bloc of countries imposes the tariff, however, the fall in demand for the imported goods will be substantial. The exporting country may then be forced to reduce the price of the goods. The possibility of lower prices for imports results from the greater market power of the bloc relative to that of a single country. The result may then be an improvement in the trade position of the bloc countries. Any gain in the trade position of bloc members, however, is offset by a deteriorating trade position for the exporting country. Again, unlike the win-win situation resulting from free trade, the scenario involving a trade bloc is instead win-lose.

Increased Competition and Economies of Scale

Integration increases market size and therefore may result in a lower degree of monopoly in the production of certain goods and services.[2] This is because a larger market will tend to increase the number of competing firms, resulting in greater efficiency and lower prices for consumers. Moreover, less energetic and productive economies may be spurred into action by competition from the more industrious bloc members.

Many industries, such as steel and automobiles, require large-scale production in order to obtain economies of scale in production. Therefore, certain industries may simply not be economically viable in smaller, trade-protected countries. However, the formation of a trading bloc enlarges the market so that large-scale production is justified. The lower per-unit costs resulting from scale economies may then be obtained. These lower production costs resulting from greater production for an enlarged market are called **internal economies of scale.**

In a common market, **external economies of scale** may also be present. Because a common market allows factors of production to flow freely across borders, the firm may now have access to cheaper capital, more highly skilled labor, or superior technology. These factors will improve the quality of the firm's product or service or will lower costs or both.

internal economies of scale lower production costs resulting from increased production for an enlarged market

external economies of scale reduced manufacturing costs resulting from a firm's access to lower cost capital, labor, and technology in other countries

Higher Factor Productivity

When factors of production are freely mobile, the wealth of the common market countries, in aggregate, will likely increase. The theory behind this contention is straightforward: Factor mobility will lead to the movement of labor and capital from areas of low productivity to areas of high productivity. In addition to the economic gains from factor mobility, there are other benefits not so easily quantified. The free movement of labor fosters a higher level of communication across cultures. This, in turn, leads to a higher degree of cross-cultural understanding; as people move, their ideas, skills, and ethnicity move with them.

Again, however, factor mobility will not necessarily benefit each country in the common market. A poorer country, for example, may lose badly needed investment capital to a richer country, where opportunities are perceived to be more profitable. Another disadvantage of factor mobility that is often cited is the brain-drain phenomenon. A poorer country may lose its most talented workers when they are free to search out better opportunities.

Regionalism versus Nationalism

Economists have composed elegant and compelling arguments in favor of the various levels of economic integration. It is difficult, however, to turn these arguments into reality in the face of intense nationalism. The biggest impediment to economic integration remains in the reluctance of nations to surrender a measure of their sovereignty. Integration, by its very nature, requires the surrender of national power and self-determinism. In order to understand the extent of regional integration, it is easiest to consider the world, as a whole, as being divided into three parts: Europe, the Americas, and Asia. Each of these parts is experiencing varying degrees of integration and will be evaluated in turn.

THE EUROPEAN UNION

Economic Integration in Europe from 1948 to the Mid-1980s

The period of the Great Depression from the late 1920s through World War II was characterized by isolationism, protectionism, and fierce nationalism. Because of the

FIGURE 5.1 **Development of the European Union**

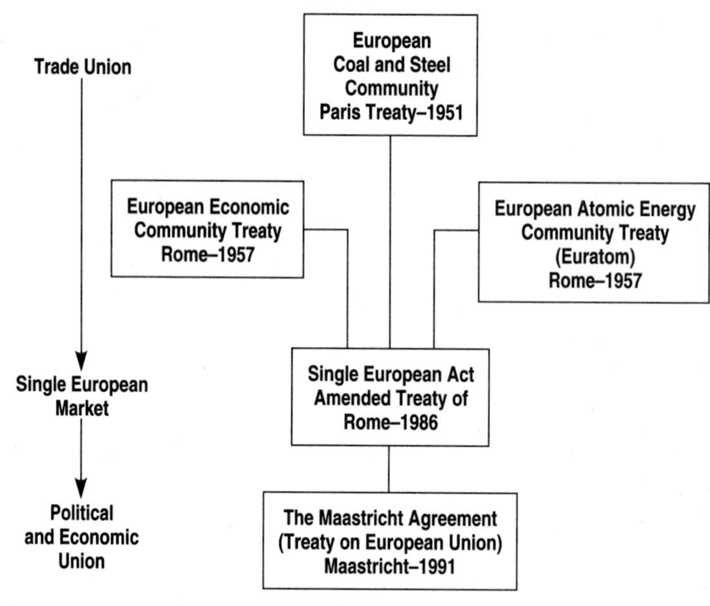

SOURCE: Adapted from Hotchkiss, Carolyn, *International Law for Business.* McGraw-Hill, Inc., New York, 1994, 103.

economic chaos and political difficulties of the period, no serious attempts at economic integration were made until the end of the war. From the devastation of the war, however, a spirit of cooperation gradually emerged in Europe.

In 1957, the European Economic Community (now called the European Union) was formally established by the Treaty of Rome. Figure 5.1 traces the development of the European Union from the formation of the European Coal and Steel Community (ECSC) to the current European Union.

In 1951, France, Germany, Italy, Belgium, the Netherlands, and Luxembourg signed the Paris Treaty establishing the ECSC. The treaty eliminated protectionist measures in the member countries; established a common market for coal, steel, coke, iron ore, and scrap steel; harmonized freight rates; and, through taxes on freight, paid for some of the human costs associated with the restructuring of the market.

The success of the ECSC in its limited sphere led the Benelux countries (Belgium, the Netherlands, and Luxembourg) to call for integration of all areas of the economy across Europe. A lengthy series of conferences and negotiations led to the establishment of more communities in 1957. The first treaty, signed in Rome in 1957, established Euratom, a European agency regulating nuclear energy. The second, more important treaty established the European Economic Community (EEC). This treaty among the six countries is known as the Treaty of Rome and is the operating constitution for the economic integration of Western Europe. The Treaty of Rome is a monumental document, composed of more than 200 articles. The main provisions of the treaty are summarized in Table 5.2. The document was (and is) quite ambitious. The cooperative spirit apparent throughout the treaty was based on the premise that the mobility of goods, services, labor, and capital (the "four freedoms") was of paramount importance for the economic prosperity of the region. Founding members envisioned

TABLE 5.2 **Main Provisions of the Treaty of Rome**

1. Formation of a free trade area: the gradual elimination of tariffs, quotas, and other barriers to trade among members
2. Formation of a customs union: the creation of a uniform tariff schedule applicable to imports from the rest of the world
3. Formation of a common market: the removal of barriers to the movement of labor, capital, and business enterprises
4. The adoption of common agricultural policies
5. The creation of an investment fund to channel capital from the more advanced to the less developed regions of the community

that the successful integration of the European economies would result in an economic power to rival that of the United States.

Some countries, however, were reluctant to embrace the ambitious integrative effort of the treaty. In 1960, a looser, less integrated philosophy was endorsed with the formation of the European Free Trade Association (EFTA). The members of the EFTA were the United Kingdom, Norway, Denmark, Sweden, Austria, Finland, Portugal, and Switzerland. As the name implies, the goal of the EFTA was to dismantle trade barriers among members. Since 1960, however, the distinctions between the EU and the EFTA have blurred considerably. Great Britain, Portugal, and Denmark have since joined the EU, and other EFTA members have formed free trade agreements with the community. For those EFTA countries not wanting to join the EU, the European Economic Area agreement will give them most of the benefits of Europe's single market. Table 5.3 shows the founding members of the community in 1957, additions to membership in 1993 and 1995, and potential new members about the year 2000 and beyond.

Another source of difficulty that intensified in the 1980s was the administration of the union's **common agricultural policy (CAP).** Most industrialized countries, including the United States, Canada, and Japan, have adopted wide-scale government intervention and subsidization schemes for the agriculture industry. In the case of the EU, however, these policies have been implemented on a communitywide, rather than national, level. The CAP includes (1) a price-support system whereby EU agriculture officials intervene in the market to keep farm product prices within a specified range, (2) direct subsidies to farmers, and (3) rebates to farmers who export or agree to store farm products rather than sell them within the union. The implementation of these policies absorbs about two-thirds of the annual EU budget.

common agricultural policy (CAP)
an integrated system of subsidies and rebates applied to agricultural interests in the European Community

The CAP has caused problems both within the EU and in relationships with nonmembers. Within the EU, the richer, more industrialized countries resent the extensive subsidization of the more agrarian economies. Outside trading partners, especially the United States, have repeatedly charged the EU with unfair trade practices in agriculture.

The European Union since the Mid-1980s

By the mid-1980s, a sense of "Europessimism" permeated most discussions of European integration. Although the members remained committed in principle to the "four freedoms," literally hundreds of obstacles to the free movement of goods, services, people, and capital remained. For example, there were cumbersome border restrictions on trade in many goods, and although labor was theoretically mobile, the professional certifications granted in one country were often not recognized in others.

TABLE 5.3 **Membership of the European Union**

1957	1993	1995*	2000** Invited to Join EU	Applied, But Not Yet Invited to Join EU
France	Great Britain (1973)	Austria (1995)	Poland	Slovakia
West Germany	Ireland (1973)	Finland (1995)	Czech Republic	Bulgaria
Italy	Denmark (1973)	Sweden (1995)	Hungary	Romania
Belgium	Greece (1981)		Slovenia	Lithuania
Netherlands	Spain (1986)		Estonia	Latvia
Luxembourg	Portugal (1986)		Cyprus	

*Norway rejected membership in the EU in a nationwide referendum on Nov. 29, 1994.
**As of July 16, 1997; no formal timetable set.

Growing dissatisfaction with the progress of integration, as well as threats of global competition from Japan and the United States, prompted the European Union to take action. Steps to remove these obstacles to free trade began in 1987 with the passage of the Single European Act, which stated that "the community shall adopt measures with the aim of progressively establishing the internal market over a period expiring on 31 December 1992." The Single European Act envisaged a true common market where goods, people, and money move between Germany and France with the same ease that they move between Wisconsin and Illinois.

The goal of free movement of goods has been achieved largely due to the move from a "common standards approach" to a "mutual recognition approach." Under the common standards approach, EU members were forced to negotiate the specifications for literally thousands of products, often unsuccessfully. For example, because of differences in tastes, agreement was never reached on specifications for beer, sausage, or mayonnaise. Under the mutual recognition approach, the laborious quest for common standards is in most cases no longer necessary. Instead, as long as a product meets legal and specification requirements in one member country, it may be freely exported to any other.

Less progress toward free movement of people in Europe has been made than toward free movement of goods. The primary difficulty is that EU members have been unable to agree on a common immigration policy. As long as this disagreement persists, travelers between countries must pass through border checkpoints. Some countries—notably Germany—have relatively lax immigration policies, while others—especially those with higher unemployment rates—favor strict controls on immigration. A second issue concerning the free movement of people is the acceptability of professional certifications across countries. In 1993, the largest EU member countries passed all of the professional worker directives. This means that workers' professional qualifications will be recognized throughout the EU, guaranteeing them equal treatment in terms of employment, working conditions, and social protection in the host country. There are, however, no guarantees on having a job as is pointed out in Global Learning Experience 5.1.

Attaining free movement of capital within the EU entails several measures. First, citizens will be free to trade in EU currencies without restrictions. Second, the regulations governing banks and other financial institutions will be harmonized. In addition, mergers and acquisitions will be regulated by the EU rather than by national governments. Finally, securities will be freely tradable across countries.

A key aspect of free trade in services is the right to compete fairly to obtain government contracts. Under the 1992 guidelines, a government should not give preference to its own citizens in awarding government contracts. However, little progress has been made in this regard.

As noted previously, project 1992 had always been part of a larger plan and a process more so than a deadline.[3] Many in the EU bureaucracy argued that the 1992 campaign required a commitment to **economic and monetary union (EMU)** and subsequently to political union. The summit in Maastricht in December 1991, which produced recommendations **(Maastricht Agreement)** for a single European currency and a single, independent central bank, did not meet unanimous approval. The Danes rejected it in the spring of 1992, the British delayed decision on it, and the French approved it by the narrowest of margins because many felt that it would create an unresponsive supranational body in Brussels. Despite these initial concerns, the ratification of the Maastricht Treaty in late 1993 by all 12 member countries of the EC created the European Union starting January 1, 1994. The treaty calls for a commitment to economic and monetary union, with the Euro to become a common European currency by 1999. (The European Monetary System is discussed in some detail in Chapter 4.)

economic and monetary union (EMU)
ideal among European leaders that economic integration should move beyond the four freedoms; specifically, it entails (1) closer coordination of economic policies to promote exchange rate stability and convergence of inflation rates and growth rates, (2) creation of a European central bank called the Eurofed, and (3) replacement of national monetary authorities by the Eurofed and adoption of the Euro as the European currency

Maastricht Agreement
established European Community citizenship and an economic union, i.e., a European central bank, a system to manage monetary policy, price stability, a European currency, and commitment by member countries to reduce excessive government deficits

Despite the uncertainties about the future of the EU, new members are waiting to join. Most EFTA countries want to join in spite of the fact that the European Economic Area treaty gives them most of the benefits of the single market. They also want to have a say in making EU laws. Access to the EU is essential for growth in Central Europe. It could also create investment opportunities for Western firms and provide cheaper goods for EU consumers.

In June 1993, the EU invited Poland, Hungary, the Czech Republic, Slovakia, Romania, and Bulgaria to join the group when their economic and political conditions permit. Conditions for membership in the EU include: a stable democracy, respect for human rights and the rights of minorities, a functioning market economy, and an economy capable of withstanding competition from the West. As shown in Table 5.3, a number of other countries have expressed interest in membership in the EU.

Implications of European Integration

Perhaps the most important implication of the four freedoms for Europe is the economic growth that is expected to result.[4] Several specific sources of increased growth have been identified. First, there will be gains from eliminating the transaction costs associated with border patrols, customs procedures, and so forth. Second, economic growth will be spurred by the economies of scale that will be achieved when production facilities become more concentrated. Third, there will be gains from more intense competition among EU companies. Firms that were monopolists in one country will now be subject to competition from firms in other EU countries.

There will be substantial benefits for those firms already operating in Europe. These firms will gain because their operations in one country can now be freely expanded into others, and their products may be freely sold across borders. In a borderless Europe, firms will have access to approximately 320 million consumers. In addition, the free movement of capital will allow these firms to sell securities, raise capital, and recruit labor throughout Europe. Substantial economies of scale in production and marketing will also result.

QUESTION *What three South American countries are along the Equator?*

Ecuador, Colombia and Brazil

For firms from nonmember countries, integration presents various possibilities depending on the firm's position within the EU.[5] Well-established U.S.-based multinational marketers such as H. J. Heinz and Colgate-Palmolive will be able to take advantage of the new economies of scale. For example, 3M plants earlier turned out different versions of the company's products for various markets. Now, the 3M plant in Wales, for example, makes videotapes and videocassettes for all of Europe.[6] Colgate-Palmolive has to watch out for competitors, like Germany's Henkel, in the brutally competitive detergent market. At the same time, large-scale retailers, such as France's Carrefour and Germany's Aldi group, are undertaking their own efforts to exploit the situation with hypermarkets supplied by central warehouses with computerized inventories. Their procurement policies have to be met by companies like Heinz. Many multinationals are developing pan-European strategies to exploit the emerging situation; that is, they are standardizing their products and processes to the greatest extent possible without compromising local input and implementation.

A company with a foothold in only one European market is faced with the danger of competitors who can use the strength of multiple markets. Furthermore, the elimination of barriers may do away with the company's competitive advantage. For example, more than half of the 45 major European food companies are in just one or two of the individual European markets and seriously lag behind broader-based U.S. and Swiss firms. Similarly, automakers PSA and Fiat are nowhere close to the cross-manufacturing presence of Ford and GM. The courses of action include expansion through acquisitions or mergers, formation of strategic alliances (for example, AT&T's joint venture with Spain's Telefonica to produce state-of-the-art microchips), rationalization by concentrating only on business segments in which the company can be a pan-European leader and, finally, divestment.

Exporters will need to worry about maintaining their competitive position and continued access to the market. Companies with a physical presence may be in a better position to assess and to take advantage of the developments. Some firms, like Filament Fiber Technology Inc. of New Jersey, have established production units in Europe. Digital Microwave Corporation of California decided to defend its market share in Europe by joining two British communications companies and setting up a digital microwave radio and optical-fiber plant in Scotland.[7] In some industries, marketers do not see a reason either to be in Europe at all or to change from exporting to more involved modes of entry. Machinery and machine tools, for example, are in great demand in Europe, and marketers in these companies say they have little reason to manufacture there.

Fortress Europe
suspicion raised by trading partners of Western Europe, claiming that the integration of the European Union may result in increased restrictions on trade and investment by outsiders

The term **Fortress Europe** has been used to describe the fears of many U.S. firms about a unified Europe. The concern is that while Europe dismantles internal barriers, it will raise external ones, making access to the European market difficult for U.S. and other non-EU firms. In a move designed to protect European farmers, for example, the EU has recently banned the import of certain agricultural goods from the United States. The EU has also called on members to limit the number of American television programs broadcast in Europe. Finally, many U.S. firms are concerned about the relatively strict domestic-content rules recently passed by the EU. These rules require certain products sold in Europe to be manufactured with European inputs. One effect of the perceived threat of Fortress Europe has been increased direct investment in Europe by U.S. firms. Fears that the EU will erect barriers to U.S. exports and of the domestic-content rules governing many goods have led many U.S. firms to initiate or expand European direct investment.

ECONOMIC INTEGRATION IN THE AMERICAS

Although the EU is undoubtedly the most well-known integrative effort, similar efforts in North America, although only a few years old, have gained momentum and attention. What started as a trading pact between two close and economically well-developed allies, the United States and Canada, (U.S.–Canada Free Trade Agreement, effective January 1, 1989) has already been expanded to include Mexico, and long-term plans call for further additions, notably Chile. However, in North American integration, the interest is purely economic; there are no constituencies for political integration.

Debate over the North American Free Trade Agreement in 1992 was complicated by difficulties associated with the existing U.S.-Canadian Free Trade Agreement. Detractors in the United States have accused Canada of subsidizing its lumber exports in order to gain an unfair advantage over the U.S. lumber industry. Disputes of this type undermine efforts toward the kind of trading partnership advocated by proponents of NAFTA.

SOURCE: © Robert Semeniuk/FIRST LIGHT, Toronto.

North American Free Trade Agreement

Negotiations on a North American Free Trade Agreement (NAFTA) began in 1991 to create the world's largest free market (consisting of the United States, Canada, and Mexico), with 367 million consumers and a total output of $6.2 trillion, 25 percent larger than the EU.[8] The pact would mark a bold departure: Never before have industrialized countries created such a massive free trade area with a developing-country neighbor. The agreement went into effect on January 1, 1994.

Since Canada stood to gain very little from NAFTA (its trade with Mexico is 1 percent of its trade with the United States), much of the controversy centered on the gains and losses for the United States and Mexico. Proponents argued that the agreement would give U.S. firms access to a huge pool of relatively low-cost Mexican labor at a time when demographic trends are indicating job shortages in many parts of the United States; at the same time, many new jobs are created in Mexico. The agreement gives firms in both countries access to millions of additional consumers, and the liberalized trade flows were to result in faster economic growth in both countries.

NAFTA suffered a serious setback due to a significant devaluation of the Mexican peso in early 1995 and the subsequent impact on trade. Critics of NAFTA argued that too much was expected too fast of a country whose political system and economy were not ready for open markets. In response, advocates of NAFTA argued that there was nothing wrong with the Mexican real economy and that the peso crisis was a political one that would be overcome with time.

Both critics and proponents of NAFTA agree on the benefits of free trade and that in the long term the agreement is likely to spur economic growth for the three countries. The real debate concerning NAFTA is on the gain or loss of American jobs. Most likely to be harmed are unskilled U.S. workers who might lose employment and/or wages because of Mexico's low-cost labor pool. As noted previously in Global Learning Experience 5.1, *economic integration does not guarantee jobs.* The extreme positions in the NAFTA debate are illustrated by President Clinton's claim that NAFTA would create 170,000 new U.S. jobs in the first year of the agreement. Presidential candidate Ross Perot took the position that NAFTA would create a one-way flow of jobs to Mexico, creating "a giant sucking sound."[9]

The answer to the debate over U.S. job gains and/or losses is not an easy one. As a practical matter, the United States (and Canada) does not have a system for measuring employment gains or losses; most of the job estimates resulting from NAFTA are based on formulas that are prone to error and on a variety of assumptions that may prove incorrect. Consider several possible scenarios, or a combination thereof, that could take place:

1. A U.S. firm moves its operations to Mexico because of lower labor costs. U.S. jobs are lost.
2. A U.S. firm moves its low-tech jobs to Mexico, keeping high-tech jobs in the United States. By including the low-cost Mexican component in the final product assembled in the United States, the company lowers its total cost. This enables

the company to lower the price of the product, which results in greater sales in all three countries. Jobs that were lost to Mexico are replaced by jobs needed to handle increased sales volume.

3. Removal of market barriers allows U.S. firms to expand into Canadian and Mexican markets at competitive prices; the increase in volume creates more U.S. jobs.
4. Suppliers to U.S. and Canadian companies set up operations in lower-labor cost Mexico instead of Asia. The "giant sucking sound" is low-cost Asian jobs being lost to Mexico. There is no reduction of U.S. employment.
5. Without trade barriers, a variety of U.S. produced products, particularly agricultural products, will become less costly to Mexican consumers, and it will be more efficient to continue to produce them in the United States. This would have the effect of increasing the U.S. demand for Mexican workers willing to do this tough, low-wage work. This would contradict the U.S. government's claim that NAFTA would reduce the floodtide of illegal immigrants by creating more job opportunities in Mexico. More U.S. jobs are created, but not for Americans.

All of the scenarios presented above could also be applied to Canadian and Mexican firms with respect to the U.S. market.

maquiladoras
plants that make goods and parts or process food for export back to the United States

The transfer of U.S. jobs to Mexico may be traced to the **maquiladora** program, which began in May 1965, allowing designated firms to import supplies and equipment free of taxation when their production is exported. The program allows maquiladoras to take advantage of low-cost Mexican labor and pay duties only on the value added in Mexico. (See Global Learning Experience 5.2 for perspectives on the cost of labor worldwide.) As of May 1996, there were 2,356 maquiladora plants located in the various states of Mexico, employing 737,386 workers.[10] Table 5.4 shows the distribution of maquiladora firms and employees by industry.

Wages for maquiladora laborers are often less than $1 dollar (U.S.) per hour, not including fringe benefits. These are formal sector jobs that make workers eligible for health, retirement, and housing benefits from the Social Security Administration. Nearly 40 percent of Mexico's exports are generated by the maquiladora sector, about 60 percent of which are concentrated along the U.S. border.[11]

Growth in Trade Among NAFTA Members

If the theoretical basis for free trade, and the gains to be realized from it, are valid, then it is expected that the total trade among nations that embrace those principles should increase. Figure 5.2 presents a summary of the combined total merchandise trade among Canada, Mexico, and the United States from 1989 (the year the Canada–U.S. Trade Agreement took effect) through 1996. This period includes the starting date, January 1, 1994, of the NAFTA pact. During the eight-year interval, the combined merchandise trade among the NAFTA group has increased from $224.8 billion in 1989 to $430.4 billion in 1996, an improvement of 91 percent.

Of particular interest is the impact that the growth in trade among the countries had on each nation's balance of trade with the other partners. In 1993, just prior to the effective date of NAFTA, the United States had a combined merchandise trade deficit of $11.1 billion with its NAFTA partners Canada ($12.1 billion deficit) and Mexico ($1.0 billion surplus). In three years, the U.S. trade deficit with its NAFTA partners increased three-and-one-half times to the 1996 level of $42.4 billion. Of this amount, the United States had a trade deficit of $24.0 billion with Canada and a deficit of $18.4 billion with Mexico. Additionally, Canada had a merchandise trade deficit of $3.5 billion with Mexico. The result was that Mexico enjoyed a combined trade surplus of $21.9 billion with Canada and the United States.

Low Labor Costs—A Global Perspective

As the reader has no doubt concluded, one of the primary causes of trade diversion is the low-cost labor of developing nations. The table below provides a perspective of hourly compensation costs for manufacturing workers in 27 selected countries. Although not all of the newly emerging and/or low-labor cost nations (i.e., China, Indonesia, Malaysia, and South American countries) are shown, the data are useful in that they convey a sense of the comparative labor costs of the most developed nations with those that are just emerging on the global industrial scene.

1995 Hourly Compensation Costs* for Production Workers in Manufacturing (in U.S. dollars)

Country	Hourly Compensation Costs	Percent of U.S. Cost	Country	Hourly Compensation Costs	Percent of U.S. Cost	Country	Hourly Compensation Costs	Percent of U.S. Costs
Germany	31.88	185	Sweden	21.36	124	Israel	10.59	62
Switzerland	29.28	170	France	19.34	112	New Zealand	10.11	59
Belgium	26.88	156	United States	17.20	100	Greece	8.95	52
Austria	25.38	148	Italy	16.48	96	Korea	7.40	43
Finland	24.78	144	Canada	16.03	93	Singapore	7.28	42
Norway	24.38	142	Australia	14.40	84	Taiwan	5.82	34
Denmark	24.19	141	Ireland	13.83	80	Portugal	5.35	31
Netherlands	24.18	141	United Kingdom	10.77	80	Hong Kong	4.82	28
Japan	20.66	138	Spain	12.70	74	Mexico	1.51	9

*Hourly compensation is defined as (1) all payments made directly to the worker, and (2) employer expenditures for legally required insurance programs and contractual and private benefit plans, and additional taxes that are regarded as labor costs. These are appropriate measures for comparing levels of employer labor costs. They do not indicate relative living standards of workers or the purchasing power of their income.

SOURCE: U.S. Department of Labor, Bureau of Labor Statistics, Report 909, September 1996.

The analysis shows Germany as having hourly compensation costs of $31.88, about 85 percent higher than that of the United States, at $17.20; from a labor-cost view, that probably makes Germany the most expensive country in the world in which to conduct manufacturing operations. At the other end of the spectrum is Mexico, with hourly compensation of $1.51, or 9 percent of the U.S. figure and significantly lower than several of the low-cost Asian countries (Korea, Singapore, Taiwan, and Hong Kong). From the data it can be seen that hourly compensation costs in Mexico are only 5 percent of those in Germany.

These facts illustrate the appeal of moving manufacturing operations from any number of nations to countries typified by Mexico. Assuming that the Mexican-type worker can be trained to do the manufacturing job and is provided with up-to-date plant and facilities, the attraction of significant labor-cost savings is understandable. It should be noted that labor costs are not the only factor in determining where a manufacturing facility is to be located—logistic costs, the availability of suppliers, and other manufacturing costs must also be considered in the location decision.

TABLE 5.4

Percentage Distribution of Maquiladora Firms and Employees by Industry, May 1996

	Firms	Employees
Total No. of Firms/Employees	**2,356**	**737,386**
Percentage Distribution in:		
Textiles	23.9%	17.2%
Furniture	12.4	5.3
Auto Equipment and Accessories	7.7	21.9
Electric Machinery	5.2	9.4
Electric Materials and Accessories	17.1	24.5
Chemicals	4.0	1.8
Toys and Sporting Goods	1.8	1.5
Services	5.2	4.2
Other	22.7%	14.2%

SOURCE: Secretaria de Comercio y Formento Industrial (SECOFI), quoted in NAFTA facts #8312, U.S. Dept. of Commerce.

FIGURE 5.2

The Results of Merchandise Trade among the Participating Countries of NAFTA, 1989–1996 (in billions of U.S. dollars)

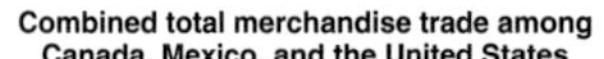

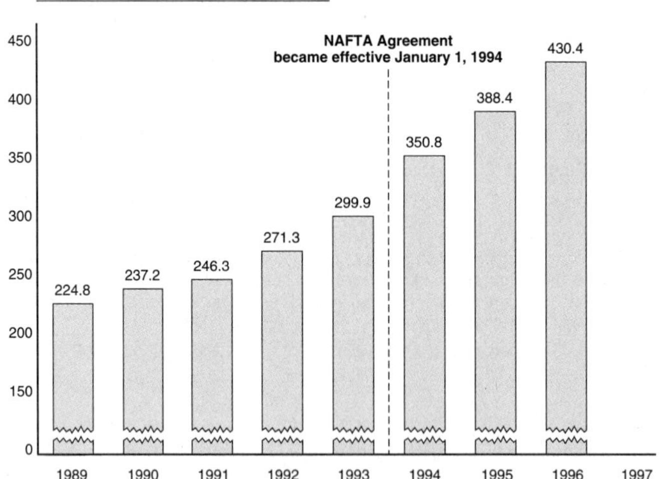

Trade Resulted in the Following Combined Trade Surplus or (Deficit) for Each Country

	1989	1990	1991	1992	1993	1994	1995	1996
Canada	7.9	8.7	5.4	7.9	9.9	13.8	17.4	19.3
Mexico	3.4	3.3	0.1	(3.3)	1.2	1.8	19.2	19.7
United States	(11.3)	(12.0)	(5.5)	(4.6)	(11.1)	(15.6)	(36.6)	(39.0)
Composition of U.S. NAFTA Trade Deficit:								
Canada	(8.8)	(9.6)	(7.1)	(9.5)	(12.1)	(16.3)	(20.5)	(22.8)
Mexico	(2.5)	(2.4)	1.6	4.9	1.0	0.7	(16.1)	(16.2)
Total	(11.3)	(12.0)	(5.5)	(4.6)	(11.1)	(15.6)	(36.6)	(39.0)

SOURCES: (A) U.S. Department of Commerce. (B) Statistics Canada.

In summary it appears that so far, in terms of merchandise trade, NAFTA has been a very good thing for Mexico and problematic for the United States. The questions now concerning NAFTA are whether or not predictions of early and quick gains for the U.S. economy were unrealistic and if year-to-year comparisons are appropriate; or if the anticipated gains should be measured in decades. Whatever the answers, one thing is clear, the integration of trade activities involves powerful and dynamic forces that will change the economic structures of the countries involved. Experience also indicates that these changes result in some degree of pain, such as lost employment and wages and relocation of plants and industries.

OTHER ECONOMIC ALLIANCES IN THE AMERICAS

Perhaps the world's developing countries have the most to gain from successful integrative efforts. Because many of these countries are also quite small, economic growth is difficult to generate internally. Many of these countries have adopted policies of **import substitution** to foster economic growth. With an import substitution policy, new domestic industries produce goods that were formerly imported. Many of these industries, however, can be efficient producers only with a higher level of production than can be consumed by the domestic economy. Their success, therefore, depends on accessible export markets made possible by integrative efforts.

import substitution new domestic industries produce goods that were formerly imported

Until a few years ago, many Latin American nations were run by military dictators who spend heavily for military projects and in doing so heightened tensions with neighboring countries. Urgently needed economic development, the improvement of living standards, and trade had a low priority in the minds of the military leaders. Now that most of these countries are under civilian rule, they are quickly discovering the benefits of free trade and that former enemies can make good trading partners. The new friendships and economic interplay among neighbors are part of a quiet revolution taking hold across a continent long dominated by militarists and trade protectionists. Military barriers are coming down, and new webs of free-trade pacts, of highways and waterways, and of oil and gas pipelines are rapidly binding South America together as never before.[12] As a result of this new sense of interdependency and cooperation, trade among members of the various trade groups has risen sharply. U.S. trade with Latin American countries is also up since 1990. By 2010, American officials calculate that the United States will export more to Latin America than to Europe and Japan combined.[13] The following sections review the major economic integration efforts in Central and South America and the Caribbean.

Southern Cone Common Market (Mercosur)

This South American trading bloc, known as *Mercosur* (Mercado Común Del Sur) in Spanish and *Mercosul* in Portuguese, includes Brazil, Argentina, Paraguay, and Uruguay. Two more countries—Chile and Bolivia—are in the process of joining the trading bloc: The agreement creating Mercosur went into effect on January 1, 1995.

The Mercosur effort has three main objectives:

1. Establishment of a free trade zone.
2. A common external tariff (a customs union).

QUESTION *The Gulf Stream flows essentially (North, Southeast or West?) along the U.S. Coast.*

The Gulf Stream flows essentially northward along the coast of the U.S. before turning eastward toward Europe.

3. Free movement of capital, labor, and services. In the future, the Mercosur group is expected to *harmonize* economic, fiscal, and trade policies.

Figure 5.3 illustrates the results of merchandise trade between the United States and the Mercosur group of four countries since 1989. During the eight-year period, U.S. exports to Mercosur increased three times—from $6.1 billion in 1989 to $18.6 billion in 1996. However, U.S. imports from the Mercosur group have not kept pace, increasing from $10.0 billion in 1989 to $11.3 billion in 1996. Of the four Mercosur countries, Brazil is the most advanced in manufacturing and technology. Saõ Paulo is one of the world's major industrial cities and is home to the affiliates and subsidiaries of many for-

FIGURE 5.3 **U.S. Merchandise Trade with Mercosur, 1989–1996 (in billions of U.S. dollars)**

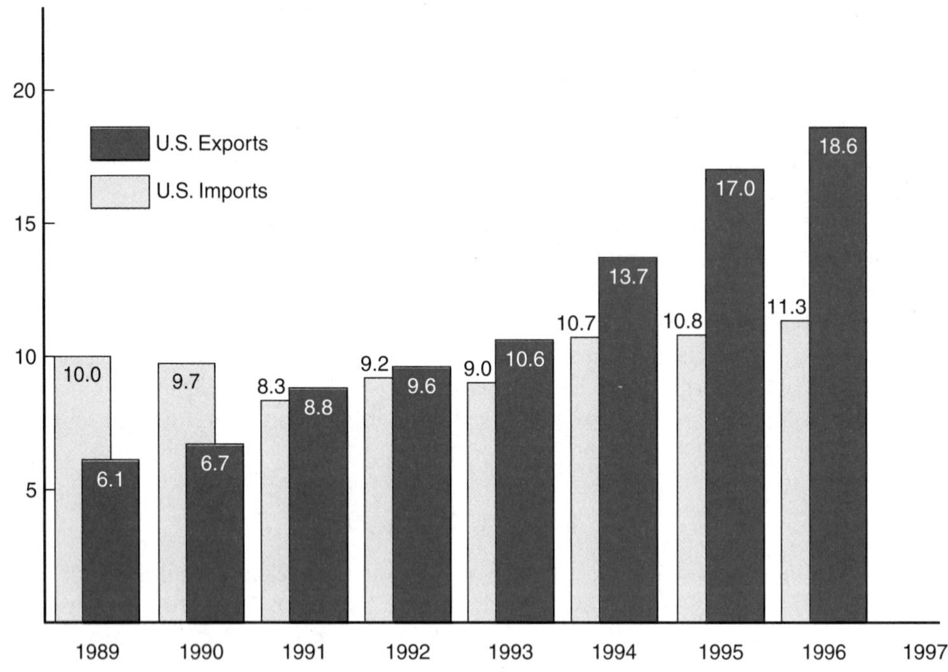

SOURCE: Analysis of U.S. Trade Data, U.S. Department of Commerce, prepared by GTI (Global Trade Information Services, Inc.).

eign corporations. Even with its significant industrial base, vast interior areas of Brazil and their rich resources remain virtually untapped. Major infrastructure improvements are under way that will permit these resources to be brought to market in a cost efficient manner.

An outgrowth of the Mercosur arrangement was a 1992 agreement with Bolivia to jointly develop the Parana and Paraguay rivers into a waterway system that will serve the needs of modern and cost-efficient trade. The *Hidrovia* (in Portuguese, the waterway) will stretch 2,150 miles from Caceres in the far west of Brazil to Nueva Palmira on the Atlantic Ocean near Buenos Aires. The waterway had been used for a limited amount of trade, but with improvements it is anticipated that it will serve as cheap transportation for large volumes of cargo. The waterway will open up Brazil's pantanal area, rich in agriculture and minerals, and will provide landlocked Bolivia with a route to the Atlantic Ocean and enable it to participate fully in international trade. Currently, it takes days and weeks to move cargo from the Brazilian interior across thousands of miles of rough terrain and roads at costs much higher than those projected for the improved waterway.[14]

The Hidrovia is only one of several ambitious projects under way in the region. Brazil alone is harnessing five river systems for a total of 5,000 miles (8000 km) of waterway; an $1.8 billion pipeline, due to start operating by 1999, will pump natural gas 2,000 miles (3,200 km) from Bolivia to Central Brazil. Additionally, the construction of a 1,072 mile railway is in its initial phase and when completed will link Pôrto VelHo in Brazil's heartland to the Port of Santos on the Atlantic, near São Paulo. In the western region of Brazil, soybean harvests are greater per acre than in the American Midwest. Brazil, a legendary coffee producer, exports more soybeans than coffee. The new railroad, often called the Soy Railroad, is expected to cut freight costs in half. Envisioned are freight trains stretching up to a half-mile hauling soybeans, grains, and tropical lumber to the Port of Santos. On their way back, the trains would carry fuel, fertilizer, and general cargo for the growing new western cities of Rondonópolis, Cuiabá, and Pôrto VelHo.[18]

As these, and other major infrastructure projects are completed, Mercosur countries will become increasingly competitive in global markets. Trading activity among the Mercosur members is up sharply. From 1992 through 1995, trade among the four nations increased 100 percent, while their exports to the rest of the world rose by 40 percent.[16] Notwithstanding these trading gains, there is growing concern in some areas that the Mercosur pact has diverted substantial trade from more efficient producers outside the region. There are indications that the most-traded products within Mercosur are generally highly capital-intensive goods that members have not been able to export competitively to outside markets.[17]

Andean Common Market (ANCom)

In May 1991, in Caracas, Venezuela, the Andean group "summit" set out the framework for an Andean Common Market to be in full operation by 1996. The Andean Common Market membership consists of Bolivia, Colombia, Ecuador, Peru, and Venezuela. Figure 5.4 summarizes the U.S. merchandise trade position with these five nations. The potential gains from free trade among themselves that could be realized by the Andean Common Market countries were further enhanced by expanded duty-free entry into the United States granted by the U.S. Congress under the **Andean Trade Preference Act (ATPA).** The ATPA went into effect on December 4, 1991, and will expire on December 4, 2001. One of the goals of ATPA is to encourage alternatives to illegal coca cultivation and production in Bolivia, Colombia, Ecuador, and Peru by offering broader duty-free

Andean Trade Preference Act provides duty-free entry into the United States for a broad range of products from Bolivia, Colombia, Ecuador, and Peru; expires Dec. 4, 2001

FIGURE 5.4

U.S. Merchandise Trade with the Andean Common Market, 1989–1996 (in millions of dollars)

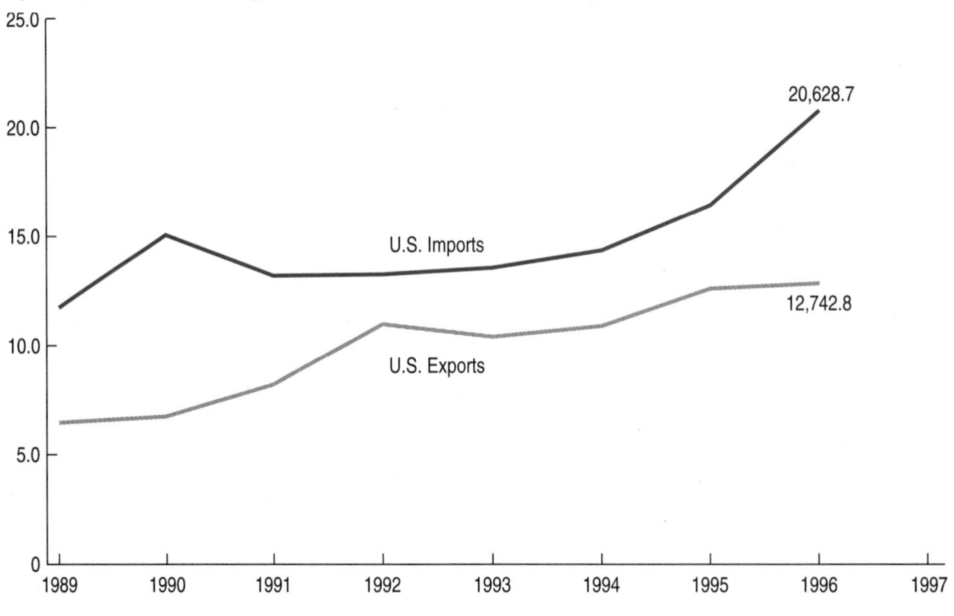

SOURCE: Global Trade Information Services, Inc.

access to the U.S. market for legal crops and other commodities, for example, flowers. Another goal is to stimulate investment in nontraditional sectors and diversify the four Andean countries' export base. To participate in ATPA, each country must meet certain criteria and be designated by the President of the United States as a "beneficiary" of the act. Bolivia and Colombia were formally designated beneficiaries in July 1992, followed by Ecuador and Peru in April and August 1993.

As a result of the act, the production and export of flowers from Colombia and Ecuador to the United States increased significantly from 1991 through 1996—up almost 600 percent. Freshly cut flowers have become Colombia's third largest export to the United States, after oil and coffee, and Ecuador's sixth largest export. In the process, cut flowers from the Andes have created 5,400 jobs in southern Florida, the major point of entry into the United States. Table 5.5 summarizes the Andean Common Market exports to the United States by commodity in 1996. Oil dominates the list of exports accounting for almost 70 percent of the total, followed by coffee, precious stones, seafood, and flowers. In total, the five commodities represent approximately 81 percent of all exports to the United States.

The desired objective of the Andean Trade Preference Act, the substitution of legal products (flowers) for illegal products (coca leaf), appears to have been unsuccessful. Colombia is growing more coca leaf for cocaine than before, and diversification into opium poppies has made Colombia a serious rival to Asia in heroin production.[18] This raises an interesting policy problem for the United States: If Colombian cut flowers are decertified under the ATPA, thousands of U.S. jobs may be lost; not to decertify the flowers might encourage additional production of coca leaf and poppies, and ultimately greater quantities of cocaine and heroin will enter the United States.

TABLE 5.5

Andean Common Market Exports to the U.S., 1996 (in millions of dollars)

Commodity	Amount	Percent of Total	Major Exporter	Amount
Mineral fuel, oil	14,392.9	69.8%	Venezuela	11,325.7
Spices, coffee	697.2	3.4	Colombia	502.3
Precious stones	685.3	3.3	Colombia	288.6
Fish and seafood	574.1	2.8	Ecuador	436.7
Live trees, plants, flowers	437.9	2.1	Colombia	367.6
Edible fruit and nuts	432.6	2.1	Ecuador	258.5
Iron and steel	365.2	1.8	Venezuela	354.2
Aluminum	289.6	1.4	Venezuela	279.3
Woven apparel	248.7	1.2	Colombia	234.7
Knit apparel	235.8	1.1	Peru	140.7
All other	2,269.4	11.0	—	—
Total	20,628.7	100.0		

SOURCE: Global Trade Information Services, Inc.

Central American Common Market (CACM)

Established by the General Treaty of Central American Economic Integration, signed in Managua in December 1960, the CACM members are Costa Rica, El Salvador, Guatemala, Honduras, and Nicaragua. The group anticipates the eventual liberalization of intra-regional trade and the establishment of a free-trade area.

The region's major trading partner is the United States. Central American exports are increasing rapidly due to production diversification, but people in the region now consume more than ever before. Being "Made in the USA" is a real plus to any product in the CACM market, and U.S. firms generally have a good reputation for providing service and support.[19]

Table 5.6 indicates that CACM exports to the United States have increased 84 percent from 1992 through 1996, while imports from the United States rose about 48 percent. This suggests that the Central American economies are becoming more competitive in global markets resulting in an improved standard of living for the peoples of the region. Leading exports to the United States in 1996 include woven and knit apparel, edible fruits, coffee, seafood, and sugar. Major imports from the United States in 1996 were textiles, machinery, cereals, mineral fuel, paper, plastic, and vehicles.

TABLE 5.6

U.S. Merchandise Trade with CACM Members, 1992, 1994, 1996 (in millions of U.S. dollars)

	1992	1994	1996	Percent change 1992 to 1996
Exports to the U.S.	3,727.3	4,803.7	6,867.0	84.2%
Imports from the U.S.	4,299.8	5,350.8	6,353.4	47.8%
U.S. trade surplus/(deficit)	572.5	547.1	(513.6)	

SOURCE: Analysis of U.S. Trade Data prepared by GTI (Global Trade Information Services, Inc.).

Caribbean Common Market (CARICOM)

CARICOM's primary mandate is to provide a framework for regional political and economic integration. The following 14 nations make up the Caribbean community:

Antigua and Barbuda	Grenada	St. Lucia
Bahamas	Guyana	St. Vincent and the Grenadines
Barbados	Jamaica	Suriname
Belize	Montserrat	Trinidad and Tobago
Dominica	St. Kitts-Nevis	

The principal objectives of CARICOM are:

1. Strengthening, consideration, and regulation of the economic and trade regulations among member states.
2. Sustained expansion and continuing integration of economic activities.
3. Achievement of a greater measure of economic independence of its member states.

Caribbean Basin Initiative

The members of CARICOM (excluding Suriname) have been designated beneficiaries of the Caribbean Basin Economic Recovery Act of 1983 (amended in 1990) which provides customs duty-free entry to the United States on a permanent basis for a broad range of products from **Caribbean Basin Initiative (CBI)** beneficiary countries. Even the advantage of duty-free entry to the U.S. market is no protection against trade being diverted to other low-cost labor countries, as illustrated in Global Learning Experience 5.3.

Caribbean Basin Initiative permits duty-free entry into the United States on a permanent basis for a broad range of products from Caribbean Basin Initiative (CBI) beneficiary countries

Other Latin American Economic Integration Efforts

In addition to the economic integration efforts previously mentioned, there are a number of initiatives in varying stages of implementation in the Americas:

Group	Type
Association of Carribean States	Trade preference association
CARICOM—Bolivia Free Trade Agreeement	Free trade in selected products
CARICOM—Venezuela Free Trade Agreement	Free trade in selected products
Group of Three (Mexico, Colombia, Venezuela)	Free trade area
Latin American Integration Association	Trade preference association
Organization of Eastern Caribbean States	Customs union

Free Trade Area of the Americas (FTAA)

In December 1994, the United States hosted the first summit of Western Hemisphere leaders. The "Summit of the Americas" concluded with an agreement by leaders of 34 nations to form a regional trading zone and set the year 2005 as the deadline for completing the necessary negotiations. When implemented, the FTAA would be a trading zone stretching from Point Barrow, Alaska, to Tierra Del Fuego at the tip of Argentina in South America.

INTEGRATION IN ASIA

The development in Asia has been quite different from that in Europe and in the Americas. While European and North American arrangements have been driven by

GLOBAL LEARNING EXPERIENCE 5.3

Trade Diversion in the Americas

While there may be concern about U.S. jobs "going south," there are indications that other countries in the Americas are experiencing an adverse economic impact as the result of NAFTA. Early in the NAFTA deliberations, it was anticipated that the Caribbean economies would suffer due to Mexico's low-cost labor and its more efficient manufacturing base. The solution was to give the Caribbean economies "NAFTA parity"—to extend the same trade preferences enjoyed by Mexico to the Caribbean nations. NAFTA parity has not been implemented, and as forecast, the Caribbean economy is feeling the impact of a classic case of trade diversion.

Changing Shares of U.S. Apparel Imports, 1992–1996 (in percent)

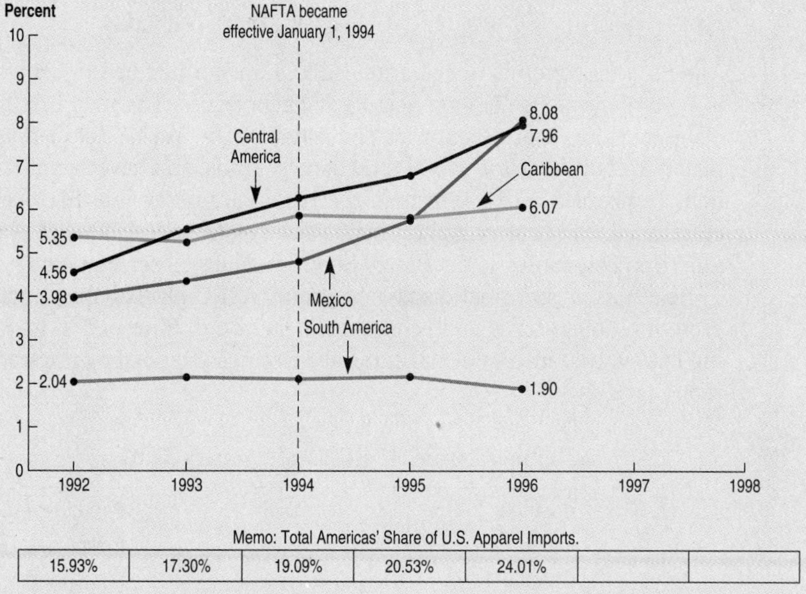

Memo: Total Americas' Share of U.S. Apparel Imports.

15.93%	17.30%	19.09%	20.53%	24.01%		

SOURCE: Analysis of U.S. trade data prepared by GTI (Global Trade Information Services, Inc.).

The Caribbean countries had become a major exporter of apparel to the United States as a result of the Caribbean Basin Initiative. However, in just two years, more than 150 Caribbean apparel plants have closed and 123,000 jobs have been lost as a direct result of trade and investment diversion to Mexico. The figure, Changing Shares of U.S. Apparel Imports, indicates the percentage shares of U.S. apparel imports received from Mexico, Central America, the Caribbean, and South American countries, which in total increased from 15.9 percent in 1992 to 24.1 percent in 1996. In the span of those five years, the Caribbean nations' share of U.S. apparel imports increased moderately from 5.4 percent in 1992 to 6.1 percent in 1996. In direct contrast, Mexico's share, which was 4.0 percent in 1992, more than doubled to 8.1 percent by 1996. As the figure shows, Mexico's major gain occurred from 1994 through 1996. A similar pattern is evident for Central American countries (primarily Honduras, El Salvador, Costa Rica, and Guatemala) which accounted for 4.6 percent of U.S. apparel imports at the beginning of the five-year period and which increased to 8.0 percent in 1996—an approximate doubling of their share. The data make it clear that the Caribbean countries are losing ground not only to Mexico, but also to several low-labor cost countries in Central America.

SOURCE: "Blows from NAFTA Batter the Caribbean Economy," L. Rohter, *New York Times,* January 30, 1997, A1.

political will, market forces may compel politicians in Asia to move toward formal integration. While Japan is the dominant force in the area to take leadership in such an endeavor, neither the Japanese themselves nor the other nations want Japan to do it. The concept of a "Co-Prosperity Sphere" of 50 years ago has made nations wary of Japan's influence.[20] Also, in terms of economic and political distance, the potential member countries are far from each other, especially compared to the EU. However, Asian interest in regional integration is increasing. First, European and American markets are significant for the Asian producers and some type of organization or bloc may be needed to maintain leverage and balance against the two other blocs. Second, given that much of the growth in trade for the nations in the region is from intra-Asian trade, having a common understanding and policies will become necessary. There are two major initiatives toward economic integration in Asia: (1) *Asia-Pacific Economic Cooperation (APEC)* and (2) *Association of Southeast Asian Nations (ASEAN).*

Asia-Pacific Economic Cooperation (APEC)

Asia-Pacific Economic Cooperation (APEC) was formed in 1989 in response to the growing interdependence among Asia-Pacific economies. The membership of APEC consists of 18 countries that account for about half of the world's total annual output, approximately half of the world's total merchandise trade, and have a combined GNP of $15 trillion. Companies with interests in the region are observing APEC-related developments closely. Global Learning Experience 5.4 suggests the market potentials that await American companies as the United States develops closer trading ties with Asian nations.

Begun as an informal discussion group, APEC has become a major organization in promoting open trade and economic cooperation. Since 1993, its major annual meeting has evolved into informal summit meetings attended by the leaders of the member economies.

Membership of APEC as of January 1997

Australia	Indonesia*	Papua New Guinea
Brunei*	Japan	Philippines*
Canada**	S. Korea	Singapore*
Chile	Malaysia*	Taiwan
China (PRC)	Mexico**	Thailand*
Hong Kong	New Zealand	United States**

**Member of ASEAN*
***Member of NAFTA*

In 1991, APEC members agreed on specific objectives:

- To sustain the growth and development of the region;
- To encourage the flow of goods, services, capital, and technology;
- To develop and strengthen an open multilateral trading system;
- To reduce barriers to trade in goods and services among participants.

Table 5.7 presents a chronology of the major APEC meetings since its inception. From 1989 through 1992, the meetings were primarily at the ministerial level. In 1993, President Clinton hosted the meeting in Seattle, which was attended by the APEC economic leaders and elevated these annual meetings to the level of an "informal summit." The practice has continued since then.

GLOBAL LEARNING EXPERIENCE 5.4

When a Foe Becomes a Friend

In December 1992, about 18 years after a humiliating withdrawal of U.S. military forces from Vietnam and a subsequent U.S. embargo on American firms doing business there, the Bush Administration permitted U.S. companies to open offices in Vietnam. The action did not allow the companies to conduct business, but only to prepare to conduct business in the event the embargo was lifted.

Vietnam, with a population of approximately 72 million people, is one of the last untapped consumer markets in Asia. Understandably, many foreign countries (Taiwan, Hong Kong, France, Australia, Britain, and Japan) were making large direct investments in Vietnam in an effort to gain market share, while U.S. companies were not permitted to participate.

On February 3, 1994, President Clinton lifted the trade embargo with Vietnam, and almost immediately U.S. businesses began sending personnel to Ho Chi Minh City (formerly Saigon). Within hours, Pepsi was handing out free samples and indicated plans to run a new TV commercial featuring Miss Vietnam; Coca-Cola has announced plans for new investments in Vietnam; American Express will soon issue its cards; and United Airlines reported that it will soon begin service from Los Angeles to Ho Chi Minh City. Other U.S. companies with offices in Vietnam include Citibank, Bank of America, General Electric, Baker Mackenzie, Philip Morris, I.B.M., Digital Equipment, Motorola, Boeing, Caterpillar, and Mobil Corporation.

"I liked it better when we were enemies."
SOURCE: Mike Peters, *Dayton Daily News,* Reprinted by permission: Tribune Media Services.

Association of Southeast Asian Nations (ASEAN)

The association of Southeast Asian Nations (ASEAN) is composed of seven member nations: Brunei, Indonesia, Malaysia, Philippines, Singapore, Thailand, and Vietnam. An additional three countries—Cambodia, Laos, and Myanmar—have been granted observer status. The aim of the group is reductions in tariffs to a maximum level of 5 percent among the members by the year 2003 under the ASEAN Free Trade Agreement (AFTA).

TABLE 5.7 **Chronology of APEC Meetings**

Year	Location	Outcome
1989	Canberra, Australia	Ministerial meeting.
1990	Singapore	Ministerial meeting.
1991	Seoul, S. Korea	Seoul APEC declaration; agreement on specific objectives.
1992	Bangkok, Thailand	Ministerial meeting.
1993	Blake Island, Seattle	APEC elevated to "summit level" discussions; agreement on economic vision for the region.
1994	Bogor, Indonesia	Announce two-step timetable to liberalize trade; industrialized countries to remove trade barriers by 2010; developing nations to remove barriers by 2020.
1995	Osaka, Japan	Each nation announced a so-called "initial action" toward lowering trade barriers; China pledges to reduce tariffs on 4,000 items in the next year.
1996	Manila, Philippines	Australia, China, United States, Mexico, Hong Kong, and Taiwan endorsement to "substantially eliminate" tariffs on computers and other information technologies by 2000.
1997	Vancouver, British Columbia	

The Malaysians have pushed for the formation of the East Asia Economic Group (EAEG), which would add Hong Kong, Japan, South Korea, and Taiwan to the list. This proposal makes sense; without Japan and the rapidly industrializing countries of the region, such as South Korea and Taiwan, the effect of the arrangement would be small. Japan's reaction has been generally negative toward all types of regionalization efforts, mainly because it has had the most to gain from free trade efforts. However, part of what has been driving regionalization has been Japan's reluctance to foster some of the elements that promote free trade, like reciprocity.[21] Should the other trading blocs turn against Japan, its only resort may be to work toward a more formal trade arrangement in Pacific Asia.

Indian Subcontinent

Economic integration has also taken place on the Indian subcontinent. In 1985, seven nations of the region (India, Pakistan, Bangladesh, Sri Lanka, Nepal, Bhutan, and the Maldives) launched the South Asian Association for Regional Cooperation (SAARC). Cooperation is limited to relatively noncontroversial areas, such as agriculture and regional development. Elements such as the formation of a common market have not been included.

Integration in Africa and the Middle East

Africa's economic groupings range from currency unions among European nations and their former colonies to customs unions between neighboring states. In 1975, 16 West African nations attempted to create a megamarket large enough to interest investors from the industrialized world and reduce hardship through economic integration. The objective of the Economic Community of West African States (ECOWAS) was to form a customs union and eventual common market. Although many of its objectives have not been reached, its combined population of 160 million represents the largest economic entity in sub-Saharan Africa. Other entities in Africa include the Afro-Malagasy Economic Union, the East Africa Customs Union, the West African Economic Community, and the Maghreb Economic Community. Many of these, however, have not been successful due to the small size of the membership and lack of economic infrastructure to produce goods to be traded inside the blocs.

Countries in the Arab world have made some progress in economic integration. The Gulf Cooperation Council (GCC) is one of the most powerful, economically speaking, of any trade groups. The per-capita income of its six member states (Bahrain, Kuwait, Oman, Qatar, Saudi Arabia, and the United Arab Emirates) is $7,690. The GCC was formed in 1980 mainly as a defensive measure due to the perceived threat from the Iran-Iraq war. Its aim is to achieve free trade arrangements with the EU and EFTA as well as bilateral trade agreements with Western European nations.

Cartels and Commodity Price Agreements

An important characteristic that distinguishes developing countries from industrialized countries is the nature of their export earnings. While industrialized countries rely heavily on the export of manufactured goods, technology, and services, the developing countries rely chiefly on the export of primary products and raw materials—for example, copper, iron ore, and agricultural products. This distinction is important for several reasons. First, the level of price competition is higher among sellers of primary products, because of the typically larger number of sellers and also because primary products are homogeneous. This can be seen by comparing the sale of computers with, for example, copper. Only three or four countries are a competitive force in the computer market, whereas at least a dozen compete in the sale of copper. Furthermore, while product differentiation and therefore brand loyalty are likely to exist in the market for computers, buyers of copper are likely to purchase on the basis of price alone. A second distinguishing factor is that supply variability will be greater in the market for primary products because production often depends on uncontrollable factors such as weather. For these reasons, market prices of primary products—and therefore developing country export earnings—are highly volatile.

Responses to this problem have included cartels and commodity price agreements. A **cartel** is an association of producers of a particular good. While a cartel may consist of an association of private firms, our interest is in the cartels formed by nations. The objective of a cartel is to suppress the market forces affecting its product in order to gain greater control over sales revenues. A cartel may accomplish this objective in several ways. First, members may engage in price fixing. This entails an agreement by producers to sell at a certain price, eliminating price competition among sellers. Second, the cartel may allocate sales territories among its members, again suppressing competition. A third tactic calls for members to agree to restrict production, and therefore supplies, resulting in artificially higher prices.

cartel
association of producers of a particular good

The most widely known cartel is the Organization of Petroleum Exporting Countries (OPEC). OPEC became a significant force in the world economy in the 1970s. In 1973, the Arab members of OPEC were angered by U.S. support for Israel in the war in the Mideast. In response, the Arab members declared an embargo on the shipment of oil to the United States and quadrupled the price of oil—from approximately $3 to $12 per barrel. OPEC tactics included both price fixing and production quotas. Continued price increases brought the average price per barrel to nearly $35 by 1981. The cartel experienced severe problems during the 1980s, however. First, the demand for OPEC oil declined considerably as the result of conservation, the use of alternative

Central Europe and Asia: The Location of Major Emerging Market Economies

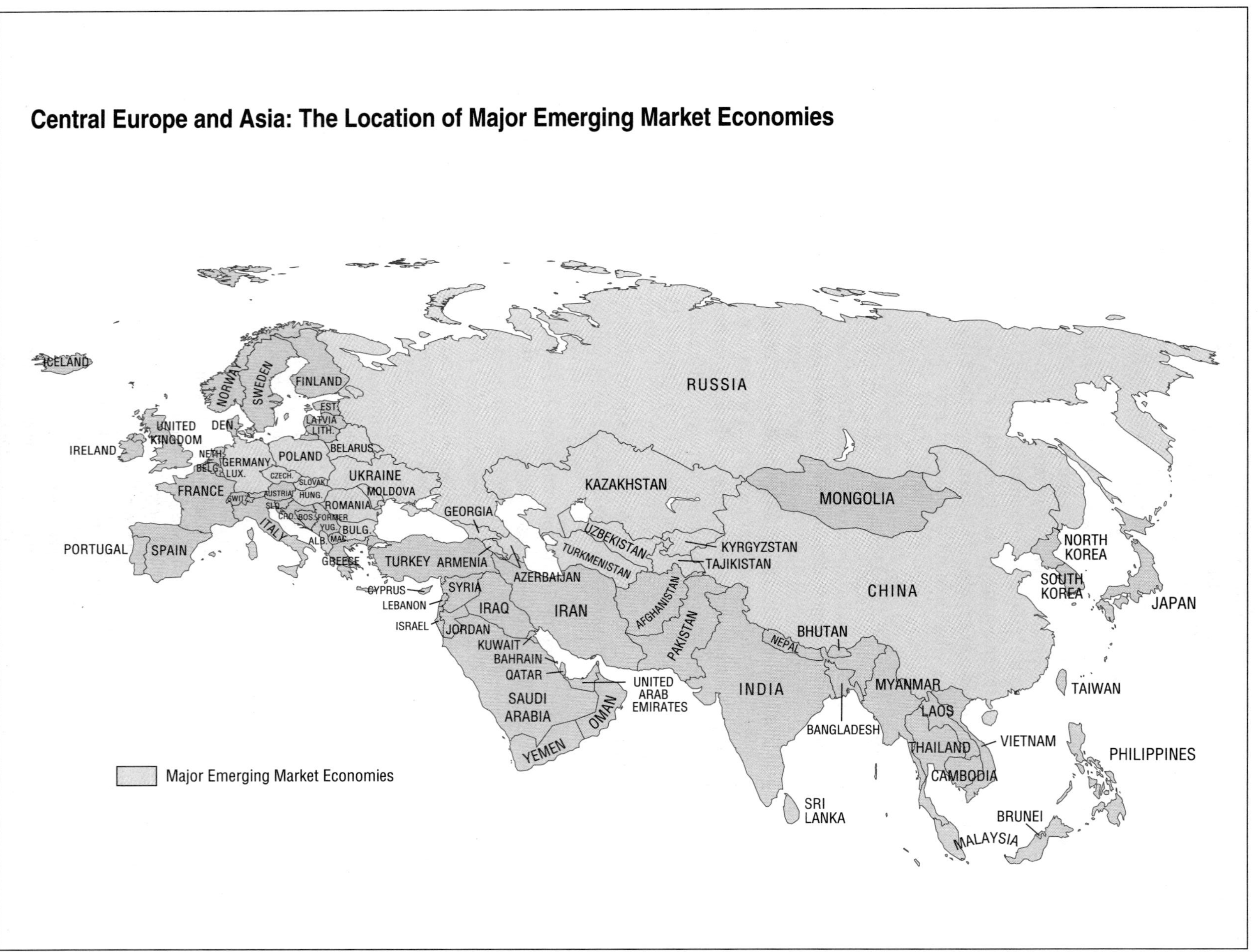

sources, and increased oil production by nonmembers. All of these factors also contributed to sharp declines in the price of oil. Second, the cohesiveness among members diminished. Sales often occurred at less than the agreed-upon price, and production quotas were repeatedly violated. The members of OPEC convened following the Persian Gulf war in early 1991 in an attempt to regain control over oil prices, but it remains to be seen whether OPEC will regain its influence as a major force in the world economy.

International **commodity price agreements** involve both buyers and sellers in an agreement to manage the price of a certain commodity. Often, the free market is allowed to determine the price of the commodity over a certain range. However, if demand and supply pressures cause the commodity's price to move outside that range, an elected or appointed manager will enter the market to buy or sell the commodity to bring the price back into the range. The manager controls the **buffer stock** of the commodity. If prices float downward, the manager purchases the commodity and adds to the buffer stock. Under upward pressure, the manager sells the commodity from the buffer stock. This system is somewhat analogous to a managed exchange rate system such as the EMS, in which authorities buy and sell to influence exchange rates. International commodity agreements are currently in effect for sugar, tin, rubber, cocoa, and coffee.

commodity price agreements involve both buyers and sellers in an agreement to manage the price of a certain commodity

buffer stock stock of a commodity kept on hand to prevent a shortage in times of unexpectedly great demand; under international commodity and price agreements, the stock controlled by an elected or appointed manager for the purpose of managing the price of the commodity

EMERGING MARKET ECONOMIES

The major emerging market economies are the Commonwealth of Independent States, East Germany (now unified with West Germany), the Eastern and Central European nations (Albania, Bulgaria, the Czech and Slovakia Republics, Hungary, Poland, and Romania), and the People's Republic of China.

It is a common belief that business ties between the Western world and these nations are a new phenomenon. That is not the case. In the 1920s, for example, General Electric and RCA helped to develop the Soviet electrical and communications industries. Ford constructed a huge facility in Gorky to build Model A cars and buses. DuPont introduced its technology to Russia's chemical industry. Conversely, Tungsram in Hungary conducted research and development for General Electric. However, by the mid-1930s, most American companies had withdrawn from the scene or were forced to leave. Since then, former centrally planned economies and Western corporations engaged in international business have had rather limited contact.[22]

Prague, Czech Republic, is coming alive with business opportunities in its newly freed economy. *SOURCE:* © 1992 Filip Horvat/ SABA.

To a large extent, this limited contact has been the result of an ideological wariness on both sides. Socialist countries often perceived international corporations as "aggressive business organizations developed to further the imperialistic aims of Western, especially American, capitalists the world over."[23] Furthermore, many aspects of capitalism, such as the private ownership of the means of production, were seen as exploitative and antithetical to communist ideology.[24] Western managers, in turn, often saw socialism as a threat to the Western world and the capitalist system in general.

Over time, these rigid stances were modified on both sides. Decision makers in former centrally planned economies recognized the need to purchase products and technology that were unavailable domestically or that could be produced only at a substantial comparative disadvantage. They were determined to achieve economic growth and improve the very much neglected standard of living in their society, deciding that the potential benefits of cooperation in many instances outweighed the risks of decentralized economic power and reduced reliance on plans. As a result, government planners in former socialist economies began to include some market considerations in their activities and opened up their countries to Western businesses.

At the same time, the greater openness on the part of these governments resulted in more flexibility of Western government control of East-West trade. The drive toward modernization of production and growing consumer demand greatly raised the attractiveness of doing business with the newly emerging democracies (NEDs). Furthermore, many Western firms experienced a need to diversify their international business activities from traditional markets because of current trade imbalances and were searching for new opportunities. The large populations and pent-up demand of the NEDs offered those opportunities.

THE DEMISE OF THE SOCIALIST SYSTEM

By late 1989, with an unexpected suddenness, the Iron Curtain disappeared, and within less than three years, the communist empire ceased to exist. Virtually overnight Eastern Europe and the former Soviet Union, with their total population of 400 million and a combined GNP of $3 trillion,[25] shifted their political and economic orientation toward a market economy. The former socialist satellites shed their communist governments. Newly elected democratic governments decided to let market forces shape their economies. East Germany was unified with West Germany. In March 1992, Hungary was admitted as an associate member of the European Union. The Czech Republic, Slovakia, and Poland announced their desire to achieve full convertibility of their currencies and to join the GATT system (the General Agreement on Tariffs and Trade, discussed in Chapter 6). By 1992, the entire Soviet Union had disappeared. Individual regions within the Commonwealth of Independent States reasserted their independence and autonomy, resulting in a host of emerging nations, often heavily dependent on one another, but now separated by nationalistic feelings and political realities.

The political changes were accompanied by major economic action. Externally, trade flows were redirected from the former Soviet Union toward the European Union, as shown in Figure 5.5. Internally, austerity programs were introduced and prices of subsidized products were adjusted upward to avoid distorted trade flows due to distorted prices. Wages were kept in check to reduce inflation. Entire industries were either privatized or closed down. These steps led to a significant decrease in the standard of living of the population. Yet the support for the internal economic transformation continued, demonstrating the great desire on the part of individuals and governments to participate in the world marketplace and the hope that these transformations would achieve a better standard of living over time.

A Reorientation of Trade **FIGURE 5.5**

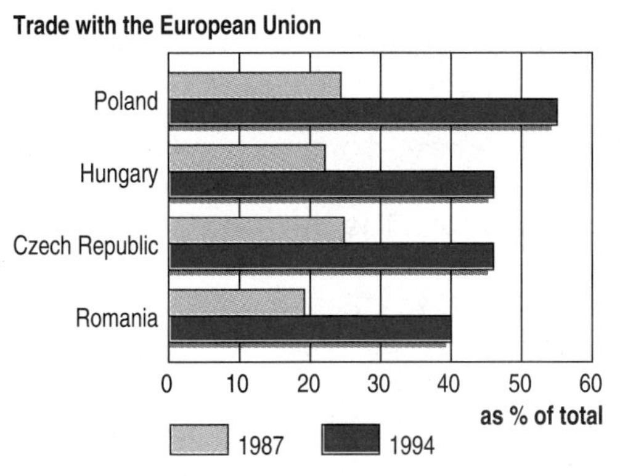

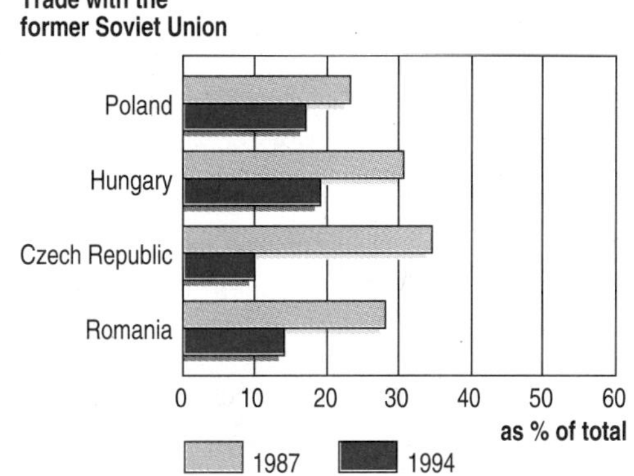

SOURCE: *Directory of Trade Statistics* (Washington, D.C.: IMF). 1994.

While China did not undergo the radical political shifts of Europe, its economic changes were of similar significance. New enterprise zones were opened, designed to produce products targeted for export. Foreign investors were invited. Individuals were permitted to translate their entrepreneurial skills into action and keep the profits. As Global Learning Experience 5.5 shows, a new perspective has begun to permeate business and the economy.

From a Western perspective, all these changes indicated the end of the Cold War and a resultant significant decrease in the need to withhold economic benefits and technology from an entire world region. It was also understood that the shouts for democracy were, to a large degree, driven not only by political but also by economic desires. Freedom meant not only the right to free elections but also the expectation of an increased standard of living in the form of color televisions, cars, and the many benefits of a consumer society. To sustain the drive toward democracy, these economic desires had to appear attainable. Therefore, it was in the interest of the Western world as a whole to contribute toward the democratization of the former communist nations by searching for ways to bring them "the good life."

A bus shelter in Moscow's Red Square advertising foreign products is evidence of business opportunities in Russia's newly freed economy.
SOURCE: Robert Harding Picture Library/London.

Private Business Clubs in China

Business club elitism seems to be an idea that goes down well in nominally socialist China where access and contacts are the keys to success. Twenty business, private, and country clubs are either open or in the works in Beijing, all vying for membership among foreign executives, Chinese tycoons, and government officials. One estimate is that there are more than 60 business and golf clubs under construction across the country.

New clubs market their prestige and facilities fiercely, advertising in print and over the radio, offering free trips and pitching enrollment in limited memberships as an investment that will pay off handsomely in the future. "I am besieged with calls from these clubs; I refuse to speak to them anymore," said an American banking executive.

The Capital Club, perched on the fiftieth floor near a north Beijing diplomatic enclave, boasts a panoramic view of the smoggy Chinese capital. This club is the latest entry, with a mini who's who of Beijing government and business. In addition to a wood-paneled ambience and dining areas designed like boardrooms, the club also has a recreation center with a glass-domed swimming pool, bowling lanes, billiard tables, and a golf simulator. The membership fees of $7,500 for corporations and $5,000 for individuals include access to 200 associated private and country clubs in 14 countries.

"We are trying to provide better opportunities for each member to do business and for foreign and Chinese businessmen to exchange views," said Robert Dedman, chairman of Club Corp. of America, the joint venture partner of China International Trust and Investment Corporation. Other facilities in Shanghai and Guangzhou are planned. In December 1994, the Changan Club opened, with entrance fees ranging from $20,000 to $28,000. The club has private tennis courts, saunas, gymnasiums, and dining rooms and happens to be located near the walled citadel of China's Communist leadership.

SOURCE: "New Business Clubs Prove Popular," *Financial Times,* November 7, 1994, IX.

The Realities of Economic Change

For Western firms, all these shifts resulted in the conversion of what had been a latent market into a market offering very real and vast opportunities. Yet these shifts are only the beginning of a process. The announcement of an intention to change does not automatically result in change itself. For example, the abolition of a centrally planned economy does not create a market economy. Laws permitting the emergence of private-sector entrepreneurs do not create entrepreneurship. The reduction of price controls does not immediately make goods available or affordable. Deeply ingrained systemic differences between the emerging democracies and Western firms continue. Highly prized, fully accepted fundamentals of the market economy—such as the reliance on competition, support of the profit motive, and the willingness to live with risk on a corporate and personal level—are not yet fully accepted. It is therefore useful to review the major economic and structural dimensions of the emerging democracies to identify major shortcomings and opportunities for international business.

The elected democratic governments in Central Europe are a completely new phenomenon. While full of good intentions, these governments are new to the tasks of governing and have either very limited experience or none at all. At the same time, they face major legal uncertainties and the existence of old, entrenched bureaucracies, whose members are still deeply suspicious of any change and less than helpful or forthcoming. These governments have precipitated the disappearance of the previous trading system but have yet to replace the old, imperfect set of trading relationships with a new one. As a result, their ability to successfully shape the competitive environment of their nations is limited.

Many of the NEDs also face major infrastructure shortages. Transportation systems, particularly those leading to the West, are either nonexistent or in disrepair. The housing stock is in need of total overhaul. Communication systems will take years to improve. Market intermediaries often do not exist. Payments and funds-transfer systems are inadequate. Even though major efforts are under way to improve the infrastructure —evidenced, for example, by the former Soviet Union's desire to obtain fiber-optic telephone lines or by Hungary's success in installing a cellular telephone system—infrastructure shortcomings will inhibit economic growth for years to come.

Capital shortages are also a major constraint. Catching up with the West in virtually all industrial areas will require major capital infusions. In addition, a new environmental consciousness will require large investments in environmentally sound energy-generation and production facilities. Even though major programs are being designed to attract hidden personal savings into the economies, NEDs must rely to a large degree on attracting capital from abroad. Continued domestic uncertainties and high demand for capital around the world make this difficult.

Firms doing business with the emerging democracies encounter very interesting demand conditions. Clearly, the pent-up demand from the past bodes well for sales. Yet buyers, in many instances, have never been exposed to the problem of decision making; their preferences are vague and undefined, and they are therefore poorly trained in making market choices.[26] As a result, buyers are unlikely to demand high levels of quality or service. Rather, their demand is driven much more by product availability than by product sophistication. Yet little accurate market information is available. For example, knowledge about pricing, advertising, research, and trading is virtually nonexistent, and few institutions are able to accurately assess demand and channel supply. As a result, corporate responsiveness to demand is quite difficult.

To the surprise of many investors, the emerging democracies have substantial knowledge resources to offer. For example, it is claimed that the former USSR and former eastern Europe possess about 35 to 40 percent of all researchers and engineers working in the world.[27] At the same time, however, these nations suffer from the drawback imposed by a lack of management skills. In the past, management mainly consisted of skillful maneuvering within the allocation process. Central planning, for example, required firms to request tools seven years in advance; material requirements needed to be submitted two years in advance. Ordering was done haphazardly, since requested quantities were always reduced, and surplus allocations could always be traded with other firms. The driving mechanism for management was therefore not responsiveness to existing needs, but rather plan fulfillment through the development of a finely honed allocation mentality.

Commitment by managers and employees to hard work is similarly nonexistent. Employees are to a large degree still caught up in old work habits, which consisted of never having to work a full shift. The notion that "they pretend to pay us, and we

QUESTION

Where is the world's largest tropical coral-reef complex?

ANSWER *The greatest reef of all is Australia's Great Barrier Reef, which extends more than 1,300 miles along the continent's Pacific Coast. This is only a third of the length of the Great Wall of China, but impressive enough when you consider its massive bulk—80,900 square miles—its 400 species of coral and 6500 species of fish.*

pretend to work" is still very strong. The current dismantling of the past policy of the "Iron Rice Bowl," which made layoffs virtually impossible, is further reducing rather than increasing such commitment.

The new environment also complicates managerial decision making. Because of the total lack of prior market orientation, even simple reforms require an almost unimaginable array of decisions about business licenses, the setting of optimal tax rates, rules of business operation, definitions of business expense for taxation purposes, safety standards, and rules concerning nondiscrimination and consumer protection.[28] All new market economies experience a gap in management skills. Improved managerial training is therefore a key building block in developing the international competitiveness of the region. Table 5.8 presents the key management skills and qualities that were found to be needed in Russia.

Adjusting to Rapid Change

Both institutions and individuals tend to display some resistance to change. The resistance grows if the speed of change increases. It does not necessarily indicate a preference for the earlier conditions but rather concern about the effects of adjustment and fear of the unknown. In light of the major shifts that have occurred both politically and

TABLE 5.8 **Top Ten Management Skills and Qualities Needed in Free-Market Russia**

	Percentage	Frequency
1. Connections and personal contacts	58	89
2. Problem-solving, crisis-handling skills	53	84
3. Marketing and sales skills	45	72
4. Leadership and communication skills	44	70
5. Action-oriented, willing to take risks	41	65
6. Technical knowledge of operation and product	38	60
7. Planning and organizing skills	37	59
8. Financial and accounting skills	30	48
9. Creativity and innovation	29	46
10. Drive and persistence	22	35

SOURCE: Clinton O. Longenecker and Serguei Popovski, "Managerial Trials of Privatization," *Business Horizons*, November–December 1994, 38.

economically in Central Europe and the former U.S.S.R., Commonwealth of Independent States (CIS), and the accompanying substantial dislocations, resistance should be expected. Deeply entrenched interests and traditions are not easily dislocated by the tender and shallow root of market-oriented thinking. The understanding of linkages and interactions cannot be expected to grow overnight. For example, greater financial latitude for firms also requires that inefficient firms be permitted to go into bankruptcy—a concept not cherished by many. The need for increased efficiency and productivity will cause sharp reductions in employment—a painful step for the workers affected. The growing ranks of unemployed are swelled by the members of the military who have been brought home or demobilized. Concurrently, wage reforms threaten to relegate blue-collar workers, who were traditionally favored by the socialist system, to second-class status while permitting the emergence of a new enterpreneurial class of the rich, an undesirable result for those not participating in the upswing. Retail price reforms may endanger the safety net of large population segments, and widespread price changes may introduce inflation. It is difficult to accept a system where there are winners and losers, particularly for those on the losing side. As a result, an increase in ambivalence and uncertainty may well produce rapid shifts in economic and political thinking, which in turn may produce another set of unexpected results.

But it is not just in the emerging democracies that major changes have come about. The shifts experienced there also have a major impact on the established market economies of the West. Initially, the immediate changes in the West were confined to the reduction of the threat of war and a redefinition of military and political strategy. Over time, however, Western governments are discovering that the formation of new linkages and dismantling of old ones will also cause major dislocations at home. For example, the change in military threat is likely to have an effect on military budgets, which for the United States alone was $300 billion annually. Budget changes in turn will affect the production of military goods and the employment level in the defense sector. A declining size of armies will only reinforce the resulting employment needs.

Over the long term, major changes will also result from the reorientation of trade flows. With traditional and "forced" trade relationships vanishing and the need for income from abroad increasing, most of the former socialist countries will exert major efforts to become partners in global trade. They will attempt to export much more of their domestic production. Many of these exports will be in product categories such as agriculture and basic manufacturing, which are precisely the economic sectors in which the Western nations are already experiencing surpluses. As a result, the threat of displacement will be high for traditional producers.

International Business Challenges and Opportunities

The pressure of change in the NEDs also presents vast opportunities for the expansion of international business activities. Their large populations offer potential consumer demand and production supply unmatched by any other region in the world. Furthermore, the knowledge of the international manager may be particularly useful to these economies where business skills are only rudimentary. These countries need assistance and contacts to reshape their domestic economies and penetrate foreign markets. For example, Russia is asking for help in areas such as business and personnel training, marketing, banking, auditing, and compilation of statistics.[29]

Of major concern are the limitations placed on goods that can be sold to emerging market economies. Although export restrictions have been eased in light of political developments, the international manager needs to consider the current and future political environments when planning long-term business commitments. A second major challenge is the lack of information about end users. Business strives to satisfy the needs and wants of individuals and organizations. Unable to ascertain their desires directly, the international manager must use secondary information such as hearsay, educated guesses, and the opinions of intermediaries.

Another major difficulty encountered in conducting business with these countries is the frequent unavailability of hard currency. Products, however necessary, often cannot be purchased by emerging market economies because no funds are available to pay for them. As a result, many of these countries resort to barter and countertrade. This places an additional burden on the international manager, who must not only market products to the clients but must also market the products received in return to other consumers and institutions.

Similar problems are encountered when attempting to source products from emerging market economies. Many firms have found that selling is not part of the economic culture of these countries. The available descriptive materials are often poorly written and devoid of useful information. Obtaining additional information about a product may be difficult and time consuming.

The quality of the products obtained can also be a major problem. In spite of their great desire to participate in the global marketplace, the NEDs still tend to place primary emphasis on product performance and, to a large extent, to neglect style and product presentation. The result is "a willingness to leave equipment rough and unfinished when a lack of finishing does not significantly affect function."[30] Therefore, the international manager needs to forge agreements that require the manufacturer to improve quality, provide for technical control, and ensure prompt delivery before sourcing products from emerging market economies.

Even when satisfactory products are obtained from emerging market economies, the marketing of these products elsewhere can be a major problem. One study revealed negative attitudes toward products sourced from emerging market economies—particularly consumer products. International managers may well "find a portion of the population [in the United States] hesitant to purchase [such] goods."[31]

Nevertheless, sufficient opportunities exist to make consideration of these international business activities worthwhile. Emerging market economies do have products that can be of use in free-market economies and that are often unique in performance. In most instances, these tend to be industrial rather than consumer products, reflecting the past orientation of centrally planned research and development.

The fall of the Berlin Wall signaled the opening of Eastern Europe, providing vast opportunities for the expansion of international marketing activities.
SOURCE: Filip Horvat/SABA.

Russian Software Firms Look Overseas

A small but growing number of Russian software companies are bringing their ideas to the global marketplace. Russian software designers, industry insiders say, are among the world's most gifted but an undeveloped sense of what consumers want and lack of financial resources hampered such firms. Today, however, some of Russia's leading software makers are finding ways to translate their skills into commercial results.

Nikolai Lebedev, the chairman of Transas Marine, is trying to develop technology the world has never seen. The Russian company is testing a system now that allows the navigation of a virtual reality cargo ship through a three-dimensional vision of actual ports around the world. The $100,000 system, used for pilot training, combines painstakingly detailed maps with state-of-the-art graphics. The 120-person, privately owned software house expects to sell about $9 million in marine-related software in 1994, mostly overseas.

Paragraph International, another Moscow software house, already made millions of dollars by licensing technology to Apple Computer Inc. for the use of the U.S. firm's Newton MessagePad. One of several new projects is a "virtual home museum," which is touted as the photo album of the future. After transferring photos onto a personal computer, the user can arrange pictures along the walls of a gallery that can be designed on screen. Other products include a three-dimensional, medical diagnostic program and a "time travel" game that lets players interact via telephone modems in computer-generated fantasy worlds.

Russian software firms are still facing troubling barriers. Most Russian designers work with primitive equipment, forcing them to accomplish results with very little power. "We needed to be ingenious," said Arkady Moreynis, general manager of Macsimum, which develops software to run on Apple's Macintosh computers.

Despite such problems, the abundance of local talent has enticed a number of Western companies to contract out work to Russian designers. The level of skill present is portrayed in one Russian software firm named Steepler Corp. Roustem Akhiarov, a co-owner, helped create a Russian version of Nintendo after observing video-game addicts in the United States. Steepler's "Dendy," a TV video game manufactured in Taiwan, now dominates the Russian market. By the beginning of 1994, Steepler was selling 83,000 units a month for about $40 apiece.

SOURCE: Adi Ignatius, "Russian Software Firms Look Overseas," *The Wall Street Journal,* July 8, 1994, A5.

Consumer products may in time play a larger role. Lower labor costs and, in some instances, the greater availability of labor may enable emerging market economies to offer consumers in free-market economies a variety of products at a lower cost. Due to their low cost, existing service capabilities may also present interesting international business possibilities. Global Learning Experience 5.6 provides an example of successful Russian software exports.

Privatization

privatization
policy of shifting operation of government-owned enterprises to private ownership to cut costs and ensure more efficient services

Governments are increasingly recognizing that it is possible to reduce the cost of governing by changing their role and involvement in the economy. Through **privatization,** governments can cut their budget costs and still ensure that more efficient services—not

Privatization Sweeps the Globe

After record privatization in Eastern Europe, Russia, Latin America, and Asia, privatization is now sweeping across Western Europe like a tidal wave. Italy is selling off giant industries that have been part of the government since the Mussolini era. State-owned industrial conglomerates have been turned into public-stock companies in fields such as oil, banking, food, power, and aerospace. France is cutting loose control over everything from computer companies to giant insurers. Even Germany is getting into the act by putting its national airline, Lufthansa, and Deutsche Bundespost Telekom on the block.

This is not an easy step to take. Says Daniel Gros of the Brussels-based Center for European Policy Studies: "Some diehards don't want to sell their state firms." They give the power to government to "give people hundreds of thousands of jobs. That's where they get their power from."

Why all the privatization? First of all, state enterprises were not very successful. Under state ownership, both managers and workers have strong incentives to "decapitalize" the enterprises that employ them by extracting as much wealth as they can for themselves. They have little or no incentive to increase the value of the firm through wise investments, increasing productivity, or restraining wages and employment, because they have little chance of sharing in the firm's future prosperity. But new rules in the European Union also helped. These rules have banned billions in state subsidies that uncompetitive state firms have relied on for decades to stay afloat. Finally, many countries see privatization as an opportunity to trim massive budget deficits and national debt.

SOURCES: Patrick Oster, "Europe Dashes to Jettison State-Owned Businesses," *The Washington Post*, July 23, 1992, D10, D14; "Owners Are the Only Answer," *The Economist*, September 21, 1991, 10.

fewer services—are provided to the people. In addition, the product or service may also become more productive and more innovative and may expand choices for the private sector.

In the mid-1970s, the United States took the lead in reducing government involvement with industry by deregulating domestic industries such as telephone service and airlines, which had been tightly controlled or regulated. Britain pioneered the concept of privatization in 1979 by converting 20 state firms into privately owned companies. In the 1980s, Chile privatized 470 enterprises, which had produced 24 percent of the country's value added.[32] By the 1990s, privatization had become a key element in governmental economic strategy around the world. In addition to Asia, Africa, Latin America, and the Eastern European nations, even Western Europe entered the privatization field on a large scale, as Global Learning Experience 5.7 shows.

The methods of privatization vary from country to country. Some nations come up with a master plan for privatization, whereas others deal with it on a case-by-case basis. The Treuhandanstalt of Germany, for example, which has been charged with disposing of most East German state property, aims to sell firms but maximize the number of jobs retained. In other countries, ownership shares are distributed to citizens and employees. Some nations simply sell to the highest bidder in order to maximize the proceeds. For example, Mexico has used most of its privatization proceeds to amortize its internal debt, resulting in savings of nearly $1 billion a year in interest payments. Figure 5.6 shows some of the large companies that originated in emerging market economies as a result of privatization.

Some Results of Privatization FIGURE 5.6

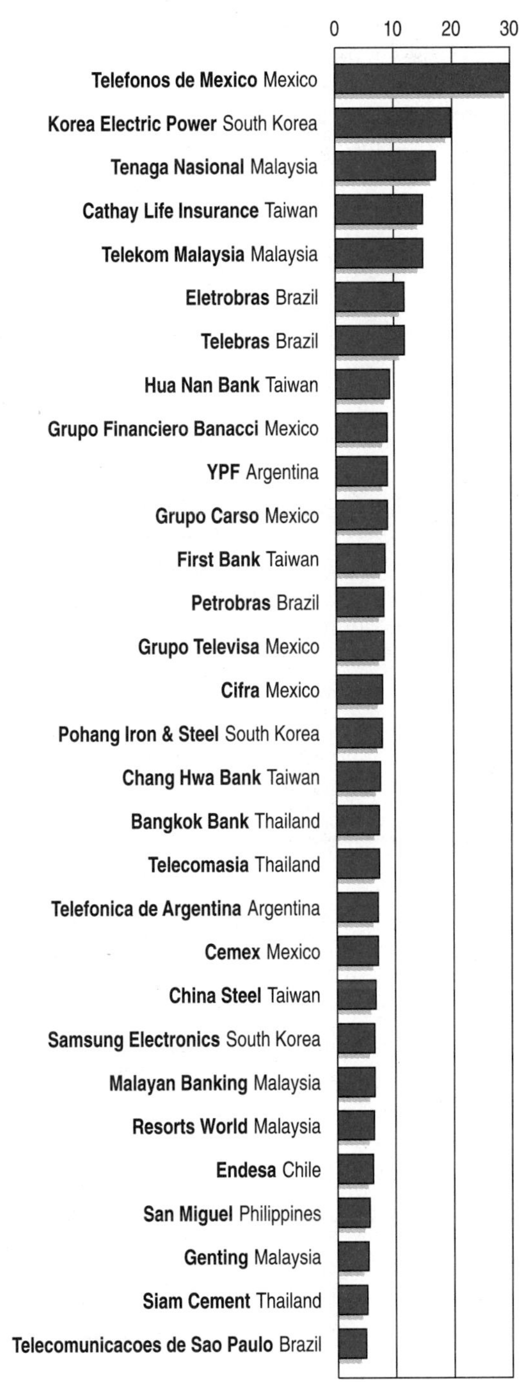

SOURCE: *The Economist,* July 16, 1994.

The purpose of many privatization programs is to improve productivity, profitability, and product quality and to shrink the size of government. It is expected that as companies are exposed to market forces and competition, they will have to produce better goods at lower costs. In most instances, privatization also intends to attract new capital for these firms so that they can carry out necessary adjustments and improvements. Since local capital is often scarce, and government budgets tight, privatization efforts increasingly aim at attracting foreign capital. Therefore, the trend toward privatization offers unique opportunities for international managers. Existing firms, both large and small, can be acquired at low cost, often with governmental support through tax exemptions, investment grants, special depreciation allowances, and low interest rate credits. The purchase of such firms enables the international firm to expand operations without having to start from scratch. In addition, since wages are often low in the countries where privatization takes place, there is a major opportunity to build low-cost manufacturing and sourcing bases. Furthermore, the international firm can also act as a catalyst by accelerating the price of transferring business skills and technology and by boosting trade prospects. In short, the very process of change offers new opportunities to the adept manager.

SUMMARY

Economic integration involves agreements among countries to establish links through the movements of goods, services, and factors of production across borders. These links may be weak or strong depending on the level of integration. Levels of integration include the free trade area, customs union, common market, and full economic union.

The benefits derived from economic integration include trade creation, economies of scale, improved terms of trade, the reduction of monopoly power, and improved cross-cultural communication. However, a number of disadvantages may also exist. Most importantly, economic integration may work to the detriment of nonmembers by causing deteriorating terms of trade and trade diversion. In addition, no guarantee exists that all members will share the gains from integration. The biggest impediment to economic integration is nationalism. There is strong resistance to surrendering autonomy and self-determinism to cooperative agreements.

The most successful example of economic integration is the European Union. The EU has succeeded in eliminating most barriers to the free flow of goods, services, and factors of production. In addition, the EU has made progress toward the evolution of a common currency and central bank, which are fundamental requirements of an economic union. In the Americas, NAFTA is paving the way for a hemispheric trade bloc.

A number of regional economic alliances exist in Africa, Latin America, and Asia, but they have achieved only low levels of integration. Political difficulties, low levels of development, and problems with cohesiveness have impeded integrative progress among many developing countries. However, many nations in these areas are seeing economic integration as the only way to prosperity in the future.

In the emerging market economies, the key to international business success will be an understanding of the fact that societies in transition require special adaptation of business skills and time to complete the transformation. It must also be recognized that the changes in these economies will in turn precipitate changes in the West, particularly in the trade sector. Adapting early to these changes can offer new opportunities to the international firm.

The current global trend toward privatization offers new opportunities to the international firm, either through investment or by offering business skills and knowledge to assist in the success of privatization.

Key Terms and Concepts

- trading blocs
- European Social Charter
- free trade area
- customs union
- common market
- Single European Act
- economic union
- harmonize
- trade creation
- trade diversion
- internal economies of scale
- external economies of scale
- common agricultural policy (CAP)
- economic and monetary union (EMU)
- Maastricht Agreement
- Fortress Europe
- maquiladoras
- import substitution
- Andean Trade Preference Act
- cartel
- commodity price agreement
- buffer stock
- privatization

Questions for Discussion

1. Explain the difference between a free trade area and a customs union.
2. What problems might a member country of a common market be concerned about?
3. What are the main provisions of the Single Europe Act?
4. How can U.S. consumer acceptance of Russian products be improved?
5. How can and should the West help Eastern European countries?
6. How can Central European managers be trained to be market oriented?
7. Where do you see the greatest potential in future trade between emerging market economies and the West?
8. What are the benefits of privatization?

Recommend Readings

Boecker, Paul M., ed. *Latin America's Turnaround: The Paths to Privatization and Foreign Investment.* San Francisco: ICS Press, 1993.

Buiter, William, and Richard Marston. *International Economic Policy Coordination.* Cambridge, England: Cambridge University Press, 1987.

Cooper, Richard. *Economic Policy in an Interdependent World.* Cambridge, Mass.: MIT Press, 1987.

Czinkota, Michael. "The EC '92 and Eastern Europe: Effects of Integration vs. Disintegration." *Columbia Journal of World Business* 26, no. 1 (1991): 20–27.

Dobek, Mariusz. *The Political Logic of Privatization: Lessons from Great Britain and Poland.* Westport, Conn.: Greenwood/Praeger, 1993.

Fogel, Daniel S. *Managing in Emerging Market Economies: Cases from the Czech and Slovak Republics.* Boulder, Colo.: Westview Press, 1994.

Hachette, Dominique, and Rolf Luders. *Privatization in Chile: An Economic Appraisal.* San Francisco: ICS Press, 1992.

Lardy, Nicholas R. *China in the World Economy.* Washington, D.C.: Institute for International Economics, 1994.

Puffer, Sheila M., ed., *The Russian Management Revolution.* Armonk, N.Y.: M.E. Sharpe, 1992.

Ryans, John K., Jr., and Pradeep A. Rau. *Marketing Strategies for the New Europe: A North American Perspective on 1992.* Chicago, Ill.: American Marketing Association, 1990.

Sapir, André, and Alexis Jacquemin, eds. *The European Internal Market.* Oxford, England: Oxford University Press, 1990.

Stoeckel, Andrew, David Pearce, and Gary Banks. *Western Trade Blocs.* Canberra, Australia: Centre for International Economics, 1990.

Suriyamongkol, Marjorie L. *Politics of ASEAN Economic Cooperation.* Oxford, England: Oxford University Press, 1988.

Notes

1. The discussion of economic integration is based on the pioneering work by Bela Balassa, *The Theory of Economic Integration* (Homewood, Ill.: Richard D. Irwin, 1961).
2. J. Waelbroeck, "Measuring Degrees of Progress in Economic Integration," in *Economic Integration, Worldwide, Regional, Sectoral,* ed. F. Machlop (London: Macmillan, 1980).
3. Various aspects of the 1992 Common Market are addressed in André Sapir and Alexis Jacquemin, eds., *The European Internal Market* (Oxford, England: Oxford University Press, 1990).
4. Economic growth effects are discussed in Richard Baldwin, "The Growth Effects of 1992," *Economic Policy* (October 1989): 248–281; or Rudiger Dornbusch, "Europe 1992: Macroeconomic Implications," *Brookings Papers on Economic Activity* 2 (1989): 341–362.
5. John F. Magee, "1992: Moves Americans Must Make," *Harvard Business Review* 67 (May–June 1989): 72–84.
6. Richard I. Kirkland, "Outsider's Guide to Europe in 1992," *Fortune,* October 24, 1988, 121–127.
7. "Should Small U.S. Exporters Take the Plunge?" *Business Week,* November 14, 1988, 64–68.
8. See *The Likely Impact on the United States of a Free Trade Agreement with Mexico* (Washington, D.C.: United States International Trade Commission, 1991).
9. J. Sterngold, "NAFTA Trade-Off: Some Jobs Lost, Others Gained," *New York Times,* October 9, 1995, A-1.
10. U.S. Department of Commerce, Office of NAFTA, Document #8312, p 4.
11. U.S. Department of Commerce. Office of NAFTA, Document #8313, p 7.
12. J. Brooke, "The New South Americans: Friends and Partners," *New York Times,* April 8, 1994.
13. J. Brooke, "More Open Latin Borders Mirror an Opening of Markets," *New York Times,* July 4, 1995, 47.
14. *The Economist,* February 17, 1996, 40.
15. J. Brooke, "Building a Railroad Deep into Brazil," *New York Times,* January 19, 1995, D-1.
16. Organization of American States, Foreign Trade Information System (SICE), March 17, 1997.
17. P. Passell, "Trade Pack by Regions: Not the Elixir As Advertised," *New York Times,* February 4, 1997, D1.
18. C. Wren, "U.S. Sours on Flowers from the Andes," *New York Times,* February 17, 1997, 8.
19. "In the Middle of It All," *World Trade,* August 1996, 72–76.
20. Emily Thornton, "Will Japan Rule a New Trade Bloc?" *Fortune,* October 5, 1992, 131–132.
21. Paul Krugman, "A Global Economy Is Not the Wave of the Future," *Financial Executive* 8 (March/April 1992): 10–13.
22. Richard M. Hammer, "Dramatic Winds of Change," *Price Waterhouse Review* 33 (1989): 23–27.
23. Peter G. Lauter and Paul M. Dickie, "Multinational Corporations in Eastern European Socialist Economies," *Journal of Marketing* 25 (Fall 1975): 40–46.
24. Alan B. Sherr, "Joint Ventures in the USSR: Soviet and Western Interests with Considerations for Negotiations," *Columbia Journal of World Business* 23 (Summer 1988): 25–37.
25. *The World Factbook 1992* (Washington, D.C.: Central Intelligence Agency, 1992).
26. Johny K. Johansson, *Marketing, Free Choice and the New International Order* (Washington, D.C.: Georgetown University, March 2, 1990), 10.
27. Mihaly Simai, *East-West Cooperation at the End of the 1980s: Global Issues, Foreign Direct Investments, and Debts* (Budapest: Hungarian Scientific Council for World Economy, 1989), 21.
28. Jerry F. Hough, *Opening Up the Soviet Economy* (Washington, D.C.: The Brookings Institution, 1988), 46.
29. Janet Porter, "Western Consultants Benefit as Soviets Restructure Business," *The Journal of Commerce* (July 12, 1988): 1A, 3A.
30. John W. Kiser, "Tapping Soviet Technology," in *Common Sense in U.S.-Soviet Trade,* eds. M. Chapman and C. March (Washington, D.C.: American Committee on East-West Accord, 1983), 104.
31. Robert D. Hisrich, Michael P. Peters, and Arnold K. Weinstein, "East-West Trade: The View from the United States," *Journal of International Business Studies* 12 (Winter 1981): 109–121.
32. "Owners Are the Only Answer," *The Economist,* September 21, 1991, 10.

National Trade and Investment Policies

LEARNING OBJECTIVES

To see how trade and investment policies have historically been a subset of domestic policies.

To examine how historical attitudes toward trade and investment policies are changing.

To see how global linkages in trade and investment have made policymakers less able to focus solely on domestic issues.

To understand the various types of trade barriers that can restrict imports.

Can California Rice Stick in Japan?

A bad summer reduced the 1993 Japanese rice harvest, so Japan was forced to import foreign rice. Now the government wants to make sure that imports do not undermine the market for domestic rice, and that Japanese consumers will keep buying subsidized, expensive Japanese rice.

The new rice accord under GATT rules out import quotas or other barriers. Therefore, Japan's Ministry of Agriculture has designed a more subtle means to maintain control of the market. Hiding behind a superficial argument of "national equality," the ministry announced in early 1994 that no specific rice could be sold separately. All rice—domestic and imported—had to be mixed, so that the resulting rice does not have a "nationality." The directive prescribed a mix formula of 30 percent Japanese; 50 percent Californian, Chinese, and Australian combined; and 20 percent Thai rice.

Different rices have different uses. For instance, the Californian variety works well when steaming while the Chinese or Thai variety are needed for a Chinese dish and the Japanese goes very well with sushi. As no doubt was intended, the resultant nationless rice was appalling. You simply cannot steam a Californian/Thai mix.

The ministry's thinking: Given a choice, every Japanese in his right mind would buy the homegrown, nonmixed product as soon as it hit the market again. There would be no need for import quotas or other nontariff barriers. While the initial reaction to the mixed rice policy was what the ministry was looking for, it wasn't long before outrage over the restricting policies grew so strong that retailers were able to ignore the mixing directive without fearing ministry action. It had become clear that the citizens had sufficiently disliked Thai rice and had not developed a taste for Chinese rice either, thus the ministry declared that foreign rice could now be sold just by itself—with one exception. The most popular of all imports, the sticky Californian rice, still could not be sold in its pure form. It is mixed with rice from other states and sold under the name "American." The official reason for this mixing is that there is not enough Californian rice for everyone. But retailers openly admit that the rice is mixed in order to lower its quality, so that they can also sell the less popular Chinese and Thai grains.

In addition to being the object of this quality-reducing policy, the "American" mix is subject to a 580 percent tariff, which makes it exactly as expensive as medium-quality Japanese rice ($15 a pound), thereby removing any price advantage. The Japanese government is expected to take in revenues of $2.7 billion from its rice-import tariffs. The revenue is used to subsidize Japanese rice farmers and improve their irrigation systems. The idea is that as the new GATT "minimum-access rule" kicks in over a seven-year period beginning in 1995, Japanese farmers will become price competitive.

SOURCE: Ulrike Schaede, "Japan Rice Move Leaves 'Em Steaming." *The Wall Street Journal,* June 1, 1994, A14.

Chapter 6 discusses the policy actions taken by countries. All nations have international trade and investment policies. These policies may be publicly pronounced or kept secret, they may be disjointed or coordinated, they may be applied consciously or determined by a hands-off attitude. In any case, they come into play when measures taken by governments affect the flow of trade and investment across national borders. As the Global Learning Experience 6.1 illustrates, nations can and will target their actions to achieve particular policy goals. In this instance, U.S. exports of rice to Japan were clearly the target.

RATIONALE AND GOALS OF TRADE AND INVESTMENT POLICIES

national sovereignty
provides a government with the right and burden to shape the environment of the country and its citizens

Government policies are designed to regulate, stimulate, direct, and protect national activities. The exercise of these policies is the result of **national sovereignty,** which provides a government with the right and burden to shape the environment of the country and its citizens. Because they are "border bound," governments focus mainly on domestic policies. Most actions taken, even if they have an international impact, are a subset of domestic policies. Nevertheless, many policy actions have repercussions on other nations, firms, and individuals abroad and are therefore a component of a nation's trade and investment policy.

Government policy can be divided into two groups of policy actions that affect international trade and investment:

Indirect—A government's domestic policy that has the side effect of influencing its foreign trade and investment situations.

Direct—A government's policy action that is specifically intended to influence its foreign trade and investment situation.

standard of living
level of material affluence of a group or nation, measured as a composite of quantities and qualities of goods

quality of life
standard of living combined with environmental factors, it determines the level of well-being of individuals

The domestic policy actions of most governments aim to increase—or at least maintain—the **standard of living** of the country's citizens; maintain or improve the **quality of life;** stimulate national development; and achieve full employment. Clearly, all of these goals are closely intertwined. An improved standard of living is likely to contribute to national development. Similarly, quality of life and standard of living are closely interlinked. Also, a high level of employment will play a major role in determining the standard of living. Yet all of these policy goals will also have international impact. For example, if foreign industries become more competitive and rapidly increase their exports, employment in the importing countries may suffer. Likewise, if a country accumulates large quantities of debt, which at some time must be repaid, the present and future standard of living will be threatened.

A country may also pursue policies of increased development that mandate either technology transfer from abroad or the exclusion of foreign industries to the benefit of domestic infant firms. Also, government officials may believe that imports threaten the culture, health, or standards of the country's citizens and thus the quality of life. As a result, officials are likely to develop regulations to protect the citizens.

foreign policy
area of public policy concerned with relationships with other countries

In more direct ways, nations institute **foreign policy** measures. They are designed with domestic concerns in mind but explicitly aim to exercise influence abroad. One major goal of foreign policy measures is often national security. For example, nations may develop alliances, coalitions, and agreements in order to protect their borders or their spheres of interest. Similarly, nations may take measures to enhance their national security preparedness in case of international conflict. Governments also wish to improve trade and investment opportunities and to contribute to the security and safety of their own firms abroad.

All of these policy aims may be approached in various ways. In order to develop new markets abroad and to increase their sphere of influence, nations may give foreign aid to other countries. This was the case when the United States generously awarded Marshall Plan funds for the reconstruction of Europe. Similarly, Japan provides development aid to nations in Asia. Governments may also feel a need to restrict or encourage trade and investment flows in order to preserve or enhance the capability of industries that are important to national security.

Not all of these measures necessarily work in favor of global trade and investment flows. Some argue, for example, that foreign policy concerns of the United States have led to consistently destructive trade-offs in U.S. trade policy. They point out that the U.S. government frequently accommodates or even bails out foreign nations for foreign policy purposes and this in turn results in detrimental repercussions for U.S. producers and workers.[1] U.S. willingness to permit Chinese textile imports is often cited as an example, even though the Chinese government may feel that its exports are strangled by U.S. quotas.

Because each country develops its own domestic policies, policy aims will vary from nation to nation. Inevitably, conflicts arise. Full employment policies in one country may directly affect employment policies in another. Similarly, the development aims of one country may reduce the development capability of another. Even when health issues are concerned, disputes may arise. One nation may argue that its regulations are in place to protect its citizens, whereas other nations may interpret these regulations as market barriers. An example for the latter situation is the celebrated hormone dispute between the United States and the European Union. U.S. cattle are treated with growth hormones. While the United States claims that these hormones are harmless to humans, many Europeans find them scary. Given these differences in perspectives, there is much room for conflict when it comes to trade policies, particularly when the United States wants to export more beef and the European Union attempts to restrict such beef imports.[2]

Conflicts among nations are also likely to emerge when foreign policy goals lead to trade and investment measures. Such conflicts can even involve international aid. For example, because of its vast current account surplus, Japan is able to grant generous **developmental aid** to countries in Asia. While few governments would criticize altruistic aid, many of them dispute the use of aid funds for purposes of trade distortions. Japanese aid payments are seen as linked to the purchases of Japanese products. Even if such linkages are not overt, the simple fact that Japanese engineers and designers may assess a project and contribute to its development can have major repercussions on trade flows. The reason is that the design determines the specifications of machines, computers, and materials that will be purchased. Obviously, if influences in the design phase come from only one nation, they will provide significant direction for future purchases.

developmental aid
international aid to developing countries

Conflicts among national policies have always existed but have only recently come to prominence. The reason lies in the changes that have taken place in the world trade and investment climate. A brief review of the global developments that led to the current environment will be useful here.

GLOBAL DEVELOPMENTS SINCE WORLD WAR II

The **General Agreement on Tariffs and Trade (GATT)** has been called a "remarkable success story of a postwar international organization that was never intended to become one."[3] It started out in 1947 as a set of rules to ensure nondiscrimination, clear procedures, the settlement of disputes, and the participation of the lesser developed countries in international trade. The main tools GATT used to increase trade consist of tariff concessions, through which member countries agree to limit the level of tariffs they will impose on imports from other GATT members, and the **most favored nation (MFN)** clause, which calls for each member country to grant every other member country the most favorable treatment it accords to any country with respect to imports and exports.[4]

General Agreement on Tariffs and Trade (GATT)
international code of tariffs and trade rules signed by 23 nations in 1947; headquartered in Geneva, Switzerland; 99 members currently

most favored nation (MFN)
term describing a GATT clause that calls for member countries to grant other member countries the most favorable treatment they accord any country concerning imports and exports

QUESTION *What is today's temperature in Quito, Ecuador?*

ANSWER *The temperature in Quito today is probably 69–71 degrees F. This is interesting because temperatures vary widely in most places on Earth, and Quito is one of those unusual spots where it does not. The explanation: Quito is at 9,300 ft. and only eight miles south of the Equator. High-altitude equatorial settings have much the same weather every day.*

The GATT was not originally intended to be an international organization but slowly became the governing body for settling international trade disputes. Gradually it evolved into an institution that sponsored various successful rounds of international trade negotiations. Headquartered in Geneva, Switzerland, the GATT Secretariat conducted work as instructed by the representatives of its member nations. Even though the GATT had no independent enforcement mechanism, it relied entirely on moral suasion and on frequently wavering membership adherence to its rules and in the process, achieved major progress for world trade.

Early in its history, the GATT achieved the reduction of duties for trade in 50,000 products, amounting to two-thirds of the value of the trade among its participants.[5] In subsequent years, special GATT negotiations such as the Kennedy Round, named after John Kennedy, and the Tokyo Round, named after the location where the negotiations were agreed upon, further reduced trade barriers and improved dispute-settlement mechanisms. The GATT also developed better provisions for dealing with subsidies and more explicit definitions of roles for import controls. Table 6.1 provides an overview of the different GATT rounds.

The latest GATT negotiations, called the Uruguay Round, were initiated in 1987. Even though tariffs still were addressed in these negotiations, their importance had been greatly diminished due to the success of earlier agreements. The main thrust of negotiations had become the sharpening of dispute-settlement rules and the integration of the trade and investment areas that were outside of the GATT. Several key areas addressed were nontariff barriers, trade in textiles, agriculture and services, intellectual property rights, and trade-related investment measures.

TABLE 6.1 **Negotiations in the GATT**

Round	Dates	Number of Countries	Value of Trade Covered	Average Tariff Cut	Average Tariffs Afterward
Geneva	1947	23	$10 billion	35%	n/a
Annecy	1949	33	Unavailable	—	n/a
Torquay	1950	34	Unavailable	—	n/a
Geneva	1956	22	$2.5 billion	—	n/a
Dillon	1960–1961	45	$4.9 billion	—	n/a
Kennedy	1962–1967	48	$40 billion	35%	8.7%
Tokyo	1973–1979	99	$155 billion	34%	4.7%
Uruguay	1986–1994	124	$300 billion	38%	3.9%

SOURCES: John H. Jackson, *The World Trading System* (Cambridge, Mass: MIT Press, 1989), and *The GATT: Uruguay Round Final Act Should Produce Overall U.S. Economic Gains,* U.S. General Accounting Office, Report to Congress, Washington, D.C., July 1994.

After many years of often contentious negotiations, a new accord was finally ratified in early 1995. As part of this ratification, the GATT was supplanted by a new institution, the **World Trade Organization (WTO),** which now administers international trade and investment accords. The accords have brought major change to the world trade and investment environment. They will gradually reduce governmental subsidies to industries and will convert nontariff barriers into more transparent tariff barriers. The textile and clothing industries eventually will be brought into the WTO regime, resulting in decreased subsidies and fewer market restrictions. An entirely new set of rules was designed to govern the service area, and agreement also was reached on new rules to encourage international investment flows.

World Trade Organization (WTO)
established on January 1, 1995; the legal and institutional foundation of the multilateral trading system

The GATT and now the WTO have made major contributions to improved trade and investment flows around the world. The latest round alone is predicted to increase global exports by more than $755 billion by the year 2002.[6] It has not been just the industrialized nations that benefited from trade liberalization, but developing countries as well.

The success of GATT and the resulting increase in welfare, particularly in the Western nations, has refuted the old postulate that "the strong is most powerful alone." Nations have increasingly come to recognize that global trade and investment activities are important to their own economic well-being.

Nations have also come to accept that they must generate sufficient outgoing export and investment activities to compensate for the inflow of imports and investment taking place. In the medium and long term, the balance of payments must be maintained. For short periods of time, gold or capital transfers can be used to finance a deficit. Such financing, however, can continue only while gold and foreign assets last or while foreign countries will accept the IOUs of the deficit countries, permitting them to pile up foreign liabilities.[7] This willingness, of course, will vary. Some countries, such as the United States, can run up deficits of hundreds of billions of dollars because of political stability, acceptable rates of return, and perceived economic security. Yet over the long term, all nations are subject to the same economic rules.

CHANGES IN THE GLOBAL POLICY ENVIRONMENT

Three major changes have occurred over time in the global policy environment: (1) a reduction of domestic policy influence; (2) a weakening of traditional global institutions; and (3) a sharpening of the conflict between industrialized and developing nations. These three changes in turn have had a major effect on global trade and foreign investment policies.

Reduction of Domestic Policy Influences

The effects of growing global linkages on the U.S. economy have been significant. Policymakers have increasingly come to recognize that it is very difficult to isolate domestic economic activity from global market events. Again and again, domestic policy measures are vetoed or counteracted by the activities of global market forces. Decisions that were once clearly in the domestic area now have to be revised due to influences from abroad. Occasionally, one can even see how global factors begin to shape or direct domestic economic policy.

Agricultural policies, for example—historically a major domestic issue—have been thrust into the global realm. Any industrial policy consideration must now be seen in light of global repercussions due to increased reliance on trade. The following examples highlight the penetration of U.S. society by foreign trade considerations:

- One of every four U.S. farm acres is producing for export.
- One of every six U.S. manufacturing jobs is producing for export.
- One of every seven dollars of U.S. sales is to someone abroad.
- One of every three cars, nine of every ten television sets, two of every three suits, and every video recorder sold in the United States is imported.
- One of every four dollars' worth of U.S. bonds and notes is issued to foreigners.[8]

currency flows
flows of currency from nation to nations, which in turn determine exchange rates

To some extent, the economic world as we knew it has been turned upside down. For example, trade flows are used to determine currency flows and therefore the exchange rate. In the more recent past, **currency flows** took on a life of their own, increasing from an average daily foreign exchange trading volume of $18 billion in 1980 to $1,260 billion in 1995. As a result, they have begun to set the value of exchange rates independent of trade. These exchange rates in turn have now begun to determine the level of trade. Governments that wish to counteract these developments with monetary policies find that currency flows outnumber trade flows by ten to one. Also, private-sector financial flows vastly outnumber the financial flows that can be marshaled by governments, even when acting in concert. Financial flows influence interest rates, and interest rates are increasingly determined by the activity of international financial markets, not by governmental financial institutions. Similarly, constant, rapid technological change and vast advances in communication permit firms and countries to quickly emulate innovation and counteract carefully designed plans. As a result, governments are often powerless to implement effective policy measures, even when they know what to do.

Governments also find that domestic regulations, which used to be established and implemented without regard for international effects, often have major international repercussions for domestic firms and industries. In the United States, the breakup of AT&T resulted in significant changes in the purchasing practices of the newly formed Bell companies. Overnight, competitive bids became decisive in a process that previously was entirely within the firm. This change opened up the U.S. market for foreign suppliers of telecommunications equipment, with only limited commensurate market developments abroad for U.S. firms. Similarly, policy measures, such as grazing rights on federal lands or subsidized water prices in dryland areas, which may appear to be only domestically focused, may bring counteraction from other nations.[9]

Throughout the world, legislation has a profound impact on the ability of firms to compete abroad. Legislators often ignore the side effects in the global marketplace because countries view it as their sovereign right to set domestic policies. Yet given the linkages between economies, this is an unwarranted and often dangerous view. It threatens to place firms at a competitive disadvantage in the global marketplace and may make it easier for foreign firms to compete in the domestic market. Trade policy changes can also assist in revitalizing industries. As Global Learning Experience 6.2 shows, the lessening of import restrictions in Brazil has been instrumental in the development of a competitive Brazilian automotive industry.

punitive tariffs
tax on an imported good or service intended to punish a trading partner

Even when policymakers want to take decisive steps, they are often unable to do so. In the late 1980s, the United States decided to impose **punitive tariffs** of 100 percent on selected Japanese imports to retaliate for Japanese nonadherence to a previously reached semiconductor agreement. The initial goal was clear. Yet the task became increasingly difficult as the U.S. government identified specific imports as targets. In many instances, the U.S. market was heavily dependent on the Japanese imports, which meant that U.S. manufacturers and consumers would be severely affected by the higher tariffs, as the cost of everything they imported from Japan would increase. As Figure 6.1 shows, many Japanese products are actually assembled in the United States. To halt the importing of components would throw Americans out of work.

GLOBAL LEARNING EXPERIENCE 6.2

Brazilian Policy Shifts Change the Auto Industry

Brazil's auto industry, Latin America's biggest industrial complex, was dead to the world in the 1980s. Once the symbol of the "Brazilian miracle" of the 1970s, the auto industry had become emblematic of Latin America's "lost decade" of the 1980s. A ban on imports meant that technological innovations passed the industry by, and consumers had no choices. A 1991 study by James P. Womack, of MIT, found that Brazil had "by far the oldest mix of products assembled anywhere in the world." Quality was the second worse and productivity took the prize for the lowest anywhere.

In 1994, the industry was booming. Production rose nearly 30 percent to 1.39 million units. Brazil had overtaken Italy and Mexico as the tenth largest auto producer in the world. The president of General Motors do Brasil believes the nation has the potential to crack the top five. Another industry executive envisions a car market of 5 million units by 2015, a market comparable to the United States, Europe, or Japan.

The turnaround began with President Fernando Collor de Mello, who called Brazilian-made cars "horse carts" when he replaced the ban in imports with a 35 percent duty. He also repealed the ban on imports of electronic goods, allowing cars to be equipped with such items as electronic fuel injection and digital clocks. Robots were put on some production lines.

Production is drastically changing in the wake of the country's policy shifts. General Motors do Brasil used to need about three years to develop a car. The Corsa model, launched in 1994, took 17 months. This quicker turnaround was possible in part because of trade liberalization. Previously, import restrictions forced GM to develop virtually all of the parts locally. The Corsa has only 70 percent of its parts locally made. While the earlier Chevette was made without a single robot and took 30 man-hours to assemble, the Corsa can now be made with 62 robots, imported from Japan and Sweden, and takes 22 man-hours. "The Corsa is a turning point for GM and for the industry," said an auto analyst. "It's the first car launched in Brazil almost at the same time as in the First World." There has also been a major effect on production quantity. GM has put out as many cars since 1992 as it did in the two preceding decades.

"This is a revolution; the industry is reinventing itself," said Pierre-Alain de Smedt, the president of Autolatina, the Latin American joint venture between Volkswagen AG and Ford Motor Co. But without the adjustment in the nation's trade policies, this revolution could never have developed.

SOURCE: Thomas Kamm, "Pedal to the Metal: Brazil Swiftly Becomes Major Auto Producer As Trade Policy Shifts," *The Wall Street Journal,* April 20, 1994, A1.

Other targeted products were not actually produced in Japan. Rather, Japanese firms had opened plants in third countries, such as Mexico. Penalizing these product imports would therefore punish Mexican workers and affect Mexican employment, an undesirable result.

More and more products were eliminated from the list before it was published. In two days of hearings, additional problems emerged. For example, law enforcement agencies testified that if certain fingerprinting equipment from Japan were subjected to the higher tariffs, law enforcement efforts would suffer significantly. Of the $1.8 billion worth of products initially considered for the higher tariff list, the government was

FIGURE 6.1 **Examples of Japanese Products Assembled in the United States**

barely able to scrape together $300 million worth. With so many product components being sourced from different countries around the world, it becomes increasingly difficult to decide what constitutes a domestic product.

Policymakers find themselves with increasing responsibilities, yet with fewer and less effective tools to carry them out. More segments of the domestic economy are vulnerable to global shifts at the same time that they are becoming less controllable. To regain some power to influence policies, some governments have sought to restrict the influence of world trade by erecting barriers, charging tariffs, and implementing import regulations. However, these measures too have been restrained by the existence of global agreements forged through institutions such as the GATT or bilateral negotiations. World trade has therefore changed many previously held notions about the sovereignty of nation-states and extraterritoriality. The same interdependence that made us all more affluent has left us more vulnerable.

Weakening of Traditional Global Institutions

nontariff barriers
barriers to trade, other than tariffs; examples include buy-domestic campaigns, preferential treatment for domestic bidders, and restrictions on market entry of foreign products such as involved inspection procedures

The intense linkages among nations and the new economic environment resulting from new market entrants and the encounter of different economic systems are weakening the traditional international institutions, and are therefore affecting their roles.

The ratification of the Uruguay Round and the formation of the WTO have provided the former GATT with new impetus. However, the organization is confronted with many difficulties. One of them is the result of the organization's success. Historically, a key focus of the WTO's predecessor was on reducing tariffs. With tariff levels at an unprecedented low level, however, attention now has to rest with areas such as **nontariff**

barriers, which are much more complex and indigenous to nations. In consequence, any emerging dispute is likely to be more heatedly contested and more difficult to resolve. A second traditional focus rested with the right to establishment in countries. Given today's technology, however, the issue has changed. Increasingly, firms will clamor for the right to operations in a country without seeking to establish themselves there. For example, given the opportunities offered by telecommunications, one can envision a bank becoming active in a country without a single office or branch.

Another key problem area results from the fact that many disagreements were set aside for the sake of concluding the negotiations. Disputes in such areas as entertainment, financial services, and intellectual property rights protection are likely to resurface in the near term and cause a series of trade conflicts among nations. If the WTO's dispute settlement mechanism is then applied to resolve the conflict, outcries in favor of national sovereignty may cause nations to withdraw from the agreement.

A final major weakness of the WTO may result from the desire of some of its members to introduce "social causes" into trade decisions. It is debated, for example, whether the WTO should also deal with issues such as labor laws, competition, and emigration freedoms. Other issues, such as freedom of religion, provision of health care, and the safety of animals are being raised as well. It will be very difficult to have the WTO remain a viable organization if too many nongermane issues are loaded onto the trade and investment mission. The 131 governments participating in the WTO have diverse perspectives, histories, relations, economies, and ambitions. Many of them fear that social causes can be used to devise new rules of protectionism against their exports. Then there is also the question as to how much companies—which, after all, are the ones doing the trading and investing—should be burdened with concerns outside of their scope.

To be successful, the WTO needs to be able to focus on its core mission, which deals with international trade and investment. The addition of social causes may appear politically expedient, but will be a key cause for divisiveness and dissent, and thus will inhibit progress on further liberalization of trade and investment. Failure to achieve such progress would leave the WTO without teeth and would negate much of the progress achieved in the Uruguay Round negotiations. It might be best to leave the WTO free from such pressures and look to increased economic ties to cross-pollinate cultures, values and ethics and to cause changes in the social arena.[10]

Similar problems have befallen international financial institutions. For example, although the IMF has functioned well so far, it is currently under severe challenge by the substantial financial requirements of less-developed countries and new entrants in world capital markets from the former Soviet bloc. So far, the IMF has been able to smooth over the most difficult problems, but has not found ways to solve them. For example, in the 1995 peso crisis of Mexico, the IMF was able to provide some relief through a stand-by credit. Yet, given the financial needs of many other nations such as Russia, the nations of central Europe, and many countries in Latin America, the IMF simply does not have enough funds to satisfy such needs. In case of multiple financial crises, it then is unable to provide its traditional function of calming financial markets in turmoil. Even the increase in capitalization agreed to in June of 1995 offers more of a temporary than a permanent solution.

Apart from its ability to provide funds, the IMF must also rethink its traditional rules of operations. For example, it is quite unclear whether stringent economic

QUESTION *There are two ice caps on Earth. Where are they?*

The world's two ice caps are in Greenland and Antarctica. The ice there may be more than ten thousand feet thick.

rules and benchmark performance measures are equally applicable to all countries seeking IMF assistance. New economic conditions that have not been experienced to date, such as the privatization of formerly centrally planned economies, may require different types of approaches. The linkage between economic and political stability also may require different considerations, possibly substantially changing the IMF's mission.

Similarly, the World Bank successfully met its goal of aiding the reconstruction of Europe but has been less successful in furthering the economic goals of the developing world and the newly emerging market economies in the former Soviet bloc. Therefore, at the same time when domestic policy measures have become less effective, international institutions that could help to develop substitute international policy measures have been weakened by new challenges to their traditional missions and insufficient resources to meet such challenges.

Sharpening of the Conflict between Industrialized and Developing Nations

In the 1960s and 1970s, it was hoped that the developmental gap between industrialized nations and many countries in the less developed world could gradually be closed. This goal was to be achieved with the transfer of technology and the infusion of major funds. Even though the 1970s saw vast quantities of petrodollars available for recycling and major growth in the borrowing by some developing nations, the results have not been as expected. Since the Mexican debt crisis of 1982, the Western world has recognized that the goals envisioned have not been achieved. Even though several less developed nations have gradually emerged as newly industrialized countries (NICs), even more nations are faced with a grim economic future.

Particularly in Latin America, nations such as Argentina and Brazil are saddled with enormous amounts of debt, rapidly increasing populations, and very fragile economies (See Figure 4.7 in Chapter 4.) The newly emerging democracies in Central Europe and the former Soviet Union also face major debt and employment problems. In view of their shattered dreams, policymakers in these nations have become increasingly aggressive in their attempts to reshape the ground rules of the world trade and investment flows. Even though many other nations share the view that major changes are necessary to resolve the difficulties that exist, no clear-cut solutions have emerged.

Lately, an increase in environmental awareness has contributed to a further sharpening of the conflict. As Global Learning Experience 6.3 shows, developing countries may place different emphasis on environmental protection. If they are to take measures that will assist the industrialized nations in their environmental goals, they expect to be assisted and rewarded in these efforts. Yet many in the industrialized world view environmental issues as "global obligation," rather than as a matter of choice.

POLICY RESPONSES TO CHANGING CONDITIONS

The word *policy* conjures up an image of a well-coordinated set of governmental activities. Unfortunately, in the trade and investment sector, as in most of the domestic

GLOBAL LEARNING EXPERIENCE

6.3

Major Industrialized Nations Give Global Warming the Cold Shoulder

Global warming was put at the top of an international agenda at the Earth Summit in Rio in 1992, in an effort to save the planet from greenhouse gas emissions. Five years later (June 1997) at Earth Summit + 5, global warming still topped the agenda with little progress achieved toward the goal of reducing emissions to 1990 levels by the year 2000.

At both of these summits, two points of view were evident. The developing nations essentially want money (a reduction in debt) and technology. The industrialized nations want to reduce greenhouse gases and conserve ecologically critical resources such as rain forests. The main problems seem to revolve around major industries of the industrialized countries that are heavy users of fossil fuels like coal and oil. A sudden change in energy usage could have serious implications for their global competitiveness as well as the jobs of the large numbers of workers they employ.

A second major sticking point is the idea of giving financial aid to developing nations "to support energy efficiency, develop alternative energy sources, and improve resource management to promote growth that does not have an adverse effect on the climate." Given the financial problems and high unemployment rates of the European countries, it is doubtful if the already resentful European voters would be happy to stay unemployed so that billions of dollars could be given to foreign governments, thousands of miles away, to ostensibly save a rain forest.

SOURCE: The U.N. conference on the environment was held in New York, June 23 through June 27, 1997, and was widely covered by the media—no one source is clearly identifiable.

SOURCE: *The New York Times* Op-Ed Section, Friday, June 27, 1997, p. A29.

policy areas, this is rarely the case. Policymakers need to respond too often to short-term problems, need to worry too much about what is politically salable to multiple constituencies, and in some countries, are in office too short a time to formulate a guiding set of long-term strategies. All too often, because of public and media pressures, policymakers must be concerned with current events—such as monthly trade deficit numbers and investment flow figures—that may not be very meaningful in the larger picture. In such an environment, actions may lead to extraordinarily good tactical measures but fail to achieve long-term realignments.

Policy responses in the foreign trade and investment area tend to consist mainly of political quick-fix reactions, which over the years have changed from concern to protectionism. This is particularly true in the United States. While in the mid-1970s most lawmakers and administration officials simply regretted the poor U.S. performance in global markets, industry pressures have forced increasing action in more recent times.

Restrictions of Imports

The U.S. Congress in recent years has increasingly been ready to provide the president with additional powers to restrict trade and investment flows. Many resolutions have also been passed and much legislation enacted admonishing the president to pay closer attention to such policy issues. However, most of these admonitions provided only for an increasing threat against foreign importers and investors, not for better conditions for U.S. exporters of goods, services, or capital. The power of the executive branch of government to improve international trade and investment opportunities for U.S. firms through international negotiations and the relaxation of rules, regulations, and laws has become increasingly restricted over time.

A tendency has existed to disregard the achievements of past international negotiations. For example, members of the 98th Congress attempted to amend protectionist legislation by stipulating that U.S. international trade legislation, when not in conformity with internationally negotiated rules, should not take effect. The amendment was voted down by an overwhelming majority, demonstrating a legislative lack of concern for such international trade agreements.

Worldwide, most countries maintain at least a surface-level conformity with international principles. However, many exert substantial restraints on free trade through import controls and barriers. A summary of the types of barriers to trade are listed in Table 6.2. In addition, Table 6.3 provides additional detail on some of the more frequently encountered barriers. They are found particularly in countries that suffer from major trade deficits or major infrastructure problems, causing them to enter into voluntary restraint agreements with trading partners or to selectively apply trade-restricting measures, such as tariffs or nontariff barriers, against trading partners.

voluntary restraint agreements trade restraint agreements resulting in self-imposed restrictions on exports from one country to another

Voluntary restraint agreements are designed to help domestic industries reorganize, restructure, and recapture production prominence. Even though officially "voluntary," these agreements are usually implemented through severe threats against trading partners. Due to this "voluntary" nature, these agreements are not subject to any previously negotiated bilateral or multilateral trade accords.

When nations do not resort to the subtle mechanism of voluntary agreements to affect trade flows, they often impose tariffs and quotas. For example, in 1983 the International Trade Commission imposed a five-year tariff on Japanese heavy motorcycles imported into the United States. The 49.4 percent duty was granted at the request of Harley-Davidson, which could no longer compete with the heavily discounted bikes being imported by companies such as Honda and Kawasaki. The gradually declining tariff gave Harley-Davidson the time to enact new management strategies without wor-

Types of Barriers to Trade — TABLE 6.2

Tariff Barriers

A tariff is a tax on imports. Duty is not charged on all products; based on the product and the country of origin, some products are permitted duty-free entry into the United States.

Protective tariffs are assessed to protect domestic products from foreign competition.

Revenue tariffs are imposed to generate tax revenue.

Punitive tariffs are intended to punish a trading partner.

Antidumping duties are assessed of merchandise that is sold in the United States at less than fair-market value.

Countervailing duties are applied to counter the effects of subsidies provided by foreign governments to merchandise that is exported to the United States.

Tariffs may be classified as to the way the duty, or tariff, is levied.

Ad valorem tariff is expressed as a fixed percentage of the customs value of the imported product, for example, 8 percent tariff on a shipment valued at $10,000.

Specific tariff is expressed as an amount of money per unit of product, for example, $2 per ton.

Compound tariff is a combination of the ad valorem and specific tariffs.

Nontariff Barriers

Nontariff barriers include a variety of measures that have the common objective of restricting imports.

Quotas limit the amount of product that may be imported during a certain period of time. Quotas are established by legislation, by directives, and by proclamations issued under the authority contained in specific legislation.

Absolute quota means that no more of a product than the amount specified may be permitted entry during a quota period. There are two types of absolute quotas:

Global quota is a limitation on the quantity that applies to all foreign countries as a group.

Country quota is an allocation of a portion of the quota to specified foreign countries.

Tariff-rate quota provides for the entry of a specified quantity of the product at a reduced rate during the quota period. Quantities entered in excess of the quota are subject to higher duty rates.

Local content regulation is a requirement that some specified portion of a product be produced locally.

Voluntary export restraints are quotas and exports set by the exporting country to forestall more severe restrictions by the importing country.

Subsidies are payments made by governments to industries or companies that essentially offset their high costs and permit them to be artificially competitive in an export market, thereby compromising the intent of free trade.

Administrative barriers are a complex of laws, regulations, administrative rulings, health and safety standards, testing certification, etc., that, when applied, make it difficult, costly, or virtually impossible to export goods to a foreign country. Even when capable of being complied with, these measures tend to raise the price of exported goods.

SOURCES: *Harmonized Tariff Schedule of the United States;* Code of Federal Regulations No. 19, Customs Duties; *Importing into the United States,* Department of the Treasury, 1991.

rying about the pressure of the Japanese imports. Within four years, Harley-Davidson was back on its feet and again had the highest market share in the heavyweight class of bikes. In 1987, Harley-Davidson officials requested that the tariff be lifted a year early. As a result, the policy was labeled a success. However, at no time were the costs of these measures to U.S. consumers even considered.

TABLE 6.3 **Trade Barriers**

There are literally hundreds of ways to build a barrier. The following list provides just a few of the trade barriers that exporters face.

- Restrictive licensing
- Special import authorization
- Global quotas
- Voluntary export restraints
- Temporary prohibitions
- Advance import deposits
- Taxes on foreign exchange deals
- Preferential licensing applications
- Excise duties
- Licensing fees
- Statistical taxes
- Sales taxes
- Consumption taxes
- Discretionary licensing
- Licenses for selected purchases
- Country quotas
- Seasonal prohibitions
- Health and sanitary prohibitions
- Foreign exchange licensing
- Licenses subject to barter and countertrade
- Customs surcharges
- Stamp taxes
- Consular invoice fees
- Taxes on transport
- Service charges
- Value-added taxes
- Turnover taxes
- Internal taxes

SOURCE: Mark Magnier, "Blockades to Food Exports Hide Behind Invisible Shields." *The Journal of Commerce* (September 18, 1989): 5A. Permission to reprint granted by the Journal of Commerce.

Tariffs are taxes based primarily on the value of imported goods and services. An *ad valorem tariff* is expressed as a fixed percentage of the value of the product. A *specific tariff* is charged on the basis of a specified amount per unit of the product. A *compound tariff* is a combination of the ad valorem and specific tariffs. Figure 6.2 is a page from the *Harmonized Tariff Schedule of the United States*, which illustrates how these three types of tariffs are applied. *Nontariff barriers* include quotas, which are restrictions on the quantity of a foreign product that can be imported.

Quotas were proposed for tuna fish packaged in water, because U.S. producers complained that Japanese processors took away their market share for the product. However, U.S. firms had forced Japanese processors to concentrate on water packed tuna by preventing them in the early 1970s from entering the U.S. market with tuna fish packed in oil. At that time, the majority of canned tuna sold in the United States was packed in oil. Only 7 percent of all canned tuna sold was water packed. Eventually, the situation was reversed; most canned tuna purchased was packed in water. The Japanese firms that had been forced to concentrate on this small market niche had grown quite successful in penetrating it. They became even more successful as it became larger. However, the market share situation changed not because of Japanese ingenuity but because of changing consumer tastes. The Japanese adapted, whereas many U.S. firms did not.

Subsidies are used by many governments to protect domestic industries from low-cost foreign competition. In providing a subsidy, the government makes payment to the domestic company or industry to offset its uncompetitiveness, thereby keeping companies in business that normally would not be able to survive the rigors of global competition. Global Learning Experience 6.4 is an interesting account of one U.S. industry and related unions that took the short-term view of subsidies and jobs now, in lieu of much greater gains in the long term.

Harmonized Tariff Schedule of the United States, 1996 (annotated for statistical reporting purposes)

FIGURE 6.2

Heading/ Subheading	Stat. Suf- fix	Article Description	Units of Quantity	Rates of Duty 1 General[a]	Rates of Duty 1 Special[b]	Rates of Duty 2[c]
2001		Vegetables, fruit, nuts and other edible parts of plants, prepared or preserved by vinegar or acetic acid:				
2001.10.00	00	Cucumbers including gherkins	kg	11.2%	Free (A, E, IL, J, MX) 2.4% (CA)	35%
2001.20.00	00	Onions	kg	6.5%	Free (A, E, IL, J, MX) 1.6% (CA)	35%
2001.90		Other:				
		Capers:				
2001.90.10	00	In immediate containers holding more than 3.4 kg	kg	8%	Free (A, E, IL, J, MX) 1.6% (CA)	20%
2001.90.20	00	Other	kg	8%	Free (E, IL, J) 1.6% (CA) 5.6% (MX)	20%
		Other:				
		Vegetables:				
2001.90.25	00	Artichokes	kg	11.4%	Free (A, E, IL, J, MX) 2.4% (CA)	35%
2001.90.30	00	Beans	kg	7.9%	Free (A, E, IL, J, MX) 1.8% (CA)	35%
2001.90.33	00	Nopalitos	kg	10.6%	Free (A, E, IL, J, MX) 2.4% (CA)	35%
2001.90.35	00	Pimientos (Capsicum anuum)	kg	9%	Free (E, IL, J) 1.9% (CA) 6.6% (MX)	38.5%
2001.90.39	00	Other	kg	11.2%	Free (A, E, IL, J) 2.4% (CA) 4.8% (MX)	35%
2001.90.42	00	Chestnuts	kg	4.9¢/kg	Free (A, E, IL, J, MX) 1.5¢/kg (CA)	55¢/kg
2001.90.45	00	Mangoes	kg	2.7¢/kg	Free (A, E, IL, J, MX) 0.6¢/kg (CA)	33¢/kg
2001.90.50	00	Walnuts	kg	9.7¢/kg	Free (A, E, IL, J, MX) 2.2¢/kg (CA)	33¢/kg
2001.90.60	00	Other	kg	16.3%	Free (E, IL, J) 3.5% (CA) 12.2% (MX)	35%
2002		Tomatoes prepared or preserved otherwise than by vinegar or acetic acid:				
2002.10.00		Tomatoes, whole or in pieces		14% 1/	Free (E, IL, J) 2.9% (CA) 10.2% (MX)	50%
	20	In containers holding less than 1.4 kg	kg			
	80	Other	kg			
2002.90.00		Other		12.9%	Free (E, IL, J) 2.7% (CA) 8% (MX)	50%
		Paste:				
	10	In containers holding less than 1.4 kg	kg			
	20	Other	kg			
		Puree:				
	30	In containers holding less than 1.4 kg	kg			
	40	Other	kg			
	50	Other	kg			
2003		Mushrooms and truffles, prepared or preserved otherwise than by vinegar or acetic acid:				
2003.10.00		Mushrooms		6.7¢/kg on drained weight + 9.5%	Free (E, IL, J) 1.4¢/kg on drained weight + 2% (CA) 4.9¢/kg on drained weight + 7% (MX)	22¢/kg on drained weight + 45%
	09	Straw mushrooms	kg			
		Other:				
		In containers each holding not more than 255 g:				
	27	Whole (including buttons)	kg			
	31	Sliced	kg			
	37	Other	kg			
		In containers each holding more than 255 g:				
	43	Whole (including buttons)	kg			
	47	Sliced	kg			
	53	Other	kg			

Column notes:
[a]General - Applies to the products of countries designated Beneficiary Developing Countries for purposes of the Generalized System of Preferences(GSP).
[b]Special - Products eligible for special tariff treatment from countries indicated by the code letter, i.e. MX indicates Mexico, CA is Canada.
[c]2 - Products imported directly or indirectly from Afganistan, Cuba, Kampuchea, Laos, North Korea and Vietnam.

SOURCE: *Harmonized Tariff Schedule of the United States,* 1996.

U.S. Shipyards on a Self-Destructive Course

International shipbuilding is estimated by the U.S. government to become a $250 billion market in the next decade. Because of the high costs of American shipyard operations and generous subsidies (up to 9 percent of cost) to Asian and European shipbuilders by their governments, U.S. shipyards are not competitive in the global marketplace. Accordingly, American trade negotiators spent many years persuading Asian and European governments to agree to an accord that would end shipbuilding subsidies and "level the playing field" for the American companies.

What appeared to be a good arrangement for U.S. shipyards quickly fell apart as the major U.S. builders, subsidized to some extent by work for the Department of Defense, realized they would lose those subsidies. Additionally, global restructuring of the shipbuilding market could lead to the loss of some U.S. jobs now, in exchange for a share in a large and profitable market a few years in the future. With intensive lobbying against the pact, U.S. shipbuilders and labor unions chose subsidies and jobs *now.* Being an election year, the U.S. congress walked away from the agreement. The outcome: Asian and European governments are still subsidizing their shipyards and U.S. shipbuilders are still uncompetitive.

SOURCE: Adapted from: David E. Sanger, "On Second Thought, U.S. Decides Shipyard Subsidies Aren't So Bad, *New York Times,* Oct. 3, 1996, D-1.

Administrative barriers are another way in which imports may be reduced. They consist of a variety of measures, such as testing, certification, or simply bureaucratic hurdles, that have the effect of restricting imports. All of these measures tend to raise the price of imported goods. They, therefore, constitute a transfer of funds from the buyers (and, if absorbed by them, the sellers) of imports to the government, and—if accompanied by price increases of competing domestic products—to the domestic producers of such products.

Probably the most famous are the measures implemented by France. In order to stop, or at least reduce, the importation of foreign video recorders, the French government ruled in 1983 that all of them had to be sent to the customs station at Poitiers. This customshouse was located away from major transport routes, woefully understaffed, and open only a few days each week. In addition, the few customs agents at Poitiers insisted on opening each package separately to inspect the merchandise. Within a few weeks, imports of video recorders came to a halt. Members of the French government, however, were able to point to the fact that they had fully adhered to the letter of international law. Global Learning Experience 6.5 indicates that the use of demanding technical requirements for products exported to foreign markets is increasing.

The discussion of import restrictions has focused thus far on merchandise trade. Similar restrictions are applicable to investment flows and, by extension, to international trade in services. In order to protect ownership, control, and development of domestic industries, many countries impose varying restrictions on investment capital flows. Most frequently, they are in the form of investment-screening agencies that decide whether any particular foreign investment project is sufficiently meritorious to warrant execution. Canada, for example, has a Foreign Investment Review Agency (FIRA) that scrutinizes foreign investments.[11] So do most developing nations where

Tariff Barriers on the Way Down; Nontariff Barriers on the Way Up

Although the GATT and WTO have been successful in bringing about reductions in tariff barriers over the years, many nations are imposing new nontariff obstacles to trade. Many of the new barriers are technical in nature and include labeling rules, insect quarantines, fumigation requirements, and lower pesticide residue tolerances and product shelf-life requirements. They are reportedly being imposed to protect local industry from U.S. exports.

Hard hit are U.S. exports of agricultural, meat, and processed products. It is estimated that these nontariff barriers are restraining almost $5 billion in exports a year. The U.S. Department of Agriculture projects that the technical barriers imposed by South Korea alone cost U.S. agricultural exporters more than $1 billion each year. Officials indicate that as many as half of the new technical barriers are not for legitimate health or safety reasons, but are attempts to restrict imports.

A section in the GATT Uruguay Round Agreement requires that nontariff import restrictions be justified scientifically; thus the skills of technical experts in disproving the fears and concerns of foreign governments is becoming increasingly important in the competition for global markets.

SOURCE: Adapted from: Peter M. Tirschwell, "Nontariff Obstacles to Trade on Rise," *The Journal of Commerce*, February 13, 1996, A-1.

special government permission must be obtained for investment projects. This permission frequently carries with it certain conditions, such as levels of ownership permitted, levels of dividends that can be repatriated, number of jobs that must be created, or the extent to which management can be carried out by individuals from abroad.

The United States restricts foreign investment in instances where national security or related concerns are at stake. Major foreign investments may be reviewed by the **Committee for Foreign Investments in the United States (CFIUS).** CFIUS became active, for example, during the intended purchase of Fairchild Semiconductor Industries by Fujitsu of Japan. The review precipitated a major national discussion and resulted in the withdrawal of the Fujitsu purchase offer. Prior to that, national attention was focused on investment strategies of Arab firms, governments, and individuals in the United States. The concern was that, because of their increased oil income in the 1970s, Arab countries and nationals would be able to take over significant portions of U.S. industry and real estate. Yet the fears of being bought out were never justified, because investor perceptions of the potential political backlash resulted in a self-regulatory mechanism.

Committee for Foreign Investments in the United States (CFIUS)
federal committee with the responsibility for reviewing major foreign investments to determine whether national security or related concerns are at stake

Foreign direct investment in the United States has steadily increased in recent years. Americans are again becoming concerned about the level of foreign direct investment in the United States. Legislators have been proposing, debating, and in some instances implementing foreign investment controls in an effort to curb "the sale of America."

If you order "Mountain Chicken" in Montserrat or Dominica (both in the West Indies) what do you get?

Frogs' legs the size of chicken's.

However, the bottom line is that although the restriction of investments may permit more domestic control over industries, it also denies access to foreign capital. This in turn can result in a tightening up of credit markets, higher interest rates, and less impetus for innovation.

The Effects of Import Restrictions Policymakers are faced with several problems when trying to administer import controls. First, most of the time such controls exact a huge price from domestic consumers. Import controls may mean that the most efficient sources of supply are not available. The result is either second-best products or higher costs for restricted supplies, which in turn cause customer-service standards to drop and consumers to pay significantly higher prices. Even though these costs may be widely distributed among many consumers and so less obvious, the social cost of these controls may be damaging to the economy and subject to severe attack from individuals. However, these attacks are countered by pressure from protected groups that benefit from import restrictions. For example, while citizens of the European Union may be forced by import controls to pay an elevated price for all the agricultural products they consume, agricultural producers in the region benefit from higher incomes. Achieving a proper trade-off is often difficult, if not impossible, for the policymaker.

A second major problem resulting from import controls is the downstream change in the composition of imports that may result. For example, if the importation of copper ore is restricted, through either voluntary restraints or quotas, producing countries may opt to shift their production systems and produce copper wire instead, which they can export. As a result, initially narrowly defined protectionistic measures may snowball in order to protect one downstream industry after another.

A final major problem that confronts the policymaker is that of efficiency. Import controls designed to provide breathing room to a domestic industry so it can either grow or recapture its competitive position often do not work. Rather than improve the productivity of an industry, such controls may provide it with a level of safety and a cushion of increased income, subsequently causing it to lag behind in technological advancements.

Restrictions of Exports

In addition to imposing restraints on imports, nations also control their exports. The reasons are short, supply foreign policy purposes, or the desire to retain capital.

The United States, for example, places major emphasis on export controls because it regards trade as a privilege of the firm, granted by the state, rather than a right or a necessity. As will be explained in more detail in Chapter 7, U.S. legislation to control exports focuses on **national security** controls—that is, the control of weapons exports or high-technology exports that might adversely affect the safety of the nation. In addition, U.S. exports are controlled for reasons of foreign policy and short supply. These controls restrict the global business opportunities of firms if an administration feels that such a restriction would send a necessary foreign policy message to another country. Such action may be undertaken regardless of whether the message will have any impact or whether similar products can easily be supplied by companies in other nations. Although perhaps valuable as a tool of global relations, such policies give U.S. firms the reputation of being unreliable suppliers and may divert orders to firms in other countries.

national security
ability of a nation to protect its internal values from external threats

Many nations restrict exports, particularly of capital, because **capital flight** is a major problem for them. Citizens who accumulate funds often believe that the return on investment or the safety of the capital is not sufficiently ensured in their own countries. The reason may be governmental measures or domestic economic factors such as inflation. These holders of capital want to invest abroad. By doing so, however, they deprive their domestic economy of much needed investment funds.

capital flight
flow of private funds abroad because investors believe that the return on investment or the safety of capital is not sufficiently ensured in their own countries

Once governments impose restrictions on the export of funds, the desire to transfer capital abroad only increases. Because companies and individuals are ingenious in their efforts to achieve capital flight, governments, particularly in developing countries, continue to suffer. In addition, few new investment funds will enter the country because potential investors fear that dividends and profits will not be remitted easily.

Export-Promotion Efforts

The desire to increase participation in global trade and investment flows has led nations to implement export-promotion programs. These programs are designed primarily to help domestic firms enter and maintain their position in global markets and to match or counteract similar export-promotion efforts by other nations.

Most governments supply some support to their firms participating or planning to participate in global trade. Typically, this support falls into one of four categories: export information and advice, production support, marketing support, or finance and guarantees.[12] Given the deterioration of the U.S. trade balance, U.S. government trade policy is focusing on export programs to improve the global trade performance of U.S. firms. The Department of Commerce has added new information services that provide data on foreign trade and market developments. The Foreign Commercial Service was reformed and is now under the aegis of the U.S. Department of Commerce; it was formerly part of the Department of State. Many new professionals were hired to provide an inward and outward link for U.S. business in terms of information flow and marketing assistance. As Global Learning Experience 6.6 shows, governments often go to great lengths to assist their firms in obtaining international orders.

Another new area of interest is export financing. Although many efforts were made in the past to reduce the activities of the Export-Import Bank of the United States (Eximbank), U.S. policymakers have increasingly recognized that U.S. business may be placed at a disadvantage if it cannot meet the subsidized financing rates of foreign suppliers. The bank, charged with a new mission of aggressively meeting foreign export financing conditions, has in recent years even resorted to offering loans composed partially of commercial interest rates and partially of highly subsidized developmental aid interest rates, resulting in very-low-interest loans.

Tax legislation that inhibited the employment of Americans by U.S. firms abroad has also been altered. In the past, U.S. nationals living abroad were, with some minor exclusions, fully subject to U.S. federal taxation. Because the cost of living abroad can often be quite high, companies frequently were not able to send U.S. employees to their foreign subsidiaries. However, a revision of the tax code now allows a substantial amount of income (up to $70,000) to remain tax free. More Americans can now be posted abroad. In their work, they may specify the use of U.S. products, thus enhancing the competitive position of U.S. firms.

Another chicken question: If you order "Bamboo Chicken" in Belize (South America), what do you get?

"Bamboo Chicken" is roast iguana.

GLOBAL LEARNING EXPERIENCE 6.6

Military Exports: To Promote or Not to Promote?

To help American defense contractors promote their products at Asian Aerospace '94 in Singapore, the Pentagon dispatched 75 U.S. military personnel and 20 top-of-the-line military aircraft. Even the aircraft carrier USS Independence was diverted so three Navy F/A-18 fighter jets could make an appearance.

Industry officials consider the strong U.S. military presence a major boost to their sales efforts in the booming Asian arms market. Joel Johnson, a vice president of the Aerospace Industries Association, said, "There's no question the services would like to be supportive. If the Malaysians are going to buy airplanes, [U.S. military officials] would rather have them be F-18s than MiG-29s. . . . The services have clearly all focused on the fact that the only thing keeping our production lines open for the next three to five years is going to be exports."

However, the Pentagon also has detractors. Some groups believe that the policy sends a wrong signal. Advocates of tighter controls on U.S. weapons exports are alarmed and say that the administration is undermining its own efforts to curb weapons exports from countries such as Russia and China while fueling a destabilizing arms race among Asian countries. "The administration sends the wrong signal to other suppliers and undercuts the prospects for controlling weapons proliferation," according to the nonprofit Arms Control Association.

An administration official answered the protests by saying, "I don't think anyone is talking about creating circumstances where all of a sudden we would be selling arms to people we didn't used to because there's money to be made." A Pentagon report asserted that "demonstration of specific U.S. equipment at exhibitions such as this will in no way undermine the careful case-by-case review that the Defense and State Departments undertake before approving the sales of U.S. defense systems."

U.S. arms exports account for nearly half of all arms sales worldwide, far more than any other nation—$32.4 billion worth in 1993. One administration official said, "Whether you like it or not, weapons are a significant export earner and one area where the U.S. remains quite competitive. What should be the role, if any, of the U.S. government in promoting, encouraging, or assisting exports by U.S. defense industries, particularly during a stage when our own military procurement is shrinking? When the President of France goes overseas, he [asks his hosts], 'Why don't you buy [French-made] Mirage jets?' The question is, should the U.S. government play a more active role in doing this sort of thing?"

SOURCE: John Lancaster, "Administration Helps Arms Makers Promote Goods at Singapore Show," *The Washington Post,* February 28, 1994, A6.

A major U.S. export-promotion effort consisted of the passage of the Export Trading Company Act of 1982. Intended to be the American response to the *sogoshosha,* the giant Japanese trading companies, this legislation permits firms to work together to form export consortia. The basic idea is to provide the foreign buyer with one-stop shopping centers in which a group of U.S. firms offers a variety of complementary and competitive products. The act exempted U.S. firms from current antitrust statutes. It also permitted banks to cooperate in the formation of the consortia through direct capital participation in the financing of trading activities. Although the legislation was originally hailed as a masterstroke, so far it has not attracted a large number of successful firms.

Import-Promotion Efforts

Increasingly, policymakers resort to import-promotion measures. The measures are implemented primarily by nations that have accumulated and maintained large balance-of-trade surpluses. They hope to allay other nations' fears of continued imbalances and to gradually redirect trade flows.

Japan, for example, has completely refurbished the operations of the Japan External Trade Organization (JETRO). This organization, which initially was formed to encourage Japanese exports, has now begun to focus on the promotion of imports to Japan. It organizes trade missions of foreign firms coming to Japan, hosts special exhibits and fairs within Japan, and provides assistance and encouragement to potential importers.

Countries such as South Korea and Taiwan sponsor buying missions to countries with which they have major trade surpluses. For example, representatives of several Korean firms, under the sponsorship of Korean government, periodically visit the United States to sign highly visible purchasing contracts. Through these measures, governments attempt to demonstrate their willingness to reduce trade imbalances.

Many countries are also implementing policy measures to attract foreign direct investment. These policies are the result of the needs of poorer countries to attract additional foreign capital to fuel economic growth without taking out more loans that call for fixed schedules of repayment.[13]

SUMMARY

Trade and investment policies historically have been a subset of domestic policies. Domestic policies in turn have aimed primarily at maintaining and improving the standard of living, the developmental level, and the employment level within a nation. Occasionally, foreign policy concerns also played a role. Increasingly, however, this view of trade and investment policies is undergoing change. While the view was appropriate for global developments that took place following World War II, changes in the world environment require changes in policies.

Increasingly, the capability of policymakers simply to focus on domestic issues is reduced because of global linkages in trade and investment. In addition, traditional global institutions concerned with these policies have been weakened, and the developmental conflict among nations has been sharpened.

Many countries place restrictions on free trade through import controls and trade barriers. These controls and barriers ultimately result in the consumer having to pay higher prices for domestically produced goods.

Key Terms and Concepts

national sovereignty
standard of living
quality of life
foreign policy
developmental aid
General Agreement on Tariffs and Trade (GATT)
most favored nation (MFN)
World Trade Organization (WTO)
currency flows
punitive tariff
voluntary restraint agreements
nontariff barriers
Committee for Foreign Investments in the United States (CFIUS)
national security
capital flight

Questions for Discussion

1. Discuss the role of voluntary import restraints in global business.
2. Discuss the differences among tariff, quota, and nontariff barriers to trade.
3. Discuss the impact of import restrictions on consumers.
4. Why would policymakers sacrifice major global progress for minor domestic policy gains?
5. Discuss the varying inputs to trade and investment restrictions of beneficiaries and of losers.

6. What is the World Trade Organization? (Tip: Check out http://www.wto.org)

Recommended Readings

Cavusgil, S. Tamer, and Michael R. Czinkota, eds. *International Perspectives on Trade Promotion and Assistance.* New York: Quorum, 1990.

Czinkota, Michael R., ed. *Improving U.S. Competitiveness.* Washington, D.C.: Government Printing Office, 1988.

Frazier, Michael. *Implementing State Government Export Programs.* New York: Praeger, 1992.

Guide to the Evaluation of Trade Promotion Programmes. Geneva, Switzerland: International Trade Centre, UNCTAD/GATT, 1987.

Howell, Thomas R., Alan William Wolff, Brent L. Bartlett, and R. Michael Gadbaw. *Conflict Among Nations: Trade Policies in the 1990's.* Boulder, Colo.: Westview Press, 1992.

Hufbauer, Gary Clyde, and Kimberely Ann Elliott. *Measuring the Costs of Protection in the United States.* Washington, D.C.: Institute for International Economics, 1994.

Krugman, Paul, and Alasdair Smith, eds. *Empirical Studies of Strategic Trade Policy.* Chicago: The University of Chicago Press, 1994.

McKibbin, Warwick, J., and Jeffrey D. Sachs. *Global Linkages: Macroeconomic Interdependence and Cooperation in the World Economy.* Washington, D.C.: Brookings Institution, 1991.

Ramdas, Ganga Persaud. *U.S. Export Incentives and Investment Behavior.* Boulder, Colo.: Westview Press, 1991.

Schott, Jeffery J. *The Uruguay Round: An Assessment.* Washington, D.C.: Institute for International Economics, 1994.

Stern, Robert M. ed. *The Multilateral Trading System: Analysis and Options for Change.* Ann Arbor: University of Michigan Press, 1993.

Wolf, Charles, Jr. *Linking Economic Policy and Foreign Policy.* New Brunswick, N.J.: Transaction Publishers, 1991.

Notes

1. D. Quinn Mills, "Destructive Tradeoffs in U.S. Trade Policy," *Harvard Business Review* 64 (November-December 1986): 199–224.
2. Peter Passell, "Tuna and Trade: Whose Rules?" *The New York Times,* February 19, 1992, D2.
3. Thomas R. Graham, "Global Trade: War and Peace," *Foreign Policy* 50 (Spring 1983): 124–127.
4. Edwin I. Barber, "Investment-Trade Nexus," in *U.S. International Economic Policy,* ed. Gary Clyde Hufbauer (Washington, D.C.: The International Law Institute, 1982), 9-5.
5. Mordechai E. Kreinin, *International Economics: A Policy Approach* (New York: Harcourt Brace Jovanovich, 1971), 12.
6. "Uruguay Round Results to Expand Trade by $755 Billion," Focus: GATT Newsletter, May 1994, 6.
7. Raymond J. Waldmann, *Managed Trade: The Competition between Nations* (Cambridge, Mass.: Ballinger, 1986); and *Ward's Automotive Report,* January 9, 1989.
8. Tobey, "Currency Trading," *The Washington Post,* September 14, 1989, E1.
9. John H. Jackson, *The World Trading System* (Cambridge, Mass.: MIT Press, 1989).
10. Michael R. Czinkota, "The World Trade Organization: Perspectives and Prospects," *Journal of International Marketing* 3, 1 (1995), 85–92.
11. The U.S.–Canada Free Trade Agreement of 1988 provides for a significant downscaling of these screening activities.
12. Lisa A. Elvey, "Export Promotion and Assistance: A Comparative Analysis," in *International Perspectives on Trade Promotion and Assistance,* S.T. Cavusguil and M.R. Czinkota, eds. (New York: Quorum, 1990), 133–146.
13. Stephen Guisinger, "Attracting and Controlling Foreign Investment," *Economic Impact* (Washington, D.C.: United States Information Agency, 1987), 18.

The War of the Bananas

The European Union (EU) is the main market in the world for bananas, constituting 37.5 percent of all world trade (see Figure 1). That is why a decision by the EU Farm Council in December of 1992 attracted attention among banana-producing nations. Up until the decision, different EU countries had different policies regarding imports of bananas. While Germany, for example, had no restrictions at all, countries such as the United Kingdom, France, and Spain restricted their imports to favor those from their current and former African, Caribbean, and Pacific (ACP) colonies. (This preferential trading agreement is known as the Lome Convention.) The decision calls for a quota of 2.1 million tons with a 20 percent tariff for all banana imports from Latin America ($126 per ton), rising to 170 percent for quantities over that limit ($1,150 per ton). Since Latin American exports to Europe were approximately 2.7 million tons in 1992, the quota would cut almost 25 percent of the countries' exports to the EU.

The main stated reason for imposing the quota and the tariffs is to protect former colonies by allowing them to enjoy preferential access to the EU market. Other reasons implied have been the $260 million in tariff revenue resulting from the measures as well as moving against the "banana dollar" (reference to the U.S. control of the Latin American banana trade through its multinationals). Belgium, Germany, and Holland objected to the measures not only because of the preference given to higher-cost, lower-quality bananas from current and former colonies, but also because of the economic impact. The Belgians estimated an immediate loss of 500 jobs in its port cities, which traditionally have handled substantial amounts of Latin American banana imports. Even in the United Kingdom, where the preferential treatment has enjoyed widespread support, there has been criticism of the decision.

Since then, the conflict has escalated and is one of the most complicated trade wars in the international trade scene. It pits EU members against one another, the United States against the EU, U.S. multinationals against European counterparts, U.S. investment interests against U.S. diplomatic concerns, Guatemala against Costa Rica, Latin American growers against Caribbean growers, and the U.S. government against four major Latin American nations.

THE LATIN AMERICAN POSITION

Bananas are the world's most-traded fruit and the $5.1 billion in banana trade makes it second only to coffee among foodstuffs. The major banana producers in the world are presented in Figure 2. For countries such as Ecuador, Costa Rica, Colombia, and Honduras the restrictions would cost $1 billion in revenues and 170,000 jobs. For countries such as Costa Rica, banana exports are vital. Bananas represent 8 percent of the country's domestic product, bring in $500 million in hard-currency earnings, and employ one-fifth of the labor force.

SOURCE: This case was prepared by Ilkka A. Ronkainen. It is based on "Banana Trouble," *The Washington Times,* November 6, 1994, A13–14; "Banana Regulations Split the European Community," *The Journal of Commerce* (October 22, 1993): 1; "The Banana War," *International Business Chronicle* 4 (February 1–15, 1993): 22; Organization of American States, "OAS Takes Note of Regional Statements on the Marketing of Bananas in Europe," *Report on the OAS Permanent Council Meeting,* February 24, 1993; and Joseph L. Brand, "The New World Order," *Vital Speeches of the Day* 58 (December 1991): 155–160. The help of Gladys Navarro with an earlier version of this case is appreciated.

FIGURE 1 **Trade in Bananas: EU Country Imports by Source**

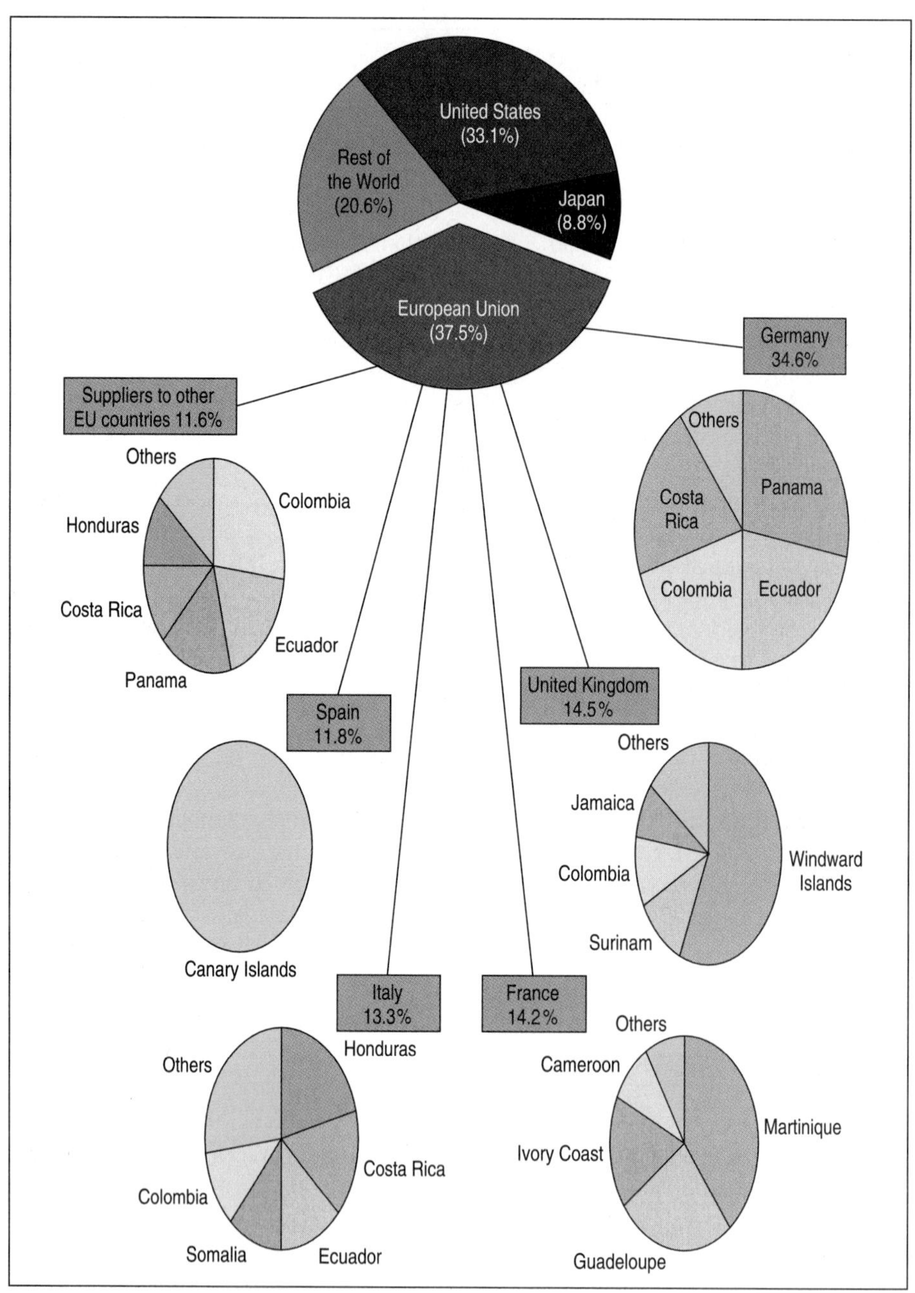

SOURCE: Brent Borrell and Sandy Cuthbertson, *EC Banana Policy 1992,* Center for International Economics, Sydney, Australia, 1991, chart 2.1.

Leading Banana Producers FIGURE 2

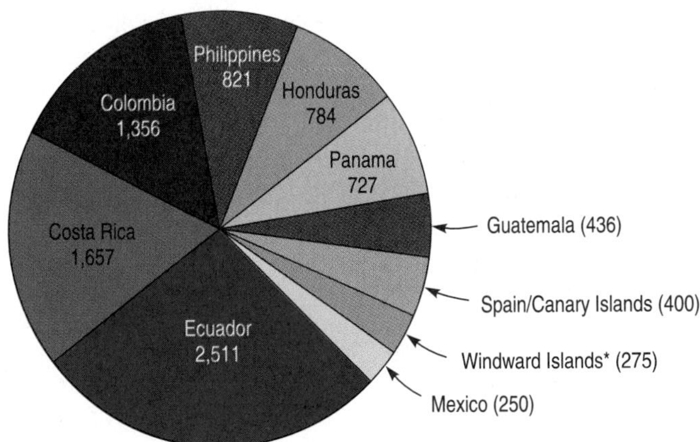

*Includes Dominica, Grenada, Saint Lucia, Saint Vincent and Grenadines.

SOURCE: United Nations Food and Agriculture Organization, Intergovernmental Group on Bananas.

The presidents of Colombia, Costa Rica, Ecuador, Guatemala, Honduras, Nicaragua, Panama, and Venezuela held a summit February 11, 1993, in Ecuador and issued a declaration rejecting the EU banana-marketing guidelines as a violation of GATT and principles of trade liberalization. The GATT has agreed with the Latin American countries twice that tariffs and quotas were indeed harmful. Following the formal adoption of the banana decision in July 1993, the EU and four Latin American nations (Costa Rica, Colombia, Nicaragua, and Venezuela) cut a deal in March 1994. The four countries agreed to drop their GATT protest in exchange for modifications in the restrictions they face. Guatemala refused to sign the agreement, and Ecuador, Panama, and Mexico lodged protests.

The economics of production are clearly in favor of the Latin producers. The unit-cost of production in the Caribbean is nearly 2.5 times what it is for Latin American producers. For some producers, such as Martinique and Guadeloupe, the cost difference is even higher. The EU quota therefore results in major trade diversion.

The affected Latin nations have used various means at the international level to get the EU to modify its position. In addition to the summit, many are engaged in lobbying in Brussels as well as the individual EU-member capitals. They have also sought the support of the United States, given its interests both in terms of U.S. multinational corporations' involvement in the banana trade as well as its investment in encouraging economic growth in the developing democracies of Latin America.

THE U.S. POSITION

Initial U.S. reaction was that of an interested observer. The United States provided support and encouragement for the Latin Americans in their lobbying efforts in Geneva, Brussels, and the European capitals. However, in October 1994, U.S. Trade Representative Mickey Kantor announced plans to start a year-long investigation of the EU's banana restrictions, with sanctions against European imports as a possibility. This action broke new ground in trade disputes. While governments traditionally have started trade wars as a means of protecting domestic jobs and key industries, the banana dispute involves

U.S. investment and overseas markets more than it does jobs at home. The probe was requested by Chiquita, the world's largest banana marketer, and the Hawaii Banana Industry Association, whose 130 small family farms constitute the entire banana-growing contingent. Although only 7,000 of the company's 45,000 employees are in the United States, Chiquita officials argued that the value added by the company's U.S. workers—marketers, shippers, and distributors—make it a major agricultural priority.

The U.S. challenge was "not politically prudent," complained Gerard Kiely, spokesperson for the EU Agricultural Commissioner, by noting that the United States does not even export bananas. However, 12 senators sent a letter to Mr. Kantor warning against the dangerous precedent if the EU banana regime went unchallenged.

THE CARIBBEAN POSITION

For many nations banana exports are the mainstay of their economies. For example, for the tiny West Indies island of Saint Lucia, which sells its bananas to its former colonial master, the U.K., banana dependence is 70 percent of the national income. Furthermore, the industry employs four out of five St. Lucians.

Therefore it was not surprising that heads of government of the 13-member Caribbean Community (CARICOM) approved a resolution February 24, 1993, supporting the EU guidelines. "No one country in this hemisphere is as dependent on bananas for its economic survival as the Windward Islands," declared Ambassador Joseph Edsel Edmunds of Saint Lucia. Referring to the criticism of the EU decision by the Latin nations, he added: "Are we being told that, in the interest of free trade all past international agreements between the Caribbean and friendly nations are to be dissolved, leaving us at the mercy of Latin American states and megablocs?" He noted that Latin American banana producers command 95 percent of the world market and more than two-thirds of the EU market.

Ambassador Kingsley A. Layne of Saint Vincent and the Grenadines asserted that the issue at stake "is nothing short of a consideration of the right of small states to exist with a decent and acceptable standard of living, self-determination, and independence. The same flexibility and understanding being sought by other powerful partners in the GATT in respect of their specific national interests must also be extended to the small island developing states."

THE CORPORATE POSITION

The dispute has also pitted U.S. multinationals (Chiquita, Dole, and Del Monte) against the Europeans (Geest and Fyffes). The two European multinationals control between them virtually all of the banana shipping and marketing from such markets as Belize, Suriname, Jamaica, and the Caribbean. U.S. companies complain that the EU is arranging insider deals for Geest and Fyffes to exempt them from export licensing fees imposed by Latin American nations that have agreed with the EU, or even to secure them a slice of the export business from Latin American markets where they have no foothold at present.

Questions for Discussion

1. If you were a member of the Organization of American States (of which all of the Caribbean and Latin American countries mentioned in the case are members) and its Permanent Council (which must react to two opposing statements concerning the EU decision), with which one would you side?
2. What can the EU do to alleviate the impact of its decision on the Latin American banana producers?
3. What types of strategic moves will an international marketing manager of a Latin American banana exporter have to take in light of the quota and the tariffs?

VIDEO CASE

North American Free Trade Agreement

The benefits of trade among nations are only available if countries are willing to relinquish some independence and autonomy. There are four basic levels of economic integration: the free-trade area, the customs union, the common market, and the economic union. This case, which looks at the trade pact developed between Canada, the United States, and Mexico, is an example of the first level of integration, the free-trade area.

Under a free-trade area, considered the least restrictive form of economic integration, all barriers to trade among members are removed. Goods and services are freely traded among members. The United States and Mexico began negotiating a free-trade agreement in the late 1980s. The pact, the North American Free Trade Agreement, also will include Canada. The Bush administration began talks with Mexico on the belief that free trade with Mexico is crucial, and it pushed for quick approval by Congress. The fast-track approach means that when the negotiating on the agreement is done, Congress can vote the bill up or down, it cannot amend the agreement and cannot hold it up. When it came to a congressional vote the agreement faced formidable opposition in the United States.

One concern raised by opponents was whether Mexico's lower wages will make it an unfair competitor. The worry is that Mexican goods and services will be priced much lower than those of Canada and the United States because Mexico's costs are so much lower. Lower wages also are viewed as a threat to U.S. jobs.

"If you take the United States, an average manufacturing worker earns about $10.57 an hour, thereabouts," said U.S. Sen Donald Riegle, D-Mich. "And down in Mexico, it's a tiny fraction of that, about 57 cents an hour. So I think with those huge differentials, if you have a free trade agreement, what's going to happen is the manufacturing jobs are going to run out of the United States and go down to Mexico," he said. Ross Perot, as presidential candidate, talked of "the giant sucking sound" created by the movement of U.S. jobs to Mexico.

Former U.S. Trade Representative Carla Hills disagrees. Jobs could have tumbled down south without a free trade agreement, she counters. "What a free-trade agreement does is to reduce the barriers to our exports to Mexico."

Meanwhile, European countries are working to create economic integration through the European Union, designed to sweep away all trade barriers. Advocates of the North American Free Trade Agreement say its members, particularly the United States, need it to compete globally.

"It isn't the United States alone that's trying to produce," said U.S. Sen John Chafee, R–R.I. "We're in a competitive position, whether we like it or not, with the European Union and with the Asian rim countries."

According to Hills, Japan has been enormously successful in developing collaborative arrangements with lower-wage countries in east Asia. Germany has created

---

SOURCE: This case was drawn from the Public Broadcasting System's television program "Adam Smith," which aired in 1991. Producer: Alvin H. Perlmutter, Inc.

successful collaborations with Spain and Portugal, she said, "And I can't imagine why the United States would not want to have a close, collaborative arrangement with a neighbor with whom we share a 2,000-mile border."

In addition to the wage differential, treatment of the environment along the U.S.–Mexico border was another major concern of opponents. John O'Connor of the National Toxics Campaign said manufacturers are "turning the border into a 2,000-mile Love Canal, the largest toxic lagoon ever known to humankind."

Lloyd Bensten of Texas, formerly a U.S. senator and treasury secretary, said he has seen enormous improvements in the way business is conducted along the border, especially with regard to environmental protection. "I was born and reared on that Mexican border, and I have never seen the kinds of changes that are happening there, such as the privatizing of industry and the lowering of tariffs," Bensten said. "I've seen moves made on environmental improvement that I have not seen in any other developing country." But Bentsen, who led the fight on Capitol Hill for fast-track consideration of the free trade agreement, concedes some environmental problems remain in that area.

"We've got a serious problem so far as the environment along the border," Bentsen said. "We've got a situation where in one of those towns they've been dumping 26 million gallons of raw sewage every day into the Rio Grande River. Well, that's a real problem. It creates problems of cholera and of water contamination generally. But now you've having a joint effort between the United States and Mexico to build the sewage plants, the treatment plants there. That's real progress."

Bentsen, the Democratic candidate for vice president in 1988, was asked what he says to labor unions, traditional supporters of the Democratic party that typically oppose the free trade accord. "I stated repeatedly during these debates for the fast track that it would depend on what came back, whether I supported it or not," Bentsen said. He would support an agreement that produces a net increase in jobs in both sides. "But if we don't get that, I'll fight it just as strongly as I worked to see that we got the fast track," he said.

In the fall of 1993, the U.S. Congress passed NAFTA by a narrow margin.

Questions for Discussion

1. Compare and contrast the other three levels of economic integration with that of NAFTA.
2. What are the central arguments for and against adopting NAFTA, as outlined in the case? Are there any noneconomic arguments for or against adopting NAFTA?
3. Should the United States have adopted NAFTA? Why or why not? Be prepared to explain your position.
4. How has NAFTA developed since this video was aired?

Protecting the Environment: The Dolphin Controversy

Marine scientists do not know why, but some kinds of dolphins swim above, or "associate with," schools of mature yellowfin, skipjack, and bigeye tuna. Thus, to catch quantities of tuna, fishermen look for the leaping dolphins and cast purse seines (nets pulled into a bag-like shape to enclose fish) around both tuna and dolphins. With this method, fishermen can efficiently and reliably catch a high number of good-sized tuna. The unfortunate side effect is that the dolphins also are caught. Because they are mammals, dolphins must surface to breathe oxygen. Entangled in the net or trapped below other dolphins, some are asphyxiated.

In the late 1960s and early 1970s, the "incidental" catch of various species of dolphins by tuna fishers in the eastern tropical Pacific (the "ETP" is a major tuna-fishing area) was in the hundreds of thousands. Because of society's growing and vociferous concern for these senseless deaths, new fishing techniques were developed to reduce dolphin mortality.

Perhaps the most important new technique is the "backdown operation." After "setting on dolphins" to catch tuna, that is, encircling both tuna and dolphins with the purse seine, the ship backs away, elongating the net, submerging the corkline in the back, and pulling the net out from under the dolphins. If the operation works correctly, and the captain and crew are willing to work with the by now sluggish and uncooperative dolphins, the tuna remain in the bottom of the net and the dolphins swim free. If, however, the operation is flawed, dolphins are injured or killed and discarded from the catch as waste.

Rather than relying on this imperfect correction of the purse seine method, some environmental groups think that entirely different methods of fishing for tuna should be employed. Alternatives could include using a pole and line or "setting" on tuna not associated with dolphins. However, according to marine scientists and fishermen, the alternative methods have serious drawbacks as well.

Some catch many sexually immature tuna, which for some reason don't associate with dolphins. Juvenile tuna often are too small to be marketed. If too many are caught, the sustainability of the population could be jeopardized. In addition, alternative methods frequently catch high numbers of other incidental species such as sharks, turtles, rays, mahi-mahi, and many kinds of noncommercial fish. Finally, all fishing methods expend energy. The practice of setting on dolphins uses the least amount of energy per volume of tuna caught.

According to many of the experts involved, including the Inter-American Tropical Tuna Commission, the U.S. National Marine Fisheries Service, and the scientific advisor to the American Tunaboat Association, the most efficient method for fishing tuna, in terms of operational cost, yield, and conservation of the tuna population, is to set on dolphins with a purse seine. From the point of view of the canning industry, only purse seine fishing provides the volume of catch necessary for growth of the industry.

SOURCES: Saul Alvarez-Borrego, "The Tuna and Dolphin Controversy," *UC Mexus News*, University of California Institute for Mexico and the United States 31 (Fall 1993): 8–13. "The Best Way to Save Dolphins," *The New York Times*, July 7, 1996, 4, 8; "Save Most of the Dolphins," *The Washington Post*, July 4, 1996, A-28: Colman McCarthy, "Dolphin Safe Claim Is in Danger," *The Washington Post*, July 23, 1996, E-18; Gary Lee, "Tuna Fishing Bill Divides Environmental Activists," *The Washington Post*, July 8, 1996, A-7.

Many experts also believe that with current technology, it is not possible to abandon the practice of setting on dolphins without falling into other, more grave, problems. While research to develop better techniques is now underway, positive results are not expected in the near future.

THE TRADE ASPECTS

This tuna-dolphin problem has engendered serious friction on the international level. The United States and Mexico, two countries sensitive to marine mammal protection and with solid laws in place for many years, have come head-to-head over the issue.

In 1988, the United States amended the U.S. Marine Mammal Act to prohibit the incidental kill of dolphins during commercial tuna fishing. The amendment requires the banning of tuna imports from any country that does not implement several specific measures to reduce dolphin mortality and achieve a kill-per-set rate (the number of dolphins killed in each casting of the fishing net) of no more than 1.25 times the U.S. rate.

In February of 1991, a U.S. trade embargo was imposed on tuna caught by foreign fishing fleets using the purse seine method in the ETP, with Mexico as a prime target. This harsh step was seen as necessary, since over the previous fifteen years, an estimated 7 million dolphins died in tuna nets. The embargo cost tuna-exporting countries such as Mexico, Costa Rica, and Ecuador hundreds of millions of dollars. To avoid future losses, the embargoed nations met with U.S. officials in 1992 to determine ways in which they could improve their fishing methods, end the embargo, and regain access to the lucrative U.S. market.

Several changes in fishing methods were introduced after these negotiations. Although foreign fishers did not abandon the purse seine method, they learned to dip their nets deeper to allow dolphins to escape. Dolphin safety panels were installed in many nets, serving as escape hatches for the dolphins. In addition, divers are now deployed to assist dolphins that cannot find their way out of the nets. The effect of these changes on dolphins survival were major. Figure 1 shows that in 1986, an average of fifteen dolphins were killed each time a Mexican boat cast its net on tuna. By 1992, the Mexican fleet had cut this rate to 1.85 deaths per cast. In all, tuna fishing-related dolphin deaths in the ETP have decreased by 96 percent. Independent estimates indicate that total dolphin deaths in the ETP have declined from 133,000 in 1986 to 3,274 in 1995.

Despite these encouraging results, fishermen from Mexico and other nations in the ETP are still restricted from selling dolphins in the United States because of their use of purse seines. In 1995, the United States and ten fishing nations negotiated the Panama declaration, an agreement which called for the United States to allow dolphins imports from these nations if their fishermen continue their efforts to improve dolphin safety measures.

Following this agreement, legislation proposing an end to the embargo was offered in both the U.S. House of Representatives and the Senate in mid-1996. The legislation was meant as a reward for the efforts already undertaken and contained a provision that would have permitted the "dolphin safe" label for certain tuna caught via purse seines, a privilege now reserved only for non-purse seine fishers.

THE ONGOING DEBATE

Proponents of the law argued that unless foreign fleets received an incentive to continue their successful efforts, they would revert back to their old and easier ways of catching fish. U.S. Vice President Al Gore, a supporter of the embargo's abolishment stated that "in recent years, we have reduced dolphin mortality in the Pacific Tuna

Incidental Dolphin Mortality Rate, Mexican Tuna Fleet (sets on dolphins, 1986–1993)

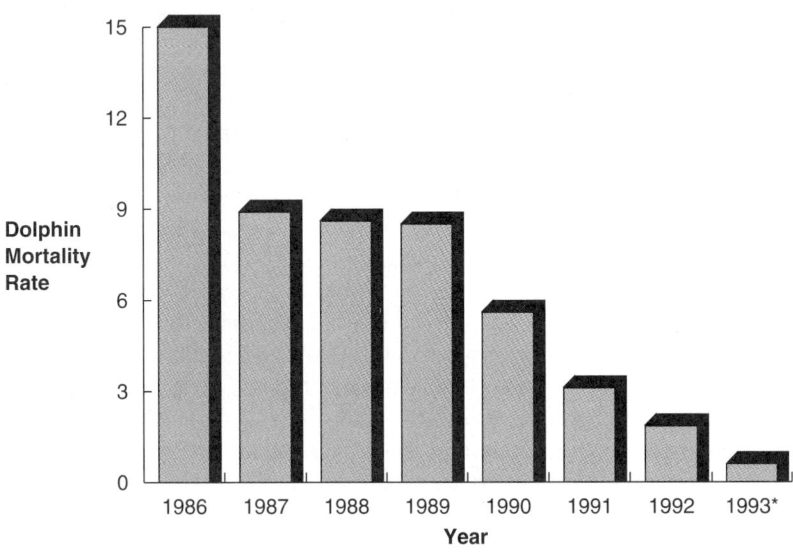

*Projected.
SOURCE: *UC Mexus News* (Fall 1993): 12.

Fishery far below historic levels. This legislation will codify an international agreement to lock these gains in place." Support for the lifting of the embargo was also expressed by Greenpeace, the Environmental Defense Fund, the World Wildlife Federation, and other environmental groups.

However, opponents of the legislation, which included several major environmental groups such as the Sierra Club and the Earth Island Institute, argued that the lifting of the embargo would bring a return to the fishing practices that led to the initial slaughter. They stated that in spite of the attempt to reduce dolphin deaths, purse seining still causes fatalities and should not be supported as an acceptable fishing method. They also labeled as not credible the threat that, if not granted access to the U.S. market, foreign fleets would revert to their old methods and sell tuna elsewhere, since over 90 percent of all tuna is consumed in the U.S., Canada, and Europe, all of which currently have anti-purse seining laws.

Some argue that it is unfair for the United States to impose unilaterally an embargo against tuna fishers only in the ETP and to disregard how tuna is fished in other oceans. The ETP hosts the best-known and best-managed tuna fishery in the world, employing scientific data to maintain a sustainable tuna yield and putting an observer on every ship to gather accurate statistics on the dolphin kill rate. It is contended that without observer programs in other oceans it is impossible to determine the number of dolphins killed in the pursuit of tuna not currently affected by the embargo.

In spite of the political tension, the Inter-American Tropical Tuna Commission has been working toward multilateral agreements on dolphin conservation. Commitments have been made by all governments represented in the ETP to adopt 100 percent observer coverage. Since 1993, a biologist is assigned to every ship to observe fishing methods and to record dolphin mortality. The participating governments also adopted a vessel quota system in which the overall yearly quota for dolphin mortality is equally divided among the boats fishing in the region. This way, each boat is individually held responsible for its dolphin kill. Otherwise, a few careless ships could destroy the entire fishery's attempts to meet lower mortality rates for the year.

Currently, the total yearly mortality for each dolphin species is under 1 percent of its population, an amount that can be sustained without reducing the total number; in fact, the populations are currently increasing. Thus, most scientists now view the mortality of dolphins incidental to tuna fishing not as an environmental problem but as one of avoiding unnecessary killing. In fact, a National Marine Fisheries Service scientist has stated that if Mexico has money for research, it would be better invested on behalf of the Vaquita, a species in real danger of extinction, than in the tuna-dolphin issue, since there is no danger to the dolphin population as a whole.

Strong opposition to current practices continues to be voiced by environmentalists. States David Philips, executive director of the Earth Island Institute: "The goal is to eliminate the killing of dolphins entirely by prohibiting the technique of setting on them to catch tuna." Even though the embargo relief passed in the U.S. House of Representatives, it was never voted on in the Senate. With the adjournment of Congress in 1996, the bill died. Supporters of the plan indicate that it will be reintroduced in 1997. In the meantime, however, purse seine fishermen are still barred from the U.S. market.

Questions for Discussion

1. Why is there such a concern about dolphins?
2. What is your view of using the technologically most advanced country's performance as a benchmark for evaluating other countries' activities?
3. Is the denial of market access an appropriate tool to enforce a country's environmental standards?
4. Is a zero-dolphin-death goal realistic?

VIDEO CASE

Lobbying in the United States

Success in the international marketplace often requires more than mere business know-how. A firm also must understand and deal with the intricacies of national politics and laws. In an era of increased business-government interaction, a firm's ability to anticipate, understand, and perhaps even shape government action may be critical for long-term market penetration. To become aware of government policies and to in-

SOURCE: This case was written by Michael R. Czinkota and is based on *America for Sale: Japan's Buy-Out Binge*, Financial News Network, and William J. Holstein, "Japan's Clout in the U.S." *Business Week*, July 7, 1988, 64–66.

fluence the government decision-making process, companies frequently use the assistance of lobbyists. Usually, these lobbyists are well connected individuals and firms that can provide access to policymakers and legislators.

In the United States, firms have for a long time ensured that their voices are heard in Washington, DC. Increasingly, foreign countries and companies have participated in this lobbying process as well. Since many government actions are likely to affect international business, numerous lobbyists have been hired to work for foreign firms.

Public attention has particularly focused on the "influence-buying" activities of Japan in the United States. Some believe that Japanese attempts at shaping or influencing U.S. trade policy are inappropriate. For example, Texas Congressman John Bryant claims that his bills, which seek more disclosure of Japanese investment activities in the United States, have repeatedly been rejected due to lobbying efforts by Japanese firms. He believes that as a result of these efforts, the U.S. government is less informed about foreign investment activities than it should be.

Another major concern to many is the fact that former U.S. policymakers often become key lobbyists for Japanese firms. Three former U.S. trade representatives, who were the heads of the government office that develops and executes U.S. international trade negotiations and policy, are now working for Japanese firms. For example, the law firm of Robert Strauss works for Fujitsu; William Brock represents Toyota; and William Eberle works for Nissan. Other examples are the former top Nixon aide Leonard Garment, who works for Toshiba, and the former national chairman of the Democratic party Charles Manatt, who now represents NEC. One Washington insider, Clyde Prestowitz, claims: "About 80 percent of former U.S. high-ranking government officials, and virtually every high-powered political lawyer in Washington, is retained in one way or another by Japanese interests. It is by far the biggest lobby in Washington, and the most well funded." States Pat Choate, author of the book *Agents of Influence:* "It is wrong, I believe, that so many Americans wind up on foreign payrolls, particularly after they have been in high positions in the U.S. government. Americans seem to be available so easily, so cheaply. This demeans us in the eyes of the world. It casts doubt in the minds of our own people about the integrity of our decision-making process."

Many believe that this easy availability of former U.S. trade negotiators to Japanese firms may undermine the U.S. policy process. It is claimed that these individuals may give away secret U.S. trade strategies or help Japanese companies find ways to circumvent existing trade legislation. Frequently cited is the case of a former U.S. negotiator in the automotive sector who applied for a position with Japanese firms while still holding his position in U.S. government.

Also of major concern are Japanese expenditures aimed at U.S. think tanks and universities. Critics argue that the funding of research projects or the endowment of chairs raises basic ethical questions. They say that Japan's wealth may tempt some of America's elite to accept Japanese funds at the expense of broader U.S. interests.

These views are vigorously disputed by others. For example, William Eberle, one of the former U.S. trade representatives mentioned earlier, maintains that his and other ex-trade officials' influence is greatly exaggerated. He states that he might be able to get the door open, but he doesn't think he has any more influence from the fact that he once held the job of U.S. trade representative. Others are more vocal. In their view, the Japanese funding provided to institutions such as the Reischauer Center of the Johns Hopkins University, or to think tanks like the Brookings Institution and the American Enterprise Institute, has no influence at all on the outcome of research projects. Scholars at these institutions are very upset at having their integrity questioned. States John Makin of the American Enterprise Institute, "This whole notion that anybody who talks about free trade is being paid off by the Japanese, which is what critics are essentially saying, is schlock."

Questions for Discussion

1. Should foreign firms be able to represent their interests in Washington, DC?
2. Should U.S. ex-policymakers be able to represent such foreign interests? How about domestic interests?
3. Should there be a cooling-off period before ex-policymakers can take on representation of foreign interests? If so, how long should such a period be? Is it fair to impose such an employment restriction burden on former government officials?
4. Do you see the donation of funds by Japanese firms to U.S. think tanks as undermining U.S. interests?

PART THREE

Environmental Considerations in Global Business Operations

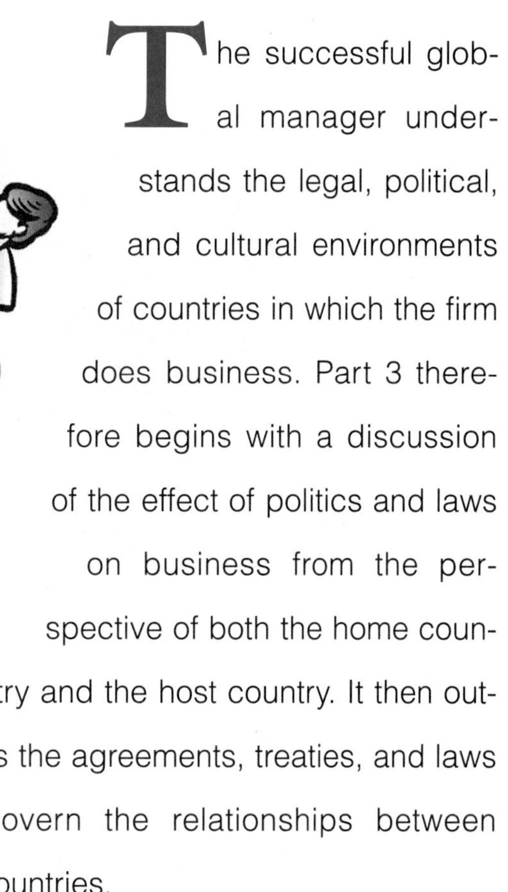

The successful global manager understands the legal, political, and cultural environments of countries in which the firm does business. Part 3 therefore begins with a discussion of the effect of politics and laws on business from the perspective of both the home country and the host country. It then outlines the agreements, treaties, and laws that govern the relationships between home and host countries.

Managing conflicts between cultures requires an understanding of cultural differences in language, religion, values, customs, and education. This knowledge is the key to developing cross-cultural competence.

Part 3 concludes with a chapter on the organization, management, and control of global operations. In the highly competitive global business arena, the manager must learn how to organize human and physical resources in ways that permit optimal responses to changes in the marketplace. Once organized, these resources must be managed and controlled on a day-to-day basis.

The Legal and Political Environment of Global Business

LEARNING OBJECTIVES

To understand the importance of the legal and political environments in both the home and host countries to the global business executive.

To learn how governments affect business through legislation and regulations.

To see how the political actions of countries expose firms to international risks.

To examine the differing laws regulating global trade found in different countries.

To understand how international political relations, agreements, and treaties can affect global business.

An understanding of the legal and political environments that a global business must be sensitive and react to is fundamental to successful worldwide competition. International law is the basis for trade in goods and services and investment in foreign companies and lands. An introductory knowledge of the international legal environment will alert executives to the potential perils and pitfalls of conducting business with organizations of, or in, foreign lands. For the global manager, "the most important question is always, how does the law affect my business plans? The emphasis is on strategic planning, keeping a business from getting into legal trouble, and learning how to ask the right questions worldwide to get the best information for making management decisions."[1]

This chapter will examine law and politics from the manager's point of view. The two subjects are considered together because both are intertwined to some extent; that is, in some instances political decisions may cause laws to be modified. On the other hand, laws may restrict the power of politicians. A single legal and political environment does not exist, but changes from country to country. Additionally, the global company may not be influenced only by the legal and political situation in a host country, but by the legal system and political realities of its home country. As a firm enters the global marketplace, it soon realizes that it must become aware of a legal environment consisting of:

- *National laws and regulations,* including the law of its own country (domestic law) and that of other countries with which it does business.
- *Private international law,* covering the rights, duties, and disputes among persons from different places.
- *Public international law,* including treaties and commercial customs.
- *International organizations,* with their laws, regulations, and guidelines.

NATIONAL LAW

Any business activity crossing a national border is subject to the **national law** of the home country and that of the foreign, or host, country. All of the categories of law applying to any domestic business transaction—such as contracts, torts, and antitrust law—will apply to the international transaction.[2] Many of the national, or domestic, laws and regulations may not specifically address global business issues, yet they can have a major impact on a firm's opportunities abroad. Minimum wage legislation has a bearing on the global competitiveness of a firm using production processes that require large amounts of labor. The cost of satisfying domestic safety regulations significantly affect the pricing policies of firms. For example, U.S. legislation creating the Environmental Superfund requires payments by chemical firms based on their production volume, regardless of whether the production is sold domestically or exported. As a result, these firms are at a disadvantage when exporting their chemical products, which are like commodities in that global competition is mainly based on price. They are required to compete against firms that have a cost advantage because their home countries do not require payment into an environmental fund.

national law
body of legal regulations that govern activities carried on inside the legal boundaries of an organization's or citizen's home country

Other legal and regulatory measures, however, are clearly aimed at companies that do business on an international basis. Some of these regulations may be designed to help firms in their global efforts. Governments may attempt to aid and protect the business efforts of domestic companies facing competition from abroad by setting standards for product content and quality. The political environment in most countries tends to provide general support for the global business efforts of firms headquartered within that country. A new government may work to reduce trade barriers or to increase trade opportunities through bilateral and multilateral negotiations. Such actions will affect individual firms to the extent that they improve the global climate for free trade.

INTERNATIONAL LAW

international law
body of rules and laws that regulate activities carried on outside the legal boundaries of states

state
political entity comprising a territory, population, a government capable of entering into international relations, and a government capable of controlling its territory and peoples

public international law
division of international law that deals primarily with the rights and duties of states and intergovernmental organizations as between themselves

International law is the body of rules and norms that regulates activities carried on outside the legal boundaries of **states.** Traditionally, international law was viewed as consisting of two distinct branches—**public international law,** the law dealing with conduct between states, and **private international law,** the name given to the rules that regulate the affairs of private persons internationally. Figure 7.1 provides examples of public and private international law. Contemporary international law now regulates organizations and individuals as well as nations, and the division between public and private law has become blurred. Today the term "international law" applies to any conduct outside the boundaries of states, whether of a public or a private nature.[3]

PRIVATE INTERNATIONAL LAW

In an expanding world market, the courts cannot possibly anticipate the "risks" of the many transactions into which traders enter. Societies, therefore, give the parties freedom of contract, allowing them to accommodate their needs to those of the world community and, in effect, to negotiate a *private law* to cover a particular transaction. Private law is not the laws of nations. The various legal systems provide the interpre-

FIGURE 7.1 **Categories of International Law**

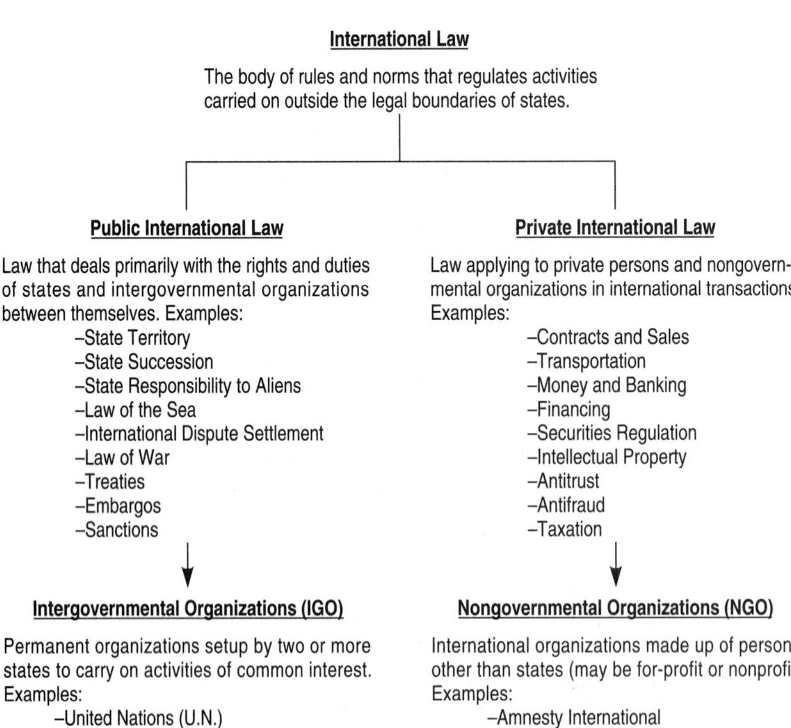

SOURCE: Adapted from August, R., *International Business Law,* 2nd ed., Prentice-Hall, Upper Saddle River, N.J.: 1997.

tation of contracts, but the courts will not make a contract for the parties. Thus, the contract is a private affair and not a social institution.[4]

Private international law is the domain of rights, duties, and disputes among persons from different places. It concerns how a nation's courts deal with a different nation's laws. Often referred to as the field of **conflict of laws,** it consists of three areas:

- choice of law (which laws apply to the transaction)
- choice of forum (who has jurisdiction or the power to hear the case)
- recognition and enforcement of judgments[5]

Consider the following situation. An American seller alleges a breach of contract by a French buyer: Which nation's law applies to the transaction? In which country will the case be heard—the United States or France? Will a French court enforce a judgment against the French company if it is obtained in an American court?

The study of conflicts of law has long been a legal theoretician's delight and, thus, a manager's nightmare. There are no universal rules for choosing the appropriate law to govern a dispute; rather, different states and countries employ a variety of techniques—these techniques have changed over time.[6]

private international law
division of international law that deals primarily with the rights and duties of individuals and nongovernmental organizations in their international affairs

conflict of laws
differences in the laws of countries as they apply to transactions among persons from different places

International Contracts

The contract is used to facilitate world trade. It is a legal document created according to a body of domestic law—sometimes more than one body of law—that attaches rights, duties, and obligations to the parties to the agreement.[7] In the event of disagreement and/or dispute among the parties to the agreement, the legal systems underlying it must be referred to in order to determine the legality of the agreement, the rights of the parties, and possible remedies for disputes. Contracts will be treated differently in different legal, cultural, and economic systems. Generally, most global business transactions fall into one of several categories:

1. The *sale of goods and services:*
   - Direct sales transaction between buyer and seller.
   - Indirect sales transaction using an intermediary such as an agent or distributor.
2. *Licensing and franchising:* a contract permitting another company to manufacture and/or sell the good or service in the foreign land.
3. *Direct investment:* the operation of a foreign branch office or facility, creation of a foreign subsidiary company, or participation in a joint venture with other business or governmental organizations.

Each of these categories of global business activity rely heavily on some form of contractual relationship. Often the contract is between parties with only a casual or no personal relationship—physically separated by thousands of miles of ocean, doing business in diverse cultures, and operating under vastly different legal systems.

International Contractual Disputes

The international legal environment affects the manager to the extent that firms must concern themselves with jurisdictional disputes. Because no single body of international law exists, firms usually are restricted by both home- and host-country laws. If

What's the name of the beer in Timbuktu? (Bomako, Tombigber, Brekhorn, Tim Buck II or Bou Bou Tou?)

Bomako is the beer of Timbuktu.

a conflict occurs between contracting parties in two different countries, a question arises concerning which country's laws are to be used and in which court the dispute is to be settled. Sometimes the contract will contain a jurisdictional clause, which settles the matter with little problem. If the contract does not contain such a clause, however, the parties to the dispute have a few choices. They can settle the dispute by following the laws of the country in which the agreement was made, or they can resolve it by obeying the laws of the country in which the contract will have to be fulfilled. Which laws to use and in which location to settle the dispute are two different decisions. As a result, a dispute between a U.S. exporter and a French importer could be resolved in Paris but be based on New York State law.

arbitration
procedure for settling a dispute in which an objective third party hears both sides and makes a decision; procedure for resolving conflict in the international business arena through the use of intermediaries, such as representatives of chambers of commerce, trade associations, or third-country institutions

In cases of disagreement, the parties can choose either **arbitration** or litigation. Litigation is usually avoided for several reasons. It often involves extensive delays and is very costly. In addition, firms may fear discrimination in foreign countries. Therefore, companies tend to prefer conciliation and arbitration, because these processes result in much quicker decisions. Arbitration procedures are often spelled out in the original contract and usually provide for an intermediary who is judged to be impartial by both parties. Frequently, intermediaries will be representatives of chambers of commerce, trade associations, or third-country institutions.

Avoiding the Pitfalls of Negotiating Contracts in an Unfamiliar Legal Environment

Many countries around the world, including some of the most significant world trading nations, have legal systems based on non-Western ways of thinking. Each country's system is unique, and traders doing business in non-Western countries need to explore several issues before they do business. First, they should inquire into the cultural traditions of each country and the significant historical events that shaped the legal system. Second, they should look at the function of law in each society and the roles of its leading institutions and its lawyers. Third, they should look to see under what circumstances traditional Western ways of thinking about business and legal issues will be adequate for resolving trade and investment problems. Equipped with this knowledge, the Western business person can improve the prospects for success in dealings with non-Western cultures.[8] Finally, armed with a general understanding of the foreign legal system in question, the global manager should seek the legal counsel of an attorney skilled in the craft of international law and thoroughly knowledgeable of the legal system involved.

Restriction of Global Business Activity

extraterritoriality
nation's attempt to set policy outside its territorial limits

Governments also have specific rules and regulations that restrict global business activity. These restrictions are particularly sensitive when they address activities outside the country. Such measures challenge the territorial sovereignty of other governments and raise the issue of **extraterritoriality**—meaning a nation's attempt to set policy outside its territorial limits (see Global Learning Experience 7.1). Yet actions implying such extraterritorial reach are common, because nations often argue that their citizens and products maintain their nationality wherever they may be, and they therefore continue to be subject to the rules and laws of their home country.

GLOBAL LEARNING EXPERIENCE 7.1

U.S. Justice Department Sues British Firm in Extraterritorial Application of U.S. Antitrust Law

In a classic example of the extraterritorial application of U.S. antitrust laws, the U.S. Justice Department sued Pilkington P.L.C., the world's largest maker of flat glass. The antitrust suit accused the British company of monopolizing the technology for making sheets of glass like those used in window panes or car windshields. The Justice Department argued that Pilkington fell under American jurisdiction because it owned 80 percent of an American glassmaker, the Libbey-Owens-Ford Company.

Pilkington developed and patented its technology for producing flat glass in the late 1950s and required licenses for the right to use the technology. It limited licensees to a certain geographical area. Although many of Pilkington's patents have expired, the company has continued to require the licenses, contending that its production processes are trade secrets. Virtually all of the world's glass factories operate under Pilkington licenses, including plants in Russia and China.

The case had little to do with the glass market in the United States; instead, it sought to make sure that American companies could operate freely abroad, by requiring that the company drop its rule that American glass concerns could not build factories outside the U.S. territory assigned in their licenses. Glass is both heavy and fragile, making it costly to export, so factories tend to be located near a market. By the terms of their licenses, American glass firms were not permitted to build factories outside the United States, effectively barring them from competing in foreign markets.

The Justice Department reached a settlement in 1996 with Pilkington in which the company would drop its geographical rules. No financial penalties were imposed and Pilkington denied any wrongdoing.

SOURCE: *New York Times,* May 27, 1994, D-6.

Of major concern to the global business manager are *antitrust laws.* The primary law which regulates business activity that restrains trade or competition in the United States is the **Sherman Antitrust Act of 1890.** The act prohibits contracts, agreements, and conspiracies that restrain interstate or international trade. A second law, the **Clayton Act of 1914** expanded the provisions of the Sherman Act, and a third law, the **Robinson-Patman Act of 1936,** made price discrimination illegal.

The courts have ruled that these laws apply to international operations beyond U.S. borders, as well as to domestic business (see Global Learning Experience 7.2). The Justice Department watches closely when a U.S. firm buys an overseas company, engages in a joint venture with a foreign firm, or makes an agreement abroad with a competing firm in order to ensure that the action does not result in restraint of competition in the United States.

Given the increase in worldwide cooperation among companies, however, the wisdom of extending U.S. antitrust legislation to international activities is being questioned. Some limitations to these tough antitrust provisions were already implemented decades ago. The Webb-Pomerene Act of 1918 excludes from antitrust prosecution firms cooperating to develop foreign markets. The exclusion of international activities from antitrust regulation was further enhanced by the Export Trading Company Act of 1982, which was designed specifically to assist small and medium-sized firms in their export efforts by permitting them to join forces. Further steps to loosen the application

Sherman Antitrust Act of 1890 forbids combinations and conspiracies in restraint of interstate and international trade, and forbids monopolies and attempts to monopolize interstate and international trade

Clayton Act of 1914 expands the enforcement provisions of the Sherman Antitrust Act; defines exclusive dealing and tying clauses as being mergers that result in monopolies, and interlocking directorates as being unfair business practices

Robinson-Patman Act of 1936 forbids price discrimination

Foreign Companies Held Liable for Non-U.S. Price Fixing

Criminal charges of price fixing can be brought against foreign companies even if the act of wrongdoing took place outside the United States. This ruling by the United States Court of Appeals for the First Circuit is believed to be the first time a federal appeals court has ruled on the legality of *criminal charges* against foreign businesses on antitrust actions taken outside the United States.

The three companies, Nippon Paper Industries and Mitsubshi Paper Mills of Japan and Arto Wiggins Appleton P.L.C. of Britain, were accused of conspiring to increase the price of jumbo rolls of fax paper between February 1990 and February 1992. Nippon Paper argued that the actions took place in Japan, beyond the reach of the Sherman Antitrust Act. The U.S. Justice Department argued that Nippon Paper's actions affected the American fax paper market.

In ruling against the foreign companies, the U.S. Appeals Court judge wrote: "We live in an age of international commerce where decisions reached in one corner of the world can reverberate around the globe in less time than it takes to tell the tale. Thus, a ruling in Nippon Paper Industries' favor would create perverse incentives for those who would use nefarious means to influence markets in the United States."

Since 1945, the U.S. Supreme Court has allowed foreign companies to be sued for acting outside the United States to block competition in this country. The right to bring such civil suits was reaffirmed by the high court in 1993.

SOURCE: *New York Times,* March 19, 1997, D-2.

of U.S. antitrust laws to international business are under consideration because of increased competition from state-supported enterprises, strategic alliances, and megacorporations from abroad.

Regulating the Moral Behavior of Global Businesses

Home countries may implement special laws and regulations to ensure that the global business behavior of firms headquartered within them is conducted within moral and ethical boundaries considered appropriate. The definition of appropriateness may vary from country to country and from government to government. Therefore, the content of such regulations, their enforcement, and their impact on firms may vary substantially between nations.

U.S. firms operating overseas are affected by U.S. laws against bribery and corruption. In many countries, payments or favors are a way of life, and "a greasing of the wheels" is expected in return for government services. As a result, many U.S. companies doing business internationally had routinely paid bribes or done favors for foreign officials in order to gain contracts. In the 1970s, a major national debate erupted about these business practices, led by arguments that U.S. firms have an ethical and moral leadership obligation and that contracts won through bribes do not reflect competitive market activity. As a result, the **Foreign Corrupt Practices Act** was passed in 1977, making it a crime for U.S. executives of publicly traded firms to bribe a foreign official in order to obtain business. Specifically, the Foreign Corrupt Practices Act prohibits U.S. firms from paying, or offering to pay, foreign officials for assistance in obtaining contracts or business. In determining whether or not a U.S. business firm has violated the

Foreign Corrupt Practices Act passed in 1977, making it a crime for U.S. executives of publicly traded firms to bribe a foreign official in order to obtain business

GLOBAL LEARNING EXPERIENCE 7.3

Paying the Price for Payoffs

The Foreign Corrupt Practices Act, which was passed in 1977, forbids the bribery of foreign government officials in order to obtain business contracts. One of the original reasons for enacting the law was that the Lockheed Corporation allegedly paid $22 million in bribes to foreign government officials to obtain contracts for its F-104 fighter plane in the mid-1970s. Some of the payoffs were made to a Dutch crown prince and a Japanese prime minister, among others. Having admitted to paying the bribes and having their business tactics exposed, the company indicated that its use of bribes would stop.

In 1986, a subsidiary of Lockheed was involved in the payment of bribes and kickbacks to New York City officials while seeking a city contract to handle collections for the city's Parking Violations Bureau. The company avoided prosecution by cooperating with legal authorities.

There is an old saying that, "A person who does not learn from his mistakes is bound to repeat them." This is apparently what happened at Lockheed.

In 1994, the company was again in the spotlight for bribing foreign officials. This time Lockheed pleaded guilty to the charge of paying $1 million to a member of the Egyptian Parliament in exchange for assistance in securing a $79 million contract for the sale of three C-130 Hercules transport planes. (A Federal District Court fined Lockheed $24.8 million.)

SOURCE: Adapted from *New York Times,* January 28, 1995, p. 475.

provisions of the FCPA, the amount of the payment, or bribe, is not important, but rather the intent. If the intent is to pay local officials "grease money" to facilitate processing of routine paperwork, the firm has not violated the law, but if the intent of the payment is to obtain business, the U.S. firm is in violation of the act. Global Learning Experience 7.3 provides a review of one U.S. company's involvement in payoffs to obtain business overseas.

Bribery and various forms of corruption are not uncommon in the global business arena, as illustrated by the Corruption Perception Index in Table 7.1. In Italy, bribes given to public officials are a time-honored, centuries-old practice. The bribe money is called a *bustarella*—small envelope filled with the money. Lately, however, numerous financial scandals involving many government officials may be changing the Italian public's attitude toward the practice. In Mexico, a bribe is a *mordida,* or the bite. In 1993, Japan was rocked by scandal after scandal of Japanese government officials being paid huge bribes. Most resigned their positions, although few, if any, have gone to jail.

A number of U.S. firms have complained about the act, arguing that it hinders their efforts to compete internationally against companies whose home countries have no such antibribery laws. The problem is one of ethics versus practical needs and, to some extent, of the amounts involved. It may be hard to draw the line between providing a generous tip and paying a bribe in order to speed up a business transaction. Many business executives believe that the United States should not apply its moral principles to other societies and cultures in which bribery and corruption are endemic. To compete internationally, executives argue, they must be free to use the most common methods of competition in the host country.

TABLE 7.1

1996 Corruption Perception Index
(Score relates to perceptions of the degree of which corruption is seen by business people. A perfect 10.0 would be a totally corrupt free country.)

Country	Score	Country	Score
Nigeria	0.69	Bolivia	3.40
Pakistan	1.00	Argentina	3.41
Kenya	2.21	Italy	3.42
Bangladesh	2.29	Turkey	3.54
China	2.43	Spain	4.31
Cameroon	2.46	Hungary	4.86
Venezuela	2.50	Jordan	4.89
Russia	2.58	Taiwan	4.98
India	2.63	Greece	5.01
Indonesia	2.65	South Korea	5.02
Philippines	2.69	Malaysia	5.32
Uganda	2.71	Czech Republic	5.37
Colombia	2.73	Poland	5.57
Egypt	2.84	South Africa	5.68
Brazil	2.96	Portugal	6.53
Ecuador	3.19	Chile	6.80
Mexico	3.30	Belgium	6.84
Thailand	3.33	France	6.96

SOURCE: Transparency International

For U.S. firms seeking business abroad, the problem of adhering to the letter and spirit of the Foreign Corrupt Practices Act is best illustrated by the way foreign governments react to bribes. In Denmark, Switzerland, and many other European countries, bribes given to foreign public officials to obtain business may be tax deductible if declared on tax returns. There are indications that nations are beginning to appreciate how bribery can distort free trade. In April 1996, the Organization for Economic Cooperation and Development (OECD)—with a membership of 26 major nations—under intense pressure from the United States, agreed to rewrite tax rules that have effectively encouraged the bribery of foreign public officials by permitting the bribes to be tax deductible.[9]

Another major issue that is critical for international business managers is that of general standards of behavior and ethics. Increasingly, public concerns are raised about such issues as environmental protection, global warming, pollution, and moral behavior. However, these issues are not of the same importance in every country. What may be frowned upon or even illegal in one nation may be customary, or at least acceptable, in others. For example, the cutting down of the Brazilian rain forest may be acceptable to the government of Brazil, but scientists and concerned consumers may object vehemently because of the effect on global warming and other climatic changes. The export of U.S. tobacco products may be legal but results in accusations of exporting death to developing nations. China may use prison labor in producing products for export, but U.S. law prohibits the importation of such products. Mexico may permit the use of low safety standards for workers, but the buyers of Mexican products may object to the resulting dangers.

International firms must understand these conflicts and should assert leadership in implementing change. Not everything that is legally possible should be exploited for profit. Although companies need to return a profit on their investments, these issues must be seen in the context of time. By acting on existing, leading-edge knowledge and standards, firms will be able to benefit in the long term through consumer goodwill and the avoidance of later recriminations.

PUBLIC INTERNATIONAL LAW

Another aspect of international law which may have significant implications on global business activity lies in the area of *public international law.* This is the area of law that deals primarily with the rights and duties of states and intergovernmental organizations between themselves. Governments may promulgate specific rules and regulations that are frequently political in nature and are based on governmental objectives that override commercial concerns and restrict global business activities. Three types of regulations are of particular interest to the global manager: export controls, boycotts, and sanctions and embargoes.

Export Controls

Many nations have **export-control systems,** which are designed to deny or at least delay the acquisition of strategically important goods to adversaries. In the United States, the export-control system is based on the Export Administration Act and the Munitions Control Act. These laws control all exports of goods, services, and ideas from the United States. The determinants for controls are national security, foreign policy, short supply, and nuclear nonproliferation. Every export from the United States requires an approval from the Department of Commerce, which administers the Export Administration Act. There are two types of approval: *no license required* (NLR) and an *export license.*

export-control systems
designed to deny or at least delay the acquisition of strategically important goods to adversaries

Most exports may be made under NLR conditions, which is a blanket permission to export. Under NLR conditions, products can be freely shipped to most trading partners provided that neither the end user nor the end use involved are considered sensitive.

When products to be exported involve sensitive, high-level technologies and/or are being exported to countries not friendly to the United States, the exporter must apply for an **export license.** After the application for the export license has been filed, specialists in the Department of Commerce check the commodity to be exported against the **Critical Commodities List,** a file containing information about products that are either particularly sensitive for national security reasons or controlled for other purposes. The product is then matched with the country of destination and recipient company. If the Department of Commerce has no concerns about these three items, an export license is issued. The decision steps in the export-licensing process are summarized in Figure 7.2.

export license
license obtainable from the U.S. Department of Commerce Bureau of Export Administration, which is responsible for administering the Export Administration Act

Critical Commodities List
file containing information about products that are either particularly sensitive to national security or controlled for other purposes

Export controls are increasingly difficult to implement and enforce for several reasons. First, the number of countries able to manufacture products of strategic importance has increased. Industrializing nations, which only a decade ago were seen as poor imitators at best, are now at the forefront of cutting-edge technology. Their products can have a significant impact on the balance of power in the world. Second, products that are in need of control are developed and disseminated very quickly. Product life cycles have been shortened to such an extent that even temporary delays in distribution may result in a significant setback for a firm. Third, because of advances in miniaturization, products that are in need of control are shrinking in size. The smuggling and diversion of such products have become easier because they are easier to conceal. Finally, the transfer of technology and know-how has increasingly taken on major

FIGURE 7.2 **U.S. Export-Control System**

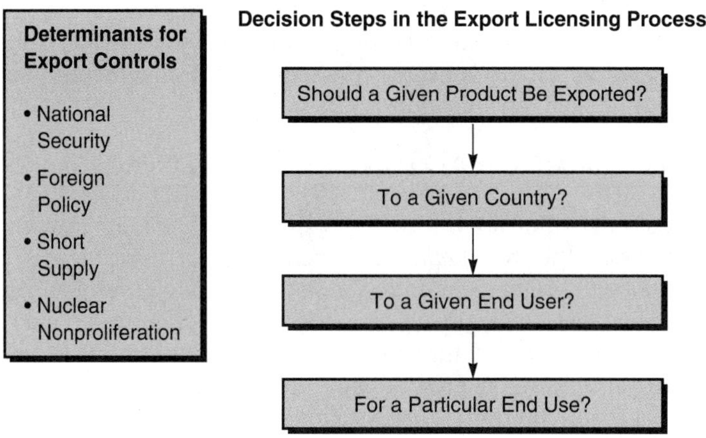

strategic significance because such services are often invisible, performed by individuals, and highly personalized. They are easy to transship and therefore difficult to trace and control.

Boycott

boycott
to combine in abstaining from, or preventing dealings with a person or organization as a means of coercion

A major way in which the United States attempts to govern international business activities is through boycotts. A **boycott** is a collaboration to prevent a country from carrying on international trade by preventing or obstructing other countries from dealing with it. In 1948, the League of Arab States began an economic boycott of Israel. Business firms that did business with, or had any ties to, Israel could be or were blacklisted and denied the opportunity to do business with the Arab States. Because of U.S. political ties to Israel, various U.S. laws were changed to make it illegal to support or comply with any boycott imposed by foreign governments against a country friendly to the United States. U.S. firms that comply with the boycott are subject to heavy fines and to denial of export privileges.

Given the nature of the boycott and the complex paperwork required to avoid violating the U.S. antiboycott laws, many U.S. firms have not vigorously pursued business opportunities in the Middle East. This has worked to the advantage of foreign competitors and may have resulted in a loss of profits for U.S. business. In November 1993, the United States announced that the U.S. International Trade Commission would begin a yearlong study into the costs of the boycott to U.S. companies that do business with Israel. Signs that the 45-year-old boycott may be slowly deteriorating were indicated by discussions between Israel and Jordan on a variety of economic and political matters, and the granting of partial autonomy for Palestinians.

Sanctions and Embargoes

sanction
action by one or more states toward another state calculated to force it to comply with legal obligations

The *International Emergency Economic Powers Act of 1977* grants wide authority to the president of the United States to regulate international economic and financial transactions, including placing restrictions on exports and imports and the seizure of foreign assets held in U.S. banks. **Sanctions** tend to consist of specific trade measures such as the cancellation of trade financing or the prohibition of high-technology trade.

Embargoes are usually much broader than sanctions in that they prohibit trade entirely. The embargo is usually reserved for political purposes. The use of such an extraordinary remedy is usually designed to implement foreign policy objectives, such as to punish another country for some offensive conduct in world affairs.

embargoes
1. an order of a government prohibiting the movement of merchant vessels from or into ports. 2. an injunction from a government control agency to refuse freight for shipment. 3. any legal restriction imposed on commerce

Over the years, economic sanctions have become a principal tool of foreign policy for many countries. Often, they are imposed unilaterally in the hope of changing a country's government or at least changing its policies. Between 1914 and 1983, there were 99 incidents in which sanctions were used to pursue political goals, 46 of which occurred after 1970.[10] Reasons for the impositions have varied, ranging from the upholding of human rights to attempts to promote nuclear nonproliferation or antiterrorism.

A 1997 study by the National Association of Manufacturers, using the broadest definition of sanctions, found that the President or Congress of the United States had enacted 61 laws and executive actions authorizing unilateral economic sanctions for foreign policy purposes from 1993–1996. Thirty-five countries were specifically targeted, which represent 2.3 billion potential consumers of U.S. goods and services (42 percent of the world's population) and $790 billion worth of export markets (19 percent of the world's total). Figure 7.3 illustrates the geographic scope of the sanctions.[11]

The problem with sanctions, however, is that frequently their unilateral imposition has not produced the desired result. Sanctions may make the obtaining of goods more difficult or expensive for the sanctioned country, yet their purported objective is almost never achieved. In order to work, sanctions need to be imposed multilaterally—a goal that is clear, yet difficult to implement. On rare occasions, however, global cooperation can be achieved. For example, when Iraq invaded Kuwait in August of 1990, virtually all members of the United Nations condemned this hostile action and joined a trade embargo against Iraq. Typically, individual countries have different relationships with the country subject to the embargo and cannot or do not wish to terminate trade relations. In this instance, however, both major and minor Iraqi trading partners—including many Arab nations—honored the United Nations trade sanctions and ceased trade with Iraq in the attempt to force it to withdraw its troops from Kuwait. Agreements were made to financially compensate those countries most adversely affected by the trade embargo.

Sanctions imposed by governments normally mean significant loss of business, and the issue of compensating the domestic firms and industries affected by these sanctions is always raised. One study examined the economic impact of U.S. sanctions in place in 1995 that targeted 26 different countries. The conclusion was that the sanctions cost $15 billion to $20 billion in lost U.S. exports and 200,000 to 250,000 U.S. jobs.[12]

The United Nations trade sanctions devastated Iraq's economy following Iraq's invasion of Kuwait because most Iraqi trading partners, including many Arab nations, honored the sanctions. However, the sanctions did not prove effective in averting the Gulf War.
SOURCE: The Bettmann Archives, Reuters/Bettmann.

FIGURE 7.3 **U.S. Unilateral Sanctions, 1993–1996**

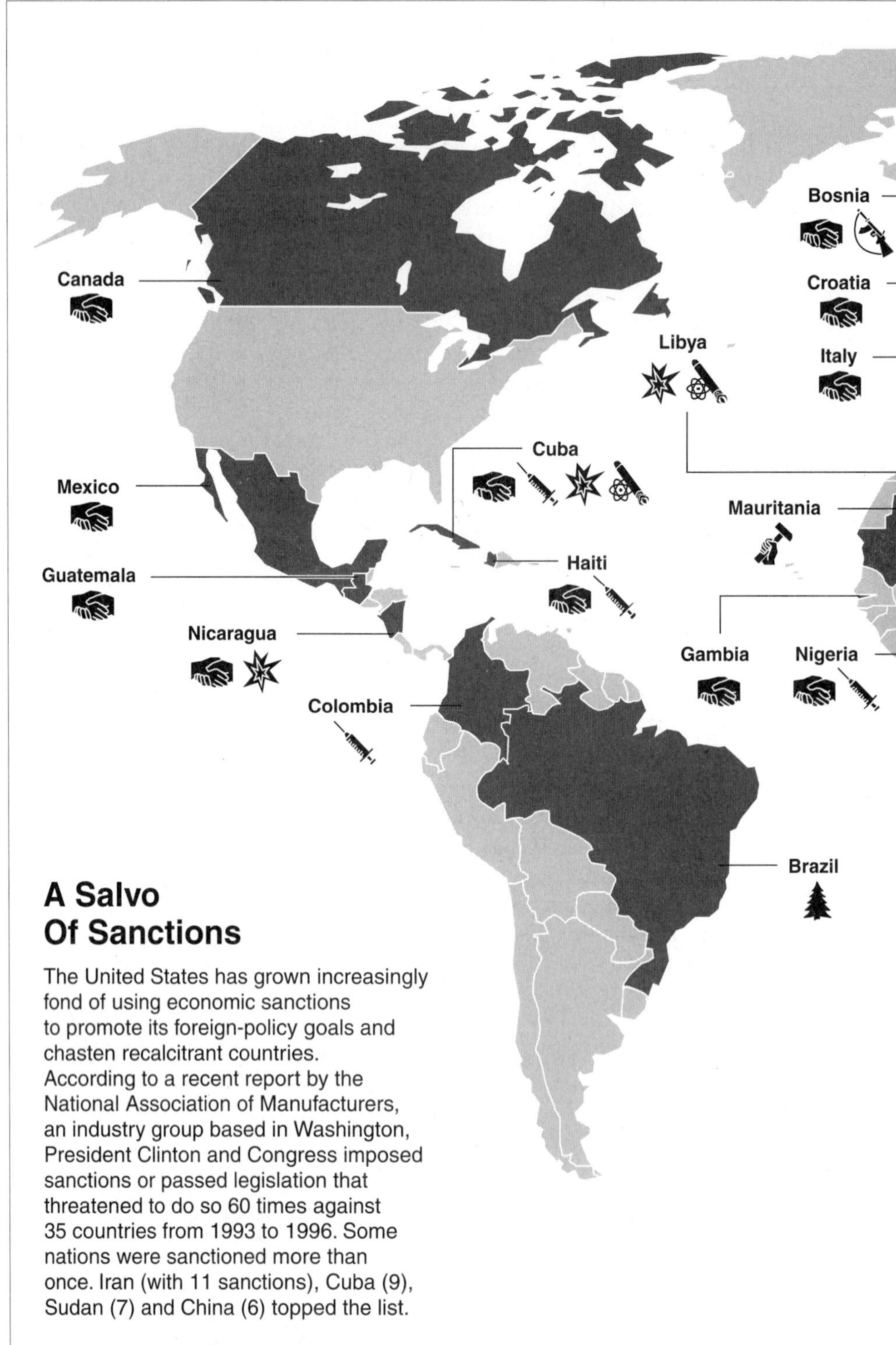

SOURCE: *The New York Times, Sunday,* April 20, 1997; National Association of Manufacturers

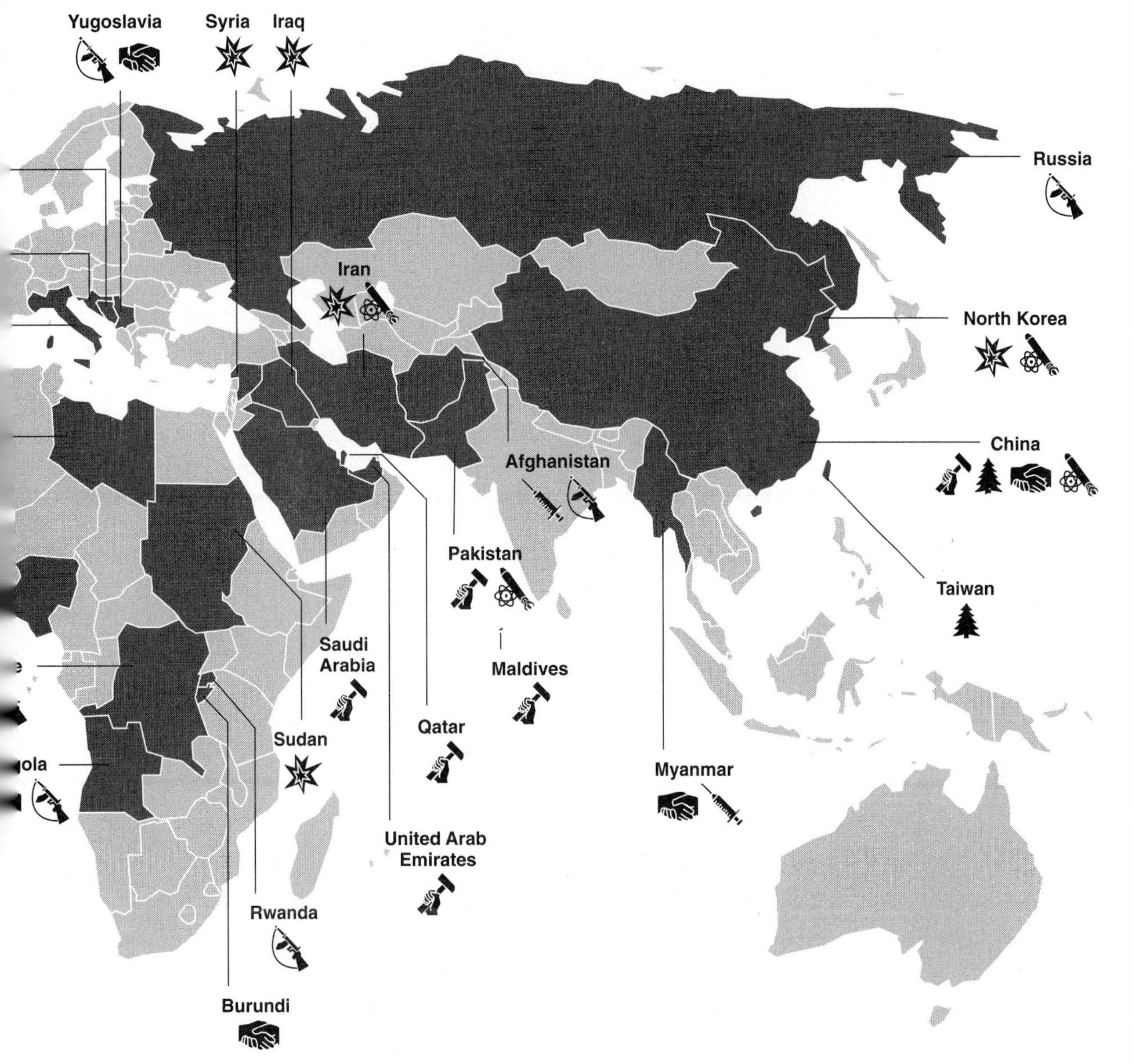

Yugoslavia

Syria

Iraq

Russia

Iran

North Korea

China

Afghanistan

Taiwan

Pakistan

Maldives

Saudi Arabia

Qatar

Sudan

ola

Myanmar

United Arab Emirates

Rwanda

Burundi

Countries subject to United States economic sanctions from 1993-96 aimed against:

Terrorism

 Abuse of workers' rights

 Drug trafficking

 Nuclear proliferation

Environmental violations

 Regional strife

 Human and political rights abuses

Unfortunately, trying to impose sanctions slowly or making them less expensive to ease the burden on these firms undercuts their ultimate chance for success. The international business manager is often caught in this political web and loses business as a result. Frequently, firms try to anticipate sanctions based on their evaluations of the international political climate. Nevertheless, even when substantial precautions are taken, firms may still suffer substantial losses.

Conventions and Regulations of Intergovernmental Organizations

intergovernmental organizations (IGO) permanent organization set up by two or more states to carry on activities of common interest

Intergovernmental organizations (IGO) are permanent organizations set up by two or more states to carry on activities of common interest. Examples are the United Nations, World Trade Organization, and the European Community. An IGO derives its legal capacity to conduct activities with other international persons and states, to sue or be sued, and so forth, by being recognized as an international personality. In the course of carrying out the duties set forth in its charter, IGOs may be empowered to promulgate regulations and conventions that effectively bind member states to some standard of performance in a particular area. When a member state is bound, so too are the business organizations in its domain. For example, if the United Nations, speaking on behalf of the world community, obtains approval of a convention to improve airport security, concurrence by the U.S. government will serve to increase U.S. airline operating costs and, thus, ticket prices with or without the consent of the airlines.

Protection of Intellectual Property Rights

International law also plays a major role in protecting intellectual property rights. Rights to intellectual property involve rights to inventions, patents, trademarks, and industrial designs, and copyrights for literary, musical, artistic, photographic, and cinematographic works. Currently, these types of intellectual property are not completely defined by any international treaty, and the laws differ from country to country on several important points. Thus the rights granted by one country's patent, trademark, or copyright may confer no protection abroad.

Some international agreements exist to ease the task of filing for intellectual property rights in those countries in which a firm wants to conduct business or ensure protection. The Paris Convention for the Protection of Industrial Property, to which 96 countries are party, sets minimum standards of protection and provides the right of national treatment and the right of priority. This means that members will not discriminate against foreigners and that firms have one year (six months for a design or trademark) in which to file an application.

The Patent Cooperation Treaty (PCT) provides procedures for filing one international application designating countries in which a patent is sought, which has the same effect as filing national applications in each of those countries. Similarly, the European Patent Office examines applications and issues national patents in any of its member countries.

Much more needs to be done to protect intellectual property. Knowledge is often the firm's most precious competitive advantage, and violation of those rights can have significant financial repercussions.

International organizations such as the United Nations and the Organization for Economic Cooperation and Development have also undertaken efforts to develop codes and guidelines that affect international business. Global Learning Experience 7.4 reviews a global agreement (160 nations) intended to widen the law to protect material that can be easily copied and distributed over computer networks.

GLOBAL LEARNING EXPERIENCE 7.4

Global Agreement to Protect Intellectual Property in the Digital Age

In December 1996, delegates to the World Intellectual Property Organization, a United Nations body, met in Geneva, Switzerland, and agreed on the most sweeping extension of international copyright law in 25 years.

The delegates approved two treaties that extend copyright protection to creative works that could be distributed on the internet. The first treaty covers literary and artistic works, including films and computer software. The second treaty provides protection for recorded music. Internet piracy can cost its American creators large amounts of revenue. The U.S. software industry is estimated to lose about $13 billion each year from piracy. The American music industry estimates that illegal copying costs $2 billion in cost revenues each year.

SOURCE: *New York Times,* December 21, 1996, p. 1, 38.

In addition to multilateral agreements, firms are affected by bilateral treaties and conventions between the countries in which they do business. For example, a number of countries have signed bilateral Treaties of Friendship, Commerce, and Navigation (FCN). The agreements generally define the rights of firms doing business in the host country. They normally guarantee that firms will be treated by the host country in the same manner in which domestic firms are treated. While these treaties provide for some sort of stability, they can also be canceled when relations worsen.

Legal Differences and Restraints

Not only are there several different systems of law in use in the world, but the actual laws, the practice and administration of the laws, and court systems are different from one country to another. Global Learning Experience 7.5 indicates the stark differences between punishment in the United States and Singapore. As a result, these differences in laws can become a legal minefield for the global business executive who does not seek appropriate legal counsel. For example, over the past decade, the United States has become an increasingly litigious society in which institutions and individuals are quick to initiate lawsuits. Court battles are often protracted and costly, and even the threat of a court case can reduce business opportunities. Interestingly, Japan has only about 12,500 fully licensed lawyers, compared with some 650,000 in the United States. Whether the number of lawyers is cause or effect, the Japanese tend not to litigate.[13] Litigation in Japan means that the parties have failed to compromise, which is contrary to Japanese tradition of consensus and results in loss of face. A cultural predisposition therefore exists to settle conflicts outside the court system, as shown in Global Learning Experience 7.6.

Basic Systems of Law

There are three basic systems of law: (1) civil law (used by approximately 70 countries); (2) common law (practiced in some 27 countries); and (3) Muslim law (the underlying philosophy for law in approximately 27 other countries). In addition to these three systems of law, one should remember that in some parts of the world, such as Somalia, there is no law at all. It should also be noted that the presence of a legal system and a body of law in a country does not guarantee uniform and equal application of the law among different groups within a country.

The Law in Singapore

The dramatic differences in law and the application of the law from country to country was brought into sharp focus in early 1994. A young American man (18 years old), living in Singapore, was sentenced to four months in prison and ordered to pay a $2,230 fine and to receive six lashes of a cane. The Singapore courts imposed the sentence after the American admitted he was part of a group that had spray-painted cars and threw eggs at other vehicles.

The decision to lash the prisoner with a cane was widely reported in the U.S. news media; even the President of the United States called the punishment extreme and asked that it be reconsidered. Caning is a form of flogging in which the prisoner is tied to a wooden trestle and struck on the bare buttocks with a rattan cane. The process is said to be so painful that it causes the victims to go into shock and leaves them with permanent scars. This type of punishment would not be permitted in the United States.

Despite the fact that the case threatened to damage relations between the United States and Singapore, the Singapore government was unforgiving and rejected the prisoner's appeal to be spared the caning. However, in a gesture of goodwill to the President of the United States, it reduced the flogging punishment to four strokes of the cane. The punishment was carried out on May 5, 1994.

In the long run, the young American may have the last laugh. Immediately after the flogging his family was inundated with television and motion picture requests and book offers. All of these offers will probably leave the victim a very wealthy individual. As shown below, political cartoonists had a field day with the incident.

SOURCE: *New York Times,* April 18, 1994. Signe Wilkinson, Cartoonists and Writers Syndicate.

SOURCE: Mike Shelton, *New York Times,* May 8, 1994. Reprinted with special permission of King Features Syndicate.

civil law
compilation of laws, or set of rules, set forth in a listing called a code

Civil law, sometimes referred to as code law, is a compilation of laws, or set of rules, set forth in a listing called a code. Civil law had its origins in the Roman code of law, the "twelve tables" developed by the consuls of the Republic in 450 B.C. Essentially, the consuls and their advisers developed a list of what they thought the laws were and published them. The Roman code was reorganized and simplified by the Emperor Justinian about

Two Air Disasters, Two Cultures, Two Remedies

When two jumbo jets crashed ten days apart in Dallas and in the mountains near Tokyo, Americans and Japanese shared a common bond of shock and grief. Soon, however, all parties in Japan—from the airline to the employers of victims—moved to put the tragedy behind them. In the United States, legal tremors will continue for years.

Lawyers hustled to the scene of the Delta Air Lines accident at Dallas—Fort Worth Airport and set up shop at an airport hotel. Proclaimed San Francisco attorney Melvin Belli: "I'm not an ambulance chaser—I get there before the ambulance." "We always file the first suit," bragged Richard Brown, a Melvin Belli associate who flew to Dallas "to get to the bottom of this and to make ourselves available." But he adds: "We never solicited anyone directly. We were called to Texas by California residents who lost their loved ones." Within 72 hours, the first suit against Delta was filed. Insurance adjusters working for Delta went quickly to work as well.

Seven thousand miles away, Japan Air Lines (JAL) President Yasumoto Takagi humbly bowed to families of the 520 victims and apologized "from the bottom of our hearts." He vowed to resign once the investigation was complete. Next of kin received "condolence payments" and negotiated settlements with the airline. Traditionally, few if any lawsuits are filed following such accidents.

Behind these differences lie standards of behavior and corporate responsibility that are worlds apart. "There is a general Japanese inclination to try to settle any disputes through negotiations between the parties before going to court," said Koichiro Fujikura, Tokyo University law professor. Added Carl Green, a Washington D.C., attorney and specialist on Japanese law, "There is an assumption of responsibility. In our adversarial society, we don't admit responsibility. It would be admitting liability."

After a JAL jet crashed into Tokyo Bay in 1982, killing 24, JAL President Takagi visited victims' families, offered gifts, and knelt before funeral altars. JAL offered families about $2,000 each in condolence payments, then negotiated settlements reported to be worth between $166,000 and $450,000, depending on the age and earning power of each victim. Only one family sued.

Japanese legal experts expected settlements in the 1985 crash to be as high as 500 million yen—about $2.1 million—apiece. Negotiations may be prolonged. But if families believe that JAL is sincerely sorry, "I think their feelings will be soothed," predicted attorney Takeshi Odagi.

Japan's legal system encourages these traditions. "Lawyers don't descend in droves on accident scenes because they barely have enough time to handle the suits they have," says John Haley, a law professor at the University of Washington who has studied and worked in Japan. "There are fewer judges per capita than there were in 1890," Haley added. Only 500 lawyers are admitted to the bar each year.

SOURCE: Clemens P. Work, Sarah Peterson, and Hidehiro Tanakadate, "Two Air Disasters, Two Cultures, Two Remedies," *U.S. News & World Report,* August 26, 1985, 25–26.

Where did coffee originate?

Coffee came originally from Ethiopia, where coffee trees still grow wild in the mountains. It spread with Islam in the seventh to tenth centuries.

534 A.D. Over many centuries, the Roman code was revised, modified, and reinterpreted and in the 1800s went into two slightly different directions. The French civil code (code Napoleon) was enacted in 1804 and became the basis for codes in Africa, Belgium, Indochina, Indonesia, Latin America, Netherlands, Poland, Portugal, Spain and Sub-Saharan Africa. The German civil code, issued in 1896, became the model for the legal systems in Austria, Czechoslovakia, Greece, Hungary, Japan, South Korea, Switzerland, Turkey, and Yugoslavia.

common law
system of law that relies on the rulings of previous cases (precedent), common usage, and customs as the basis for court decisions

Common law is a system of law that relies on the rulings of previous cases (precedent), common usage, and customs as the basis for court decisions. Common law dates to England in the year 1066 and William the Conqueror. The name *common law* is derived from the idea that the king's courts represented the common custom of the country. Unlike civil law, which is a straightforward listing of the law that remains fairly consistent from day to day, common law is an ever-changing mixture of previous rulings, statutes, jury actions, and complex terminology. Common law has been adopted by many of the countries that trace their origins to, or had ties with, England, such as Australia, Canada, many Caribbean nations, India, Ireland, New Zealand, and the United States.

Muslim or Islamic law
the Sunnah (writings and sayings of the Prophet Muhammad), Islamic scholars, and the Islamic legal community

Muslim or **Islamic Law,** known as *Sharía,* is derived from the Koran, the Sunnah (teachings and practices of the prophet Muhammad (A.D. 570–632), Islamic scholars, and the Islamic legal community. In the 10th century, Islamic legal scholars decided that the Divine Law had been sufficiently interpreted and that *Ijtihad,* or further independent reasoning, was unnecessary. This effectively closed the *Sharía* to modern interpretation based on events since the 10th century. Accordingly, judges and legal scholars apply the law as it was written in the 10th century. For the organization trying to conduct modern, 21st century business in a legal climate that is frozen in the 10th century, it can be somewhat difficult and requires sensitivity, ingenuity, and local assistance with such a legal system.

Although the *Sharía* is basically a moral code, its content is such that it contains many similarities to common and civil law. Approximately one quarter of the world's population is Muslim, living primarily in the Middle East, North Africa, and Southern Asia. As shown in the table below, Islam is the principal religion in some 32 countries. The use of Islamic Law as the underlying foundation for national law in Muslim countries varies from strict adherence to the *Sharía,* as in Saudi Arabia, to varying combinations of the *Sharía* and civil law in other countries.

Countries where Islam is the Principal Religion

Afghanistan	Kyrgyzstan	Somalia
Algeria	Libya	Sudan
Azerbaijan	Mali	Syria
Bangladesh	Malaysia	Tajikstan
Egypt	Mauritania	Tunisia
Indonesia	Morocco	Turkey
Iran	Niger	Turkmenistan
Iraq	Oman	United Arab Emirates
Jordan	Pakistan	Uzbekistan
Kazakhistan	Qatar	Yemen
Kuwait	Saudi Arabia	

Host countries may adopt a number of laws that affect the firm's ability to do business, as discussed in Chapter 6. Tariffs and quotas, for example, can affect the entry of goods. Special licenses for foreign goods may be required.

Other laws may restrict entrepreneurial activities. In Argentina, for example, pharmacies must be owned by the pharmacist. This legislation prevents an ambitious businessperson from hiring druggists and starting a pharmacy chain.[14]

Specific legislation may also exist regulating what does and does not constitute deceptive advertising. Many countries prohibit specific claims that compare products to the competition, or they restrict the use of promotional devices. Even when no laws exist, regulations may hamper business operations. For example, in some countries, firms are required to join the local chamber of commerce or become a member of the national trade association. These institutions in turn may have internal sets of regulations that specify standards for the conduct of business that may be quite confining.

Finally, seemingly innocuous local regulations that may easily be overlooked can have a major impact on the firm's success. For example, Japan has an intricate process regulating the building of new department stores or supermarkets. Because of the government's desire to protect smaller merchants, these regulations brought the opening of new, large stores to a virtual standstill. As department stores and supermarkets serve as the major conduit for the sale of imported consumer products, the lack of new stores severely affected opportunities for market penetration of imported merchandise.[15] Only after intense pressure from the outside did the Japanese government decide in early 1991 to reconsider these regulations.

To succeed in a market, the international manager needs much more than business know-how. He or she must also deal with the intricacies of national politics and laws. Although to fully understand another country's legal political system will rarely be possible, the good manager will be aware of its importance and will work with people who do understand how to operate within the system.

THE GLOBAL POLITICAL ENVIRONMENT

The effect of politics on global business is determined by both the bilateral political relations between home and host countries and by multilateral agreements governing the relations among groups of countries.

The government-to-government relationship can have a profound influence on business activities in a number of ways, particularly if it becomes hostile. Among numerous examples in recent years of the relationship between international politics and global business, perhaps the most notable involves U.S.-Chinese relations following the Tiananmen Square uprising in 1989.

International political relations do not always have harmful effects. If bilateral political relations between countries improve, business can benefit. One example is the improvement in U.S. relations with Eastern Europe following the official end of the Cold War. The political warming opened the potentially lucrative former Eastern bloc markets to U.S. businesses. For example, the IBM Corporation is now able to develop actively the market for computers, particularly personal computers, in Eastern Europe.

The overall international political environment has effects, whether good or bad, on global business. For this reason, the good manager will strive to remain aware of political currents worldwide and will attempt to anticipate changes in the international political environment so that his or her firm can plan for them.

political risk
the risk of loss by an international corporation of assets, earning power, or managerial control as a result of political actions by the host country

ownership risk
the risk inherent in maintaining ownership of property abroad. The exposure of foreign-owned assets to governmental intervention

operating risk
the danger of interference by governments or other groups in one's corporate operations abroad

transfer risk
the danger of having one's ability to transfer profits or products in and out of a country inhibited by governmental rules and regulations

Political Action and Risk

Firms usually prefer to conduct business in a country with a stable and friendly government, but such governments are not always easy to find. Managers must therefore continually monitor the government, its policies, and its stability to determine the potential for political change that could adversely affect corporate operations.

There is **political risk** in every nation, but the range of risks varies widely from country to country. In general, political risk is lowest in countries that have a history of stability and consistency. Political risk tends to be highest in nations that do not have this sort of history. In a number of countries, however, consistency and stability that were apparent on the surface have been quickly swept away by major popular movements that drew on the bottled-up frustrations of the population. Three major types of political risk can be encountered: **ownership risk,** which exposes property and life; **operating risk,** which refers to interference with the ongoing operations of a firm; and **transfer risk,** which is mainly encountered when attempts are made to shift funds between countries. Firms can be exposed to political risk due to government actions or even outside the control of governments. The type of actions and their effects are classified in Figure 7.4.

A major political risk in many countries is that of conflict and violent change. A manager will want to think twice before conducting business in a country in which the

FIGURE 7.4 **Exposure to Political Risk**

Contingencies May Include:	**Loss May Be the Result of:** The actions of legitimate government authorities	Events caused by factors outside the control of government
The involuntary loss of control over specific assets without adequate compensation	• Total or partial expropriation • Forced divestiture • Confiscation • Cancellation or unfair calling of performance bonds	• War • Revolution • Terrorism • Strikes • Extortion
A reduction in the value of a stream of benefits expected from the foreign-controlled affiliate	• Nonapplicability of "national treatment" • Restriction in access to financial, labor, or material markets • Controls on prices, outputs, or activities • Currency and remittance restrictions • Value-added and export performance requirements	• Nationalistic buyers or suppliers • Threats and disruption to operations by hostile groups • Externally induced financial constraints • Externally imposed limits on imports or exports

SOURCE: José de la Torre and David H. Neckar, "Forecasting Political Risks for International Operations." International Journal of Forecasting, Vol. 4 (1988), pp. 221–241, as reprinted in H. Vernon-Wortzel and L. Wortzel, *Global Strategic Management: The Essentials.* 2d ed. (New York: John Wiley and Sons, 1991), 194–214.

likelihood of such change is high. To begin with, if conflict breaks out, violence directed toward the firm's property and employees is a strong possibility. Guerrilla warfare, civil disturbances, and terrorism often take an anti-industry bent, making companies and their employees potential targets. U.S. corporations or firms linked to the United States are often subject to major threats, even in countries that boast of great political stability. For example, on December 12, 1996, a Cuban-inspired guerrilla group, the Tupac Amaru Revolutionary Movement (M.R.T.A.) of Peru, attacked the Japanese ambassador's residence in Lima during a party. The rebels seized the residence and took 600 guests hostage. The guest list included many ambassadors and international dignitaries, business leaders, and Peruvian legislators. The Tupac Amaru guerrillas were demanding freedom for 400 of their comrades held in Peruvian prisons.

After four months, the crisis which had threatened Peru's economic and political stability came to a violent end on April 22, 1997, when Peruvian troops raided the Japanese Diplomatic Residence, killing the rebels and rescuing the remaining hostages. The irony of this event is that Peru is one of the major recipients of Japanese foreign aid in the world, with pledges of nearly $600 million in loans to the country. A number of Japanese firms have begun operations in Peru, and some of the hostages that had been taken were executives of those firms.

Less drastic, but still worrisome, are changes in government policies that are not caused by changes in the government itself. These occur when, for one reason or another, a government feels pressured to change its policies toward foreign businesses. The pressure may be the result of nationalist or religious factions or widespread anti-Western feeling. In any case, the aware manager will work to anticipate such changes and plan for ways to cope with them.

The Doctrine of Sovereign Immunity

As a member of the world system, nations (1) are presumed "equal," (2) are sovereign, in that they are able to act independently of other nations in world affairs, (3) have exclusive rights to manage their internal affairs, and (4) are not subject, without their consent, to a compulsory jurisdiction of international law.[16] These understandings have resulted in the development of the **Doctrine of Sovereign Immunity.** This doctrine holds that sovereign states are immune from lawsuits concerning their laws and regulations, including laws expropriating property, acts of their armed forces or diplomatic service, and public loans.[17]

Doctrine of Sovereign Immunity
holds that sovereign states are immune from lawsuits covering their laws and regulations, including laws expropriating property, acts of their armed forces or diplomatic service, and public loans

In essence, the recognition and acceptance of the Doctrine of Sovereign Immunity by the nations of the world implies that a nation may do almost anything it wants to do within its borders without fear of reprisal by other nations. The situation highlights the dilemma of investing in foreign lands—if anything goes wrong politically, there is little that the government of the United States can do directly to solve the company's problem.

Seizure of Company Assets

While there are many types of political risk involved in doing business globally, the ultimate risk is that a foreign government might take control and ownership of a company's assets without paying full or reasonable compensation.

There is only one city inside the Arctic Circle. Can you name it?

Murmansk, Russia. (There are no cities inside the Antarctic Circle.)

The legal basis for the government taking of private property is the doctrine of *eminent domain,* which permits the taking of the property for public use and requires the payment of just compensation. Often referred to as the modern traditional theory in international law, this concept is generally accepted by Western European and North American nations.

Modern Traditional Theory
doctrine that recognizes a sovereign state's right to nationalize foreign-owned property, to be accompanied by prompt, adequate, and effective compensation

Calvo Doctrine
doctrine that embraces the idea that the state is supreme over foreign investors within the state's territory, challenges any intervention by foreign states in investment disputes as a violation of its territorial jurisdiction, and rejects the concept of prompt and adequate compensation for the property seized

expropriation
taking of foreign-owned property by the state

confiscation
similar to expropriation in that it results in a transfer of ownership from the firm to the host country, but differs in that it does not involve compensation for the firm

Not all states, however, follow the **modern traditional theory** of just compensation for the seizure. Another theory, the **Calvo Doctrine,** views the seizure of private property as a legitimate exercise of a state's right to restructure its economy without interference from other states or the jurisdiction of international law. The Calvo Doctrine was embraced by the developing nations of Latin America and Asia, which have limited finances to pay for seized property, so that under this doctrine, payment is not required. Even if some level of payment is granted, it may be a schedule of payments over time or, in lieu of cash, the issuance of national bonds in the local currency, which subject the former owner of the assets to the further risks of devaluation and the country's ability to pay.

Expropriation is the taking of foreign-owned property by the state. According to the World Bank, from the early 1960s through the 1970s, a total of 1,535 firms from 22 different countries were expropriated in 511 separate actions by 76 nations.[18] Expropriation was an appealing action to many countries because it demonstrated their nationalism and transferred a certain amount of wealth and resources from foreign companies to the host country immediately. It did have costs to the host country, however, to the extent that it made other firms more hesitant to invest there. Expropriation does not relieve the host government of providing compensation to the former owners. However, these compensation negotiations are often protracted and frequently result in settlements that are unsatisfactory to the owners.

Confiscation is similar to expropriation in that it results in a transfer of ownership from the firm to the host country. It differs in that it does not involve compensation for the firm. Some industries are more vulnerable than others to confiscation and expropriation because of their importance to the host country's economy and their lack of agility to shift operations. For this reason, sectors such as mining, energy, public utilities, and banking have frequently been targets of such government actions.

domestication
a government demands transfer of ownership and management responsibility

local content
regulations to gain control over foreign investment by ensuring that a large share of the product is locally produced or a larger share of the profit is retained in the country

Confiscation and expropriation constitute major political risk for foreign investors. Other government actions, however, are equally detrimental to foreign firms. Many countries are turning from confiscation and expropriation to more subtle forms of control, such as **domestication.** The goal of domestication is the same—that is, to gain control over foreign investment—but the method is different. Through domestication, the government demands transfer of ownership and management responsibility. It can impose **local-content** regulations to ensure that a large share of the product is locally produced or demand that a larger share of the profit is retained in the country. Changes in labor laws, patent protection, and tax regulations are also used for purposes of domestication.

Most businesses operating abroad face a number of other risks that are less dangerous, but probably more common, than the drastic ones already described. A host government's political situation or desires may lead it to impose regulations or laws to restrict or control the international activities of firms. Global Learning Experience 7.7 indicates how sensitive political issues may influence the ability of a company to do business in a foreign land.

GLOBAL LEARNING EXPERIENCE 7.7

Disney's Dalai Lama Film Imperils Company's Future in China

The interrelationship between global business and politics was highlighted once again by the announcement that the Chinese government would be forced to reconsider the Walt Disney Company's plans for extensive investment in China's growing entertainment market. The problem was not entertainment but politics. Disney is in the process of producing a film, *Kundun,* about the life of the Dalai Lama, the exiled religious leader of Tibet. Even though the movie is not being filmed in China, or is intended to be shown in China, Beijing authorities view the film as being intended to glorify the Dalai Lama and, thus, is an interference in China's internal affairs.

Disney had ambitious plans for operating in the huge and growing Chinese market. Not only is the acceptance of animated features like *The Lion King* increasing, but sales of merchandise at the company-owned Mickey's Corner stores are growing, and the company has been discussing the possibility of a Disney theme park in Southern China. Disney executives faced a difficult choice—bend to Chinese political pressure and ruin the studio's reputation or risk the loss of huge potential profits in China. The company indicated that it would honor its commitments and distribute the film. The warning from Beijing is clear and will cause the Hollywood film industry to rethink any future plans of films with reference to China.

SOURCE: *New York Times* cartoon Mickey vs. Tanks. Sunday—November 27, 1996.

Nations that face a shortage of foreign currency sometimes will impose controls on the movement of capital in and out of the country. Such controls may make it difficult for a firm to remove its profits or investments from the host country. Sometimes **exchange controls** are also levied selectively against certain products or companies in an effort to reduce the importation of goods that are considered to be a luxury or to be sufficiently available through domestic production. Such regulations are often difficult for the international manager to deal with because they may affect the importation of parts, components, or supplies that are vital to production operations in the country.

exchange controls
controls on the movement of capital in and out of a country, sometimes imposed when the country faces a shortage of foreign currency

price controls
government regulation of the prices of goods and services; control of the prices of imported goods and services as a result of domestic political pressures

The international executive also has to worry about **price controls.** In many countries, domestic political pressures can force governments to control the prices of imported products or services, particularly in sectors considered highly sensitive from a political perspective, such as food or health care. A foreign firm involved in these areas is vulnerable to price controls because the government can play on citizens' nationalistic tendencies to enforce the controls.

Actions Available in the Event of Expropriation or Confiscation

Assuming that there is inadequate or no compensation for the seizure of company assets, what steps are available to global management to recover the value of expropriated or confiscated assets? There are basically three steps that may be utilized.

1. *Exhaust all local legal remedies.* This is a fundamental step; before a firm may go forward with a complaint against a state, it must first seek relief from that state in the local courts.
2. If the firm does not receive satisfaction in the courts of the foreign state, the matter may then be referred to the *U.S. Department of State* in anticipation of settling the dispute through diplomacy.
3. Finally, if diplomacy does not achieve a satisfactory outcome, the dispute may then be directed to an international tribunal, such as the *International Court of Justice,* the *Permanent Court of Arbitration,* or the *International Center for the Settlement of Investment Disputes.*

For the global manager, the best course of action may be to avoid or minimize political risk, to the extent that this is possible.

Minimizing Political Risk

There are a number of ways to minimize political risk, they are:

1. *Insure against the risk.* Several forms of insurance are available to protect the firm against political risk. The *Overseas Private Investment Corporation (OPIC)* offers programs to cover the risks associated with expropriation, currency inconvertibility (transfer risk), and the hazards of political violence. The *Multilateral Investment Guarantee Agency (MIGA)* insures foreign investors against expropriation, war, revolution, or other noncommercial risks. In addition some private insurance companies offer insurance to protect against various political risks.
2. *Create a* **structured operating environment.** For those companies that have numerous foreign operations, the idea is to make foreign investments in such a way that seizure of the firm's assets by a foreign government results in no gain (or loss) to the government. For example, if a U.S. automobile firm sets up a foreign plant to make one component of a car, and the plant is confiscated, the automaker will shift production elsewhere. The foreign government is then left with a plant, but no customer for the product.

structured operating environment
distribution of foreign investments in a way that prevents gain by a foreign government in the event of seizure

3. *Develop an "early warning" risk-monitoring system.* Expropriation or confiscation rarely happen overnight; rather foreign control tends to take the form of **creeping expropriation.** This is a slow, but gradual, series of acts by the foreign state that collectively take away the right to control ownership of the firms assets. Accordingly, the prudent global manager would develop a procedure to systematically monitor the political risk level in countries in which the company is operating. Such a procedure could provide early indications of expropriation, and thus, time for the organization to develop strategies that would mitigate or avoid the expropriation.

creeping expropriation
series of acts or regulations that gradually and together limit the exercise of ownership rights

Despite the risks, the global business executive should not feel overwhelmed. Many research groups and publications, such as the Economist Intelligence Unit and Global Risk Assessments, Inc., devote major efforts to the assessment of country risk.

Country-risk Ratings

Figure 7.5 presents a view of the riskiness of doing business in a selected group of countries. As shown, Russia is deemed to be most risky of the economies shown, having a combined economic and political risk score of 75, compared to the maximum of 100. Mexico is in second place with a score of 65, followed by Brazil with 60.

Country-risk ratings (Fourth quarter 1996) FIGURE 7.5

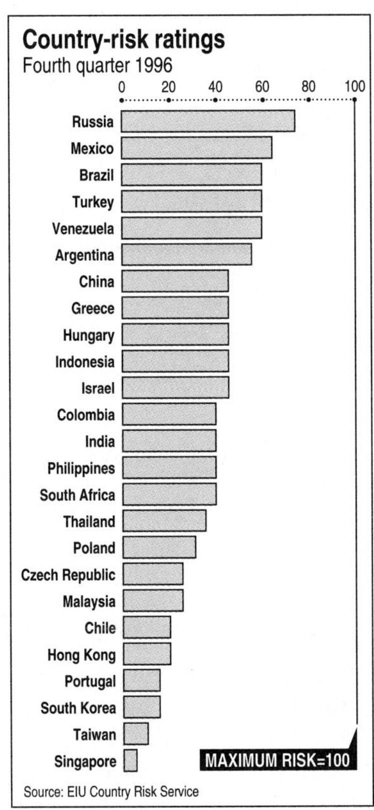

SOURCE: "Emerging-Market Indicators," *The Economist,* March 22, 1997, p. 980.

The Prophet of Profit: British Accounting Practices

"The book they tried to ban," trumpets the cover. This time the forbidden topic is not the spooks of *Spycatcher* or the erotica of *Lady Chatterly's Lover,* but the somewhat duller subject of massaging corporate results to make them look better. *Accounting for Growth* by Terry Smith, a top analyst at UBS Phillips & Drew, a London brokerage house, is the chilling tale of "creative" accounting in the boardrooms of Britain's 200 biggest firms. The book has made national headlines and won an unrepentant Smith suspension from his job.

The 12 techniques identified by Smith are perfectly legal but, he argues, can be used to mislead investors. They include the inconsistent use of extraordinary and exceptional items, some tricks of acquisition and disposal accounting, off-balance-sheet financing, disguising debt as equity, changing depreciation rules, and capitalizing costs. These practices all tend to do one of two things: increase reported profits or make a company's balance sheet look stronger. So the shares of companies using such ploys may be overvalued. As a crude rule of thumb, investors should steer clear of firms that use the criticized techniques, says Smith.

Many economists have a more fundamental objection to Smith's views. In an efficient market, they argue, accounting tricks should have no effect on share prices. Provided a handful of clever analysts can find a way through the accounting jungle to the firm's true financial position, and there are big investors willing to trade on that information, share prices will reflect the firm's true value because the canny investors will continue to buy or sell the shares until the right price is reached. In other words, a few informed people can set the correct price for everyone, including investors who cannot tell a profit-and-loss account from a balance sheet.

Does this mean that the market sees through creative accounting? Most of these studies looked at large firms and well-publicized accounting changes. The market might take longer to spot subtler massaging of profits, especially by small and medium-sized firms.

When a firm uses accounting tricks to boost earnings, it usually means that there is a lot more bad news to come, says Mr. Lev (of the University of California at Berkeley). Smith's advice to avoid firms that practice creative accounting may not be so crude after all.

SOURCE: Abstracted from "The Prophet of Profit," *The Economist,* August 22, 1992, 57.

ACCOUNTING PRACTICE AND TAX LAWS

Domestic law is highly relevant to how firms do their accounting and pay taxes. The methods used in the measurement of company operations, accounting principles and practices, vary across countries. These methods have a very large impact on how firms operate, how they compare against domestic and international competitors, and how governments view their respective place in society. Accounting principles are, however, moving toward more standardization across countries.

Taxation and accounting are fundamentally related. The principles by which a firm measures its sales and expenses, its assets and liabilities, all go into the formulation of profits, which are subject to taxation. The tax policies of more and more governments, in conjunction with accounting principles, are also becoming increasingly similar. Many of the tax issues specifically in the mind of officials, such as the avoidance of taxes in high-tax countries or by shielding income from taxation by holding profits in so-called

GLOBAL LEARNING EXPERIENCE 7.9

The Father of Accounting: Luca Pacioli Who?

Doctors have Hippocrates and philosophers have Plato. But who is the father of accounting? Knowing that accountants have long had inferiority complexes, two Seattle University professors have decided that the profession should have a father and that he should be Luca Pacioli.

But their anointing of the Renaissance scholar occasions an identity crisis. Hardly anyone—accountants included—has ever heard of Pacioli (pronounced pot-CHEE-oh-lee).

Five centuries ago, Pacioli published *Summa de Arithmetica, Geometria, Proportioni et Proportionalita.* It contained a slender tract for merchants on double-entry bookkeeping, which had been in wide use in Venice for years. Because of that, some accounting historians, including Professors Weis and Tinius, credit Pacioli with codifying accounting principles for the first time. That would seem to establish paternity.

Professor Vangermeersch (University of Rhode Island) says the origins of double-entry bookkeeping are open to question. "If you're crediting people of past centuries for contributions to accounting, you should include Leonardo of Pisa, who brought Arabic numerals to the West; James Peele, who initiated journal-entry systems; and Emile Garcke and J. M. Fells, who applied accounting to factory use," he says. All these men have another thing in common, he adds: They are just as obscure as Luca Pacioli.

Even in literature, says Vangermeersch, the only famous accountant was Daniel Defoe, who wrote *Robinson Crusoe.* Unfortunately, Defoe was a terrible businessman and failed in a series of ventures, the professor observes. "Even as a dissenter and pamphleteer, he was tarred and feathered by the public."

SOURCE: Abstracted from "Father of Accounting is a Bit of a Stranger To His Own Progeny," *The Wall Street Journal,* January 29, 1983, A1, A6.

tax havens, are slowly being eliminated by increasing cooperation between governments. Like the old expression of "death and taxes," they are today, more than ever, inevitable.

Principal Accounting Practice Differences Across Countries

Global **accounting diversity** can lead to any of the following errors in global business conducted with the use of financial statements: (1) poor or improper business decision making; (2) hinder the ability of a firm or enterprise to raise capital in different or foreign markets; (3) hinder or prevent the monitoring of competitive factors across firms, industries, and countries. Examples of these problems abound in international business literature. For example, it is widely believed that much of the recent trend of British firms acquiring U.S. companies is primarily a result of their ability to completely expense "goodwill" (the added cost of a firm purchased over and above the fair market value of its constituent components). Global Learning Experience 7.8 identifies some creative accounting techniques.

accounting diversity The range of differences in national accounting practices.

Origins of Differences in Accounting Practice

Accounting standards and practices are in many ways no different from any other legislative or regulatory statutes in their origins. Laws reflect the people, places, and events of their time (see Global Learning Experience 7.9). Most accounting practices and laws are linked to the objectives of the parties who will use this financial information. These end-users are investors, lenders, and governments.

National accounting principles are also frequently affected by other environmental factors, such as the dominance of one country's trade and financial activity over the trade and financial activity of another country. Although there are substantial differences between U.S. and Canadian accounting practices, many of the recent changes forced on Canadian firms have their origins in U.S. practice.

Classification Systems

There are several ways to classify and group national accounting systems and practices. Figure 7.6 illustrates one such classification based on a statistically based clustering of practices across countries by C. W. Nobes. The systems are first subdivided into micro-based (characteristics of the firms and industries) and macro-uniform (following fundamental government or economic factors per country). The micro-based national accounting systems are then broken down into those that follow a theoretical principle or pragmatic concerns. The latter category includes the national accounting systems of countries as diverse as the United States, Canada, Japan, the United Kingdom, and Mexico.

The macro-uniform systems, according to Nobes, are primarily European countries. The continental Europeans are typified by accounting systems that are formulated in secondary importance to legal organizational forms (Germany) or for the apportion-

FIGURE 7.6 Nobes Classification of National Accounting Systems

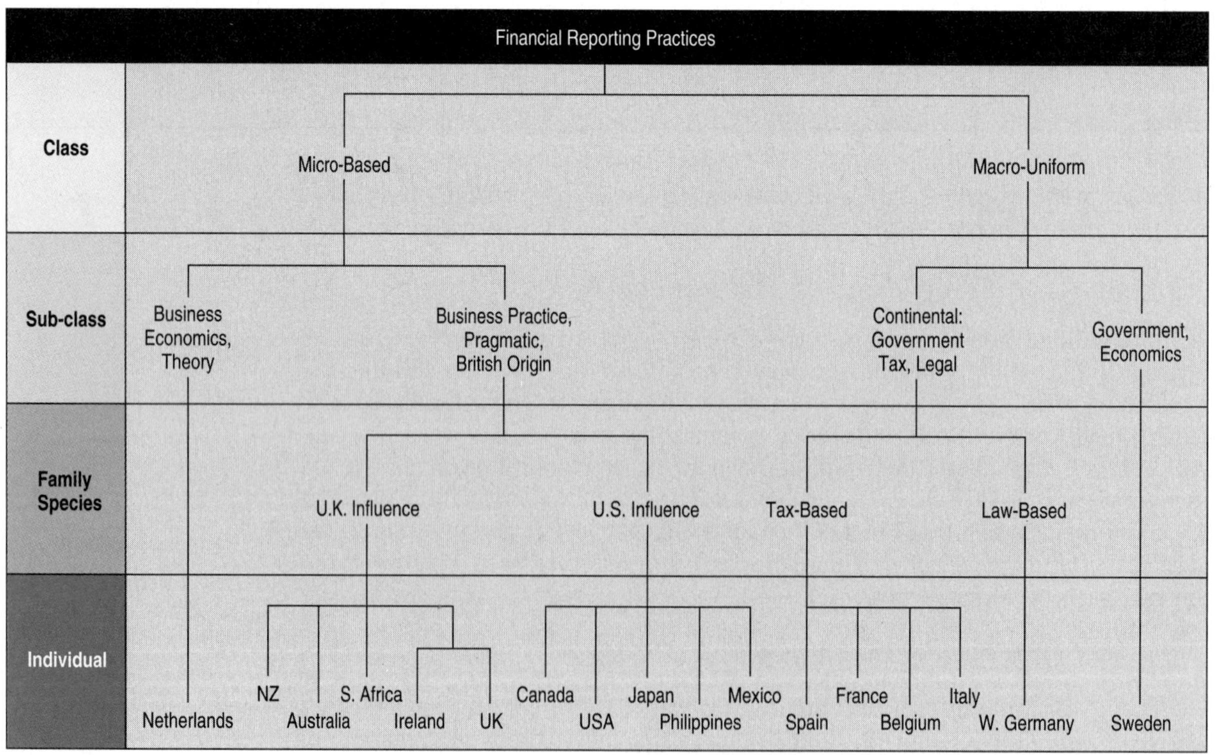

SOURCE: C. W. Nobes, "International Classification of Accounting Systems," unpublished paper, April 1980, Table C, as cited in Choi and Mueller, 1992, p. 34.

ment and application of national tax laws (France, Spain, Italy), or the more pure forms of government and economic models (Sweden). An alternative approach to these in the European classification would be those such as Sweden and Germany, which have pushed their firms to adopt more widespread uniform standards. However, as with all classification systems, the subtle differences across countries can quickly make such classifications useless in practice. As the following sections will illustrate, slight differences can also yield significant competitive advantages or disadvantages to companies organized and measured under different financial reporting systems.

Table 7.2 provides an overview of nine major areas of significant differences in accounting practices across countries. There are, of course, many more hundreds of differences, but these nine serve to highlight some of the fundamental philosophical differences across countries. Accounting differences are real and persistent, and there is still substantial question of competitive advantages and informational deficiencies that may result from these continuing differences across countries.

Accounting for Income Taxes All countries require the payment of income taxes on earnings; however, the definition and timing of earnings can constitute a problem. In many countries, the definition of earnings for financial accounting purposes differs from earnings for tax purposes. The question then focuses on whether the tax effect should be recognized during the period in which the item appears on the income statement or during the period in which the item appears on the tax return.

If the expense is recognized during the period in which the item appears on the income statement, the tax gives rise to an associated asset or liability referred to as deferred tax. Some countries do not suffer this debate (whether this deferred tax should actually appear on the balance sheet of the firm) by having all financial reporting follow tax rules. Examples include Germany, France, and Japan. However, most countries must deal with the timing mismatch of the deferred tax.

INTERNATIONAL TAXATION

Governments alone have the power to tax. Each government wants to tax all companies within its jurisdiction without placing burdens on domestic or foreign companies

Differences in depreciation methods used in accounting for fixed assets, such as this Arco chemical plant under construction in Marseille, France, result in different expensing schedules across countries.
SOURCE: Larry Lee 1987.

TABLE 7.2 Summary of Principal Accounting Differences around the World

Accounting Principle	United States	Japan	United Kingdom	France	Germany
1. Capitalization of R&D costs	Not allowed	Allowed in certain cases	Allowed in certain cases	Allowed in certain cases	Not allowed
2. Fixed-asset revaluations stated at amount in excess of cost	Not allowed	Not allowed	Allowed	Allowed	Not allowed
3. Inventory valuation using LIFO	Allowed	Allowed	Allowed but rarely done	Not allowed	Allowed in certain cases
4. Finance leases capitalized	Required	Allowed in certain cases	Required	Not allowed	Allowed in certain cases
5. Pension expense accrued during period of service	Required	Allowed	Required	Allowed	Required
6. Book and tax timing differences on balance sheet as deferred tax	Required	Allowed in certain cases	Allowed	Allowed in certain cases	Allowed but rarely done
7. Current rate method of currency translation	Required	Allowed in certain cases	Required	Allowed	Allowed
8. Pooling method used for mergers	Required in certain cases	Allowed in certain cases	Allowed in certain cases	Not allowed	Allowed in certain cases
9. Equity method used for 20–50 percent ownership	Required	Required	Required	Allowed in certain cases	Allowed

SOURCE: Adapted from "A Summary of Accounting Principle Differences Around the World," Phillip R. Peller and Frank J. Schwitter, 1991, p. 4.3.

that would restrain trade. Each country will state its jurisdictional approach formally in the tax treaties that it signs with other countries. One of the primary purposes of tax treaties is to establish the bounds of each country's jurisdiction to prevent double taxation of international income.

Tax Jurisdictions

Nations normally follow one of two basic approaches to international taxation: a residential approach or a territorial or source approach. The residential approach to international taxation taxes the international income of its residents without regard to where the income was earned. The territorial approach to transnational income taxes all parties, regardless of country of residency, within its territorial jurisdiction.

Most countries in practice must combine the two approaches to tax foreign and domestic firms equally. For example, the United States and Japan both apply the resi-

TABLE 7.2 *continued*

Netherlands	Switzerland	Canada	Italy	Brazil
Allowed in certain cases	Allowed in certain cases	Allowed in certain cases	Allowed in certain cases	Allowed in certain cases
Allowed in certain cases	Not allowed	Not allowed	Allowed in certain cases	Allowed
Allowed	Allowed	Allowed	Allowed	Allowed but rarely done
Required	Allowed	Required	Not allowed	Not allowed
Required	Allowed	Required	Allowed	Allowed
Required	Allowed	Allowed	Allowed but rarely done	Allowed
Required	Required	Allowed in certain cases	Required	Required
Allowed but rarely done	Allowed but rarely done	Allowed but rarely done	Not allowed	Allowed but rarely done
Required	Required	Required	Allowed	Required

dential approach to their own resident corporations and the territorial approach to income earned by nonresidents within their territorial jurisdictions. Other countries, like Germany, apply the territorial approach to dividends paid to domestic firms from their foreign subsidiaries (such dividends are assumed taxed abroad and are exempt from further taxation). Global Learning Experience 7.10 considers the tax implications of transfer pricing regulations.

Within the territorial jurisdiction of tax authorities, a foreign corporation is typically defined as any business that earns income within the host country's borders but is incorporated under the laws of another country. Normally, the foreign corporation must surpass some minimum level of activity (gross income) before the host country assumes primary tax jurisdiction. However, if the foreign corporation owns income-producing assets or a permanent establishment, the threshold is automatically surpassed.

GLOBAL LEARNING EXPERIENCE 7.10

All the President's Taxmen

Bill Clinton's vow to make foreign businesses pay "their fair share" of U.S. taxes, set against the backdrop of the need to raise $300 billion of extra revenue between 1993 and 1996 to fund his domestic programs, could mean substantial new tax burdens on British businesses investing in the United States.

As part of a package of corporate "loophole closers," Clinton claims that he will raise $45 billion over four years by combating "tax avoidance" by foreign-owned corporations and branches that shift profits outside the United States, largely by juggling with transfer prices. Transfer prices are those charged within families of companies for goods, services, or intangibles. Clinton maintains that foreign-owned firms set these prices artificially high in order to reduce their U.S. taxable income.

The Treasury and U.S. Congress have provided Clinton with some statistical support for this perception, but not for the revenue estimate. President Bush's Commissioner of the Internal Revenue Service (IRS) stated in recent congressional hearings that 72 percent of foreign-controlled corporations operating in the United States pay no U.S. taxes. The U.S. Treasury released a study showing that in 1988 U.S.–controlled foreign corporations reported $890 billion in revenues and paid more than $25 billion in taxes to foreign governments. In contrast, in the same year, foreign-controlled corporations in the United States had revenues of $825 billion but paid only $7 billion in U.S. taxes.

The draft transfer-pricing regulations the IRS issued in 1993 caused a storm of international protest; they are widely thought to introduce a different notion of what is "arm's length" from that generally accepted by other tax authorities. Although the draft rules may be toned down in theory, overseas tax authorities are well aware of their likely effect and Clinton's intended enforcement. The United States is not the only country with economic problems that is looking to transfer pricing to provide additional tax revenues. Japan, Australia, Korea, the U.K., and Germany have all introduced new rules, allocated extra resources to transfer pricing, or both.

SOURCE: Abstracted from Terry Symons, "All the President's Taxmen," *Accountancy,* January 1993, 64.

Accounting practices for the costs of environmental contamination treatment and restoration, such as Amoco Corporation's reclamation of the dunes of Coatham Sands, Great Britain, are an evolving issue in international business.
SOURCE: Photo Courtesy of Amoco Corporation.

Tax Types

Taxes are generally classified as direct and indirect. **Direct taxes** are calculated on actual income, either individual or firm income. **Indirect taxes,** like sales taxes, severance taxes, tariffs, and value-added taxes, are applied to purchase prices, material costs, quantities of natural resources mined, and so forth. Although most countries still rely on income taxes as the primary method of raising revenue, tax structures vary widely across countries.

The **value-added tax (VAT)** is the primary revenue source for the European Union. A value-added tax is applied to the amount of product value added by the production process. The tax is calculated as a percentage of the product price less the cost of materials and inputs used in its manufacture, which have been taxed previously. Through this process, tax revenues are collected literally on the value added by that specific stage of the production process. Under the existing World Trade Organization (WTO) regulations, the legal framework under which international trade operates, value-added taxes may be levied on imports into a country or group of countries (like the European Union) in order to treat foreign producers entering the domestic markets equally with firms within the country paying the VAT. Similarly, the VAT may be refunded on export sales or sales to tourists who purchase products for consumption outside the country or community. For example, an American tourist leaving London may collect a refund on all value-added taxes paid on goods purchased within the United Kingdom. The refunding usually requires documentation of the actual purchase price and amount of tax paid.

direct taxes
calculated on actual income, either individual or firm income

indirect taxes
like sales taxes, severance taxes, tariffs, and value-added taxes, are applied to purchase prices, material costs, quantities of natural resources minded, and so forth

value-added tax (VAT)
a tax on the value added at each stage of the production and distribution process; a tax assessment in most European countries and also common among Latin American countries

LABOR LAW

The laws pertaining to labor vary widely from country to country. In the United States, employers have a great deal of control over the pay and benefits received by their employees. With the exception of employees covered by union contracts, the minimum-wage law, and safety and health regulations, U.S. employers make the decisions regarding pay, hours worked, overtime work and pay, vacation, paid holidays, health benefits, pension plans, and termination. In many foreign countries, these items are a matter of national law and are beyond the control of the employer. A few general points in Sweden's and Brazil's labor laws provide good examples of the differences.

Sweden

By Swedish law, an employee may not work more than 40 hours a week, and overtime, when permitted, is regulated. All employees are entitled by law to a 5-week paid vacation in addition to 11 statutory holidays. Four other holidays are customary, but not statutory. The law also requires employers to give written notice of termination, including factual reasons for the termination. The period between notice and termination depends on the employer's age and length of service and may be as much as six months. Further, the law voids any reason for termination if the employee can reasonably be given another job by the employer, and it provides for court reinstatement of employees who are unjustly dismissed. The law also covers social security, national health insurance, and pension plans.

QUESTION *Where is the world's highest commercial airport?*

It is at LaPaz, Bolivia at an altitude of 15,500 feet.

Brazil

The terms of employment must be stated on a mandatory employee's work card. Employers are obliged to provide dining accommodations on premises when more than 300 persons are employed, a work week of 44 hours, paid vacation of 30 days each year, and a vacation bonus of one-third of the monthly salary. Employers are obligated to pay an annual bonus equal to one month's salary—in effect 13 months of salary. The law also mandates annual salary increases, special allowances for each child under 14, and a 20 percent premium on night work. Dismissal requires giving 30 days written notice and severance payments of one month's salary for each year of service.

These brief highlights of foreign labor laws are indicative of their social character, which tend to put the immediate social well-being of workers ahead of long-term corporate profitability and, thus, long-term labor security. Generally speaking, it is easy to hire and difficult to fire. Accordingly, the labor laws of a country require careful analysis prior to commencing foreign operations.

Legal Forms of Business Organization

In the United States, the legal forms of business are the sole proprietorship, the partnership, and the corporation. While the legal forms of business in other countries are similar to these three forms, important and subtle differences exist. Therefore, professional legal and tax advice is required in the selection of the business form to ensure adherence to the laws of the host country and to avoid unnecessary taxation or delay in the formation of the company.

SUMMARY

The legal and political environment in the home and host countries and the laws and agreements governing relationships between nations are important to the global business executive. Compliance is mandatory in order to do business successfully abroad. To avoid the problems that can result from changes in the legal and political environment, it is essential to anticipate changes and to develop strategies for coping with them. Whenever possible, the manager must avoid being taken by surprise and letting events control business decisions.

Governments affect global business through legislation and regulations, which can support or hinder business transactions. An example is when export sanctions or embargoes are imposed to enhance foreign policy objectives. Similarly, export controls are used to preserve national security. Nations also regulate the global business behavior of firms by setting standards that relate to bribery and corruption, boycotts, and restraint of competition.

Through political actions such as expropriation, confiscation, or domestication, countries expose firms to international risk. Management therefore needs to be aware of the possibility of such risk and alert to new developments.

Managers need to be aware that different countries have different laws. One clearly pronounced difference is between civil-law countries, where all possible legal rules are spelled out, and common-law countries such as the United States, where the law is based on tradition, precedent, and custom.

Managers must also pay attention to international political relations, agreements, and treaties. Changes in relations or rules can mean major new opportunities and occasional threats to global business.

Accounting practices differ substantially across countries. The efforts of a number of international associations and agencies in the past two decades have, however, led to increasing cooperation and agreement among national accounting authorities. Real accounting differences remain, and many of these differences still contribute to the advantaged competitive position of some countries' firms over global competitors.

International taxation is a subject close to the pocketbook of every multinational firm. Although the tax policies of most countries are theoretically designed to not change or influence financial and business decision making by firms, they often do. Labor laws in foreign countries may vary significantly and have important implications for the rate of pay, vacation pay, bonuses, overtime, and so forth, all of which affect the ability of the global company to remain cost competitive.

Key Terms and Concepts

national law
international law
state
public international law
private international law
conflict of laws
arbitration
extraterritoriality
Sherman Antitrust Act
Clayton Act
Robinson-Patman Act
Foreign Concept Practices Act
export-control systems
export license
boycott
critical commodities list
sanction
embargo
intergovernmental organizations
structured operating environment
accounting diversity
direct taxes
indirect taxes
value added tax
civil law
common law
Muslim or Islamic Law
political risk
ownership risk
operating risk
transfer risk
Doctrine of Sovereign Immunity
modern traditional theory
Calvo Doctrine
expropriation
confiscation
domestication
local content
exchange controls
price controls
Overseas Private Investment Corporation
Multilateral Investment Guarantee Agency
creeping expropriation

Questions for Discussion

1. After you hand your passport to the immigration officer in country X, he misplaces it. A small "donation" would certainly help him find it again. Should you give him the money? Is this a business expense to be charged to your company? Should it be tax deductible?
2. Discuss this potential dilemma: "High political risk requires companies to seek a quick payback on their investments. Striving for a quick payback, however, exposes firms to charges of exploitation and results in increased political risk."
3. Discuss this statement: "The national security that our export-control laws seek to protect may be threatened by the resulting lack of international competitiveness of U.S. firms."

4. Discuss the advantages and disadvantages of common law and civil law.
5. The United States has been described as a litigious society. How does frequent litigation affect international business?
6. Do you think all firms, in all economic environments, should operate under the same set of accounting principles?
7. What is the nature of the purported benefit that accounting principles provide British firms over American firms in the competition for mergers and acquisitions?
8. Comment on the statement that hiring an employee in a foreign land is the same as in the United States.

Recommended Readings

August, Ray. *International Business Law: Texts, Cases and Readings,* 2d ed. Upper Saddle River, N.J.: Prentice Hall, 1997.

Bertsch, G. K., and S. E. Gowen, eds. *Export Controls in Transition: Perspectives, Problems, and Prospects.* Durham, N.C.: Duke University Press, 1992.

Carter, Barry E. *International Economic Sanctions.* New York: Cambridge University Press, 1988.

Choate, Pat. *Agents of Influence.* New York: Knopf, 1990.

De la Torre, José, and David H. Neckar. "Forecasting Political Risks for International Operations." In *Global Strategic Management: The Essentials,* 2d ed. H. Vernon-Wortzel and L. Wortzel, eds. New York: John Wiley and Sons, 1990.

United States General Accounting Office, GAO/NSIAD-92-167. *Export Controls: Multilateral Efforts to Improve Enforcement.* Washington, D.C.: Government Printing Office, 1992.

Finding Common Ground: U.S. Export Controls in a Changed Global Environment. Washington, D.C.: National Academy Press, 1991.

Heinz, John. *U.S. Strategic Trade: Export Control Systems for the 1990's.* Boulder, Colo.: Westview Press, 1991.

Hotchkiss, Carolyn. *International Law for Business.* New York, NY: McGraw-Hill, Inc., 1994.

Litka, Michael. *The Legal Environment of Business,* 2d ed. Boston, MA: PWS-Kent Publishing Co., 1991.

Schaffer, R., B. Earle, and F. Agusti. *International Business Law and Its Environment.* 3d ed. St. Paul, Minn.: West Publishing, 1996.

Notes

1. Hotchkiss, C., *International Law for Business,* McGraw-Hill, Inc.: New York, 1994, p. 5.
2. *Ibid.,* pp. 24–25.
3. August, Ray, *International Business Law,* 2d ed., Upper Saddle River, N.J.: Prentice Hall, 1993, p. 1.
4. Litka, Michael, *The Legal Environment of Business,* 2d ed., Boston, M.A.: PWS-Kent Publishing Co., 1991, pp. 6–7.
5. Schaffer, R., Earle, B., and Agusti, F., *International Business Law and Its Environment,* 3d ed., St. Paul, M.N.: West Publishing Co., 1996, p. 61.
6. Hotchkiss, C., *ibid.,* p. 39.
7. Litka, M. *ibid.,* p. 97.
8. Hotchkiss, C., *ibid.,* p. 96.
9. "U.S. enlists rich nations in move to end business bribes," *New York Times,* April 12, 1996, A-10.
10. Hufbauer, Gary Clyde, and Schott, Jeffrey J., "Economic Solutions," an often used and occasionally effective tool of foreign policy in *Export Controls,* ed. Michael R. Czinkota.
11. A catalog of new U.S. unilateral economic sanctions for foreign policy purposes, 1993–1996, National Association of Manufacturers, March 1997, p. 1.
12. U.S. engage transcript of press conference, April 16, 1997, p. 9; http://USA engage.org.
13. "Japan Still Has Only 12,500 Lawyers," *The Exporter* 6 (September 1986): 18.
14. Rowe, James L., Jr., "Inflation Slowed, Argentina's Alfonsin Now Tackling Economic Stagnation," *The Washington Post,* July 13, 1986, G-1, G-8.
15. Czinkota, Michael R., and Woronoff, Jon, *Unlocking Japan's Market,* Chicago: Probus Publishing, 1991.
16. Litka, M., *ibid.,* p. 3.
17. Hotchkiss, C., *ibid.,* p. 323.
18. Miscallef, Joseph V., "Political Risk Assessment," *Columbia Journal of World Business* 16 (January 1981): 47.

The Cultural Environment

LEARNING OBJECTIVES

To define and demonstrate the effect of culture's various dimensions on global business.

To examine ways in which cultural knowledge can be acquired and individuals and organizations prepared for cross-cultural interaction.

To illustrate ways in which cultural risk poses a challenge to the effective conduct of business communications and transactions.

To suggest ways in which global businesses act as change agents in the diverse cultural environments in which they operate.

GLOBAL LEARNING EXPERIENCE 8.1

Using Culture to Achieve Success

Thousands of European and U.S. companies have entered or expanded their operations in the fastest growing region in the world—Asia. In the 1990s, the region outpaced the growth of the world's 24 leading industrial economies by more than six times. A total of 400 million Asian consumers have disposable incomes at least equal to the rich-world average.

Few businesses have had as much experience—or success—as the 3M Company. The maker of everything from heart-lung machines to Scotch tape, the company's revenues for 1996 from international sales reached $7,590 billion (53.3 percent of total), a full third coming from the Asia-Pacific. At the root of the company's success are certain rules that allow it both to adjust to and exploit cultural differences.

- *Embrace local culture*—3M's new plant near Bangkok, Thailand, is one example of how the company embraces local culture. A gleaming Buddhist shrine, wreathed in flowers, pays homage to the spirits Thais believe took care of the land prior to the plant's arrival. Showing sensitivity to local customs helps sales and builds employee morale, officials say. It helps the company understand the market and keeps it from doing something inadvertently to alienate people.
- *Employ locals to gain cultural knowledge*—The best way to understand a market is to have grown up in it. Of the 7,500 3M employees in Asia, fewer than 10 are Americans. The rest are locals who know the customs and buying habits of their compatriots. 3M also makes grants of up to $50,000 available to its Asian employees to study product innovations, making them equals with their U.S. counterparts.
- *Build relationships*—3M executives started preparing for the Chinese market soon after President Nixon's historic visit in 1972. For ten years, company officials visited Beijing and invited Chinese leaders to 3M headquarters in St. Paul, Minnesota, building contacts and trust along the way. Such efforts paid off when, in 1984, the government made 3M the first wholly owned foreign venture on Chinese soil, 3Mers call the process FIDO ("first in defeats other") which is a credo built on patience, and long-term perspective.
- *Adapt products to local markets*—Examples of how 3M adapts its products read like insightful lessons on culture. In the early 1990s, sales of 3M's famous Scotchbrite cleaning pads were languishing. Company technicians interviewed maids and housewives to determine why. The answer: Filipinos traditionally scrub floors by pushing around a rough shell of coconut with their feet. 3M responded by making the pads brown and shaping them like a foot. In China, a big seller for 3M is a composite to fill tooth cavities. In the United States, dentists pack a soft material into the hole and blast it with a special beam of light, making it hard as enamel in five seconds. But in the People's Republic, dentists cannot afford the light. The solution is an air-drying composite that does the same thing in two minutes; it takes a little longer but is far less expensive.
- *Help employees understand you*—At any given time, more than 30 Asian technicians are in the United States, where they learn the latest product advances while gaining new insight into how the company works. At the same time, they are able to contribute by infusing their insight into company plans and operations.
- *Coordinate by region*—When designers in Singapore discovered that consumers wanted to use 3M's Nomad household floor mats in their cars, they spread the word to their counterparts in Malaysia and Thailand. Today, the specially made car mats with easy-to-clean vinyl loops are big sellers across Southeast Asia. The company encourages its product managers from different Asian countries to hold regular meetings and share insights and strategies. The goal is to come up with regional programs and "Asianize" a product more quickly.

SOURCE: John R. Engen, "Far Eastern Front," *World Trade,* December 1994, 20–24; "A Survey of Asia," *The Economist,* October 30, 1993; 3M Annual Report 1996. For more information, see http://www.3M.com/intl/.

The world has become smaller as a result of improvements in transportation and information systems, but the behavioral patterns, values, and attitudes that govern human interaction may still remain relatively unchanged. Technological innovation is bringing about the globalization of business, and individuals at all levels of the firm are becoming involved in cross-cultural interaction. Firms expanding globally acquire foreign clients as well as foreign personnel with whom regular communication is necessary, with the result that day-to-day operations require significant cross-cultural competence. As the distinction between domestic and global activities diminishes, cultural sensitivity in varying degrees is required from every employee. Global Learning Experience 8.1 illustrates how one company achieved success in the global market place by thoroughly understanding local cultures.

In the past, business managers who did not want to worry about the cultural challenge could simply decide not to do so and concentrate on domestic markets. In today's business environment, a company has no choice but to face global competition. In this new environment, believing that concern about cultural elements is a waste of time often proves to be disastrous.

Cultural differences often are the subject of anecdotes, and business blunders may provide a good laugh. Cultural diversity must be recognized not simply as a fact of life but as a positive benefit; that is, differences may actually propose better solutions to challenges shared across borders. Cultural competence must be recognized as a key management skill.[1] Adjustments will have to be made to accommodate the extraordinary variety in customer preferences and work practices by cultivating the ability to detect similarities and to allow for differences. Ideally, this means that successful ideas can be transferred across borders for efficiency and adapted for local conditions for effectiveness. For example, in one of his regular trips to company headquarters in Switzerland, the general manager of Nestlé Thailand was briefed on a promotion for a cold coffee concoction called Nescafe Shake.[2] The Thai group swiftly adopted and adapted the idea. It designed plastic containers to mix the drink and invented a dance, the Shake, to popularize the product. Cultural incompetence, however, can easily jeopardize millions of dollars through wasted negotiations, lost purchases, sales, and contracts, and poor customer relations. Furthermore, the internal efficiency of a multinational corporation may be weakened if managers and workers are not "on the same wavelength." **Cultural risk** is just as real as political risk in the global business arena.

cultural risk
the risk of business blunders, poor customer relations, and wasted negotiations that results when firms fail to understand and adapt to the cultural differences between their own and host countries' cultures

The intent of this chapter is first to analyze the concept of culture and its various elements and then to provide suggestions for meeting the cultural challenge. Culture does, after all, affect each and every aspect of business.

CULTURE DEFINED

Culture is learned, shared, and transmitted from one generation to the next. Culture is primarily passed on from parents to their children but also transmitted by social organizations, special interest groups, the government, the schools, and the church. Common ways of thinking and behaving that are developed are then reinforced through social pressure. Hofstede calls this the "collective programming of the mind.[3] Culture is also multidimensional, consisting of a number of common elements that are interdependent. Changes occurring in one of the dimensions will affect the others as well.

SOURCES for Culture Tips throughout Chapter 8: (axt)—Roger E. Axtell, *Do's and Taboos,* 3rd Edition, Wiley, New York, 1993.
(mcd)—P. B. Harris, and R. T. Moran, *Managing Cultural Differences,* 2nd Edition, Gulf Publishing Company, Houston, 1987.

For the purposes of this text, culture is defined as an integrated system of learned behavior patterns that are characteristic of the members of any given society. It includes everything that a group thinks, says, does, and makes—its customs, language, material artifacts, and shared systems of attitudes and feelings.[4] The definition, therefore, encompasses a wide variety of elements from the materialistic to the spiritual. Culture is inherently conservative, resisting change and fostering continuity. Every person is encultured into a particular culture, learning the "right way" of doing things. Problems may arise when a person encultured in one culture has to adjust to another one. The process of **acculturation**—adjusting and adapting to a specific culture other than one's own—is one of the keys to success in global operations.

acculturation
adjusting and adapting to a specific culture other than one's own

Edward T. Hall, who has made some of the most valuable studies on the effects of culture on business, makes a distinction between high- and low-context culture.[5] In **high-context cultures,** such as Japan and Saudi Arabia, context, or the intention and unspoken meaning, is at least as important as what is actually said. The speaker and the listener rely on a common understanding of the context. In **low-context cultures,** however, most of the information is contained in the words. North American cultures engage in low-context communications. Unless one is aware of this basic difference, messages and intentions can easily be misunderstood, as shown in Global Learning Experience 8.2. One of the interesting differences in performance appraisals is that the U.S. system emphasizes the individual's development, whereas the Japanese system focuses on the group within which the individual works. In the United States, criticism is more direct and recorded formally, whereas in Japan it is more subtle and verbal. What is not being said can carry more meaning than what is said.

high-context cultures
cultures in which context is at least as important as what is actually said

low-context cultures
most of the information is contained explicitly in the words

Few cultures today are as homogeneous as those of Japan and Saudi Arabia. Elsewhere, intracultural differences based on nationality, religion, race, or geographic areas have resulted in the emergence of distinct subcultures. The global manager's task is to distinguish relevant cross-cultural and intracultural differences and then to isolate potential opportunities and problems. Good examples are the Hispanic subculture in the United States and the Flemish and the Walloons in Belgium. On the other hand, borrowing and interaction between national cultures may lead to narrowing gaps between cultures. Here the global business entity will act as a **change agent** by introducing new products or ideas and practices. Although this may consist of no more than shifting consumption from one product brand to another, it may lead to massive social change in the manner of consumption, the type of products consumed, and social organization. Consider, for example, that in a ten-year period the international portion of McDonald's annual sales grew from 13 percent to 23 percent.

change agent
person or institution who facilitates change in a firm or in a host country

In bringing about change or in trying to cater to increasingly homogeneous demand across markets, the global business entity may be accused of "cultural imperialism," especially if the changes brought about are dramatic or if culture-specific adaptations are not made in management or marketing programs.

The example of Kentucky Fried Chicken in India illustrates the difficulties marketers may have in entering culturally complex markets. Even though the company opened its outlets in two of India's most cosmopolitan cities (Bangalore and New Delhi), it found itself the target of protests by a wide range of opponents. KFC could have

CULTURE TIP

Latin Americans are often late according to North American standards, but expect North Americans to be on time. Dinner usually begins at 8 P.M. or later. As a guest, never arrive on time; a 30 minute delay is customary. (mcd 375; axt 99)

GLOBAL LEARNING EXPERIENCE

8.2

U.S. Foreign Policy Toward China—Tangled in Words

As U.S. firms expand abroad, they will encounter different cultures that require patience and an understanding of how business is conducted in those foreign lands. This is especially true when the low-context culture of the United States, only some 300 years old, encounters the high-context cultures of Asia and the Middle East, steeped in thousands of years of tradition and rituals. U.S. marketers can learn a lesson of the importance of words and the context in which they are used from the world of diplomacy. There, words are used very carefully and the context in which they are used is thoroughly considered. Even a seemingly slight change in words can have a significant impact on the meaning and interpretation of the thought they convey.

An interesting illustration of the importance of words and their context occurred when former U.S. Secretary of State Warren Christopher visited Shanghai in late 1996 to give a speech at Fudan University. The speech was titled "Building a Partnership for the 21st Century." Those words, based on an early draft of the speech, were painted on a big blue sign above the podium to advertise Mr. Christopher's speech, and people had seen it. A Chinese official commented: "Christopher is using the word 'partnership' in the title of his talk. This is the first time we've heard this word. It's much better than 'cooperation.' It means we have a real chance to improve relations now, and I'm very optimistic."

Apparently unaware of the favorable interpretation of the word 'partnership' and the subtle change of diplomatic policy it signaled to the Chinese, Mr. Christopher's address was revised by senior staff members, who removed the word "partnership" and replaced it with "cooperation." The officials objected to the "hackneyed" use of "partnership" and questioned the credibility of a partnership between the United States and a China that is still cited for human rights abuses.

The Chinese were anticipating a "partnership" but were given "cooperation," which implied a significantly different relationship between the two countries. To add to the confusing and unfortunate policy implications of the change in words, President Clinton used the word "partnership" in regard to China at a news conference in Canberra, Australia. Speaking of various areas of cooperation between the two nations, Mr. Clinton said, "But I see this in the context of building a partnership with China, not isolating it."

SOURCE: "Diplomacy vs. Semantics on China Visit," *New York Times,* Nov. 22, 1996.

alleviated or eliminated some of the anti-Western passions by taking a series of preparatory steps. First, rather than opting for more direct control, KFC should have allied with local partners for advice and support. Second, KFC should have tried to appear more Indian rather than using high-profile advertising with Western ideas. Indians are quite ambivalent toward foreign cultures, and ideas usable elsewhere do not work well in India. Finally, KFC should have planned for reaction by competition, which came from small restaurants with political clout at the local level.[6]

CULTURE TIP

South of the border, nobody rushes into business. As a foreign businessperson, take your time and ask about your colleague's family's health or make a few comments about the weather. The local sports team is a good beginning point of conversation. (mcd 37)

THE ELEMENTS OF CULTURE

The study of culture has led to generalizations that may apply to all cultures. These include such elements as bodily adornments, courtship rituals, etiquette, concept of family, gestures, joking, mealtime customs, music, personal names, status differentiation, and trade customs.[7] The major elements of culture are summarized in Table 8.1. The sensitivity and adaptation to these elements by an international firm depends on the firm's level of involvement in the market—for example, licensing versus direct investment—and the product or service marketed. Naturally, some products and services or management practices require very little adjustment, while some have to be adapted dramatically.

Language

Language has been described as the mirror of culture. Language itself is multidimensional by nature. This is true not only of the spoken word but also of what can be called the nonverbal language of international business. Messages are conveyed by the words used, by how the words are spoken (for example, tone of voice), and through nonverbal means such as gestures, body position, and eye contact.

Very often mastery of the language is required before a person is accultured to a culture other than his or her own. Language mastery must go beyond technical competency because every language has words and phrases that can be readily understood only in context. Such phrases are carriers of culture; they represent special ways a culture has developed to view some aspect of human existence.

Language capability serves four distinct roles in global business.[8] Language is important in information gathering and evaluation. Rather than rely completely on the opinions of others, the manager is able to see and hear personally what is going on.

TABLE 8.1 **Elements of Culture**

Elements of Culture
Language
Verbal
Nonverbal
Religion
Values and attitudes
Manners and customs
Material elements
Aesthetics
Education
Social institutions

CULTURE TIP

As a foreigner, be prepared for Latin men to flirt with all wives, but men should be careful not to flatter or flirt with a South American wife. Also be aware that a Latin may have a public wife (legal) and a private wife (mistress). (mcd 3)

People are far more comfortable speaking their own language, and this should be treated as an advantage. The best intelligence on a market is gathered by becoming part of the market rather than observing it from the outside. Local managers of a multinational corporation should be the firm's primary source of political information to assess potential risk. Second, language provides access to local society. Although English may be widely spoken and may even be the official company language, speaking the local language may make a dramatic difference. Third, language capability is increasingly important in company communications, whether within the corporate family or with channel members. Imagine the difficulties encountered by a country manager who must communicate with employees through an interpreter. Finally, language provides more than the ability to communicate. It extends beyond mechanics to the interpretation of contexts.

The manager's command of the national language(s) in a market must be greater than simple word recognition. Consider how dramatically different English terms can be when used in Australia, the United Kingdom, or the United States. In negotiations, U.S. delegates "tabling a proposal" mean that they want to delay a decision, while their British counterparts understand the expression to mean that immediate action is to be taken. If the British promise something "by the end of the day," this does not mean within 24 hours, but rather when they have completed the job. Additionally, they may say that negotiations "bombed," meaning that they were a success, which to an American could convey exactly the opposite message.

An example of this separation of Americans and British by the same language is provided in Figure 8.1. Electrolux's theme in marketing its vacuum cleaners is interpreted in the United Kingdom without connotations, while in the United States the slang implications would earn the campaign blunder honors. Similar problems occur with other languages and markets. Swedish is spoken as a mother tongue by 8 percent of the population in Finland, where it has idioms that are not well understood by Swedes.

Difficulties with language usually arise through carelessness, which is manifested in a number of translation blunders. The old saying, "If you want to kill a message, translate it," is true. A classic example involves GM and its "Body by Fisher" theme; when translated into Flemish, this became "Corpse by Fisher." There is also the danger of sound-alikes. For example, Chanel No. 5 would have fared poorly in Japan had it been called Chanel No. 4, because the Japanese word for four (shih) also sounds like the word for death. This is the reason that IBM's series 44 computers had a different number classification in Japan than in any other market. The danger of using a translingual homonym also exists; that is, an innocent English word may have strong aural resemblance to a word not used in polite company in another country. Examples in French-speaking areas include Pet milk products and a toothpaste called Cue. A French firm trying to sell pâté to a Baltimore importer experienced a problem with the brand name Tartex, which sounded like shoe polish. Kellogg renamed Bran Buds in Sweden, where the brand name translated roughly to "burned farmer."

Another consideration is the capability of language to convey different shades of meaning. As an example, a one-word equivalent to "aftertaste" does not exist in many languages and in others is far-fetched at best. To communicate the idea may require a lengthy translation of "the taste that remains in your mouth after you have finished eating or drinking."

✹ CULTURE TIP

North Americans begin getting to know people by asking a lot of questions. In Latin America, it is safer to talk about local things. Questions are often interpreted as prying. (mcd 3)

Example of an Ad That Will Transfer Poorly **FIGURE 8.1**

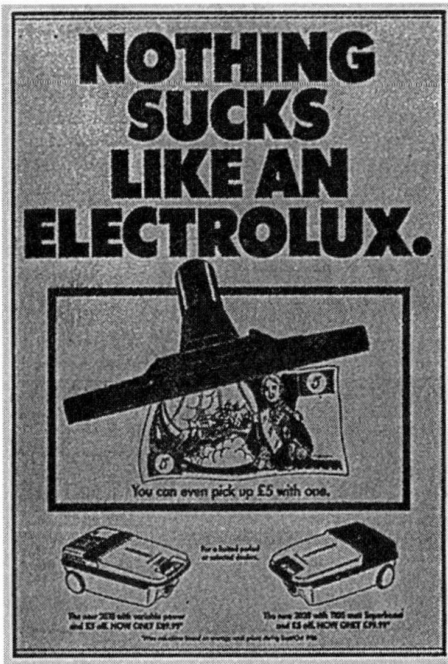

SOURCE: "Viewpoint: Letters," *Advertising Age,* June 29, 1987, 20.

The role of language extends beyond that of a communications medium. Linguistic diversity often is an indicator of other types of diversity. In Quebec, the French language has always been a major consideration of most francophone governments, because it is one of the clear manifestations of the identity of the province vis-à-vis the English-speaking provinces. The Charter of the French Language states that the rights of the francophone collectivity are (1) the right of every person to have the civil administration, semipublic agencies, and business firms communicate with him or her in French: (2) the right of workers to carry on their activities in French; and (3) the right of consumers to be informed and served in French. The Bay, a major Quebec retailer, spends $8 million annually on its translation operations. It has even changed its name to La Baie in appropriate areas.

If a brand name or an advertising theme is to be extended, care has to be taken to make sure of a comfortable fit. Kellogg's Rice Krispies snap, crackle, and pop in most markets; the Japanese, who have trouble pronouncing these words, watch the caricatures "patchy, pitchy, putchy" in their commercials.

Dealing with the language problem invariably requires local assistance. A good local advertising agency and a good local market research firm can prevent many problems. When translation is required, as when communicating with suppliers or customers, care should be taken in selecting the translator. One of the simplest methods of control is **backtranslation**—the translating of a foreign language version back to the original language by a different person than the one who made the first translation.

backtranslation
translating of a foreign language version back to the original language by a different person than the one who made the first translation

✷ CULTURE TIP

Latin Americans tend to stand close during conversation. If you want to do business in this part of the world, learn to accept your host's distance. (axt 98)

Nonverbal Language

Managers also must analyze and become familiar with the hidden language of foreign cultures. Five key topics—time, space, material possessions, friendship patterns, and business agreements—offer a starting point from which managers can begin to acquire the understanding necessary to do business in foreign countries. In many parts of the world, time is flexible and not seen as a limited commodity; people come late to appointments or may not come at all. In Hong Kong, it is futile to set exact meeting times, because getting from one place to another may take minutes or hours depending on the traffic situation. Showing indignation or impatience at such behavior would astonish an Arab, Latin American, or Asian. Understanding national and cultural differences in the concept of time is critical for the global business manager.

In some countries, the feeling is that one should know one's business partner on a personal level before transactions can occur. Therefore, rushing straight to business will not be rewarded, because deals are made on the basis of not only the best product or price but also the entity or person deemed most trustworthy. Contracts may be bound on handshakes, not lengthy and complex agreements—a fact that makes some, especially Western, businesspeople uneasy.

Individuals vary in the amount of space they want separating them from others. Arabs, and Latin Americans like to stand close to people they are talking with. If an American, who may not be comfortable at such close range, backs away from an Arab, this might incorrectly be taken as a negative reaction. Also, Westerners are often taken aback by the more physical nature of affection between Slavs—for example, being kissed squarely on the lips by a business partner, regardless of sex.

Body language must be included in the nonverbal language of global business. For example, an American manager may, after successful completion of negotiations, impulsively give a finger-and-thumb OK sign. In Southern France, the manager will have indicated that the sale is worthless, and in Japan, that a little bribe has been asked for; the gesture is grossly insulting to Brazilians. An interesting exercise is to compare and contrast the conversation styles of different nationalities. Northern Europeans are quite reserved in using their hands and maintain a good amount of personal space, whereas Southern Europeans involve their bodies to a far greater degree in making a point.

Religion

In most cultures, people find in religion a reason for being and legitimacy in the belief that they are of a larger context. To define religion requires the inclusion of the supernatural and the existence of a higher power. Religion defines the ideals for life, which in turn are reflected in the values and attitudes of societies and individuals. Such values and attitudes shape the behavior and practices of institutions and members of cultures.

Religion has an impact on international marketing that is seen in a culture's values and attitudes toward entrepreneurship, consumption, and social organization. The impact will vary depending on the strength of the dominant religious tenets. While religion's impact may be quite indirect in Protestant Northern Europe, its impact in countries where Islamic fundamentalism is on the rise (such as Algeria) may be profound.

CULTURE TIP

When invited to the home of an Arab businessman for dinner, skip your previous meal so that you have a keen appetite. Proper appreciation of a meal is shown by eating large quantities. (axt 83)

Religion provides the basis for transcultural similarities under shared beliefs and behavior. The impact of these similarities will be assessed in terms of the dominant religions of the world: Christianity, Islam, Hinduism, Buddhism, and Confucianism. While some countries may officially have secularism, such as Marxism-Leninism as a state belief (for example, in China, Vietnam, and Cuba), traditional religious beliefs still remain as a powerful force in shaping behavior.

Christianity has the largest following among world religions, with more than 1.8 billion people.[9] While there are many significant groups within Christianity, the major ones are Catholicism and Protestantism. A prominent difference between the two of them is the attitude toward making money. While Catholicism has questioned it, the Protestant ethic has emphasized the importance of work and the accumulation of wealth for the glory of God. At the same time, frugality is stressed and the residual accumulation of wealth from hard work formed the basis for investment. It has been proposed that this is the basis for the development of capitalism in the Western world, and the rise of predominantly Protestant countries into the world economic leadership in the 20th century.[10]

Major holidays are often tied to religion. The holidays will be observed differently from one culture to another to the next, to the extent that the same holiday may have different connotations. Christian cultures observe Christmas and exchange gifts on either December 24 or 25, with the exception of the Dutch, who exchange gifts on St. Nicholas Day, December 6. Global Learning Experience 8.3 illustrates the cultural and religious significance of the **Day of the Dead** in Mexico. Tandy Corporation, in its first year in the Netherlands, targeted its major Christmas promotion for the third week of December with less than satisfactory results. The international marketing manager must see to it that local holidays are taken into account in the scheduling of events ranging from fact-finding missions to marketing programs.

Dia De los Muertos (Day of the Dead)
Central and South American observance of All Saints Day (Nov. 1) and All Souls Day (Nov. 2)

Islam, which reaches from the west coast of Africa to the Philippines and across a wide band that includes Tanzania, Central Asia, Western China, India, and Malaysia, has more than a billion followers.[11] Islam is also a significant minority religion in many parts of the world, including Europe. Islam has a pervasive role in the life of its followers, referred to as Muslims, through the Shariá (law of Islam). This is most obvious in the five stated daily periods of prayer, fasting during the holy month of Ramadan, and the **Hajj,** the pilgrimage to Mecca, Islam's holy city. While Islam is supportive of entrepreneurship, it nevertheless strongly discourages acts that may be interpreted as exploitation. Islam is also absent of discrimination, except to those outside the religion. Some have argued that Islam's basic fatalism (that is, nothing happens without the will of Allah) and traditionalism have deterred economic development in countries observing the religion.

Hajj
annual Muslim pilgrimage to Mecca, required of all Muslims at least once in their lifetime

The role of women in business is tied to religion, especially in the Middle East, where they are not able to function as they would in the West. The effects of this are numerous; for example, a firm may be limited in its use of female managers or personnel in these areas, and women's role as consumers and influencers in the consumption process may be different. Except for food purchases, men make the final purchase decisions.[12] Access to women in Islamic countries may only be possible through the use of female sales personnel, direct marketing, and women's specialty shops.[13]

CULTURE TIP

In the Arab world, be careful about admiring your host's watch, cuff links, or other possessions. An Arab businessman is often very magnanimous. He might give them to you on the spot and be offended if you refuse them. (axt 83)

Dia De los Muertos—Day of the Dead

The subject of death and dying is an unhappy and morbid one for most people around the world. When Christian traditions and pre-Columbian Indian rituals meet, as they often do in Central and South America, the cultural response to death can be a strange one indeed.

Many of the predominantly Christian countries recognize, in varying degrees, the religious observance of All Saints' Day (November 1)—a day when the saints are revered—and All Souls' Day (November 2)—when deceased relatives and friends are remembered. In a number of countries, either one or both of these religious days are national legal holidays.

Probably nowhere do death and the remembrance of departed souls take on more significance than in Mexico. There pre-Columbian Zapotec Indian rituals fuse with those of Spanish Roman Catholicism in the celebration of *Dia De los Muertos,* Day of the Dead.

From dusk on October 31 through November 2, most Mexicans participate in a huge festive event, one that reaffirms life and celebrates death. During *Dia De los Muertos,* families visit the graves of their loved ones to pray, picnic, drink, and sing. The dead are remembered with an array of flowers and foods placed on the graves intended to nourish the deceased on their way to heaven. Some families construct an altar, or *ofrenda,* in the home and laden it with the favorite foods, drink, and personal belongings of the departed relative. Bakeries and food vendors join in the celebration by selling cookies in the shape of skeletons, sugar confections shaped like skulls and coffins, and the bread of the dead, *Pan De los Muertos,* which are loaves of bread with sugar-coated faces baked on them—a special treat for the holidays.

The Mexican poet Octavio Paz sums up the subject of death in this clash of cultures: "Death also lacks meaning for the modern Mexican. It is no longer a transition, an access to another life more alive than our own. But although we do not view death as a transcendence, we have not eliminated it from our daily lives. The word death is not pronounced in New York, in Paris, in London, because it burns the lips. The Mexican, in contrast, is familiar with death, jokes about it, caresses it, sleeps with it, celebrates it; it is one of his favorite toys and his most steadfast love." Paz also says, "In a closed world where everything is death, only death has value. But our affirmation is negative. Sugar-candy skulls, and tissue-paper skulls and skeletons strung with fireworks. . . . Our popular images always poke fun at life, affirming the nothingness and insignificance of human existence. We decorate our houses with death's heads, we eat bread in the shape of bones on the day of the dead, we love the songs and stories in which death laughs and cracks jokes, but all this boastful familiarity does not rid us of the question we all ask: What is death? We have not thought up a new answer. And each time we ask, we shrug our shoulders: Why should I care about death if I have never cared about life?"

SOURCE: Octavio Paz, *The Labyrinth of Solitude,* translated by C. Kemp, Y. Milos, and R. Belash, Chapter 3, "The Day of the Dead," p. 57–59, Grove Press, Inc., New York, 1985.

✷ CULTURE TIP

In the Middle East, it is an insult to sit in such a way as to face your host with the soles of your shoes showing. Do not place your feet on a desk, table, or chair. (axt 79)

Religion impacts the marketing of products and service delivery. When beef or poultry is exported to an Islamic country, the animal must be killed in the *halal* method and certified appropriately. Recognition of religious restrictions on products (for example, pork products and alcoholic beverages) can reveal opportunities, as evidenced by successful launches of several nonalcoholic beverages in the Middle East. Other restrictions may call for innovative solutions. A challenge of the Swedish firm that had the primary responsibility for building a traffic system to Mecca was that non-Muslims are not allowed access to the city. The solution was to use closed-circuit television to supervise the work. Given that Islam considers interest payments usury, bankers and Muslim scholars have worked to create interest-free banking products that rely on lease agreements, mutual funds, and other methods to avoid paying interest[14] as shown in Global Learning Experience 8.4.

Hinduism has 750 million followers, mainly in India, Nepal, Malaysia, Guyana, Suriname, and Sri Lanka. It actually is not a religion, but a way of life predicated on which caste, or class, into which one is born. While the caste system has produced social stability, its impact on business can be quite negative. For example, if one cannot rise above one's caste, individual effort is hampered. Problems in workforce integration and coordination may become quite severe. Furthermore, the drive for business success may not be forthcoming because of the fact that followers place value mostly on spiritual rather than materialistic achievement.

The family is an important element in Hindu society, with extended families being the norm. The extended family structure will have an impact on the purchasing power and consumption of Hindu families. Market researchers, in particular, must take this into account in assessing market potential and consumption patterns.

Buddhism, which extends its influence throughout Asia from Sri Lanka to Japan, has 334 million followers. Although it is an offspring of Hinduism, it has not caste system. Life is seen as an existence of suffering with achieving nirvana, a state marked by an absence of desire, as the solution to the suffering. The emphasis in Buddhism is on spiritual achievement rather than worldly goods.

Confucianism has 150 million followers throughout Asia, especially among the Chinese, and has been characterized as a code of conduct rather than a religion. However, its teachings that stress loyalty and relationships have been broadly adopted. Loyalty to central authority and placing the good of a group before that of the individual may explain the economic success of Japan, South Korea, Singapore, and the Republic of China. It also has led to cultural misunderstandings: In Western societies there has been a perception that the subordination of the individual to the common good has resulted in the sacrifice of human rights. The emphasis on relationships is very evident in developing business ties in Asia. The preparatory stage may take years before the needed level of understanding is reached and actual business transactions can take place.

Values and Attitudes

Values are shared beliefs or group norms that have been internalized by individuals.[15] Attitudes are evaluations of alternatives based on these values. The Japanese culture raises an almost invisible—yet often unscalable—wall against all *gaijin* (foreigners).

CULTURE TIP

Remember to respect Ramadan (the ninth month of the Islamic calendar). No work is done after noon during Ramadan. (axt 78)

GLOBAL LEARNING EXPERIENCE 8.4

Financing Purchases the Islamic Way

As American business organizations expand globally, particularly to countries with large Muslim populations, they quickly learn that religion and finance are interrelated. In the United States, home, automobiles, appliances, and just about everything else are usually purchased with loans—the monthly payments being part payment of principal and part payment of interest. For U.S. consumers, the financial arrangement is, in many instances, the element that clinches the sale.

Dealing with Muslims, however, requires creativity in designing the financing portion of the product offering. Muslims who follow Islamic Law are forbidden to pay or receive interest because the body of the law of the Koran, called *Shariá,* prohibits them from making a guaranteed profit on capital. Investors can get around the ban by making investments that involve risk or by arranging leases rather than loans for homes and automobiles.

In its most basic form, Islamic banking covers both savings and credit. Instead of being paid interest, Islamic bank depositors are considered shareholders and receive dividends when the bank earns a profit and lose money when it has a loss. In essence, Islamic banking is an interest-free banking system that relies on lease arrangements, mutual funds, and other methods to avoid paying interest. The following example illustrates how an Islamic bank might design a lease arrangement that gets around interest payments.

For a house that costs $200,000, a buyer puts down $40,000 or 20 percent. In a partnership agreement, the bank puts up the remaining $160,000 and leases its portion of the house to the buyer.

The buyer, called the resident owner, pays rent based on the portion of the home that the finance company owns plus a little more to increase equity. As the portion of the home that the bank owns decreases the resident owner's equity increases (as it does with a standard mortgage).

The home's value is reassessed every year and rental payments are adjusted accordingly. If the real estate market is doing well, the resident owner's rent will increase. Although he loses no money invested, his equity will be diluted. If the home's value falls, so do rent payments, cutting into the bank's income.

If the resident owner defaults on the deal and the bank sells the house, the owner does not lose his equity, as could happen with a conventional mortgage. The bank and the owner split the proceeds, depending on the percentage each owns of the house.

SOURCE: "Islamic Banking: Faith and Creativity," *New York Times,* April 8, 1994, D-1, D-6.

CULTURE TIP

When you don't talk business can be as important as when you do. In Britain, for instance, as soon as the day is done, so is business, and nothing will turn your hosts off faster than continuing shoptalk over drinks and dinner. (axt 20)

Many middle-aged bureaucrats and company officials feel that buying foreign products is downright unpatriotic. The resistance therefore is not so much to foreign products as to those who produce and market them. Similarly, foreign-based corporations have had difficulty in hiring university graduates or mid-career personnel because of bias against foreign employers.

Even under these adverse conditions, the race can be run and won through tenacity, patience, and drive. As an example, Procter & Gamble has made impressive inroads with its products by adopting a long-term, Japanese-style view of profits. Since the mid-1970s, the company has gained some 20 percent of the detergent market and made Pampers a household word among Japanese mothers. The struggle toward such rewards can require foreign companies to take big losses for five years or more.

The more rooted that values and attitudes are in central beliefs (such as religion), the more cautiously the global business manager has to move. Attitudes toward change are basically positive in industrialized countries, whereas in more tradition-bound societies, change is viewed with great suspicion—especially when it comes from a foreign entity. These situations call for thorough research, most likely a localized approach, and a major commitment at the top level for a considerable period of time. Global Learning Experience 8.5 outlines how the H. J. Heinz Co. approaches foreign markets.

Cultural differences in themselves can be a selling point suggesting luxury, prestige, or status. Sometimes U.S. companies use domestic marketing approaches when selling abroad because they believe the American look will sell the product. In Japan, Borden sells Lady Borden ice cream and Borden cheese deliberately packaged and labeled in English, exactly as they are in the United States. Similarly, in France, General Foods sells a chewing gum called Hollywood with an accompanying Pepsi-generation type of ad campaign that pictures teenagers riding bicycles on the beach.

Occasionally, U.S. firms successfully use American themes abroad that would not succeed at home. In Japan, Levi Strauss promoted its popular jeans with a television campaign featuring James Dean and Marilyn Monroe, who represent the epitome of Japanese youth's fantasy of freedom from a staid, traditional society. The commercials helped to establish Levi's as *the* prestige jeans, and status-seeking Japanese youth now willingly pay 40 percent more for them than for local brands. Their authentic Levi's, however, are designed and mostly made in Japan, where buyers like a tighter fit than do Americans.[16] Similarly, many global brands, such as Nike and Reebok, are able to charge premium prices for their products due to the loyal following.[17] At the same time, in the U.S. market, many companies have been quite successful emphasizing their foreign, imported image.

Manners and Customs

Changes occurring in manners and customs must be carefully monitored, especially in cases that seem to indicate a narrowing of cultural differences between peoples. Phenomena such as McDonald's and Coke have met with success around the world, but this does not mean that the world is becoming Westernized. Modernization and Westernization are not at all the same, as can be seen in Saudi Arabia, for example.

✷ CULTURE TIP

To the Japanese there is almost no distinction between the business day and the business night. They consider it part of both their personal and professional lives to spend virtually every evening with business associates. "You get through to a man's soul at night," is a saying among Japanese businessmen. (axt 20)

Understanding manners and customs is especially important in negotiations, because interpretations based on one's own frame of reference may lead to a totally incorrect conclusion as noted in Global Learning Experience 8.6. To negotiate effectively abroad, all types of communication should be read correctly. Americans often interpret inaction and silence as negative signs. As a result, Japanese executives tend to expect that their silence can get Americans to lower prices or sweeten the deal. Even a simple agreement may take days to negotiate in the Middle East because the Arab party may want to talk about unrelated issues or do something else for a while. The abrasive style of Russian negotiators and their usual last-minute change requests may cause astonishment and concern on the part of ill-prepared negotiators. As another example, consider the reaction of an American businessperson if a Finnish counterpart were to propose the continuing of negotiations in the sauna.

In many cultures, certain basic customs must be observed by the foreign businessperson. One of them concerns use of the right and left hands. In so-called right-hand societies, the left hand is the "toilet hand," and using it to eat, for example, is considered impolite. While many managers have caught on to cultural differences in the past decade or so, continued attention to details when approaching companies or when negotiating with their officials is necessary.

Managers must be concerned with differences in the ways products are used. For example, General Foods' Tang is positioned as a breakfast drink in the United States; in France, where orange juice usually is not consumed at breakfast, Tang is positioned as a refreshment. The questions that the global manager must ask are: "What are we selling?" and "What are the use benefits we should be providing?"

Usage differences have to be translated into product form and promotional decisions. Maxwell House coffee is a worldwide brand name. It is used to sell coffee in both ground and instant form in the United States. In the United Kingdom, Maxwell House is available only in instant form. In France and Germany, it is sold in freeze-dried form only, while in the Scandinavian countries, Maxwell House is positioned as the top-of-the-line entry. As a matter of fact, Maxwell House is called simply Maxwell in France and Japan, because "House" is confusing to consumers in those countries. In one South American

Campbell Soup positioned Swanson Chicken Broth as a base for Chinese meals in order to gain consumer acceptance in Hong Kong, Taiwan, and mainland China.
SOURCE: Courtesy of Campbell Soup Company.

✷ CULTURE TIP

In Thailand, doorsills must never be stepped on, for Thais believe that kindly spirits dwell below them. To open a window at night is to let evil spirits in. (axt 22)

GLOBAL LEARNING EXPERIENCE 8.5

Pitching Ketchup in 57 Ways

H.J. Heinz Co., like most of its competitors, is betting on overseas markets for growth. Since 1886, when Henry J. Heinz made his first overseas sale to England's Fortnum & Mason, the company's international participation has expanded to 3,000 products in over 200 countries and territories. More than 43 percent of Heinz's sales of $7 billion came from outside the United States in 1996. International sales are especially expected of some of its mature domestic product lines and brands, such as ketchup. With Americans consuming three pounds of ketchup a year and Heinz's market share at 53 percent, additional growth potential at home is not easily forthcoming.

Heinz uses focus groups to determine what consumers want in the way of taste and image. In some regions, the company alters the spices it uses in the product. Americans prefer a relatively sweet ketchup, but Europeans go for a spicier, more piquant variety. In Central Europe and Sweden, Heinz sells a hot ketchup, a Mexican ketchup, and a curry ketchup in addition to the classic sweet ketchup.

In addition to changes in the product, Heinz will have to adjust to consumption differences. In some cases, this may mean promoting new usage situations; for example, in Greece this means running advertisements showing how ketchup can be poured on pasta, eggs, and cuts of meat. In Tokyo, Heinz offers cooking lessons to Japanese homemakers on using ketchup as an ingredient in Western-style foods such as omelets, sausages, and pasta.

While the product may be the same in most markets, global marketers have to figure out which countries are receptive to which messages. Heinz's image does not function the same in all

✷ CULTURE TIP

Remember that every culture has its own holidays, which are considered truly holy days. To schedule a business trip during Ramadan, Carnival in Rio, Chinese New Year, etc., is like a foreigner's asking you to attend a meeting on Christmas morning. (axt 22)

continued

countries. For example, Heinz lost its market leadership in France to BSN's Amora ketchup, which was able to cater to market needs (especially of the largest segment, youngsters) better by introducing plastic bottles resembling rocket ships and running TV ads featuring kids painting smiling faces on fried eggs. Meanwhile, Heinz was using glass bottles and running ads featuring a cowboy on horseback lassoing a Heinz ketchup bottle.

While some markets consider Heinz's American origin a plus, there are others where it has to be played down. In Sweden, where ketchup is served as an accompaniment to traditional meatballs and fishballs, Heinz deliberately avoids reminding consumers of its heritage. Its ads instead reflect distinctly Swedish concerns, such as those about health. The positioning of the brand is more cosmopolitan to differentiate the brand from the local competition. In Finland, Heinz has run ads with health-related messages similar to those aired in Sweden. But the company takes care to run ads that reflect Finnish culture. "The Finns are more down to earth than Swedes," says Barry Tilley, London-based general manager of Heinz's Western Hemisphere trading division.

American themes work well in markets like Germany. In Heinz's TV ad, American football players in a restaurant become irritated when the 12 steaks they ordered arrive without ketchup. The ad ends on a positive note, of course, with plenty of Heinz ketchup to go around.

SOURCE: "The New Life of O'Reilly," *Business Week,* June 13, 1994, 64–66; and "Heinz Aims to Export Taste for Ketchup," *The Wall Street Journal,* November 20, 1992, B-1, B-10. For additional information, see www.hjheinz.com.

WWW

market, a shampoo maker was concerned about poor sales of the entire product class. Research uncovered the fact that many women wash their hair with bars of soap and use shampoo only as a brief rinse or topper.

Many Western companies have stumbled in Japan because they did not learn enough about the distinctive habits of Japanese consumers. Purveyors of soup should know that the Japanese drink it mainly for breakfast. Johnson & Johnson had relatively little success in selling baby powder until research was conducted on the use conditions of the product. In their small homes, mothers fear that powder will fly around and get into their spotlessly clean kitchens. The company now sells baby powder in flat boxes with powder puffs so that mothers can apply it sparingly. Adults will not use it at all. They wash and rinse themselves before soaking in hot baths; powder would make them feel dirty again. Another classic case involves General Mills' Betty Crocker cake mix. The company designed a mix to be prepared in electric rice cookers. After the product's costly flop, the company found that the Japanese take pride in the purity of their rice, which they thought would be contaminated by cake flavors. General Mills' mistake was comparable to asking an English housewife to make coffee in her teapot.

Package sizes and labels must be adapted in many countries to suit the needs of the particular culture. In Mexico Campbell's sells soup in cans large enough to serve four or five because families are generally large. In Britain, where consumers are more

✷ CULTURE TIP

Shoes are forbidden within Muslim mosques and Buddhist temples. Never wear them into Japanese homes or restaurants unless the owner insists. In Indian and Indonesian homes, if the host goes shoeless, do likewise. (axt 15)

GLOBAL LEARNING EXPERIENCE

8.6

Negotiating in Europe: Watch Out for the Differences

While the European Union is an economic dynamo with 370 million people and economic power to match any other bloc, it is also a patchwork quilt of different languages and national customs, which makes it far less homogeneous than Japan, the United States, or even Asia as a whole. All of this can make negotiating in Europe a challenge. Businesspeople tend to be relatively reserved and quite formal (especially as compared to their U.S. counterparts). One has to be prepared to wait for the work to begin and for an atmosphere of trust to be created. While any stereotyping of negotiators can be dangerous, broad characterizations do help negotiators as sensitization tools.

Even among the Europeans, if two partners have not taken the trouble to get acquainted or complete their homework, the results can be disastrous. In one case, the Italian director of a construction company went to Germany to negotiate for a project. He began the discussion with a presentation of his company that vaunted its long history and its achievements. The German managers first looked startled, then they excused themselves and walked out the door, without even listening to the offer. The explanation: Germans typically do all the necessary background research before walking in the door. They thought the Italian manager was engaged in idle boasting about his company and they found that offensive. Yet the Italian manager thought he was engaged in a vague preliminary to any real negotiations. Real negotiating, as far as he was concerned, would not start at least for another day.

The example also illustrates the stark differences between the business styles of the Northern and Southern Europeans. Northern Europe, with its Protestant tradition and indoor culture, tends to emphasize the technical, the numerical, the tested. Southern Europe, on the other hand, with its Catholic background and open-air lifestyle, tends to favor personal networks, social context, innovation, and flair. Meetings in the south are often longer, but the total decision process may be faster.

The French do not neatly fit into the north-south dichotomy. In a way, the French still embrace the art of diplomatic negotiating invented in France in the 14th century. French managers will have carefully prepared for the negotiations, but they generally will begin with some light, logical sparring. Throughout the preliminary and middle stages of negotiating, the French manager will judge the partners carefully on their intellectual skills and their ability to reply quickly and with authority. The details come last in French negotiations, so the finalizing stage can prove to be tricky. French managers tend to slip in little extras when finalizing, like executive bonuses. It is therefore important to insist on what one wants at this stage, even if days have been spent getting to this point.

SOURCE: Alex Blackwell, "Negotiating in Europe," *Hemispheres*, July 1994, 43–47.

✳ CULTURE TIP

The Japanese obsession with pleasing guests does not mean they make quick friends. Naniwabushi *(to get on such close personal terms with someone that they will have to do you a favor) is standard Japanese operating procedure. Hence, accepting lavish gifts from a Japanese business acquaintance can lead to obligations that may later prove awkward, if not downright painful. (axt 3)* accustomed to ready-to-serve soups, Campbell's prints "one can makes two" on its condensed soup labels to ensure that shoppers understand how to use it.

Managers must be careful of myths and legends. One candy company had almost decided to launch a new peanut-packed chocolate bar in Japan, aimed at giving teenagers quick energy when cramming for exams. The company then found out about the Japanese old wives' tale that eating chocolate with peanuts can cause a nosebleed. The launch never took place. Similarly, approaches that would not be considered in the United States or Europe might be recommended in other regions, as shown in Global Learning Experience 8.7. Meticulous research plays a major role in avoiding these types of problems.

Material Elements

economic infrastructure
transportation, energy, and communication systems in a country

social infrastructure
housing, health, educational, and other social systems in a country

financial infrastructure
facilitating financial agencies in a country, for example, banks

marketing infrastructure
facilitating marketing agencies in a country, for example, market research firms, channel members

cultural convergence
exposure to foreign cultures accelerated by technological advances

Material culture refers to the results of technology and is directly related to how a society organizes its economic activity. The basic **economic infrastructure** consists of transportation, energy, and communications systems. **Social infrastructure** refers to housing, health, and educational systems prevailing in the country of interest. **Financial** and **marketing infrastructures** like banks and marketing research firms can aid the global firm's operation in a given market. In some parts of the world, the global firm may have to be a partner in developing the various infrastructures before it can operate, whereas in others it may greatly benefit from their high level of sophistication.

The level of material culture can aid in developing products for individual markets. For companies selling industrial goods, such as General Electric, this can provide a convenient starting point. In developing countries, demand may be highest for basic energy-generating products. In fully developed markets, time-saving home appliances may be more in demand.

Technological advances have probably been the major cause of cultural change in many countries. The increase in leisure time so characteristic in Western cultures has been a direct result of technological development. With technological advancement comes also **cultural convergence.** Black-and-white television sets extensively penetrated U.S. households more than ten years before similar levels occurred in Europe and Japan. With color television, the lag was reduced to five years. With videocassette recorders, the difference was only three years, but this time the Europeans and the Japanese led the way while the United States was concentrating on cable systems. With the compact disc, penetration rates were equal in only one year. Today, with MTV available by satellite across Europe, no lag exists.[18] An interesting example of cultural convergence is the observance of Christmas in Instanbul—Globle Learning Experience 8.8.

Material culture—mainly the degree to which it exists and how it is esteemed—will have an impact on business decisions. Many exporters do not understand the degree to which Americans are package conscious: for example, cans must be shiny and beautiful. In foreign markets, packaging problems may arise due to the lack of certain materials, different specifications when the material is available, and immense differences in quality and consistency of printing ink, especially in South America and the Third World. Ownership levels of television sets and radios will have an impact on the ability of media to reach target audiences.

✷ **CULTURE TIP**

The Chinese are painfully cautious in business matters. A transaction that would take one week in New York, two in Paris, and three in Rio may take months in Beijing. (axt 3)

In Asia, It's Best to Check with the Spirits First

Western companies eager to enter the vast markets of Asia face many formidable tasks, from the logistic to the political. But if they want their great efforts to succeed, they had better pay attention to another business factor, and a very un-Western one at that: the supernatural. From Japanese ghosts and Chinese card-reading to Filipino healing techniques and the chanting of Mantras in Bali, the supernatural attracts many Asians. Thus, in naming products, running ad campaigns, and even deciding which way their office buildings face, wise management will heed these beliefs.

Feng Shui (pronounced Fung Shway) is a good example. This practice is widely followed in China, Hong Kong, and Singapore, and it also is a force in Japan, Vietnam, and elsewhere. Feng Shui, which means "wind and water," is the Chinese art of harmonizing people and their environment. A Feng Shui practitioner will recommend the most favorable conditions for any venture.

Houses are built only after consultations with Feng Shui masters to ensure appropriate orientation with the landscape. Funerals are often scheduled, deals struck, investments made, office buildings placed, and desks, doors, and other items arranged within only after approval of a Feng Shui master.

To have good Feng Shui, a building should face the water and be flanked by mountains. At the same time, it should not block the view of the mountain spirits. Thus, many Hong Kong office buildings have see-through lobbies. Similarly, elevators are often placed on a diagonal to the front of a building to prevent its own good spirits from escaping. On the other hand, sharp angles give off bad Feng Shui. Thus, when Tung Cheehwa, the shipping tycoon chosen by Beijing to run Hong Kong, selected the location of his offices, he rejected the British governor's office at government house because it was crowded, its Feng Shui was not good, and it was surrounded by tall buildings that blocked its spirit.

In Asia, numbers, names, and colors can be lucky or unlucky. There are a group of lucky numbers: 8, 11, 13, 25, and 39. Some numbers are unlucky in different countries. Four is unlucky in Japan; their word for the number four is shi and is associated with death. In Cambodia, even numbers are lucky, odd numbers are unlucky.

Names have luck, too. Pepsi-Cola's Chinese name is lucky; it means "one hundred happy things." Names are also lucky if they have the right balance of yin and yang, roughly, feminine and masculine qualities. In Chinese handwriting, yang characters have an odd number of strokes, while yin characters have an even number. Lucky names and lucky numbers can intersect. A name is lucky if its total number of strokes equals a lucky number.

The luckiest color in Asia is red. While blue is clearly a favorite corporate choice in the United States for logos, etc., in Asia, that color is linked to the sinister. In China, white, blue, or black gifts are associated with death; red, pink, and yellow are joyful colors. Yet, a message written in red implies the severing of a relationship. In Japan, white is also associated with death.

SOURCES: "3 Things Matter: Location, Location and Feng Shui," *New York Times* Jan. 27, 1997, A.4; "Demons Get a Fast Checkout on Bali," *New York Times,* Dec. 10, 1995, 29; "In Asia, the Supernatural Means Sales," *New York Times* February 19, 1995, 11.

✷ CULTURE TIP

The Chinese are masters of the multicourse dinner and will keep refilling your dish. To stop the flow, leave some food in your dish to indicate that your host was so generous you could not possibly finish. (axt 12)

Aesthetics

Each culture makes a clear statement concerning good taste, as expressed in the arts and in the particular symbolism of colors, form, and music. What is and what is not acceptable may vary dramatically even in otherwise highly similar markets. Sex, for example, is a big selling point in many countries. In an apparent attempt to preserve the purity of Japanese womanhood, however, advertisers frequently turn to blond, blue-eyed foreign models to make the point. In the same vein, Commodore International, a former U.S.-based personal computer manufacturer, chose to sell computers in Germany by showing a naked young man in ads that ran in the German version of *Cosmopolitan*. Needless to say, approaches of this kind would not be possible in the United States because of regulations and opposition from consumer groups.

Color is often used as a mechanism for brand identification, feature reinforcement, and differentiation. In international markets, colors have more symbolic value than in domestic markets. Black, for instance, is considered the color of mourning in the United States and Europe, whereas white has the same symbolic meaning in Japan and most of the Far East. A British bank was interested in expanding its operations to Singapore and wanted to use blue and green as its identification colors. A consulting firm was quick to tell the client that green is associated with death in that country. Although the bank insisted on its original choice of colors, the green was changed to an acceptable shade.[19] Similarly, music used in broadcast advertisements is often adjusted to reflect regional differences.

Education

Education, either formal or informal, plays a major role in the passing on and sharing of culture. Educational levels of a culture can be assessed using literacy rates, enrollment in secondary education, or enrollment in higher education available from secondary data sources. Global firms also need to know about the qualitative aspects of education, namely, varying emphases on particular skills and the overall level of the education provided. Japan and South Korea emphasize the sciences, especially engineering, to a greater degree than do Western countries.

Educational levels will have an impact on various business functions. Employee training programs for a production facility will have to take the educational backgrounds of trainees into account. For example, a high level of illiteracy will suggest the use of visual aids rather than printed manuals. In some cases, global firms routinely send locally recruited personnel to headquarters for training.

The global manager may also have to be prepared to overcome obstacles in recruiting a suitable sales force or support personnel. The Japanese culture places a premium on loyalty, and employees consider themselves members of the corporate family. If a foreign firm decides to leave Japan, its employees may find themselves stranded in mid-career, unable to find their place in the Japanese business system. Therefore, university graduates are reluctant to join any but the largest and most well-known of foreign firms.[20]

✵ CULTURE TIP

Shark's fin soup is often the highlight of a Chinese multicourse dinner, served somewhere in the middle, and is the polite time for making toasts. Also, the second-to-last course is often plain boiled rice— which you should refuse! To eat it signifies you are still hungry and is an insult to the host. (axt 12)

GLOBAL LEARNING EXPERIENCE 8.8

Christmas in Istanbul?

As businesses go global and individuals travel extensively in foreign lands, an exchange of cultures occurs. Values and customs regarding food, wearing apparel, housing, and seasonal celebrations are adopted or adapted in whole or in part—in a slow movement toward better understanding among peoples.

Istanbul, Turkey, is one of the world's great Islamic cities; the population is more than 95 percent Muslim. The country has been steadily adopting Western habits, and in large cities like Istanbul, taboos against liquor and unveiled women have long since fallen away and attendance at mosques is spotty. A sure sign that Turkey is starting to turn to Western ways is its embrace of the Christian celebration of Christmas. This trend, which emerged about a decade ago, is becoming stronger each year. Rather than being a religious observance, many people in Istanbul have come to view Santa Claus, Christmas trees, and the exchange of gifts as harmless symbols of friendship and good cheer. The differences between Christmas celebrations in Istanbul and those in Christian countries are minor and hard to spot at first. There are no scenes of Jesus in a manager, although cherubic golden angels adorn many trees, and the exchange of gifts usually takes place on New Year's Eve rather than on December 25. In the shopping areas, Santa's rosy cheeks and broad smile beam from store windows and the strains of "Jingle Bells" and "Silent Night" waft through the air in cafes and shops.

During the holiday season, Istanbul's garden shops do a booming business in mistletoe and evergreen trees and wreaths decorated with bright red bows and frosted pine cones. In the city's big hotels, Christmas parties attract throngs of Turks. The holiday season is now celebrated in Istanbul as much as it is in Vienna or New York.

SOURCE: "Strange, That's Santa in the Seat of Sultans!" *New York Times,* Dec. 21, 1996.

Social Institutions

Social institutions affect the ways people relate to each other. The family unit, which in Western industrialized countries consists of parents and children, in a number of cultures is extended to include grandparents and other relatives. This will have an impact on consumption patterns and must be taken into account, for example, when conducting market research.

The concept of kinship, or blood relations between individuals, is defined in a very broad way in societies such as those in sub-Saharan Africa. Family relations and a

✷ CULTURE TIP

A vital concept to understand in Korea is kibun, which means inner feelings. If one's kibun is good, then one functions smoothly. If one's kibun is bad, then one feels depressed. Keeping kibun in good order often takes precedence over all other considerations. Damaging a person's kibun may cut off the relationship and create an enemy. (mcd 410) strong obligation to family are important factors to be considered in human resource management in those regions. Understanding tribal politics in countries such as Nigeria may help the global manager avoid unnecessary complications in executing business transactions.

social stratification division of a particular population into classes

reference groups group such as the family, coworkers, and professional and trade associations that provide the values and attitudes that influence and shape behavior, including consumer behavior

primary reference groups small, intimate groups that are in a position to influence a person's behavior

secondary reference groups larger, less intimate groups that, because of a relationship with an individual, may influence behavior

The division of a particular population into classes is termed **social stratification.** Stratification ranges from the situation in Northern Europe, where most people are members of the middle class, to highly stratified societies, such as India, in which the higher strata control most of the buying power and decision-making positions.

An important part of the socialization process of consumers worldwide is **reference groups.**[21] These groups provide the values and attitudes that influence and shape behavior. **Primary reference groups** include the family and coworkers and other intimate acquaintances, while **secondary reference groups** are social organizations where less continuous interaction takes place, such as professional associations and trade organizations. In addition to providing socialization, reference groups also provide a baseline for compliance with group norms, which may be reflected in the choice of products used.

Social organization also determines the roles of managers and subordinates and how they relate to one another. In some cultures, managers and subordinates are separated explicitly and implicitly by various boundaries ranging from social class differences to separate office facilities. In others, cooperation is elicited through equality. Nissan USA has no privileged parking spaces and no private dining rooms, everyone wears the same type of white coveralls, and the president sits in the same room with a hundred other white-collar workers.[22] The fitting of an organizational culture to the larger context of a national culture has to be executed with care. Changes that are too dramatic may cause disruption of productivity or, at the minimum, suspicion.

While Western business practice has developed impersonal structures for channeling power and influence through reliance on laws and contracts, the Chinese emphasize getting on the good side of someone and storing up political capital with them. Things can get done without this capital, *or guanxi,* only if one invests enormous personal energy, is willing to offend even trusted associates, and is prepared to see it all melt away at a moment's notice.[23] For the Chinese, contracts form a useful agenda and a symbol of progress, but obligations come from relationships. McDonald's found this out in Beijing where it was evicted from a central building after only two years despite having a twenty-year contract. The incomer had a strong *guanxi,* whereas McDonald's had not kept its in good repair.[24]

A variety of sources and methods are available to the manager for extending his or her knowledge of specific cultures. Most of these sources deal with factual information that provides a necessary basis for market studies. Beyond the normal business literature and its anecdotal information, specific country studies are published by the U.S. government, private companies, and universities. *Country Studies* are available for 108 countries from the U.S. Government Printing Office, while *Country Updates,* produced by Overseas Briefing Associates, features 22 countries. *Information Guide for Doing Business in X* is the basic title for a series of publications produced by the accounting firm of Price Waterhouse and Co. (similar series are published by the accounting firms of Ernst & Young and KMPG–Peat Marwick); so far, 48 countries are included. *Brief Culturegrams* for 63 countries and the more extensive *Building Bridges for Understanding with the People of X* are published by the Language and Intercultural

✷ CULTURE TIP

An important concept in Indonesian social and business activities is to avoid making someone feel malu, or ashamed or embarrassed. Criticizing or contradicting a person in front of others will cause you to lose face with the group and the person will feel malu as a result of your action. (mcd 424)

Research Center of Brigham Young University.[25] Many facilitating agencies—such as banks, advertising agencies, and transportation companies—provide background information for their clients on the markets they serve. One of the more attractive sources is provided by the Hong Kong and Shanghai Banking Corporation, which has a *Business Profile Series* that is especially good for the Middle East.

Blunders in foreign markets that could have been avoided with factual information are generally inexcusable. A manager who travels to Taipei without first obtaining a visa and is therefore turned back has no one else to blame. Other oversights may lead to more costly mistakes. Brazilians are several inches shorter than the average American, but this was not taken into account when Sears erected American-height shelves that block Brazilian shoppers' view of the rest of the store.

Global business success requires not only comprehensive fact finding and preparation but also an ability to understand and appreciate fully the nuances of different cultural traits and patterns. Gaining this readiness requires "getting one's feet wet" over a sufficient length of time.

Any analysis of cultural knowledge is incomplete without the basic recognition of cultural differences. Adjusting to differences requires putting one's own cultural values aside. James A. Lee proposes that the natural **self-reference criterion**—the unconscious reference to one's own cultural values—is the root of most international business problems.[26] However, recognizing and admitting this are often quite difficult. The following analytical approach is recommended to reduce the influence of one's own cultural values:

self-reference criterion
unconscious reference to one's own cultural values

1. Define the problem or goal in terms of the domestic cultural traits, habits, or norms.
2. Define the problem or goal in terms of the foreign cultural traits, habits, or norms. Make no value judgments.
3. Isolate the self-reference criterion influence in the problem and examine it carefully to see how it complicates the problem.
4. Redefine the problem without the self-reference criterion influence and solve for the optimum-goal situation.

This approach can be applied to product introduction. If Kellogg's wants to introduce breakfast cereals into markets where breakfast is traditionally not eaten or where consumers drink very little milk, managers must consider very carefully how to instill this new habit. The traits, habits, and norms concerning the importance of breakfast are quite different in the United States, France, and Brazil, and they have to be outlined before the product can be introduced. In France, Kellogg's commercials are aimed as much at providing nutrition lessons as they are at promoting the product. In Brazil, the company advertised on a soap opera to gain entry into the market, because Brazilians often emulate the characters of these television shows.

Analytical procedures require constant monitoring of changes caused by outside events as well as the changes caused by the business entity itself. Controlling **ethnocentrism**—the tendency to consider one's own culture superior to others—can be achieved only by acknowledging it and properly adjusting to its possible effects in managerial decision making. The international manager needs to be prepared and able to put that preparedness to effective use.[27]

ethnocentrism
tendency to consider one's own culture superior to others

CULTURE TIP

The Russians are renowned for their negotiating ability. They will stall for time if they think they can get a better deal. They are famous for unnerving Western negotiations by continuously delaying and hassling. (mcd 461)

THE TRAINING CHALLENGE

Global managers face a dilemma in terms of international and intercultural competence. The lack of adequate foreign language and global business skills has cost U.S. firms lost contracts, weak negotiations, and ineffectual management. A UNESCO study of 10- and 14-year-old students in nine countries placed Americans next to last in their comprehension of foreign cultures. A sad 61 percent of U.S. business schools offer few or no courses in international business.[28] The increase in the overall global activity of firms has increased the need for cultural sensitivity training at all levels of the organization. Further, today's training must take into consideration not only outsiders to the firm but interaction within the corporate family as well. However inconsequential the degree of interaction may seem, it can still cause problems if proper understanding is lacking. Consider the date 11/12/93 on a telex; a European will interpret this as the 11th of December, an American as the 12th of November.

Some companies try to avoid the training problem by hiring only nationals or well-traveled Americans for their international operations. This makes sense for the management of overseas operations but will not solve the training need, especially if transfers to a culture unfamiliar to the manager are likely. Global experience may not necessarily transfer from one market to another.

To foster cultural sensitivity and acceptance of new ways of doing things within the organization, management must institute internal education programs. These programs may include (1) culture-specific information (data covering other countries, such as videopacks and culturegrams), (2) cultural-general information (values, practices, and assumptions of countries other than one's own), and (3) self-specific information (identifying one's own culture including values, assumptions, and perceptions about others).[29] One study found that Japanese assigned to the United States get mainly language training as preparation for the task. In addition, many companies use mentoring, whereby an individual is assigned to someone who is experienced and who will spend the required time squiring and explaining. Talks given by returnees and by visiting lecturers hired specifically for the task round out the formal part of training.[30]

The objective of formal training programs is to foster the four critical characteristics of preparedness, sensitivity, patience, and flexibility in managers and other personnel. These programs vary dramatically in terms of their rigor, involvement, and, of course, cost.[31] A summary of these programs is provided in Figure 8.2.

area briefings
training programs that provide factual preparation prior to an overseas assignment

Environmental briefings and cultural orientation programs are types of **area briefings** programs. These programs provide factual preparation for a manager to operate in, or work with people from, a particular country. Area briefings should be a basic prerequisite for other types of training programs. Alone, area briefings serve little practical purpose because they do not really get the manager's feet wet. Other, more involved, programs contribute the context in which to put facts so that they can be properly understood.

cultural assimilator
program in which trainees for overseas assignments must respond to scenarios of specific situations in a particular country

The **cultural assimilator** is a program in which trainees must respond to scenarios of specific situations in a particular country. These programs have been developed for the Arab countries, Iran, Thailand, Central America, and Greece.[32] The results of the trainees' assimilator experience are evaluated by a panel of judges. This type of program has been used in particular in cases of transfers abroad on short notice.

✹ CULTURE TIP

When in Russia, it is a good idea to have a large supply of business cards to hand out. They should be printed in Cyrillic, and the university degree of the Western businessperson should be included. At negotiations, be sure to hand out one to everyone present, in order not to overlook someone who might turn out to be important. (mcd 463)

Cross-Cultural Training Methods FIGURE 8.2

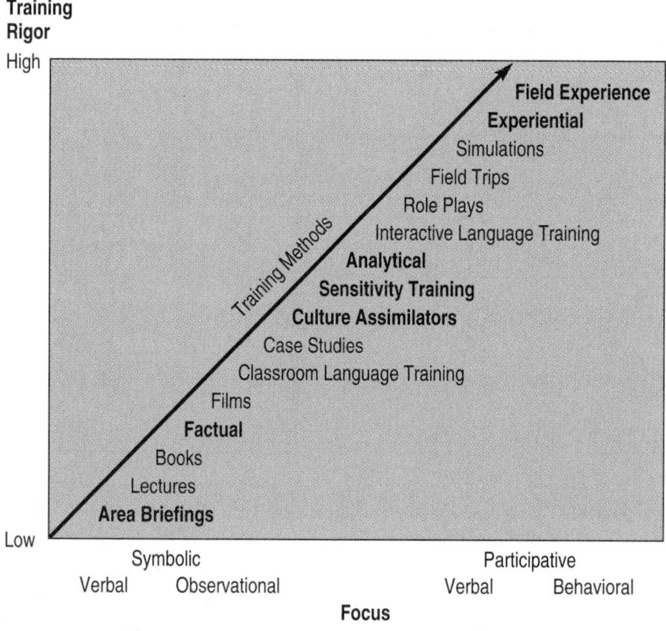

SOURCE: Reproduced from J. Stewart Black and Mark Mendenhall, "A Practical but Theory-based Framework for Selecting Cross-Cultural Training Methods," in *International Human Resource Management,* eds. Mark Mendenhall and Gray Oddou, 1991, p. 188, with the permission of South-Western College Publishing. All rights reserved.

When more time is available, managers can be trained extensively in language. This may be required if an exotic language is involved. **Sensitivity training** focuses on enhancing a manager's flexibility in situations that are quite different from those at home. The approach is based on the assumption that understanding and accepting oneself is critical to understanding a person from another culture. Finally, training may involve **field experience,** which exposes a manager to a different cultural environment for a limited amount of time. While this approach is expensive, it is used by some companies.

One field experience technique that has been suggested when the training process needs to be rigorous is the host-family surrogate. This technique places a trainee (and possibly his or her family) in a domestically located family of the nationality to which they are assigned.[33]

Regardless of the degree of training, preparation, and positive personal characteristics, a manager will always remain foreign. A manager should never rely on his or her own judgment when local managers can be consulted. In many instances, a manager should have an interpreter present at negotiations, especially if the manager is not completely bilingual. Overconfidence in one's language capabilities can create problems.

sensitivity training
training in human relations that focuses on personal and interpersonal interactions; training that focuses on enhancing an expatriate's flexibility in situations quite different from those at home

field experience
experience acquired in actual rather than laboratory settings; training that exposes a corporate manager to a different cultural environment for a limited amount of time

✳ CULTURE TIP

No other Eastern European country is as protocol-conscious as Russia. Russian officials expect to do business with only the highest-ranking executives—so the Western firm is advised to send its top managers to ensure a favorable first impression. (mcd 462)

FIGURE 8.3 **Culture Shock Cycle for an Overseas Assignment**

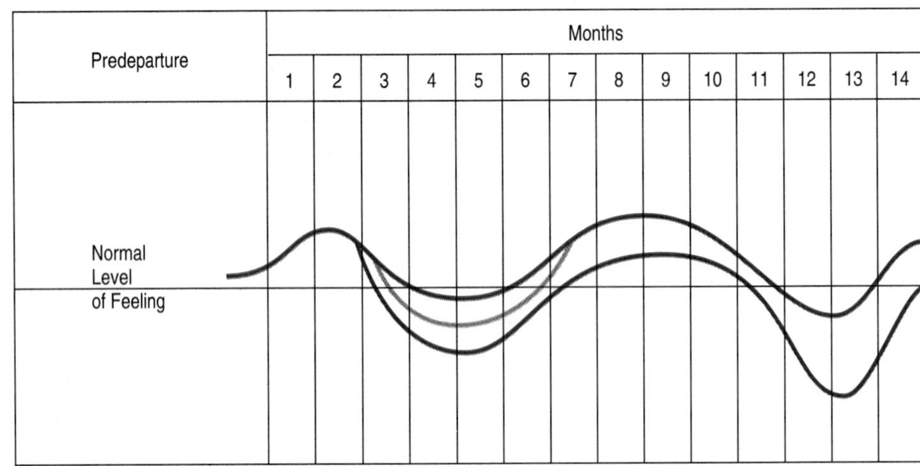

NOTE: Lines indicate the extreme severity with which culture shock may attack.
SOURCE: L. Robert Kohls, *Survival Kit for Overseas Living* (Yarmouth, Maine: Intercultural Press, 1984), 68.

Culture Shock

The effectiveness of orientation procedures can be measured only after managers are overseas. A unique phenomenon they face is **culture shock.** Although they all feel it, individuals differ widely in how they allow themselves to be affected by it.

culture shock
the more pronounced reactions to the psychological disorientation that most people feel when they move for an extended period of time in a markedly different culture

Causes and Remedies Culture shock is the term used for the more pronounced reactions to the psychological disorientation that most people experience when they move for an extended period of time into a culture markedly different from their own.[34] Culture shock and its severity may be a function of the individual's lack of adaptability but may equally be a result of the firm's lack of understanding of the situation into which the manager was sent. Often, goals set for a subsidiary or a project may be unrealistic or the means by which they are to be reached may be totally inadequate. All of these lead to external manifestations of culture shock, such as bitterness and even physical illness. In extreme cases, they can lead to hostility toward anything in the host environment.

The culture shock cycle for an overseas assignment is presented in Figure 8.3. Four distinct stages of adjustment exist during a foreign assignment. The length of the stages is highly individual. The four stages are:

1. *Initial euphoria*—enjoying the novelty, largely from the perspective of a spectator

CULTURE TIP

Connections is a key word in conducting business in Saudi Arabia. Well-connected people find their progress is made much faster. Connections in the Middle East are vital to gain access to public and private decision makers. (mcd 474)

2. *Irritation and hostility*—experiencing cultural differences, such as the concept of time, through increased participation
3. *Adjustment*—adapting to the situation, which in some cases leads to biculturalism and even accusations from corporate headquarters of "going native"
4. *Reentry*—returning home

The manager may fare better at the second stage than other members of the family especially if their opportunities for work and other activities are severely restricted. The fourth stage may actually cause a reverse culture shock when the adjustment phase has been highly successful and the return home is not desired.

Firms themselves must take responsibility for easing one of the causes of culture shock: isolation. By maintaining contact with the manager beyond business-related communication, some of the shock may be alleviated. Exxon assigns each expatriate a contact person at headquarters to share general information.

SUMMARY

Culture is one of the most challenging elements of the global marketplace. This system of learned behavior patterns characteristic of the members of a given society is constantly shaped by a set of dynamic variables: language, religion, values and attitudes, manners and customs, aesthetics, technology, education, and social institutions. To cope with this system, a global manager needs both factual and interpretive knowledge of culture. To some extent, the factual knowledge can be learned; its interpretation comes only through experience.

The most complicated problems in dealing with the cultural environment stem from the fact that one cannot learn culture—one has to live it. Two schools of thought exist in the business world on how to deal with cultural diversity. One is that business is business the world around, following the model of Pepsi and McDonald's. In some cases, globalization is a fact of life; however, cultural differences are still far from converging.

The other school proposes that companies must tailor business approaches to individual cultures. Setting up policies and procedures in each country has been compared to an organ transplant; the critical question centers around acceptance or rejection. The major challenge to the international manager is to make sure that rejection is not a result of cultural myopia or even blindness.

Fortune examined the global performance of a dozen large companies that earn 20 percent or more of their revenue overseas.[35] The globally successful companies all share an important quality: patience. They have not rushed into situations but rather built their operations carefully by following the most basic business principles. These principles are to know your adversary, know your audience, and know your customer.

✷ CULTURE TIP

In Saudi Arabia, the system of hospitality is based on mutuality. An invitation must be returned; an equal gift must be offered in return. The offer of hospitality to visit an Arab's home must be accepted. Today, you may be the guest, but tomorrow you must play the host. (mcd 475)

Key Terms and Concepts

cultural risk
acculturation
high-context cultures
low-context cultures
change agent
backtranslation
Hajj
Dia De los Muertos
economic infrastructure
social infrastructure
financial infrastructure
marketing infrastructure
cultural convergence
social stratification
reference groups
primary reference groups
secondary reference groups
self-reference criterion
ethnocentrism
cultural assimilator
area briefings
sensitivity training
field experience
culture shock

Questions for Discussion

1. Comment on the assumption, "If people are serious about doing business with you, they will speak English."
2. You are on your first business visit to Germany. You feel confident about your ability to speak the language (you studied German in school and have taken a refresher course), and you decide to use it. During introductions, you want to break the ice by asking "Wie geht's?" and insisting that everyone call you by your first name. Speculate as to the reaction.
3. Q: "What do you call a person who can speak two languages?"

   A: "Bilingual."

   Q: "How about three?"

   A: "Trilingual."

   Q: "Excellent. How about one?"

   A: "Hmmmmm. . . . American!"

   Is this joke malicious, or is there something to be learned from it?
4. What can be learned about a culture from reading and attending to factual materials?
5. Given the tremendous increase in global business, where will companies in a relatively early stage of the globalization process find the personnel to handle the new challenges?
6. Management at a U.S. company trying to market tomato paste in the Middle East did not know that, translated into Arabic, "tomato paste" is "tomato glue." How could it have known in time to avoid problems?

Recommended Readings

Axtell, Roger E. *Do's and Taboos around the World.* New York: John Wiley & Sons, 1993.

Bache, Ellyn. *Cultural Clash.* Yarmouth, ME: Intercultural Press, 1990.

Brislin, R.W., W.J. Lonner, and R.M. Thorndike. *Cross-Cultural Research Methods.* New York: Wiley, 1973.

Copeland, Lennie, and L. Griggs. *Going International: How to Make Friends and Deal Effectively in the Global Marketplace.* New York: Random House, 1985.

Hall, Edward T., and Mildred Reed Hall. *Understanding Cultural Differences.* Yarmouth, ME: Intercultural Press, 1990.

Hoecklin, Lisa. *Managing Cultural Differences.* Workingham, England: Addison-Wesley, 1995.

Hofstede, Geert. *Culture's Consequences.* London: Sage Publications, 1981.

O'Hara-Devereux, Mary and Robert Johansen. *Global Work: Bridging Distance, Culture, and Time.* San Francisco: Jossey-Bass Publishers, 1994.

Terpstra, Vern, and K. David. *The Cultural Environment of International Business.* Cincinnati, OH: Southwestern, 1991.

Trompenaars, Fons. *Riding the Waves of Culture.* New York: Irwin, 1994.

U.S. Department of Commerce. *International Business Practices.* Washington, D.C.: U.S. Government Printing Office, 1993.

Notes

1. Mary O'Hara-Devereaux and Robert Johansen, *Global Work: Bridging Distance, Culture, and Time* (San Francisco: Jossey-Bass Publishers, 1994), 11.
2. Carla Rapoport, "Nestlé's Brand Building Machine," *Fortune,* September 19, 1994, 147–156.
3. Geert Hofstede, "National Cultures Revisited," *Asia-Pacific Journal of Management* 1 (September 1984): 22–24.
4. Robert L. Kohls, *Survival Kit for Overseas Living* (Chicago: Intercultural Press, 1979), 3.
5. Edward T. Hall, *Beyond Culture* (Garden City, N.Y.: Anchor Press, 1976), 15.
6. Marita von Oldenborgh, "What's Next for India?" *International Business,* January 1996, 44–47; and Ravi Vijh, "Think Global, Act Indian," *Export Today,* June 1996, 27–28.
7. George P. Mundak, "The Common Denominator of Cultures," in *The Science of Man in the World,* ed. Ralph Linton (New York: Columbia University Press, 1945), 123–142.
8. David A. Ricks, *Big Business Blunders* (Homewood, Ill.: Irwin, 1983), 4.
9. *Statistical Abstract of the United States* (Washington, D.C.: U.S. Government Printing Office, 1994): 855.
10. David McClelland, *The Achieving Society* (New York: Irvington, 1961): 90.
11. *World Almanac and the Book of Facts* (Mahwah, NJ: Funk & Wagnalls, 1995): 734.
12. Nora Fitzgerald, "Oceans Apart, but Closer than You Think," *World Trade,* February 1996, 58.
13. Mushtaq Luqmami, Zahir A. Quraeshi, and Linda Delene, "Marketing in Islamic Countries: A Viewpoint," *MSU Business Topics* 23 (Summer 1980): 17–24.
14. "Islamic Banking: Faith and Creativity," *New York Times,* April 8, 1994, D-1, D-6.
15. James F. Engel, Roger D. Blackwell, and Paul W. Miniard, *Consumer Behavior* (Hinsdale, Ill.: Dryden, 1986), 223.
16. "Learning How to Please the Baffling Japanese," *Fortune,* October 5, 1981, 122.
17. "Latest Nike Sneakers Fly Off Tokyo Shelves Even at $1,300 a Pair" *The Washington Post,* November 7, 1996, A1, 10.
18. Kenichi Ohmae, "Managing in a Borderless World," *Harvard Business Review* 67 (May–June 1989): 152–161.
19. Joe Agnew, "Cultural Differences Probed to Create Product Identity," *Marketing News,* October 24, 1986, 22.
20. Joseph A. McKinney, "Joint Ventures of United States Firms in Japan: A Survey," *Venture Japan* 1 (1988): 14–19.
21. Engel, Blackwell, and Miniard, *Consumer Behavior,* 318–324.
22. "The Difference That Japanese Management Makes," *Business Week,* July 14, 1986, 47–50.
23. Peter MacInnis, "Guanxi or Contract: A Way to Understand and Predict Conflict Between Chinese and Western Senior Managers in China-Based Joint Ventures," in Daniel E. McCarthy and Stanley J. Hille, eds., *Multinational Business Management and Internationalization of Business Enterprises* (Nanjing, China: Nanjing University Press, 1993), 345–351.
24. Tim Ambler, "Reflections in China: Re-Orienting Images of Marketing," *Marketing Management* 4(Summer 1995): 23–30.
25. Lennie Copeland, "Training Americans to Do Business Overseas," *Training,* July 1984, 22–23.
26. James A. Lee, "Cultural Analysis in Overseas Operations," *Harvard Business Review* 44 (March–April 1966): 106–114.
27. Peter D. Fitzpatrick and Alan S. Zimmerman, *Essentials of Export Marketing* (New York: American Management Organization, 1985), 16.
28. Copeland, "Training Americans to Do Business Overseas," 22–33.
29. W. Chan Kim and R. A. Mauborgne, "Cross-Cultural Strategies," *Journal of Business Strategy* 7 (Spring 1987): 28–37.
30. Mauricio Lorence, "Assignment USA: The Japanese Solution," *Sales & Marketing Management* 144 (October 1992): 60–66.
31. Rosalie Tung, "Selection and Training of Personnel for Overseas Assignments," *Columbia Journal of World Business* 16 (Spring 1981): 68–78.
32. Philip R. Harris and Robert T. Moran, *Managing Cultural Differences* (Houston: Gulf, 1987), 267–295.
33. Simcha Ronen, "Training the International Assignee," in *Training and Career Development,* ed. I. Goldstein (San Francisco: Jossey-Bass, 1989), 426–440.
34. L. Robert Kohls, *Survival Kit for Overseas Living* (Yarmouth, Maine: Intercultural Press, 1979), 62–68.
35. Kenneth Labich, "America's International Winners," *Fortune,* April 14, 1986, 34–46.

Organization, Management, and Control of Global Operations

LEARNING OBJECTIVES

To describe alternative organizational structures for global operations.

To highlight factors affecting decisions about the structure of global organizations.

To indicate roles for country organizations in the development of strategy and implementation of programs.

To define the concept of a multinational corporation and assess its various dimensions.

To compare arguments for and against foreign direct investment from various viewpoints.

To describe the challenges of managing managers and labor personnel both in individual international markets and in worldwide operations.

To examine the training and compensation of global managers.

To illustrate the different roles of labor in global markets, especially that of labor participation in management.

GLOBAL LEARNING EXPERIENCE 9.1

Borderless Management

Ford Motor Co. has been an international enterprise from the days of Henry Ford selling the Model A. Five years after its founding in 1903, it set up its first overseas sales branch in France and by 1911 it was making cars in Britain. But more than 80 years and dozens of overseas endeavors later, Ford still is trying to figure out what it means to be a global company.

The latest reorganization at Ford in April of 1994 was dramatic: Ford merged its large and culturally distinct European and North American auto operations and plans later to fold in its Latin American and Asia-Pacific operations. The rationale, according to Ford's Chairman Alexander J. Trotman, is to make more efficient use of its engineering and product development resources against rapidly globalizing rivals in the "all out global car race." The potential advantages are considerable. If resources can be pooled and turf wars between national entities eliminated, Ford estimates that its savings can reach $3 billion a year. Planning and implementation have to work, however. When a company such as Ford centralizes all product development, a mistake that would have been confined to one country in the former organizational structure could become a global disaster. "If you misjudge the market, you are wrong in 15 countries rather than only one," said one European executive.

Ford's move makes one thing clear: With world markets rapidly merging and converging, companies that have been slow to globalize their operations will now have to scramble to catch up. In May, 1994, IBM reorganized its marketing and sales organizations into 14 worldwide industry groups, such as banking, retail, and insurance. In moving away from an organization based on geography, IBM hoped to enhance its responsiveness to customers, many of which themselves are global operators. Soon after IBM's announcement, drug giant Bristol-Myers Squibb Co. revamped its consumer business by installing a new chief responsible for its worldwide consumer medicines such as Excedrin and Bufferin. A new unit was also formed to have worldwide responsibility for its Clairol and other hair-care products.

Globalization is not taking any one form. Indeed, most companies have adopted mixed organizational formats. Unilever plc uses a classic regional structure with local managers in three areas of the world: Africa/Middle East, Latin America, and East Asia/Pacific. But in Europe and North America, where consumer preferences are more similar, the structure is different. The president of Lever Brothers Co. in New York, for example, reports to the Unilever worldwide detergents-products coordinator in London.

Simply redrawing lines on an organization chart will not make a company global. Building trust and creating a common vision among the entities that will now cooperate rather than work independently is the critical task. The effort will focus on eliminating headquarters myopia and use of cross-cultural teams to foster a one-company culture.

SOURCE: "Borderless Management: Companies Strive to Become Truly Stateless," *Business Week,* May 23, 1994, 24–25; "IBM Revamps Sales Teams," *Advertising Age,* May 9, 1994, 2; Regina Fazio Maruca, "The Right Way to Go Global: An Interview with Whirlpool CEO David Whitwam," *Harvard Business Review* 72 (March–April 1994): 134–145; and "The Global Firm: R.I.P.," *The Economist,* February 6, 1993, 69.

ORGANIZING THE GLOBAL ENTERPRISE

The process of managing a business, domestic or international, may be divided into four areas of activity: planning, organizing, directing, and controlling. Planning a firm's entry into global markets is covered in Chapters 10 and 11 of this text. This chapter deals with the various approaches to organizing the global firm, the direction and management of personnel, and finally a discussion and evaluation of techniques useful in controlling the organization.

As companies evolve from purely domestic to multinational, their organizational structure and control systems must change to reflect new strategies. With growth comes diversity in terms of products and services, geographic markets, and people in the company itself, bringing along a set of challenges for the company. Two critical issues are basic to all of these challenges: (1) the type of organization that provides the best framework for developing worldwide strategies and maintaining flexibility with respect to individual markets and operations and (2) the type and degree of control to be exercised from headquarters to maximize total effort. To achieve the optimal impact in these decision areas may result in dramatic decisions, such as seen in this chapter's opening Global Learning Experience 9.1.

This chapter will focus on the advantages and disadvantages of various organizational structures, as well as their appropriateness at different stages of globalization. A determining factor is where decision-making authority within the organizational structure will be placed. Also, the roles of the different entities that make up the organization need to be defined. The chapter will also outline the need for devising a control system to oversee the global operations of the company, emphasizing the additional control instruments needed beyond those used in domestic business and the control strategies of multinational corporations. The appropriateness and eventual cost of the various control approaches will vary as the firm expands its global operations. The overall objective of the chapter is to study the intraorganizational relationships critical to the firm's attempt to optimize its competitiveness.

ORGANIZATIONAL STRUCTURE

The basic functions of an organization are to provide (1) a route and place of decision making and coordination and (2) a system for reporting and communications. Authority and communication networks are typically depicted in the formal organization chart.

The design of an organization's structure engaged in global business will depend, in large measure, on three factors: (1) the stage, or degree, of internationalization; (2) the most desirable way to group people and resources to achieve organization goals; and (3) the type and degree of control to be exercised by headquarters.

TABLE 9.1 **How an Organization's Structure Changes As It Becomes More Involved in Global Business Activities**

	Degree of Company Globalization	Unit Typically Responsible	Typical Title of Unit Manager
1.	Occasional export order	Domestic sales department	Domestic sales manager
2.	Increasing volume of foreign sales	Newly formed unit—export sales department	Manager/director—export sales
3.	Major corporate effort to extend reach into foreign markets	International division (may involve some joint ventures or direct foreign investment)	Vice president
4.	Total corporate commitment to conduct operations on a global basis	Wholly-owned foreign subsidiaries; joint ventures, and/or other forms of interfirm cooperation	Senior vice president

Organizational Designs

The basic configurations of global organizations correspond to those of purely domestic ones; the greater the degree of globalization, the more complex the structures can become. The types of structures that companies use to manage foreign activities can be divided into four broad categories, based on the degree of globalization, as shown in Table 9.1. Table 9.1 indicates that as the company becomes more and more involved in global activities, its organizational structure and level of management responsibility will change.

Stages 1 and 2—Little or No Formal Organization In these stages, there is little or no formal organizational recognition of the global activities of the firm. This category ranges from domestic operations handling an occasional international transaction on an ad hoc basis to firms with separate export departments.

In the very early stages of global involvement, domestic operations assume responsibility for international activities. The role of international activities in the sales and profits of the corporation is initially so minor that no organizational adjustment takes place. No consolidation of information or authority over international sales is undertaken or is necessary. Transactions are conducted on a case-by-case basis, either by the resident expert or quite often with the help of facilitating agents, such as freight forwarders.

As demand from the global marketplace grows and interest within the firm expands, the organizational structure will reflect it. As shown in Figure 9.1, an export department appears as a separate entity. This may be an outside export management company

Export Department Structure FIGURE 9.1

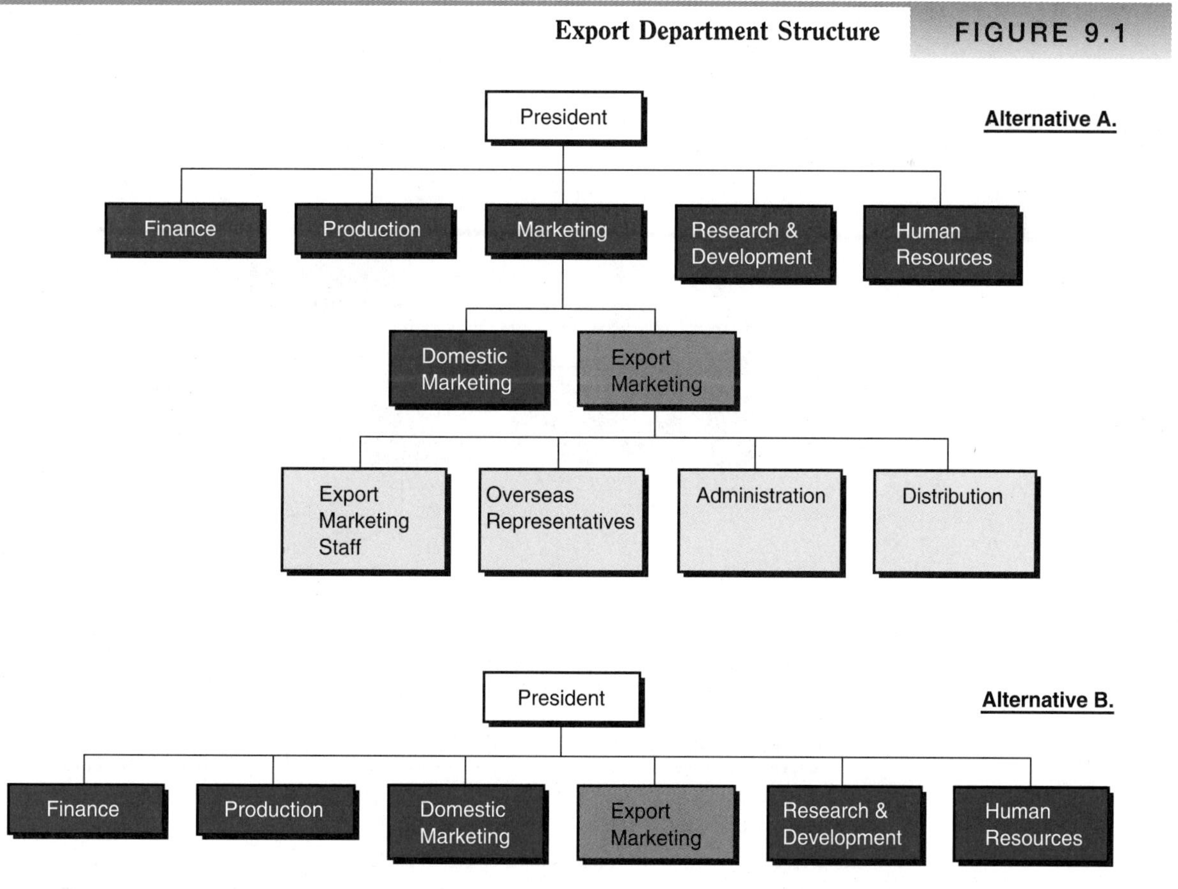

—that is, an independent company that becomes the de facto export department of the firm. This is an indirect approach to international involvement in that very little experience is accumulated within the firm itself. Alternatively, a firm may establish its own export department, hiring a few seasoned individuals to take responsibility for international activities. Organizationally, the department may be a subdepartment of marketing (alternative B. in Figure 9.1) or may have equal ranking with the various functional departments (alternative A.). This choice will depend on the importance assigned to overseas activities by the firm. Because the export department is the first real step toward globalizing the organizational structure, it should be a full-fledged marketing organization and not merely a sales organization.

Licensing as an international entry mode may be assigned to the R&D function despite its importance to the overall global strategy of the firm. A formal liaison among the export, marketing, production, and R&D functions has to be formed for the maximum utilization of licensing.[1] If licensing indeed becomes a major activity for the firm, a separate manager should be appointed.

Stage 3—The International Division The more the firm becomes involved in foreign markets, the more quickly the export department structure will become obsolete. For example, the firm may undertake joint ventures or direct foreign investment, which require those involved to have functional experience. The firm therefore typically establishes an international division.

The international division centralizes in one entity, with or without separate incorporation, all of the responsibility for international activities, as illustrated in Figure 9.2. The approach aims to eliminate a possible bias against global operations that may exist if domestic divisions are allowed to serve international customers independently. The international division concentrates international expertise, information flows con-

FIGURE 9.2 **The International Division Structure**

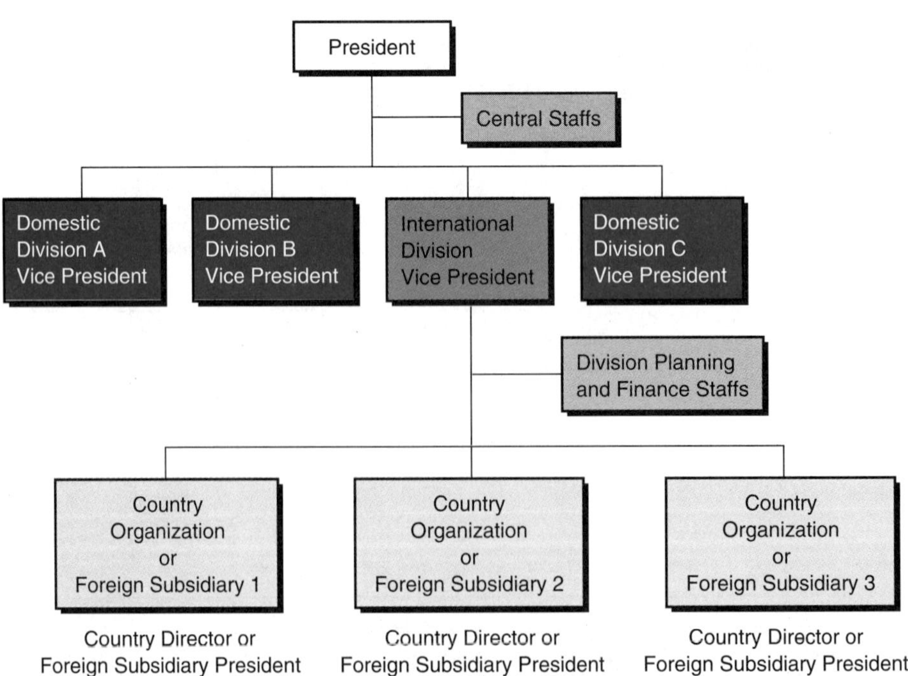

cerning foreign market opportunities, and authority over international activities. However, manufacturing and other related functions remain with the domestic divisions in order to take advantage of economies of scale.

To avoid putting the international division at a disadvantage in competing for products, personnel, and corporate services, coordination between domestic and international operations is necessary. Coordination can be achieved through a joint staff or by requiring domestic and international divisions to interact in strategic planning and to submit the plans to headquarters. Further, many corporations require and encourage frequent interaction between domestic and international personnel to discuss common problems in areas such as product planning.

International divisions best serve firms with few products that do not vary significantly in terms of their environmental sensitivity and with international sales and profits that are still quite insignificant compared with those of the domestic divisions. Companies may outgrow their international divisions as their global sales grow in significance, diversity, and complexity. A number of U.S.-based companies in the 1970s shifted from a traditional organizational structure with an independent international division to entities built around worldwide or global structures with no differentiation between "domestic" and "international" operations.[2]

Size in itself is not a limitation on the use of the international division structure. Some of the world's largest corporations rely on international divisions. The management of these companies believes that specialization is needed, primarily in terms of the environment.

Stage 4—The Global Organization As a company commits itself to global operations, new challenges arise. The most important challenges are communication among, and the coordination of, distant parts of the organization. In many industries, competition is on a global basis, with the result that companies must be able to react to a competitor simultaneously in many parts of the world.

Grouping People and Physical Resources to Achieve Organizational Goals

A major consideration in forming a global organization is how employees (human resources) and related physical resources of the company should be grouped, or arranged, in order to accomplish the tasks assigned to them, efficiently.

It should be noted that there is no perfect organizational structure. A structure that seems to work for one company may be inappropriate for another organization. There are a number of reasons for this, which will be discussed later in this chapter.

As a practical matter, the global organization chart is committed to paper, ideally with research and a number of individuals "thinking the problem through." At some point the organizational changes necessary to achieve the new structure are implemented. After a period of time, conclusions are drawn as to how the new organization structure is working. If it is not working as planned, then it is changed. In some cases only "fine tuning" is required. In more extreme instances, the structure is considered totally ineffective and an entire new organizational structure must be devised. In

QUESTION *What river flows between the twin cities of Buda and Pest in Hungary?*

Danube River

arranging people to do work, five basic approaches are available: *product, geographic, function, process,* and *customer.* In the application of these approaches, the reader is reminded that several of the five approaches may be (and usually are) used in various parts of the organizational structure.

1. *Product*—Workers are organized according to the *type of product.* In this case, product divisions are responsible for all manufacture and marketing of given products worldwide.
2. *Geographic*—Human resources are organized on the basis of *where the work is to be done.* This approach features geographic divisions that are responsible for all manufacture and marketing in their respective geographic area or region.
3. *Function*—In a functional approach, personnel are organized according to the *type of work to be done,* such as marketing, engineering, finance, or production. Thus, the production department, for example, would be responsible for the company's worldwide production operations.
4. *Process*—Employees and resources are organized on the basis of the *type of manufacturing process* involved. This approach is common in the energy and mining industries, where one division may be in charge of the worldwide exploration for energy sources, while another division may be responsible for the actual mining.
5. *Customer*—Firms may also organize their operations according to the *type of customer,* especially if the customer groups they serve are dramatically different; for example, consumers, businesses, and governments. Catering to these diverse groups may require concentrating specialists in particular divisions. The product may be the same, but the buying processes of the various customer groups may differ. Governmental buying is characterized by a formalized bidding procedure, in which price plays a larger role than when non-governmental businesses are the buyers.

product structure
organizational structure in which product divisions are responsible for all manufacturing and marketing

Product Structure The **product structure** is the one most often used by multinational corporations.[3] This approach gives worldwide responsibility to strategic business units for the marketing of their product lines, as shown in Figure 9.3. Most consumer product firms utilize some form of this approach, mainly because of the diversity of their products. One of the major benefits of the approach is improved cost efficiency through centralization of manufacturing facilities. This is crucial in industries in which competitive position is determined by world market share, which in turn is often determined by the degree to which manufacturing is rationalized.[4] Adaptation to this approach may cause problems because it is usually accompanied by consolidation of operations and plant closings.

Other benefits of the product structure are the ability to balance the functional inputs needed for a product and the ability to react quickly to product-specific problems in the marketplace. Even smaller brands receive individual attention. Product attention is important because products vary in terms of the adaptation they need for different foreign markets. All in all, the product approach is ideally suited to the development of a global strategic focus in response to global competition.

The Global Product Structure FIGURE 9.3

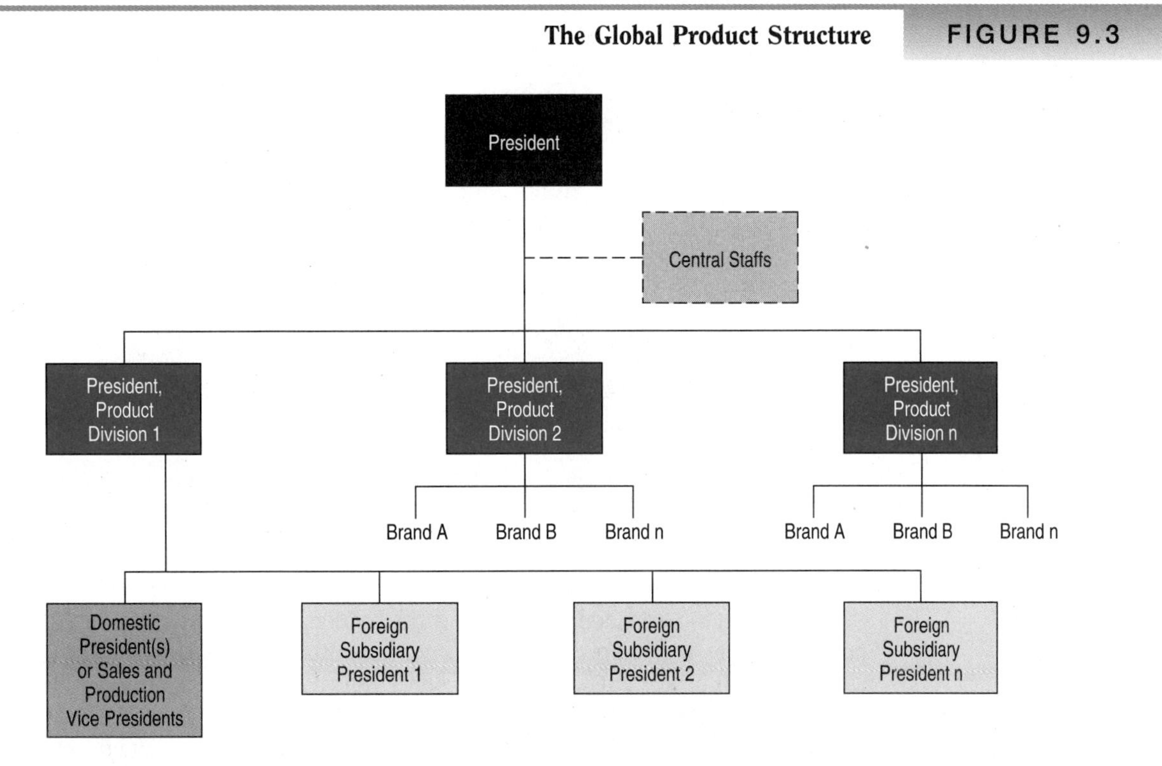

At the same time, this structure fragments global expertise within the firm because a central pool of global experience no longer exists. The structure assumes that managers will have adequate regional experience or advice to allow them to make balanced decisions. Coordination of activities among the various product groups operating in the same markets is crucial in order to avoid unnecessary duplications of basic tasks. For some of these tasks, such as market research, special staff functions may be created and then filled by the product divisions when needed. If they lack an appreciation for the global dimension, product managers may focus their attention only on the larger markets, or only on the domestic, and fail to take the long-term view.

Geographic Area Structure The approach adopted second most frequently is the **geographic area structure,** illustrated in Figure 9.4. Such firms are organized on the basis of geographical areas; for example, operations may be divided into those dealing with North America, the Far East, Latin America, and Europe. Regional aggregation may play a major role in this structuring; for example, many multinational corporations have located their European headquarters in Brussels, where the EU has its headquarters. In the case of Campbell Soup Co. the inevitability of a North American trading bloc (NAFTA) led to the creation of the North American division in 1990, which replaced the U.S. operation as the power center of the company.[5] Similarly, many U.S. companies have their headquarters for Latin American operations in Miami. Ideally, no special preference is given to the region in which the headquarters is located—for example, North America or Europe. Central staffs are responsible for providing coordination support for worldwide planning and control activities performed at headquarters. Organizational changes made at 3M Company as a result of NAFTA are outlined in Global Learning Experience 9.2.

geographic area structure organizational structure in which geographic divisions are responsible for all manufacturing and marketing in their respective areas

FIGURE 9.4 The Geographic Area Structure

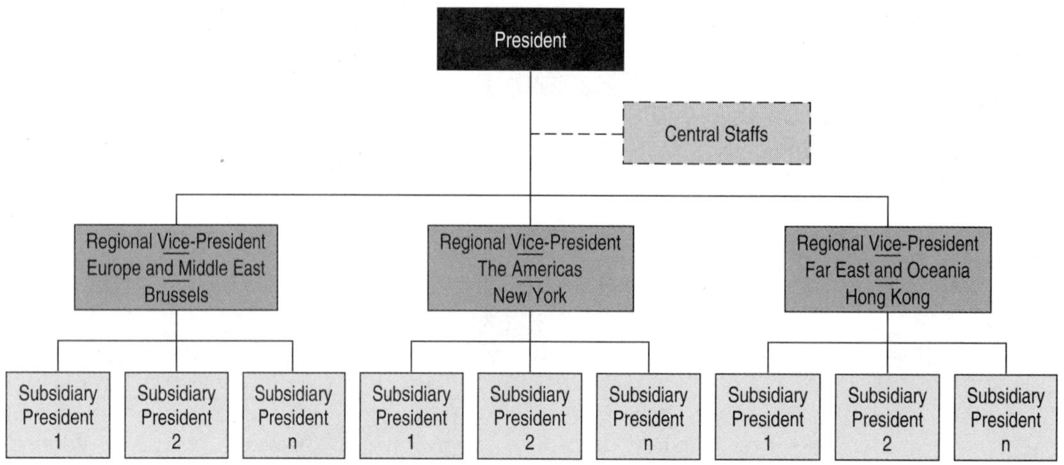

The geographic area approach follows the marketing concept most closely because individual areas and markets are given concentrated attention. If market conditions with respect to product acceptance and operating conditions vary dramatically, the geographic area approach is the one to choose. Companies opting for this alternative typically have relatively narrow product lines with similar end uses and end users. However, expertise is needed in adapting the product and its marketing to local market conditions. Once again, to avoid duplication of effort in product management and in functional areas, staff specialists—for product categories, for example—may be used.

Without appropriate coordination from the staff, essential information and experience may not be transferred from one regional entity to another. Also, if the company expands its product lines and if end markets begin to diversify, the area structure may become inappropriate.

Within the context of a geographic structure are the role and significance of organization on a country-by-country basis. It is important to remember that a company's subsidiary in another country, Germany, for example, is incorporated and authorized under German law, records all financial transactions in Deutschemarks, does business according to German practices, speaks German, and operates in the German culture. This situation raises concerns about the relationship between country organizations and headquarters.

A truckload of tires from Vienna arrives in Budapest, site of Goodyear's first sales office in Central Europe. *source:* Peter Komiss/Black Star, Peter Komiss.

GLOBAL LEARNING EXPERIENCE 9.2

Restructuring for NAFTA

A number of businesses are adopting strategic plans to take full advantage of the trilateral free trade pact of NAFTA. 3M's North American operational plan centers on organizational restructuring based on three concepts: simplification, linkage, and empowerment. The plan was fully implemented in the United States and Canada in 1992; Mexico was added in 1994.

"We always treated Mexico as a far off, foreign country," said David Olsen, 3M's manager of customs and chairman of the company's task force on NAFTA. Now, the company intends to manage by area rather than by country. Key goals of the operational plan are:

- Eliminate the role of 3M International Operations in cross-border activities within North America. All business units in Canada and Mexico will deal directly with 3M's divisions in the United States.
- Redefine management functions. Each general sales and marketing manager in Canada and Mexico will have a new title—business manager—and will serve as the key link between local customers and the corresponding U.S. general managers. The business managers also will be members of 3M U.S.'s planning, pricing, and operating committees, will participate in the early stages of the global business planning, and will execute the global strategy in Canada and Mexico.
- Coordinate functions and share resources among the three countries, especially in marketing, advertising, and sales. New-product launches will be synchronized throughout North America, with standardized sizing and part numbers wherever possible. Distribution strategies and agreements will be coordinated. Sales literature, packaging, and labeling will be uniform and written in the appropriate local language.
- Establish North American tactical teams. Members of the groups will be drawn from all three countries and will work on projects such as market research, new-product development, and competitor monitoring.
- Set up centers of excellence. To maximize efficiency and to avoid duplication of effort, each country will specialize in the function or process that it does best and eliminate those that can be performed elsewhere. The centers may be built around manufacturing of a product or product line, market niches, customer service, or technical skills.
- Modify performance-measurement criteria. North American performance will be gauged by North American—not U.S., Canadian, or Mexican—market share, earnings growth, and income.

At 3M Canada, major changes have taken place. Layers of management have been trimmed, communication and coordination have been enhanced, and the requirement to go through the international division removed. Incorporating Mexico into the plan has presented some unique challenges, however. For 3M U.S. headquarters, meeting or communicating electronically with Canadian counterparts is far easier than doing the same with Mexico. Language and cultural barriers also present potential challenges. Given that only products—not people—are free to cross borders, sales personnel cannot solicit business across borders and direct cross-border reporting may not be possible.

SOURCE: "3M Restructuring for NAFTA," *Business Latin America,* July 19, 1993, 6–7.

Country organizations should be treated as a source of supply as much as a source of demand. Quite often, however, headquarters managers see their role as the coordinators of key decisions and controllers of resources and perceive subsidiaries as implementors and adaptors of global strategy in their respective local markets. Furthermore, they may see all country organizations as the same. This view severely limits utilization of the firm's resources and deprives country managers of the opportunity to exercise their creativity.[6]

The role that a particular country organization can play naturally depends on that market's overall strategic importance as well as its organizational competence. The role of a **strategic leader** can be played by a highly competent national subsidiary located in a strategically critical market. Such a country organization serves as a partner of headquarters in developing and implementing strategy. Procter & Gamble's Eurobrand teams, which analyze opportunities for greater product and marketing program standardization, are chaired by a brand manager from a "lead country."[7]

strategic leader
highly competent national subsidiary located in a strategically critical market

A **contributor** is a country organization with a distinctive competence, such as product development. Increasingly, country organizations are the source of new products. These range from IBM's recent breakthrough in superconductivity research, generated in its Zurich lab, to low-end innovations like Procter & Gamble's liquid Tide, made with a fabric-softening compound developed in Europe.[8]

contributor
country organization with a distinctive competence, such as product development

Implementors provide the critical mass for the international marketing effort. These country organizations may exist in smaller, less developed countries in which corporate commitment for market development is less. Although most entities are given this role, it should not be slighted, since the implementors provide the opportunity to capture economies of scale and scope that are the basis of a global strategy.

implementor
typical subsidiary role, which involves implementing strategy that originates with headquarters

The **black hole** situation is one in which the international marketer has a low-competence country organization—or no organization at all—in a highly strategic market. In strategically important markets such as the European Union, a local presence is necessary to maintain the company's global position and, in some cases, to protect others. One of the major ways of remedying the black hole situation is to enter into strategic alliances. In the 1980s, AT&T, which had long restricted itself to its domestic market, needed to go global fast. Some of the alliances it formed were with Philips in telecommunications and Olivetti in computers and office automation.[9] In some cases, firms may use their presence in a major market as an observation post to keep up with developments before a major thrust for entry is executed.

black hole
situation that arises when an international marketer has a low-competence subsidiary—or none at all—in a highly strategic market

Depending on the role of the country organization, its relationship with headquarters will vary from loose control based mostly on support to tighter control to ensure that strategies get implemented appropriately. Yet in each of these cases, it is imperative that country organizations have enough operating independence to cater to local needs and to provide motivation to country managers. For example, an implementor's ideas concerning the development of a regional or global strategy or program should be heard. Strategy formulators should make sure that appropriate implementation can be achieved at the country level.

functional structure
arranges employees based on the type of work to be done

Functional Structure Of all the approaches, the **functional structure** is the simplest from the administrative viewpoint because it emphasizes the basic tasks of the firm—for example, manufacturing, sales, and research and development. This approach, illustrated in Figure 9.5, works best when both products and customers are relatively few and similar in nature. Because coordination is typically the key problem, staff functions have been created to interact between the functional areas. Otherwise, the company's marketing and regional expertise may not be exploited to the fullest extent possible.

process structure
a variation of the functional structure in which departments are formed on the basis of production processes

A variation of this approach is one that uses manufacturing processes as a basis for structure. The **process structure** is common in the energy and mining industries, where one corporate entity may be in charge of exploration worldwide and another may be responsible for the actual mining operation.

customer structure
organizational structure that groups human resources according to the type of customer or customer category

The **customer structure** is based on differences in the types of customers that the firm serves. Customers may be categorized in a number of ways—large versus small, government versus non-government, industrial versus consumer, and so forth. These distinctions imply differences in purchasing procedures which may require an organizational structure that can be responsive to the customers' needs, wants, and desires.

The Global Functional Structure **FIGURE 9.5**

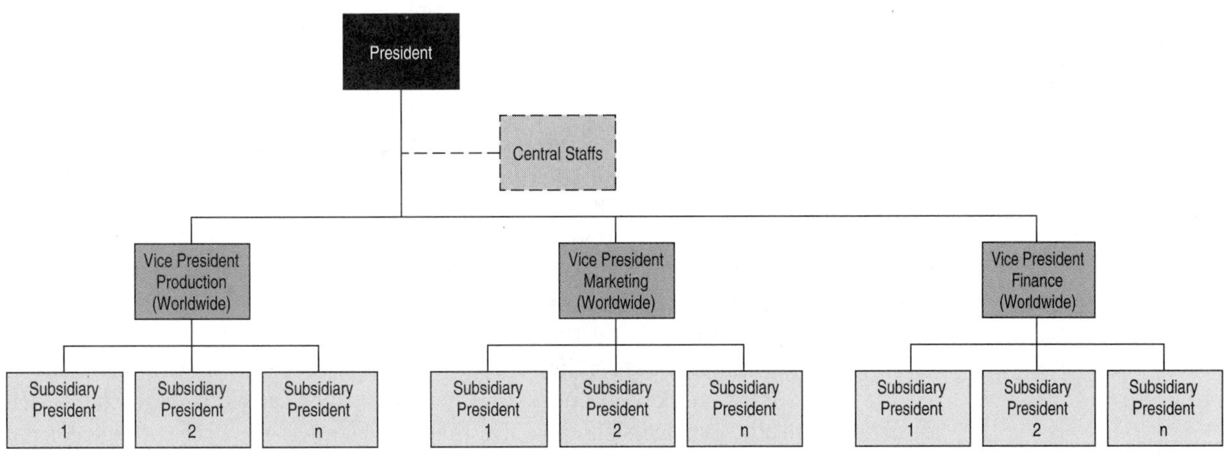

Mixed Structure In some cases, mixed, or hybrid, organizations exist. A **mixed structure** combines two or more organizational dimensions simultaneously. It permits adequate attention to product, area, or functional needs as it is needed by the company. This approach may only be a result of a transitional period after a merger or an acquisition, or it may come about due to a unique customer group or product line (such as military hardware). It may also provide a useful structure before the implementation of the matrix structure.[10]

mixed structure
an organizational structure that combines two or more organizational dimensions, for example, products, areas, or functions

Naturally, organizational structures are never as clear-cut and simple as presented here. Whatever the basic format, product, functional, and area inputs are needed. Alternatives could include an initial product structure that would subsequently have regional groupings or an initial regional structure with subsequent product groupings. However, in the long term, coordination and control across such structures become tedious.

For the largest global companies, the sheer size, complexity, and scope of their operations presents unusual challenges in organizing, managing, and controlling hundreds of thousands of employees at numerous locations about the world.

Matrix Structure Some multinational corporations, in an attempt to facilitate planning for, organizing, and controlling interdependent businesses, critical resources, strategies, and geographic regions, have adopted the **matrix structure.**[11] Eastman Kodak shifted from a functional organization to a matrix system based on business units. Business is driven by a worldwide business unit (for example, photographic products or commercial and information systems) and implemented by a geographic unit (for example, Europe or Latin America). The geographical units, as well as their country subsidiaries, serve as the "glue" between autonomous product operations.[12]

matrix structure
organizational structure that uses functional and divisional structures simultaneously

QUESTION *In what city is the Taj Mahal?*

The Taj Mahal is in Agra, the ancient Mogul capital of India. The world's most beautiful building is a mausoleum, built in the middle 1600s.

Organizational matrices integrate the various approaches already discussed. The matrix manager will have functional, product, and resource managers reporting to him or her. The whole approach is based on team building and multiple command, with each manager specializing in his or her own area of expertise. The matrix approach will provide a mechanism for cooperation between country managers, business managers, and functional managers on a worldwide basis through increased communication, control, and attention to balance in the organization.

Many companies have found the matrix arrangement problematic.[13] The dual reporting channel easily causes conflict, complex issues are forced into a two-dimensional decision framework, and even minor issues may have to be solved through committee discussion. Ideally, managers should solve these problems themselves through formal and informal communication; however, physical and psychic distance often make that impossible. The matrix structure, with its inherent complexity, may actually increase the reaction time of a company, a potentially serious problem when competitive conditions require quick responses.

Decentralized versus Centralized Organizational Structures

The third major factor to be considered in the design of the global organizational structure is the type and degree of control to be exercised by headquarters.

Organizational structures themselves do not indicate where the authority for decision making and control rests within the organization. If subsidiaries are granted a high degree of autonomy, with a good deal of decision making made at the local level, the system is called **decentralization.** In decentralized systems, controls are relatively loose and simple, and the flows between headquarters and subsidiaries are mainly financial; that is, each subsidiary operates as a profit center. On the other hand, if controls are tight and the strategic decision making is concentrated at headquarters, the system is described as **centralization.** Firms are typically neither completely centralized nor decentralized; for example, some functions of the firm—such as finance—lend themselves to more centralized decision making; others—such as promotional decisions—do so far less. Research and development in organizations is typically centralized, especially in cases of basic research work. Some companies have, partly due to governmental pressures, added R&D functions on a regional or local basis. In many cases, however, variations are product and market based; for example, Corning Glass Works' TV tube marketing strategy requires global decision making for pricing and local decision making for service and delivery.

decentralization
granting of a high degree of autonomy to subsidiaries

centralization
concentrating control and strategic decision making at headquarters

The basic advantage of allowing maximum flexibility at the subsidiary level is that subsidiary management knows its market and can react to changes more quickly. Problems of motivation and acceptance are avoided when decision makers are also the implementors of the strategy. On the other hand, many multinationals faced with global competitive threats and opportunities have adopted global strategy formulation, which by definition requires a higher degree of centralization. What has emerged as a result can be called **coordinated decentralization.** This means that overall corporate strategy is provided from headquarters, while subsidiaries are free to implement it within the range agreed on in consultation with headquarters.

coordinated decentralization
overall corporate strategy is provided from headquarters, while subsidiaries are free to implement it within the range agreed on in consultation with headquarters

Guanxi—The Web of Relationships

There is a fundamental difference in the way Western and Asian firms approach business. Basically, for Western companies the business comes first and then the relationship follows. With Asian firms the relationship is developed first and the business flows from the relationship. Thus, a basic strategy for Asian organizations is the development of a web of relationships, or *guanxi,* that will eventually pay off with business opportunities. The development of long-term relationships requires time and patience, but in them Asians find commercial security. An Asian firm that really knows the people and companies it is doing business with reduces its business risks, as opposed to dealings with unknown, untried individuals and business organizations.

Western companies, on the other hand, seem not to have the desire, patience, or time necessary for Asian-style networking. Part of the reason may be traced to the relatively short stay of Western executives in Asian assignments. The typical stay of 2–4 years is not sufficient for the development and nurturing of long-term relationships. A more desirable strategy would be for Western firms to consider investing human resources over a 10–20 year time span. In a similar manner, many Western firms position executives in Asia without giving them decision-making authority. This requires the executives to constantly confer with headquarters for advice and approvals—undermining how they are viewed by Asian business leaders and causing, in effect, a "loss of face" in a land where "saving face" is everything.

SOURCE: *The Economist,* March 29th, 1997

Other Factors Affecting Organizational Structure and Decision Making

The firm's country of origin and the political history of the area can also affect organizational structure and decision making. For example, Swiss-based Nestlé, with only 3 to 4 percent of its sales from its small domestic market, has traditionally had a highly decentralized organization. Moreover, European history for the past 75 years—particularly the two world wars—has often forced subsidiaries of European-based companies to act independently to survive.

The type and variety of products marketed will affect organizational decisions. Companies that market consumer products typically have product organizations with high degrees of decentralization, allowing for maximum local flexibility. On the other hand, companies that market technologically sophisticated products—such as GE, which markets turbines—display centralized organizations with worldwide product responsibilities.

Apart from situations requiring the development of an area structure for an organization, the characteristics of certain markets or regions may require separate arrangements for the firm. For many Japanese and European companies, the North American market has been given priority, manifested by direct organizational links to top management at headquarters. For many U.S. firms, a key objective is to gain entry into Asian markets, which may involve a special allocation of human resources and a corresponding change in the organizational structure, as noted in Global Learning Experience 9.3.

The human factor in any organization is critical. Management personnel both at headquarters and in the subsidiaries have to bridge the physical and psychic distances separating them. If subsidiaries have competent management that does not have to rely on headquarters consultation to solve the majority of its problems, they may be granted high degrees of autonomy. In the case of global organizations, subsidiary management has to understand the corporate culture of the firm to be an efficient part of the corporation, especially when decisions are called for that are not optimum for the local market but meet the long-term objectives of the firm as a whole.

The Networked Global Organization

There seems to be no ideal global structure, and some have challenged the wisdom of even looking for one. They have recommended attention to new processes that would, in a given structure, help to develop new perspectives and attitudes that reflect and respond to the complex, opposing demands of global integration and local responsiveness.[14] The question thus changes from which structural alternative is best to how the different perspectives of various corporate entities can better be taken into account when making decisions. In structural terms, nothing may change.

Companies that have adopted the approach have incorporated the following three dimensions into their organizations: (1) the development and communication of a clear corporate vision, (2) the effective management of human resource tools to broaden individual perspectives and develop identification with corporate goals, and (3) the integration of individual thinking and activities into the broad corporate agenda.[15] The first dimension relates to a clear and consistent long-term corporate mission that guides individuals wherever they work in the organization. Examples of this are Johnson & Johnson's corporate credo of customer focus and NEC's C&C (= computers and communications). The second relates both to the development of global managers who can find opportunities in spite of environmental challenges as well as creating a global perspective among country managers. The last dimension relates to the development of a cooperative mindset among country organizations to ensure effective implementation of global strategies. Managers may feel that global strategies are intrusions on their operations if they do not have an understanding of the corporate vision, if they have not contributed to the global corporate agenda, or if they are not given direct responsibility for its implementation. Defensive, territorial attitudes can lead to the emergence of the **not-invented-here syndrome;** that is, country organizations objecting to or rejecting an otherwise sound strategy.

not-invented-here syndrome wherein local or subordinate organizational units reject strategies and/or firm initiatives solely because they were initiated elsewhere in the organization

The network avoids the problems of effort duplication, inefficiency of operations, and nonacceptance of ideas developed elsewhere by giving subsidiaries the latitude, encouragement, and tools to pursue local business development within the framework of the global strategy. Headquarters considers each unit a source of ideas, skills, capabilities, and knowledge that can be utilized for the benefit of the entire organization. This means that subsidiaries must be upgraded from mere implementors and adaptors to contributors and partners in the development and execution of worldwide strategies. Efficient plants may be converted into international production centers, innovative R&D units converted into centers of excellence (and thus role models), and leading subsidiary groups given the leadership role in developing new strategies for the entire corporation. The main tool of implementation used in this approach is global teams of managers who meet regularly to develop strategy. While final direction may come from headquarters, it has been informed of local conditions, and implementation of the strategy is enhanced since local-country managers were involved in its development.

THE MULTINATIONAL CORPORATION

Once a firm establishes a production facility abroad, its global operations take on new meaning. The firm has typically evolved to this stage through exporting and/or licensing, which no longer can satisfy its growth objectives. Many companies have found their exports dramatically curtailed because of unfavorable changes in exchange rates or trade barriers. Moreover, for firms in small domestic markets, physical presence through manufacturing is a must in the world's largest markets if the firm is to survive in the long term. Direct investment makes the firm's commitment to the international marketplace more permanent.

At the same time, the firm also becomes a corporate citizen in another nation-state, subject to its laws and regulations as well as its overall environmental influences. To remain effective and efficient as an entity, the firm has to coordinate and control its activities in multiple environments, making decisions that may not be optimal for one or more of the markets in which it operates. As a result, the firm may come under scrutiny by private and public organizations, ranging from consumer groups to supranational organizations such as the United Nations.

In today's environment—with no single country dominating the world economy or holding a monopoly on innovation—technologies, capital, and talents flow in many different directions, driving the trend toward a form of "stateless" corporation.

The Multinational Corporation Defined

Different terms abound for the multinational corporation. They include global, world, transnational, international, supernational, and supranational corporation. The term *multinational enterprise* is used by some when referring to internationally involved entities that may not be using a corporate form. In this book, we use the term *multinational corporation* (MNC) to describe the type of stateless corporation mentioned in the Global Learning Experience 9.4.

Similarly, there is an abundance of definitions. The United Nations defines multinational corporations as "enterprises which own or control production or service facilities outside the country in which they are based."[16] Although this definition has been criticized as being oriented too much to the economist,[17] it nevertheless captures the quantitative and qualitative dimensions of many of the other definitions proposed.

Quantitatively, certain minimal criteria have been proposed that firms must satisfy before they can be regarded as multinational. The number of countries of operation is typically two, although the Harvard multinational enterprise project required subsidiaries in six or more nations.[18] Another measure is the proportion of overall revenue generated from foreign operations. Although no agreement exists over the exact percentage to be used, 25 to 30 percent is the one most often cited.[19] One proposal is that the degree of involvement in foreign markets has to be substantial enough to make a difference in decision making. Another study proposed that several nations should be owners of the corporation, as is the case with Royal Dutch Shell Group and Unilever or, more recently, as in the merger between Swiss Brown Boveri and Swedish Asea to form ABB.[20]

However, production abroad does not necessarily indicate a multinational corporation. Qualitatively, the behavior of the firm is the determining factor. If the firm is to be categorized as a multinational corporation, its management must consider it to be multinational and must act accordingly. In terms of management philosophies, firms can be categorized as **ethnocentric** (home-market oriented), **polycentric** (oriented toward individual foreign markets), or **regiocentric** or **geocentric** (oriented toward larger

ethnocentric
tending to regard one's own culture as superior; tending to be home-market oriented

polycentric
tending to regard each culture as a separate entity; tending to be oriented toward individual foreign markets

regiocentric or geocentric
tending to be oriented toward regions larger than individual countries as markets

The Stateless Corporation

As cross-border trade and investment flows reach new heights, big global companies are effectively making decisions with little regard to national boundaries. The European, U.S., and Japanese giants heading in this direction are learning how to juggle multiple identities and multiple loyalties. Worried by the emergence of regional trading blocs in Europe, North America, and East Asia, these world corporations are building insider capabilities no matter where they operate. At the same time, factories and laboratories are moved around the world freely. Given the wave of mergers, acquisitions, and strategic alliances, the question of national control has become even more unclear.

A fitting example of such a corporation is ABB (Asea Brown Boveri), a $28 billion electrical engineering giant. From headquarters in Zurich, Swedish, German, and Swiss managers shuffle assets around the globe, keep the books in dollars, and conduct most of their business in English. Yet the companies that make up their far-flung operations tailor ABB's turbines, transformers, robots, and high-speed trains to local markets so successfully that ABB looks like an established domestic player everywhere.

Statelessness does provide certain environmental advantages. Among the benefits are the ability to avoid trade and political problems, to sidestep regulatory hurdles, to achieve labor concessions, to balance costs, and to win technology breakthroughs.

The Canadian telecommunications giant, Northern Telecom, has moved so many of its manufacturing functions to the United States that it can win Japanese contracts on the basis of being a U.S. company. Japan favors U.S. over Canadian telecommunications companies because of the politically sensitive U.S.–Japanese trade gap.

When Germany's BASF launched biotechnology research at home, it confronted legal and political challenges from the environmentally conscious Green movement. As a result, the company moved its cancer and immune-system research to Cambridge, Massachusetts, because of the availability of engineers and scientists and because the state has better resolved controversies involving safety, animal rights, and the environment.

One of the main factors that prompted U.S. pharmaceutical maker SmithKline and Britain's Beecham to merge was that they needed to guarantee that they could avoid licensing and regulatory hassles in their largest markets, Western Europe and the United States. The new company can now identify itself as an inside player on both sides of the Atlantic.

When Xerox Corp. started moving copier rebuilding work to Mexico, its union in Rochester, New York, objected. The risk of job loss was clear, and the union agreed to undertake the changes in work style and productivity needed to keep the jobs.

Some world companies make almost daily decisions on where to shift production. When Dow Chemical saw European demand for a certain solvent decline recently, the company scaled back its production in Germany and shifted to producing another chemical there, one previously imported from Louisiana and Texas.

Otis Elevator Inc.'s latest product, the Elevonic 411, benefited from the company's global operations. The elevator was developed by six research centers in five countries. Otis's group in Farmington, Connecticut, handled the systems integration, Japan designed the special motor devices that make the elevators ride smoothly, France perfected the door systems, Germany handled the electronics, and Spain took care of the small-geared components. The international process saved more than $10 million in design costs and cut the development cycle from four years to two.

Some analysts have suggested that today's global firms will be superseded by a new form, the "relationship enterprise." These are networks of strategic alliances among big firms, spanning different industries and countries, but held together by common goals that encourage them to act almost as a single firm. For example, early in the twenty-first century, Boeing, British Airways, Siemens, TNT (an Australian parcel delivery firm), and SNECMA (a French aircraft engine maker) might together win a deal to build new airports in China. British Airways and TNT would receive preferential routes and landing slots, Boeing and SNECMA would win aircraft contracts, and Siemens would provide the air traffic control systems.

SOURCES: "The Global Firm: R.I.P.," *The Economist,* February 6, 1993, 69; "Cooperation Worth Copying," *The Washington Post,* December 13, 1992, H1, H6; "The Euro-Gospel According to Percy Bamevik," *Business Week,* July 23, 1990, 64–66; and "The Stateless Corporation," *Business Week,* May 14, 1990, 96–106.

areas, even the global marketplace).[21] Even ethnocentric firms would qualify as multinational corporations if production were the sole criterion. However, the term should be reserved for firms that view their domestic operation as a part of worldwide (or regionwide) operations and direct an integrated business system. The definition excludes polycentric firms, which may be comparable to holding companies.

Both quantitative and qualitative criteria are important in the defining task. Regardless of the definition, the key criteria are that the firm controls its production facilities abroad and manages them (and its domestic operations) in an integrated fashion in pursuit of global opportunities.

The World's Multinational Corporations

Many of the world's largest corporate entities, listed in Table 9.2, are larger economically than most of their host nations. Some operate in well over 100 countries; for example, IBM has operations in 132 nations. Of the 50 firms listed, 22 are headquartered in the United States, 16 in Western Europe, and 12 in East Asia. The economic power they command is enormous; according to one estimate, the 500 largest industrial corporations account for 80 percent of the world's direct investment and ownership of foreign affiliates.[22]

Although dominated by certain countries, the multinational corporate phenomenon has spread worldwide. For example, corporate headquarters for the 500 largest industrial corporations are in 32 different nations. Direct investment by firms from Africa, Asia, and Latin America has increased dramatically, especially by firms from more industrialized nations such as the Republic of Korea, Mexico, and Brazil.[23] Samsung, Korea's largest company, has assets of $16 billion and operations in 55 countries.[24]

The impact of multinationals varies by industry sector and by country. In oil, multinational corporations still command 30 percent of production, despite strong national efforts by some countries.[25] Their share in refining and marketing is still 45 percent. In several agribusiness sectors, such as pineapples, multinationals account for approximately 60 percent of the world output. Similarly, the contribution of multinational corporations' affiliates may account for more than one-third of the output of the marketing sector in certain countries.[26] For example, U.S. companies owned 32 percent of the paper and pulp industry, 36 percent of the mining and smelting industry, and 39 percent of manufacturing overall in Canada before the foreign direct investment climate changed in the early 1980s.[27] Despite a tightening of investment regulations, 40 percent of Canadian manufacturing was foreign owned in 1990, with U.S. firms accounting for 80 percent of that share.

TABLE 9.2 The World Super Fifty Corporations

Rank	Company	Business	Country	Revenue ($mil)	Net Income ($mil)	Assets ($mil)	Market Value ($mil)	Employees (thou)
1	**Royal Dutch/ Shell Group**	energy	Netherlands	128,186	8,888	124,373	169,123[2]	101.0
2	**General Electric**	elec & electron	United States	79,179	7,280	272,402	198,578	230.5
3	**Exxon**	energy	United States	116,728	7,510	95,527	147,141	80.5
4	**International Business Machines**	computer systems	United States	75,947	5,429	81,132	87,881	233.0
5	**Toyota Motor**	automobiles	Japan	108,702	3,426	102,417	108,899	146.9
6	**Ford Motor**	automobiles	United States	146,991	4,446	262,867	44,550	371.7
7	**General Motors**	automobiles	United States	164,069	4,963	222,142	49,057	648.0
8	**British Petroleum**	energy	United Kingdom	69,858	3,986	55,307	67,295	53.7
9	**Bank of Tokyo-Mitsubishi**	banking	Japan	46,451	362	647,781	81,071	19.3
9	**Wal-Mart Stores**	retailing	United States	104,859	3,056	39,604	68,336	701.5
11	**AT&T**	telecommunications	United States	52,184	5,770	55,026	59,663	129.4
12	**Citicorp**	banking	United States	32,605	3,788	281,018	52,980	87.4
13	**Mobil**	energy	United States	71,129	2,964	46,408	55,083	46.7
14	**El du Pont de Nemours**	chemicals	United States	38,349	3,636	37,987	61,216	101.0
14	**Fannie Mae**	leasing & finance	United States	25,054	2,754	351,041	46,433	3.3
14	**Procter & Gamble**	food, household	United States	35,212	3,237	28,120	93,681	103.0
17	**Nippon Tel & Tel**	telecommunications	Japan	78,321	1,330	115,865	151,895	222.1
18	**Philip Morris Cos**	tobacco	United States	54,553	6,303	54,871	35,309	152.5
19	**HSBC Group**	banking	United Kingdom	28,863	4,860	401,666	27,078	102.5
20	**American International Group**	insurance	United States	28,205	2,897	148,431	63,215	35.6
20	**Unilever**	food, household	Netherlands	52,076	2,500	30,993	52,687[3]	306.0
22	**Nestlé**	food, household	Switzerland	48,939	2,752	37,906	49,059	221.1
23	**Allianz Worldwide**	insurance	Germany	55,397	1,096	200,362	48,616	65.8
23	**Lloyds TSB Group**	banking	United Kingdom	20,375	2,460	250,228	53,938	82.5

[1]Figures are latest available. [2]Combined market value for Royal Dutch Petroleum and Shell Transport & Trading. [3]Combined market value for Unilever NV and Unilever Plc.

The above table ranks the 50 largest U.S. and foreign firms on a composite score based on each company's best three out of four rankings for sales, profits, assets and market value.

SOURCE: *Forbes,* July 28, 1997, 180.

FOREIGN DIRECT INVESTMENT

To understand the multinational corporate phenomenon, one must analyze the rationale for foreign direct investment. Foreign direct investment represents one component of the international business flow and includes start-ups of new operations as well as purchases of more than 10 percent of existing companies. The other component is portfolio investment—that is, the purchase of stocks and bonds internationally—which was discussed in Chapter 4.

TABLE 9.2 *continued*

Rank	Company	Business	Country	Revenue ($mil)	Net Income ($mil)	Assets ($mil)	Market Value ($mil)	Employees (thou)
25	Chase Manhattan	banking	United States	27,421	2,461	336,099	40,712	70.2
26	Hewlett-Packard	computer systems	United States	39,427	2,708	27,156	52,196	107.2
27	Chevron	energy	United States	37,580	2,607	34,854	45,728	41.9
28	Deutsche Bank Group	banking	Germany	41,033	1,418	569,906	27,762	74.4
28	ENI	energy	Italy	37,384	2,885	58,856	40,095	83.4
30	Indl Bank of Japan	banking	Japan	38,694[1]	−659[1]	361,372[1]	30,576	5.3
31	Barclays	banking	United Kingdom	19,694	2,560	315,830	29,435	87.4
32	ING Group	financial svcs	Netherlands	35,942	1,970	277,528	34,745	58.1
33	Daimler-Benz Group	automobiles	Germany	70,707	1,835	72,331	39,672	291.3
34	Deutsche Telekom	telecommunications	Germany	41,916	1,168	112,121	60,946	236.8
35	Amoco	energy	United States	32,150	2,834	32,100	44,444	42.2
36	Sanwa Bank	banking	Japan	27,973	230	427,438	37,180	13.9
37	Novartis Group	personal care	Switzerland	29,314	1,864	43,098	93,501	116.2
38	Intel	computer peripherals	United States	20,847	5,157	23,735	124,382	45.1
39	NationsBank	banking	United States	17,509	2,375	185,794	33,579	60.6
39	Siemens Group	elec & electron	Germany	63,716	1,877	57,310	31,749	378.8
41	Chrysler	automobiles	United States	61,397	3,720	56,184	22,124	126.0
42	ABN-Amro Holding	banking	Netherlands	27,656	1,959	341,396	25,398	65.4
43	Travelers Group	insurance	United States	21,345	2,331	151,067	35,269	51.9
44	Honda Motor	automobiles	Japan	46,994	1,964	33,787	28,657	101.1
45	British Telecom	telecommunications	United Kingdom	23,695	3,295	40,834	46,185	129.6
45	Johnson & Johnson	medical supplies	United States	21,620	2,887	20,010	79,949	85.8
47	Fuji Bank	banking	Japan	24,071	968	432,738	37,379	15.2
47	Merck	personal care	United States	19,829	3,881	24,293	107,933	47.2
47	Texaco	energy	United States	44,561	2,018	26,963	28,341	28.6
50	Matsushita Electric Indl	appliances	Japan	68,148	1,224	70,100	39,761	265.5

Reasons for Foreign Direct Investment

Firms expand internationally for a variety of reasons. An overview of the major determinants of foreign direct investment is provided in Table 9.3.

Marketing Factors Marketing considerations and the corporate desire for growth are major causes of the increase in foreign direct investment. Even a sizable domestic market may present limitations to growth. Firms therefore need to seek wider market access in order to maintain and increase their sales. Some firms make investments in order to be closer to and better serve some of their major clients, such as Siemens with its $4.3 billion investment in the U.S. market. The growth objective can be achieved most quickly through the acquisition of foreign firms. Other reasons for foreign direct investment include the desire to gain know-how and the need to add to existing sales force strength.

TABLE 9.3 Major Determinants of Direct Foreign Investment

Marketing Factors	Cost Factors	Investment Climate
1. Size of market	1. Desire to be near source of supply	1. General attitude toward foreign investment
2. Market growth	2. Availability of labor	2. Political stability
3. Desire to maintain share of market	3. Availability of raw materials	3. Limitation on ownership
4. Desire to advance exports of parent company	4. Availability of capital/technology	4. Currency exchange regulations
5. Need to maintain close customer contact	5. Lower labor costs	5. Stability of foreign exchange
6. Dissatisfaction with existing market arrangements	6. Lower other production costs	6. Tax structure
7. Export base	7. Lower transport costs	7. Familiarity with country
8. Desire to follow customers	8. Financial (and other) inducements by government	
9. Desire to follow competition	9. More favorable cost levels	**General**
		1. Expected higher profits
Barriers to Trade		2. Other
1. Government-erected barriers to trade		
2. Preference of local customers for local products		

SOURCE: Adapted from Organization for Economic Cooperation and Development, *International Investment and Multinational Enterprises* (Paris: OECD, 1983.), 41.

A major cause for the recent growth in foreign direct investment is derived demand. Often, as large multinational firms move abroad, they are quite interested in maintaining their established business relationships with other firms. Therefore, they frequently encourage their suppliers to follow them and continue to supply them from the new foreign location. For example, advertising agencies often move abroad in order to service foreign affiliates of their domestic clients. Similarly, engineering firms, insurance companies, and law firms often are invited to provide their services abroad. Yet not all of these developments come about from co-optation by client firms. Often, firms invest abroad for defensive reasons, out of fear that their clients may find other sources abroad, and this eventually might jeopardize their status even in the domestic market. To preserve quality, Japanese automakers have urged more than 40 of their suppliers from Japan to establish production in the United States.[28]

For similar reasons, firms follow their competitors abroad. Competitive firms influence not only their engaging in foreign direct investment, but even where the investments are made.[29] Many firms have found that even their competitive position at home is affected by their ability to effectively compete in foreign markets.

Barriers to Trade Foreign direct investment permits firms to circumvent barriers to trade and operate abroad as domestic firms, unaffected by duties, tariffs, or other import restrictions. The enormous amount of U.S. investment would not have been attracted to Canada had it not been for the barriers to trade erected by the Canadian government to support domestic industry.

In addition to government-erected barriers, barriers may also be imposed by customers through their insistence on domestic goods and services, either as a result of nationalistic tendencies or as a function of cultural differences. Furthermore, local buyers may wish to buy from sources that they perceive to be reliable in their supply, which means buying from local producers. For some products, country-of-origin effects may force a firm to establish a plant in a country that has a built-in positive stereotype for product quality.[30]

Cost Factors Servicing markets at sizable geographic distances and with sizable tariff barriers has made many exporters' offerings in foreign markets prohibitively expensive. Many manufacturing multinationals have established plants overseas to gain cost advantages in terms of labor and raw materials. Many of the border plants in Mexico provide their U.S. parents with low-cost inputs and components through the *maquiladora* program.

Investment Climate Foreign direct investment by definition implies a degree of control over the enterprise.[31] yet this may be unavailable because of environmental constraints, even if the firm owns 100 percent of the subsidiary. The general attitude toward foreign investment and its development over time may be indicative of the long-term prospects for investment. For example, if asked to choose, 48 percent of Americans would discourage Japanese investment and only 18 percent would encourage it.[32] In many countries, foreign direct investment tends to arouse nationalistic feelings. Political risk has to be defined broadly to include not only the threat of political upheaval but also the likelihood of arbitrary or discriminatory government action that will result in financial loss. This could take the form of tax increases, price controls, or measures directed specifically at foreign firms such as partial divestment of ownership, local-content requirements, remittance restrictions, export requirements, and limits on expatriate employment.[33] The investment climate is also measured in terms of foreign currency risk. The evaluations will typically focus on possible accounting translation exposure levels and cash flows in foreign currency.

In a survey of 108 U.S.-based multinational corporations, foreign direct investment was found to be profit and growth driven.[34] The influence of the other variables will vary depending on the characteristics of the firm and its management, on its objectives, and on external conditions.

The Host-Country Perspective

The host government is caught in a love-hate relationship with foreign direct investment.[35] On the one hand, the host country has to appreciate the various contributions, especially economic, that the foreign direct investment will make. On the other hand, fears of dominance, interference, and dependence are often voiced and acted upon. The major positive and negative impacts are summarized in Table 9.4.

The Positive Impact Foreign direct investment capital flows are especially beneficial to countries with limited domestic sources and restricted opportunities to raise funds in the world's capital markets.

The role of foreign direct investment has been seen as that of technology transfer.[36] Technology transfer includes the introduction of not only new hardware to the market but also the techniques and skills to operate it. An integral part of technology transfer is managerial skills, which are the most significant labor component of foreign direct investment. With the growth of the service sector, many economies need skills rather than expatriate personnel to perform the tasks.

Foreign direct investment can be used effectively in developing a geographical region or a particular industry sector. Foreign direct investment is one of the most expedient ways in which unemployment can be reduced in chosen regions of a country.

TABLE 9.4 Positive and Negative Impacts of Foreign Direct Investment on Host Countries

Positive Impact	Negative Impact
1. Capital formation	1. Industrial dominance
2. Technology and management skills transfer	2. Technological dependence
3. Regional and sectoral development	3. Disturbance of economic plans
4. Internal competition and entrepreneurship	4. Cultural change
5. Favorable effect on balance of payments	5. Interference by home government of multinational corporation
6. Increased employment	

SOURCE: Jack N. Behrman, *National Interests and the Multinational Enterprise* (Englewood Cliffs, N.J.: Prentice-Hall, 1970), chapters 2 through 5; Jack N. Behrman, *Industrial Policies: International Restructuring and Transnationals* (Lexington, Mass.: Lexington Books, 1984), chapter 5; and Christopher M. Korth, *International Business* (Englewood Cliffs, N.J.: Prentice-Hall, 1985), chapters 12 and 13.

In many developing countries, foreign direct investment may be a way to diversify the industrial base and thereby reduce the country's dependence on one or a few sectors.

At the company level, foreign direct investment may intensify competition and result in benefits to the economy as a whole as well as to consumers through increased productivity and possibly lower prices. Competition typically introduces new techniques, products and services, and ideas to the markets. It may improve existing patterns of how business is done.

Jobs are often the most obvious reason to cheer about foreign direct investment. The creation of jobs translates also into the training and development of a skilled workforce.

All of the benefits discussed are indeed possible advantages of foreign direct investment. Their combined effect can lead to an overall enhancement in the standard of living in the market as well as an increase in the host country's access to the world market and its international competitiveness. It is equally possible, however, that the impact can be negative rather than positive.

Foreign direct investment creates jobs. Even developed nations such as the United States benefit from additional employment opportunities provided by foreign investment in production facilities such as the Toyota–GM plant in California.
SOURCE: Courtesy of New United Motor Manufacturing, Inc.

The Negative Impact

Although some of the threats posed by multinational corporations and foreign direct investment are exaggerated, in many countries some industrial sectors are dominated by foreign-owned entities.

Because foreign direct investment in most cases is concentrated in technology-intensive industries, research and development account for another area of tension. With its technology transfer, the multinational corporation can assist the host country's economic development, but it may leave the host country dependent on flows of new and updated technology. Furthermore, the multinational firm may contribute to the **brain drain** by attracting scientists from host countries to its central research facility. Many countries have demanded, and won, research facilities on their soil, the results of which they can control to a better extent. Many countries are weary of the technological dominance of the United States and Japan and see this as a long-term threat.

brain drain
migration of professional people from one country to another, usually for the purpose of improving their incomes or living conditions

Many of the economic benefits of foreign direct investment are controversial as well. Capital inflows may be accompanied by outflows in a higher degree and over a longer term than is satisfactory to the host government. Many officials also complain that the promised training of local personnel, especially for management positions, has never taken place. Rather than stimulate local competition and encourage entrepreneurship, multinationals with their often superior product offering and marketing skills have stifled competition. Many countries, including the United States, have found that multinational companies do not necessarily want to rely on local suppliers but rather bring along their own from the domestic market.

Many governments see multinationals as a disturbance to their economic planning. Decisions are made concerning their economy over which they have little or no control.

Multinational companies are, by definition, change agents. They bring about change not only in the way business may be conducted but also, through the products and services they generate and the way they are marketed, cause change in the lifestyles of the consumers in the market. The extent to which this is welcomed or accepted varies by country.

The multinational corporation will also have an impact on business practices. They may engage in practices that are alien to the local workforce, such as greater work-rule flexibility. Older operators, for example, may be removed from production lines to make room for more productive employees.

Some host nations have expressed concern over the possibility of interference, economically and politically, by the home government of the multinational corporation; that is, they fear that the multinational may be used as an instrument of influence.

Fixed investments by multinationals can be held hostage by a host country in trying to win concessions from other governments. In an increasing number of cases, host governments insist on quid pro quo deals in which foreign direct investment is contingent on adherence to specified requirements, such as export targets.

Countries engage in formal evaluation of foreign direct investment, both outbound and inbound. Canada uses the Foreign Investment Review Agency to determine whether foreign-owned companies are good corporate citizens. Sweden reviews outbound foreign direct investment in terms of its impact on the home country, especially employment.

QUESTION *What is the last course in an authentic Chinese meal?*

Soup is the last course in a Chinese meal.

The Home-Country Perspective

Most of the aspects of foreign direct investment that concern host countries apply to the home country as well. Foreign direct investment means addition to the home country's gross national product from profits, royalties, and fees remitted by affiliates. In many cases, intracompany transfers bring about additional export possibilities.[37] Many countries, in promoting foreign direct investment, see it as a means to stimulate economic growth—an end that would expand export markets and serve other goals, such as political motives, as well. Some countries, such as Japan, have tried to gain preferential access to raw materials through firms that owned the deposits. Other factors of production can be obtained through foreign direct investment as well.

The major negative issue centers on employment. Many unions point not only to outright job loss but also to the effect on imports and exports. The most controversial have been investments in plants in developing countries that export back to the home countries. Multinationals such as electronics manufacturers, who have moved plants to Southeast Asia and Mexico, have justified this as a necessary cost-cutting competitive measure.

Another critical issue is that of technological advantage. Some critics state that, by establishing plants abroad or forming joint ventures with foreign entities, the country may be giving away its competitive position in the world marketplace. This is especially true when the recipients may be able to avoid the time and expense involved in developing new technologies.

The U.S. government has also taken a position on the behavior of U.S.-based firms overseas by the passage of the Foreign Corrupt Practices Act in 1977. (The FCPA was discussed in Chapter 7.)

Management of the Relationship

Arguments for and against foreign direct investment are endless. Costs and benefits must be weighed. Only the multinational corporation itself can assess expected gains against perceived risks in its overseas commitments. At the same time, only the host and home countries can assess benefits realized against costs in terms of their national priorities. If these entities cannot agree on objectives because their most basic interests are in conflict, they cannot agree on the means either. In most cases, the relationship between the parties is not necessarily based on logic, fairness, or equity, but on the relative bargaining power of each.[38] Furthermore, political changes may cause rapid changes in host-government MNC relations.

Host countries try to enhance their role by instituting control policies and performance requirements on affiliates. Governments attempt to prevent the integration of activities among affiliates and control by the parent. In this effort, they exclude or limit foreign participation in certain sectors of the economy and require local participation in the ownership and management of the entities established. The extent of this participation will vary by industry, depending on how much the investment is needed by the host economy. Performance requirements typically are programs aimed at established foreign investors in an economy. These often are such discriminatory policies as local content requirements, export requirements, limits on foreign payments (especially profit repatriation), and demands concerning the type of technology transferred or the sophistication and level of operation engaged in. In some cases, demands of this type have led to firms' packing their bags. For example, Coca-Cola left India when the government demanded access to what the firm considered to be confidential intellectual property. Cadbury Schweppes sold its plant in Kenya because price controls made its operation unprofitable.[39] On their part, governments can, as a last resort, expropriate the affiliate, especially if they see that the benefits are greater than the cost.[40]

The approaches and procedures that have been discussed are quite negative by nature. However, relations between the firm and its host country, or the home country for that matter, by no means need to be adversarial. The multinational corporation can satisfy its own objectives and find local acceptability by implementing activities that contribute to the following six goals: (1) efficiency, by applying appropriate technologies to different markets; (2) equity, by reinvesting earnings; (3) participation, by establishing local training programs; (4) creativity, by introducing indigenous R&D capabilities in local affiliates; (5) stability, by consistently and openly explaining behavior; and (6) diversity, by developing product lines specifically for local demand.[41]

Environmental concerns are emerging as an important part of a multinational's normal business operations. Multinationals have extensive involvement in many pollution-intensive industries and have, by definition, mobility to seek attractive locations for production sites. However, multinationals give rise to higher expectations and often are expected to assume leadership roles in environmental protection due to their financial, managerial, and technological strength. Studies have found that although multinationals may have adopted lower environmental standards in their developing-country operations, they maintain overall a better record than their local counterparts.[42]

Dealing with Other Constituents

Multinational corporations also have to manage their relations with various other constituencies. This is crucial because even small, organized groups of stockholders may influence control of the firm, particularly if the ownership base is wide. Companies must, therefore, adopt policies that will allow them to effectively respond to pressure and criticism, which will continue to surface. Oliver Williams suggests that these policies have the following traits: (1) openness about corporate activities with a focus on how these activities enhance social and economic performance; (2) preparedness to utilize the tremendous power of the multinational corporation in a responsible manner and, in the case of pressure, to counter criticisms swiftly; (3) integrity, which very often means that the marketer must avoid not only actual wrongdoing but the mere appearance of it; and (4) clarity, because it will help ameliorate hostility if a common language is used with those pressuring the corporation.[43] He proposes that the marketer's role is one of enlightened self-interest: Reasonable critics understand that the business cannot compromise the bottom line.

Complicating the situation very often is the fact that groups in one market criticize what the marketer is doing in another market. For example, the Interfaith Center on Corporate Responsibility urged Colgate-Palmolive to stop marketing Darkie toothpaste under that brand name in Asia because of the term's offensiveness elsewhere in the world. Darkie toothpaste has been sold in Thailand, Hong Kong, Singapore, Malaysia, and Taiwan, packaged in a box that features a likeness of Al Jolson in blackface.[44]

Organizations have two general human resource objectives.[45] The first is the recruitment and retention of a workforce made up of the best people available for the jobs to be done. The recruiter in international operations will need to keep in mind both cross-cultural and cross-national differences in productivity and expectations when selecting employees. Once they are hired, the firm's best interest lies in maintaining a stable and experienced workforce.

The second objective is to increase the effectiveness of the workforce. This depends to a great extent on achieving the first objective. Competent managers or workers are likely to perform at a more effective level if proper attention is given to factors that motivate them.

To attain the two major objectives, the activities and skills needed include:

1. Personnel planning and staffing, the assessment of personnel needs, and recruitment.
2. Personnel training to achieve a perfect fit between the employee and the assignment.
3. Compensation of employees according to their effectiveness.
4. An understanding of labor-management relations in terms of how these two groups view each other and how their respective power positions are established.

This section of the chapter will examine the management of human resources in international business from two points of view, first that of managers and then that of labor.

MANAGING MANAGERS

The importance of the quality of the workforce in global business cannot be overemphasized, regardless of the stage of globalization of the firm. As seen in the Global Learning Experience 9.5, global business systems are complex and dynamic and require competent people to develop and direct them.

Early Stages of Globalization

The marketing or sales manager of the firm typically is responsible for beginning export activities. As foreign sales increase, an export manager will be appointed and given the responsibility for developing and maintaining customers, interacting with the firm's intermediaries, and planning for overall market expansion. The export manager also must champion the international effort within the company because the general attitude among employees may be to view the domestic market as more important. Another critical function is the supervision of export transactions, particularly documentation. The requirements are quite different for international transactions than for domestic ones, and sales or profits may be lost if documentation is not properly handled. The first task of the new export manager, in fact, is to hire a staff to handle paperwork that typically had previously been done by a facilitating agent, such as a freight forwarder.

The firm starting international operations will usually hire an export manager from outside rather than promote from within. The reason is that knowledge of the product or industry is less important than international experience. The cost of learning through experience to manage an export department is simply too great from the firm's standpoint.

The manager who is hired will have obtained experience through Foreign Service duty or with another corporation. In the early stages, a highly entrepreneurial spirit with a heavy dose of trader mentality is required. Even then, management should not expect the new export department to earn a profit for the first year or so.

Advanced Stages of Globalization

As the firm progresses from exporting to an international division to foreign direct involvement, manpower-planning activities will initially focus on need vis-à-vis various

GLOBAL LEARNING EXPERIENCE 9.5

Global Talent Search

Many corporate decision makers have realized that human resources play at least as significant a role as advanced technology and economies of scale when it comes to competing successfully in the new global world order.

According to a 1994 *International Business* survey of 1,200 mid-size U.S. multinationals with annual sales of $1 billion or less, senior executives seek managers who are culturally diverse but responsive to the direction of headquarters. Most U.S.–based companies try to fill senior positions abroad with locals, using expatriates only for such specific projects as technology transfer. However, the same companies send their U.S. middle managers the clear message that overseas operations are so important to corporate welfare that solid international experience is needed for advancement.

While major markets in Europe and Asia possess deeper pools of managerial talent than ever before, many of the nationals prefer to work for domestic rather than foreign firms. In particularly short supply are marketing managers and it is especially hard to find people who have the cross-cultural experience to make good regional managers.

Very few global leaders are born that way; that is, with an international childhood, command of several languages, and an education from an institution with an international focus. In most cases, they have to be trained and nurtured carefully. To achieve this goal, companies are using various approaches.

Gaynor Kelley, chairman, and Riccardo Pigliucci, president and COO, of Perkin-Elmer Corp., which makes analytical instruments, frequently attend monthly meetings of senior executives held at production and sales locations around the world. The meetings permit the two men to assess the performance of company managers—be they nationals or expatriates. Pigliucci is a prime example of Perkin-Elmer's desire to breed global managers. He joined the company as a chemist from the University of Milan, and served stints in product development and sales and marketing in Europe and North America.

NetFRAME Systems Inc., a maker of networking computers, gathers its expatriate and non–U.S. managers at its California headquarters every quarter. The idea is to encourage joint planning and problem solving on a global basis. By building cross-border employee cooperatives, companies not only can design solutions to better meet the needs of various customer constituencies, they can develop organizations where the sun never sets on innovation.

Some companies take what can be called the "Dutch uncle" approach. They pair a key overseas manager with one at headquarters. This helps top management to keep tabs on the manager's progress and helps the manager stay in tune with what is going on back at the source of power. Such mentoring can also provide vital input into management succession strategizing.

Companies spending time and money creating and training global talent naturally want to retain it for as long as possible. Loctite Corp., maker of industrial adhesives, offers global opportunity, professional challenge, and a competitive compensation package to keep its rising stars. Of the three approaches, claims the company, compensation is the least important to the managers.

SOURCES: "Globe Trotter: If It's 5:30, This Must Be Tel-Aviv," *Business Week,* October 17, 1994, 102; and Lori Ioannou, "It's a Small World After All," *International Business,* February 1994, 82–88.

FIGURE 9.6 An Example of a Global Management Development System

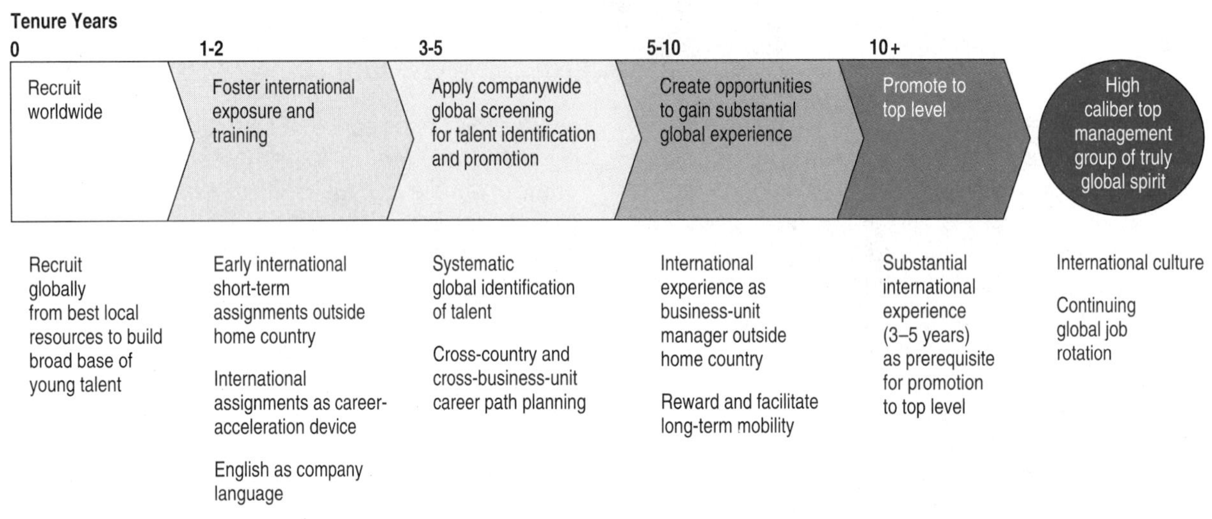

SOURCE: Ingo Theuerkaut, "Reshaping the Global Organization," *McKinsey Quarterly* No. 3 (1991): 103–119.

markets and functions. Existing personnel can be assessed and plans made to recruit, select, and train employees for positions that cannot be filled internally. The four major categories of overseas assignments are: (1) CEO, to oversee and direct the entire operation; (2) functional head, to establish and maintain departments and ensure their proper performance; (3) troubleshooters, who are utilized for their special expertise in analyzing, and thereby preventing or solving, particular problems; and (4) white- or blue-collar workers.[46] International oil companies typically assign a great many employees overseas when the available pool is small, such as in Saudi Arabia.

One of the major sources of competitive advantage of global corporations is their ability to attract talent around the world. These corporations need systematic management-development systems, with the objective of creating and carefully allocating management personnel. An example of this is provided in Figure 9.6. In global corporations, there is no such thing as a universal global manager, but a network of global specialists in four general groups of managers has to work together.[47] Global business (product) managers have the task to further the company's global-scale efficiency and competitiveness. Country managers have to be sensitive and responsive to local market needs and demands but, at the same time, be aware of global implications. Functional managers have to make sure that the corporation's capabilities in technical, manufacturing, marketing, human resource, and financial expertise are linked and can benefit from each other. Corporate executives at headquarters have to manage interactions between these three groups of managers as well as identify and develop the talent to fill these positions.

Global companies should show clear career paths for managers assigned overseas and develop the systems and the organization for promotion. This approach serves to eliminate many of the perceived problems and thus motivates managers to seek out foreign assignments. Foreign assignments can occur at various stages of the manager's tenure. In the early stages, assignments may be short term, such as a membership in an international task force or 6 to 12 months at headquarters in a staff function. Later, an individual may serve as a business-unit manager overseas. Many companies use cross-postings to other countries or across product lines to further an individual's acculturation to the corporation.[48] A period in a head-office department or a subsidiary will not only provide an understanding of different national cultures and attitudes but also improve an individual's "know-who" and therefore establish unity and common sense of purpose necessary for the property implementation of global programs.

Compensation

A firm's international compensation program has to be effective in (1) providing an incentive to leave the home country on a foreign assignment, (2) maintaining a given standard of living, (3) taking into consideration career and family needs, and (4) facilitating reentry into the home country.[49] To achieve these objectives, firms pay a high premium beyond base salaries to induce managers to accept overseas assignments. The costs to the firm are 2 to 2.5 times the cost of maintaining a manager in a comparable position at home. U.S. firms traditionally offer their employees more high-value perks, such as bigger apartments.[50]

The compensation of the manager overseas can be divided into two general categories: (1) base salary and salary-related allowances and (2) nonsalary-related allowances. Although incentives to leave home are justifiable in both categories, they create administrative complications for the personnel department in tying them to packages at home and elsewhere. As the number of transfers increases, firms develop general policies for compensating the manager rather than negotiate individually on every aspect of the arrangement.

Base Salary and Salary-Related Allowances A manager's **base salary** depends on qualifications, responsibilities, and duties, just as it would for a domestic position. Furthermore, criteria applying to merit increases, promotions, and other increases are administered as they are domestically. Equity and comparability with domestic positions are important, especially in ensuring that repatriation will not cause cuts in base pay.[51] For administrative and control purposes, the compensation and benefits function in multinational corporations is most often centralized.[52]

base salary
salary not including special payments such as allowances paid during overseas assignments

The cost of living varies considerably around the world. The purpose of the **cost of living allowance (COLA)** is to enable the manager to maintain as closely as possible the same standard of living that he or she would have at home.

cost of living allowance (COLA)
allowance paid during assignment overseas to enable the employee to maintain the same standard of living as at home

The **foreign service premium** is actually a bribe to encourage a manager to leave familiar conditions and adapt to new surroundings. Although the methods of paying the premium vary, as do its percentages, most firms pay it as a percentage of the base salary. The percentages range from 10 to 25 percent of base salary. One variation of the straightforward percentage is a sliding scale by amount—15 percent of the first $20,000, then 10 percent, and sometimes a ceiling beyond which a premium is not paid. Another variation is by duration, with the percentages decreasing with every year the manager spends abroad. Despite the controversial nature of foreign service premiums paid at some locations, they are a generally accepted competitive practice. Global Learning Experience 9.6 illustrates the various compensation adjustments necessary to relocate an U.S. executive to Tokyo.

foreign service premium
bribe to encourage a manager to leave familiar conditions and adapt to new surroundings

The environments in which a manager will work and the family will live vary dramatically. To compensate for this type of expense and adjustment, firms pay **hardship allowances.** These allowances are based on U.S. State Department Foreign Post Differentials. The percentages vary from zero (for example, the manager in Helsinki) to 50 percent (as in Monrovia). The higher allowances typically include a danger pay extra added to any hardship allowance.[53]

hardship allowances
allowance paid during an assignment to an overseas area that requires major adaptation

Housing costs and related expenses are typically the largest expenditure in the expatriate manager's budget. Firms usually provide a **housing allowance** commensurate with the manager's salary level and position. When the expatriate is the country

housing allowance
allowance paid during assignment overseas to provide living quarters

Getting Compensated for the Overseas Assignment

The cost of sending an American executive to an overseas location can be staggering compared to a relocation in the United States. In many parts of the world, the basic cost of living and maintaining the same quality of life as in the United States is much higher than stateside. This requires that any individual agreeing to an overseas transfer fully understand beforehand the nature and costs of living in a particular city to ensure that he or she will be adequately compensated.

Consider housing. In the United States, because of its large middle-class population, housing of all types and costs is reasonably available. Overseas, however, some locations do not have a middle class to speak of, so adequate housing that maintains the U.S. quality of life is expensive.

An extremely important item is healthcare. It is only when people leave the country that they appreciate how good the U.S. healthcare system really is. If first-class medical assistance is not available at the overseas location, then some provision must be made for the cost of transferring a sick or injured expatriate to it.

What currency will you be paid in? Even if your U.S. salary is increased by a cost-of-living allowance and you are paid in dollars, you could be in for a problem if the value of the dollar falls against the currency of the foreign land.

The U.S. expatriate will usually be paying taxes in two countries. Some allowance must be made to offset, or equalize, the additional tax burden.

Then there is the cost of education for the children. Unless the transfer is to an English-speaking country, private English-speaking schools will be required—at a cost.

Often overlooked is the cost of "socializing." In some cities of the world, most of the U.S. expatriates belong to the "American Club"—an oasis of American culture in what can seem a sometimes inhospitable foreign land. Being a member of the club offers a refuge of friendly surroundings, as well as social and business contacts, and can be the difference between a happy and an unhappy tour of duty in a foreign land. But membership also has a price tag.

Additional Compensation that Enabled One U.S. Executive to Cover Living Costs in Tokyo

Cost of living increase:	25 percent of base salary.
Housing:	$68,000 for a four bedroom apartment.
Education:	$52,000 for two children to attend English-speaking private school.
Automobile:	Provided by the company.
Parking allowance:	$7,200
Health insurance:	Kept company health plan, understanding that he would return to the U.S. in the event of a major health problem.
Taxes:	Company reimbursement for extra tax costs.
Currency:	Paid in U.S. dollars, which fell in value against the yen, causing some hardship.

SOURCE: Data from "Financial Survival in Tokyo," *New York Times,* Your Money Section, December 10, 1994.

manager for the firm, the housing allowance will provide for suitable quarters in which to receive business associates. In most cases, firms set a range within which the manager must find housing. For common utilities, firms either provide an allowance or pay the costs outright.

One of the major determinants of the manager's lifestyle abroad is taxes. A U.S. manager earning $100,000 in Canada would pay nearly $40,000 in taxes—in excess of $10,000 more than in the United States. For this reason, 90 percent of U.S. multinational corporations have **tax-equalization** plans. When a manager's overseas taxes are higher than at home, the firm will make up the difference. However, in countries with a lower rate of taxation, the company simply keeps the difference. The firms' rationalization is that "it does not make any sense for the manager in Hong Kong to make more money than the guy who happened to land in Singapore."[54]

tax-equalization
reimbursement by the company when an employee in an overseas assignment pays taxes at a higher rate than if he or she were at home

Nonsalary-Related Allowances Other types of allowances are made available to ease the transition into the period of service abroad.[55] Typical allowances during the transition stage include (1) a relocation allowance to compensate for the additional expense of a move, such as purchase of electric converters; (2) a mobility allowance as an incentive to managers to go overseas, usually paid in a lump sum and as a substitute for the foreign service premium (some companies pay 50 percent at transfer, 50 percent at repatriation); (3) allowances related to housing, such as home sale or rental protection, shipment and storage of household goods, or provision of household furnishings in overseas locations; (4) automobile protection in terms of covering possible losses on the sale of a car or cars at transfer and having to buy others overseas, usually at a higher cost; (5) travel expenses, using economy-class transportation except for long flights (for example, from Washington to Taipei); and (6) temporary living expenses, which may become substantial if housing is not immediately available—as for the expatriate family that had to spend a year at a hotel in Beijing, for example.

Education for children is one of the major concerns of expatriate families. Free public schooling may not be available and the private alternatives expensive. In many cases, children may have to go to school in a different country. Firms will typically reimburse for such expenses in the form of an **education allowance.** In the case of college education, firms reimburse for one round-trip airfare every year, leaving tuition expenses to the family.

education allowance
reimbursement by the company for dependent educational expenses incurred while a parent is assigned overseas

Repatriation

Returning home may evoke mixed feelings on the part of the **expatriate** and the family. Their concerns are both professional and personal. Even in two years, dramatic changes may have occurred not only at home but also in the way the individual and the family perceive the foreign environment. At worst, reverse culture shock may emerge.

expatriate
one living in a foreign land; a corporate manager assigned to an overseas location

The most important professional issue is finding a proper place in the corporate hierarchy. See Global Learning Experience 9.7. If no provisions have been made, a returning manager may be caught in a holding pattern for an intolerable length of time. For this reason, Dow Chemical, for example, provides each manager embarking on an overseas assignment with a letter that promises a job at least equal in responsibility upon return. Furthermore, because of their isolation, assignments abroad mean greater autonomy and authority than similar domestic positions. Both financially and psychologically, many expatriates find the overseas position difficult to give up. Many executive perks, such as club memberships, will not be funded at home. For financial reasons, for example, many officers of the U.S. and Foreign Commercial Service dread a summons for a two-year tour in the United States.

The Foreign Assignment—Will It Help Your Career or Hinder It?

It is commonly believed that a successful foreign assignment is a sure-fire ticket to the ranks of senior management. Magazine and newspaper articles, corporate presidents, industry organizations, international business courses and textbooks (including this one) all extol the virtues and advantages of gaining overseas experience. It all sounds so logical—an executive with broad global experience should be worth his or her weight in gold. This Global Learning Experience presents a balanced perspective—a reality check on the subject.

A Conference Board study of 152 U.S. corporations found that 80 percent of the executives who had completed foreign assignments felt that their companies did not value the experience they gained overseas. Upon return to the United States, these executives felt ignored and isolated from the company mainstream. The study indicated that about 15 percent of these executives leave their companies within 12 to 18 months and nearly 40 percent leave after three years. Two-thirds of the companies do not have procedures or plans for dealing with their returned employees. About 75 percent of expatriate executives expect a successful overseas assignment to enhance their careers, but only 10 percent are actually promoted upon return.

The problem seems to be the classic one of "out of sight, out of mind." Once the manager leaves on the foreign assignment, he or she is effectively out of the mainstream of corporate activity and decision making. Others quickly move into the void, and in due course the expatriate executive may be all but forgotten.

Complicating the problem is the continual restructuring and/or downsizing of the corporate world. Human resource professionals are faced with the challenge of expatriate career reinsertion into smaller home operations. Indeed, 60 percent of the respondents to the Conference Board study reported that less than 25 percent of expatriates know what their return position will be four months prior to their return.

This doesn't mean that overseas assignments are of no value—they are. It really means that before leaving, the manager should have clear agreement on: (1) the specific objectives to be achieved overseas, (2) when the assignment is to be concluded, and most important (3) the position that successful achievement of the assignment will lead to. Is this too much to ask of the company? The answer is that even if you have the agreement, there is no guarantee that it will be honored three or four years hence, but at least it is the basis for discussions and is a moral obligation of the firm. Without the agreement, you're likely to become another statistic in a future Conference Board study.

Finally, once overseas, keep in frequent contact with headquarters and offset the out of sight, out of mind syndrome. In any event, make the most of the foreign assignment and gather as much experience as possible. If it turns out that your company doesn't appreciate your contributions, don't worry—there are many other firms who are willing to pay dearly for a seasoned executive with in-depth foreign experience.

SOURCE: Data from The Conference Board, *Managing Expatriates' Return.* Report No. 1148-96-RR.

WWW

The family, too, may be reluctant to give up their special status. In India, expatriate families have servants for most of the tasks they perform themselves at home. Many longer-term expatriates are shocked by increases in the prices of housing and education in the United States. For the many managers who want to stay abroad, this may mean a change of company or even career—from employee to independent businessperson. According to one study, 20 percent of the employees who complete overseas assignments want to leave the company upon their return.[56]

This alternative is not an attractive one for the company, which stands to lose valuable individuals who could become members of an international corps of managers. Therefore, planning for repatriation is necessary.[57] A four-step process can be used for this purpose. The first step involves an assessment of foreign assignments in terms of environmental constraints and corporate objectives, making sure that the latter are realistically defined. The second stage is preparation of the individual for an overseas assignment, which should include a clear understanding of when and how repatriation takes place. During the actual tour, the manager should be kept abreast of developments at headquarters, especially in terms of career paths. Finally, during the actual reentry, the manager should receive intensive organizational reorientation, reasonable professional adjustment time, and counseling for the entire family on matters of, for example, finance. A program of this type allows the expatriate to feel a close bond with headquarters regardless of geographical distance.

MANAGING LABOR PERSONNEL

None of the firm's objectives can be realized without a labor force, which can become one of the firm's major assets or its major problems depending on the relationship that is established. Because of local patterns and legislation, headquarters' role in shaping these relations is mainly advisory, limited to setting the overall tone for the interaction. Many of the practices adopted in one market or region may easily come under discussion in another, making it necessary for multinational corporations to set general policies concerning labor relations. Often, multinational corporations have been instrumental in bringing about changes in the overall work environment in a country.

Labor strategy can be viewed from three perspectives: (1) the participation of labor in the affairs of the firm, especially as it affects performance and well-being; (2) the role and impact of unions in the relationship; and (3) specific human resource policies in terms of recruitment, training, and compensation.

Labor Participation in Management

Over the past quarter century, many changes have occurred in the traditional labor-management relationship as a result of dramatic changes in the economic environment and the actions of both firms and the labor force. The role of the worker is changing both at the level of the job performed and in terms of participation in the decision-making process. To enhance workers' role in decision making, various techniques have emerged: self-management, codetermination, minority board membership, and work councils. In striving for improvements in quality of work life, programs that have been initiated include flextime, quality circles, and work-flow reorganization. Furthermore, employee ownership has moved into the mainstream.

Labor Participation in Decision Making The degree to which workers around the world can participate in corporate decision making varies considerably. Rights of information, consultation, and codetermination develop on three levels:

1. The shop-floor level, or direct involvement; for example, the right to be consulted in advance concerning transfers.

2. The management level, or through representative bodies; for example, work council participation in setting of new policies or changing of existing ones.
3. The board level, for example, labor membership on the board of directors.[58]

codetermination management approach in which employees are represented on supervisory boards to facilitate communication and collaboration between management and labor

minority participation participation by a group having less than the number of votes necessary for control

In some countries, employees are represented on the supervisory boards to facilitate communication between management and labor by giving labor a clearer picture of the financial limits of management and by providing management with new awareness of labor's point of view. This process is called **codetermination.** In Germany, companies have a two-tiered management system with a supervisory board and the board of managers, which actually runs the firm. The supervisory board is legally responsible for the managing board. Reactions to codetermination vary. Six European nations—Sweden, the Netherlands, Norway, Luxembourg, Denmark, and France—have introduced their own versions and report lower levels of labor strife.[59] In some countries, labor has **minority participation.** In the Netherlands, for example, work councils can nominate (not appoint) board members and can veto the appointment of new members appointed by others. In other countries, such as the United States, codetermination has been opposed by unions as an undesirable means of cooperation, especially when management-labor relations are confrontational.

A tradition in labor relations, especially in Britain, is *work councils.* These bodies provide labor a say in corporate decision making through a representative body, which may consist entirely of workers or of a combination of managers and workers. The councils participate in decisions on overall working conditions, training, transfers, work allocation, and compensation. In some countries, such as Finland and Belgium, workers' rights to direct involvement, especially as it involves their positions, are quite strong.

The countries described are unique in the world. In many countries and regions, workers have few if any of these rights. The result is long-term potential for labor strife. A good example is the Republic of Korea, where, during 1987, riots by workers demanding better overall work conditions disrupted an economy noted for its dependence on export trade.

The Role of Labor Unions The role of labor unions varies from country to country, often because of local traditions in management-labor relations. The variations include the extent of union power in negotiations and the activities of unions in general. In Europe, especially in the Northern European countries, collective bargaining takes

Team building at Avery Label Systems in the United Kingdom, a division of Avery Dennison Corporation, has created "work cell teams" that have full product responsibility throughout the production process. Each team member can perform every other team member's job. *SOURCE:* Courtesy of Avery Dennison Corporation.

place between an employers' association and an umbrella organization of unions, on either a national or a regional basis, establishing the conditions for an entire industry. On the other end of the spectrum, negotiations in Japan are on the company level, and the role of larger-scale unions is usually consultative. Another striking difference emerges in terms of the objectives of unions and the means by which they attempt to attain them. In the United Kingdom, for example, union activity tends to be politically motivated and identified with political ideology. In the United States, the emphasis has always been on improving workers' overall quality of life.

Human Resource Policies

The objectives of a human resource policy pertaining to workers are the same as for management: to anticipate the demand for various skills and to have in place programs that will ensure the availability of employees when needed. For workers, however, the firm faces the problem on a larger scale and does not have, in most cases, an expatriate alternative. This means that, among other things, when technology is transferred for a plant, it has to be adapted to the local workforce.

Although most countries have legislation and restrictions concerning the hiring of expatriates, many of them—for example, some of the EU countries and some oil-rich Middle Eastern countries—have offset labor shortages by importing large numbers of workers from countries such as Turkey and Jordan. The EU by design allows free movement of labor. A mixture of backgrounds in the available labor pool of course puts a strain on personnel development. As an example, the firm may incur considerable expense to provide language training to employees. In Sweden, a certain minimum amount of language training must be provided for all "guest workers" at the firm's expense.

Bringing a local labor force to the level of competency desired by the firm may also call for changes. As an example, managers at Honda's plant in Ohio encountered a number of problems: Labor costs were 50 percent higher and productivity 10 percent lower than in Japan. Automobiles produced there cost $500 more than the same models made in Japan and then delivered to the United States. Before Honda began to produce the Accord in the United States, it flew 200 workers representing all areas of the factory to Japan to learn to build Hondas the Sayama way and then to teach their coworkers these skills.[60]

Compensation of the workforce is a controversial issue. Of course, payroll expenses must be controlled in order for the firm to remain competitive; on the other hand, the firm must attract in appropriate numbers the type of workers it needs. The compensation packages of U.S.-based multinational companies have come under criticism, especially when their level of compensation is lower in developing countries than the United States. Criticism has occurred even when the salaries or wages paid were substantially higher than the local average.[61]

Comparisons of compensation packages are difficult because of differences in the packages that are shaped by culture, legislation, collective bargaining, taxation, and individual characteristics of the job. In Northern Europe, for example, new fathers can accompany their wives on a two-week paternity leave at the employer's expense.

QUESTION *If you spent a week in Beijing, about how many dogs would you see on the streets? One or two, perhaps one hundred to one thousand, many more than one thousand?*

ANSWER! *You'd see only a handful of dogs in Beijing. The Chinese government discourages their presence in the cities. Also, many Chinese favor a good boiled dog on a cold winter's evening. At the Ye Wei Xiang (Wild Fragrance) restaurant in Beijing, a house specialty is fragrant dog meat stew.*

CONTROL

The function of the organizational structure is to provide a framework in which objectives can be met. A set of instruments and processes is needed, however, to influence the performance of organizational members so as to meet the goals. Controls focus on means to verify and correct actions that differ from established plans. Compliance needs to be secured from subordinates through different means of coordinating specialized and interdependent parts of the organization.[62] Within an organization, control serves as an integrating mechanism. Controls are designed to reduce uncertainty, increase predictability, and ensure that behaviors originating in separate parts of the organization are compatible and in support of common organizational goals despite physical, psychic, and temporal distances.[63]

The critical issue here is the same as with organizational structure: What is the ideal amount of control? On the one hand, headquarters needs controls to ensure that international activities contribute the greatest benefit to the overall organization. On the other hand, they should not be construed as a code of laws and subsequently allowed to stifle local initiative.

This section will focus on the design and functions of control instruments available for international business operations, along with an assessment of their appropriateness. Emphasis will be placed on the degree of formality of controls used by firms.

In the design of the control systems, a major decision concerns the object of control. Two major objects are typically identified: output and behavior.[64] Output controls consist of balance sheets, sales data, production data, product-line growth, or a performance review of personnel. Measures of output are accumulated at regular intervals and forwarded from the foreign locale to headquarters, where they are evaluated and critiqued based on comparisons to the plan or budget. Behavioral controls require the exertion of influence over behavior after—or, ideally, before—it leads to action. These can be achieved through the preparation of manuals on such topics as sales techniques, to be made available to subsidiary personnel, or through efforts to fit new employees into the corporate culture.

In order to institute either of these measures, instruments of control have to be decided upon. The general alternatives are either formalized control or cultural control.[65] Formal controls consist of regulations and rules that outline the desired levels of performance. Cultural controls, on the other hand, are much less formal and are the results of shared beliefs and expectations among the members of an organization. Table 9.5 provides examples of various formal and cultural control mechanisms.

Formalized Control The elements of a formalized control system are (1) an international budget and planning system, (2) the functional reporting system, and (3) policy manuals used to direct functional performance.

Budgets refers to shorter-term guidelines regarding investment, cash, and personnel policies, while *plans* refers to formalized plans with more than a one-year horizon.

TABLE 9.5

Examples of Control Mechanisms

Formal Controls	Cultural Controls
Financial and operating plans	Company language
Budgets (operating expenses, advertising, and capital budgets)	Dress codes
Standards of performance	Employee recruiting and selection process
Periodic financial reports, i.e., cash flow, inventories, etc.	Employee indoctrination process
Monthly financial statements, i.e., income statement and balance sheet	Company creed and philosophy
Comparison of planned vs. actual results	Companywide and regional meetings
Sales reports (orders received, sales call reports)	Criteria for promotion
Reports of manufacturing operations	Bonus payment plans
Standard operating procedures	
Company policies concerning expense accounts	
Individual performance evaluations	
Marketing and management information systems	
Customer complement and complaint analyses	

The budget and planning process is the major control instrument in headquarters-subsidiary relationships. Although systems and their executives vary, the objective is to achieve as good a fit as possible with the objectives and characteristics of the firm and its environment.

The budgetary period is typically one year, since it is tied to the accounting systems of the multinational. The budget system is used for four main purposes: (1) allocation of funds among subsidiaries, (2) planning and coordination of global production capacity and supplies, (3) evaluation of subsidiary performance, and (4) communication and information exchange among subsidiaries, product organizations, and corporate headquarters.[66] Long-range plans vary dramatically, ranging from two years to ten years in length, and are more qualitative and judgmental in nature. However, shorter periods, such as two years, are the norm, considering the added uncertainty of diverse foreign environments.

Functional reports are another control instrument used by headquarters in managing subsidiary relations. These vary in number, complexity, and frequency. The structure and elements of these reports are typically highly standardized to allow for consolidation at the headquarters level.

Since the frequency of reports required from subsidiaries is likely to increase due to the globalization trend, it is essential that subsidiaries see the rationale for this often time-consuming exercise. Two approaches, used in tandem, can facilitate this process: participation and feedback. The first refers to avoiding the perception at subsidiary levels that reports are "art for art's sake" by involving the preparers in the actual use of the reports. When this is not possible, feedback about their consequences is warranted. Through this process, communication is enhanced as well.

On the behavioral front, headquarters may want to guide the way in which subsidiaries make decisions and implement agreed upon strategies. U.S.-based multinationals tend to be far more formalized than their Japanese and European counterparts, with a heavy reliance on manuals for all major functions.[67] These manuals discuss such items as recruitment, training, motivation, and dismissal policies. The use of manuals is in direct correlation with the required level of reports from subsidiaries, discussed in the previous section.

Cultural Controls Cultural controls require an extensive socialization process to which informal, personal interaction is central. Substantial resources have to be spent to train the individual to share the corporate cultures, or "the way things are done at the company."[68] To build common vision and values, managers spend a substantial share of their first months at Matsushita in what the company calls "cultural and spiritual training." They study the company credo, the "Seven Spirits of Matsushita," and the philosophy of the founder, Konosuke Matsushita. Then they learn how to translate these internalized lessons into daily behavior and operational decisions. Although more prevalent in Japanese organizations, many Western entities have similar programs, such as Philips's "organization cohesion training" and Unilever's "indoctrination."[69]

The primary instruments of cultural control are the careful selection and training of corporate personnel and the institution of self-control. The choice of cultural controls can be justified if the company enjoys a low turnover rate; they are thus applied when companies can offer and expect lifetime or long-term employment, as many firms do in Japan.

Corporations rarely use one pure control mechanism. Rather, most use both quantitative and qualitative measures. Corporations are likely, however, to place different levels of emphasis on different types of performance measures and on how they are derived.

Exercising Control

In their global operations, U.S.-based multinationals place major emphasis on obtaining quantitative data. Although this allows for good centralized comparisons against standards and benchmarks or cross-comparisons among different corporate units, it entails several drawbacks. In the global environment, new dimensions—such as inflation, differing rates of taxation, and exchange rate fluctuations—may distort the performance evaluation of any given individual or organizational unit. For the global corporation, measurement of whether a business unit in a particular country is earning a superior return on investment relative to risk may be irrelevant to the contribution an investment may make worldwide, or to the long-term results of the firm. In the short term, the return may even be negative.[70] Therefore, the control mechanism may quite inappropriately indicate reward or punishment. Standardizing the information received may be difficult if the various environments involved fluctuate and require frequent and major adaptations. Further complicating the issue is the fact that although quantitative information may be collected monthly, or at least quarterly, environmental data may be acquired annually or "now and then," especially when a crisis seems to loom on the horizon. In order to design a control system that is acceptable not only to headquarters but also to the organization and individuals abroad, great care must be taken to use only relevant data. Major concerns, therefore, are the data collection process and the analysis and utilization of data. Evaluators need management information systems that provide for greater comparability and equity in administering controls. The more behaviorally based and culture oriented controls are, the more care needs to be taken.[71]

In designing a control system, management must consider the costs of establishing and maintaining it versus the benefits to be gained. Any control system will require investment in a management structure an in systems design. Consider, for example, costs associated with cultural controls: Personal interaction, use of expatriates, and training programs are all quite expensive. Yet these expenses may be justified by cost savings through lower employee turnover, an extensive worldwide information system, and an improved control system.[72] Moreover, the impact goes beyond the administrative component. If controls are misguided or too time consuming, they can slow or undermine the strategy implementation process and thus the overall capability of the firm. The result will be lost opportunities or, worse yet, increased threats. In addition, time spent on reporting takes time from everything else, and if the exercise is seen as mundane, results in lowered motivation. A parsimonious design is therefore imperative. The control system should collect all the information required and trigger all the intervention necessary; however, it should not lead to the pulling of strings by a puppeteer.

The impact of the environment has to be taken into account as well, in two ways. First, the control system must measure only those dimensions over which the organization has actual control. Rewards or sanctions make little sense if they are based on dimensions that may be relevant to overall corporate performance but over which no influence can be exerted, such as price controls. Neglecting the factor of individual performance capability would send wrong signals and severely harm motivation. Second, control systems have to be in harmony with local regulations and customs. In some cases, however, corporate behavioral controls have to be exercised against local customs even though overall operations may be affected negatively. This type of situation occurs, for example, when a subsidiary operates in markets in which unauthorized facilitating payments are a common business practice.

SUMMARY

This chapter discussed three of the four functions of management: organizing, directing and managing personnel, and controlling.

Global firms can choose from a variety of organizational structures, ranging from a domestic organization that handles ad hoc export orders to a full-fledged global organization. The choice will depend heavily on the degree of globalization of the firm, the diversity of global activities, and the relative importance of product, area, function, and customer variables in the process. A determining factor is also the degree to which headquarters wants to decide important issues concerning the whole corporation and the subsidiaries individually. Organizations that function effectively still need to be revisited periodically in order to ensure that they remain responsive to a changing environment. Some of this responsiveness is showing up not as structural changes, but rather in how the entities conduct their internal business.

Multinational corporations are probably among the most powerful economic institutions of all time. They not only have production facilities in multiple countries but also look beyond their own domestic markets for opportunities. They scan the globe to expand their operations. Multinational corporations are no longer the monopoly of the United States, Western Europe, and Japan; many developing countries have a growing amount of foreign direct investment.

Foreign direct investment is sought by nations and firms alike. Nations are looking to foreign direct investment for economic development and employment, firms for new markets, resources, and increased efficiency. The relationship between the entities involved—the firm, the host government, and the home government—has to be managed to make it mutually beneficial. The critical role of foreign direct investment is technology transfer, which means the transfer of a combination of hardware, software, and skills for production processes.

Firms attract global managers from a number of sources, both internal and external. In the earlier stages of globalization, recruitment must be external. Later, an internal pool often provides candidates for transfer. The decision then becomes whether to use home-country, host-country, or third-country nationals.

Labor can no longer be considered as simply services to be bought. Increasingly, workers are taking an active role in the decision making of the firm and in issues related to their own welfare. Various programs are causing dramatic organizational change, not only by enhancing the position of workers but by increasing the productivity of the workforce as well. Workers employed by the firm usually are local, as are the unions that represent them. Their primary concerns in working for a multinational firm are job security and benefits. Unions are therefore cooperating across national boundaries to equalize benefits for workers employed by the same firm in different countries.

The control function takes on major importance for multinationals, due to the high variability in performance resulting from divergent local environments and the need to reconcile local objectives with the corporate goal of synergism. While it is important to grant autonomy to country organizations so that they can be responsive to local market needs, it is of equal importance to ensure close cooperation among units to optimize corporate effectiveness.

Control can be exercised through either bureaucratic means emphasizing formal reporting and evaluation of benchmark data or cultural means, in which norms and values are understood by the individuals and entities that make up the corporation. U.S. firms typically rely more on the bureaucratic controls, while MNCs from other countries frequently run operations abroad through informal means and rely less on stringent measures.

Key Terms and Concepts

product structure
geographic area structure
strategic leader
contributor
implementor
black hole
functional structure
process structure
customer structure
mixed structure
matrix structure
decentralization
centralization
coordinated decentralization
not-invented-here syndrome
ethnocentric
polycentric
regiocentric
geocentric
brain drain
base salary
cost of living allowance (COLA)
foreign service premium
hardship allowance
housing allowance
tax equalization
education allowance
expatriate
codetermination
minority participation

Questions

1. Explain what is meant by organizing by function, geography, product, and customer.
2. What are some of the factors that might influence the design of the organizational structure?
3. What changes in the firm and/or environment might cause a firm to abandon the functional approach?

4. Discuss the various criteria that have been suggested for determining if a company is an MNC. Which do you think is appropriate?
5. Develop a list of advantages and disadvantages of direct foreign investment based on the perspective of the host country.
6. Design a program for the training and development of global managers.
7. a. Discuss the role of labor unions in Europe compared with those in the United States.

   b. Comment on the idea of labor participation in management.
8. Distinguish between formalized and cultural controls. Give a few examples of each.

Recommended Readings

Alknafaji, Abbass F. *Competitive Global Management.* Delray Beach, Fla.: St. Lucie Press, 1995.

Austin, James. *Managing in Developing Countries.* New York: Free Press, 1990.

Badaracoo, Joseph L. *The Knowledge Link: Competing Through Strategic Alliances.* Boston: Harvard Business School Press, 1991.

Beamish, Paul W., Allen Morrisson, and P. Rosenzweig, *International Management,* 3rd ed. Barr Ridge, Ill.: Irwin, 1997.

Black, J. Stewart, Hal B. Gregsen, and Mark E. Mendenhall. *Global Assignments.* San Francisco, Calif.: Jossey-Bass Publishers, 1992.

Casse, Pierre. *Training for the Multicultural Manager.* Washington, D.C.: SIETAR, 1987.

Casson, Mark. *Multinational Corporations.* New York: Stockton Press, 1989.

Collins, Timothy, and Thomas Doorley. *A Guide to International Joint Ventures and Strategic Alliances.* Homewood, Ill.: Richard D. Irwin, 1990.

Costin, Harry. *Managing in the Global Economy.* Fort Worth, Tex.: Harcourt Brace & Co., 1996.

Culpan, Refik, ed. *Multinational Strategic Alliances.* Binghampton, N.Y.: International Business Press, 1993.

Davidson, William H., and José de la Torre. *Managing the Global Corporation.* New York: McGraw-Hill, 1989.

Deresicy, Helen. *International Management,* 2nd ed. New York, N.Y.: Addison-Wesley, 1997.

Dowling, Peter J., and Randall S. Schuler, *International Dimensions of Human Resource Management.* Boston: PWS-Kent, 1990.

Dunning, John H., ed. *The United Nations Library on Transnational Corporations.* Volumes 1–20. New York: Routledge, 1993.

Fatehi, Kamal. *International Management.* Upper Saddle River, N.J.: Prentice-Hall, 1996.

Goehle, Donna D. *Decision-Making in Multinational Corporations.* Ann Arbor, Mich.: UMI Research Press, 1980.

Harris, Philip, and Robert T. Moran. *Managing Cultural Differences.* Houston, Tex.: Gulf, 1990.

Hodgetts, Richard, and Fred Luthans. *International Management,* 3rd ed. New York: McGraw-Hill, 1997.

Lewis, Jordan D. *Partnerships for Profit: Structuring and Managing Strategic Alliances.* New York: The Free Press, 1990.

Luostarinen, Reijo, and Lawrence Welch. *International Business Operations.* Helsinki, Finland: Kyriiri Oy, 1990.

Marquardt, Michael J., and Dean W. Engel. *Global Resource Development.* Englewood Cliffs, N.J.: Prentice-Hall, 1993.

Mendenhall, Mark, and Gary Oddou. *International Human Resource Management.* Boston: PWS–Kent, 1991.

Porter, Michael E., ed. *Competition in Global Industries.* Boston: Harvard Business School Press, 1986.

Pucik, Vladimir, Noel M. Tichy, and Carole K. Barnett. *Globalizing Management: Creating and Leading the Competitive Organization.* New York: John Wiley, 1992.

Rubner, Alex. *The Might of the Multinationals.* Westport, Conn.: Quorum Books, 1990.

Strafford, David C., and Richard H. A. Purkis. *Director of Multinationals.* New York: Stockton Press, 1989.

Walmsley, John. *The Development of International Markets.* Higham, Mass.: Graham & Trotman, 1990.

Notes

1. Michael Z. Brooke, *International Management: A Review of Strategies and Operations* (London: Hutchinson, 1986), 173–174.

2. William H. Davidson and Philippe Haspeslagh, "Shaping a Global Product Organization," *Harvard Business Review* 59 (March/April 1982): 69–76.
3. See Joan P. Curhan, William H. Davidson, and Suri Rajan, *Tracing the Multinationals* (Cambridge, Mass.: Ballinger, 1977); M. E. Wicks, *A Comparative Analysis of the Foreign Investment Evaluation Practices of U.S.-based Multinational Corporations* (New York: McKinsey & Co., 1980); and Lawrence G. Franko, "Organizational Structures and Multinational Strategies of Continental European Enterprises," in *European Research in International Business*, eds. Michel Ghertman and James Leontiades (Amsterdam, Holland: North Holland Publishing Co., 1977).
4. Davidson and Haspeslagh, "Shaping a Global Product Organization."
5. Bill Saporito, "Campbell Soup Gets Piping Hot," *Fortune,* September 9, 1991, 94–98.
6. Christopher A. Bartlett and Sumantra Ghoshal, "Tap Your Subsidiaries for Global Research," *Harvard Business Review* 64 (November–December 1986): 87–94.
7. John A. Quelch and Edward J. Hoff, "Customizing Global Marketing," *Harvard Business Review* 64 (May–June 1986): 59–68.
8. Richard I. Kirkland, Jr., "Entering a New World of Boundless Competition," *Fortune,* March 14, 1988, 18–22.
9. Louis Kraar, "Your Rivals Can Be Your Allies," *Fortune,* March 27, 1989, 66–76.
10. Daniel Robey, *Designing Organizations: A Macro Perspective* (Homewood, Ill.: Richard D. Irwin, 1982), 327.
11. Thomas H. Naylor, "International Strategy Matrix," *Columbia Journal of World Business* 20 (Summer 1985): 11–19.
12. "Kodak's Matrix System Focuses on Product Business Units," *Business International,* July 18, 1988, 221–223.
13. Thomas J. Peters, "Beyond the Matrix Organization," *Business Horizons* 22 (October 1979): 15–27.
14. Christopher Bartlett, "MNCs: Get Off the Reorganization Merry-Go-Round," *Harvard Business Review* 60 (March/April 1983): 138–146.
15. Christopher A. Bartlett and Sumantra Ghoshal, "Matrix Management: Not a Structure, A Frame of Mind," *Harvard Business Review* 68 (July–August 1990): 138–145.
16. United Nations, *Multinational Corporation in World Development* (New York: United Nations, 1973), 23.
17. Alan M. Rugman, *Inside the Multinationals* (London: Croom Helm, 1981), 31.
18. Raymond Vernon, *Sovereignty at Bay: The Multinational Spread of United States Enterprises* (New York: Basic Books, 1971), 11.
19. Alan M. Rugman, "Risk Reduction by International Diversification," *Journal of International Business Studies* 7 (Fall 1976): 75–80.
20. Donald Kircher, "Now the Transnational Enterprise," *Harvard Business Review* 42 (March–April 1964): 6–10, 172–176.
21. Howard V. Perlmutter, "The Tortuous Evolution of the Multinational Corporation," *Columbia Journal of World Business* 4 (January–February 1969): 9–18; Howard V. Perlmutter and David A. Heenan, "How Multinational Should Your Top Managers Be?" *Harvard Business Review* 52 (November–December 1974): 121–132; and Yoram Wind, Susan P. Douglas, and Howard V. Perlmutter, "Guidelines for Developing International Marketing Strategies," *Journal of Marketing* 37 (April 1973): 14–23.
22. John M. Stopford, *The World Directory of Multinational Enterprises* (London: Macmillan, 1982), xii.
23. Krishna Kumar and Maxwell G. McLeod, *Multinationals from Developing Countries* (Lexington, Mass.: Lexington Books, 1981), xv–xxv.
24. "Korea's Biggest Firm Teaches Junior Execs Strange Foreign Ways," *The Wall Street Journal,* December 30, 1992, 1.
25. George Chandler, "The Innocence of Oil Companies," *Foreign Policy* 27 (Summer 1977): 60.
26. United Nations Economic and Social Council, *Transnational Corporations in World Development: A Reexamination* (New York: United Nations, 1978), 13.
27. Herbert E. Meyer, "Trudeau's War on U.S. Business," *Fortune,* April 6, 1981, 74–82.
28. "The Difference Japanese Management Makes," *Business Week,* July 14, 1986, 47–50.
29. Edward B. Flowers, "Oligopolistic Reactions in European and Canadian Direct Investment in the United States," *Journal of International Business Studies* 7 (Fall–Winter 1976): 43–55.
30. Philip D. White and Edward W. Cundiff, "Assessing the Quality of Industrial Products," *Journal of Marketing* 42 (January 1978): 80–86.
31. Frank G. Vukmanic, Michael R. Czinkota, and David A. Ricks, "National and International Data Problems and Solutions in the Empirical Analysis of Intra-Industry Direct Foreign Investment," *Multinationals as Mutual Invaders: Intra-Industry Direct-Foreign Investment,* ed. A. Erdilek (Beckenham, Kent: Croom Helm Ltd., 1985), 160–184.
32. "Japan, U.S.A.," *Business Week,* July 14, 1986, 45–46.
33. Stephen Kobrin, "Assessing Political Risk Overseas," *The Wharton Magazine* 6, No. 2 (1981): 6–14.
34. Marie E. Wicks Kelly and George C. Philippatos, "Comparative Analysis of the Foreign Investment Evaluation Practices by U.S.-based Manufacturing Multinational Companies," *Journal of International Business Studies* 13 (Winter 1982): 19–42.
35. Jack N. Behrman. *National Interests and the Multinational Enterprise* (Englewood Cliffs, N.J.: Prentice-Hall, 1970), 7.

36. Casson, *Alternatives to the Multinational Enterprise,* 4.
37. Lawrence Franko, "Foreign Direct Investment in Less Developed Countries: Impact on Home Countries," *Journal of International Business Studies* 9 (Winter 1978): 55–65.
38. Peter P. Gabriel, "MNCs in the Third World: Is Conflict Unavoidable?" *Harvard Business Review* 50 (July–August 1972): 91–102.
39. Victor H. Frank, "Living with Price Control Abroad," *Harvard Business Review* 62 (March–April 1984): 137–142.
40. Thomas W. Shreeve, "Be Prepared for Political Changes Abroad," *Harvard Business Review* 62 (July–August 1984): 111–118.
41. Jack N. Behrman, *Industrial Policies: International Restructuring and Transnationals* (Lexington, Mass.: Lexington Books, 1984), 114–115.
42. William C. Frederick, "The Moral Authority of Transnational Corporations," *Journal of Business Ethics* 10 (March 1991): 165–178; and United Nations, *World Investment Report: An Executive Summary* (New York: United Nations, 1993), 11–12.
43. Oliver Williams, "Who Cast the First Stone?" *Harvard Business Review* 62 (September–October 1984): 151–160.
44. "Church Group Gnashes Colgate-Palmolive," *Advertising Age,* March 24, 1986, 46.
45. Herbert G. Heneman and Donald P. Schwab, "Overview of the Personnel/Human Resource Function," in *Perspectives on Personnel/Human Resource Management,* eds. Herbert G. Heneman and Donald P. Schwab (Homewood, Ill.: Irwin, 1986), 3–11.
46. Richard D. Hays, "Expatriate Selection: Insuring Success and Avoiding Failure," *Journal of International Business Studies* 5 (Summer 1974): 25–37.
47. Christopher A. Bartlett and Sumantra Ghoshal, "What Is a Global Manager?" *Harvard Business Review* 70 (September–October 1992): 124–132.
48. Floris Majlers, "Inside Unilever: The Evolving Transnational Company," *Harvard Business Review* 70 (September–October 1992): 46–52.
49. Raymond J. Stone, "Compensation: Pay and Perks for Overseas Executives," *Personnel Journal* (January 1986): 64–69.
50. "Americans Lead the HK Perks Race," *Sunday Morning Post,* July 12, 1992, 14.
51. *1987 Professional Development Seminar: International Compensation* (Phoenix, Ariz.: American Compensation Association, 1987), module 1.
52. Brian Toyne and Robert J. Kuhne, "The Management of the International Executive Compensation and Benefits Process," *Journal of International Business Studies* 14 (Winter 1983): 37–49.
53. U.S. Department of State, *Indexes of Living Costs Abroad, Quarters Allowances, and Hardship Differentials,* January 1993, Table 1.
54. "How to Make a Foreign Job Pay," *Business Week,* December 23, 1985, 84–85.
55. *1987 Professional Development Seminar: International Compensation,* modules 4 and 5.
56. Nancy J. Adler, *International Dimensions of Organizational Behavior* (Boston: PWS-Kent, 1990), chapter 4.
57. Michael G. Harvey, "The Other Side of Foreign Assignments: Dealing with the Repatriation Dilemma," *Columbia Journal of World Business* 16 (Spring 1981): 79–85.
58. Industrial Democracy in Europe International Research Group, *Industrial Democracy in Europe* (Oxford, England: Clarendon Press, 1981), chapter 14.
59. Richard D. Robinson, *Internationalization of Business* (Hinsdale, Ill.: Dryden, 1986), chapter 3.
60. Rice, "America's New No. 4 Automaker — Honda."
61. Oliver Williams, "Who Cast the First Stone?" *Harvard Business Review* 62 (September–October 1984): 151–160.
62. Amitai Etzioni, *A Comparative Analysis of Complex Organizations* (Glencoe, England: Free Press, 1961).
63. William G. Egelhoff, "Patterns of Control in U.S., U.K., and European Multinational Corporations," *Journal of International Business Studies* 15 (Fall 1984) 73–83.
64. William G. Ouchi, "The Relationship between Organizational Structure and Organizational Control," *Administrative Science Quarterly* 22 (March 1977): 95–112.
65. B. R. Baliga and Alfred M. Jaeger, "Multinational Corporations: Control Systems and Delegation Issues," *Journal of International Business Studies* 15 (Fall 1984): 25–40.
66. Laurent Leksell, *Headquarters-Subsidiary Relationships in Multinational Corporations* (Stockholm, Sweden: Stockholm School of Economics, 1981), chapter 5.
67. Anant R. Negandhi and Martin Welge, *Beyond Theory Z* (Greenwich, Conn.: JAI Press, 1984), 16.
68. Richard Pascale, "Fitting New Employees into the Company Culture," *Fortune,* May 28, 1984, 28–40.
69. Bartlett and Ghoshal, "Matrix Management: Not a Structure, A Frame of Mind."
70. John J. Dyment, "Strategies and Management Controls for Global Corporations," *Journal of Business Strategy* 7 (Spring 1987): 20–26.
71. Hans Schoellhammer, "Decision-Making and Intraorganizational Conflicts in Multinational Companies," presentation at the Symposium on Management of Headquarter-Subsidiary Relationships in Transnational Corporations, Stockholm School of Economics, June 2–4, 1980.
72. Alfred M. Jaeger, "The Transfer of Organizational Culture Overseas: An Approach to Control in the Multinational Corporation," *Journal of International Business Studies* 14 (Fall 1983): 91–106.

Parker Pen Company

Parker Pen Company, the manufacturer of writing instruments based in Janesville, Wisconsin, is one of the world's best-known companies in its field. It sells its products in 154 countries and considers itself number one in "quality writing instruments," a market that consists of pens selling for $3 or more.

In early 1984, the company launched a global marketing campaign in which everything was to have "one look, one voice," and with all planning to take place at headquarters. Everything connected with the selling effort was to be standardized. This was a grand experiment of a widely debated concept. A number of international companies were eager to learn from Parker's experiences.

Results became evident quickly. In February 1985, the globalization experiment was ended, and most of the masterminds of the strategy either left the company or were fired. In January 1986, the writing division of Parker Pen was sold for $100 million to a group of Parker's international managers and a London venture-capital company. The U.S. division was given a year to fix its operation or close.

GLOBALIZATION

Globalization is a business initiative based on the conviction that the world is becoming more homogeneous and that distinctions between national markets are not only fading but, for some products, they will eventually disappear. Some products, such as Coca-Cola and Levi's, have already proven the existence of universal appeal. Coke's "one sight, one sound, one sell" approach is a legend in the world of global marketers. Other companies have some products that can be "world products," and some that cannot and should not be. For example, if cultural and competitive differences are less important than their similarities, a single advertising approach can exploit these similarities to stimulate sales everywhere, and at far lower cost than if campaigns were developed for each individual market.

Compared with the multidomestic approach, globalization differs in three basic ways:

1. The global approach looks for similarities between markets. The multidomestic approach ignores similarities.
2. The global approach actively seeks homogeneity in products, image, marketing, and advertising message. The multidomestic approach produces unnecessary differences from market to market.
3. The global approach asks, "Should this product or process be for world consumption?" The multidomestic approach, relying solely on local autonomy, never asks the question.

Globalization requires many internal modifications as well. Changes in philosophy concerning local autonomy, concern for local operating results rather than corporate performance, and local strategies designed for local—rather than global—competitors are all delicate issues to be solved. By design, globalization calls for centralized deci-

---

SOURCE: This case was prepared by Ilkka A. Ronkainen for discussion purposes and not to exemplify correct or incorrect decision making. The case draws facts from Joseph M. Winski and Laurel Wentz, "Parker Pen: What Went Wrong?" *Advertising Age,* June 2, 1986, 1, 60–61, 71, and Lori Kesler, "Parker Rebuilds a Quality Image," *Advertising Age,* March 21, 1988, 49.

sion making; therefore, the "not-invented-here" syndrome becomes a problem. This can be solved by involving those having to implement the globalization strategy at every possible stage as well as keeping lines of communication open.[1]

GLOBALIZATION AT PARKER PEN COMPANY

In January 1982, James R. Peterson became the president and CEO of Parker Pen. At that time, the company was struggling, and global marketing was one of the key measures to be used to revive the company. While at R. J. Reynolds, Peterson had been impressed with the industry's success with globalization. He wanted for Parker Pen nothing less than the writing instrument equivalent of the Marlboro man.

For most of the 1960s and 1970s, a weak dollar had lulled Parker Pen into a false sense of security. About 80 percent of the company's sales were abroad, which meant that when local currency profits were translated into dollars, big profits were recorded.

The market was changing, however. The Japanese had started marketing inexpensive disposable pens with considerable success through mass marketers. Brands such as Paper Mate, Bic, Pilot, and Pentel each had greater sales, causing Parker's overall market share to plummet to 6 percent. Parker Pen, meanwhile, stayed with its previous strategy and continued marketing its top-of-the-line pens through department stores and stationery stores. Even in this segment, Parker Pen's market share was eroding because of the efforts of A. T. Cross Company and Montblanc of Germany.

Subsidiaries enjoyed a high degree of autonomy in marketing operations, which resulted in broad and diverse product lines and forty different advertising agencies handling the Parker Pen account worldwide.

When the dollar's value skyrocketed in the 1980s, Parker's profits plunged and the loss of market share became painfully evident.

Peterson moved quickly upon his arrival. He trimmed the payroll, chopped the product line to 100 (from 500), consolidated manufacturing operations, and ordered an overhaul of the main plant to make it a state-of-the-art facility. Ogilvy & Mather was hired to take sole control of Parker Pen advertising worldwide. The logic behind going with one agency instead of the forty formerly employed was cost savings and the ability to coordinate strategies on a worldwide basis. Among the many agencies terminated was Lowe Howard-Spink in London, which had produced some of the best advertising for Parker Pen's most profitable subsidiary. The immediate impact was a noticeable decline in employee morale and some expressed bitterness at the subsidiary being dictated to by a subsidiary that had been cross-subsidizing the American operations over the years.

A decision was also made to go aggressively after the low end of the market. The company would sell an upscale line called Premier, mainly as a positioning device. The biggest profits were to come from a roller-ball pen called Vector, selling for $2.98. Plans were drawn to sell an even cheaper pen called Itala—a disposable pen never thought possible at Parker.

Three new managers, to be known as Group Marketing, were brought in. All three had extensive marketing experience, most of it in international markets. Richard Swart, who became marketing vice president for writing instruments, had handled 3M's image advertising worldwide and taught company managers the ins and outs of marketing planning. Jack Marks became head of writing instruments advertising. At Gillette, he had orchestrated the worldwide marketing of Silkience hair care products. Carlos

[1]Laurence Farley, "Going Global: Choices and Challenges," presented at the American Management Association Conference, June 10, 1985. Chicago, Illinois.

Del Nero, brought in to be Parker's manager of global marketing planning, had gained broad international experience at Fisher-Price. The concept of marketing by centralized direction was approved.

The idea of selling pens the same way everywhere did not sit well with many Parker subsidiaries and distributors. Pens were indeed the same, but markets, they believed, were different: France and Italy fancied expensive fountain pens; Scandinavia was a ballpoint market. In some markets, Parker could assume an above-the-fray stance; in others it had to get into the trenches and compete on price. Nonetheless, headquarters communicated to them all:

> Advertising for Parker Pens (no matter model or mode) will be based on a common creative strategy and positioning. The worldwide advertising theme, "Make Your Mark With Parker," has been adopted. It will utilize similar graphic layout and photography. It will utilize agreed-upon typeface. It will utilize the approved Parker logo/design. It will be adapted from centrally supplied materials.

Swart insisted that the directives were to be used only as "starting points" and that they allowed for ample local flexibility. The subsidiaries perceived them differently. The U.S. subsidiary, especially, fought the scheme all the way. Ogilvy & Mather London strongly opposed the "one world, one brand, one advertisement" dictum. Conflict arose, with Swart allegedly shouting at one of the meetings: "Yours is not to reason why, yours is to implement." Local flexibility in advertising was out of the question. (see Figure 1).

The London-created "Make Your Mark" campaign was launched in October 1984. Except for language, it was essentially the same: long copy, horizontal layout, illustrations in precisely the same place, the Parker logo at the bottom, and the tag line or local equivalent in the lower right-hand corner. Swart once went to the extreme of suggesting that Parker ads avoid long copy and use just one big picture.

Problems arose on the manufacturing side. The new $15 million plant broke down repeatedly. Costs soared, and the factory turned out defective products in unacceptable numbers. In addition, the new marketing approach started causing problems as well. Although Parker never abandoned its high-end position in foreign markets, its concentration on low-priced, mass distribution products in the United States caused dilution of its image and ultimately losses of $22 million in 1985. Conflict was evident internally, and the board of directors began to turn against the concept of globalization.

In January 1985, Peterson resigned. Del Nero left the company in April; Swart was fired in May, Marks in June. When Michael Fromstein became CEO of the company, he assembled the company's country managers in Janesville and announced: "Global marketing is dead. You are free again."

Questions for Discussion

1. Should the merits of global marketing be judged by what happened at Parker Pen Company?
2. Was the globalization strategy sound for writing instruments? If yes, what was wrong in the implementation? If not, why not?
3. What marketing miscalculations were made by the advocates of the globalization effort at Parker Pen?
4. The task is to "fix it or close it." What should be done?

Ads for Parker's Global Campaign **FIGURE 1**

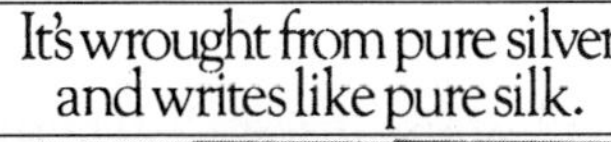

It's wrought from pure silver and writes like pure silk.

Our Sterling Silver Fountain Pen is an instrument made for beautiful writing. Important facts. Lovely thoughts. Notable notes. Masterful memos.

Its smoothness never impedes the flash of inspiration from mind to page.

Its uniquely styled grip graces a body that balances effortlessly in the hand.

A body made from solid sterling silver, the finest that can be worked.

But thoughts can flow only as smoothly as ink. So we made its nib from 18-carat gold, split and shaped by hand and subjected to 131 separate checks.

A truly magnificent pen from Parker, earning its own certificate of quality from the craftsmen who made it.

Buy one, and even if you never write anything magnificent, you'll never write anything but magnificently.

Make your mark with a Parker

PARKER

Avec le Parker en argent, même vos mémos seront des petits chefs-d'œuvre.

Tout pourrait porter à croire que le Parker Premier a été pensé pour écrire des chefs-d'œuvre.

Une femme qui a pardonné à son homme, ne doit pas lui réchauffer ses péchés pour le petit-déjeuner

Venise... c'est comme avaler d'un seul coup une entière boîte de bonbons liquoreux.

Ainsi, il ne nous étonnerait pas que Truman Capote en ait usé pour écrire des perles telles que: 'Venise,... c'est comme avaler d'un seul coup une entière boite de bonbons liquoreux.' Ou Marlène Dietrich quand elle écrivit que 'Une femme qui a pardonné à son homme ne doit pas lui réchauffer ses péchés pour le petit-déjeuner'.

Laissez transparaître votre personnalité jusque dans vos notes les plus brèves. Bien sûr, il n'est pas donné à tout le monde d'écrire des chefs-d'œuvre, mais même un simple mémo peut être rédigé avec style.

Notre Premier Rollerball en argent massif est l'instrument par excellence qui vous permettra de jeter vos idées soudaines sur le papier, ou d'écrire vos idées les plus profondes. Le Parker Premier est si bien équilibré qu'écrire n'impose plus aucun effort.

C'est avec une fluidité extrême que les idées s'en échappent et qu'elles viennent impeccablement se poser sur le papier. Même l'encre du Rollerball a été l'objet d'une attention particulière: à base d'eau, elle est mieux absorbée par le papier que d'autres encres qui ont tendance à rester à sa surface.

Prenez le Premier Rollerball de Parker entre vos doigts. Essayez-le. Et si vous n'êtes pas de ceux qui écrivent des chefs-d'œuvre, sachez que c'est avec un chef-d'œuvre que vous écrivez.

Exprimez-vous avec un Parker

PARKER

VIDEO CASE

The Culture of Commerce

The world has always been a diverse place. So it's no surprise that each country has its own way of doing business. That's particularly true of the capitalistic global giants Germany, Japan, and the United States.

In the Japanese culture, employees enter what has customarily been regarded as a lifetime agreement. They pledge their best efforts, and are loyal to their companies almost as though a familial bond existed. This sentiment endures because company objectives are regarded as morally correct. Often, ceremonies play an important part in reinforcing these ties. The company's side of the bargain is fulfilled by a defacto guarantee of lifetime employment. Recently, this implied contract has been tested. Difficult economic times have made employee cutbacks unavoidable. But most workers who were laid off saw their companies honor the spirit of this agreement. Instead of offering severance pay or job counseling, many companies actually found their workers new positions.

Hard economic times have also come to Germany. But in Germany's capitalistic system, government and private industries work in close cooperation. The law requires companies to come up with written plans detailing how layoffs can be minimized, if not avoided completely. And within the companies themselves, labor and management also closely coordinate activities. Generally, all parties—government, industry, and labor—give input on how best to keep workers employed.

The approach of U.S. companies to layoffs is quite different. Workers are often given only two weeks notice—some are shown the door without even being allowed to clean out their desks—once the company no longer needs them. Retraining and job placement help is spotty. Management focuses instead on daily stock prices and quarterly profits.

Three cultures, all capitalistic, but with very different value systems and approaches to dealing with employees. A closer look inside some actual companies can shed even more light on the issue.

The midsized German steelmaker, VSG, is a recent example of the cooperation between the government and private industry. The company had to cut costs to stay competitive. But simply turning the workers out on the street was not considered an option. Instead, a joint group of company managers and state officials retrained the workers who would have been laid off. In Germany, this is viewed as managing structural changes in the economy.

The German approach contrast sharply with how things are done in the U.S. steel industry. Take the Monongahela Valley Works Steel Co. in Pittsburgh. It spent $250 million in capital improvements for the specific purpose of cutting labor costs. US Steel put off similar reinvestment in automation so long that it was forced to lay off huge numbers of workers when the plan was finally implemented. Many steelworkers have been unemployed as long as two years, and it's estimated that as many as 80 percent have left the region for good. Those that remain have often had to take a two-thirds cut in pay for the work they can find.

US Steel CEO Tom Usher's view of the company's responsibilities to terminated workers offers insight into the U.S. mentality. Essentially, he thinks economic fluctuations that put people out of work are simply the reality of capitalism. Finding another job is the worker's own problem. And if they require retraining, the company has no obligation to offer assistance. According to Usher, management's primary responsibility is to maximize returns to shareholders.

Questions for Discussion

1. Would the German model of cooperation between government and industry work in the United States? Why or why not?
2. What long-term repercussions, if any, do U.S. companies face as a result of their hard-line approach to layoffs?
3. Who should management feel primarily responsible to: the workforce or the stockholders?

The way things work at Daimler Benz in Germany would probably give a U.S. executive like Usher heartburn. The automaker's board is divided evenly between owners and representatives for the company's 360,000 employees. The workforce is the nation's highest paid, and it also has the most benefits. Cooperation between labor and management is smooth and fluid. Work councils determine the best and most efficient method of getting work done. Strikes are extremely rare. The system is known as codetermination.

The actual way power is shared at Daimler Benz might well give Usher a heart attack. Labor can veto the appointment of any top executive, including the CEO. Not surprisingly, this set-up has led to fair and evenhanded dealings between the company's top brass and the rank and file. Power sharing also has led to strong alliances between executives and labor representatives. It helps that most German companies, including Daimler Benz, don't focus on the short term, but instead have business plans that stretch as long as seven years.

Again, things are different in the United States, and a couple of companies graphically illustrate this fact. Probably nowhere else in the world are labor-management relations as poisoned as at Caterpillar Inc. In 1992, CEO Don Fites, arguing that labor costs had to be reduced or the company could not compete in the world market, effectively declared war on labor. The bitterness that ensued is unmatched in anything seen since the early 1900s. Many union workers are back on the job, but they are resentful of the company and most put forth only the minimum level of effort.

Recent problems at General Motors can be attributed in large part to a compliant board of directors. This hand-picked group of cronies failed in their function as overseers under the assumption that CEO Roger Smith knew how to run the business. But Smith spent $77 billion in capital improvements that made the auto maker inflexible and inefficient because of overcapacity. As for employees, GM management doesn't have any labor representatives on the board. Most executives never even see actual workers.

The Mitsubishi company is a good example of why multinationals from anywhere else in the world find it tough to crack the Japanese market. Mitsubishi literally has millions of products and processes. But the major difference between Mitsubishi and its overseas competitors is this: Its executives will seldom do business with any company not underneath their corporate umbrella. These groups, called keiretsus, work together and provide complimentary services, including manufacturing processes, marketing, distribution, and the like. Often, banks are part of the process as well. And when governmental assistance is also thrown in, a formidable entity is created. Few outside companies can effectively compete.

Capitalistic purists may scream foul, but the governments of many countries now actively support their private industries. A while back, and much to the chagrin of the Boeing Corporation and other U.S. aircraft manufacturers, the governments of France, Germany, Britain, and Spain cooperated on the development of the Airbus. They soon captured nearly a third of the world market. They eclipsed McDonnell Douglas and were closing in on Boeing, both of which were still smarting from Defense Department contract cutbacks.

Boeing counterpunched with its 777 aircraft. The plane represented a leap forward for the company. The old-line approach was scrapped, and the plane was largely designed by computer. Teams of engineers, factory hands, marketing personnel, and even financial people all assisted. And in the biggest break with tradition, Boeing permitted eight other airline manufacturers to offer input on how best to create the jet.

Top executives came away from the experience convinced that a cooperative effort between government and industry is the only way to keep the playing field level and to give United States a chance to be competitive in world markets.

Even a quick overview of various economies and companies leaves little doubt that capitalistic systems differ greatly. Culture and customs are huge factors in how capitalism evolves. But some fundamentals can be pinned down. Just as companies must stay close to their customer base, so too must they stay close to their employees. U.S. management and labor may never develop the rapport that exists in Japan or Germany, but it certainly would appear they could benefit from a closer relationship than now exists.

Questions for Discussion

4. List what you think are the three primary strengths of the Japanese and German systems. What are the principal shortcomings?
5. If you were a U.S. executive, what approach would you take to out-maneuver the keiretsu groups and crack the Japanese market?
6. What are the biggest differences in the way Boeing designed and built the 777 from the traditional design and manufacturing process?

Ecological Cooling: The Fridge from Eastern Germany

In March of 1993, mass production of the world's first refrigerator that works without damaging the earth's vital ozone layer began in Niederschmiedeberg, the hometown of a small eastern German firm. FORON Domestic Appliances GmbH offers the first "green" refrigerator, completely free of chlorofluorocarbons (CFCs). The road to this achievement, however, was not easy.

CFCS AND THE MONTREAL AGREEMENT

For decades, chlorofluorocarbons (CFCs) were the refrigerants of choice worldwide. They were nontoxic, nonflammable, and energy-efficient. The price of \$.57 per pound in 1980 also made CFCs quite inexpensive. Introduced in the 1930s, CFCs by 1985 represented a worldwide market of \$1.5 billion a year.

SOURCE: This case was written by Michael R. Czinkota based on discussions with Dr. Juergen Lembke, head of marketing, FORON GmbH, and reports by German and U.S. media. Financial and logical support from the U.S. Information Agency (USIA) is gratefully acknowledged.

Since 1974, scientists had theorized that CFCs could deplete the earth's ozone layer, which shields the earth from the sun's harmful ultraviolet rays. As a result of these implications, and due to public pressure, the U.S. government banned the use of CFCs in aerosol propellants in 1978. Due to the nonavailability of reasonable substitutes, however, the use of CFCs in refrigerators and air conditioners continued to be permitted.

After scientists observed a hole in the ozone layer over Antarctica, nations from around the world enacted the 1987 Montreal Protocol, which called for a 50 percent cut in CFC use by mid-1998. Given the growing public concern with environmental issues, the protocol was subsequently revised twice: in 1990, it was agreed that the 50 percent reduction in most CFCs was to be achieved by 1995 and the 1992 revision banned all CFC use by 1996.

The ban had a chilling effect on the producers of cooling devices since they depended heavily on CFCs. For example, to reduce energy consumption, refrigerators are insulated with polyurethane foam. During manufacture, the foam is saturated with 300 to 600 grams of CFCs. The gas remains in the foam and because it insulates better than air, the gas provides for heat insulation. The disadvantage of CFC-formed polyurethane is that the CFCs gradually diffuse out of the foam and are replaced by air. The CFC escapes into the atmosphere and destroys the ozone layer. The energy efficiency of the refrigerators also deteriorates considerably over the years due to the CFC-air exchange.

CFCs also contribute to the actual refrigeration process. Due to their thermodynamic properties, CFCs are highly temperature responsive to compression and expansion, therefore allowing an efficient cooling process to take place. Even though hermetically sealed, a leaky pipe or uncontrolled disposal can result in the gradual release of up to 250 grams of CFCs.

DKK SCHARFENSTEIN

Deutsche Kilma and Krafmaschinen AG was founded in the German state of Saxony in 1927. The firm concentrated on producing heating and cooling devices together with compressors. In the 1950s the East German communist regime took over the firm as state property and renamed it dkk Scharfenstein. As the only firm in Eastern Europe producing both refrigerators and compressors, dkk Scharfenstein (DKK) soon achieved a leadership position in the region. By 1989, the firm's 5,200 employees produced more than 1 million refrigerators and 1.5 million compressors. Every apartment built by the East Germany regime had a refrigerator made by DKK. Ten million East German households had a DKK fridge; 80 percent of households had its freezers.

With the fall of the Berlin Wall on November 9, 1989, and the collapse of communism in Eastern Europe, DKK's markets collapsed as well. Long-term export contracts were rescinded. At the same time, domestic demand declined precipitously as stylish new products from West Germany became available. By 1992, production had declined to 200,000 refrigerators, and employment had shrunk to 1,000. In light of the continuing decline of its business, dkk Scharfenstein was taken over by Germany's Treuhandanstalt, the German government's privatization arm.

DEVELOPMENT OF THE ECO-FRIDGE

dkk Scharfenstein had been familiar with the ecological problems of CFCs since the mid-eighties. At that time, the firm had considered a switch of hydrofluorocarbon (HFC) 134a. This new chemical did not contain chlorine, but still made use of fluor, which contributes to the greenhouse effect and to global warming. However, these plans were abandoned for two reasons. First, the price of HFC 134a was far more than that of CFC. Second, unlike its Western counterparts, Scharfenstein was unable to obtain the product from Western markets due to export control regulations promulgated by the Multilateral Committee for Export Controls (COCOM). While HFC 134a was available in the Soviet Union, only very limited quantities were offered for sale.

After 1990, HFC 134a became freely available in eastern Germany. By that time, however, the Scharfenstein staff already was working on a different project. In conjunction with Professor Harry Rosin, head of the Dortmund Institute for Hygiene, Scharfenstein had focused on a mix of butane and propane gases to cool its refrigerators. The ingredients were environmentally friendly and, with newly designed compressors, the equipment operated with less electrical power.

Management presented the new product to Treuhand, in an effort to stave off the liquidation of the firm. Treuhand attempted to interest a consortium consisting of the German firms Bosch and Siemens in acquiring Scharfenstein. After a cursory review, however, both firms decided that the new technology was too radical, unproven, and flammable and withdrew from all discussions. They, like major competitors such as Whirlpool and AEG, would continue to concentrate on HFC 134a research and production. Although expensive, HFC 134a now was competitive because new taxes had increased CFC prices to more than $5 per pound. In addition, major investments had already been made into HFC production. For example, in its race against DuPont and Elf Atochem, the British firm Imperial Chemical Industries PLC alone already had invested nearly $500 million into HFC development. To ensure that retailers would share their perspective, major producers of refrigerators supplied leaflets that warned about the dangers of explosion of fridges filled with propane and butane.

Truehand did not approve the production of the new fridge. In light of mounting losses, an additional 3,560 Scharfenstein employees were laid off and Treuhand announced plans to liquidate the firm.

Facing the shutdown of its operations, Scharfenstein's management decided to go public with its new product. Information on the CFC-free fridge was sent to all manufacturers of refrigeration equipment, none of whom showed any interest. However, interest did materialize from unexpected quarters: The leadership of the Greenpeace organization. This worldwide environmental nonprofit group quickly recognized the benefits of the new fridge. It commissioned ten prototype models to be produced, and after finding them satisfactory, mounted a $300,000 advertising campaign in favor of the production of "greenfreeze." Intense negotiations with retailers brought in orders and options for 70,000 of the refrigerators.

The future of Scharfenstein brightened immediately. The German Ministry for the Environment supported a capital infusion of $3 million into the company. Shortly thereafter, Treuhand rescinded the layoffs that had been announced. By 1993, the firm was acquired by a consortium of British, Kuwaiti, and German investors and renamed FORON Household Appliances GmbH.

Since then, FORON has received various environmental prizes and labels. The firm was awarded the government's coveted Blue Angel symbol for environmental friendliness. The German Technical Society awarded its safety seal of approval. The business magazine *DM* named the fridge its product of the year.

The giant German appliance manufacturers, which once scorned the new technology as "impossible, dangerous, and too energy-consuming," now are scrambling to put out their own green refrigerators. Major efforts for CFC-free refrigerators are also being undertaken by U.S. and Japanese manufacturers. In the United States, a group of utilities offered $30 million to the manufacturer that designed the most energy efficient refrigerator without using CFCs.

FORON expects to produce more than 160,000 eco-fridges per year and actively is exploring the possibility of exports. Inquiries have been received from China, Japan, the United States, India, Australia, and New Zealand. Even though the product is priced some 5 to 10 percent more than conventional models, the firm believes that "consumers who are environmentally aware will pay the price."

Questions for Discussion

1. Why is the acceptance of innovation sometimes inhibited by established industry players?
2. Evaluate the role of Greenpeace in promoting the eco-fridge. Is such an activity appropriate for a nonprofit organization?
3. What motivated Scharfenstein's investment in environmentally friendly technology?
4. How can governments encourage the development of environmentally responsive technology?

VIDEO CASE

ESPRIT

"Europe now has a position in technologies where we are no longer in danger of losing the pace." This statement by a European executive underlines the fact that Europe's experiment in cooperative research and development (R&D) is paying off. Since the mid-1980s, companies and research institutes from Denmark to Spain have pooled their resources on megaprojects ranging from genetic engineering to thermonuclear fusion. One of the most ambitious efforts is ESPRIT (European Strategic Programs for Research in Information Technologies). In the first period of ESPRIT (ESPRIT 1), 1984–1989, a total of 1.5 billion ECU ($2 billion) were spent; in the second period (ESPRIT 2), 1987–1991, an additional 3.2 billion ECU ($4.4 billion) was made available,

SOURCE: This case was compiled by Ilkka A. Ronkainen. It is based on "Screened Out," *The Economist,* September 24, 1994, 66; Marc Van Wegberg, Arjen Van Witteloostuijin, and Michiel Roscam Abbing, "Multimarket and Multiproject Collusion," *De Economist* 142 (Number 3, 1994): 253–285; Willem A. Ledeboer and Tjerk R. Gorter, "ESPRIT: Successful Industrial R&D Cooperation in Europe," *International Journal of Technology Management* 8 (Numbers 6, 7, 8, 1993): 528–543; "Do Not Adjust Your Set Yet," *The Economist,* February 27, 1993, 65–66; "Sematech Claims Major Advance by Halving Size of Chip Circuits," *The Wall Street Journal,* January 22, 1992, B5; Louis Kraar, "Your Rivals Can Be Your Allies," *Fortune,* March 27, 1989, 63–76; Les Smith, "Can Consortiums Defeat Japan?" *Fortune,* June 5, 1989, 215–254; Jonathan B. Levine, "Hanging Tough by Teaming Up," *Business Week,* October 22, 1990, 121; and Jeremy Main, "Making Global Alliances Work," *Fortune,* December 17, 1990, 121–126. Thanks to Boyd J. Miller for his assistance with an earlier version of this case.

and for ESPRIT 3, which ended in 1994, another 2.7 billion ECU ($3.7 billion) was allocated. ESPRIT 4, which started January 1, 1995, and will have a duration of four years, already has had 1.9 billion ($2.5 billion) proposed for its projects to "contribute toward the construction of a European information infrastructure in order to ensure the future competitiveness of all European industry and to improve the quality of life."

BACKGROUND

The history of intra-European cooperation had a shaky beginning at best. The rising costs of research in aerospace, electronics, and chemicals, as well as the substantial technological gap between European and U.S. firms in the 1960s, provided the impetus for greater intra-European collaboration. In April 1970, the European Commission proposed the creation of an EC office to coordinate development contracts in advanced technology. Although the number of mergers did rise in the 1970s, the decade was marked by a series of failures in intra-European cooperation. Most prominent was the failure of UNIDATA, a computing resource venture by Bull, Philips, and Siemens.

In 1980, Étienne Daignon, then Commissioner of Industry in the EC, invited 12 of Europe's largest information technology firms (Siemens, AEG, and Nixdorf of Germany; Plessey, GEC, and STC of the United Kingdom; CGE, Thomson, and Bull of France; Philips of the Netherlands; and Olivetti and Stet of Italy) to help create a cooperative work program for their industry to be called ESPRIT. The objectives of the effort were (1) to promote intra-European industrial cooperation, (2) to furnish European industry with the basic technologies that it would need to bolster its competitiveness over the next five to ten years, and (3) to develop European norms and standards. Five major themes were agreed upon: advanced micro electronics, software technology, advanced information processing, office systems, and computer integrated manufacture. The European Commission wanted to make clear from the beginning that ESPRIT was not meant as an industrial policy on a regional level, but rather a technology policy that had the task of identifying key areas of technology. ESPRIT launched a pilot program in 1983 and began full-scale operations a year later.

The involved parties and the influences in the decision-making process of European R&D projects are summarized in Figure 1. Industry specifies the subject areas and priorities, while the European Commission makes a coherent work plan, acts as a program director and contract manager, and makes the selection of projects and monitors their progress. The Commission is obligated to report to the Council of Ministers, the European Parliament, and the Economic and Social Committee.

Today, roughly half of ESPRIT's budget is paid for by the EU. The other half is provided by the participating companies. Specific measures, such as actions to encourage standardization and measures to provide general service tools to research centers and universities, may qualify for an EU contribution of up to 100 percent of total costs. ESPRIT's project rules require that at least two firms located in two different EU countries be represented. This rule ensures that ESPRIT is an intercontinental program. Initially, the vast majority of programs included the Big-12 firms. Over time, smaller firms, research institutes, and universities have become significant contributors. Since a significant amount of financing comes from taxpayers, officials must disperse funds equitably rather than to the strongest competitors. This has allowed smaller firms, such as IMEC, to collaborate with multinational giants such as Philips. The results are discussed and exhibited annually during "ESPRIT Week" in Brussels.

ESPRIT plays different roles for the participating entities. For firms already engaged in alliances, ESPRIT has helped complement them. Commitment levels to R&D and to individual projects have also improved. For example, European information technology

The Decision-Making Process of European R&D Programs **FIGURE 1**

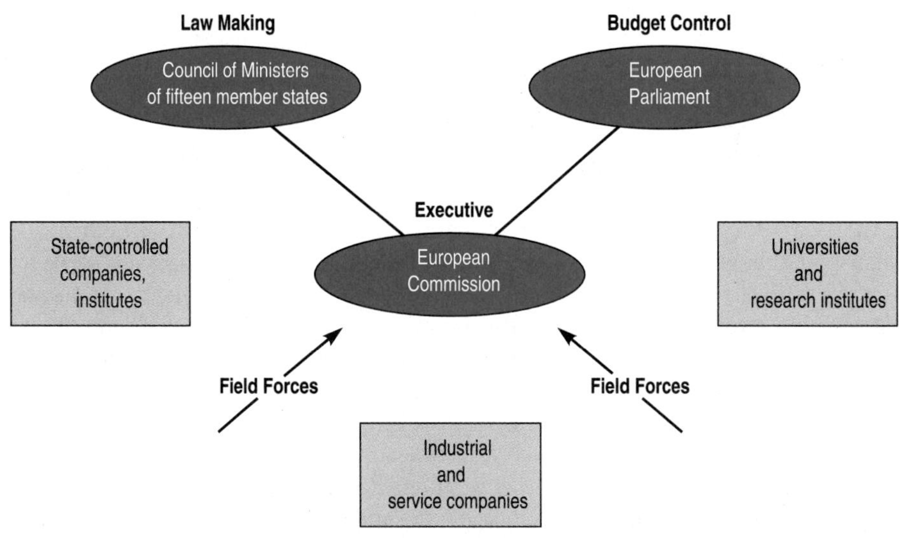

SOURCE: Willem A. Ledeboer and Tjerk R. Gorter, "ESPRIT: Successful Industrial R&D Cooperation in Europe," *International Journal of Technology Management* 8, 6, 7, 8 (1993): 530.

companies increased their R&D and capital spending by 5 percent in the four years ended in 1990, to 19.2 percent of revenues from 14.5 percent, nearly matching the level of U.S. companies. Furthermore, ESPRIT has allowed participants to work together in the development of new European standards of technology to ensure, for example, that computer systems are able to work together.

By subsidizing the costs of R&D, facilitating the emergence of complementary technologies between firms, and promoting standardization, the ESPRIT program enhances interfirm cooperation without requiring explicit, formal, long-term contractual arrangements. A total of 1,027 projects have been started under ESPRIT's auspices: 241 with ESPRIT 1, 433 with ESPRIT 2, and 353 with ESPRIT 3 (many of which are still under execution). Fewer than 5 percent have been terminated because of poor results or trouble within the consortium.

INDUSTRY CHALLENGES

Both the computer and telecommunications industries suffer from rising R&D costs, relatively short product life cycles, rapid product obsolescence, and extensive capital requirements. As product development costs soar, small and medium-sized firms especially come under considerable financial pressure to keep up with technological developments.

It is estimated that it takes nearly $1 billion to develop a new telecommunications switching system or a new generation of semiconductor. For this investment to be profitable, markets of nearly $14 billion are needed. New production lines also require considerable capital investment. In semiconductors, for example, the minimum investment for a new microelectronics production line is approaching the total value of annual output for that plant.

With rising R&D costs and shortened product life cycles, competition has intensified, and firms see little future in becoming national monopolies. Securing access to foreign markets and reducing costs and risks are essential to long-term survival in the industry.

COOPERATIVE EFFORTS IN JAPAN AND THE UNITED STATES

The success of the Ministry of International Trade and Industry (MITI) in Japan in including the private sector in public planning decisions was the inspiration for ESPRIT. In the late 1970s, a consortium of six companies, including NTT, Mitsubishi, and Matsushita, that was designed to overtake the United States in producing very large scale integrated (VLSI) circuits—high-powered memories-on-a-chip—functioned so well that the U.S. government pressured the Japanese government to stop giving the consortium money. It was too late: by the mid-1980s, Japanese companies dominated the market. Since then, the Japanese have launched other consortia. One of them consists of nine companies (including Hitachi, Toshiba, and NEC) whose mission is to develop advanced computer technologies such as artificial intelligence and parallel processing.

Activities are organized under three headings: (1) underpinning technologies: software technologies, technologies for components and subsystems (e.g., semiconductors, microsystems, and peripherals), and multimedia; (2) long-term research to ensure potential for next-generation solutions; and (3) focused research on projects such as high-performance computing and networking and integration in manufacturing.

In the United States, well over 100 R&D consortia have registered with the Justice Department to pool their resources for research into technologies ranging from artificial intelligence to those needed to overtake the Japanese lead in semiconductor manufacturing. The major consortia are MCC (Microelectronics and Computer Technology Corp.) and Sematech, which boast as members the largest U.S. companies such as AT&T, GE, IBM, Motorola, and 3M. Sematech, founded in 1988, was formed to rescue an ailing U.S. computer chip industry. Funded jointly by the U.S. government and member companies, the consortium is credited with slowing the market-share drop of U.S. chip-equipment makers, who now control 53 percent of a $10 billion world market, up from less than 40 percent five years earlier. Although in theory most consortia have no real limitations on membership, barriers may exist. Sematech, for example, refuses to accept foreign firms, worrying that if Europeans were allowed to join, there would be no way to keep out the Japanese.

The race for developing the standard for high-definition television (HDTV) in the United States created interesting alliances. The government entity involved, the Federal Communications Commission (FCC), did not finance or participate actively in the choice of the standard; it formed a private sector advisory committee to pick the technically best system in an open contest. One team formed for this contest included the U.S. subsidiaries of France's Thomson and Holland's Philips (backed by the EU to develop Europe's standard) as well as NBC, one of the major U.S. broadcast networks. The other two teams included Zenith and AT&T in one and General Instrument (a maker of cable TV gear) and the Massachusetts Institute of Technology in the other one. In the spring of 1993, the FCC was encouraging all three teams to form a "grand alliance," combining all systems for a final round of testing. In late May of 1993, the three teams decided to join forces in a single approach, a move that was strongly supported by top federal officials. While many expected the agreement to hasten the introduction of HDTV (because it reduces the likelihood of protracted disputes and litigation and represents a broad technical consensus for the next generation of television sets), it has been delayed because of the reluctance of television networks to re-equip their studios and the forecast that consumers would not switch to HDTV until set prices would drop to around $500—an impossibility with today's technology.

MANAGEMENT OF COLLABORATIVE EFFORTS

Three factors have been shown to make collaborative efforts succeed: leaders who are inspired, angry, or even scared; goals that are limited and well defined; and a dependable source of revenue. Some never overcome inherent problems. As cooperative ventures, they are intrinsically anticompetitive, so they risk becoming sluggish and stifling.

The broader and more formal the collaborative effort, the greater the hazard that it will get bogged down in bureaucracy. Management by committee could be a problem if it results in a lack of responsiveness to the marketplace. Some also decry the participation of governments in these efforts, pointing to possible meddling in the choice of programs and the way they are run.

Culture clash can also threaten collaborative efforts, since the efforts are often staffed at least partly by people on the payrolls of their members. Mixing corporate cultures may result in conflict. "Consortia are the wave of the future, but they sure are hard to manage," said a former consortium chief operating officer. Furthermore, if dominant companies refuse to join in an effort, and those participating remain aloof and suspicious of each other, the effort will not succeed.

The bottom line is that entities participating in collaborative efforts have to be as attentive to executing and maintaining them as they are to initiating them. Since working with former competitors is frequently a new experience, it requires new ground rules: from domestic market to a global economic and cultural perspective, from blanket secrecy and suspicion to judicious trust and openness, and from win-lose to win-win relationships.

Questions for Discussion

1. Can collaborative efforts, such as ESPRIT, really do things no single company could—or would—undertake?
2. What additional challenges are introduced when R&D collaboration is across national borders; i.e., will ESPRIT prove to be more problematic than Sematech (which does not allow non-U.S. members)?
3. How will ESPRIT's development of pan-European standards help Europe and European companies?
4. Will small and medium-sized firms benefit more from their participation in projects such as ESPRIT than the large, multinational corporation?

PART FOUR

Global Marketing

Marketing is the process of planning and executing the conception, pricing, promotion, and distribution of ideas, goods, and services to create exchanges that satisfy individual and organizational objectives.[1]

Satisfaction and exchange are at the core of marketing. For an exchange to occur, two or more parties have to come together, communicate, and deliver things of perceived value. Customers are information seekers who evaluate marketers' offerings in terms of their own needs. When an offering is consistent with their needs, they tend to choose the product or service; if not, they look elsewhere. A key task of marketers is to recognize ever-changing customer needs and wants.

The marketing manager's task is to plan and execute programs to ensure a company's long-term competitive advantage. This task has two parts: (1) determination of target markets (covered in Chapters 10 and 11) and (2) marketing management—manipulating product, price, promotion, and distribution (discussed in Chapters 12 and 13) to satisfy the needs of target markets. Regardless of the market, these basics do not vary; they have been called the technical universals of marketing.[2]

---

[1] "AMA Board Approves New Marketing Definition," *Marketing News,* March 1, 1985, 1.
[2] Robert Bartels, "Are Domestic and International Marketing Dissimilar?" *Journal of Marketing* 36 (July 1968): 56–61.

Global Business and Marketing Research

LEARNING OBJECTIVES

To gain an understanding of the need for research.

To explore the differences between domestic and international research.

To learn where to find sources of secondary information.

To gain insight into the gathering of primary data.

GLOBAL LEARNING EXPERIENCE 10.1

Some First Steps in International Research

Most company executives know that they need to conduct careful research before they prepare to market abroad. But knowing what to do is not the same as knowing how to get it done. Because many small and medium-sized firms are looking at international markets for the first time these days, they frequently go charging off in the wrong direction or spend tremendous sums on research. In reality, a great deal of international research can be accomplished for very little money, if you know where to look.

When my firm is asked to help answer international research questions, we try very hard not to reinvent the wheel or redo research that is already available. One of the first things we do is check established sources of information. Typically, that involves several steps.

First, we check reference information on countries, products, markets, and competitors. We look at reference guides, country directories, and publications of industrial development organizations. We also use international sources, including the United Nations, the World Bank, and the Food and Agriculture Organization, where the right kind of digging can pay off with useful information. The same is true of U.S. government agencies.

Next, we conduct secondary research on-line and in the library. Here we check all secondary information that may help answer client questions regarding products, markets, opportunities, competitors, and the wisdom of alternative business strategies. Typically, we conduct on-line research through Dialog, Nexis, and other services. The trick here is knowing which of the hundreds of databases to check for appropriate questions, key words, and subjects. After appropriate articles and published references have been identified, we spend time in the library reviewing abstracts and getting copies of pertinent articles and other references.

A third step then consists of identifying multiclient studies that have already been conducted that answer some of the questions we have. At this point, we know what is available. However, it is not cost efficient or wise to purchase every possible study, so some additional research is necessary. This involves contacting the publishers of the studies, requesting copies of the contents page and the prospectus for each study of interest.

Only after reviewing all the material obtained will we start developing a plan for proprietary primary research.

SOURCE: Ian MacFariane, "Do-It-Yourself Marketing Research," *Management Review,* May 1991, 34–37.

The single most important cause for failure in global business is insufficient preparation and information. The failure of managers to comprehend cultural disparities, the failure to remember that customers differ from country to country, and the lack of investigation into whether or not a market exists prior to market entry has made global business a high-risk activity.[1] Global business research is therefore instrumental to global business success. As noted in Global Learning Experience 10.1, research does not always have to consist of packing one's bags and traveling to foreign countries at great cost in time and money. A library nearby or simply access to good databases can be very useful in starting up the research process.

QUESTION *Why is it easy for a stranger to get lost in Tokyo?*

ANSWER *It's easy to get lost in Tokyo because this is one of the biggest, most populous cities in the world. It has grown with virtually no zoning, so that factories stand next to houses, next to schools, next to bars, next to ancient Shinto Temples, and there are almost no street names, numbers, or signs. The best way to tell a stranger how to find you is to memorize the locations of coffee shops in various parts of the city, rehearse giving directions to them, and then describe their location to your visitors. Then you can go and meet them there.*

This chapter discusses data collection and provides a comprehensive overview of how to obtain general screening information on global markets, to evaluate business potential, and to assess current or potential opportunities and problems. Data sources that are low cost and that take little time to accumulate—in short, secondary data—are considered first. The balance of the chapter is devoted to more sophisticated forms of global research, including primary data collection and the development of an information system.

RECOGNIZING THE NEED FOR GLOBAL RESEARCH

Many firms do little research before they enter a foreign market. Often, decisions concerning entry and expansion in overseas markets and selection and appointment of distributors are made after a cursory, subjective assessment of the situation. The research done is less rigorous, less formal, less quantitative than for domestic activities. Furthermore, once a firm has entered a foreign market, it is likely to discontinue researching that market.[2,3] Many business executives appear to view foreign research as relatively unimportant.

A major reason why managers are reluctant to engage in global research is their lack of sensitivity to differences in culture, consumer tastes, and market demands. A second reason is limited appreciation for the different environments abroad. Often, firms are not prepared to accept that labor rules, distribution systems, the availability of media, or advertising regulations may be entirely different from those in the home market. Because of the pressure to satisfy short-term financial goals, managers are unwilling to spend money to find out about the differences.

A third reason is lack of familiarity with national and global data sources and inability to use global data once they are obtained. As a result, the cost of conducting global research is seen as prohibitively high and therefore not a worthwhile investment relative to the benefits to be gained.[4]

Finally, firms often build up their international business activities gradually, frequently based on unsolicited orders. Over time, actual business experience in a country or with a specific firm may then be used as a substitute for organized research.[5]

Despite the reservations firms have, research is as important globally as it is domestically. Firms must learn where the opportunities are, what customers want, why they want it, and how they satisfy their needs and wants so that the firm can serve them efficiently. Firms must obtain information about the local infrastructure, labor market, and tax rules before making a plant-location decision. Doing business abroad without the benefit of research places firms, their assets, and their entire global future at risk.

Research allows management to identify and develop global strategies. This task includes the identification, evaluation, and comparison of potential foreign business opportunities and the subsequent target-market selection. In addition, research is necessary for the development of a business plan that identifies all the requirements necessary for market entry, market penetration, and expansion. On a continuing basis, research provides the feedback needed to fine-tune various business activities. Finally, research can provide management with the intelligence to help anticipate events, take appropriate action, and adequately prepare for global changes.

TARGET-MARKET SELECTION

The process of target-market selection involves narrowing down potential country markets to a feasible number of countries and market segments within them. Rather than try to appeal to everyone, firms best utilize their resources by (1) identifying potential markets for entry and (2) expanding selectively over time to those deemed attractive.

Identification and Screening

A four-stage process for screening and analyzing foreign markets is presented in Figure 10.1. It begins with very general criteria and ends with product-specific market analyses. The data and the methods needed for decision making change from secondary to primary as the steps are taken in sequence. Although presented here as a screening process for choosing target markets, the process is also applicable to change of entry mode or even divestment.

If markets were similar in their characteristics, the global marketer could enter any one of the potential markets. However, differences between markets exist in three dimensions: physical, psychic, and economic.[6] Physical distance is the geographic distance between home and target countries; its impact has decreased as a result of recent technological developments. Psychic, or cultural, distance refers to differences in language, tradition, and customs between the two countries. Economic distance is created by differences in the economic environments of the host country and the target market. Generally, the greater the overall distance—or difference—between the two countries, the less knowledge the marketer has about the target market. The amount of information that is available varies dramatically. For example, although the marketer can easily learn about the economic environment from secondary sources, invaluable interpretive information may not be available until the firm actually operates in the market.

The four stages in the screening process are: preliminary screening, estimation of market potential, estimation of sales potential, and identification of segments.[7] Each stage should be given careful attention. The first stage, for example, should not merely reduce the number of alternatives to a manageable few for the sake of reduction, even though the expense of analyzing markets in depth is great. Unless care is taken, attractive alternatives may be eliminated.

Preliminary Screening The preliminary screening process must rely chiefly on secondary data for country-specific factors as well as product- and industry-specific factors. Country-specific factors typically include those that would indicate the market's overall buying power; for example, population, gross national product in total and per capita, total exports and imports, and production of cement, electricity, and steel.[8] Product-specific factors narrow the analysis to the firm's specific areas of operation. A company such as Motorola, manufacturing for the automotive aftermarket, is interested in the number of passenger cars, trucks, and buses in use. These statistical analyses must be accompanied by qualitative assessments of the impact of cultural elements and the overall climate for foreign firms and products. A market that satisfies the levels set becomes a prospective target country. Global trade databases are an important method of scanning secondary data to identify potential markets. See Global Learning Experience 10-2.

FIGURE 10.1 **The Screening Process in Target-Market Choice**

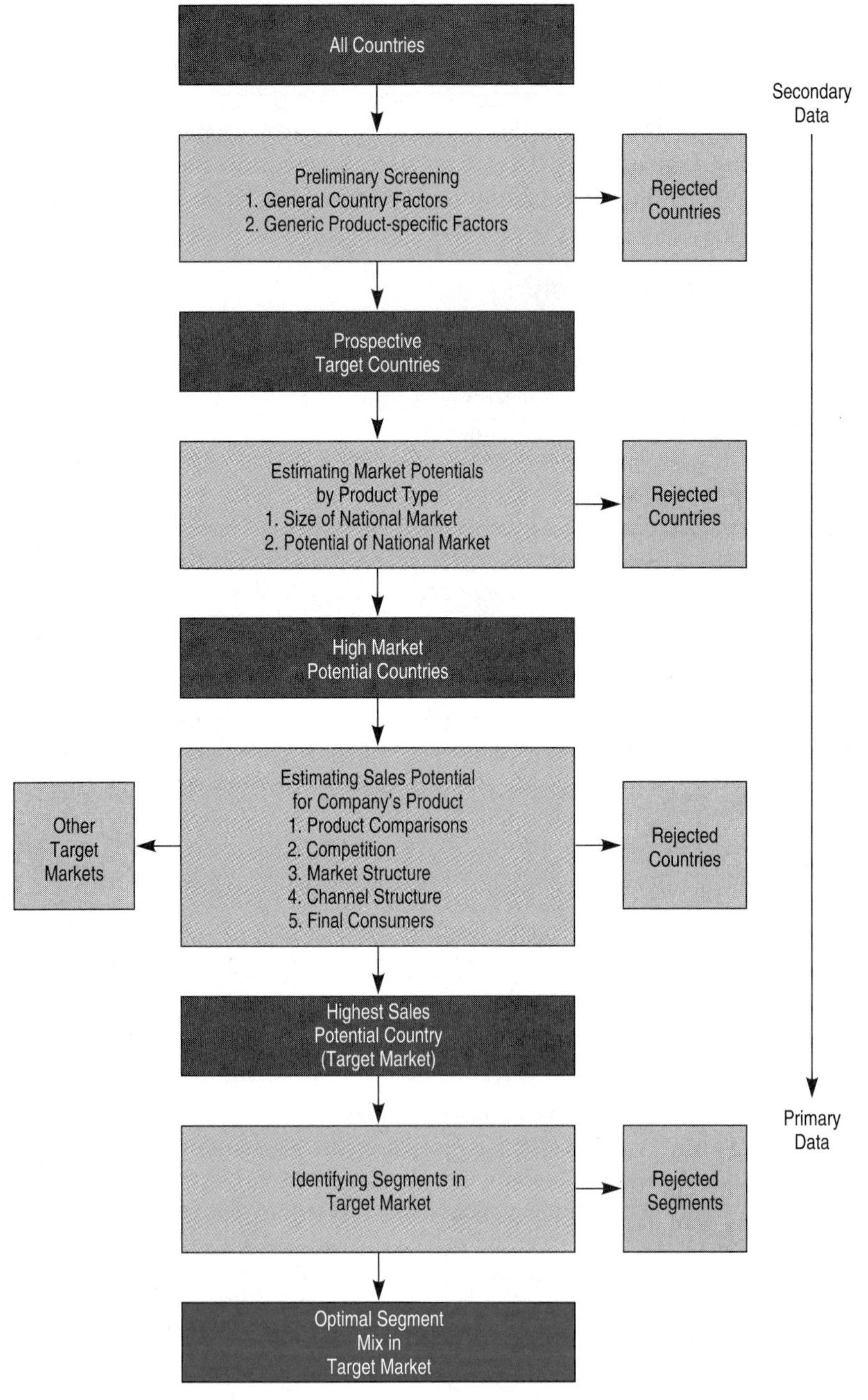

SOURCE: Reprinted by permission of Lexington Books, an imprint of Macmillan Publishing Company from *Entry Strategies for International Markets,* by Franklin R. Root, p. 34. Copyright © 1987 by Lexington Books.

GLOBAL LEARNING EXPERIENCE 10.2

Building Export Markets

Companies that export are more profitable and innovative, on average, than companies that do not. Yet, the majority of U.S. manufacturers do not export, and the most common reason is they simply do not know where to start. Lack of knowledge about foreign markets is one of the major barriers which conspire to anchor far too many companies to the U.S. market. However, potential exporters can save considerable time and money by using international trade data to answer one of the most essential questions: Where should I sell my products? Specifically, potential exporters need to know:

- Which are the largest and fastest growing markets for their product over the past three to five years? Has market growth been consistent or subject to fluctuations? Continuous growth in demand in a large market indicates the market would be receptive to the company's products, but also indicates a highly competitive import market.
- What smaller markets are fast emerging. High rates of import growth suggest the market is opening up for a product. While this also suggests a competitive market, the likelihood that competition will be entrenched is less.

Let's take an example. Assume you are a manufacturer of compressors for refrigeration equipment wanting to export. Using *The World Trade Atlas,*® a highly useful CD-ROM database on U.S. foreign trade, one learns that the top ten nations account for 72 percent of U.S. exports of compressors and five of these markets—Korea, Hong Kong, China, Japan, and Brazil—have registered strong multiyear growth. Canada, the largest market, is not growing rapidly, while the Mexican market may or may not be creating increasing demand for compressors. Saudi Arabia offers declining near term potential. Using this data, the manufacturer can quickly determine which are the largest markets for its product and which nations among these evidence increased future demand.

The World Trade Atlas
841430 COMPRESSOR REFR EQP—U.S. Exports

		January–December						
		Millions of U.S. Dollars			% Share			% Change
Rank	Partner Country	1994	1995	1996	1994	1995	1996	96/95
	WORLD	719.930	833.368	947.932	100.00	100.00	100.00	13.75
1	Canada	132.161	159.017	161.772	18.36	19.08	17.07	1.73
2	Korean Republic	52.214	73.451	117.556	7.25	8.81	12.40	60.05
3	Hong Kong	27.000	65.699	84.421	3.75	7.88	8.91	28.50
4	Mexico	67.748	43.525	70.236	9.41	5.22	7.41	61.37
5	Thailand	62.907	62.686	69.417	8.74	7.52	7.32	10.74
6	Saudi Arabia	88.593	68.881	49.691	12.31	8.27	5.24	−27.86
7	China	4.689	8.340	36.085	0.65	1.00	3.81	332.66
8	Japan	13.475	26.031	33.051	1.87	3.12	3.49	26.97
9	Brazil	12.999	19.170	31.564	1.81	2.30	3.33	64.66
10	United Kingdom	16.535	25.181	27.269	2.30	3.02	2.88	8.30

continued

There is an additional $267 million going to other nations that may offer less competition and a better chance for the company to penetrate the market. The company further identifies the following countries as potential export candidates:

The World Trade Atlas
841430 COMPRESSOR REFR EQP—U.S. EXPORTS

		January–December						
		Millions of U.S. Dollars			% Share			% Change
Rank	Partner Country	1994	1995	1996	1994	1995	1996	96/95
13	Malaysia	11.996	16.981	19.020	1.67	2.04	2.01	12.01
15	Egypt	5.755	6.794	17.559	0.80	0.82	1.85	158.45
22	Philippines	2.727	4.307	9.623	0.38	0.52	1.02	123.45
23	Germany	3.256	6.014	8.797	0.45	0.72	0.93	46.27
24	United Arab Emirates	5.149	4.212	6.110	0.72	0.51	0.64	45.06
26	Colombia	4.419	4.693	5.955	0.61	0.56	0.63	26.88
29	Turkey	1.051	2.029	4.070	0.15	0.24	0.43	100.55

These nations may have been overlooked by other exporters and are growing fast enough to potentially absorb new market entrants.

From a universe of over 200 countries, the company has narrowed the field for further investigation to 12 demonstrating high demand for refrigeration compressors. Because new exporters need to concentrate on one to two markets initially, this field must be narrowed further through market research on individual national markets. The next steps require examining:

- Factors affecting demand in each country including the importance of imports to total product consumption, the market share held by other exporting nations, the size and sophistication of domestic producers, and economic and demographic factors affecting the long-term market for compressors.
- Analyzing how compressors are marketed in each country, including the channels of distribution, and which channel affords the most cost effective access to most buyers. Analysis should also address understanding common business practices and idiosyncrasies.
- What tariff regulatory barriers currently exist or are likely to be imposed? What informal barriers also exist?

Answers to these questions will probably not provide a neat, clear picture of the top export candidate, but some markets will appear more attractive than others because of size, growth, competition, and accessibility. From the above nations, there is probably not a wrong choice, and the selection will also reflect the level of resources the firm is willing to commit to its initial export effort, the comfort level and perceived learning curve associated with that market, and the sophistication of the firm's export plan and strategy. Most new to export companies are advised to focus on one to two countries initially. However, the choice of country may also reflect regional growth. From the above examples, it would be logical for the exporter to explore the Chinese and Thai markets if Hong Kong emerged as the top initial choice.

Once chosen, the company needs to further understand how this market operates through attending trade shows in-country; meeting with exporters of similar, but noncompeting products and with end users and different marketing channel intermediaries to better understand how the market operates, and product adaptation and marketing support requirements. Once accomplished, the company is finally in a position to determine how it will approach the market, with what products, and how it will sell into the market. This is far from making a quick export sale, but reflects an approach that should position the company to become a long-term player in its chosen market and provides a basis for subsequent expansion into additional export markets.

SOURCE: Global Trade Information Services.

Estimating Market Potential Total market potential is the sales, in physical or monetary units, that might be available to all firms in an industry during a given period under a given level in industry marketing effort and given environmental conditions.[9] The global marketer needs to assess the size of existing markets and forecast the size of future markets.

Because of the lack of resources, and frequently the lack of data, market potentials are often estimated using secondary data-based analytical techniques.[10] These techniques focus on or utilize demand patterns, income elasticity measurements, multiple-factor indexes, and estimation by analogy.

Demand pattern analysis indicates typical patterns of growth and decline in manufacturing. At early stages of growth, for example, manufacturing is concentrated in food, beverage, and textile industries, and some light industry. An awareness of trends in manufacturing will enable the marketer to estimate potential markets for input, such as raw materials or machinery. Income elasticity of demand describes the relationship between demand and economic progress as indicated by growth in income. The share of income spent on necessities will provide both an estimate of the market's level of development and an approximation of how much money is left for other purchases.

Multiple-factor indexes measure market potential indirectly by using proxy variables that have been shown (either through research or intuition) to correlate closely with the demand for the particular product. An index for consumer goods might involve population, disposable personal income, and retail sales in the market or area concerned. Estimation by analogy is used when data for a particular market do not exist. The market size for a product in country A is estimated by comparing a ratio for an available indicator (such as disposable income) for country A and country B, and using this ratio in conjunction with detailed market data available for country B.

Despite the valuable insight generated through these techniques, caution should be used in interpreting the results. All of these quantitative techniques are based on historical data that may be obsolete or inapplicable because of differences in cultural and geographic traits of the market. Further, with today's technological developments, lags between markets are no longer at a level that would make all of the measurements valid. Moreover, the measurements look at a market as an aggregate; that is, no regional differences are taken into account. In an industrialized country like Sweden, the richest 10 percent of the population receives 20 percent of the income, while the respective income figures for the richest 10 percent in the middle-income countries such as Brazil (46 percent) and low-income countries such as Sri Lanka (43 percent) are much

QUESTION *What country do the Galapogos Islands belong to?*

Ecuador owns the Galapogos Islands.

higher.[11] Therefore, even in the developing countries with low GNP figures, segments exist with buying power rivaled only in the richest developed countries.

In addition to these quantitative techniques that rely on secondary data, international marketers can use various survey techniques. They are especially useful when marketing new technologies. A survey of end-user interest and responses may provide a relatively clear picture of the possibilities in a new market.

Estimating Sales Potential Even when the global marketer has gained an understanding of markets with the greatest overall promise, the firm's own possibilities in those markets are still not known. Sales potential is the share of the market potential that the firm can reasonably expect to get over the longer term. To arrive at an estimate, the marketer needs to collect product- and market-specific data. These will have to do with:

1. *Competition*—strength, likely reaction to entry.
2. *Market*—strength of barriers.
3. *Consumers*—ability and willingness to buy.
4. *Product*—degree of relative advantage, compatibility, complexity, trialability, and communicability.
5. *Channel structure*—access to retail level.

The marketer's questions can never be fully answered until the firm has made a commitment to enter the market and is operational. The mode of entry has special significance in determining the firm's sales potential.[12]

market segmentation grouping of people based on the common characteristics shared by members of the group; i.e., demographics, geographic, psychographics (lifestyles), degree of product usage, and desired benefit from the product

Identifying Segments Within the markets selected, individuals and organizations will vary in their wants, resources, geographical locations, buying attitudes, and buying practices. Initially, the firm may cater to one or only a few segments and later expand to others, especially if the product is innovative. **Market segmentation** is indicated

Tyson Foods customizes more than 5,000 products to satisfy local taste preferences in 57 countries. Targeted research helps Tyson identify opportunities globally.
SOURCE: Courtesy of Tyson Foods.

when segments are indeed different enough to warrant individualized attention, are large enough for profit potential, and can be reached through the methods that the international marketer wants to use.

Once the process is complete for a market or group of markets, the global marketer may begin again for another one. When growth potential is no longer in market development, the firm may opt for market penetration.

Concentration versus Diversification

Choosing a market expansion policy involves the allocation of effort among various markets. The major alternatives are concentration on a small number of markets or diversification, which is characterized by growth in a relatively large number of markets in the early stages of global market expansion.[13]

Expansion Alternatives Either concentration or diversification is applicable to market segments or to total markets, depending on the resource commitment the international marketer is willing and able to make. One option is a dual-concentration strategy, in which efforts are focused on a few segments in a limited number of countries. Another is a dual-diversification strategy, in which entry is to most segments in most available markets. The first is a likely strategy for small firms or firms that market specialized products to clearly definable markets, for example, ocean-capable sailing boats. The second is typical for large consumer-oriented companies that have sufficient resources for broad coverage. Market concentration/segment diversification opts for a limited number of markets but for wide coverage within them, putting emphasis on company acceptance. Market diversification/segment concentration usually involves the identification of a segment, possibly worldwide, to which the company can market without major changes in its marketing mix.

Factors Affecting Expansion Expansion strategy is determined by the market-, mix-, and company-related factors listed in Table 10.1. In most cases, the factors are interrelated.

Market-Related Factors These factors are the ones that were influential in determining the attractiveness of the market in the first place. In the choice of expansion strategy, demand for the firm's products is a critical factor. With high and stable growth rates in certain markets, the firm will most likely opt for a concentration strategy. If the demand is strong worldwide, diversification may be attractive.

TABLE 10.1 **Factors Affecting the Choice between Concentration and Diversification Strategies**

Factor	Diversification	Concentration
Market growth rate	Low	High
Sales stability	Low	High
Sales response function	Concave	S Curve
Competitive lead time	Short	Long
Spillover effects	High	Low
Need for product adaptation	Low	High
Need for communication adaptation	Low	High
Economies of scale in distribution	Low	High
Extent of constraints	Low	High
Program control requirements	Low	High

SOURCE: Igal Ayal and Jehiel Zif, "Marketing Expansion Strategies in Multinational Marketing," *Journal of Marketing* 43 (Spring 1979): 89.

The uniqueness of the firm's offering with respect to competition is also a factor in the expansion strategy. If lead time over competition is considerable, the decision to diversify may not seem urgent. Complacency can be a mistake in today's competitive environment, however; competitors can rush new products into the market in a matter of days.

In many product categories, marketers will be, knowingly or unknowingly, affected by spillover effects. Consider, for example, the impact that satellite channels have had on advertising in Europe, where ads for a product now reach most of the Western European market. Where geographic (and psychic) distances are short, spillover is likely, and marketers are most likely to diversify. Governmental constraints—or the threat of them—can be a powerful motivator in a firm's expansion. For example, a firm may feel compelled to enter a foreign market through direct foreign investment, if there are fears that the government of that market is likely to impose import restrictions.

Mix-Related Factors These factors relate to the degree to which marketing mix elements—primarily product, promotion, and distribution—can be standardized. The more that standardization is possible, the more diversification is indicated. Overall savings through economies of scale can then be utilized in marketing efforts.

Depending on the product, each market will have its own challenges. Whether constraints are apparent (such as tariffs) or hidden (such as tests or standards), they will complicate all of the other factors. Nevertheless, regional integration has allowed many marketers to diversify their efforts.

Company-Related Factors These include the objectives set by the company for its global operations and the policies it adopts in those markets. As an example, the firm may require—either by stated policy or because of its products—extensive interaction with intermediaries and clients. When this is the case, the firm's efforts will likely be concentrated because of resource constraints.

CONDUCTING RESEARCH

Identifying Sources of Data

Typically, the information requirements of firms will cover both information about countries and trade, as well as information specific to the firm's activities. Table 10.2

TABLE 10.2 **Most Critical International Information for U.S. Firms**

Country and Trade Data

- Tariff information
- U.S. export/import data
- Nontariff measures
- Foreign export/import data
- Data on government trade policy

Business Activity Data

- Local laws and regulations
- Size of market
- Local standards and specifications
- Distribution system
- Competitive activity

SOURCE: Michael R. Czinkota, "International Information Needs for U.S. Competitiveness," *Business Horizons* 34, 6 (November-December 1991): Table 1, p. 83. Copyright 1991 by the Foundation for the School of Business at Indiana University. Used with permission.

provides an overview of the types of information that, according to a survey of U.S. executives, are most crucial for international business.

Before discussing international business research any further, it is appropriate to distinguish between data and information and to outline the various sources of data. **Data** are the accumulation of raw facts and figures, whereas **information** is data put into useable form.

data
the accumulation of raw facts and figures

information
data put into useable form

The two types of data are primary and secondary. **Primary data** are the collection of original facts and figures. Because this type of data is original, not having been done before, developing primary data can be a costly and time-consuming effort. The basic methods used to collect primary data include: experimentation, observation, and survey techniques (personal interview, telephone, mail, and focus groups).

primary data
collection of original fact and figures

secondary data
data that have been collected by others

Secondary data are data that have been collected by others. Secondary data are usually less expensive and easier to collect. For these reasons, most international business researchers usually attempt to gather secondary data first, before expending time and money collecting primary data. Appendix A at the end of this chapter presents an array of important sources that should be considered as a starting point in the accumulation of secondary data. Basic sources should include:

Governments (United States, foreign, and state and local)
United Nations
Other International Organizations
Trade Associations
Trade Publications, Directories, and Newsletters
Service Organizations
Nonprofit Research Organizations
Commercial Databases
Other Firms

U.S. Government The U.S. government has a great variety of data available. Most of them are collected by the Department of Commerce, the Department of Agriculture, the Department of State, the Department of the Treasury, and by U.S. embassies abroad.

Typically, the information provided by the U.S. government addresses either macro or micro issues or offers specific data services. Macro information includes data on population trends, general trade flows between countries, and world agricultural production. Micro information in turn includes materials on specific industries in a country, their growth prospects, and their foreign trade activities. Specific data services might provide custom-tailored information responding to the detailed needs of a firm. Alternatively, some data services may concentrate on a specific geographic region. More information on selected U.S. government publications and research services is presented in Appendix B to this chapter. Global Learning Experience 10.3 explains some of the information services offered by the European union.

Other Governments Most countries have a wide array of national and international trade data available. Unfortunately, the data are often published only in their home countries and in their native languages. These publications mainly present numerical data, however, and so the translation task is relatively easy. In addition, these information sources are often available at embassies and consulates, whose mission includes the enhancement of trade activities. The commercial counselor or commercial attaché can provide the information available from these sources. The user should be

GLOBAL LEARNING EXPERIENCE 10.3

Electronic Information Sources on the EU

With the expanding economic and political union occurring within Europe, official information resources are becoming more centralized. A short sampling of government sources of information helpful to international marketers targeting the EU are reviewed below.

EUROBASES

Eurobases is an Internet service that provides access to bibliographic, legal, and statistical databases offered by the European Commission. Many databases are available on Eurobases, including RAPID, SCAD, EUROCRON, and ECLAS. RAPID provides full text of press materials issued each day by the Commission and the Council of Ministers, weekly summaries of Court actions, and speeches by Commission members. In addition to the texts, a list of items released each day may be downloaded. SCAD is a bibliographic database with references to official legislative documents and publications, as well as secondary periodical literature on the EU. EUROCRON provides a menu-guided presentation of general macroeconomic statistics and farm data. ECLAS is an on-line catalog of the Central Library of the Commission.

EUROSTAT

The Statistical Office of the Euoprean Communities (EUROSTAT) offers information on disketts, tapes, and CD-ROMs. EUROSTAT's COMEXT is a CD-ROM product with detailed internal and external trade statistics of the EU based on the Harmonized System of product classification. An annual subscription includes 11 updates with monthly data. Each update contains the most current monthly data and two years of annual retrospective data. COMEXT offers software for graphs and other presentations, as well as downloading into standard spreadsheet programs. The Electronic Statistical Yearbook of the European Community, offered by EUROSTAT, has macro, micro, and regional economic data for the EU and individual member states, including map and graph capabilities. Eurofarm, a EUROSTAT CD-ROM database, has statistics on farm structure, wine cultivation, and orchard fruit trees.

EPOQUE

EPOQUE is the documentary database of the European Parliament. It operates with a user-friendly menu. Its files cover the status of legislation in progress, citations for session documents, debates, resolutions, and opinions, bibliographic references to studies done by the Parliament and national parliaments, and a catalog of the Parliament's library.

SOURCE: *The European Union: Electronic Information,* the Delegation of the European Commission, Washington, D.C., June 1995.

cautioned, however, that the information is often dated and that the industry categories used abroad may not be compatible with industry categories used at home.

International Organizations Some international organizations provide useful data for the researcher. The *Statistical Yearbook* produced by the United Nations (UN) contains international trade data on products and provides information on exports and imports by country. However, because of the time needed for worldwide data collection, the information is often quite dated. Additional information is compiled and made available by specialized substructures of the United Nations. Some of these are the

United Nations Conference on Trade and Development (UNCTAD), which concentrates primarily on global issues surrounding developing nations, such as debt and market access, and the United Nations Center on Transnational Corporations. The *World Atlas* published by the World Bank provides useful general data on population, growth trends, and GNP figures. The Organization for Economic Cooperation and Development (OECD) also publishes quarterly and annual trade data on its member countries. Finally, organizations such as the International Monetary Fund (IMF) and the World Bank publish summary economic data and occasional staff papers that evaluate region- or country-specific issues in depth.

Trade Associations Associations such as world trade clubs and domestic and international chambers of commerce (such as the American Chamber of Commerce abroad) can provide good information on local markets. Often, files are maintained on international trade flows and trends affecting global managers. Valuable information can also be obtained from industry associations. These groups, formed to represent entire industry segments, often collect from their members a wide variety of data that are then published in an aggregate form. Because most of these associations represent the viewpoints of their member firms to the federal government, they usually have one or more publicly listed representatives in Washington. The information provided is often quite general, however, because of the wide variety of clientele served.

Trade Publications, Directories, and Newsletters A large number of industry trade publications and directories are available on local, national, and international levels. These publications primarily serve to identify firms and to provide very general background information, such as the name of the chief executive officer, the level of capitalization of the firm, the location, the address and telephone number, and some description of a firm's products. In the past few years, a host of newsletters has sprung up discussing specific global business issues, such as global trade finance, legislative activities, countertrade, international payment flows, and customs news. Usually, these newsletters cater to narrow audiences but can provide important information to the firm interested in a specific area.

Service Organizations A wide variety of service organizations that provide information include banks, accounting firms, freight forwarders, airlines, global trade consultants, foreign research firms, and publishing houses located abroad. Frequently, they are able to provide information on business practices, legislative or regulatory requirements, and political stability, as well as basic trade and financial data. Although this information is available without charge, its basic intent is to serve as an "appetizer." Much of the initial information is quite general in nature, as Figure 10.2 suggests. More detailed and up-to-date answers are also available from these sources, but they will require payment of an appropriate fee.

Databases Increasingly, electronic databases also provide international business information. For example, information can be found on financial markets, the latest in trade press and academic writings, and political developments, among other topics. Information services are provided through various media, including on-line interactive delivery, compact disc read-only memory, magnetic tape, floppy disk, interactive

---

QUESTION *If a person in South America is referred to by the following terms, where is he or she from?*
A. Carioca B. Limeño C. Porteño D. Paceño
E. Paulistano F. Caricaeño

A. Rio De Janiero, Brazil
B. Lima, Peru
C. Buenos Aires, Argentina
D. La Paz, Bolivia
E. São Paulo, Brazil
F. Caracas, Venezuela

voice/audiotext, and on-line broadcast. Figure 10.3 provides an example of a database particularly useful to the international marketer.

On-line databases and, in particular, the Internet link computer users worldwide. Rapidly growing information and communication media allow firms to find out about new developments in their fields of interest and also permits them to gather information through bulletin boards and discussion groups. For example, some firms use search engines or software programs to comb through thousands of newsgroups for mention of a particular product. If they find frequent references to the product, they can find out what customers are saying.[14] In a further step, some

FIGURE 10.2 **Advertisement Offering Global Services**

SOURCE: *Forbes*, June 21, 1993.

Information Services on CD-ROM **FIGURE 10.3**

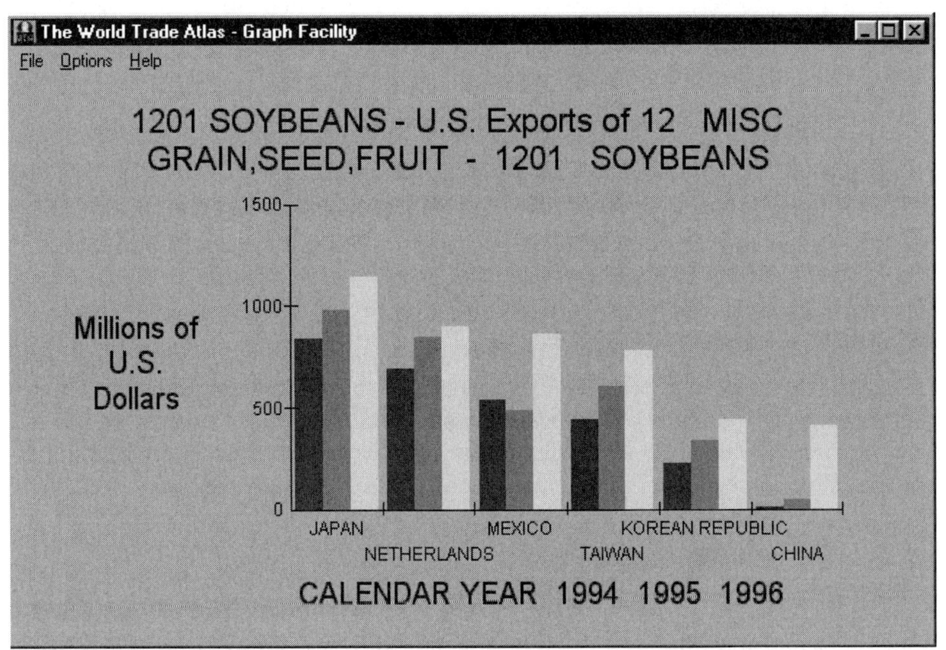

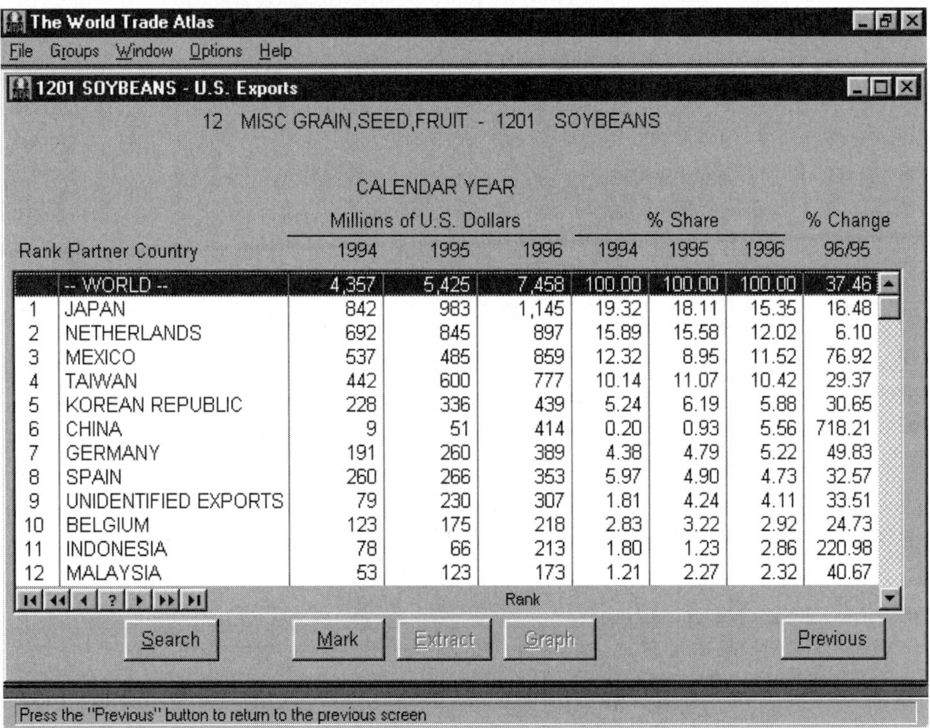
The World Trade Atlas

File Groups Window Options Help

1201 SOYBEANS - U.S. Exports

12 MISC GRAIN,SEED,FRUIT - 1201 SOYBEANS

CALENDAR YEAR

Rank	Partner Country	Millions of U.S. Dollars 1994	1995	1996	% Share 1994	1995	1996	% Change 96/95
	-- WORLD --	4,357	5,425	7,458	100.00	100.00	100.00	37.46
1	JAPAN	842	983	1,145	19.32	18.11	15.35	16.48
2	NETHERLANDS	692	845	897	15.89	15.58	12.02	6.10
3	MEXICO	537	485	859	12.32	8.95	11.52	76.92
4	TAIWAN	442	600	777	10.14	11.07	10.42	29.37
5	KOREAN REPUBLIC	228	336	439	5.24	6.19	5.88	30.65
6	CHINA	9	51	414	0.20	0.93	5.56	718.21
7	GERMANY	191	260	389	4.38	4.79	5.22	49.83
8	SPAIN	260	266	353	5.97	4.90	4.73	32.57
9	UNIDENTIFIED EXPORTS	79	230	307	1.81	4.24	4.11	33.51
10	BELGIUM	123	175	218	2.83	3.22	2.92	24.73
11	INDONESIA	78	66	213	1.80	1.23	2.86	220.98
12	MALAYSIA	53	123	173	1.21	2.27	2.32	40.67

Rank

Search Mark Extract Graph Previous

Press the "Previous" button to return to the previous screen

Databases, such as the Annual Summary of the World Trade Atlas® pictured, provide businesses with valuable information on the global market. The screens shown here are from a database on CD-ROM that contains global merchandise trade data from 1989 forward. Users can sort the data by country or product and view tables and charts.
SOURCE: Courtesy of Global Trade Information Services, Inc., Columbia, SC.

firms, such as Digital Equipment Corporation, Silicon Graphics, and Sun Microsystems, systematically use the Internet to get closer to their customers by developing and interacting with discussion groups about their products. Not only do these activities shed light on customer thinking, but the interaction can also save large amounts of money be reducing customer service calls.[15] Appendix C of this chapter lists a series of Web sites that can be particularly useful to the international market researcher.

Other Firms Often, home-country competitors can provide useful information for global business purposes. Firms appear to be more open about their international than about their domestic business activities. On some occasions, valuable information can also be obtained from foreign firms and distributors.

Selection of Secondary Data

Just because secondary information has been found to exist does not mean that it has to be used. Even though one key advantage of secondary data over primary research is that they are available relatively quickly and inexpensively, the researcher should still assess the effort and benefit of using them. Secondary data should be evaluated regarding the quality of their source, their recency, and their relevance to the task at hand. Clearly, since the information was collected without the current research requirements in mind, there may well be difficulties in coverage, categorization, and comparability. An "engineer" in one country may differ substantially in terms of training and responsibilities from a person in another country holding the same title. It is therefore important to use such data carefully when getting ready to analyze and interpret them.

Analysis and Interpretation of Secondary Data

proxy information
data used as a substitute for more desirable data that are unobtainable

Once secondary data have been obtained, the researcher must creatively convert them into information. Secondary data were originally collected to serve another purpose than the one in which the researcher is currently interested. Therefore, they can often be used only as **proxy information** in order to arrive at conclusions that address the research objectives. The market penetration of television sets may be used as a proxy variable for the potential demand for video recorders. Similarly, in an industrial setting, information about plans for new port facilities may be useful in determining future containerization requirements. The researcher should proceed with caution when comparing secondary data across borders.

The researcher must use creative inferences, and such creativity brings risks. Therefore, once analysis and interpretation have taken place, a consistency check must be conducted. The researcher should always cross-check the results with other possible sources of information or with experts. Yet if properly implemented, such creativity can open up one's eyes to new market potential.

CONDUCTING PRIMARY RESEARCH

Even though secondary data are useful to the researcher, on many occasions primary information will be required. Primary data are obtained by a firm to fill specific information needs. Firms do specialize in primary global research, even under difficult circumstances, as indicated in Figure 10.4. Although the research may not be conducted by the company with the need, the work must be carried out for a specific research purpose in order to qualify as primary research. Typically, primary research intends to answer such clear-cut questions as:

An Example of Primary Research under Difficult Conditions FIGURE 10.4

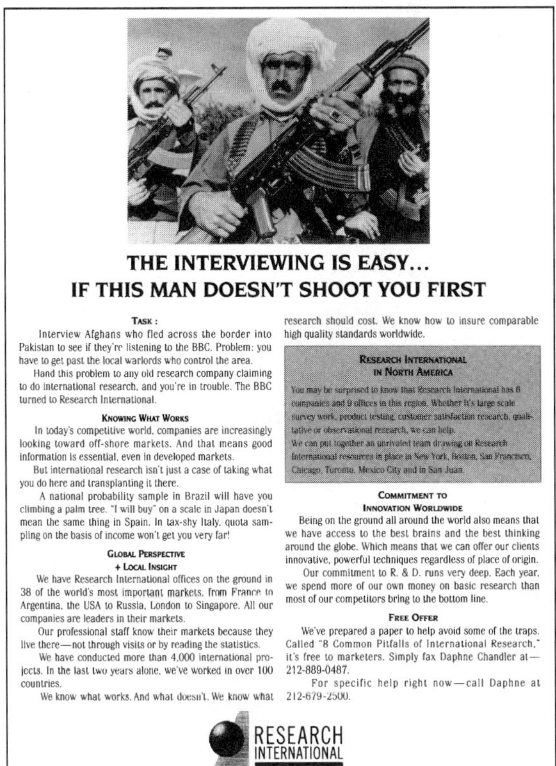

SOURCE: Research International. The Leading Worldwide Research Company.

- What is our sales potential in market X?
- How skilled is the labor force in this region?
- What will happen to demand if we raise the price by 10 percent?
- What effect will a new type of packaging have on our sales?

When extending his or her efforts abroad, the researcher must determine the specific country or region to be investigated. Conducting research in an entire country may not be necessary if, for example, only urban centers are to be penetrated. Multiple regions of a country need to be investigated, however, if a lack of homogeneity exists because of different economic, geographic, or behavioral factors. The researcher must, of course, have a clear idea of what the population under study should be and where it is located before deciding on the country or region to investigate. Conducting primary research internationally can be complex due to different environments, attitudes, and market conditions. Yet it is precisely because of these differences that such research is necessary. Global Learning Experience 10.4 provides an example of such a situation.

Industrial versus Consumer Sources of Data

The researcher must decide whether research is to be conducted in the consumer or the industrial product area, which in turn determines the size of the universe and respondent accessibility. Consumers usually are a very large group, whereas the total

GLOBAL LEARNING EXPERIENCE 10.4

Information Obstacles in Russia

Russian pollsters and information specialists face a gauntlet of obstacles. Russia has the largest land mass in the world, stretching across 11 time zones. Random telephone polls, commonly used in the United States, are virtually impossible in Russia. Millions of rural villagers are beyond the reach of telephones, and often urban phone networks are not reliable. For a nationwide survey, pollsters must set up stationary points across the country from which to launch person-to-person interviews, a time-consuming and expensive effort. The pollsters send their workers into the field, usually to conduct 20- to 30-minute interviews. But in trying to capture a representative sample of such a vast country, the pollsters face many unknown factors. The last Russian census was in 1988, making it extraordinarily difficult to sample the population accurately.

"Quite often it is difficult to reach some rural areas, and we must make a selection of 3,000 people to poll," said Vsevolod Vilchek, director of sociological research for Russia's public television channel. "These 3,000 must be an exact model of society. Very often we fail to do that. Inevitably there is a big margin of error." On average, 15 percent of Russians approached for a poll refuse to participate. "We still have these fears living in us," said Vilchek. "They are fears from the Communist times. People still do not believe these polls are really anonymous, that they won't be used to inform on somebody, and later on they won't be arrested. It is difficult to convince people that we are . . . not KGB agents."

Many people do not know how to answer complex questions. "If you ask difficult questions, you can't count on the answer being what people really think," according to the head of Russia's Public Opinion Foundation. He says, "For example, 'What is your attitude toward privatization?' Twenty percent say positive, 30 percent say negative, and the rest don't know what to say. People don't understand the word *privatization,* or what it means." Pollsters and market researchers, attempting to overcome such obstacles, often add indirect questions to their surveys in the hope of detecting hidden intentions and trends. "You have to be a psychologist here," according to Vilchek, "to image the hidden part of the iceberg."

SOURCE: David Hoffman, "Russian Voters' Poll Position: Fear, Uncertainty," *The Washington Post,* May 23, 1996, A-31.

population of industrial users may be fairly limited. Cooperation by respondents may also vary, ranging from very helpful to very limited. In the industrial setting, differentiation between users and decision makers may be important because their personalities, their outlooks, and their evaluative criteria may differ widely. Determining the proper focus of the research is therefore of major importance to its successful completion.

Determining the Research Technique

experimentation
research method in which all but one variable is held constant and a new, single variable is introduced; any change in the market as a result of the test is ascribed to the new variable

Once the type of data sought is determined, the researcher must choose a research technique. As in domestic research, the types available are experimentation, observation, and surveys. Each one provides a different depth of information and has its unique strengths and weaknesses.

Experimental Techniques **Experimentation** determines the effect of an intervening variable and helps establish precise cause-and-effect relationships. However, it is difficult to implement in global research. The researcher faces the task of designing an experiment in which most variables are held constant or are comparable across cultures. An experiment to determine a causal effect within the distribution system of one country may be very difficult to transfer to another country because the distribution system may be quite different. For this reason, experimental techniques are only rarely used, even though their potential value to their global researcher is recognized.

Observation **Observation** requires the researcher to play the role of a nonparticipating observer of activity and behavior. In a global setting, observation can be extremely useful in shedding light on practices not previously encountered or understood. This aspect is especially valuable to the researcher who has no knowledge of a particular market or market situation. It can help in understanding phenomena that would have been difficult to assess with other techniques. For example, Toyota sent a group of its engineers and designers to southern California to nonchalantly "observe" how women get into and operate their cars. They found that women with long fingernails have trouble opening the door and operating various knobs on the dashboard. Toyota engineers and designers were able to "understand" the women's plight and redesign some of their automobile exterior and interior, producing more desirable cars.[16]

observation
research method that relies on observation of an activity as it occurs

All the research instruments discussed so far are useful primarily for the gathering of qualitative information. The intent is not to amass data or to search for statistical significance, but rather to obtain a better understanding of given situations, behavioral patterns, or underlying dimensions. The researcher using these instruments must be cautioned that even frequent repetition of the measurements will not lead to a statistically valid result. However, statistical validity often may not be the major focus of corporate research. Rather, it may be the better understanding, description, and prediction of events that have an impact on decision making. When quantitative data are desired, surveys and experimentation are more appropriate research instruments.

Surveys **Survey** research is useful in quantifying concepts. In the social sciences, it is generally accepted that the cross-cultural survey is scientifically the most powerful method of hypothesis testing.[17] Surveys are usually conducted via questionnaires that are administered *personally,* by *mail,* or by *telephone.* Use of the survey technique presupposes that the population under study is accessible—able to comprehend and respond to the question posed through the chosen medium.

surveys
research method that gathers data by soliciting answers to carefully framed questions from a group of participants in the market

Often **personal interviews** with knowledgeable people can be of great value for the corporation desiring international information. Because bias from the individual may be part of the findings, the intent should be to obtain not a wide variety of data, but rather in-depth information. Particularly when specific answers are sought to very narrow questions, interviews can be most useful.

personal interview
survey technique in which an interviewer personally calls on a respondent in an effort to complete a questionnaire

For **mail** and **telephone surveys,** a major precondition is the feasibility of using the postal system or the widespread availability of telephones. Obviously, this is not a given in all countries. In many nations, only limited records about dwellings, their location, and their occupants are available. In Venezuela, for example, most houses are not numbered but rather are given individual names like Casa Rosa or El Retiro. In some countries, street maps are not even available. As a result, reaching respondents by mail is virtually impossible. Global Learning Experience 10.5 summarizes this type of problem in one of the world's major cities—Tokyo. In other countries, obtaining a correct address may be easy, but the postal system may not function well. The Italian postal service, for example, repeatedly has suffered from scandals that exposed such practices as selling undelivered mail to paper mills for recycling.

mail survey
survey technique in which the questionnaire is mailed to a selected group of respondents

telephone survey
survey technique in which a selected group of respondents are contacted by telephone and asked questions about some activity

GLOBAL LEARNING EXPERIENCE 10.5

In Tokyo, Finding the Correct Address Is Not Easy

Conducting consumer research using personal interviews or mail surveys is easy—all you need is an accurate mailing address so that the local postal service or interviewer can find the respondent and deliver the survey package or conduct the interview. Surprisingly, it's not that simple, as many places in the world do not have street names and there are not rules for numbering the houses; large Japanese cities are good examples.

Tokyo is one of the largest metropolitan centers in the world, but very few of the streets have names. The streets themselves are confusing as they wander in every direction. A Tokyo address includes the name of the area and numbers representing the district, block, and house. The house closest to the Imperial Palace is supposed to be No. 1, and all other houses are supposed to be numbered from that point clockwise around the block. The problem is that many times these rules are not followed. In some instances, all of the houses on the block have the same number.

How, then, does one find a specific house in the maze of unnamed streets and houses numbered in odd ways? The answer—with great difficulty. Tokyo residents try to get around the problem by describing the house location relative to some conspicuous landmark; even then it's not easy to find the house.

For the market researcher, conducting surveys in cities like Tokyo presents special problems. The problems can be minimized by a comprehensive understanding of the market and careful preplanning of the research.

In Japanese cities, finding a street address can be a time-consuming task. Shuichi Abe, a delivery man at Express Company, looked for a house in an alley in central Tokyo to deliver a package.
SOURCE: "Tokyo; Where Streets Are Noodles," *New York Times*, July 16, 1996, A-6.

Telephone surveys may also be inappropriate if telephone ownership is rare. In such instances, any information obtained would be highly biased even if the researcher randomized the calls. In some cases, inadequate telephone networks and systems, frequent line congestion, and a lack of telephone directories may also prevent the researcher from conducting surveys. Yet, with today's communication capabilities, some research firms are able to conduct telephone research around the world from a single location.

Since surveys deal with people, who in a global setting are likely to display major differences in culture, preference, education, and attitude, just to mention a few factors, the use of the survey technique must be carefully examined. For example, in some regions of the world, recipients of letters may be illiterate.[18] Others may be very literate, but totally unaccustomed to some of the standard research scaling techniques used in the United States and therefore unable to respond to the instrument. Other recipients of a survey may be reluctant to respond to writing, particularly when sensitive questions are asked. This sensitivity, of course, also varies by country. In some nations, any questions about income, even in categorical form, are considered highly proprietary; in others, the purchasing behavior of individuals is not easily divulged.

The researcher needs to understand these constraints and prepare a survey that is responsive to them. For example, surveys can incorporate drawings or even cartoons to communicate better. Personal administration or collaboration with locally accepted intermediaries may improve the response rate. Indirect questions may need to substitute for direct ones in sensitive areas. Questions may have to be reworded to ensure proper communication.

Focus Groups **Focus groups** are a useful research tool resulting in interactive interviews. A group of knowledgeable people is gathered for a limited period of time (two to four hours). Usually, seven to ten participants is the ideal size for a focus group. A specific topic is introduced and thoroughly discussed by all group members. Because of the interaction, hidden issues are sometimes raised that would not have been detected in an individual interview. The skill of the group leader in stimulating discussion is crucial to the success of a focus group. Focus groups, like in-depth interviews, do not provide statistically significant information; however, they can be helpful in providing information about perceptions, emotions, and attitudinal factors. In addition, once individuals have been gathered, focus groups are highly efficient means of rapidly accumulating a substantial amount of information.

focus groups
research technique in which representatives of a proposed target audience contribute to marketing research by participating in a supervised unstructured discussion

When planning global research using focus groups, the researcher must be aware of the importance of language and culture in the discussion process. Not all societies encourage frank and open exchange and disagreement among individuals. Status consciousness may result in the opinion of one participant being reflected by all others. Disagreement may be seen as impolite, or certain topics may be taboo. Unless a native focus group leader is used, it also is possible to completely misread the interactions among group participants and to miss out on nuances and constraints participants feel when commenting in the group situation. Before deciding on a focus group in a global setting, the researcher must be fully aware of these issues. See Global Learning Experience 10.6.

Summary of Survey Methods

In spite of all the potential difficulties, the survey technique remains a useful one because it allows the researcher to rapidly accumulate a large quantity of data amenable to statistical analysis. With constantly expanding technological capabilities, global researchers will be able to use this technique even more in the future.

Table 10.3 summarizes the major advantages and disadvantages of each survey method. The reader should note the possible additional disadvantages of using these methods globally.

Scenario Building

scenario building
identification of crucial variables and determining their effects on different cases or approaches

The information obtained through research efforts can then be used to conduct a scenario analysis. One approach involves the development of a series of plausible

GLOBAL LEARNING EXPERIENCE 10.6

Market Research in Mexico

Learning which products Mexicans want is difficult because marketing research in Mexico is unpopular. Reliable information often cannot be obtained because of a lack of experience in data collection and supervision of fieldwork. In addition, Mexican consumers are not accustomed to someone calling on the phone or knocking at the door and asking for an opinion.

Market researchers must carefully consider data collection methods in order to obtain honest opinions. For instance, it is almost impossible to conduct phone surveys in Mexico. Telephone penetration in Mexico City is between 55 percent and 60 percent; in the large cities of Monterrey and Guadalajara it is less than 50 percent. In other cities, as few as 35 percent of the people have phones. Collecting data that fully represent the population is nearly impossible.

House-to-house research is believed to be the only truly reliable method in Mexico. The importance of sampling and fieldwork are crucial in this instance. Some Mexican research firms don't realize the importance of sampling. For example, when a client requires 1,000 completed interviews, many firms pick anyone from anywhere to interview and hire people to do the job as quickly as possible.

Controlling the quality of the interviewer can be difficult. When a house-to-house survey is done, usually large numbers of untrained and inexperienced interviewers are conducting it. A company representative may want to be present for the training of those who will be doing the work in order to make an evaluation.

It is possible to conduct focus groups almost anywhere in Mexico, but many major cities do not have the facilities. Sessions have to be conducted in a hotel or in a place where viewers can watch on closed-circuit TV. It is important to supervise the recruitment of participants. Many focus group facilities allow those involved to bring friends and relatives who do not meet the requirements of the screener. To avoid this problem, the facility can be asked to provide a daily progress report with the names, addresses, and phone numbers of the participants. On the day of the focus group, the moderator should reevaluate the participants before accepting them into the group.

SOURCE: Naghi Namakforoosh, "Data Collection Methods Hold Key to Research in Mexico," *Marketing News,* August 29, 1994, 28.

scenarios that are constructed from trends observed in the environment. Another method consists of formally reviewing assumptions built into existing business plans and positions.[19] Subsequently, some of these key assumptions such as economic growth rates, import penetration, population growth, and political stability can be varied. By projecting variations for medium- to long-term periods, completely new environmental conditions can emerge. These conditions can then be analyzed for their potential domestic and international impact on corporate strategy.

The identification of crucial variables and the degree of variation are of major importance in scenario building. Frequently, key experts are used to gain information about potential variations and about the viability of certain scenarios.

A wide variety of scenarios must be built in order to expose corporate executives to a number of potential occurrences. Ideally, even farfetched scenarios deserve some consideration, if only to address worst-case possibilities. A scenario for Union Carbide Corporation, for example, could have included the possibility of a disaster as it occurred in Bhopal.

Advantages and Disadvantages of Survey Methods TABLE 10.3

Advantages	Domestic Disadvantages	Additional Potential International Disadvantages
Personal Interview		
• High response rate—50%–80% • High rate of properly completed questionnaires • Complex questions can be asked	• Expensive • Moderately slow • Interviewer fraud • Interviewer may bias results personally or in interpreting answers • Necessity to "call back"	• Cultural resistance to answering questions, particularly by women • Inability of respondents to express feelings or opinions about a product or service • Problem of physically reaching and finding respondents in rural areas
Telephone		
• Moderately low cost • Fast • High response rate—40%–75% • Works well with short questionnaire • Respondents more likely to answer phone than admit interviewer into their home	• No phone • Unlisted phone number • People not at home • Refusal to answer/hang ups • Possibility of interviewer bias	• Relatively few people with telephones • Poor telephone service • Lack of telephone directories
Mail		
• Low cost • No interviewer bias	• Low response rate • Slow • Old mailing list, incorrect addresses • Not recommended for complex questions • Frequent blanks or "don't know" responses • Funny/joke responses—not useable • May be treated as junk mail	• No mail delivery • Theft of mail • Mail is "postage due" • Lack of street numbers or names • Literacy of respondents • Lack of mailing lists
Focus Groups		
• Cost-efficient interviewing method —one interviewer and 10–12 respondents • Inexpensive • Fast • Flexibility in obtaining meaningful responses • Interaction among respondents can stimulate response from shy respondents	• Respondents may not be typical of universe being researched • If respondents are typical, group is too small to be an accurate statistical sample • Success of interview depends on skill of interviewer • Single individual may try to dominate group	• All of personal interview disadvantages listed above • Cultural problem in mixing genders and different social levels in one group

QUESTION

Why is it said that the Gauchos, cowboys of the Argentine Pampas, don't use forks?

Advances in Telephone and Data Transmission Technology Facilitate the Collection of Data for International Business Research

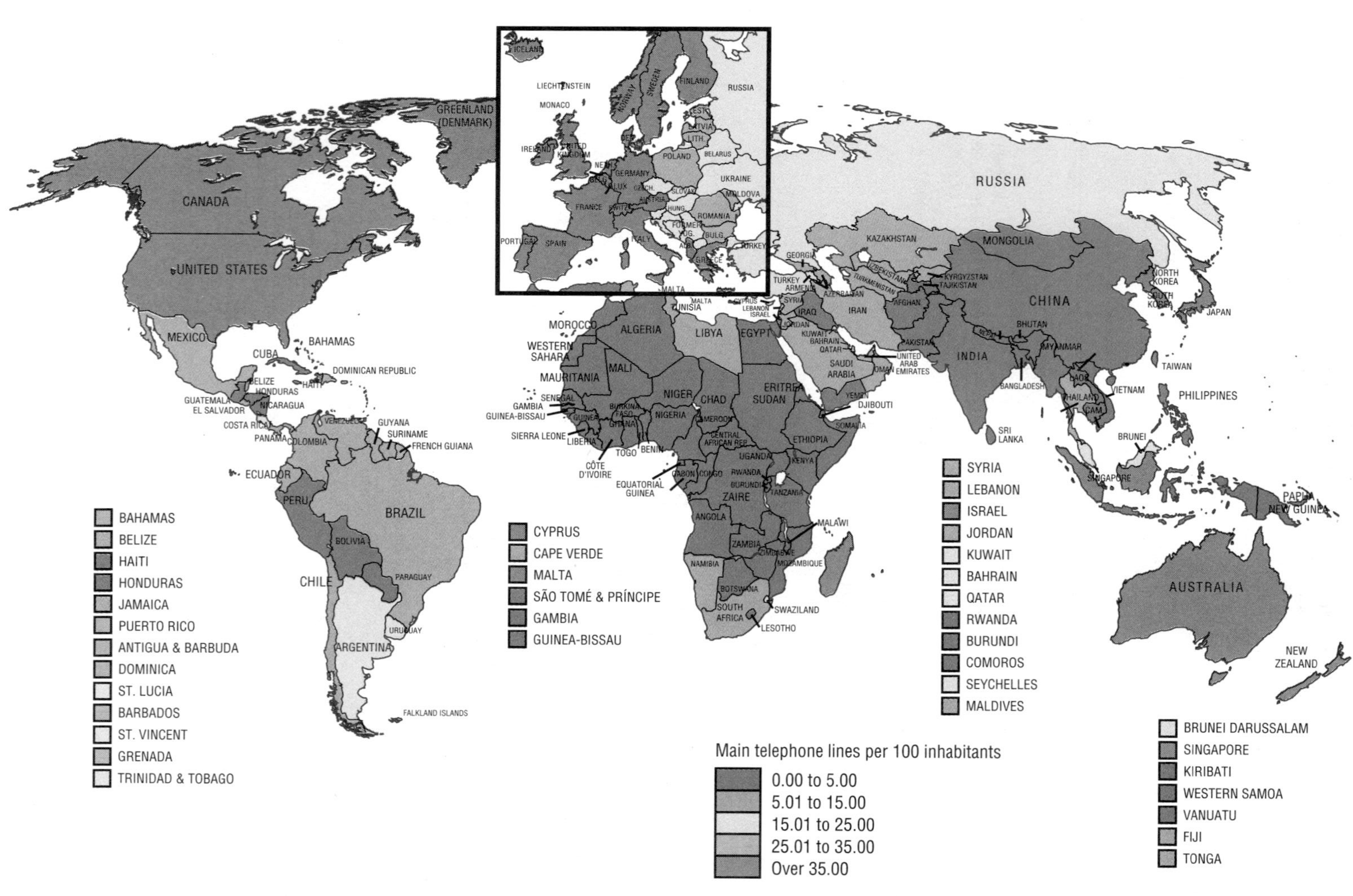

SOURCE: *Peters Atlas of the World*, 1990; *The New Book of World Rankings*, 1991.

ANSWER *The Gauchos say that if you need a fork, then you need a plate, you need a table, and then you need a chair, and before long you're living in a house with a woman and a bunch of kids and a dog that kills your chickens. So forget the forks. Stick with your* caballo *(horse) and eat with your* manos *(hands), say the Gauchos.*

In order for scenarios to be useful, management must analyze and respond to them by formulating contingency plans; such planning will broaden horizons and may prepare managers for unexpected situations. By anticipating possible problems, managers hone their response capability and in turn shorten response times to actual problems.

SUMMARY

Constraints of time, resources, and expertise are the major reasons not to conduct global research. Nevertheless, firms need to carry out planned and organized research in order to explore foreign market opportunities and challenges successfully. Such research must be linked closely to the decision-making process.

Global research differs from domestic research in that the environment—which determines how well tools, techniques, and concepts apply—is different abroad. In addition, the global manager must deal with duties, exchange rates, and international documentation; a greater number of interacting factors; and a much broader definition of the concept of competition.

The research process starts by recognizing the need for research which is often not well understood. When the firm is uninformed about global differences in consumer tastes and preferences or about foreign market environments, the need for global research is particularly great. Research objectives need to be determined based on the corporate mission, the level of international expertise, and the business plan. These objectives will enable the research to identify the information requirements.

Given the scarcity of resources, companies beginning their global effort must rely on data that have already been collected. These secondary data are available from sources such as governments, international organizations, directories, or trade associations.

To fulfill specific information requirements, the researcher may need to collect primary data. An appropriate research technique must be selected to collect the information. Sensitivity to different international environments and cultures will aid the researcher in deciding whether to use interviews, focus groups, observation, surveys, or experimentation as data-collection techniques.

Key Terms and Concepts

market segmentation
data
information
proxy information
primary data
secondary data
experimentation
observation
surveys
personal interview
mail survey
telephone survey
focus group
scenario building

Questions

1. What is the difference between domestic and global research?
2. You are employed by National Engineering, a U.S. firm that designs subways. Because you have had a course in global business, your boss asks you to spend the next week exploring global possibilities for the company. How will you go about this task?
3. Discuss the possible shortcomings of secondary data.
4. Identify the major sources of secondary data.
5. Why should a firm collect primary data in its global research?
6. How is global research affected by differences in language and culture?
7. Is highly priced personalized advice from an individual really worth the money?

Recommended Readings

Barbuta, Domenica M., *The International Financial Statistics Locator: A Research and Information Guide,* New York, Garland Publishers, 1995.

Churchill, Gilbert A. *Marketing Research: Methodological Foundations,* 6th ed. Fort Worth, TX, Dryden Press, 1995.

Delphos, William A. *Inside Washington: Government Resources for International Business,* Washington D.C., Venture Publishing, 1995.

Directory of Online Databases, Santa Monica, CA: Cuadra Associates, published annually.

Palvia, Prashant, Anil Kumar, Nadesan Kumar and Rebecca Hendon, "Information Requirements of a Global EIS: An Exploratory Macro Assessment," *Decisions Support Systems,* 16, 2 1996: 169–179.

Patzer, Gordon L., *Using Secondary Data in Marketing Research: United States and Worldwide,* Westport, Connecticut, Quorum Books, 1995.

Notes

1. David A. Ricks, *Blunders in International Business* (Cambridge, Mass.: Blackwell, 1993).
2. Vinay Kothari, "Reseaching for Export Marketing," in *Export Promotion: The Public and Private Sector Interaction,* ed. M. Czinkota (New York: Praeger, 1983), 155.
3. S. Tamer Cavusgil, "International Marketing Research: Insights into Company Practices," in *Research in Marketing,* vol. 7, ed. J. N. Sheth (Greenwich, Conn.: JAI Press, 1984), 261–288.
4. Susan P. Douglas and C. Samuel Craig, *International Marketing Research* (Englewood Cliffs, N.J.: Prentice-Hall, 1983), 2.
5. Cavusgil, "International Marketing Research," 261–288.
6. Reijo Luostarinen, *Internationalization of the Firm* (Helsinki, Finland: The Helsinki School of Economics, 1979), 124–33.
7. Franklin R. Root, *Entry Strategies for International Markets:* (Lexington, Mass.: Lexington Books, 1994), 15–20.
8. For one of the best summaries, see Business International, *Indicators of Market Size for 109 Countries* (New York: Business International, 1986).
9. Philip Kotler, *Marketing Management: Analysis, Planning and Control* (Englewood Cliffs, N.J.: Prentice-Hall, 1984), 234.
10. Reed Moyer, "International Market Analysis," *Journal of Marketing Research* 16 (November 1968): 353–360.
11. The World Bank, *World Development Report* (Oxford, England: Oxford University Press, 1990), 236–237.
12. Root, *Entry Strategies for International Markets,* 19.
13. Igal Ayal and Jehiel Zif, "Marketing Expansion Strategies in Multinational Marketing," *Journal of Marketing* 43 (Spring 1979): 84–94.
14. David J. Andzlman, "Betting on the Net," *Sales and Marketing Management* (June 1995): 47–59.
15. Stephanie Losee, "How to Market on the Digital Frontier," *Fortune* (May 1, 1995): 88.
16. Michael R. Czinkota and Masaaki Kotabe, "Product Development the Japanese Way," *The Journal of Business Strategy,* 11,6 (November/December 1990): 31–36.
17. Lothar G. Winter and Charles R. Prohaska, "Methodological Problems in the Comparative Analysis of International Marketing Systems," *Journal of the Academy of Marketing Science* 11 (Fall 1983): 421.
18. Douglas and Craig, *International Marketing Research*, 200.
19. William H. Davidson, "The Role of Global Scanning in Business Planning," *Organizational Dynamics* (Winter 1991): 5–16.

APPENDIX

Monitors of International Issues

Selected Organizations

American Bankers Association
1120 Connecticut Avenue N.W.
Washington, D.C. 20036

American Bar Association
750 N. Lake Shore Drive
Chicago, IL 60611
and
1800 M Street N.W.
Washington, D.C. 20036

American Management Association
440 First Street N.W.
Washington, D.C. 20001

American Marketing Association
250 S. Wacker Drive Suite 200
Chicago, IL 60606

American Petroleum Institute
1220 L Street N.W.
Washington, D.C. 20005

Asian Development Bank
2330 Roxas Boulevard
Pasay City, Philippines

Chamber of Commerce of the United States
1615 H Street N.W.
Washington, D.C. 20062

Commission of the European Communities to the United States
2100 M Street N.W. Suite 707
Washington, D.C. 20037

Conference Board
845 Third Avenue
New York, NY 10022
and
1755 Massachusetts Avenue N.W.
Suite 312
Washington, D.C. 20036

Electronic Industries Association
2001 I Street N.W.
Washington, D.C. 20006

European Community Information Service
200 Rue de la Loi
1049 Brussels, Belgium
and
2100 M Street N.W. 7th Floor
Washington, D.C. 20037

Export-Import Bank of the United States
811 Vermont Avenue N.W.
Washington, D.C. 20571

Federal Reserves Bank of New York
33 Liberty Street
New York, NY 10045

Inter-American Development Bank
1300 New York Avenue N.W.
Washington, D.C. 20577

International Bank for Reconstruction and Development (World Bank)
1818 H Street N.W.
Washington, D.C. 20433

International Monetary Fund
700 19th Street N.W.
Washington, D.C. 20431

Marketing Research Society
111 E. Wacker Drive Suite 600
Chicago, IL 60601

National Association of Manufacturers
1331 Pennsylvania Avenue
Suite 1500
Washington, D.C. 20004

National Federation of Independent Business
600 Maryland Avenue S.W.
Suite 700
Washington, D.C. 20024

Organization for Economic Cooperation and Development
2 rue Andre Pascal
75775 Paris Cedex Ko, France
and
2001 L Street N.W. Suite 700
Washington, D.C. 20036

Organization of American States
17th and Constitution Avenue N.W.
Washington, D.C. 20006

Society for International Development
1401 New York Avenue N.W.
Suite 1100
Washington, D.C. 20005

United Nations

Conference of Trade and Development
Palais des Nations
1211 Geneva 10
Switzerland

Department of Economic and Social Affairs
1 United Nations Plaza
New York, NY 10017

Industrial Development Organization
1660 L Street N.W.
Washington, D.C. 20036
and

United Nations (continued)

Post Office Box 300
Vienna International Center
A-1400 Vienna, Austria

Publications
Room 1194
1 United Nations Plaza
New York, NY 10017

Statistical Yearbook
1 United Nations Plaza
New York, NY 10017

U.S. Government

Agency for International Development
Office of Business Relations
Washington, D.C. 20523

Customs Service
1301 Constitution Avenue N.W.
Washington, D.C. 20229

Department of Agriculture
12th Street and Jefferson Drive S.W.
Washington, D.C. 20250

Department of Commerce
Herbert C. Hoover Building
14th Street and Constitution Avenue N.W.
Washington, D.C. 20230

Department of State
2201 C Street N.W.
Washington, D.C. 20520

Department of the Treasury
15th Street and Pennsylvania Avenue N.W.
Washington, D.C. 20220

Federal Trade Commission
6th Street and Pennsylvania Avenue N.W.
Washington, D.C. 20580

International Trade Commission
701 E. Street N.W.
Washington, D.C. 20436

Small Business Administration
Imperial Building
1441 L Street N.W.
Washington, D.C. 20416

Trade Development Program
1621 North Kent Street
Rosslyn, VA 22209

World Trade Center Association
1 World Trade Center Suite 7701
New York, NY 10048

Indexes to Literature

Business Periodical Index
H.W. Wilson Co.
950 University Avenue
Bronx, NY 10452

New York Times Index
University Microfilms International
300 N. Zeeb Road
Ann Arbor, MI 48106

Public Affairs Information Service Bulletin
11 W. 40th Street
New York, NY 10018

Readers' Guide to Periodical Literature
H.W. Wilson Co.
950 University Avenue
Bronx, NY 10452

Wall Street Journal Index
University Microfilms International
300 N. Zeeb Rd.
Ann Arbor, MI 48106

Periodic Reports, Newspapers, Magazines

Advertising Age
Crain Communications Inc.
740 N. Rush Street
Chicago, IL 60611

Advertising World
Directories International Inc.
150 Fifth Avenue Suite 610
New York, NY 10011

Arab Report and Record
84 Chancery Lane
London WC2A 1DL, England

Barron's
University Microfilms International
300 N. Zeeb Road
Ann Arbor, MI 48106

Business America
U.S. Department of Commerce
14th Street and Constitution Avenue N.W.
Washington, D.C. 20230

Business International
Business International Corp.
One Dag Hammarskjold Plaza
New York, NY 10017

Business Week
McGraw-Hill Publications Co.
1221 Avenue of the Americas
New York, NY 10020

Commodity Trade Statistics
United Nations Publications
1 United Nations Plaza
Room DC2-853
New York, NY 10017

Periodic Reports, Newspapers, Magazines (continued)

Conference Board Record
Conference Board Inc.
845 Third Avenue
New York, NY 10022

Customs Bulletin
U.S. Customs Service
1301 Constitution Avenue N.W.
Washington, D.C. 20229

Dun's Business Month
Goldhirsh Group
38 Commercial Wharf
Boston, MA 02109

The Economist
Economist Newspaper Ltd.
25 St. James Street
London SW1A 1HG, England

Europe Magazine
2100 M Street N.W. Suite 707
Washington, D.C. 20037

The Financial Times
Bracken House
10 Cannon Street
London EC4P 4BY, England

Forbes
Forbes, Inc.
60 Fifth Avenue
New York, NY 10011

Fortune
Time, Inc.
Time & Life Building
1271 Avenue of the Americas
New York, NY 10020

Global Trade
North American Publishing Co.
401 N. Broad Street
Philadelphia, PA 19108

Industrial Marketing
Crain Communications Inc.
740 N. Rush Street
Chicago, IL 60611

International Financial Statistics
International Monetary Fund
Publications Unit
700 19th Street N.W.
Washington, D.C. 20431

Investor's Daily
Box 25970
Los Angeles, CA 90025

Journal of Commerce
110 Wall Street
New York, NY 10005

Sales & Marketing Management
Bill Communications Inc.
633 Third Avenue
New York, NY 10017

Wall Street Journal
Dow Jones & Company
200 Liberty Street
New York, NY 10281

World Agriculture Situation
U.S. Department of Agriculture
Economics Management Staff
Information Division
1301 New York Avenue N.W.
Washington, D.C. 20005

World Development
Pergamon Press Inc.
Journals Division
Maxwell House
Fairview Park
Elmsford, NY 10523

World Trade Center Association (WTCA) Directory
World Trade Center Association
1 World Trade Center
New York, NY 10048

Directories

American Register of Exporters and Importers
38 Park Row
New York, NY 10038

Arabian Year Book
Dar Al-Seuassam Est.
Box 42480
Skuwakh, Kuwait

Directors of American Firms Operating in Foreign Countries
World Trade Academy Press
Uniworld Business Publications Inc.
50 E. 42nd Street
New York, NY 10017

Encyclopedia of Associations
Gale Research Co.
Book Tower
Detroit, MI 48226

Polk's World Bank Directory
R.C. Polk & Co.
2001 Elm Hill Pike
P.O. Box 1340
Nashville, TN 37202

Verified Director of Manufacturers' Representatives
MacRae's Blue Book Inc.
817 Broadway
New York, NY 10003

World Guide to Trade Associations
K.G. Saur & Co.
175 Fifth Avenue
New York, NY 10010

Encyclopedias, Handbooks, and Miscellaneous

A Basic Guide to Exporting
U.S. Government Printing Office
Superintendent of Documents
Washington, D.C. 20402

Doing Business in . . . Series
Price Waterhouse
1251 Avenue of the Americas
New York, NY 10020

Economic Survey of Europe
The United Nations
United Nations Publication Division
1 United Nations Plaza
Room DC-0853
New York, NY 10017

Economic Survey of Latin America
United Nations
United Nations Publishing Division
1 United Nations Plaza
Room DC-0853
New York, NY 10017

Encyclopedia Americana, International Edition
Grolier Inc.
Danbury, CT 06816

Encyclopedia of Business Information Sources
Gale Research Co.
Book Tower
Detroit, MI 48226

Europa Year Book
Europa Publications Ltd.
18 Bedford Square
London WC1B 3JN, England

Export Administration Regulations
U.S. Government Printing Office
Superintendent of Documents
Washington, D.C. 20402

Export Shipping Manual
U.S. Government Printing Office
Superintendent of Documents
Washington, D.C. 20402

Exporters' Encyclopedia—World Marketing Guide
Dun's Marketing Services
49 Old Bloomfield Road
Mountain Lake, NJ 07046

Export-Import Bank of the United States Annual Report
U.S. Government Printing Office
Superintendent of Documents
Washington, D.C. 20402

Exporting for the Small Business
U.S. Government Printing Office
Superintendent of Documents
Washington, D.C. 20402

Exporting to the United States
U.S. Government Printing Office
Superintendent of Documents
Washington, D.C. 20402

Foreign Business Practices: Materials on Practical Aspects of Exporting, International Licensing, and Investing
U.S. Government Printing Office
Superintendent of Documents
Washington, D.C. 20402

A Guide to Financing Exports
U.S. Government Printing Office
Superintendent of Documents
Washington, D.C. 20402

Handbook of Marketing Research
McGraw-Hill Book Co.
1221 Avenue of the Americas
New York, NY 10020

International Encyclopedia of the Social Sciences
Macmillan and the Free Press
866 Third Avenue
New York, NY 10022

Market Share Reports
U.S. Government Printing Office
Superintendent of Documents
Washington, D.C. 20402

Marketing and Communications Media Dictionary
Media Horizons Inc.
50 W. 25th Street
New York, NY 10010

Media Guide International: Business/Professional Publications
Directories International Inc.
150 Fifth Avenue Suite 610
New York, NY 10011

Overseas Business Reports
U.S. Government Printing Office
Superintendent of Documents
Washington, D.C. 20402

Trade Finance Report
U.S. Department of Commerce
International Trade Administration
Washington, D.C. 20230

World Economic Conditions in Relation to Agricultural Trade
U.S. Government Printing Office
Superintendent of Documents
Washington, D.C. 20402

Yearbook of International Trade Statistics
United Nations
United Nations Publishing Division
1 United Nations Plaza
Room DC-0853
New York, NY 10017

APPENDIX

Description of Selection U.S. Government Publications and Services

Macro Data

World Population is issued by the U.S. Bureau of the Census, which collects and analyzes worldwide demographic data. Information is provided about total population, fertility, mortality, urban population, growth rate, and life expectancy. Also published are detailed demographic profiles, including an analysis of the labor force structure of individual countries.

Foreign Trade Highlights are annual reports published by the Department of Commerce. They provide basic data on U.S. merchandise trade with major trading partners and regions. They also contain brief analyses of recent U.S. trade developments.

Foreign Trade Report FT410 provides a monthly statistical record of shipments of all merchandise from the United States to foreign countries, including both the quantity and dollar value of exports to each country. It also contains cumulative export statistics from the first of the calendar year.

World Agriculture, a publication of the U.S. Department of Agriculture, provides production information, data, and analyses by country along with a review of recent economic conditions and changes in agricultural and trade policies. Frequent supplements provide an outlook of anticipated developments for the coming year.

Country Information

National Trade Data Bank, a key product of the U.S. Department of Commerce, provides monthly CD-ROM disks that contain overseas market research, trade statistics, contact information, and other reports that may assist U.S. exporters in their international marketing efforts.

Country Marketing Plan reports on commercial activities and climate in a country and is prepared by the Foreign Commercial Service staffs abroad. It also contains an action plan for the coming year, including a list of trade events and research to be conducted.

Industry SubSector Analyses are market research reports, ranging from 5 to 20 pages, on specific product categories, for example, electromedical equipment in one country.

Overseas Business Reports (OBR) present economic and commercial profiles on specific countries and provide background statistics. Selected information on the direction and the volume and nature of U.S. foreign trade is also provided.

Background Notes, prepared by the Department of State, present a survey of a country's people, geography, economy, government, and foreign policy. The reports also include important national economic and trade information.

Foreign Economic Trends presents recent business and economic developments and the latest economic indicators of more than 100 countries.

Product Information

Export Statistics Profiles analyze exports for a single industry, product by product, country by country, over a five-year period. Data are rank-ordered by dollar value for quick identification of the leading products and industries. Tables show the sales of each product to each country as well as competitive information, growth, and future trends. Each profile also contains a narrative analysis that highlights the industry's prospects, performance, and leading products.

U.S. Industrial Outlook, an annual publication of the U.S. Department of Commerce, provides an overview of the domestic and international performance of all major U.S. industries, complete with employment and shipment information and a forecast of future developments.

Export Information System Data Reports, available from the U.S. Small Business Administration, provide small businesses with a list of the 25 largest importing markets for their products and the 10 best markets for U.S. exporters of the products. Trends within those markets and the major sources of foreign competition are also discussed.

Services

Agent Distributor Service (ADS): The Foreign Commercial Service (FCS) provides a customized search for interested and qualified foreign representatives for a firm's product.

Aglink: Collaborative effort between the Foreign Agricultural Service and the Small Business Administration to match foreign buyers with U.S. agribusiness firms.

Catalog Exhibitions: The Department of Commerce organizes displays of product literature and videotape presentations overseas.

Comparison Shopping Service: The FCS provides a custom foreign market survey on a product's overall marketability, names of competitors, comparative prices, and customary business practices.

Economic Bulletin Board: The Department of Commerce provides access to the latest economic data releases, including trade opportunities, for on-line users.

Foreign Agricultural Service: Employees of the U.S. Department of Agriculture, stationed both abroad and in the United States with the mission to facilitate agricultural exports from the United States. Provides counseling, research, general market information, and market introduction services.

Foreign Buyer Program: The FCS brings foreign buyers to U.S. trade shows for industries with high export potential.

Going Global: A computerized, on-line information system which lists market opportunities, information on foreign countries and export intermediaries. Primarily focused on agricultural firms.

Matchmaker Events: The Department of Commerce introduces U.S. companies to new markets through short visits abroad to match the U.S. firm with a representative or prospective partner.

Seminar Missions: The Department of Commerce sponsors technical seminars abroad designed to promote sales of sophisticated products and technology.

Trade Missions: Groups of U.S. business executives, led by Commerce Department staff, meet with potential foreign buyers, agents, and distributors.

Trade Opportunity Program: The FCS daily collection of trade opportunities worldwide is published and electronically distributed to subscribers.

World Traders Data Reports: The FCS publishes background research conducted by FCS officers abroad on potential trading partners, such as agents, distributors, and licensees.

APPENDIX

Internet Addresses for Global Marketing Research

Selected Organizations

American Bankers Association
http:/www.aba.com

American Bar Association
http://www.abanet.org

American Management Association
http://www.tregistry.com/ttr/ama

American Petroleum Institute
http://www.api.org

Asian Development Bank
http://www.asiandevbank.org

Commission of the European Union to the United States
http://www.eurunion.org

Electronic Industries Association
http://www.eia.org

European Community Information Service
http://www.europa.eu.int

Export-Import Bank of the United States
http://www.exim.gov

Federal Reserve Bank of New York
http://www.ny.frb.org

Inter-American Development Bank
http://iadb.6000.iadb.org

International Bank for Reconstruction and Development (World Bank)
http://www.worldbank.org

International Monetary Fund
http://www.imf.org

National Association of Manufacturers
http://www.nam.org

National Federation of Independent Business
http://www.nfibonline.com

Organization for Economic Cooperation and Development
http://www.oecd.org (France) AND
http://www.oecdwash.org (Washington, DC)

Organization of American States
http://www.oas.org

Society for International Development
http://www.waw/be/sid

United Nations

All listings at:
http://www.un.org

Industrial Development Organization
http://www.unido.org

U.S. Government

Agency for International Development
http://www.info.gov.usaid.gov

Customs Service
http://www.customs.ustreas.gov

Department of Agriculture
http://www.usda.gov

Department of Commerce
http://www.doc.gov

Department of State
http://www.state.gov

Department of Treasury
http://www.ustreas.gov

Federal Trade Commission
http://www.ftc.gov

International Trade Commission
http://www.usitc.gov

Small Business Administration
http://www.sbaonline.gov

World Trade Centers Association
http://www.wtca.org

Indexes to Literature

New York Times Index
http://www.nytimes.com

Public Affairs Information Service Bulletin
http://www.pais.org

Reader's Guide to Periodical Literature
http://www.tulane.edu/~horn.rdg.html

Wall Street Journal Index
http://www.wsj.com

Periodic Reports, Newspapers, Magazines

Advertising Age
http://www.adage.com

Barron's
http://www.barrons.com

Business Week
http://www.businessweek.com

The Economist
http://www.economist.com

The Financial Times
http://www.ft-se.co.uk

Forbes
http://www.forbes.com

Fortune
http://fortune.com

International Financial Statistics
http://www.imf.com

Wall Street Journal
http://www.wsj.com

World Agricultural Situation
http://www.econ.ag.gov

Some Other Helpful Internet Sites

U.S. Business Advisor
http://www.business.gov

National Trade Data Bank
http://www.stat-usa.gov

Office of the U.S. Trade Representative
http://www.ustr.gov/index.html

The White House
http://www.whitehouse.gov

Fed World:
http://www.fedworld.gov

Central Intelligence Agency
http://www.cia.gov

Global Business Entry

LEARNING OBJECTIVES

To see how firms gradually progress through a globalization process.

To examine the differing reasons why firms may globalize.

To study the various ways of entering the global market.

To understand the role and functions of international intermediaries.

To learn about the multiple problems and challenges of export trading.

Some Keys to Export Success

Since 1985, the United States has experienced an export boom unprecedented in history. Never before had a developed nation accomplished such rapid export growth of manufactured goods. Considering that in 1985 the United States was already the world's top exporter, the growth is extremely impressive. This success seems in stark contrast to the recent domestic recession. Although the volume of annual export growth has slowed down during the past couple years, unless the world economy takes a significant slump, exports of U.S. manufactured goods are expected to continue to do well.

What factors account for the success of U.S. exporters? Peter Drucker identifies characteristics consistent across many of the successful U.S. exporters.

1. *Don't compete based on price:* All of the export powerhouses sold a high-value-added product in the foreign market. In only very few cases is the product sold primarily on price competition. Instead, the product is often unique and occupies a distinct niche position in the marketplace. One clear example is 3M's Post-its.
2. *Know your foreign customers:* Successful exporters know their customers well. Drucker argues that even with the huge geographical separation, this intimacy is easy to achieve. Take the example of Boeing, for instance, whose business is to know and track all the world's airlines. When Boeing enters a foreign market, it has good insight into the customer's marketplace, needs, and resources. Similarly, a U.S. rock-and-roll producer, after performing some market research, is likely to have good insight into whether or not a hit U.S. tape will also be a hit in Germany. Says Drucker: "The world market is a 'foreign' market only in terms of trade statistics. For successful businesspeople, these are all 'familiar' markets, at least for knowledge-intensive products." This proposition is supported by an exporting heart valve manufacturer who said: "I do not sell to the world market. I sell to cardiac surgeons."
3. *Bigness is not an advantage:* Many of the winners of the U.S. export boom are mid-size or small companies boasting a particular expertise in a specific field. Even the large companies doing business abroad often create independent business units responsible for exporting and marketing a specific product abroad. General Electric is an example. Although GE is engaged in a variety of businesses, its European medical electronics division only sells medical electronics, and its European jet engine division only sells jet engines.

SOURCE: Peter Drucker, "Secrets of the U.S. Export Boom," *The Wall Street Journal,* August 1, 1991, p. A12.

Global business holds out the promise of large new market areas, yet firms cannot simply jump into the global marketplace and expect to be successful. They must adjust to needs and opportunities abroad, have quality products, understand their customers, and do their homework, as this chapter's opening learning experience shows. The rapid globalization of markets, however, reduces the time available to adjust to new market realities.[1]

This chapter is concerned with the activities of firms preparing to enter global markets. Primary emphasis is placed on export activities. Global Learning Experience 11.1

identifies some of the strategies used by successful exporters. The chapter focuses on the role of management in starting up global operations and describes the basic stimuli for global activities. Ways of entering the global arena are highlighted, and the problems and benefits of each way are discussed. Finally, the role of facilitators and intermediaries in global business is described.

THE ROLE OF MANAGEMENT

The type and quality of its management are the keys to whether or not a firm will enter the international marketplace. Researchers have found that *management commitment* is crucial in the first steps toward international operations.[2] The management of firms that have been successful internationally is usually described as active rather than passive[3,4] or as aggressive rather than nonaggressive.[5] Conversely, the managers of firms that are unsuccessful or inactive globally usually exhibit a lack of determination or devotion to global business. The issue of managerial commitment is a crucial one because foreign market penetration requires a vast amount of market development activity, sensitivity toward foreign environments, research, and innovation.

Initiating global business activities takes the firm in an entirely new direction, quite different from adding a product line or hiring a few more people. Going global means that a fundamental strategic change is taking place. Research has shown that the decision to export, for example, usually comes from the highest levels of management. Typically, the president, chairman, or vice president of marketing is the chief decision maker.[6] A survey of the fastest growing mid-sized companies in the United States showed that for all global operations, the personal commitment and vision of the chief executive officer played a forceful role.[7]

The carrying out of the decision—that is, the initiation of global business transactions and their implementation—is then the primary responsibility of marketing personnel. However, in the final decision stage of evaluating global activities, the responsibility again rests with senior management. It therefore appears that, in order to influence a firm to go global, the president first needs to be convinced. Once the decision to globalize is made, the marketing department becomes active in global business.

The first step in acquiring global commitment is to become aware of global business opportunities. Management may then decide to enter the global marketplace on a limited basis and evaluate the results of the initial activities. Global business orientation develops over time.

Management in the majority of firms is much too preoccupied with short-term, immediate problems to engage in sophisticated long-run planning. As a result, most firms are simply not interested in global business. Yet certain situations may lead a manager to discover and understand the value of going global and to decide to pursue global business activities. Trigger factors frequently are foreign travel, during which new business opportunities are discovered, or the receipt of information that leads management to believe that such opportunities exist. Managers who have lived abroad and have learned foreign languages or are particularly interested in foreign cultures are more likely to investigate whether global business opportunities would be appropriate for their firms.

New management or new employees can also bring about a global orientation. For example, managers entering a firm may already have had some international business experience and may try to use this experience to further the business activities of the firm where they are currently employed.

REASONS TO GO ABROAD

Normally, management will consider global activities only when stimulated to do so. A variety of motivations can push and pull individuals and firms along the international path.[8] An overview of the major reasons that have been found to make firms go global is provided in Table 11.1. Some of the reasons come from within the firm (internal) while other reasons are the result of events outside (external) the firm.

Proactive Reasons

Profits are the major proactive motivation for seeking global business. Management may see global sales as a potential source of higher profit margins or of more added-on profits. Of course, the profitability anticipated when planning to go global is often quite different from the profitability actually obtained. Recent research has indicated that, particularly in global start-up operations, initial profitability may be quite low.[9]

Unique products or a technological advantage can be another major reason. A firm may produce goods or services that are not widely available from global competitors. Again, real and perceived advantages must be differentiated. Many firms believe that theirs are unique products or services, even though this may not be the case globally. If products or technologies are unique, however, they certainly can provide a competitive edge. What needs to be considered is how long such an advantage will last. The length of time is a function of the product, its technology, and the creativity of competitors. In the past, a firm with a competitive edge could often count on being the sole supplier to foreign markets for years to come. This type of advantage has shrunk dramatically because of competing technologies and the frequent lack of global patent protection.

Special knowledge about foreign customers or market situations may be another reason. Such knowledge may result from particular insights by a firm, special contacts an individual may have, in-depth research, or simply from being in the right place at the right time (for example, recognizing a good business situation during a vacation trip). Although such exclusivity can serve well as an initial stimulus for global business, it will rarely provide prolonged motivation because competitors—at least in the medium run—can be expected to catch up with the information advantage. Only if firms build up global information advantage as an ongoing process, through, for example, broad market scanning or assured informational exclusivity, can prolonged corporate strategy be based on this motivation.

Another reason reflects the desire, drive, and enthusiasm of management toward global business activities. This managerial commitment can exist simply because managers like to be part of a firm that engages in global business. Often, however, the

TABLE 11.1 **Major Reasons to Globalize Small and Medium-Sized Firms**

Proactive Reasons	Reactive Reasons
Profit advantage	Competitive pressures
Unique products	Overproduction
Technological advantage	Declining domestic sales
Exclusive information	Excess capacity
Managerial commitment	Saturated domestic markets
Tax benefit	Proximity to customers and ports
Economies of scale	

GLOBAL LEARNING EXPERIENCE 11.2

An Accidental Exporter

Sceptic-turned-exporter Maynard Saunder, president and CEO of ready-to-assemble furniture maker Saunder Woodworking Company of Archibold, Ohio, thought for the longest while that exporting was not for him. The do-it-yourself household furnishings market in the United States had been gathering steam in the late 1980s, and Saunder Woodworking was a supplier to national general merchandisers such as Wal-Mart, Kmart, Sears, and J.C. Penney. It was supplying retailers with products in the $19 to $399 range and had just cracked the $200 million sales point. Annual growth was humming at 12 percent to 15 percent. Exports at this time were negligible and occurred almost by accident. For instance, the firm started to sell products in the Caribbean because a salesman vacationed there.

How times have changes. The company expected to chalk up $50 million in exports in 1996. Domestic volume has gone flat over the past few years, while international accounts have posted an average annual increase of 30 percent. It wasn't until Jerry Paterson, a former export manager for Owens-Corning Fiberglass Corp., caught Saunder's attention that the company became serious about exporting. "I questioned our ability to compete in foreign markets," Saunders says. "I wasn't sure we could make it on price, and then I wondered if customers outside the U.S. would accept our designs." But the cost-benefit analysis, plus Paterson's presence, made it worth a try. "If Jerry Paterson can bring our export sales up to a million and a half to two million dollars a year, it will more than pay his expenses," Saunder recalls figuring. "It took us three to four years to reach a critical mass in exporting, but I knew after a year or so that we were going to give our program full support, and that we were in it for the long pull, not casually and not lukewarm."

Paterson quickly went to work and allayed Saunder's initial fears about jumping into exporting. Soon he realized that the company's proximity to particle board suppliers in Central Ohio, would help it keep prices competitive worldwide. Concerns over decor preferences also evaporated. "Our styles and colors have proved very acceptable, especially in France, where our penetration has been remarkable. But we're doing very well in Turkey, too." Add to this a positive outlook for sales in India and plans to ship to China via Hong Kong.

"We proved in a very short time that we can compete anywhere in the world," Saunder said. Many U.S. exporters are discovering that American labor can compete with workers anywhere in the world, thanks to increased efficiency and the higher quality of the finished product. Our made-in-the-U.S.A. products are a great sales booster for us the world over."

SOURCE: Daniel McConville, "An Accidental Exporter Turns Serious," *World Trade*, March 1996, 28.

managerial commitment to globalize is simply the reflection of a general entrepreneurial motivation, that is, a desire for continuous growth and market expansion.[10] Global Learning Experience 11.2 indicates how a change in management thinking led to success in the global marketplace.

Tax benefits can also play a major motivating role. In the United States, for example, a tax mechanism called a foreign sales corporation (FSC) provides firms with certain tax deferrals and makes global business activities more profitable. As a result of the tax ben-

Economies of scale help mass marketers like Coca-Cola stay competitive in both domestic and international markets.
SOURCE: © 1994 Arthur Meyerson/Courtesy of Coca-Cola.

efits, firms either can offer their product at a lower cost in foreign markets or can accumulate a higher profit.

A final major proactive reason involves economies of scale. Global activities may enable the firm to increase its output and therefore lower its average cost for each unit produced. The Boston Consulting Group has shown that the doubling of output can reduce production costs up to 30 percent. Increased production for global markets can therefore help to reduce the cost of production for domestic sales and make the firm more competitive domestically as well.[11]

Reactive Reasons

A second set of reasons, primarily characterized as reactive, influences firms to respond to environmental changes and pressures rather than to attempt to blaze trails. Competitive pressures are one example. A company may fear losing domestic market share to competing firms that have benefited from the economies of scale gained through global business activities. Further, it may fear losing foreign markets permanently to competitors that have decided to focus on these markets. Because market share usually is most easily retained by firms that obtained it initially, companies frequently enter the global market head over heels. Quick entry, however, may result in similarly quick withdrawal once the firm recognizes that its preparation has been inadequate.

Similarly, overproduction can result in a major reactive force to globalize. During downturns in the domestic business cycle, foreign markets have historically provided an ideal outlet for excess inventories. Global business expansion motivated by overproduction usually does not represent full commitment by management, but rather a safety-valve activity.[12] As soon as domestic demand returns to previous levels, global business activities are curtailed or even terminated. Firms that have used such a strategy once may encounter difficulties when trying to employ it again because many foreign customers are not interested in temporary or sporadic business relationships.

QUESTION *Off the Venezuelan coast are three islands whose official name is the Netherlands Antilles. They are sometimes called the ABC islands. What are their individual names?*

Aruba, Bonaire, Curaçao are the ABC islands.

Declining domestic sales, whether measured in sales volume or market share, have a similar motivating effect. Products marketed domestically may be at the declining stage of their product life cycle. Instead of attempting to push back the life cycle process domestically, or in addition to such an effort, firms may opt to prolong the product life cycle by expanding the market. In the past, such efforts by firms in industrialized countries often met with success because customers in less developed countries only gradually reached the level of need and sophistication already obtained by customers in the developed countries. Increasingly, however, because of the more rapid diffusion of technology, these lags are shrinking.

Excess capacity can also be a powerful motivator. If equipment for production is not fully utilized, firms may see expansion abroad as an ideal way to achieve broader distribution of fixed costs.

fixed costs
costs that remain constant regardless of the level of production, i.e., officer salaries, security staff, rent, etc.

variable cost
cost of production; it varies with the level of production, i.e., labor, raw materials, parts and assemblies, etc.

contribution margin
difference between selling price (per unit) and variable cost (per unit)

Alternatively, if all **fixed costs** are allocated to, or borne by, domestic operations, the firm can penetrate foreign markets with a pricing scheme that focuses mainly on **variable costs.** The resultant **contribution margin** can be used to increase profits (or help pay for domestic fixed costs—overhead). Table 11.2 illustrates this concept.

The amounts shown in Table 11.2 will help to illustrate the cost and profit implications of doing business internationally. If we assume that 100 percent of the company's fixed costs (overhead), amounting to $100,000, is allocated to domestic operations, then any selling price for product units sold internationally that is greater than the out-of-pocket cost of manufacturing and shipping (variable costs) will increase the company's profit.

The table also shows that if the company can sell the product overseas without incurring any additional fixed costs, it stands to improve profits (or, alternatively, help pay for domestic fixed costs) by an additional $7 for each unit sold. It can lower its international selling price to any price that is more than the variable costs ($13), for example, a selling price of $14, and still increase profits by $1 per unit.

Variable cost pricing is a short-term solution because as production increases to meet global demands, the related manufacturing equipment will wear out faster. It will have to be replaced sooner, thus increasing the company's variable costs.

TABLE 11.2 **Use of Variable Cost Pricing to Enter Foreign Markets**

Cost Category	Domestic Operations	International Operations
A. Fixed costs (overhead)—100% allocated to domestic operations	$100,000	—
B. Selling price (per unit)	$20	$20–14
C. Variable costs (per unit)		
Labor	5	5
Raw material	2	2
Purchased parts	3	3
Exporting costs	—	3
Total variable costs	10	13
D. Contribution margin (per unit)	$10	$7–1

A Model for Going Global FIGURE 11.1

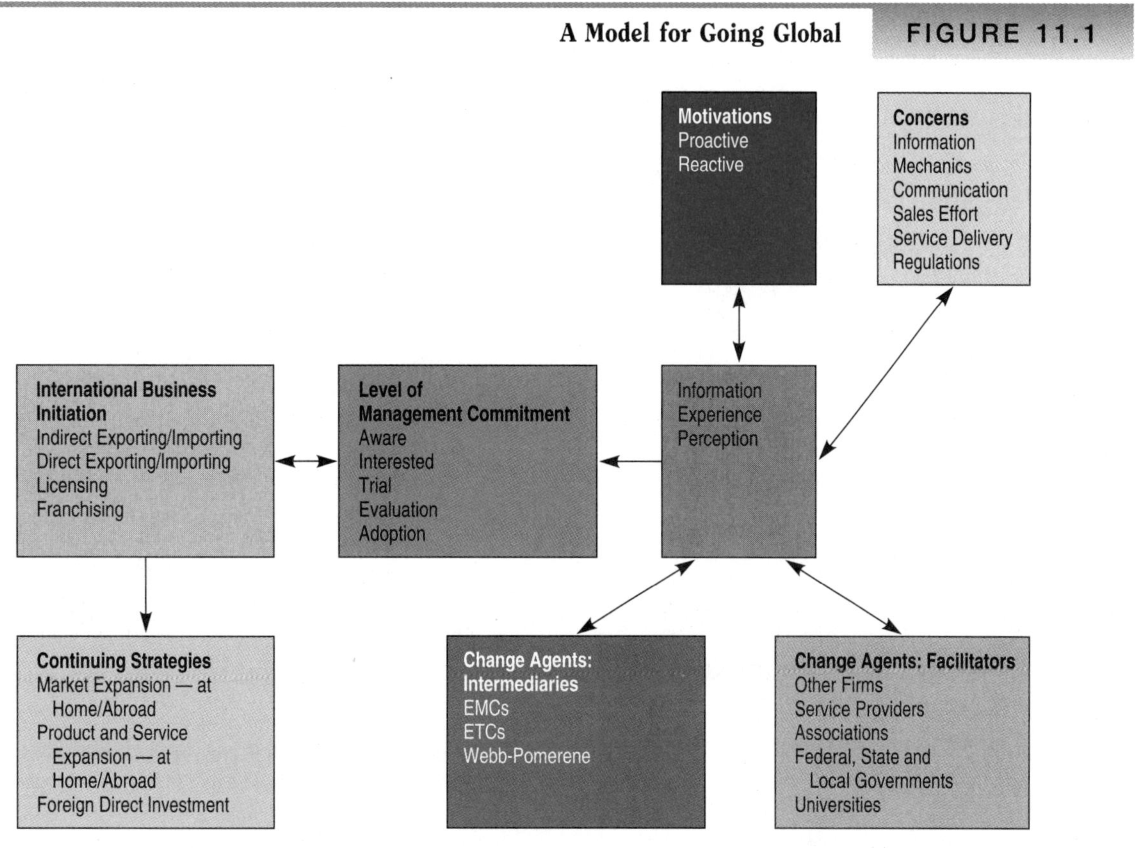

A saturated domestic market has similar results to that of declining domestic sales. Again, firms in this situation can use the global market to prolong the life cycle of their product and even of their organization.

A final major reactive reason is that of proximity to customers and ports. Physical and psychological closeness to the global market can often play a major role in the global business activities of the firm. A firm established near a border may not even perceive itself as going abroad if it does business in the neighboring country. Except for some firms close to the Canadian or Mexican border, however, this factor is much less prevalent in the United States than in many other nations. Most European firms automatically go abroad simply because their neighbors are so close.

In general, firms that are most successful in global business are usually motivated by proactive—that is, firm internal—factors. Proactive firms are also frequently more service oriented than reactive firms. Further, proactive firms are more marketing and strategy oriented than reactive firms, which have as their major concern operational issues. The clearest differentiation between the two types of firms can probably be made ex post facto by determining how they initially entered global markets. Proactive firms are more likely to have solicited their first international order, whereas reactive firms frequently begin international activities after receiving an unsolicited order from abroad. The developments, processes, and factors involved in the overall process of going global are presented schematically in Figure 11.1.

TABLE 11.3 **Summary of Methods for Entering Global Markets**

Method	Basic Approach
Exporting/Importing Direct Indirect	Firm enters international markets by manufacturing in home country and shipping and selling goods in foreign country. Minimizes risk and is a valuable way to learn about international business.
Contractual Methods	
Licensing	Company permits foreign firm to use its technology, patents, trademarks, copyrights for a fee (royalty).
Franchising	Specialized form of licensing in which a company allows another individual or company to use its complete business system, usually for some type of fee or royalty.
Contract manufacturing	Contract under which domestic firm has its products manufactured overseas by a foreign company.
Management contracts	Firm sells its expertise; manages a foreign-owned company.
Turnkey operations	Specialized type of management contract, usually found in the construction industry. Requires manager to provide owner with a completely operational facility.
Complementary marketing (piggyback)	Agreement between partners with noncompeting products, permitting access to each other's markets.
Ownership/Equity Methods	
Equity participation	Minority ownership in strategically important supplier or partner.
Joint venture	Two or more companies contribute assets, own some equity, and share risk to achieve a common business objective.
Wholly owned subsidiary	Full ownership (100%) of foreign subsidiary.
Other Methods of Interfirm Cooperation	
Informal cooperation	No binding agreement; partners exchange information, technologies, personnel, etc. Based on mutual trust and friendship.
Consortia	Strategic alliance of companies that pool their resources, usually in research or manufacturing.

METHODS OF ENTERING GLOBAL MARKETS

There are a number of ways to enter the global business area. Deciding which method to use is a key management decision, as each method has advantages and disadvantages. Some methods are more appropriate for small to medium-sized companies while others favor larger, more experienced firms. Table 11.3 summarizes the various methods and provides a short description of each.

Indirect and Direct Exporting and Importing

Firms can be involved in exporting and importing in an indirect or direct way. *Indirect exporting* means that the firm participates in international business through an intermediary and does not deal with foreign customers or firms. Direct exporting means that the firm works with foreign customers or markets with the opportunity to develop a relationship. The end result of exporting and importing is similar whether the activities are direct or indirect. In both cases, goods and services either go abroad or come to the domestic market from abroad, and goods may have to be adapted to suit the targeted market.

TABLE 11.4

Exporting in Your Own Backyard: A Dozen Segments of the United States for Export Markets

1. Large U.S. companies purchasing U.S. goods for their own foreign affiliates
2. Large design and construction firms purchasing U.S. goods for foreign projects awarded to them
3. U.S. branches of gigantic foreign trading companies purchasing U.S. goods for their affiliates
4. Export merchants buying for their own account
5. Large foreign companies purchasing U.S. goods through their U.S. buying office or agents
6. U.S. military purchasing for use abroad
7. U.S. exporters seeking U.S. goods to round out their own lines
8. United Nations members purchasing for development projects
9. Foreign governments purchasing U.S. goods
10. Foreign department stores purchasing U.S. goods through U.S. buying offices
11. Foreign buyers on purchasing trips
12. Aid-financed transactions requiring U.S. goods

SOURCE: Nelson Joyner, Georgetown University, teaching notes, 1997.

Many firms are indirect exporters and importers, often without their knowledge. As an example, merchandise can be sold to a domestic firm that in turn sells it abroad. This is most frequently the case when smaller suppliers deliver products to large multinational corporations, which use them as input to their foreign sales.

Similarly, firms may sell products to a government agency, for example, the Department of Defense, and they may ultimately be shipped to military outposts abroad. Or foreign buyers purchase products locally and then send them immediately to their home country. More examples of "exporting in your own backyard" are given in Table 11.4. While indirect exports may be the result of unwitting participation, many firms also choose this method of global entry as a strategic alternative that conserves effort and resources while still taking advantage of foreign opportunities.

At the same time, many firms that perceive themselves as buying domestically may in reality buy imported products. They may have long-standing relations with a domestic supplier who, because of cost and competitive pressures, has begun to source products from abroad rather than produce them domestically. In this case, the buyer firm has become an indirect importer.

Firms that participate indirectly in global business rarely are able to gather much experience and knowledge about how to do business abroad. Therefore, while indirect activities represent a form of global market entry, they are unlikely to result in growing management commitment to global markets or increased capabilities in serving them.

Firms that opt to export or import directly have more opportunities ahead of them, they learn much quicker the competitive advantages of their products and can therefore expand more rapidly. They also have the ability to control their global activities better and can forge relationships with their trading partners, which can lead to further global growth and success. Global Learning Experience 11.3 outlines an on-line system designed to assist smaller companies in locating potential export customers.

However, these firms also are faced with obstacles that those who access global markets indirectly avoid. These hurdles include identifying and targeting foreign suppliers and/or customers and finding retail space, which can be very costly and time

GLOBAL LEARNING EXPERIENCE 11.3

Exporting On-line

Small and medium-size business owners can now sell their products and source components anywhere in the world with just a few keystrokes on their personal computers. This is possible through an on-line system called IBEX (the International Business Exchange), launched by a group including AT&T, Dun & Bradstreet, General Electric, Microsoft, and the U.S. Chamber of Commerce. "The way people conduct international trade today is by looking in directories, getting on planes, and receiving unsolicited letters," says Peter Sandiford, chief executive and president of the Global Business Alliance, Inc., which manages IBEX. "(IBEX) allows businesses to locate, qualify, and negotiate with business partners around the world from a PC."

The IBEX software allows companies to anonymously sign on and submit requests for goods or services, using an array of categories, including location, product type, payment, and shipping terms. Customer then receive bids from businesses hoping to land contracts. Once a bid is chosen, the identities of the businesses are disclosed and negotiations may begin. IBEX allows users to attach documents, such as confidentiality agreements, contracts, and purchase orders. The participation of Dun & Bradstreet permits users to check each others' company profiles by tapping into D&B's vast international database of company information and references. The system can also do a basic translation of terms of a deal from English into Spanish, French, or any of 10 other languages. After a deal is completed, IBEX allows users to locate freight forwarders, bankers, accountants, or customs brokers.

The IBEX system is based on communications networks provided by AT&T and GE. Digital Equipment handles software orders and provides the IBEX package in its PCs, while the Chamber of Commerce serves a reseller of the service through more than 3,000 offices worldwide. Such corporate backing gives the service the strength it needs to build business-to-business electronic relationships. "They're working with the right people," says Brian O'Connell, staff editor at Technologic Partners, a high-tech publishing and consulting firm. Companies such as Dun & Bradstreet and AT&T "are as close to global organizations as you can get."

The system is meant to benefit smaller companies. Its launch coincides with a small business trend toward increasing exports and rapid integration of computers and technology. "Thanks to IBEX, the benefits of electronic commerce and a global reach are no longer the monopoly of big business," says Mark Van Fleet, the U.S. Chamber of Commerce's IBEX manager. Bruce Valley, president of Globalnet, Inc., a transportation equipment supplier, was involved in IBEX test simulations and is very enthusiastic: "It has the potential of allowing me to be a General Electric or a Boeing on my computer screen here in my 11-person business." The IBEX service is a good, quick way to engage in true electronic commerce without the baggage of Internet security concerns. While potential users can learn about and subscribe to IBEX through the Internet, actual business negotiations are conducted on a more private and secure electronic mail network. Additionally, users avoid the relatively high cost of commercial on-line services—IBEX costs only $250 to register. The system has several thousand users in approximately 25 countries and has achieved more than 2,000 matches between buyers and sellers in its first year. An estimated 1.5 million users are expected to sign on within five years.

SOURCES: Jared Sandberg, "On-Line Service to Assist Global Trade," *The Wall Street Journal,* September 26, 1995, James Worsham, "A Global Reach for Small Firms," *Nation's Business,* October 1995, 40; Interview with U.S. Chamber of Commerce officials, November, 1996.

consuming. Some firms are overcoming these barriers through the use of mail-order catalogs ("storeless" distribution networks) or video brochures. In Japan, for example, "high-cost rents, crowded shelves, and an intricate distribution system have made launching new products via conventional methods an increasingly difficult and expensive proposition. Direct marketing via catalog short-circuits the distribution train and eliminates the need for high-priced shop space."[13] Entrepreneurs are becoming creative in other ways to avoid the high cost of land and labor in Japan. Taking advantage of the fact that the Japanese are used to vending machines (there are more than 5.4 million machines in the country), a San Diego meat-packing firm is thinking of entering the Japanese market by selling steaks in vending machines located outside train stations and convenience stores.[14]

Direct importers and exporters frequently make use of intermediaries who can assist with troublesome yet important details such as documentation, financing, and transportation. The intermediaries may also identify foreign suppliers or customers. Facilitators in this process will be discussed later in this chapter. After firms have acquired some experience, however, they may carry out all export and import transactions on their own.

Licensing

Under a **licensing agreement,** one firm permits another to use its intellectual property for compensation designated as *royalty.* The recipient firm is the licensee. The property licensed might include patents, trademarks, copyrights, technology, technical know-how, or specific business skills. For example, a firm that has developed a bag-in-the-box packaging process for milk can permit other firms abroad to use the same process. Licensing therefore amounts to exporting intangibles.

licensing agreement
one firm permits another to use its intellectual property for compensation designated as royalty

Assessment of Licensing Licensing has intuitive appeal to many would-be global managers. As an entry strategy, it requires neither capital investment nor detailed involvement with foreign customers. By generating royalty income, licensing provides an opportunity to exploit research and development already conducted. After initial costs, the licensor can reap benefits until the end of the license contract period. Licensing also reduces the risk of expropriation because the licensee is a local company that can provide leverage against government action.

Licensing may help to avoid host-country regulations that are more prevalent in equity ventures. Licensing also may provide a means by which foreign markets can be tested without major involvement of capital or management time. Similarly, licensing can be used as a strategy to preempt a market before the entry of competition, especially if the licensor's resources permit full-scale involvement only in selected markets.

Licensing is not without disadvantages. It is the most limited form of foreign market participation and does not in any way guarantee a basis for future expansion. As a matter of fact, quite the opposite may take place. In exchange for the royalty, the licensor may create its own competitor not only in the market for which the agreement was made but for third-country markets as well.

Licensing has also come under criticism from many governments and supranational organizations. They have alleged that licensing provides a mechanism for corporations in industrialized countries to capitalize on older technology. These accusations have been made even though licensing offers a foreign entity the opportunity for immediate market entry with a proven concept. It therefore eliminates the risk of R&D failure, the cost of designing around the licensor's patents, or the fear of patent infringement litigation.

A special form of licensing is trademark licensing, which has become a substantial source of worldwide revenue for companies that can trade on well-known names and

GLOBAL LEARNING EXPERIENCE 11.4

Finding Success in China Through Licensing

Playboy magazine may be banned in China, but Playboy clothes are more than welcomed. That paradox amuses John Chan, founder and chairman of Chaifa Holdings Company, which holds the exclusive license to sell Playboy-brand garments and accessories on the mainland. Chan has managed to make the Playboy rabbit silhouette one of the most popular emblems on shirts, sweaters, shoes, leather belts, key chains, and neckties sold in China.

In the four years since Chaifa entered China, the number of outlets selling Playboy goods has mushroomed from a handful to nearly 320. Chaifa has plans for dozens more. "What Chaifa has done in four years might take a more experienced, better-connected retailer 10 to 20 years to do," said one industry analyst. In contrast to the company's impressive sales and profit growth, the China operations of some larger Hong Kong garment retailers have rung up losses over the past several years.

Chan founded Chaifa, which means "going to be rich" in Chinese, in 1986. Unlike most Hong Kong retailers, Chaifa concentrates on mainland China, where 318 of its 338 outlets are located. To sell to mainland shoppers, Chan decided to operate franchised outlets, including boutiques and department store counters. The Playboy outlets sell only garments and accessories made by Chaifa's factory in Shantou, China. This way, capital outlay and business risks are minimized and the headache of managing hundreds of stores with thousands of employees is avoided. Chaifa pays Playboy Enterprises, Inc., U.S. owner of the trademark, royalties based on sales.

To find suitable dealers, Chan visits duty-free shops, department stores, and other retailers all over the country. "It was hard work at first, getting a cold shoulder here and there. But without contacts, that was the only way," he says. He recalls those early years when he traveled with only a briefcase stocked with goods to show potential retailers. These days, Chan advertises for prospective dealers in mainland newspapers and trade magazines. He visits all potential business partners and often helps them search for retail space.

Chan, often dressed in business suits, socks, and shoes emblazoned with the Playboy logo, attributes his company's success to choosing mid-priced brand-name products that he knows will appeal to Chinese consumers. "Many Chinese still prefer buying Western brand-name products to generic goods because of the cachet," Chan said. "And I go for mid-price goods, because to make money, one has to sell China's growing middle class, not the few elites," he adds.

Chaifa spends an average 3 percent to 4 percent of sales on advertising and promotion through the media, fashion shows, exhibitions, and trade events all across China. Because most Chinese have never seen Playboy magazine, the company tries to project a healthy, youthful image for the name. "I always explain that Playboy is a lifestyle, a culture, not sex," Chan says. Chaifa also promotes Garfield the Cat, as a children's buddy, and Arnold Palmer, as a model of success for mature men. "I intend to make Playboy, Garfield, and Arnold Palmer household names in China," explains Chan.

SOURCE: Lotte Chow, "Chinese Consumers Embrace Market for Attire Emblazoned by Playboy," *The Wall Street Journal*, August 25, 1995, A5E.

characters. Trademark licensing permits the names or logos of designers, literary characters, sports teams, or movie stars to appear on clothing, games, foods and beverages, gift and novelties, toys, and home furnishings. A classic example of this approach to market entry is presented in Global Learning Experience 11.4. Licensors can make millions of dollars with little effort, while licensees can produce a brand or product that consumers will recognize immediately. Trademark licensing is possible, however, only if the trademark name indeed conveys instant recognition.

Franchising

Another global entry strategy, **franchising,** is the granting of the right by a parent company (the franchisor) to another, independent entity (the franchisee) to do business in a prescribed manner. This right can take the form of selling the franchisor's products; using its name, production, and marketing techniques; or using its general business approach.[15] Usually, franchising involves a combination of many of these elements. The major forms of franchising are manufacturer-retailer systems (such as a car dealership), manufacturer-wholesaler systems (such as soft drink companies), and service firm-retailer systems (such as lodging services and fast-food outlets).

franchising
granting of the right by a parent company (the franchisor) to another independent entity (the franchisee) to do business in a prescribed manner

Typically, to be successful in international franchising, the firm must be able to offer unique products or unique selling propositions. If such uniqueness can be offered, growth can be rapid and sustained. Global Learning Experience 11.5 provides an example of how a U.S. franchised restaurant chain used its uniqueness to achieve success in foreign markets.

International franchising has grown strongly in the past decade. In 1996, more than 400 franchising companies in the United States operated about 40,000 outlets in international markets,[16] and the units abroad often make significant contributions to corporate income. For example, McDonald's generates 65 percent and Coca-Cola 80 percent of income from international operations.[17] Foreign franchisors are penetrating global markets as well. Examples include Holiday Rent-a-Car of Canada and Descamps, a French firm selling linens and tablecloths.

The reasons for global expansion of franchise systems are market potential, financial gain, and saturated domestic markets. U.S. franchisors expanded dramatically in 1984, taking advantage of the strong U.S. dollar. Foreign market demand was also very high for franchises. For example, the initial impetus for ComputerLand's expansion into the Asia-Pacific region was that "Asian entrepreneurs [were] coming knocking on our door asking for franchises."[18] From a franchisee's perspective, the franchise is beneficial because it reduces risk by implementing a proven concept. From a governmental perspective, there are also major benefits. The source country does not see a replacement of exports or export jobs. The recipient country sees franchising as requiring little outflow of foreign exchange, since the bulk of the profits generated remains within the country.[19]

Franchising is one way to expand into international markets. The Dunkin' Donuts franchise in Thailand operates some 50 stores like this one.
SOURCE: Courtesy of Allied Lyons.

Franchising Americana Abroad

Europeans are into Americana. That's good news for Swedish nightclub owner Staffan Linder and Applebee International's foreign franchising executive director, Gilbert Simon. Linder runs BZ, his family's 65-year-old discotheque in downtown Stockholm. A graduate of Cornell University's hotel management school, he first explored Applebee's franchising in 1988. The restaurant didn't head abroad until 1993, at which time Simon felt the U.S. market was saturated. Today, the company has franchises in the United States, Canada, Europe, and the Caribbean. Linder is

An example of franchising in Hungary.
SOURCE: Courtesy Ilona Czinkota.

set to open 10 restaurants in Sweden by the turn of the century.

As with any global expansion, there have been hurdles. Never mind that domestically, Applebee's restaurants insist on a highly attentive, "in your face" serving style. "Inattentive service is the norm in Europe. Culturally, that's a huge gap," said Simon. There's another cultural barrier: "Applebee's what?" (The complete restaurant name is Applebee's Neighborhood Grill & Bar.) A U.S. franchise has no brand identity when it moves into a new country. "You have to be very skilled at being able to explain what the concept is. 'American-style dining' doesn't translate well," said Simon. "You then have to persuade the franchisee that they can make money, and that this is a good thing."

But that's why Linder chose Applebee's—Americana sells. The franchise has a versatile menu and the tone of the place matches the Swedes' informal approach to business. Plus, Linder likes franchising's low-risk proposition: a proven concept and the support of a parent company. "We are going to sell an American restaurant with a big advantage over the United States: the Americana concept is more popular in Europe than it is in America," says Linder.

For Simon, Linder has the properties he admires in a potential franchisee—and that's only true of one in 100 inquiries. Linder is a restaurateur. He has substantial backers, including a prominent Swedish economist and an owner of a large resort and conference center. They are seeking an international opportunity in a targeted market. And Linder and company meet Simon's most important, toughest criterion for potential franchisees: "I have to like them," he said.

Simon believes franchising is a growth industry for many businesses, though he is more enthusiastic about the international scene than the highly regulated U.S. franchise market. Yet the global market is no playground, he said. Beware the franchiser with a string of restaurants in the eastern United States who wants to grant franchises in Egypt, Australia, and Chile. Supporting such far-flung franchisees as those would be an unwieldy and expensive proposition. Said Simon: "We invested over $1 million of our own money to get Europe up and operating, but we don't own it. Give me three years and we may break even. You've got to be prepared to make the investment to provide the service. I think too many companies franchising in the U.S. don't make that investment."

SOURCE: Ian Jones, "Where Everybody Knows Your Name" *World Trade,* June 1996, 40.

Franchising by its very nature calls for a great degree of standardization. In most cases, this does not mean 100 percent uniformity but, rather, global recognizability. Fast-food franchisors will vary the products and product lines offered depending on local market conditions and tastes.

Even though franchising has been growing rapidly, problems are often encountered in global markets. Some of them are summarized in Table 11.5. A major problem is foreign government intervention. In the Philippines, for example, government restrictions on franchising and royalties hindered ComputerLand's Manila store from offering a broader range of services, leading to a separation between the company and its franchisee. Selection and training of franchisees represents another problem area. The lag of McDonald's behind Burger King in France was the result of the company's suing to revoke the license of its largest franchisee for failure to operate 14 stores according to McDonald's standards.

Which of these is the real "Banana Republic": Costa Rica, Nicaragua, Guatemala, Saint Lucia, Belize, or Honduras?

ANSWER

None of the Central American countries mentioned have bananas as their primary crop, if that's what you mean by Banana Republic. But bananas are the primary crop on Saint Lucia, an island in the lesser Antilles. Saint Lucia's luscious bananas are all shipped to Europe.

Many franchise systems have run into difficulty by expanding too quickly and granting franchises to unqualified entities. Although the local franchisee knows the market best, the franchisor still needs to understand the market for product adaptation and operational purposes. The franchisor, in order to remain viable in the long term, needs to coordinate the efforts of individual franchisees—for example, to share ideas and engage in joint undertakings, such as cooperative advertising.

Contract Manufacturing

An alternative to licensing or foreign direct investment is *contract manufacturing.* In this situation, the global firm contracts with a local manufacturer in the foreign market to manufacture the firm's products or to perform partial manufacturing operations, such as final assembly of imported parts. The advantages of contract manufacturing are that the global marketer does not lose control of the product, as might happen in a licensing arrangement, and it does not incur the risk or expense of a direct investment. The potential problem with contract manufacturing is the reliability and quality control standards of the foreign manufacturer—a potential problem with domestic suppliers as well. Contract manufacturing may be viewed as a low-cost, low-risk first step of "testing the waters" prior to major investment in the foreign market.

TABLE 11.5 **Rank Order of Problems Encountered in Global Markets by U.S. Franchise Systems**

1. Host government regulations and red tape
2. High import duties and taxes in foreign environment
3. Monetary uncertainties and royalty remission to franchisor
4. Logistical problems in operation of international franchise system
5. Control of franchisees
6. Location problems and real estate costs
7. Patent, trademark, and copyright protection
8. Recruitment of franchisees
9. Training of foreign franchisee personnel
10. Language and cultural barriers
11. Availability of raw materials for company product
12. Foreign ownership limitations
13. Competition in foreign market areas
14. Adaptation of franchise package to local markets

SOURCE: Donald W. Hackett, "The International Expansion of U.S. Franchise Systems," in *Multinational Product Management,* eds. Warren Keegan and Charles Mayer (Chicago: American Marketing Association, 1979), 78.

Management Contracts

In some parts of the world and in certain industries, governments insist on complete or majority ownership of firms, which has caused multinational companies to turn to an alternative method of enlarging their overseas business.[20] The alternative is a **management contract,** in which the firm sells its expertise in running a company while avoiding the risk or benefit of ownership. Depending on the extensiveness of the contract, it may even permit some measure of control. As an example, the manufacturing process may have to be relinquished to foreign firms, yet global distribution may be required for the product. A management contract could serve to maintain a strong hold on the operation by ensuring that all distribution channels remain firmly controlled.

management contract
a firm sells its expertise in running a company while avoiding the risk or benefit of ownership

Management contracts may be more than a defensive measure. Although they are used to protect existing investment interests when they have been partly expropriated by the local government, an increasing number of companies are using them as a profitable opportunity to sell valuable skills and resources. Companies in the service sector often have independent entities with the sole task of seeking out opportunities and operating management contracts.[21]

Often, a management contract is the critical element in the success of a project. For example, financial institutions may gain confidence in a project because of the existence of a management contract and may sometimes even make it a precondition for funding.[22]

Turnkey Operations

One specialized form of management contract is the **turnkey operation.** Here, the arrangement permits a client to acquire a complete global system, together with skills investment sufficient to allow unassisted maintenance and operation of the system following its completion.[23] The client need not search for individual contractors or subcontractors or deal with scheduling conflicts or with difficulties in assigning responsibilities or blame. Instead, a package arrangement permits the accumulation of responsibility in one entity, thus greatly easing the negotiation and supervision requirements and subsequent accountability. When the project is online, the system will be totally owned, controlled, and operated by the customer. An example of such an arrangement is the Kama River truck plant in Russia, built mainly by U.S. firms.

turnkey operation
specialized form of management contract, where the arrangement permits a client to acquire a complete global system together with skills investment sufficient to allow unassisted maintenance and operation of the system following its completion

Management contracts have clear benefits for the client. They provide organizational skills not available locally, expertise that is immediately available rather than built up, and management assistance in the form of support services that would be difficult and costly to replicate locally. For example, hotels managed by the Sheraton Corporation have access to Sheraton's worldwide reservation system. Management contracts today typically involve training of locals to take over the operation after a given period.

Similar advantages exist for the supplier. The risk of participating in a global venture is substantially lowered, while significant amounts of control are still exercised. Existing know-how that has been built up through substantial investment can be commercialized, and frequently the impact of fluctuations in business volume can be reduced by making use of experienced personnel who otherwise would have to be laid off. In industrialized countries such as the United States, with economies that are increasingly service based, accumulated service knowledge and comparative advantage should be used globally. Management contracts permit firms to do so.

Management contracts require an attitude change on two accounts: Control must be shared, and the time involvement may be limited. Establishing a working relationship with the owner in which both understand and respect their roles is essential. Even though the management contractor may be training local personnel to eventually take over, this by no means signifies the end of the relationship. For example, the hotel once managed by Sheraton may well remain in the system to buy reservation services, thus providing Sheraton with additional revenue.

From the client's perspective, the main drawbacks to consider are overdependence and potential loss of some essential control. If the management contractor maintains all of the global relationships, little if any experience may be passed on to the local operation. Instead of gradual transfer of skills leading to increasing independence, the client may have to rely more and more on the performance of the contractor.

Complementary Marketing

complementary marketing arrangement between two companies for the sharing of facilities and/or marketing activities; allows firms to achieve objectives that they cannot reach efficiently by themselves

Strategic-alliance partners may join forces for joint R&D, joint marketing, or joint production. Similarly, their joint efforts might include licensing, cross-licensing, or cross-marketing activities. Nestlé and General Mills have signed an agreement whereby Honey Nut Cheerios and Golden Grahams are made in General Mills's U.S. plants, shipped in bulk to Europe for packaging at a Nestlé plant, and then marketed in France, Spain, and Portugal by Nestlé.[24] This arrangement—**complementary marketing** (also known as **piggybacking**)—allows firms to reach objectives that they cannot reach efficiently by themselves.[25] Firms also can have a reciprocal arrangement whereby each partner provides the other access to its markets for a product. AT&T and Olivetti have had such a cross-marketing agreement covering the United States and Europe. In the service sector, global airlines have started to share hubs, coordinate schedules, and simplify ticketing. SAS has entered into joint-marketing deals with All Nippon Airways, Lan-Chile, and Canadian Airlines International to provide links to routes and hubs in Tokyo, Latin America, and Toronto.[26] Contractual agreements also exist for outsourcing; for example. General Motors buys cars and components from Korea's Daewoo, and Siemens buys computers from Fujitsu.

Ownership/Equity Methods

equity participation multinational minority ownership in companies that have strategic importance to them

Equity Participation

With **equity participation** alliances, multinational corporations acquire minority ownerships in companies that have strategic importance for them to ensure supplier viability and build formal and informal working relationships. Examples include IBM's 12 percent share of Intel and Ford Motor Company's 33 percent share of Mazda. The partners continue operating as distinctly separate entities, but each enjoys the strengths the other partner provides. For example, thanks to Mazda, Ford has excellent support in the design and manufacture of subcompact cars, while Mazda has improved access to the global marketplace. Similar arrangements abound in the automotive sector: Mitsubishi Motors owns 10.2 percent of Chrysler, while Honda owns 20 percent of Britain's Rover.[27]

joint venture participation of two or more companies in an enterprise to achieve a common goal

Joint Ventures

A **joint venture** can be defined as the participation of two or more companies in an enterprise in which each party contributes assets, owns the entity to some degree, and shares risk.[28] The venture is also considered long term.[29] The reasons for establishing a joint venture can be divided into three groups: (1) government suasion or legislation, (2) one partner's needs for other partner's skills, and (3) one partner's needs for other partners' attributes or assets.[30] Equality of the partners is not necessary. In some joint ventures, each partner holds an equal share; in others, one partner has the majority of shares. The partners' contributions—typically consisting of funds, technology, plant, or labor—also vary. Global Learning Experience 11.6 shows how a joint venture can benefit both partners.

The key to a joint venture is the sharing of a common business objective, which makes the arrangement more than a customer-vendor relationship but less than an outright acquisition. The partners' rationales for entering into the arrangement may vary. An exam-

GLOBAL LEARNING EXPERIENCE 11.6

Forming a Joint Venture in China

In the early 1990s, Fedders, America's largest manufacturer of room air-conditioners, decided that the best way to grow was to venture abroad. The company concluded that China was the best option for investment. Annual sales of room air-conditioners in China, barely 500,000 five years ago, had risen to over 4 million by 1995, making it as big as the American market, but one that is still growing. By some estimates, only about 12 percent of homes in the main Chinese cities, such as Beijing, Shanghai, and Guangzhou, have an air-conditioner. By contrast, in Hong Kong, it is hard to find a home that does not have one or more.

From the start, it was clear that Fedders needed a local partner. It compiled a list of about 120 air-conditioning producers in China. However, most were small and weak, so the list was eventually whittled down. Fedders eventually found the Ningbo General Air Conditioner Factory, which was, like Fedders, worried about its future. It was facing mounting competition, both from local companies and from a growing number of formidable looking joint ventures with Japanese, South Korean, and American firms.

The two sides reached a preliminary agreement on a capital structure for a joint venture. The goal was to boost Ningbo's production to 500,000 units within three years, half of which would be exported. The joint venture would be responsible for sales inside China, while Fedders would handle all the exports. The efforts made by Fedders to understand their partner greatly impressed Ningbo's Mr. Cai. He says that both sides recognized how badly they needed one another. When problems did crop up, they were usually solved in the traditional Chinese manner—over dinner.

In July 1995, Fedders and the Ningbo General Air Conditioner Factory signed a contract establishing their joint venture. Despite all the difficulties, this had been one of the fastest joint-venture deals ever to be put together in China.

Now, the most urgent task facing Fedders Xinle is to ramp up its production to 200,000 units, launch its new high-tech product, and then hit its target of 500,000 within two years. Meanwhile, it also has to make some money. Mr. Laurent says he is confident of receiving a quick return on his investment. His optimism stems partly from the sales potential in China, and partly from exports to other parts of Asia, to Japan, and (with its new product) to America itself.

There is, though, another way for the joint-venture to return its investment. Entering China has created an entirely new group of potential suppliers for the parent company: companies that used to supply the Chinese partner. Provided these firms can meet the right quality standards, they will also be able to supply parts to Fedders' two factories back home. If just one of those Chinese suppliers can shave $1 off the cost of an air-conditioner in America, Fedders will save up to $1.5 million a year, and the Chinese suppliers will have found a huge new market.

SOURCE: "Keeping Cool in China," *The Economist*, April 6, 1996, 73.

ple is New United Motor Manufacturing Inc. (NUMMI), the joint venture between Toyota and GM. Toyota needed direct access to the U.S. market, while GM benefited from the technology and management approaches provided by the Japanese partner.

Joint ventures may be the only way in which a firm can profitably participate in a particular market. For example, India restricts equity participation in local operations by foreigners to 40 percent. Other entry modes may limit the scale of operation substantially; for example, exports may be restricted because of tariff barriers. Many Western firms are using joint ventures to gain access to Eastern and Central European markets.

Joint ventures are valuable when the pooling of resources results in a better outcome for each partner than if each were to conduct its activities individually. This is particularly the case when each partner has a specialized advantage in areas that benefit the venture. A firm may have new technology yet lack sufficient capital to carry out foreign direct investment on its own. Through a joint venture, the technology can be used more quickly and market penetration achieved more easily. Similarly, one of the partners may have a distribution system already established or have better access to local suppliers, either of which permits a greater volume of sales in a shorter period of time.

Joint ventures also permit better relationships with local government and other organizations, such as labor unions. Government-related reasons are the major rationale for joint ventures in less developed countries four times more frequently than in developed countries.[31] Particularly if the local partner is the government, or the local partner is politically influential, the new venture may be eligible for tax incentives, grants, and government support. Negotiations for certifications or licenses may be easier because authorities may not perceive themselves as dealing with a foreign firm. Relationships between the local partner and the local financial establishment may enable the joint venture to tap local capital markets. The greater experience (and therefore greater familiarity) with the local culture and environment of the local partner may enable the joint venture to benefit from greater insights into changing market conditions and needs.

A final major commercial reason to participate in joint ventures is the desire to minimize the risk of exposing long-term investment capital, while at the same time maximizing the leverage on the capital that is invested.[32] Economic and political conditions in many countries are increasingly volatile. At the same time, corporations tend to shorten their investment planning time span more and more. This financial rationale therefore takes on more importance.

A joint venture with Sterch Controls enabled Honeywell to enter the potentially vast markets of Central Europe and the former Soviet Union. *SOURCE:* © Jim Sims for Honeywell.

Full Ownership

For many firms, the foreign direct investment decision is, initially at least, considered in the context of 100 percent ownership. The reason may have an ethnocentric basis; that is, management may feel that no outside entity should have an impact on corporate decision making. Alternatively, it may be based on financial concerns. The management of IBM believes that by relinquishing a portion of its ownership abroad, it would be setting a precedent for shared control with local partners that would cost more than could possibly be gained.[33] In some cases, IBM has withdrawn operation from a country rather than agree to government demands for local ownership. Global Learning Experience 11.7 indicates that multinational companies are investing heavily to acquire competitors in industrialized countries and set up operations in emerging markets.

In order to make a rational decision about the extent of ownership, management must evaluate the extent to which total control is important to the success of its global marketing activities. Often full ownership may be a desirable, but not a necessary, prerequisite for global success. At other times, it may be essential particularly when strong linkages exist within the corporation. Interdependencies between and among local operations and headquarters may be so strong that nothing short of total coordination will result in an acceptable benefit to the firm as a whole.[34]

Increasingly, however, the global environment is hostile to full ownership by multinational firms. Government action through outright legal restrictions or discriminatory actions is making the option less attractive. The choice is either to abide by existing restraints and accept a reduction in control or to lose the opportunity to operate in the country. In addition to formal action by the government, the general conditions in the market may make it advisable for the firm to join forces with local entities.

Multinationals Invest at a Record Pace

Multinational companies invested a record $325 billion in 1995 to acquire competitors in industrialized countries and set up operations in emerging markets. This spending level represented a 46 percent increase over the prior year. While foreign direct investments in developing countries continued to grow strongly during the year, to nearly $97 billion, the flow into developed countries jumped at a more surprising rate. According to the United Nation's World Investment Report, foreign direct investment inflows to developed countries totaled $216 billion in 1995, up from about $130 billion in each of the two previous years.

The United States was both the largest host country for investments ($74.7 billion) and the largest initiator of investments in other countries ($97 billion). Germany went from a net reduction of foreign direct investment in 1994 to an inflow of $9 billion. Similarly, the United Kingdom showed an increase to $30 billion from $10 billion in 1994. Karl Sauvant, research director for a division of the UN Council on Trade and Development, said Western Europe and Germany in particular are attracting more attention because their economies are expected to improve over the coming years. He also said many multinational companies want to "globalize production" to become more competitive.

"The trend among companies is to get closer to their customers and become a major presence in the markets where they sell," said Robert Hormats, vice chairman of Goldman Sachs International. The acquisitions and expansion of operations abroad allow quicker delivery of products, greater flexibility to adapt to local markets, and access to local technology and skills, he added.

Large acquisitions accounted for much of the increase in foreign direct investment. Hoechst, a big German pharmaceutical company, acquired Marion Merrell Dow of Kansas City, Missouri, for $7.1 billion. Cadbury Schweppes of the United Kingdom purchased Dr. Pepper/Seven-Up Cos. of Dallas for $2.6 billion. U.S. packaging giant Crown, Cork & Seal of Philadelphia acquired France's CarnaudMetalbox, a large paper and plastic company, for $5.2 billion. Increased political and currency stability throughout the world, plus greater relaxation of trade and investment restrictions, were other important factors that encouraged companies to go beyond their borders, noted Arthur Andersen Co.'s Andrew Kane. "It allows capital to flow to where the best opportunities are, including the Asian Pacific countries, which are beginning to mature as consumer markets," he added.

This fast pace of investment continued into 1996, with Ford Motor Co.'s purchase of Mazda as one prime example. Hormats sees the trend lasting, if for no other reason than that "countries all want foreign investment. The old porcupinish days of nationalism haven't gone away but countries increasingly realize they need to have an appealing (foreign direct investment) environment to attract jobs."

SOURCE: Fred Bleakley, "Multinational Firms Spent $325 Billion in 1995 on Foreign Direct Investment," *The Wall Street Journal,* June 5, 1996, A2.

Interfirm Cooperation

The world is too large and the competition too strong for even the largest multinational corporations to do everything independently. Technologies are converging and markets becoming integrated, thus making the costs and risks of both product and market

Where is Timbuktu?

Timbuktu is in Mali.

development ever greater. Partly as a reaction to and partly to exploit these developments, management in multinational corporations has become more pragmatic about what it takes to be successful in global markets.[35] The result has been the formation of **strategic alliances** with suppliers, customers, competitors, and companies in other industries to achieve multiple goals.

strategic alliance
new term for collaboration among firms, often similar to joint ventures

A strategic alliance (or partnership) is an informal or formal arrangement between two or more companies with a common business objective. It is something more than the traditional customer-vendor relationship but something less than an outright acquisition. These alliances can take forms ranging from informal cooperation to joint ownership of worldwide operations. For example, Texas Instruments has reported agreements with companies such as IBM, Hyundai, Fujitsu, Alcatel, and L. M. Ericsson, using such terms as "joint development agreement," "cooperative technical effort," "joint program for development," "alternative sourcing agreement," and "design/exchange agreement for cooperative product development and exchange of technical data.[36]

Reasons for Interfirm Cooperation Strategic alliances are being used for many different purposes by the partners involved. Market development is one common focus. Penetrating foreign markets is a primary objective of many companies. In Japan, Motorola is sharing chip designs and manufacturing facilities with Toshiba to gain greater access to the Japanese market. Some alliances are aimed at defending home markets. With no orders coming in for nuclear power plants, Bechtel Group has teamed up with Germany's Siemens to service existing U.S. plants.[37] Another focus is the spreading of the cost and risk inherent in production and development efforts. Texas Instruments and Hitachi have teamed up to develop the next generation of memory chips. The costs of developing new jet engines are so vast that they force aerospace companies into collaboration; one such consortium was formed by United Technologies' Pratt & Whitney division, Britain's Rolls-Royce, Motoren-und-Turbinen Union from Germany, Fiat of Italy, and Japanese Aero Engines (made up of Ishikawajima Heavy Industries and Kawasaki Heavy Industries).[38] Finally, some alliances are formed to block and co-opt competitors.[39] For example, Caterpillar formed a heavy equipment joint venture with Mitsubishi in Japan to strike back at its main global rival, Komatsu, in its home market. In many cases, companies have used most of these rationales to justify their alliances. Figure 11.2 provides examples of how the complementary strengths of two companies can be combined to achieve joint objectives.

Informal Cooperation In informal cooperative deals, partners work together without a binding agreement. This arrangement often takes the form of visits to exchange information about new products, processes, and technologies or may take the more formal form of the exchange of personnel for limited amounts of time. Often, such partners are of no real threat in each other's markets and of modest size in comparison to the competition, making collaboration necessary.[40] The relationships are based on mutual trust and friendship, and they may lead to more formal arrangements, such as contractual agreements or joint projects.

Consortia A new drug can cost $200 million to develop and bring to market; a mainframe computer or a telecommunications switch can require $1 billion. Some $4 billion went into creating the generation of computer chips in the early 1990s;

Complementary Strengths Create Value **FIGURE 11.2**

Partner *Strength...*	+ Partner *Strength...*	= Joint Objective
Pepsico *marketing clout for canned beverages*	**Lipton** *recognized tea brand and customer franchise*	*To sell canned iced tea beverages jointly*
Coca-Cola *marketing clout for canned beverages*	**Nestle** *recognized tea brand and customer franchise*	*To sell canned iced tea beverages jointly*
KFC *established brand and store format, and operations skills*	**Mitsubishi** *real estate and site-selection skills in Japan*	*To establish a KFC chain in Japan*
Siemens *presence in range of telecommunications markets worldwide and cable-manufacturing technology*	**Corning** *technological strength in optical fibers and glass*	*To create a fiber-optic-cable business*
Ericsson *technological strength in public telecommunications networks*	**Hewlett-Packard** *computers, software, and access to electronics channels*	*To create and market network management systems*

SOURCE: Joel Bleeke and David Ernst, "Is Your Strategic Alliance Really a Sale?" *Harvard Business Review* 73 (January–February 1995): 97–105; and Melanie Wells, "Coca-Cola Proclaims Nestea Time for CAA," *Advertising Age*, January 30, 1995, 2.

up to $7 billion will be needed to develop the next generation.[41] To combat the high costs and risks of research and development, research consortia have emerged in the United States, Japan, and Europe. Since the passage of the Joint Research and Development Act of 1984 (which allows both domestic and foreign firms to participate in joint basic research efforts without the fear of antitrust action), well over 100 consortia have been registered in the United States. These consortia pool their resources for research into technologies ranging from artificial intelligence to those needed to overtake the Japanese lead in semiconductor manufacturing. (The major consortia in those fields are MCC and Sematech.)[42] The Europeans have five megaprojects to develop new technologies registered under the names EUREKA, ESPRIT, BRITE, RACE, and COMET. The Japanese consortia have worked on producing the world's highest-capacity memory chip and advanced computer technologies. On the manufacturing side, the formation of Airbus Industrie secured European production of commercial jets. The consortium, backed by France's Aerospatiale, Germany's Messerschmitt Boklow Blohm, British Aerospace, and Spain's Construcciones Aeronauticas, has become a prime global competitor.

Strategic Alliances

A strategic alliance, by definition, also means a joining of two corporate cultures, which can often be quite different. To meet this challenge, partners must have frequent communication and interaction at three levels of the organization: the top management, operational leaders, and workforce levels. Trust and relinquishing control are difficult not only at the top but also at levels where the future of the venture is determined. A dominant partner may determine the corporate culture, but even then the other partners should be consulted.

Strategic alliances operate in a dynamic business environment and must therefore adjust to changing market conditions. The agreement between partners should provide for changes in the original concept so that the venture can flourish and grow. The trick is to have an a priori understanding as to which party will take care of which pains and problems so that a common goal is reached.

INTERNATIONAL INTERMEDIARIES

Intermediaries can provide significant assistance to firms engaged in global business. Three major types of international intermediaries are export management companies, Webb-Pomerene associations, and export trading companies.

Export Management Companies

export management companies (EMCs) domestic firms that specialize in performing global business services as commission representatives or as distributors

Domestic firms that specialize in performing global business services as commission representatives or as distributors are known as **export management companies (EMCs).** Although few directories listing EMCs are available, more than 1,000 of these firms are estimated to be operating in the United States. A study conducted by the National Federation of Independent Businesses found that more than 20 percent of all manufactured goods exporters in the United States are EMCs.[43] Most EMCs are quite small. Many were formed by one or two principals with experience in global business or in a particular geographic area. Their expertise enables them to offer specialized services to domestic corporations.

EMCs have two primary forms of operation: They either take title to goods and operate globally on their own account, or they perform services as agents. Because they often serve a variety of clients, their mode of operation may vary from client to client and from transaction to transaction. An EMC may act as an agent for one client and as a distributor for another. It may even act as both for the same client on different occasions.

The EMC as an Agent When working as an agent, the EMC is primarily responsible for developing foreign business and sales strategies and establishing contact abroad. Because the EMC does not share in the profits from a sale, it depends heavily on a high sales volume, on which it charges commission.

EMCs that have specific expertise in selecting markets because of language capabilities, previous exposure, or specialized contacts appear to be the ones most successful and useful in aiding client firms in their global business efforts. For example, they can cooperate with firms that are already successful in global business but have been unable to penetrate a specific region. By sticking to their area of expertise and representing only a limited number of clients, such agents can provide quite valuable services.

The EMC as a Distributor When operating as a distributor, the EMC purchases products from the domestic firm, takes title, and assumes the trading risk. Selling in its own name, it has the opportunity to reap greater profits than when acting as an agent. The potential for greater profit is appropriate, because the EMC has drastically reduced the risk for the domestic firm while increasing its own risk. The burden of the merchandise acquired provides a major motivation to complete an international sale successfully. The domestic firm selling to the EMC is in the comfortable position of having sold its merchandise and received its money without having to deal with the complexities of the global market. On the other hand, it is less likely to gather much global business expertise.

For the concept of an export management company to work, both parties must fully recognize the delegation of responsibilities; the costs associated with these activities; and the need for information sharing, cooperation, and mutual reliance. Use of an EMC should be viewed just like domestic channel commitment. This requires a thorough investigation of the intermediary and the advisability of relying on its efforts, a willingness to cooperate on a relationship rather than on a transaction basis, and a willingness to properly reward its efforts. The EMC in turn must adopt a flexible approach to managing the export relationship. It must continue to upgrade the levels of services offered, constantly highlighting for the client the dimensions of postsales service and providing in-depth information, since these are its biggest sources of differential advantage.[44] By doing so, the EMC lets the client know that the cost charged is worth the service and thereby reduces the desire for circumvention.

Webb-Pomerene Associations

Legislation enacted in 1918 that led to Webb-Pomerene associations permits firms to cooperate in terms of global sales allocation, financing, and pricing information. The associations must take care not to engage in activities that would reduce competition within the United States. To more successfully penetrate global markets, however, they can allocate markets, fix quotas, and select exclusive distributors or brokers.

In spite of this early effort to encourage joint activities by firms in the international market, the effectiveness of Webb-Pomerene associations has not been substantial. At their peak, from 1930 to 1934, 50 Webb-Pomerene associations accounted for about 12 percent of U.S. exports. By 1991, only 22 associations were active and accounted for less than 2 percent of U.S. exports.[45] In addition, it appears that most of the users of this particular form of export intermediary are not the small and medium-size firms the act was initially intended to assist, but rather the dominant firms in their respective industries.

The lack of success of this particular intermediary has mainly been ascribed to the fact that the antitrust exemption granted was not sufficiently ironclad. Further, specialized export firms are thought to have more to offer to a domestic firm than does an association, which may be particularly true if the association is dominated by one or two major competitors in an industry. This makes joining the association undesirable for smaller firms.

Trading Companies

A third major intermediary is the trading company. The most famous ones are the general trading companies, or *sogoshosha,* of Japan. Names like Mitsubishi, Mitsui, and C. Itoh have become household words in the United States. The nine trading company giants of Japan in 1995 acted as intermediaries for about one-third of the country's exports and two-fifths of its imports.[46] These general trading companies play a unique role in world commerce by importing, exporting, countertrading, investing, and manufacturing. Because of their vast size, they can benefit from economies of scale and perform their operations at high rates of return even though their profit margins are very low. Global Learning Experience 11.8 examines the global scope of operations of one *sogoshosha*—the Mitsubishi Co.

Four major reasons have been given for the success of the Japanese *sogoshosha.* First, by concentrating on obtaining and disseminating information about market opportunities and by investing huge funds in the development of information systems, these firms now have the mechanisms and organizations in place to gather, evaluate, and translate market information into business opportunities. Second, economies of scale permit the firms to take advantage of their vast transaction volume to obtain preferential treatment by negotiating transportation rates or even opening up new transportation routes and distribution systems. Third, these firms serve large internal markets, not only in Japan but also around the world, and can benefit from opportunities for countertrade. Finally, *sogoshosha* have access to vast quantities of capital, both within Japan and in the global capital markets. They can therefore carry out transactions that are too large or risky to be palatable or feasible for other firms.[47]

GLOBAL LEARNING EXPERIENCE 11.8

Sogoshosha: Surviving in Changing Times

Mitsubishi, one of the Japan's largest *sogoshosha,* has annual revenues in excess of $150 billion. Imagine a company whose sales equal those of GM, the largest U.S. corporation, with Dow Chemical's revenues piled on top. Mitsubishi's revenues are bigger than those of AT&T, Dupont, Citicorp, and Proctor & Gamble combined. In serving its 45,000 customers, Mitsubishi moves as many as 100,000 products, from kernels of corn to huge power generators, around the world. Among the dozens of properties it owns outright are cattle feedlots and coal mines in Australia, pulp mills and iron ore mines in Canada, copper mines in Chile, a resort in Hawaii, and liquefied natural gas fields off the coast of Brunei.

Ironically enough, Mitsubishi is scraping by on a meager profit margin of approximately 0.10 percent. The other *sogoshosha* suffer similarly—even at their best in the 1960s and 1970s, these trading companies had profit margins of never more than 3 percent. Now, rising costs threaten to swallow earnings altogether. The core business that built the companies, hauling raw materials into Japan and speeding finished goods out into the world, has been declining for more than a decade. Experts believe that worldly wise Japanese manufacturers, who once depended on the *sogoshosha,* no longer need a trading company. They now make their own arrangements with shippers, dealers, and advertising agencies.

Luckily for Mitsubishi, a portion of its import business is protected from erosion because it has bought all or a slice of many supply sources. Take the corn trade it runs between the United States and Japan. It owns three grain elevators in central Nebraska where it stores the corn it buys locally. Back home, Mitsubishi owns Japan's largest livestock operation, so it feeds some of that American corn to its own chickens and pigs. A number of those chickens, in turn, end up on the tables of Japan's 1,050 Kentucky Fried Chicken restaurants, of which Mitsubishi is a proprietor.

Mitsubishi's greatest strength for the long haul, however, is its ability to continually attract top talent. The company ranks among the most desired employers among Japanese university students. So Mitsubishi can dispatch some of the brightest and the best of Japan's graduates to its 108 overseas offices which comprise one of the world's great information-gathering networks. (During the Gulf War, Mitsubishi's expatriates in the Middle East sent the home office more political and economic intelligence than foreign service officers provided the Japanese government.) How and where should this and other trading companies focus their talent as they struggle for a new role? The prevailing wisdom as to the "where" is simple—fast-growing Southeast Asia, China, and India. "As Japanese companies increase their direct investment in the region, they're going to travel in caravans," says Victor Fung, head of one of the largest Overseas China trading companies in Hong Kong. "And they're going to need someone to show them the way. That should make this a golden age for traders."

SOURCE: Lee Smith, "Does the World's Biggest Company Have a Future?" *Fortune,* August 7, 1995, 124.

export trading company (ETC) result of 1982 legislation to improve the export performance of small and medium-size firms, the export trading company allows businesses to band together to export or offer export services; additionally, the law permits bank participation in trading companies and relaxes antitrust provisions

In the United States, **export trading company (ETC)** legislation designed to improve the export performance of small and medium-sized firms was implemented in 1982. In order to improve export performance, bank participation in trading companies was permitted and the antitrust threat to joint-export efforts was reduced through precertification of planned activities by the U.S. Department of Commerce. Businesses were encouraged to join together to export or offer export services.

Permitting banks to participate in ETCs was intended to allow ETCs better access to capital and therefore permit more trading transactions and easier receipt of title to goods.

The relaxation of antitrust provisions in turn was meant to enable firms to form joint ventures more easily. The cost of developing and penetrating global markets would then be shared, with the proportional share being, for many small and medium-sized firms, much easier to bear. As an example, in case a warehouse is needed in order to secure foreign market penetration, one firm alone does not have to bear all the costs. A consortium of firms can jointly rent a foreign warehouse. Similarly, each firm need not station a service technician abroad at substantial cost. Joint funding of a service center by several firms makes the cost less prohibitive for each one. The trading company concept also offers a one-stop shopping center for both the firm and its foreign customers. The firm can be assured that all global functions will be performed efficiently by the trading company, and at the same time, the foreign customer will have to deal with few individual firms.

The legislation permits a wide variety of possible structures for an ETC. General trading companies may handle many commodities, perform import and export services, countertrade, and work closely with foreign distributors. Regional trading companies may handle commodities produced in only one region, specializing in products in which that region possesses a comparative advantage. Product-oriented trading companies may concentrate on a limited number of products and offer their market penetration services for only these products. Trading companies may also be geographically oriented, targeting one particular foreign nation, or may be focused on certain types of projects, such as turnkey operations and joint ventures with foreign investors. Finally, trading companies may develop an industry-oriented focus, handling only goods of specific industry groups, such as metals, chemicals, or pharmaceuticals.[48]

Independent of its form of operation, an ETC can engage in a wide variety of activities. It can purchase products, act as a distributor abroad, or offer services. It can provide information on distribution costs and even handle domestic and international distribution and transportation. This can range from identifying distribution costs to booking space on ocean or air carriers and handling shipping contracts.

Although ETCs seem to offer major benefits to many U.S. firms wishing to go abroad, they have not been very extensively used. By 1996, only 162 individual ETC certificates had been issued by the U.S. Department of Commerce. Since some of these certificates covered all the members of trade associations, more than 5,000 companies were part of an ETC.[49]

ETCs may still become the major vehicle for the generation of new global business entry activities by small and medium-sized firms. The concepts of synergism and cooperation certainly make sense in terms of enhancing the global competitiveness of firms. Yet the focus of ETCs should perhaps not be pure exporting. Importing and third-country trading may also generate substantial activity and profit. Through the carrying out of a wide variety of business transactions, global market knowledge is obtained. This management and consulting expertise may in itself be a salable service.

INTERNATIONAL FACILITATORS

Facilitators are entities outside the firm that assist in the process of going global by supplying knowledge and information but not participating in the transaction. A major

QUESTION *This small, important island, adjacent to the mainland of China, has an area of 23 sq. miles and is one of the most densely populated places on earth with 247,500 people per square mile.*

ANSWER *Hong Kong. For comparison purposes here are the population densities per square mile of some other cities around the world. Lagos, Nigera—142,821; Dhaka, Bangladesh—138,108; Jarkata, Indonesia—130,026; Bombay, India—127,461; Seoul, S. Korea—49,101; São Paulo, Brazil—41,466; Mexico City, Mexico—40,037 and New York City, U.S.A.—11,480.*

facilitator consists of the statements and actions of other firms in the same industry. Information that would be considered proprietary, if it involved domestic operations, is often freely shared by competing firms when it concerns global business. This information not only has source credibility but is viewed with a certain amount of fear, because a too-successful competitor may eventually infringe on the firm's domestic business.

A second, quite influential group of facilitators is distributors. Often, a firm's distributors are engaged, through some of their business activities, in global business. In order to increase their global distribution volume, they encourage purely domestic firms to participate in the global market. This is true not only for exports but also for imports. For example, a major customer of a manufacturing firm may find that materials available from abroad, if used in the domestic production process, would make the product available to him or her at lower cost. In such instances, the customer may approach the supplier and strongly encourage foreign sourcing.

Banks and other service firms, such as accounting and consulting firms, can serve as major facilitators by alerting their clients to global opportunities. While these service providers historically follow their major multinational clients abroad, increasingly they are establishing a foreign presence on their own. Frequently, they work with domestic clients on expanding market reach in the hope that their service will be used for any global transaction that results. Given the extensive information network of many service providers—banks often have a wide variety of correspondence relationships—the role of these facilitators can be major. Like a mother hen, they can take firms under their wings and be pathfinders in foreign markets.

Chambers of commerce and other business associations that interact with firms can frequently heighten their interest in global business. Yet in most instances, these organizations function only as secondary intermediaries, because true change is brought about by the presence and encouragement of other managers. Increasingly, however, associations recognize the importance of international business, and they produce and disseminate materials that can be useful in the development of entry strategies.

Government offices, such as the U.S. Department of Commerce, can also serve as major facilitators. The Commerce Department has district offices across the country that are charged with increasing the global business activities of U.S. firms. District officers, with the help of voluntary groups such as export councils, visit firms in the district and attempt to analyze their global business opportunities. Such activities raise questions about market and product knowledge. Only rarely will government employees have expertise in all areas. However, they can draw on the vast resources of their agency to provide more information to an interested firm.

Increasingly, nonfederal entities—primarily at the state and local level—also are active in encouraging firms to participate in global business. Many states have formed agencies for economic development that provide information, display products abroad, conduct trade missions, and sometimes even offer financing. Similar services can also be offered by state and local port authorities and by some of the larger cities. Most of these efforts are too recent to evaluate; however, it appears that, because of their closeness to firms, state and local authorities can become a major factor in facilitating global activities.

SUMMARY

The driving force of globalization is the level of managerial commitment to it. This commitment will grow gradually from an awareness of global potential to the realization that global business is a strategic option for the company. Management's commitment and its view of the firm's capabilities will then trigger various global business activities, which can range from exporting/importing to licensing and franchising. Eventually, the firm may then expand further through measures such as joint ventures, various strategic alliances, or foreign direct investment.

For the small firm, or one that is new to global business, exporting, licensing, or franchising would appear to be the prudent choice of entry. As the firm acquires knowledge and experience, it could then consider some of the other methods of global business entry.

Different operational modes are possible for the multinational corporation. Full ownership is becoming more unlikely in many markets as well as industries, and the firm has to look at alternative approaches. The main alternative is interfirm cooperation, in which the firm joins forces with other business entities, possibly even a foreign government. In some cases, when the firm may not want to make a direct investment, it will offer its management expertise for sale in the form of management contracts.

In going abroad, firms encounter multiple problems and challenges. These range from a lack of information to mechanics and documentation. In order to gain assistance in its initial global experience, the firm can make use of either intermediaries or facilitators. Intermediaries are outside companies that actively participate in a global transaction. They are export management companies, Webb-Pomerene associations, or export trading companies. In order for these intermediaries to perform global business functions properly, however, they must be compensated. This will result in a reduction of profits.

International facilitators do not participate in a global business transaction, but they contribute knowledge and information. Increasingly, facilitating roles are played by private-sector groups, such as industry associations, banks, accountants, or consultants and by federal, state, and local government authorities.

Key Terms and Concepts

fixed costs
variable costs
contribution margin
licensing agreement
franchising
management contract
turnkey operations
complementary marketing
equity participation
joint venture
strategic alliances
export management companies (EMCs)
export trading company (ETC)

Questions for Discussion

1. Discuss the difference between a proactive and a reactive firm, focusing your answer on global business.
2. Why is management commitment so important to export success?

3. Explain the benefits that global sales can have for domestic business activities.
4. Discuss the benefits and the drawbacks of treating global market activities as a safety-valve mechanism.
5. Give some of the reasons why distributors would want to help a firm gain a foothold in the global market.
6. Comment on the stance that "licensing is really not a form of global involvement because it requires no substantial additional effort on the part of the licensor."
7. Suggest reasons for the explosive global expansion of U.S.-based franchised systems.
8. What is the purpose of export intermediaries?
9. Is there a need for export trading companies?
10. What makes a U.S. export trading company different from Japanese trading companies?

Recommended Readings

Agmon, Tamir, and Richard Drobnick. *Small Firms in Global Competition.* York: Oxford University Press, 1994.

Blaine, Michael James. *Co-operation in International Business: The Use of Limited Equity Arrangements.* Brookfield, Vt.: Avebury, 1994.

Buckley, Peter J. *Foreign Direct Investment and Multilateral Enterprises.* New York: Macmillan, 1995.

Cavusgil, S. Tamer, and Michael R. Czinkota, eds. *Trade Promotion and Assistance: International Perspectives.* Westport, CT: Quorum Books, 1990.

Contractor, Farok J. *Licensing in International Strategy: A Guide for Planning and Negotiations.* Westport, Conn.: Quorum Books, 1985.

Czinkota, Michael R., and Ilkka A. Ronkainen. *International Marketing Strategy: Environmental Assessment and Entry Strategies.* Fort Worth: Dryden Press, 1994.

Czinkota, Michael R., Ilkka Ronkainen, and John Tarrant. *The Global Marketing Imperative.* Lincolnwood, Ill.: NTC Business Books, 1995.

Dunning, John H. and Rajneesh Narula, eds. *Foreign Direct Investment and Governments: Catalysts for Economic Restructuring.* New York: Routledge, 1996.

Eli, Max. *Japan Inc: Global Strategies of Japanese Trading Corporations.* Chicago: Probus, 1991.

The Export Yellow Pages. Washington, D.C.: U.S. West Publishing, 1997.

Foreign Direct Investment, Trade and Employment. Paris: Organization for Economic Cooperation and Development, 1995.

Graham, Edward M., and Paul R. Krugman. *Foreign Direct Investment in the United States,* 3rd ed. Washington, D.C.: Institute for International Economics, 1995.

International Direct Investment Statistics Yearbook. Paris: Organization for Economic Co-operation and Development, 1994.

James, Harvey S., and Murray Weidenbaum. *When Businesses Cross International Borders: Strategic Alliances and Their Alternatives.* Westport, CT: Praeger, 1993.

Joyner, Nelson. *How to Build an Export Business,* 2nd ed. Reston, Virginia: Federation of International Trade Associations, 1995.

Kaynak, Erdener, ed. *The Global Business: Four Key Marketing Strategies.* New York: International Business Press, 1993.

Kotabe, Masaaki, Arvind Sahay, and Preet S. Aulakh. "Emerging Role of Technology Licensing in the Development of Global Product Strategy: Conceptual Framework and Propositions." *Journal of Marketing* 60, 1, 1996: 73–88.

Leonidou, Leonidas C., and Constantine S. Katsikeas. "The Export Development Process: An Integrative Review of Empirical Models." *Journal of International Business Studies* 27, 3, 1996: 517–551.

Lewis, Jordan D. *Partnerships for Profit: Structuring and Managing Strategic Alliances.* New York: Free Press, 1990.

Luostarinen, Reijo, and Lawrence Welch. *International Business Operations,* Helsinki, Finland: Helsinki School of Economics, 1990.

—, *Metropolitan Area Exports: An Export Performance Report on Over 250 U.S. Cities.*" Washington, D.C.: U.S. Department of Commerce, 1996.

Nothdurft, William E. *Going Global: How Europe Helps Small Firms Export,* Washington, D.C.: Brookings Institution, 1992.

Nye, William W. "An Economic Profile of Export Trading Companies." *The Antitrust Bulletin* (Summer 1993): 309–325.

Paliwoda, Stanley. *New Perspectives on International Marketing.* London: Routledge, Chapman, & Hall, Inc. 1991.

Perry, Anne C. *The Evolution of Selected U.S. Trade Intermediaries.* Westport, Conn.: Quorum Books, 1992.

Richardson, David J., and Karin Rindal, *Why Exports Matter: More!,* Washington D.C.: Institute for International Economics and The Manufacturing Institute, 1996.

Root, Franklin. *Entry Strategies for International Markets.* New York: Lexington Books, 1994.

Seringhaus, F. H., Rolf and Philip J. Rosson. *Export Development and Promotion: The Role of Public Organizations.* Boston: Kluwer Academic Publishers, 1991.

Stanworth, John, and Patrick Kaufmann. "Similarities and Differences in UK and US franchise research data: Towards a dynamic model of franchisee motivation." *International Small Business Journal* 14, April/June 1996: 57–70.

Tomas, Michael J., and Donald G. Howard. "The Export Trading Company Act: An Update." *Journal of Marketing Channels* 2, 1 (1993): 105–119.

Towards Multilateral Investment Rules, Paris: Organization for Economic Cooperation and Development, 1996.

United National Centre on Transnational Corporations. *The Determinants of Foreign Direct Investment: A Survey of the Evidence.* New York: United Nations, 1992.

U.S. Department of Commerce, *A Basic Guide to Exporting.* Washington, D.C., Government Printing Office, 1992.

Whitney, James D. "The Causes and Consequences of Webb-Pomerene Associations: A Reappraisal." *The Antitrust Bulletin* (Summer 1993): 395–418.

Yoshino, M. Y., and U. S. Rangan. *Strategic Alliances: An Entrepreneurial Approach to Globalization.* Boston: Harvard Business School Press, 1995.

Notes

1. Theodore Levitt, "The Globalization of Markets," *Harvard Business Review* 61 (May–June 1983): 92–102.
2. Warren J. Bilkey and George Tesar, "The Export Behavior of Smaller Sized Wisconsin Manufacturing Firms," *Journal of International Business Studies* 8 (Spring–Summer 1977): 93–98.
3. William C. Pavord and Raymond G. Bogart, "The Dynamics of the Decision to Export," *Akron Business and Economic Review* 6 (Spring 1975): 6–11.
4. Finn Wiedersheim-Paul, H. C. Olson, and L. S. Welch, "Pre-Export Activity: The First Step in Internationalization," *Journal of International Business Studies* 9 (Spring–Summer 1978): 47–58.
5. George Tesar and Jesse S. Tarleton, "Comparison of Wisconsin and Virginia Small and Medium-Sized Exporters: Aggressive and Passive Exporters," in *Export Management,* eds. Michael R. Czinkota and George Tesar (New York: Praeger, 1982), 85–112.
6. Michael R. Czinkota, *Export Development Strategies* (New York: Praeger, 1982), 10.
7. *Winning in the World Market* (Washington, D.C.: American Business Conference Inc., November 1987), 20.
8. S. Tamer Cavusgil, "Global Dimensions of Marketing," in *Marketing,* eds. Patrick E. Murphy and Ben M. Enis (Glenview, Ill.: Scott, Foresman, 1985), 577–599.
9. Masaaki Kotabe and Michael R. Czinkota, "State Government Promotion of Manufacturing Exports: A Gap Analysis," *Journal of International Business Studies,* (Winter 1992).
10. Yoo S. Yang, Robert P. Leone, and Dana L. Alden, "A Market Expansion Ability Approach to Identify Potential Exporters," *Journal of Marketing* 56 (January 1992): 84–96.
11. Michael R. Czinkota and Michael L. Ursic, "An Experience Curve Explanation of Export Expansion," *Journal of Business Research* 12 (Spring 1984): 159–168.
12. Wesley J. Johnston and Michael R. Czinkota, "Managerial Motivations as Determinants of Industrial Export Behavior," in *Export Management: An International Context,* eds. Michael R. Czinkota and George Tesar (New York: Praeger, 1982), 3–7.
13. "New 'Storeless' Market Gateways," *Focus Japan,* August 1989, 3.
14. Fred Hiatt, "Vending U.S. Steak on Japanese Corners," *International Herald Tribune,* April 5, 1990, 13.
15. Donald W. Hackett, "The International Expansion of U.S. Franchise Systems," in *Multinational Product Management,* eds. Warren J. Keegan and Charles S. Mayer (Chicago: American Marketing Association, 1979), 61–81.
16. Nancy Womack, International Franchise Association, October 11, 1996.
17. Andrew E. Seruser, "McDonald's Conquers the World," *Fortune,* October 17, 1994: 103–116.
18. "ComputerLand Debugs Its Franchising Program for Asia/Pacific Region," *Business International,* September 13, 1985, 294–295.

19. Nizamettin Aydin and Madhav Kacker, "International Outlook of U.S.-based Franchisers," *International Marketing Review* 7 (1990): 43–53.
20. Lawrence S. Welch and Anubis Pacifico, "Management Contracts: A Role in Internationalization?" *International Marketing Review* 7, (1990): 64–74.
21. Richard Ellison, "An Alternative to Direct Investment Abroad," *International Management* 31 (June 1976): 25–27.
22. Michael Z. Brooke, *Selling Management Services Contracts in International Business* (London: Holt, Rinehart and Winston, 1985), 7.
23. Richard W. Wright and Colin S. Russel, "Joint Ventures in Developing Countries: Realities and Responses," *Columbia Journal of World Business* 10 (Spring 1975): 74–80.
24. Richard Gibson, "Cereal Venture Is Planning Honey of a Battle in Europe," *The Wall Street Journal,* November 14, 1990, B1, B8.
25. Vern Terpstra and Chwo-Ming J. Yu, "Piggbacking: A Quick Road to Internationalization," *International Marketing Review* 7, (1990): 52–53.
26. "Can SAS Keep Flying with the Big Birds?" *Business Week,* November 27, 1989, 142–146.
27. "Mitsubishi Is Taking a Back Road into Europe," *Business Week,* November 19, 1990, 64.
28. Kathryn Rudie Harrigan, "Joint Ventures and Global Strategies," *Columbia Journal of World Business* 19 (Summer 1984): 7–16.
29. W. G. Friedman and G. Kalmanoff, *Joint International Business Ventures* (New York: Columbia University Press, 1961), 5.
30. J. Peter Killing, *Strategies for Joint Venture Success* (New York: Praeger, 1983), 11–12.
31. Paul W. Beamish, "The Characteristics of Joint Ventures in Developed and Developing Countries," *Columbia Journal of World Business* 20 (Fall 1985): 13–19.
32. Charles Oman, *New Forms of International Investment in Developing Countries* (Paris: Organization for Economic Cooperation and Development, 1984), 79.
33. Dennis J. Encarnation and Sushil Vachani, "Foreign Ownership: When Hosts Change the Rules," *Harvard Business Review* 63 (September–October 1985): 152–160.
34. Richard H. Holton, "Making International Joint Ventures Work" (Paper presented at the seminar on the Management of Headquarters/Subsidiary Relationships in Transnational Corporations, Stockholm School of Economics, June 2–4, 1980), 4.
35. *Collaborative Ventures: An Emerging Phenomenon in the Information Industry* (New York: Coopers & Lybrand, 1984), 3.
36. Thomas Gross and John Neuman, "Strategic Alliances Vital in Global Marketing," *Marketing News,* June 19, 1989, 1–2.
37. Louis Kraar, "Your Rivals Can Be Your Allies," *Fortune,* March 27, 1989, 66–76.
38. "MD-90 Airliner Unveiled by McDonnell Douglas," *The Washington Post,* February 14, 1993, A4.
39. Jordan D. Lewis, *Partnerships for Profit: Structuring and Managing Strategic Alliances* (New York: The Free Press, 1990), 85–87.
40. Gary Hamel, Yves L. Doz, and C. K. Prahalad, "Collaborate with Your Competitors—and Win," *Harvard Business Review* 67 (January–February 1989): 133–139.
41. "Can Europe Catch Up in the High-Tech Race?" *Business Week,* October 23, 1989, 142–154.
42. Lee Smith, "Can Consortiums Defeat Japan?" *Fortune,* June 5, 1989, 245–254.
43. Economic Consulting Services, *A Study of the Feasibility of Using Export Associations to Promote Increased Exports by Small Businesses* (Washington, D.C.: Economic Consulting Services, 1982), 29.
44. Daniel C. Bello, David J. Urban, and Bronislaw J. Verhage, "Evaluating Export Middlemen in Alternative Channel Structures," *International Marketing Review* 8 (1991): 49–64.
45. Carl Hevener, Federal Trade Commission, Washington, D.C., 1992.
46. Lee Smith, "Does the World's Biggest Company Have a Future?" *Fortune,* August 7, 1995: 125.
47. Yoshi Tsurumi, *Sogoshosha: Engines of Export-Based Growth* (Montreal: The Institute for Research on Public Policy, 1980).
48. *The Export Trading Company Act of 1982* (Washington, D.C.: Chamber of Commerce of the United States of America, 1983), 4.
49. Office of Export Trading Companies, U.S. Department of Commerce, Washington, D.C., October 15, 1996.

The Marketing Mix for Products and Services

LEARNING OBJECTIVES

To describe how environmental differences generate new challenges for the global marketing manager.

To compare and contrast the merits of standardization versus localization strategies for country markets and of regional versus global marketing efforts.

To discuss market-specific and global challenges within each of the marketing functions: product, price, promotion, and place (distribution).

MARKETING MANAGEMENT

After target markets are selected, the next step is the determination of marketing efforts at appropriate levels. A key question in global marketing concerns the extent to which the elements of the marketing mix—product, price, promotion, and place (distribution) should be standardized. The marketer also faces the specific challenges of adjusting each of the mix elements in the global marketplace.

Standardization versus Adaptation

The global marketer must first decide what modifications in the mix policy are needed or warranted. Three basic alternatives in approaching global markets are available:

1. Make no special provisions for the global marketplace but, rather, identify potential target markets and then choose products that can easily be marketed with little or no modification.
2. Adapt to local conditions in each and every target market (the multidomestic approach).
3. Incorporate differences into a regional or global strategy that will allow for local differences in implementation (globalization approach).

In today's environment, standardization usually means cross-national strategies rather than a policy of viewing foreign markets as secondary and therefore not important enough to have products adapted for them. Ideally, the global marketer should think globally and act locally,[1] focusing on neither extreme: full standardization or full localization. Global thinking requires flexibility in exploiting good ideas and products on a worldwide basis, as noted in Global Learning Experience 12.1.

The question of whether to standardize or to custom tailor marketing programs in each country has continued to trouble practitioners and academics alike and has produced many and varied opinions. In the 1960s, Robert Buzzell stated that it depends on the strengths of the barriers to standardization, such as national differences in consumer preferences and legal restrictions, and on the potential payoffs of standardizing marketing strategy.[2] Studies on how firms view standardization have found that arguments in favor of standardizing whenever possible fall into two categories: better marketing performance and lower marketing cost.[3] Factors that encourage standardization or adaptation are summarized in Table 12.1.

The World Customer Controversy The world customer[4] identified by Ernest Dichter more than 20 years ago has gained new meaning with Theodore Levitt's suggestion that inexpensive air travel and new technologies have led consumers the world over to think and shop increasingly alike.[5] In addition, Kenichi Ohmae has identified a new group of consumers that is emerging in a triad composed of the United States, Japan, and Western Europe. Marketers can treat the triad as a single market with the same spending habits.[6] Approximately 600 million in number, these consumers have similar educational backgrounds, income levels, lifestyles, use of leisure time, and aspirations. One reason given for the similarities in their consumer demand is a level of purchasing power that is ten times greater than that of less developed countries (LDCs) or newly industrialized countries (NICs). This translates into higher diffusion rates for certain products. Another reason is that developed infrastructures—ownership of telephones and an abundance of paved roads—lead to attractive markets for other products. Products can be designed to meet similar demand conditions throughout the triad. Whirlpool, after conducting consumer research throughout Europe, entered the fast-growing microwave market with a product that offered various product

GLOBAL LEARNING EXPERIENCE 12.1

Thinking Globally, Acting Locally

Automakers around the world are trying to figure out what automotive customers in 200 countries want—and to beat their competitors to the punch. However, they are faced by the most fundamental global marketing challenge in their quest: while the customer's desire for cost savings drives the automakers' idea for global automobiles, the danger is that the resulting vehicles will be too compromised to appeal to specific markets.

Ignoring local marketing input is a sure way to imperil a marketer's international aspirations. For example, Germany's Volkswagen AG operated for years with the philosophy that only one car was good enough for all of the world. VW marketing executives in the United States tried in vain to include items such as cupholders and American-style seatback release levers in cars destined for the U.S. market. VW is now rethinking this strategy, as are many of its competitors that have seen their sales and profitability slip as a result of not paying enough attention to what its customers want.

Nissan determined that it cannot afford to build, design, and market completely distinct models, such as the Infiniti Q45 and J30, just for the U.S. market. Instead, future Infiniti models will be variations of cars designed for affluent Japanese customers as well as U.S. buyers. Nissan strategists look at the marketing requirements of Japan, the United States, and Europe to determine which customer preferences overlap. Then Nissan's export, research and development, and accounting departments decide which car model to manufacture for each market. There is still a strong economic need to manufacture similar products even when working in different markets, of course.

France's Renault has taken the middle road between developing a world car and one for a single market. More than 90 percent of the company's sales are generated in Europe. Minor alterations—such as better air conditioning in southern markets and stronger heaters in the Nordic countries—are made, but the body, engine, transmission, and chassis are identical for each model.

Ford's approach is best seen in its introduction of the Mondeo in Europe and its sister cars, the Ford Contour and Mercury Mystique, in the North American market. The Mondeo varies slightly for the different European markets; for example, for some markets a sun roof is standard, while for others, an air conditioner may be included. The Mondeo's image will vary from market to market, since the economies of scale do not carry over to positioning. In Italy, where the Mondeo competes against Fiat, the Mondeo is not seen as an upmarket car. But in Germany, where the Mondeo competes with Mercedes and BMW, Ford advertises with quotations from car industry publications to make the Mondeo appear more upscale.

SOURCE: Ray Serafin, "Auto Marketers Gas Up for World Car Drive," *Advertising Age,* January 16, 1995, I–16; "Another New Model . . ." *The Economist,* January 7, 1995, 52–53; and Alex Taylor III, "New Ideas from Europe's Automakers," *Fortune,* December 12, 1994, 159–172.

features with different appeal in different countries clearly targeted at the Euroconsumer.[7]

Even companies that are famous for following the same methods worldwide that they follow domestically have made numerous changes in their marketing programs, however. For instance, McDonald's serves abroad the same menu of hamburgers, soft drinks, and other foods it does in the United States, and the restaurants look the same. But in Japan, Ronald McDonald is called Donald McDonald because it is easier to pronounce. Menu adjustments include beer in Germany and wine in France. Of course,

TABLE 12.1 **Standardization versus Adaptation**

Factors Encouraging Standardization	Factors Encouraging Adaptation
• Economies in product R&D	• Differing use conditions
• Economies of scale in production	• Government and regulatory influences
• Economies in marketing	• Differing buyer behavior patterns
• Control of marketing programs	• Local initiative and motivation in implementation
• "Shrinking" of the world marketplace	• Adherence to the marketing concept

similar situations may occur in domestic markets; for example, U.S. fast-food restaurants in the South offer iced tea, but those in the Northeast do not.

Globalization *Globalization* is a business initiative based on the belief that the world is becoming more homogeneous; further, distinctions between national markets are not only fading but, for some products, will eventually disappear. As a result, companies need to globalize their international strategy by formulating it across country markets to take advantage of underlying market, cost, environmental, and competitive factors.[8]

About 20 percent of large U.S. corporations now consider themselves global marketers.[9] Companies such as Coca-Cola and Levi Strauss have proven that universal appeal exists. Coke's "one sight, one sound, one sell" approach is a legend among global marketers. Other companies have some "world products" and some products that are not. If cultural and competitive differences are less important than similarities, a single advertising approach can exploit the similarities to stimulate sales everywhere. This can be done at far lower cost than if campaigns were developed for each market.

Globalization differs from the multidomestic approach in these three basic ways:

1. The global approach looks for similarities between markets. The multidomestic approach ignores similarities.
2. The global approach actively seeks homogeneity in products, image, marketing, and advertising message. The multidomestic approach results in unnecessary differences from market to market.
3. The global approach asks, "Is this product or process suitable for world consumption?" The multidomestic approach, relying solely on local autonomy, never asks the question.[10]

In a globalization strategy, marketing is typically the most "localized" of the business functions. Even within marketing, however, differences exist in marketing mix elements and between companies. Elements that are strategic—such as positioning—are more easily globalized, while tactical elements—such as sales promotions—are typically determined locally. Notice that adaptation is present even at Coca-Cola, which is acknowledged to be one of the world's most global marketers. The key is the worldwide use of good ideas rather than absolute standardization of all facets of the marketing programs.

Globalization, by definition, means the centralization of decision making. Changes in philosophy concerning local autonomy are delicate issues, and the "not invented here" syndrome may become a problem. It can be solved by utilizing various motivational policies:

1. Encourage local managers to generate ideas.
2. Ensure that local managers participate in the development of marketing strategies and programs for global brands.

3. Maintain a product portfolio that includes local as well as regional and global brands.
4. Allow local managers control over their marketing budgets so they can respond to local consumer needs and counter local competition.[11]

Finding the balance between overglobalizing and underglobalizing is indeed difficult. While the benefits of cost reduction and improved quality and competitiveness of products and programs are attractive, there are pitfalls that can leave the marketing effort catering to no one.[12] For example, Lego A/S, the Danish toy manufacturer, tried American-style consumer promotions, which had proven highly successful in North America, unaltered in Japan. Subsequent research showed that Japanese consumers considered them wasteful, expensive, and not very appealing.

Some firms approach markets regionally, and some have bridged local and global strategies through a regionalization policy.[13] As an example, Colgate-Palmolive considered using a "one sight, one sound" approach and hiring one advertising agency for all brands. Eventually, management settled on a regional approach, with one agency in Europe, another in Asia, and another for Latin America.

PRODUCTS AND SERVICES

Products or services from the core of the firm's international operations. Its success depends on how well those products or services satisfy the needs and wants of global customers and how well they are differentiated from those of the competition.

Services often accompany products, but they are also, by themselves, an increasingly important part of our economy. One author has contrasted services and products by stating that "a good is an object, a device, a thing; a service is a deed, a performance, an effort."[14] This definition, although quite general, captures the essence of the difference between products and services. Services tend to be more intangible, personalized, and custom made than products. In addition, services are the fastest-growing sector in world trade. These major differences bring with them the need for a major differentiation, because they add dimensions to services that are not present in products.

While the growth in international merchandise trade over the past 25 years has been phenomenal, the increase in international services trade has been equally remarkable. Figure 12.1 indicates the rapid rise in U.S. exports and imports of merchandise and services since 1970. It is interesting to note that in 1996 U.S. exports of services were equivalent to 37 percent of merchandise exports, illustrating clearly the important role that services have in U.S. global trade activities.

The first portion of this chapter will discuss considerations in the global marketing of physical products. The last section of the chapter will cover the marketing of services.

Product Policy

Factors Affecting Adaptation Even when marketing programs are based on highly standardized ideas and strategies, they depend on three sets of variables: (1) the market(s) targeted, (2) the product and its characteristics, and (3) company characteristics, including factors such as resources and policy.[15]

Factors affecting product adaptation to foreign market conditions are summarized in Figure 12.2. The changes vary from minor ones, such as translation of a user's manual, to major ones, such as a more economical version of the product. Many of the factors have an impact on product selection as well as product adaptation for a given market.

A detailed examination of 174 consumer packaged goods destined for developing countries showed that, on the average, 4.1 changes per product were made in terms of

U.S. Exports, Imports and Trade Balance of Merchandise and Services. 1970, 1980, 1990 and 1996 (in millions of U.S. dollars)

FIGURE 12.1

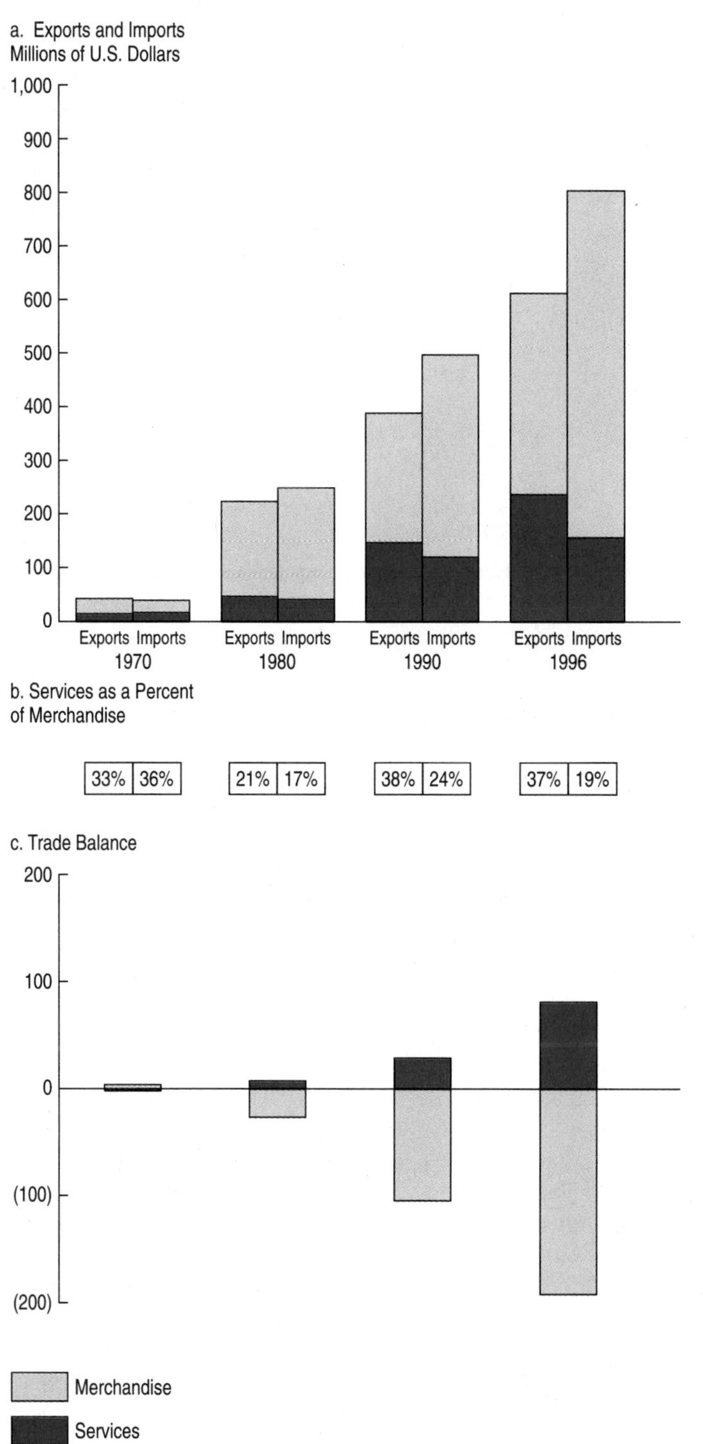

SOURCE: U.S. Department of Commerce, *Survey of Current Business,* July 1997. Table 1, 67.

FIGURE 12.2 Factors Affecting Product Adaptation Decisions

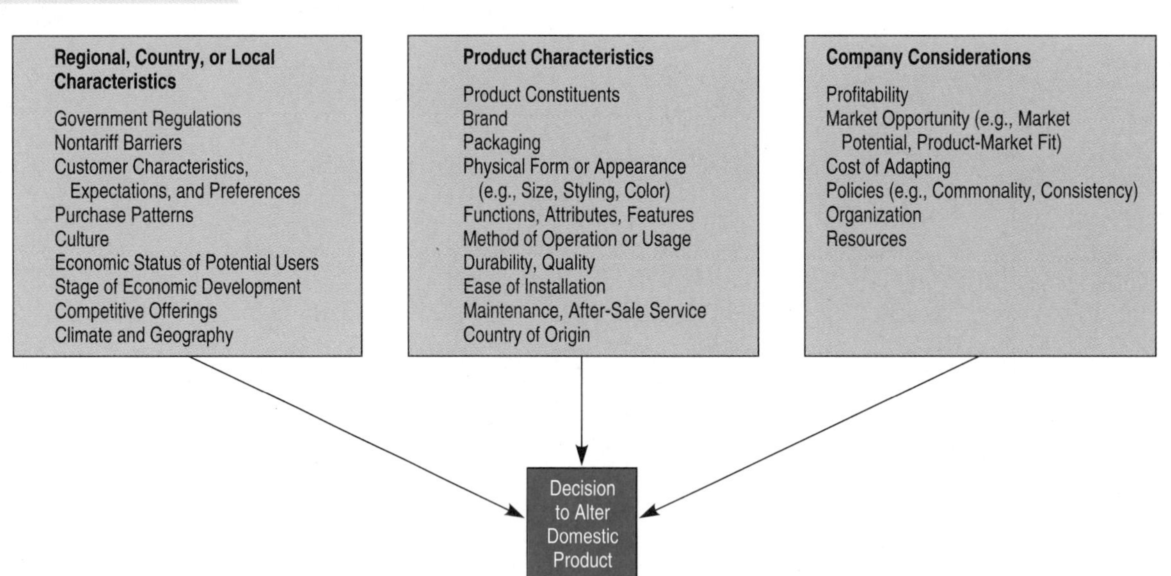

SOURCE: V. Yorio, *Adapting Products for Export* (New York: The Conference Board, 1983), 7. Reprinted with permission of the Conference Board.

brand name, packaging, measurement units, labeling, constituents, product features, and usage instructions. Only one out of ten products was transferred without modification. Some of the changes were mandatory, some discretionary.[16]

Questions of adaptation have no easy answers. Marketers in many firms rely on decision-support systems to aid in program adaptation, while others consider every situation independently. All products must, of course, conform to environmental conditions over which the marketer has no control. Further, the global marketer may use adaptation to enhance its competitiveness in the marketplace.

The Market: Regional, Country, or Local Characteristics Typically, the market environment mandates the majority of product modifications. However, the most stringent requirements often result from government regulations. Some of the requirements may serve no purpose other than a political one (such as protection of domestic industry or response to political pressures). Because of the sovereignty of nations, individual firms must comply, but they can influence the situation by lobbying directly or through industry associations to have the issue raised during trade negotiations. Government regulations may be spelled out, but firms need to be ever vigilant for changes and exceptions. The 18 member countries of the European Economic Area are imposing standards in more than 10,000 product categories ranging from toys to tractor seats. While companies like Murray Manufacturing have had to change their products to comply with these standards (in Murray's case, making its lawnmowers quieter), they will be able to produce one European product in the future. Overall, U.S. producers may be forced to improve quality of all their products because some product rules require adoption of an overall system approved by the International Standards Organization (ISO).[17]

Product decisions made by marketers of consumer products are especially affected by local behavior, tastes, attitudes, and traditions—all reflecting the marketer's need to gain the customer's approval. Global Learning Experience 12.2 indicates how a well-

The Sharper Image Focuses on the World

The Sharper Image, a San Francisco-based retailer with a high-end, off-beat reputation and designs on global markets, is facing a steep learning curve overseas. Consider the "Saucer Launcher," an aptly named device that lets children propel toy saucers through the air. The Sharper Image sold 89,000 of the $22 items in the United States in 1995, but watched it crash-land in Scandinavia, where parents thought it wasn't durable enough. Likewise with a pinball machine that was a hit in the U.S. but flopped in Norway, where folks are steadfast in demanding educational value from toys.

The company hasn't been shut out since launching its international division at the behest of CEO Richard Thalheimer two years ago. Although only 2 percent of its $200 million in annual sales are international, the Sharper Image has stores in Australia, Japan, Sweden, and South Korea and is negotiating for deals in Saudi Arabia, the United Kingdom, Canada, Indonesia, and France. Also in the works are a roll-out in Germany and "a major assault" on South America, centered on Brazil, Colombia, Argentina, Chile, and Peru.

Thalheimer wants the international division to claim 10 percent of sales within the next two years and has some success stories to build upon. In South Korea, the company's top international market so far, a licensee has opened a store on prime real estate in Seoul. The Korean operation was launched with a mail-order catalog last year and has seen sales climb steadily.

The Sharper Image put up big numbers in Mexico, selling 30,000 motorized tie racks, until the peso crash of 1994. In Switzerland, sculptures of an alien made popular by Hollywood have been selling briskly at $3,500 apiece. And thousands of snore detectors, which prod wearers to turn over by emitting a pulse when they start to snore, have been sold in Italy.

Alas, the peso crash forced the company's Mexican licensees to close five stores. Back in Norway, a test store in Oslo recently was shuttered after Norwegian shoppers found its wares too "frivolous" for their tastes. And in the Middle East, company executives are searching for a product mix that won't offend Islamic standards—which leaves out such items as massage tapes.

SOURCE: Marcy Burstiner, "The Sharper Image Focuses on the World," *World Trade,* April 1996, 14.

known U.S. mail order and retail company is having difficulty in selecting the right products in different cultures. A knowledge of cultural and psychological differences may be the key to success. For example, Brazilians rarely eat breakfast; therefore, Dunkin' Donuts markets doughnuts as snacks, as dessert, and for parties. To further appeal to Brazilians, doughnuts are made with local fruit fillings like papaya and guava.

Often, no concrete product changes are needed, only a change in the product's **positioning.** Positioning is the perception by consumers of the firm's brand in relation

positioning
perception by consumers of a firm's product in relation to competitors' products

There is more than one United States in the Western Hemisphere. There are three. Can you name them?

The United States of America, Los Estados Unidos Mexicanos, y Estados Unidos de Venezuela.

to competitors' brands; that is, the mental image a brand, or the company as a whole, evokes. Coca-Cola took a risk in marketing Diet Coke in Japan because the population is not overweight by Western standards. Further, Japanese women do not like to drink anything clearly labeled as a diet product. The company changed the name to Coke Light and subtly shifted the promotional theme from "weight loss" to "figure maintenance."

Nontariff barriers include product standards, testing or approval procedures, subsidies for local products, and bureaucratic red tape. The nontariff barriers affecting product adjustments usually concern elements outside the core product. For example, France requires the use of the French language "in any offer, presentation, advertisement, written or spoken, instructions for use, specification or guarantee terms for goods or services, as well as for invoices and receipts." Because nontariff barriers are usually in place to keep foreign products out or to protect domestic producers, getting around them may be the single toughest problem for the international marketer.

The monitoring of competitors' product features, as well as determining what has to be done to meet and beat them, is critical to product adaptation decisions. Competitive offerings may provide a baseline against which resources can be measured—for example, they may help to determine what it takes to reach a critical market share in a given competitive situation. American Hospital Supply, a Chicago-based producer of medical equipment, adjusts its product in a preemptive way by making products that are hard to duplicate. As a result, the firm increased sales and earnings in Japan about 40 percent a year over a ten-year period.

Product decisions are affected by cultural variables discussed in Chapter 8. Reflecting the social, political, and religious heritage of the country, culture often presents the most difficult variable for any company to change. An example is the experience of the Coca-Cola Company when it introduced Mellow Yellow in Thailand. Because "yellow" in Thai means "pus," the name was shortened to Mello.[18] Chinese and Western consumers share similar standards when it comes to evaluating brand names. Both appreciate a brand name that is catchy, memorable, distinct, and says something indicative of the product. But, because of cultural and linguistic factors, Chinese consumers expect more in terms of how the names are spelled, written, and styled, and whether they are considered lucky. In 1994, PepsiCo, Inc., introduced Cheetos in the Chinese market under a Chinese name, *qi duo,* roughly pronounced "chee-do," that translates as "many surprises."[19]

Management must take into account the stage of economic development of the overseas market. As a country's economy advances, buyers are in a better position to buy and to demand more sophisticated products and product versions. On the other hand, the situation in some developing markets may require backward innovation; that is, the market may require a drastically simplified version of the firm's product because of lack of purchasing power or of usage conditions. As noted in Global Learning Experience 12.3, creative research may uncover new product opportunities. Economic conditions may affect packaging decisions. Pillsbury packages its products in six- and eight-serving sizes for developing-country markets, while the most popular size in the North American market is two servings.[20]

The target market's physical separation from the host country and its climatic conditions will usually have an effect on the total product offering: the core product; tan-

Different Cultures Open New Export Markets

For many years, American poultry producers had been disposing of chicken feet and the inedible parts of the bird by rendering the material into a type of animal feed. In recent years, however, the U.S. producers have discovered that the lowly chicken foot is a popular food dish in Chinese cuisine. In Guangdong Province, which borders Hong Kong, chicken feet are one of the many dishes eaten for breakfast. Chicken feet are also appreciated in Hong Kong where they are prepared in a number of ways, from being transformed into gelatinous delights by master chefs to crunchy, deep-fried snacks sold by street vendors.

Almost every major U.S. poultry producer is exporting chicken feet to Hong Kong and China—the shipping volume is estimated at 300 to 500, 40-feet intermodal containers each month. The dollar value of these exports are shown below.

U.S. Exports of Chicken Cuts and Edible Offal (except livers), Frozen Harmonized Classification #02074,0000, 1994–1996 (in millions of dollars)

	1994	1995	1996
Hong Kong	$253.8	$373.8	$351.2
China	22.2	30.9	55.1
Total	$276.0	$404.7	$406.3

Note: A large portion of chicken parts shipped to Hong Kong are reshipped to China.

U.S. commercial fishermen, like their poultry counterparts, found a new export product in the despised sea urchin. Japanese gourmets enjoy eating the sea urchin's golden eggs, or roe, on top of rice, seaweed, or noodles. Depending on the quantity of the roe in a catch, urchins can bring as much as $1 a pound dockside; the golden roe itself can bring as much as $100 a pound. In several years, the sea urchin has moved from being a despised scavenger of bait to a valuable seafood export, as shown in the following export data.

U.S. Exports of Sea Urchin Roe to Japan (in millions of dollars)

1991	1992	1993	1994	1995	1996
67.9	65.6	98.0	120.8	129.5	105.7

In both of these cases, in-depth research of a cultural variable—eating and foods—uncovered export and new product opportunities.

Sources: Adapted from Brian Johns, "U.S. Chicken Producers Find Feet Have Wings in China," *Journal of Commerce,* March 29, 1995, A-1; Andrew C. Revkin, "The Despised Urchin Enriches Maine Coast," *New York Times,* January 2, 1996, C-33; export data provided by Global Trade Information Services.

gible elements, mainly packaging; and the augmented features. The global marketer must consider two sometimes contradictory aspects of packaging. On the one hand, the product itself has to be protected against longer transit times and possibly longer shelf life. On the other hand, care has to be taken not to use proscribed preservatives. Initial attempts to sell Colombian guava paste in the United States were not successful because the original packaging could not withstand the longer distribution channels and the longer time required for distribution.

Product Characteristics Product characteristics are the inherent features of the product offering, whether actual or perceived. The inherent characteristics of products, and the benefits they provide to consumers in the various markets in which they are marketed, make certain products good candidates for standardization—and others not.

The global marketer has to make sure that products do not contain ingredients that might violate legal requirements or religious or social customs. DEP Corporation, a Los Angeles manufacturer with $19 million in annual sales of hair and skin products, takes particular pains to make sure that no Japan-bound products contain formaldehyde, an ingredient commonly used in the United States, but illegal in Japan.[21] Where religion or custom determines consumption, ingredients may have to be replaced for the product to be acceptable. In Islamic countries, for example, vegetable shortening has to be substituted for animal fats.

Packaging is an area where firms generally do make modifications.[22] Because of the longer time that products spend in channels of distribution, global companies, especially those marketing food products, have used more expensive packaging materials and/or more expensive transportation modes for export shipments. Food manufacturers have solved the problem by using airtight, reclosable containers that seal out moisture and other contaminants.

The promotional aspect of packaging relates primarily to labeling. The major adjustments concern legally required bilinguality, as in Canada (French and English), Belgium (French and Flemish), and Finland (Finnish and Swedish). Other governmental requirements include more informative labeling of products for consumer protection and education. Inadequate identification, failure to use the required languages, or inadequate or incorrect descriptions printed on the labels may all cause problems.

brand name
the part of the brand that can be vocalized, or spoken

brand
name, term, symbol, sign, design or combination thereof used to differentiate a firm's products from competitors

Brand names convey the image of the product or service. The term **brand** refers to a name, term, symbol, sign, or design used by a firm to differentiate its offerings from those of its competitors. Offhand, brands may seem to be one of the most standardizable items in the product offering. However, the establishment of worldwide brands is difficult; how can a marketer of consumer products establish world brands when the firm sells 800 products in more than 200 countries and most of them under different names? This is the situation of Gillette. A typical example is Silkience hair conditioner, which is sold as Soyance in France, Sientel in Italy, and Silkience in Germany. Standardizing the name to reap promotional benefits is difficult because names have become established in each market, and the action would lead to objections from local managers.

In some markets, brand-name changes are required by the government. In Korea, unnecessary foreign words are barred from use; for example, Sprite has been renamed Kin. The same situation has emerged in Mexico, where the reason for local branding is primarily to control the marketing leverage that foreign companies would have with a universal brand.

Adjustments in product styling, color, size, and other appearance features are more common in consumer marketing than in industrial marketing. Color plays an important role in how consumers perceive a product, and marketers must be aware of what signal their product's color is sending. Color can be used for brand identification—for example, the yellow of Hertz, red of Avis, and green of National. It can be used for feature reinforcement; for example, Rolls-Royce uses a dazzling silver paint that spells luxury. Colors communicate in a subtle way in developed societies, whereas they have direct meaning in more traditional societies.

The product offered in the domestic market may not be operable in the foreign market. One of the major differences faced by appliance manufacturers is electrical power systems. In some cases, variations may exist within a country, such as Brazil. An exporter can find out about these differences through local government regulations or various trade publications such as *Electric Current Abroad,* published by the U.S. Department of Commerce. Some companies have adjusted their products to operate in different systems; for example, VCR equipment can be adjusted to record and play back on different color systems.

When a product that is sold globally requires repairs, parts, or service, the problems of obtaining, training, and holding a sophisticated engineering or repair staff are not easy to solve. If the product breaks down, and the repair arrangements are not up to standard, the product image will suffer. In some cases, products abroad may not even be used for their intended purpose and may thus require not only modifications in product configuration but also in service frequency. For instance, snowplows exported from the United States are used to remove sand from driveways in Saudi Arabia.

The country of origin of a product, typically communicated by the phrase "made in (country)," has considerable influence on quality perceptions. The perception of products manufactured in certain countries is affected by a built-in positive or negative assumption about quality. One study of machine-tool buyers found that the United States and Germany were rated higher than Japan, with Brazil rated below all three of them.[23] These types of findings indicate that steps must be taken by the global marketer to overcome or at least neutralize biases. This issue is especially important to developing countries, which need to increase exports, and for importers, who source products from countries different from where they are sold.[24]

Company Considerations Company policy will often determine the presence and degree of adaptation. Discussions of product adaptation often end with the question, "Is it worth it?" The answer depends on the company's ability to control costs, to correctly estimate market potential and, finally, to secure profitability. The decision to adapt should be preceded by a thorough analysis of the market. Formal market research with primary data collection and/or testing is warranted. From the financial standpoint, some companies have specific return on investment levels (for example, 25 percent) to be satisfied before adaptation. Others let the requirement vary as a function of the market considered and also the time in the market—that is, profitability may be initially compromised for proper market entry.

Most companies aim for consistency in their market efforts. This means that all products must fit in terms of quality, price, and user perceptions. Consistency may be difficult to attain in, for example, the area of warranties. Warranties can be uniform only if use conditions do not vary drastically and if the company is able to deliver equally on its promise anywhere it has a presence.

Product Line Management Global marketers' product lines consist of local, regional, and global brands. In a given market, an exporter's **product line,** typically shorter than domestically, concentrates on the most profitable products. Product lines may vary dramatically from one market to another depending on the extent of the firm's operations. Some firms at first cater only to a particular market segment and eventually expand to cover an entire market. For example, Japanese auto manufacturers moved into the highly profitable luxury car segment after establishing a strong position in the world small-car segment.[25]

product line
series of related products offered by a company

GLOBAL LEARNING EXPERIENCE 12.4

Gillette Tries to Stop Counterfeit Razor Blades in China

The Gillette Company entered the Chinese market with a 70-percent ownership in a joint venture with the Shanghai Razor Blade factory in 1992. The factory produces Gillette's Chinese Flying Eagle, Atra, and Sensor brands of razors.

About one year later, Gillette learned that the Huaxing Razor Blade factory, also in Shanghai, was making an imitation of the Flying Eagle single-edged razor, sold in copied Gillette packages. It took months of legal action, police raids, and some nominal fines to stop the counterfeiters. In the interim, Gillette lost an estimated $10 million in sales.

Gillette is only one of many U.S. companies who are finding out that the counterfeiting of consumer products has grown rapidly and is taking a significant portion of their profits in China. DuPont, Minnesota Mining and Manufacturing, S.C. Johnson, and McDonald's are among dozens of other companies that are fighting trademark infringements by counterfeiters. The problem is illustrated in the case of McDonald's; it competes with another nearby fast-food restaurant that uses a sign with golden arches on a red background.

As a result of pressure from American negotiators, China has agreed to the protection of intellectual property rights, but the legal system in China moves slowly. Part of the problem appears to be fines and penalties so minimal that they actually invite more counterfeiting. One legal expert on counterfeiting in China argued that "if nobody's going to jail and fines are negligible, you just invite more piracy." Thus, the need for stiffer penalties that will be enforced.

SOURCE: Seth Faison, "Razors, Soap, Cornflakes: Pirating Spreads in China," *New York Times*, Feb. 17, 1995, 1.

The domestic market is not the only source of new-product ideas for the global marketer, nor is it the only place where they are developed.[26] Some products may be developed elsewhere for worldwide consumption because of an advantage in skills, for example. Mazda, which is 33 percent owned by Ford, has designed and engineered cars to be produced by others in the Ford empire. In fact, many firms have benefited greatly from subsidiaries' local or regional product lines when demand conditions changed in the domestic market to favor new product characteristics. U.S. car manufacturers, for example, have used products from their European operations to compete in the small-sized and sports-style segments.

Sensitivity to local tastes has to also be reflected in the company's product line. In Brazil, Levi Strauss developed the Femina line of jeans exclusively for women there, who prefer ultratight jeans. However, what is learned in one market can often be adopted in another. Levi's line of chino pants and casual wear originated in the company's Argentine unit and was applied to loosely cut pants by its Japanese subsidiary. The company's U.S. operation adopted both in 1986, and the line generated $550 million in North American Revenues in 1990.[27]

product counterfeiting illegal manufacture, use, or patent and copyright infringement of a product or intellectual property

Product Counterfeiting About $20 billion in domestic and export sales are estimated to be lost by U.S. companies annually because of **product counterfeiting** and trademark patent infringement of consumer and industrial products. Counterfeit goods are any goods bearing an unauthorized representation of a trademark, patented invention, or copyrighted work that is legally protected in the country where it is marketed.

In today's environment, firms are taking more aggressive steps to protect themselves. Victimized firms are losing not only sales (see Global Learning Experience 12.4). They are also losing goodwill in the longer term if customers, believing they are getting the real product, unknowingly end up with a copy of inferior quality. In addition to the normal measures of registering trademarks and copyrights, firms are taking steps in product development to prevent copying of trademarked goods. For example, new authentication materials in labeling are virtually impossible to duplicate. Jointly, companies have formed organizations to lobby for legislation and to act as information clearninghouses.

PRICING POLICY

Pricing is the only element in the marketing mix that is revenue generating; all of the others are costs. It should therefore be used as an active instrument of strategy in the major areas of marketing decision making. Pricing in the global environment is more complicated than in the domestic market, however, because of such factors as government influence, different currencies, and additional costs. International pricing situations can be divided into three general categories: export pricing, foreign market pricing, and intracompany, or transfer, pricing.[28]

Export Pricing Three general price-setting strategies in global marketing are a standard worldwide price; dual pricing, which differentiates between domestic and export prices; and market-differentiated pricing.[29] The first two are cost-oriented pricing methods that are relatively simple to establish, easy to understand, and cover all of the necessary costs. **Standard worldwide pricing** is based on average unit costs of fixed, variable, and export-related costs.

In **dual pricing,** the export price is often based on **marginal cost pricing,** resulting in a lower export price than the domestic price. This method, based on incremental costs, considers the direct costs of producing and selling products for export as the floor beneath which prices cannot be set, while the firm considers other fixed costs (such as basic R&D) to have been recaptured by domestic operations. (See Chapter 11, Figure 11.1, and the related discussion on this point.) This may open the company to dumping charges, because determination of dumping has generally been based on average total costs, which can be considerably higher. Lower export prices are common, especially among Western European companies, which have a heavier tax burden (value-added tax) on their domestically sold products than on exported products because the tax is refunded for exported products. Cost-oriented pricing creates some major problems because it (1) is based on arbitrary cost allocations, (2) does not take into consideration highly differing market conditions, and (3) is subject to differing internal conditions in the various markets, such as entry mode and stage of the product's life cycle in the respective markets.

On the other hand, **market-differentiated pricing** is based on a demand-oriented strategy. This method also allows consideration of competitive forces in setting export price. The major problem is the exporter's perennial dilemma: lack of information. Therefore, in most cases, marginal costs provide a basis for competitive comparisons, on which the export price is set.

In preparing an export quotation, the exporter must be careful to take into account the unique costs related to exporting and include them in pricing the product. Many exporters use some form of export quotation worksheet (or checklist) to ensure that no costs are overlooked when making the quotation. The worksheet then becomes the basis for preparing the pro forma invoice (see Chapter 13). Figure 12.3 illustrates the format and costs included in a typical export quotation worksheet.

In addition, the expense incurred in operating the export department/function should be reflected in the product pricing. Examples of these expenses are personnel, market research, communication costs with foreign customers, travel expense, and overseas promotional costs. When shipping overseas to company offices or agents for inventory

standard worldwide pricing
price-setting strategy based on average unit costs of fixed, variable, and export-related costs

dual pricing
price-setting strategy in which the export price may be based on marginal cost pricing, resulting in a lower export price than domestic price; may open the company to dumping charges

marginal cost pricing
pricing based on the additional out-of-pocket cost or incremental costs

market-differentiated pricing
price-setting strategy based on demand rather than cost

FIGURE 12.3 **XYZ Manufacturing Co.: Export Quotation Worksheet**

Reference Number__________ Date__________

Customer Information

Name __________ Customer Reference Number__________

Address __________ Terms of Sale__________

__________ Destination__________

Telephone__________ Payment Terms__________

Product Information

Product__________ Dimensions _____ × _____ × _____

No. of Units__________ Cubic Measure (Per Unit) _____ sq. in.

Units Per Master Carton__________ _____ sq. ft.

Net Weight _____ lbs _____ kg _____ m

Gross Weight _____ lbs _____ kg Total Measurement__________

A. Product Pricing

Price/Cost per Unit $_____ Total $_____

Cost of Modifications for Export _____

Sales/Agent Commission _____

Profit Margin _____

Selling Price _____

B. Miscellaneous Charges

Freight Forwarding Fees $_____

Bank Fees (Letter of Credit/Collection) _____

Export Packing/Labeling/Marking _____

Other Charges _____

C. Documentation Fees

Certificate of Origin $_____

Consular Invoice Fees _____

Export License _____

Notary _____

Other _____

Total Selling Price-Exfactory $_____

D. Inland Freight to _____ $_____

E. Port Charges

Unloading (Heavy Lift) _____

Terminal _____

Other _____

Total Price F.A.S. Vessel or Aircraft $_____

F. Ocean Freight _____

G. Marine Insurance _____

Total-CIF $_____

purposes, the firm may incur the cost of tariffs and taxes and subject the organization to some degree of political risk. The combined effect of both clear-cut and hidden costs results in export prices far in excess of domestic prices. This is called **price escalation.**

price escalation
establishing of export prices far in excess of domestic prices—often due to a long distribution channel and frequent markups

Inexpensive imports often trigger accusations of **dumping**—that is, selling goods overseas for less than in the exporter's home market, or at a price below the cost of production, or both. Cases that have been reported include charges by Florida tomato growers that Mexican vegetables were being dumped across the border and the ruling of the Canadian Anti-Dumping Tribunal that U.S. firms were dumping radioactive diagnostic reagents in Canada.[30]

dumping
selling goods overseas at a price lower than in the exporter's home market, or at a price below the cost of production, or both

Dumping ranges from predatory to unintentional. Predatory dumping is the tactic of a foreign firm that intentionally sells at a loss in another country in order to increase its market share at the expense of domestic producers. This amounts to an international price war. Unintentional dumping is the result of time lags between the date of sales transactions, shipment, and arrival. Prices, including exchange rates, can change in such a way that the final sales price is below the cost of production or below the price prevailing in the exporter's home market.

In the United States, domestic producers may petition the government to impose antidumping duties on imports alleged to be dumped. The remedy is a duty equal to the dumping margin. International agreements and U.S. law provide for countervailing duties. They may be imposed on imports that are found to be subsidized by foreign governments. They are designed to offset the advantages imports would otherwise receive from the subsidy.

Foreign Market Pricing Pricing within the individual markets in which the firm operates is determined by (1) corporate objectives, (2) costs, (3) customer behavior and market conditions, (4) market structure, and (5) environmental constraints. Because all of these factors vary from country to country, pricing policies of the multinational corporation must vary as well. Despite arguments in favor of uniform pricing in multinational markets, price discrimination is an essential characteristic of the pricing policies of firms conducting business in differing markets.[31] In a study of 42 U.S.-based multinational corporations, the major problem areas they reported in making pricing decisions were meeting competition, cost, lack of competitive information, distribution and channel factors, and governmental barriers.[32]

Of great importance to multinational corporations is the control and coordination of pricing to intermediaries. When currency exchange rate discrepancies widen, **gray markets** emerge. The term refers to brand-name imports that enter a country legally but outside regular, authorized distribution channels. The gray market is fueled by companies that sell goods in foreign markets at prices that are far lower than prices charged to, for example, U.S. distributors, and by one strong currency, such as the dollar or the yen. This phenomenon not only harms the company financially but also may harm its reputation, because authorized distributors often refuse to honor warranties on items bought through the gray market. Cars bought through the gray market, for example, may not pass EPA inspections and thus may cause major expense to the unsuspecting buyer.[33]

gray market
a market entered in a way not intended by the manufacturer of the goods

Transfer Pricing Transfer, or intracompany, pricing is the pricing of sales to members of the same corporate family. The overall competitive and financial position of the

transfer pricing
intracompany pricing; pricing of sales to members of the same corporate family

What is the most widely spoken language on Earth?

ANSWER *About 726 million speak Mandarin Chinese, most of them in China. About 397 million speak English and another 400 million use English as a second language. About 274 million speak Russian, 254 million speak Hindi and 251 million speak Spanish.*

firm forms the basis of any pricing policy. In this, transfer pricing plays a key role. Intracorporate sales can easily change consolidated global results because they often are one of the most important ongoing decision areas in a company.

Doing business overseas requires coping with many complexities, the effect of which can be alleviated by manipulating transfer prices. Factors that call for price adjustments include taxes, import duties, inflationary tendencies, unstable governments, and other regulations.[34] For example, high transfer prices on goods shipped to a subsidiary and low ones on goods imported from it will result in minimizing the tax liability of a subsidiary operating in a country with a high income tax. Tax liability thus results not only from the absolute tax rate but also from differences in how income is computed. On the other hand, a higher transfer price may have an effect on the import duty to be paid.

In the hypothetical example below, the German subsidiary of the Global Automobile Co. is manufacturing and shipping automobile engines to the American subsidiary. Under "normal pricing" conditions, the Germany subsidiary would record a profit of $200 and invoice the American subsidiary for $1,200. Instead of earning its normal profit and paying taxes in Germany, the corporation directs the German subsidiary to ship and invoice the U.S. subsidiary at cost. This allows the U.S. subsidiary to earn the profit in the United States where it will be taxed at a rate of 20 percent, compared with the 50 percent rate in Germany. The result is a tax savings of $60 ($100–$40) on each engine. Sixty dollars doesn't look like a large number, but consider the savings on 1,000,000 engines. Table 12.2 provides an example of how transfer pricing can affect tax liability.

The main concerns with transfer pricing are both internal and external to the multinational corporation. Manipulating intracorporate prices complicates internal control measures and, without proper documentation, will cause major problems. If the firm operates on a profit-center basis, some consideration must be given to the effect of transfer pricing on the subsidiary's apparent profit and its actual performance. An adjustment in the control mechanism is called for to give appropriate credit to the divi-

TABLE 12.2 **An Example of How Transfer Pricing Can Affect Corporate Profits**

	Global Automobile Co.		
	German Subsidiary		U.S. Subsidiary
	Normal Pricing	Corporate Directed Pricing	(Earns Profit in U.S. Instead of Germany)
Manufacturing Cost	$1,000	$1,000	$1,000
Mark-up 20%	200	—	200
Selling Price	1,200	1,000	1,200
Taxable Profit	200	—	200
Corporate Tax Rate	50%	50%	20%
Taxes on $200 Profit	$100	—	$40

sions for their actual contributions. The method called for may range from dual bookkeeping to compensation in budgets and profit plans. Regardless of the method, proper organizational communication is required to avoid unnecessary conflict between subsidiaries and headquarters.

Transfer prices will by definition involve tax and regulatory jurisdiction of the countries in which the company does business. Typically, authorities try to establish or approximate an *arm's length level of pricing.* Quite often, the multinational corporation is put in a difficult position. U.S. authorities may think the transfer price is too low, whereas the foreign entity (especially a less developed country) may perceive it to be too high.

In the host environments, the concern of the multinational corporation is to maintain its status as a good corporate citizen. Many corporations, in drafting multinational codes of conduct, have specified that intracorporate pricing will follow the arm's length principle. Multinationals have also been found to closely abide by tax regulations governing transfer pricing.[35]

PROMOTIONAL POLICY

The global marketer must choose a proper combination of the various promotional tools—personal selling, advertising, publicity, and sales promotion—to create images among the intended target audience. The choice of **promotional mix** will depend on the target audience, company objectives, the product or service marketed, the resources available for the endeavor, and the availability of the tool in a particular market.

promotional mix
the mix, or combination, of personal selling, advertising, publicity, and sales promotion activities

Personal Selling Although advertising is often equated with the promotional effort, in many cases promotional efforts consist of personal selling. In the early stages of globalization, exporters rely heavily on personal contact. The marketing of industrial goods, especially of high-priced items, requires strong personal selling efforts. In some cases, personal selling may be truly global; for example, Boeing or Northrop salespeople engage in sales efforts around the world. However, in most cases, personal selling takes place at the local level. The best interests of any company in the industrial area lie in establishing a solid base of dealerships staffed by local people. Personal selling efforts can be developed in the same fashion as advertising. For the multinational company, the primary goal again is the enhancement and standardization of personal selling efforts, especially if the product offering is standardized.

As an example, Eastman Kodak has developed a line-of-business approach to allow for standardized strategy throughout a region.[36] In Europe, one person is placed in charge of the entire copier-duplicator program in each country. That person is responsible for all sales and service teams within the country. Typically, each customer is served by three representatives, each with a different responsibility. Sales representatives maintain ultimate responsibility for the account; they conduct demonstrations, analyze customer requirements, determine the right type of equipment for each installation, and obtain orders. Service representatives install and maintain the equipment and retrofit new-product improvements to existing equipment. Customer service representatives are the liaison between sales and service. They provide operator training on a continuing basis and handle routine questions and complaints. Each team is positioned to respond to any European customer within four hours.

media strategy
strategy applied to the selection of media vehicles and the development of a media schedule

Advertising The key decision-making areas in advertising are (1) media strategy, (2) the promotional message, and (3) the organization of the promotional program.

media mix
the mix, or combination of various types of advertising media, i.e., newspapers, magazines, radio, TV, outdoor, and transit advertising

Media strategy is applied to the selection of available advertising (the **media mix**) media and the development of a media schedule. In some cases, the international marketer may find that the choice is limited. For example, the J. Walter Thompson advertising agency has estimated that advertising expenditures on Western European television would be $2.4 to $3.3 billion more if regulations were completely eased.[37] Some of the regulations include limits on the amount of time available for advertisements, ranging from complete prohibition (as in Sweden) to 15 to 20 minutes per day in blocks of 3 to 5 minutes (as in Germany). France and Italy limit the percentage of revenues that the state monopoly systems can derive from advertising. Strict separation between programs and commercials is almost a universal requirement, preventing U.S.-style sponsored programs. Restrictions on items such as comparative claims and gender stereotypes are prevalent; for example, Germany prohibits the use of superlatives such as "best."

Consumer protection dominated the regulatory scene of the 1980s and is expected to continue in the 1990s.[38] Tobacco products and alcoholic beverages are the most heavily regulated products in terms of promotion; however, the manufacturers of these products have not abandoned their promotional efforts. Philip Morris engages in corporate image advertising via its cowboy spokesperson. John Player sponsors sports events, especially Formula-One car racing. What is and is not allowable is very much a reflection of the country imposing the rules.

Some media vehicles have been developed that have target audiences on at least three continents and for which the media buying takes place through a centralized office. Global media have traditionally been publications that, in addition to the worldwide edition, have provided advertisers the option of using regional editions. For example, *Time* provides 133 editions, enabling advertising to reach a particular country, continent, or the world. Other global publications include *The International Herald Tribune, The Wall Street Journal,* and *National Geographic.*

In broadcast media, pan-regional radio stations have been joined in Europe by television as a result of satellite technology. By the end of the 1990s, approximately half of the households in Europe will have access to additional television broadcasts either through cable or direct satellite, and television will no longer be restricted by national boundaries. As a result, marketers need to make sure that advertising works not only within markets but across countries as well.[39]

promotional message content of an advertisement, publicity release, or sales promotion activity.

Developing the **promotional message** is referred to as creative strategy. The marketer must determine what the consumer is really buying—that is, the consumer's motivations. They will vary, depending on:

1. The diffusion of the product into the market. For example, to penetrate Third World markets with business computers is difficult when potential customers may not be able to type.
2. The criteria on which the consumer will evaluate the product. For example, in traditional societies, the time-saving qualities of a product may not be the best ones to feature, as Campbell Soups learned in Italy and in Brazil, where housewives felt inadequate as homemakers if they did not make soups from scratch.
3. The product's positioning. For example, Parker Pen's upscale image around the world may not be profitable enough in a market that is more or less a commodity business. The solution is to create an image for a commodity product and make the public pay for it—for example, the positioning of Perrier in the United States as a premium mineral water.

The ideal situation in developing message strategy is to have a world brand—a product that is manufactured, packaged, and positioned the same around the world. However, a number of factors will force companies to abandon identical campaigns in favor of recognizable campaigns. These factors are culture, of which language is the main manifestation, economic development, and lifestyles. Consider, for example, the campaign for Conner Peripherals presented in Figure 12.4. The images in the Southeast Asia and Japanese ver-

A Campaign Adapted to Local Conditions in Japan and Southeast Asia **FIGURE 12.4**

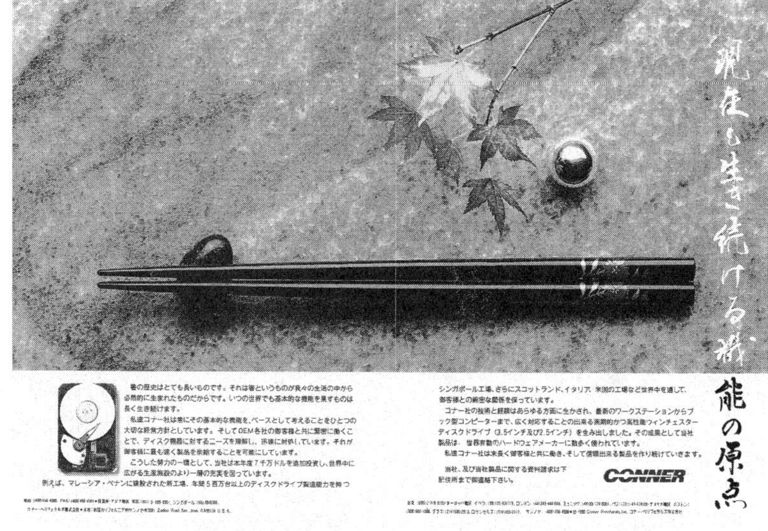

Japan

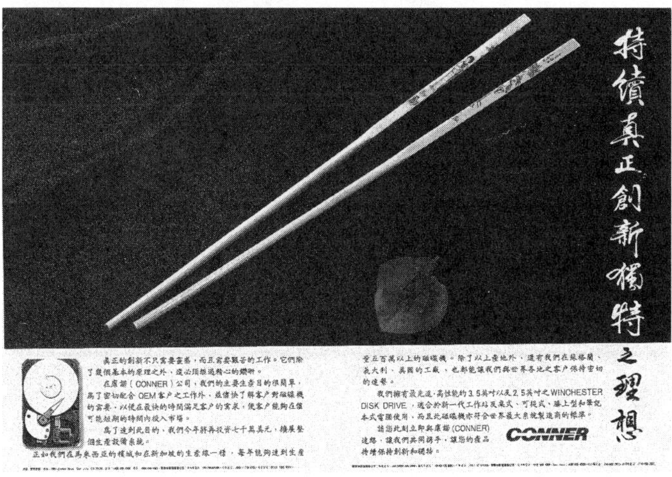

Southeast Asia

SOURCE: Michael Field, "Fragrance Marketers Sniff Out Rich Aroma," *Advertising Age,* January 30, 1986, 10.

sions of the company's "Unique Ideas" ad differ in subtle but important ways. The Southeast Asian execution pictures bone Chinese chopsticks on black cloth; the Japanese version shows enameled pointed chopsticks on a marble slab to appeal to a different aesthetic.[40] Global Learning Experience 12.5 presents a checklist of the most important things to know about a foreign market prior to developing an advertising campaign.

Many multinational corporations are staffed and equipped to perform the full range of promotional activities. In most cases, however, they rely on the outside expertise of advertising agencies and other promotions-related companies such as media-buying companies and specialty marketing firms. According to a Grey Advertising survey of 50 multinational marketers, 76 percent believe the ideal situation is to use the same agency worldwide, with some local deviation as necessary. The same percentage believes an ad agency should be centrally run, and 72 percent believe in using the same

An Advertising Checklist for Entering New Markets

To avoid advertising that becomes a cultural disaster when crossing borders, experts suggest some points to check out carefully.

Context A determination should be made whether or not the country is high or low context. In a high-context country, the surroundings and atmosphere are just as important as the message. Asian and Arabic countries tend to be high context. Examples of low-context countries are Switzerland, Germany, and the United States.

The Significance of Color and Music There are many cultural meanings to color and music, hand motions, and gestures. Finding out what they are requires some research; for example, white stands for purity in Western cultures but stands for death in China. In Korea, designs with red circles have a strong Japanese image and may summon up a lot of bad blood.

Translate Ads from English Very Carefully What is straightforward and simple in one language may be offensive and embarrassing in another. For example, "The Pepsi Generation," once translated into Chinese, seemed to imply that the beverage would bring your ancestors back from the dead. The backtranslation method is recommended.

Is Your Target Audience Ad Literate? Many advertisers are having problems in emerging nations because those audiences are just getting used to watching advertising. Some TV commercials assume the audience has a level of experience and understanding that will enable them to make a subtle connection between the symbolic images on the TV tube and the underlying advertising message. Failure to make the connection will leave the audience confused.

Global advertising requires common sense, an eye for detail, and an understanding of context.

SOURCE: Adapted from Nora Fitzgerald, "Transactional Faux Pas," *World Trade,* September, 1996, 92.

advertising strategy worldwide.[41] Local agencies will survive, however, because of governmental regulations. In Peru, for example, a law mandates that any commercial aired on Peruvian television must be 100 percent nationally produced. Local agencies tend to forge ties with foreign ad agencies for better coverage and customer service and thus become part of the general globalization effort.

Publicity/Public Relations Public relations is the marketing communications function charged with executing programs to earn public understanding and acceptance, which means both internal and external communication. Internal communication is important, especially in multinational companies, to create an appropriate corporate culture. External campaigns can be achieved through the use of corporate symbols, corporate advertising, customer relations programs, and the generation of publicity. Some material on the firm is produced for special audiences to assist in personal selling. A significant part of public relations activity focuses on portraying multinational corporations as good citizens of their host markets.

Public relations activity includes anticipating and countering criticism. The criticisms range from general ones against all multinational corporations to specific complaints. They may be based on a market; for example, a company's presence in China. They may concern a product; for example, Nestlé's practices in advertising and promoting infant formula in developing countries where infant mortality is unacceptably high. They may center on the company's conduct in a given situation; for example, Union Carbide's perceived lack of response in the Bhopal disaster. If not addressed, these criticisms can lead to more

GLOBAL LEARNING EXPERIENCE 12.6

How *Not* to Run a Promotion

In what turned out to be a classic case of how *not* to run a promotion, several senior executives of the Maytag Company of Europe lost their jobs and the company was forced to take a $48.8 million pretax charge against 1993 first-quarter earnings.

The problem began when the company offered free airline tickets from the United Kingdom and Ireland to European destinations and New York or Orlando, Florida, to customers who purchased $375 worth of the company's Hoover brand appliances. As many as 200,000 customers responded. Apparently, the executives in charge neglected to pretest the promotion. If they had conducted a pretest, they would have discovered that the promotion was mispriced. The result was that the more appliances the company sold, the more money it lost.

To make matters worse, the company was not prepared administratively to handle 200,000 unexpected ticket applications, which led to considerable customer frustration and negative feelings about the company. Finally, adding insult to injury, newspapers in the United Kingdom and Ireland ran unfavorable news reports about the program's failure. What started out as a clever idea became a promotional and financial disaster, resulting in a loss of customer goodwill and a bad publicity nightmare.

The lesson to be learned from the Maytag Europe experience is clear. Before undertaking a major advertising or promotional campaign, it is prudent to pretest it on a small, carefully controlled sample of the market. The results of the pretest can then be used to estimate the effectiveness or impact of the campaign on the whole market.

significant problems, such as a globally orchestrated boycott of products. The six-year boycott of Nestlé did not so much harm earnings as it harmed image and employee morale.

Sales Promotion Sales promotion has been used as the catchall term for promotion that is not advertising, personal selling, or publicity. Sales promotion directed at consumers involves such activities as couponing, sampling, premiums, consumer education and demonstration activities, cents-off packages, point-of-purchase materials, and direct mail. The success in Latin America of Tang, General Foods' presweetened powdered juice substitute, is for the most part traceable to successful sales promotion efforts. One promotion involved trading Tang pouches for free popsicles from Kibon (General Foods' Brazilian subsidiary). Kibon also placed coupons for free groceries in Tang pouches. In Puerto Rico, General Foods ran Tang sweepstakes. In Argentina, instore sampling featured Tang poured from Tang pitchers by girls in orange Tang dresses. Decorative Tang pitchers were a hit throughout Latin America.

For sales promotion to work, the campaigns planned by manufacturers or their agencies have to gain the support of the local retailer population. As an example, retailers must redeem coupons presented by consumers and forward them to the manufacturer or to the company handling the promotion. A. C. Nielsen tried to introduce cents-off coupons in Chile and ran into trouble with the nation's supermarket union, which notified its members that it opposed the project and recommended that coupons not be accepted. The main complaint was that an intermediary, like Nielsen, would unnecessarily raise costs and thus the prices to be charged to consumers. Also, some critics felt that coupons would limit individual negotiations, because Chileans often bargain for their purchases. A classic case of a sales promotion effort that resulted in a corporate financial disaster is discussed in Global Learning Experience 12.6.

Sales promotion directed at intermediaries, also known as trade promotion, includes activities such as trade shows and exhibits, trade discounts, and cooperative advertising. For example, attendance at an appropriate trade show is one of the best ways to make contacts with government officials and decisions makers, work with present intermediaries, or attract new ones.

PLACE (DISTRIBUTION) POLICY

The last of the four Ps—place, or distribution—includes two important components: (1) channels of distribution and (2) physical distribution and international logistics (covered in Chapter 13). Combined they create "place" and "time" utility; that is, they result in the product being where the customer wants it (place), when the customer wants it (time). This is the final stop in the transfer of the product from the manufacturer to the consumer or user. All previous efforts in developing the product, pricing it, and promoting it are wasted if the product is not on the shelf when the customer enters the store or the service is not available when the customer requests it.

The channel decision is the most inflexible of the marketing mix decisions in that it cannot be readily changed. In addition, it involves relinquishing some of the control the firm has over the marketing of its products. These two factors make choosing the right channel structure a crucial decision. Properly structured and staffed, the distribution system will function more as one rather than as a collection of often quite different units.

Channels of Distribution

channel design
length and width of the distribution channel

demographics
characteristics of people, i.e., age, income, sex, marital status, occupation, level of education, etc.

psychographics
study of people based on their lifestyles, i.e., their activities, interests, and opinions

Channel Design The term **channel design** refers to the length and width of the channel employed. Channel design is determined by factors that can be summarized as the 11 C's: customer, culture, competition, company, character, capital, cost, coverage, control, continuity, and communication. The international marketer can use the 11 C's as a checklist to determine the proper approach to reach target audiences before selecting channel members to fill the roles. The first three factors are givens in that the company must adjust its approach to the existing structures. The other eight are controllable to a certain extent by the marketer.

The **demographic** and **psychographic** characteristics of targeted *customers* will form the basis for channel design decisions. Answers to questions such as what customers need as well as why, when, and how they buy are used to determine ways in which prod-

Pepsi expands its channels of distribution with a system of vending stands in the Moscow subway system.
SOURCE: PepsiCo.

GLOBAL LEARNING EXPERIENCE 12.7

The Problem of Finding Channels of Distribution in Japan

In Japan, U.S. automakers (GM, Ford, and Chrysler) have the right products—high-quality automobiles (with the steering wheel on the right-hand side). They have adequate promotional dollars allocated to educating the Japanese consumer, and they have prices that make American cars look very reasonable and fairly cheap compared the Japanese makes. Their real problem is with the channels of distribution—they are learning that car dealers willing to sell American-made cars are difficult to find.

Traditionally, Japanese car dealers have very close ties to the Japanese automakers. Many of the automakers own a portion of the dealership. This effectively ties the dealers' hands when it comes to adding new lines of cars. The ties between dealer and company are so close that many of the dealers tend to consider themselves as employees of the Japanese automakers, making it difficult for them to sell cars that compete against Nissan or Toyota.

The extremely high price of real estate in Japan makes it prohibitively expensive for the American auto companies to set up their own dealership networks, so they need to use the existing networks—which are effectively controlled by their competitors.

With respect to Ford, dealers that sell Toyota and Nissan are reluctant to sell the smaller Ford cars (small cars account for 20 percent of the Japanese market) because they are made by Mazda, a competitor of Toyota and Nissan, and Ford owns 33 percent of Mazda.

The Japanese automakers also apply pressure on the car dealers in a variety of subtle ways. For example, they require that the dealers have separate showrooms for Japanese and American cars—increasing the dealers' cost of doing business. If a dealer switches from a Japanese automaker to a U.S. automaker, the dealer must give up its sales records. In Japan, cars are often sold by visiting customers in their homes. Without past sales records, the dealer must start from scratch.

All of these factors make it difficult for dealers to earn a profit on American-made cars. A Japanese dealer taking on a line of American autos can expect to endure two or three years of losses before there is any hope of profit.

SOURCES: Adapted from Andrew Pollack, "A Tough Sell for Detroit," *New York Times,* December 12, 1996, D-1; Andrew Pollack, "In Japan's Showrooms Barely," *New York Times,* June 3, 1995, 31.

ucts should be made available in order to generate a competitive advantage. When PepsiCo began expanding its operations in Russia, it noted that many Moscow residents purchased breakfast or luncheon snacks while traveling on the city's subway system. This led to the development of large mobile vending stands positioned on the subway platforms—exactly where the customers wanted them.

Customers characteristics may cause one product to be distributed through two different types of channels. All sales of Caterpillar's earthmoving equipment are handled by independent dealers, except that sales are direct to the U.S. government and the People's Republic of China.

The marketer must analyze existing channel structures, or what might be called the distribution *culture* of a market. In most cases, the global marketer must adjust to existing structures (see Global Learning Experience 12.7). In Finland, for example, 92

QUESTION *Name two landlocked countries in Western Europe.*

ANSWER *No part of Western Europe is farther than three hundred miles from the ocean. Four of the larger landlocked ones are Austria, Switzerland, Hungary and Czech Republic. The mini-states of Luxembourg, San Marino, Andorra, Liechtenstein and Vatican City are also inland.*

percent of all distribution of nondurable consumer goods is through four wholesale chains. In the United Kingdom, major retail chains control markets. Without their support, no significant penetration of the market is possible.

Foreign legislation affecting distributors and agents is an essential part of the distribution culture of a market. Legislation may require foreign companies to be represented only by firms that are 100 percent locally owned. Some countries have prohibited the use of dealers so as to protect consumers from abuses in which intermediaries have engaged.

Channels used by *competitors* form another basis for plans. First, channels utilized by the competition may make up the only distribution system that is accepted both by the trade and by consumers. In this case, the global marketer's task is to use the structure more effectively and efficiently. An alternate strategy is to use a totally different distribution approach from the competition and hope to develop a competitive advantage in that manner.

No channel of distribution can be properly selected unless it meets the requirements set by overall *company* objectives for market share and profitability. Sometimes, management may simply want to use a particular channel of distribution, even though no sound business basis exists for the decision. Some management goals may have conflicting results.

The *character* of the product will have an impact on the design of the channel. Generally, the more specialized, expensive, bulky, or perishable the product and the more it may require after-sale service, the more likely the channel is to be relatively short. Staple items, such as soap, tend to have longer channels. The type of channel chosen has to match the overall positioning of the product in the market. Changes in overall market conditions, such as currency fluctuations, may require changes in distribution as well. An increase in the value of the dollar may cause a repositioning of the marketed product as a luxury item, necessitating an appropriate channel (such as an upscale department store) for its distribution.

The term *capital* is used to describe the financial requirements in setting up a channel system. The global marketer's financial strength will determine the type of channel and the basis on which channel relationships will be built. The stronger the marketer's finances, the more able the firm is to establish channels it either owns or controls. Intermediaries' requirements for beginning inventories, selling on a consignment basis, preferential loans, and need for training all will have an impact on the type of approach chosen by the global marketer.

Closely related to the capital dimension is *cost*—that is, the expenditure incurred in maintaining a channel once it is established. Costs will naturally vary over the life cycle of the relationship as well as over the life cycle of the products marketed. Costs may also be incurred in protecting the company's distributors against adverse market conditions. A number of U.S. manufacturers helped their distributors maintain competitive prices through subsidies when the exchange rate for the U.S. dollar caused pricing problems.

The term *coverage* is used to describe both the number of areas in which the marketer's products are represented and the quality of that representation. The number of areas to be covered depends on the demand in the market and also the time elapsed since the product's introduction to the market. A company typically enters a market with one local distributor but, as volume expands, the distribution base often has to be adjusted.

The use of intermediaries will automatically lead to loss of some *control* over the marketing of the firm's products. The looser the relationship is between the marketer and the intermediaries, the less control can be exerted. The longer the channel, the more difficult it becomes for the marketer to have a final say over pricing, promotion, and the types of outlets in which the product will be made available.

Nurturing long-term *continuity* in the relationship with channel members rests heavily on the marketer because foreign distributors may have a more short-term view of the relationship. For example, Japanese wholesalers believe that it is important for manufacturers to follow up initial success with continuous improvement of the product. If such improvements are not forthcoming, competitors are likely to enter the market with similar, but lower-priced, products, and the wholesalers of the imported product will turn to the Japanese suppliers.[42]

Communication provides the exchange of information that is essential to the functioning of the channel. Proper communication helps convey the marketer's goals to the distributors, helps solve conflict situations, and aids in the overall marketing of the product. Communication is a two-way process that does not permit the marketer to dictate to intermediaries. Sometimes, the planned program may not work because of a lack of communication. Prices may not be competitive; promotional materials may be obsolete or inaccurate and not well received overall.[43]

Selection and Screening of Intermediaries Once the basic design of the channel has been determined, the global marketer must begin a search to fill the roles defined with the best available candidates. Choices will have to be made within the framework of the company's overall philosophy on distributors versus agents, as well as whether the company will use an indirect or direct approach to foreign markets.

Firms that have successful international distribution attest to the importance of finding top representatives. The undertaking should be held in the same regard as recruiting and hiring within the company because "an ineffective foreign distributor can set you back years; it is almost better to have no distributor than a bad one in a major market."[44]

Various sources exist to assist the marketer in locating intermediary candidates. One of the easiest and most economical ways is to use the services of governmental agencies. The U.S. Department of Commerce has various services that can assist firms in identifying suitable representatives abroad; some have been designed specifically for that purpose. A number of private sources are also available to the global marketer. Trade directories, many of them published by Dun & Bradstreet, usually list foreign representatives geographically and by product classification. Telephone directories, especially the yellow page sections or editions, can provide distributor lists. Although not detailed, these listings will give addresses and an indication of the products sold. The firm can solicit the support of some of its facilitating agencies, such as banks, advertising agencies, shipping lines, and airlines. The marketer can take an even more direct approach by buying advertising space to solicit representation. These advertisements typically indicate the type of support the marketer will be able to give to its distributor.

Managing the Channel Relationship A channel relationship can be likened to a marriage in that it brings together two independent entities that shared goals. For the relationship to work, each party has to be open about its expectations and openly communicate changes perceived in the other's behavior that might be contrary to the agreement.

The complicating factors that separate the two parties fall into three categories: ownership, geographic and cultural distance, and different rules of law. Rather than lament their existence, both parties must take strong action to remedy them. Often, the first major step is for both parties to acknowledge that differences exist.

Services Policy

Linkage between Services and Products Services may complement products; at other times, products may complement services. The offering of products that are in need of substantial technological support and maintenance may be useless if no proper assurance for service can be provided. For this reason, the initial contract of sale often includes the service dimension. This practice is frequent in aircraft sales. When an aircraft is purchased, the buyer contracts not only for the physical product—namely, the plane—but often for the training of personnel, maintenance service, and the promise of continuous technological updates. Similarly, the sale of computer hardware depends on the availability of proper servicing and software. In an international setting, the proper service support can often be crucial. Particularly for newly opening markets or for products new to market, the provision of the product alone may be insufficient. Rather, to be successful, communication services need to accompany the product in order to inform and prepare the potential market.

Services can be just as dependent on products. An airline that prides itself on providing an efficient reservation system and excellent linkups with rental cars and hotel reservations could not survive if it were not for its airplanes. As a result, many offerings in the marketplace consist of a combination of products and services.

The simple knowledge that services and products interact, however, is not enough. Successful managers must recognize that different customer groups will frequently view the service-product combination differently. The type of use and the usage conditions will also affect evaluations of the market offering. For example, the intangible dimension of "on-time arrival" by airlines may be valued differently by college students than by business executives. Similarly, a 20-minute delay will be judged differently by a passenger arriving at his or her final destination than by one who has just missed an overseas connection. As a result, adjustment possibilities in both the service and the product areas emerge that can be used as a strategic tool to stimulate demand and increase profitability. The manager must identify the role of each and adjust all of them to meet the desires of the target customer group. By rating the offerings on a scale ranging from dominant tangibility to dominant intangibility, the manager can compare offerings and also generate information for subsequent market-positioning strategies.

Stand-Alone Services Services do not always come in unison with products. Increasingly, they compete against products and become an alternative offering. For example, rather than buy an in-house computer, the business executive can contract computing work to a local or foreign service firm. Similarly, the purchase of a car (a product) can be converted into the purchase of a service by leasing the car from an agency.

Services may also compete against one another. As an example, a store may have the option of offering full service to customers or of converting to the self-service format. The store may provide only checkout services, with customers engaging in other activities such as selection, transportation, and sometimes even packaging and pricing.

Services differ from products most strongly in their **intangibility:** They are frequently consumed rather than possessed. One major difference concerns the storing of services. Because of their nature, services are difficult to inventory. If they are not used, the "brown around the edges" syndrome tends to result in high **perishability.** Unused capacity in the form of an empty seat on an airplane, for example, becomes nonsalable quickly. Once the plane has taken off, selling an empty seat is virtually impossible—except for an in-flight upgrade from coach to first class—and the capacity cannot be stored for future usage. Similarly, the difficulty of inventorying services makes it troublesome to provide service backup for peak demand. To maintain **service capacity** constantly at levels necessary to satisfy peak demand would be very expensive. The busi-

intangibility
inability to be seen, tasted, or touched in a conventional sense; the characteristic of services that most strongly differentiates them from products

perishability
susceptibility to deterioration; the characteristic of services that makes them difficult to inventory

service capacity
maximum level at which a service provider is able to provide services to customers

GLOBAL LEARNING EXPERIENCE

12.8

Educating the World

Corporations aren't the only organizations looking for new markets abroad. American colleges and universities have taken their search for students overseas as well. One of the primary reasons is educational. Colleges and universities need to prepare students to compete in a global economy, prompting more international recruiting—particularly by business schools. "If you're going to provide an MBA environment that is heavily case-oriented, it really relies on the experience of the classmates," said Mark H. Wellman, assistant dean of the College of Business and Management at the University of Maryland, which aggressively markets itself overseas. "You need people from those cultures who know the business environment, who know the culture, who essentially know how things get done in that environment."

Another reason for the international focus is financial. With a decline in state and federal funds for college aid, schools find themselves providing more financial support for students by way of reduced tuition and aid. One way to build revenue is by recruiting foreign students, who are often able to pay the full sticker price for a degree. "This is one way to ease the budget pressure," said B. Ann Wright, dean of enrollment management at Smith College.

Many colleges and universities began recruiting abroad during the 1980s, when the number of 18-year-olds in the United States dipped. The global economy and increasing financial pressures are more recent factors. "There are nearly 450,000 foreign students in the United States bringing in more than $6 billion to our economy," said Richard M. Krasno, president of the Institute of International Education.

Foreign enrollment in U.S. schools rose 0.6 percent last year, the smallest increase in the past 10 years. Krasno said the slowdown might suggest that other countries have realized the benefits of international recruitment and are going after some of the same students that U.S. colleges and universities are targeting. "The Japanese have become much more aggressive in terms of recruiting," he said. "There's no question about it, other countries are realizing the advantages."

Most of the foreign students in U.S. schools come from Asia. Charles A. Deacon, dean of undergraduate admissions at Georgetown University, said the number of applicants from Asia has increased by about 50 percent since 1991. Georgetown recruiters travel to Asia with those from Harvard University and Yale University, and to Europe with those from Dartmouth College and Duke University. The University of Maryland gets applications from about 8,000 foreign students a year, about 1,500 of which are admitted. Maryland has students from 135 different countries.

Linda Heaney is the president of Linden Educational Services, a Washington, D.C.-based company that helps colleges and universities market themselves abroad. The company organizes recruitment tours to Asia, Latin America, the Middle East, and India. "This year, we'll do eight different tours," she said. The company started 14 years ago, working with 10 colleges. "This year, we'll work with 150, and we've expanded the number of trips and the number of people on the trips," Heaney said. "The need for diversity, quality, and fully paid tuitions" is driving the increase, she said.

SOURCE: Martha Hamilton, "Studying Locally, Recruited Globally," *The Washington Post,* March 7, 1996, D9.

ness manager must therefore attempt to smooth out demand levels in order to optimize overall use of capacity. Global Learning Experience 12.8 reviews one high quality U.S. service that foreigners really want—U.S. education—and indicates how U.S. colleges and universities are marketing their services world-wide.

customer involvement active participation of customers; a characteristic of services in that customers often are actively involved in the provision of services they consume

For the services offering, the time of production is usually very close to or even simultaneous with the time of consumption. This frequently means close **customer involvement** in the production of services. Customers frequently either service themselves or cooperate in the delivery of services. As a result, the service provider often needs to be physically present when the service is delivered. This physical presence creates both problems and opportunities, and it introduces a new constraint that is seldom present in the marketing of products.

At the same time, however, some services have become "delocalized" as advances in modern technology have made it possible for firms to unlink production and service processes and move labor-intensive service performance to areas where qualified, low-cost labor is plentiful.

The close interaction with customers also points to the fact that services often are custom made. This contradicts the desire of the firm to standardize its offering: Yet at the same time, it offers the service provider an opportunity to differentiate the service. The concomitant problem is that, in order to fulfill customer expectations, *service consistency* is required. For anything offered on-line, however, consistency is difficult to maintain over the long run. Therefore, the human element in the service offering takes on a much greater role than in the product offering. Errors may enter the system, and unpredictable individual influences may affect the outcome of the service delivery. The issue of quality control affects the provider as well as the recipient of services because efforts to increase control through uniform service may sometimes be perceived by customers as the limiting of options. It may therefore have a negative market effect.[45]

Services often require entirely new forms of distribution. Traditional channels frequently have multiple levels and are therefore long and slow. They often cannot be used at all because of the perishability of services. A weather news service, for example, either reaches its audience quickly or rapidly loses value. As a result, direct delivery and short distribution channels are required. When they do not exist, which is often the case domestically and even more so globally, service providers need to be distribution innovators in order to reach their market.

Because services are delivered directly to the user, they are frequently much more sensitive to cultural factors than are products. Their influence on the individual abroad may be welcomed or greeted with hostility. For example, Walt Disney, the first studio guaranteed a time slot on Polish television, began broadcasting Disney animated shows and live-action features in September 1990.[46] On the other hand, countries that place a strong emphasis on cultural identity have set barriers inhibiting market penetration by foreign films. For instance, Brazil imposed the CONCINE Resolution 98, which, among other restrictions, requires all Brazilian home video distributors and outlets to carry a minimum inventory of 25 percent Brazilian titles. As Brazil is the tenth largest foreign market in revenue for all media, this barrier severely restricts the number of foreign film titles imported into the country.[47]

THE ROLE OF SERVICES IN THE U.S. ECONOMY

Since the Industrial Revolution, the United States has seen itself as a primary international competitor in the production of goods. In the past few decades, however, the U.S. economy has increasingly become a service economy, as Figure 12.5 shows. The service sector now produces 75 percent of the GNP and employs 79 percent of the workforce. The major segments that compose the service sector are communications, transportation, public utilities, finance, insurance and real estate, wholesale and retail businesses, government, and "services" (a diverse category including business services,

Employment in Industrial Sectors as a Percentage of the Total Labor Force FIGURE 12.5

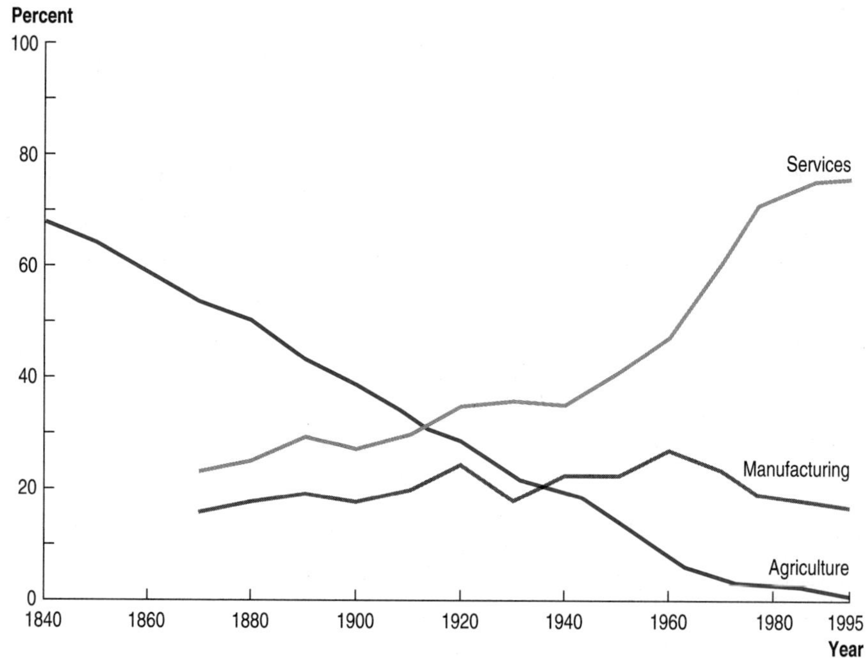

SOURCES: Quarterly Labor Force Statistics, Paris, Organization for Economic Cooperation and Development, 1996, No. 2; J. B. Quinn, "The Impacts of Technology on the Service Sector," *Technology and Global Industry: Companies and Nations in the World Economy* (Washington, D.C.: National Academy of Sciences, 1987).

personal services, and professional and health services). The service sector accounts for most of the growth in total nonfarm employment.

Only a limited segment of the total range of U.S. services is sold internationally. Federal, state, and local government employees, for example, sell few of their services to foreigners. U.S. laundries and restaurants only occasionally service foreign tourists. Many service industries that do sell abroad often have at their disposal large organizations, specialized technology, or advanced professional expertise. Strength in these characteristics has enabled the United States to become the world's largest exporter of services. Total U.S. services exported grew from $14 billion in 1970 to almost $237.0 billion in 1996.[48]

Global service trade has had very beneficial results for many U.S. firms. Citibank, for example, receives 65 percent of its total revenues from foreign operations. Most of the large management consulting firms derive more than half of their revenue from international sources. The largest advertising agencies serve customers around the globe, some of them in 107 countries. Table 12.3 shows how many countries are served by these agencies and how many accounts they service in 10 or more countries. Interesting is also the fact that six of the firms have the term "worldwide" in their name. After many years of increasing activity by foreign insurance companies in the United States, U.S. firms are now aggressively beginning to enter the $1.4 trillion world insurance market. These facts demonstrate that many service firms have become truly international and formidable in size.

However, dramatic global growth is not confined to U.S. firms. The import of services into the United States is also increasing dramatically. In 1996, the United States

TABLE 12.3 **The Globalization of Advertising Agencies**
Number of countries served and number of client accounts serviced in 10 or more countries (1996 data).

Agency	Countries Served	Single Accounts in 10+ Countries
Ammirati Puris Lintas Worldwide	58	12
	68	23
Bates Worldwide	69	17
DDB Needham Worldwide	86	21
D'Arcy Masius Benton & Bowles	98	15
Grey Advertising	78	43
J. Walter Thompson Co.	67	25
Leo Burnett Co.	65	14
McCann Erickson Worldwide	107	49
Ogilvy & Mather Worldwide	79	26
Saatchi & Saatchi Advertising Worldwide	93	21
Young & Rubicam Advertising	64	24

SOURCE: Laurel Wentz and Sasha Emmons, "'AAI' charts show yearly growth, consolidation," *Advertising Age International*, September, 1996: 133

imported more than $156.0 billion worth of services.[49] Competition in global services is rising rapidly at all levels, as Global Learning Experience 12.9 indicates; Hong Kong, Singapore, and Western Europe are increasingly active in service industries such as banking, insurance, and advertising. Years ago, U.S. construction firms could count on a virtual monopoly on large-scale construction projects. Today, firms from South Korea, Italy, and other countries are taking a major share of the international construction business. Furthermore, the United States has long been recognized as the leader in software development; yet, this lead may be challenged soon. The overall result of these developments is that the U.S. share of global service trade is estimated to have declined in relative terms—from 25 to 20 percent of the world market—within a decade.

THE ROLE OF GLOBAL SERVICES IN THE WORLD ECONOMY

The United States is not unique in its conversion to a service economy. Similar changes have taken place globally, and several developed countries have service sectors that produce more than 50 percent of their gross domestic products. At the present time, services trade is taking place mainly among the industrialized countries. However, this trend appears to be changing.

The economies of developing countries have traditionally first established a strong agricultural and then a manufacturing sector to meet basic needs such as food and shelter before venturing into the services sector. Some developing countries, such as Mexico, Singapore, Hong Kong, Bermuda, and the Bahamas, are steering away from the traditional economic development pattern and are concentrating on developing strong service sectors.[50] The reasons vary from a lack of natural resources with which to develop agricultural and/or manufacturing sectors to recognition of the strong demand for services and the ability to provide them through tourism and a willing, skilled, and

GLOBAL LEARNING EXPERIENCE

12.9

The Global Temp

The temporary-help business is going global. Once a business that consisted almost exclusively of local orders for secretaries and assembly-line workers, big temp-help companies routinely scramble for huge national contracts to supply all the temporary help needs of big corporations. Now, some of those same employment-services companies are gearing up for the next big battle—a fight over international business, as the demand for "flexible staffing" crosses borders.

"We're going to see more of this," predicts Erik Vonk, who heads the U.S. operations of Randstad Holding NV of the Netherlands. Randstad, which entered the U.S. with two acquisitions in 1993, has used its U.S. foothold to gain stateside business from European customers, such as Philips Electronics NV and Stork NV, an industrial machinery maker. It cemented its international reputation in 1996 by supplying 17,000 temps to the Summer Olympics in Atlanta.

While one-stop global contracts are still rare, it is increasingly common for big contracts in one country to lead to new business in others. Temporary-help companies are finding that far-flung networks outside their home countries are big assets as their customers expand internationally. "We like to be a preferred supplier, and if it's on a global scale, we have the horses out there," says Manpower Chairman Mitchell Fromstein.

Increasingly, that means taking staffing services to the doorsteps of international clients. In an office opposite Northern Telecom Ltd.'s headquarters in Toronto, Manpower fields toll-free calls for temporary workers from Northern Telecom managers in the United States, Canada, and Mexico. Manpower also stations managers at five other Northern Telecom locations in the United States and Canada to coordinate the hiring of temps.

That service enabled Northern Telecom to shrink its list of North American temporary-help suppliers from 125 in the early 1990s to 1. On any given day, Manpower might supply Northern Telecom with some 2,000 temporaries, ranging from office workers to telecommunications equipment installers. Instead of hundreds of invoices each month, Northern Telecom now deals with "one bill, one company, and one point of contact," says Joe Simeone, the company's director of supply and services. Now, Manpower and Northern Telecom are talking about extending their relationship overseas—something Manpower has already done with computer giant Hewlett-Packard Co.

Industry giants aren't the only ones finding a need to cross borders with their temporary help and other staffing needs. W.H. Brady Co., a Milkwaukee-based maker of identification and specialty tape products, recently hired Manpower to supply temporary workers and help recruit new full-time workers in about a dozen countries in which the company does business. Turning the work over to Manpower allowed Brady to redeploy some human-resource workers into other jobs. "For the first time, we know what it costs to do recruiting, because we pay Manpower," says Katherine Hudson, Brady's chief executive officer. It also fits a goal of Hudson and a growing number of executives in the United States and Europe: to create a "buffer" of temporary workers to help shield full-time workers from dismissal should times get tough or markets change.

In Europe, rigid rules on hiring and firing full-time workers make temporary help an attractive alternative. From Madrid to Manchester, England, temporary help offices are sprouting up as the leading players rush to build market share. Industry experts in Europe expect annual revenue growth of 10 percent to 15 percent over the next decade.

For the most part, temporary-help companies export their expertise, not their workers. But even that is changing. Randstad says it recently signed a contract to send about 20 aircraft engineers from the Netherlands to temporary jobs with Boeing Co. in Seattle. And when phone calls flood a customer-service center that Manpower staffs for a big computer company in Britain, Manpower sends the overflow to the United States. For callers, the only thing that changes is the accent at the end of the line.

SOURCE: Robert Rose, "Temporary-Help Firms Start New Game: Going Global," *The Wall Street Journal,* May 16, 1996, B4.

inexpensive labor force. As a result, it is anticipated that services trade will continue to grow. However, as more countries enter the sector, the global services business will become more competitive.

GLOBAL TRANSFORMATIONS IN THE SERVICES SECTOR

What changes account for the dramatic rise in services trade? Two major factors that seem to be responsible are environmental and technological change.

One primary environmental change is reduced governmental regulation of services, particularly within the United States. In the mid-1970s, a philosophical decision was made to reduce government interference in the marketplace in the hope of enhancing competition. The primary deregulated industries in the United States have been transportation, banking, and telecommunications. As a result of regulatory changes, new competitors participate in the marketplace. Some service sectors have benefited and others have suffered from this withdrawal of government intervention. Regulatory changes were initially thought to have primarily domestic effects, but they have rapidly spread internationally. For example, the 1984 **deregulation** of AT&T has given rise to competition not only in the United States. Japan's telecommunication monopoly, NT&T, was deregulated in 1985. Today, domestic and global competition in the telecommunications sector has increased dramatically. Growth for all U.S. long-distance carriers typically has been stronger internationally than domestically. Apart from AT&T, firms such as MCI and Sprint now offer their services worldwide. As MCI President Bert C. Roberts stated: "I can't overemphasize the importance of the international market to the growth of this business."[51]

deregulation
removal of the government regulation of a company or industry to stimulate competition, i.e., the U.S. airline industry

Similarly, deregulatory efforts in the transportation sector have had global repercussions. New air carriers have entered the market to compete against established truck carriers and have done so successfully by pricing their services differently both nationally and internationally. The deregulatory movement that originated in the United States has spread globally, particularly to Europe, and fostered new competition and new competitive practices. Because many of these changes resulted in lower prices, demand has been stimulated, leading to a rise in the volume of global services trade.

Another major environmental change in the United States has been the decreased regulation of service industries by their service groups. Business practices in fields such as health care, law, and accounting are becoming increasingly competitive and aggressive. New economic realities require firms in these industries to search for new ways to attract market share and expand their markets. Global markets are one frequently untapped possibility for market expansion and have therefore become a prime target for such firms.

Technological advancement is the second major change that has taken place. Increasingly, progress in technology is offering new ways of doing business and is permitting businesses to expand their horizons globally. Through computerization, for instance, service exchanges that previously would have been prohibitively expensive are now feasible. Ford Motor Company uses one major computer system to carry out its new car designs in both the United States and Europe. This practice not only lowers expenditures on hardware but also permits better utilization of existing equipment by allowing design groups in different time zones to use the equipment around the clock. Of course, this development could take place only after advances in data-transmission procedures. Similarly, more rapid data transmission also enabled financial institutions to expand their service delivery through a worldwide network.

Another result of technological advancement is that service industry expansion is not confined to those services that are labor intensive and therefore better per-

This driver's mobile radio equipment operates on Motorola's Japan Specialized Mobile Radio System, which is among the world's most advanced services of its type.
SOURCE: Courtesy of Motorola, Inc.

formed in areas of the world where labor possesses a comparative advantage. Rather, technology-intensive services are becoming the sunrise industries of the 1990s.

Starting to Offer Services Globally

For services that are delivered mainly in support of or in conjunction with products, the most sensible approach for the global novice is to follow the path of the product. For years, many large accounting and banking firms have done this by determining where their major multinational clients have set up new operations and then following them. Smaller service providers who cooperate closely with manufacturing firms can determine where the manufacturing firms are operating globally. Ideally, of course, it would be possible to follow clusters of manufacturers abroad in order to obtain economies of scale globally while simultaneously looking for entirely new client groups.

Service providers whose activities are independent from products need a different strategy. These individuals and firms must search for market situations abroad that are similar to the domestic market. Such a search should be concentrated in their area of expertise. For example, a design firm learning about construction projects abroad can investigate the possibility of rendering its design services. Similarly, a management consultant learning about the plans of a foreign country or firm to computerize can explore the possibility of overseeing a smooth transition from manual to computerized activities. What is required is the understanding that similar problems are likely to occur in similar situations.

Another opportunity consists of identifying and understanding points of transition abroad. Just as U.S. society has undergone change, foreign societies are subject to a changing domestic environment. If new transportation services are introduced, an expert in containerization may wish to consider whether to offer his or her service to improve the efficiency of the new system.

Leads for global service opportunities can also be gained by keeping informed about international projects sponsored by domestic organizations such as the U.S. Agency for

QUESTION

One of the smallest nations in the world is also the oldest country in Europe, and the oldest Republic in the world. Most of its citizens earn their living making and selling postage stamps. Name it.

San Marino, on the slopes of the Apennines entirely within Italy, has been an independent Republic since 1631. It covers twenty-four square miles.

International Development or the Trade Development Program as well as international organizations such as the United Nations, the International Finance Corporation, or the World Bank. Frequently, such projects are in need of support through services. Overall, the global service provider needs to search for similar situations, similar problems, or scenarios requiring similar solutions in order to formulate an effective global expansion strategy.

Strategic Indications

To be successful in the global service offering, the manager must first determine the nature and the aim of the services-offering core—that is, whether the service will be aimed at people or at things and whether the service act in itself will result in tangible or intangible actions. Table 12.4 provides examples of such a classification strategy that will help the manager to better determine the position of the services effort.

During this determination, the manager must consider other tactical variables that have an impact on the preparation of the service offering. For example, in the field of

TABLE 12.4 Understanding the Nature of the Service Act

	Direct Recipient of the Service	
Nature of the Service Act	**People**	**Things**
Tangible actions	Services directed at people's bodies:	Services directed at goods and other physical possessions:
	Health care	Freight transportation
	Passenger transportation	Industrial equipment repair and maintenance
	Beauty salons	Janitorial services
	Exercise clinics	Laundry and dry cleaning services
	Restaurants	Landscaping/lawn care
	Haircutting	Veterinary care
Intangible actions	Services directed at people's minds:	Services directed at intangible assets:
	Education	Banking
	Broadcasting	Legal services
	Information services	Accounting
	Theaters	Securities
	Museums	Insurance

SOURCE: Christopher H. Lovelock, *Managing Services,* © 1988, p 47. Reprinted by permission of Prentice-Hall, Inc., Englewood Cliffs, N.J.

research, the measurement of capacity and delivery efficiency often remains highly qualitative rather than quantitative. In the field of communications, the intangibility of the service reduces the manager's ability to provide samples. This makes communicating the service offered much more difficult than communicating a product offer. Brochures or catalogs explaining services often must show a proxy for the service in order to provide the prospective customer with tangible clues. A cleaning service, for instance, can show a picture of an individual removing trash or cleaning a window. However, the picture will not fully communicate the performance of the service. Because of the different needs and requirements of individual consumers, the manager must pay attention to the two-way flow of communication. Mass communication must be supported by intimate one-on-one follow-up.

The role of personnel deserves special consideration in global service delivery. Because the customer interface is intense, proper provisions need to be made for training of personnel both domestically and internationally. Major emphasis must be placed on appearance. Most of the time, the person delivering the service—rather than the service itself—will communicate the spirit, value, and attitudes of the service corporation.

This close interaction with the consumer will also have organizational implications. For example, while tight control over personnel may be desired, the individual interaction that is required points toward the need for an international decentralization of service delivery. This, in turn, requires delegation of large amounts of responsibility to individuals and service "subsidiaries" and requires a great deal of trust in all organizational units. This trust, of course, can be greatly enhanced through proper methods of training and supervision.

The areas of pricing and financing require special attention. Because services cannot be stored, much greater responsiveness to demand fluctuation must exist, and therefore much greater pricing flexibility must be maintained. At the same time, flexibility is countered by the desire to provide transparency for both the seller and the buyer of services in order to foster an ongoing relationship. The intangibility of services also makes financing more difficult. Frequently, even financial institutions with large amounts of global experience are less willing to provide financial support for global services than for products. The reasons are that the value of services is more difficult to assess, service performance is more difficult to monitor, and services are difficult to repossess. Therefore, customer complaints and difficulties in receiving payments are much more troublesome for a lender to evaluate in the area of services than for products.

Finally, the distribution implications of global services must be considered. Usually, short and direct channels are required. Within these channels, closeness to the customer is of overriding importance in order to understand what the customer really wants, to trace the use of the service, and to aid the customer in obtaining a truly tailor-made service.

SUMMARY

A critical decision in global marketing concerns the degree to which the overall marketing program should be standardized or localized. The ideal is to standardize as much as possible without compromising the basic task of marketing: satisfying the needs and wants of the target market. Many multinational marketers are adopting globalization strategies that involve the standardization of good ideas, while leaving the implementation to local entities.

The technical side of marketing management is universal, but environments require adaptation within all of the mix elements. The degree of adaptation will vary by market, product or service marketed, and overall company objectives.

Services are taking on an increasing importance in global trade. They need to be considered separately from trade in merchandise because they no longer simply complement products. Often, products complement services or are in competition with them. Because of service attributes such as their intangibility, their perishability, their custom design, and their cultural sensitivity, international trade in services is frequently more complex than trade in goods.

Services play an increasing role in the economies of the United States and of other industrialized nations. As a result, global growth and competition in this sector have begun to outstrip that of merchandise trade and are likely to intensify in the future. Even though services are unlikely to replace production, the sector will account for the shaping of new competitive advantages globally.

The many service firms now operating domestically need to investigate the possibility of going global. Historical patterns of service providers following manufacturers abroad have become obsolete as stand-alone services become more important to world trade. Management must therefore assess its vulnerability to service competition from abroad and explore opportunities to provide its services globally.

Key Terms and Concepts

positioning
brand
brand name
product line
product counterfeiting
standard worldwide pricing
dual pricing
marginal cost pricing
market-differentiated pricing
price escalation
dumping
gray markets
transfer pricing
promotional mix
media strategy
media mix
promotional message
channel design
demographics
psychographics
intangibility
perishability
service capacity
customer involvement
deregulation

Questions for Discussion

1. Is globalization ever a serious possibility, or is the regional approach the closest the global marketer can ever hope to get to standardization?
2. Is a "world car" a possibility?
3. Argue for and against gray marketing.
4. What courses of action are open to a global marketer who finds all attractive intermediaries already under contract to competitors?
5. You are planning a pan-European advertising campaign for calculators with a back-to-school theme. The guideline specifies illustrating the various models sold in the market along the margins of the advertisement and using a title that suggests calculators help students to do better in school and college. What type of local adjustments do you expect to make to the campaign?
6. Discuss the major reasons for the growth of global services.
7. Why does the United States have a comparative advantage in many services sectors?
8. How does the global sale of services differ from the sale of goods?

9. What are some ways for a firm to expand its services globally?

10. Which services would you expect to migrate abroad in the next decade? Why?

Recommended Readings

Aharoni, Yair. *Coalitions and Competition: The Globalization of Professional Business Services.* London and New York: Routledge, 1993.

Bateson, John E. G. *Managing Services Marketing* 3rd ed. Fort Worth, Tex.: Dryden Press, 1995.

Berry, Leonard L., David R. Bennett, and Carter W. Brown, *Service Quality.* Homewood, Ill.: Dow Jones-Irwin, 1989.

Cateora, Phillip R. *International Marketing* 9th ed. Chicago, Ill.: Irwin, 1996.

Czinkota, Michael R., and Ilkka A. Ronkainen. *Global Marketing Imperative: Positioning Your Company for the New World of Business.* Lincolnwood, Ill.: NTC, 1995.

Czinkota, Michael R., and Ilkka A. Ronkainen. *Global Marketing.* Fort Worth, Tex.: Dryden, 1996.

Czinkota, Michael R., and Jon Woronoff. *Unlocking Japan's Market.* Chicago: Probus Publishers, 1991.

Feketekuty, Geza. *International Trade in Services.* Cambridge, Mass.: Ballinger, 1988.

Hoekman, Bernard M. *Liberalizing Trade in Services.* Washington, D.C.: The World Bank, 1994.

Jeannet, Jean-Pierre, and H. David Hennessey. *Global Marketing Strategies,* Boston, Mass.: Houghton-Mifflin, 1995.

Johansson, Johny K. *Global Marketing.* Chicago, Ill.: Irwin, 1997.

Keegan, Warren J., and Mark C. Green. *Marketing.* 3rd ed. Upper Saddle River, N.J.: Prentice-Hall, 1997.

Lanvin, Bruno. *Trading in a New World Order: The Impact of Telecommunications and Data Services on International Trade in Services.* Boulder and Oxford: Westview Press, 1993.

Leo Burnett. *Worldwide Advertising and Media Fact Book.* Chicago, IL: Triumph Books, 1994.

Lovelock, Christopher H. *Services Marketing.* 2nd ed. Englewood Cliffs, N.J.: Prentice-Hall, 1991.

McKee, David L., and Don E. Garner. *Accounting Services, The International Economy and Third World Development.* New York: Praeger, 1992.

Smith, N. Craig, and John A. Quelch. *Ethics in Marketing.* Homewood, Ill.: Irwin, 1993.

United States Congress. *International Competition in Services.* Washington, D.C.: Congress of the United States, Office of Technology Assessment, undated.

U.S. Department of Commerce. *A Basic Guide to Exporting.* Washington, D.C.: U.S. Government Printing Office, 1989.

Walmsley, James. *The Development of International Markets.* Hingham, Mass.: Graham & Trotman, 1990.

Yip, George S. *Total Global Strategy.* Englewood Cliffs, N.J.: Prentice-Hall, 1992.

Notes

1. Alice Rudolph, "Standardization Not Standard for Global Marketers," *Marketing News,* September 27, 1985, 3–4.
2. Robert Buzzell, "Can You Standardize Multinational Marketing?" *Journal of Marketing* 46 (November–December 1968): 98–104.
3. Ralph Z. Sorenson and Ulrich E. Wiechmann, "How Multinationals View Marketing Standardization," *Harvard Business Review* 53 (May–June 1975): 38–56.
4. Ernest Dichter, "The World Customer," *Harvard Business Review* 40 (July–August 1962): 113–122.
5. Theodore Levitt, *The Marketing Imagination* (New York: The Free Press, 1983), 20–49.
6. Kenichi Ohmae, *Triad Power—The Coming Shape of Global Competition* (New York: The Free Press, 1985), 22–27.
7. Warren Strugatch, "Make Way for the Euroconsumer," *World Trade,* February 1993, 46–50.
8. George Yip, "Global Strategy . . . In a World of Nations," *Sloan Management Review* 31 (Fall 1989): 29–41.
9. Anne B. Fisher, "The Ad Biz Gloms onto 'Global,' " *Fortune,* November 12, 1984, 77–80.
10. Laurence Farley, "Going Global: Choices and Challenges" (paper presented at the American Management Association Conference, Chicago, Ill., June 10, 1985).
11. John A. Quelch and Edward J. Hoff, "Customizing Global Marketing," *Harvard Business Review* 64 (May–June 1986): 59–68.
12. Kamran Kashani, "Beware the Pitfalls of Global Marketing," *Harvard Business Review 67* (September–October 1989): 91–98.
13. John Daniels, "Bridging National and Global Marketing Strategies through Regional Operations," *International Marketing Review* 4 (Autumn 1987): 29–44.

14. Leonard L. Berry, "Services Marketing Is Different," in *Services Marketing,* ed. Christopher H. Lovelock (Englewood Cliffs, N.J.: Prentice-Hall, 1984), 30.
15. V. Yorio, *Adapting Products for Export* (New York: The Conference Board, 1983), 1.
16. John S. Hill and Richard R. Still, "Adapting Products to LDC Tastes," *Harvard Business Review* 62 (March–April 1984): 92–101.
17. Cyndee Miller, "U.S. Firms Lag in Meeting Global Quality Standards," *Marketing News,* February 15, 1993, 1, 6; and "Europe's Standards Blitz Has Firms Scrambling," *The Washington Post,* October 18, 1992, H1, H4.
18. "One Mello, Please," *Advertising Age,* August 1, 1983, 26.
19. "The Puff, the Magic, the Dragon," *The Washington Post,* September 2, 1994, B1, B3; and "Big Names Draw Fine Line on Logo Imagery," *South China Morning Post,* July 7, 1994, 3.
20. Hill and Still, "Adapting Products to LDC Tastes," 92–101.
21. "Going through Customs," *Inc.,* December 1984, 180–184.
22. Bruce Seifert and John Ford, "Are Exporting Firms Modifying Their Product, Pricing and Promotion Policies?" *International Marketing Review* 6 (Number 6, 1989): 53–68.
23. Phillip D. White and Edward W. Cundiff, "Assessing the Quality of Industrial Products," *Journal of Marketing* 42 (January 1978): 80–86.
24. Warren J. Bilkey and Erik Nes, "Country-of-Origin Effects on Product Evaluations," *Journal of International Business Studies* 13 (Spring–Summer 1982): 89–99.
25. "Detroit Beware: Japan Is Ready to Sell Luxury," *Business Week,* December 9, 1985, 114–118.
26. Ikka A. Ronkainen, "Product Development in the Multinational Firm," *International Marketing Review* 1 (Winter 1983): 24–30.
27. "For Levi's, a Flattering Fit Overseas," *Business Week,* November 5, 1990, 76–77.
28. Helmut Becker, "Pricing: An International Marketing Challenge," in *International Marketing Strategy,* eds. Hans Thorelli and Helmut Becker (New York: Pergamon Press, 1980), 201–215.
29. Richard D. Robinson, *Internationalization of Business: An Introduction* (Hinsdale, Ill.: Dryden, 1984), 49–54.
30. Steven Plaut, "Why Dumping Is Good for Us," *Fortune,* May 5, 1980, 212–222.
31. Peter Kessler, "Is Uniform Pricing Desirable in Multinational Markets?" *Akron Business and Economic Review 2* (Winter 1971): 3–8.
32. James C. Baker and John K. Ryans, "Some Aspects of International Pricing: A Neglected Area of Management Policy," *Management Decisions* (Summer 1973): 177–182.
33. Ilkka A. Ronkainen and Linda Van de Gucht, "Making a Case for Gray Markets," *Journal of Commerce,* January 6, 1987, 13A.
34. James Shulman, "When the Price Is Wrong—By Design," *Columbia Journal of World Business* 4 (May–June 1967): 69–76.
35. Mohammad F. Al-Eryani, Pervaiz Alam, and Syed H. Akhter, "Transfer Pricing Determinants of U.S. Multinationals," *Journal of International Business Studies* 21 (Fall 1990): 409–425.
36. Joseph A. Lawton, "Kodak Penetrates the European Copier Market with Customized Marketing Strategy and Product Changes," *Marketing News,* August 3, 1984, 1, 6.
37. D. Pridgen, "Satellite Television Advertising and Regulatory Conflict in Western Europe," *Journal of Advertising* 14 (Winter 1985): 23–29.
38. Jean J. Boddewyn, "Advertising Regulation in the 1980s," *Journal of Marketing* 46 (Winter 1982): 22–28.
39. John Clemens, "Television Advertising in Europe," *Columbia Journal of World Business* 22 (Fall 1987): 35–41.
40. Kate Bertrand, "Conner's Japanese Success Drive," *Business Marketing,* December 1991, 18–20.
41. Dennis Chase, "Global Marketing: The New Wave," *Advertising Age,* June 25, 1984, 49, 74.
42. Michael R. Czinkota, "Distribution of Consumer Products in Japan," *International Marketing Review* 2 (Autumn 1985): 39–51.
43. Philip J. Rosson, "Success Factors in Manufacturer-Overseas Distributor Relationships in International Marketing," in *International Marketing Management,* ed. Erdener Kaynak (New York: Praeger, 1984), 91–107.
44. "How to Evaluate Foreign Distributors: A *BI* Check-list," *Business International,* May 10, 1985, 145–149.
45. G. Lynn Shostack, "Service Positioning through Structural Change," *Journal of Marketing* 51 (January 1987): 38.
46. "Mickey and Co. Go to Poland," *Journal of Commerce* (July 20, 1990): 5A.
47. *1989 National Trade Estimate Report on Foreign Trade Barriers* (Washington, D.C.: Office of the United States Representative, 1989), 21–22.
48. U.S. Department of Commerce, *Survey of Current Business,* June 1997.
49. Ibid.
50. Allen Sinai and Zaharo Sofianou, "Service Sectors in Developing Countries: Some Exceptions to the Rule," *The Service Economy,* July 1990, 13.
51. Cindy Skrzycki, "China Answers a Ringing Need," *The Washington Post,* July 30, 1991, E1, E4.

Physical Distribution

LEARNING OBJECTIVES

To examine the escalating importance of international physical distribution as competitiveness becomes increasingly dependent on cost efficiency.

To learn about inbound materials management and outbound distribution, both part of international physical distribution.

To learn why international physical distribution is more complex than domestic physical distribution.

To see how the transportation infrastructure in host countries often dictates the options open to the global manager.

To learn why inventory management is crucial for global success.

GLOBAL LEARNING EXPERIENCE 13.1

Shipping Cherries to Japan

For the past 10 years, the annual ripening of cherries in West Coast orchards has touched off a frantic scramble in the airfreight industry. Each year from mid-May through mid-July, growers push 25 million pounds of cherries into airports from Los Angeles to Vancouver, British Columbia, most in search of the first available cargo space bound for Japan. "Even with the lousy weather we had this year, there are so many cherries in such a short period that it's hard to find enough air capacity," said Craig Ruess, president of Kaimac International Air Cargo Marketing in Palo Alto, California.

The Japanese crave cherries and routinely pay such high prices for them that U.S. growers can afford cargo rates running $3 per kilogram, instead of the normal $2 per kilogram for the trans-Pacific trip. At such premium rates, cherries can bump other cargo off normal schedules, forcing shippers to squeeze freight onto other flights, often at higher-than-normal rates.

"There's a real crap shoot when it comes to air shipment of cherries," said Jim Culbertson, manager of the California Cherry Advisory Board in Lodi, California. "We could have 1.2 million 18-pound cartons like we did in 1994 or we could have only 600,000 cartons, the way we will this year." California orchards normally produce about 75 percent of the U.S. cherries sold overseas, with nearly all of the balance coming from orchards in the Pacific Northwest.

Cherries that miss a flight and sit a day in the California sun risk losing $1 per carton in value once they reach Japan. Growers say they sometimes find themselves pleading for available cargo space on charter flights. Airfreight companies expecting a heavy crop may arrange a number of charters, only to discover that they aren't needed, Ruess said. Cherry harvests in California and Washington create such sharp, brief spikes in the year-round flow of air cargo that it's difficult for airlines to create the cargo space just when it's needed.

"When the cherries are moving, other freight may get pushed off planes going to Japan, so those other trans-Pacific planes have less space and can charge more for it," Ruess said. "The cherries affect everything." But cherry growers in California and the Pacific Northwest said they are starting to wonder if there aren't alternatives to the high cost and unpredictability of air transport. Some growers are setting up their own chill facilities to keep cherries in top condition until they're ready to fly.

Stemilt Growers of Wenatchee, Washington, and Freshold Inc. of Salinas, California, have pioneered an alternative approach by experimenting with special packing that allows cherries to cross the Pacific by ship. Stemilt is using Freshold modified atmosphere bags to deliver cherries across the Pacific as sea freight with airfreight quality. Shelly Karam, technical sales manager at Freshold, said 20 pounds of cherries are sealed in a bag with a mix of carbon dioxide and oxygen that slows ripening for the 12 to 14 days that a ship takes to cross the Pacific. A special membrane keeps the gas mix balanced as the fruit breathes during the trip.

SOURCE: John Davies, "Growers Search for Cargo Space," *Journal of Commerce—Air Commerce,* June 24, 1996: 10.

In Chapter 12 we discussed the importance of creating place and time utility in completing the marketing task of providing customers with the goods and services they want, where they want them, when they want them. Channels of distribution, the organizations involved in transferring ownership of goods and services from the manufacturer to the ultimate consumer, were explained and evaluated. This chapter deals with a second important function in creating place and time utility, physical distribution (also referred to as logistics).

For the international firm, customer locations and sourcing opportunities are widely dispersed. The physical distribution aspects of international business therefore have great importance. To obtain and maintain favorable results from the complex international environment, the international manager must coordinate distribution activities and gain the cooperation of all departments. Neglect of distribution issues brings not only higher costs but eventual noncompetitiveness, which will result in diminished market share, more expensive supplies, or lower profits. As we saw in Global Learning Experience 13.1, distribution problems can prevent exporters from fully exploiting a potentially profitable market overseas. Worse yet, different distribution regulations based on environmental concerns may even preclude any market participation.

This chapter will focus on international physical distribution activities. Primary areas of concern are transportation, inventory, packaging, storage, and environmental issues. The physical distribution problems and opportunities that are peculiar to international business will also be highlighted.

THE FIELD OF PHYSICAL DISTRIBUTION

Physical distribution (logistics) costs currently comprise between 10 and 25 percent of the total landed cost of an international order, and they continue to increase.[1] International firms have already achieved many of the cost reductions that are possible in financing, communication, and production, and they are now beginning to look at international distribution as a competitive tool. Managers realize that "competition is the name of the game" in global business and that distribution "is key to making—and keeping—customers."[2] They also believe that future sales growth in the international market will come mainly from the development of wider and better physical distribution systems.[3]

A Definition of International Physical Distribution

International physical distribution is defined as the designing and managing of a system that controls the flow of materials into, through, and out of the international corporation. It encompasses the total movement concept by covering the entire range of operation concerned with product movement, including therefore both exports and imports simultaneously. An overview of the system is provided in Figure 13.1.

Two major phases in the movement of materials are of importance. The first phase is inbound *materials management,* or the timely movement of raw materials, parts, and supplies into and through the firm. The second phase is outbound *distribution,* which involves the movement of the firm's finished product to its customers. In both phases, movement is seen within the context of the entire process. Stationary periods (storage and inventory) are therefore included. The basic goal of physical distribution management is the effective coordination of both inbound and outbound phases to achieve a given level of customer service at the lowest total cost.

The growth of physical distribution as a field has brought to the forefront three major new concepts: the systems concept, the total cost concept, and the trade-off concept. The **systems concept** is based on the notion that materials-flow activities within and outside the firm are so extensive and complex that they can be considered only in the context of their interaction. Instead of each corporate function, supplier, and customer operating with the goal of individual optimization, the systems concept stipulates that some components may have to work suboptimally in order to maximize

systems concept
concept of logistics based on the notion that materials-flow activities are so complex that they can be considered only in the context of their interaction

The Physical Distribution System FIGURE 13.1

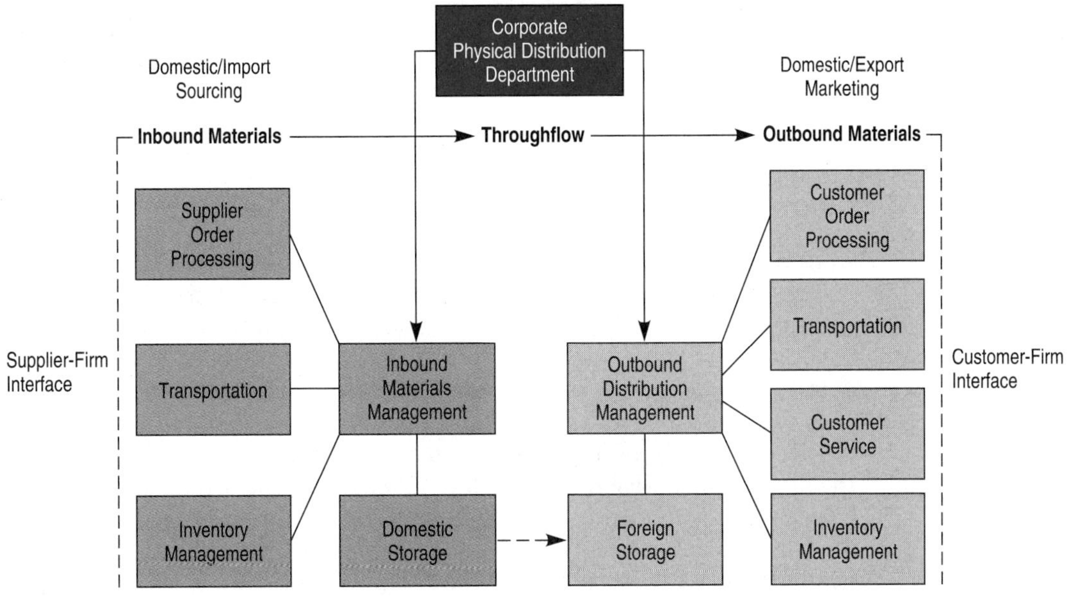

the benefits of the system as a whole. Clearly, the systems concept intends to provide the firm, its suppliers, and its customers, both domestic and foreign, with the benefits of synergism expected from size.

A logical outgrowth of the systems concept is the development of the **total cost concept.** In order to evaluate and optimize logistical activities, cost is used as a basis for measurement. The purpose of the total cost concept is to minimize the firm's overall physical distribution cost by implementing the systems concept appropriately. Increasingly, however, the total cost concept is being partially supplanted by a **total after-tax profit concept.** This takes into account the impact of national tax policies on the physical distribution function and has the objective of maximizing after-tax profits rather than minimizing total cost. Because tax variations in the international arena often have major consequences, this new focus appears quite appropriate.[4]

total cost concept
decision concept that uses cost as a basis for measurement in order to evaluate and optimize logistical activities

total after-tax profit concept
decision concept that takes into account the impact of national tax policies on the logistics function

trade-off concept
decision concept that recognizes linkages within the decision system

The **trade-off concept,** finally, recognizes that an improvement or gain in one area may result in a loss in another area. Thus, it is necessary to consider both the gain and the loss. The idea of giving up something to get something—the give and take—is the basis of the trade-off concept. For example, locating a warehouse near the customer may reduce the cost of transportation. However, additional costs are associated with new warehouses. Similarly, a reduction of inventories will save money but may increase the need for costly emergency shipments. Managers can maximize performance of physical distribution systems only by formulating decisions based on the recognition and analysis of these trade-offs.

QUESTION

How many oceans are there?

ANSWER *There are four oceans; the Pacific is the largest with 46 percent of the Earth's water, next is the Atlantic with about 23 percent, the Indian Ocean with 20 percent of the world's water, and the Arctic Ocean with 4 percent of the Earth's water. The oceans cover about 70 percent of the Earth's surface.*

Differences between Domestic and International Physical Distribution

In the domestic environment, physical distribution decisions are guided by the experience of the manager, possible industry comparisons, an intimate knowledge of trends, and rules of thumb. The distribution manager in the international firm, on the other hand, frequently has to depend on educated guesses to determine the steps required to obtain a desired service level. Variations in location mean variations in environment. Lack of familiarity with these variations leads to uncertainty in the decision-making process. By applying decision rules based only on the environment encountered at home, the firm will be unable to adapt well to new circumstances and the result will be inadequate profit performance. The long-term survival of international activities depends on an understanding of the differences inherent in the international physical distribution field. These variations can be classified as basic differences and country differences.[5]

Basic Differences Basic differences in international physical distribution emerge because the corporation is active in more than one country. One example of a basic difference is distance. Global business activities frequently require goods to be shipped farther to reach final customers. These distances in turn result in longer lead times, more opportunities for things to go wrong, more inventories—in short, greater complexity. Currency variation is a second basic difference. The corporation must adjust its planning to incorporate the existence of different currencies and changes in exchange rates. The border-crossing process brings with it the need for conformity with national regulations, an inspection at customs, and proper documentation. As a result, additional intermediaries participate in the international distribution process. They include freight forwarders, customs agents, customs brokers, banks, and other financial intermediaries. Finally, the **transportation modes** may also be different. Most transportation within the United States is either by truck or by rail, whereas the multinational corporation quite frequently ships its products by air or by sea. Airfreight and ocean freight have their own stipulations and rules that require new knowledge and skills.

transportation modes forms of transportation

Country Differences Within each country, the multinational corporation faces specific distribution attributes that may be quite different from those experienced at home. Transportation systems and intermediaries may vary. The computation of freight rates may be unfamiliar. Packaging and labeling requirements differ from country to country. Management must consider all of these factors in order to develop an efficient international physical distribution operation.

INTERNATIONAL TRANSPORTATION

International transportation is of major concern to the global firm because transportation determines how and when goods will be received. Additionally, transportation is a significant element of cost, representing 7 to 15 percent of the total landed cost of an international order.[6] Improvements in the overall logistics system that reduce transportation costs represent an opportunity to increase profits. Transportation can be divided into three parts: infrastructure, availability of different forms of transportation, and choice of transportation mode.

Infrastructure

In the United States, firms can count on an established transportation network, that is, superhighways, bridges, tunnels, ports, air, and rail facilities. Internationally, however, it is possible to encounter significant weaknesses in the infrastructure. Some countries may have excellent inbound and outbound port facilities but lack a comparable network of internal highways and roads. In such instances, shipping to the market may be easy, but delivery to a final inland destination may represent a very difficult and time-consuming task.

Due to political changes that have occurred recently, new and/or growing routes of commerce have also opened up. Without the proper infrastructure, the opening of markets between the former East and West political blocs is being accompanied by major new infrastructure bottlenecks. A similar situation is appearing in trade between the United States and Mexico: major border-crossing points were overwhelmed with truck traffic prior to NAFTA. Now that NAFTA is in place and trucking volume is expected to increase significantly, it appears that major improvements in highways will be necessary if both countries are to realize the full benefits of the trade agreement.

Closely related to potential infrastructure difficulties are the speed and conditions of loading or unloading at a foreign destination. The port at Santos, Brazil, is an enlightening example. Santos is Latin America's largest port. Union work rules and government regulations require that each stevedore gang (who load/unload containers) includes someone schooled in the ancient art of sewing torn coffee sacks. To load a container on a ship in Santos requires a labor crew of 31 people and costs $525. To unload the same container in Rotterdam, Netherlands, requires a crew of ten and costs $130. The Dutch workers move an average of 28 containers an hour, twice as many as are moved in Santos.[7]

Other problems, such as theft of cargo, is a constant problem at most ports. More ominous is the increasing number of incidents of piracy by armed bands who board ships at sea, at anchor, or dockside and make off with millions of dollars of cargo. Global

This Sea-Land container ship approaching Dubai exemplifies the primary difference between the transportation modes of national and international trade. Ocean freight and airfreight are essential to international trade.
SOURCE: © 1991 Charles Crowell/Black Star.

GLOBAL LEARNING EXPERIENCE 13.2

Pirates Still Roam the Seas

There are many potential hazards involved in ocean shipping: fire and collisions at sea, storms, sinkings, and water damage to cargo are only a few. However, a new danger—piracy—appears to be on an upward trend in certain parts of the world. The International Marine Bureau recorded 224 incidents of piracy worldwide in 1996, up from 170 in 1995, the majority in or near the South China Sea.

The modern-day pirates use speedboats and hand guns to ambush and board smaller, slower freighters. Once the vessel is under their control, the pirates sail the ship to a Chinese port and sell the cargo, seemingly with the approval of local government officials. In an incident in June 1995, a Panamanian freighter sailing from Singapore to Cambodia was hijacked by Chinese in army uniforms. They made off with the ship's cargo of $2 million worth of cigarettes and photo equipment. Before the 14-member crew were freed, the Chinese forced them to sign documents saying they were smuggling cargo into China.

Another area noted for piracy is the Brazilian Coast near the ports of Santos and Rio de Janeiro. Shippers and ship lines believe that the pirates there are receiving inside information regarding the cargo being carried on specific ships. Many of the attacks occur while the ships are at the dock and calls to the police go unanswered. Because the Port of Santos is quite crowded, ships will often be required to anchor outside the port for several days while waiting for a berth. There, they become easy prey for the pirates. Eventually, the higher costs associated with cargo losses, added security, and higher insurance rates will be passed on to shippers.

Learning Experience 13.2 provides a perspective of this peril. Theft and piracy add to the cost of ocean shipping and hamper the free flow of goods.

Reaching markets conveniently under favorable cost conditions is a key component of a firm's competitive position. Because different countries and regions may have different infrastructures, the firm must recognize that such differences can become the margin between success and failure.

Extreme variations also exist in the frequency of transportation services. A particular port may not be visited by a ship for weeks or even months. Sometimes only carriers with particular characteristics, such as small size, will serve a given location. All of these infrastructural concerns must be taken into account in the initial planning of the firm's location and transportation framework.

Availability of Modes

land bridge
transfer of ocean freight on land among various modes of transportation

sea bridge
transfer of freight among various modes of transportation at sea

intermodal movements
transfer of freight from one mode or type of transportation to another

Even though some goods are shipped abroad by rail or truck, international transportation frequently requires ocean or airfreight modes, which many U.S. corporations only rarely use domestically. In addition, combinations such as **land bridges** or **sea bridges** frequently permit the transfer of freight among various modes of transportation, resulting in **intermodal movements.** The international distribution manager must understand the specific characteristics of the different modes of transportation in order to use them intelligently.

Ocean Shipping The most common types of vessels operating in ocean shipping are the conventional (break bulk) cargo vessel, container ships (lift-on, lift-off vessels), and combination container and roll-on, roll-off vessels.

Conventional cargo vessels are useful for oversized and unusual cargoes but may be less efficient in the way they are loaded or unloaded.

Container ships carry standardized steel containers that greatly facilitate the loading and unloading of containers onto waiting truck trailers (chassis), railroad cars, or barges. As a result, the time the ship has to spend in port is reduced. The standard containers used in international trade measure 8 × 8 feet in height and width and are available in lengths of 20 and 40 feet. The 20-foot container is sometimes referred to as the ton equivalent unit (TEU). A container ship's capacity is rated in TEUs. The larger ships rated at 2,000 TEUs are capable of transporting 2,000 20-foot containers or its equivalent, 1,000 40-foot containers. When containers are loaded or unloaded, huge gantry cranes lift an outbound container from its truck chassis alongside the vessel and place it on board. The cranes then lift an inbound container from the vessel and place it on the truck chassis. This method of alternately lifting on and off gives rise to the term **lift-on, lift-off** operations.

container ships
ships designed to carry standardized containers, which greatly facilitate loading and unloading as well as intermodal transfers

Container traffic has increased steadily since its introduction by the Sea-Land Service Co. Figure 13.2 indicates the recent trend in U.S. containerized exports and imports. In 1989, U.S. containerized exports and imports totaled 8.7 million TEUs; by 1996, the total had increased to 13.1 million TEUs—a gain of 50 percent in seven years and is projected to increase through 1998. Table 13.1 identifies the top 20 ocean container carriers for 1996, ranked by TEUs (ton equivalent units). Not content with the recent trend in containerized shipments, the ocean carriers are using advanced technology to expand the capabilities of the container to ship more competitively, as indicated in Global Learning Experience 13.3.

lift-on, lift-off
method of loading and unloading containers by alternately lifting an outbound container on board the vessel and then in the same cycle of the crane lifting an inbound container off the vessel

Combination vessels, generally referred to as **third-generation ships,** feature both container and *roll-on, roll-off* capabilities. In **roll-on, roll-off (RORO),** a portion of the ship below deck is essentially a parking garage. Trucks, autos, buses, construction equipment, and anything on wheels enters the vessel via a built-in ramp, usually at the rear of the ship. When a ship pulls into port, container loading (or unloading) is in

third-generation ships
ships that carry containers on the weather deck and roll-on, roll-off cargo below in the hold of the vessel

roll-on, roll-off (RORO)
ship-loading operation in which cargo with wheels are driven on board the vessel and parked

FIGURE 13.2

Growth of U.S. Containerized Exports and Imports 1989–1996 Actual, 1997 and 1998 Projected (in millions of TEUs)

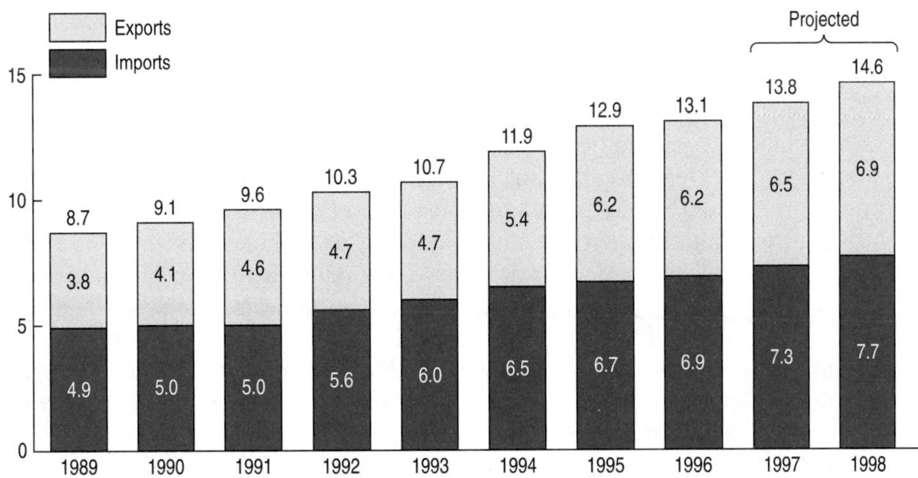

SOURCE: Port Import Export Reporting Service (PIERS), New York.

TABLE 13.1 **Top 20 Ocean Container Carriers, 1996 (in TEUs)**

Rank	Carrier	Total	Exports	Imports
1.	Sea-Land Service	1,301,370	584,822	716,548
2.	Evergreen Line	1,118,175	554,462	563,713
3.	Maersk Line	859,550	344,435	515,115
4.	Hanjin Shipping Co.	713,692	333,502	380,190
5.	APL	631,944	223,392	408,552
6.	Hyundai Merchant Marine	527,896	247,447	260,451
7.	Orient Overseas Container Line	478,427	224,151	254,276
8.	Nippon Yusen Kalsha	476,407	204,687	271,720
9.	China Ocean Shipping	454,156	248,519	205,637
10.	Kawasaki Kleen Kalsha	439,164	190,218	248,946
11.	Mitsui O.S.K. Line	414,861	195,966	218,895
12.	Yang Ming Marine Line	407,692	170,908	236,785
13.	Crowley American Transport	294,761	179,464	115,297
14.	Hapag-Lloyd	268,442	122,860	145,582
15.	Zim Container	265,902	133,282	132,620
16.	P&O Containers Ltd.	260,105	136,928	123,178
17.	DSR Senator Line	256,805	123,052	133,753
18.	Mediterranean Shipping	250,186	127,198	122,987
19.	Neptune Orient Lines	243,042	91,494	151,548
20.	Dole Fresh Fruit Co.	205,646	55,368	150,278
	Total U.S.	13,061,673	6,209,088	6,852,585

SOURCE: U.S. Global Container Report 1996, *Journal of Commerce,* May, 1997.

operation on the weather deck while, at the same time, roll-on, roll-off operations are underway below deck. The third-generation vessel provides unusual flexibility in international ocean shipping. Figure 13.3 is a cutaway illustration of this type of vessel.

Another vessel used in international shipping is the lighter aboard ship (LASH) vessel. LASH vessels consist of barges stored on the ship that are lowered to the water at the point of destination. These individual barges can then operate on inland waterways, a feature that is particularly useful in shallow water.

The availability of a certain type of vessel, however, does not automatically mean that it can be used. The greatest constraint in international ocean shipping is the lack of ports and port services. Modern container ships cannot serve some ports because the local equipment cannot handle the resulting traffic. This problem is often found in developing countries, where local authorities lack the funds to develop facilities. In some instances, nations may purposely limit the development of ports to impede the inflow of imports. Increasingly, however, governments have begun to recognize the importance of an appropriate port facility structure and are developing such facilities in spite of the large investments necessary. If such investments are accompanied by concurrent changes in the overall infrastructure, transportation efficiency should, in the long run, more than recoup the original investment. The investment may be even more profitable if ports of neighboring countries are not adequate. Merchants may opt to use neighboring ports with port facilities that are up to their standards and then transport the goods over land to their final destination. For example, with the opening of the Eastern

Keeping Exported Produce Fresh

From the outside, the intermodal steel container may not appear to be a very exciting piece of transportation equipment, but inside, some of them incorporate advanced technology that maintain the condition and value of the cargo. Such is the case of Sea-Land Service's "Fresh Mist" humidity-controlled refrigerated containers, designed to prevent dehydration of fresh produce during long ocean voyages. It does this by maintaining the moisture inside a refrigerated container at optimal levels, which keeps the produce fresh longer. The fresh produce arrives heavier and better looking, with a longer shelf-life and commands a higher price in overseas markets.

Inside the container, sophisticated microprocessor technology atomizes water into minute particles and injects them into the air stream—maintaining optimal humidity levels without damage to the product packaging.

Temperature and Humidity Requirements for Selected Fruits and Vegetables

Fresh Fruits and Vegetables	Percent Water Content	Expected Shelf Life	Optimum Temperature	Optimum Humidity
Artichoke	83.7	2–3 weeks	32–33	90–95%
Asparagus	93.0	2–3 weeks	32–35	90–95%
Broccoli	89.9	10–14 days	32–33	90–95%
Cabbage (early)	92.4	3–6 weeks	32–33	95–100%
Celery	93.7	2–3 months	32–33	90–95%
Grapes	81.9	8–26 weeks	32–33	90–95%
Green onions	89.4	2–3 weeks	32–33	95–100%
Leeks	85.4	2–3 months	32–33	95–100%
Lettuce	94.8	2–3 weeks	32–33	90–95%

SOURCE: Sea-Land Service, Inc., July 1997.

European markets, the German ports of Hamburg, Bremen, and Bremerhaven are in an ideal location. Because larger vessels would have to sail around Denmark to reach Eastern European ports, thereby adding at least a couple of days of voyage time, the German ports expect to snare a good portion of the anticipated increases in trade.[8]

Large investments in infrastructure are always necessary to produce results. Selective allocation of funds to transportation usually results only in the shifting of bottlenecks to some other point in the infrastructure. If these bottlenecks are not removed, the consequences may be felt in the overall economic performance of the nation.

airfreight
transport of goods by air; accounts for less than one percent of the total volume of international shipments

Air Shipping To and from most countries, **airfreight** is available. This includes the developing world, where it is often a matter of national prestige to operate a national airline. The tremendous growth in international airfreight over past decades is shown in Figure 13.4. However, the total volume of airfreight in relation to total shipping

FIGURE 13.3 **A Third-Generation RORO Container Ship**

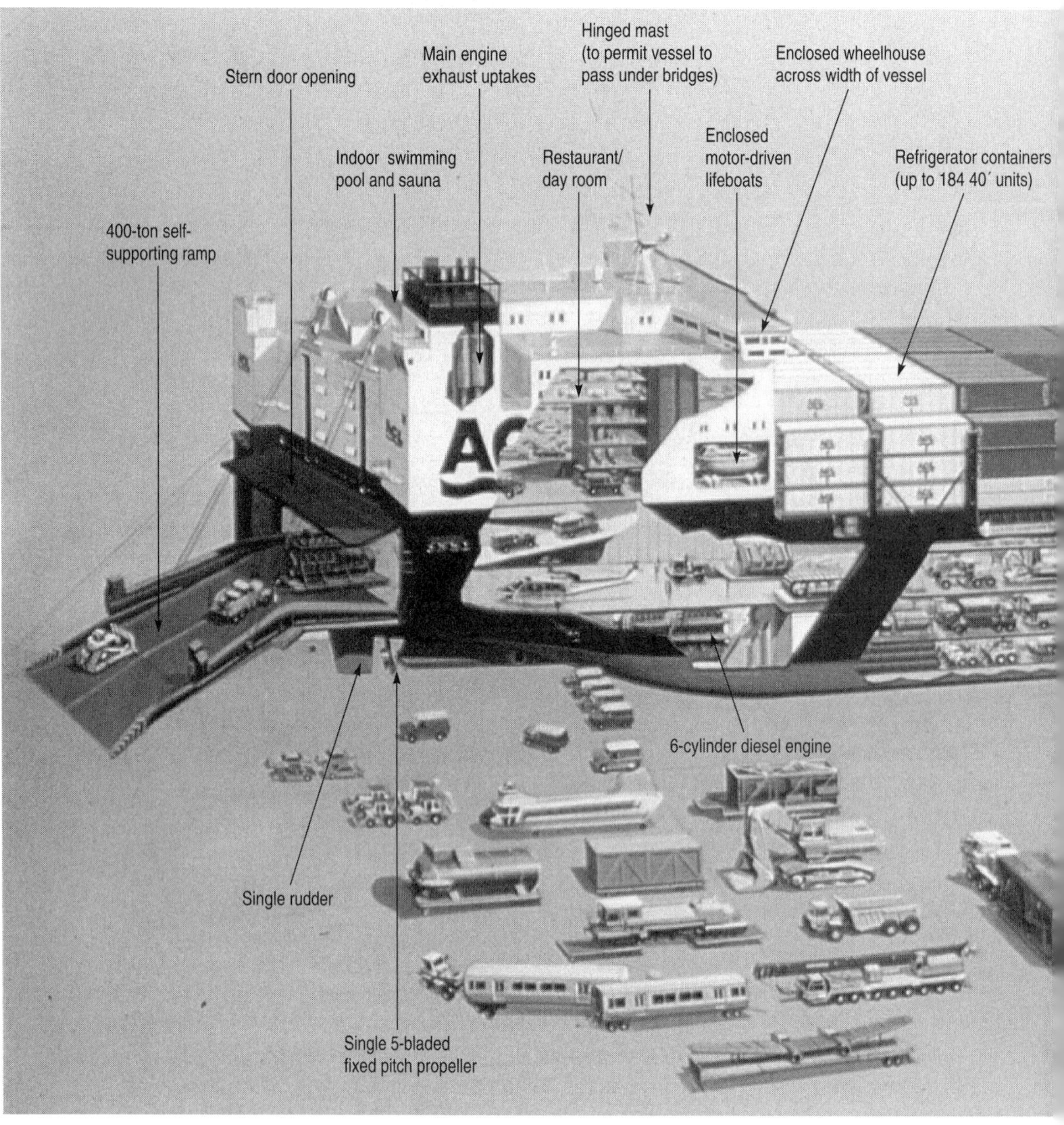

volume in international business remains quite small. It accounts for less than 1 percent of the total volume of international shipments, although it often represents more than 20 percent of the value shipped by industrialized countries.[9] Clearly, high-value items are more likely to be shipped by air, particularly if they have a high *density,* that is, a high weight-to-volume ratio.

Over the years, airlines have made major efforts to increase the volume of airfreight. Many of these activities have concentrated on developing better, more efficient ground fa-

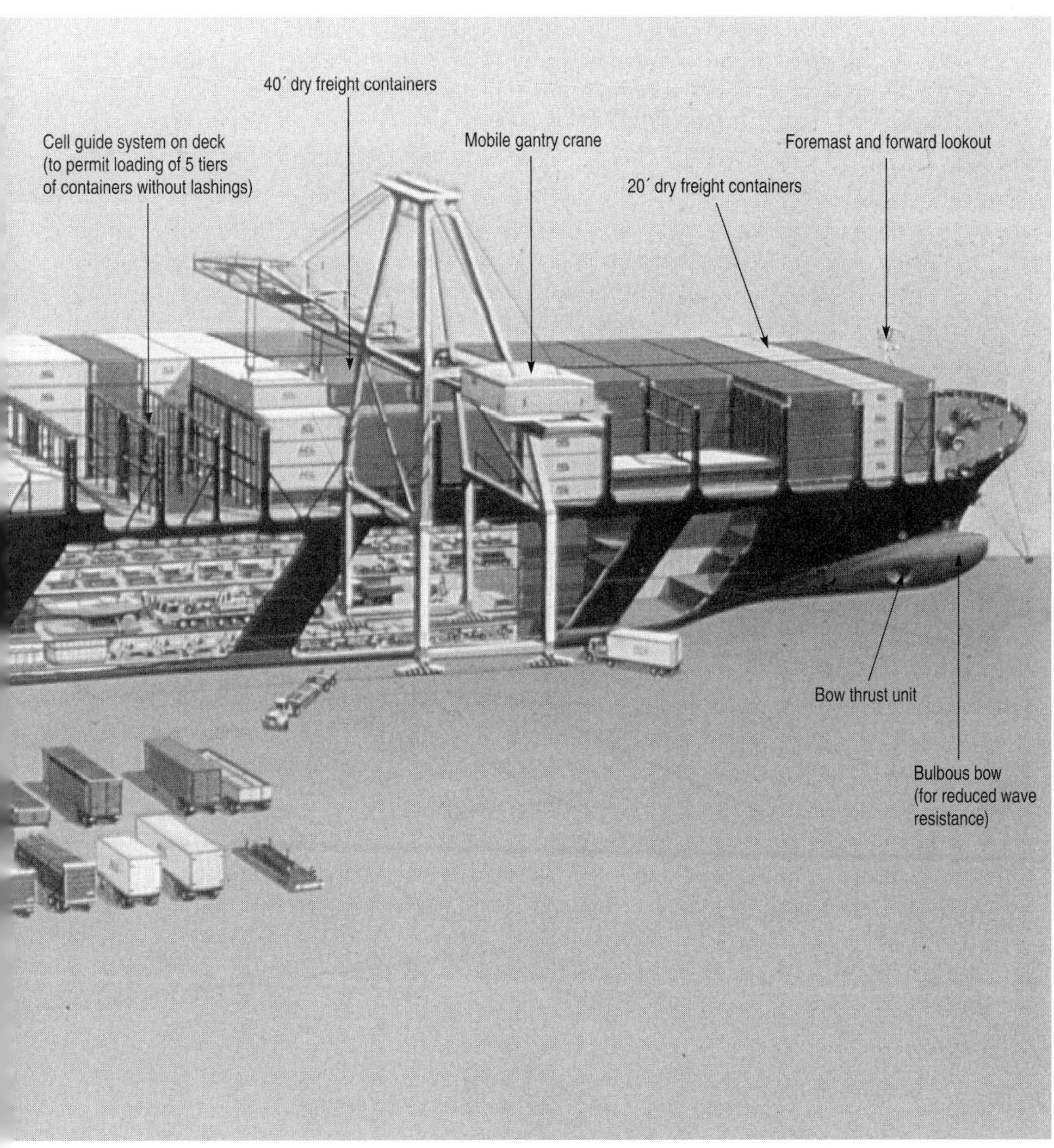

SOURCE: Courtesy of Atlantic Container Line

cilities, automating air waybills, introducing airfreight containers, and providing and marketing a wide variety of special services to shippers. In addition, some airfreight companies and ports have specialized and become partners in the international distribution effort.

QUESTION *What is the difference between an ocean and a sea?*

ANSWER *Basically, a sea refers either to a smaller division of the oceans or to a large saltwater bay partially enclosed by land. There are many seas in the world; the principal ones are (in order of size): South China, Caribbean, Mediterranean, Bering, Gulf of Mexico, Sea of Okhotsk, East China, Hudson Bay, Sea of Japan, North Sea, and Baltic Sea.*

Changes have also taken place within the aircraft. As an example, 30 years ago, the holds of large propeller aircraft could take only about 10 tons of cargo. Today's jumbo jets can hold more than 30 tons and can therefore transport bulky products. In addition, aircraft manufacturers have responded to industry demands by developing both jumbo cargo planes and combination passenger and cargo aircraft. The latter carry passengers in one section of the main deck and freight in another. These hybrids can be used by carriers on routes that would be uneconomical for passengers or freight alone.[10]

From the shipper's perspective, the products involved must be appropriate for air shipment in terms of their size. In addition, the market situation for any given prod-

FIGURE 13.4 **International Airfreight, 1960–1995***

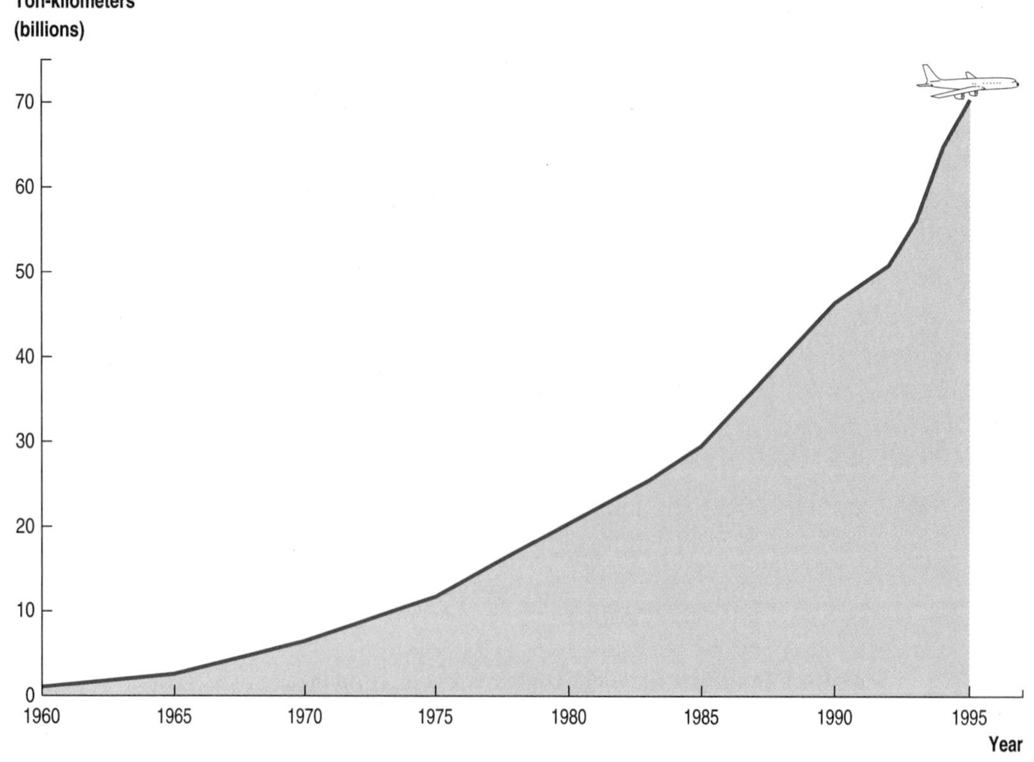

*Based on data supplied by member states of the International Civil Aviation Organization (ICAO). As the number of member states increased from 116 in 1970 to 150 in 1983, there is some upward bias in the data, particularly from 1970 on when data for the USSR were included for the first time.

SOURCE: *Civil Aviation Statistics of the World* (Montreal: ICAO 1996).

uct must be evaluated. Airfreight may be needed if a product is perishable or if, for other reasons, it requires a short transit time. The level of customer-service needs and expectations can also play a decisive role. The shipment of an industrial product that is vital to the ongoing operations of a customer is usually much more urgent than the shipment of most consumer products.

Choice of Transportation Modes

The international distribution manager must make the appropriate selection from the available modes of transportation. This decision, of course, will be heavily influenced by the needs of the firm and its customers. The manager must consider the performance of each mode on four dimensions: transit time, predictability, cost, and noneconomic factors.

Transit Time The period between departure and arrival of the carrier varies significantly between ocean freight and airfreight. The 45-day **transit time** of an ocean shipment can be reduced to 24 hours if the firm chooses airfreight. The length of transit time will have a major impact on the overall logistical operations of the firm. As an example, a short transit time may reduce or even eliminate the need for an overseas depot. Also, inventories can be significantly reduced if they are replenished frequently. As a result, capital can be freed up and used to finance other corporate opportunities. Transit time can also play a major role in emergency situations. If the shipper is about to miss an important delivery date because of production delays, a shipment normally made by ocean freight can be made by air.

transit time
period between departure and arrival of a carrier

Perishable products require shorter transit times. Transporting them rapidly prolongs the shelf life in the foreign market. As shown in Figure 13.5, air delivery may be the only way to successfully enter foreign markets with products that have a short life span. International sales of cut flowers have reached their current volume only as a result of airfreight.

Predictability Providers of both ocean freight and airfreight service wrestle with the issue of reliability. Both modes are subject to the vagaries of nature, which may impose delays. Yet because **reliability** is a relative measure, the delay of one day for airfreight tends to be seen as much more severe and "unreliable" than the same delay for ocean freight. However, delays tend to be shorter in absolute time for air shipments. As a result, arrival time via air is more predictable. This attribute has a major influence on corporate strategy. Because of the higher predictability of airfreight, inventory safety stock can be kept at lower levels. Greater predictability also can serve as a useful sales tool for foreign distributors, which can make more precise delivery promises to their customers. If inadequate port facilities exist, airfreight may again be the better alternative. Unloading operations from oceangoing vessels are more cumbersome and time consuming than for planes. Finally, merchandise shipped via air is likely to suffer less loss and damage from exposure of the cargo to movement. Therefore, once the merchandise arrives, it is more likely to be ready for immediate delivery—a facet that also enhances predictability.

reliability
dependability; the predictability of the outcome of an action

Cost of Transportation A major consideration in choosing international transportation modes is the cost factor. International transportation services are usually priced on the basis of both cost of the service provided and value of the service to the shipper. Because of the high value of the products shipped by air, airfreight is often priced according to the value of the service. In this instance, of course, price becomes a function of market demand and the monopolistic power of the carrier.

The manager must decide whether the clearly higher cost of airfreight can be justified. In part, this will depend on the cargo's properties. The physical density and the

FIGURE 13.5 **Advertisement for Cut Flowers**

SOURCE: Courtesy of Customer and Marketing Services Division, Aviation Department, Port Authority of New York and New Jersey.

value of the cargo will affect the decision. Bulky products may be too expensive to ship by air, whereas very compact products may be more appropriate for airfreight transportation. High-priced items can absorb transportation costs more easily than low-priced goods because the cost of transportation as a percentage of total product cost will be lower. As a result, sending diamonds by airfreight is easier to justify than sending coal.

Most important, however, are the overall distribution considerations of the firm. The manager must determine how important it is for merchandise to arrive on time. The need to reduce or increase international inventory must be carefully measured. Related to these considerations are the effect of transportation cost on price and the need for product availability abroad. Some firms may wish to use airfreight as a new tool for aggressive market expansion. Airfreight may also be considered a good way to begin operations in new markets without making sizable investments.

Although costs are the major consideration in modal choice, the overall cost perspective must be explored. Simply comparing transportation modes on the basis of price alone is insufficient. The manager must factor in all corporate activities that are affected by the modal choice and explore the total cost effects of each alternative.

Noneconomic Factors Often, noneconomic dimensions will enter into the selection process for a proper form of transportation. The transportation sector, nationally and internationally, both benefits and suffers from government involvement. Carriers may be owned or heavily subsidized by governments. As a result, governmental pressure is exerted on shippers to use national carriers, even if more economical alternatives exist. Such **preferential policies** are most often enforced when government cargo is being transported. Restrictions are not limited to developing countries. For example, in the United States, the federal government requires that all cargo and official travelers use national flag carriers when available.

preferential policies
government policies that favor certain (usually domestic) firms; for example, the use of national carriers for the transport of government freight even when more economical alternatives exist

For balance of payments reasons, international quota systems of transportation have been proposed. The United Nations Conference on Trade and Development (UNCTAD), for example, has recommended that 40 percent of the traffic between two nations be allocated to vessels of the exporting country, 40 percent to vessels of the importing country, and 20 percent to third-country vessels. However, stiff international competition among carriers and the price sensitivity of customers frequently render such proposals ineffective, particularly for trade between industrialized countries.

Although many justifications are possible for such national policies, ranging from prestige to national security, they may distort the economic choices of the international corporation. Yet these policies are a reflection of the international environment within which the firm must operate. Proper adaptation is necessary.

EXPORT DOCUMENTATION

Nothing moves internationally without accompanying paperwork; that is, all international shipments require some form of documentation. The actual documents required depend on the requirements of buyer and seller; local and foreign government regulations; bank financing of the transaction, if any; and type of merchandise being exported.

The number of documents required can be quite cumbersome and costly, creating a deterrent to trade. For example, it was estimated that the border-related red tape and controls within the European Union cost European companies $9.2 billion in extra administrative costs and delays annually.[11] In order to eliminate the barriers posed by all this required documentation, the EU introduced the Single Administrative Document (SAD) in 1988. The SAD led to the elimination of nearly 200 customs forms required of truckers throughout the EU when traveling from one member country to another.

To ensure that all documentation required is accurately completed and to minimize potential problems, firms entering the international market should consider using *freight forwarders,* specialists in handling export documentation.

A **bill of lading** is a contract between the exporter and the carrier indicating that the carrier has accepted responsibility for the goods and will provide transportation in return for payment. The bill of lading can also be used as a receipt and to prove ownership of the merchandise. There are two types of bills, negotiable and nonnegotiable. **Straight bills of lading** are nonnegotiable and are usually used in prepaid transactions. The goods are delivered to a specific individual or company. **Shipper's order** bills of

bill of lading
contract between the exporter and the carrier indicating that the carrier has accepted responsibility for the goods and will provide transportation in return for payment

straight bill of lading
nonnegotiable bill of lading usually used in prepaid transactions in which the transported goods involved are delivered to a specific individual or company

shipper's order
negotiable bill of lading that can be bought, sold, or traded while the subject goods are still in transit and that is used for letter of credit transactions

QUESTION *How did the Yellow, Red and Black Seas get their names?*

ANSWER *The Yellow Sea is named for the yellow silt deposited by the Yellow River in its waters; the Red Sea gets its name from the masses of reddish seaweed found in its waters; the Black Sea is quite dark and stormy, thus the name Black Sea.*

lading are negotiable; can be bought, sold, or traded while the goods are still in transit; and are used for letter-of-credit transactions. The customer usually needs the original or a copy of the bill of lading as proof of ownership to take possession of the goods.[12]

commercial invoice bill for the goods stating basic information about the transaction, including a description of the merchandise, total cost of the goods sold, addresses of the shipper and seller, and delivery and payment terms

A **commercial invoice** is a bill for the goods stating basic information about the transaction, including a description of the merchandise, total cost of the goods sold, addresses of the shipper and seller, and delivery and payment terms. Some governments use the commercial invoice to assess customs duties.

A variety of other export documents may be required. These are summarized in Table 13.2.

TERMS OF SHIPMENT AND SALE

At the beginning of discussions or negotiations relative to an international transaction, it is essential that the seller, and the buyer agree on the *terms of sale,* that is, what is and what is not included in the price quotation and when the seller's responsibility for goods ends and the buyer's responsibility begins.

TABLE 13.2 Summary of Common Export Documents

Document	Issued by	General Purpose
Pro forma invoice	Seller	Quotation to buyer; used to obtain import license and letter-of-credit financing
Sales contract	Seller or buyer	Confirms all details of transaction
Export license	U.S. government	Required by U.S. law
Carrier's receipt	Truck or rail carrier	Acknowledgment that carrier has accepted cargo for transportation to pier or airport
Dock/warehouse receipt	Pier or warehouse	Acknowledgment that cargo has been received
Ocean bill of lading/airway bill	Steamship company or airline	Contract between shipper and shipping company for transport of cargo
Insurance certificate	Insurance company	Evidence that cargo is insured against stated risks
Inspection certificate	Inspection company	Confirms to financing bank and buyer that cargo meets specifications set forth in sales contract and/or letter of credit
Packing lists	Seller	Required by shipping company and foreign customs
Commercial invoice	Seller	Actual invoice for goods
Consular invoice	Foreign government	Used to control imports and identify goods
Certificate of origin	U.S. Chamber of Commerce	Required by foreign government
Shipper's export declaration	Seller	Required by U.S. government to control exports and compile trade statistics

Incoterms are the internationally accepted standard definitions for terms of sale by the International Chamber of Commerce (ICC). The Incoterms 1990 went into effect on July 1, 1990, with significant revisions to better reflect changing transportation technologies and to facilitate electronic data interchange.[13] Although the same terms may be used in domestic transactions, they gain new meaning in the international arena. The most common of the Incoterms used in international marketing are summarized in Figure 13.6.

It should be noted that several of the documents mentioned previously are proof of performance of terms of sale and thus become justification for payment regardless of what may have happened to the cargo in the interim.

Prices quoted **ex-works (EXW)** apply only at the point of origin, and the seller agrees to place the goods at the disposal of the buyer at the specified place on the date or within the fixed period. All other charges are for the account of the buyer.

One of the new Incoterms is **free carrier (FCA),** which replaced a variety of FOB terms for all modes of transportation except vessel. FCA (named inland point) applies only at a designated inland shipping point. The seller is responsible for loading goods into the means of transportation; the buyer is responsible for all subsequent expenses. If a port of exportation is named, the costs of transporting the goods to the named port are included in the price. Under ex-works and free carrier terms, the responsibility of the seller ends when the buyer (or designated inland carrier) picks up the cargo. The carrier's receipt is proof of performance.

Free alongside ship (FAS) at a named U.S. port of export means that the exporter quotes a price for the goods, including charges for delivery of the goods alongside a vessel at the port. The seller handles the cost of unloading and wharfage; loading, ocean transportation, and insurance are left to the buyer. The dock receipt is proof of performance of FAS delivery.

Free on board (FOB) applies only to vessel shipments. The seller quotes a price covering all expenses up to and including delivery of goods on an overseas vessel provided by or for the buyer. The ocean bill of lading is proof that the cargo has been placed on board the designated vessel and that ownership of the goods has been passed from seller to buyer. Regardless of what happens to the ship and its cargo from that point on, the seller is entitled to payment.

Under **cost and freight (CFR)** to a named overseas port of import, the seller quotes a price for the goods, including the cost of transportation to the named port of debarkation. The cost of insurance and the choice of insurer are left to the buyer.

With **cost, insurance, and freight (CIF)** to a named overseas port of import, the seller quotes a price including insurance, all transportation, and miscellaneous charges to the point of debarkation from the vessel or aircraft. Items that may enter into the calculation of the CIF cost are (1) port charges: unloading, wharfage (terminal use) handling, storage, cartage, heavy lift, and demurrage; (2) documentation charges: certification of invoice, certificate of origin, weight certificate, and consular forms; and (3) other charges, such as fees of the freight forwarder and freight (inland and ocean) insurance premiums (marine, war, credit).

With **delivery duty paid (DDP),** the seller delivers the goods, with import duties paid, including inland transportation from import point to the buyer's premises. With **delivered duty unpaid (DDU),** only the destination customs duty and taxes are paid by the consignee. Ex-works signifies the maximum obligation for the buyer; delivered duty paid puts the maximum burden on the seller.

The careful determination and clear understanding of terms used and their acceptance by the parties involved are vital if subsequent misunderstandings and disputes are to be avoided.

Incoterms
internationally accepted standard definitions for terms of sale by the International Chamber of Commerce (ICC)

ex-works (EXW)
price quotes that apply only at the point of origin; the seller agrees to place the goods at the disposal of the buyer at the specified place on the date or within the fixed period

free carrier (FCA)
applies only at a designated inland shipping point; seller is responsible for loading goods into the means of transportation; buyer is responsible for all subsequent expenses

free alongside ship (FAS)
applies only at a designated inland shipping point; seller is responsible for loading goods into the means of transportation; buyer is responsible for all subsequent expenses

free on board (FOB)
applies only to vessel shipments; seller quotes a price covering all expenses up to and including delivery of goods on an overseas vessel provided by or for the buyer

cost and freight (CFR)
seller quotes a price for the goods, including the cost of transportation to the named port of debarkation; cost and choice of insurance are left to the buyer

cost, insurance, and freight (CIF)
seller quotes a price including insurance, all transportation, and miscellaneous charges to the point of debarkation from the vessel or aircraft

delivery duty paid (DDP)
seller responsible for delivery to buyer's premises, including payment of import duties and inland transportation

delivered duty unpaid (DDU)
seller responsible for delivery to buyer, excluding customs duties and taxes

FIGURE 13.6 Selected Trade Terms

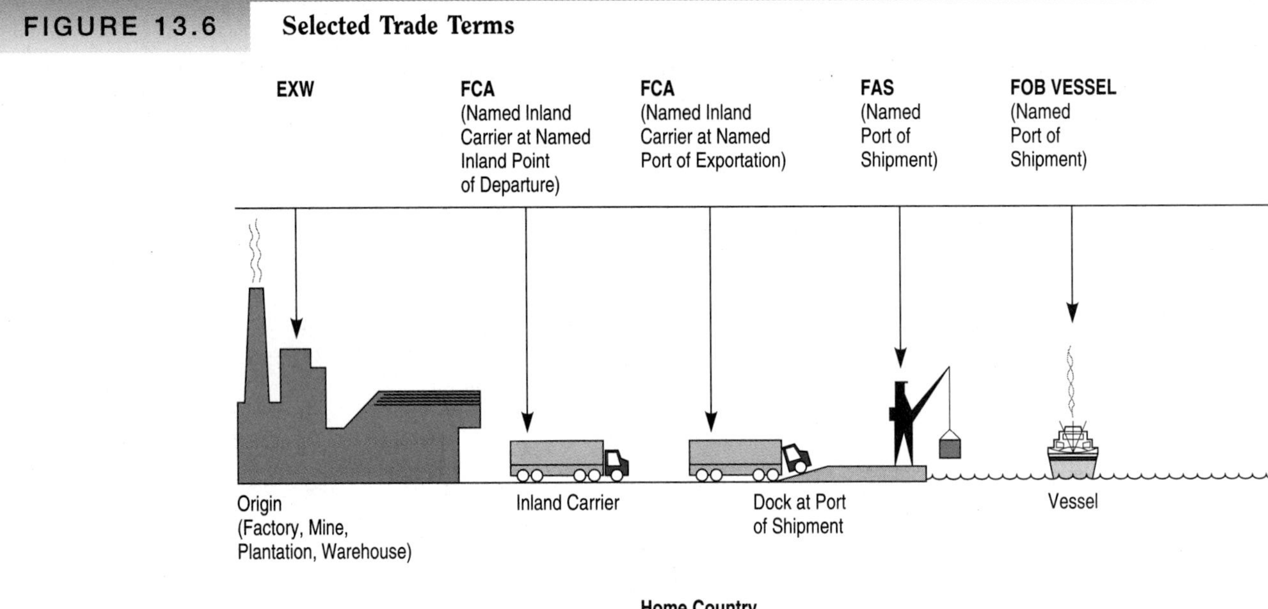

SOURCE: Ann Dwyer Maffry, *Foreign Commerce Handbook* (Washington, D.C.: Chamber of Commerce of the United States, 1981), 126–129.

These terms are also powerful competitive tools. The exporter should therefore learn what importers usually prefer in the particular market and what the specific transaction may require. An exporter should quote CIF whenever possible because it clearly shows the buyer the cost to get the product to a port in or near a desired country.

An inexperienced importer might be discouraged from further action by a quote such as ex-plant Jessup, Maryland, whereas CIF Kotka will enable the Finnish importer to handle the remaining costs because they are incurred at home.

INTERNATIONAL INVENTORY ISSUES

inventory carrying costs expense of maintaining inventories

just-in-time inventory materials scheduled to arrive precisely when they are needed on a production line

Inventories tie up a major portion of corporate funds. Capital used for inventory is not available for other corporate opportunities. Because annual **inventory carrying costs** (the expense of maintaining inventories) can easily account for 25 percent or more of the value of the inventories themselves[14] proper inventory policies should be of major concern to the international logistician. In addition, **just-in-time inventory** policies are increasingly being adopted by multinational manufacturers. These policies minimize the volume of inventory by having suppliers deliver it only when it is needed for the production process. Firms using such a policy will choose suppliers on the basis of their delivery and inventory performance. Proper inventory management may therefore become a key item in obtaining a sale.

In its international inventory management, the multinational corporation is faced not only with new situations that affect inventories negatively but also with new opportunities and alternatives.

The purpose of establishing *inventory* systems—to maintain product movement in the delivery pipeline—is the same for domestic and international operations. The international environment, however, includes unique factors such as currency exchange rates,

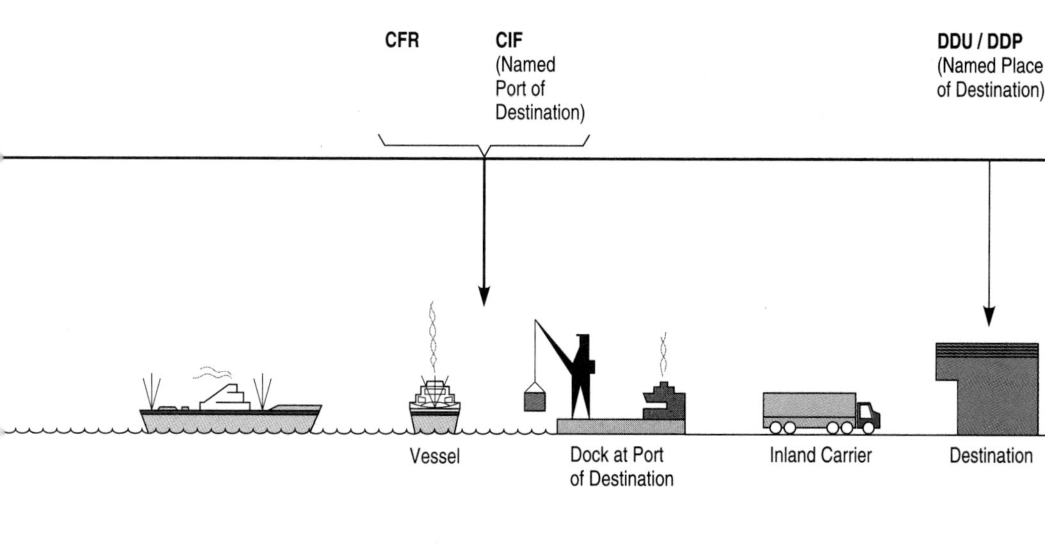

greater distances, and duties. At the same time, international operations provide the corporation with an opportunity to explore alternatives not available domestically, such as new sources of supply. In international operations, the firm can make use of currency fluctuations by placing varying degrees of emphasis on inventory operations, depending on the stability of the currency of a specific country. Entire operations can be shifted to different nations to take advantage of new opportunities. International inventory management can therefore be much more flexible in its response to environmental changes.

In deciding the level of inventory to be maintained, the international manager must consider three factors: the order cycle time, desired customer-service levels, and use of inventories as a strategic tool.

Order Cycle Time The total time that passes between the placement of an order and the receipt of the merchandise is referred to as **order cycle time.** Two dimensions are of major importance to inventory management: the length of the total order cycle and its consistency. In international business, the order cycle is frequently longer than in domestic business. It comprises the time involved in order transmission, order filling, packing and preparation for shipment, and transportation. Order transmission time varies greatly internationally depending on whether facsimile, telex, telephone, or mail is used in communicating. The order-filling time may also be increased because lack of familiarity with a foreign market makes the anticipation of new orders more difficult. Packing and shipment preparation requires more detailed attention. Finally, of course, transportation time increases with the distances involved. As a result, total order cycle time frequently approaches 100 days or more.[15] Larger inventories may have to be maintained both domestically and internationally in order to bridge these time gaps.

order cycle time
total time that passes between the placement of an order and the receipt of the merchandise

Consistency, the second dimension of order cycle time, is also more difficult to maintain in international business. Depending on the choice of transportation mode, delivery times may vary considerably from shipment to shipment. This variation requires the maintenance of larger safety stocks in order to be able to fill demand in periods when delays occur.

The international inventory manager should attempt to reduce order cycle time and increase its consistency without an increase in total costs. This can be accomplished by altering methods of transportation, changing inventory locations, or improving any of the other components of the order cycle time, such as the way orders are transmitted. Shifting order placement from a mail to a facsimile system can significantly reduce the order cycle time. Yet because such a shift is likely to increase the cost of order transmittal, offsetting savings in other inventory areas must be achieved.

customer service
total corporate effort aimed at customer satisfaction; customer services levels in terms of responsiveness that inventory policies permit for a given situation

Customer-Service Levels The level of **customer service** denotes the responsiveness that inventory policies permit to any given situation. A customer-service level of 100 percent would be defined as the ability to fill all orders within a set time—for example, three days. If within the same three days only 70 percent of the orders can be filled, the customer-service level is 70 percent. The choice of customer-service level for the firm has a major impact on the inventories needed. Higher service levels require the company to keep more inventory on hand, thus raising inventory carrying costs. In their domestic operations, U.S. companies frequently aim to achieve customer-service levels of 90 to 95 percent. Often, such "homegrown" rules of thumb are then used in international inventory operations as well.

Many managers do not realize that standards determined by rule of thumb and based on competitive activity in the home market are often inappropriate abroad. Different locales have country-specific customer-service needs and requirements. Service levels should not be oriented primarily around cost or customary domestic standards. Rather, the level chosen for use internationally should be based on expectations encountered in each market. These expectations are dependent on past performance, product desirability, customer sophistication, and the competitive status of the firm.

Because high customer-service levels are costly, the goal should not be the highest customer-service level possible, but rather an acceptable level. If, for example, foreign customers expect to receive their merchandise within 30 days, for the international corporation to promise delivery within 10 or 15 days does not make sense. Customers may not demand or expect such quick delivery. Indeed, such delivery may result in storage problems. In addition, the higher prices associated with higher customer-service levels may reduce the competitiveness of a firm's product.

Inventory as a Strategic Tool International inventories can be used by the international corporation as a strategic tool in dealing with currency valuation changes or hedging against inflation. By increasing inventories before an imminent devaluation of a currency instead of holding cash, the corporation may reduce its exposure to devaluation losses. Similarly, in the case of high inflation, large inventories can provide an important inflation hedge. In such circumstances, the international inventory manager must balance the cost of maintaining high levels of inventories with the benefits accruing to the firm from hedging against inflation or devaluation. Many countries charge a property tax on stored goods. If the increase in tax payments outweighs the hedging benefits to the corporation, it would be unwise to increase inventories before a devaluation.

Despite the benefits of reducing the firm's financial risk, inventory management must still fall in line with the overall corporate market strategy. Only by recognizing the trade-offs, which may result in less than optimal inventory policies, can the overall benefit to the corporation be maximized. Operations-research models can be very helpful in modeling such trade-offs.

Stresses in Intermodal Movement FIGURE 13.7

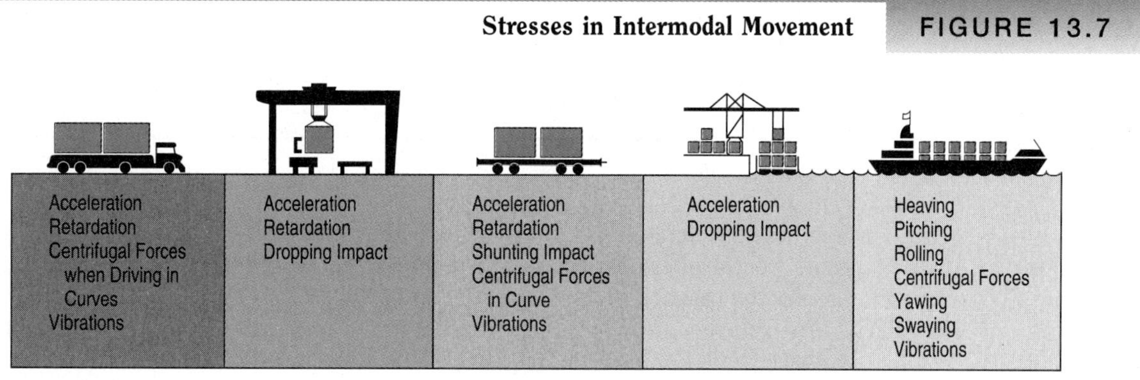

NOTE: Each transportation mode exerts a different set of stresses and strains on containerized cargoes. The most commonly overlooked are those associated with ocean transport.

SOURCE: David Greenfield, "Perfect Packing for Export," from *Handling and Shipping Management* (now *Transportation and Distribution*), September 1980 (Cleveland, Ohio: Penton Publishing), 47.

INTERNATIONAL PACKAGING ISSUES

Packaging is of particular importance in international distribution because it is instrumental in getting the merchandise to the ultimate destination in a safe, maintainable, and presentable condition. Packaging that is adequate for domestic shipping, such as the corrugated carton, would be inadequate for international transportation because the shipment will be subject to the motions of the vessel on which it is carried. Added stress in international shipping also arises from the transfer of goods among different modes of transportation. Figure 13.7 provides examples of some sources of stress in intermodal movement that are most frequently found in international transportation.

The responsibility for appropriate packaging rests with the shipper of goods. The U.S. Carriage of Goods by Sea Act of 1936 states: "Neither the carrier nor the ship shall be responsible for loss or damage arising or resulting from insufficiency of packing." The shipper must therefore ensure that the goods are prepared appropriately for international shipping. This is important because it has been found that "the losses that occur as a result of breakage, pilferage, and theft exceed the losses caused by major maritime casualties, which include fires, sinkings, and collision of vessels. Thus, the largest of these losses is a preventable loss."[16]

Packaging decisions must also take into account differences in environmental conditions—for example, climate. When the ultimate destination is very humid or particularly cold, special provisions must be made to prevent damage to the product. In humid climates, the air in a ship's hold may contain hundreds of gallons of water. A drop in temperature caused by sailing into a cooler climate will cause the humid air to turn into drops of water which will fall on the cargo below. If not properly protected, the cargo can be stained, rusted, or ruined.

The weight of packaging must also be considered, particularly when airfreight is used, as the cost of shipping is often based on weight. At the same time, packaging material must be sufficiently strong to permit stacking in international transportation.

How deep is the ocean?

The average depth of the ocean is more than 3,600 feet. The greatest known depth is in the Pacific Ocean, Mariana Trench. It's 36,198 feet deep.

Another consideration is that, in some countries, duties are assessed according to the gross weight of shipments, which includes the weight of packaging. Obviously, the heavier the packaging, the higher the duties will be.

The shipper must pay sufficient attention to instructions provided by the customer for packaging. For example, requests by the customer that the weight of any one package should not exceed a certain limit, or that specific package dimensions should be adhered to, usually are made for a reason. Often, they reflect limitations in transportation or handling facilities at the point of destination. It is also necessary to put handling instructions on packages in two languages, one being the language at the port of destination.

Although the packaging of a product is often used as a form of display abroad, international packaging can rarely serve the dual purpose of protection and display. Therefore double packaging may be necessary. The display package is for future use at the point of destination; another package surrounds it for protective purposes.

One solution to the packaging problem in international distribution has been the development of intermodal containers—large metal boxes that fit on trucks, ships, railroad cars, and airplanes and ease the frequent transfer of goods in international shipments. In addition, containers offer greater safety from pilferage and damage. Ironically, theft-resistant containers sometimes work to the advantage of the thief. Global Learning Experience 13.4 illustrates how U.S. auto thieves are using intermodal containers to reach global markets. Developed in different forms for both sea and air transportation, containers also offer better utilization of carrier space because of standardization of size. The shipper therefore may benefit from lower transportation rates.

Container traffic is heavily dependent on the existence of appropriate container handling facilities, like dockside Gantry cranes and/or shipboard cranes, both domestically and internationally. In addition, the quality of inland transportation equipment must be considered. If transportation for containers is not available and the merchandise must be removed from the container and shipped loose, the expected cost reductions may not materialize.

In some countries, rules for the handling of containers may be designed to maintain employment. For example, U.S. union rules obligate shippers to withhold containers from firms that do not employ members of the International Longshoremen's Association for the loading or unloading of containers within a 50-mile radius of Atlantic or Gulf ports. Such restrictions can result in an onerous cost burden. Packaging issues also need to be closely linked to overall strategic plans. The international distribution manager should focus on the total delivery picture to ensure customer satisfaction. The type of packaging, method of transportation, route, country of destination, port facilities, customs procedures, identification markings, final destination, and customer specifications all need to be taken into consideration when packing goods for export.

Overall, close attention must be paid to international packaging. The customer who ordered and paid for the merchandise expects it to arrive on time and in good condition. Even with replacements and insurance, the customer will not be satisfied if there are delays. This dissatisfaction will usually translate directly into lost sales.

GLOBAL LEARNING EXPERIENCE

13.4

U.S. Auto Thieves Go Global

If automobile theft were a legitimate business, it would rank No. 56 on the Fortune 500 list—somewhere between Coca-Cola and Union Carbide. Because of improved law enforcement activity, business is getting tighter in the domestic market so, like executives in any competitive industry, car thieves are looking for markets abroad.

Each year, approximately 1.5 million motor vehicles are stolen in the United States and about 62 percent are recovered. Of the unrecovered 38 percent, or 570,000 vehicles, it is estimated that 200,000 to 300,000 are exported. Most exported vehicles are late-model luxury and 4-wheel-drive models.

U.S. car thieves have been quick to utilize modern physical distribution methods—particularly the use of the intermodal container. The National Insurance Crime Bureau indicates that a large number of stolen vehicles exported are containerized. In some cases, the thieves change the identification numbers on the cars and drive them straight onto a roll-on, roll-off ship. A single 40-foot container can hold two to four stolen autos.

There are model preferences for stolen cars in various parts of the world. The Chinese in Hong Kong go for luxury cars—Mercedes, Jaguar, Porsche, Lexus, etc. In the Middle East, it's BMW, Cadillac, and Lincoln Town Car. The Poles and Russians prefer Oldsmobiles and Ford Escorts. Mexico, one of the top markets for illegal auto exports, seems to crave Ford Explorers and Nissan Pathfinders.

In a recent case (April 1997), U.S. and Hong Kong officials found four Lexus LS 400s in one container. The vehicles had been stolen in New York. The container was shipped to the West Coast by rail and then by sea to Hong Kong. Valued at approximately $53,000 each, the vehicles could have been sold for $100,000 to $180,000 apiece in the Hong Kong market.

The U.S. Customs Service is not staffed to cope with the volume of inbound and outbound containers and most of the stolen exports go undetected. However, when U.S. Customs does discover a stolen car hidden in a container before it leaves the country, they remove the car and tape a matchbox model car to the bottom of the container and send it on. At the other end, the recipient—expecting a $50,000 Mercedes—finds instead a huge space occupied by a toy car.

SOURCE: Adapted from "Squeezed at Home, Car Thieves Wheel and Deal Overseas," *Journal of Commerce,* August 8, 1995: 1A; and data provided by National Insurance Crime Bureau.

INTERNATIONAL STORAGE ISSUES

Although international distribution is discussed as a movement or flow of goods, a stationary period is involved when merchandise becomes inventory stored in warehouses. On the one hand, customers may expect quick responses to orders and rapid delivery. Accommodating the customer's expectations may require locating many distribution centers around the world. On the other hand, warehousing space is expensive. In addition, the larger volume of inventory increases the inventory carrying cost. The international distribution manager must consider the trade-offs between service and cost to determine the appropriate levels of warehousing. Other trade-offs also exist within the logistics function. As an example, fewer warehouses will allow for consolidation of transportation and therefore lower transportation rates to the warehouse. However, if the warehouses are located far from customers, the cost of outgoing transportation from them will increase.

Storage Facilities

location decision
decision as to the number of distribution centers that should be utilized and where they are to be located

Distribution management is faced with the **location decision** of how many distribution centers to have and where to locate them. The availability of facilities abroad will differ from the domestic situation. While public storage is widely available in the United States, such facilities may be scarce or entirely lacking abroad. Also, the standards and quality of facilities abroad are often not comparable to those available in the United States. As a result, the storage decision of the firm is often accompanied by the need for large-scale, long-term investments. Despite the high cost, international storage facilities should be established if they support the overall distribution effort. In many markets, adequate storage facilities are imperative in order to satisfy customer demands and to compete successfully.

Once the decision is made to utilize storage facilities abroad, the warehouses must be carefully analyzed. In some countries, warehouses have low ceilings. Packaging developed for the high stacking of products is therefore unnecessary. In other countries, automated warehousing is available. Proper bar coding of products and the use of package dimensions acceptable to the warehousing system are basic requirements. In contrast, in warehouses still stocked manually, weight limitations will be of major concern.

To optimize the distribution system, the management should analyze international product sales and then give priority to products according to warehousing needs. Products that are most sensitive to delivery time may be classified as "A" products. "A" products would be stocked in all distribution centers, and safety stock levels would be kept high. Products for which immediate delivery is not urgent may be classified as "B" products. They would be stored only at selected distribution centers around the world. Finally, products for which short delivery time is not important, or for which there is little demand, would be stocked only at headquarters. Should an urgent need for delivery arise, airfreight could be considered for rapid shipment. Classifying products enables the international distribution manager to substantially reduce total international warehousing requirements and still maintain acceptable service levels.

Special Trade Zones

foreign trade zones
areas where foreign goods may be held or processed and then reexported without incurring duties

Areas where foreign goods may be held or processed and then reexported without incurring duties are called **foreign trade zones.**[17] These zones can be found at major ports of entry and also at inland locations near major production facilities. For example, Kansas City, Missouri, has one of the largest foreign trade zones in the United States.

The existence of trade zones can be quite useful to the international firm. In a particular country, the benefits derived from lower factor costs, such as labor, may be offset by high duties and tariffs. As a result, location of manufacturing and storage facilities in that country may prove uneconomical. Foreign trade zones are designed to exclude the impact of duties from the location decision. This is done by exempting merchandise in the foreign trade zone from duty payment. The international firm can therefore import merchandise; store it in the foreign trade zone; and process, alter, test or demonstrate it—all without paying duties. If the merchandise is subsequently shipped abroad (that is, reexported), no duty payments are ever due. Duty payments become due only if the merchandise is shipped into the country from the foreign trade zone.

All parties to the arrangement benefit from foreign trade zones. The government maintaining the trade zone achieves increased employment and investment. The firm using the trade zone obtains a spearhead in the foreign market without incurring all of the costs customarily associated with such an activity. As a result, goods can be reassembled, and large shipments can be broken down into smaller units. Also, goods can be repackaged when packaging weight becomes part of the duty assessment. Finally,

Mobil Aims for Safety

Mobil Corporation's fleet of oil tankers navigates the world's oceans, delivering about 2 million barrels of crude oil and refined petroleum products each day to ports around the globe. That amounts to about 5 percent of the petroleum products transported worldwide by sea—or enough oil to power 30 million cars for a day. Gerhard Kurz, president of Mobil's shipping subsidiary, says that not a day goes by that he doesn't ponder lessons learned from the huge Exxon Valdez oil spill. Amazingly, Mobil's ships spilled a mere 8 barrels of oil in 1995.

Kurz and other industry executives say that the improving numbers on spills reflect a new emphasis on safety that has sharply reduced the risk of major oil spills, at least within U.S. waters. A key is to focus on prevention, they say, requiring modernized tankers, constant inspections, and a well-trained crew. Like any corporate executive, Mobil is also striving for profitability—and this can create tough decisions.

In Kurz's view, the high costs of new safety measures and building expensive but safer tankers are dwarfed by the potentially larger costs of oil spill cleanups and punitive lawsuits. "We do our shipping for safety and environmental reasons," said Kurz. "Our goal is to have a high quality operation that sets a benchmark . . . but we also want to provide safe, cost-effective transportation for the corporation."

So can Mobil provide safety and a sizable profit? Kurz believes that over the long run, Mobil's decision to spend heavily on more expensive, double-hull tankers may pay off in profits, partly because these ships are vastly more efficient than cheaper ones and require much less maintenance. Even the simplest of these large tankers will cost at least $80 million to build. This means that a shipowner must earn about $38,000 a day throughout the ship's life span to simply break even. This compares to about $20,000 a day for cheaper, single-hull ships.

Kurz foresees a time not too far off when shipowners will have to scrap many of their old takers and rush to build new, double-hull ones. (Under international rules, 25-year-old ships must be retired or replaced with double-hull ships.) At that point, the price of the ships will probably go up as a limited number of shipyards try to meet demand. Tanker scrappings will exceed new ship deliveries, and the world's demand for oil will expand. Then Mobil, with four double-hull ships already under construction or in service, will have an edge. Kurz believes, at this point, that Mobil will have it all—safety and profit.

SOURCE: Daniel Sutherland, "Mobilizing the Fleet," *The Washington Post,* June 23, 1996: H1.

goods can be given domestic "made-in" status if assembled in the foreign trade zone. Thus, duties may be payable only on the imported materials and component parts rather than on the labor that is used to finish the product.

For the distribution manager, the decision whether to use such zones is mainly framed by the overall benefit for the distribution system. Clearly, often transport and retransport are required, warehousing facilities need to be constructed, and material-handling frequency will increase. However, these costs may well be balanced by the preferential government treatment or by lower labor costs.

DISTRIBUTION AND THE ENVIRONMENT

Apart from the nature of the distribution function, major changes are also occurring in the strategic orientation of the function. The distribution manager plays an increasingly important role in allowing the firm to operate in an environmentally conscious way. Environmental laws, expectations, and self-imposed goals set by firms are difficult to adhere to without a distribution orientation that systematically takes these concerns into account. Since laws and regulations differ across the world, the firm's efforts need to be responsive to a wide variety of requirements. One new distribution orientation that has grown in importance due to environmental concerns is the development of **reverse distribution** systems. Such systems are instrumental in ensuring that the firm not only delivers the product to the market, but also can retrieve it from the market for subsequent use, recycling, or disposal. The ability to develop such a reverse distribution system is a key determinant for market acceptance and profitability.

reverse distribution system responding to environmental concerns that ensures a firm can retrieve a product from the market for subsequent use, recycling, or disposal

Society is also beginning to recognize that retrieval should not be restricted to short-term consumer goods, such as bottles. Rather, it may be even more important to devise systems that enable the retrieval and disposal of long-term capital goods, such as cars, refrigerators, air conditioners, and industrial goods, with the least possible burden on the environment. The design of such long-term systems across the world may well be one of the key challenges and opportunities for management and will require close collaboration with all other functions in the firm, such as design, production, and marketing.

On the transportation side, distribution managers will need to expand their involvement in carrier and routing selection. For shippers of oil or other potentially hazardous materials, it will be increasingly expected to ensure that the carriers used have excellent safety records and use only double-hulled ships. Society may even expect corporate involvement in choosing the route that the shipment will travel, preferring routes that are far from ecologically important and sensitive zones. Global Learning Experience 13.5 indicates how one oil company is handling these environmental concerns.

The distribution function will also need to consider trade-offs between distribution performance and the resulting environmental burden. For example, even though a just-in-time inventory system may connote highly desirable inventory savings, the resulting cost of frequent delivery, additional highway congestion, and incremental air pollution also need to be factored into the planning horizon. Despite the difficulty, firms will need to assert leadership in such trade-off considerations in order to provide society with a better quality of life.

SUMMARY

The relevance of international distribution was not widely recognized in the past. As competitiveness is becoming increasingly dependent on cost efficiency, however, the field is emerging as one of major importance, because international distribution accounts for between 10 and 25 percent of the total landed cost of an international order.

International distribution is concerned with the flow of materials into, through, and out of the global corporation and therefore includes materials management as well as physical distribution. The distribution manager must recognize the total systems demands of the firm in order to develop trade-offs between various distribution components.

International distribution differs from domestic activities in that it deals with greater distances, new variables, and greater complexity because of national differences. One major factor to consider is transportation. The global manager needs to understand transportation infrastructures in other countries and modes of transportation such as ocean shipping and airfreight. The choice among these modes will depend on the customer's demands and the firm's transit time, predictability, and cost requirements. In addition, noneconomic factors such as government regulations weigh heavily in this decision.

Inventory management is another major consideration. Inventories abroad are expensive to maintain yet often crucial for international success. The distribution manager must evaluate requirements for order cycle times and customer-service levels in order to develop an international inventory policy that can also serve as a strategic management tool.

International packaging is important because it ensures arrival of the merchandise at the ultimate destination in safe condition. In developing packaging requirements, environmental conditions such as climate and handling conditions must be considered.

The distribution manager must also deal with international storage issues and determine where to locate inventories. International warehouse space will have to be leased or purchased and decisions made about utilizing foreign trade zones.

International distribution management is increasing in importance. Connecting the distribution function with overall corporate strategic concerns will increasingly be a requirement for successful global competitiveness.

Key Terms and Concepts

systems concept
total cost concept
total after-tax profit concept
trade-off concept
transportation modes
land bridges
sea bridges
intermodal movements
container ships
lift-on, lift-off
roll-on, roll-off
third-generation ships
airfreight
transit time
reliability
preferential policies
bill of lading
straight bill of lading
shipper's order
commercial invoice
Incoterms
ex-works (EXW)
free carrier (FCA)
free alongside ship (FAS)
free on board (FOB)
cost and freight (CFR)
cost, insurance, and freight (CIF)
delivery duty paid (DDP)
delivery duty unpaid (DDU)
inventory carrying costs
just-in-time inventory
order cycle time
customer service
location decision
foreign trade zones
reverse distribution

Questions for Discussion

1. Why do global firms pay so little attention to global physical distribution issues?
2. Contrast the use of ocean shipping and airfreight.
3. Explain the meaning and impact of transit time in global distribution.
4. How and why do governments interfere in "rational" freight carrier selection?
5. How can a global firm reduce its order cycle time?
6. Why should customer-service levels differ globally? Is it, for example, ethical to offer a lower customer-service level in developing countries than in industrialized countries?
7. What role can the global distribution manager play in improving the environmental performance of the firm?

Recommended Readings

Ballou, Ronald H. *Business Logistics Management,* 3rd ed. Englewood Cliffs, N.J.: Prentice-Hall, 1992.

Bowersox, Donald J., Patricia J. Daugherty, Cornelia L. Droege, Richard N. Germain, and Dale S. Rogers. *Logistical Excellence.* Burlington, MA: Digital Press, 1992.

Christopher, Martin. *Logistics: The Strategic Issues.* New York: Chapman and Hall, 1992.

Coyle, John J., Edward J. Bardi, and C. John Langley Jr. *The Management of Business Logistics,* 6th ed. Minneapolis: West Publishing Company, 1996.

Johnson, James C., and Donald F. Wood. *Contemporary Logistics,* 6th ed. Upper Saddle River, N.J.: Prentice-Hall, 1996.

Kotabe, Masaaki. *Global Sourcing Strategy: R&D, Manufacturing and Marketing Interfaces.* New York: Quorum Books, 1992.

O'Laughlin, Kevin A., James Cooper, and Eric Cabocel. *Reconfiguring European Logistics Systems.* Oak Brook, Ill.: Council of Logistics Management, 1993.

Ross, Frederick David, *Distribution Planning and Control.* New York: Chapman & Hall, 1996.

Schary, Philip B., and Tage Skjott-Larsen. *Managing the Global Supply Chain.* Copenhagen Studies in Economics and Management: Copenhagen, 1995.

United Nations Conference on Trade and Development (UNCTAD), Review conference on the United Nations Convention on a Code of Conduct for Liner Conferences, Geneva, July 11, 1991.

Wood, Donald E. (ed.). *International Logistics.* New York: Chapman & Hall, 1994.

Notes

1. "Distribution's Vital Role," *Distribution* 79 (October 1980).
2. Dennis Davis, "New Involvement in the Orient," *Distribution* 78 (October 1979).
3. U.S. Department of Commerce, *Survey of Export Management Companies on the Export Trading Company Concept* (Washington, D.C.: Government Printing Office, 1977).
4. Paul T. Nelson and Gadi Toledano, "Challenges for International Logistics Management," *Journal of Business Logistics* 1, No. 2 (1979): 7.
5. Ibid., 2.
6. Robert L. Vidrick, "Transportation Cost Control—The Key to Successful Exporting," *Distribution* 79 (March 1980).
7. "Exporters Fight Costs and Rules of Brazil's Ports," *New York Times,* June 25, 1991.
8. William Armbruster, "W. German Ports Hope to Win East Bloc Trade," *The Journal of Commerce* (December 27, 1989): 1A.
9. Gunnar K. Sletmo and Jacques Picard, "International Distribution Policies and the Role of Air Freight," *Journal of Business Logistics* 6, No. 1 (1984): 35–52.
10. Klaus Wittkamp, "Rickshaws for Taiwan or Cattle for China, It's All Air Freight," *The German Tribune,* June 26, 1983, 10.
11. Julie Wolf, "Help for Distribution in Europe," *Northeast International Business,* January 1989, 52.
12. *A Basic Guide to Exporting* (Washington, D.C.: U.S. Department of Commerce, 1986), 64.
13. Kevin Maloney, "Incoterms: Clarity at the Profit Margin," *Export Today* 6 (November–December 1990): 45–46.
14. Bernard J. LaLonde and Paul H. Zinszer, *Customer Service: Meaning and Measurement* (Chicago: National Council of Physical Distribution Management, 1976).
15. Michael R. Czinkota, Harvey J. Iglarsh, Richard L. Seeley, and James Sood, "The Role of Order Cycle Time for the Latin American Exporting Firm," (presentation at the Annual Meeting of the Academy of International Business, New Orleans, La., October 21, 1980), 9.
16. Charles A. Taft, *Management of Physical Distribution and Transportation,* 7th ed. (Homewood, Ill.: Irwin, 1984), 324.
17. Ronald H. Ballou, *Basic Business Logistics* (Englewood Cliffs, N.J.: Prentice-Hall, 1978), 445.

Lakewood Forest Products

Since the 1970s, the United States has had a merchandise trade deficit with the rest of the world. Up to 1982, this deficit mattered little because it was relatively small. As of 1983, however, the trade deficit increased rapidly and became, due to its size and future implications, an issue of major national concern. Suddenly, trade moved to the forefront of national debate. Concurrently, a debate ensued on the issue of the international competitiveness of U.S. firms. The onerous question here was whether U.S. firms could and would achieve sufficient improvements in areas such as productivity, quality, and price to remain successful international marketing players in the long term.

The U.S.–Japanese trade relation took on particular significance because it was between those two countries that the largest bilateral trade deficit existed. In spite of trade negotiations, market-opening measures, trade legislation, and other governmental efforts, it was clear that the impetus for a reversal of the deficit through more U.S. exports to Japan had to come from this private sector. Therefore, the activities of any U.S. firm that appeared successful in penetrating the Japanese market were widely hailed. One company whose effort to market in Japan aroused particular interest was Lakewood Forest Products, in Hibbing, Minnesota.

COMPANY BACKGROUND

In 1983, Ian J. Ward was an export merchant in difficulty. Throughout the 1970s, his company, Ward, Bedas Canadian Ltd., had successfully sold Canadian lumber and salmon to countries in the Persian Gulf. Over time, the company had opened four offices worldwide. However, when the Iran-Iraq war erupted, most of Ward's long-term trading relationships disappeared within a matter of months. In addition, the international lumber market began to collapse. As a result, Ward, Bedas Canadian Ltd. went into a survivalist mode and sent employees all over the world to look for new markets and business opportunities. Late that year, the company received an interesting order. A firm in Korea urgently needed to purchase lumber for the production of chopsticks.

Learning about the Chopstick Market

In discussing the wood deal with the Koreans, Ward learned that in the production of good chopsticks, more than 60 percent of the wood fiber is wasted. Given the high transportation cost involved, the large degree of wasted materials, and his need for new business, Ward decided to explore the Korean and Japanese chopstick industry in more detail.

He quickly determined that chopstick making in the Far East is a fragmented industry, working with old technology and suffering from a lack of natural resources. In Asia, chopsticks are produced in very small quantities, often by family organizations. Even the largest of the 450 chopstick factories in Japan turns out only 5 million chopsticks

SOURCE: This case was written by Michael R. Czinkota based on the following sources: Mark Clayton, "Minnesota Chopstick Maker Finds Japanese Eager to Import His Quality Waribashi," *Christian Science Monitor,* October 16, 1987, 11; Roger Worthington, "Improbable Chopstick Capital of the World," *Chicago Tribune,* June 5, 1988, 39; Mark Gill, "The Great American Chopstick Master," *American Way,* August 1, 1987, 34, 78–79; "Perpich of Croatia," *Economist,* April 20, 1991, 27; interview with Ian J. Ward, president, Lakewood Forest Products.

a month. This compares with an overall market size of 130 million pairs of disposable chopsticks a day. In addition, chopsticks represent a growing market. With increased wealth in Asia, people eat out more often and therefore have a greater demand for disposable chopsticks. The fear of communicable diseases has greatly reduced the utilization of reusable chopsticks. Renewable plastic chopsticks have been attacked by many groups as too newfangled and as causing future ecological problems.

From his research, Ward concluded that a competitive niche existed in the world chopstick market. He believed that if he could use low-cost raw materials and ensure that the labor cost component would remain small, he could successfully compete in the world market.

The Founding of Lakewood Forest Products

In exploring opportunities afforded by the newly identified international marketing niche for chopsticks, Ward set four criteria for plant location:

1. Access to suitable raw materials
2. Proximity of other wood product users who could make use of the 60 percent waste for their production purposes
3. Proximity to a port that would facilitate shipment to the Far East
4. Availability of labor

In addition, Ward was aware of the importance of product quality. Because people use chopsticks on a daily basis and are accustomed to products that are visually inspected one by one, he would have to live up to high quality expectations in order to compete successfully. Chopsticks could not be bowed or misshapen, have blemishes in the wood, or splinter.

To implement his plan, Ward needed financing. Private lenders were skeptical and slow to provide funds. This skepticism resulted from the unusual direction of Ward's proposal. Far Eastern companies have generally held the cost advantage in a variety of industries, especially those as labor-intensive as chopstick manufacturing. U.S. companies rarely have an advantage in producing low-cost items. Further, only a very small domestic market exists for chopsticks.

However, Ward found that the state of Minnesota was willing to participate in his new venture. Since the decline of the mining industry, regional unemployment had been rising rapidly in the state. In 1983, unemployment in Minnesota's Iron Range peaked at 22 percent. Therefore, state and local officials were eager to attract new industries that would be independent of mining activities. Of particular help was the enthusiasm of Governor Rudy Perpich. The governor had been boosting Minnesota business on the international scene by traveling abroad and receiving many foreign visitors. He was excited about Ward's plans, which called for the creation of over 100 new jobs within a year.

Hibbing, Minnesota, turned out to be an ideal location for Ward's project. The area had an abundance of aspen wood, which, because it grows in clay soil, tends to be unmarred. The fact that Hibbing was the hometown of the governor also did not hurt. In addition, Hibbing boasted an excellent labor pool, and both the city and the state were willing to make loans totaling $500,000. Further, the Iron Range Resources Rehabilitation Board was willing to sell $3.4 million in industrial revenue bonds for the project. Together with jobs and training wage subsidies, enterprise zone credits, and tax increment financing benefits, the initial public support of the project added up to about 30 percent of its start-up costs. The potential benefit of the new venture to the region was quite clear. When Lakewood Forest Products advertised its first 30 jobs, more than 3,000 people showed up to apply.

THE PRODUCTION AND SALE OF CHOPSTICKS

Ward insisted that in order to truly penetrate the international market, he would need to keep his labor cost low. As a result, he decided to automate as much of the production as possible. However, no equipment was readily available to produce chopsticks because no one had automated the process before.

After much searching, Ward identified a European equipment manufacturer that produced machinery for making popsicle sticks. He purchased equipment from this Danish firm in order to better carry out the sorting and finishing processes. However, because aspen wood was quite different from the wood the machine was designed for, as was the final product, substantial design adjustments had to be made. Sophisticated equipment was also purchased to strip the bark from the wood and peel it into long, thin sheets. Finally, a computer vision system was acquired to detect defects in the chopsticks. This system rejected over 20 percent of the production, and yet some of the chopsticks that passed inspection were splintering. However, Ward firmly believed that further fine-tuning of the equipment and training of the new work force would gradually take care of the problem.

Given this fully automated process, Lakewood Forest Products was able to develop capacity for up to 7 million chopsticks a day. With a unit manufacturing cost of $0.03 and an anticipated unit selling price of $0.057, Ward expected to earn a pretax profit of $4.7 million in 1988.

Due to intense marketing efforts in Japan and the fact that Japanese customers were struggling to obtain sufficient supplies of disposable chopsticks, Ward was able to presell the first five years of production quite quickly. By late 1987, Lakewood Forest Products was ready to enter the international market. With an ample study of raw materials and an almost totally automated plant, Lakewood was positioned as the world's largest and least labor-intensive manufacturer of chopsticks. The first shipment of six containers with a load of 12 million pairs of chopsticks was sent to Japan in October 1987.

Questions for Discussion

1. What are the future implications of continuing large U.S. trade deficits?
2. What are the important variables for the international marketing success of chopsticks?
3. Rank the variables in Question 2 according to the priority you believe they have for foreign customers.
4. Why haven't Japanese firms thought of automating the chopstick production process?
5. How long will Lakewood Forest Products be able to maintain its competitive advantage?

Water from Iceland[1]

Stan Otis was in a contemplative mood. He had just hung up the phone after talking with Roger Morey, vice president of Citicorp. Morey had made him a job offer in the investment banking sector of the firm. The interviews had gone well, and Citicorp management was impressed with Stan's credentials from a major northeastern private university. "I think you can do well here, Stan. Let us know within a week whether you accept the job," Morey had said.

The three-month search had paid off well, Stan thought. However, an alternative plan complicated the decision to accept the position.

Stan had returned several months before from an extended trip throughout Europe, a delayed graduation present from his parents. Among other places, he had visited Reykjavik, Iceland. Even though he could not communicate well, he found the island enchanting. What particularly fascinated him was the lack of industry and the purity of the natural landscape. In particular, he felt the water tasted extremely good. Returning home, he began to consider making the water available in the United States.

THE WATER MARKET IN THE UNITED STATES

In order to consider the possibilities of importing Icelandic water, Stan knew that he first had to learn more about the general water market in the United States. Fortunately, some former college friends were working in a market research firm. Owing Stan some favors, these friends furnished him with a consulting report on the water market.

The Consulting Report

Bottled water has almost a 10 percent market share of total beverage consumption in the United States. The overall distribution of market share is shown in Figure 1. Primary types of water available for human consumption in the United States are treated or processed water, mineral water, sparkling or effervescent water, spring well water, club soda, and tonic water.

Treated or processed water comes from a well stream or central reservoir supply. This water usually flows as tap water and has been purified and fluoridated.

Mineral water is spring water that contains a substantial amount of minerals, which may be injected or occur naturally. Natural mineral water is obtained from underground water strata or a natural spring. The composition of the water at its source is constant, and the source discharge and temperature remain stable. The natural content of the water at the source is not modified by an artificial process.

Sparkling or effervescent water is water with natural or artificial carbonation. Some mineral waters come to the surface naturally carbonated through underground gases but lose their fizz on the surface with normal pressure. Many of these waters are injected with carbon dioxide later on.

Club soda is obtained by adding artificial carbonation to distilled or regular tap water. Mineral content in this water depends on the water supply used and the purifica-

[1]*SOURCE:* This study was prepared by Michael R. Czinkota and Veronika Cveckova, using the following background material: International Bottled Water Association statistics; "Top 10 Bottled Water Companies: 1994," *Beverage World,* March 1995; "Water in Order," *Beverage World*, September 1996; Ann Arbor, "Consumers Reach for Bottled Water," *Arroyo,* March 1996.

FIGURE 1

Retail Market Shares of Beverage Products in 1995

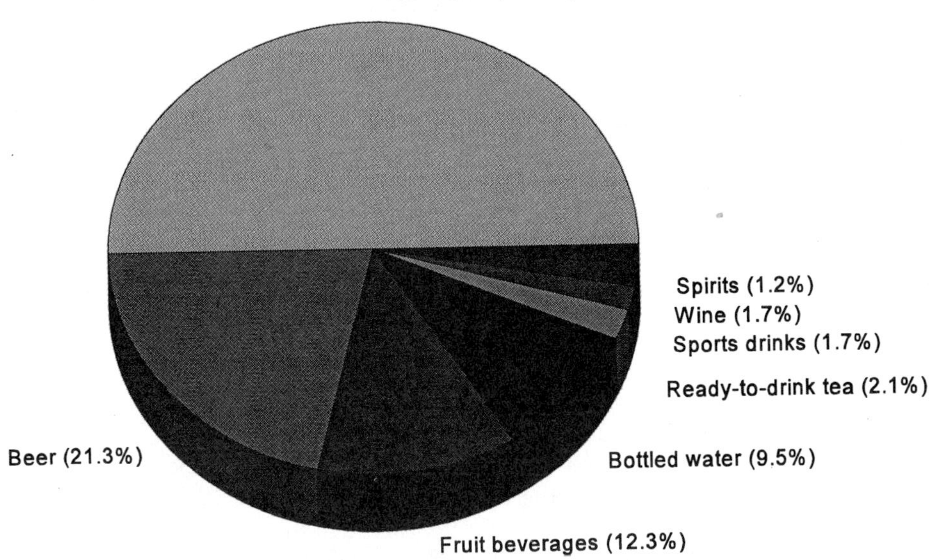

SOURCE: *Beverage World.*

tion process the water has undergone. Tonic water is derived from the same process as club soda, but has bitters added to it.

Minerals are important to the taste and quality of water. The type and variety of minerals present in the water can make it a very healthy and enjoyable drink. The combination of minerals present in the water determines its relative degree of acidity. The level of acidity is measured by the pH factor. A pH 7 rating indicates a neutral water. A higher rating indicates that the water contains more solids, such as manganese calcium, and is said to be "hard." Conversely, water with a lower rating is classified as "soft." Most tap water is soft, whereas the majority of commercially sold waters tend to be hard.

Water Consumption in the United States

Tap water has generally been inexpensive, relatively pure, and plentiful in the United States. Traditionally, bottled water has been consumed in the United States by the very wealthy. In the past several years, however, bottled water has begun to appeal to a wider market. The four reasons for this change are:

1. An increasing awareness among consumers of the impurity of city water supplies
2. Increasing dissatisfaction with the taste and odor of city tap water
3. Rising affluence in society
4. An increasing desire to avoid excess consumption of caffeine, sugar, and other substances present in coffee and soft drinks

Bottled water consumers are found chiefly in the states of California, Florida, Texas, New York, and Illinois. Combined, these states represent 52 percent of nationwide bottled water sales. California alone represents over 29 percent of industry sales. Nationwide, bottled water is drunk by one out of every fifteen households. The per

TABLE 1 **U.S. Beverage Consumption in 1995**

	Retail Receipts in Billions of Dollars	Per Capital Consumption in Gallons
Soft drinks	52.1	52.1
Beer	51.6	22.1
Spirits	32.4	1.2
Fruit beverages	12.5	12.6
Wine	12.1	1.8
Bottled Water	4.0	9.9
Ready-to-drink tea	2.8	2.2
Sports drinks	1.8	1.7

SOURCE: *Beverage World.*

capita consumption in 1995 was estimated at 9.9 gallons. (For comparison of per capita consumption of bottled water and other beverages see Table 1.)

Before 1976, bottled water was considered primarily a gourmet specialty, a luxury item consumed by the rich. Today, there are over 700 brands of bottled water available on the U.S. market. Since the entry of Perrier Group into the U.S. market, bottled water consumption has shown exceptional growth. The volume of bottled water sold rose from 255 million gallons in 1976 to 2.7 billion gallons in 1995. Over the past decade, the U.S. consumption of bottled water increased by over 200 percent, taking market share from beverages such as coffee, tea, milk, juice, and alcoholic drinks.

In 1995, the industry's receipts totaled $2.9 billion in the wholesale and $4.1 billion at the retail level, an 8 percent increase from 1994. While bottled water gallonage increased by 8 percent between 1994 and 1995, nonsparkling bottled water volume was up by 9.7 percent for the same period. For more information on the growth of bottled water consumption in the United States, see Figures 2 and 3. Nonsparkling water accounts for over 90 percent of total bottled water gallonage.

As Figure 4 shows, in 1995, imported water held a 3.6 percent share of the domestic market in terms of volume but a 14.4 percent share in terms of wholesale prices (see Table 2). The leading country importing water to the U.S. is France, with a 61.6 percent share of total bottled water imports. Canada is second with 25.5 percent, and Italy third with 7 percent of the imported gallonage (see Figure 5).

Among producers, Perrier is a strong leader with a 25 percent market share. The Perrier Group's top three selling bottled water brands are Arrowhead, Poland Spring, and Ozarka. McKesson holds 8 percent of the market and Anjou International 5.2 percent.

Overall, a cursory analysis indicates good potential for success for a new importer of bottled water in the United States. This is especially true if the water is exceptionally pure and can be classified as mineral water.

ADDITIONAL RESEARCH

Further exploring his import idea, Stan Otis gathered information on various other marketing facets. One of his main concerns was government regulations.

Bottled Water Regulations in the United States

The bottled water industry in the United States is regulated and controlled at two levels—by the federal government and various state governments. Some states, such

U.S. Bottled Water Sales in Billions of Wholesale Dollars FIGURE 2

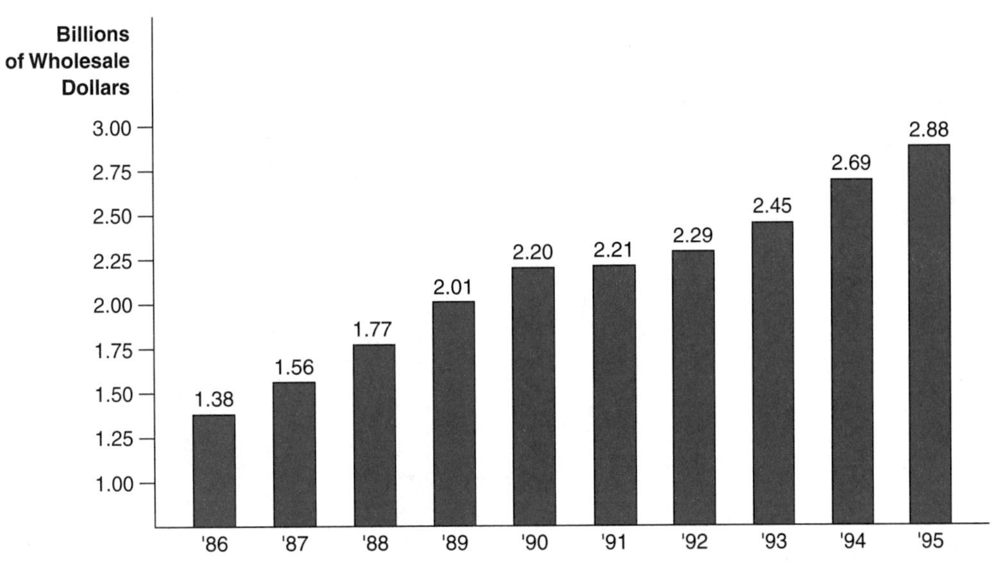

SOURCE: Beverage Marketing Corporation.

U.S. Beverage Consumption: Growth Over the Past Ten Years FIGURE 3

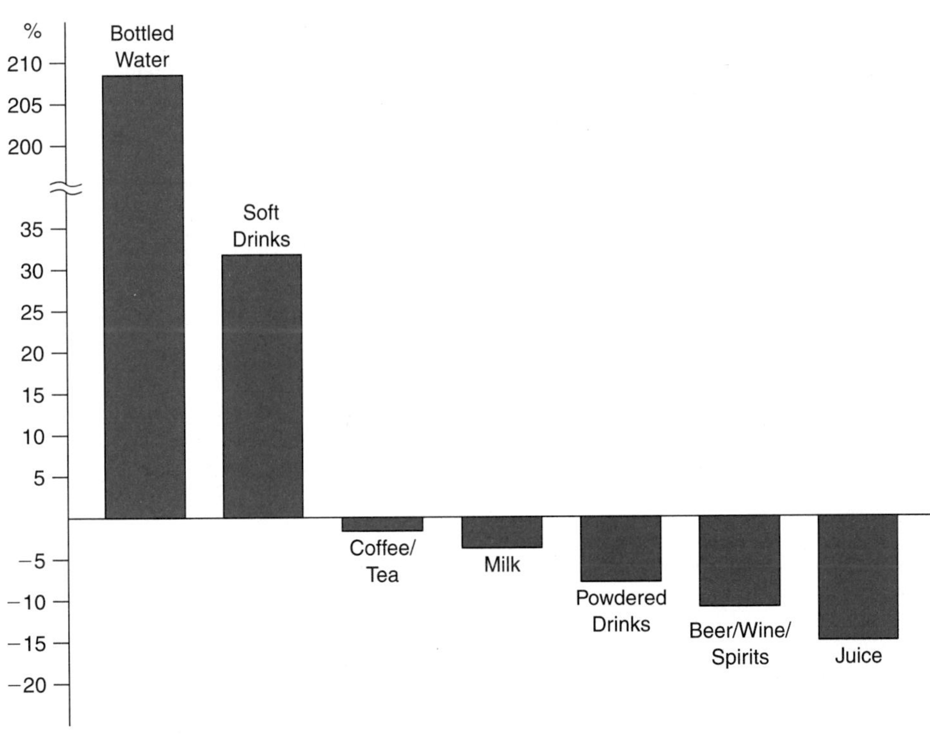

SOURCE: Norland International, Inc.

FIGURE 4 **Market Share of Bottled Water by Segment in 1995 (Based on Volume)**

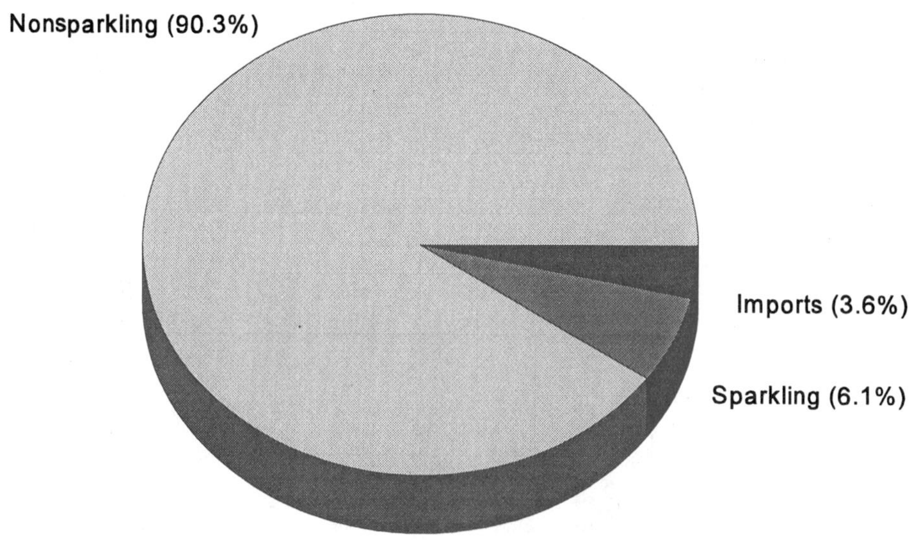

SOURCE: International Bottled Water Association.

as California and Florida, impose even stricter regulations on bottled water than they are required to follow under the federal regulations. Others, such as Arizona, do not regulate the bottled water industry beyond the federal requirements. About 75 percent of bottled water is obtained from springs, artesian wells, and drilled wells. The other 25 percent comes from municipal water systems which are regulated by the Environmental Protection Agency (EPA). All bottled water is considered food and is thus regulated by the Food and Drug Administration (FDA). Under the 1974 Safe Drinking Water Act, the

TABLE 2 **Share of Imports in U.S. Bottled Water Market**

	Estimated Wholesale Dollars	Gallonage
1984	8%	1.8%
1985	11.7%	2.8%
1986	10%	2.6%
1987	11%	2.7%
1988	12.1%	3.1%
1989	11.9%	3.1%
1990	13%	3.7%
1991	11.2%	3.5%
1992	12.6%	4.1%
1993	15%	4.1%
1994	16.2%	4.2%
1995	14.4%	3.6%

SOURCE: International Bottled Water Association.

Bottled Water Imports by Country in 1995 (Based on Volume) FIGURE 5

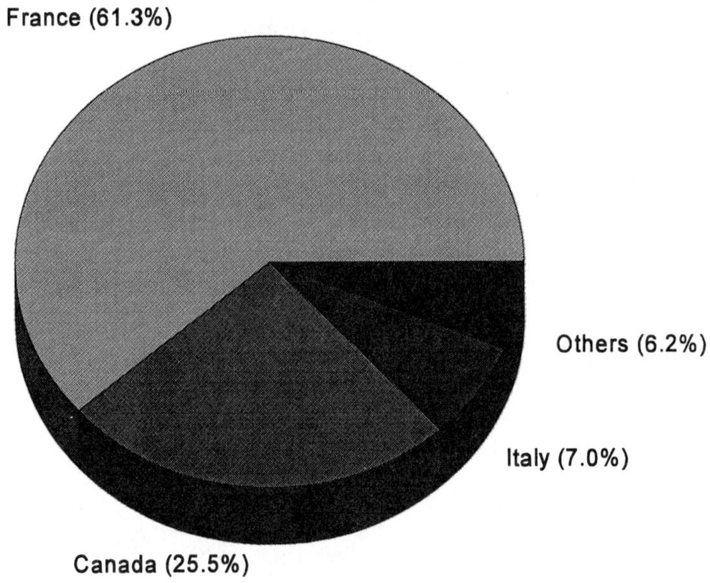

SOURCE: Beverage Marketing Corporation.

FDA adopted bottled water standards compatible with EPA's standards for water from public water systems. As the EPA revises its drinking water regulations, the FDA is required to revise its standards for bottled water or explain in the Federal Register why it decided not to do so. The FDA requires bottled water products to be clean and safe for human consumption, processed and distributed under sanitary conditions, and produced in compliance with FDA good manufacturing practices. In addition, domestic bottled water producers engaged in interstate commerce are subject to periodic, unannounced FDA inspections.

In 1991, an investigation by the U.S. House Energy and Commerce Committee found that 25 percent of the higher-priced bottled water comes from the same sources as ordinary tap water, another 25 percent of producers were unable to document their sources of water, and 31 percent exceeded limits of microbiological contamination. The Committee faulted the FDA with negligent oversight. In response, the FDA established, in November of 1995, definitions for artesian water, groundwater, mineral water, purified water, sparkling bottled water, sterile water, and well water in order to ensure fair advertising by the industry. These rules went into effect in May 1996. They include specification of the mineral content of water which can be sold as mineral water. Previously, mineral water was not regulated by the FDA, which resulted in varying standards for mineral water across states. In addition, under these rules, if bottled water comes from a municipal source, it must be labeled to indicate its origin.

The Icelandic Scenario

Iceland is highly import-dependent. In terms of products exported, it has little diversity and is dangerously dependent on its fish crop and world fish prices. The government, troubled by high inflation rates and low financial reserves, is very interested in diversifying its export base. An Icelandic Export Board has been created and charged with developing new products for export and aggressively promoting them abroad.

The Ministry of Commerce, after consulting the Central Bank, has the ultimate responsibility in matters concerning import and export licensing. The Central Bank is responsible for the regulation of foreign exchange transactions and exchange controls, including capital controls. It is also responsible for ensuring that all foreign exchange due to residents is surrendered to authorized banks. All commercial exports require licenses. The shipping documents must be lodged with an authorized bank. Receipts exchanged for exports must be surrendered to the Central Bank.

All investments by nonresidents in Iceland are subject to individual approval. The participation of nonresidents in Icelandic joint venture companies may not exceed 49 percent. Nonresident-owned foreign capital entering in the form of foreign exchange must be surrendered.

Iceland is a member of the United Nations, the European Free Trade Association, and the World Trade Organization. Iceland enjoys "most favored nation" status with the United States. Under this designation, mineral and carbonated water from Iceland is subject to a tariff of 0.33 cents per liter, and natural (still) water is tariff-free.

Questions for Discussion

1. Do you have enough information to determine whether importing water from Iceland would be a profitable business? If not, what additional information do you need?
2. Do you think the market climate in the United States is favorable to water imports from Iceland?
3. How would you interpret the fluctuation in the market share held by imports over the past ten years?
4. Should the U.S. government be involved in regulating bottled water products?

Toys 'Я' Us Japan

ABSTRACT

The cases describe the growth of Toys 'Я' Us (TRU) as the leading U.S. toy retailer to its international expansion and entry into Japan. Access to the Japanese market was made possible by adjustments to the Daitenho or "Big Store Law." TRU expanded rapidly to twenty-seven stores, but as the case ends, management needs to respond quickly to the crisis of losing its distribution center in Kobe.

SOURCE: The "Toys 'Я' Us Japan" case was written by Mark J. Kay, Ph.D., Montclair State University, Upper Montclair, New Jersey, as the basis for class discussion rather than to illustrate either the effective or ineffective handling of an administrative situation.

TOYS 'Я' US JAPAN

Tuesday, January 6, 1992, Toys 'Я' Us (TRU) Grand Opening in Kashihara, Naraken, Japan. Arriving by helicopter, U.S. President George Bush appeared at the opening ceremonies for the second TRU store in Japan. Attending were Minister Kozo Watanabe of Japan's Ministry of International Trade and Industry (MITI), U.S. Commerce Secretary Robert Mosbacher, U.S. Ambassador to Japan Michael Armacost, Japanese Ambassador to the United States Ryohei Murata, Toys 'Я' Us Chairman Charles Lazarus, and the local governor and mayor. About 2,000 Nara-ken policemen and students from local police academies were mobilized in a massive security measure. About 5,000 people came to witness the event; many of them waved small Japanese and American flags.[1]

President Bush thanked the gathered officials and praised the progress of the Structural Impediments Initiative (SII) to remove economic barriers to trade, create more jobs in America, and bring the Japanese consumer world-class goods. He continued,

> And what makes me so happy here today is that we see here the beginning of a dynamic, new economic relationship. One of greater balance. There is much that we can do for the world based on a forward-looking global partnership between two great nations, two powerful economies and two resourceful innovative peoples. And together we will go far . . .[2]

Few Americans would attach a great deal of significance to the public appearance of politicians at ceremonies such as these. Surprising to TRU, however, the showcase appearance of the U.S. president at Nara had an immediate impact upon Japanese toy industry vendors in the weeks following the event. Negotiations suddenly improved between TRU Japan and its Japanese suppliers. Japanese vendors apparently began to take seriously the previous announcement that TRU Japan intended to open 100 stores in the next ten years and become the major toy retailer in Japan.

Company Background

The first TRU store was opened in Washington, DC in 1957 by Charles Lazarus. Three stores opened over the next ten years and Lazarus sold his ownership stake for $7.5 million to Interstate Stores in 1966. When problems with other Interstate divisions drove the corporation into bankruptcy proceedings, Lazarus regained control in 1978 through a management-led buyout.

The TRU strategy is based upon price, selection, and keeping stores in-stock. As Lazarus explained, "When a customer walks through our doors with a shopping list, we better have 95 percent of what's on her list or we're in trouble."[3] The EDLP (every day low prices) strategy and in-stock image stimulates purchasing year-round instead of primarily during the Christmas season. Baby diapers and formula are sold at or below cost, in hopes of winning over new parents and keeping them as customers as their children mature. This strategy has won TRU a steadily increasing share of the retail toy market, rising to about 22 percent in 1995.

TRU shifted its goals for expansion dramatically in 1983. The firm entered the children's clothing market with Kids 'Я' Us and established the International Division. Joseph Baczko was recruited from his job as chief executive of the European operations of Max Factor to lead international expansion.

---

[1]Kazuo Nagata, "Bush Plays Tough at Toys 'Я' Us," *Daily Yomiuri,* January 8, 1992, 8.

[2]Ibid.

[3]Reda, Susan, "1995 NRF Gold Medal Award Winner: Charles Lazarus, Chairman of Toys 'Я' Us," *Stores,* January 77 (1, 1995): 131–136.

Baczko perceived that there were increasing global opportunities in the toy business. In an article in 1986 for the industry trade magazine, *Playthings,* he noted that customers overseas had higher disposable income, were more educated, and had more free time. Moreover, these buyers were more price conscious and tended to prefer specialty retailers, factors that favored the international expansion of TRU.[4]

The first international store opened in 1984 in Canada. In 1986, TRU struck joint venture deals in Singapore and Hong Kong. The company next expanded to the United Kingdom in 1987, into Germany in 1988, and into France and Taiwan in 1989. By 1994, TRU had penetrated the Nordic countries and developed new franchise relationships with Top-Toy A/S, the leading Scandinavian toy retailer. The franchise division also led to the entry of TRU to Israel, Saudi Arabia, and the United Arab Emirates, markets which would otherwise be prohibitive because of both cultural differences and restrictive laws.

TRU learned to adapt to the different competitive retail situations in each country that it entered. Different countries can have drastically different competitive environments. For example, supermarket toy sales as a percentage of all toy sales range from about 4 percent in the United Kingdom to 48 percent in France. High costs in land, labor, and distribution created problems in maintaining the TRU price and selection strategy. Low-cost retail sites proved difficult to find in England, leading TRU to try smaller store formats. In Germany, competing retailers initially pressured vendors not to sell to TRU. Nevertheless, sales increased and store expansion was rapid. Even in England, where British parents spend less on toys, the number of shoppers per store was very high. New store openings attracted 40,000 shoppers in Hong Kong and 20,000 to a one-acre site in Frankfurt. International sales grew to about one-quarter of company revenues by 1994.

Customer preferences can vary enormously among countries, hence TRU had to control its product mix carefully. Porcelain dolls are carried in Japan, while Germans prefer wooden ones. TRU sells a version of Monopoly in Hong Kong that replaces "Boardwalk" and "Park Place" with "Sheko" and "Repulse Bay," and those in France stock scale models of the French high-speed train. While about 70 to 80 percent of its European toy sales are the same items as those in America, in Japan, this number is only about 30 to 40 percent.

TRU has constantly worked to refine the warehouse toy store concept in its home market. To better service customers, TRU linked store managers' pay to customer service activities and tried "store within a store" or "boutique" concepts. These included Lego shops, "plush" or stuffed animal shops, learning centers, and entertainment software sections. The most successful of these was the book department, called "Books "Я" Us," a joint effort with Western Publishing that requires special chairs, lights, carpets, and tables. Though it may not have as wide a selection of books as bookstores, the book department enables TRU to pick up sales from parents supplementing a toy purchase with a book having better "educational" value.

As a specialty store "category killer," TRU competes across retail categories, not just with toy stores. To better compete with discounters, in 1994 TRU developed coupon books to offer deeper price savings. A "Big Toy Book Catalogue," a "Video Game & Electronic Toys Catalogue," and an internet connection were introduced as shopping aids. Additionally, the "Toy Guide for Differently Abled Kids" offers professional evaluations of toys for families of disabled children; this complements the TRU corporate giving program which focuses on improving the health care needs of children.

---

[4]Baczko, Joseph, "Toymakers Should Adopt a Global Strategy," *Playthings* 86 (2, 1986): 307.

Going to Japan

Japan was a particularly attractive target for TRU for several reasons. Japan was the second largest toy market in the world. The "Statistics of Toys" of the Japan Toy Association estimated the size of the overall Japanese toy market on a retail price basis at ¥932 to ¥950 billion in 1991. By the 1980s, Japan had developed a particularly high per capita income, and toy sales had been growing despite the low birthrate. Spending on children was particularly high, particularly in the early years of childhood, yet toy shops in Japan tended to have small selections and high prices.

As TRU formulated plans to enter the Japanese market, it first had to deal with the barrier posed by local laws and politics. The biggest impediment was the Daitenho or "Big Store law," which went into effect in 1974. The law stated that local store owners must give their consent before a retail outlet with floor space larger than roughly 5,400 square feet can be opened in their locale. Under the guise of protecting the community, the law granted small local businesses the authority to force new competitors into a review process which could last more than ten years. The Daitenho effectively enabled local shopkeepers to block the establishment of TRU stores in Japan beginning in late 1988.

Though originally intended to protect the small shops, the Daitenho effectively made the retail network of stores rather rigid, benefiting the large incumbent stores established before the law was created. Store chains such as Yaohan could not expand in Japan, and Yaohan eventually moved its headquarters to Hong Kong to concentrate upon international expansion. Opponents of the Daitenho included Shinji Shimiju, CEO of the Lion supermarket convenience store chain who sued MITI in the mid-1980s on the basis that the law barred competition. While lawsuits are uncommon in Japan, press coverage on the suit helped focus public attention to the fact that chains such as Daiei and Ito-Yokado were unfairly benefiting from the law.

Widespread publicity about the TRU difficulties to open new stores gained attention in both the American and Japanese press. Being unable to get approval for any of its stores, TRU appealed for help directly through the U.S. trade representative and other channels. Lobbying efforts by Japanese business had been taking place for several years to change the Daitenho and American negotiation pressure reinforced this effort.

In 1989, TRU International Division president Joseph Baczko had met Takuro Isoda of Daiwa Securities America while sitting on Georgetown University's forum on Japan. Isoda introduced Baczko to Den Fujita, President of McDonald's Japan, which by that time had already developed a network of 700 shops yielding $1.2 billion in sales. Their compatibility led McDonald's Japan to take a 20 percent stake in the TRU Japan subsidiary. Den Fujita had substantial experience with real estate and numerous government contacts, many of them fellow alumni of the University of Tokyo's law department.[5]

MITI had shown it was receptive to the relaxation of the Daitenho in the spring of 1989 in a report it circulated entitled "Vision of the Japanese Retail Industry in the 1990s." As Kabun Muto rose to become the minister of MITI, he encouraged the idea of formally revising the Daitenho, not just altering MITI's interpretation of the law.

As discussions were taking place within the Japanese government, Fujita traveled to the United States to meet with Trade Representative Carla Hills in 1990. Fujita urged her office to take diplomatic efforts to push for changes in the Daitenho. Fujita knew that the time was right for a change in the law. MITI was ready to be persuaded by the Americans to publicly take action.

[5]Grover, Martha. "The Team Approach," *Los Angeles Times,* Nov. 13, 1989.

Japan: Distribution and Retail Environment

Japanese society is hierarchical and group-oriented; there is a strong emphasis on maintaining harmony and avoiding confrontations. Sensitivity to social practices is of great importance in establishing successful business relationships in Japan. The view of the individual differs significantly in comparison to European or American standards.

It is important to acknowledge and respect obligations, created through educational ties, employment, favors, or assistance. Obligations tend to be mutually felt and bind business partners to each other. Failure to repay a perceived debt or recompense for an obligation can bring about a "loss of face" for a person who perceives himself as indebted. Since business in Japan tends to be conducted on the basis of long-term relationships and trust, entry into the Japanese market generally requires a long-term commitment. Proper introduction and personal contacts can be highly important. This has fueled the claim that the Japanese business system gives inordinate advantages to entrenched incumbents to the detriment of newcomers. The web of overlapping relationships which constitutes the distribution sector of the economy is particularly difficult for foreign firms to penetrate.

In addition, many Japanese business sectors, such as telecommunications, financial services, and construction, remain heavily regulated. In the retail sector, laws restrict the size of buildings that retailers can erect and dictate store layouts and construction materials. Rules and regulations apply to all companies, Japanese included, but government ties and relationships can sometimes give established firms an edge in getting past the red tape.

With 124 million people residing in a mountainous country, 70 percent of Japan's population are concentrated in coastal areas constituting about 20 percent of the country. Densely populated Japanese cities have high real estate prices. As a consequence, homes and stores are small. Japanese households have small kitchen areas with little room to store fresh foods and shopping tends to occur on a daily basis.

The Japanese distribution system involves many middlemen and includes 1.6 million "mom and pop" stores, half of which sell only food items. The average Japanese retail store has only about 3,200 square feet of floor space and limited storage capacity. Distributors make small deliveries of less than full case quantities. Japanese consumers tend to make frequent small purchases from shop owners whom they know within their neighborhood setting, particularly in the food sector. Small shops account for 56 percent of retail sales in Japan as compared with 3 percent for the United States and 5 percent for Europe. The number of retail outlets in Japan is nearly the same as the United States, despite the fact that its population is roughly half that of the United States and Japan is slightly smaller than California.

Mom and pop stores are closely connected with neighborhood and community events. Every shopping street or district in Japan has its own retailer's union which puts up seasonal decorations in the streets, hold storefront sales, and organize special events. Most events coincide with matsuri (festivals) such as summer festivals in August, the hottest month of the year, that can draw substantial crowds. Some groups run drawings or coupon shopping schemes that are aimed at encouraging local residents to patronize their neighborhood stores.

Cultural values can serve to reinforce the complex network of wholesalers. Small stores may not be able to secure credit by themselves and often are provided financial, ownership, or other exclusive arrangements with major Japanese manufacturers, industrial groups, or trading companies. Japanese wholesalers have become powerful through their capacity to provide financial support to smaller manufacturers and retailers who have limited resources. Having limited space and high storage costs, retailers rely on wholesalers to maintain inventories, obligating them further to wholesalers. Since one of every five Japanese workers is employed in distribution, change is likely to entail political problems.

Changing the Daitenho

The rising level of wealth in the 1980s permitted many more Japanese to travel outside the country. Exposed to new cultures, Japanese consumers begin to question high prices, government regulation, and distribution practices within Japan. Popular opinion toward many traditional aspects of business changed.

As Japan entered the 1990s, it was troubled by economic and political problems. The so-called "bubble economy" of the 1980s burst in 1991, plunging Japan into a recession. The Liberal-Democratic party (LDP), which had been in control since the early 1950s, began to lose its grip on power as a result of scandals amongst its leadership. A parade of "revolving door" prime ministers even included the advancement of the Socialist party leader, Tomichi Murayama, to the prime minister's office in 1994.

The Structural Impediments Initiative (SII), a set of discussions between the United States and Japan, was launched in July 1989 to address the underlying causes of the bilateral trade imbalance, examining macroeconomic policies and business practices as trade barriers. In June 1990, the two sides released a report in which they made commitments to reduce structural impediments and meet for follow-up discussions from 1990 to 1993. Japan's multilayered distribution sector became an issue in these discussions.

MITI agreed, in April 1990, to limit to eighteen months the application process under the Daitenho. This eighteen-month period included six months for consultation with local small store owners, eight months for negotiating details with those stores, and four months for adjustments. Further changes came on January 31, 1992, as MITI reduced the waiting period to twelve months and upgraded membership of the local "advisory councils." These councils reviewed applications for new stores and could demand certain reductions in store size.

For "type 1" large stores, which includes supermarkets and department stores, the maximum size was enlarged to 3,000 square meters (about 30,000 square feet) from the previous 1,500 square meters. For "type 2" specialty stores like TRU, the maximum size was enlarged from 500 square meters to 3,000 square meters. Exceptions to size regulations applied to those stores opening in Tokyo's twenty-three wards and in major cities, where the maximum was set to 6,000 square meters.[6] Finally, on May 1, 1994, MITI made two further concessions. Large stores were allowed to extend their closing time to 8 PM; and the number of days stores were required to close for holidays was reduced to twenty-four, from forty-four.[7]

Getting Started in Japan

TRU Japan established an office in Kawasaki and targeted development of store sites in Niigata, Chiba, Sagamihara, and Fukuoka. While MITI had agreed to revisions to shorten the approval process, TRU also had to deal with local and regional ordinances. For example, certain changes in the Daitenho agreed to by MITI required the approval of the Ministry of Home Affairs. In January 1990, TRU Japan submitted the paperwork to open a store in Niigata on the northern coast of Japan. To win local approval from the Niigata Chamber of Commerce and Industry, TRU agreed to shrink the size of its originally planned store by 30 percent and the opening became further delayed.

---

[6]"Japan Enacts Amended Large-Store Law Reducing Waiting Period for Applications," *International Trade Reporter* (vol. 9, no. 6) February 5, 1992, 228.

[7]Ohashi, Yoshimitsu, "Economic Perspective," *The Daily Yomiuri,* May 9, 1994, 8.

In May 1990, TRU Japan started talks on opening a store in Sagamihara, a Tokyo suburb of 520,000, submitting applications to the ministry, Kanagawa Prefecture, Sagamihara City, and the Chamber of Commerce. In August, TRU participated in an "explanation meeting" at the local public hall and later made presentations to the Sagamihara Commercial Activities Council, a MITI-inspired body of eighteen consumers, merchants, professionals, and academics. After four meetings, the council gave approval in June 1991 to allow TRU to open its store some time after December first. The requirement was that, like other stores, TRU had to close every day by 8 PM and not open on at least thirty days of the year. In addition, TRU had to consult with regulatory bodies over possible traffic congestion problems. By September, those consultations and construction delays forced a postponement of the Sagamihara opening until March, 1992. Determined to open one store in 1991, TRU tried to hasten a similar approval process of its planned store in Ibaraki.[8]

Meanwhile, other obstacles had surfaced. Takashigi Seki, of the group called the All Japan Associated Toys, cited with alarm to the press that British toy stores had decreased from 6,000 to 1,500 after the TRU entry. In Japan, the total number of toy stores, which had peaked at about 8,000, had recently declined to about 6,000.

Next, in September 1990, 520 small toy retailers formally announced forming the Japan Association of Specialty Toy Shops, to "protect its members from the likes of TRU Japan" by lobbying and other means. Public statements indicated that the association intended to provide members research on toy retailing, employee education, sales promotion, and management techniques.[9] Eleven major retailers led the lobbying association, including Kiddy Land in Tokyo, Pelican in Osaka, and Angel in Fukuoka. Toshikazu Koya, leader of the association, practicing attorney, and president of the fifty-three store Kiddy Land chain, explained that he planned to pool purchases with other Japanese retailers to buy large lots of inventory at competitive prices.[10]

Japanese toy retailers and wholesalers bitterly complained that TRU would put them out of business. In seeking retail space to lease, TRU found that some were reluctant to lease TRU space which could upset local business clients. Most seriously, toy vendors, worried about their long-established relationships with toy retailers, refused to sell to TRU or deal directly with them.

TRU vice chairman, Robert Nakasone, himself an American of Japanese descent, confidently remarked to the press that disputes with Japanese toy makers could be resolved. TRU had been dealing with many Japanese companies for years. Large toy manufacturers such as Nintendo, having established a long-term business relationship with TRU, could not "lose face" by refusing to do business with TRU in Japan. Eventually Nintendo publicly announced their intention to directly supply TRU Japan, negotiating prices that would not offend other retailers. Other manufacturers began to follow.

On its part, however, TRU was committed to working with local suppliers. One reason for this was to stock toys carrying the "ST" mark. The "ST" or Safety Toy mark is a voluntary quality mark that can be applied to toys that meet the safety standards set by the Japanese toy industry through the Toy Safety Control Administration, a self-regulatory commission composed of toy manufacturers, consumers, and health professionals. The Japan Toy Association established the "ST" mark and had long engaged in information campaigns aimed at educating Japanese consumers about the merits of

[8]"Guess Who's Selling Barbies in Japan Now?" *Business Week,* December 9, 1991, 60.

[9]"Japan Toy Shops Unite to Fight Foreign Competition," *The Reuter Business Report,* September 28, 1990.

[10]Schoenberger, Karl, "Selling Toys to Japanese Anything but Child's Play," *The Toronto Star,* October 9, 1990, C5.

buying toys affixed with the "ST" mark. Over 95 percent of toys sold in Japan, whether domestic or imported, carry the "ST" mark.

While cooperating with Japanese vendors in many respects, TRU rebelled against the Japanese practice of selling at manufacturers' suggested retail prices. TRU maintained that prices should not be decided by their manufacturers or wholesalers, and initiated direct dealings with manufacturers. For the most part, TRU was forced to go through established distribution channels. Although TRU was a large distributor in America, this had little importance to most Japanese toy vendors since it was regarded as a small company within Japan.

TRU moved forward with its plans aggressively. As Joseph Baczko left to become CEO of Blockbuster, Larry Bouts was brought in from PepsiCo Foods to head the TRU International Division. Den Fujita announced to the press a plan to link McDonald's Japan with TRU Japan and Blockbuster in a large suburban store concept, calling the group the "MTB Rengo." With a bit of marketing flourish, Fujita referred to the plan as the "Meiji Ishin of distribution," comparing the idea to the Japanese political revolution at the end of the samurai period.[11]

On December 20, 1991, TRU Japan opened its first retail store in Japan in Amimachi, Ibaraki-ken, about 40 miles northeast of Tokyo. With the colorful, English language TRU sign in front of the store and an 850-car parking lot, the store is similar to those in the United States. It is smaller than was hoped, with retail floor space of about 3,000 square meters or 32,400 square feet as opposed to the average of 46,000 square feet in the United States—but still, this is about ten times larger than the average toy store in Japan. While the typical small Japanese toy store stocks between 1,000 and 2,000 different items, TRU Japan started out with about 8,000 and eventually increased this number to 15,000 items. With all the publicity that TRU had gotten in the newspapers, a crowd of 17,000 jammed the store on opening day and set a TRU grand-opening sales record.[12]

Questions for Discussion

1. What advantages did TRU have that helped it to enter the Japanese market?
2. How did the 20 percent stake taken by McDonald's help TRU to gain entry?
3. What problems do you anticipate that TRU will have in the next few years as it expands?

---

[11] *Yomiuri News,* Report From Japan, October 8, 1991.

[12] "Japanese 'Я' Us," *Los Angeles Times,* December 25, 1991, 6.

McDonnell Douglas: The F-18 Hornet Offset

In May of 1992, the Finnish government's selection of the F/A-18 Hornet over the Swedish JAS-39 Gripen, the French Mirage 2000-5, and fellow American F-16 to modernize the fighter fleet of its air force was a major boost to McDonnell Douglas (MDC) in an otherwise quiet market. The deal would involve the sale of 57 F/A-18 Cs and 7 F/A-18 Ds at a cost of FIM 9.5 billion (approximately $2 billion). Deliveries would take place between 1995 and 2000.

Winning the contract was critical since MDC had been on the losing side of two major aircraft competitions in the United States in 1991. In addition, one of its major projects with the U.S. Navy had been terminated (the A-12), and the government of the Republic of Korea had changed its mind to buy F-16 aircraft after it already had an agreement with MDC for F/A-18 Hornets.

However, the $2 billion will not be earned without strings attached. Contractually, McDonnell Douglas and its main subcontractors (Northrop, General Electric, and General Motor's subsidiary Hughes), the "F-18 Team," are obligated to facilitate an equivalent amount of business for Finnish industry over a ten-year period (1992–2002) using various offset arrangements.

OFFSETS

Offsets are various forms of industrial and business activities required as a condition of purchase. They are an obligation imposed on the seller in major (and often military hardware) purchases by or for foreign governments to minimize any trade imbalance or other adverse economic impact caused by the outflow of currency required to pay for such purchases. In wealthier countries, it is often used for establishing infrastructure. Two basic types of offset arrangements exist: direct and indirect (as seen in Figure 1). Although offsets have long been associated only with the defense sector, there are now increasing demands for offsets in commercial sales where the government is the purchaser or user.

Direct offset consists of product-related manufacturing or assembly either for the purposes of the project in question only or for a longer-term partnership. The purchase, therefore, enables the purchaser to be involved in the manufacturing process. Various Spanish companies produce dorsal covers, rudders, aft fuselage panels, and speed brakes for the F/A-18s designated for the Spanish Air Force. In addition to coproduction arrangements, licensed production is prominent. Examples include Egypt producing U.S. M1-A1 tanks, China producing MDC's MD-82 aircraft, and Korea assembling the F-16 fighter. An integral part of these arrangements is the training of the local employees. Training is not only for production/assembly purposes but also for maintenance and overhaul of the equipment in the longer term. Some offsets have buy-back

SOURCE: This case study was written by Ilkka A. Ronkainen and funded in part by a grant from the Business and International Education Program of the U.S. Department of Education. The assistance of the various organizations cited in the case is appreciated. Special thanks to David Danjczek of Western Atlas, Inc. For more information, see http://www.dac.mdc.com/

FIGURE 1 **The Offset Process**

Offset Obligation	Offset Initiatives → / ← Accreditation	Offset Credits (direct) • Licensing • Coproduction/Subassembly • Training • Buyback • Maintenance • Overhaul
		Offset Credits (indirect) • Direct Purchases • Marketing Assistance • Finance Assistance • Investment • Technology Transfer

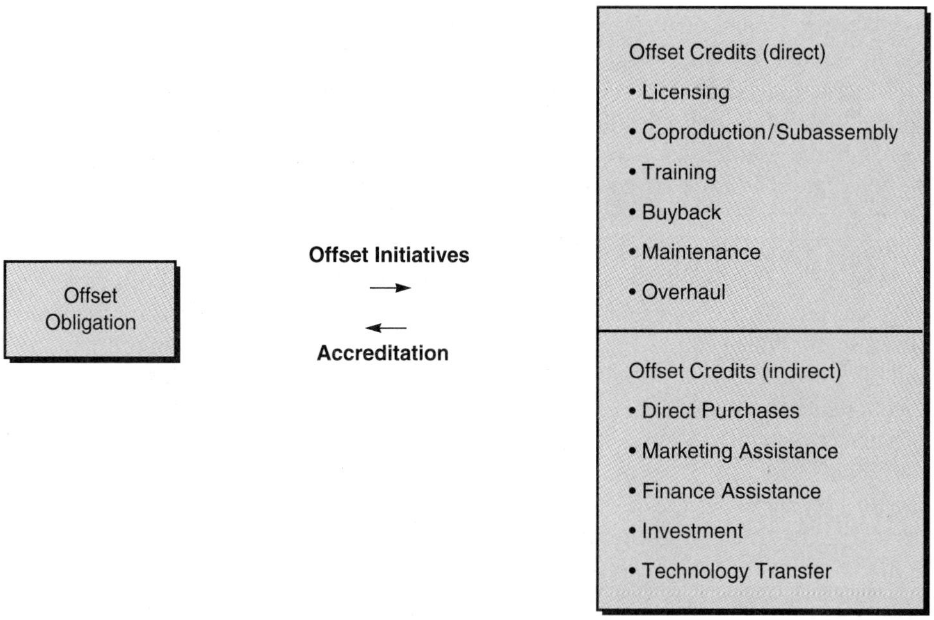

provisions; that is, the seller is obligated to purchase output from the facility or operations it has set up or licensed. For example, Westland takes up an agreed level of parts and components from the Korean plant that produces Lynx Helicopters under license. In practice, therefore, direct offsets amount to technology transfer.

Indirect offsets are deals that involve products, investments, and so forth which are not to be used in the original sales contract but that will satisfy part of the seller's "local" obligation. Direct purchases of raw materials, equipment, or supplies by the seller or its suppliers from the offset customer country present the clearest case of indirect offsets. These offset arrangements are analogous to counterpurchases and switch trading. Sellers faced with offset obligations work closely with their supplier base, some having goals of increasing supplier participation in excess of 50 percent. Teamwork does make the process more effective and efficient. There are various business activities taking place and procurement decisions being made by one of the sellers or its suppliers without offset needs that others may be able to use as offset credit to satisfy an indirect obligation.

Many governments see offsets as a mechanism to develop their indigenous business and industrial sectors. Training in management techniques may be attractive to both parties. The upgrading of humanware may be seen by the government as more critical for improving international competitiveness than efforts focused only on hardware. For the seller, training is relatively inexpensive, but it provides good credits because of its political benefit.

An important dimension of the developmental effort will relate to exports. This may involve the analysis of business sectors showing the greatest foreign market potential, improving organizational and product readiness, conducting market research (e.g., estimating demand or assessing competition), identifying buyers or partners for foreign market development, or assisting in the export process (e.g., company visits, support in negotiations and reaching a final agreement, facilitating trial/sample shipments, handling documentation needs).

Sales are often won or lost on the availability of financing and favorable credit terms to the buyer. Financing packages put together by one of the seller's entities, if it is critical in winning the bid, will earn offset credits.

Buyer nations focusing on industrial development and technology transfer have negotiated contracts that call for offsetting the cost of their purchases through investments. Saudi Arabian purchases of military technology have recently been tied to sellers' willingness to invest in manufacturing plants, defense-related industries, or special interest projects in the country. British Aerospace, for example, has agreed to invest in factories for the production of farm feed and sanitary ware.

Most often, the final offset deal includes a combination of activities, both direct and indirect vis-à-vis the sale, and no two offset deals are alike. With increasing frequency, governments may require "pre-deal counterpurchases" as a sign of commitment and ability to deliver should they be awarded the contract. Some companies, such as United Technologies, argue that there is limited advantage in carrying out offset activities in advance of the contract, unless the buyer agrees to a firm commitment. While none of the bidders may like it, buyer's market conditions give them very little choice to argue. Even if a bidder losses the deal, it can always attempt to sell its offset credits to the winner or use the credits in conjunction with other sales that one of its divisions may have. Some of the companies involved in the bidding in Finland maintain offset accounts with the Finnish government.

McDonnell's Deal with the Finnish Air Force

The F/A-18 Hornet is a twin-engine, twin-tail, multimission tactical aircraft that can be operated from aircraft carriers or from land bases (see Table 1). It is both a fighter (air-to-air) and an attack (air-to-ground) aircraft. McDonnell Aircraft Company, a division of MDC, is the prime contractor of the F/A-18. Subcontractors include General Electric for the Hornet's smokeless F404 low-bypass turbofan engines, Hughes Aircraft Company for the APG-73 radar, and Northrop Corporation for the airframe. Approximately 1,100 F/A-18s have been delivered worldwide. Although it had been in use by the United States since 1983, it had been (and can continue to be) upgraded during its operational lifetime. Furthermore, it had proven its combat readiness in the Gulf War.

Only since June of 1990 has the F/A-18 been available to countries that are not members of the North Atlantic Treaty Organization (NATO). The change in U.S. government position resulted from the rapidly changed East-West political situation. The attractive deals available in neutral countries such as Switzerland and Finland helped push the government as well. When the Finnish Air Force initiated its program in 1986, MDC was not invited to (and would not have been able to) offer a bid because of U.S. government restrictions.

THE FINNISH GOVERNMENT POSITION

The Finnish government's role in the deal had two critical dimensions: one related to the choice of the aircraft, the other related to managing the offset agreement in a fashion to maximize the benefit to the country's industry for the long term.

Selecting the Fighter

In 1986, the Finnish Air Force (FAF) decided to replace its aging Swedish-made Drakens and Soviet-made MIG-21s, which made up three fighter squadrons. At that time, the re-

TABLE 1 F/A-18 Hornet Strike Fighter

Prime contractor	McDonnell Douglas
Principal subcontractor	Northrop Corporation
Type	Single- (C) and two-seat (D), twin-turbofan for fighter and attack missions
Power plant	Two General Electric F404-GE-402 (enhanced performance engine)
Thrust	4800 kp each (approx.)
Afterburning thrust	8000 kp each (approx.)
Dimensions	
Length	17.07 m
Span	11.43 m
Wing area	37.16 m^2
Height	4.66 m
Weights	
Empty	10 455 kg
Normal takeoff	16 650 kg
Maximum takeoff	22 328 kg
Wing loading	450 kg/m^2
Fuel (internal)	6 435 litre (4925 kg)
Fuel (with external tanks)	7 687 litre
Armament	
Cannon	One General Electric M61A-1 Vulcan rotary-barrel 20-mm
Missiles	Six AIM-9 Sidewinder air-to-air
	Four AIM-7 Sparrow
	Six AIM-120 AMRAAM
Radar	AN/APG-73 multi-mode air-to-air and air-to-surface
Performance	
Takeoff distance	430 m
Landing distance	850 m
Fighter-mission radius	$>$ 740 km
Maximum speed	1.8 Mach (1 915 km/h) at high altitude
	1.0 Mach at intermediate power
Service ceiling	15 240 m
Payload	7 710 kg
Used since	1983
Expected manufacturing lifetime	2000+
Users	USA, Australia, Canada, Spain, and Kuwait
Ordered quantity	1,168

maining service life of these aircraft was estimated to be fifteen years, calling for the new squadrons to be operational by the year 2000 and to be up-to-date even in 2025. Finland, due to its strategic geographic location, has always needed a reliable air defense system. The position of neutrality adopted by Finland had favored split procurement between Eastern and Western suppliers until the collapse of the Soviet Union in December of 1991 made it politically possible to purchase fighters from a single Western supplier.

The first significant contacts with potential bidders were made in 1988 and in February 1990, the FAF requested proposals from the French Dassault-Breguet, Sweden's Industrigruppen JAS, and General Dynamics in the United States for forty fighters and a trainer aircraft. In January 1991, the bid was amended to sixty fighters and seven trainers. Three months later, MDC joined the bidding, and by July 1991, binding bids were received from all of the four manufacturers.

During the evaluative period, the four bidders tried to gain favor for their alternative. One approach was the provision of deals for Finnish companies as "pre-deal counterpurchases." For example, General Dynamics negotiated for Vaisala (a major Finnish electronics firm) to become a subcontractor of specialty sensors for the F-16. Before the final decision, the Swedish bidder had arranged for deals worth $250 million for Finnish companies, the French for over $100 million, and General Dynamics for $40 million. MDC, due to its later start, had none to speak of. Other tactics were used as well. The Swedes pointed to long ties that the countries have had, and especially to the possibilities to develop them further on the economic front. As a matter of fact, offsets were the main appeal of the Swedish bid since the aircraft itself was facing development cost overruns and delays. The French reminded the Finnish government that choosing a European fighter might help in Finland's bid to join the European Union (EU) in 1995. Since the FAF prefers the U.S. AMRAAM missile system for its new fighters, the U.S. government cautioned that its availability depended on the choice of the fighter. The companies themselves also worked on making their bid sweeter: Just before the official announcement, General Dynamics improved its offer to include sixty-seven fighters for the budgeted sum and a guarantee of 125 percent offsets; that is, the amount of in-country participation would be 125 percent of the sale price paid by the Finnish government for the aircraft.

After extensive flight testing both in the producers' countries and in Finland (especially for winter conditions), the Hornet was chosen as the winner. Despite the high absolute cost of the aircraft (only 57 will be bought versus 60), the Hornet's cost-effectiveness relative to performance was high. The other alternatives were each perceived to have problems: The JAS-39 Gripen had the teething problems of a brand-new aircraft; the Mirage's model 2000-5 has not yet been produced; and the F-16 may be coming to the end of its product life cycle. The MIG-29 from the Soviet Union/Russia was never seriously in the running due to the political turmoil in that country. Some did propose purchasing the needed three squadrons from the stockpiles of the defunct East Germany (and they could have been had quite economically), but the uncertainties were too great for a strategically important product.

Working out the Offsets

Typically, a specific committee is set up by the government to evaluate which arrangements qualify as part of the offset. In Finland's case, the Finnish Offset Committee (FOC) consists of five members with Ministries of Defense, Foreign Affairs, as well as Industry and Trade represented. Its task is to provide recommendations as to which export contracts qualify and which do not. The Technical Working Group was set up to support its decision making, especially in cases concerning technology transfer. From

FIGURE 2 **Offset: Finnish Industry Input**

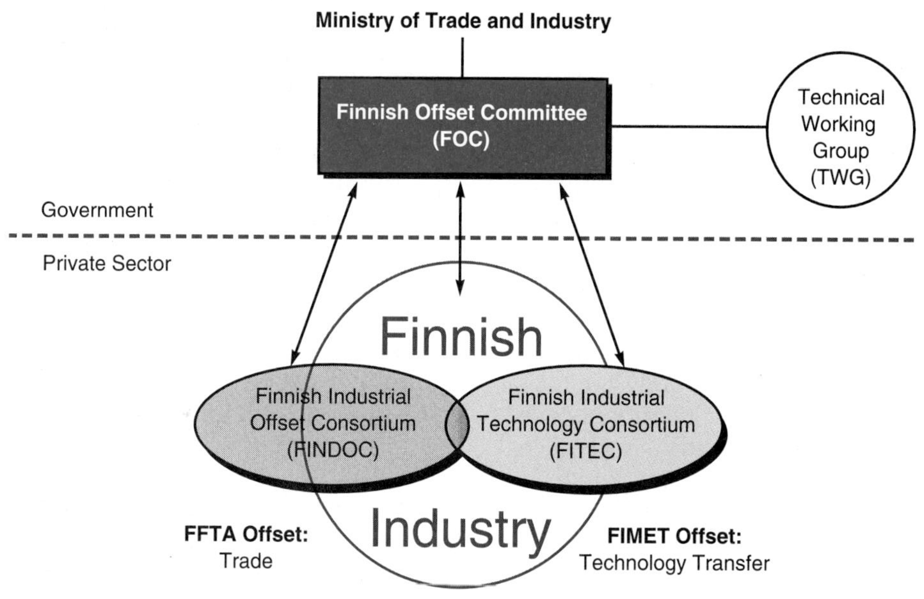

1977 to 1991, the procedures and final decisions were made by the Ministry of Defense; since then the responsibility has been transferred to the Ministry of Trade and Industry (see Figure 2). The transfer was logical given the increased demands and expectations on the trade and technology fronts of the F/A-18 deal.

When the committee was established in 1977 in conjunction with a major military purchase, almost all contracts qualified until an export developmental role for offsets was outlined. The Finnish exporter is required to show that the offset agreement played a pivotal role in securing its particular contract.

Two different approaches are taken by the government to attain its developmental objective. First, the government will not make available (or give offset credit) for counterpurchasing goods that already have established market positions unless the counterpurchaser can show that the particular sale would not have materialized without its support (e.g., through distribution or financing). Second, the government will use compensation "multipliers" for the first time. While previous deals were executed on a one-on-one basis, the government now wants, through the use of multipliers, direct purchases to certain industries or types of companies. For example, in the case of small- or medium-sized companies, a multiplier of two may be used; that is, a purchase of $500,000 from such a firm will satisfy a $1 million share of the counterpurchaser's requirement. Attractive multipliers also may be used which may generate long-term export opportunities or support Finland's indigenous arms or other targeted industry. Similarly, the seller may also insist on the use of multipliers. In the case of technology transfer, the seller may request a high multiplier because of the high initial cost of research and development that may have gone into the technology licensed or provided to the joint venture as well as its relative importance to the recipient country's economic development.

Finnish industry is working closely with the government on two fronts. The Finnish Industrial Offset Consortium (FINDOC) was established to collaborate with the Finnish

Foreign Trade Association (a quasi-governmental organization) on trade development. FINDOC's twenty-one members represent fifteen main business areas (e.g., aircraft, shipbuilding, pulp and paper machinery, and metal and engineering) and are among the main Finnish exporters. Their consortium was set up to take advantage of offset opportunities more efficiently and to provide a focal point for the F-18 Team's efforts. For example, MDC and FINDOC arranged for a familiarization trip to the United States for interested Finnish businesses in the fall of 1992. For those companies not in FINDOC, it is the task of the FFTA to provide information on possibilities to benefit from the deal. The Finnish Industrial Technology Consortium (FITEC) was established to facilitate technology transfer to and from the Finnish metal and engineering industries.

THE F-18 TEAM'S POSITION

The monies related to offset management and associated development are not generally allowed as a separate cost in the sales contract. Profit margins for aircraft sales are narrow, and any additional costs must be watched closely. Extraordinary demands by the buyer make bidding more challenging and time-consuming. For example, the customer may want extensive changes in the product without changes in the final price. Switzerland wanted major alterations made to the airframe and additional equipment which made its total cost per plan higher than the price in Finland. In the experience of high-tech firms, the add-on for direct offsets range from 3 to 8 percent, which has to be incorporated into the feasibility plans. Offsets have to make good business sense and, once agreed to, successfully executed.

Competing for the Deal

In accepting the offer to bid for the FAF deal, the F-18 Team believed it had only a 5 percent chance to win the deal but, given its size, decided to go ahead. From the time it received a request to bid from the FAF, MDC had three months to prepare its proposal. The only main negative factor from the short preparation time was MDC's inability to arrange for "prepurchase" deals and generate goodwill with the constituents.

After two fact-finding missions to Finland, MDC established an office in Helsinki in August 1991. The decision to have a full-time office in Finland (compared to the competitors whose representatives were in Helsinki two days a week on the average) was made based on the experiences from Korea and Switzerland. MDC's approach was to be ready and able to help the customer in terms of information and be involved with all the constituents of the process, such as the testing groups of the FAF, the Ministry of Defense (owners of the program), and the Parliament (supporters of the program).

Beyond the technical merits of the Hornet, MDC's capabilities in meeting the pending offset obligations were a critical factor in winning the deal. MDC had by 1992 a total of 100 offset programs in twenty-five countries with a value of $8 billion, and its track record in administering them was excellent. Another factor in MDC's favor was its long-term relation with Finnair, the national airline. Finnair's aircraft have predominantly come from MDC, starting with the DC-2 in 1941 to the MD-11 aircraft delivered in 1991.

Satisfying the Offset Obligation

Offset deals are not barter where the seller and the buyer swap products of equal value over a relatively short time period. The F-18 Team members have to complete the offset program by the year 2002 through a number of different elements including marketing assistance, export development, technology transfer, team purchases, and investment financing. One of the major beneficiaries of the offset arrangement is Valmet, the only major aircraft manufacturer in Finland. Valmet will assemble the fifty-seven C-versions in Finland and is also counting on the F-18 Team's connections to open markets for its Redigo trainer aircraft. The F-18 Team works with Finnish companies to develop exports for their products and services by identifying potential buyers and introducing the two parties to each other. Purchases can come from within the contractor companies, suppliers to the F-18 contractors, and third parties. The motivation for completing offset projects is financial penalties for the prime team members if they do not meet contract deadlines.

However, no one in the F-18 Team or among its suppliers is obligated to engage in a given transaction just because Finland purchased fighters from McDonnell Douglas. The key point is that products must meet specifications, delivery dates, and price criteria to be successfully sold in any market. After an appropriate purchase has taken place, the F-18 Team receives offset credit based on the Finnish-manufactured content of the transaction value as approved by the Finnish Offset Committee. For example, when Finnyards won the bid to build a passenger ferry for the Danish Stena Line, Northrop received offset credits due to its role in financing Finnyard's bid.

The offset obligations are not limited to the United States. The Team has offset partners all over the world because the members operate worldwide. Furthermore, given the long time frame involved, there are no pressing time constraints on the members to earn offset credits.

Since 1992, the MDC office in Helsinki has had two officers: one in charge of the aircraft, the other focused on offsets. Due to the worse recession in recent Finnish history, the response to the offset program has been unprecedented, and the office has been inundated with requests for information.

ONE COMPANY'S EXPERIENCE

Hackman, one of Finland's leading exporters in the metal sector, started its cooperation with McDonnell Douglas by putting together a portfolio of Hackman products which offer the best offset potential. The proposal ended up covering a wide range of products ranging from tableware to turnkey cheese plants. Disinfecting machines and food processors created the most interest because of McDonnell Douglas' contracts in the hospital and construction sectors.

The first project identification came in July 1992 when word came from McDonnell Douglas that a $187 million hotel being planned for Denver, Colorado, was a potential offset target. The contractor was seeking export financing (e.g., through GE Finance) in exchange for sourcing products through offset from Finland for which offset credits could be used by MDC. Ideally, the contractor would get attractive financing, the F-18 Team would get offset credits, and Finnish participants would get a shot at a huge deal worth up to $40 million in total.

Questions for Discussion

1. Why would the members of the F-18 Team, McDonnell Douglas, Northrop, General Electric, and Hughes agree to such a deal rather than insist on a money-based transaction?
2. After the deal was signed, many Finnish companies expected that contracts and money would start rolling in by merely calling up McDonnell Douglas. What are the fundamental flaws of this thinking?
3. Why do Western governments typically take an unsupportive stance on countertrade arrangements?

4. Comment on this statement: "Offset arrangements involving overseas production that permit a foreign government or producer to acquire the technical information to manufacture all or part of a U.S.–origin article trade short-term sales for long-term loss of market position."

References

"Countertrade's Growth Continues," *BarterNews* 27 (1993): 54–55.

"Offsets in the Aerospace Industry," *BarterNews* 27 (1993): 56–57.

"Investing, Licensing, and Trading Conditions Abroad: Saudi Arabia." *Business International* May 15, 1990, 5.

Jakubik, Maria, Irina Kabirova, Tapani Koivunen, Päivi Lähtevänoja, and Denice Stanfors. *Finnish Air Force Buying Fighters*. Helsinki School of Economics, September 24, 1993.

VIDEO CASE

A Taste of the West

In the mid-1980s, Mikhail Gorbachev introduced a new program called "perestroika" in the Soviet Union. Perestroika was to reform the Soviet economy fundamentally by improving the overall technological and industrial base as well as improving the quality of life for Soviet citizens through increased availability of food, housing, and consumer goods. It was hoped that this program would stimulate the entrepreneurial spirit of Soviet citizens and help the country and its government overcome crucial shortcomings. These shortcomings were the result of decades of communist orientation, which had led to significant capital and management shortages and inhibited the development of a market orientation and of consumer-oriented technology.

In subsequent years, a number of joint ventures between Western firms and Soviet institutions were either contemplated or even formed. However, many of these ventures, due to internal difficulties, met with only limited success. Nevertheless, the efforts of one firm, McDonald's—an icon of free enterprise—were hailed as a spectacular success.

The January 31, 1990, grand opening of McDonald's in the center of Moscow represented an important milestone for McDonald's Corporation and for the food service industry in the Soviet Union. The state-of-the-art renovated building, formally a café and a cultural gathering place, has indoor seating for over 700 people, has outside seating

SOURCES: McDonald's corporate information, 1994; "A Month Later, Moscow McDonald's Is Still Drawing Long and Hungry Lines," *Houston Post,* March 1, 1990; background information from McDonald's Restaurants of Canada, Ltd.; Jeffrey A. Tannenbaum, "Franchisers See a Future in East Bloc," *The Wall Street Journal,* June 5, 1990, B1; Kevin Maney and Diane Rinehart, "McDonald's in Moscow Opens Today," *USA Today,* January 31, 1990, B1; "McDonald's on the Volga," *Employment Review 3* (1990); Moscow McDonald's videotape produced for Dryden Press, 1990; Oliver Wates, "Crowds Still Gather at Lenin's Tomb, but Lineups Are Longer at McDonald's," *London Free Press,* June 9, 1990. For information see http://www.mcdonalds.com/.

for 200, and is fully accessible to the handicapped. It currently employs over 1,000 people—the largest McDonald's crew in the world—and has served over 30,000 people per day. The original plans were to serve between 10,000 and 15,000 customers per day. The Soviet Union became the 52nd country to host the world's largest quick-service food restaurant company, and the Russian language is the 28th working language in which the company operates. McDonald's Corporation, based in Oak Brook, Illinois, serves over 22 million people daily in 11,000 restaurants in fifty-two countries. The Soviet population of over 291 million represented a major potential market of new customers for McDonald's.

THE NEGOTIATIONS

George A. Cohon, vice chairman of Moscow McDonald's and president and chief executive officer of McDonald's Restaurants of Canada, Limited, provided the leadership for the company's successful venture. His personal commitment and energy were irreplaceable during the long period of joint-venture discussions with the Soviet Union. Cohon's Canadian team spent over twelve years negotiating the agreement for McDonald's to enter into the Soviet market. In April 1988, agreement was reached on the largest joint venture ever made between a food company and the Soviet Union. This concluded the longest new territory negotiations by the company since it was founded in 1955.

Cohon and his Canadian team had spent thousands of hours in Moscow making presentations to hundreds of senior trade officials, staff at various ministries, and countless other groups within the Soviet Union. Despite numerous setbacks and requests for endless submissions of and revisions of their proposals, Cohon persisted because many Soviets appeared to genuinely want to establish closer ties with the West. According to Cohon, McDonald's negotiations "outlived three Soviet premiers."

The historic joint venture contract provided for an initial twenty McDonald's restaurants in Moscow and a state-of-the-art food production and distribution center to supply the restaurants. McDonald's accepts only rubles; future restaurants may accept hard currency. McDonald's Canada is managing the new venture in partnership with the Food Service Administration of the Moscow City Council in a 51 to 49 percent Soviet-Canadian partnership.

INTERNATIONAL TECHNOLOGY TRANSFER

Cohon stated that what ultimately sold the Soviets on McDonald's was the food technology it had to offer. In addition, the company's emphasis on quality, service, cleanliness, and value convinced the Moscow city officials that McDonald's could work in their city. Vladimir Malyshkov, chairman of the board of Moscow McDonald's, stated that McDonald's "created a restaurant experience like no other in the Soviet Union. It demonstrates what can be achieved when people work together."

Moscow McDonald's was clearly an international venture. McDonald's personnel from around the world helped prepare for the opening. Dutch agricultural consultants assisted in improving agricultural production. For example, they helped plant and harvest a variety of potato needed to make french fries that met McDonald's quality standards. Other international consultants assisted in negotiating contracts with farmers throughout the country to provide quality beef and other food supplies, including onions, lettuce, pickles, milk, flour, and butter. Once the Soviet farmers learned to trust the consultants, they became eager to learn about the new Western production technologies.

This technology transfer provided important long-term benefits to the Soviet citizenry. For example, through the transfer of agricultural technology and equipment, the Soviet potato farm Kishira increased its yield by 100 percent. According to the Kishira chairman, farmers from all over the Soviet Union requested technical training in production methods to increase their crop yields. Also, since the Soviet machinery lagged fifteen to twenty years behind Western technology, new machinery from Holland was used to harvest the potatoes used to make french fries. However, according to a Dutch agricultural consultant, because of the McDonald's venture, it may not take the Soviets twenty years to catch up to Western production methods.

The development of a 10,000-square-meter food production and distribution center, located in the Moscow suburb of Solntsevo, was also an international effort involving equipment and furnishings from Austria, Canada, Denmark, Finland, Germany, Holland, Italy, Japan, Spain, Sweden, Switzerland, Taiwan, Turkey, the United Kingdom, the United States, and Yugoslavia. The center provides a state-of-the-art food-processing environment that meets McDonald's rigid standards.

At full capacity, the center employs over 250 workers. Also at full capacity, the meat line produces 10,000 patties per hour from locally acquired beef. Milk delivered in McDonald's refrigerated dairy trucks from a local farm is pasteurized and processed at the center. Flour, yeast, sugar, and shortening are used to produce over 14,000 buns per hour on the center's bakery line. Storage space at the center holds 3,000 tons of potatoes, and the pie line produces 5,000 apple pies per hour, made from fruit from local farmers.

MANAGEMENT TRAINING

Training for McDonald's crew and managers is essential to the customer service that the company provides. According to Bob Hissink, vice president of operations for Moscow McDonald's, hiring was just the beginning of assembling the largest McDonald's crew in the world. Over 25,000 applications were sorted, and 5,000 of the most qualified candidates were interviewed. Finally, the 630 new members of the first Moscow McDonald's team were selected. Initial training sessions were compressed into a four-week period with four or five shifts twelve hours a day. Seasoned McDonald's staff from around the world assisted the Soviet managers with crew training. The new crew of 353 women and 277 men was trained to work in several different capacities at the restaurant and had accumulated over 15,000 hours of skills development by opening day. During restaurant operating hours, about 200 crew members at a time are on duty.

The training requirements were more extensive for McDonald's managers. Four Soviets selected as managers of Moscow McDonald's spent more than nine months in North American training programs that must be completed by any McDonald's manager in the world. The Soviets graduated from the Canadian Institute of Hamburgerology after completing over 1,000 hours of training. Their studies included classroom instruction, equipment maintenance techniques, and on-the-job restaurant management.

Their training also included a two-week, in-depth study program at Hamburger University, McDonald's international training center in Oak Brook, Illinois. With more than 200 other managers from around the world, they completed advanced restaurant operations studies in senior management techniques and operating procedures. The Soviet managers were thus qualified to manage any McDonald's restaurant in the world.

THE GRADUAL EXPANSION

Initially, McDonald's Corporation had expected a rather quick expansion of restaurants. However, political and economic difficulties slowed down progress. In 1991, the Soviet

Union ceased to exist. From then on, the firm had to deal with the new Russian government. But at the original McDonald's on Pushkin Square, the twenty-seven cash registers at the seventy-foot service counter kept on ringing. In spite of all the political changes, by June 1993, over 50 million customers had been served at a rate of 40,000 to 50,000 a day. The original staff of 630 had grown to 1,500, and the initial eighty expatriates working in Moscow had dwindled to less than a dozen.

On June 1, 1993, the McDonald's office building opened in Moscow. The twelve-story building had cost the equivalent of $50 million. It was the most modern office building in Moscow and had prestige tenants such as Coca-Cola, American Express, Mitsui, and the Upjohn Company. On its main floor was the second McDonald's restaurant, which was opened by Russian president Boris Yeltsin. Only one month later, the third McDonald's restaurant opened in Moscow's Arbat district. Like its predecessors, this restaurant too accepted only rubles. Ten thousand people waited in line for the opening to taste the food and see the restoration of the historic building in which the restaurant was located. By the end of the first day, this new restaurant had served 60,000 people. The day's receipts, an estimated 50 million rubles, were presented to Mrs. Yeltsin, in support of child health care.

THE LONG-TERM VISION

According to Cohon, "McDonald's is a business, but also is a responsible member of the communities it serves. The joint venture should help foster cooperation between nations and a better understanding among people. When individuals from around the world work shoulder-to-shoulder, they learn to communicate, to get along, and to be part of a team. That's what we call burger diplomacy." There is a Russian expression that says that you must eat many meals with a person before you come to know him. At 70,000 meals per day, it may not take long for the Russians to better understand the West through its corporate ambassador, McDonald's.

Questions for Discussion

1. Was Cohon's negotiation effort worth the success? Why or why not?
2. Discuss the extent of infrastructural investment necessary to start the first McDonald's restaurant in Moscow.
3. What is the effect of the "ruble only" policy?
4. How can McDonald's use the acquired rubles?

PART FIVE

International Finance and the Future

This final part of this text examines the various techniques for making payment in global business transactions and explores the role and growth of countertrade. The methods of financing foreign operations and the scope and availability of foreign debt and equity markets are analyzed. Chapter 15 provides an outlook for the future of global business. Career opportunities with global business organizations are discussed with some special observations regarding global management positions for women.

International Finance

LEARNING OBJECTIVES

To understand the various methods used in the financing of global trade transactions.

To examine why countertrade transactions are becoming increasingly common.

To become acquainted with the types of countertrade options available to the firm.

To understand the strategies and financial techniques used to manage cash flows of the modern multinational firm.

To evaluate the factors that can influence the structure of overseas subsidiaries.

To examine multinational firms' exposure to exchange rates over time.

Chinese Banks Holding Up Payments on Delivered Goods

HONG KONG—Some foreign exporters say they are being forced to wait as long as six months for payment on goods delivered to customers in China. And the culprits are cash-strapped Chinese banks, according to analysts and company executives in Hong Kong.

Under a system that foreign companies and U.S. trade negotiators have long decried, any foreign enterprise exporting goods to China must sell through a state-owned import-export company. Customers, from retailers to factories, must pay this middleman in renminbi for the goods. The import-export company's bank then remits the money to the foreign supplier in foreign exchange.

While extricating money from Chinese banks has never been easy, the delays have lengthened in recent months. Ultronics International Holdings, Ltd., a Hong Kong medical equipment distributor that relies on China for 90 percent of its sales, has faced increasing delays in payments since the end of last year. The wait used to be one or two months; now it is as long as six months, said Leo Lam, the company's financial controller.

There are ways for companies to cushion themselves. Goldlion Holdings Ltd., which has close to 70 percent of its sales in China, insists on letters of credit for almost all of its transactions on the mainland. Under this system, when Goldlion delivers its goods—men's ties, leather goods and accessories—it receives a letter of credit, which it then presents to the customer's bank. That bank must transfer money to Goldlion within a set time, which can range from several days to several weeks, said Louis Lau, Goldlion's financial controller. "With a letter of credit, the risk is basically none," Lau said.

However, both men concede that it can be difficult to negotiate such payment terms with customers and remain competitive. And others scoff at the idea that China's banks will honor a letter of credit more readily than another contract. "Getting a letter of credit in China is practically useless," said a Hong Kong exporter whose company rarely uses them. "Under international practice, banks are supposed to pay (when a letter of credit is presented). But in China, they can refuse payment if they don't have the money."

SOURCE: Extracted from Leslie Chang, "Exporters Say Struggling Chinese Banks Hold Up Payments on Delivered Goods," *The Wall Street Journal,* November 22, 1994, A17.

This chapter is divided into two major sections, Financing Exports and Imports, and Financial Management. The first section is designed to acquaint the reader with the various methods used in making payment in global trade transactions. The section also includes a review of countertrade techniques and how new variations of one of the oldest methods of payment now make possible global trade that ordinarily would not take place. The second section deals with the various tools and techniques used by international financial executives in managing the cash flows of their companies, in making capital structure decisions, and in managing risks inherent in global business.

FINANCING EXPORTS AND IMPORTS

Export/Import Financing

This portion of the chapter deals with the most common methods of financing exports or imports. Unlike most domestic business, global business often occurs between two parties that do not know each other very well and who may be physically separated from each other by thousands of miles. Lack of a relationship, extended distances, time differences, communication problems, and differing legal systems all tend to aggravate the problem of receiving payment for merchandise shipped, as shown in Global Learning Experience 14.1. We now review the various payment options available to the exporter and importer.

Cash The best of all worlds would be for the exporter to receive payment prior to shipping goods. Unfortunately, it would be a rare importer who would be willing to part with money without first seeing the merchandise.

Open Account With this option, the exporter ships merchandise and sends the importer an invoice, allowing some period of time for the importer to make payment. But what would a U.S. exporter do if an importer in Hong Kong refused to make payment? The exporter would first have to find the importer in Hong Kong (assuming the importer and the merchandise were still there) and then proceed to sue the importer under Hong Kong law. Understandably, because of the potential for problems, few exporters will ship merchandise unless they have the importers' money up front.

At this point there seems to be an impasse; under cash and open account options, either the importer or exporter is exposed to severe financial risk. Fortunately, there are ways around this dilemma. The reader will recall from Chapter 13 that two of the properties of the ocean bill of lading are that it is negotiable and that it is evidence of ownership. These properties result in two other methods of collecting funds that minimize the financial risk of exporting and importing.

documentary collection
use of financial intermediaries to collect funds; documents are used to control merchandise until payment is made

Documentary Collection Sometimes referred to as documents against payment, the **documentary collection** method uses financial intermediaries (usually banks) to facilitate the collection of funds. Figure 14.1 indicates how this type of collection works. The names of the parties shown in the figure tell you what they do.

FIGURE 14.1 **The Collection Procedure**

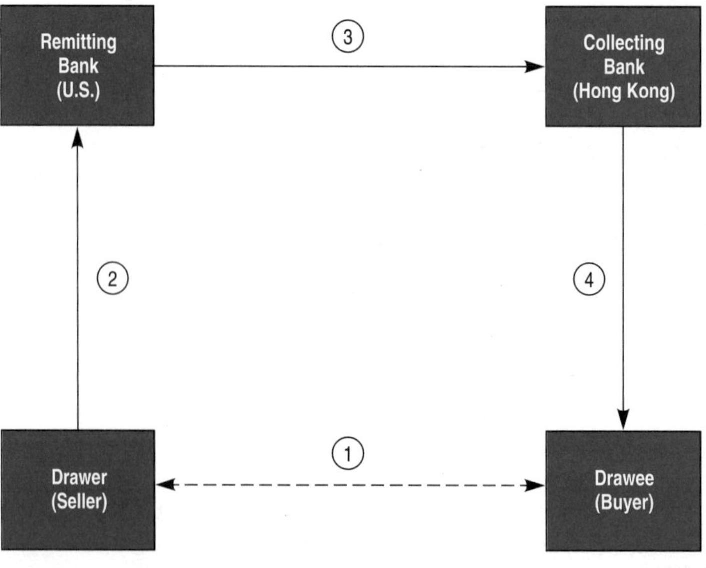

Step 1. The buyer and seller agree on the terms of a contract, including the buyer's obligation to pay on delivery (sight) of the required documents, including the ocean bill of lading.

Step 2. The seller ships the merchandise and has a collecting bank named as the consignee on the ocean bill of lading. The seller (drawer) draws a draft (also called a bill of exchange), payable by the drawee on sight of the documents. The draft and all documents are delivered to a U.S. bank.

Step 3. A U.S. bank sends the documents with instructions to the collecting bank in the foreign country (Hong Kong).

Step 4. When the cargo arrives in Hong Kong, the steamship company notifies the consigner (collecting bank). The collecting bank advises the buyer that the cargo is in and that payment is due. The buyer accepts the draft and makes payment. The collecting bank then endorses the ocean bill of lading to the buyer, which permits the buyer to remove the cargo from the pier. The collected funds are then forwarded to the seller.

Operating in conjunction with the banking intermediaries, the seller is able to control the merchandise until payment is made. In the event that the buyer does not come forward to accept the draft and make payment (a nonacceptance), the seller is left with only a few options: ship the merchandise back to the United States; try to find another buyer in the foreign market; abandon the cargo at the pier, or attempt to renegotiate the contract with the original buyer in the hope of arriving at a selling price that will cover costs.

Since the documentary collection process presents some degree of risk for the seller, it is probably best reserved for use between subsidiaries of the same company or with a customer with whom the seller has had a long history of excellent relations.

Letter of Credit The **letter of credit** overcomes the risk inherent in a documentary collection. The letter of credit is an undertaking by a bank to make payment to the seller (exporter) upon completion of the tasks set forth in the letter. The tasks usually include the presentation of required shipping and export documents. As in the documentary collection, the ocean bill of lading is the key document.

letter of credit
undertaking by a bank to make payment to a seller upon completion of the conditions set forth in the letter of credit

Figure 14.2 illustrates a letter of credit transaction. (Remember that the names of the parties shown in the figure tell you what they do.)

The reader will observe that the parties to the letter of credit may be the same as those to a documentary collection. There is, however, a big difference between the relationships. With a documentary collection, the banks are merely financial intermediaries; with a letter of credit arrangement, the banks are parties to the transaction.

Step 1. The buyer and seller agree on the terms of a contract, including the buyer's obligation to furnish the seller with a confirmed, irrevocable letter of credit.

Step 2. The applicant (buyer) applies to a bank in his or her area for a letter of credit. (Banks evaluate an application for a letter of credit the same way they evaluate a loan application.)

Step 3. If the foreign bank approves the letter of credit application, it will issue its letter of credit, guaranteeing payment to the seller if the terms of the letter are met. At this point, the issuing bank becomes a party to the transaction. The letter of credit is then forwarded to a corresponding bank in the vicinity of the seller.

Step 4. The corresponding bank (the advising bank) advises the selling company that it is the beneficiary of the issuing bank's letter of credit. The confirming bank adds its guarantee of payment to that of the issuing bank's. The net effect of the

FIGURE 14.2 **The Export Letter of Credit Procedure**

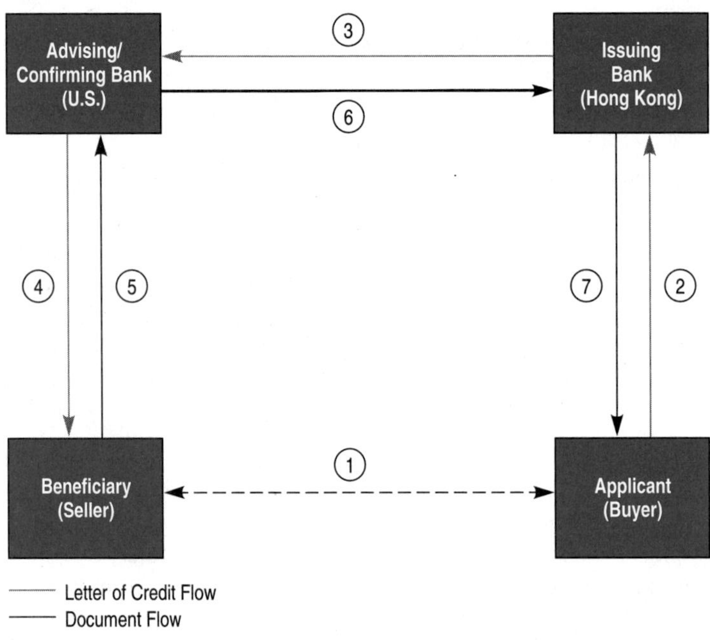

transaction so far is that the seller is dealing with two banks, both promising to make payment upon delivery of the specified documents (the arrangement between the applicant and the issuing bank is of no interest to the seller).

Step 5. The seller ships the merchandise and presents the confirming bank with the documents specified in the letter of credit. When the confirming bank accepts the documents, the seller will be paid.

Steps 6 and 7. The confirming bank forwards the documents, including the ocean bill of lading consigned to the issuing bank. The issuing bank then endorses the bill of lading over to the buyer.

The reader might wonder what happens if the buyer refuses to make payment to the issuing bank. The answer is that this is a problem for the issuing bank; that is, as long as the seller has provided the documents specified in the letter of credit, the transaction is completed and the seller is entitled to payment.

forfaiting
exporter discounts bills of exchange received from an importer

Forfaiting Although not common in the United States, **forfaiting** is widely used to finance export transactions in Europe. Essentially, forfaiting involves the exporter discounting bills of exchange or promissory notes received as an obligation to pay from an importer. Normally, the importer must provide for a third party, that is, a bank, to guarantee payment. Most forfaiting involves capital goods of high value with payments spread out from 18 months to as many as 10 years.

export receivable factor
assignment of invoices and documents related to a shipment to a factor who then pays exporter with a discounted amount

Export Receivable Factoring The **export receivable factor** method of trade financing, when it can be arranged, gives the exporter the benefit of being able to sell on what amounts to open account terms but with the guarantee of predictable cash flows from the sale. Export orders are preapproved by the factor. When the merchandise is shipped

TABLE 14.1 A Sample of Barter Agreements

Country		Exported Commodity	
A	B	A	B
Hungary	Ukraine	• Food stuffs • Canned foods • Pharmaceuticals	• Timber
Austria	Ukraine	• Power station emissions control equipment	• 800 megakilowatts/year for 15 years
U.S. (Chrysler)	Jamaica	• 200 pickup trucks	• Equivalent value in iron ore
Ukraine	Czech Republic	• Iron ore	• Mining equipment
U.S. (Pierre Cardin)	China	• Technical advice	• Silks and cashmeres
U.K. (Raleigh Bicycle)	CIS	• Training CIS scientists in mountain-bike production	• Titanium for 30,000 bike frames per year
Indonesia	Uzbekistan	• Indian tea • Vietnamese rice • Miscellaneous Indonesian products	• 50,000 tons of cotton/year for three years
Zaire	Italy	• Scrap iron	• 12 locomotives
China	Russia	• 212 railway trucks of mango juice	• Passenger jet
Morocco	Romania	• Citrus products	• Several large ports/ small harbors

SOURCES: American Countertrade Association, http://www.i-trade.com, December 1996; Aspy P. Palia and Oded Shenkar, "Countertrade Practices in China," *Industrial Marketing Management,* 1991, 58.

by the exporter, the invoices and related documentation are assigned to the factor. The factor pays the exporter with a discounted amount and accepts the responsibility of collecting the receivable.

countertrade payment for goods and services with other goods and services

Countertrade The basic idea of **countertrade** is to pay for goods or services with other goods or services. The earliest and most fundamental form of countertrade is barter—a direct exchange of goods of approximately equal value between parties with no money involved. As Table 14.1 shows, such transactions can encompass the exchange of a wide variety of goods, for example, bananas for cars or airplane parts for training, and are carried out both in developing and industrialized countries.

Countertrade transactions have always arisen when economic circumstances made it more acceptable to exchange goods directly rather than to use money as an intermediary. Conditions that encourage such business activities are lack of money, lack of value of or faith in money, lack of acceptability of money as an exchange medium, or greater ease of transaction by using goods.

What would happen if the Earth's polar ice caps were to melt, let's say as a result of extreme global warming?

If they melt, the average sea level would rise by about 60 feet, a catastrophe that would submerge half of the world's population.

Increasingly, countries are deciding that countertrade transactions are more beneficial to them than transactions based on financial exchange alone. A primary reason is that the world debt crisis has made ordinary trade financing very risky. Many countries, particularly in the developing world, simply cannot obtain the trade credit or financial assistance necessary to pay for desired imports. Heavily indebted countries, faced with the possibility of not being able to afford imports at all, hasten to use countertrade in order to maintain at least a trickle of product inflow. Furthermore, the use of countertrade permits the covert reduction of prices and therefore allows the circumvention of price and exchange controls.[1]

A second reason for the increase in countertrade is that many countries are again responding favorably to the notion of bilateralism. Thinking along the lines of "you scratch my back and I'll scratch yours," they prefer to exchange goods with countries that are their major business partners.

Countertrade is also often viewed by firms and nations alike as an excellent mechanism to gain entry into new markets. The producer often hopes that the party receiving the goods will serve as a new distributor, opening up new international marketing channels and ultimately expanding the original market.

Conversely, because countertrade is highly sought after in many enormous, but hard-currency poor emerging market economies such as China, and the former Eastern bloc countries, as well as in other cash-strapped countries in South America and the Third World, engaging in such transactions can provide major growth opportunities for firms. In increasingly competitive world markets, countertrade can be a good way to attract new buyers. By providing countertrade services, the seller is in effect differentiating its product from those of its competitors.[2]

Finally, countertrade can provide stability for long-term sales. For example, if a firm is tied to a countertrade agreement, it will need to source the product from a particular supplier, whether it wishes to do so or not.

Types of Countertrade

Increasingly, participants in countertrade have resorted to more sophisticated versions of exchanging goods that often also include some use of money. Table 14.2 provides a summary of the different forms of countertrade. One such refinement of simple barter is the counterpurchase, or parallel barter, agreement. In order to unlink the timing of contract performance, the participating parties sign two separate contracts that specify the goods and services to be exchanged. In this way, one transaction can go forward even though the second transaction needs more time. Such an arrangement can be particularly advantageous if delivery performance is dependent on a future event—for example, the harvest. Frequently, the exchange is not of precisely equal value; therefore, some amount of cash will be involved. However, despite the lack of linkage in terms of timing, an exchange of goods for goods does take place. A special case of parallel barter is that of reverse reciprocity, "whereby parallel contracts are signed, granting each party access to needed resources (for example, oil in exchange for nuclear power plants)."[3] Such contracts are useful when long-term exchange relationships are desired.

Another common form of countertrade is the buy-back, or compensation arrangement. One party agrees to supply technology or equipment that enables the other party

TABLE 14.2 **Types of Countertrade**

Barter	Direct exchange of goods of approximately equal value
Counterpurchase, or Parallel Barter	Two separate contracts for exchange of goods or services. Permits one side of the transaction to go forward, with the other side to follow at a later time.
Buy-back, or Compensation Arrangement	First party supplies technology or equipment, permitting second party to begin production. First party is then paid with goods produced.
Clearing Account Barter	Parties establish clearing accounts, such as a bank account, which keeps track of purchases made by each party. Long-term goal is equalization of purchases on both sides. Additional flexibility given by *switch trading,* in which credits in the account can be sold or transferred to a third party.
Offset	Requires that portions of the product be produced or assembled in buying country.
Debt Swaps	Countries with large amounts of external debt agree to exchange debt for some other asset of the country.
Debt-for-Debt Swap	Loan held by one creditor is exchanged for a loan held by another creditor.
Debt-for-Equity Swap	Debt is converted into foreign equity (ownership) in a domestic firm.
Debt-for-Product Swap	Debt is exchanged for products.
Debt-for-Nature Swap	Debt is exchanged for agreement by debtor nation to preserve natural resources.
Debt-for-Education Swaps	Proposal to cancel debt in exchange for education of U.S. students in debtor country.

to produce goods with which the price of the supplied products or technology is repaid. These arrangements often "include larger amounts of time, money, and products than straight barter arrangements."[4] They originally evolved "in response to the reluctance of communist countries to permit ownership of productive resources by the private sector—especially by foreign private sectors."[5] One example of such a buy-back arrangement is an agreement entered into by Levi Strauss and Hungary. The company transferred know-how and the Levi's trademark to Hungary. A Hungarian firm began to produce Levi's products. Some of the output was sold domestically, and the rest was marketed in Western Europe by Levi Strauss, in compensation for the know-how. In the past decade, buy-back arrangements have been extended to encompass many developing and newly industrialized nations.

Another form of more refined barter, which tries to reduce the effect of bilateralism and the immediacy of the transaction, is called clearing account barter. Here, clearing accounts are established to track debits and credits of trades. These entries merely represent purchasing power, however, and are not directly withdrawable in cash. As a result, each party can agree in a single contract to purchase goods or services of a specified value. Although the account may be out of balance on a transaction-by-transaction basis, the agreement stipulates that over the long term, a balance in the account will be restored. Frequently, the goods available for purchase with clearing account funds are tightly stipulated. In fact, funds have on occasion been labeled "apple clearing dollars" or "horseradish clearing funds." Sometimes, additional flexibility is given to the clearing account by permitting switch-trading, in which credits in the account can be

Preferred Items for Export in Countertrade Transactions

Preferred Items for Export in Countertrade Transactions

- Industrial goods
- Industrial machinery
- Equipment
- Manufactured goods
- Construction
- Engineering goods
- Computer software
- Plastic products
- Sporting goods
- Hides, skins & leather
- Textiles
- Animals
- Foodstuffs
- Timber & wood products
- Minerals
- Gems & jewelry
- Metals
- Chemicals & allied products
- Tobacco
- Fish Meal
- Grain
- Rice
- Wool
- Salt
- Oil Seeds
- Rum
- Molasses
- Fruits & vegetables
- Agriculture
- Coffee
- Sugar
- Cotton
- Shrimp
- Bauxite
- Gold
- Alumina
- Copper
- Iron ore
- Refined silver
- Lead
- Zinc
- Coal
- Natural gas
- Petroleum
- Petroleum products
- Crude oil

SOURCE: International Countertrade, Individual Country Practices, August 1992.

Offsets Help International Sales

To clinch the sale of $250 million worth of Apache helicopters to the United Arab Emirates, McDonnell Douglas recently agreed to equip the nation against a pesky airborne enemy: the whitefly. McDonnell Douglas is helping to install an insect trap system in the U.A.E. capital Abu Dhabi to fight a major infestation of the whitefly, which is decimating important vegetable crops there. "(Countertrade) is a marketing tool that we use to help facilitate our sales overseas," says Gary Pacific, manager of countertrade for McDonnell Douglas. The aircraft giant is one of the United States' most active participants in countertrade, with total transactions of several billion dollars each year.

Most countertrade is conducted by big companies with foreign markets to defend, such as McDonnell Douglas, Pepsi-Cola International, General Motors, and Caterpillar. Many of these firms have in-house countertrade departments. (McDonnell Douglas has a countertrade staff of 50.) Other countertraders employ independent trading companies to assist in completing deals.

Chicago-based Inland Steel Industries, Inc., plans to include countertrade in a joint venture with China. Inland will set up centers in China to distribute steel and other metals for U.S. and Chinese firms. When needed, Inland will accept Chinese-made coke and other raw materials as payment for its services. "The PRC (People's Republic of China) is looking for inflows of U.S. dollars," says Robert Weidner, head of investor and commercial relations at Inland. "If the optimal return is through a barter arrangement rather than hard currency, that's how we'll go."

More foreign governments are requiring countertrade to offset the cost of large procurements in the civil and defense sectors. Countertrade is used increasingly by companies as a marketing strategy in areas where sophisticated bargaining is part of the business culture. Recently, for example, McDonnell Douglas won an $800 million sale of Apache AH-64 helicopters to the Netherlands after offering to offset the cost through technology transfer and helping to sell Dutch ships around the world. "We were competing with the French," Pacific said. "We won because, besides the best helicopter, we had the best offset."

SOURCE: Ann Scott Tyson, "Countertrade Flourishes: Steel Centers for Coke," *The Christian Science Monitor,* May 2, 1995: 8.

sold or transferred to a third party. Doing so can provide creative intermediaries with opportunities for deal making by identifying clearing account relationships with major imbalances and structuring business transactions to reduce them.

Another major form of countertrade arrangement is called offset. These arrangements are most frequently found in the defense-related sector and in sales of large-scale, high-priced items such as aircraft and were designed to "offset" the negative effects of large purchases from abroad on the current account of a country. For example, a country purchasing aircraft from the United States might require that certain portions of the aircraft be produced and assembled in the purchasing country. As Global Learning Experience 14.2 indicates, large international sales often hinge on the ability to provide an attractive offset. See Table 14.3 for examples of direct and indirect offsets.

QUESTION *What is the distance around the Earth at the Equator?*

ANSWER

The circumference of the Earth at the Equator is 24,901.45 miles. The Earth rotates counter clockwise on its axis at approximately 1,000 miles per hour, making one complete revolution each day. If you could fly westward at a speed greater than 1,000 miles per hour, you would outrace the rotation of the Earth (and time) and arrive at your destination before you left.

A final, newly emerging form of countertrade, chiefly used as a financial tool, consists of debt swaps. These swaps are carried out particularly with less developed countries in which both the government and the private sector face large debt burdens. Because the debtors are unable to repay the debt anytime soon, debt holders have increasingly grown amenable to exchange of the debt for something else. The following five types of swaps are most prevalent: debt-for-debt swaps, debt-for-equity swaps, debt-for-product swaps, debt-for-nature swaps, and debt-for-education swaps.

A debt-for-debt swap is when a loan held by one creditor is simply exchanged for a loan held by another creditor. For example, a U.S. bank may swap Argentine debt for

TABLE 14.3 **Samples of Direct and Indirect Offset Practices**

Type	Description
Direct Offsets	
Coproduction	Overseas production based on government-to-government or producer agreements that permit a foreign government to acquire the technical information and tooling to manufacture all or part of a defense article.
Directed Subcontracting	The procurement of domestic-made components for incorporation or installation in the items sold to that same nation under direct commercial contracts.
Concessions	Commercial compensation practices whereby capabilities and items are given free of charge to the buyer.
Technology transfers/ Licensed production	Helping countries establish defense industry capabilities by providing valuable technology and manufacturing know-how.
Investments in defense firms	Capital invested to establish or expand a company in the purchasing country.
Indirect Offsets	
Procurements	Purchases of parts/components from the purchasing country which are unrelated to the military system being acquired.
Investments in nondefense firms	Establishing corporations in the purchasing countries to invest capital in the nations' companies.
Trading of commodities	Using brokers to link buyers with commodities sellers in the purchasing country.
Foreign defense-related projects	Assisting the recipient country's military services.

SOURCE: United States General Accounting Office. *Report to Congressional Requesters, Military Exports: Concerns Over Offsets Generated with U.S. Foreign Military Financing Program Funds,* June 1994: 18–19.

Chilean debt with a European bank. Through this mechanism, debt holders are able to consolidate their outstanding loans and concentrate on particular countries or regions.

Debt-for-equity swaps arise when debt is converted into foreign equity in a domestic firm. The swap therefore serves as the vehicle for foreign direct investment. Although the equity itself is denominated in local currency, the terms of the conversion may allow the investor future access to foreign exchange for dividend remittances and capital repatriation.[6] In some countries, these debt-for-equity swaps have been very successful.

A third form of debt swap consists of debt-for-product swaps. Here, debt is exchanged for products. Usually, these transactions require that an additional cash payment be made for the product. For example, First Interstate Bank of California concluded an arrangement with Peruvian authorities whereby a commitment was made to purchase $3 worth of Peruvian products for every $1 of products paid for by Peru against debt.[7]

An emerging form of debt swap is that of the debt-for-nature swap. Firms or entities buy what are otherwise considered to be nonperforming loans at substantial discounts and return the debt to the country in exchange for the preservation of natural resources. As repayment of debt becomes more and more difficult for an increasing number of nations, the swap of debt for social causes is likely to increase.

Debt-for-education swaps have been suggested in the U.S. government by one of the authors as a means to reduce the debt burden and to enable more U.S. students to study abroad, which could greatly enhance the international orientation, foreign-language training, and cultural sensitivity of the U.S. education system.[8] As Global Learning Experience 14.3 shows, some universities are already taking advantage of this form of countertrade.

With the increasing sophistication of countertrade, the original form of straight barter is less used today. Most frequently used is the counterpurchase agreement. Because of high military expenditures, offsets are the second most frequently used form. Figure 14.3 presents the results of a survey of U.S. firms that showed—for U.S. firms at least—the relatively low use of barter, findings confirmed by other research.[9]

FINANCIAL MANAGEMENT

Financial management is a broad term that covers all business decisions regarding cash flows. These cash flows extend from the funding of the entire enterprise to the preservation of firm liquidity given the gaps in time between when products are produced, sold, and shipped, to when payment is received. International financial management is the extension of this same set of concerns to the cross-border activities of the enterprise.

OVERVIEW OF INTERNATIONAL FINANCIAL MANAGEMENT

International financial management is not a separate set of issues from domestic or traditional financial management, but the additional levels of risk and complexity introduced by the conduct of business across borders. Business across borders introduces different laws, different methods, different markets, different interest rates, and most of all, different currencies.

The many dimensions of international financial management are most easily explained in the context of a firm's financial decision-making process of evaluating a potential foreign investment.

- *Working capital and cash flow management*—the management of operating and financial cash flows passing in and out of a specific investment project.

GLOBAL LEARNING EXPERIENCE
14.3

Swapping Debt for Education

Struggling to finance a college education? If your debt grows large enough, a debt-for-education swap might be the answer. Harvard University agreed to sponsor a program that converts Ecuadorian debt into a fund providing scholarships to Ecuadorian students and research grants for U.S. students and professors. There are four steps in the conversion process:

1. Harvard purchases $5 million of nonperforming Ecuadorian loans from banks at 15 percent of face value, or $750,000. The banks, faced with the possibility of having to swallow the defaulted loans, are happy to sell at the heavily discounted rate.
2. Harvard then presents the debt to Fundacion Capacitar, an educational foundation in Ecuador. The foundation sells the debt to the Ecuadorian government in exchange for bonds worth $2.5 million, or 50 percent of the original face value of the debt. The transaction reduces the government's outstanding debt by 50 percent.
3. Fundacion Capacitar then sells the bonds, which are valued in Ecuadorian currency, to local investors.
4. Income from the sale of the bonds is converted back into American dollars, invested in the United States, and used to set up a scholarship fund primarily for Ecuadorian students. Secondarily, the fund finances research grants to American students and professors.

The scholarship is expected to cover tuition and living expenses at Harvard for about 70 Ecuadorian students over the next 10 years. But who will actually receive the scholarship? Miguel Falconi, president of Fundacion Capacitar, claims that the fund "is mainly addressed to students without economic resources for studies." Critics of the program question whether the large landowners who dominate the countryside will support the program. They also question whether the rural student is equipped to handle life in Harvard yard.

Other American universities are actively negotiating similar agreements with the Ecuadorian government. Indeed, more than eight universities are expected to be involved in an exchange program that will provide study abroad financing to non-U.S. and U.S. students and teachers.

SOURCE: Laurel Shaper Walters, "Debt Funds Scholars," *Christian Science Monitor,* July 30, 1990, 14.

- *Capital structure*—the determination of the relative quantities of debt capital and equity capital that will constitute the funding of the investment.
- *Raising long-term capital*—the acquisition of equity or debt for the investment. This requires the selection of the exact form of capital, its maturity, its reward or repayment structure, its currency of denomination, and its source.

International financial management means that all the above financial activities will be complicated by the differences in markets, laws, and especially currencies. This is the field of financial risk management. Firms may intentionally borrow foreign currencies, buy forward contracts, or price their products in different currencies in order to manage their cash flows which are denominated in foreign currencies.

Changes in interest and exchange rates will affect each of the above steps in the international investment process. All firms, no matter how "domestic" they may seem in structure, are influenced by exchange rate changes. The financial managers of a firm

Countertrade Usage by Types FIGURE 14.3

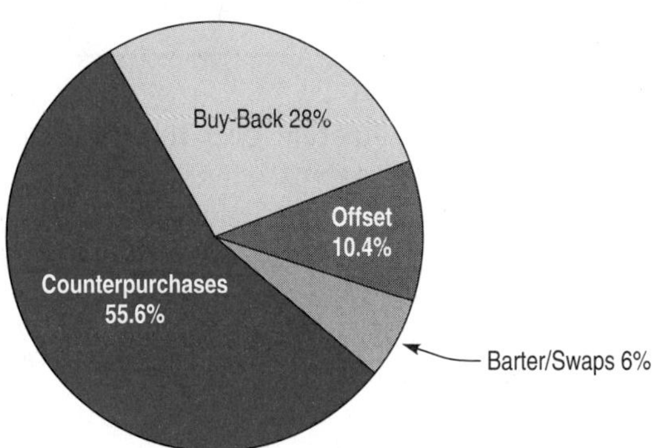

SOURCE: Richard Fletcher, "Australian Countertrade in The Global Economy," *Working Proper Series*1/96, University of Technology, Sydney, 1996.

that has any dimension of international activity, imports or exports, foreign subsidiaries or affiliates, must pay special attention to these issues if the firm is to succeed in its international endeavors.

Operating and Financial Cash Flows

A fundamental objective of financial management, domestic or international, is the management and maximization of **cash flows;** that is, the amount of cash that the company has. To the extent that the company can maximize its cash position by internal means, it reduces the need to go outside the company for external funds.

cash flow
the amount of cash (on hand or in banks) that a company has

INTERNATIONAL WORKING CAPITAL AND CASH FLOW MANAGEMENT

Working capital management is the financing of short-term or current assets, but the term is used here to describe all short-term financing and financial management of the firm. Even a small multinational firm will have a number of different cash flows moving throughout its system at one time. The maintenance of proper liquidity, the monitoring of payments, and the acquisition of additional capital when needed require a great degree of organization and planning in international operations.

Firms have both operating cash flows and financial cash flows. Operating cash flows arise from the everyday business activities of the firm, such as paying for materials or resources (accounts payable) or receiving payments for items sold (accounts receivable). In addition to the direct cost and revenue cash flows from operations, there are a number of indirect cash flows. These indirect cash flows are primarily license fees paid to the owners of particular technological processes and royalties to the holders of patents or copyrights. Many multinational firms also spread their overhead and

QUESTION

What is the world's deepest lake?

The deepest lake in the world is Lake Baikal in Siberia, which is 5,715 feet deep.

management expenses incurred at the parent over their foreign affiliates and subsidiaries that are utilizing the parent's administrative services.

Financial cash flows arise from the funding activities of the firm. The servicing of funding sources, interest on debt, and dividend payments to shareholders constitute potentially large and frequent cash flows. Periodic additions to debt or equity through new bank loans, new bond issuances, or supplemental stock sales may constitute additional financial cash flows in the international firm.

Cash Flow Management

The structure of the firm dictates the ways cash flows and financial resources can be managed. The trend in the past decade has been for the increasing centralization of most financial and treasury operations. The centralized treasury is often responsible for both funding operations and cash flow management. The centralized treasury may often enjoy significant economies of scale, offering more services and expertise to the various units of the firm worldwide than the individual units themselves could support. However, regardless of whether the firm follows a centralized or decentralized approach, there are a number of operating structures that aid the multinational firm in managing its cash flows.

Managing the Payment of Receivables and Their Conversion into Cash

When a company chooses to do business in a foreign country or region through a wholly owned subsidiary or some form of cooperative venture, the need to secure payment through export letters of credit is eliminated. In its place the more traditional method of payment (payment against delivery of goods and presentation of an invoice) becomes operable. In attempting to design a system that will speed up the conversion of accounts receivable into cash, the following items will require analysis for each country in which the company does business:

- The bank(s) or financial institution used by each customer for effecting payment
- The method of payment used by customers; unlike the United States where checks are the usual method of payment, a variety of other methods are in use in foreign countries
- Banking regulations and clearing practices and times
- Mail delivery times
- Value-dating practices, that is, when the bank actually recognizes the availability of funds

Assuming the analyses just mentioned have been performed, the following basic techniques might be used to expedite the receipt of payments in order to convert those payments into cash.

Electronic Transfers *Cable remittance* is the transfer of funds from one bank to another bank using communication systems owned by others, for example, telex or telegram. Funds can be transferred globally, commonly with next-day delivery.

Wire transfer is the bank-to-bank transfer of funds using the SWIFT system (Society of Worldwide Interbank Financial Telecommunications). The SWIFT system is owned and operated by approximately 900 banks in the United States, Europe, and the Far East. SWIFT is less costly and more efficient than cable remittance.

Mobilization Centers Customers can be instructed to mail their payment to the sellers' regional office, which would then consolidate funds and expedite transfer to the home office or an appropriate subsidiary. Payments may also be deposited directly into the seller's account at a branch of the bank working with the mobilization center.

Lock Boxes The lock box is a technique with wide domestic and international use. Customers mail payments to a lock box, a post office box to which the seller's bank is given access. The bank removes and deposits checks frequently. If analysis indicates that a large number of customers in a given area are using branches of the same bank, consideration should be given to establishing a lock box account in the customers' bank. This may result in the same-day clearing of funds.

Techniques to Minimize the Need for Cash or Cash Outflows

Cash Pooling A large firm with a number of units operating within an individual country and across countries may be able to economize on the amount of firm assets needed in cash if the cash holding is operated through one central pool. With one pool of capital and up-to-date information on the cash flows in and out of the various units, the firm spends much less in terms of lost interest on cash balances that are held in safekeeping against unforeseen cash flow shortfalls. A single large pool may also be able to negotiate better financial service rates with banking institutions for clearing purposes.

Netting Many of the cash flows between units of a multinational firm are two-way and may result in unneeded transfer costs and transaction expenses. Coordination between units simply requires some planning and budgeting of intrafirm cash flows in order that two-way flows are **netted** against one another, with one smaller cash flow replacing two opposed flows. This is particularly helpful if the two-way flow is in two different currencies, as each would be suffering currency exchange charges for intrafirm transfers.

netting
coordination of two opposite cash flows between subsidiaries of a firm so that only the net balance of the two is actually exchanged

Leads and Lags The timing of payments between units of a multinational is somewhat flexible. This flexibility allows the firm to not only position cash flows where they are needed most, but may actually aid in currency risk management. A foreign subsidiary that is expecting its local currency to fall in value relative to the U.S. dollar may try to speed up, or "lead," its payments to the parent. Similarly, if the local currency is expected to rise versus the dollar, the subsidiary may want to wait, or "lag," payments until exchange rates are more favorable.

Reinvoicing Multinational firms with a variety of manufacturing and distribution subsidiaries scattered over a number of countries within a region may often find it more economical to have one office or subsidiary taking ownership of all invoices and payments between units. This subsidiary literally buys from one unit and sells to a second unit, therefore taking ownership of the goods and reinvoicing the sale to the next unit. Once ownership is taken, the transaction can be redenominated in a different currency, netted against other payments, hedged against specific currency exposures, or repriced in accordance with potential tax benefits of the reinvoicing center's host country. The additional flexibility achievable in cash flow management, product pricing, and profit placement may be substantial.

Internal Banks Some multinational firms have found that their financial resources and needs are becoming either too large or too sophisticated for the financial services that are available in many of their local subsidiary markets. One solution to this has been the establishment of an "internal bank" within the firm. This bank actually buys and sells payables and receivables from the various units. This frees the units of the firm from struggling for continual working capital financing and allows them to focus on their primary business activities.

These structures and procedures are often combined in different ways to fit the needs of the individual multinational firm. Some techniques are encouraged or prohibited by laws and regulations, depending on the host country's government and stage of capital market liberalization. In fact, it is not uncommon to find one system at work in one hemisphere of firm operations with a different system in use in the other hemisphere. Multinational cash flow management requires flexible thinking on the part of managers.

CAPITAL STRUCTURE: INTERNATIONAL DIMENSIONS

equity capital
capital normally raised by selling shares in the company stock to investors

debt capital
capital raised by borrowing money from investors, i.e., bonds

The choice of how to fund the firm is called capital structure. Capital is needed to open a factory, build an amusement park, or even start a hot dog stand. If capital is provided by owners of the firm, it is called **equity.** If capital is obtained by borrowing from others, like commercial banking institutions, it is termed **debt.** Debt must be repaid with interest over some specified schedule. Equity capital, however, is kept in the firm. Because owners are risking their own capital in the enterprise, they are entitled to a proportion of the profits.

The Capital Structure of the Firm

The trade-offs between debt and equity are easily seen by looking at extreme examples of capital structures. If a firm had no debt, all capital would have to come from the owners. This may limit the size of the firm, as the owners do not have bottomless pockets. The primary benefit is that all net operating revenues are kept. There are no principal or interest payments to make. A firm with a large debt (highly leveraged), however, would have the capital of others with which to work. The scale of the firm could be larger, and all net profits would still accrue to the equity holders alone. The primary disadvantage of debt is the increasing expense of making principal and interest payments. This could prove to be an ever increasing proportion of net cash flows at the extreme.

Any firm's ability to grow and expand is dependent on its ability to acquire additional capital as it grows. The net profits generated over previous periods may be valuable but are rarely enough to provide needed capital expansion. Firms therefore need access to capital markets, both debt and equity. It is important to remember that the firm must have access to these markets in order to enjoy their fruits. Smaller firms operating in the smaller markets are generally unable to tape these larger international capital markets. These markets are still the domains of the multinational firms, the behemoths of multinational business.

The Capital Structure of Foreign Subsidiaries

The choice of what proportions of debt and equity to use in international investments is usually dictated by either the debt-equity structure of the parent firm or the debt-equity structure of the competitive firms in the country where the investment is to be made. The parent firm sees equity investment as capital at risk; it therefore would normally prefer to provide as little equity capital as possible. Although funding the foreign subsidiary primarily with debt would still put the parent's capital at risk, debt service pro-

TABLE 14.4 **Financing Alternatives for Foreign Affiliates**

Foreign Affiliate Can Raise Equity Capital	Foreign Affiliate Can Raise Debt Capital
1. From the parent	1. From the parent
2. From a joint-venture partner in the parent's country, a joint-venture partner in the host country, or a share issue in the host country	2. From a bank loan or bond issue in the host country or the parent firm's home country
3. From a third-country market such as a share issue in the Euro-equity market	3. From a third-country bank loan, bond issue, Euro-syndicated credit, or Euro-bond issue

vides a strict schedule for cash flow repatriation to the lender—regular principal and interest payments according to the debt agreement. Equity capital's return, dividends from profits, depends on managerial discretion. It is this discretion, the proportion of profits returned to the parent versus profits retained and reinvested in the project or firm, that often leads to conflict between host-country authorities and the multinational firm.

The sources of debt for a foreign subsidiary are theoretically quite large, but in reality they are often quite limited. The alternatives listed in Table 14.4 are often reduced radically in practice because many countries have relatively small capital markets. These countries often either officially restrict the borrowing by foreign-owned firms in their countries or simply do not have affordable capital available for the foreign firms's use. The parent firm is then often forced to provide not only the equity but also a large proportion of the debt to its foreign subsidiaries. If the project or subsidiary is a new project, it has no existing line of business or credit standing. The parent must then represent the subsidiary's credit worth and provide the debt capital at least until the project is operating and showing (hopefully) positive net cash flows.

The larger international firms will often have their own financial subsidiaries, companies purely for the purpose of acquiring the capital needed for the entire company's continuing growth needs. These financial subsidiaries will often be the actual unit extending the debt or equity capital to the foreign project or subsidiary. Hopefully, with time and success, the foreign investment will grow sufficiently to establish its own credit standing and acquire more and more of its capital needs from the local markets in which it operates, or even from the international markets which become aware of its growth.

INTERNATIONAL CAPITAL MARKETS

Just as with the money markets, the international capital markets serve as links between the capital markets of the individual countries, as well as constituting a separate market of its own, the capital that flows into the Euromarkets. Firms can now raise capital, debt or equity, fixed or floating interest rates, in any of a dozen currencies, for maturities ranging from 1 month to 30 years, in the international capital markets. Although the international capital markets have traditionally been dominated by debt instruments, international equity markets have shown considerable growth in recent years.

The international financial markets can be subdivided in a number of different ways. The following sections will describe the international debt and equity markets for securitized and nonsecuritized capital. This is capital which is separable and tradable, like a bond or a stock. Nonsecuritized, a fancy term for bank loans, was really the original source of international capital (as well as the international debt crisis).

FIGURE 14.4 **Categories of Financial Transactions**

	Domestic Currency	Foreign Currency
Domestic Borrower	1. General Motors issues a bond in the United States raising $100 million.	3. British firm Allied-Lyons issues a bond in London to raise United States $40 million.
Foreign Borrower	2. Germany BMW issue bonds in the United States to raise $50 million in capital.	4. French firm issues United States-dollar-denominated bond in London. This is a Eurodollar bond.

Defining International Financing

The definition of what constitutes an international financial transaction is dependent on two fundamental characteristics: (1) whether the borrower is domestic or foreign and (2) whether the borrower is raising capital denominated in the domestic currency or a foreign currency. These two characteristics form four categories of financial transactions, as illustrated in Figure 14.4.

Using this classification system, it is possible to categorize any individual international financial transaction. For example, the distinction between an international bond and a Eurobond is simply that of a Category 2 transaction (foreign borrower in a domestic currency market) and a Category 3 or 4 transaction (foreign currency denominated in a single local market or many markets).

Category 1: Domestic Borrower/Domestic Currency This is a traditional domestic financial market activity. A borrower that is resident within the country raises capital from domestic financial institutions denominated in local currency. For example, if a U.S. firm such as General Motors issues a bond in the United States, raising $100 million, the transaction would be classified as purely domestic. All countries with basic market economies have their own domestic financial markets, some large and some quite small. This is still by far the most common type of financial transaction.

Category 2: Foreign Borrower/Domestic Currency This is when a foreign borrower enters another country's financial market and raises capital denominated in the local currency. For example, if a large foreign firm such as the German automaker BMW comes to the United States and issues a bond, raising $50 million in capital, it is conducting a Category 2 financial transaction. The international dimension of this transaction is only who the borrower is. This is a relatively common type of financial transaction. Many borrowers, both public and private, increasingly go to the world's largest financial markets to raise capital for their enterprises. The ability of a foreign firm to raise capital in another country's financial market is sometimes limited by government restrictions on who can borrow, as well as the market's willingness to lend to foreign governments and companies that it may not know as well as domestic borrowers.

Category 3: Domestic Borrower/Foreign Currency Many borrowers in today's international markets need capital denominated in a foreign currency. A domestic firm may actually issue a bond to raise capital in its local market where it is known quite well, but raise the capital in the form of a foreign currency. For example, if a large British firm such as Allied-Lyons issued a bond in London to raise US$40 million, it would be classified as a domestic borrower of a foreign currency. This type of financial transaction occurs less often than the previous two types because it requires a local market in foreign currencies, a Eurocurrency market. A number of countries such as the United States highly restrict the amount and types of financial transactions in foreign currency. International financial centers such as London and Zurich have been the traditional centers of these types of transactions.

Category 4: Foreign Borrower/Foreign Currency This is the strictest form of the traditional Eurocurrency financial transaction, a foreign firm borrowing foreign currency. For example, a French firm that issues a U.S. dollar–denominated bond in London would be issuing a Eurodollar bond. Once again, this type of activity may be restricted by which borrowers are allowed into a country's financial markets and which currencies are available. This type of financing dominates the activities of many banking institutions in the offshore banking market.

Using this classification system, it is possible to categorize any individual international financial transaction. For example, the distinction between an international bond and a Eurobond is simply that of a Category 2 transaction (foreign borrower in a domestic currency market) and a Category 3 or 4 transaction (foreign currency denominated in a single local market or many markets).

Driving Forces in the International Financial Markets

The rapid growth of the international financial markets over the past 30 years is the result of four different but complementary forces: deregulation, innovation, securitization, and internationalization. Although one normally thinks of the world's largest industrial countries when describing financial markets, all four forces are visible in differing degrees the world over. In fact, the newly opened economies of the former Eastern European bloc such as Czechoslovakia (now split into the Czech Republic and Slovakia), Hungary, Poland, and many others are now seeing the impacts of these four forces at something approaching the speed of light.

Deregulation is the first and most important force in opening financial markets. As governments continue to allow foreign firms to enter their markets for the buying and selling of goods, they have also become more willing to allow foreign firms to participate in their local financial markets.

One of the major areas still restricted by many governments is the ability to conduct financial transactions in foreign currencies. Only the true international financial centers like London allow the types of transactions described in Categories 3 and 4, Euromarket transactions.

Innovation has been the second major driving force. While product markets have grown increasingly competitive, so has the market for financial services. Financial institutions worldwide continue to innovate new and more efficient and effective services for their public and private clients alike. The creation of new types of financial instruments, like floating-rate loans and notes and bonds in the 1970s, was a logical market

Locations of the World's Most Important Financial Centers

SOURCES: *Financial Market Trends,* Oct. 1992; *Fortune,* July 30, 1990.

reaction to a world in which inflation was generally rising across all countries and currencies. Floating interest rates allowed lenders like banks to shift more of the risk of rising interest rates to the borrowers of capital while still allowing the markets to operate and provide much needed financing for growth.

Securitization has been a remarkably important force in just the past decade. Securitization is the process of turning an illiquid loan into a tradable, asset-backed security. For example, a bank loan is a highly customized contract between a bank and a borrower. Because each loan is so different, it is difficult for the bank to sell its loans. Securitization is the process of creating new ways to make these types of financial agreements liquid (salable in a secondary market).

Many firms have shifted away from traditional bank loan markets to securitized debt markets. Large firms in the United States, for example, used to acquire most of the long- and short-term capital from banks. As bond markets have grown in size, however, corporations have started funding their long-term capital needs through bonds, debt securities.

The fourth and final force is *internationalization.* Internationalization of business activity has forced many firms to acquire capital in many different markets in many different currencies. The growth of the multinational firm, a firm with subsidiaries and affiliates in 10, 20, or 30 countries, has provided an incentive for domestic financial markets to deregulate, innovate, and even securitize financial transactions to compete. Financial services in today's technologically sophisticated information age are considered by many to be more competitive than any product market.

INTERNATIONAL BANKING

Banks have existed in different forms and roles since the Middle Ages. Bank loans provided nearly all of the debt capital needed by industry since the start of the Industrial Revolution. Even in this age in which securitized debt instruments (bonds, notes, and other types of tradable paper) are growing as sources of capital for firms worldwide, banks still perform a critical role by providing capital for medium and smaller firms, which dominate all economies.

Structure of International Banking

A bank that wants to conduct business with clients in other countries but does not want to open a banking operation in that country can do so through **correspondent banks or representative offices.** A correspondent bank is an unrelated bank (by ownership) based in the foreign country. By the nature of its business, the correspondent bank has knowledge of the local market and access to clients, capital, and information, which a foreign bank does not. For example, a U.S. bank may maintain correspondent bank relationships with several banks in other major industrial countries. This would require that the U.S. bank keep a small amount of capital on deposit at the individual banks, as would the foreign banks with the U.S. bank. If there are financial services to be provided in the foreign country, the U.S. bank would communicate by phone, telex, or fax the appropriate directions and transactions to be undertaken.

correspondent banks or representative offices
banks located in different countries and unrelated by ownership that have a reciprocal agreement to provide services to each other's customers

Can you name the wettest spot on Earth?

If you like walking or singing in the rain visit Mount Waialeale, Hawaii. It has an annual rainfall of 471 inches.

A second way that banks may access foreign markets without actually opening a banking operation is through representative offices. A representative office is basically a sales office for a bank. It provides information regarding the financial services of the bank, but it cannot deliver the services itself. It cannot accept deposits or make loans. The foreign representative office of a U.S. bank will typically sell the bank's services to local firms that may need banking services for trade or other transactions in the United States.

If a bank wants to conduct banking business within the foreign country, it may open a branch banking office, banking affiliate, or even a wholly owned banking subsidiary. A branch banking office is an extension of the parent bank and is not independently financed from the parent. Because the branch office is not independently incorporated, it is commonly restricted in the types of banking activities that it may conduct. Any business conducted by the branch office is a legal liability of the parent bank. Branch banking is by far the most common form of international banking structure used by banks, particularly by banks based in the United States. Although branches are commonly limited in their capabilities due to the restrictions placed upon them by local governments, they are also relatively cheap ways of accessing foreign markets.

A foreign banking affiliate or banking subsidiary is a locally and separately incorporated bank from the parent bank. If the local bank is wholly owned by the parent, it is a subsidiary; if only partially owned, it is an affiliate. Because these are for all intents and purposes local banks, they normally can provide all the same financial services just like any other banks in that country.

Offshore Banking

Most governments regulate the degree of financial activity in a foreign currency that can take place. This has encouraged the growth of what is generally referred to as offshore banking. Offshore banking is the name given to Category 4 transactions, foreign borrowers of foreign currencies.

The primary motivation of offshore banking is avoiding banking and taxes regulations. Because governments do not normally regulate banking activity that does not affect their domestic markets, countries that have historically allowed unregulated foreign banking activity have been the centers of offshore banking. Many tropical islands, such as the Caymans, the Bahamas, and the Netherlands Antilles, have been the center of much of offshore banking activity, although countries such as Luxembourg and Switzerland have also provided many of the same services. Although these transactions are officially "booked" through these offshore centers, most of the activity is on paper or telex only as most of the capital never reaches these remote locales.

International Bank Lending

Bank lending internationally consists of two types of financial credits: (1) loans extended by a single bank and (2) loans extended by a collection or syndicate of banks. These loans are international loans if they are extended to a foreign borrower or are denominated in a foreign currency.

International bank lending has grown significantly since the early 1980s when net lending was dominated by syndicated loans extended to developing countries. After the decline of the syndicated loan market in 1983–1986, the growth in international bank lending was in the more traditional form of a simple loan arranged between a single bank and a corporate (not government) borrower.

INTERNATIONAL SECURITY MARKETS

Although banks continue to provide a large portion of the international financial needs of government and business, it is the international debt-securities markets that have experienced the greatest growth in the past decade. The international debt-securities market is composed of the **Euronote** market and the international bond market.

Euronote
a short- to medium-term debt instrument sold in the Eurocurrency markets

The Euronote Market

The **Euronote** market is a collective term for a variety of short- to medium-term types of financing. The true source of sustained financing in the Euronote market came from a financial export of the United States, commercial paper (CP). Commercial paper is a short-term note, typically 30, 60, 90, or 180 days in maturity, sold directly into the financial markets by large corporations. The market originated in the United States in the 1970s when a number of major firms realized they were actually larger and more creditworthy than many of the banks they were borrowing from. The solution was to sell their own debt notes directly to the market and bypass the costs of banks. These notes were called commercial paper.

The international version, Euro–commercial paper (Euro-CP), arrived in the European markets with a splash in the early 1980s. One of the primary reasons for its rapid growth was the lack of anything similar in most national financial markets. Domestic commercial paper markets were legalized in many major countries only in the middle to late 1980s; before the domestic markets arose, the Euro-CP market served most of the large industrial borrowers. Although the growth of domestic CP markets has taken a little steam out of the Euro-CP market of late, it has continued to provide the majority of the financing in the general Euronote market since the mid-1980s.

The third and final type of financing available in the Euronote market is the Euro–Medium-Term Note (EMTN). Another export of the rapidly innovating financial markets in the United States, the EMTN is the Euromarket version of a method of selling short- to medium-maturity bonds when needed. Unlike a bond issue, which is the sale of a large quantity of long-term debt all at one time, medium-term notes can be sold gradually into the market as the firm decides it needs additional debt financing. This is the result of having a "shelf-registration," in which the government authorities (in the United States the Securities and Exchange Commission) allow a large quantity of debt (the notes) to be registered but to be held "on the shelf" and sold as needed by the firm. The MTN has filled a maturity gap in debt-security issuance between the short-term commercial paper and the traditional longer maturities of bonds. The Euromarket version, the EMTN, has been just as successful for the very same reasons.

The International Bond Market

Even with all these strange and innovative ways of raising capital in the international financial markets, it is still the **international bond** market that provides the bulk of financing.

international bond
bond issued in domestic capital markets by foreign borrowers (foreign bonds) or issued in the Eurocurrency markets in currency different from that of the home currency of the borrower (Eurobonds)

The four categories of international debt financing discussed previously (Figure 14.4) particularly apply to the international bond markets. Foreign borrowers have been using the large, well-developed capital markets of countries like the United States and the United Kingdom for many years. These issues are classified generally as foreign bonds as opposed to Eurobonds. Each has gained its own pet name for foreign bonds issued in that market. For example, foreign bond issues in the United States are called Yankee bonds, in the United Kingdom Bulldogs, in the Netherlands Rembrandt bonds, and in Japan they are called Samurai bonds. When bonds are issued by foreign borrowers in these markets, they are subject to the same restrictions that apply to all domestic borrowers. If a Japanese firm issues a bond in the United States, it still must comply with all rules of the U.S. Securities and Exchange Commission, including the fact that it must be dollar-denominated.

Eurobond
a bond that is denominated in a currency other than the currency of the country in which the bond is sold

Bonds that fall into Categories 3 and 4 are termed **Eurobonds.** The primary characteristic of these instruments is that they are denominated in a currency other than that of the country where they are sold. For example, many U.S. firms may issue Euro-yen bonds on world markets. These bonds are sold in international financial centers such as London or Frankfurt, but they are denominated in Japanese yen.

Aside from the foreign bond-Eurobond distinction, international bonds are also classified by the way the buyer is repaid: (1) straight or fixed-rate bonds, (2) floating-rate bonds, and (3) bonds with equity links. As in any domestic market, the type of bond issued reflects what the firm thinks is the type that will be most acceptable to the market and easiest for the firm to repay.

The majority of bonds issued internationally are still the traditional fixed-rate bond. This is a debt issuance typically between four and ten years in maturity with a fixed coupon payment (interest payment) to the buyer of the bond annually. Because the timing and amount of all interest and principal repayments are known at the time of sale, the fixed-rate issue is always considered a solid and attractive investment. The continued growth of the international bond market is dependent on the continued use of the fixed-rate issue.

The second type of international bond, the floating-rate bond or floating-rate note (FRN), continues to make up a small but stable portion of the total market. The floating-rate note is structured so that its interest payments to the holders of the bonds are adjusted on an annual or semiannual basis with current market conditions.

The third type of international bond that has had some degree of success in the late 1980s is the equity-linked bond. There are two major types of equity-linked bonds: (1) convertible bonds and (2) bonds with equity warrants. An equity-linked bond is convertible into the common stock of the company issuing it. This provides the buyer of the bond two ways to achieve a return: the interest payment that the bond will still guarantee over its life, and the possibility of converting the bond into common stock (equity) if the firm's stock price rises far enough to make the conversion worthwhile. The major advantage to the issuer of such a convertible bond is that the interest rate that must be promised to investors is smaller when convertibility is present.

The bond with equity-warrant attached is much the same. A warrant is an option given to the buyer (literally attached to the bond) to purchase shares in the firm at a specified price. Like the convertible bond, the price is normally 20 to 30 percent higher than the price when issued. If the stock price does rise substantially over the coming years, the warrant would allow the investor to buy a share of the stock at the specified price, which would then be cheaper than the market price. Once again, attaching the warrant to the bond allows the issuer to save by promising a lower interest rate than without the warranty.

International Equity Markets

Firms are financed with both debt and equity. Although the debt markets have been the center of activity in the international financial markets over the past three decades, there are signs that international equity capital is becoming more popular.

Again using the same categories of international financial activities, the Category 2 transaction of a foreign borrower in a domestic market in local currency is the predominant international equity activity. Foreign firms often issue new shares in foreign markets and list their stock on major stock exchanges such as those in New York, Tokyo, or London. The purpose of foreign issues and listings is to expand the investor base, hopefully gaining access to capital markets in which the demand for shares of equity ownership is strong.

There has been considerable growth in the Euro-equity markets. A Euro-equity issue is the simultaneous sale of a firm's shares in several different countries, with or without listing the shares on an exchange in that country. The sales take place through investment banks. Once issued, most Euro-equities are listed at least on the computer screen quoting system of the International Stock Exchange in London, the SEAQ. One of the most globalized of major equity exchanges is the Frankfurt Stock Exchange; almost half of the firms listed on that exchange are foreign.

Private Placements

One of the largest and largely unpublicized capital markets is the private placement market. A private placement is the sale of debt or equity to a large investor. The sale is normally a one-time-only transaction in which the buyer of the bond or stock purchases the investment and intends to hold it until maturity (if debt) or until repurchased by the firm (if equity). How does this differ from normal bond and stock sales? The answer is that the securities are not resold on a secondary market like the domestic bond market or the New York or American stock exchanges. If the security was intended to be publicly traded, the issuing firm would have to meet a number of disclosure and registration requirements with the regulatory authorities. In the United States, this would be the Securities and Exchange Commission.

FINANCIAL RISK MANAGEMENT

All firms are in some way influenced by three financial prices: exchange rates, interest rates, and commodity prices. The management of these prices, these risks, is termed financial risk management. Interest rates have always received, deservedly, much of management's attention in business; it is only recently that many firms have chosen to acknowledge their financial health is also affected by exchange rates and commodity prices. The following analysis focuses on the exchange rate risks suffered by firms operating internationally.

Financial Price Risk and Firm Value

Risk is a word that deserves more respect than is commonly afforded it. Most dictionaries will refer to risk as the possibility of suffering harm or loss, danger; or a factor or element involving uncertain danger or hazards. These are negative definitions. Yet in the field of finance, the word *risk* has a neutral definition: a value or result that is at present unknown. This means that risk can be either positive or negative in impact.

There are three categories of financial price risk: interest rate risk, exchange rate risk, and commodity price risk. Each can have potentially positive or negative impacts on the profitability or value of the firm. For example, a U.S. exporter like Eastman Kodak pays specific attention to the value of the U.S. dollar. If the dollar were to appreciate against other major currencies like the Japanese yen, Kodak's products would be more expensive to foreign buyers, and it may lose market share to foreign competitors (like Fuji).

The negative relationship between Kodak's firm value and the yen-dollar exchange rate is illustrated in Figure 14.5. As the dollar appreciates versus the yen (for example,

FIGURE 14.5 **Financial Price Risks and the Value of the Firm**

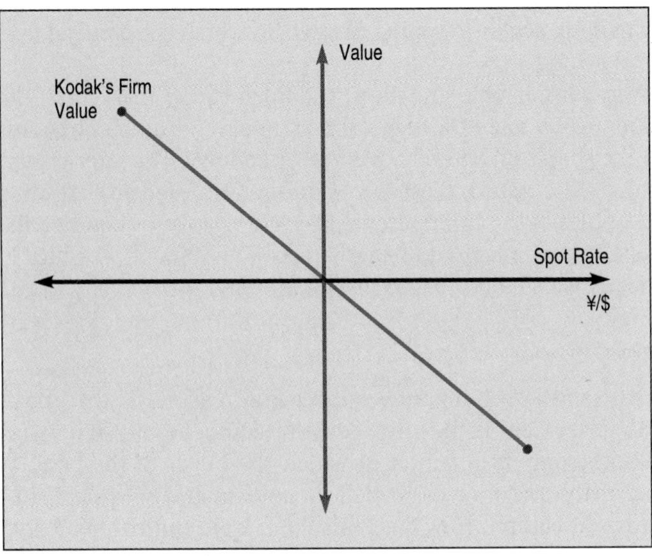

if the spot rate moved from ¥125/$ to ¥140/$), Kodak would suffer falling sales in Japan, and possibly also in the United States, because Fuji's comparable products would be relatively cheaper. The result is a fall in the value of Kodak. Corporate management expects financial managers to control these risks and protect the firm against exchange rate risks as best they can.

But this same firm-value sensitivity also exists for interest rates and commodity prices. Most firms are at least partially financed with short-term floating-rate debt. Therefore, whenever interest rates rise, these firms suffer higher financing costs, reducing the value of the firms.

Similarly, an increase in the price of commodities like oil or coal, which are inputs into the production processes of many firms, will also reduce the value of those firms. But it does vary across firms. For example, a company like Kidder Peabody, which mines coal, will see rising profits and firm value when coal prices rise. Each firm is different. It simply depends on the markets and makeup of each company. Although the following sections will focus on the measurement and management of exchange rate risk, it is important to remember that other financial price risks, such as those of interest rates and commodity prices, are fundamentally the same. They too can be measured and managed by firms.

Classification of Foreign Currency Exposures

Companies today know the risks of international operations. They are aware of the substantial risks to balance sheet values and annual earnings that interest rates and exchange rates may inflict on any firm at any time. And as is the case with most potential risks or problems to the firm, senior management expects junior management to do something about it. Financial managers, international treasurers, and financial officers of all kinds are expected to protect the firm from these risks. But before you can manage a risk, you must be able to measure it. There are three types of foreign currency exposures that firms have in varying degrees:

1. *Transaction exposure*—This is the risk associated with a contractual payment of foreign currency. For example, a U.S. firm that exports products to France will receive a guaranteed (by contract) payment in French francs in the future. Firms that buy or sell internationally have **transaction exposures** if any of the cash flows are denominated in foreign currency.
2. *Economic exposure*—This is the risk to the firm that its long-term cash flows will be affected, positively or negatively, by unexpected future exchange rate changes. Although many firms that consider themselves to be purely domestic may not realize it, all firms have some degree of **economic exposure.**
3. *Translation exposure*—This risk arises from the legal requirement that all firms consolidate their financial statements (balance sheets and income statements) of all worldwide operations annually. Therefore, any firm with operations outside its home country, operations that will be either earning foreign currency or valued in foreign currency, has **translation exposure.**

transaction exposure
potential for losses or gains when a firm is engaged in a transaction denominated in a foreign currency

economic exposure
potential for long-term effects on a firm's value as the result of changing currency values

translation exposure
potential effect on a firm's financial statements of a change in currency values

Transaction exposure and economic exposure are "true exposures" in the financial sense. This means they both present potential threats to the value of a firm's cash flows over time. The third exposure, translation, is a problem that arises from accounting. Under the present accounting principles in practice across most of the world's industrialized countries, translation exposure is not the problem it once was. For the most part, few real cash resources should be devoted to a purely accounting-based event.

TRANSACTION EXPOSURE

Transaction exposure is the most commonly observed type of exchange rate risk. Only two conditions are necessary for a transaction exposure to exist: (1) a cash flow that is denominated in a foreign currency; (2) the cash flow to occur at a future date. Any contract, agreement, purchase or sale that is denominated in a foreign currency and will be settled in the future constitutes a transaction exposure.[10]

The risk of a transaction exposure is that the exchange rate might change between the present date and the settlement date. The change may be for the better or for the worse. For example, an American firm signs a contract to purchase heavy rolled-steel pipe from a South Korean steel producer for 21,000,000 Korean won. The payment is due in 30 days upon delivery. This 30-day account payable, so typical of international trade and commerce, is a transaction exposure for the U.S. firm. If the spot exchange rate on the date the contract is signed is Won 700/$, the U.S. firm would expect to pay

$$\frac{\text{Won } 21{,}000{,}000}{\text{Won } 700/\$} = \$30{,}000$$

But the firm is not assured of what the exchange rate will be in 30 days. If the spot rate at the end of 30 days is Won 720/$, the U.S. firm would actually pay less. The payment would then be $29,167. If, however, the exchange rate changed in the opposite direction, for example, to Won 650/$, the payment could just as easily have increased to $32,308. This type of price risk, transaction exposure, is a major problem for international commerce.

Transaction-Exposure Management

Management of transaction exposures is usually accomplished by either natural hedging or contractual hedging. Natural hedging is the term used to describe how a firm

GLOBAL LEARNING EXPERIENCE 14.4

Lost in a Maze of Hedges

Volatile exchange rates in recent weeks have sent many a nervous boss scurrying to his finance department to check up on its currency-hedging strategy. Few of them will emerge much the wiser, for the typical multinational's strategy can seem impenetrable.

Hedging is simple enough in theory. Just doing business exposes many firms to foreign exchange risk: If an exchange rate moves the wrong way, profit or the balance sheet suffers. Suppose a British exporter sells goods that will be paid for in dollars three months later. If the dollar weakens against the pound, the exporter will get less in sterling than it expected. Hedging lets firms reduce or eliminate this risk by using a financial instrument that moves in the opposite way when exchange rates change. For the British exporter, that means one that is worth more pounds as the dollar falls.

The best way to hedge is to do it "naturally." Firms can design their trading, borrowing, and investment strategies to match their sales and assets in a particular currency with their purchases and liabilities in it. If, say, a British firm owns an asset valued in dollars, it can hedge by borrowing in dollars. No matter what happens to the pound-dollar exchange rate, there will be no net effect on the firm's balance sheet.

Few firms can hedge all, or even most, of their risk naturally. So many hedge actively in the financial markets, mainly using forward contracts and options. Forward contracts, agreements to buy or sell a given amount of a currency at an agreed exchange rate on a particular date, get rid of all exchange rate risk, and are often thought of as the perfect hedge. If the British exporter is going to be paid $1m in three months, it can make a forward contract to sell the $1m on that date and know exactly how many pounds it will get in return even if exchange rates fluctuate in the spot market.

The trouble with forward contracts is that they are irrevocable. If the dollar strengthens against sterling, the British exporter with a forward contract is worse off than it would have been with no hedge at all. Options, which give firms the right, but not the obligation, to use a particular forward contract, are more flexible. Imagine that the British exporter buys an option to sell dollars in three months at the forward rate. If the exchange rate moves against the firm, it can use its option and limit the damage; if the rate goes in its favor, it can let the option lapse and enjoy the windfall.

Firms seem to use forward contracts at least twice as much as options. One reason is cost. Forward contracts are no dearer than an ordinary trade in the spot market. Options, by contrast, are expensive and must be paid for whether or not they are used. Option prices can jump about wildly, depending on which currencies are involved and how volatile the market is. Prices have gone through the roof recently: On September 29, 1992, Swiss Bank Corporation priced a three-month option to sell dollars at 2.7 percent of the contract, a hefty $27,000 for a British exporter wanting to hedge $1 million.

SOURCE: Abstracted from "Lost in a Maze of Hedges," *The Economist,* October 3, 1992, 84. Distributed by the New York Times Special Features/Syndication Sales.

might arrange to have foreign currency cash flows coming in and going out at roughly the same times and same amounts. This is referred to as natural hedging because the management or hedging of the exposure is accomplished by matching offsetting foreign currency cash flows and therefore does not require the firm to undertake unusual financial contracts or activities to manage the exposure. For example, a Canadian firm that generates a significant portion of its total sales in U.S. dollars may acquire U.S. dollar debt. The U.S. dollar earnings from sales could then be used to service the dol-

Economic Exposure: Foreign Automakers in Mexico

Foreign automakers in Mexico enjoyed double-digit sales growth throughout 1993 and 1994, in the transition years of the North American Free Trade Agreement (NAFTA). Volkswagen (Germany), Chrysler (USA), Nissan (Japan), and Ford (USA), just to name a few, all saw record sales in the rapidly expanded deregulated Mexican consumer market. Then, in December 1994, the peso fell.

The peso crisis immediately sent much of the domestic market down. Increasingly tight monetary policies, cuts in government spending, and emergency measures to shore up the falling peso all contributed to a sudden and drastic drop in domestic automobile sales. Within the first two weeks of 1995, the automakers shifted the focus of their sales from domestic to export. The devalued peso made exported automobiles attractive to buyers worldwide, and increasing exports was a commercial policy definitely supported by the anxiety-ridden Mexican government.

lar debt as needed. In this way, regardless of whether the C$/US$ exchange rate goes up or down, the firm would be naturally hedged against the movement. If the U.S. dollar went up in value against the Canadian dollar, the U.S. dollars needed for debt service would be generated automatically by the export sales to the United States. U.S. dollar cash inflows would match U.S. dollar cash outflows.

Contractual hedging is when the firm uses financial contracts to hedge the transaction exposure. The most common foreign currency contractual hedge is the forward contract, although other financial instruments and derivatives, such as currency futures and options, are also used. The forward contract (see Chapter 4) would allow the firm to be assured a fixed rate of exchange between the desired two currencies at the precise future date. The forward contract would also be for the exact amount of the exposure. Both natural hedging and contractual hedging are discussed in Global Learning Experience 14.4.

ECONOMIC EXPOSURE

Economic exposure, also called operating exposure, is the change in the value of a firm arising from unexpected changes in exchange rates. Economic exposure emphasizes that there is a limit to a firm's ability to predict either cash flows or exchange rate changes in the medium to long term. All firms, either directly or indirectly, have economic exposure.

It is customary to think of only firms that actively trade internationally as having any type of currency exposure (like Lufthansa or Eastman Kodak described previously). But actually all firms that operate in economies affected by international financial events such as exchange rate changes are affected by these events. A barber in Ottumwa, Iowa, seemingly isolated from exchange rate chaos, is still affected when the dollar rises as it did in the early 1980s. U.S. products become increasingly expensive to foreign buyers, American manufacturers like John Deere & Co. in Iowa are forced to cut back production and lay off workers, and businesses of all types decline. Even the business of barbers. The impacts are real, and they affect all firms, domestic and international alike. Global Learning Experience 14.5 indicates how foreign automakers in Mexico responded to the peso crisis.

Impact of Economic Exposure

The impacts of economic exposure are as diverse as are firms in their international structure. Take the case of a U.S. corporation with a successful British subsidiary. The British subsidiary manufactured and then distributed the firm's products in Great Britain, Germany, and France. The profits of the British subsidiary are paid out annually to the American parent corporation. What would be the impact on the profitability of the British subsidiary and the entire U.S. firm if the British pound suddenly fell in value against all other major currencies (as it did in September and October 1992)?

If the British firm had been facing competition in Germany, France, and its own home market from firms from those other two continental countries, it would now be more competitive. If the British pound is "cheaper," so are the products sold internationally by British-based firms. The British subsidiary of the American firm would, in all likelihood, see rising profits from increased sales.

But what of the value of the British subsidiary to the U.S. parent corporation? The same fall in the British pound that allowed the British subsidiary to gain profits would also result in substantially fewer U.S. dollars when the British pound earnings are converted to U.S. dollars at the end of the year. It seems that it is nearly impossible to win in this situation. Actually, from the perspective of economic-exposure management, the fact that the firm's total value, subsidiary and parent together, is roughly a wash as a result of the exchange rate change is desirable. Sound financial management assumes that a firm will profit and bear risk in its line of business, not in the process of settling payments on business already completed.

Economic Exposure Management

Management of economic exposure is being prepared for the unexpected. A firm such as Eastman Kodak (U.S.), which is highly dependent on its ability to remain cost competitive in markets both at home and abroad, may choose to take actions now that would allow it to passively withstand any sudden unexpected rise of the dollar. This could be accomplished through diversification—diversification of operations and diversification of financing.

Diversification of operations would allow the firm to be desensitized to the impacts of any one pair of exchange rate changes. For example, many multinational firms such as Hewlett-Packard produce the same products in manufacturing facilities in Singapore,

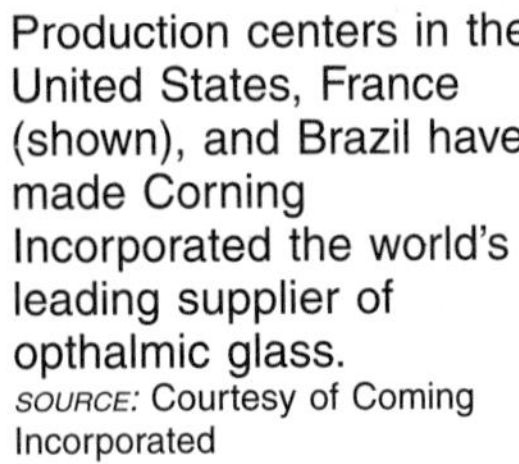
Production centers in the United States, France (shown), and Brazil have made Corning Incorporated the world's leading supplier of opthalmic glass.
SOURCE: Courtesy of Coming Incorporated

the United States, Puerto Rico, and Europe. If a sudden and prolonged rise in the dollar made production in the United States prohibitively expensive and uncompetitive, they are already positioned to shift production to a relatively cheaper currency environment. Although firms rarely diversify production location for the sole purpose of currency diversification, it is a substantial additional benefit from such global expansion.

Diversification of financing serves in hedging economic exposure much in the same way as it did with transaction exposures. A firm with debt denominated in many different currencies is sensitive to many different interest rates. If one country or currency experiences rapidly rising inflation rates and interest rates, a firm with diversified debt will not be subject to the full impact of such movements. Purely domestic firms, however, are actually somewhat captive to these local conditions and are unable to ride out such interest rate storms as easily.

It should be noted that in both cases, diversification is a passive solution to the exposure problem. This means that without knowing when or where or what the problem may be, the firm simply spreads its operations and financial structure out over a variety of countries and currencies to be prepared.

TRANSLATION EXPOSURE

Translation or accounting exposure results from the conversion or translation of foreign currency-denominated financial statements of foreign subsidiaries and affiliates into the home currency of the parent. This is necessary in order to prepare consolidated financial statements for all firms as country law requires. The purpose is to have all operations worldwide stated in the same-currency terms for comparison purposes. Management often uses these translated statements to judge the performance of foreign affiliates and their personnel on the same currency terms as the parent itself.

The problem, however, arises from the translation of balance sheets in foreign currencies into the domestic currency. Which assets and liabilities are to be translated at current exchange rates (at the current balance sheet date) versus historical rates (those in effect on the date of the initial investment)? Or should all assets and liabilities be translated at the same rate? The answer is somewhere in between, and the process of translation is dictated by financial accounting standards.

Translation-Exposure Management

At present in the United States, the proper method for translating foreign financial statements is given in Financial Accounting Standards Board statement No. 52 (FASB 52). According to FASB 52, if a foreign subsidiary is operating in a foreign currency functional environment,[11] most assets, liabilities, and income statement items of foreign affiliates are translated using current exchange rates (the exchange rate in effect on the balance sheet date). For this reason, it is often referred to as the current-rate method.

Translation exposure under FASB 52 results in no cash flow impacts under normal circumstances. Although consolidated accounting does result in cumulative translation adjustment (CTA) losses or gains on the parent's consolidated balance sheet, these accounting entries are not ordinarily realized. Unless liquidation or sale of the subsidiary is anticipated, neither the subsidiary nor the parent firm should expend real resources

What is El Niño?

ANSWER

Short for "El Niño de Navidad," or the Christ Child, El Niño is a huge pool of extra-warm seawater that flows out of the tropical eastern Pacific Ocean. It seems to occur very strongly about once a decade, usually in December, before Christmas; hence the name. It usually wreaks havoc with the Earth's climate and can be extremely destructive.

on the management of an accounting convention. In the event that the realization of the CTA translation gain or loss is imminent, traditional currency-hedging instruments can be used.

SUMMARY

International financial management is both complex and critical to the multinational firm. All traditional functional areas of financial management are affected by the internationalization of the firm. Capital budgeting, firm financing, capital structure, and working capital and cash flow management, all traditional functions, are made more difficult by business activities that cross borders and oceans, not to mention currencies and markets.

The most fundamental job of financial management is to obtain payment for goods shipped. For typical export shipments, a confirmed, irrevocable letter of credit is preferred to all other payment arrangements except cash with order.

Countertrades are business transactions in which the sale of goods is linked to other goods or performance rather than only to money. In spite of their inefficiency, such transactions are emerging with increasing frequency due to hard currency shortfalls in many nations around the world.

Concurrent with their increased use, countertrade transactions have also become more sophisticated. Rather than exchange goods for goods in a straight barter deal, companies and countries now structure counterpurchase agreements, compensation arrangements, clearing accounts, offset agreements, and debt swaps to promote their industrial policies and encourage development.

As the company expands into the global business arena and establishes wholly owned subsidiaries abroad, new financial challenges appear: (1) managing cash flow across international borders and (2) financing the subsidiary using international security markets.

In addition to the traditional areas of financial management, international financial management must deal with the three types of currency exposure: (1) transaction exposure, (2) economic exposure, and (3) translation exposure. Each type of currency risk confronts a firm with serious choices regarding its exposure analysis and its degree of willingness to manage these inherent risks. This chapter described not only the basic types of risk, but also outlined a number of the basic strategies employed in the management of these exposures.

Key Terms and Concepts

documentary collection
letter of credit
forfaiting
export factor receivable
countertrade
cash flow
netting
equity capital
debt capital
correspondent bank

- Euronote
- international bond
- Eurobond
- transaction exposure
- economic exposure
- translation exposure

Questions for Discussion

1. Discuss the differences between a documentary collection and a letter of credit.
2. What are the advantages of a confirmed, irrevocable letter of credit?
3. What are some of the major causes for the resurgence of countertrade?
4. What forms of countertrade exist and how do they differ?
5. Discuss the advantages and drawbacks of countertrade.
6. Why would a buyer insist on countertrade transactions?
7. Discuss several techniques for expediting the payment of receivables and converting them into cash.
8. What is the difference between debt financing and equity financing?
9. Why have international financial markets grown so fast in the past decade?
10. What are the major types of securities traded on the international financial markets?
11. Distinguish among transaction, economic, and translation exposure.

Recommended Readings

Ahn, Mark J., and William D. Falloon. *Strategic Risk Management: How Global Corporations Manage Financial Risk for Competitive Advantage.* Chicago: Probus Publishing, 1991.

Brigham, Eugene F., and Louis C. Gapenski. *Intermediate Financial Management.* Fort Worth, Tex.: Dryden, 1993.

Directory of Organizations Providing Countertrade Services 1996–97, 7th ed. Fairfax Station: DP Publications Co., 1996.

Eaker, Mark; Frank Fabozzi, and Dwight Grant. *International Corporate Finance.* Fort Worth, Tex.: Dryden, 1996.

Eiteman, David K., Arthur I. Stonehill, and Michael H. Moffett. *Multinational Business Finance,* seventh edition. Reading, Mass.: Addison-Wesley Publishing, 1995.

Giddy, Ian H. *Global Financial Markets.* Lexington, Mass.: Elsevier, 1994.

Grabbe, J. Orlin. *International Financial Markets,* 3rd. edition. Lexington, Mass.: Elsevier, 1996.

Guild, I., and R. Harris. *Forfaiting.* New York: Universe Books, 1986.

Howcroft, Barry, and Christopher Storey. *Management and Control of Currency and Interest Rate Risk.* Chicago: Probus Publishing, 1989.

Martin, Stephen (ed.). *The Economics of Offsets: Defense Procurement and Countertrade.* Amsterdam: Harwood Academic Publishers. 1996.

Offsets in Defense Trade. Bureau of Export Administration, U.S. Department of Commerce. Washington D.C., May 1996.

Shapiro, Alan C. *Foundations of Multinational Financial Management,* 2nd. edition. Allyn & Bacon, 1994.

Smith, Clifford W., Charles W. Smithson, and D. Sykes Wilford. *Managing Financial Risk,* The Institutional Investor Series in Finance. New York: Harper Business, 1990.

Smith, Roy C., and Ingo Walter. *Global Financial Services.* New York: Harper & Row Publishers. 1990.

Verzariu, Pompiliu. *International Countertrade: A Guide for Managers and Executives.* Washington, D.C.: U.S. Department of Commerce, 1995.

Verzariu, Pompiliu. *International Countertrade: Individual Country Practices.* Washington, D.C.: U.S. Department of Commerce, 1995.

Wunnicke, Diane B., David R. Wilson, and Brooke Wunnicke. *Corporate Financial Risk Management.* New York: John Wiley & Sons, 1992.

Zurawicki, Leon, and Louis Suichmezian. *Global Countertrade: An Annotated Bibliography.* New York: Garland Publishers, 1991.

Notes

1. Jean-François Hennart, "Some Empirical Dimensions of Countertrade," *Journal of International Business Studies* 21, 2 (Second Quarter, 1990): 243–270.
2. Jong H. Park, "Is Countertrade Merely a Passing Phenomenon? Some Public Policy Implications," in *Proceedings of the 1988 Conference,* ed. R. King (Charleston, S.C.: Academy of International Business, Southeast Region, 1988), 67–71.
3. Christopher M. Korth, "The Promotion of Exports with Barter," in *Export Promotion,* ed. M. Czinkota (New York: Praeger, 1983), 42.
4. Donna U. Vogt, *U.S. Government International Barter,* Congressional Research Service, Report No. 83-211ENR (Washington, D.C.: Government Printing Office, 1983), 65.
5. Korth, "The Promotion of Exports with Barter," 42.
6. Richard A. Debts, David L. Roberts, and Eli M. Remolona, *Finance for Developing Countries* (New York: Group of 30, 1987), 18.
7. Pompiliu Verzariu, "An Overview of Nontraditional Finance Techniques in International Commerce," in *Trade Finance: Current Issues and Developments* (Washington, D.C.: Government Printing Office, 1988), 48.
8. Michael R. Czinkota and Martin J. Kohn, *A Report to the Secretary of Commerce: Improving U.S. Competitiveness—Swapping Debt for Education* (Washington, D.C.: Government Printing Office, 1988).
9. Donald J. Lecraw, "The Management of Countertrade: Factors Influencing Success," *Journal of International Business Studies* 20 (Spring 1989): 41–59.
10. Many firms only acknowledge the existence of a transaction exposure when they "book" the receivable, when they ship the order to the customer and issue the account receivable. In fact, whether they realize it or not, when they accepted the order at a fixed price in terms of foreign currency, they gave birth to a transaction exposure.
11. The distinction as to what the "functional currency" of a foreign subsidiary or affiliate operation is depends on a number of factors, including the currency that dominates expenses and revenues. If the foreign subsidiary's dominant currency is the local currency, the current-rate method of translation is used. If, however, the functional currency of the foreign subsidiary is identified as the currency of the parent, the U.S. dollar in the example, the temporal method of translation is used. The temporal method is the procedure that was used in the United States from 1975 to 1981 under FASB 8.

The Future

LEARNING OBJECTIVES

To understand the many changing dimensions that shape global business.

To learn about and evaluate the global business forecasts made by a panel of experts.

To be informed about different career opportunities in global business.

The Demise of the Global Firm?

Cyrus Freidheim, vice chairman of the consulting firm Booz, Allen & Hamilton, has a provocative perspective of the global firm. He predicts that current economic and political developments mean that global firms will be superseded by the "relationship-enterprise," a network of strategic alliances among big firms, spanning different industries and countries, but held together by common goals that encourage them to act almost as a single firm. He envisions the enterprises to be corporate juggernauts, with total revenues approaching $1 trillion by early next century, larger than all but the world's six biggest economies.

He suggests that early in the twenty-first century, Boeing, British Airways, Siemens, TNT (an Australian parcel delivery firm), and SNECMA (a French aero-engine maker) might together win a deal to build ten new airports in China. As part of the deal, British Airways and TNT would receive preferential routes and landing slots, the Chinese government would buy all state aircraft from Boeing-SNECMA, and Siemens would provide the air traffic control systems for all ten airports.

While this may sound farfetched, consider that Boeing, members of the airbus consortium, McDonnell Douglas, Mitsubishi, Kawasaki, and Fuji already are talking about jointly developing a new super-jumbo jet. Mitsubishi and Daimler-Benz already share engineers. General Motors and Toyota are discussing the possibility of Toyota's building light trucks in a GM plant.

According to Friedheim, the conventional model of the global firm is flawed. Most so-called global companies are still perceived as having a home base. For example, in 1991, only 2 percent of the board members of big American companies were foreigners. In Japanese companies, foreign directors are as rare as British sumo wrestlers. Firms therefore have a natural home-country bias, with the big decisions kept firmly at home.

This bias, together with various other constraints, hinders companies' efforts to become truly global. For instance, when capital is limited, firms tend to protect their home market at the expense of developing untapped markets overseas. Second, antitrust laws limit the ability of global firms to expand through takeovers. But most important of all is the problem of nationalism. No country likes foreigners controlling its industries. By contrast, a relationship enterprise can sidestep these constraints. Such an alliance can draw on lots of money; it can dodge antitrust barriers; and with home bases in all the main markets, it has the political advantage of being a local firm almost everywhere.

SOURCE: "The Global Firm: R.I.P." *The Economist,* February 6, 1993, 69.

All global businesses face constantly changing world economic conditions. This is not a new situation nor one to be feared, because change provides the opportunity for new market positions to emerge and for managerial talent to improve the competitive position of the firm. Recognizing the importance of change and adapting creatively to new situations are the most important tasks of the global business executive. This would include possible changes in the nature of the global firm itself, as discussed in Global Learning Experience 15.1.

QUESTION *What is the driest place on Earth?*

Atacama, on the Pacific Coast of North Central Chile, between Arica and Antofagosta, receives less than 1/16 of an inch of precipitation annually.

Recently, changes are occurring more frequently, more rapidly, and have a more severe impact. The past has lost much of its value as a predictor of the future. What occurs today may not only be altered in short order but be completely overturned or reversed. For example, some countries find their major exports, which have increased steadily over decades, shrinking markedly in a brief period. Political stability can be completely disrupted over the course of a few months. Countries that have been considered enemies for decades, and with which no executive would dream of doing business, become close allies and offer a wealth of business opportunities. A major, sudden decline in world stock markets leaves corporations, investors, and consumers with strong feelings of uncertainty. An overnight currency decline of 40 percent results in an entirely new business climate for international suppliers and their customers. In all, global business managers today face complex and rapidly changing economic and political conditions.

This chapter will discuss possible future developments in the global business environment, highlight the implications of the changes for global business management, and offer suggestions for a creative response to the changes. The chapter also will explore the meaning of strategic changes as they relate to career choice and career path alternatives in global business.

THE INTERNATIONAL BUSINESS ENVIRONMENT

This section analyzes the global business environment by looking at political, financial, societal, and technological conditions of change and providing a glimpse of possible future developments as envisioned by an international panel of experts.* The impact of these factors on doing business abroad, on global trade relations, and on government policy is of particular interest to the global manager.

The Political Environment

The global political environment is undergoing a substantial transformation characterized by the reshaping of existing political blocs, the formation of new groupings, and the breakup of old coalitions.

The East-West Relationship From 1945 to 1985, the adverse relationship between the dominant powers in the East and West changed little. Within a few years, however, the relationship was transformed. The communist empire briefly reshaped itself into a socialist league, only to emerge shortly thereafter as individual, distinct entities. The former eastern Europe satellite nations of the Soviet Union reasserted their independence and implemented market-oriented economies. The Soviet Union itself has been replaced by a loose confederation of independent states. Politically and economically, the repercussions of the changes have been far reaching. The key collaborative military mechanism in the East—the Warsaw Pact—ceased to exist. The economic agreement among the socialist countries—the Council for Mutual Economic Assistance (CMEA or COMECON)—has been disbanded.

*The information presented here is based largely on an original Delphi study by Michael R. Czinkota and Ilkka A. Ronkainen utilizing an international panel of experts.

Such rapid transformations cause major internal adjustments and economic dislocations, which in turn have political repercussions. A rapid rise of inflation in these nations is accompanied by deepening individual dissatisfaction due to unmet expectations of economic progress. Employment, domestic markets, and trade volumes are shrinking due to necessary adjustments in production capabilities based on market forces. Both the countries and companies involved suffer from deteriorating liquidity positions and a growing number of insolvencies.

The raising of the Iron Curtain has brought two separate economic and business systems closer together. A reduction of export controls, direct linkages with economic blocs, and the West's desire to help are transforming the business relations of the past.

As a result of easing political tensions, firms are presented with new opportunities. Demand—particularly for consumer products, which had been repressed in the past—now can be met with goods from the West. Yet, due to very limited consumer choice skills and knowledge levels, firms entering the new markets need to develop demand from the ground up—a difficult task.

Concurrently, central Europe emerges as a significant source of products and services destined for export. An increase in the formation of international joint ventures and cooperative alliances is taking place. Yet many Western nations still are unprepared to accept an inflow of goods from a new source of competition. The inflow could throw carefully balanced trade relationships out of kilter and results in heated political discussions. To protect themselves against an avalanche of supplies from new quarters, governments frequently slow down the dismantling of old trade barriers, and sometimes even erect new ones. In doing so, they inhibit the development of a market orientation in the nations in transition by robbing them of incentive for change.[1]

Overall, many business activities will be subject to regional economic and political instability, increasing the risk of foreign business partners. Progress toward the institution of market-based economies may be halted or even reversed as large population segments are exposed to growing hardship during the transformation process. Still, large pools of untapped potential customers and production opportunities that are enhanced by the availability of a relatively cheap and well-trained labor force, may help offset the risk. To manage risks and operations, it will be crucial for corporations to find capable executives who can organize operations in these countries. As Global Learning Experience 15.2 shows, finding such executives is not easy, but the fact that they are needed is an incentive for new talent to adopt a global vision.

The North-South Relationship The distinction between developed and less-developed countries (LDCs) is unlikely to change. Some theoreticians argue that the economic gap between the two groups will diminish, whereas others hold that the gap will increase. Both arguments lead to the conclusion that a gap will endure for some time. The ongoing disparity between developed and developing nations is likely to be based, in part, on continuing debt burdens and problems with satisfying basic needs. As a result, political uncertainty may well result in increased polarization between the haves and have-nots, with growing potential for political and economic conflict. Demands for political solutions to economic and financial problems are likely to increase. Some countries may consider migration as a key solution to population-growth problems, yet many emigrants may encounter government barriers to their migration. As a result, there may well be more investment flows by firms bringing their labor and skill-intensive manufacturing operations to these countries.[2] In addition, new approaches to international development taken by multilateral institutions may be effective in strengthening the grass roots of developing economies. Global Learning Experience 15.3 provides an example.

GLOBAL LEARNING EXPERIENCE
15.2

The Struggle to Fill Positions in China

With demand for executives outstripping supply, salary levels and job-hopping are spiraling out of control in China. Few local managers in that land of 1.2 billion boast Western business experience. Expatriates, wary about harsh living conditions in parts of China, seek lavish compensation packages.

Five U.S. executive search firms recently have opened offices in China. Executive Access Ltd. in Hong Kong, one of Asia's largest search firms, expects to conduct about 120 China assignments for corporate clients in 1994. But the task is not easy. Ranjan Marwah, chief executive, spent seven fruitless months seeking a $100,000-a-year agricultural manager in China for a major U.S. food producer. The candidate had to speak English and Mandarin, have business experience in China, and be able to negotiate with farmers and government officials. "Such a collection of experience doesn't exist at this point," said Marwah.

A senior U.S. executive relocating to China can command an expatriate package that typically includes a hardship allowance ranging between 20 percent and 35 percent of base salary, free housing, frequent "rest and relaxation" trips to Hong Kong, and a chauffeur-driven car.

The hottest candidates for China assignments are "bicultural" Asian managers, typically born outside the mainland but with both Western and Asian work experience. Certain bicultural executives can even get a dual-housing benefit—living in China during the week and rejoining families on the weekend in Hong Kong.

Local managers who have international experience are valuable to companies. Indigenous managers provide contacts and knowledge of the Chinese market, and also cost companies only one tenth of the salary of expatriates. A mid-level government functionary recently agreed to run a big Canadian company's office in Beijing for a pay package that totaled 200,000 Hong Kong dollars (about US$26,000). The sum was one-tenth the size of a package rejected by an American expatriate with three other job offers. But the former bureaucrat now earns about 27 times what he had made working for the government.

The intense demand for talent in China has provoked considerable job-hopping by both local and foreign managers. Francis Kwong, a Hong Kong native, has worked for AT&T in China for less than a year. He previously worked for IBM in Hong Kong and Beijing. Several search firms approached him before he accepted AT&T's bid. Headhunters still call at least once a month.

Avon tends to lose locally hired Chinese managers to the lure of doubled salaries, free housing, promotions, training, and travel offered by U.S. consumer product makers. "These people are in a race to better their lives," said one Avon executive.

SOURCE: Joann S. Lublin and Craig S. Smith, "U.S. Companies Struggle With Scarcity of Executives to Run Outposts in China," *The Wall Street Journal,* August 23, 1994, B1.

The issue of environmental protection will also be a major force shaping the relationship between the developed and the developing world. In light of the need and desire to grow their economies, however, there may be much disagreement on the part of the industrializing nations as to what approaches to take. Three possible scenarios emerge.

One scenario is that of continued global cooperation. The developed countries could relinquish part of their economic power to less-developed ones, thus contributing actively to their economic growth through a sharing of resources and technology. Although such cross-subsidization will be useful and necessary for the development of

GLOBAL LEARNING EXPERIENCE

15.3

Lenders Target Women in the Developing World

The developing world's women are gaining a measure of economic autonomy as perceptions of them and their role in developing economies change. Even the big development agencies and multilateral banks are increasingly funding women-led small businesses and farming projects based on an assumption that women, more than men, are the critical players in the fight to relieve poverty. Agencies such as the World Bank, Agency for International Development, and Inter-American Development Bank say women are usually better at repaying their loans and less prone to waste or loot development money.

The motivation to target women has less to do with sexual politics than with the economic reality that women do much of the work in developing countries. "All over the developing world, in rural areas, the women are the mainstay of the local economy," said Gustave Speth, administrator of the United Nations Development Programme. A recent World Bank study found that women head half the households in sub-Saharan Africa. A study of village life in Cameroon found that women work an average of 64 hours a week, compared with 32 for men. And women's earnings are more likely to be used for the health and education of the next generation.

The focus on women's economic activities coincides with a growing interest in financing the thousands of tiny businesses that make up the developing world's vast "informal sector." Many of these so-called microenterprises, ranging from food sellers on street corners to one-person apparel makers, are run by women. Though statistics are shaky, it is estimated that informal-sector businesses make up as much as half of all economic activity in many developing countries. Yet, until recently, the international institutions have funneled nearly all development funds to governments and state enterprises for projects that often did little for the poorest population segments.

In the Dominican Republic, the marriage between the large international agencies and grass roots groups is helping to get money into the hands of more poor women running businesses. To some extent, the small Caribbean state is seen as a model for others working on programs to lend to the poor. Within a year, development experts from Botswana, Brazil, Colombia, Jamaica, Mexico, and Senegal visited and studied how Dominican lenders extend credit to the poorest segments of society but still cover costs and stay afloat. Pedro Jimenez, the executive director of the largest small-enterprise lender in the Dominican Republic, argued that bankers to the poor have to avoid a "charity window" mentality. To stay in business, he says, lenders must charge real interest rates, usually about 30 percent, that cover the lenders' costs plus any inflation risk. Jimenez's bank grants loans for an average amount of $800 and has a 98.6 percent repayment rate.

In Niger, CARE is helping establish women's savings groups in about 45 villages. "They haven't had access to banking systems anywhere," said Ann Duval, the program's overseer. About 35 women contribute 50 cents per week. Two-week loans are made, with an interest rate of about 10 percent. Periodically the women liquidate their banks and distribute the money for certain needs. But the banks always start up again. Once they have had a bank, the women don't want to go without one.

SOURCE: Tim Carrington, "Gender Economics: In Developing World, International Lenders Are Targeting Women," *The Wall Street Journal,* June 22, 1994, A1.

LDCs, it may reduce the rate of growth of the standard of living in the more developed countries. It would, however, increase trade flows between developed and less developed countries and precipitate the emergence of new global business opportunities.

A second scenario is that of confrontation. Due to an unwillingness to share resources and technology sufficiently (or excessively, depending on the point of view), the developing and the developed areas of the world may become increasingly hostile toward one another. As a result, the volume of global business, both by mandate of governments and by choice of the private sector, could be severely reduced.

A third scenario is that of isolation. Although there may be some cooperation between them, both groups, in order to achieve their domestic and global goals, may choose to remain economically isolated. This alternative may be particularly attractive if each region believes that it faces unique problems and therefore must seek its own solutions.

Emergence of New Economic Blocs Some foresee the realignment of global strategic power through the emergence of new economic blocs. One such bloc would consist of a reshaped Europe, which would include political and economic membership of the 15 European Union nations, the central European nations, and possibly even some of the former Soviet republics. A second bloc would be led by Japan and would be mainly trade based; members would come mainly from the Pacific Rim. A third bloc could emerge in the Western Hemisphere, led by the United States and including Canada, Mexico, and several Central and South American nations. Such a bloc would be primarily trade based, but could eventually also incorporate political dimensions.

The bloc formations could result in heightened business stability and cooperation within each arrangement. Yet a concurrent danger might be the emergence of bloc-based competition and protectionism. Such a development could force global firms to choose a "home bloc" and could introduce new inefficiencies into global trade relations. On the positive side, however, due to their relative equality of power, the blocs could also be the precursors of global cooperation, resulting in an even more open and free global business environment.

A Divergence of Values It might well be that different nations or cultures become increasingly disparate in terms of values and priorities. For example, in some countries, the aim for financial progress and an improved quantitative standard of living may well give way to priorities based on religion or the environment. Even if nations share similar values, their priorities among these values may differ strongly. For example, within a market-oriented system, some countries may prioritize profits and efficiency, while others may place social harmony first, even at the cost of maintaining inefficient industries.

Such a divergence of values will require a major readjustment of the activities of the international corporation. A continuous scanning of newly emerging national values thus becomes imperative for the global executive.

The International Financial Environment

Even though the international debt problem of the developing world appears temporarily subdued, it will remain a major global trade and business issue into the 2000s. Debt constraints and low commodity prices create slow growth prospects for many developing countries. They will be forced to reduce their levels of imports and to exert more pressure on industrialized nations to open up their markets. Even if the markets are opened, however, demand for most primary products will be far lower than supply. Ensuing competition for market share will therefore continue to depress prices.

Developed nations have a strong incentive to help the debtor nations. The incentive consists of the market opportunities that economically healthy developing countries can offer and of national security concerns. As a result, industrialized nations may very well be in a situation in which a funds transfer to debtor nations, accompanied by debt-relief measures such as debt forgiveness, are necessary to achieve economic stimulation at home.

The dollar will remain one of the major international currencies with little probability of gold returning to its former status in the near future. However, global transactions in both trade and finance are increasingly likely to be denominated in nondollar terms, using regional currencies such as the new European currency (Euro). The system of floating currencies will likely continue, with occasional attempts by nations to manage exchange rate relationships or at least reduce the volatility of swings in currency values. However, given the vast flows of financial resources across borders, it would appear that market forces rather than government action will be the key determinant of a currency's value. Factors such as investor trust, economic conditions, earnings perceptions, and political stability are therefore likely to have a much greater effect on the international value of currencies than domestic monetary and fiscal experimentation.

Given the close linkages among financial markets, shocks in one market will quickly translate into rapid shifts in others and easily overpower the financial resources of individual governments. Even if there should be a decision by governments to pursue closely coordinated fiscal and monetary policies, they are unlikely to be able to negate long-term market effects in response to changes in economic fundamentals.

international debt load
total accumulated negative net investment of a nation

A looming concern in the international financial environment will be the **international debt load** of the United States. Both domestically and internationally, the United States is incurring debt that would have been inconceivable only a few decades ago. For example, in the 1970s the accumulation of financial resources by the Arab nations was of major concern in the United States. Congressional hearings focused on whether Arab money was "buying out America." At that time, however, Arab holdings in the United States were $10 billion to $20 billion. Today the accumulation of dollar holding inside and outside of the United States has led to much more significant shifts in foreign holdings.

In 1985, the United States became a net negative investor globally. The United States entered 1996 with an international debt burden of more than $1.3 trillion, making it the largest debtor nation in the world, owing more to other nations than all the developing countries combined. Mitigating this burden are the facts that most of the debts are denominated in U.S. dollars and that, even at such a large debt volume, U.S. debt-service requirements are only a small portion of GNP. Yet this accumulation of foreign debt may very well introduce entirely new dimensions into the global business relationships of individuals and nations. Once debt has reached a certain level, the creditor as well as the debtor is hostage to the loans.

Since foreign creditors expect a return on their investment, a substantial portion of future U.S. global trade activity will have to be devoted to generating sufficient funds for such repayment. For example, at an assumed interest rate or rate of return of 10 percent, the international U.S. debt level—without any growth—would require the annual payment of $130 billion, which amounts to about 15 percent of current U.S. exports. Therefore, it seems highly likely that global businesses will become a greater priority than it is today and will serve as a source of major economic growth for firms in the United States.

QUESTION *Can you guess the hottest and coldest places ever recorded?*

Hottest: Azizia, Libya, 136.4°F. in 1922. Coldest: Vostok Station, Antarctica, minus 128.6°F in 1983.

To some degree, foreign holders of dollars may also choose to convert their financial holdings into real property and investments in the United States. This will result in an entirely new pluralism in U.S. society. It will become increasingly difficult and, perhaps, even unnecessary to distinguish between domestic and foreign products—as is already the case with Hondas made in Ohio. Senators and members of Congress, governors, municipalities, and unions will gradually be faced with conflicting concerns in trying to develop a national consensus on global trade and investment. National security issues may also be raised as major industries become majority owned by foreign firms.

At the same time, U.S. international debt will, among other things, contribute to an increasingly tight money supply around the world. When combined with the financial needs of the emerging central and eastern European market economies, the fund flows to the former Soviet Union, and the aid requirements of many developing nations, a more heated competition for capital is likely to emerge, with continuing scarcity leading to relatively high real interest rates worldwide. Industrialized countries are likely to attempt to narrow the domestic gap between savings and investments through fiscal policies. Without concurrent restrictions on international capital flows, such policies are likely to meet with only limited success. Lending institutions can be expected to become more conservative in their financing, a move that may hit smaller firms and developing countries the hardest. Comparatively easier access to better financial resources will become a key competitive determinant and perhaps even be critical to the survival of many companies. At the same time, firms must strive to become best in their class. Given the increasing competition worldwide, products and services that only offer me-too features and capabilities will be hard pressed to stay in the market.

The Effects of Population Shifts

population growth
effect on economic matters of changes in countries' populations

The population discrepancy between less-developed nations and the industrialized countries will continue to increase. In the industrialized world, an increase in **population growth** will become a national priority, given the fact that in many countries, particularly in Western Europe, the population is shrinking rather than increasing. The shrinkage may lead to labor shortages and to major societal difficulties in providing for a growing elderly population.

In the developing world, the reduction of population growth will continue to be one of the major challenges of governmental policy. In spite of well-intentioned economic planning, continued rapid increases in population will make it more difficult to ensure that the pace of economic development exceeds population growth. If the standard of living of a nation is determined by dividing the GNP by its population, any increase in the denominator will require equal increases in the numerator to maintain the standard of living. Therefore, if the population's rate of growth continues at its current pace, even greater efforts must be made to increase the economic activity within these nations. With an annual increase in the world population of 100 million people, the task is daunting. It becomes even more complex when one considers that within countries with high population increases, large migration flows take place from rural to urban areas. As a result, by the end of this decade, most of the world's 10 largest metropolitan areas will be in the developing world.[3]

The Technological Environment

The concept of the global village is commonly accepted today and indicates the importance of communication in the technological environment. Satellite dishes can be built out of easily obtainable components. The rapidly expanding use of fax machines, portable telephones, and personal communication devices points to the evolution of unrestricted information flows. The importance of these technologies is driven home when one considers that, since 1991, the fax traffic between the United States and Europe has exceeded voice traffic.[4] Concurrently, the availability of information to be communicated has increased dramatically. Since all this information includes details about lifestyles, opportunities, and aspirations, global communication will be a great equalizer in the future.

Changes in other technologies will be equally rapid and will have a major effect on business in general. For example, the appearance of superconductive materials and composite materials has made possible the development of new systems in fields such as transportation and electric power, pushing the frontiers of human activity into as yet unexplored areas such as outer space and the depths of the oceans. The development of biotechnology is already leading to revolutionary progress not only in agriculture, medicine, and chemistry but also in manufacturing systems within industry.[5]

High technology is expected to become one of the more volatile areas of economic activity. Order of magnitude changes in technology can totally wipe out private and public national investment in a high-technology sector. In the hard-hitting race toward technological primacy, some nations will inevitably fall behind and others will be able to catch up only with extreme difficulty.

Even firms and countries that are at the leading edge of technology will find it increasingly difficult to marshal the funds necessary for further advancements. For example, investments in semiconductor technology are measured in billions rather than millions of dollars and do not bring any assurance of success. Not to engage in the race, however, will mean falling behind quickly in all areas of manufacturing when virtually every industrial and consumer product is "smart" due to its chip technology.

As this chapter's opening Global Learning Experience showed, it is likely that firms will join forces through cooperative agreements, joint ventures, and strategic partnerings to compete for major projects, spread the necessary financial commitments, and reduce the risk of technology development. Concurrently, governments will increase their spending on research and development in order to further "techno-nationalism" through the creation of more sources of technological innovation within their boundaries. Government-sponsored collaborative research ventures are likely to increase across industries and country groupings. However, difficulties may emerge when global firms threaten to rapidly internationalize any gains from such regionalized research ventures.

CHANGES IN TRADE RELATIONS

The formation of the World Trade Organization (WTO) has brought to conclusion a lengthy and sometimes acrimonious round of global trade negotiations. However, key disagreements among major trading partners are likely to persist, particularly in the areas of financial and information services. Ongoing major imbalances in trade flows will tempt nations to apply their own national trade remedies, particularly in the antidumping field. Even though WTO rules permit for a retaliation against unfair trade practices, such actions would only result in an ever-increasing spiral of adverse trade relations.

multilateral trade negotiations trade negotiations among more than two parties; the intricate relationships among trading countries

A key question will be whether nations are willing to abrogate some of their sovereignty even during difficult economic times. An affirmative answer will strengthen the **multilateral trade negotiations** system and enhance the flow of trade. However, if key trading nations resort to the development of insidious nontariff barriers, unilateral actions, and bilateral negotiations, protectionism will increase on a global scale and the volume of global trade is likely to decline.

Global trade relations also will be shaped by new participants whose market entry will restructure the composition of global trade. For example, new players with exceptionally large productive potential, such as the People's Republic of China and Central Europe will substantially alter world trade flows. And while both governments and firms will be required to change many trading policies and practices as a result, they will also benefit in terms of market opportunities and sourcing alternatives.

Finally, the efforts of governments to achieve self-sufficiency in economic sectors, particularly in agriculture and heavy industries, have ensured the creation of long-term, worldwide oversupply of some commodities and products, many of which historically had been traded widely. As a result, after some period of intense market share competition aided by subsidies and governmental support, a gradual and painful restructuring of these economic sectors will have to take place. This will be particularly true for agricultural cash crops such as wheat, corn, and dairy products and industrial products such as steel, chemicals, and automobiles.

GOVERNMENTAL POLICY

Global trade activity now affects domestic policy more than ever. For example, trade flows can cause major structural shifts in employment. Linkages between industries spread these effects throughout the economy. Fewer domestically produced automobiles will affect the activities of the steel industry. Shifts in the sourcing of textiles will affect the cotton industry. Global productivity gains and competitive pressures will force many industries to restructure their activities. In such circumstances, industries are likely to ask their governments to help in their restructuring efforts. Often, such assistance includes a built-in tendency toward protectionist action.

Such restructuring is not necessarily negative. Since the turn of the century, farm employment in the United States has dropped from more than 40 percent of the population to less than 3 percent. Yet today, the farm industry feeds 270 million people in the United States and still produces large surpluses. A restructuring of industries can greatly increase productivity and provide the opportunity for resource allocation to emerging sectors of an economy.

Governments cannot be expected, for the sake of the theoretical ideal of "free trade," to sit back and watch the effects of deindustrialization on their countries. The most that can be expected is that they will permit an open-market orientation subject to the needs of domestic policy. Even an open-market orientation is maintainable only if governments can provide reasonable assurances to their own firms and citizens that the openness applies to foreign markets as well. Therefore, unfair trade practices such as governmental subsidization, dumping, and industrial targeting will be examined more closely, and retaliation for such activities is likely to be swift and harsh.

trigger mechanisms
specific acts or stimuli that set off reactions

Increasingly, governments will need to coordinate policies that affect the international business environment. The development of international indexes and **trigger mechanisms,** which precipitate government action at predetermined intervention points, will be a useful step in that direction. Yet, for them to be effective, governments will need to muster the political fortitude to implement the policies necessary for cooperation. For example, international monetary cooperation will work in the long term only if domestic fiscal policies are responsible to the achievement of the coordinated goals.

At the same time as the need for collaboration among governments grows, it will become more difficult to achieve a consensus. In the Western world, the time from 1945 through 1990 was characterized by a commonality of purpose. The common defense against the communist enemy remanded trade relations to second place, and provided a bond that encouraged collaboration. With the common threat gone, however, the bonds have been diminished—if not dissolved—and the priority of economic performance has increased. Unless a new key jointness of purpose can be found by governments, collaborative approaches will become increasingly difficult.[6]

Governmental policymakers must take into account the global repercussions of domestic legislation. For example, in imposing a special surcharge tax on the chemical industry designed to provide for the cleanup of toxic waste products, they need to consider its repercussions on the global competitiveness of the chemical industry. Similarly, current laws such as antitrust legislation need to be reviewed if the laws hinder the global competitiveness of domestic firms.

Policymakers also need a better understanding of the nature of the global trade issues confronting them. Most countries today face both short-term and long-term trade problems. Trade balance issues, for example, are short term in nature, while competitiveness issues are much more long term. All too often, however, short-term issues are attacked with long-term **trade policy mechanisms,** and vice versa. In the United States, for example, the desire to "level the international playing field" with mechanisms such as vigorous implementation of import restrictions or voluntary restraint agreements may serve long-term competitiveness well, but it does little to alleviate the publicly perceived problem of the trade deficit. Similarly, a further opening of Japan's market to foreign corporations will have only a minor immediate effect on that country's trade surplus or the trading partners' deficit. Yet it is the expectation and hope of many in both the public and the private sectors that such instant changes will occur. For the sake of the credibility of policymakers, it therefore becomes imperative to precisely identify the nature of the problem and to design and use policy measures that are appropriate for its resolution.

trade policy mechanisms
measures used to influence and alter trade relationships

In the years to come, governments will be faced with an accelerating technological race and with emerging problems that seem insurmountable by individual firms alone, such as pollution of the environment and global warming. As market gaps emerge and times becomes crucial, both governments and the private sector will find that even if the private sector knows that a lighthouse is needed, it may still be difficult, time-consuming, and maybe even impossible to build one with private funds alone. As a result, it seems likely that the concepts of administrative guidance and government-corporate collaboration will increasingly become part of the policy behavior of governments. The global manager in turn will have to spend more time and effort dealing with governments and with macro rather than micro issues.

THE FUTURE OF GLOBAL BUSINESS MANAGEMENT

Global change results in an increase in risk. One short-sighted alternative for risk-averse managers would be the termination of global activities altogether. However, businesses will not achieve long-run success by engaging only in risk-free actions. Further, other factors make the pursuit of global business mandatory.

Global markets remain a source of high profits, as a quick look at a list of multinational firms would show.[7] Global activities help cushion slack in domestic sales resulting from recessionary or adverse domestic conditions and may be crucial to the very survival of the firm. Global markets also provide firms with foreign experience that helps them compete more successfully with foreign firms in the domestic market.

International Planning and Research

Firms must continue to serve customers well to be active participants in the global marketplace. One major change that will come about is that the global manager will need

Ford Motor Co. currently sponsors "Ocean Planet," an exhibition focusing on ocean conservation. This exhibit opened in Washington, D.C. and will travel to 11 cities before the year 2000. The motivation prompting its creation is to create awareness now, through education, regarding ocean conservation before this issue becomes "the rain forest" of the '90s.
SOURCE: Courtesy Ford Motor Co.

CARS AREN'T THE ONLY BODIES WE'RE CONCERNED ABOUT.

That's why Ford Motor Company is proud to be a sponsor of Ocean Planet. *Glorious in scope, the Smithsonian Institution's traveling exhibition dramatically illustrates how all life is affected by the health of the ocean and highlights the urgent need for ocean conservation. Our support of* Ocean Planet *underscores an ongoing commitment to ENVIRONMENTAL concerns. Back in 1903 Henry Ford himself designed suppliers' shipping crates so they could be dismantled and used as running boards and wooden trim, reducing packing waste. Since then our engineers have continued to create INNOVATIVE ways of protecting our environment such as recycling and reducing harmful emissions, as well as developing cars that run on electricity and NATURAL gas. We're honored to be a part of* Ocean Planet, *and we urge everyone to visit the exhibition and learn what we can do to assure our world's survival. A topic that's a concern to us all.*

QUALITY IS JOB 1

to respond to general governmental concerns to a greater degree when planning a business strategy. Further, societal concern about macro problems needs to be taken into account directly and quickly because societies have come to expect more social responsibility from corporations. Taking on a leadership role regarding social causes may also benefit corporations' bottom lines, since consumers appear more willing than ever to act as significant pressure points for policy changes and to pay for their social concerns.

Another trend consists of increased competition in global markets. The trend will create a need for more niches in which firms can create a distinct international competence. As a result, increased specialization and segmentation will let firms fill very narrow and specific demands or resolve very specific problems for their global customers.[8] Identifying and filling the niches will be easier in the future because of the greater availability of global research tools and information. The key challenge to global firms will be to build and manage decision-making processes that allow quick responses to multiple changing environmental demands. This capability is important since firms face a growing need for worldwide coordination and integration of internal activities,

FIGURE 15.1 **Long-Term Planning**

SOURCE: *The Economist,* October 24, 1992, 29.

such as logistics and operations, while being confronted with the need for greater national differentiation and responsiveness at the customer level.[9]

In spite of the frequent short-term orientation by corporations and investors, companies will need to learn to prepare for long-term horizons. Particularly in an environment of heated competition and technological battles, of large projects and slow payoffs, companies, their stakeholders, and governments will need to find avenues that not only permit but encourage the development of strategic perspectives. Figure 15.1 provides an example of such a long-term view.

If you really know your geography, you'll be able to estimate the number of active volcanoes in the world.

There are approximately 600 active volcanoes.

Governments both at home and abroad will demand that private business practices not increase public costs and that businesses serve customers equally and nondiscriminately.[10] The concept directly counters the desire to serve first the markets that are most profitable and least costly. Global executives will therefore be torn in two directions and, to provide results that are acceptable both to customers and to the societies they serve, they must walk a fine line, balancing the public and the private good.

Global Product Policy

Two major trends are emerging in the product policies of multinational corporations. On one hand, automation and the search for increasing economies of scale demand that firms serve more markets. Even large domestic markets such as the United States or Japan may be "too small to absorb the output of the world-class automated plants needed for economies of scale in many product areas."[11] Europe, Japan, and the United States harbor the greatest buying power and concentration of demand in the world for many products. For example, the three regions account for nearly 85 percent of the world's demand for consumer electronic goods; they also consumed 85 percent of the computers and 70 percent of the machine tools produced in the world.[12] According to these facts, production should be concentrated in one of the regions and output widely distributed.

Although this trend would argue for greater exports and greater standardization of products, a counterargument holds that, because of increasing protectionist policies and the desire of nations to obtain and develop their own technology, foreign direct investment and multiple plant locations will replace exports.[13] As long as firms have the flexibility of choice of location, managers will have substantial leverage over domestic legislation and regulations that would affect their global effort. Governments will run the risk of unemployment growth if domestic firms, because of an unsatisfactory **competitive platform,** move their operations abroad.

competitive platform
business environment provided by a nation to its firms, which affects their international competitiveness

Regardless of which avenue firms use to take their products and services abroad, it appears certain that worldwide introduction of products will occur much more rapidly in the future. As a result of the ever-quickening pace of technological change, the life cycles of most products will be greatly shortened. To stay ahead of the competition, firms will need to constantly adapt, adjust, and incrementally improve their products.[14] As a result, new products will be developed based on a system-oriented integration within the firm, where management, marketing, research, and development are joint rather than separate activities. Due to a more rapid commercialization of new technology, firms will have to develop more efficient, faster, and better targeted marketing strategies around the world, accompanied by better and shorter distribution channels. The homogenization of patterns of consumption will assist these efforts through the emergence of global or regional consumer segments, which will accelerate the penetration of global brands. Overall, product introduction will grow more complex, more expensive, and riskier, and the rewards to be reaped from a successful product will need to be accumulated more quickly.

Factor endowment advantages have a significant impact on the decisions of international managers. Given the acceleration of **product life cycles,** nations with low production costs will be able to develop and offer products more cheaply. Countries such as India, Israel, or the Philippines offer large pools of skilled people at labor rates much

product life cycle
theory that views products as passing through four stages: introduction, growth, maturity, decline

U.S. Utility Patents Granted in 1996 FIGURE 15.2

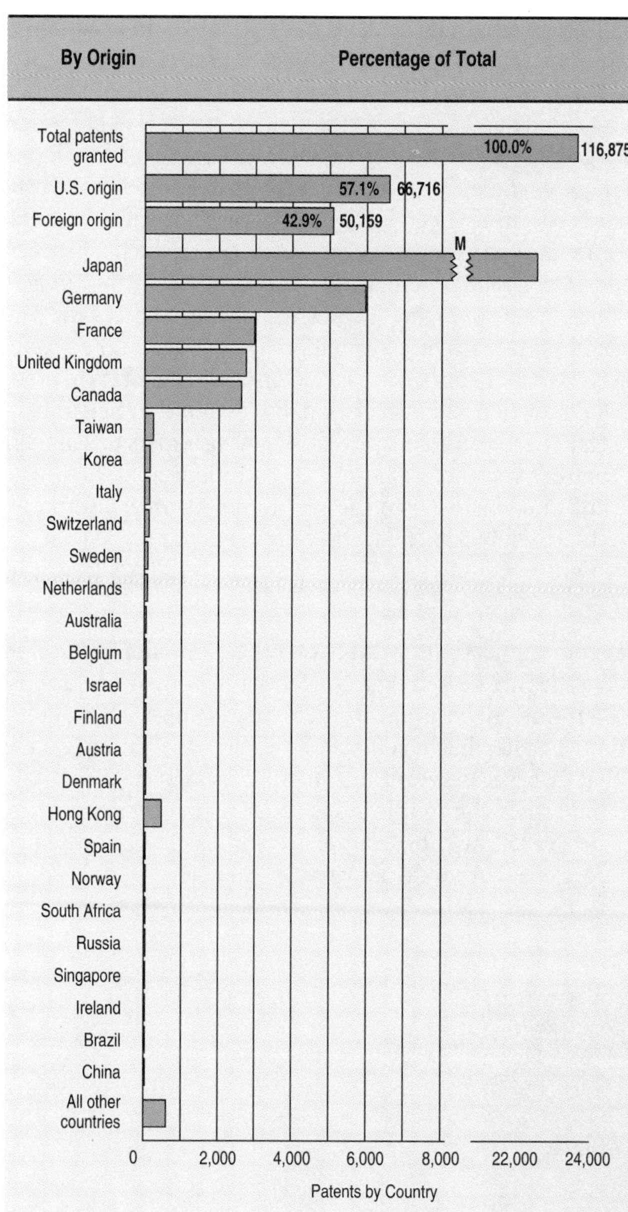

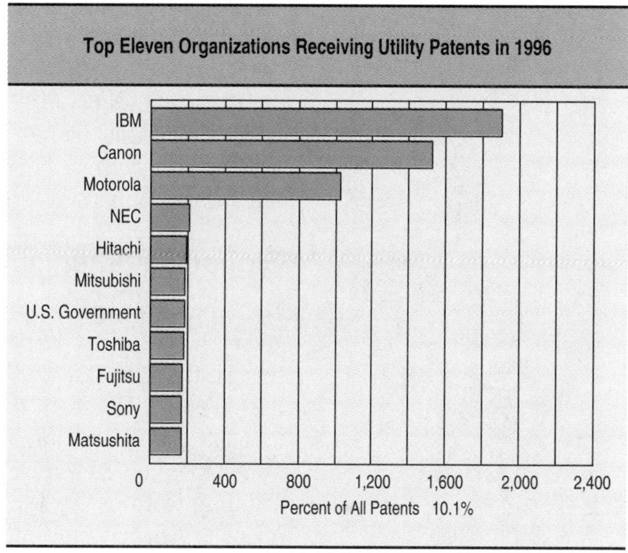

SOURCE: U.S. Department of Commerce, U.S. Patent and Trademark Office. *Technology Assessment and Forecast Report,* February, 1997.
NOTES: The origin of a patent is determined by the residence of the first-named inventor.

lower than in Europe, Japan, or the United States. For example, India has the third largest number of engineers after the United States and the CIS. All this talent also results in a much wider dissemination of technological creativity, a factor that will affect the innovative capability of firms. For example, in 1996, 43 percent of all the patents in the United States were granted to foreign inventors. Figure 15.2 shows the countries of origin of patent recipients in 1996. The single largest recipient of patents was IBM with 1,867 patents of the 116,875 total. Additionally, nine corporations (one American and eight Japanese) together with the U.S. Government accounted for 11,814 of the patents granted—10.1 percent of the total.

Firms need to make global knowledge and advantages part of their production strategies—or they need to develop consistent comparative advantages in production technology—to stay ahead of the game. Similarly, workers engaged in the productive process must attempt, through training and skill enhancement, to stay ahead of foreign workers who are willing to charge less for their time. The need to stay ahead highlights the importance, for governments, companies, and workers alike, to invest in human capital so that the interest from such investment can be drawn on for competitive success.

Firms also will need to evaluate the formation of collaborative arrangements between nominally competing companies and search for complementary strengths, be they in personnel availability, specialized skills, access to capital markets, or technical know-how. The partners do not need to be large to make a major contribution. Depending on the type of product, very small firms can serve as coordinating subcontractors and collaborate in product and service development and production and distribution. For example, in Belgium, in the center of Europe, sits European Telecom, a company that allows customers to dial their international calls by remote control by way of California, using American carriers. The service saves customers one-third in comparison to the stiff European rates. European Telecom has only three employees and only $50,000 worth of equipment.[15]

Global Communications

The advances made in global communications will also have a profound impact on global management. Entire industries are becoming more footloose in their operations; that is, they are less tied to their current location in their interaction with markets; Best Western Hotels in the United States has channeled its entire reservation system through a toll-free number that is being serviced out of the prison system in Utah. Companies could even concentrate their communications activities in other countries. Communications for worldwide operations, for example, could easily be located in Africa or Asia without impairing global corporate activities.

Advances in telecommunications allow staff in different countries to talk together and share pictures and data on their computer screens. In the state-of-the-art video conference center at Hoffmann-LaRoche's U.S. headquarters in Nutley, N.J., scientists discuss research goals and results with Roche colleagues in Basel, Switzerland.
SOURCE: Courtesy of Hoffmann-LaRoche, Inc.

Staff in different countries can not only talk together but can also share pictures and data on their computer screens. Worldwide rapid product development has therefore become feasible. Technology also makes it possible to merge the capabilities of computers, televisions, and telecommunications. Communication costs are decreasing significantly at the same time that the capabilities of communication tools increase. As a result firms have the opportunity for worldwide data exchange and benefit from virtually unlimited availability of detailed market and customer data. The challenge is to see who can use and apply information technology best.

Distribution Strategies

Worldwide distribution systems are assisting global business development. Integrated systems, labeled sea bridges or land bridges, already are operational. Major trading routes that offer substantial distribution economies of scale are being developed. The global manager will experience relative ease in planning distribution as long as he or she stays within established routes but will encounter difficulties when attempting to deviate from them. Customers who are on the routes benefit from the low cost of distribution and see a widening in their choice of products. Off-route customers have fewer product choices and pay increased prices for foreign products. Market access is also a crucial component in determining a firm's capability to develop new products since lack of customers will sharply reduce the economic benefits derived from new products. Therefore, the distribution systems may often become the deciding factor in whether markets can be served and whether industry will develop. Communications advances will ensure that the customers in different markets are informed about product availability, making distribution limitations even more painful.

More sophisticated distribution systems will also offer new management opportunities to firms but, at the same time, will introduce new uncertainties and fragilities into corporate planning. For example, the development of just-in-time delivery systems makes firms more efficient yet, on a global basis, also exposes them to more risk due to distribution interruptions. A strike in a faraway country may therefore be newly significant for a company that depends on the timely delivery of supplies.

Global Pricing

Global price competition will become increasingly heated. As their distribution spreads throughout the world, many products will take on commodity characteristics, as semiconductors did in the 1980s. Therefore, price differentials of one cent per unit may become crucial in making an international sale. However, since many new products and technologies will address completely new needs, forward pricing will become increasingly difficult and controversial as demand levels are impossible to predict with any kind of accuracy.

Even for consumer products, price competition will be substantial. Because of the increased dissemination of technology, the firm that introduces a product will no longer be able to justify higher prices for long; domestically produced products will soon be of similar quality. As a result, exchange rate movements may play more significant roles in maintaining the competitiveness of the international firm. Firms can be expected to prevail on their government to manage the country's currency to maintain a favorable exchange rate.

Through subsidization, targeting, government contracts, or other hidden forms of support, nations will attempt to stimulate their worldwide competitiveness. Due to the price sensitivity of many products, the global manager will be forced to identify such unfair practices quickly, communicate them to his or her government, and insist on either similar benefits or government action to create an internationally level playing field.

The Cost of Living in the World's Major Business Cities

(in U.S. dollars)

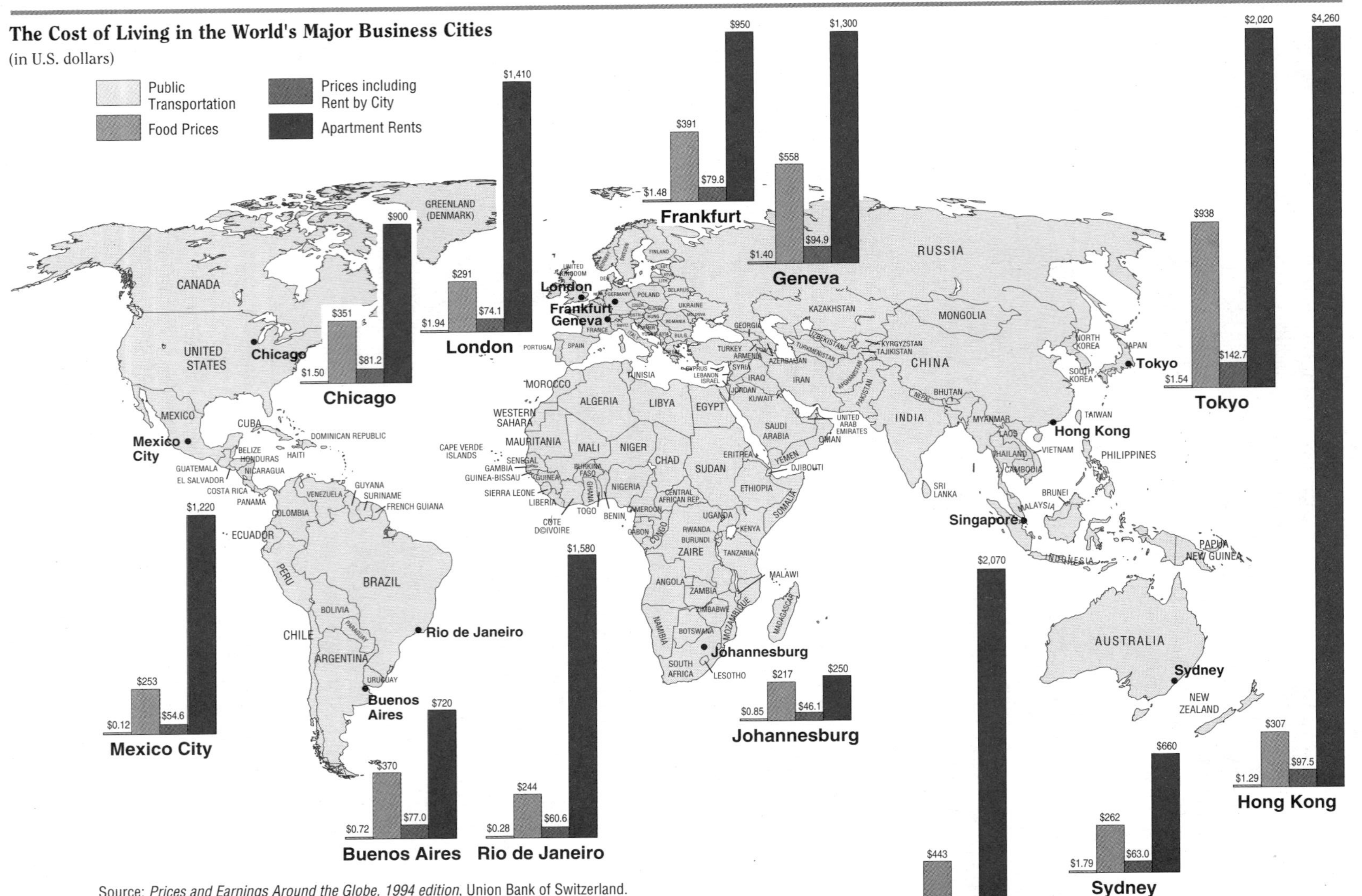

Source: *Prices and Earnings Around the Globe, 1994 edition*, Union Bank of Switzerland.

Note: Prices including rent by city are indexed, with Zurich = 100. The cost of a basket of 111 goods and services, including 3 rent categories, based on European consumer habits is between 31 and 96% higher in Lagos, Oslo, Zurich, Geneva, Copenhagen, Singapore, and Tokyo. The indexed average for all cities surveyed was 67.2 points. Food prices are based on a basket consisting of 39 food and beverage items. Apartment rents reflect medium local monthy rent for unfurnished 3-room apartment. Public transportation based on single ticket for bus, streetcar, or subway for a 10-kilometer (6-mile) trip.

At the same time, many firms will work hard to reduce the price sensitivity of their customers. By developing relationships with their markets rather than just carrying out transactions, other dimensions such as loyalty, consistency, the cost of shifting suppliers, and responsiveness to client needs may become much more important than price in future competition.

CAREERS IN GLOBAL BUSINESS

By studying this book you have learned about the intricacies, complexities, and thrills of global business. Of course, a career in global business is more than jet-set travel between New Delhi, Tokyo, Frankfurt, and New York. It is hard work and requires knowledge and expertise. Yet, in spite of the difficulties, global business allows an individual to break away from set patterns and offers new horizons, new experiences, and new opportunities for growth.

To prepare, you should be well versed in a specific functional business area and take summer internships abroad. You should take language courses and travel, not simply for pleasure but to observe business operations abroad and gain a greater appreciation of different peoples and cultures. The following pages provide an overview of principal further training and employment opportunities in the global business field.

Further Training

One option for the student on the road to more global involvement is to obtain further in-depth training by enrolling in graduate business school programs that specialize in international business education. Even though the global orientation of U.S. universities is relatively recent, a substantial number of schools have developed specific international programs. Many universities around the world also specialize in training global managers. A review of college catalogues and of materials from groups such as the Academy of International Business will be useful here.

In addition, as the world becomes more global, many organizations are able to assist students interested in studying abroad or in gathering foreign work experience. Over time, an increasing number of scholarships and exchange programs have become available. Table 15.1 lists some key international exchange and training programs and the eligible participants.

For those ready to enter or rejoin the "real world," different employment opportunities need to be evaluated.

Employment with a Large Firm

One career alternative in global business is to work for a large multinational corporation. These firms constantly search for personnel to help them in their international operations. For example, a Procter & Gamble recruiting advertisement published in a university's study newspaper is reproduced in Figure 15.3.

Many multinational firms, while seeking specialized knowledge such as languages, expect employees to be firmly grounded in the practice and management of business. Rarely, if ever, will a firm hire a new employee at the starting level and immediately place him or her in a position of international responsibility. Usually, a new employee is expected to become thoroughly familiar with the company's internal operations before being considered for an international position. Reasons a manager is sent abroad include that the company expected him or her to reflect the corporate spirit, to be tightly wed to the corporate cultures, and to be able to communicate well with both

TABLE 15.1 U.S.-Funded International Exchange and Training Programs

	Eligible Participants						
Agency and Name of Program	**Undergraduate Students**	**Graduate Students**	**Other Students**	**Teachers**	**Professors**	**Researchers**	**Post-Doctorate Scholars**
Agency for International Development							
Thomas Jefferson Fellowship Program	X	X		X	X	X	X
Participant Training Program Europe	X	X		X	X	X	X
Regional Human Resources Program	X	X		X			
Department of Agriculture							
Research and Scientific Exchange Program		X		X	X	X	X
Department of Commerce							
Exchange Visitor Program						X	
Special American Business Internship Training Program							
Department of Defense							
International Military Education and Training Program		X		X	X		
National Security Education Program	X	X					X
Navy Exchange Scientist Program							
Professional Military Education Exchanges							
U.S. Military Academies Exchanges	X						
Department of Education							
Foreign Language and Area Studies Fellowship Program		X					
Fulbright-Hays Group Projects Abroad	X	X		X	X		
Fulbright-Hays Doctoral Dissertation Research Abroad		X					
Fulbright-Hays Faculty Research Abroad					X	X	X
Fulbright-Hays Seminars Abroad				X	X		
Department of Health and Human Services							
International Research Fellowships						X	
Senior International Fellowships					X	X	
Scholars in Residence					X	X	
National Research Service Awards							
Visitor and Training Program							
Individual Health Scientist Exchanges and Biomedical Research Exchange Programs					X	X	
Visiting Program						X	
National Institutes of Health-French Postdoctoral Fellowship					X	X	
Inter-American Foundation							
Academic Fellowship Program		X					
Department of the Interior							
U.S.–Russia Environmental Agreement						X	
U.S.–China Nature Conservation Protocol						X	

TABLE 15.1 *continued*

Agency and Name of Program	Eligible Participants						
	Undergraduate Students	Graduate Students	Other Students	Teachers	Professors	Researchers	Post-Doctorate Scholars
Japan–U.S. Friendship Commission							
Japan–U.S. Friendship Commission Grants		X		X	X	X	
Department of Labor							
International Visitors Labor Studies							
National Endowment for the Arts							
U.S. Artists at International Festivals and Exhibitions							
U.S.–Japan Artist Exchanges							
International Projects Initiative							
Travel Grants Program							
U.S.–Mexico Artist Residencies							
British America Arts Association Fellowships							
National Endowment for the Humanities							
Elementary and Secondary Education in the Humanities				X			
Higher Education in the Humanities					X		
NEH Teachers-Scholars				X	X		
Foreign Language Education				X	X		
Travel to Collections					X		X
Interpretive Research					X	X	X
Summer Seminars for School Teachers				X			
International Research							X
Summer Stipends				X	X		X
Humanities Projects in Museums and Historical Organizations						X	
Summer Seminars for College Teachers					X	X	X
Fellowship for College Teachers and Independent Scholars				X	X	X	X
Humanities Projects in Media					X	X	
Public Humanities Projects					X	X	
Centers for Advanced Study							X
Fellowship for University Teachers			X	X			X
Humanities Projects in Libraries and Archives						X	
National Science Foundation							
Summer Institute in Japan		X					
U.S.–India Exchange of Scientists					X	X	X
Smithsonian Institution							
Bureau Appointments	X	X					X
Wildlife Conservation and Management Training	X	X		X	X	X	X

continued

TABLE 15.1 ***continued***

Agency and Name of Program	Eligible Participants						
	Undergraduate Students	Graduate Students	Other Students	Teachers	Professors	Researchers	Post-Doctorate Scholars
Department of State							
Russian, Eurasian, and Eastern European Studies Program		X			X	X	X
U.S. Information Agency							
Fulbright Academic Program	X	X		X	X	X	X
International Visitors Program					X		
Citizens Exchanges	X	X		X	X		
Hubert H. Humphrey Fellowship							
Youth Programs	X		X				
University Affiliations Program					X	X	X
Performing Arts Exchanges							
Study of the United States				X	X		
Academic Specialist Program					X		
U.S. Speakers					X	X	
Media Training Program							
Arts America Program							
Fulbright Teacher Exchange				X			
Library Fellows Program							
English Teaching Fellow				X			
American Cultural Specialists							
Artistic Ambassadors							
Arts America Speakers							

SOURCE: U.S. General Accounting Office, *Exchange Programs: Inventory of International Educational, Cultural and Training Programs,* Washington, D.C., June 1993.

local and corporate management personnel. In this liaison position, the manager will have to be exceptionally sensitive to both headquarters and local operations. As an intermediary, the expatriate must be empathetic, understanding, and yet fully prepared to implement the goals set by headquarters.

It is very expensive for companies to send an employee overseas. As this chapter's map shows, the annual cost of maintaining a manager overseas is often a multiple of the cost of hiring a local manager. Companies want to be sure that the expenditure is worth the benefit they will receive. Failure not only affects individual careers, but also sets back the business operations of the firm. Therefore, firms increasingly develop training programs for employees destined to go abroad.

Even if a position opens up in global operations, there is some truth in the saying that the best place to be in global business is on the same floor as the chief executive at headquarters. Employees of firms that have taken the international route often come back to headquarters to find only a few positions available for them. After spending time in foreign operations, where independence is often high and authority significant, a return to a regular job at home, which sometimes may not even call on the many skills acquired abroad, may turn out to be a difficult and deflating experience. Such encounters lead to some disenchantment with international activities as well as to financial

An Advertisement Recruiting New Graduates for Employment in Global Operations **FIGURE 15.3**

EN BUSCA DE SU TALENTO

Procter & Gamble
División de Peru / Latino America

¤ Más de 40 productos de consumo en Latino America como Pampers, Ace, Ariel, Crest, Head & Shoulders, Camay y Vicks.

¤El area tiene el mayor volumen de ventas entre todas las divisiones Internacionales de P&G.

¤Oportunidades de desarrollar una carrera profesional en areas como Mercadeo, Finanzas, Computación, Ventas, etc.

Buscamos individuos con Talento, Empuje, Liderazgo, y continuo afán de superación para posiciones permanentes o practicas de verano en Peru, Puerto Rico, México, Colombia, Venezuela, Brazil, Chile, etc.

Es muy importante que envies tu RESUME pronto ya que estaremos visitando tu Universidad en la primera semana de Noviembre.

¿QUE DEBES HACER?
Envia tu resume tan pronto como sea posible a la atencion de Ms. Cynthia Huddleston (MBA Career Services) antes del 18 de Octubre.

SOURCE: *The Hoya,* Georgetown University, October 6, 1989, 2.

QUESTION *Do you know the difference between a rain forest and a jungle?*

A rain forest typically has a high canopy of vegetation with very little undergrowth, while a jungle is densely undergrown.

pressures and family problems, all of which may add up to significant executive stress during reentry.[16] Although many firms depend on their global operations for a substantial amount of sales volume and profits, reentry programs are often viewed as an unnecessary expense. The decision is difficult for the internationalist who wants to go abroad, make his or her mark, and return home to an equivalent or even better position. However, as firms begin to recognize the importance of global operations, more efforts toward proper personnel management are likely to be made. Eventually, most firms will make global experience a requirement for further moves upon the corporate ladder.

Sources for Management Recruitment

The location and the nationality of candidates for a particular job are the key issues in recruitment. The advantage of internal recruitment is that candidates already know the corporate system and corporate culture. In fact, internal candidates may have been slated for certain positions when they entered the organization and have been trained accordingly.

When global operations are expanded, a management-development dilemma may result. Through internal recruitment, young managers will be offered interesting new opportunities. However, some senior managers may object to the constant drain of young talent from their units. Selective recruitment from the outside will help to maintain a desirable combination of inside talent and fresh blood. Furthermore, with dynamic market changes or new markets and new-business development, outside recruitment may be the only available approach.

A firm has three alternative sources for recruitment. All of them are typically used to some degree, depending on the characteristics of the firm and the industry. The first source is local, that is, citizens of the host country. The other two are home-country nationals and third-country nationals (citizens of countries other than the home or the host country). The factors that influence the choice are summarized in Table 15.2. They fall into three general categories: (1) the availability and equality of the local pool, (2) corporate policies and their cost, and (3) environmental constraints.

Currently, most managers in subsidiaries are host-country nationals. The reasons include an increase in availability of local talent, corporate relations in the particular market, and the economies realized by not having to maintain a corps of managers overseas. Local managers are generally more familiar with environmental conditions

TABLE 15.2 **Factors Determining the Choice between Local and Expatriate Managers**

• Availability of managers	• Corporate objectives	• Cost
• Competence	Control	• Environment
Market	Management development	Legal
Technical	Corporate citizenship	Cultural

and how they should be interpreted. By employing local management, the multinational is responding to host-country demands for increased localization and providing advancement as an incentive to local managers. In this respect, however, localization can be carried too far. If the firm does not subscribe to a global philosophy, the manager's development is tied to the local operation or to a particular level of management in that operation.

Local managers, if not properly trained and indoctrinated, may see things differently from the way they are viewed at headquarters. As a result, both control and the overall coordination of programs may be jeopardized. For the corporation to work effectively, of course, employees must first of all understand each other. Most corporations have adopted a common corporate language, with English as the **lingua franca;** that is, the language habitually used among people of diverse speech to facilitate communication.

lingua franca
language habitually used among people of diverse speech to facilitate communication

Cultural differences that shape managerial attitudes must be considered when developing multinational management programs. For example, British managers place more emphasis than most other nationals on individual achievement and autonomy. French managers, however, value competent supervision, sound company policies, fringe benefits, security, and comfortable working conditions.[17]

The decision as to whether to use home-country nationals in a particular operation depends on such factors as the type of industry, the life cycle stage of the product, the availability of managers from other sources, and the functional areas involved. The number of home-country managers is typically higher in the service sector than in the industrial sector. However, some overseas assignments, particularly in the service sector, may be quite short term.

The number of home-country nationals in an overseas operation rarely rises above 10 percent of the workforce and is typically only 1 percent. The reasons are both internal and external. In addition to the substantial cost of transfer, a manager may not fully adjust to foreign working and living conditions. Good corporate citizenship today requires multinational companies to develop the host country's workforce at the management level. Legal impediments to manager transfers may exist, or other difficulties may be encountered. Many U.S.-based hotel corporations, for example, have complained about delays in obtaining visas to the United States not only for managers but also for management trainees.

The use of third-country nationals is most often seen in large multinational companies that have adopted a global philosophy. An advantage is that third-country nationals may contribute to the firm's overall international expertise. However, many third-country nationals are career global managers, and they may become targets for raids by competitors looking for high levels of talent. They may be a considerable asset in regional expansion; for example, established subsidiary managers in Singapore might be used to start up a subsidiary in Malaysia. On the other hand, some transfers may be inadvisable for cultural or historical reasons, with transfers between Turkey and Greece as an example.

All firms use a similar pattern of recruitment during the internationalization process.[18] During the export stage, outside expertise is at first sought, but the firm then begins to develop its own personnel. Foreign entry through manufacture reverses this trend. The firm's reliance on home-country personnel diminishes as host-country nationals are prepared for management positions. The use of home-country nationals and third-country nationals is increasingly restricted to special assignments, such as transfer of technology or expertise. They will continue to be used as a matter of corporate policy to internationalize management and to foster the infusion of a particular corporate culture.

Selection Criteria for Overseas Assignments

The traits that have been suggested as necessary for the global manager range from the ideal to the real. One characterization describes "a flexible personality, with broad intellectual horizons, attitudinal values of cultural empathy, general friendliness, patience and prudence, impeccable educational and professional (or technical) credentials —all topped off with immaculate health, creative resourcefulness, and respect of peers. If the family is equally well endowed, all the better."[19] Although this would seem to describe a supermanager, a number of companies believe that the qualities that make a successful international manager are increasingly the traits needed at headquarters.[20] Traits typically mentioned in the choosing of managers for overseas assignments are listed in Table 15.3. Their relative importance may vary dramatically, of course, depending on the firm and the situation.

Competence Factors An expatriate manager usually has far more responsibility than a manager in a comparable domestic position and must be far more self-sufficient in making decisions and conducting daily business. To be selected in the first place, the manager's technical competence level has to be superior to local candidates'; otherwise, the firm would in most cases have chosen a local person. The manager's ability to do the job in the technical sense is one of the main determinants of ultimate success or failure in an overseas assignment.[21] However, management skills will not transfer from one culture to another without some degree of adaptation. This means that, regardless of the level of technical skills, the new environment still requires the ability to adapt them to local conditions. Technical competence must also be accompanied by the ability to lead subordinates in any situation or under any conditions.

cultural knowledge
knowledge about other cultures that can be defined by the way it is acquired: *objective* or *factual knowledge* is obtained from others through communication, research, and education; *experimental knowledge* is acquired by being directly involved in a culture

area expertise
knowledge of the basic systems in a particular region or market

The role of factual **cultural knowledge** in the selection process has been widely debated. **Area expertise** includes a knowledge of the basic system in the region or market for which the manager will be responsible—such as the roles of various ministries in international business, the significance of holidays, and the general way of doing business. None of these variables is as important as language, although language skill is not always highly ranked by firms themselves.[22] A manager who does not know the language of the country may get by with the help of associates and interpreters but is not in a position to assess the situation fully. Of the Japanese representing their companies in the United States, for example, almost all speak English. Of the Americans representing U.S. companies in Japan, however, few speak Japanese well.[23] Some companies place language skills or aptitude in a larger context; they see a strong correlation between language skills and adaptability. Another reason to look for language competence in managers considered for assignments overseas is that all managers spend most of their time communicating.

TABLE 15.3 **Criteria for Selecting Managers for Overseas Assignment**

Competence	Adaptability	Personal Characteristics
Technical knowledge	Interest in overseas work	Age
Ledership ability	Relational abilities	Education
Experience, past performance	Cultural empathy	Sex
Area expertise	Appreciation of new management styles	Health
Language	Appreciation of environmental constraints	Marital relations
	Adaptability of family	Social acceptability

In Tokyo, Merck representative Satomi Tomihari confers with Yasumasa Nakamura, M.D. Tomihari is one of 25 women recruited by Merck affiliate Banyu Pharmaceutical, Ltd.
SOURCE: Griffiths, Photographer for Magnum Photo. Courtesy of Merck & Co., Inc.

Adaptability Factors The manager's own motivation to a great extent determines the viability of an overseas assignment and consequently its success. The manager's interest in the foreign culture must go well beyond that of the average tourist if he or she is to understand what an assignment abroad involves. In most cases, the manager will need counseling and training in order to comprehend the true nature of the undertaking.

Adaptability means a positive and flexible attitude toward change. The manager assigned overseas must progress from factual knowledge of culture to interpretive cultural knowledge, trying as much as possible to become part of the new scene. This scene may be quite different from the one at home. The work habits of middle-level managers may be more lax, productivity and attention to detail less, and overall environmental restrictions far greater. The manager on a foreign assignment is part of a multicultural team, in which both internal and external interactions determine the future of the firm's operations. For example, a manager from the United States may be used to an informal, democratic type of leadership that may not be applicable in countries such as Mexico or Japan, where employees expect more authoritarian leadership.[24]

The characteristics of the family as a whole are important. Screeners look for family cohesiveness and check for marital instability or for behavioral difficulties in children. Abroad, the need to work together as a family often makes strong marriages stronger and causes the downfall of weak ones.

Personal Characteristics Despite all of the efforts made by multinational companies to recruit the best person available, demographics still play a role in the selection process. Because of either a minimum age requirement or the level of experience needed, many foreign assignments go to managers in their mid-30s or older. Normally, companies do not recruit candidates from graduating classes for immediate assignment overseas. They want their global people first to become experienced and familiar with the corporate culture, and this can best be done at the headquarters location.

In the selection process, firms are concerned about the health of the people they may send abroad. Some assignments are in host countries with dramatically different environmental conditions from the home country, and they may aggravate existing health problems. Moreover, if the candidate selected is not properly prepared, foreign assignments may increase stress levels and contribute to the development of peptic ulcers, colitis, or other problems.

Social acceptability varies from one culture to another and can be a function of any of the other personal characteristics. Background, religion, race, and sex usually become critical only in extreme cases in which a host environment would clearly reject a candidate based on one or more of these variables. The Arab boycott of the state of Israel, for example, puts constraints on the use of managers of Jewish and Arab origin. Women cannot negotiate contracts in many Middle Eastern countries. This would hold true even if the woman were president of the company.

The Selection and Orientation Challenge Because of the cost of transferring a manager overseas, many firms go beyond standard selection procedures and use adaptability screening as an integral part of the process. During the screening phase, the method most often used involves interviewing the candidate and the family. The interviews are conducted by senior executives, human relations specialists within the firm, or outside firms. Interviewers ask the candidate and the family to consider the personal issues involved in the transfer; for example, what each will miss the most. In some cases, candidates themselves will refuse an assignment. In others, the firm will withhold the assignment on the basis of interviews that clearly show a degree of risk.

The candidate selected will participate in an orientation program on internal and external aspects of the assignment. Internal aspects include issues such as compensation and reporting. External aspects are concerned with what to expect at the destination in terms of customers and culture. Typically, these programs last from a few days to two weeks. Some last several months, especially when language training is involved. The emphasis is on enhancing the individual's capability to handle cross-cultural encounters.

The attrition rate in overseas assignments averages 40 percent among companies with neither adaptability screening nor orientation programs, 25 percent among companies with cultural orientation programs, and 5 to 10 percent among companies that use both kinds of programs.[25] Considering the cost of a transfer, catching even one potentially disastrous situation pays for the program for a full year. Most companies have no program at all, however, and others provide them for higher-level management positions only. Companies that have the lowest failure rates typically employ a four-tiered approach to expatriate use: (1) clearly stated criteria, (2) rigorous procedures to determine the suitability of an individual across the criteria, (3) appropriate orientation, and (4) constant evaluation of the effectiveness of the procedures.[26] Global Learning Experience 15.4 provides an interesting perspective of the challenges in being an expatriate manager.

Employment with a Small or Medium-Size Firm

A second alternative is to begin work in a small or medium-size firm. Very often, these firms have only recently developed a global outlook, and the new employee will arrive on the "ground floor." Initial involvement will normally be in the export field—evaluating potential foreign customers, preparing quotes, and dealing with activities such as shipping and transportation. With a very limited budget, the export manager will only occasionally visit foreign markets to discuss business strategies with foreign distributors. Most of the work will be done by mail, via telex, by fax, or by telephone. The hours are often long because of the need, for example, to reach a contact during business hours in Hong Kong. The main obstacle encountered in the small firm is the lack of an adequate budget—a phenomenon always found in business—yet the possibilities for implementing creative business transactions are virtually limitless. It is also gratifying and often rewarding that one's successful contribution will be visible directly through the firm's growing export volume.

GLOBAL LEARNING EXPERIENCE

15.4

Preparing for an International Assignment

Up to 40 percent of expatriate managers terminate their assignments early, costing their companies between $50,000 and $150,000 and derailing their careers. Moreover, 50 percent of those who do not terminate their assignments early function at a low level of effectiveness.

Many expatriates fail primarily because they neglect to prepare for such assignments. Prospective expatriates can better the chances of success if they determine whether an overseas assignment is really for them. After a short period of entrancement by the new culture and the excitement of traveling, a period of disillusionment develops during which the expatriate no longer finds it romantic to converse with a limited vocabulary or navigate around a new city without proper directions. After three to six months, expatriates either have terminated the assignment or have begun to adjust to life in the host country. Research indicates that individuals with such personal characteristics as adaptability, flexibility, and tolerance for ambiguity are more likely to pass through the stage of disillusionment and successfully complete the assignment. They must be able to recognize and accept societal and business norms that may seem alien.

Since experts and support systems usually available to managers often are not present at foreign locations, expatriates often must have all the technical skills necessary to complete the assignment by themselves. Further, expatriate managers are usually their own bosses, having to make decisions that at home typically would be made by their supervisors. Therefore, expatriate managers must be able to complete their assignments with little or no help from above or below in the organizational hierarchy.

An understanding of nonverbal communications will help to avoid costly errors and assist in the analysis of business transactions. For example, in the United States the spoken word is heavily relied upon, while in Japan, China, and the Middle East, the external environment, the situation, and nonverbal behavior are crucial to accurate communication. A knowledge of business etiquette helps avoid problems. Although the Germans, French, British, and Italian will discuss the general details of business over lunch, the Swiss instead use the time to strengthen relationships and do not discuss business. Before departing on an international assignment, a basic knowledge is needed in such things as acceptable greetings, the proper use of business cards, the country's dress code, the concept of time, proper dining manners, gift-giving protocol, and religious and political taboos.

Expatriates need to discard the myth that says, "If you're effective in New York, you'll be effective in Hong Kong." Simulation training can help trainees; presented with a number of vignettes about international situations and judged by a panel of experts, they learn to interact with people of other cultures and are provided with models of appropriate and inappropriate behaviors

Courses that provide information about a particular country are also available. Some of the programs begin with a training exercise called BaFa BaFa. In the exercise, two teams try to trade with each other without knowing the negotiation rules. Most participants in the exercise make inaccurate assumptions about the other team's behaviors and motives. The exercise encourages trainees to reserve judgment about other cultures until they have more information.

SOURCE: Howard Tu and Sherry E. Sullivan, "Preparing Yourself for an International Assignment," *Business Horizons*, January–February 1994, 67.

QUESTION *Where is the world's largest rain forest?*

ANSWER! *The Amazon in South America is the world's largest rain forest. It is an area almost as big as forty-eight of the fifty states of the U.S. and contains more species of plants and animals than any other place on Earth. Unfortunately it's being burned and cleared at the rate of about 4 percent each year.*

Alternatively, global work in a small firm may involve importing; that is, finding low-cost sources that can be substituted for domestically sourced products. Decisions often must be based on limited information, and the manager is faced with many uncertainties. Often, things do not work out as planned. Shipments are delayed, letters of credit are canceled, and products almost never arrive in exactly the form and shape anticipated. Yet the problems are always new and offer an ongoing challenge.

As a training ground for global activities, probably no better starting place exists than a small or medium-sized firm. Later on, the person with some experience may find work with an export-trading or export-management company, resolving other people's problems and concentrating almost exclusively on the global arena.

OPPORTUNITIES FOR WOMEN IN GLOBAL MANAGEMENT

As U.S. business firms become more and more involved in global business activities, the need for skilled global managers is growing. Concurrent with this increase in business activity is the ever growing presence and managerial role of women in U.S. industry. A variety of data support this trend:

- From 1970 to 1995, civilian employment in the United States grew by 46.2 million. Of this increase, 27.8 million, or 60.2 percent, is accounted for by women.
- In 1970, women comprised 37.7 percent of the employed workforce; by 1995, the percentage had risen to 46.1 percent.
- In 1995, approximately two-thirds (64.8 percent) of women 15 to 64 years old were working. This compares favorably with 46 percent in 1970.
- The number and percentage of degrees in business and management conferred on women have increased significantly. At the bachelor's degree level in 1971, 10,440 women received 9.1 percent of degrees awarded; by 1993, the number had increased to 121,229, or 47.2 percent of the total. Similar gains were also noted with respect to graduate degrees. Only 1,013 women received a master's degree in business and management in 1971 (3.9 percent of the total). In 1993, 31,992 master's degrees were conferred on women, representing 35.7 percent of the total. At the Ph.D. level, women received 2.8 percent of the degrees in 1971, compared with 28.0 percent in 1993.
- In 1995, women were employed in 48.0 percent of the executive, administrative, and managerial positions in the United States, up sharply from 32.4 percent only 13 years earlier.[27]

Research conducted during the mid-1980s[28] indicated that women held only 3.3 percent of the overseas positions in U.S. business firms and that five years prior to that time, almost no women were global managers in either expatriate or professional travel status. Thus, the 3.3 percent figure should be viewed as a significant increase, not a poor showing. The reason for the past low participation of women in global management roles seems to have been the assumption that because of the subservient roles of women in Japan, Latin America, and the Middle East, neither local nor expatriate women would be allowed to succeed as managers. The error is that expatriates are not seen as local women, but rather as "foreigners who happen to be women," thus solving many of the problems that would be encountered by a local woman manager.

There appear to be some distinct advantages for a woman in a management position overseas. Among them are the advantages of added visibility and increased access to clients. Foreign clients tend to assume that "expatriate women must be excellent, or else their companies would not have sent them."

It also appears that companies that are larger in terms of sales, assets, income, and employees send more women overseas than smaller organizations. Further, the number of women expatriates are not evenly distributed among industry groups. Industry groups that utilize greater numbers or percentages of women expatriates include banking, electronics, petroleum, publishing, diversified corporations, pharmaceuticals, and retailing and apparel.

For the future, it is anticipated that the upward trends previously cited reflect the forthcoming increased participation of women in global management roles.

SUMMARY

This final chapter has provided an overview of the environmental changes facing global managers and alternative managerial responses to these changes. International business is a complex and difficult activity, yet it affords many opportunities and challenges. Observing changes and analyzing how to best incorporate them in the global business mission is the most important task of the global manager. If the international environment were constant, there would be little challenge to global business. The frequent changes are precisely what makes global business so fascinating and often highly profitable for those who are active in the field.

Key Terms and Concepts

international debt load
population growth
multilateral trade negotiations
trigger mechanisms
trade policy mechanisms
competitive platform
product life cycle
lingua franca
cultural knowledge
area expertise

Questions for Discussion

1. For many developing countries, debt repayment and trade are closely linked. What does protectionism mean to them?
2. Should we worry about the fact that the United States is a debtor nation?
3. How can a U.S. firm compete in light of low wages paid to workers abroad?
4. Is international segmentation ethical if it deprives poor countries of products?
5. How would our lives and our society change if imports were banned?

Recommended Readings

Adler, Nancy J., and Dafna N. Izraeli, eds. *Competitive Frontiers: Women Managers in a Global Economy.* Cambridge, Mass.: Blackwell, 1994.

Czinkota, Michael R., and Ilkka Ronkainen. "Global Marketing 2000: A Marketing Survival Guide." *Marketing Management.* Winter 1992: 36–45.

de Vries, Andre. *The Directory of Jobs and Careers Abroad.* Oxford: Gresham Press, 1993.

Kocher, Eric. *International Jobs: Where They Are and How to Get Them.* Reading, Mass.: Addison-Wesley, 1993.

Naisbitt, John. *Global Paradox.* New York: Morrow and Co., 1994.

Phillips, Nicola. *Managing International Teams.* Burr Ridge, Ill.: Irwin, 1994.

Pinto Carland, Maria, and Daniel H. Spatz. *Careers in International Affairs.* Washington, D.C.: School of Foreign Service, Georgetown University, 1991.

Rossman, Marlene L. *The International Businesswoman of the 1990's: A Guide to Success in the Global Marketplace.* New York: Praeger, 1990.

Work Study Travel Abroad 1992–1993. 11th ed. New York: St. Martins Press, 1992.

Notes

1. Michael R. Czinkota, Ilkka Ronkainen, and John Tarrant, *The Global Marketing Imperative* (Lincolnwood, Ill: NTC Publishing, 1995), 9.
2. William B. Johnston, "Global Workforce 2000: The New World Labor Market," *Harvard Business Review* (March–April 1991): 115–127.
3. *State of World Population,* London: United Nations Population Fund, 1993.
4. John Naisbitt, *Global Paradox* (New York: Morrow and Co., 1994), 97.
5. Shinji Fukukara, *The Future of U.S.-Japan Relationship and Its Contribution to New Globalism* (Tokyo: Ministry of International Trade and Industry, 1989), 10–11.
6. Michael R. Czinkota, "Rich Neighbors, Poor Relations," *Marketing Management* (Spring 1994): 46–52.
7. *U.S. Manufacturers in the Global Marketplace* (New York: The Conference Board, 1994).
8. Sudhir H. Kale and D. Sudharshan, "A Strategic Approach to International Segmentation," *International Marketing Review* 4 (Summar 1987): 60.
9. Benn R. Konsynski and Jahangir Karimi, "On the Design of Global Information Systems," in eds. S. Bradley, J. Hausman, and R. Nolan, *Globalization, Technology, and Competition: The Fusion of Computers and Telecommunications in the 1990s* (Boston: 1993), 81–108.
10. Robert Bartels, *Global Development and Marketing* (Columbus, Ohio: Grid, 1981), 111.
11. Kenichi Ohmae, "Only Triad Insiders Will Succeed," *The New York Times,* November 2, 1984, 2f.
12. Ibid.
13. Bartels, *Global Development and Marketing,* 112.
14. Michael R. Czinkota and Masaaki Kotabe, "Product Development the Japanese Way," in eds. M. Czinkota and I. Ronkainen, *International Marketing Strategy* (Fort Worth, Tex.: The Dryden Press, 1994), 285–291.
15. Naisbitt, *Global Paradox,* 18.
16. Michael G. Harvey, "Repatriation of Corporate Executives: An Empirical Study," *Journal of International Business Studies* 20 (Spring 1989): 131–144.
17. Rabindra Kanungo and Richard W. Wright, "A Cross-Cultural Comparative Study of Managerial Job Attitudes," *Journal of International Business Studies* 14 (Fall 1983): 115–129.
18. Lawrence G. Franko, "Who Manages Multinational Enterprises?" *Columbia Journal of World Business* 8 (Summer 1973): 30–42.
19. Jean E. Heller, "Criteria for Selecting an International Manager," *Personnel* (May–June 1980): 18–22.
20. Walter Kiechel, "Our Person in Pomparippu," *Fortune,* October 17, 1983, 213–218.
21. Richard D. Hays, "Ascribed Behavioral Determinants of Success-Failure among U.S. Expatriate Managers," *Journal of International Business Studies* 2 (Summer 1971): 40–46.
22. *Compensating International Executives* (New York: Business International, 1970), 35.
23. Lennie Copeland, "Training Americans to Do Business Overseas," *Training,* July 1984, 22–33.
24. Lee Smith, "Japan's Autocratic Managers," *Fortune,* January 7, 1985, 14–23.
25. "Gauging a Family's Suitability for a Stint Overseas," *Business Week,* April 16, 1979, 127–130.
26. Rosalie Tung, "Selection and Training of Personnel for Overseas Assignments," *Columbia Journal of World Business* 16 (Spring 1981): 68–78.
27. 1996 Statistical Abstract of the United States, (Washington, D.C.: U.S. Government Printing Office) Tables 14, 320, 303, 616, 628, and 637.
28. Nancy J. Adler, "Women in International Management: Where Are They?" *California Management Review,* Vol. xxvi, No. 4, (Summer 1984): 78–89.

ENGLISH GLOSSARY

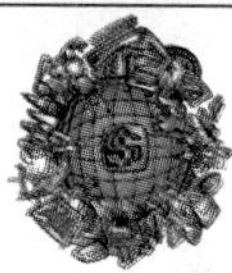

absolute advantage The ability to produce a good or service more cheaply than it can be produced elsewhere.

accounting diversity The range of differences in national accounting practices.

acculturation Adjusting and adapting to a specific culture other than one's own.

affiliates of foreign corporations Affiliates are United States companies owned ten percent or more by foreigners.

airfreight Transport of goods by air; accounts for less than one percent of the total volume of international shipments.

Andean Trade Preference Act Provides duty-free entry into the United States for a broad range of products from Bolivia, Colombia, Ecuador, and Peru; expires Dec. 4, 2001.

antitrust laws Laws that prohibit monopolies, restraint of trade, and conspiracies to inhibit competition.

arbitration The procedure for settling a dispute in which an objective third party hears both sides and makes a decision; a procedure for resolving conflict in the international business arena through the use of intermediaries such as representatives of chambers of commerce, trade associations, or third-country institutions.

area briefings Training programs that provide factual preparation prior to an overseas assignment.

area expertise A knowledge of the basic systems in a particular region or market.

autarky A country that does not participate in international trade.

backtranslation The translating of a foreign language version back to the original language by a different person than the one who made the first translation.

backward innovation The development of a drastically simplified version of a product.

balance of payments International economic transactions between one country and another.

barter Direct exchange of goods of approximately equal value.

barter economy A system of trading one economy for another.

base salary Salary not including special payments such as allowances paid during overseas assignments.

basic balance The sum of the current account and the long-term capital account of a country's balance of payments.

bill of lading A contract between the exporter and the carrier indicating that the carrier has accepted responsibility for the goods and will provide transportation in return for payment.

black hole The situation that arises when an international marketer has a low-competence subsidiary—or none at all—in a highly strategic market.

boycott A collaboration to prevent a country from carrying on international trade by preventing or obstructing other countries from dealing with it.

brain drain A migration of professional people from one country to another, usually for the purpose of improving their incomes or living conditions.

brand The name, term, symbol, sign, or design or combination thereof used to differentiate a firm's product from competitors.

brand name The part of the brand that can be vocalized or spoken.

brokers Professionals who assist in the transfer of funds between banks and find the most favorable prices for currencies.

buffer stock Stock of a commodity kept on hand to prevent a shortage in times of unexpectedly great demand; under international commodity and price agreement, the stock controlled by an elected or appointed manager for the purpose of managing the price of the commodity.

bulk service Ocean shipping provided on contract either for individual voyages or for prolonged periods of time.

buy-back or compensation arrangement First party supplies technology or equipment permitting second party to begin production. First party is then paid with goods produced.

Calvo Doctrine Doctrine that embraces the idea that the state is supreme over foreign investors within the state's territory, and challenges any intervention by foreign states in investment disputes as a violation of its territorial jurisdiction, and rejects the concept of prompt and adequate compensation for the property seized.

capital account Transfers of capital assets and debt forgiveness among nations without compensation.

capital flight The flow of private funds abroad because investors believe that the return on investment or the safety of capital is not sufficiently ensured in their own countries.

Caribbean Basin Initiative (CBI) Permits duty-free entry into the United States on a permanent basis for a broad range of products from Caribbean Basin Initiative (CBI) beneficiary countries.

cartel An association of producers of a particular good.

cash flow The amount of cash (on hand or in banks) that a company has.

central banks National banks that implement governmental policies regarding the value of their currencies.

centralization The concentrating of control and strategic decision making at headquarters.

change agent A person or institution that facilitates change in a firm or in a host country.

channel design The length and width of the distribution channel.

civil law A compilation of laws, or set of rules, set forth in a listing called a code.

Clayton Act of 1914 Expands the enforcement provisions of the Sherman Antitrust Act; defines exclusive dealing and tying clauses as being mergers that result in monopolies, and interlocking directorates as being unfair business practices.

clearing account barter Parties establish clearing accounts, like a bank account, which keeps track of purchases by each. The long-term goal is equalization of purchases on both sides.

codetermination A management approach in which employees are represented on supervisory boards to facilitate communication and collaboration between management and labor.

commercial invoice A bill for the goods stating basic information about the transaction, including a description of the merchandise, total cost of the goods sold, addresses of the shipper and seller, and delivery and payment terms.

Committee for Foreign Investments in the United States (CFIUS) A federal committee with the responsibility for reviewing major foreign investments to determine whether national security or related concerns are at stake.

commodity price agreements Involve both buyers and sellers in an agreement to manage the price of a certain commodity.

common agricultural policy (CAP) An integrated system of subsidies and rebates applied to agricultural interests in the European community.

common law A system of law which relies on the rulings of previous cases (precedent), common usage, and customs as the basis for court decisions.

common market Like a customs union, has no barriers to trade among members and a common external trade policy; and further, removes restrictions on the movement of factors of production across member borders.

comparative advantage The ability to produce a good or service more cheaply, relative to other goods and services, than other countries can.

competitive platform The business environment provided by a nation to its firms which affects their international competitiveness.

complementary marketing An arrangement between two companies for the sharing of facilities and/or marketing activities; allows firms to achieve objectives that they cannot reach efficiently by themselves.

concentration The market expansion policy that involves concentrating on a small number of markets.

conference pricing The establishment of prices by a cartel; used in shipping.

confiscation Similar to expropriation in that it results in a transfer of ownership from the firm to the host country, but differs in that it does not involve compensation for the firm.

conflict of laws Differences in the laws of countries as they apply to transactions among persons from different places.

container ships Ships designed to carry standardized containers, which greatly facilitate loading and unloading as well as intermodal transfers.

contribution margin The difference between selling price (per unit) and variable cost (per unit).

contributor A country organization with a distinctive competence, such as product development.

coordinated decentralization The overall corporate strategy is provided from headquarters, while subsidiaries are free to implement it within the range agreed on in consultation with headquarters.

correspondent banks or representative offices Banks located in different countries and unrelated by ownership that have a reciprocal agreement to provide services to each other's customers.

cost and freight (CFR) Seller quotes a price for the goods, including the cost of transportation to the named port of debarkation. Cost and choice of insurance are left to the buyer.

cost of living allowance (COLA) An allowance paid during assignment overseas to enable the employee to maintain the same standard of living as at home.

cost, insurance, and freight (CIF) Seller quotes a price including insurance, all transportation, and miscellaneous charges to the point of debarkation from the vessel or aircraft.

counterpurchase or parallel sorter Two separate contracts for exchange of goods and services. Permits one side of the transaction to go forward, with the other side to follow at a later time.

countertrade Payment for goods and services with other goods and services.

credit Created whenever an asset is decreased, a liability is increased, or an expense is decreased.

creeping expropriation A series of acts or regulations that gradually and together limit the exercise of ownership rights.

Critical Commodities List A file containing information about products that are either particularly sensitive to national security or controlled for other purposes.

cross rate Exchange rate quotations that do not use the U.S. dollar.

cultural assimilator A program in which trainees for overseas assignments must respond to scenarios of specific situations in a particular country.

cultural convergence Exposure to foreign cultures accelerated by technological advances.

cultural knowledge Knowledge about other cultures that can be defined by the way it is acquired: *Objective or factual knowledge* is obtained from others through communication, research, and education; *experiential knowledge* is acquired by being directly involved in a culture.

cultural risk The risk of business blunders, poor customer relations, and wasted negotiations that results when firms fail to understand and adapt to the cultural differences between their own and host countries' cultures.

culture shock The more pronounced reactions to the psychological disorientation that most people feel when they move for an extended period of time in a markedly different culture.

currency flows The flows of currency from nation to nation, which in turn determine exchange rates.

current transfers Transfers, gifts or grants of humanitarian goods and services.

customed structure An organizational structure that groups human resources according to the type of customer or customer category.

customer involvement The active participation of customers; a characteristic of services in that customers often are actively involved in the provision of services they consume.

customer service A total corporate effort aimed at customer satisfaction; customer service levels in terms of responsiveness that inventory policies permit for a given situation.

customs union Elimination of tariff and quota barriers among member countries; member countries establish *common* tariff and quota barriers against nonmember countries.

data The accumulation of raw facts and figures.

debit Created whenever an asset is increased, a liability is decreased, or an expense is increased.

debt capital Capital raised by borrowing money from investors, i.e., bonds.

debt swaps Countries with large amounts of external debt agree to exchange debt for some other asset of the country.

decentralization The granting of a high degree of autonomy to subsidiaries.

delivered duty unpaid (DDU) Seller is responsible for delivery to buyer, excluding customs duties and taxes.

delivered duty paid (DDP) Seller is responsible for delivery to buyer's premises, including payment of import duties and inland transportation.

demand pattern analysis Indicated typical patterns of growth and decline in manufacturing.

demographics The characteristics of people, i.e., age, income, sex, marital status, occupation, level of education, etc.

developmental aid International aid to developing countries.

Dia de los Muertos (Day of the Dead) Central and South American observances of All Saints Day (Nov. 1) and All Souls Day (Nov. 2).

direct investment Transactions between investors and enterprises in the control or ownership of assets in a foreign economy.

direct quotation A foreign exchange quotation that specifies the units of home country currency needed to purchase one unit of foreign currency.

direct taxes Calculated on income, either individual or firm income.

deregulation Removal of the government regulation of a company or industry to stimulate competition, i.e., the United States airline industry.

diversification A market expansion policy characterized by growth in a relatively large number of markets or market segments.

division of labor assigning stages of production to several individuals rather than each producing an entire good or service.

dock receipt Proof of performance of FAS delivery.

Doctrine of Sovereign Immunity Holds that sovereign states are immune from lawsuits covering their laws and regulations, including laws expropriating property, acts of their armed forces or diplomatic service, and public loans.

documentary collection Use of financial intermediaries to collect funds; documents are used to control merchandise until payment is made.

domestic company A company that operates only within its own country.

domestic law Body of legal regulations that govern activities carried on inside the legal boundaries of an organization's or citizen's home country.

domestication The government demands transfer of ownership and management responsibility.

double entry bookkeeping A method of accounting in which every transaction produces both a debit and a credit of the same amount.

dual pricing Price-setting strategy in which the export price may be based on marginal cost pricing, resulting in a lower export price than domestic price; may open the company to dumping charges.

dumping Selling goods overseas at a price lower than in the exporter's home market, or at a price below the cost of production, or both.

economic and monetary union (EMU) Ideal among European leaders that economic integration should move beyond the four freedoms; specifically, it entails 1) closer coordination of economic policies to promote exchange rate stability and convergence of inflation rates and growth rates, 2) creation of a European central bank called the Eurofed, and 3) replacement of national monetary authorities by the Eurofed and adoption of the ECU as the European currency.

economic exposure The potential for long-term effects on a firm's value as the result of changing currency values.

economic infrastructure The transportation, energy, and communication systems in a country.

economic union Has all the characteristics of a common market and, in addition, the integration of economic policies; harmonized monetary policies, taxation, government spending, and common currency.

education allowance Reimbursement by the company for dependent educational expenses incurred while a parent is assigned overseas.

embargo Usually much broader than sanctions in that they prohibit trade entirely.

equity capital Capital normally raised by selling shares in the company stock to investors.

equity participation Multinational minority ownership in companies that have strategic importance to them.

estimation by analogy Used when data for a particular market do not exist.

ethnocentric Tending to regard one's own culture as superior; tending to be home-market oriented.

ethnocentrism The tendency to consider one's own culture superior to others.

Euro Name of currency to be introduced as part of the implementation of the European Monetary Union (EMU).

Euro-commercial paper (ECP) A short-term debt instrument, typically 30, 60, 90, or 180 days in maturity, sold in the Eurocurrency markets.

Eurobond A bond that is denominated in a currency other than the currency of the country in which the bond is sold.

Eurocurrency Any foreign currency-denominated deposit or account at a financial institution outside the country of the currency's issuance.

Eurodollars U.S. dollars deposited in banks outside the United States; not confined to banks in Europe.

Euromarkets Money and capital markets in which transactions are denominated in a currency other than that of the place of the transaction; not confined to Europe.

Euronote A short to medium-term debt instrument sold in the Eurocurrency markets. The three major classes of Euronotes are Euro-commercial paper, Euro-medium term notes, and Euronotes.

European Monetary System (EMS) Fixed parity rates among member countries.

European Social Charter Establishes and guarantees economic, social, and cultural rights for the nationals of the member states of the council of Europe.

ex-works (EXW) Price quotes that apply only at the point of origin; the seller agrees to place the goods at the disposal of the buyer at the specified place on the date or within the fixed period.

exchange controls Controls on the movement of capital in and out of a country, sometimes imposed when the country faces a shortage of foreign currency.

exchange economy A system of trading in which a commodity is exchanged for precious metal equal to the worth of the commodity.

Exchange-Rate Mechanism (ERM) The acceptance of responsibility by a European Monetary System member to actively maintain its own currency within agreed-upon limits versus other member currencies established by the European Monetary System.

expatriate One living in a foreign land; a corporate manager assigned to an overseas location.

experiential knowledge Knowledge acquired through involvement (as opposed to information, which is obtained through communication, research, and education).

experimentation Research method in which all but one variable is held constant and a new, single variable is introduced; any change in the market as a result of the test is ascribed to the new variable.

export factor receivable Assignment of invoices and documents related to a shipment to a factor who then pays exporter with a discounted amount.

export trading company (ETC) The result of 1982 legislation to improve the export performance of small and medium-size firms, the export trading company allows businesses to band together to export or offer export services; additionally, the law permits bank participation in trading companies and relaxes antitrust provisions.

export license A license obtainable from the U.S. Department of Commerce Bureau of Export Administration, which is responsible for administering the Export Administration Act.

export management companies (EMC) Domestic firms that specialize in performing international business services as commission representatives or as distributors.

export-control systems Designed to deny or at least delay the acquisition of strategically important goods to adversaries.

exporting The sale and delivery of tangible goods to another country.

expropriation The taking of foreign-owned property by the state.

external economies of scale Reduced manufacturing costs resulting from a firm's access to lower cost capital, labor, and technology in other countries.

extraterritoriality A nation's attempt to set policy outside its territorial limits.

factors of production All inputs into the production process, including capital, labor, land, and technology.

field experience Experience acquired in actual rather than laboratory settings; training that exposes a corporate manager to a different cultural environment for a limited amount of time.

financial assets The exchange of financial claims (stocks, bonds, loans, purchases, or sales of companies) in exchange for other financial claims or money.

financial infrastructure Facilitating financial agencies in a country; for example, banks.

financial risk management The management of a firm's cash flows associated with the three basic financial prices of interest rates, exchange rates, and commodity prices.

fixed costs Costs which remain constant regardless of the level of production, i.e., officer salaries, security staff, rent, etc.

fixed foreign exchange rate Under the Gold Exchange Standard, foreign currencies linked to each other based on gold.

floating foreign exchange rate Foreign exchange rates that respond quickly to market forces of supply and demand.

focus groups Research technique in which representatives of a proposed target audience contribute to marketing research by participating in a supervised, unstructured discussion.

Foreign Corrupt Practices Act Passed in 1977, making it a crime for U.S. executives of publicly traded firms to bribe a foreign official in order to obtain business.

foreign direct investments The establishment or expansion of operations in a foreign country with a transfer of capital.

foreign exchange market An international market that exchanges financial instruments in a variety of different currencies.

foreign policy The area of public policy concerned with relationships with other countries.

foreign service premium A bribe to encourage a manager to leave familiar conditions and adapt to new surroundings.

foreign trade zones Areas where foreign goods may be held or processed and then reexported without incurring any duties.

forfeiting Exporter discounts bills of exchange received from an importer.

Fortress Europe Suspicion raised by trading partners of Western Europe, claiming that the integration of the European Union may result in increased restrictions on trade and investment by outsiders.

forward contract Agreements between firms and banks which assure the firm of either selling or buying a specific foreign currency at a future date at a known price.

forward outright Transactions for maturities of 30, 90, 120, 180 and 360 days (from the present date).

forward swaps Exchange of currency for an agreed length of time at an agreed rate.

forward transaction Exchange of currencies on a future date at an agreed upon exchange rate.

franchising The granting of the right by a parent company (the franchisor) to another, independent entity (the franchisee) to do business in a prescribed manner.

free alongside ship (FAS) Applies only at a designated inland shipping point; seller is responsible for loading goods into the means of transportation; buyer is responsible for all subsequent expenses.

free on board (FOB) Applies only to vessel shipments. Seller quotes a price covering all expenses up to and including delivery of goods on an overseas vessel provided by or for the buyer.

free trade area Elimination of quota barriers among member countries, while each country establishes its own tariff and quota barriers against nonmember countries.

functional structure Arranges employees based on the type of work to be done.

fundamental disequilibrium Persistent imbalances in BOP.

gap analysis Analysis of the difference between market potential and actual sales.

General Agreement on Tariffs and Trade (GATT) An international code of tariffs and trade rules signed by 23 nations in 1947; headquartered in Geneva, Switzerland; 99 members currently.

geographic area structure An organizational structure in which geographic divisions are responsible for all manufacturing and marketing in their respective areas.

global company A business organization that operates in more than one country.

gray market A market entered in a way not intended by the manufacturer of goods.

Group of Five The G5 countries, composed of the United States, Japan, West Germany, United Kingdom and France.

Group of Seven The G7 is the G5 countries, plus Canada and Italy.

Hajj The annual Muslim pilgrimage to Mecca, required of every Muslim at least once in their lifetime.

hardship allowance An allowance paid during an assignment to an overseas area that requires major adaptation.

harmonize The merging of the policies of several countries into a common, unified policy.

high-context cultures Cultures in which context is at least as important as what is actually said.

housing allowance An allowance paid during assignment overseas to provide living quarters.

implementor The typical subsidiary role, which involves implementing strategy that originates with headquarters.

import substitution Restriction of imports in order to allow domestic firms an opportunity to grow and prosper.

importing The purchase and receipt of tangible goods from another country.

income elasticity of demand Describes the relationship between demand and economic progress as indicated by growth in income.

Incoterms The internationally accepted standard definitions for terms of sale by the International Chamber of Commerce (ICC).

indirect quotation Foreign exchange quotation that specifies the units of foreign currency needed to chase one unit of the home currency.

indirect taxes Like sales taxes, severance taxes, tariffs, and value-added taxes, are applied to purchase prices, material costs, quantities of natural resources mined, and so forth.

industrial policy Official planning for industry as a whole or for a particular industry; in the United States, occurs only indirectly.

information Data put into useable form.

input-output analysis Provides a method of estimating market potentials, especially in the industrial sector.

intangibility The inability to be seen, tasted, or touched in a conventional sense; the characteristic of services that most strongly differentiates them from products.

Interbank Market Banks dealing with other banks in large volumes with transactions exceeding one million dollars.

intergovernmental organizations (IGO) Permanent organization set up by two or more states to carry on activities of common interest.

intermodal movements The transfer of freight from one mode or type of transportation to another.

internal economies of scale Lower production costs resulting from increased production for an enlarged market.

internalization Action by a firm to keep all production related to a product inside the organization in order to protect manufacturing know-how or secrets from competitors.

International Bank for Reconstruction and Development The World Bank intended for reconstruction and development.

international bond Bond issues in domestic capital markets by foreign borrowers (foreign bonds) or issued in the Eurocurrency markets in currency different from that of the home currency of the borrower (Eurobonds).

international competitiveness The ability of a firm, an industry, or a country to compete in the international marketplace at a stable or rising standard of living.

international debt load Total accumulated negative net investment of a nation.

international law Body of rules and laws that regulates activities carried on inside the legal boundaries of an organization's or citizen's home country.

International Monetary Fund Gold and constituent currencies available to members for currency stabilization.

intervention Government buying and selling of the country's own currency on the open market.

intra-industry trade The two-way exchange of the same goods.

inventory carrying costs The expense of maintaining inventories.

isolationism A policy that a nation can exist without interacting with other nations.

joint occurrence Occurrence of a phenomenon affecting the business environment in several locations simultaneously.

Joint Research and Development Act of 1984 A 1984 act that allows both domestic and foreign firms to participate in joint basic-research efforts without fear of U.S. antitrust action.

joint venture Participation of two or more companies in an enterprise to achieve a common goal.

just-in-time inventory Materials scheduled to arrive precisely when they are needed on a production line.

land bridge Transfer of ocean freight on land among various modes of transportation.

Law of One Price The exchange rate between two currencies based on just one good or service.

Leontief Paradox The general belief that the United States was capital-abundant against Leontief's finding that the country is labor-abundant.

letter of credit Undertaking by a bank to make payment to a seller upon completion of the conditions set forth in the letter of credit.

licensing agreement One firm permits another to use its intellectual property for compensation designated as royalty.

lift on-lift off The method of loading and unloading containers by alternately lifting an outbound container on board the vessel and then in the same cycle of the crane lifting an inbound container off the vessel.

liner service Ocean shipping characterized by regularly scheduled passage on established routes.

lingua franca The language habitually used among people of diverse speech to facilitate communication.

local content Regulations to gain control over foreign investment by ensuring that a large share of the product is locally produced or a larger share of the profit is retained in the country.

location decision Decision as to the number of distribution centers that should be utilized and where they are to be located.

logistics platform Vital to a firm's competitive position, it is determined by a location's ease and convenience of market reach under favorable cost circumstances.

low-context cultures Most of the information is contained explicitly in the words.

mail survey Survey technique in which the questionnaire is mailed to a selected group of respondents.

management contract A firm sells its expertise in running a company while avoiding the risk or benefit of ownership.

maquiladoras Plants that make goods and parts or process food for export back to the United States.

marginal cost pricing Pricing based on the additional out-of-pocket or incremental costs.

market-differentiated pricing Price-setting strategy based on demand rather than cost.

market segmentation Grouping of people based on the common characteristics shared by members of the group; i.e., demographics, geographics, psychographics (lifestyles), degree of product usage and desired benefit from the product.

market transparency Availability of full disclosure and information about key market factors such as supply, demand, quality, service, and prices.

marketing infrastructure Facilitating marketing agencies in a country; for example, market research firms, channel members.

Maastricht Agreement Established European Community (EC) citizenship and an economic union, i.e., a European central bank, a system to manage monetary policy, price stability, a European currency, and commitment by member countries to reduce excessive government deficits.

matrix structure An organizational structure that uses functional and divisional structures simultaneously.

media mix The mix or combination of various types of advertising media, i.e., newspapers, magazines, radio, TV, outdoor, and transit advertising.

media strategy Strategy applied to the selection of media vehicles and the development of a media schedule.

mercantilism Political and economic policy encouraging the export of goods in return for gold.

merchandise Tangible goods such as automobiles, machinery and chemicals.

merchandise trade Funds used for merchandise imports and funds obtained from merchandise exports.

minority participation Participation by a group having less than the number of votes necessary for control.

mixed structure An organizational structure that combines two or more organizational dimensions; for example, products, areas, or functions.

Modern Traditional Theory Doctrine that recognizes a sovereign state's right to nationalize foreign-owned property, to be accompanied by prompt, adequate, and effective compensation.

Most-Favored Nation (MFN) A term describing a GATT clause that calls for member countries to grant other member countries the most favorable treatment they accord any country concerning imports and exports.

multilateral trade negotiations Trade negotiations among more than two parties; the intricate relationships among trading countries.

multinational company (MNC) A company that operates internationally to earn profits on a global basis.

multiple-factor indexes Measure market potential indirectly by using proxy variables that have been shown (either through research or intuition) to correlate closely with the demand for a particular product.

Muslim or Islamic law The Sunnah (writings and sayings of the Prophet Muhammed), Islamic scholars, and the Islamic legal community.

NAFTA North American Free Trade Agreement; agreement among Canada, the United States and Mexico to lower and or eliminate tariff barriers among the three countries in order to stimulate trade.

national security The ability of a nation to protect its internal values from external threats.

national sovereignty Provides a government with the right and burden to shape the environment of the country and its citizens.

natural hedging or contractual hedging The structuring of a firm's operations so that cash flows by currency, inflows against outflows, are matched.

netting Coordination of two opposite cash flows between subsidiaries of a firm so that only the net balance of the two are actually exchanged.

nongovernmental organizations (NGO) International organization made up of persons other than states.

nontariff barriers Barriers to trade, other than tariffs. Examples include buy-domestic campaigns, preferential treatment for domestic bidders, and restrictions on market entry of foreign products such as involved inspection procedures.

not-invented-here syndrome Wherein local or subordinate organizational units reject strategies and/or firm initiates solely because they were initiated elsewhere in the organization.

observation A research method that gathers information that relies on observation of an activity as it occurs.

ocean shipping The forwarding of freight by ocean carrier.

official reserves account The total currency and metallic reserves held by official monetary authorities within the country.

official settlements balance A summary measure of a country's balance of payments which is the sum of the current account, long-term and short-term capital accounts, and the net balance on errors and omissions.

offset Requires that portions of the product be produced or assembled in buying country.

offshore banking The use of banks or bank branches located in low-tax countries, often Caribbean islands, to raise and hold capital for multinational operations.

operating risk The danger of interference by governments or other groups in one's corporate operations abroad.

opportunity cost The additional cost of taking one action as compared to another.

order cycle time The total time that passes between the placement of an order and the receipt of the merchandise.

ownership risk The risk inherent in maintaining ownership of property abroad. The exposure of foreign owned assets to governmental intervention.

Pacific Rim Developed and newly industrialized countries (N.I.C.) of the Far East, including Japan, China, Hong Kong, South Korea, Singapore, Taiwan, Indonesia, Malaysia, Philippines, Thailand, Australia, New Zealand, Brunei, Macao, and Papua New Guinea.

per capita The average dollar value of exports and imports for each person in a country.

per capita income The income of a country divided by the number of its citizens.

personal interview Survey technique in which an interviewer personally calls on a respondent in an effort to complete a questionnaire.

perishability Susceptibility to deterioration; the characteristic of services that makes them difficult to inventory.

physical distribution The movement of finished products to customers.

political risk The risk of loss by an international corporation of assets, earning power, or managerial control as a result of political actions by the host country.

polycentric Tending to regard each culture as a separate entity; tending to be oriented toward individual foreign markets.

population growth The effect on economic matters of changes in a country's population.

portfolio capital Flows of money resulting from financial investments.

portfolio investment The net balance of capital that flows in and out of the United States less than ten percent ownership.

positioning The perception by consumers of a firm's product in relation to competitors' products.

preferential policies Government policies that favor certain (usually domestic) firms; for example, the use of national carriers for the transport of government freight even when more economical alternatives exist.

price controls Government regulation of the prices of goods and services, control of the prices of imported goods and services as a result of domestic political pressures.

price escalation The establishing of export prices far in excess of domestic prices—often due to a long distribution channel and frequent markups.

primary data The collection of original facts and figures.

primary reference groups Small, intimate groups that are in a position to influence a person's behavior.

private international law Division of international law that deals primarily with the rights and duties of individuals and nongovernmental organizations in their international affairs.

private placement The sale of debt securities to private or institutional investors without going through a public issuance like that of a bond issue or equity issue.

privatization A policy of shifting operation of government-owned enterprises to private ownership to cut costs and ensure more efficient services.

process structure A variation of the functional structure in which departments are formed on the basis of production processes.

product counterfeiting Illegal manufacture, use, or patent and copyright infringement of a product or intellectual property.

product cycle theory Views the manufacturing of products as passing through three stages: new product, maturing product, and standardized product.

product life cycle theory Marketing theory illustrating that a product goes through four stages: introduction, growth, maturity, and decline.

product line A series of related products offered by a company.

product structure An organizational structure in which product divisions are responsible for all manufacturing and marketing.

production possibilities curve A curve designed to show all possible combinations of two products (or output) that can be produced with a nation's limited resources; how much of one product is "traded off" in order to produce another.

promotional message The content of an advertisement or publicity release.

promotional mix The mix, or combination, of personal selling, advertising, publicity, and sales promotion activities.

proxy information Data used as a substitute for more desirable data that are unobtainable.

psychographics The study of people based on their lifestyles; i.e., their activities, interests, and opinions.

public international law Division of international law that deals primarily with the rights and duties of states and intergovernmental organizations as between themselves.

punitive tariffs A tax on an imported good or service intended to punish a trading partner.

purchasing power parity (PPP) A theory that the prices of tradable goods will tend to equalize across countries.

quality of life The standard of living combined with environmental factors, it determines the level of well-being of individuals.

R&D cost Research and development cost; the costs incurred in developing technology.

real assets The exchange of physical goods and all types of services for the payment of money.

recognizability The characteristic of appearing to be previously known; the ability of a product to be recognized even though it has been adapted to local market conditions.

reference groups Groups such as the family, co-workers, and professional and trade associations that provide the values and attitudes that influence and shape behavior, including consumer behavior.

regiocentric or geocentric Tending to be oriented toward regions larger than individual countries as markets.

reliability Dependability; the predictability of the outcome of an action.

reverse distribution A system responding to environmental concerns that ensures a firm can retrieve a product from the market for subsequent use, recycling, or disposal.

Robinson-Palman Act of 1936 Forbids price discrimination.

roll on-roll off Ship loading operation in which cargo with wheels are driven on board the vessel and parked.

sanction Specific trade measures such as the cancellation of trade financing or the prohibition of high technology trade.

scenario building Identifying crucial variables and determining their effects on different cases or approaches.

sea bridge The transfer of freight among various modes of transportation at sea.

secondary data Data that has been collected by others.

secondary reference groups Larger, less intimate groups that, because of a relationship with an individual, may influence behavior.

securitization The conversion of developing country bank debt into tradable securities.

self-reference criterion The unconscious reference to one's own cultural values.

selling forward The forward contract has a rate for purchasing marks that is cheaper than the present spot rate.

sensitivity training Training in human relations that focuses on personal and interpersonal interactions; training that focuses on enhancing an expatriate's flexibility in situations quite different from those at home.

services The export and import of all types of services.

service capacity The maximum level at which a service provider is able to provide service to customers.

service trade The international exchange of personal or professional services.

Sherman Antitrust Act of 1890 Forbids combinations and conspiracies in restraint of interstate and international trade, and forbids monopolies and attempts to monopolize interstate and international trade.

shipper's order A negotiable bill of lading that can be bought, sold, or traded while the subject goods are still in transit and that is used for letter of credit transactions.

Single European Act Amended the Treaty of Rome; mandates the removal of physical, technical and tax barriers to the free movement of persons, goods, services, and capital.

social infrastructure The housing, health, educational, and other social systems in a country.

social stratification The division of a particular population into classes.

sogoshasha A large Japanese general trading company.

Special Drawing Right (SDR) An index of currencies available to each member country.

spot transaction The exchange of currencies for immediate delivery.

standard of living The level of material affluence of a group or nation, measured as a composite of quantities and qualities of goods.

standard worldwide pricing Price-setting strategy based on average unit costs of fixed, variable, and export-related costs.

state Political entity comprising a territory, population, a government capable of entering into international relations, and a government capable of controlling its territory and peoples.

state-owned enterprise A corporate form that has emerged in non-Communist countries, primarily for reasons of national security and economic security.

straight bill of lading A nonnegotiable bill of lading usually used in prepaid transactions in which the transported goods involved are delivered to a specific individual or company.

strategic alliance A new term for collaboration among firms, often similar to joint ventures.

strategic leader A highly competent national subsidiary located in a strategically critical market.

structured operating environment Distribution of foreign investments in a way that prevents gain by a foreign government in the event of seizure.

surveys A research method that gathers data by soliciting answers to carefully framed questions from a group of participants in the market.

switch trading Credits in the clearing account that can be sold or transferred to a third party.

syndicated loan An arrangement in which between 20 and 50 banks in many different countries contribute to the funding of a single large loan.

systems concept A concept of logistics based on the notion that materials-flow activities are so complex that they can be considered only in the context of their interaction.

tax-equalization Reimbursement by the company when an employee in an overseas assignment pays taxes at a higher rate than if he or she were at home.

telephone survey Survey technique in which a selected group of respondents are contacted by telephone and asked questions about some activity.

third-generation ships Ships that carry containers on the weather deck and roll on-roll off cargo below in the hold of the vessel.

total after-tax profit concept A decision concept that takes into account the impact of national tax policies on the logistics function.

total cost concept A decision concept that uses cost as a basis for measurement in order to evaluate and optimize logistical activities.

trade creation Benefit of economic integration; the benefit to a particular country when a group of countries trade a product freely among themselves but maintain common barriers to trade with nonmembers.

trade diversion Cost of economic integration; the cost to a particular country when a group of countries trade a product freely among themselves.

trade-off concept A decision concept that recognizes linkages within the decision system.

trade policy mechanisms Measures used to influence and alter trade relationships.

trademark licensing A special form of licensing that permits the name or logos of recognizable individuals or groups to be used on products.

trading blocs Preferential economic arrangement among a group of countries.

trading partners Other countries with which a country does business.

tramp service Ocean shipping via irregular routes, scheduled only on demand.

transaction exposure The potential for losses or gains when a firm engages in a transaction denominated in a foreign currency.

transfer cost All variable costs incurred in transferring technology to a licensee and all ongoing costs of maintaining the licensing agreement.

transfer pricing Intracompany pricing; pricing of sales to members of the same corporate family.

transfer risk The danger of having one's ability to transfer profits or products in and out of a country inhibited by governmental rules and regulations.

transit time The period between departure and arrival of a carrier.

translation exposure The potential effect on a firm's financial statements of a change in currency values.

transportation modes Forms of transportation.

Treaty of Rome The original agreement that established the European Economic Community (now called the European Community, or EC) in 1957.

trigger mechanisms Specific acts or stimuli that set off reactions.

turnkey operation A specialized form of management contract, where the arrangement permits a client to acquire a complete international system together with skills investment sufficient to allow unassisted maintenance and operation of the system following its completion.

unilateral transfer Gifts from one country to another.

value-added tax (VAT) A tax on the value added at each stage of the production and distribution process; a tax assessed in most European countries and also common among Latin American countries.

variable cost The cost of production; it varies with the level of production, i.e., labor, raw materials, parts and assemblies, etc.

voluntary restraint agreements Trade restraint agreements resulting in self-imposed restrictions on exports from one country to another.

Webb-Pomerene associations Permit firms to cooperate in terms of international sales allocation, financing, and pricing information.

Webb-Pomerene Act of 1918 Excludes from antitrust prosecution, firms cooperating to develop foreign markets.

working-capital management The financing of short-term or current assets, but also describes all short-term financing and financial management of the firm.

World Trade Organization (WTO) Established on Jan. 1, 1995, the legal and institutional foundation of the multilateral trading system.

GLOSARIO EN ESPAÑOL

Acta de Clayton de 1914 Expande las provisiones de cumplimiento del Acta de Sherman contra los Trusts; define negocios exclusivos y cláusulas amarrantes como fusión que resultan en monopolios y atentados a monopolizar el comercio interestatal e internacional.

Acta de Europa singular Tratado de Roma enmendado; requiere la eliminación de barreras físicas, técnicas, y de impuestos que impidan el libre movimiento de bienes, personas, servicios, y capital.

Acta de Robinson-Patman de 1936 Prohibe la discriminación de precios.

Acta de Sherman de 1890 contra los trusts Prohibe combinaciones y conspiraciones para restringir comercio interestatal e internacional, y prohibe monopolios y atentados para monopolizar el comercio interestatal e internacional.

Acta sobre prácticas corruptas en el extranjero Aprobada en 1977, esta ley declara ser un crimen que ejecutivos de una empresa social estadounidense sobornen a oficiales extranjeros para obtener negocios.

Acta del Tratado de Preferencia Andino Provee entrada, libre de aranceles, en Estados Unidos a productos de varias categorías provenientes de Bolivia, Colombia, Ecuador, y Perú.

Acuerdo General Sobre Aranceles y Comercio (GATT) Código internacional de aranceles y reglas de comercio firmado por 23 naciones en 1947; domiciliado en Ginebra, Suiza; tiene 99 miembros actualmente.

Acuerdo de licencia Una firma le permite a otra usar su propiedad intelectual en cambio de compensación designada como derechos de pago.

Acuerdo de Maastricht Estableció la ciudadanía en la CE y una unión económica, i.e., un banco central europeo, un sistema para manejar la política monetaria, una moneda europea, y obliga a los miembros a reducir déficites gubernamentales excesivos.

Acuerdos de precio de mercadería Involucra al comprador y al vendedor juntos en un acuerdo para controlar el precio de cierta mercancía.

Adelantada cabal Transacciones por períodos de madurez de 30, 90, 180, y 360 días.

Adopción de cultura Ajustarse y adaptarse a una cultura otra que la propia.

Afiliadas de empresas extranjeras Empresas de Estados Unidos pertenecientes en un diez por ciento o más a una(s) entidad(es) extranjera(s)

Agente de cambio Una persona o institución que facilita el cambio (cultural) en una empresa en un país anfitrión.

Aislacionismo Política por la que una nación dice poder existir sin interactuar con ningunas otras naciones.

Alianza estratégica Nuevo término para la colaboración entre empresas, con frecuencia similar a las venturas juntas.

Aranceles de castigo Impuestos sobre un bien o servicio importados cuya intención es la de castigar a un socio comercial.

Arbitraje Proceso para resolver una disputa por el cual un árbitro objetivo escucha a ambos disputantes y hace una decisión: un proceso para resolver un conflicto en la arena de negocios internacionales a través del uso de intermediarios tales como representantes de las cámaras de comercio, asociaciones de negocios, o instituciones de un tercer país.

Area de comercio libre Eliminación de barreras de cuota entre países miembros, mientras que cada país establece sus propias barreras de cuota contra países que no son miembros.

Areas de comercio exterior Zonas de comercio donde bienes extranjeros pueden ser retenidos o procesados y luego reexportados sin incurrir aranceles adicionales.

Aro del Pacífico Países desarrollados y recientemente industrializados (P. R. I.) del Lejano Oriente y que incluye al Japón, China, Hong Kong, Corea del Sur, Singapore, Taiwan, Indonesia, Malasia, Filipinas, Tailandia, Australia, Nueva Zelandia, Brunei, Macao, y Papúa Nueva Guinea.

Armonizar La fusión de políticas de varios países en una política común y unificada.

Asimilador cultural Programa por el que candidatos para trabajo fuera del país, son entrenados para responder a situaciones específicas en un país específico.

Autarquía Un país que no participa en el comercio internacional.

Ayuda para el desarrollo Ayuda iternacional para los países en desarrollo.

Balance de pagos: Transacciones económicas internacionales entre un país y otro.

Banco Internacional para la Reconstrucción y el Desarrollo El Banco Mundial para la reconstrucción y el desarrollo.

Bancos centrales Bancos nacionales que implementan las políticas gubernamentales que tienen que ver con el valor de sus monedas.

Bancos correspondientes u oficinas representativas Bancos localizados en diferentes países y no relacionados por pertenencia que tienen un acuerdo recíproco para proveer sevicios a los respectivos clientes.

Barreras no arancelarias Barreras al comerciono basadas en aranceles aduaneros. Ejemplos pueden incluír campañas para la compra doméstica, tratamiento preferencial a postores domésticos, y restricciones al mercado de entrada de bienes extranjeros a través de estrategias como un largo proceso de inspecciones complicadas.

Bloques de comercio Arreglo económico preferencial entre un grupo de países.

Boicot Combinarse en la abstención y prevención de tratar con una persona u organización como medio de coerción.

Bonificación por servicio en el extranjero Un soborno para animar a un administrador a que deje atrás las condiciones familiares y se adapte a un ambiente nuevo y diferente en otro país.

Buques de recipientes Diseñados para llevar recipientes normados que facilitan el cargue y descargue así como transferencias intermodales.

Calidad de vida El nivel de vida combinado con factores ambientales, determina el nivel de bienestar de los individuos.

Cambistas Profesionales que ayudan en la transferencia de fondos entre bancos y encuentran los precios más favorables para moneda corriente.

Capacidad de servicios Nivel máximo al que el proveedor de servicios puede proveerlos a sus clientes.

Capital de cartera Flujo de dinero como resultado de inversiones financieras.

Capital de deuda Capital levantado por dinero prestado de inversionistas, i.e., bonos.

Capital de valor Capital normalmente levantado al vender acciones de la compañía a inversionistas.

Cargo aéreo Transporte de bienes por aire; da cuenta de menos del uno por ciento del volumen total de cargamento internacional.

Carta constitucional social europea Establece y garantiza derechos económicos, sociales y culturales de los países miembros del consejo de Europa.

Carta de crédito Cargo que se hace un banco de hacer pago a un vendedor, una vez que las condiciones adelantadas en la carta de crédito han sido cumplidas.

Cartel Asociación de productores de un bien específico.

Caudal de Reserva Reserva de un producto guardado y accesible para prevenir su falta en tiempos de gran demanda inesperada; bajo acuerdos internacionales sobre precios, el caudal es controlado por un administrador elegido o nombrado para manejar el precio de un producto tal.

Cavidad negra Situación que se desarrolla cuando un comerciante internacional tiene un subsidiario de baja competencia- o ninguna en absoluto- en un mercado altamente estratégico.

Centralización Concentración de controles y decisiones estratégicas en la sede principal de una empresa.

Ciclo de tiempo para pedidos El tiempo total que pasa entre el emplazamiento de un pedido y el recibo de la mercancía.

Ciclo de vida de un producto Teoría que considera productos como teniendo cuatro fases: introducción, crecimiento, madurez, y declino.

Cobro documentario Uso de intermediarios fiduciarios para cobrar fondos. Los documentos se usan para controlar mercancía hasta que el pago sea hecho.

Codeterminación Estilo de administración en el cual los empleados están representados en juntas supervisorias para facilitar la comunicación entre el labor y los administradores.

Combinación promocional Combinación de ventas personales, publicidad y actividades de promoción de ventas.

Combinación publicitaria Combinación de varios tipos de medios publicitarios tales como avisos en periódicos, revistas, radio, TV, carteles y vehículos de tránsito.

Comercio intraindustrial Intercambio mutuo de los mismos productos.

Comercio de mercancía Fondos usados para la importación de mercancías y fondos obtenidos de la exportación de mercancía.

Comercio de servicio Intercambio iternacional de servicios profesionales o personales.

Comité para Inversiones Extranjeras en Estados Unidos Comité federal con la responsabilidad de revisar inversiones extranjeras mayores para determinar si la seguridad nacional u otros asuntos relacionados van a ser afectados.

Compañía doméstica Empresa que opera únicamente dentro de las fronteras de su propio país.

Compañía global Una organización de negocios que opera en más de un país.

Compañía multinacional Una empresa que opera internacionalmente para realizar ganancias por base global.

Compañías de comercio exportador Resultado de legislación pasada en 1982 (EU) para mejorar el desenlace exportador de compañías pequeñas y medianas; las compañías de comercio exportador, les permiten a los negocios juntarse para exportar o para ofrecer servicios de exportación. En adición, la ley les permite a los bancos participar en estas compañías y limita las provisiones contra trusts.

Compañías de manejo de exportación Firmas domésticas que se especializan en realizar servicios de negocios globales como representantes por comisión, o como distribuidores.

Concepto de costo total Concepto de decisión que utiliza el costo con base de medida para evaluar y optimizar las actividades de logística.

Concepto de ganancia total después de impuestos Concepto de decisión que toma en cuenta el el impacto que las políticas nacionales de impuestos tienen sobre las funciones de la logística.

Concepto de sistemas Concepto de logística basado en la noción de que las actividades del flujo de material son tan complejas que pueden sólo ser consideradas dentro del contexto de su interacción propia.

Concepto de trueque Concepto de decisión que reconoce acoplamientos dentro del sistema de decisiones.

Confiabilidad Dependabilidad; la predictabilidad del resultado de una acción.

Confiscación Similar a la expropiación en que resulta en la transferencia de pertenencia de una empresa al estado.

Conocimiento cultural Conocimiento de otras culturas — puede ser definido por la manera en que se adquiere. Conocimiento objetivo o de hecho, obtenido a través de otros, por comunicación, investigación, y educación. Conocimiento experiencial, obtenido por estar directamente envuelto en la cultura.

Conocimiento de embarque Contrato entre el exportador y el transportador indicando que el transportador ha aceptado la responsabilidad por bienes cargados y proveerá el transporte a cambio de pago.

Conocimiento de embarque sencillo No negociable; generalmente se usa en transacciones pagadas de antemano en las que el cargo se entrega específicamente a un individuo o empresa.

Construcción de escenario La identificación de variables cruciales y la determinación de sus efectos en casos o tentativas diferentes.

Contabilidad de doble partida Un método de contaduría por el que cada transacción produce al mismo tiempo un débito y un crédito por exactamente la misma cantidad.

Contracomercio Pago por bienes y servicios con otros bienes y servicios.

Contrato de manejo Firma vende su pericia en manejar una compañía y así evita los riesgos y beneficios de pertenencia.

Contribuidor Organización en un país con una competencia distintiva, tal como desarrollo de productos.

Controles de intercambio Controles del movimiento de capital dentro y fuera de un país, a veces impuestos cuando el país enfrenta una falta de divisas extranjeras.

Convergencia cultural Exposición a otras culturas acelerada por la tecnología.

Costo, seguros, y cargo El vendedor cotiza un precio que incluye seguros, todo el transporte, y gastos misceláneos hasta el punto de desembarque del barco o el avión.

Costo y cargo El vendedor cotiza un precio por los bienes, incluyendo el costo de transporte al nombrado punto de desembarque. Costo y tipo de seguros lo asume el comprador.

Costos fijos Costos que permanecen constantes prescindiendo de los niveles de producción, i.e., salarios ejecutivos, seguridad, arriendo, etc.

Costos de llévada de inventario Gastos por mantener inventario.

Costos variables El costo de producción: varía con el nivel de producción. i.,e., labor, materias crudas, partes, asemblaje, etc.

Cotización directa Una cotización de intercambio extranjero que especifica las unidades de moneda doméstica necesarias para la compra de una unidad de moneda extranjera.

Cotización indirecta Cotización de intercambio extranjero que especifica las unidades de moneda extranjera necesarias para la compra de una unidad de moneda doméstica.

Cotización de precios de exportación (CPE) Cotizaciónes de precios que se aplican sólo al punto de origen; el vendedor acuerda poner a la disposición del comprador los bienes en un lugar y fecha prescritos o dentro de un período de tiempo fijo.

Creación de comercio Beneficio de la integración económica; el beneficio a un país particular cuando un grupo de países comercia un producto libremente entre sí mismos pero mantienen barreras comunes para el comercio con los que no son miembros.

Crecimiento de la población Efecto que tiene los cambios en la población de los países en cuestiones económicas.

Crédito Creado cuando un bien se disminuye, una desventaja se aumenta, o un gasto se disminuye.

Criterio de referencia propia La referencia inconsciente que se hace a los valores de la cultura propia.

Cuenta de capital Transferencias de bienes de capital y subvención de deudas sin indemnización.

Cuenta oficial de reservas Total de reservas de moneda y metálicas guardadas por la autoridad monetaria dentro de un país.

Culturas de alto contexto Culturas en las que el contexto es por lo menos tan importante como lo que actualmente se dice.

Culturas de bajo contexto La mayoría de la información se contiene explícitamente en las palabras mismas.

Choque cultural Las más pronunciadas reacciones a la desorientación psicológica experimentada por la mayoría de la gente que se desenvuelve por un período de tiempo extendido en una cultura marcadamente diferente de la suya propia.

Débito Creado cuando un bien se aumenta, una desventaja se disminuye, o un gasto se aumenta.

Decentralización Dotar de gran autonomía a los subsidiarios.

Decentralización coordinada La estrategia general empresaria se provee de la sede principal, mientras que los subsidiarios tienen libertad de implementarla dentro de límites acordados, o en consulta con la sede principal.

Decisión de localización Decisión en cuanto al número total de centros de distribuición a ser utilizados, y dónde deben estar localizados.

Demográfica Las características de la gente tales como edad, ganancias, género, estado civil, ocupación, nivel de educación, etc.

Derecho civil Compilación de leyes, o grupo de ellas contenidas en una lista llamada un código.

Derecho de cobre especial Un índice de valor monetario disponible a cada miembro del Fondo Internacional Monetario. (FIM)

Derecho común Un sistema de leyes que se basa en las declaraciones de casos previos (precedentes), uso común, y costumbres, para las decisiones de las cortes.

Derecho doméstico Cuerpo de regulaciones legales llevadas a cabo dentro de las fronteras legales del país de una organización o de un ciudadano.

Derecho internacional Cuerpo de reglas y leyes que regulan las actividades que tienen lugar fuera de las fronteras legales de los estados.

Derecho internacional privado División de derecho internacional que se ocupa principalmente de los derechos y deberes de individuos y organizaciones no gubernamentales en sus asuntos internacionales.

Derecho internacional público División de derecho internacional que se ocupa pricipalmente de los derechos y deberes mutuos de estados y organizaciones intergubernamentales.

Desregulación Remover regulaciones gubernamentales de una compañía o industria para estimular la competición, i.e., en E.U. las aerolíneas.

Día de los muertos Celebración en Centro y Sudamérica del Día de Todos los Santos (1 de noviembre) y del Día de las Almas (2 de noviembre).

Diseño de canal Lo ancho y largo de un canal de distribuición.

Distribución reversa Sistema que responde a intereses ambientales que aseguran que una firma puede recoger un producto del mercado para uso subsecuente, reciclo, o disposición.

Diversidad de contabilidad Grado de diferencias en las prácticas contabiliarias nacionales.

Diversión de comercio Costo de integración económica; el costo a un país particular cuando un grupo de países comercia un producto libremente entre sí mismos.

División de labor Asignar etapas de producción a varios individuos en lugar de que cada uno produzca un servicio o producto entero.

Doctrina de Calvo Doctrina que abraza la idea de que el estado es supremo sobre inversionistas extranjeros dentro del territorio de dicho estado; impugna cualquier intervención por parte de estados foráneos en disputas sobre inversiones como violación de su jurisdicción territorial, y rechaza el concepto de pronta y adecuada compensación por la propiedad decomisada.

Doctrina de inmunidad soberana Mantiene que estados soberanos tienen inmunidad de demandas legales que cubren sus códigos legales y regulaciones, incluyendo leyes de expropiación de propiedad, actos de sus fuerzas armadas o servicio diplomático, y préstamos públicos.

Domesticación Un gobierno demanda que se transfieran pertenencia y responsabilidad de manejo.

Drenado de cerebros Emigración de profesionales de un país a otro, usualmente con el propósito de mejorar sus ganancias o su nivel de vida.

"Dumping" Venta de bienes fuera del país a un precio más bajo que el del país de origen del exportador, o a precio menor que el de costo de producción.

Economías de escala externas Costos de producción reducidos como resultado del acceso de una empresa a costo más bajo de capital, labor, y tecnología que en otros países.

Economías de escala internas Costos de producción más bajos debido al incremento de producción para un mercado agrandado.

Embargo 1. Orden de un gobierno prohibiendo el movimiento de barcos mercantiles de o a puertos. 2. Mandamiento restrictivo de la agencia de control de un gobierno para rehusar cargo para salida. 3. Cualquier restricción impuesta al comercio.

Entrenamiento para la sensibilidad Entrenamiento en relaciones humanas que se enfoca en en la interacción personal e interpersonal; entrenamiento que se enfoca en acrecentar la flexibilidad del expatriado en situaciones bastante diferentes de las que encontraba en su propia cultura.

Entrevista personal Técnica de medición en el cual un entrevistante llama personalmente al respondiente en el esfuerzo de completar un cuestionario.

Envolvimiento de clientes Participación activa de los clientes: una de las características de los servicios ya que los clientes están activamente envueltos en los servicios que reciben.

Escalación de precios Establecimiento de precios de exportación demasiado en exceso de los precios domésticos, con frecuencia debido al largo canal de distribución, y subidas frecuentes.

Estado Una entidad política que comprende un territorio, población, un gobierno capaz de entrar en relaciones exteriores, y un gobierno capaz de controlar a sus gentes y su territorio.

Estrategias de publicidad Aplicada a la selección de medios de publicidad y al desarrollo del programa para implementarla.

Etnocentrismo Tendencia a considerar la cultura propia como superior a las demás; tender exclusivamente hacia el mercado doméstico.

Estratificación social La división en clases sociales de una población específica.

Estructura de clientela Organización estructural que agrupa sus recursos humanos de acuerdo con el tipo o categoría de clientela.

Estructura funcional Organiza a los empleados de acuerdo con el tipo de trabajo a hacer.

Estructura geográfica Estructura organizacional en la cual las divisiones geográficas tienen la responsabilidad por la manufactura y mercadería en sus áreas respectivas.

Estructura matriz Estructura organizacional que utiliza estructuración funcional y divisional simultáneamente.

Estructura mixta Estructura organizacional que combina dos o más dimensiones organizacionales, por ejemplo, productos, áreas, o funciones.

Estructura por proceso Variación de la estructura funcional en la cual los departamentos se forman a base de procesos de producción.

Estructura por producto Estructura organizacional en la que las divisiones de producción tienen la responsabilidad de toda manufactura y mercado.

Euro Nombre de la moneda que va a ser introducido como parte de la implementación de la Unión Monetaria Europea (EMU).

Eurobono Bono denominado en moneda otra de la del país en donde se vende.

Expatriado Alguien que vive en una tierra extranjera; administrador de empresa asignado a una posición fuera del país.

Experiencia de campo Experiencia adquirida en el campo de actividad y nó en laboratorio; entrenamiento que expone al gerente de empresa a un ambiente cultural diferente del suyo propio, por un período de tiempo limitado.

Experimentación Método de investigación por el cual todas menos una variable se conservan constantes, y una nueva variable singular se introduce. Cualquier cambio en el mercado como resultado del experimento se le adscribe a la nueva variable.

Exposición económica Potencia de efectos a largo plazo en el valor de una firma como resultado de cambios en la moneda extranjera.

Exposición traduccional El efecto potencial sobre las declaraciones financieras de una firma con el cambio de valores de moneda extranjera.

Exposición transaccional Potencia de pérdidas o ganancias cuando una firma se involucra en una transacción denominada en moneda extranjera.

Expropiación Decomiso de propiedad extranjera por el estado.

Expropiación progresiva Una serie de actos y regulaciones que gradualmente y tomados juntos, limitan el ejercicio de derechos de pertenencia.

Extraterritorialidad El intento de una nación de implementar una política fuera de sus límites fronterizos.

Factor de exportación por cobrar Asignación de facturas y documentos relacionados a un cargo, a un agente o factor quien paga al exportador una cantidad descontada.

Factores de producción Todo lo introducido al proceso de producción, incluyendo el capital, el labor, la tierra, y la tecnología.

Factura comercial Factura por los bienes declarando información básica sobre la transacción, incluyendo una descripción de la mercancía, costo de los bienes vendidos, direcciones del transportador y el vendedor, y términos de entrega y pago.

Falsificación de productos Manufactura ilegal de un producto; el mal uso de un patente o transgresión de una marca registrada.

Flujo en efectivo La cantidad total (a mano y en bancos) que una compañía tiene de dinero en efectivo.

Flujo de moneda Flujo de moneda de nación a nación que a su vez determina las tasas de intercambio.

Forfaiting Exportador descuenta cuentas de cambio recibidas de un importador.

Fortaleza Europa Sospecha levantada por socios comerciales de Europa occidental que mantenían que la integración de la Unión Europea podría resultar en restricciones de comercio e inversiones, por parte de otros fuera de la Unión.

Franquicia Compañía principal le otorga derechos a otra entidad independiente para hacer negocios en forma prescribida.

Fragilidad Susceptibilidad a la deterioración; la característica de servicios que los hace difíciles de inventariar.

Grupo de Cinco Los países del G5 son: Estados Unidos, Japón, Alemania, el Reino Unido, y Francia.

Grupo secundarios de referencia Grupos más grandes que, por relación al individuo, pueden influenciar su comportamiento.

Grupo de Siete Los países del G5 más el Canadá e Italia.

Grupos de enfoque Técnica de medición en la cual representantes de una audiencia objeto contribuyen a la medición de un mercado, participando en una discusión supervisada pero no estructurada.

Grupos primarios de referencia Grupos pequeños, íntimos, que están en la posición de influír el comportamiento de alguien.

Grupos de referencia Grupos tales como la familia, compañeros de trabajo, y asociaciones profesionales y obreras que proveen valores y actitudes que influencian y forman el comportamiento, incluyendo el de los consumidores.

Haaj El peregrinaje musulmán anual a Meca, obligatorio para todo musulmán al menos una vez en la vida.

Igualamiento de impuestos Reembolso por una empresa cuando un empleado, asignado a una posición en el extranjero, tiene que pagar una tasa mayor de impuesto que si estuviera viviendo en su propio país.

Implementador Función típica de un subsidiario, generalmente envuelve la implementación de estrategias desarrolladas en la oficina principal.

Impuesto al valor agregado (VAT) Un impuesto al valor agregado a cada etapa del proceso de producción y distribuición de de un producto; un impuesto gravado en la mayoría de los países europeos y también común en los países latinoamericanos.

Impuestos directos Calculado en ganancias actuales tanto de un individuo como de una empresa.

Impuestos indirectos Tales como sobre la venta, impuestos de separación, tarifas, e impuestos de valor agregado que se aplican a precios de compra, costos de material, cantidades de reservas naturales manejadas, y demás.

Incotérminos Definiciones normadas por la Cámara Internacional de Comercio y aceptadas internacionalmente como términos de venta.

Información por proxi Datos utilizados como sustitutos por mejores que no son obtenibles.

Infraestructura económica El sistema de transporte, energía, y comunicaciones de un país.

Infraestructura financiera Facilita las agencias de mercadería en un país, como por ejemplo, los bancos.

Infraestructura de mercado Facilita a agencias mercaderas en un país, como por ejemplo, firmas de investigación de mercados, canalizadores.

Infraestructura social Sistemas de vivienda, salud, educación y sociales en general, de un país.

Iniciativa de la Cuenca Caribe Permite la entrada libre de una variedad de productos provenientes de países beneficiarios de la Iniciativa de la Cuenca Caribe.

Instrucciones sobre área Programas de entrenamiento para preparar a quienes van a ser mandados fuera del país.

Intangibilidad Inhabilidad de ser visto, gustado o tocado en un sentido convencional; la característica de servicios que más fuertemente los diferencian de los productos.

Intervención La compra y venta de su propia moneda por el gobierno de un país en el mercado libre.

Inventario justo a tiempo Materiales programados para llegar exactamente cuando se necesitan en la línea de producción.

Inversión directa (1) Propiedad y control de una empresa en otro país. (2) Transacciones entre inversionistas y empresas en el control o posesión de bienes en una economía extranjera.

Inversión extranjera directa El establecimiento o expansión de operaciones en un país extranjero con transferencia de capital.

Levantadentro, levantafuera Método de cargar y descargar recipientes alternativamente levantando uno, poniéndolo a bordo del barco a salir, y sacando, en el mismo ciclo de la grúa, otro a llegar.

Ley islámica Derivada del Sunnah (dichos y escritos de profeta Mahoma), sabios islámicos, y la comunidad legal islámica.

Ley de precio único La tasa de intercambio entre dos monedas basada en sólo un bien o servicio.

Libre abordo Se aplica sólo a transportes de barco. El vendedor cotiza un precio que cubre todos los gastos hasta e incluyendo la entrega de bienes en un barco de ultramar proveído por o para el comprador.

Libre al lado del barco Se aplica sólo a un punto designado de transporte interior. El vendedor se responsabiliza por la carga y transporte de los bienes; el comprador se responsabiliza por todos los gastos subsecuentes.

Licencia de importación Licencia obtenible de la Oficina para la Administración de Exportaciones del Departamento de Comercio de Estados Unidos, quien es responsable por la ejecución del Acta de Adminitración de Exportaciones.

Líder estratégico Subsidiario nacional altamente competente, localizado en un mercado estratégicamente crítico.

Línea de productos Serie de productos relacionados ofrecidos por una empresa.

Lingua franca Lengua habitualmente usada por gente de habla diferente para facilitar la comunicación.

Lista de bienes críticos Archivo que contiene información sobre productos que son, o particularmente sensitivos para la seguridad de la nación, o controlados por algún otro propósito.

Marca Nombre, término, símbolo o diseño, o cobinación de tales usados para diferenciar los productos de una firma de los de otros competidores.

Marca de fábrica La que se puede vocalizar o decir.

Margen de contribución La diferencia entre el precio de venta (por unidad) y el costo variable (por unidad).

Más Favorecida Nación (MFN) Término que describe una cláusula del código GATT de que un miembro le extienda a otro el trato más favorable acordado a cualquier otro país en cuanto a exportaciones e importaciones.

Mecanismo de gatillo Actos o estímulos específicos que desatan reacciones.

Mecanismos de política comercial Medidas utilizadas para influír y alterar relaciones comerciales.

Mecanismo de tasa de intercambio Mantenimiento del Sistema Monetario Europeo en la moneda de un miembro verso la moneda de los otros miembros.

Medición Método de investigación que recoge datos por medio de la solicitud de respuestas a preguntas cuidadosamente enmarcadas de un grupo de participantes en el mercado.

Medición por correo Técnica de medición por la que se envía un cuestionario por correo a un grupo selecto de respondientes.

Medición por teléfono Técnica de medición por la cual un grupo selecto de respondientes son llamados por teléfono y se les hacen preguntas sobre alguna actividad.

Mensaje promocional Contenido de un aviso, o entrega publicitaria, o actividad de promoción de ventas.

Mercado complementario Arreglo entre dos empresas para compartir facilidades y actividades mercantiles. Les permite así llevar a a cabo objetivos que no podrían alcanzar solas.

Mercado común Como la unión de aduanas, no tiene barreras para el comercio entre países miembros, si no una política común para el comercio exterior; más aún, remueve las restricciones del movimiento de factores de producción a través de las fronteras de los países miembros.

Mercado interbancario Bancos negociando con otros bancos en gran volumen con transacciones excediendo un millón de dólares.

Mercado de intercambio extranjero Un mercado internacional que intercambia instrumentos financieros en una variedad de monedas.

Mercancía Efectos tangibles tales como automóviles, maquinaria y productos químicos.

Mercantilismo Política económica y social que alienta la exportación de bienes a cambio de oro.

Negociaciones multilaterales de comercio Negociaciones de comercio entre más de dos partes; las complicadas relaciones entre países que comercian.

Netar Coordinación de dos flujos en efectivo opuestos entre subsidiarios de una empresa así que sólo el balance neto de los dos es actualmente intercambiado.

Nivel de vida El nivel de afluencia material de un grupo o de una nación, medido como el compuesto de cantidades y calidad de bienes materiales.

No se inventó aquí Síndrome por el que unidades locales o subordinadas rechazan estrategias o iniciativas de empresa sólo porque fueron iniciadas en otra sección de la firma.

Observación Método de investigación que se basa en la observación de una actividad así que ocurre.

Operación de vuelta de llave Forma especializada de contrato de manejo en la que el arreglo permite al cliente adquirir un sistema global junto con la inversión de habilidad suficiente para permitir mantenimiento inasistido y la operación del sistema al punto de completación.

Orden de remitente Conocimiento de embarque negociable, que puede ser comprado, vendido, o trocado mientras que el cargo está en tránsito y se usa en transacciones de carta de crédito.

Organización mundial de Comercio Establecida el 1 de enero de 1995; la base legal e institucional del Sistema Multilateral de Comercio.

Organizaciones intergubernamentales Organización permanente establecida por dos o más estados para llevar a cabo actividades de interés común.

Organizaciones no gubernamentales Organización internacional constituída por personas que no son estados.

Paradoja de Leontief La creencia generalizada de que Estados Unidos era un país con abundancia de capital en contra de lo que encontró Leontief indicando que el país lo que tenía era abundancia de labor.

Paridad de habilidad de compras Una teoría que indica que los precios de bienes comerciales tienden a igualarse a través de los países.

Participación minoritaria Participación por un grupo que tiene menos del número necesario de votos para adquirir control.

Participación al valor Pertenencia multinacional minoritaria en compañías que tienen importancia estratégica.

Per cápita El promedio valor en dólares de exportaciones e importes por cada persona de un país.

Pericia de área Conocimiento de los sistemas básicos de una región o mercado específico.

Plataforma competitiva El ambiente comercial proveído por una nación a sus firmas, lo que afecta su competividad internacional.

Policéntrico Tender a considerar cada cultura como una entidad separada; tender a orientarse hacia mercados extranjeros individualmente.

Política agraria común Sistema integrado de subsidios y descuentos aplicado a los intereses agrarios en la Comunidad Europea.

Política extranjera Area de política pública que tiene que ver con las relaciones con otros países.

Políticas preferenciales Políticas gubernamentales que favorecen a ciertas empresas (usualmente domésticas); por ejemplo, el uso de transporte nacional para cargo gubernamental aún cuando existan alternativas más económicas.

Posicionamiento Percepción por el consumidor del producto de una firma en relación a los productos de los competidores.

Precio de costo marginal Basado en costos adicionales o incrementales.

Precio dual Estrategia para establecer precios en la cual el precio de exportación está basado en el precio de costo marginal, resultando en un costo de exportación más bajo que el precio doméstico; puede resultar en un cargo de practicar "dumping."

Precio de mercado diferenciado Estrategia para establecer precios basada en la demanda en lugar del costo.

Precio regulador mundial Estrategia para establecer precios basada en el promedio de costo por unidad considerando los costos fijos, variables y los relacionados a la exportación.

Precio de transferencia Precio intraempresario; precio de venta a entidades de la misma sociedad o empresa.

Privatización Política de transferir la operación y manejo de empresas pertenecientes al gobierno a manos privadas para bajar costos y asegurar sevicios más eficientes.

Psicografía Estudio de la gente basado en su estilo de vida, i.e., sus actividades, intereses y opiniones.

Regiocéntrico o geocéntrico Tender a orientarse en el mercado hacia regiones mayores más que hacia países individuales.

Riesgo cultural Riesgo de mal acabar un negocio, malas relaciones con la clientela, y negociaciones perdidas que pueden resultar cuando una empresa falla en comprender y adaptarse a las diferencias culturales entre las propias y las del país anfitrión.

Riesgo de operación El peligro de interferencia por el gobierno u otros grupos en las operaciones empresarias propias fuera del país.

Riesgo de pertenencia El riesgo inherente al mantener propiedad fuera del país. La exposición a la pérdida de activos en el extranjero por intervenciones gubernamentales.

Riesgo político El riesgo de pérdida por una empresa internacional de activos, posibilidad de ganancias, o control de manejo debido a acciones políticas llevadas a cabo por el país anfitrión.

Riesgo de transferencia El peligro de la inhibición de la habilidad de transferir ganancias o productos dentro o fuera de un país debido a reglas y regulaciones gubernamentales.

Rodando adentro, rodando afuera Método de operación para cargar y descargar un barco por el cual recipientes con ruedas son conducidos y estacionados en la cala del barco.

Salario de base Salario que no incluye pagos especiales tales como subsidios pagados durante asignaciones fuera del país.

Sanción Acción de uno o más estados hacia otro estado calculada para forzarlo a cumplir con sus obligaciones legales.

Segmentación del mercado Agrupar a la gente de acuerdo con las características comunes del grupo participatorio, i.e., demográficas, psicográficas (estilo de vida), grados de uso del producto, y beneficios deseados del producto.

Seguridad nacional La habilidad de una nación para proteger sus valores internos de amenazas externas.

Servicio de clientes Esfuerzo total de una empresa para satifacer al cliente; el servicio de clientes se nivela en términos de soluciones inmediatas permitidas por las políticas del iventario en una situación dada.

Servicios La exportación e importación de todo tipo de servicios.

Sistema monetario europeo Tasas fijas de paridad entre las monedas de los países miembros.

Sistemas de control para la exportación Diseñadas para negar o retrasar la adquisición de bienes estratégicamente importantes por adversarios.

Soberanía nacional Provee a un gobierno con el derecho y la responsabilidad de formar a sus ciudadanos y al medio ambiente.

Socios de comercio Otros países con los que un país comercia.

Subsidio para el costo de vida Subsidio pagado durante asignaciones fuera del país para permitir al empleado mantener el mismo nivel de vida que el de su propio país si viviera allí.

Subsidio para la educación Reembolso por una empresa por los gastos incurridos en la educación de la prole mientras los responsables están asignados fuera del país.

Subsidio para vivienda Subsidio pagado durante asignaciones en el extranjero para proveer vivienda adecuada.

Subsidio por dureza Subsidio pagado durante asignación en el extranjero cuando tal requiere una adaptación de grandes proporciones.

Tasa cruzada Cotizaciones de tasa de intercambio que no utilizan como base el dólar estadounidense.

Tasa de intercambio extranjero fija Monedas extranjeras vinculadas a sí mismas cuyo valor está basado en el oro.

Tasa de intercambio extranjero flotante Tasa de intercambio extranjero que responden rápidamente a las fuerzas mercantiles de oferta y demanda.

Teoría Moderna Tradicional Doctrina que reconoce el derecho de un estado soberano anacionalizar propiedad perteneciente a extranjeros, acompañada de pronta, adecuada y efectiva compensación.

Tiempo de tránsito Período entre la salida y llegada de un transporte.

Traducción de vuelta Traducir una versión en lengua extranjera a la lengua original por otra persona diferente de la que la hizo la primera vez.

Transacción adelantada El intercambio de monedas para una fecha futura: una tasa pre-acordada.

Transacción de sitio El intercambio de monedas para entrega inmediata.

Transferencias corrientes Transferencias, regalos o subvenciones de bienes o servicios humanitarios.

Tratado de Libre Comercio (NAFTA) Acuerdo bajo el cual Estados Unidos, Canadá y México bajan o eliminan aranceles de importación y exportación entre los tres países para estimular el comercio.

Trueques adelantados Intercambio de monedas por un período de tiempo acordado, a una tasa acordada.

Unión de Aduanas Eliminación de aranceles y barreras de cuota entre países miembros; países miembros establecen aranceles y barreras de cuota comunes contra los países que no son miembros.

Unión económica Tiene todas las características de un mercado común y, además la integración de políticas económicas: políticas monetarias armonizadas, impuestos, gastos gubernamentales y moneda común.

Ventaja absoluta La habilidad de producir un producto o un servicio más barato de lo que puedan ser producidos en cualquiera otra parte.

Ventaja comparativa La habilidad de producir un producto o un servicio, en relación a otros bienes y servicios, más barato que cualquier otro país.

Ventura junta Participación de dos o más compañías en un negocio para alcanzar objetivos comunes.

Vuelo de capital El flujo de capital fuera del país porque los inversionistas creen que las ganancias realizadas por inversiones o la seguridad del capital no están suficientemente aseguradas en su propio país.

CREDITS

5 Copyright © 1995 Time Inc. All rights reserved. Reprinted by permission **6-7** Reprinted by permission of FORBES Magazine © Forbes Inc., 1997. **10** Courtesy of Taco Bell. **11** Courtesy of All American Television, Inc. **13** Courtesy of The Ford Motor Company. **14** Courtesy of The Ford Motor Company. **16** Reprinted by permission of *The Wall Street Journal* © 1993 Dow Jones & Company, Inc. All Rights Reserved Worldwide. **19** Courtesy of Avon Products, Inc. **23** Courtesy of Integraph. **83** Reprinted by permission of *The Wall Street Journal* © 1992 Dow Jones & Company, Inc. All Rights Reserved Worldwide. **93** Reprinted by permission of *The Wall Street Journal* © 1995 Dow Jones & Company, Inc. All Rights Reserved Worldwide. **113** Reprinted by permission of *The Wall Street Journal* © 1994 Dow Jones & Company, Inc. All Rights Reserved Worldwide. **126** ROB ROGERS reprinted by permission of United Features Syndicate, Inc. **127** Copyright © 1995. Reprinted with permission Knight-Ridder/Tribune Information Services. **144** Copyright © 1994. Reprinted by permission of the McGraw-Hill Companies. **168** Copyright © 1994. Reprinted by permission of *The Financial Times.* **173** Reprinted by permission of *The Wall Street Journal* © 1994 Dow Jones & Company, Inc. All Rights Reserved Worldwide. **187** Reprinted by permission of *The Wall Street Journal* © 1994 Dow Jones & Company, Inc. All Rights Reserved Worldwide. **191** Reprinted by permission from EdSubitzky. **200** © 1994 *The Washington Post.* Reprinted with permission. **209** *UC Mexus News,* University of California Institute for Mexico and the United States, © 1993, The Regents of the University of California. **230** Copyright © 1997 The New York Times Company. Reprinted by permission. **235** Copyright 1995 *US News & World Report.* Reprinted with permission. **241** MATT DAVIES reprinted by permission of United Features Syndicate, Inc. **245** Reprinted by permission of *The Wall Street Journal* © 1993 Dow Jones & Company, Inc. All Rights Reserved Worldwide. **266** Copyright 1985 Grove/Atlantic, Inc. Reprinted by permission. **273** Reprinted by permission of *Hemispheres,* the magazine of United Airlines. **282** Reprinted with permission of Intercultural Press, Inc., Yormouth, ME. Copyright 1996. **285** Reproduced by permission of The Economist Intelligence Unit, 111 West 57 Street, New York, NY 10019. **304** Reprinted by permission of FORBES Magazine © Forbes, Inc. 1996. **318** Reprinted by permission of The Conference Board. **347** © 1991 American Management Association, New York. All rights reserved. **364** © 1996 *The Washington Post.* Reprinted with permission. **366** Noboru Hashimot/New York Times Pictures. **368** Reprinted with permission from *Marketing News,* published by the American Marketing Association, August 29, 1994. **394** Reprinted by permission of *The Wall Street Journal* © 1995 Dow Jones & Company, Inc. All Rights Reserved Worldwide. **403** Reprinted by permission of *The Wall Street Journal* © 1996 Dow Jones & Company, Inc. All Rights Reserved Worldwide. **405** Reprinted by permission of *Harvard Business Review* from Joel Bleeke and David Ernst, "Is Your Strategic Alliance A Sale?" *Harvard Business Review* 73 (January/February 1995). Copyright © 1995 by the President and Fellows of Harvard College; all rights reserved. Reprinted with permission from the January 30, 1995 issue of *Advertising Age.* Copyright Crain Communications Inc. 1995. **408** Copyright © 1995 Time, Inc. All rights reserved. Reprinted by permission. **443** © 1996 *The Washington Post.* Reprinted with permission. **481** © 1996 *The Washington Post.* Reprinted with permission. **517** Reprinted by permission of *The Wall Street Journal* © 1994 Dow Jones & Company, Inc. All Rights Reserved Worldwide. **525** Copyright © 1995 The Christian Science Publishing Society. All rights reserved. Reprinted with permission. **528** Copyright © 1990 the Christian Science Publishing Society. All rights reserved. Reprinted with permission. **529** Reprinted by permission of Richard Fletcher. **556** Reprinted by permission of *The Wall Street Journal* © 1994 Dow Jones & Company, Inc. All Rights Reserved Worldwide. **559** Reprinted by permission of *The Wall Street Journal* © 1994 Dow Jones & Company, Inc. All Rights Reserved Worldwide. **581** Copyright © 1994 by the Foundation for the School of Business at Indiana University. Used with permission.

Name Index

Subject Index